THE OXFORD HANDBOOK OF

ETHICS AND ART

THE OXFORD HANDBOOK OF

ETHICS AND ART

Edited by
JAMES HAROLD

OXFORD
UNIVERSITY PRESS

Oxford University Press is a department of the University of Oxford. It furthers
the University's objective of excellence in research, scholarship, and education
by publishing worldwide. Oxford is a registered trade mark of Oxford University
Press in the UK and certain other countries.

Published in the United States of America by Oxford University Press
198 Madison Avenue, New York, NY 10016, United States of America.

© Oxford University Press 2023

Library of Congress Cataloging-in-Publication Data
Names: Harold, James (James Edward), editor.
Title: The Oxford handbook of ethics and art / James Harold.
Description: New York, NY : Oxford University Press, [2023] |
Includes bibliographical references and index.
Identifiers: LCCN 2023014257 (print) | LCCN 2023014258 (ebook) |
ISBN 9780197539798 (hardback) | ISBN 9780197539811 (epub) | ISBN 9780197539828
Subjects: LCSH: Art—Moral and ethical aspects.
Classification: LCC N72.E8 O94 2023 (print) | LCC N72.E8 (ebook) |
DDC 175—dc23/eng/20230503
LC record available at https://lccn.loc.gov/2023014257
LC ebook record available at https://lccn.loc.gov/2023014258

DOI: 10.1093/oxfordhb/9780197539798.001.0001

Printed by Integrated Books International, United States of America

CONTENTS

II. THEORETICAL APPROACHES
TO ETHICS AND ART

III. ETHICAL ISSUES IN INDIVIDUAL ARTS

IV. ETHICAL PROBLEMS IN THE ARTS

Acknowledgments

EDITING this volume has been a group effort from the very beginning.

First of all, I want to thank Lucy Randall for inviting me to submit a proposal to edit this volume, and for guiding me for more than two years through the process of revising the proposal, contacting authors, making changes, and so on. Thanks are also owed to the anonymous reviewers whose detailed and helpful feedback led me to substantially revise and expand the topics covered and the contributors invited. I am grateful to Paloma Escovedo and Lauralee Yearly at Oxford University Press for all of their editorial expertise, and for seeing the volume through each stage of production.

I am deeply grateful to all of the authors for their carefully researched, exciting, and insightful chapters. The process of reading drafts of these chapters has been deeply rewarding. I cannot overstate how much I have learned from reading their contributions. I also need to thank all of the authors for being so patient throughout this process, and for their capacity to forgive my mistakes along the way.

Nils Hennes-Stear has been a great help to me during the process of putting this together. When I was stuck puzzling out some questions about whom to ask to write what, he listened well, provided wise advice, and offered to help in all kinds of ways. (He also wrote a terrific chapter.)

Laura Sizer took the time to read through my introduction and to offer helpful feedback. I am extremely grateful for her time and effort, and I believe that the final product is better as a result of her input.

I need to thank Mount Holyoke College, which has supported this project by funding a student assistant, Sabryna Coppola, to aid me in every stage of editing.

Most important, I want to thank Sabryna Coppola, the student who has served as my unofficial assistant editor. (I deeply regret that it is not possible to give them this title officially.) For more than six months, Sabryna worked diligently on this project. They read every chapter draft very carefully, making minor corrections, attending to details of reference formatting, and offering other insights and suggestions. Sabryna created and maintained a master spreadsheet, tracking chapter submissions, abstracts, keywords, and word counts. They were constantly reminding me what needed to be done, and half the time, they simply did it themselves. I have been told that it is not worth employing undergraduate students as research assistants, but Sabryna has proved this to be completely false. Their contributions have been essential.

And, as always, I am grateful to my family for supporting me patiently through every stage of this project.

CONTRIBUTORS

Sondra Bacharach is associate professor of philosophy at Victoria University of Wellington.

Christopher Bartel is professor of philosophy at Appalachian State University and adjunct research fellow at Charles Sturt University.

Nalini Bhushan is Andrew W. Mellon Professor in the Humanities and professor of philosophy at Smith College.

Jeanette Bicknell is an independent scholar in Toronto, Canada.

Paul Butterfield is assistant professor of philosophy at Alfred University.

Noël Carroll is Distinguished Professor of philosophy and film studies at the CUNY Graduate Center.

Jacoby Adeshi Carter is associate professor of philosophy at Howard University.

Adriana Clavel-Vázquez is assistant professor of philosophy at Tilburg University.

Timothy M. Costelloe is professor of philosophy at the College of William & Mary.

Anthony Cross is assistant professor of philosophy at Texas State University.

Pierre Destrée is associate research fellow at the Fonds National belge de la Recherche Scientifique and associate professor at the Université catholique de Louvain.

A. W. Eaton is professor of philosophy and associate dean for faculty affairs and interdisciplinary programs at University of Illinois, Chicago.

Saul Fisher is associate provost for research, grants, and academic initiatives and associate professor of philosophy at Mercy College.

Michalle Gal is professor of philosophy at Shenkar College of Engineering, Design, and Art.

Karen Gover is a law student at Harvard Law School.

Barry Hallen is the director of Southern Crossroads Academic in Sarasota, Florida.

James R. Hamilton is professor of philosophy emeritus at Kansas State University.

James Harold is professor of philosophy at Mount Holyoke College.

Darren Hudson Hick is assistant professor of philosophy at Furman University.

Kathleen Higgins is professor of philosophy at the University of Texas at Austin.

Eric L. Hutton is professor of philosophy at the University of Utah.

Daniel Jacobson is Bruce D. Benson Professor of Philosophy and director of the Benson Center for the Study of Western Civilization at the University of Colorado, Boulder.

Eileen John is professor of philosophy at the University of Warwick.

Jennifer Judkins is adjunct professor of music (retired) at the University of California, Los Angeles.

Alex King is associate professor of philosophy at Simon Fraser University.

Carolyn Korsmeyer is research professor of philosophy at the University at Buffalo.

Peter Lamarque is professor of philosophy at the University of York.

Oliver Leaman is professor of philosophy at the University of Kentucky.

Shen-yi Liao is associate professor of philosophy at the University of Puget Sound.

Eva Kit Wah Man is Kiriyama Professor at the University of San Francisco and professor emeritus at Hong Kong Baptist University.

Sheena Michele Mason is assistant professor of English at SUNY Oneonta.

Erich Hatala Matthes is associate professor of philosophy and director of the Camilla Chandler Frost '47 Center for the Environment at Wellesley College.

Arvind Krishna Mehrotra is professor of English (retired) at the University of Allahabad.

Amy Mullin is professor of philosophy at the University of Toronto.

Ted Nannicelli is associate professor in the School of Communication and Arts at the University of Queensland.

C. Thi Nguyen is associate professor of philosophy at the University of Utah.

Carl Plantinga is professor of film and media at Calvin University.

Becca Rothfeld is a PhD candidate in philosophy at Harvard University.

Yuriko Saito is professor of philosophy emerita at the Rhode Island School of Design.

Elisabeth Schellekens is chair professor of aesthetics at Uppsala University.

Sandra Shapshay is professor of philosophy at Hunter College and the Graduate Center, CUNY.

Joy Shim is a PhD candidate in philosophy at Princeton University.

Nancy E. Snow is professor of philosophy at the University of Kansas.

Moonyoung Song is assistant professor of philosophy at the National University of Singapore.

Brian Soucek is professor of law and Chancellor's Fellow at the University of California, Davis.

Nils-Hennes Stear is associate lecturer at Uppsala University.

Matthew Strohl is professor of philosophy at the University of Montana.

Paul C. Taylor is Presidential Professor of Philosophy at University of California, Los Angeles.

Aili Whalen is director of development and planned giving at Bellarmine University.

Mary Beth Willard is professor of philosophy at Weber State University.

Scott Woodcock is associate professor of philosophy at the University of Victoria.

CHAPTER 1

....

INTRODUCTION

....

JAMES HAROLD

ART has not always had the same salience in philosophical discussions of ethics that many other elements of our lives have. There are well-defined areas of "applied ethics" corresponding to nature, business, healthcare, war, punishment, animals, and more, but there is no recognized research program in "applied ethics of the arts" or "art ethics." Art often seems to belong to its own sphere of value, separate from morality. The first questions we ask about art are usually not about its moral rightness or virtue, but about its beauty or originality. However, it is impossible to do any serious thinking about the arts without engaging in ethical questions.

Leo Tolstoy begins his *What Is Art?* by describing a day he spent at an opera house, watching rehearsals. He is horrified by the cruel behavior of the conductor toward the performers, and by the vast quantity of time and money that have been poured into staging a piece which is, he thinks, merely a mildly pleasing entertainment. To Tolstoy, this seems incredible—why would we sacrifice so much to make and consume art?

> In every large town enormous buildings are erected for museums, academies, conservatoires, dramatic schools, and for performances and concerts. Hundreds of thousands of workmen, carpenters, masons, painters, joiners, paperhangers, tailors, hairdressers, jewellers, moulders, type-setters, spend their whole lives in hard labour to satisfy the demands of art, so that hardly any other department of human activity, except the military, consumes so much energy as this.
>
> Not only is enormous labour spent on this activity, but in it, as in war, the very lives of men are sacrificed. Hundreds of thousands of people devote their lives from childhood to learning to twirl their legs rapidly (dancers), or to touch notes and strings very rapidly (musicians), or to draw with paint and represent what they see (artists), or to turn every phrase inside out and find a rhyme to every word. And these people, often very kind and clever, and capable of all sorts of useful labour, grow savage over their specialised and stupefying occupations, and become one-sided and self-complacent specialists, dull to all the serious phenomena of life, and skillful only at rapidly twisting their legs, their tongues, or their fingers. (Tolstoy 1904, 2)

What is most striking about Tolstoy's discussion is not the specifics of his moral concerns, but the strength of his passion. Tolstoy is *furious* that art asks so much from us, that we give so much of ourselves to the production of art, and he wants to know what value we can get out of it beyond entertainment. For Tolstoy, art is *itself* an ethical problem that needs our attention.

Artworks do have moral costs and sometimes convey moral meaning. In some cases, art has appeared so morally dangerous that it seemed like the only reasonable thing to do is to ban it. And in other cases, art can seem like one of the key elements of living a good and meaningful life. What makes art morally good or morally bad? How do these judgments vary across history, culture, and different art forms? What does it *mean* for art to be morally good or bad? What, if anything, does morality have to do with art's aesthetic value, or its value *qua* art? How does art affect and engage us in ways that matter morally?

Through much of the twentieth century, Anglophone philosophers mostly ignored the questions that mattered so much to Tolstoy. The relationship between ethics and art was barely discussed. This neglect was partly due to early analytic philosophers' general disinterest in evaluative questions, and partly due to the dominance of formalist aesthetics in art criticism, which treated ethical questions as irrelevant to art evaluation (though see Gal's chapter in this volume). Then, in the 1980s and early 1990s, work by Martha Nussbaum, Marcia M. Eaton, Noël Carroll, and Berys Gaut, among others, reminded Anglophone philosophers that there were important and difficult philosophical problems surrounding the intersection of art and ethics. In the immediate aftermath of this work, philosophers turned their attention to questions such as "Can we gain moral knowledge from artwork?" and "Do moral flaws in artworks affect artworks' aesthetic worth?" They also reached back to earlier figures in the Western tradition, particularly Plato, Aristotle, Hume, and Kant, to think anew about ethics and art.

In recent years, the conversation has broadened even further. Some of these interests follow changes in society as a whole. The #MeToo movement put new emphasis on the problem of how to treat artworks by creators who have done morally awful things. The artworld has also become more aware of how racial, ethnic, and other identities are represented in artworks, and on who is doing the representing, as shown by public campaigns like #OscarsSoWhite. Public arguments about what to do with monuments and memorials that distort history or eulogize racists have focused attention on the moral meanings of these works. New, richly interactive artforms, such as video games, public art, and interactive online media, have posed moral problems of privacy and ownership in sharp and challenging ways. Academic philosophy is just beginning to struggle with these kinds of cases, and to confront philosophy's own limitations, cultural biases, and other blind spots.

In recent years, philosophers have also begun to think about the connections between thinking about ethics and art and other philosophical questions. Is there a universal moral basis for judging art to be morally good or bad? For example, is it appropriate to judge ancient artworks by our moral standards? What is the difference, after all, between judging something to be morally wrong and aesthetically bad? Can traditional moral theories offer any resources for thinking about ethics in art?

OVERVIEW OF THIS HANDBOOK

The aim of this volume is to give an overview of some of the most significant and exciting philosophical controversies concerning ethics and the arts. The aim is not to be *complete*; even a volume as long as this one cannot possibly hope to cover everything. Instead, this volume aims to be "comprehensive" in the older meaning of that term: that of offering an extensive grasp of a subject matter. Each section samples a mix of topics that have been widely discussed alongside those that have been less noticed by philosophers. What emerges is a sense of the great variety of different problems and approaches as well as some recurring and overlapping themes.

A deliberate effort has been made to stretch beyond some of the debates and problems most familiar to Anglophone philosophers. Familiar topics and positions have been placed side by side with new and neglected ones, sometimes suggesting surprising connections and conflicting approaches.

The volume is divided into four sections: Historical Perspectives, Theoretical Approaches, Individual Arts, and Problems.

SECTION I: HISTORICAL PERSPECTIVES

Chapters in this section cover significant historical and cultural periods in which philosophical debates about ethics and art became salient. Some chapters (e.g., Saito's chapter on Japan) span hundreds of years; others focus on briefer historical eras (e.g., the Harlem Renaissance). These chapters show the wide variety of different concrete practices that were associated with the idea of "art," as well as the great range of approaches to thinking about what constitutes an "ethical" concern. In many cases the latter includes political meanings such as racialized conceptions of the self. These chapters also make clear how larger historical, economic, and political circumstances have shaped how people think about ethics and art. The chapters appear in more or less chronological order, though there is often considerable overlap in the times covered across different cultural traditions.

We begin with the debates over the value of the arts, and especially music, in pre–Han China. The usual picture has it that Confucians defended the value of the arts in developing virtue (*de*), while the Mohists condemned elaborate musical performances as wasteful and dangerous. (The Mohists' arguments anticipate Tolstoy's in surprising ways!) To this picture, Eric Hutton adds further richness: for example, the Confucians take music's value to lie in its role in transmitting human tradition and culture, whereas the Daoists Laozi and Zhuangzi emphasize music's connection to nonhuman nature. There are different conceptions at work here in thinking about what counts as "moral" when evaluating music. Hutton also notes the ways in which classical Chinese conceptions of "the arts" differ from contemporary Western thought.

Pierre Destrée's chapter on ancient Greece has some new things to say about familiar figures like Plato and Aristotle, as well as in his discussions of Plutarch and Epicurus, whose contributions to this debate have been largely neglected. Destrée shows that Plato's well-known condemnation of poetry also reveals a new possibility: that grappling with art's moral dangers can itself, apparently paradoxically, result in moral learning. There is more complexity and depth to the Greek tradition than the traditional story of the quarrel between the philosophers and the poets.

Oliver Leaman's chapter on morality and arts in Islamic tradition emphasizes a tension between two moral themes. On the one hand, many Islamic thinkers hold that there is a very close relationship between beauty and goodness, and Sufi thinkers have forged a similar link between goodness and the use of the imagination. On the other hand, Islamic thinkers have often been suspicious of the moral status of certain art forms, like pictorial images. Leaman also interrogates what is meant by "Islamic" when we speak of Islamic tradition, and shows both the variety of Islamic thought as well as how many features of Islamic thought draw from pre-Islamic sources and traditions.

In her wide-ranging chapter, Yuriko Saito examines Japanese ideas about ethics and art both pre-and post-Westernization (1868 CE). As we will see in many of the other chapters in this section, Western colonization and expansion impacted not only the practice of art, but also the moral possibilities expressed through art. Among other traditions, Saito discusses the mixed moral inheritance of *Wabi* aesthetics, which emphasizes imperfection and difficulty. On the one hand, *Wabi* aesthetics can cultivate open-mindedness; on the other hand, it can also be used to justify keeping imperfect or even unjust moral and political systems. Saito also shows how the Japanese traditional aesthetic attitude of attending to details of the everyday is also itself a moral attitude of cultivating careful attention toward others.

Timothy Costelloe's chapter on the modern period in Europe shows that philosophers of this period were very interested in the connections between morality and aesthetics, but did not have as much to say about "the arts" as such (with some exceptions, such as Reid and Kant). Instead, they explored topics such as: moral and aesthetic beauty; the faculty of taste both in appreciating art and in morality; the picturesque, which seems to deny moral reality in favor of the pretty; and the role of deception in writing. The great variety and richness of this period goes well beyond the most famous passages from Hume, Shaftesbury, and Kant.

Barry Hallen's chapter on Yorùbá tradition grapples with the picture of Yorùbá art and thought in the context of colonial narratives that regard Yorùbá as merely "traditional" or primitive. Hallen argues that in Yorùbá practice, art is intricately interconnected to both ethics and epistemology: in assessing art, we also assess its moral insight. He further argues for a kind of existential moral theme in Yorùbá art-making: a norm that art should authentically represent human life as it is.

In their discussion of the arts in India, Nalini Bhushan and Arvind Krishna Mehrotra, like Hallen, emphasize existential themes. In precolonial India, they argue, art and ethics had a close relationship, but the fact of British colonialization raised new dilemmas for artists about what counted as ethical engagement with the arts. They examine how artists grappled with this problem by looking closely at some examples of poetry and painting.

The art-critical movement known as formalism has long played the antagonist role in narratives about ethics and art. The figure of the formalist denies any role for ethics in thinking about art, or so we are told. In her chapter, Michalle Gal challenges this narrative, showing that in the writings of the nineteenth- and twentieth-century formalists there is a subtle but important connection between art and ethics in formalist thought, through the internal normativity of the work, that art is a model for moral life.

Jacoby Adeshei Carter and Sheena Michele Mason's chapter on the debates over art and ethics in the Harlem Renaissance emphasizes the complex and dynamic relationships between ethical ideas and the problems of racialization. The "great debate" between W. E. B. Du Bois and Alain LeRoy Locke over whether Black artists should make anti-racist art also implicates a wider variety of moral, artistic, and political issues having to do with what Blackness is in the first place, and whether and how it can be represented in the arts. One example they examine is the case of racial passing and narratives about the so-called mulatto/a in which the boundaries of racial categories are explored and challenged.

The last chapter in this section also focuses on how political questions shape ethical ones. Eva Kit Wah Man's chapter traces the development of thought in modern China about the role art and artists should play in Chinese society. Man begins with Mao Zedong's famous speeches in 1942 and takes us all the way up to the present day. In this chapter we see rival conceptions of art's power to reshape society as well as questions about government control of the arts.

SECTION II: THEORETICAL APPROACHES

In the next section, we move from considerations of particular historical moments to a discussion of the theoretical issues in judging artworks morally. Here by far the most discussed question is the "value interaction debate"—do moral judgments affect aesthetic judgments, and vice versa? Four of the chapters in this section are devoted to discussing this important question. But there are other important theoretical questions here too, having to do with the nature of moral and aesthetic judgments in the first place, and with the grounds for judging artworks morally good or bad.

The section begins with four chapters that we might think of as "meta-evaluative": chapters that ask about the objectivity and nature of the kinds of evaluative judgments that we make of artworks. Next, we look at how art might be evaluated morally given four different kinds of moral-theoretical approaches: Kantian, consequentialist, virtue theoretic, and feminist. Last, we turn to the value interaction debate, covering the familiar positions of autonomism, moralism, and contextualism, as well as less-discussed position, aestheticism.

The first meta-evaluative chapter is Alex King's. King focuses on the question of realism and anti-realism in aesthetics. Her approach takes the debates in metaethics over moral realism as a model for meta-aesthetics, by way of classic arguments for and against cognitivism. King takes moral realism to mean that there are genuine moral facts. Aesthetic realism, therefore, is the view that there are genuine aesthetic facts, and aesthetic anti-realism is the denial of this view. Cognitivism is the view that aesthetic or moral judgments are belief-like—they aim to represent the world as it is. She argues that while aesthetic anti-realism might *appear* to be the more intuitive view, aesthetic realism is much more plausible than it has often been thought to be, and so is a view worth taking seriously.

All debates about the interaction between moral and aesthetic value seem to assume that there is in fact some difference between the two types of value. In her chapter, Moonyoung Song examines the characteristics of aesthetic value, as well as artistic value, if that is distinct from aesthetic value. She considers the possibility such distinctions might not be invariant, or that there might not be any determinate answer to this problem.

In his chapter, Ted Nannicelli takes up the problem of moral relativism in the ethical evaluation of art. Many people are moved to condemn historical artworks that include sexist or racist elements, even if those sentiments were more widely accepted in the time of the work's creation. Nannicelli questions this tendency, and defends a moderate version of moral relativism, which builds on Bernard Williams's "relativism of distance."

Sandra Shapshay offers the first of four accounts of what might make art morally good or bad: Kant's own. According to Shapshay, the usual view of Kant on art that takes him to endorse an autonomist or formalist approach is wrong, or at the least, incomplete. Shapshay shows that according to Kant, art has moral value because of its role as a symbol of morality and its connection to the sublime, among other reasons.

A chapter on consequentialist approaches to art would seem to be quite straightforward: a consequentialist can judge art according to its morally significant consequences, just like anything else. But Scott Woodcock's discussion illustrates the complexity and difficulty of applying different versions of consequentialism to evaluating art. He argues that these difficulties, rather than showing any weakness in consequentialism, are appropriate to the complexities inherent in the subject matter.

In her chapter on virtues and the arts, Nancy Snow explores the recent literature on virtue aesthetics. She shows the connections between virtue ethics, virtue epistemology, and virtue aesthetics in order to cast light on how the creation and appreciation of the arts might reinforce or undermine the development of various virtues.

In her chapter, Amy Mullin surveys the range of ethical perspectives that might be called "feminist" in connection with the evaluation of art. She concludes that there is no one approach or criterion for judging art that should be called feminist, but rather a great variety. Feminist approaches to art, in fact, seem to be distinguished by their resistance to narrowness or pigeon-holing—they are inclusive, intersectional, and political.

The debate over "value interaction" is far and away the most thoroughly studied and discussed problem in contemporary Anglophone discussions of ethics and art. The question, put simply, is whether the moral judgment one makes of an artwork and the aesthetic judgment one makes of that artwork interact in some way, or whether they are independent or autonomous of one another. The first chapter on this topic, by Nils-Hennes Stear, takes up and evaluates the autonomist view (or set of views). Stear begins by reviewing autonomism's history and its connection to formalism (though see Gal's discussion here too). Stear argues that the existing arguments for autonomism suffer from a number of weaknesses, and that it should not be considered the default view.

Noël Carroll's 1996 article "Moderate Moralism" was one of the first, and one of the most cited and discussed, contemporary forays into this debate. Here Carroll expands on the view he set out in that article and defends it against a wide variety of objections. Moralism, Carroll says, is the family of views that says that ethical evaluation of art *qua* art is appropriate. Carroll defends his preferred version of moralism not only from autonomism, but also from Berys Gaut's ethicism, which Carroll understands as a particularly strong version of moralism. He also defends moralism against the view that has often been called "immoralism," which is the topic of the next chapter.

In his chapter, Daniel Jacobson also revisits and defends a position first set out by him more than twenty years ago. Jacobson prefers the term "contextualism" to describe the view that many have sometimes called "immoralism": the view that sometimes the moral defects in an artwork contribute to its aesthetic virtue. Paying careful attention to details of particular cases, Jacobson argues, shows that sometimes certain aesthetically valuable features of works are nonetheless morally flawed, but others wherein the opposite is true. Contextualism, according to Jacobson, relies on some very modest and plausible assumptions about art and ethics.

The final chapter in this section takes up a position that has been largely overlooked. Becca Rothfeld here defends aestheticism: the view that ethical judgments of artworks are sometimes at least partly grounded in aesthetic ones—that is, for example, a work of art can be morally bad *because* it is ugly. She surveys some historical precedents for this position, but the main goal is to show that the view is both plausible and attractive as an alternative to the three standard views of autonomism, moralism, and contextualism.

SECTION III: THE INDIVIDUAL ARTS

The third section of the *Handbook* takes up a number of individual art forms, and here authors consider ways in which the distinctive features of each art form give rise to specific sorts of ethical questions and problems. The list of art forms here is of course highly selective, but it includes both traditional "high" arts, as well as some forms of mass or popular art, and new art forms that have received less philosophical scrutiny. The aim in this section is to see how these ethical evaluations are made in different kinds of cases, and to see how different approaches to ethical judgments emerge from these different art forms.

Elisabeth Schellekens's chapter on ethics in paintings dives into particular cases. Schellekens offers a taxonomy of different ways in which paintings pictorially engage with ethics, such as the representation of a moral ideal, a moral emotion, or an ethical event that implicates the viewer. She focuses on what she calls ethical issues "internal" to painting, relating to the experience of the work itself and its thematic content. The value of these ethical elements of painting, she argues, is far from straightforward, involving problems of interpretation, reception, and more.

It is hard to think of an artform where ethics is more often discussed than literature. In his chapter, Peter Lamarque defends a conception of literature that recognizes that does not reduce literature to morality. Looking closely at a range of literary examples, Lamarque makes a robust case for literary autonomism. Attending to ethical issues in literature is not the same as thinking that what makes a work ethically good is the same as what makes it good as literature.

In his chapter on film, Carl Plantinga focuses on the ethical salience of film's engaging the audience's emotions. Reviewing the history of this relatively new art form, Plantinga concludes that an ethical approach to film must focus on the phenomenon of spectatorship. He argues that film has both positive moral potential, as when it engages and increases our empathy, and negative potential, as when it plays into and amplifies harmful stereotypes.

Kathleen Higgins's approach to thinking about music is attentive to the range and variety of musical traditions from around the world. She maintains that a philosophical focus on music "itself" is not fruitful; we need to be attentive to contextual factors, including music's social and psychological roles. Like Plantinga, Higgins recognizes the moral risks as well as benefits present in music. She argues that music in its fullest sense offers indirect contributions to human flourishing, as well as posing some moral dangers.

The art of theater is an ancient one and has long been a center of moral attention. In his chapter, James Hamilton attends closely to the moral problems that theatrical performers have grappled with. That is, in contrast to Plantinga's chapter on film, the focus is not only on the ethics of being a spectator but also on the morally salient elements of performing. Hamilton considers the moral risks of acting, including the risks of preparing for a role and the moral challenges of cooperation with others. He concludes with a discussion of the moral obligations that performers have to spectators, arguing that there is nothing morally wrong with plays that merely "invite" audiences to imagine something immoral.

Like theater, dance faces ethical questions about performers who must interact with one another and with an audience in the same space, but there is also much that is distinctive. In her chapter, Aili Whalen reviews a variety of specific issues that arise from performers sharing space, touching one another, and interacting in highly intimate ways. She also discusses political aspects of dance, including problems of cultural appropriation and discrimination, which illustrate some of the issues discussed on the fourth section. She closes with a discussion of the impact of the COVID-19 pandemic and the awareness it has brought to public health considerations in the ethics of dance performance.

Saul Fisher's discussion of ethics in architecture centers on a provocative idea: that works of architecture can be thought of as though they were agents, which then can have moral virtues or vices. Fisher notes that we *live* with architecture, that architecture has a life span, and that it both shapes and is shaped by our behavior. Works of architecture— our homes, our places of work and worship, and so on—serve as moral partners in our lives, and this service can be done well or badly.

Christopher Bartel takes up the ethics of video games, an artform that is the recurring subject of much moral hand-wringing in the popular press. While much of this public discussion is focused on the rather narrow question of whether playing video games is bad for the players, Bartel takes a broader view. He distinguishes between moral questions that are internal to gameplay, such as players imaginatively absorbing the values of a game while they play it, and those that are external to gameplay itself, which includes a wide variety of issues such as the environmental impact of the game industry. He also takes up moral issues on the border between internal and external, such as the role of "trolling" in games, and the ethics of multiplayer games.

A. W. Eaton offers an overview and assessment of pornography and erotic art. She begins by arguing that the attempts to distinguish between the two is itself an immoral project, as the works that are generally classified as "erotic art" and thereby superior are also those produced by and for upper-class white men. In her study of the ethics of por- nography and erotic art, Eaton attends to the moral dangers of inegalitarian works, as well as the morally possibilities of egalitarian, sex-positive works of pornography and erotic art.

Paul Butterfield's chapter on humor takes up three main questions: whether humor can be morally wrong at all, why humor might be morally wrong when it is wrong, and how humor's moral status might affect its funniness. In doing so, Butterfield gives us an- other look at the value interaction problem. Throughout, Butterfield stresses the ambi- guity inherent in humor, and how this complicates efforts to assess humor morally.

Jeanette Bicknell, Jennifer Judkins, and Carolyn Korsmeyer take up another topic that is perennially important but seems to be especially salient in recent years: the ethics of monuments and memorials. Monuments and memorials are built to endure, and the people who build them typically hope that their messages will last. But Bicknell, Judkins, and Korsmeyer argue that inevitably, the meanings and audiences for these works change. That fact, and the fact that such works have an inherently public character, complicates our ethical relationship to them.

In the final chapter of this section, Anthony Cross considers a group of new forms of cultural expressions that make use of the internet and social media, including viral videos and gifs. Cross emphasizes the radical nature of these new media, which allow nearly everyone to participate as creators and audience simultaneously. The communities that form around these practices can strengthen commitments to moral values, for good or ill. And such media also challenge traditional conceptions of artistic ownership.

SECTION IV: PROBLEMS

The final section of this *Handbook* takes up moral problems in ethics and art that are not specific to any one artform. Some of these problems have to do with artists and ownership: what are the limits of artists' rights, and how should we understand the moral claims arising from the ownership of art? What role do governments and audiences play here? Some of these problems arise from art's role in society and how it can advance or set back a political movement. How are different marginalized groups represented in art? What counts as cultural appropriation in the arts, and under what conditions is it wrong? And some of these problems have important psychological aspects. How does art engage our moral imagination, and what can we learn from art, morally speaking? Each of the chapters in this section looks at some of these legal, political, and psychological questions, often all at once.

The first chapter in this section, by Karen Gover, is about artistic authorship. Gover studies the limits of the moral rights of artists, and discusses how this intersects with other moral rights, including that of the owner of the artwork and of the public. Gover argues that the rights of artists cannot always take precedence over other moral considerations.

Mary Beth Willard picks up some of the problems discussed in Anthony Cross's chapter on internet art as well as those discussed in Jeanette Bicknell, Jennifer Judkins, and Carolyn Korsmeyer's chapter on monuments and memorials. Willard is interested in the problems that arise when an artwork is public and its meaning is publicly contested. While Gover focuses on the rights of individual artists, Willard considers the role and value of group agency in fixing moral meanings. She shows that such art poses problems for our conceptions of democracy that we have only just begun to explore.

What should we do with the work of immoral artists? Some people think that we must "separate the art from the artist" while others find a grave moral wrong in continuing to enjoy artworks made by vicious people. In his chapter, Erich Hatala Matthes attempts to find a middle ground between these two positions. He argues that whether or not to engage with the work of immoral artists is not a yes or no question, but that we must instead think about *how* we engage with such works.

In the following chapter, C. Thi Nguyen and Matthew Strohl also take on another highly polarizing issue—the appropriation of artistic style—and they try to find a middle ground. Some philosophers have argued for highly restrictive approaches, according to which members of outgroups should not ever participate in artistic forms belonging to another group. Others have argued for a more permissive approach that minimizes the alleged wrongs or harms suffered by group members. Nguyen and Strohl stress the dangers of paternalistic approaches to this issue, and defend a view built around group intimacy and consent.

Whereas many people disagree about whether cultural appropriation is wrong at all, the moral questions about forgery do not focus on whether it is wrong, but on what exactly constitutes forgery, and on what makes it wrong. Darren Hudson Hick, through careful discussion of individual cases, argues that the wrong of forgery is not one thing, but a constellation of wrongs of varying degrees of moral seriousness, and they include not merely harms to specific persons, but also issues of moral integrity and trust.

As in the case of forgery, it is widely accepted that the vandalism of art is morally wrong. In her chapter, Sondra Bacharach looks more closely at the variety of vandalism and comes to the surprising conclusion that vandalism is not always morally bad, and may sometimes be morally good. Bacharach carefully distinguishes between different types of vandalism, including "invisible" and "additive" vandalism, where the vandal is also a kind of artist.

As we saw in a number of chapters in the first section (such as Man's chapter on modern China), the question of the government's role in regulating and even censoring art is highly controversial. In his chapter, Brian Soucek considers the ethics of government regulation and sponsorship, but also goes on to discuss various kinds of nongovernmental power, including corporate power and popular movements, such as "cancel culture" and its backlash. In doing so, Soucek argues that the question of *who* is doing the regulation may be the most important moral question.

Many of the chapters in this volume discuss race and racism: the arts have been one of the most contested sites for thinking about race (shown most vividly in Carter and Mason's chapter on the Harlem Renaissance). Adriana Clavel-Vázquez's chapter on race and racism in art explores a central tension between two competing ideas. On the one hand, art can be a vehicle for resisting racism and asserting a positive racial identity; on the other, art can reinforce and strengthen existing racial hierarchies. Understanding the ethical value of race in art will mean connecting the moral with the political.

Paul C. Taylor's chapter on ethics and representation in art considers the ways in which we ask of art that it be appropriately representative. He distinguishes between four different senses of representation: a work's subject matter (aboutness), the interests that a work serves (fiduciary), how a group of persons is portrayed (exemplarity), and the sense in which a work captures a cultural moment (expressiveness). Through an examination of a couple of recent examples, including the treatment of Black characters in *Hamilton*, Taylor argues that an understanding of the ethical meanings of representation is essential to our thinking about a host of other ethical questions involving the arts.

In their chapter on the imagination, Joy Shim and Shen-yi Liao survey a wide range of interrelated topics. Some of these debates are quite familiar to Anglophone philosophers, such as the problem of imaginative resistance, in which audiences fail to imaginatively engage with artworks that ask them to accept an immoral idea. But Shim and Liao also direct our attention to a variety of other important questions about the imagination, such as whether and how imagination exercised through art can help to bring about political change.

The final chapter of the volume, by Eileen John, is on the topic of moral learning from art. While much of the attention on ethics and art has been negative (e.g., Mozi, Plato, Tolstoy), one very old idea is that the arts have a central role to play in one's moral education. John distinguishes between four ways that moral learning might happen in the arts: protesting the moral *status quo*, expanding our moral circle, bearing moral witness, and starting a moral conversation. John defends the claim that art has a role to play in moral learning, while acknowledging the risks that go along with it.

CONCLUSION

The forty-five chapters in this volume, taken together, cover a lot of ground. If there is any common theme to be found here, it is likely to be just how fertile that ground is. Whether taking on old problems or new ones, well-known art forms with centuries of philosophical scholarship or still-evolving new forms, there is more to these moral questions than it seems at first. Collectively, the authors of these chapters issue an invitation to think and argue about these problems carefully and deeply.

As noted at the outset, there is no recognized subfield of applied ethics called "art ethics" or the like. And, looking at the contributions in this volume, it seems that there should not be. Such a classification would likely be too limiting. To think about ethics and the arts is not merely to apply ethical thinking to the arts: it means being ready to rethink our own assumptions about ethics, about the arts, about politics, history, and more.

Tolstoy was certainly right about one thing: art *matters* to morality. We just need to figure out how.

REFERENCE

Tolstoy, Leo. 1904. *What is Art?* Translated by Almeyer Maude. New York: Funk & Wagnalls Company.

PART I

HISTORICAL PERSPECTIVES ON ETHICS AND ART

CHAPTER 2

ETHICS AND THE ARTS IN EARLY CHINA

ERIC L. HUTTON

INTRODUCTION

CONCERNING the relations between ethics and the arts, China provides such abundant material for reflection that no short essay can do it justice, not even one confined to just the early, formative period of Chinese philosophy (the sixth to third centuries BCE). So instead of presenting a comprehensive overview, this chapter will give nonspecialists a highly selective introduction to some relevant discussions. Hopefully, some of my observations will also interest specialists in Chinese thought. Since uncertainty surrounds the dating of various texts, my analysis will be organized topically, rather than chronologically. I aim to equip readers to see both where debates in the Chinese tradition may overlap those of other traditions and where Chinese views about ethics and the arts are relatively distinctive.

To begin with, one must use caution in applying the categories of "ethics" and "the arts" to ancient Chinese discourse, as neither maps neatly onto how the Chinese themselves tended to talk about things. In the former case, while contemporary philosophers often distinguish ethics from political philosophy rather sharply, most ancient Chinese thinkers do not, and they also do not particularly treat aesthetics as a third, distinct subject matter. On the other hand, what constitutes "the arts" is a complicated question even among current Western thinkers, and the groupings of practices and products given in ancient Chinese texts do not correspond well with the category of "the arts" nowadays.[1] Addressing these methodological problems adequately would require more space than

---

[1] For example, one ancient Chinese term, *liu yi* 六藝, is typically translated as "the Six Arts" in English, and it refers to (1) ritual, (2) music, (3) archery, (4) horsemanship/charioteering, (5) calligraphy, and (6) counting/mathematics. While the second and fifth of these will fit comfortably within many people's notion of "the arts," the rest may not. That discrepancy raises a question about the extent to which the term *yi* 藝 corresponds to the notion of an "art." As noted in the main text, however, due to constraints of space here I have chosen not to examine Chinese categories such as *yi* 藝 and other similar

is available, and so lest we get mired in those questions, here I will simply focus on some concrete cases that would on many accounts be considered relevant to understanding the relations between "ethics" and "the arts" in ancient Chinese thought. I will also highlight how Chinese views might prompt adjustments to those categories themselves.

Now, archaeological and textual evidence shows that many of the arts as currently conceived were practiced in ancient China: visual arts (such as painting and calligraphy, and production of objects from clay, metal, stone, wood, or bone), literary arts (especially poetry), performing arts (such as signing, music, and dance), textile arts (such as weaving and embroidery), culinary arts (especially in the form of fine dining), and architecture. Of these, what figures most frequently in philosophical discussions is a combination of poetry, song, the playing of instruments, and dance, which were often simply subsumed under the label of "music" (*yue* 樂). Therefore, most of the examples discussed here will concern that art.

To orient the discussion, let us start from *Analects* 3.25, which depicts Confucius evaluating two pieces of music:

> The Master [i.e., Confucius] said of the *Shao* that "It is completely beautiful, and moreover completely good." He said of the *Wu* that "It is completely beautiful, yet not completely good."[2]

These comments raise three issues relevant for the present chapter. First is the appraisal of music in terms of how "good" (*shan* 善) it is, where this is distinct from—and potentially out of alignment with—how "beautiful" (*mei* 美) it is. While the term *shan* should not uncritically be taken as simply equivalent to the Western notion of what is morally "good," that term's role in Chinese discussions is nevertheless highly analogous to "goodness" in Western ethical discourse, which makes translating *shan* as "good" a reasonable first approximation of its sense, even if in other ways it is not a perfect match (and *mutatis mutandis* for rendering *mei* as "beautiful").[3] To that extent, this passage provides a fairly clear instance of the idea that at least some artworks can be bearers of ethical value.

Second, in the *Analects,* Confucius serves as a moral exemplar. Thus, the very fact that he comments on this difference between the *Shao* and *Wu* casts listening to and properly appreciating music (and potentially other artworks, too) as a facet of ethical life. While *Analects* 3.25 does not specify what one should *do* given this difference, other passages clearly indicate that some pieces of music should not be heard (*Analects* 15.11), such that living ethically is portrayed as also involving knowing which music ought to be criticized and avoided.

A third point emerges from considering the particular pieces of music mentioned in *Analects* 3.25. Namely, the *Shao* and *Wu* were believed to have been composed by or

---

notions. My approach focusing on particular examples can hopefully demonstrate that one can still offer useful observations without such an examination.

[2]   All translations here are my own, unless noted otherwise.

[3]   For further discussion of how *shan* differs from "goodness" and the implication of this difference, see Hutton (2008).

at the direction of ancient sage kings, whom Confucius idolized as moral paragons. (Hence, although he deems the *Wu* not completely good, he likely does not think it is worthless or should not be heard.) With this history presumed, Confucius thus implicitly endorses the notion that the ethical life includes *making* music, a commitment illustrated and reinforced by other instances in the *Analects* (e.g., 7.32 and 17.20) that portray Confucius himself as singing and playing instruments.

Analects 3.25 thus touches on two concerns at the intersection between ethics and the arts, which are at least partly connected to values that artworks can have or lack: namely, concerns about (1) the consumption of the arts and (2) the production of the arts. The *Analects* may not have initiated the Chinese debates about these matters, but it is clear that various early Chinese thinkers disagreed about both, for various reasons. In what follows, I will structure my survey around these two concerns, then conclude by considering one element of the Chinese tradition that may stretch our notions of "the arts" and "ethics."

ETHICS AND CONSUMPTION OF THE ARTS

The music favored in the *Analects* is what at that time resembled our notion of "classical" music, namely elegant music from a past age, deriving largely from the royal court or other aristocratic settings. However, the idea that listening to and appreciating such music (and other arts) is an important part of an ethical life was challenged by some, which prompted defenses by others who articulated justifications that are absent or underdeveloped in the *Analects*.

One such challenge came from Mozi (fl. c. fifth to fourth century BCE). That challenge is largely consequentialist in character and focuses on the material resources and time sacrificed for musical performances, while bypassing the issue of music's ethical content (or lack thereof). The following passage exemplifies several features of Mozi's view:

> Our teacher Mozi says, "The benevolent (*ren* 仁) surely are those who devote themselves to finding ways to promote what is beneficial to the world while eliminating what is harmful. . . . If something benefits the world then they will do it. If it does not benefit the world then they will stop doing it. Moreover, . . . if there is something that attracts their eyes, delights their ears, pleases their palates, and gives comfort to their bodies but this thing can only be gotten by sacrificing the people's stock of food and clothing, they will not engage in it."
>
> And so our teacher Mozi does not condemn music because he thinks that the sounds of bells, drums, zithers, and pipes are not pleasing, nor because he thinks that inlaid and carved patterns and designs are not fine, nor because he thinks that roasts of grain- and grass-fed meat are not delicious, nor because he thinks that high towers, lofty halls, and secluded pavilions are not comfortable. Though his body knows the comfort of such places, his mouth the relish of such food, his eye the fineness of such patterns, and his ears the pleasure of such sounds, nevertheless, he sees

that it does not . . . promote the benefit of the people in the world today. And so our teacher Mozi says, "Musical performances are wrong!"

Our teacher Mozi says, "These days, kings, dukes, and other persons of high rank . . . must heavily tax the people in order to enjoy the sounds of bells, drums, zithers, and pipes. . . . [And so] those who are hungry are unable to get food, those who are cold are unable to obtain clothing, and those who toil are not afforded a chance to rest. These are the three greatest hardships upon the people. But what if we play the great bells, strike up the drums, sound the zithers, blow the pipes, and dance with shields and battle axes? Will this enable the people to procure food or clothing? I believe that such performances will not produce such results."[4]

As the third paragraph makes clear, Mozi's argument targets primarily the powerful, and the performances they are criticized for consuming are elaborate productions involving several instruments, multiple musicians, singers, and dancers, which was characteristic of the aristocratic music commended in the *Analects*. However, the passage opens by invoking general ethical considerations about the behavior of one who is "benevolent," and hence the reasoning here potentially applies to anyone: if partaking of music causes some to go without basic necessities, then that action is wrong. Moreover, although the focus here is music, the second paragraph implies that the argument can apply to other arts as well. At the same time, the argument's consequentialist standard is curiously narrow, appealing only to relatively concrete, physical goods such as food, clothing, and rest, while ignoring or discounting less tangible goods. For that reason, as scholars have noted, despite how Mozi's conclusion is framed in terms seeming to attack *all* musical performances, the argument does not actually prohibit all music, because some performances will require no sacrifice of physical goods or productive time (e.g., farmers listening to songs without instrumental accompaniment, at night before bedtime during winter, when it is too cold and too dark to do any other work) (Van Norden 2007, 172–174).[5] The argument is also vulnerable to refutation—as we shall see—by appeal to a broader consequentialist standard that considers how listening to music has beneficial effects for human psychology and for society more broadly that may outweigh the costs of producing musical performances (and likewise for other arts).

Other challenges to the notion that one should partake of the "classical" music favored in the *Analects* are presented in the *Laozi* and the *Zhuangzi*. Those challenges focus on what might be called the "conventionality" or "artificiality" of the standards embodied in such music. Chapter 12 of the *Laozi* provides a succinct example:

The five colors blind our eyes.
The five notes deafen our ears.
The five flavors deaden our palates.[6]

---

[4] Translation from Ivanhoe and Van Norden (2006, 105–106).

[5] This view—which is arguably the consensus among Anglophone interpreters of Mozi—is rejected by Park (2020). I think her textual arguments are unsound, but lack space to rebut them here.

[6] Translation from Ivanhoe and Van Norden (2006, 168).

The "five notes" represent the conventionally recognized elements for composing "proper" music like that praised by Confucius, and the remark that they "deafen" the ears is best not taken literally, but rather as a figurative way of warning that rigid adherence to these standards and preference for music conforming to them will impair one's ability to appreciate other sorts of sounds and music that do not fit this conventional mold but which nonetheless deserve to be appreciated (and as the other lines indicate, the point can be extended to the visual and culinary arts). In particular, the *Laozi* hints at two such alternatives. One is what we might think of as "rustic" music that is simple and humble, as opposed to "elegant" music following the "classical" standards. The *Laozi* diagnoses many of humanity's troubles as deriving from a mistaken scheme of conventional values that lead people to pursue unnecessary goods, and the pursuit of these goods is unfulfilling, self-defeating, or leads to destructive competition. As an antidote, the text elsewhere (in Chapter 80) extols a primitive form of village life as ideal, and although that chapter does not discuss music specifically, a "rustic" sort of music would fit quite naturally with the other simple enjoyments it prescribes.[7] The other alternative at which the text hints (in Chapter 41)[8] is a form of "music" that is not man-made at all, and may not even be audible, at least in any ordinary sense.

While the *Laozi* offers only the barest hint of this latter alternative, a more explicit version of the idea appears in the *Zhuangzi*, though there, too, it remains only a sketch. Chapter 2 begins:

> Master Dapple . . . sat leaning on his armrest. He looked up and sighed, vacant, as though he'd lost his counterpart. Yancheng Ziyou stood before him in attendance. "What's this?" he said. "Can the body really be turned into dried wood? Can the mind really be turned into dead ashes? The one leaning on the armrest now is not the one who leaned on it before!"
>
> Master Dapple said, "My, isn't that a good question you've asked, Ziyou! Just now I lost myself. Do you know? You've heard the pipes of humans, but not the pipes of earth. Or if you've heard the pipes of earth, you haven't heard the pipes of Heaven."
>
> "May I ask what you mean?"
>
> "The Big Lump belches breath and it's called wind. . . . When it starts, the ten thousand holes begin to hiss. Don't you hear the *shsh-shsh*? In the mountain vales there are great trees a hundred spans around with knots like noses, like mouths, like ears, like sockets. . . . Gurgling, humming, hooting, whistling, shouting, shrieking, moaning, gnashing! . . . In a light breeze it's a little chorus, but in a gusty wind it's a huge orchestra. . . . Haven't you witnessed the brouhaha?"

---

[7] The *Laozi* is famously ambiguous, and the idea I mention here depends on a particular reading of the latter half of Chapter 80, such as that in the Heshang Gong commentary. For a translation, see Tadd 2013.

[8] Again, this point depends on a particular reading of Chapter 41. The commentaries by Wang Bi and Cheng Xuanying are two such examples. For a translation of the former, see Lynn (2004), and for the latter, see Assandri (2021).

> Ziyou said, "So the pipes of earth are those holes, and the pipes of humans are bamboo flutes. May I ask about the pipes of Heaven?"
>
> Master Dapple said, "Blowing the ten thousand differences, making each be itself and all choose themselves—who provokes it?"[9]

This passage may be parodying the *Analects,* which features a disciple of Confucius named Ziyou (who, among other things, tries to teach the common people music at *Analects* 17.4). More important, though, is that here Master Dapple has special abilities, and when asked about these, he replies by mentioning three different "pipings." How this answers Ziyou's question is rather unclear, but that problem need not detain us, as it is apparent enough that part of what gives Master Dapple his abilities and qualifies him as teacher is his grasp of the three pipings, especially the third. What is the piping of Heaven? Here, Heaven (*tian* 天, lit. "sky") seems—as it often does in the *Zhuangzi*— to refer metonymically to the processes of nature broadly. The piping of Heaven thus designates the way these processes generate the world's myriad things, each unique to some degree ("the ten thousand differences" mentioned in the passage). The passage labels those processes as music and portrays the ability to "hear" and appreciate that music—even though those processes are often soundless—as part of the ideal that Master Dapple represents. In comparison, the piping of humans—and by extension, the music favored by Confucians—seems paltry.

As noted earlier, these rival views about whether to partake of music and which sorts of music one should consume (and likewise for the other arts) provoked rebuttals from later Confucians. Here we will review one such response from the *Xunzi*. That text's extended defense of music explicitly targets Mozi, but also contains elements that, when taken together with other parts of the *Xunzi*, outline a response to the challenges from the *Laozi* and *Zhuangzi* as well.

The *Xunzi*'s refutation of Mozi adopts precisely the potential strategy mentioned above, namely pointing to the psychological effects of listening to music and other social consequences flowing from those effects, in order to defend the value of listening to music. Chapter 20 states:

> Music is joy, an unavoidable human disposition. So, people cannot be without music; if they feel joy, they must express it in sound and give it shape in movement . . . but if it takes shape and does not accord with the Way, then there will inevitably be chaos. The former kings [i.e., the sage kings] hated such chaos, and therefore they established the sounds of the *Ya* and the *Song* in order to guide them. They caused the sounds to be enjoyable without becoming dissolute. They caused the patterns to be distinctive without becoming degenerate. . . . This is the manner in which the former kings created music, and so what is Mozi doing denouncing it?

---

[9] References to the *Zhuangzi* will be given according to the numbering system in Lau and Chen (2000) (hereafter referred to as *Zhuangzi*, HKCS). This passage is from 2/3/14–24. Translation modified slightly from Ivanhoe and Van Norden (2006, 213–214).

And so, when music is performed in the ancestral temple and the ruler and ministers, superiors and inferiors, listen to it together, none fail to become harmoniously respectful. When it is performed within the home and father and sons, elder and younger brothers listen to it together, none fail to become harmoniously affectionate. And when it is performed in the village, and old and young people listen to it together, none fail to become harmoniously cooperative. Thus, music . . . is sufficient to lead people in a single, unified way, and is sufficient to bring order to . . . them. This is the method by which the former kings created music, and so what is Mozi doing denouncing it?[10]

Here, music is a means to guide people's emotions in constructive ways, and, especially as the second paragraph indicates, listening to music together becomes a means to encourage harmony, respect, affection, and cooperation among people. Thus, consuming (the right kind of) music has nonmaterial benefits that can potentially more than make up for the time and resources spent on it. That is especially so if, as the *Xunzi* suggests elsewhere,[11] such harmony, respect, affection, and cooperation among people actually facilitate producing those goods that Mozi worries about sacrificing for musical performances.[12]

The passage just quoted also stresses music as the product of sage kings, and we can use this point to begin reconstructing its response to the challenges expressed in the *Laozi* and *Zhuangzi*. In numerous ways, the *Xunzi* argues that human artifice is a crucial element in the life proper for human beings, and the text explicitly criticizes a recurrent viewpoint in the *Zhuangzi* we noted earlier. Namely, in that *Zhuangzi* passage, the piping of humans and of Heaven—which represents nature more broadly—are distinguished from one another, and (knowledge of) the latter is associated with a higher state. The *Xunzi* complains that such a view "was fixated on the Heavenly and did not understand the value of the human" (*Xunzi*, HKCS 21/103/9; Hutton 2014, 227).[13] In the case of music, the complaint would amount to denying that the "music" produced by nature, though coming from a more powerful and pervasive force, is thereby more worthy of human attention than human music that arises from and answers to human psychological needs. Furthermore, insofar as the *Xunzi* thus defends what might be considered a moderate anthropocentrism,[14] its focus on the music created by the sage kings suggests another, more straightforward objection to the idea of a nonhuman, even soundless

---

[10] References to the *Xunzi* will be given according to the numbering system in Lau and Chen (1996) (hereafter referred to as *Xunzi*, HKCS). This passage is from 20/98/14 – 20/99/2. Translation from Hutton (2014, 218).

[11] See *Xunzi*, HKCS 10/44/20 – 10/45/14; Hutton (2014, 88–90). Part of this passage is quoted later in the main text of this chapter, on p. 22.

[12] Due to constraints of space, here I offer only the barest sketch of the *Xunzi*'s argument. For more thorough analysis, see Hutton and Harold (2016).

[13] For more discussion of this criticism, see Kjellberg (1996).

[14] I call this view "moderate anthropocentrism" because the *Xunzi* emphasizes the value of *human* concerns and the adoption of a *human* perspective in addressing them. It also deems human beings superior to all other animals, at least when people are morally cultivated (see *Xunzi*, HKCS 9/39/10;

music proposed in the *Laozi* and *Zhuangzi*, which is that the phenomena in question—no matter how beautiful—simply should not be labeled "music," precisely because they are not human products. That response is not explicitly articulated in the *Xunzi*, but Chapter 22 extensively criticizes abuses of language by rival thinkers, and such an objection would be a very natural extension of its arguments.[15]

Regarding the other challenge raised by the *Laozi*, namely that prizing "refined," "classical" music (and other such arts) leads people to strive after such goods in harmful ways while failing to appreciate humbler, simpler goods that are more readily available, the *Xunzi* provides two responses. On the one hand, it insists that a properly cultivated person *will* be able to delight in more minimal sights and sounds—someone incapable of enjoying anything other than the "highest" arts would be judged as incorrectly developed (*Xunzi*, HKCS 22/112/9–21; Hutton 2014, 246–247).[16] On the other hand, the *Xunzi* claims that people naturally desire the "utmost" sights, sounds, flavors, and so on (*Xunzi*, HKCS 11/51/24–11/52/1; Hutton 2014, 104) and it implies that the sage kings' elaborate musical pieces (and other arts) will, by their very magnificence, provide greater satisfaction for these desires (*Xunzi*, HKCS 22/109/17–18; Hutton 2014, 240).[17] Such artworks are thus liable to become objects of pursuit and competition, just as the *Laozi* worries, but the *Xunzi* proposes that with the right sort of education and social structures, people's desires for these goods not only can be managed so as to avoid destructive consequences, but moreover can be used to build a system of incentives that actually conduces to social order benefitting all:

> [In] the matter of being a lord and superior to others, to lack beautiful things and ornaments will leave one incapable of uniting the people. . . . Thus, the former kings were sure to strike great bells, beat sounding drums, blow on reeds and pipes, and play lyres and zithers, in order to fill up their ears. They were sure to have carving, polishing, engraving, and inlay, insignias and ornaments, in order to fill up their eyes. They were sure to have fine meats and good grains, the five flavors and various spices, in order to fill up their mouths. . . . They thereby caused all the people in the world to know that what they wished for and desired lay here with the kings. Thus, their rewards worked. . . . When rewards work . . . then the

---

Hutton 2014, 76). However, the *Xunzi* also stresses that the proper moral perspective regards human beings as a partner to (rather than master of) Heaven and Earth, and stresses the need for human beings to take care of (rather than simply exploit) the natural world. For more on these issues, see Ivanhoe (2014).

[15] For detailed discussion of these arguments, see Fraser (2016).

[16] Despite the text's claims, it remains an empirical question whether consuming some forms of music will unavoidably interfere with one's ability to appreciate other sorts of music, so the *Xunzi*'s response to the *Laozi* on this point does not fully resolve the issue.

[17] This latter passage attacks the claims that "Fine meats are not any more flavorful [i.e., than other foods]" and "Great bells are not any more entertaining [than other sounds]." Who propounded these claims is not known, but these ideas may have circulated alongside the sort of complaint in the *Laozi* against "high" arts. In rejecting those claims, the *Xunzi* thus implies that refined arts do indeed provide greater satisfaction for the natural human desires for the "utmost" sounds, flavors, and so on.

worthy can be gotten to advance . . . and the capable . . . can be accorded their proper offices. When it is like this, then the myriad things will obtain what is appropriate to them . . . and . . . one will obtain harmony among mankind. (*Xunzi*, HKCS 10/45/16–22; Hutton 2014, 90)

Apart from rejecting the *Laozi*'s objections (and those of Mozi as well) to elaborate music and other arts, one further feature of this passage merits attention. Elsewhere, the *Xunzi* clearly advocates for structuring government around a hierarchy of virtue, with the most virtuous at the top (*Xunzi*, HKCS 9/35/3–6, 12/59/18 – 12/60/1, 18/89/18; Hutton 2014, 68, 123, 200). When understood in light of that idea, this passage presents consumption of the finest arts not just as a fitting reward for virtue, but moreover as something to be undertaken as a *model* for others. In other words, the virtuous person should enjoy the arts as a means to encourage others to be virtuous as well—such enjoyment is not merely an aesthetic experience, but is itself an ethical act, insofar as it represents to others how a good person lives.[18]

Regrettably, the preceding discussion has had to omit several other aspects of early Chinese debates over consumption of the arts, but it must suffice for now. At this point, let us turn to the other side of the coin, and consider early Chinese views about producing art.

ETHICS AND PRODUCTION OF THE ARTS

To start, let me emphasize the difference between practicing the arts as *part* of the ideal life versus making the arts one's *profession*. This point is important, because some disagreements among Chinese thinkers play out in terms of this difference. Mozi's arguments against consuming music, on the grounds that the resources and time spent on it would be better used elsewhere, apply straightforwardly with equal force (of lack thereof) to producing music and other arts, whether as one's profession or not, so we need not discuss his views further.

The early Confucians' ethical ideal is a life dedicated to bringing about a harmonious, orderly, and prosperous society, which they consider best pursued through government service. Consequently, they do not hold up as ethical models those people who practice the arts as their profession. They allow that professional artists will be a necessary part of the ideal society, but the Confucians' view of how that society should function, namely

---

[18] One important topic that I lack space to discuss here is the issue of enjoying art by oneself versus in front of others. The *Xunzi* passage quoted in the main text presupposes that the king's enjoyment of the arts is quite public and widely known. While in other cases, a person might enjoy some artworks out of view of others, the *Xunzi* (like some other Confucian texts) stresses that "[a virtuous person's] slightest word, his most subtle movement, all can serve as a model for others" (*Xunzi*, HKCS 1/3/14–15; Hutton 2014, 5). On such a view, enjoying arts in solitude also sets a standard.

according to the hierarchy of virtue mentioned earlier, implies that those most virtuous will not be professional artists.

On the other hand, as noted earlier, the Confucians *do* consider practicing the arts an important part of the ethically ideal life, even if it should not be one's occupation. The *Xunzi*'s discussion of music again provides perhaps the clearest articulation of their rationale for that view. In a passage quoted previously, the text explains that music arises from and expresses certain emotions, but in virtue of that feature, music can guide the emotions and the actions resulting from them. By that token, performing music oneself can serve as a method of self-cultivation, and hence it figures prominently in early Confucians' moral curriculum.[19] Beyond that, however, Confucian texts stress the importance of expressing one's values, which also provides a reason for performing music as part of the ideal life, namely that it makes manifest (and reinforces) one's commitments to what is proper. Consider the *Xunzi*'s description of the "gentleman" (*junzi* 君子), who in Confucian texts represents the virtuous person: "[As] for bells, drums, pipes, chimes, zithers, and mouth-organs, the *Shao, Xia, Hu, Wu, Zhuo, Huan, Xiao*, and *Xiang*, these are the forms used by the gentleman when he is moved by what he finds delightful and enjoyable" (*Xunzi*, HKCS 19/98/3–5; Hutton 2014, 216). The gentleman *ex hypothesi* delights in what is proper, and so in performing these pieces of music, he conveys his devotion to the correct way of life and simultaneously highlights the content of that life. Notice as well that two pieces of music in this list, the *Shao* and *Wu*, are the same pieces we saw Confucius appraising, and the others were either likewise thought to be derived from the sage kings or to celebrate their achievements. While the *Xunzi* does not evaluate these musical pieces individually like *Analects* 3.25, various passages suggest that the *Xunzi*, too, sees them as bearers of ethical value. To that extent, its view is that an ethical person will express their ethical values through performing music that is ethical itself.

So stated, this view has two features deserving comment. One is that although performing music is made part of the ideal life, creativity and originality are not emphasized. While the gentleman's performances *may* display creativity and originality, the performances are not valued for that: the gentleman need not devise new compositions, nor offer new interpretations of old compositions. The other point to note is that while the aim of practicing the arts to cultivate and express one's ethical values could in theory be satisfied by many different arts, the Confucians do not

---

[19] See, for example, *Analects* 8.8, and the multiple references to music appearing *passim* in the first two chapters of the *Xunzi*, which focus on self-cultivation. Some of these remarks are ambiguous about whether one is to study music merely through listening to and appreciating it, or whether one should also learn to perform it. For the Confucians, such ambiguity is natural, since either method can aid one's moral development, but given the multiple depictions in the *Analects* of Confucius singing or playing music, the references to studying music there are typically taken as including learning to perform it. For a clear example from the *Xunzi*, see HKCS 20/100/6–7, Hutton (2014, 221 [especially lines 121–126]).

embrace that possibility, and instead focus almost exclusively on music as the art that a virtuous person will practice. In this respect, the Confucians' view evinces a somewhat curious asymmetry—while they promote consumption of numerous arts by the virtuous person, they do not promote a similarly wide range of arts for the virtuous person to practice. Exactly why this asymmetry exists is unclear, since the Confucian texts do not argue for practicing music *over* other arts. Perhaps the asymmetry may derive from cultural norms of the time that led the Confucians to disregard the potential value of practicing other arts. For example, textile arts were generally women's work, whereas most Confucian texts were written by men and for men. Likewise, other arts (e.g., ceramics) were the province of commoners, whereas Confucians belonged mainly to the *shi* 士 class, which was composed of low-ranking aristocrats. Apart from such explanations based on cultural bias though, the Confucians may have a more substantial reason for favoring music over other arts, but in order to appreciate what that might be, it will be helpful first to consider a rival view.

As before, the *Zhuangzi* provides one of the most noteworthy contrasts in early China to the views of the Confucians (and Mozi) on these topics. The following anecdote from Chapter 19 illustrates that contrast strikingly:

> Woodworker Qing . . . made a bell stand, and . . . everyone who saw it marveled, for it seemed to be the work of gods or spirits. When the marquis of Lu saw it, he asked, "What art is it you have?"
>
> Qing replied, "I am only a craftsman—how would I have any art? There is one thing, however. When I am going to make a bell stand, ... I always fast in order to still my mind. When I have fasted for three days, I no longer have any thought of congratulations or rewards, of titles or stipends. When I have fasted for five days, I no longer have any thought of praise or blame, of skill or clumsiness. And when I have fasted for seven days, I am so still that I forget that I have four limbs and a form and body. By that time, . . . [my] skill is concentrated and all outside distractions fade away. After that, I go into the mountain forest and examine the Heavenly nature of the trees. If I find one of superlative form, and I can see a bell stand there, I put my hand to the job of carving; if not, I let it go. This way I am simply matching up 'Heaven' with 'Heaven.' That's probably the reason that people wonder if the results were not made by spirits." (*Zhuangzi*, HKCS 19/52/4–8; translation from Watson 2013, 152–153)

Insofar as Woodworker Qing serves as an exemplar, one divergence from the Confucian view is immediately apparent: the ideal way of life can be realized by someone who produces artworks as a profession. Moreover, note that his product is not music, but rather a carved wood object. The *Zhuangzi* thus suggests that the Confucians' preference for practicing music over other arts is unjustified. In addition to those contrasts, even though Qing is not particularly trying to be creative or original, the passage subtly celebrates the distinctiveness of his products: the implication of people mistaking his bell stands for the work of super-human entities is that *they look like no other human-made bell stands.*

The *Zhuangzi* should not, though, be understood as advocating the polar oppo-site of the Confucian view. The text presents several exemplars, a number of whom do not have the arts as their profession, and so it does not encourage taking the ideal life to require such a profession, and even less does it promote any partic-ular art over others. Some of its exemplars do make music at times, perhaps most (in)famously, the figure Zhuangzi himself—after whom the text is named—who drums on a tub and sings after his wife dies (*Zhuangzi*, HKCS 18/48/9–13; Ivanhoe and Van Norden 2006, 247). However, the text does not endorse any specific pro-gram of self-cultivation involving the performance of music or any other arts for de-veloping desirable dispositions or expressing them, and, at points, it even suggests that there is nothing particularly inevitable or even valuable about the emotion of joy (or any other emotion) that the *Xunzi* uses as the basis for arguing that a vir-tuous person will practice music (*Zhuangzi*, HKCS 3/8/21, 6/17/30; Ivanhoe and Van Norden 2006, 226, 238).[20] Hence, while the *Zhuangzi* allows that practicing music or other arts *may* be part of the ideal life, neither does it make such practices a crucial element of that life.

To understand the basis for this view, let us examine Woodworker Qing's closing remarks in the passage quoted earlier. He says he is "simply matching up 'Heaven' with 'Heaven.'" In light of the point noted previously (p. 20) that "Heaven" in the *Zhuangzi* often represents what is "natural," Burton Watson's footnote to this phrase decently captures its basic meaning by explaining that Qing is "matching his own innate nature with that of the tree" (Watson 2013, 153). To put that point less succinctly but perhaps more clearly, Qing is following certain deep-seated natural sensitivities and impulses within him that become operative after his "fasting" has removed various psychological obstacles impeding them. These sensitivities and impulses help him identify those trees whose natural structure is suited to becoming a marvelous bell stand, and he then follows that natural structure in his carving. In turn, *that* process is roughly the sort of approach that the *Zhuangzi* advocates for living in general. When to that we add the idea that things all naturally differ from one another (recall the "ten thousand differences" resulting from Heaven's piping), we can see why the text would suggest that practicing the arts, either occasionally or as one's profession, *can* be one manifestation of that approach to living, but is not to be prescribed for all. Much less, then, is there reason to favor practicing any particular art.

With these points in mind, we can return to the Confucians' reasons for prioritizing the practice of music, because the contrast with the *Zhuangzi* can help us see better what may motivate their preference. To frame the contrast, note that virtually all early Chinese thinkers present themselves as instructing us about "the Way" (*dao* 道) to live. In the *Zhuangzi*, as we saw, "the Way" is repeatedly portrayed as involving sensitivity to and conformity with certain natural patterns. Even more strongly, the text at times treats "the Way" as not just an ideal manner of living, but as an independent force that is

---

[20]   See also *Zhuangzi*, HKCS 15/42/3; Watson (2013, 120).

constituted by the various natural processes of the world or that generates and regulates them.[21] (The notion of "Heaven" thus comes to be nearly synonymous with "the Way" in the text.) On this latter usage, "the Way" is a possible way to live but is also "the Way" that the world operates at some deep level, which people may either resist—usually to their own detriment—or with which they may harmonize and thereby derive benefit. To restate the conclusion of the previous paragraph in slightly different terms, then, since human life is not the sole or even primary focus of this "cosmic" Way, it is unsurprising that no human art is especially important for following it, though following it *may* take the form of practicing the arts.

In early Confucian texts like the *Analects* and the *Xunzi*, on the other hand, the Way is generally not conceived in this second, "cosmic" sense. Instead, they mostly speak about the Way as just the proper manner for human beings to live. They take this Way to have been discovered (or perhaps invented) and made manifest by the ancient sage kings, and believe that it is preserved in the various legacies handed down from them. To follow this Way is thus not merely to live properly, but also to participate in and maintain the traditions initiated by the sages. When the Confucian Way is conceived in terms of carrying on a tradition, we can see one possible reason (though surely not the only reason) why music might become more important to early Confucians than most other arts, which is that, as in other places and times where literacy was rare and writing materials or other material means of recording tradition were difficult to acquire or reproduce, the combination of poetry, song, playing of instruments, and dance that fell under the category of "music" was one of the most easy and effective methods for transmitting that tradition to others. Indeed, as already noted, several musical pieces especially favored by the Confucians were compositions believed to be by the sages or compositions that celebrated their achievements, and teaching was a main method by which they aimed to realize the ideal society, so the Confucians' stress on performing music may have another, better justification than just mere cultural bias.[22]

In this light, the differences between the *Zhuangzi* and the Confucians on the need to practice the arts reflect their broader ethical positions, but also reflect more particularly the extent to which they consider (or do not consider) the arts as vehicles of tradition and education. That question of how we ought to conceive the arts brings me back to a problem I mentioned at the outset but delayed discussing, and with which I will now conclude.

---

[21] The *Zhuangzi* is notoriously difficult to interpret, and some scholars would contest my characterization of it. I cannot engage in those controversies here. Suffice it to say that my account follows one common interpretation. For a review and criticism of some alternative readings, see Ivanhoe (1996), whose view I endorse.

[22] Note that in *Analects* 17.4, when Confucius jokes about Ziyou's attempts to teach the common people to perform music, Ziyou defends himself by describing the situation as one where the common people are "learning the Way," and, moreover, claims he learned his approach from Confucius himself.

RECONSIDERING THE CATEGORIES OF "ETHICS" AND "THE ARTS"

I have focused on music because it provides (among other things) a convenient reference point for comparing early Chinese debates about ethics and the arts with those of other traditions. However, Confucian texts often link music with another concept, *li* 禮, which is standardly translated as "ritual." That translation conveys some of its sense, but can also mislead. For many English speakers, "ritual" refers just to ceremonies performed on specific and special occasions, whereas *li* refers to standards for behavior covering a much wider range of situations, including day-to-day scenarios, which in English more ordinarily fall under the label of "etiquette." The Confucians believe that a major component of the tradition of the ancient sages is constituted by and contained in certain rituals that they initiated, and hence practicing these rituals is one of the most important elements in following the Way.

The early Confucians had good reason to discuss music hand-in-hand with ritual, since musical performances were often part of important Chinese ceremonies, just as they are in many ceremonies around the world even today. Indeed, the use of music within ritual is certainly also one reason why the Confucians prize learning to perform music (though again, that fact by itself would not necessarily justify prioritizing that art over nearly all others, many of which also feature in rituals). The Confucian discussions, however, invite one to consider ritual itself as an art, since music and ritual are often treated nearly on a par conceptually, and the *Xunzi*, for instance, uses many of the same arguments to defend both music and ritual.

When viewed this way, the notion of ritual can prompt reconsideration of both "ethics" and "the arts" as categories. On the one hand, many have thought that ethics rests in universal principles quite distinct from and superior to "merely conventional etiquette." The Confucian notion of ritual militates against so sharply distinguishing etiquette from morality, suggesting instead that etiquette is *also* a moral matter, and potentially quite important.[23] On the other hand, insofar as the rituals are relatively fixed prescriptions for how to behave, following them may not seem much like practicing an art. Yet since the rituals not only have an expressive function but also serve to "beautify" the performance of one's obligations (*Xunzi*, HKCS 19/94/8; Hutton 2014, 209 [lines 304–307]), they have aesthetic aspects comparable to other arts.[24]

To the extent that the rituals are simultaneously ethical norms and artistic forms, Confucianism demands that one practice a particular art, but unlike performing music, which is limited to a set of discrete episodes, the practice of ritual is supposed to be pervasive in one's life, with ritual governing almost everything one does. In that sense,

---

[23] For further discussion of this point, see Olberding (2016) and Cline (2016).
[24] I cannot explore that similarity here, but Radice (2017), for example, insightfully compares ritual and dramaturgy.

Confucian ethics requires not merely that one practice a particular art, but moreover that one practice it nearly all the time; the ethical life and this artistic practice wind up mostly coextensive. While we have reached this description by starting from the two separate categories of "ethics" and "the arts" and asking how they might intersect, had we started from the perspective of a Confucian gentleman, perhaps the more appropriate questions would be: How—if at all—should we divide "the arts" from "ethics" in the first place? And if we do make that distinction, why think that an ethical life might possibly be *devoid* of all arts?

Answering these questions or assessing the usefulness of asking them lies beyond the scope of this chapter. I hope, though, that they (along with the other issues surveyed here) can indicate some of the interesting perspectives on the topic of this book to be found in the Chinese tradition.

See also: Man, Higgins, Song, this volume.

REFERENCES

Assandri, Friederike, tr. 2021. *The* Daode jing *Commentary of Cheng Xuanying: Daoism, Buddhism, and the* Laozi *in the Tang Dynasty*. New York: Oxford University Press.

Cline, Erin M. 2016. "The Boundaries of Manners: Ritual and Etiquette in Early Confucianism and Stohr's *On Manners*." *Dao* 15, no. 2: 241–255.

Fraser, Chris. 2016. "Language and Logic in the *Xunzi*." In *Dao Companion to the Philosophy of Xunzi*, edited by Eric L. Hutton, 291–321. Dordrecht: Springer.

Hutton, Eric L. 2008. "Un-Democratic Values in Plato and Xunzi." In *Polishing the Chinese Mirror: Essays in Honor of Henry Rosemont, Jr.*, edited by Martha Chandler and Ronnie Littlejohn, 313–330. New York: Global Scholarly Publications.

Hutton, Eric L., tr. 2014. *Xunzi: The Complete Text*. Princeton, NJ: Princeton University Press.

Hutton, Eric L., and James Harold. 2016. "Xunzi on Music." In *Dao Companion to the Philosophy of Xunzi*, edited by Eric L. Hutton, 269–289. Dordrecht: Springer.

Ivanhoe, P. J., and Bryan Van Norden, eds. 2006. *Readings in Classical Chinese Philosophy*, 2nd ed. Indianapolis: Hackett Publishing Co.

Ivanhoe, Philip J. 1996. "Was Zhuangzi a Relativist?" In *Essays on Skepticism, Relativism, and Ethics in the Zhuangzi*, edited by Philip Ivanhoe and Paul Kjellberg, 196–214. Albany: SUNY Press.

Ivanhoe, Philip J. 2014. "A Happy Symmetry: Xunzi's Ecological Ethic." In *Ritual and Religion in the Xunzi*, edited by T. C. Kline III and Justin Tiwald, 43–60. Albany: SUNY Press.

Kjellberg, Paul. 1996. "Sextus Empiricus, Zhuangzi, and Xunzi on 'Why be skeptical?'" In *Essays on Skepticism, Relativism, and Ethics in the Zhuangzi*, edited by Philip Ivanhoe and Paul Kjellberg, 1–25. Albany: SUNY Press.

Lau, D. C., and F. C. Chen, eds. 1996. *A Concordance to the Xunzi* 荀子逐字索引. Hong Kong: The Commercial Press 商務印書館. (Cited as *Xunzi*, HKCS.)

Lau, D. C., and F. C. Chen, eds. 2000. *A Concordance to the Zhuangzi* 莊子逐字索引. Hong Kong: The Commercial Press 商務印書館. (Cited as *Zhuangzi*, HKCS.)

Lynn, Richard J., tr. 2004. *The Classic of the Way and Virtue: A New Translation of the* Tao-te Ching *of Laozi as Interpreted by Wang Bi*. New York: Columbia University Press.

Olberding, Amy. 2016. "Etiquette: A Confucian Contribution to Moral Philosophy." *Ethics* 126, no. 2: 422–446.

Park, So-Jeong. 2020. "Danger of Sound: Mozi's Criticism of Confucian Ritual Music." *The Philosophical Forum* 51, no. 1: 49–65.

Radice, Thomas. 2017. "Method Mourning: Xunzi on Ritual Performance." *Philosophy East and West* 67, no. 2: 466–493.

Tadd, Misha. 2013. "Alternatives to Monism and Dualism: Seeking Yang Substance with Yin Mode in *Heshanggong's Commentary on The Daodejing*." PhD diss., Boston University.

Van Norden, Bryan. 2007. *Virtue Ethics and Consequentialism in Early Chinese Philosophy*. New York: Cambridge University Press.

Watson, Burton, tr. 2013. *The Complete Works of Zhuangzi*. New York: Columbia University Press.

CHAPTER 3

....

ANCIENT GREEK
PHILOSOPHERS ON ART
AND ETHICS

How Can Immoral Art Be Ethically Beneficial?

....

PIERRE DESTRÉE

THROUGHOUT the long history of ancient Greek culture, Homer was considered the emblematic figure of poetry, and art more generally. He was not only (taken to be) the author of the *Iliad* and the *Odyssey* as well as of a parodic epic poem, the *Margites* (meaning: the *Fool*), but also considered the origin of all subsequent literature, notably tragedy and comedy. As children, citizens were taught by heart entire passages from his poems; as adults they regularly attended readings of poetry in private banquets and participated in the numerous civic festivals where Homeric recitations, as well as tragedies and comedies were performed. And everywhere in Greek cities, statues and wall paintings abounded, often depicting memorable scenes from the Iliad or the odyssey.[1] People were constantly exposed to art, and as all our testimonies report, art was widely considered an incomparable source of pleasure and joy. This is how Homer himself presents poetry in the iconic scene of the Sirens in the *Odyssey*: they sing the *Iliad* in such a delightful manner that any listener would prefer to adjourn her way home and continue to enjoy it until death (12.39–54; 154–201).

But most Greek art was anything but peaceful, dispassionate, or morally uplifting. As Homer announces at the very beginning of the *Iliad*, this poem is about Achilles's wrath, which begins with harshly insulting the Greek army's commander in chief Agamemnon

---

[1] Such scenes can still be seen today in numerous painted pots, as well as in mosaics and frescos in Pompeii.

and ends as a foolish obstinacy that will cause the deaths of many of his comrades and finally of his best friend (and presumably lover) Patroclus, which he would avenge by desecrating the corpse of the Trojan Hector in a horrific way.

It is therefore not surprising that Greek philosophers have tried to solve an urgent dilemma. If (most) art is full of evil deeds and inappropriate words, and yet the pleasures of art are something no one is ready to miss, how can regular exposure to art go on without dire consequences to our lives?

Homer invented the fascinating image of Odysseus protecting himself from any such threat by being fixed to the mast of his ship passing by the Sirens' shore while his crew continues to row forward with their ears firmly plugged with wax. In the *Phaedrus*, in the pastoral setting of a hot summer day, Socrates encourages his interlocutor Phaedrus, a great admirer of sophisticated rhetoric and poetry, "to sail past" the cicadas singing (rhetoric and poetry) all around "as though they were Sirens, and to *remain unenchanted*," that is, to resist the temptation "to fall asleep under their spell," and "to pursue discussion" instead, that is, to practice philosophy (259a–b).

In the ethical context of the *Republic*, Plato radicalized that paradoxically poetic image into what has become the most (in)famous motto in the history of philosophy, the "banishment of the poets." If regular exposure to such art may influence your own views or behavior in harmful ways, shouldn't we give it up once and for all, and replace it with ethically correct art?[2] But for all its morally dubious features Plato himself actually recognizes the importance of that art in human existence. When Socrates first envisages the ideal of a "healthy city" where there would be neither banqueting nor art except for dull poems that would only praise virtue, Plato's own brother Glaucon replies graphically: "It is a city for pigs," where no human being would ever choose to live (*Rep.* 2, 372d). And indeed, in another iconic passage in the *Odyssey*, celebrated throughout antiquity, one hears Odysseus enthusiastically declaring that listening to a bard singing (Homeric) poetry accompanied by his lyre at a rich banquet is quite simply "the most beautiful thing" making a human life worth living (9.3–11). Hence the notorious challenge Plato addresses at the end of his critique of art: poetry and the arts will be allowed to come back to the city, once they have been proven to be not only pleasurable but also of benefit to what the Greeks called "*eudaimonia*," a "flourishing life," or "happiness" (*Rep.* 10, 607d).

All subsequent ancient Greek philosophical aesthetics has tried to meet this challenge. Let's first get into some of the details of this dilemma, and Plato's "banishment of the poets," before reviewing how philosophers, from Plato himself to Plutarch, Aristotle, and Epicurus, have dealt with it.

---

[2] For a contemporary discussion of these issues, see Soucek, "Censorship and Selective Support for the Arts," this volume.

PLATO'S CRITIQUE OF THE ARTS

It's probably with Heraclitus that the ethical criticism of poetry is born: "Homer deserves to be thrown off the stage and beaten with a stick, and so does Archilochus" (Fgt B42 DK). The context is clearly the theatre, where police slaves charged with maintaining order could beat disorderly spectators. So Heraclitus urges that the police should turn their stick against the poets themselves. Heraclitus wants theater goers to be turned away from the poets they admire and enjoy listening to. The reason is arguably their visions of war: for Homer, a gruesome vision of battlefields with brutal and reckless warriors; in Archilochus's parodic poems, cowardice and lack of patriotism are presented as a kind of standard.[3] Since courage was considered an essential virtue of citizens, and courage should be conceived as the virtue of fighting for the rule of law ("The people must fight for the law as for their city wall," Fgt B44 DK), what Homer and Archilochus seem to be accused of is transmitting their morally dubious conceptions of war to all the citizens of a city.

It's against this background that Plato's attack against poetry, and art more generally, must be understood. Three features seem to be key in this critique. First, it's because he considered art to be such a powerful provider of emotions and pleasure that Plato so vigorously condemns art when it conveys morally dubious images. Second, it's because Homer is generally taken to be a *sophos* that his poetry is all the more dangerous: enjoying his poetry all the while one is fully persuaded that its author is a wise and a truth purveyor is how one can be imbued by the wrong values his poetry conveys. And third, characters of the stories that make the poems and visual artworks are considered "heroes," that is, people we very much admire.

In the *Republic*, the "banishment of the poets" is expressly called for twice (3, 398a–b; 10, 607a). Scholars commonly speak of the "first critique" of art in books 2 and 3, while book 10 offers a "second critique." The first critique is presented as part of the education of the youth in the ideal city of Kallipolis, but it is fairly obvious that Plato has in mind poetry and the other arts as they are consumed by children and adults alike; the second critique presents more detailed arguments to defend the banishment of the poets. Let's review some of their most central features.

As Plato emphasizes at the beginning of his critique, what readers or viewers of art focus on are the main characters, the gods and the heroes. Despite all their differences in status, they share one fundamental property: they are our "superiors" in the sense that we are doomed to admire them. There is nothing that they would do or say that we would not approve of, however repulsive that may be. Take the horrendous example of

---

[3] One of his most often cited, and often blamed, poems reads: "One of the Saians now delights in the shield I discarded/Unwillingly near a bush, for it was perfectly good,/But at least I got myself safely out. Why should I care for that shield?/Let it go. Some other time I'll find another no worse" (Fgt 5; tr. Gerber).

the castration of Kronos by his own son Zeus: "No young person should hear it said," Plato writes, "that if he were to commit the worst crimes, he would be doing nothing amazing, or that if he were to inflict every sort of punishment on an unjust father, he would only be doing the same as the first and greatest of the gods" (378b; tr. Reeve). Seeing the gods commit such acts can only lead the child to be ultimately persuaded that such behavior is morally right.

Now, how does this "persuasion" actually work? The key word in Plato's approach is *mimesis*, "imitation," or "representation." The word has two main related usages. From the perspective of the receiver, a *mimesis* (which is also called a *mimema*) is an "object," whatever it may be, that is recognized as such and such, whether a portrait (or a "representation") of a man that happens to be Socrates, or the accent of a person (or an "imitation") who is from Crete, not from Athens. From the perspective of the agent, a *mimesis* is the active imitation of such and such accent, the rendering of Socrates's traits, or the performance of actors who impersonate or play such and such characters (which may in turn "represent" such and such people).

In his "first critique," Plato seems to use *mimesis* mostly in the latter sense. Homeric poetry is mainly composed of dialogues in which the poet himself takes a back seat to his characters. Similarly, when the *Iliad* or the *Odyssey* are staged, the rhapsode impersonates, or enacts all the characters of the tales he is reciting (or actually, chanting accompanied by his lyre). And, in learning passages from Homer, children took on the different voices of the characters when they spoke them out (ancient reading was mostly aloud).

Interpreters usually tend to read this presentation as if Plato had a very strong theory of "identification."[4] When "imitating," or "enacting" one character, the child would be supposed to "become like that character," and feel and think as if she had become that character. This seems to be an overinterpretation of what Plato describes. After all, a child who wholeheartedly recites what Achilles is saying knows very well that he is not Achilles. And Plato very much insists on the pleasure of impersonating one character after another. Thus, it might be more accurate to speak of "playing" the way we say that an actor plays Achilles.[5]

What is the problem that Plato sees in such a *mimesis*? After all, playing is one of the most natural features of childhood, and a very benign activity for adults. The problem is that when they play Achilles, they take it *seriously* (388d; 397a). Again, this should not mean that they think they are Achilles, but that in speaking like Achilles, they take what Achilles says earnestly. And since Achilles is presented as a hero, they also take it that what he says is good. That is, very roughly, how the values that Achilles's sayings and deeds manifest, are transmitted. It's not that in "imitating," or "playing" an angry Achilles one learns how to behave angrily, but in taking pleasure in playing Achilles, one

---

[4] For a sophisticated version of such a reading, see Halliwell (2002), chapter 2: "Romantic Puritanism: Plato and the Psychology of Mimesis."

[5] On the importance of play in ancient aesthetics, see Kidd (2019).

unconsciously absorbs the values Achilles embodies, such as obstinacy, vengefulness, or disrespect.

This all applies not only to children, but to adults equally. We often say that a good show "absorbs" its audience. Plato makes the same point: when I follow the action of the characters on stage, it's as if I'm participating in that action, at least in the form of a game. And if I take it "seriously," and hold that Achilles is a hero to be admired, and take great pleasure in it, it can only reinforce my propensity to accept, or "absorb," the values Achilles represents. As to visual art, it may seem odd to apply that concept of play. But ancient Greeks considered a good painting or sculpture as giving its recipient the illusion that its characters were alive. It is quite telling that the word for "living being," or "animal," *zôon*, could also be used for "picture." Thus a painting of Achilles desecrating the corpse of Hector was meant to make viewers assist at such a scene, that is, somehow "participate" in it. And here too, the more I enjoy it, the more I may be persuaded that such revenge for the death of a loved one must be perfectly admissible after all.

If one takes most deeds and sayings of the Homeric heroes to be morally flawed, and the power of his art seriously into account, Plato was only consistent in condemning Homer to exile. But, one might say, that wouldn't condemn art as such, would it? As perhaps most interpreters nowadays take it, it is the poetry of Homer and a few other poets that Plato would denounce, not poetry as such. But perhaps Plato was much more radical than one may wish to admit.

Actually, it might well be the case that Plato not only condemns poetry as he knew it, but also every kind of art that would follow the same pattern. Indeed, when he embarks on his so-called second critique of art in book 10 of the *Republic*, it is *mimesis* as such that is at stake. Again, many interpreters have tended to understand "mimesis as such" in a specific way as if Plato only wanted to condemn the enactive *mimesis* that is at stake in Homer and which would culminate in the theater; and it has become standard in the literature to speak of "imitativeness," which would be opposed to a good kind of "imitation."[6] But Plato does not explicitly draw such a distinction. And since *mimesis* is the common Greek word for art, any ancient reader would have immediately understood that art as such, and not any particular conception or genre, was under consideration.

Plato's critique of "mimesis as such" contains two main arguments, one usually called "epistemological," and the other "psychological." But the two arguments are intimately linked, the second one giving the first its actual meaning. The first argument is constituted by the famous three bed analogy. While a carpenter takes a plan (which Plato calls a Form) to build an actual bed, the painter composes an image of that bed. Two consequences follow. What the painter makes is obviously no "real" bed, that is, not a bed you can take a nap in, but an image of a bed, an "appearance of a bed." And quite obviously too, the painter does make a bed from his own perspective: he paints a bed as he sees it, and not as a plan imposed to build it. This by itself is an apt (if very rough) description of what a (realistic) painter does. But the problem is with the viewer: when in

---

[6] See especially Belfiore (1983), and Moss (2007).

the Metropolitan Museum you are in front of Cezanne's *Still Life with Apples and a Pot of Primroses*, don't you commonly say, "these are apples and primroses?" Of course, no one would confuse those painted apples with apples one could eat. But the very fact of saying that these are apples, and not "a representation of apples," risks misleading us as to what apples are. Of course, this example is perfectly harmless. But Plato's example is much less so.

As can be seen on many ancient pots, painters did not hesitate in depicting workers, such as carpenters or blacksmiths. "If he is a good painter," Plato warns, "by painting a carpenter and displaying him at a distance, he might deceive children and foolish adults into thinking it is a true carpenter" (598b–c)—that is, thinking this is an accurate depiction of how a carpenter looks like and works. So the problem is that, like fools and children, we all tend to believe that if he can represent what a carpenter and his work are like, the painter must have knowledge of carpentry. And similarly with Homer: when he depicts Achilles as such and such a hero speaking and acting in such and such a way, he must know what a hero's like. When following the deeds of an Achilles, we tend to forget that his deeds are only the creation of one mind, that of Homer, who, like the painter, only narrates things from his own perspective. This we tend to forget because of the charm Homer's poetry exercises on our mind:

> The poet uses words and phrases to paint colored pictures of each of the crafts, even though he knows only how to imitate them; so that others like himself, who look at things in terms of words, will think he speaks extremely well about shoemaking or generalship or anything else, provided he speaks with meter, rhythm, and harmony. That is how great a natural spell these things cast. (601a–b)

Now why should that be so? After all, any educated adult could easily realize that painting a carpenter does not necessarily make you think the painter indeed possesses such carpentry knowledge. And Plato himself insists (not without humor) that if Homer or any other poet would have been thought useful to their fellow citizens, they would not have been allowed to travel but would have been kept in their native cities (600c–d); no one ever speaks of a "Homeric way of life" (600a–b), which is what one would have expected if Homer truly had a moral knowledge to share. So why is it that we tend to consider Homer as a wise person, or even as the "educator of Greece" (606e)? Why is it that we take so seriously the images we see in paintings, or that when participating in the play of the actors on stage, we take it as something of "serious" importance?

The answer to this set of questions comes from Plato's second, so-called psychological argument. As we have seen, art, and theater in particular, has a powerful effect on us. But how does it affect us, and up to what degree? Or as Plato puts it, which "element," or "part of our soul," does poetry and art affect? Here again, an analogy is at the center of Plato's argument. Take a straight stick: when submerged in water, it looks bent, and however you may reason that it's actually straight, it's just impossible to see it as otherwise than bent. Painting, and art more generally, is like such optical illusions: it gives you something to see as x or y, and even if you know that it's not x or y, but z, you can't help but see it as x or y. This is why mimesis, or art, is a trickery: "It is because it exploits this weakness in our nature that illusionist painting is nothing short of sorcery" (602d). But if one easily understands that a painter can create some illusion, how would this apply to the case of poetry? The answer seems to be this: seeing Achilles as a morally good hero while he is not is analogous to the stick being seen as bent while it is actually straight. But how, one may ask, can we be led to believe this while, if we reason, we could easily understand that that is not the case?

It's here that we come to the core of Plato's critique of art. In the case of the bent stick, clearly the illusion affects the vision, not the reason. In the case of poetry, the part of us that it affects must be what Plato calls the irrational part of our soul, or what we might call, very roughly, our desires and our emotions. At first sight, this may sound strange: why should art necessarily address these instead of our reason? We all like stories where the main characters are passionate lovers and wrathful avengers: these characters make for stories that are exciting and gripping. Plato was fully aware of this: "The wise and quiet character, who always remains pretty much his own self, is neither easy to imitate nor easy to understand when imitated—especially not at a festival where multifarious people are gathered together in theaters" (604e). A wise and quiet character might in principle be put on stage but it would be difficult for the poet to make him attractive, and even if he managed it, his audience wouldn't quite get what he's up to. As we still would say nowadays, people gathered in a theater expect to get their passions stirred up by complex and passionate characters, which is what gives them great pleasure. As Plato puts it, "the imitative poet, then, clearly does not naturally relate to this best element in the soul, and his wisdom is not directed to pleasing it—not if he is going to attain a good reputation with the masses—but to the irritable and complex character, because it is easy to imitate" (605a). For Plato, this is not without consequences: the imitative poet "arouses and nourishes this element in the soul and, by making it strong, destroys the rational one" (605b). This may sound rather excessive a claim. Why on earth should one have their reason not only corrupted but literally "destroyed" by merely reading poetry, or going to the theater? But that is to neglect the power of the pleasure that comes from such poetry. If it is true that no one would be willing to miss such pleasures, and you firmly believe these characters are to be considered our "heroes," wouldn't your reason be rendered incapable of standing firm against such views?

In the optical illusion of the submerged stick, you can easily adjust your reason and calculate how to grab it. But when you are in a theater or in front of a painting, you are enjoying it—actually, like Odysseus's listening to the Sirens singing, taking an immense pleasure, so immense that you would do whatever it took not to miss it. Here is the problem: since you enjoy it, you are not quite willing to be told that all you are seeing or following is not "real," or not, morally speaking, as it should be. And the characters who are doing all those things, you can't help but admire them precisely because you so much enjoy attending their story, even somehow "participating" in it.

Plato describes all this with an admirable clarity:

> When even the best of us hear Homer, or some other tragic poet, imitating one of the heroes in a state of grief and making a long speech of lamentation, or even chanting and beating his breast, you know we enjoy it and give ourselves over to it. We suffer along with the hero and take his sufferings seriously. And we praise the one who affects us most in this way as a good poet. (605c–d)

This passage gives us the very reason why even morally good persons are easily trapped by poetry. It's because we take such a great pleasure in the *mimesis* game, which consists in "suffering all along" with the man grieving immoderately that we tend to congratulate the poet who affords us such a pleasure, and that we tend to admire the grieving hero: "it is when you enjoy very much hearing them that you don't hate them as something bad" (606c). Of course, morally good people may very well know that this man is not to be admired, but the pleasure is just so great that their reason can't resist it.

ANCIENT RESPONSES TO PLATO'S CHALLENGE

Plato's critique of art is radical. If you admit that art aims at providing pleasure, and that pleasure is best provided when reckless and wanton characters make up the story, you must conclude that, from a moral perspective, it's best to avoid it altogether. "Wherever the wind of argument blows us, so to speak, that is where we must go," as Plato firmly says (3, 394d). But perhaps life isn't that reasonable and completely submissible to rational argument? It is quite telling that at the beginning and the end of his second critique of poetry, Socrates himself, who earlier advocated the ideal of a healthy city devoid of any exposure to arts, now admits to being a "lover of Homer" (10, 595b; 607e), which should probably be taken not as a personal note, but as a general recognition that indeed you can't live without poetry and art. Hence, the challenge Plato makes to all of whom would be ready to defend the value of art in a happy life: how shall we conceive it as both pleasurable and beneficial?

Plato: Enjoying Art in a Detached Way

Plato never forbade people from going to the theater, or reading Homer's poetry. What he expressly recommends is that "whenever we listen to her, we will chant to ourselves the argument we just now put forward as a counter-charm to prevent us from slipping back into the childish passion that the masses have" (608a). What does he mean? Whenever you go to the theater, the recommendation clearly is to repeat to yourself all the arguments of book 10 in order to make sure you don't participate in the dangerous game of mimesis, and you have no share in the emotional pleasure such a game provides. But would Plato also recommend that we should aim at renouncing for good any sort of exposure to Homer and other poetic genres, as is often concluded? One may doubt this.

As we have seen, the problem of reading Homer arises when one reads his poetry seriously. But it is also possible, as Plato quickly suggests in *Rep.* 3, to listen to the morally doubtful passages *not* seriously, that is "in laughing at them as not worth saying" (388d). Plato does not elaborate on this suggestion, but later in the same book, talking about comedy, he advocates that people "must know about mad and evil men and women, but they must not do or imitate anything they do" (396a). And indeed, in one passage of the *Laws*, he even recommends citizens attend comedies so they can better understand how wretched people behave (7.816d–e). But how shall we stay safe all the while watching such plays? The *Republic* passage just quoted recommends to attend it all the while "laughing at" it "as not worth saying," that is, in a sort of "detached" way. If it would be morally dangerous to read the famous scene where Achilles is desecrating Hector's body "seriously," reading it in a "detached" way would help discern how far an obstinate and wrathful person could go. And in the case of comedy, if it is dangerous to indulge in some malicious laughter toward fellow citizens (what Aristophanes often provokes), which could only fuel our natural propensity for malice, it might be useful to learn what the ridiculous character and her misdeeds look like. And since understanding is pleasurable, this constitutes one way of considering poetry to be both pleasurable and useful. To be sure, this is a very intellectualized way of enjoying poetry, which might perhaps be considered paradoxical in the case of tragedy (where emotional pleasure seems to be crucial). But are not many of our contemporary artworks meant to address our intellect rather than our emotions? After all, Bertolt Brecht meant his plays to be viewed in a similar "detached" way, in order to promote social and political criticism by the audience.

Plutarch: The Critical Consumer of Art

Plutarch, a late first–early second century AD Platonist philosopher, offers a fascinating variant of Plato's proposal. His main treatise on our topic, *How to Listen to Poetry*, aims at advising educators how they should teach the young to read poetry safely; but it also has the wider scope of answering Plato's challenge. Following Plato, Plutarch is fully aware that "it is changes which give stories elements of emotion and surprise and the unexpected, and it is these which provide the greatest effects of amazement and charm" (7, 25c–d; tr. Hunter); heroes must not only be subject to capricious changes of fortune, but also be themselves erratic and everything but measured people. And yet being himself also a great admirer of poetry and art, he cannot accept the definitive banishment of the poets: "Shall we then stop the ears of the young, Plutarch ironically asks, as those of the Ithacans were stopped, with a hard and unyielding wax . . . and avoid poetry and steer their course clear of it?" (1, 15d; tr. Russell). So how to escape the perils of poetry all the while enjoying it?

Plato suggested that we safely enjoy it in a "detached" manner. Plutarch proposes a quite different way of reading poetry and of appreciating art more generally: the recipient of a poem or a visual artwork must become a *critical* reader or viewer of the work's content. "These sayings touch the soul and cause confusion in life, because they produce bad decisions and unworthy opinions, unless we accustom ourselves always to ask *why*" such and such a character took such and such a decision or said such and such; "if you react and resist like this, Plutarch concludes, instead of bowing to every word as to a gust of wind . . . , you will soon be free of many of these false and detrimental statements" (9, 28c–d). One should not blindly read poetry (11, 30d, 31d) and foolishly accept everything that art depicts as if it were true or morally good, but remain constantly awake (32a) and exercise our critical judgment, so one can resist against those morally irrelevant or inappropriate statements or actions.[7] In other words, recipients must constantly exercise their judgment all the while they enjoy poetry: instead of having one's body attached to the mast of a boat, Plutarch exhorts that one "attaches his judgment to the mast of correct reasoning" (1, 15d).

Such correct reasoning is essentially about the two main principles of art. Those principles are descriptive, not normative, but we tend to forget them, which is the very cause of our problems. One, which is in line with Plato, is that telling lies or fictions is inherent to poetry: "we don't know poetry that would be without fiction or without lies" (16c). Hence we must fully recognize that the poets tell lies, and never attribute to them any knowledge that they would mean to teach:

> Whenever in a poem a man of note and repute makes some strange and disconcerting statement either about gods . . . or about virtue, he who accepts the statement as true is carried off his feet, and has his opinions perverted; whereas he who always remembers and keeps clearly in mind the sorcery of the poetic art in dealing with falsehood . . . will not suffer any dire effect or even acquire any false belief. (16d)

Second (and following Aristotle against Plato; see below), Plutarch urges art recipients to reason that "imitating something beautiful is not the same as imitating it beautifully" (18d). Exactly in the same way they admire and enjoy how a good painter has "beautifully" depicted an ugly animal, they admire an imitation or a representation of a wretched action because of the art of the poet who perfectly narrates how that action took place. And in the same way they won't be led to see the actual animal as being worth our admiration, that is, "beautiful," they should not consider such an action as "admirable," or morally good.

But how shall the recipient implement this critical reasoning in practice? Plutarch offers numerous means to do so. One consists in comparing various passages in order to highlight inconsistencies, which would make us see that asking a poet for truth is just a hopeless request. As to the second principle, Plutarch takes it that Homer usually gives us a hint as to how to take such and such a statement, when he adds, even if implicitly, that what was said was not right. In the many cases where Homer does not give such a hint, readers can

---

[7] Konstan (2004) intriguingly suggests that Plutarch anticipates Judith Fetterly's notion of the "resisting reader."

rely on contradictory voices, and try to discriminate by themselves which action or state-ment is right, and which is not. And if there's no such contradictory statements in the same poem, readers should never hesitate to draw passages from other writers, whether poets, or even philosophers, in order to critically assess what is said or done.

This critical stance allows to derive moral benefit from exposure to art: "The bee finds the sweetest and most useful honey among the most stinging flowers and the roughest thorns; so children, if properly nurtured on poetry, will in some way or other learn to draw a useful and beneficial lesson even from passages suspected of being vile and inap-propriate" (12, 32e; tr. Babbitt mod.). In all these cases, Plutarch says, art provides us with a kind of first philosophical reflection. And such a critical appreciation will also provide us with a true pleasure, the pleasure of exercising our critical reflection.

Aristotle: The Pleasures of Connoisseurship

Aristotle offered a totally different response to Plato's challenge. If he followed Plato in recommending that the youth should be forbidden from attending spectacles of comedy and satirical poetry where characters insult one another and act foolishly, he doesn't see any problem in adults attending such spectacles, at least after they have been rightly edu-cated, and have become "immune" to poetry's dangers (*Politics* 7.17, 1336b20–23). Aristotle never explains what such an "immunity" might consist in, but he most certainly could not have accepted Plato's suggestion of a "detached" reading or attendance at a play. Aristotle is adamant on this: in the case of tragedy, the aim of the poet is to provide an emotional pleasure, that which "comes from pity and fear" (*Poetics* 14, 1453b11–12); attending a play without being moved by these emotions would not be pleasurable. But how could one enjoy a tragic play and "suffer along with the hero lamenting on stage" as Plato said, and not become oneself a man prone to immoderate pity and fear? When defining tragic pleasure as "coming from pity and fear," Aristotle immediately adds "though mimesis" (1453b12). This addition seems to be crucial: since pity and fear are normally painful emotions, it is mimesis that transforms our pain into pleasure. It is then, more generally, the theater, or what we call the "aesthetical distance," that allows us to enjoy those emotions without damage. Plato seemed to think that it is precisely because morally good people believe that in the theater they can safely enjoy seeing bad behaviors that "they put down their guard" (606a), and thus are exposed to having their irrational desires nourished.[8] Aristotle most likely replied that that could only be true of morally poorly educated people, who would then need further moral education before going to the theater.

It's quite remarkable how Aristotle read the Sirens scene. Instead of talking of Odysseus enjoying their singing while his crew have their ears stopped up with wax, he refers to "the men enchanted by the Sirens" as if no one has been put in real danger: they all enjoyed their beautiful singing "for itself," that is without any other desire than the desire to listen (*Eudemian Ethics* 3.2, 1230b33–35). If one applies this to the case of

---

[8] See Belfiore (1983).

tragedy, one can infer that tragic pleasure "coming from pity and fear through mimesis" amounts to enjoying those emotions for themselves.

To be sure, these emotions suppose an epistemic content: one must be aware that those we are pitying are morally good people who haven't merited their fate—otherwise, it wouldn't be possible to feel pity. So many interpreters, from Lessing on up to Martha Nussbaum, have argued for an ethical reading of such a defense of tragedy: wouldn't such an experience of pity be a kind of help for better appreciating the value of pity in the real, human world (Nussbaum 1986)?[9] But Aristotle himself never ever hints at such an ethicist reading of tragedy. Actually, the only time he explicitly mentions ethics, he states that "what is right is not the same in politics and in poetry, nor is it the same in other arts as it is in the art of poetry" (*Poetics* 25, 1460b13–15). For example, when a painter depicts a horse galloping "with two right legs stretched out towards the front" (b18–20), it is a mistake from the perspective of biology, but not from an art-centered view in so far as it helps create a strong effect of awe and amazement. The same should go for ethical mistakes: the scene of Achilles desecrating Hector's corpse may be terribly wrong, but if this is meant to awaken our pity toward King Priam who will soon arrive to implore Achilles to recover his son's body, this is exactly how Homer had to write that scene. As Plutarch will conclude, one can depict something ugly in a beautiful way.

The aim of the poet is to provide his audience pleasure, not any sort of moral edification. The case of comedy confirms this. If experiencing pity and fear in the theatre is what typically constitutes tragic pleasure, the amusement that comes from incongruous and unexpected scenes or sayings is what makes for the pleasure proper to comedy. Aristotle gives the example of a scene from a comedy which seems to be a parody of a tragedy where Orestes, instead of killing Aegisthus (who had murdered Orestes's father Agamemnon) as he normally does in the myth and in tragedies, makes friends with him (*Poet.* 13, 1453a35–39). From an ethical perspective, such a scene is, of course, outrageous, as a son is expected to kill the murderer of his father. There's no reason to think that Aristotle would have not condemned Orestes's inaction in the real world, and he may have advised that no child be allowed to attend such a play. But he does not believe for a moment that we therefore ought not enjoy it in the theatre; nor does he think that we might gain any moral benefit such as a better understanding of how a son should behave in such circumstances—any average morally upright spectator knows this!

That is not to say though that there's no ethical restriction to be respected when one writes a comedy. One virtue Aristotle argues for in his *Ethics* is the "sense of humour," or "wittiness" (*Nic. Eth.* 4.8; *Eud. Eth.* 3.7). A key principle of such a virtue is that the joker does not hurt the butt of his joke. But this is not to say that jokes should not be immoral; it only means that if you make such a joke, you must make sure you don't hurt the person you are teasing, or the audience present. A good joke is a joke that is witty and refined and, provided no one is hurt, succeeds in making an audience laugh.

---

[9] See also S. Halliwell's numerous studies on Aristotle's *Poetics*, most recently Halliwell (2011), specifically Chapter 5, "Aristotle and the Experience of Tragic Emotion."

One may wonder how Aristotle actually responded to Plato's challenge to poetry's being both pleasurable and beneficial. What value does art have, if it has no ethical value? Aristotle seems to have offered two related responses. One is that laughing and lamenting are two important, inescapable human features that need to be satisfied from time to time, and the theatre is just designed to be the best place for expressing such emotional reactions. But he also believed that we can enjoy these artworks in a more sophisticated way.

In his *Politics*, when dealing with the place of music in his own ideal city in book 8, Aristotle fully admits that music can be ethically useful in some cases (on a battlefield, marshal music was regularly played to encourage soldiers to stand firm in front of the enemy); but it can also be listened to "for its own sake" (as stated in the *Eud. Eth.* passage quoted below), which he here labels "for the sake of leisure" (8. 5, 1339a25). "Leisure" should not be confused with sheer entertainment, or what Aristotle calls "relaxation"; rather, it is the general term for any disinterested activity, which requires a certain knowledge as to how to best appreciate that activity's relevant objects. In the case of music, Aristotle recommends that children learn to play an instrument so they become "judges" of music (8.6, 1340b33–39), or what we call "connoisseurs," which should allow them to appreciate music at its right value. And this is what he seems to be doing in his *Poetics*, which provides theatre goers with an understanding of how a good play is to be composed. Thus, being able to appreciate a good tragedy or comedy, or a good piece of music, and to give reasons for our aesthetic judgment, is a further benefit of art.

Epicurus: The Sensuous Pleasures of Art

In antiquity, Epicurus was often accused (notably by Plutarch) of being a kind of philistine. For, on the one hand, he seems very fond of the arts, to the point of advising philosophers to go to the theatre: "The wise man is a lover of sight and more than anyone enjoys hearing and seeing theatre performances" (Fgt 20 Usener). But, on the other hand, he unambiguously rejects all art as being a source of wisdom. In evoking the scene of the Sirens, he does so in a very odd way: "Hoist every sail, he advises his disciples, and flee from all education" (Fgt 163 Usener), as if listening to the Sirens, or enjoying art, would be just a waste of time for the philosopher. However, Epicurus does not recommend fleeing from culture or art, but "from education"; he thus means that should we think that art is of any educational or ethical benefit, we should indeed flee from the Sirens singing the *Iliad*, which mostly relates morally wrong deeds. But this should not prevent anyone from enjoying reading the *Iliad* for the sheer pleasure of reading it, provided they don't seek any ethical message or warning.

Epicurus seems to be taking the path Aristotle had shown: one must enjoy artworks independently of any kind of education or edification. But his reasons are quite different. For Epicurus, discussing poetry or learning how to play a musical instrument in order to better understand how music is constructed would be a waste of time. The only thing that really counts is philosophical discussion, which is based on arguments that aim at assuring *ataraxia*, "absence of trouble," which procures the highest sort of pleasure and happiness. And yet especially for those who have obtained (or are on the right path to obtaining) happiness, there is something to gain in going to the theatre. As one of Epicurus's first-century BC followers, Philodemus, will bluntly say in reply to Plato's challenge: "Pleasure *is* what is beneficial." But what kind of pleasure do we experience in the theatre, or during a music concert?

We have no explicit answer from Epicurus's own surviving works, or fragments. But Philodemus wrote an entire work, *On Music*, to prove (somehow anticipating Hanslick's much acclaimed study *On the Musically Beautiful*) that music had no moral content whatsoever, and that the only pleasure, yes benefit, we can hope for from music is the sensuous pleasure of the sounds and rhythms. Since it is an unnecessary pleasure, it is probably not essential to a happy human life, but, like tasting fine wines, it certainly adds zest to a life that is, for the rest, untroubled, and perfectly happy. Some modern interpreters have taken this to be a rather poor and purely materialistic approach to art (Halliwell 2002). But, to take another example, it is for no other reason that we are so keen to read detective stories or watch crime movies than for the mere pleasure of suspense. Nevertheless, that does not prevent some of them to be highly sophisticated: who would deny that George Simenon's exquisitely written novels or Alfred Hitchcock's brilliant movies count as artworks? No doubt, an Epicurean philosopher would appreciate such artworks for the enthralling stories they offer, as well as for all their formal qualities. To be sure, they don't offer much for moral improvement or philosophical reflection—but if you admit that pleasure constitutes happiness, and such artworks offer nondetrimental pleasures, why shouldn't we recognize that they are worth our engagement?

Heraclitus caustically urged that Homer and Archilochus should be beaten with a stick off the stage. In his book *On Poems*, opposing the Platonist philosopher Heraclides of Pontus who wanted to definitely condemn poems whose moral utility could not be proven, Philodemus asserts: "He beats with the stick the most beautiful poets because they provide no benefit whatsoever!" (5, col. v 10–15 Mangoni) Philodemus meant it to be caustic, too, turning the table on the whole history of the rejection of poets, from Heraclitus up to Heraclides and some stoic philosophers, who were obsessed with the moral usefulness that poetry, and art more generally, had to provide for their consumers.[10]

As Homer himself meant to convey, enjoying art is something no one would be ready to miss, and should count as something highly beneficial, or valuable, in any truly happy human life. But if one takes that benefit to be "moral" in the strict sense of the term, wouldn't we end up killing all great art? This is a question ancient Greek philosophers have left to their heirs to ponder.

See also: Soucek, Shim and Liao, Lamarque, Nannicelli, Leaman, this volume

---

[10] One may think of the Stoic Diogenes of Babylon who held very strong didactic moral views, which Philodemus harshly criticizes in his *On Music*. See Asmis (2017).

REFERENCES

Asmis, Elizabeth. 2017. "The Stoics on the Craft of Poetics." *Rheinisches Museum* 160, no. 2: 113–151.

Belfiore, Elizabeth. 1983. "Plato's Greatest Accusation against Poetry." *Canadian Journal of Philosophy* Supplementary Volume 9: 39–62.

Halliwell, Stephen. 2002. *The Aesthetics of Mimesis: Ancient Texts and Modern Problems.* Princeton, NJ: Princeton University Press.

Halliwell, Stephen. 2011. *Between Ecstasy and Truth: Interpretations of Greek Poetics from Homer to Longinus.* Oxford: Oxford University Press.

Kidd, Stephen E. 2019. *Play and Aesthetics and Ancient Greece.* Cambridge: Cambridge University Press.

Konstan, David. 2004. "'The Birth of the Reader': Plutarch as a Literary Critic." *Scholia* 13, no. 1: 3–27.

Moss, Jessica. 2007. "What Is Imitative Poetry and Why Is It Bad?" In *The Cambridge Companion to Plato's Republic,* edited by G. R. F. Ferrari, 415–444. Cambridge: Cambridge University Press.

Nussbaum, Martha. 1986. *The Fragility of Goodness: Luck and Ethics in Greek Tragedy and Philosophy.* Cambridge: Cambridge University Press.

FURTHER READING

Asmis, Elizabeth. 1995. "Epicurean Poetics." In *Philodemus and Poetry: Poetic Theory and Practice in Lucretius, Philodemus, and Horace,* edited by Dirk Obbink, 15–34. New York: Oxford University Press.

Denham, A. E, ed. 2012. *Plato on Art and Beauty.* New York: Palgrave MacMillan.

Destrée, Pierre, and Fritz-Gregor Herrmann, eds. 2011. *Plato and the Poets.* Leiden: Brill.

Destrée, Pierre, and Penelope Murray, eds. 2015. *The Blackwell Companion to Ancient Aesthetics.* Malden, MA: Wiley.

Destrée, Pierre. 2018. "Aristotle on Music for Leisure." In *Music, Text, and Culture in Ancient Greece,* edited by Armand D'Angour and Tom Phillips, 183–202. Oxford: Oxford University Press.

Destrée, Pierre. 2021. "Aristotle's Aesthetics." *The Stanford Encyclopedia of Philosophy.* Winter 2021 edition, edited by Edward N. Zalta. https://plato.stanford.edu/archives/win2021/entries/aristotle-aesthetics/

Ferrari, G. R. F. 1999. "Aristotle's Literary Aesthetics." *Phronesis* 44, no. 3: 181–198.

Ford, Andrew. 2015. "The Purpose of Aristotle's *Poetics*." *Classical Philology* 110, no. 1: 1–21.

Heath, Malcolm. 2013. *Ancient Philosophical Poetics.* Cambridge: Cambridge University Press.

Heath, Malcolm. 2014. "Aristotle and the Value of Tragedy." *British Journal of Aesthetics* 54, no. 2: 111–123.

Hunter, Richard. 2009. *Critical Moments in Classical Literature. Studies in the Ancient Views of Literature and its uses.* Cambridge: Cambridge University Press.

Janaway, Christopher. 1995. *Images of Excellence: Plato's Critique of the Arts.* Oxford: Clarendon Press.

CHAPTER 4

....

ART AND ETHICS IN ISLAM

....

OLIVER LEAMAN

THE QUR'AN AND BEAUTY

THERE is a significant link made between art and ethics in the Qur'an itself. One of the puzzles of the Book is that although much of it is very beautiful, and self-consciously so, it constantly denies it is poetry. Poetry was a very valued activity in the early Arab world, we are told, and so the fact that the style of the text fits in with that cultural feature is hardly surprising, but its defensiveness is. The point here is that the Qur'an wants to distinguish itself from what it sees as the sort of expression that cares more for how it says what it says rather than the truth of what is expressed. Poetry, and art in general, is seen as being more about style than content, as distracting us rather than helping us concentrate on what is important, and for that reason a barrier is immediately constructed between the aesthetic and religion, something that largely persists throughout Islamic thought. At the same time, the Islamic world created some of the most beautiful works of art, and often within a directly religious context also, and yet the dichotomy between art and religion persists, especially with respect to the ethical aspects of religion. There is nothing unusual in this: many thinkers and religions have defended that separation between art and ethics. In some ways it is just a reflection of common sense that something may be beautiful and yet not good, and vice versa.

In the Qur'an, aesthetic qualities are taken to apply very much to the order of the world, as laid out by the Creator. The verses of the Qur'an represent and reproduce that order (Kermani 2015). It is appropriate then that when people pray and carry out their religious duties in general, this is done gracefully and in a manner that embodies the delightfulness of those actions. Islam insists that there is no difficulty in finding out what we are supposed to do and how to do it, the religion of Islam fits in with our natural disposition. So there is a natural congruence of what we ought to do and what we find pleasant. To take some examples, the call to prayer, the *adhan*, is often regarded as very fine acoustically, the physical aspects of prayer are graceful and economical forms of speech and movement, the buildings in which prayer takes place may be graceful and awe inspiring. There is a traditional story that some nonbelievers heard the call to prayer and, although they did not understand the words, immediately announced their desire to become Muslims, so overcome were they by its beauty. This is not an uncommon experience among converts to Islam, and it might be thought to be problematic. After all, beauty does not guarantee the truth of what is being expressed, but on the other hand, the idea is perhaps that people sense the truth behind what they hear and see and make an emotional commitment to find out and accept that truth and so change their religious affiliation. The Qur'an itself advises its followers to speak and debate in a pleasant way (16:125), since that is likely to be successful in attracting adherents. A whole way of life developed later called *adab*, which emphasized the significance of not only following the rituals of Islam, but also what people wore, how they spoke to each other, and how they behaved in general, the idea being that these should all be both ethical and aesthetic, virtuous and graceful.

Early Islam

The cultural environment in which the Prophet Muhammad arose was rather limited, many Arabs were not urban and the material culture of the cities seems not to have been very developed. Within a short time though, the armies of Islam came to control a much wider area, and one in which the arts flourished, in particular ceramics, architecture and design in its broadest sense. The one art which did earn great respect in the early Arab world is poetry, and it is said that the tribes would compete with each other over who could produce the most beautiful verses, the competitions taking place where today the Ka'ba is in Mecca. The poet's products presumably had a high status, but the poet himself perhaps not so much, since the Qur'an refers to poets as being unclear (26: 221–6, 36: 69) and likely to lead people astray. It is as if they set themselves up to be alternatives to religion, and so are roundly condemned in the text. In any case, while poetry has a style designed to attract and fascinate an audience, the Qur'an does the same thing, but better, and has the additional advantage of actually being true and not just fanciful. The style is said not only to be superior to human poetry, but to be inimitable, work that could only have been produced by God. It challenges anyone to produce even a verse quite as good (2: 23), possibly harking back to the time when the Arab tribes competed with each other poetically. One of the main features of poetry in the pre-Islamic period was supposed to be its *hija'* form, a sort of poetic curse that was thought to have magical powers, and since it appealed to a deity quite other than God and so obviously not something that Muslims would be expected to repeat. Poetry was then labelled as powerful and dangerous, hence the disinclination to describe the Qur'an as poetic.

CALLIGRAPHY

It is often said that the paradigmatic Islamic art is calligraphy (Schimmel 1984). This places the focus on the Qur'an, the word of God. It is certainly true that from the relatively early years of Islam, the illumination of Qur'ans reached extraordinary heights, with highly artistic work going into the actual writing of the text and also the leaves on which those texts appear, along with the bindings. A variety of writing styles appeared and are variously spare and ornate. The beauty of the design has actually nothing to do with the beauty of the text itself, since the calligraphy is no less striking for those who have no idea what the writing actually means. This is a point worth emphasizing in general, since calligraphy often appears in buildings like mosques and palaces in places and styles that make them impossible or at the very least difficult to read. This goes against the pious interpretation of calligraphy as owing much of its effect to the meaning of the words that appear. One might point to opera, where the appreciation of the singing and acting may be entirely separated from the meaning of the words, which are often famously banal or incomprehensible to the audience.

Writing did often become a symbol of Islam, since the Prophet could not really be the figurehead. In contrast to major figures in other religions, he was presenting a message from God, and it is not the Prophet's message. So coins in the growing Islamic empire would replace the symbol of the ruler or king with some words in Arabic, representing the new authority in command. It is sometimes argued that the emphasis on calligraphy is because of the general iconophobia of Islam, but this is difficult to defend. There are plenty of images in Islam, even of the Prophet and those close to him (Grabar and Natif 2003), but there is a prolonged attack in the Qur'an on *shirk* or idolatry, and images in art might appear to offend this rule. There is a famous *hadith* or traditional saying in which the Prophet is supposed to have said that an angel does not come into a house containing a picture or a dog. The idea of a picture in the early years of Islam might have been a Christian religious image, of course (Grabar 1977).

Robert Irwin strikingly calls the Alhambra in Grenada "an inhabitable book" (Irwin 2011, 88), since it is full of Arabic writing from the Qur'an. The point is that for Muslims it is the word, and especially the word of the Qur'an, that is to be displayed and celebrated everywhere. It is often said that Islam is holistic and so Muslims have God and His work at the forefront of their minds at all times. On the other hand, when words are used as decoration, are they really operating as words in a text, or as impressive signs and images? They are there to impress, amaze, intrigue, and so on, not necessarily to be read like words in a book. The words in the Alhambra are there to project the idea of a particular language and its religion having a special status. They represent power, the power of the Nasrids, at a time when the power of Islam in what is today Spain was in decline, and being surrounded by them on the interior surface of a building is not like reading a book.

On a rather romantic view of Islam, those words are there to represent the power of God and His message, and are supposed to make the inhabitants of the space feel humble before their creator (Gonzalez 2001). We often need to remind ourselves of God, and displaying His words is one way of doing this. It is a nice story, but unlikely. Were the Nasrids walking humbly through their magnificent palace, a palace they had themselves commissioned? This was a difficult time politically, the surrounding Christian rulers were expanding their influence and would eventually expel them from the peninsula. But human beings do not build huge palaces to express their humility, even in difficult times. On the contrary, the intention is usually to project power and authority, and hope it lasts.

Carpet Controversies

It is often tempting to place emphasis on religion or indeed nationality when considering an art object. We tend to think that its origins and cultural context have a lot to tell us about it. There are problems with this approach, however. To give an example, there are a number of carpets based on designs originally made in al-Andalus, although the design no doubt came from the Near East, that have come to be known as Spanish Holbeins. They have that name because they are often represented in European paintings, and express wealth and luxury. An issue that arises is why Christian countries would give such prominence to objects from the Islamic world. The interesting feature of these carpets is that the originals of course no longer exist, carpets do not last that long, so the only record we have of them is from the paintings of the period in Europe, paintings in which they play an enormous role in adding to the perspective. It has been argued that these carpets are actually based on Christian and Armenian designs, and that their margins consist not of Arabic kufic writing but rather crosses (Gantzhorn 1998). The unlikely claim that Europeans were attracted to the Spanish Holbein carpets because of their Christian iconography is based on no evidence at all. It ignores the fact that for many centuries trade between the Islamic and Christian world flourished, especially in items of luxury like textiles, and these paintings come from long after the major period of conflict in the Middle Ages. Even then, many Islamic cultural forms entered the Christian world, in architecture for example. What attracted the Europeans at the time was the radiant beauty of the carpets which are lovingly represented by the artists, almost thread by thread, and no doubt also their exoticism. They were luxurious things and displayed the wealth and status of those who possessed them. In some of the paintings they are not on the floor but obviously on display, with the hands of their owners stroking them in a proprietary manner. In some ways, this was the case for the carpets originally, since they first came from further east and their production was developed locally by those with the skills to produce them for some time after the Reconquista with mudejar textile workers. Should the new political and religious authorities in Spain have rejected them because they were based on Islamic art? But they are so beautiful that they survived, and indeed came to be reproduced under the new regime.

In recent years the hostility between the now independent countries Azerbaijan and Armenia has developed into carpet wars, with the former saying that what are generally known as Armenian carpets are really Azeri (and the technical term for them is Karabagh, confusingly an Armenian territory in what is today Azerbaijan), and the Armenians arguing that what are called Turkish or oriental carpets are really Armenian, in that they are based on Armenian, and ultimately Christian, designs. Unfortunately the hostility has not been limited to an exchange of disputes solely about carpets, but it reminds us of the importance of not overplaying the role of the context within which an art object is produced. As we have seen, during the Renaissance we find a lot of use of the oriental carpet motif in paintings, they tend to move over time off the wall and table onto the floor, but after a time they entirely disappear. Was this because they suddenly were discovered to be Islamic? Surely not, rather an artistic theme that is popular at one time is felt perhaps to have come to an end and something else tends to dominate, perhaps because the aesthetic possibilities of that theme are felt to have become exhausted. In art as in everything things change and it is simplistic to relate those changes to direct influences from religion and/or politics.

How Islamic Is Islamic Aesthetics?

Here we get to a central issue in the discussion of Islamic aesthetics, and that is how far is it dependent on Islam as a religion and how far on its regional and cultural setting (Leaman 2006). There is a tendency to look for a definition of Islamic art that makes it essentially religious, since after all the property that art has is, we are told, Islamic. There is also a tendency to make it basically Eastern or oriental, exotic and different from other forms of art. All these tendencies should be resisted. Much of what we call Islamic art was actually made by non-Muslims, albeit under the direction no doubt of Muslims, and employed a variety of motifs and designs that existed at the time and place of construction. Like all cultures the growing Islamic world sought to express itself in public and define itself and its power through its products, and certainly what was distinctive about it was its religion, a religion that came from outside and sought to impose itself on the local communities which it now dominated. That does not mean that the local inhabitants were forced to convert to Islam or even suffered huge penalties by sticking to their existing ideas and beliefs; the move to convert certainly existed right from the start of the Muslim conquests but often were slow to take effect. After all, the fact that non-Muslims paid more taxes might have been a disinclination to push conversion more rigorously. As the dominant culture, Islam definitely saw art and design as a means to state publicly its hegemony, and at the same time, divergent communities were generally able to use their own forms of artistic expression within their own houses of worship and public and private buildings. The idea of different communities doing different things became especially engraved in the Ottoman Empire, provided those communities accepted a subsidiary role. Some churches became mosques, for example, but not all churches suffered that fate, and similarly for Hindu temples in the Indian subcontinent. Although such changed structures often underwent internal changes to remove the specifically non-Muslim iconography, there was usually no general ban on such iconography in buildings not used by Muslims.

It is often said that there is a universal disapproval of the use of images in Islam. This really needs to be challenged (Flood 2002). It is true that there is little decoration within a mosque, apart from writing and the structure of the building itself. But within Islamic art there are many images, even sometimes of the Prophet Muhammad and his Companions (Gruber 1977, 2017; Soucek 1988), although they are sometimes veiled or represented in very distinct ways. Even in countries such as Saudi Arabia that are particularly enthusiastic, or were in the past, in forbidding the use of images in religion, images themselves are ubiquitous, especially of the King. To a degree this antipathy toward images is based on what is taken to be pre-Islamic culture, where images predominated in Mecca and the Qur'an classes idolatry as a sin for which forgiveness will never be available (4:116, 39:65). The Qur'an is particularly constant in its critique of any deviation from the idea of God being one and alone, and the Wahhabi movement based on Hanbalism saw itself as purifying the practice of Islam from a sort of degenerate pantheism that had arisen over time. Indeed, Islam sees itself as the original religion that had over time become far less monotheistic until the revelations made to the Prophet Muhammad, the last message from God to humanity. As in some forms of Judaism, art was treated with suspicion as advocating the idea that things have power all their own, and not just an influence on us that ultimately derives from God (Cresswell 1946).

SUFISM ON ART

The intellectual movement in the Islamic world that really emphasized the significance of art was Sufism, a movement treated with great suspicion in the Wahhabi environment of what is today Saudi Arabia and some of its neighbors. Sufis are fond of the hadith that whoever has within himself love for God loves the face of a beautiful person, and that God is beautiful and loves beauty (Zargar 2011). Hence the aesthetic enterprise becomes part of religion itself, at least its esoteric and hidden part. Ruzbihan Baqli quotes with approval the hadith that someone who becomes close to God becomes close to every beautiful thing (1958, 9). According to Ruzbihan, all created things are ultimately beautiful (*hasan*) because they are the product of a beautiful God. The human perception of beauty or ugliness then varies to the extent that any individual sees God in any particular created thing. Beauty as *husn* is one of the attributes of God's essence and so has to be present in every act. In contrast, beauty as *jalal* is an attribute of His acts, and links God with His creation. God's *jamal* suggests a loving relationship toward His creation, which should be contrasted with His *jalal*, his majesty and awe. As a result, although some acts of the creator might not appear to be beautiful (*jamil*), they are all beautiful acts (*hasan*) as signs of God and His beauty. Sufis explain how our task is to return to God by moving through a series of stations along a path of spiritual growth throughout our lives. Beauty plays an important role in this return, since appreciating the beauty (*husn*) of created things allows us to see the creator behind the external form of His creation. Everything may be contemplated in this way since they represent and reveal their creator but human beings do it best because only they possess all the divine attributes. Ruzbihan thus argues that cultivating passionate love (*'ishq*) for beautiful people is necessary to develop love for, and intimacy with, the beautiful God who created them. Some human beings are more beautiful than others, in particular the prophets that best represent God's beauty. Ruzbihan points to Adam and Muhammad as the most perfect mirrors of divine beauty. As Murata puts it when explaining his views, "to love beauty . . . is simply to follow the most perfect human being, who has set down for humankind a beautiful model" and the route for returning to a beautiful God (2018, 127).

Sufis and those close to them, like Said Nursi, speak of Muslims linking the beauty of the world to the beauty of its Creator:

> All the beautiful creatures which display the manifestations of an eternal beauty and loveliness especially in the spring. . . . for instance the flowers, fruits, small birds, and flies . . . shows their craftsman's wondrous proficiency . . . those fine artefacts are adorned in a way so agreeable, are decorated in a way so sweet, display a beauty and art so attractive, that their maker could create these works only through an infinite knowledge. (2007, 619)

God is described as someone who makes most excellent everything that he creates (32:7), where the word used for "excellent" is *ahsanu*, bringing it with it the idea of aesthetic perfection. After all, just as the verses of the Qur'an are called *ayat*, signs, what we see around us in the world of nature are also signs of the intelligence who created them. On the other hand, not just anything can be regarded as an appropriate work of art on the religious view. It has to be uplifting, moral, inspiring and, in short, positive in its impact on its audience. This might be thought to be rather limiting aesthetically since it would seem to rule out forms of art that do not fit this sort of description, and that is true also of our interpretation of what we see in the natural world, much of which is not exciting or beautiful. We would normally say that there are plenty of gloomy artists who concentrate on the negative aspects of the world around them, and it is not clear how they fit in with this religious attitude to reality and ways of depicting it.

IMAGINATION AND PERSPECTIVE

In its early years, Islamic philosophy was interested in defining clearly what the differences are between aesthetic and other types of language, and their paradigm of the aesthetic was, not surprisingly, poetry. This was a cultural form well known and appreciated in the Arab world. Using Aristotle's arrangement of different kinds of reasoning (Leaman 2009), they argued that poetry is a form of argument, but a very weak one in what it can be taken to establish. It works on emotions, and is one down from rhetoric, which does the same but has some general public purpose in mind, so is at a higher intellectual level. Poetry uses techniques to move us emotionally and so it is structured in such a way to affect our emotions, and we can examine the art form accordingly and see how it operates. This seems a strange way of assessing poetry, as a form of argument, and it has come in for much criticism, and it is certainly true that the early writers on aesthetics in Islam had a limited number of forms of art in their environment which they could examine and discuss. On the other hand, the idea that poetry makes statements and those can be logically assessed is not unreasonable.

The problem with poetry epistemologically is that it appeals to our passions and not to our reason, according to the Peripatetic thinkers, and so is often loose and inaccurate. It employs the faculty of imagination and that is problematic since the imagination is irretrievably bound up with the body and its sense equipment. Since knowledge in the Aristotelian view is universal, it does not come close to the imagination, since the basis of imagination is our individuality. Yet on the Sufi accounts of beauty it is often represented as something quite objective. It is an external sign of something internal and inaccessible, except perhaps by acknowledging beauty. There is a hadith which tells us that God is beautiful and loves beauty (Blair and Bloom 2013), and that can be taken to imply that not caring about beauty is like not caring about God. *Ihsan* is the term at issue here, and it has both an aesthetic and a moral dimension. Translating always brings with it problems, and the Arabic for imagination also, *khayal* is often used rather differently from imagination in English, since the latter sometimes implies the unreality of the object of the experience. The Peripatetic thinkers definitely treat it in this way. Perhaps imagination does not necessarily deal with the unreal but it is not a source of secure knowledge since it is based on the senses and all that that implies in terms of partiality and error. For the Sufis though, imagination is a powerful form of knowledge. It enables us to bring things together in our minds and apply emotion to what we find there. It is not enough to understand things rationally, there is a need also to bring experiences together and apply feeling to what we perceive. This might seem to introduce subjectivity into the analysis of beauty, but many Islamic thinkers deny this and insist that there is a common moral and aesthetic principle running through Islamic art and that is revelation, or at least religious feeling of some kind. There is then a concentration on general principles such as *tawhid* or the unity of God, developing in art as symmetry, harmony, and order, which are easy to experience in much traditional Islamic art. The forms of representation are frequently not realistic of the everyday world but rather of the inner world, hence the emphasis on order and proportion that we find in the designs and even writing in Arabic. This is taken to represent the inner unity of everything, and so of course is very different from the things we see around us.

In the novel *My Name is Red,* Orhan Pamuk uses this idea to contrast the traditional Islamic artist who eschews individual features and just reproduces stereotypical images, albeit very skillfully, as representing a traditional view of what Islamic art ought to be. It should go for interior meanings, and not be obsessed with the realistic portrayal of life. In the novel, the encroaching Western forms of painting are threatening to overwhelm tradition, and the participants can understand and experience the temptation to explore physicality in that more direct way at the expense of the perspective that had over the centuries become the normal way of doing things in the Islamic world. It might be said that this is to refer back to the Qur'an, which also is relatively concise by comparison with the Bible, and just represents the main characters in schematic and fairly abstract ways. One does not usually get a sense of who they are as people, but of their relationship with God as really the only important fact about them. Even with Musa, who in his journey with Khidr does appear to be fallible and constantly so, there is not much notion of how he developed as a person as a consequence of his experiences. He becomes the stereotype of someone who is impatient, who learns little from his experiences and who also does not stick to the agreement he made with Khidr right at the start of the journey. Like the Moses in the Bible, he comes to be seen as very much a human being, but unlike that Moses, he seems to be a paradigm of someone who just constantly gets things wrong. As in what we often think of as Islamic art we find repetition, a description of a pattern, a fascination with the whole picture and not so much with its individual parts, by contrast in particular with Christian art and its emphasis on individuals and their individual feelings and emotions. This may seem a strange comment given the often highly stylized crucifixion scenes in Christian art, and anyone who has walked through galleries of such art may find them repetitive and similar. Yet there is often an emphasis on the emotions of the individuals in the picture, not just Jesus but those around him, and ways of varying the use of light to draw contrasts and project a mood. As Shaw (2019) suggests when referring to Bihzad, one of the greatest book illustrators, his use of geometry denies "propriety to the gaze and thereby does not implicate a human subject as its master" (267). He presents a perspicuous view, the sort of view that God would have, were He to have any view at all, because it captures everything that is happening all at once.

Is the suggestion here that one form of painting is superior to another? Not at all, and that comes out nicely in Pamuk's book; there are different ways of representation available to the artist at different times and places. When new ways of dealing with painting become available, some artists immediately try them and adopt them as part of their repertoire. Others resist and maintain the old techniques. We are familiar with artists trying to represent something in their work by not seeking to reproduce what they see directly in front of them. They are trying to capture something else, many art movements avoid just trying to reproduce what we take to be real. After all, what we take to be real may often be wrong and is it not more interesting aesthetically to try to capture what is behind appearance? That is certainly the case from a religious point of view and brings in another aspect of a general wariness by some Muslims toward art, namely, whether it is serious enough. The Qur'an is critical of frivolity and wasting time and not paying attention to God, *ghafla*. Like most religious texts, it is a serious work, and yet it would be wrong to see Islam as opposed to pleasure. After all, the descriptions of paradise are very sensual, and the Qur'an is generally not in favor of what it sees as the rather extreme ascetic practices of Christianity. In the sayings attributed to the Prophet, the hadith, there are often discussions of what people should be allowed to do and there is no proscription of fun. On the other hand, there are certainly firm views on what is appropriate and what is not with respect to representations of the human figure, for example, and the idea of art for art's sake is not one that any religion could really countenance. In particular, Islam is usually very critical of the use of art to criticize religion and major religious figures, and some Muslim have even responded to such art with violence and murder. There is again nothing exclusively Islamic about taking religion seriously, and criticizing as a consequence activities and products that appear to not fall into this view of the world.

ISLAMIC ART: THE DEFINITION ISSUE

Museums and art galleries have huge difficulties in knowing how to label their sections on Islamic art, as it used to be called (Porter et al. 2020). Arab art will not work as a label, there is so much Persian and Indian Islamic art of course, and then other parts of the world have artists and larger Muslim populations than the Middle East, and much of the art anyway seems to have nothing to do with religion of any kind. Some Christian and Jewish artists produce work in the style of their Muslim peers, and the whole issue of identity has now become so complex and fluid. The outstanding Arab sculptor for the last few decades has been Dia Azzawi, originally from Iraq, and his work represents a profound secular nationalism. This is not a dilemma limited to Islamic art, of course, and even labels like Irish art or American art are difficult to apply precisely, although for some reason museums and galleries like to have a national affiliation attached to their exhibits.

We need to distinguish between art for Muslims, art by Muslims, art produced within a Muslim context, and Islamic art. Art for Muslims tends to be crudely conceived, like all art designed to pull on the heart strings it aims at evoking nostalgia and ducking challenges. Middle Eastern collectors have been enthusiastic about orientalist art, despite the widespread criticism it has suffered at the hands of Edward Said and his many followers in the art history field. They blamed that form of art which flourished during colonial times for strengthening the idea of the Arabs as the Other, both noble and treacherous, and with strange ways of treating women. The latter were represented as both lascivious and lovely, often confined and available for the Western gaze. The Middle East becomes exotic and mysterious and apparently open for domination and exploitation. One can appreciate these criticisms and yet it is not surprising that there has been a lively market for paintings from that period since the artists are often spectacularly good at their work and present a very positive image of the local culture. Handsome Arab men on fine stallions with fierce hawks on their wrists and swords at their sides, gorgeous women wearing ever more luxurious silks glance casually at their viewers through lustrous eyelashes. (It is often remarked that the models were not usually in fact Muslims who would not have wanted, or been allowed, to display themselves in such ways for paintings.) It is not surprising despite the widespread critique of orientalism that in the Middle East at least some inhabitants are attracted to such images of their predecessors as both gallant and sensuous, living in an environment of savage beauty or shameless luxury.

So art for Muslims sometimes has this Middle Eastern historical flavor, but often it is more apologetic and feels it needs to express more explicitly its Islamic roots. After all, the audience is one that might be suspicious of art and wonder how licit it really is. This has given rise to a great deal of kitsch, images of important Islamic shrines and buildings, significant people (often directed at the Shiʿa), and a lot of playing around with calligraphy. The attempt is to create images that when put on the Muslim wall will be nonthreatening and nostalgic. There is nothing wrong with this, and all communities are enthusiastic purchasers of art that reflects their culture, but it is worth pointing to the lack of creativity that such work exhibits. It tends to be dull, unimaginative and obvious. It is true that calligraphy is an important Islamic art, but there is no magic in the Arabic letters themselves, despite their use in the Qurʾan. Manipulating Arabic letters, writing them very large and in unusual ways is not a particularly exciting form of art-making. Many modern artists do it and hark back to calligraphy in the past in Islam as a vindication of what they do, and yet this manipulation of the form of the letters is very different from the precise and highly controlled nature of the major writing styles in the past. It is not exciting to have an Arabic word written in the shape of what it represents, for example, as though this were the height of creativity.

Art by Muslims can be any sort of art at all. It is often thought that our religious views must enter into other areas of our lives, and sometimes they do. Often they do not, and in any case, saying someone is a Muslim says almost nothing about them, religious labels can mean anything at all. It may mean they have Muslim parents, a Muslim name or were brought up Muslim, it says nothing really about their views on a whole range of other subjects. Like all communities Muslims are often very divided in their views on things, and art is no exception. Some artists of a Muslim background seem to be trying to involve their art in that background, while others ignore it, or apparently ignore it. It is naïve to think that just because someone comes from a certain community they are going to think in a certain way, or indeed create art accordingly. Even devout Muslims may not use or reflect their religion in their art, in just the same way that Muslim scientists of varying degrees of piety operate. Aesthetic style and scientific method can be influenced by religion, but often are not.

It is difficult to know how to distinguish between art produced in an Islamic context and Islamic art. Many of the skilled craftsmen and artists in the Islamic world were not Muslims at all, but their art followed the style then prevailing in the culture. They wanted to be paid, after all, for what they did. We are familiar with the motifs, patterns, designs, and so on that for many centuries prevailed in the Islamic world. Often they have been given a deep religious explanation; they reflect *tawhid*, the unity of God, they express the symmetry and balance existing in the world, they illustrate the wonder of the divinely created universe. There is no evidence that this is what the artists actually thought they were doing or that artists with different religious views could not have created art in the same way.

Referring to the *Word into Art* 2006 exhibition at the British Museum, a commentator suggests that

> the exhibition . . . is an invaluable intervention in the usual clichés and stereotypes that dominate Western understanding of the Arab and Persian world. The overall message is straightforward: a belief in poetry, humanity, and reverence as an alternative to materialism, capitalism, and power struggles. (Platt 2007)

Here we have an orientalism in reverse: in the West we have conflict and competition, and in the East, it is all love and respect. The exhibition itself had a vast poster at the entrance with a quote from Ibn al-ʿArabi about love, and for emphasis the word for love in Arabic was written in red. Yet for most attendees at such exhibitions there is an experience of often excellent art well within the various styles of modern art today, with all its variety and vibrancy (Ali 1994). There is a difficult balance here between respecting the ways in which a local culture structures the sorts of artistic product that emerges out of it, and at the same time using universal aesthetic criteria to assess the work. When it comes to modern art it is difficult to see any cultural context except that of the world as a whole, given the fact that the world nowadays is available to everyone through modern and inexpensive media devices and the ubiquity of travel and training.

On the other hand, there is also a limited enthusiasm for a kind of revival of traditional Islamic art skills, fostered by institutions like the Prince of Wales School that are very much oriented toward the archaic. Not just Islamic art is involved here, but every kind of traditional religious artistic activity is fostered, including Byzantine art, icon making, and so on. This is based on the idea that we have already discussed, of a perennialism in art which has always existed and which comes from a deep spiritual source (Nasr 1987). It represents the authentic in art as a whole, since all genuine art is seen as religious. It is the sort of approach to art which is like a similar approach to religion that sees mysticism as at its core; in Islam, this translates as Sufism being at the heart of Islam. Classical shapes, certain proportions, geometrical outlines and similar aspects of design are seen as essentially sacred and unchanging, since they reflect an inner reality which itself is unchanging.

Fortunately, we do not have to accept this very limited notion of what counts as art; we do not have to accept it even as a description of what may be called Islamic art. We have noted how a wide variety of work can come under this label and bringing different examples under a religious label does not mean we can insist that all those examples are in fact religious. On the other hand, the introduction of religion into the discussion of art does alert us to the fact that art has a wider focus than merely to be beautiful or any other aesthetic property that we wish to apply to an object. It may have a social function or even reflect some aspect of religious commitment, and acknowledging that wider reference makes Islamic art more than just the art from a particular geographical region.

To try to define it as having some common quality shared by all the very diverse artists and their equally distinct cultural environments is a futile project. This is true of most attempts at finding a nice neat description for any general term applied to art and should disincline us from pursuing such a chimera when discussing Islamic art.

See also: Schellekens, Destrée, this volume

REFERENCES

Ali, Wijdan. 1994. "Modern Arab Art: An Overview." In *Forces of Change: Artists of the Arab World*, edited by Salwa Mikdad Nashsashibi, 72–116. Washington, DC: The International Council for Women in the Arts and the National Museum of Women in the Arts.

Baqli, Ruzbihan. [1337] 1958. *Kitab ʿAbhar al-ʿAshiqin*, edited by Henry Corbin and Muhammad Muʿin, 1–113. Tehran: Dep. d'iranologie de l'Institut francoiranien.

Blair, Sheila, and Jonathan Bloom. 2013. *God Is Beautiful and Loves Beauty: The Object in Islamic Art and Culture*. New Haven, CT: Yale University Press.

Creswell, K. A. C. 1946. "The Lawfulness of Painting in Early Islam." *Ars Islamica* 11–12: 159–166.

Flood, Barry. 2002. "Between Cult and Culture: Bamiyan, Islamic Iconoclasm, and the Museum." *The Art Bulletin* 84, no. 4: 641–659.

Gantzhorn, Volkmar. 1998. *Oriental Carpets: Their Iconology and Iconography, from Earliest Times to the 18th Century*. Cologne: Taschen.

Gonzelez, Valerie. 2001. *Beauty and Islam: Aesthetics in Islamic Art and Architecture*. London: I. B. Tauris.

Grabar, O. 1977. "Islam and Iconoclasm." In *Iconoclasm: Papers Given at the Ninth Spring Symposium of Byzantine Studies*, edited by Anthony Bryer and Judith Herrin, 45–52. Birmingham, UK: Centre for Byzantine Studies, University of Birmingham.

Grabar, Oleg, and M. Natif. 2003. "The Story of the Portraits of the Prophet Muhammad." *Studia Islamica* 96, 19–38.

Gruber, Christiane. 2017. "Images of the Prophet Muhammad: Brief Thoughts on Some European-Islamic Encounters." In *Seen and Unseen: Visual Cultures of Imperialism*, edited by Sanaz Fotouhi and Esmaeil Zeiny, 34–52. Leiden: Brill.

Irwin, Robert. 2011. *The Alhambra*. Cambridge, MA: Harvard University Press.

Kermani, Navid. 2015. Translated by Tony Crawford. *God is Beautiful: The Aesthetic Experience of the Quran*. Cambridge: Polity.

Leaman, Oliver. 2006. *Islamic Aesthetics: an Introduction*. Edinburgh: Edinburgh University Press.

Leaman, Oliver. 2009. *Islamic Philosophy: An Introduction*. Cambridge: Polity.

Murata, Kazuyo. 2018. *Beauty in Sufism: The Teachings of Ruzbihan*. Albany: SUNY Press.

Nasr, Seyyed Hossein. 1987. *Islamic Art and Spirituality*. Albany: SUNY Press.

Nursi, Said. 2007. *The Rays*. Translated by Ş. Vahide. Istanbul: Sösler.

Pamuk, Orhan. 2001. *My Name Is Red*. Translated by Erdağ Göknar. New York: Knopf.

Platt, Susan. 2007. "World into Art: Art and Artists of the Modern Middle East." *Art and Politics Now*. https://www.artandpoliticsnow.com/2007/06/word-into-art-artists-of-the-modern-middle-east/

Porter, Venetia, Natasha Morris, and Charles Tripp. 2020. *Reflection: Contemporary Art in the Middle East and North Africa*. London: British Museum Press.

Schimmel, Annemarie. 1984. *Calligraphy and Islamic Culture*. New York: New York University Press.

Shaw, Wendy. 2019. *What Is "Islamic" Art? Between Religion and Perception*. Cambridge: Cambridge University Press.

Soucek, Prisilla. 1988. "The Life of the Prophet: Illustrated Versions." *Content and Context of Visual Arts in the Islamic World*. London and University Park: The College Art Association of America and Penn State University Press.

Zargar, Cyrus. 2011. *Sufi Aesthetics: Beauty, Love, and the Human Form in the Writings of Ibn 'Arabi and al-'Iraqi*. Columbia: University of South Carolina Press.

CHAPTER 5

THE ETHICALLY GROUNDED NATURE OF JAPANESE AESTHETIC SENSIBILITY

YURIKO SAITO

INTRODUCTION

IN the history of Japan, major political changes gave rise to distinct aesthetic concepts and artistic practices of each period. During the Heian court period (794–1185), the literary arts by aristocrats flourished. The most notable among them are *The Tale of Genji* (1008–1020), a long novel narrating the life of Prince Genji written by a court lady Murasaki Shikibu; *The Pillow Book* (ca. 1002), a series of short essays and vignettes depicting nature and court life penned by another court lady, Sei Shōnagon; and the court-commissioned anthologies of poems by aristocrats and Buddhist priests. The medieval warrior culture starting in 1185 with the Kamakura period gave rise to the Zen garden, flower arrangement, Noh theater, calligraphy, brush ink painting, and tea ceremony, often regarded as quintessentially Japanese arts. This was followed by the popular culture of the Edo period (1603–1868) that gave rise to Kabuki theater, puppet theater, woodblock prints, and haiku. After ending the two and half centuries of self-isolation from the world, the rapid Westernization process that began in 1868 ushered in the modern period.

Despite these changes, however, there are consistent threads that form Japan's aesthetic sensibility. One of these is the ethically grounded nature of aesthetics, both in creative practices and aesthetic experiences. The classical works that constitute the great books tradition in Japanese aesthetics are primarily artists' accounts of art-making. What may initially appear to be training manuals for artistic practices are ultimately treatises on how to live an ethical life. Paralleling the practitioners' aesthetics is an equally ethically grounded response expected of those who gain aesthetic experiences.

In what follows, I will first explain the Japanese aesthetic tradition as a form of self-cultivation by reference to the pre-Westernization sources. This will be followed by examining how this focus on cultivating oneself made the Japanese aesthetic sensibility vulnerable to political exploitation, particularly after Westernization began. Despite such problematic historical consequences, however, the final section will explore the timely relevance of the Japanese aesthetic tradition and the positive contributions it can make to the contemporary world.

ETHICALLY GROUNDED AESTHETIC ACTIVITIES

The most dominant strand that forms the long-held Japanese aesthetic sensibility is the "other-regarding" attitude toward the materials, subject matters, and the experiencing agents when making art. Creative acts are driven by minimizing the creator's own ideas, often referred to as emptying one's mind and listening to the other's voice. Such a stance is thought not only to generate a satisfying aesthetic experience for the spectator but also to help cultivate a virtuous life for the creator.

Respect for the Material and Subject Matter

The earliest statement regarding this attitude is found in the eleventh-century treatise on garden-making, *Sakuteiki* (*Book on Garden Making*), written by an aristocrat, Tachibana-no-Toshitsuna. He emphasizes the principle of "obeying (or following) the request" (*kowan ni shitagau*乞はんに従う) of rocks, the primary ingredients of the garden at the time, which means that each rock's individual characteristics should dictate its placement and arrangement. For example, a stone with an upward thrust should be erected upright and accompanied by a flat stone placed horizontally (Tachibana-no-Toshitsuna [eleventh century] 1985).

The same design strategy developed later for shaping plant materials. Japanese gardeners work closely *with* the natural endowments of trees and bushes, instead of allowing their free growth or imposing a predetermined form, by eliminating those parts considered to be adventitious, thereby accentuating their essential characteristics (Zōen 1991). Robert Carter characterizes this attitude as "emptying" one's mind (Carter 2008, 65) by quoting Masuno Shunmyo, a contemporary master gardener: "The most important thing in executing a design is to talk to the plants and stones and hear what they themselves have to say about how they want to be laid out. In other words, I engage in a kind of dialogue with them" (63).[1]

---

[1] In this chapter I follow the Japanese order by placing the family name before the given name. Hence, Masuno is his family name. For the Japanese authors whose work have been published in English or those who are well-known outside of Japan, such as Tadao Andō and Issey Miyake, I follow the English order.

The art of flower arrangement (*ikebana*), elevated to an artistic status through its contribution to the tea ceremony during the sixteenth century, similarly aims to "let flower live," literally the translation of *ikebana*, which means to "let flower express itself" (*ikasu*) (Ōhashi 1998, 553), or "to represent nature in its inmost essence" (Ueda 1967, 86). This can be achieved by further cutting of branches, leaves, and blossoms to clearly delineate only the defining form of the particular plant. According to a contemporary master teacher cited by Carter, "when the students themselves become *empty*, they do very well at *ikebana*" (Carter 2008, 102; emphasis added).

The same principle applies to the art of representation. For example, haiku, a 5-7-5 syllable verse established in the seventeenth century by Matsuo Bashō (1644–1694), aims at articulating what characterizes the subject matter. He teaches that the poet must overcome his personal feelings and concerns and "enter into" the object with what he calls "the slenderness of mind," summarized in his well-known saying: "Of the pine-tree learn from the pine-tree. Of the bamboo learn from the bamboo" (Hattori 1981, 162–163).[2] Painters such as Tosa Mitsukuni (1617–1691) and Tsubaki Chinzan (1800–1854) also emphasize depicting the essential characteristics of the object by eliminating certain elements (Ueda 1967; Tsubaki 1990).

This mode of creative act extends to everyday activities. In Japanese cooking, the cook tries to bring out the ingredient's characteristics through specific ways of cutting, cooking, seasoning, and arranging. Kenji Ekuan observes that the mission of Japanese "culinary artifice" is "to render fish more fishlike and rice more ricelike" (Ekuan 2000, 77), and the Japanese lunch box illustrates well how the inherent appeal of each ingredient is enhanced through careful preparation and arrangement.

These accounts from classical treatises and today's practitioners together articulate that art-making is premised upon respecting the material's or the subject matter's specific characteristics. This requires carefully listening to the other's voice by emptying one's mind. "The other" here does not have to be natural objects, such as rocks and plants. Some noted contemporary designers adopt the same stance toward manufactured materials. For example, Tadao Andō's architecture often emphasizes the concreteness of concrete, while Issey Miyake explores synthetic materials and rubber in his apparel design.

Respect for the Experiencing Agent

The other-regarding attitude in art-making is also directed toward the experiencing agent. In addition to listening to the materials, Japanese garden-making follows Toshitsuna's recommendation of *suji kaete* (すじかへて), changing the axis, meaning avoiding symmetry. This strategy provides continuous nourishments for stimulating

---

[2] It should be noted that something akin to the disinterestedness required for a spectator in Western aesthetics applies to the creator in Japanese aesthetics.

imagination through meandering paths and partially hidden vistas that unfold gradually. This constantly shifting experience is punctuated by a rhythm of anticipation, surprise, and fulfillment of expectation, as well as multiperspectival views, in contrast to a one-directional view prominent in European formal gardens.[3]

Stepping stones, ubiquitous presence in Japanese gardens, are also arranged not only to ensure safety and easy walkability but also to maximize the aesthetic experience, for example by placing the stones of differing colors, textures, sizes, and shapes next to each other for mutual illumination. Sometimes the arrangement is intentionally made awkward in order to encourage the visitor to slow the pace and appreciate what she is stepping on.

By far the most eloquent expression of respect for the experiencing agent is found in the tea ceremony, established in the sixteenth century by Sen no Rikyū (1522–1591) and still practiced as a mode of cultural refinement by many. This participatory art embodies consummate thoughtfulness and care by the host toward the guest through elegant body movements and selection, arrangement, and handling of various implements and preparation of the tea hut. Despite the basic rules to guide these considerations, orchestrating various aspects of the tea ceremony to render a memorable experience of a one-time event, *ichigo ichie* (一期一会), requires utmost sensibility, flexibility, improvisational skills, imagination, and "vigilant consideration of others" (Surak 2013, 52; also see Kumakura and Varley 1989).

For both modes of respecting the other, the materials and the recipient of creation, minimizing one's self and ideas is considered paramount. The emphasis is placed on being open- or empty-minded so that the creator can listen to the other and imagine what the experience will be like on the receiving end. Creativity comes from working collaboratively as a humble partner, instead of a lone genius engaging in self-expression.

The Role of Zen Buddhism

Sakuteiki predates the introduction of Zen Buddhism to Japan from the late twelfth century to the early thirteenth century by priests Eisai (1141–1215) and Dōgen (1200–1253). However, it is no accident that the practitioners of other arts were often Zen adepts, and they practiced art-making as a form of Zen discipline.[4] Zen teaches the thoroughgoing rejection of egocentric and anthropocentric worldview, as stated by Dōgen: "Acting on and witnessing myriad things *with the burden of oneself* is 'delusion.' Acting on and witnessing oneself *in the advent of myriad things* is enlightenment." He continues, "studying the Buddha Way is studying oneself. Studying oneself is *forgetting oneself.* Forgetting oneself is *being enlightened by all things*" (Dōgen 1988, 32; emphases added).

---

[3] Alexander Pope ridicules the symmetrical, hence one-directional, view of formal gardens. (Pope [1731] 1990).

[4] It should be noted that Masuno, a contemporary master gardener, whom I cited earlier, is a Zen priest.

This transcendence of ego is facilitated by recognizing and overcoming self-centered and all-too-human schemes that govern perception. Zen is optimistic about being able to directly experience the thus-ness or being-such-ness (*immo* 恁麼) of the other-than-self. Thus, the Japanese artists' practice of respectfully listening to the other's voice and directing their creative activity accordingly is not simply an aesthetic exercise but also a spiritual discipline.

In Zen Buddhism, art-making is not the only vehicle for practicing transcending ego. Daily mundane activities, such as cooking, eating, and cleaning, also offer an opportunity. Dōgen left detailed instructions on these activities, including cleansing oneself during bathing and voiding oneself in the lavatory, all promoting self-care to cultivate a virtuous self as well as an awareness of the relational mode of human existence in this world (Dōgen 1977; 1983; 1992b). Regarding cooking, serving, and eating food, he instructs the disciples to pay respect to the raw materials used and the other people involved. To give only one example, he suggests that "fruit seeds and other similar waste must be put in a place where it will give no offence to others," so that "others must never be allowed to become disgusted by such a sight" (Dōgen 1992a, 161).[5] This expresses the need for adjusting one's action according to the other-regarding aesthetic consideration.

Reciprocal Ethically Grounded Aesthetic Experience

The aesthetic gifts created with an ethically grounded attitude call for reciprocity by the person gaining an aesthetic experience. Dōgen's many instructions for eating are applicable beyond the religious context. Well-known for the attention to details and beautiful presentation, Japanese food encourages attentive appreciation and slow eating, as pointed out by Graham Parkes: "The care with which the food has been prepared and presented invites corresponding care and attention in the handling and eating of it" (Parkes 2018, 111).

In a similar manner, a tea ceremony succeeds if the guest carefully attends to the various details expressive of the host's care and shows appreciation nonverbally, such as by cradling the tea bowl with both hands to honor the bowl and tea inside or by properly bidding farewell (Ii [1858] 1979; Sen 1965; Surak 2013). Today's tea master, Sen Genshitsu XV, explains that the primary purpose of the tea ceremony is a tacit communication whereby "the guests will 'feel' what the host intended to 'give' them in and through the ceremony. An intense level of kindness prevails, and the guests learn through this enveloping atmosphere to be kind to one another in turn" (Carter 2008, 90). Ultimately, as stated by Eiko Ikegami, "the deepest human communication took place through silent *aesthetic* communion" (Ikegami 2005, 227; emphasis added).

---

[5] A contemporary commentator also encourages gathering together remnants, such as fish bones, tail, and head, into a neat bundle to spare the server and eating companions of an unsightly sight (Shiotsuki 1983).

Also consider the act of opening a gift, a part of daily life in a gift-giving culture like Japan. Japanese gift packaging is known for embodying a "deep *respect* for material and process, and . . . for the intended user," as well as "*care* for the object inside, and . . . for the recipient" (Hendry 1993, 63; emphases added). If the receiver rips apart the package in order to reach the item fast, creating the noise of tearing paper and the unsightly torn pieces, her act cannot help but convey a failure to recognize and appreciate the thoughtful and considerate preparation by the giver (Saito 1999).

Finally, if someone rushes through a garden designed with the utmost regard for the visitors' aesthetic experience, he not only impoverishes his aesthetic life but also fails to acknowledge the gardener's care and thoughtfulness. In all these examples, a grateful acknowledgment of the aesthetic gift is expressed aesthetically: the ways of walking, drinking, eating, and opening a package. Although the verbal expression of gratitude is not irrelevant, the emphasis is on the nonverbal aesthetic embodiment.

In this way, Japanese aesthetic sensibility is regarded as an effective means of cultivating other-regarding respectful attitudes, whether toward other people or the material world. It promotes minimizing one's self and adjusting one's interactions with the other-than-self according to its lead.

MIXED LEGACY OF *WABI* AESTHETICS

The deferential attitude toward others discussed so far helps one to be open-minded by accepting and appreciating that which is commonly regarded negatively. *Wabi* aesthetics specifically challenges one to develop such an appreciation.[6] Although *wabi* aesthetics was established in the sixteenth century along with the tea ceremony, the aesthetics of the difficult-to-accept was already seen as a mark of a moral character, personified by Prince Genji, the protagonist of *The Tale of Genji*. As Ivan Morris observes (Morris 1994), the ideal man during the Heian court period possesses a delicate aesthetic sensibility not only toward other people, in particular his lovers, but also toward the *ephemeral* beauty of nature, *mono no aware*, translated as sensitivity to things, pathos of things, or tears of things (*lacrimae rerum*). Impermanence of everything is the foundation of Buddhism that had spread among the Heian aristocrats. This posed a challenge because humans generally want to maintain things, including themselves. The aristocrats sought refuge from this difficulty by aestheticizing transience. The almost cult-like aesthetics of falling cherry blossoms developed during the court period is a prime example of celebrating something that is otherwise difficult to accept. Rather than lamenting or fighting against fate, it provides an aesthetically appealing means of accepting the human existential predicament.

---

[6] *Wabi*, which means impoverishment, is often coupled with *sabi*, which means rust and loneliness and is associated with the aesthetics of haiku. For my purpose here, I am decoupling them to emphasize the notions of imperfection associated with *wabi*. I thank Arnold Berleant for raising this question.

Wabi aesthetics goes further by not only appreciating the signs of transience but also by engaging with them through using cracked bowls, lacquerwares showing wear and tear, and jugs and vases with chipped rims and missing handles in the tea ceremony. By elevating the aesthetic status of these imperfect and defective objects through active interactions, *wabi* aesthetics helps one to practice emptying one's ego by celebrating what at first may be difficult to accept, let alone appreciate. It enriches a person's aesthetic life by expanding her aesthetic palette and cultivates a respectful attitude toward what the other can offer.

At the same time, however, this aesthetics can also encourage acceptance of the imperfections of life that are brought about by social injustice. For example, a nineteenth-century tea master, Sōtaku Jakuan, claims that "*wabi* means lacking things, having things run entirely contrary to our desires, being frustrated in our wishes" and suggests: "Always bear in mind that *wabi* involves not regarding incapacities as incapacitating, not feeling that lacking something is deprivation, not thinking that what is not provided is deficiency" (*Zencharoku* (*Record of Zen Tea*) [1828], cited by Haga 1989, 195–196). Ii Naosuke, a powerful nineteenth-century statesman, specifically justifies the rigidly stratified feudal society:

> If pleasure is not gratification accompanied by a sense of contentment, it is not real pleasure ... if each individual is satisfied with his lot and is not envious, he will enjoy life ... if the art of drinking tea were widely practiced throughout the country ... both high and low would be content with their lots, would enjoy but not grieve, and would do no wrong ... The country would become peaceful and tranquil spontaneously. (*Sadō no seidō no tasuke to narubeki o agetsuraeru bun* (*An Essay on the Tea Cult as an Aid to Government*) [1846], cited by Minami 1971, 88)

The problematic nature of this aestheticization of poverty did not escape criticism by some intellectuals after the tea ceremony became popular. For example, Dazai Shundai (1680–1747), a Confucian scholar, characterizes the penchant for cracked tea implements, meager amounts of snacks, and impoverished-looking tea huts as a dilettantish amusement for the rich and powerful, the patrons and practitioners of the tea ceremony at the time.[7]

> Whatever tea dilettantes do is a copy of the poor and humble. It may be that the rich and noble have a reason to find pleasure in copying the poor and humble. But why should those who are, from the outset, poor and humble find pleasure in further copying the poor and humble? (*Dokugo* (*Solitary Words*) [1816], cited by Minami 1971, 90)[8]

---

[7] The same aesthetics of poverty and its criticism can be found today in grunge aesthetics, shabby chic, and the so-called poverty tourism.

[8] I changed Ikoma's translation to be more faithful to the original Japanese. The translation reads: "Why should those who are, from the outset, poor and humble further copy the poor and humble and make fun of them?"

However, this kind of criticism seems to have remained a minority voice, as the exploitation of *wabi* aesthetics to justify the societal status quo continued into the twentieth century, as suggested by a twentieth-century postwar writer:

> The tea cult stresses "accordance with one's lot" and "knowing contentment and resting upon complacency" . . . When this state of mind shifts to a positive state of loving privation and taking delight in poverty, *wabicha* (*wabi* tea) arises. . . . In the state of finding beauty in imperfect things, modesty begins to function and a love of privation and simplicity develops. (*Sadō kyōshitsu* (*Tea Cult Classroom*) [1950], cited by Minami 1971, 88–89)

Here *wabi* aesthetics is used unapologetically to justify the societal *status quo* that includes the results of socioeconomic injustice.

Perhaps the most striking example of appreciating the difficult-to-accept by mobilizing the long-held aesthetic sensibility toward transience and impermanence concerns the ephemeral beauty of *falling* cherry blossoms. This aesthetic legacy held since the Heian period continued to exert its power not only for the aesthetic appeal but also for symbolically signifying the virtue of accepting one's fate (Ohnuki-Tierney 2002). For example, Nishi Amane, said to be the major architect of the Japanese military of late nineteenth century, frequently lectured on the "virtue" of cherry blossoms for "not clinging to their blooming" (cited by Ohnuki-Tierney 2002, 107). Nitobe Inazō starts his *Bushidō* (*The Way of the Warriors* 1908) by declaring that "chivalry (*Bushidō*) is a flower no less indigenous to the soil of Japan than its emblem, the cherry blossom," which is contrasted with roses that cling to life as symbolizing European chivalry (cited by Ohnuki-Tierny 2002, 13).[9] Ultimately, this aestheticization of falling cherry blossoms served as a potent and poignant symbol for falling Kamikaze pilots, whose death was praised and celebrated by the wartime nation.

While various causes lead people world-over to perform suicide missions, this Japanese case is noteworthy for praising those soldiers' sacrifice not only for emptying their self to serve the country but also for committing a *beautiful* act. Their sacrifice was regarded as fulfilling *bitoku* (美徳 beauty and virtue). Indeed, in a postwar critique, Sakaguchi Ango repudiates the *bitoku* ethos imposed by the military in the name of the Emperor that instilled perseverance in hardship, inconvenience, insufficiency, and poverty, despite people's natural inclination against them. He objects to forcing people to suppress their desires and likes because it denies their humanity (Sakaguchi 1987, 247). Demanding sacrifice and perseverance during the time of war is of course common, but the Japanese wartime strategy had a particular potency because of its aesthetic appeal, underscoring both the power and the potential danger of aesthetic persuasion when utilized for a political agenda.

---

[9] In addition, a rose generally receives attention to the individual flower, while cherry blossoms' beauty is derived from a harmonious aggregate of many small flowers.

HISTORICAL CONSEQUENCES OF JAPANESE AESTHETIC SENSIBILITY

Wabi aesthetics thus illustrates a problematic consequence of transcending one's natural inclinations and desires, when *indiscriminately* applied to socioeconomic and political contexts. A further problem with this aesthetic sensibility as a form of self-discipline is its inherent paradox: developing an *other*-regarding attitude as a means of *self*-cultivation. It is true that through such an aesthetic-ethical practice one can develop respectful interactions with *the other*, but the ultimate goal is *self*-enlightenment. This paradox of the long-held virtue-centric Japanese aesthetics manifests its problematic implications in its response to the modern process of Westernization.

Circumstances Surrounding Westernization

The year 1868 marks the beginning of modernization of Japan when it opened its door to the rest of the world after more than two and half centuries of self-isolation. The sudden and rapid Westernization process challenged many aspects of Japanese society and culture. At first, dazzled by an array of ideas and items from the West considered to be both universal and advanced, the government and the populace made a concerted effort to adopt everything Western, including diet, clothing, architecture, technology, various intellectual discourses, infrastructure, medicine, arts, and the economic, judicial, governmental, military, and educational systems. However, many intellectuals soon started to challenge this indiscriminate worship of the West and the self-imposed inferiority complex by asking whether there is nothing that Japan can take pride in. They found the answer in Japan's aesthetic legacy.

This "discovery" or "construction" of Japan as a nation of aesthetics resulted from efforts on many fronts, both within Japan and directed toward the world. The turn of the century saw a proliferation of writings extolling the "unique," "distinctive," and even "superior" aesthetics of Japan. The following are representative of the works written to enlighten the Japanese populace of their native aesthetic treasures: Shiga Shigetaka's *Niohn Fūkeiron* (*A Theory of Japanese Landscape*, 1894) praising the unparalleled beauty of Japanese landscape, followed by Kojima Usui's *Nihon Sansuiron* (*A Theory of Japanese Mountains and Waters*, 1905) credited for introducing mountaineering as a physical and aesthetic activity, and Haga Yaichi's *Nihon Kokuminsei Jūron* (*A Theory of Ten National Characteristics of the Japanese*, 1907) that designated the love of nature as one of the national characteristics. These works on nature aesthetics were joined by studies on folk traditions as an effort to highlight those aspects of Japan still untouched by Western modernity. Yanagi Sōetsu (1889–1961) established the genre of Japanese folk crafts and initiated the Mingei (Folk Crafts 民芸) movement, while Yanagita Kunio (1875–1962) compiled ethnographic reports on various folk traditions throughout Japan. While these writings targeted Japanese readers, others introduced Japan's cultural and aesthetic heritage to the world by writing and publishing in English. The most notable are Okakukra Tenshin's *The Ideals of the East with Special Reference to the Art of Japan* (1903) and *The Book of Tea* (1906), followed by Nitobe Inazō's *Bushidō* (*The Way of the Warrior*, 1908).

These works and efforts together generated a cultural nationalism comprising Japanese aesthetic exceptionalism. It was easy for this aesthetics-based cultural nationalism to develop into political nationalism, given the political climate at the time. Shiga intended his landscape aesthetics to instill love of the native land among the Japanese after having witnessed firsthand the European colonization of Southeast Asia, particularly an important mission for him as a member of the ultra-nationalist party that called for the preservation and protection of the so-called pure essence of Japan. As for the other intellectuals, there are considerable disagreements among contemporary scholars whether they intended to promote Japanese nationalism (see Iida 2002). However, there is no denying that their works together served as a de facto supporter and promoter of Japanese exceptionalism.

This cultural and aesthetic exceptionalism, ironically, was made possible by both Western ideas and the colonization of Asian countries. For example, Kōjin Karatani points out that the late nineteenth-century European discovery of Japanese art created the image of Japan as an aesthetic nation and popularized *japonisme*, the Orientalist assessment that was subsequently shared by the Japanese art historians at the time (Karatani 2001).[10] Shiga's landscape aesthetics was also mediated by Western ideas, including the aesthetic categories then popular in Europe, namely beauty, sublimity, and the picturesque, as well as geology, the Western discipline in which he was trained. Kojima's praise of Japanese mountains was made possible by Walter Weston (1861–1940), a British missionary, who transformed this topography from an object of fear and awe as a spiritual presence during religious pilgrimage to an aesthetic object.[11]

In addition to its indebtedness to European ideas, the formation of the Japanese cultural identity also relied upon an uneasy relationship with the other parts of Asia. For example, by celebrating Japan, located at the far eastern edge of Asia, as "the real repository of the trust of Asiatic thought and culture" and declaring that "Asia is One" at the beginning of *The Ideals of the East*, Okakura's work contributed to appointing Japan as the leader and protector of the greater Asia through its rich legacy of aesthetics (Okakura 2007, 11 and 9). In the meantime, Yanagi's "discovery" of Japanese folk crafts, initially inspired by his early exposure to the Korean Yi dynasty's crafts, was an attempt to search for the *Japaneseness* shared by craft traditions not only from Japan but also from Korea, Okinawa, Taiwan, and Ainu people (the indigenous population in the northern island of Hokkaidō), all put under Japan's political control. Although Yanagi distinguished crafts

[10] The construction of the Japanese aesthetic legacy seen from the lens of European Orientalism is often referred to as "Oriental Orientalism" or "reverse Orientalism." See Karatani's work cited here, Karatani and Kohso (1998), and Kikuchi (2004).

[11] In fact, Weston named the mountain range that forms the spine of the Japanese main island "Japanese Alps," the name still in use today.

from the high art tradition in Japan, we find the same theme of a spiritual discipline marked by self-surrender in characterizing crafts-making, no doubt reflecting his affinity with Zen Buddhism (Yanagi 1982; Yanagi 2018). Similarly, while Yanagi's ethnographic work attends to the diversity of folk traditions, customs, and practices based upon localities, his consistent quest was to find "Japanese culture" as a contrast to the Western ethos characterized by the rational, progressive, individualistic, and scientific orientations (Morris-Suzuki 1995).

Neglect of Attention to the Sociopolitical Implications

Against the background of rapid Westernization, the successive victories over China and Russia,[12] and European colonization of many parts of Asia, Japan needed to define its nationhood in a relatively short period of time and its aesthetic heritage played a major role in the construction of cultural nationalism. The irony is that in the pretext of combatting European Imperialism as a self-appointed leader of Asia, Japan itself developed its own imperialist agenda and colonized other parts of Asia, symbolically planting cherry trees on their soils. Such exploitation of the aesthetic legacy was possible because of its inherent paradox of encouraging other-regarding appreciation as a means of self-cultivation, mentioned previously. With its emphasis on emptying one's ego and adopting a respectful attitude toward the other, this sensibility is inward-oriented, almost exclusively focused on one's self. The perceived importance of disciplining oneself to accept and appreciate the difficult-to-accept eclipsed the equally important task of critically examining that which one is accepting and appreciating, in particular the sociopolitical ramifications unfolding in real time. It is one thing to practice this attitude within the tea ceremony and nature appreciation, but it is quite another to maintain the same attitude when the object of appreciation is the society, its political agenda, and lives within. Because submitting oneself to whatever one is experienceing is regarded as a moral virtue mediated by aesthetic sensibility, we can see how it was both easy and effective for the military to harness its power to justify and promote political nationalism in support of the war.

Indeed, Zen-influenced thinkers like those who taught at Kyoto University, a group called the Kyoto school, most prominent being Nishida Kitarō (1870–1945), were later criticized for being silent, or even complicit, in the Japanese military wartime missions. Nishida and the Kyoto school thinkers were concerned with the alienation felt by many Japanese who were caught between Western modernity with its emphasis on rationalistic and scientific orientation and Japan's historical and cultural legacy that favors an aesthetic mode of being in the world. Fully aware that it is impossible to turn back the clock to the pre-Westernization state, they sought to reconfigure the Zen Buddhist worldview to offer a foundation that can also accommodate Western modernity and

---

[12] Sino-Japanese War (1894–1895); Russo-Japanese War (1904–1905).

scientific worldview. According to them, the most fundamental mode of being in the world is the pure experience of absolute nothingness that is prior and superior to the dualistic framework characteristic of the Western modernist and scientific worldview. They appointed Japan with its Zen Buddhist tradition to offer a universal and inclusive vision, fueling the ever-intensifying nationalistic sentiment. Although debates ensue over the extent to which these scholars intended and/or were aware of the political implications of their philosophical view, the recent so-called critical Buddhist thinkers criticize them for ignoring or abandoning the social and political responsibility from which philosophers should not be exempt (see Heisig and Maraldo 1995; Hubbard and Swanson 1997).

We can find the contrast between the Japanese aesthetic sensibility without regard to its social, political, and historical implications and the challenge to such aesthetics in the two Japanese recipients of the Nobel prize in literature: Kawabata Yasunari (1889–1972) and Ōe Kenzaburō (1935–2023). Kawabata's 1968 acceptance speech titled "Japan, the Beautiful and Myself" lists various examples of classical Japanese art as the inspiration behind his own work, characterizing them as "transmit(ting) the very essence of Japan" (Kawabata 1968).[13] By frequently referencing Zen teaching that favors nonverbal or nonsensical means of communication, Kawabata suggests that he aims to express something ineffable, subtle, and quiet, lying "outside words." Citing a biography of Myōe (1173–1232), Kawabata concludes that this Zen monk's eyes and ears were filled with "emptiness" when experiencing cherry blossoms, the cuckoo, the moon, and snow. He declares that "here we have the emptiness, the nothingness of the Orient," while hastening to distinguish this kind of emptiness also underlying his own work from Western nihilism. We can interpret Kawabata's speech as a summation of the Zen-inspired, ethically grounded aesthetic attitude particularly toward nature handed down through Japanese cultural history. Experienced as a form of self-cultivation and Zen-like practice, his attention is decidedly turned inward as well as toward nature, with no mention of other people or society at large.[14]

Ōe's 1994 acceptance speech titled "Japan, The Ambiguous, and Myself" challenges this aesthetics celebrated by Kawabata from the postwar generation's point of view (Ōe 1994).[15] He states at the beginning that his writing "has been to start from my personal matters and then to link it up with society, the state and the world" and pronounces that "I cannot utter in unison with Kawabata the phrase 'Japan, the Beautiful and Myself,'" in light of the atrocities Japan has committed during the World War II. For Ōe, Japan, after Westernization began, is "dubious" or "ambiguous," rather than "beautiful," as it

[13] The subsequent passages are from the same source. There are no page numbers.

[14] In a similar vein, Yuko Kikuchi points out that while Sōetsu Yanagi and William Morris shared their passion for folk crafts and started the movement to promote them, Morris was ultimately concerned with improving the society while Yanagi, who based his aesthetics largely on Zen Buddhism, was more concerned with individual enlightenment (Kikuchi 204, 80–88).

[15] The subsequent passages are from the same source. There are no page numbers. The original term *aimai* is translated as "ambiguous" in this Nobel version, but another version uses "dubious" in the translation included in Fu and Heine (1995).

has been caught in a precarious relationship both with the West and the rest of Asia. By presenting the aesthetics of emptiness as a shared vision of the Orient, Ōe points out, Kawabata is continuing the narrative formulated by Okakaura that self-appoints Japan as the protector of Asian arts and cultures. Moreover, by emphasizing the ineffability of the Japanese aesthetic sensibility, Kawabata is insulating this aesthetics from the rest of the world, rendering it exclusionary.

Thus, the long-held legacy of Japanese aesthetic sensibility played an essential, if unwitting, role in promoting Japanese nationalism and elevating its nationhood in the face of the rapid modernization and Western imperialism. Although this development was in response to the historical circumstances, the aesthetic sensibility itself harbored vulnerability to this exploitation because it was inward-looking and focused on self without enough attention or vigilance toward the social and political ramifications. However, this (negative) historical legacy should not minimize Japanese aesthetics' contemporary relevance both within and beyond Japan. The concluding section will explore how the Japanese aesthetic sensibility can help promote an ethical human relationship with the artifactual world today.

CONTEMPORARY RELEVANCE AND SIGNIFICANCE

In addition to urging his contemporary writers to address their social and political responsibility, Ōe also warns against rampant consumerism's "ominous consequence emerging out of the present prosperity" and "the expanding potential powr of both production and consumption in Asia at large" (Ōe 1994).

Japan, like other affluent industrialized nations, is responsible for overconsumption and a host of environmental problems. Today's leading Japanese designers respond to these problems by harnessing the long-held aesthetic legacies that emphasize emptiness, other-regarding attitude, imperfection, and transience. One idea they share is to avoid imposing their ego onto the design process. For example, Hara Kenya, whose writings indicate a deep indebtedness to the traditional Japanese arts, characterizes his attitude toward design by the notion of emptiness:

> "Emptiness" (*utsu*) and "completely hollow" (*karappo*) are among the terms I pondered while trying to grasp the nature of communication. When people share their thoughts, they commonly listen to each other's opinions rather than throwing information at each other. In other words, successful communication depends on how well we listen, rather than how well we push our opinions on the person seated before us. People have therefore conceptualized communication techniques using terms like "empty vessel" to try to understand each other better. (Hara 2010, Prologue)[16]

---

[16] Hara's discussion of emptiness is also found in Maruo (2015, 50, 67–69), and the chapter on "Simple and Empty—Genealogy of Aesthetic Sensibility" in Hara (2012).

Applied to the design process, this notion of emptiness encourages the designers to re-frain from forming a preconceived design, empty their mind, and listen to the users, materials, and the cumulative wisdom behind similar objects that have endured the test of time. Designers' creativity is enacted by listening to and collaborating with these others.

Another leading designer, Fukasawa Naoto, also states that he is against the kind of design that calls attention to itself with "expression of self" and recommends "get(ting) rid of the ego that says, 'I designed this object'" (Fukasawa and Morison 2008, 110). He fully embraces the seeming paradox of the creative act of "design" that is at the same time anti-design, minimizing or even erasing the signs of human manipulation. Accordingly, his kitchen utensils and appliances are characterized as "quietly being there as if it was not designed and blend in with living" (Maruo 2015, 25).[17]

Uchida Shigeru also argues against the common understanding of "design" as some-thing special, unexpected, or standing out, which promotes self-expression (Uchida 2008, 93). Instead, he advocates the kind of design that is "ordinary" by challenging its rather pejorative connotation for being boring (Uchida 2008, 103 and 92). By citing Okakura's statement in *The Book of Tea* that the tea ceremony encourages courtesy to worship beauty in the everyday life, Uchida celebrates the ordinary as an understated, modest quality that is born out of the longevity of use in everyday life (Uchida 2008, 102).

The objects designed with such an attitude are characterized by minimalism, or in Hara's word, emptiness. By drawing analogies to the empty spaces of monochrome ink paintings, the sparse interiors of traditional Japanese rooms, the tearoom being the quintessential example, and the use of only one flower or a few petals to express a season, he argues that such minimalist design provides a fertile ground for engaging the imagi-nation: "Emptiness provides a space within which our imaginations can run free, vastly enriching our powers of perception and our mutual comprehension" (Hara 2010, 60). When interacting with an object featuring emptiness, the user is encouraged to forge an intimate and individual relationship with it.

This kind of active engagement not only offers an aesthetic pleasure but also places a responsibility on the users, similar to the way in which the ethically grounded aesthetic experience in the Japanese legacy invites a reciprocal relationship between creation and reception, as mentioned in the first section. Many people in affluent societies, including Japan, have become used to material abundance and disposable culture. When an object shows its age and is considered no longer perfect or stylish, consumers tend to throw it away and purchase a new one with a more stylish and up-to-date appearance. This ethos of fast fashion and throw-away culture results from the industry strategy of planned ob-solescence accompanied by what one scholar calls "productionist bias," whereby a man-ufactured object is identified at the end stage of production, right off the belt, so to speak, where its life stops, rendering any changes afterward a deterioration (Jackson 2014).

---

[17] For examples of Hara's and Fukasawa's products and designers' own comments, see Kanai et al. (2013) and Maruo (2015).

However, empty design invites the user to regard the so-called finished product off the assembly line as an empty vessel which continues to be filled and morphed by use. Through repeated use, a relationship develops between the user and the object. The inevitable wear and tear, aging effect, and accidental happenstance come to be appreciated as an aesthetic embodiment of their history together, instead of signs of imperfection and defect. Fukasawa points out that living with the object through use involves appreciating its service to us and facilitates accrual of the "beauty that occurs with time when an object survives constant use" (Fukasawa and Morrison 2008, 111). He refers to this interaction as *shutaku* (手沢 worn or spoiled by handling), "a metaphor for something that has taken on a personality of its own, or improved with age," which he identifies as the aesthetic value of *wabi* (Fukasawa and Morrison 2008, 110 and 106). Furthermore, through "the deepening of a relationship . . . we may discover its beauty not just in how it ages but in how we age with it" (Fukasawa and Morrison 2008, 111). Here, the long-held other-regarding ethical attitude that guides art-making and art appreciation in Japan finds a contemporary application in one's relationship with the objects of daily use.

CONCLUSION

This chapter explored an intimate relationship between the aesthetic and the ethical in the Japanese cultural tradition. The aesthetic experience gained both in creation and reception is regarded as a way of cultivating a virtuous self by emptying one's self and listening to the other-than-self. While this lineage gave rise to a number of artistic practices and modes of aesthetic experience, thereby enriching the aesthetic palette for the Japanese, its almost exclusive emphasis on self-cultivation lacked a critical awareness of its possible social and political implications. As such, it was vulnerable to political exploitation to serve nationalistic and militaristic purposes in the aftermath of rapid Westernization leading to the World War II. Thus, any assessment of Japanese aesthetic sensibility should not ignore this vulnerability and the need to develop vigilance. At the same time, we can extend this ethically grounded aesthetic practice to an intimate and ongoing engagement and relationship with the material world. By sharing our life together with the objects and appreciating the beauty, rather than deterioration, in their vicissitude and impermanence, we can reshape our interactions with the material world and help mitigate today's fast fashion and throwaway culture.

See also: Song, Snow, this volume

REFERENCES

Carter, Robert E. 2008. *The Japanese Arts and Self-Cultivation*. Albany: SUNY Press.
Dōgen. [1231–1253]1988. *Shōbōgenzō: Zen Essays by Dōgen*. Translated by Thomas Cleary. Honolulu: University of Hawai'i Press.

Dōgen. [1243] 1992a. *Fushuku-Hampō (Meal-Time Regulations)*. In *Cooking, Eating, Thinking: Transformative Philosophies of Food*, edited by Deane W. Curtin and Lisa M. Heldke, 153–163. Bloomington: Indiana University Press.

Dōgen. [1237] 1992b. *Tenzo Kyōkun (Instruction for the Tenzo)*. In *Cooking, Eating, Thinking: Transformative Philosophies of Food*, edited by Deane W. Curtin and Lisa M. Heldke, 280–285. Bloomington: Indiana University Press.

Dōgen Zenji. [1231–1253] 1977. *Shōbōgenzō: The Eye and Treasury of the True Law*. Vol. 2. Translated by Kōsen Nishiyama and John Stevens. Tokyo: Nakayama Shobō.

Dōgen Zenji. [1231–1253] 1983. *Shōbōgenzō: The Eye and Treasury of the True Law*. Vol. 4. Translated by Kōsen Nishiyama, edited by John Stevens, Steve Powell, Ian Reader, and Suzan Wick. Tokyo: Nakayama Shobō.

Ekuan, Kenji. 2000. *The Aesthetics of the Japanese Lunchbox*. Translated by Don Kenny. Cambridge, MA: The MIT Press.

Fu, Charles Wei-hsui, and Steven Heine, eds. 1995. *Japan in Traditional and Postmodern Perspectives*. Albany: SUNY Press.

Fukasawa, Naoto, and Jasper Morrison. 2008. *Super Normal: Sensations of the Ordinary*. Translated by Mardi Miyake. Baden: Lars Müller Publishers.

Haga, Kōshirō. 1989. "The *Wabi* Aesthetic Through the Ages." In *Tea in Japan: Essays on the History of Chanoyu*, edited by Paul Varley and Kumakura Isao, 195–230. Honolulu: University of Hawai'i Press.

Hara, Kenya. 2010. *White*. Translated by Jooyeon Rhee. Baden: Lars Müller Publishers.

Hara, Kenya. 2012. *Nihon no Dezain—Biishiki ga Tsukuru Mirai (Japanese Design—Future Created by Aesthetic Sensibility)*. Tokyo: Iwanami Shoten.

Hattori, Dohō. [Eighteenth century] 1981. *The Red Booklet*. In *The Theory of Beauty in the Classical Aesthetics of Japan*. Edited and translated by Toshihiko and Toyo Izutsu, 159–167. The Hague: Martinus Nijhoff Publishers.

Heisig, James W., and John Maraldo, eds. 1995. *Rude Awakenings: Zen, the Kyoto School, and the Question of Nationalism*. Honolulu: University of Hawai'i Press.

Hendry, Joy. 1993. *Wrapping Culture: Politeness, Presentation, and Power in Japan and Other Societies*. Oxford: Clarendon Press.

Hubbard, Jamie, and Paul L. Swanson, eds. 1997. *Pruning the Bodhi Tree: The Storm Over Critical Buddhism*. Honolulu: University of Hawai'i Press.

Iida, Yumiko. 2002. *Rethinking Identity in Modern Japan: Nationalism as Aesthetics*. Oxon, UK: Routledge.

Ikegami, Eiko. 2005. *Bonds of Civility: Aesthetic Networks and the Political Origins of Japanese Culture*. Cambridge: Cambridge University Press.

Jackson, Steven. 2014. "Rethinking Repair." In *Media Technologies: Essays on Communication, Materiality, and Society*, edited by Tarleton Gillespie, Pablo J. Boczkowski, and Kirsten A. Foot., 221–239. Cambridge, MA: The MIT Press.

Kanai, Masaaki, Kazuko Koike, Naoto Fukasawa, Kenya Hara, and Takashi Sugimito. 2013. *Muji*. New York: Rizzoli.

Karatani, Kōjin, and Sabu Kohso. 1998. "Uses of Aesthetics: After Orientalism." *Boundary 25*, no. 2 (Summer): 145–169.

Karatani, Kōjin. 2001. "Japan as Art Museum: Okakura Tenshin and Fenollosa." In *A History of Modern Japanese Aesthetics*. Translated by Michael F. Marra, 43–52. Honolulu: University of Hawai'i Press.

Kawabata, Yasunari. 1968. "Japan, the Beautiful and Myself." Nobel Prize.org. https://www.nob
elprize.org/prizes/literature/1968/kawabata/lecture/ (accessed February 6, 2023).

Kikuchi, Yuko. 2004. *Japanese Modernisation and Mingei Theory: Cultural Nationalism and Oriental Orientalism*. London: Routledge.

Kumakura, Isao, and Paul Varley, eds. 1989. *Tea in Japan: Essays on the History of* Chanoyu. Honolulu: University of Hawai'I Press.

Maruo, Hiroshi, ed. 2015. *Mujirushi Ryōhin no Dezain (Mujirushi Ryōhin's Design)*. Tokyo: Nikkei BP sha.

Minami, Hiroshi. 1971. *Psychology of the Japanese People*. Translated by Albert R. Ikoma. Toronto: University of Toronto Press.

Morris, Ivan. 1994. *The World of the Shining Prince: Court Life in Ancient Japan*. New York: Kodansha International.

Morris-Suzuki, Tessa. 1995. "The Invention and Reinvention of 'Japanese Culture.'" *Journal of Asian Studies* 54, no. 3 (August 1995): 759–780.

Ōe, Kenzaburō. 1994. "Japan, The Ambiguous and Myself." Nobel Prize.org. https://www.nob
elprize.org/prizes/literature/1994/oe/lecture/ (accessed February 6, 2023).

Ōhashi, Ryōsuke. 1998. "Kire and Iki." In *Encyclopedia of Aesthetics*, Vol. 2, edited by Michael Kelly, 553–555. New York: Oxford University Press.

Ohnuki-Tierney, Emiko. 2002. *Kamikaze, Cherry Blossoms, and Nationalisms: The Militarization of Aesthetics in Japanese History*. Chicago: University of Chicago Press.

Okakura, Kakuzo. [1903] 2007. *The Ideals of the East: with Special Reference to the Art of Japan*. San Diego: Stone Bridge Press.

Parkes, Graham. 2018. "Savoring Taste." In *New Essays in Japanese Aesthetics*, edited by A. Minh Nguyen, 109–120. Lanham, MD: Lexington Books.

Pope, Alexander. [1731] 1990. *An Epistle to Lord Burlington*. In *The Genius of the Pace: The English Landscape Garden 1620–1820*, edited by John Dixon Hunt and Peter Willis, 211–214. Cambridge, MA: The MIT Press.

Saito, Yuriko. 1999. "Japanese Aesthetics of Packaging." *Journal of Aesthetics and Art Criticism* 57, no. 2 (Spring 1999): 257–265.

Sakaguchi, Ango. [1946] 1987. "Zoku Darakuron" (Additional Theory of Decadence). In *Shōwa Bungaku Zenshū (Collection of Shōwa Period Literature)*, Vol. 12, 245–250. Tokyo: Shōgakukan.

Sen, Sōshitsu. 1965. *Shoho no Sadō (Introductory Way of Tea)*. Kyoto: Tankōsha.

Shiotsuki, Yaeko. 1983. *Washoku no Itadaki kata: Oishiku, Tanoshiku, Utsukushiku (How to Eat Japanese Meals: Deliciously, Enjoyably, and Beautifully)*. Tokyo: Shinchōsha.

Surak, Kristin. 2013. *Making Tea, Making Japan: Cultural Nationalism in Practice*. Stanford, CA: Stanford University Press.

Tachibana-no-Toshitsuna. [Eleventh century] 1985. *Sakuteiki: The Book of Garden-Making, Being a Full Translation of the Japanese Eleventh Century Manuscript: Memoranda on Garden Making Attributed to the Writing of Tachibana-no-Toshitsuna*. Translated by S. Shimoyama. Tokyo: Town & City Planners.

Tsubaki, Chinzan. [Nineteenth century] 1990. *Chinzan Shokan (Correspondence of Chinzan)*. In *Nihon no Geijutsuron (Theories of Art in Japan)*, edited by Yasuda Ayao, 251. Tokyo: Sōgensha.

Uchida, Shigeu. 2008. *Futsū no Dezain: Nichijō ni Yadoru Bi no Katachi (Ordinary Design: Form of Beauty Dwelling in the Everyday)*. Tokyo: Kōsakusha.

Ueda, Makoto. 1967. *Literary and Art Theories in Japan*. Cleveland: The Press of Case Western Reserve University.

Yanagi, Sōetsu. 1982. *The Unknown Craftsman: A Japanese Insight into Beauty*. Adapted by Bernard Leach. Tokyo: Kōdansha International.

Yanagi, Sōetsu. 2018. *The Beauty of Everyday Things*. Translated by Michael Brase. New York: Penguin.

Zōen. [Fifteenth century] 1991. *Illustrations for Designing Mountains, Water, and Hillside Field Landscape*. In *Secret Teachings in the Art of Japanese Gardens: Design Principles, Aesthetic Values*, edited and translated by D. A. Slawson, 142–175. Tokyo: Kodansha International.

FURTHER READING

Hume, Nancy, ed. 1995. *Japanese Aesthetics and Culture: A Reader*. Albany: SUNY Press.

Izutsu, Toshihiko, and Toyo, ed. 1981. *The Theory of Beauty in the Classical Aesthetics of Japan*. The Hague: Martinus Nijhoff Publishers.

Marra, Michael F., ed. 2001. *A History of Modern Japanese Aesthetics*. Honolulu: The University of Hawai'i Press.

Marra, Michael F., ed. 1999. *Modern Japanese Aesthetics: A Reader*. Honolulu: The University of Hawai'i Press.

Nguyen, A. Minh, ed. 2018. *New Essays in Japanese Aesthetics*. Lanham, MD: Lexington Books.

Saito, Yuriko. 2007. "The Moral Dimension of Japanese Aesthetics." *Journal of Aesthetics and Art Criticism* 65, no. 1 (Winter 2007): 85–97.

Tansman, Alan. 2009. *The Aesthetics of Japanese Fascism*. Berkeley: University of California Press.

CHAPTER 6

....

ART, ETHICS, AND VALUE IN THE MODERN EUROPEAN AESTHETIC TRADITION

....

TIMOTHY M. COSTELLOE

ART, MORALS, AND THE AESTHETIC IN THE MODERN PERIOD

....

To the contemporary consciousness, the claim that there might be some connection between art and aspects of practical life will hardly register, so accustomed is it to seeing image and sound pressed into the service of some moral cause, religious dogma, or political campaign. The same is true, though one might not be offended personally, when a work of art is castigated for its corrupting effects on the same. Art, it appears, is courted as supporter or lambasted as foe, employed variously as it suits commitments, prejudices, and a point of view of the person or group concerned. Later writers—John Ruskin (1903–1912, vol. 1) and Leo Tolstoy ([1904] 1996) come to mind—had to expend time and energy making the case, but in their wake, nobody would seriously doubt the idea that art and morality are linked in tight and obvious ways.

To speak of "art and morals" in the modern period, by contrast, has an unavoidably anachronistic ring, the specific issues that philosophers routinely associate with the connection now (see Gaut 2013) likely not occurring to most writers of the time. This is due in part to the historical contingency that the now-familiar category of "art" or "the fine arts" (*les beaux arts*, *die schöne Künste*)—drawing, painting, sculpture, literature, music, dance, architecture, theater, and (at the time) gardening—was still, in the early decades of the eighteenth century, a protean idea (Kristeller 1951 and 1952); even philosophers writing later in the period who "had a firm grasp on the concept of the fine arts," as Peter Kivy observes, did not feel the need to have a philosophy of them (Kivy 2004, 268). When writers do take up any of the arts—with the extent to which they do so and the particular ones they choose varying widely—it is often for purposes of illustration rather than as a subject matter in their own right. For a significant number of leading contributors to the tradition, moreover, "art" is tantamount to "literature," or "poetry" broadly conceived, and that stained deeply by the rhetorical tradition running back through (pseudo-) Longinus (author of *On the Sublime*) to the Ancients.

That "art" or "the arts" (terms I shall use interchangeably) remains a less than fully formed concept in the period is reflected in the history of the discipline of "aesthetics," the title first used in its modern sense by Alexander Gottlieb Baumgarten ([1735] 1954 and [1750] 2007) with Lord Shaftesbury's *Characteristicks* ([1711] 2001) and Joseph Addison's essays in the *Spectator* ([1712] 1965) competing contenders for being its founding text. Though routinely collapsed (as in Eaton 2004), the discipline can be usefully divided into two distinct parts. The first part concerns the *nature and origin of art* and involves the explicit attempt to isolate some specific art-relevant feature (or features) shared by at least some (or perhaps all) objects collected under that heading. Given its clear explanandum, it is relatively easy to identify its founding texts and the feature they isolate, Jean-Baptiste (l'Abbé) DuBos's *Critical Reflections on Poetry, Painting and Music* (1719) (emotional arousal) being the main contender with Charles Batteux's *The Fine Arts Reduced to a Single Principle* (1746) (imitation) running a close second; other writers—*inter alia* Francis Hutcheson (1728) (representation), Baumgarten (applied rules of a science of sensibility), William Hogarth (1750) (the "line of beauty"), and Sir Joshua Reynolds (Reynolds 1797) (art in the "Grand Style")—are due at least an honorable mention.

This is not to say that the arts were *never* taken, individually or, over the course of time, collectively, as an object of inquiry, nor that they did not figure into discussions of and reflections on moral life. This is certainly a pronounced theme among German Enlightenment thinkers, some of whom shared the conviction, more or less explicitly articulated, that the fine arts might be married happily with morals. Moral truths are learned from independent sources but, the thought goes, they can be enlivened and made more easily accessible by representing them in such a way as to elicit a sensuous and edifying response in an audience. This view was born initially of the "perfectionist aesthetics" inspired by the early-modern rationalists (especially Gottfried Wilhelm Leibniz), given its first full articulation by Christian Wolff in the early decades of the eighteenth century, and expressed in later writers, including Moses Mendelsohn and Johan George Sulzer (Guyer 2014, Part 3). The same is visible in Immanuel Kant's treatment of beauty and the fine arts in his *Critique of the Power of Judgment* (1790), though refracted through the peculiarities of his Critical System.

Faith in the morally enlightening character of art reaches a hopeful and dramatic dénouement near century's end with Friedrich Schiller's "Aesthetic Letters" (1795), its author entrusting "Fine Art" with redemptive power, it being the best "instrument" for reviving and developing the corrupted human "capacity for feeling" (Schiller [1967] 1982, 55 and 53); in the Romantic period that follows, this conviction extends to the idea that art might be a means for attaining insight into ultimate reality more generally. In Britain, Hogarth's works on "modern moral subjects" are plausibly interpreted as the fruit of moralizing as well as satirical intentions, and among the French one cannot ignore Jean-Jacques Rousseau's unrelenting attack on the dramatic arts, pressing Plato's famous arguments against the arts of imitation (Plato 1992, 392a-403c and 595a-608b; see also Destrée, this volume) into service on behalf of the virtuous citizenry of a provincial republic (Geneva) as a bulwark against the decadence of city life (Paris) (Rousseau [1758] 1968).

Indeed, it is fitting that two philosophers with whom "philosophy of art" appears fully for the first time are also those who draw the closest connection between art and morals. The first is Thomas Reid, who is widely accepted as developing an early version of expressionism, a view associated with the twentieth century, and, paradigmatically, R. G. Collingwood (Collingwood 1938), which holds that the principal aim of art is to express the emotions of the artist that, embodied in the object created, are communicated to the audience. Reid's view might not fit exactly the contours of later versions, but he certainly articulates the idea that artists express the states of mind of the subjects they represent, an effect they achieve through their own "style" or "manner" (Kivy 2004; cf. Gallie 1998, 174–180). As part of his argument, Reid claims that although "beauty" and "sublimity" are routinely predicated of objects, including works of art, these only possess such characteristics "figuratively" or in a "derived" sense, such qualities belonging properly and "originally" to qualities of mind that belong to the artists concerned (Homer is a favorite example [587.23–32])[1] and are seen in the subject matter they choose and mode of presentation they employ (599.1–6). Thus power, knowledge, wisdom, fortitude, self-command, generosity, public spirit, friendship, and noble emulation—all qualities Reid cites (584.28–32)—possess "real and intrinsic excellence" for which reason they merit our esteem or admiration (587.33–34). Reid himself does not appear to make the claim explicitly, but if one takes these qualities as virtues and their opposites as vices, it is easy to see how works of art might be considered carriers or expressions of moral value. One might say of such objects that they are beautiful or ugly, but their material forms are really "signs" of something more fundamental and objectively real.

The second philosopher for whom the arts figure prominently and explicitly in connection to morals is Kant, for whom all "beautiful art" requires "genius" (5:307),[2] the singular capacity of artists to animate otherwise inanimate material with "soul" or "spirit" (*Geist*) (5:313). (See also Shapshay, this volume.) They accomplish this feat through articulating an "aesthetic idea," a "representation of the imagination" that effectively functions as a central image or motif of the artwork in question, making what are "ideas of reason," and thus beyond possible experience, sensible to an audience (5:314). An aesthetic idea thus "occasions much thought," Kant contends, because the cognitive powers are quickened (with imagination roused in particular) and experience consequently enriched in ways that presentation of a determinate concept could never inspire. Among rational ideas that are amenable to such aesthetic representation

---

[1] Reid ([1785] 2002). All references are to page and line numbers.
[2] Kant ([1790] 2000). References are to the volume and pagination of Kant (1900–).

Kant includes moral concepts, which artists render visible in their work, such as poets, who present readers with images of heaven, hell, eternity and creation, as well as of particular things of which we have some experience—"death, envy, . . . all sorts of vices, . . . love [and] fame"—but with a completeness that experience alone could never provide (5:314–15). In this way, the artistic products of genius—and artistic genius of poets in particular (5:326–27)—can make morality manifest and almost palpable in otherwise impossible ways.

For many other writers in the period, however, the arts as a cohesive concept plays no such clear role. The reason for this lacuna—as it might appear to a contemporary reader looking back—is that many of them were concerned more directly with the second part of "aesthetics," namely, the inquiry into a specific *kind of value*, denoted by (the master categories of) "beauty" (a positive value) and its opposite "deformity" (a negative value) and the affective states (in the form of pleasure or pain) connected to them. It is not the arts as such, then, that are the carriers of moral value, but *taste*, a term (along with its cognates) employed to isolate a capacity or actual faculty, a potentiality given by nature but in need of actualization, that is sensitive to and can discover (depending on its different theoretical manifestations) the properties that underlie the aesthetic beauty of art and nature, on the one side, and the moral beauty of virtue on the other. These inquiries, moreover, formed part of and were informed by the more general "science of man," the dominant paradigm of the period that oriented and guided writers in their wide-ranging investigations into the form and content of human nature.

This is not to say that reason and reflection were not given due place in the explanations that ensued; even Dubos, for whom *sens* and *sentiment* work primarily at the level of sensation—art plays on the "natural sensibility of the heart," he writes, and our "proclivity to be moved" (Dubos 1748, 1:32)—finds a place for judgment to intervene when artistic faults hinder the feeling of pleasure. Most writers, in fact, identified some element to limit and correct the hedonic excess of the passions, including, for example, Dubos's contemporary Jean-Pierre de Crousaz who finds it in the distinction between "ideas" and "feelings" ([1715] 2000: 391–392); Shaftesbury, who emphasizes the place of self-consciousness; Addison, who locates it in the "secondary pleasure" of the imagination; and, most forcefully perhaps, Reid, for whom the clear contrast between judgment and perception runs through his philosophy as a whole. At the same time, the focus on the aesthetic is really the defining feature of the nascent discipline, and even Baumgarten, his indisputably rational credentials notwithstanding, sought a science of *sensual* cognition, such that, as Kai Hammermeister puts it, among the Germans too "philosophical aesthetics originated as advocacy of sensibility, not as theory of art" (Hammermeister 2002, 4). It was fitting, then, that a discipline driven by an inquiry into human nature and the affective capacities of human beings should come to adopt—though its road was rocky and full recognition was conveyed only in the next century (Costelloe 2013, 1–8)—*aesthetics* as its title: a term with its origin in the Greek noun *aesthetikos* (sensitive or sentient) from the verb *aesthanesthai* (to perceive, feel, sense), which, in its nominal form, gives *aestheta* (things perceived by the senses or taste).

AESTHETIC AND MORAL VALUE

Against this background, it is not surprising to find leading writers focusing less on the arts directly and more oriented toward *spheres of value*, aesthetic and moral (see Song, this volume), and asking how the good (and bad) in one—the beautiful (and ugly) in objects of nature and art—might be connected to the right (and wrong) in the other—the virtuous (and vicious) with respect to actions and character. The former we can call *aesthetic beauty*, and the latter—following the conventions of the time—*moral beauty*. One might be forgiven for seeing the latter as the opaque result of the aesthetic bleeding into the moral, but the convention at least was to treat the spheres as distinct, a point Walter Hipple makes about the British specifically, though it surely applies to the period more generally (Hipple 1957, 314); as such, any connections between them are not direct but worked out in terms of parallels and analogies. There is a marked tendency, moreover, to rank the latter above than the former, aesthetic value often appearing as the model for and a normative steppingstone to the moral. The extent to which writers connect these spheres varies a good deal: Hutcheson, at one extreme, does so explicitly and systematically, while Edmund Burke, at the other, despite writing the century's most important treatment of aesthetics (until eclipsed by Kant's third *Critique*), barely addresses the issue at all, and then only indirectly. In the *Enquiry*, he defines beauty as the effect of qualities in objects that "cause love" (III.I.91), the latter being a feeling of affection or tenderness related to the "social passions" (sympathy, imitation, and ambition) that connect people "in the great chain of society" (1.XII.44).[3]

As some examples will show, other leading figures fall somewhere in between these extremes. Kant, for instance, provides one of the clearest expressions of the connection. (See Shapshay, this volume.) He recognizes the similarities between the two spheres, aesthetic judgments ("judgments of taste") and moral judgments both involving valuations (the good/bad and the right/wrong) and feelings on the part of the subject (a "liking of taste" and a "feeling of respect"), but insists they are independent, a conviction he maintains throughout, even if he vacillated over whether the cultivation of moral feeling should be considered a preparation for aesthetics or aesthetic experience for the cultivation of virtue (he decided, albeit ambiguously, for the latter) (see Kant [1790] 2000, 5:300–301, 326, 353–354 and 5:356). Kant expresses this conviction nowhere more forcefully than in the first of the Four Moments that constitute the "Analytic of the Beautiful," arguing that while taste is the power of judging through satisfaction or dissatisfaction—from the free play or harmony of the faculties—"without any interest" (5:211) and involves a liking, morality has an "objective value," and the objects of its judgments are esteemed or approved (5:210). Judgments of taste can be *combined* with interest, but whether that is "empirical" (where one communicates one's feeling of pleasure to everybody else) (4:297) or "intellectual" (paying attention to the beauty of forms), there

---

[3] Burke ([1757] 1958). References are to part, section, and page number.

cannot be any actual transition from one sphere to the other: the first indulges inclination and blends with the passions in general, and the second at best "indicates a disposition of the mind that is favorable to the moral feeling, if it is gladly combined with the viewing of nature" (5:299). The latter realization, however, shows that "the beautiful is a symbol of the morally good" (5:353), an indirect presentation of morality that involves a rule for reflecting on each side and their respective origins (5:353–354).

A century earlier, in Britain, Shaftesbury had already uncoupled the aesthetic from the moral sphere conceptually, claiming his *Characteristicks* as an attempt to "assert the Reality of a Beauty and Charm in *moral* as well as *natural* Subjects" (3:303).[4] Shaftesbury describes them as "*one and the same*" (2:399), an obnubilation until one realizes that something is "good" only in so far as it contributes as part to whole, a "*system* compleat, according to one *simple, consistent,* and *uniform* DESIGN" (2:286) with an ordering principle—Nature, God, Divine Mind, or the One—that explains it. Beauty is manifest as different faces of the universe, aesthetically as "*Three* Degrees or Orders of Beauty"— "dead forms," "*Forms that form,*" and the "Principle, Source, and Fountain of all Beauty" (2.408)—and morally as "virtue" or "merit," qualities predicated of "sensible" creatures who are (if good) motivated by their affections or passions directly and deliberately (or [if bad] accidentally and thus indirectly), to further the well-being of the system. Virtue is thus a meta-affect, premised on apperception, where "Affections themselves"—pity, kindness, gratitude and the like—"become Objects" and, ideally, the motives of action (2:28). There are grounds for thinking, like Reid, that for Shaftesbury, "beauty originally dwells" in the "moral and intellectual perceptions of mind" (Reid 602.19–20), though this might have more do with Reid's own views than with the details of Shaftesbury's actual position.

This same division between aesthetic and moral beauty is evident in Hutcheson's *Inquiry* advertised (in its first edition but dropped subsequently) as an explanation and defense of the "principles of the late Earl of Shaftesbury."[5] On each side, Hutcheson discovers some real (primary) quality that produces sentiments in an observer fitted by nature (and the grace of God) to receive them. In the aesthetic realm, this is *uniformity* (or *unity) amidst variety* (or *number*), at once an explanatory principle and placeholder for some "real Quality in the Objects" (I.I.IX) that excites the idea of beauty in response to shapes, the natural world, theorems, or art. In the moral realm, Hutcheson (like Shaftesbury) finds a place for self-consciousness and, specifically, the capacity of subjects to reflect on actions, through which they transcend self-interest and feel a disinterested regard for others, be it to further the good of family, friends, partners, or one's native country. Hutcheson claims that different sentiments attach to inanimate objects, which we use or possess for our own advantage, than to rational agents who have our interests and happiness (or the opposites) at heart, feel benevolence (or ill-intent) toward us, and to whom we respond with admiration and love (or the opposites). Other

---

[4] Shaftesbury ([1711] 2001). References are to the volume and parenthetical pagination of the 1732 edition on which the Liberty Fund version is based.

[5] Hutcheson ([1725/1726] 2004). References are to treatise, section, and paragraph number.

people are "parts of ourselves" (II.II.IX) such that we feel joy, admiration, and delight in *their* happiness when we see that the action flows from love, humanity, gratitude, compassion, or abhorrence and aversion when the motives reveal delight in ingratitude and the misery of others.

David Hume too draws a parallel between morals and aesthetics, and most clearly in the *Enquiry Concerning the Principles of Morals*, where his appeal to utility and agreeableness to explain moral value transfers easily to the case of aesthetic value as well.[6] In the case of "qualities useful to others" (or "general utility"), for example, beauty arises because we find pleasure in objects that promote the good of the whole, as in a "cornfield and loaded vineyards" that involves flourishing and provides for food, plenty, and happiness to others, while "briars and brambles" produce the opposite (2.9). With "qualities useful to ourselves" (the possessor), beauty arises because we see that qualities of the object that possesses them are useful for furthering the end in question: a machine, a house, furniture, clothes, a knife are beautiful because they are "well contrived for use and conveniency" (2.10). For Hume, then, virtue (and vice) and beauty (and deformity) are secondary qualities that arises in individuals as a result of their being affected by qualities of an object that produce pleasure (or pain), either by an action or character (moral sphere) or an object of nature or art (aesthetic sphere). Approval or disapproval follows, and actions and objects are rendered virtuous or vicious (moral sphere) or beautiful or deformed (aesthetic sphere). Thus "moral beauty" is really a metaphorical extension of aesthetic language to the sphere of morals, but each has its own sentiments and remains distinct.

TASTE IN BEAUTY AND OF MORALS

In demarcating and describing the aesthetic and moral realms, modern writers also formed notions of a mechanism to explain how one might detect and discern the value of each; one can *appreciate* houses, gardens, and clothes as being "convenient, fruitful, warm, easy," as Hutcheson observes, but without the existence of some prior faculty one could never find them "beautiful"; without the same in the moral realm, similarly, one could not distinguish love for a friend from the "natural good" one receives from the advantage of a commodious dwelling (Hutcheson [1725/1726] 2004 I.I.XVI; II.I.I). As noted above, the solution to which many turned was to posit some faculty or—the most suggestive notion—sense, the internal analog of those external powers through which one perceives the qualities of physical objects. These might be collected generically under the idea of "taste," a concept with its distant origins in Aristotle and, more immediately, in mid-seventeenth-century Spanish (*gusto*) whence it entered other European languages (*goût* in French, *Geschmack* in German) to become, by the eighteenth century,

---

[6] Hume ([1751/1772] 1998). References are to section and paragraph number.

a ubiquitous term of art to explain how the relevant features of the world—be they aesthetically or morally valenced—impact the subject (Townsend 2001, 47–62). Writers do not always use the *term* "taste"—in the French tradition, Dominique Bouhours, Crousaz, and Dubos (and Hume, likely under their influence) appeal to "sentiments," for example—but the concept is never far from their concerns. For Kant, taste does not name a *faculty*, but delineates a form of judgment (*Geschmacksurteil*) *involving* the faculties in their harmony or free play. The idea that it might belong, as one among the other faculties, however, is expressed early by Shaftesbury, for whom such a "reflected sense" (2.28) detects the real order of the universe: in the aesthetic sphere it appears as the "Idea or Sense of *Order* and *Proportion*" (2:284) and, in the moral, a "sense of right and wrong" (2.40–41) and "first Principle in our Constitution and Make" (2.44).

Shaftesbury's "sense" appears more metaphorical than literal, but later writers take seriously the analogy with the external senses, and it becomes subsequently a literal, internal counterpart to sight and hearing. Bouhours, for instance, speaks of it in terms of *le bon esprit* (true wit), which he characterizes as a combination of vivacity and common sense ([1671] 2000, 207–208); DuBos specifies it as a "sixth sense we have within us, without feelings its organs" (1710/1748: 2.239); and Hutcheson, more systematically, proposes both a "Sense of Beauty" and a "Moral Sense," a "Determination of the Mind, to receive any Idea from the presence of an Object which occurs to us, independent of Will" ([1725/1726] 2004, II.I.I). Others, such as Addison, Hume, Hogarth, and Reynolds, look to the "imagination"; others still—notably Alexander Gerard, Lord Kames, Archibald Alison, Dugald Stewart, and James Beattie—emphasize principles of association, effectively treating imagination and taste as a single faculty. The "*powers of the imagination*," as Gerard puts it, just are what "modern philosophers" call the "*internal or reflex senses*," which work upon the material provided by perception (Gerard 1780/1759, 1–2n). Toward century's end, even Reid, though railing against Locke's doctrine of secondary qualities and those same "modern philosophers," appeals, conventionally, to the concept of taste as the "power of the mind by which we are capable of discerning and relishing the beauties of Nature, and whatever is excellent in the fine arts" (Reid [1785] 2002 573.9–11).

The extension of the concept of "taste" or "sense" to explain the origin of beauty and morals has intuitive appeal, though it also leads to obscurity, especially in its tendency to reduce either to a master faculty under which other powers are mysteriously arranged or, in the spirit of DuBos, to duplicate its number relative to the number of phenomena in need of explanation. Hutcheson cannot resist this temptation, and, observing there to be "some *Sense* or other suited to every sort of Objects which occurs to us," goes on to enumerate five separate "classes," including a "Publick Sense" and a "sense of Honour" (Hutcheson [1728] 2002, I.I). Gerard too "resolves" taste into no fewer than seven "simple principles," each named for a different sense—novelty, sublimity, beauty, imitation, harmony, oddity and ridicule, and virtue; when these become the same with "powers of the imagination," one reaches a tautology where the "nature of *taste*" is explicable through the way in which these "tastes" cooperate (Gerard 1780/1759, Part 1). The identification of taste with sentiment promises to avoid the problem, though others arise. Dubos's *sens*, for example, is really identical with sensory pleasure, and Hume, though avoiding that eventuality by balancing sentiments with reflection, must appeal in the end to the phenomenology of the matter: since sentiments of moral *and* aesthetic beauty (and deformity) are "agreeable" (or "disagreeable"), only experiencing how those affects feel will enable one to mark the difference.

These problems are exacerbated by the fact that "taste" is inherently ambiguous, especially as it collapses "two temporalities" into one (Noggle 2012: 1–5). This is discernible even in what (as writers from Addison to Kant never tire of emphasizing) is its original home of gustatory flavors and relishes, where the organs respond instantly and untutored to the presence of sweet and bitter but, at the same time, require reflection and judgment—*education*—if they are to be sensitive or delicate to the complexity of flavors. It is at once a fixed state *and* a work in progress. This dual nature of taste is reflected perfectly in the story of Sancho's oenological kinsmen at the hogshead of wine—the episode Hume borrows from *Don Quixote* to illustrate the point—both of whom are ridiculed for detecting the one leather and the other iron, until a key with a leather thong was found at the bottom (Hume 1985, 234–235). Taste is really a balancing act of competing forces, automatic against intentional, natural opposed to acquired, so that it both reacts (as a faculty) immediately to the stimuli it detects while its operations are always expressed in activity and extended temporally.

This ambiguity persists when "taste" migrates from the external to the internal world, where it operates magically and transcendently; we are "struck, we know not how" and "without any previous consideration," as Addison puts it, ([1712] 1965, 538, 542), echoing an attitude that goes back at least to the "*je ne sais quoi*" of Bouhours ([1671] 1970, 228–238) and shared by many. At the same time, for Addison, this wondrous sense does not obviate the prosaic workings of memory and reflection ([1712] 1965, 561–562, 568) nor, above all, the passage of time and tedium of practice, all displayed in Hume's "true judge in the finer arts," that rarest of characters even in the "most polished ages," an ideal figure who almost impossibly combines strong sense, delicate sentiment, practice, comparison and freedom from prejudice (Hume 1985, 241). In the hands of some, the magical element takes control, as in Gerard, whose "sense of virtue" explains the perception of "fairness, beauty, and loveliness of virtue, of the ugliness, deformity, and hatefulness of vice" along with the obligatory nature ot the former, the faculty being no less than "our internal governour prescribing a law of life" (Gerard 1780/1759, 76–77). Alison, after him, and without much fanfare, simply reduces the aesthetic to the moral (Alison 1790, 268, 294).

Reid, for one, was suspicious of the too-easy extension of the language of taste and sense to the moral sphere, a move, he urges, that is purely metaphorical because the power of mind it denotes is only *analogous* to the "taste of the palate" (573.20–23). He too uses the language of internal sense, but (in his constant attitude of sustained horror at the very notion of secondary qualities) always refers beauty or deformity to the "real excellence" of the object or action, yielding pleasure or pain in one case but approbation or disapprobation in the other; one *loves* or *likes* beautiful things, but one feels *benevolence* toward morally good agents. Stewart too hints at the same, pointing out that so varied are the objects to which aesthetic terms are applied, that it is difficult to discern any "common or coincident meaning." The mistake—he cites Denis Diderot as a case in point—is that philosophers take all references to be species of the same genus when, in fact, aesthetic terms are "transitive": pairs in a sequence might share a property, though not terms at either extreme, so *beauty* will be predicated of dissimilar objects but appear to share a common feature (Stewart 1856–1860/1810, 191, 196). Many writers, however, are content with Lockean epistemology, and happy to move uncritically from foody relishes to the beauty of objects and on to "moral beauty," even if it owes more to the seduction of language than the power of argument. Even so, Reid is willing to admit a universal feature, that "all objects we call beautiful" produce an "agreeable emotion or feeling" along with the "opinion or belief" about some perfection or excellence belonging to them (592.5–9), and Stewart, likewise, finds the term always denotes a "certain *refined* species of pleasure," and that of an "intellectual" sort since we do not apply the "taste" to the "grosse indulgences" related to bodily sense (Stewart 1856–1860/1810, 191–192).

Another appealing aspect of "taste," and its cognates, is how handily it provides a cultural context with a normative terminology to match: it is "perfected," "refined," "delicate," in a word, *civilized*, and thus comes to define a way of being, whether of an individual, group, epoch, or nation. If taste is an achievement, moreover, it is also something for which one might be praised as a "True Critic," a "Fine Genius" "Man of Taste," "virtuoso," "connoisseur," and "polished" individual, or condemned for being the opposite, a purveyor of a "false taste," as in "love for the Gothick," a phrase that captures all things confused, foreign, and uncivilized. In the French tradition, this extends to drawing a tight connection between artistic taste and politeness, a beauty of manners or etiquette, knowing how, when, and where to behave appropriately. Needless to say, it is a short step from approving or condemning a false taste in matters of art and beauty to the same in morals where the language of "good" and "bad" translates easily into that of "right" and "wrong," "refined" and "barbaric," which too often has the ring of naïvete, at best, and, at worst, of privilege, elitism, and cultural hegemony. Thus one finds Kames moving lightly from aesthetic taste (French women using red blush and Alpine dwellers who prize an "unnatural swelling in the neck") to moral practice (exposing of infants to wild boars or punishing children for the crimes of their parents), both condemned as "aberrations" of the "standard of nature" ([1762] 2005, 2:497/724). "To ascertain the rules of morality, we appeal not to the common sense of savages," Kames intones, "but of men in their more perfect state: and we make the same appeal in forming the rules that ought to govern the fine arts: in neither can we safely rely on a local or transitory taste; but on what is the most general and the most lasting among polite nations" (2:498/725).

Kames's appeal to nature or some foundational equivalent is hardly uncommon, and one response, albeit crude in his hands, to the general difficulty with which many felt the need to contend, namely, that claims in favor of "true taste," whether aesthetic or moral, come up against the empirical fact of diversity. The sting is doubly felt given that most took taste and sense to be (like its gustatory and visual counterparts) an inseparable part of human nature and therefore, in principle, universal. The "variety of Taste, as well of opinion, which prevails in the world," as Hume writes in the most famous statement of the dilemma, makes it "natural for us to seek a *Standard of Taste*; a rule, by which the various sentiments of men may be reconciled" (Hume 1985, 226, 228). One response, favored by internal sense theorists, is to draw out further the analogy with external sense and explain diversity as a matter of impairment: as the eye fails through faulty function or external circumstance so the internal sense is corrupted through "contrary Habit and Custom" (Shaftesbury [1711] 2001, 2:44), prejudices of education (Hutcheson [1725/ 1726] 2004, I.VI.III; I.VII.III) or "wrong associations" (Reid [1785] 2002, 576.11–14). Free from such interference, the sense works unimpeded to detect the underlying order, uniformity amidst variety, real excellence, or whatever other candidate principle one prefers for a standard, and approves and condemns as the nature of the object demands. Hume's solution is more subtle; in both aesthetic beauty and morals, he argues, works and actions that stand the test of time deserve approbation even if contingencies of circumstance prevent persons, groups or nations from recognizing it. The contradiction between two "species" of common sense, however, the articulation and solution of which drives his argument—one accepting, the other denying, that a standard exists— still resolves, in the final analysis, to a claim about what pleases and displeases and can be approved or rejected by one who has "delicacy of taste" (see also Hume 1985: 3–8).

This apparent refusal to acknowledge the reality of genuine diversity might be considered a kind of cultural indifference born of turning "taste" and "nature" into abstractions that codify a particular and dominant perspective, which is then generalized through time and across place. There is another kind of indifference built into taste and its linguistic idiom, however, that takes a different path, toward *moral* indifference since it is, at bottom, as Ronald Paulson describes the position he takes Hogarth's *Analysis* to undermine, a "substitute for morals," because it replaces "moral imperatives" with "sensibility" (Hogarth [1753] 1997, xlviii; see de Bolla 2003, 80–81). One might add that it is *aesthetic* sensibility at that, taste being hedonic and hedonistic, tied fundamentally to emotional arousal and the celebration of pleasure or "amusement," which often means the trifles of the noble classes at play. If writers in the tradition are (as I have emphasized) largely focused on finding parallels and tracing analogies and thus hold the spheres apart, it is doubtful that this line of criticism hits its target head on—aesthetic value *illuminates* moral value, it does not *constitute* it—but the appeal to taste certainly has the effect of aestheticizing morality, and contains the permanent possibility of pulling a veil over the very phenomena to which the faculty of taste is supposedly sensitive, namely, sentiments of a "morally beautiful" sort; the danger, one might note, is not so acute when moving the other way, where moralizing aesthetic life at worst shows the limits of usefully considering beauty to have some moral analogue.

One might generate from this observation a general critique of the tradition as a whole, and the tendency of exclusion on which, one might argue, it is founded: "In the transcendental project of aesthetic practice and judgment," as Simon Gikandi observes, "materials that were considered anterior to the process of European self-fashioning, such as slaves, Indians, and the poor, were confined to notational margins and footnotes" (Gikandi 2011, 21). A more specific and modest case of the tendency is found in "the picturesque" (see Hipple 1957, Part II; Costelloe 2013, ch. 4), though it has less to do with cultural hegemony than with the aesthetic itself, destined from the outset to be hoisted with its own petard, premised as it is, on an insatiable imperative to rearrange the world in its own image and make it look, as its name triumphantly advertises, more "like a picture" (the Baroque landscape painters of France and Italy provided its perspective and terminology). The gaze of the "picturesque eye" works its magic on canvas and in description, and on actual landscapes themselves (the aesthetic being entwined historically with the development of landscape gardening), and does so in accordance with a particular species of beauty, "picturesque beauty," as William Gilpin, the first to treat the category philosophically, terms it, defined by "roughness" of surface and "ruggedness" of outline and producing a singular kind of pleasure (Gilpin 1794/1792, 6). Any object can please in this way if *rendered* picturesque, seen or physically remade in terms of the qualities it champions. At one level this is merely absurd—as Jane Austen's gentle parodies of the genre show (Austen [1817] 2006, 111–112 and 113)—but in its more sinister moments it inserts distance and neutralizes objects that properly demand moral evaluation. Gilpin himself discovered these limits when on his journey down the Wye he was confronted by the "poverty and wretchedness" of people he discovered living in the ruins of Tintern Abbey (Gilpin 1800/1782, 50–52). Gilpin fled in search of further pleasures, and it took the finely calibrated moral compass of Ruskin, some half a century later, to realize, in a moment of surreal insight at a scene on the Somme, how "many suffering persons must pay for [his] picturesque subject and happy walk"; on the surface it was "all exquisitely picturesque," but shifting his gaze revealed its reality, a "miserable" scene of foul waterways, rotten timbers, and grinding poverty (Ruskin 1903–1911, vol. 6, 20n).

WRITING AND THE ART OF DECEPTION

The moral indifference of the picturesque highlights the hedonic and hedonistic nature of taste: Gilpin's *pleasure* is disturbed by the destitute at Tintern Abbey, and Ruskin cannot justify the same in face of the suffering that makes it possible. The picturesque might lie at an extreme in deliberately rearranging the world in its own image—the *aim* of picturesque travel is "*searching after effects*" and of sketching picturesque landscapes to "*fix* and *communicate*" its ideas (Gilpin 1794/1792, 41, 61)—but it is really only a particular outcome and application of the more general and widely held view (its origins in Plato) that art is fundamentally imitative and always *represents* reality. On the one hand, this is to be celebrated as art's secret power and source of a particular kind of beauty— "relative" as Hutcheson calls it ([1726] 2004: I.IV.I)—and pleasure—"secondary" in Addison's terminology ([1711] 1965, 540, 559–560)—that can only arise from the act of comparison between original and copy. On the other hand, this gives art a "borrowed" life (Dubos 1719/1748, 23), and demands the spectator achieve a state of self-deception, realizing that its artifacts deceive but affirming their strange truth nonetheless. The product of art requires embracing a paradox, where, as Kant writes, albeit refracted through the structure of his Critical System, "one must be aware that it is art, and not nature" and yet still see it "*as if it were* a mere product of nature" (5:306, emphasis added).

This paradox is nowhere more apparent than in reflections on literature, the art form that receives most attention in the period, including in one manifestation, the "paradox of tragedy," the problem inherited from Aristotle of how emotions felt at depictions of awful events are pleasurable while the same in real life would bring only pain. From Addison and Dubos onward, one finds authors trying to balance the dual requirements of verisimilitude and originality, that the truth of art lies in capturing its originals, but all art—to be *art*—must lie: slavish copies are double failures since they reproduce imperfections *and* leave an audience cold and unmoved. To avoid the first, art must produce *la belle nature*, "not the reality that is" as Batteux expresses the idea that echoes long and loud until century's end, but the "reality that could be, the truly beautiful, which is represented as if it actually existed, with all the perfections it could have" ([1746] 2015, 13). To avoid the second, artists must carefully select their objects to connect with their readers: the "chitchat of the tea-table, copied faithfully, and at length," as Hume expresses the worry, would make an "insipid comedy" (Hume 1985, 191–192), and nobody wants to know every time Achilles ties his shoelaces (Hume [1751/1772] 1998, 3.11). This produces a curious dilemma when one turns to the declared literary intentions of many—the likes of Bouhours, Addison, and Shaftesbury set the tone—since achieving virtues of the civilized involves embracing the vices of mendacity and deception: taste requires placing things in the "best possible light" (Batteux [1746] 2015: 11) rather than the cold light of day.

This will to persuade, as one might call it, brings with it a will to linguistic purity as well, a working out of Locke's rejection of "figurative speeches" in favor of "*natural* and *simple*" expression (Locke 1975, 3.10.34). The art of writing itself becomes a bearer of moral value, good aesthetic taste calculated to further good moral taste, with both amenable to the same calculus of virtue and vice: affectation, embellishment, ornamentation, and rhetorical flourish are faults of writing *and* corruptions of character. Philosophical writing does not escape the calculus either, as it too moves in an ambiguous space between explanation and persuasion, anatomy and painting, dividing, as Hume marks the difference, into "different species," the "accurate and obtuse" that regards human nature as a "subject of speculation," and the "easy and obvious" that aims to "please the imagination, and engage the affections" thus "alluring us into the paths of virtue" by making us "*feel* the difference between virtue and vice" (1.1–3).[7] Attuned to the art of writing and the deception of writing, Hume opts for a middle way that seeks to pursue the former by means of the latter. This is a reconciliation of sorts, though the competing forces of art and the aesthetic remain; in attempting to control them, Hume, like others of the period, must be judged finally to have met with only limited success.

See also: Shapshay, Song, Destrée, this volume

---

[7] Hume ([1772/1748] 1999). References are to section and paragraph number.

REFERENCES

Addison, Joseph. [1712] 1965. "The Pleasures of the Imagination." In *The Spectator*, edited by Donald F. Bond, vol. 1, 535–582. Oxford: Clarendon Press.

Alison, Archibald. 1790. *Essays on the Nature and Principles of Taste*. Dublin: Byrne et al.

Austen, Jane. [1817] 2006. *Northanger Abbey*, edited by Barbara M. Benedict and Deirdre Le Faye. Cambridge: Cambridge University Press.

Batteux, Charles. [1746] 2015. *The Fine Arts Reduced to a Single Principle*. Translated by James O. Young. Oxford: Oxford University Press.

Baumgarten, Alexander Gottlieb. [1750] 2007. *Aesthetica/Ästhetik*, edited by Dagmar Mirbach, 2 vols. Hamburg: Felix Meiner Verlag.

Baumgarten, Alexander Gottlieb. [1735] 1954. *Reflections on Poetry: Alexander Gottlieb Baumgarten's Meditationes philosophicae de nonnullis ad poema pertinentibus*. Translated by Karl Aschenbrenner and William B. Holther. Berkeley: University of California Press.

Beattie, James. 1783. "Of Taste, and its Improvement." In *Dissertations: Moral and Critical*, 165–193. London: W. Strahan and T. Cadell.

Bouhours, Dominque. [1671] 1970. *Entretiens d'Ariste et Eugène*. Paris: Mabre-Cramois. Partly translated (Entretiens IV and V) as *The Conversations of Aristo and Eugene*, in *The Continental Model: Selected French Critical Essays of the Seventeenth Century in English Translation*, edited by Scott Elledge and Donald Schier, 206–238. Ithaca, NY: Cornell University Press.

Burke, Edmund. [1757] 1958. *A Philosophical Enquiry into the Origin of Our Ideas of the Sublime and Beautiful*, edited by James T. Boulton. London: Routledge & Kegan Paul.

Collingwood, R. G. 1938. *The Principles of Art*. Oxford: Clarendon Press.

Costelloe, Timothy M. 2013. *The British Aesthetic Tradition: From Shaftesbury to Wittgenstein*. Cambridge: Cambridge University Press.

Crousaz, Jean-Pierre de. [1715/1714] 2000. *Traité du beau, Où l'on montre en quoi consiste ceque l'on nomme ainsi, par des exemples tirez de la plûpart des arts & des sciences*. Amsterdam: Chez François L'Honoré. Partly translated as *Treatise on Beauty*, in *Art in Theory, 1648–1815: An Anthology of Changing Ideas*, edited by Charles Harrison, Paul Charles, Paul Wood, and Jason Gaigereds, 389–393. Oxford: Blackwell Publishers.

de Bolla, Peter. 2003. *The Education of the Eye. Painting, Landscape, and Architecture in Eighteenth Century Britain*. Stanford, CA: Stanford University Press.

DuBos, Jean-Baptiste. 1719/1748. *Réflexions critiques sur la poésie et sur la peinture*, Paris: Mariette. *Critical reflections on poetry, painting and music. With an inquiry into the rise and progress of the theatrical entertainments of the ancients. Written in French by the Abbé Du Bos. Translated into English by Thomas Nugent, gent. From the fifth edition revised, corrected, and inlarged by the author*, 3 vols. London: John Nourse.

Eaton, Marcia Muelder. 2004. "Art and the Aesthetic." In *The Blackwell Guide to Aesthetics*, edited by Peter Kivy, 63–77. Oxford: Blackwell.

Gallie, Roger D. 1998. *Thomas Reid: Aesthetics, Ethics and the Autonomy of the Self*. Dordrecht: Kluwer.

Gaut, Berys. 2013. "Art and Ethics." In *The Routledge Companion to Aesthetics*, edited by Berys Gaut & Dominic McIver Lopes, 3rd ed., 394–403. New York: Routledge.

Gerard, Alexander. 1780/1759. *An Essay on Taste. To Which Is Now Added Part Fourth, Of the Standard of Taste; with Observations Concerning the Imitative Nature of Poetry*, 3rd ed. London: T. Cadell.

Gikandi, Simon. 2011. *Slavery and the Culture of Taste*. Princeton, NJ: Princeton University Press.

Gilpin, William. 1800/1782. *Observations on the River Wye and Several Parts of South Wales, &c. Relative Chiefly to Picturesque Beauty; made in the summer of the year 1770*, 5th ed. London: A. Strahan.

Gilpin, William. 1794/1792. *Three Essays: On Picturesque Beauty; On Picturesque Travel; and On Sketching Landscape to which is added a poem, On Landscape Painting*, 2nd ed. London: R. Blamire.

Guyer, Paul. 2014. *A History of Modern Aesthetics, Volume 1: The Eighteenth Century*. Cambridge: Cambridge University Press.

Hammermeister, Kai. 2002. *The German Aesthetic Tradition*. Cambridge: Cambridge University Press.

Hipple, Walter J. 1957. *The Beautiful, the Sublime, and the Picturesque in Eighteenth-Century British Aesthetic Theory*. Carbondale: Southern Illinois University Press.

Hogarth, William. [1753] 1997. *The Analysis of Beauty*, edited by Ronald Paulson. New Haven, CT: Yale University Press.

Hume, David. [1748/1772] 1999. *An Enquiry Concerning Human Understanding*, edited by Tom Beauchamp. Oxford: Oxford University Press

Hume, David. [1772/1751] 1998. *An Enquiry Concerning the Principles of Morals*, edited by Tom Beauchamp. Oxford: Oxford University Press.

Hume, David. 1985. *Essays: Moral, Political, and Literary*, edited by Eugene F. Miller. Indianapolis: Liberty Fund.

Hutcheson, Francis. [1725/1726] 2004. *An Inquiry into the Original of Our Ideas of Beauty and Virtue in Two Treatises*, 2nd ed. Indianapolis: Liberty Fund.

Hutcheson, Francis. [1728] 2002. *An Essay on the Nature and Conduct of the Passions and Affections, with Illustrations on the Moral Sense*. Indianapolis: Liberty Fund.

Home, Henry, Lord Kames. [1762] 2005. *Elements of Criticism. The Sixth Edition. With the Author's Last Corrections and Additions*, 2 vols. Indianapolis: Liberty Fund.

Kant, Immanuel. [1790] 2000. *Kritik der Urteilskraft. Kants gesammelte Schriften*. Königlichen Preussischen (later Deutschen) Akademie der Wissenschaften, 29 vols. Berlin: Reimer (later de Gruyter, 1900–), vol. 5. *Critique of the Power of Judgment*, translated by Paul Guyer and Eric Matthews. Cambridge: Cambridge University Press.

Kivy, Peter. 2004. "Reid's Philosophy of Art." In *The Cambridge Companion to Thomas Reid*, edited by Terence Cuneo and René van Woudenberg, 267–288. Cambridge: Cambridge University Press.

Kristeller, P. O. 1951. "The Modern System of the Arts: A Study in the History of Aesthetics Part I." *Journal of the History of Ideas* 12, no. 4: 496–527.

Kristeller, P. O. 1952. The Modern System of the Arts: A Study in the History of Aesthetics Part II." *Journal of the History of Ideas* 13, no. 1: 17–46.

Locke, John. [1690] 1975. *An Essay Concerning Human Understanding*, edited by Peter H. Nidditch. Oxford: Clarendon Press.

Noggle, James. 2012. *The Temporality of Taste in Eighteenth-Century British Writing*. Oxford: Oxford University Press.

Plato. 1992. *Republic*, translated by G. M. A. Grube. Indianapolis: Hackett.

Reid, Thomas. [1785] 2002. "Of Taste." In *Essays on the Intellectual Powers of Man*, 572–614. University Park: Penn State University Press.

Reynolds, Joshua. [1797] 1997. *Discourses on Art*, edited by Robert R. Wark. New Haven, CT: Yale University Press.

Rousseau, Jean-Jacques. [1758] 1968. *Politics and the Arts. Letter to M. D'Alembert on the Theatre*. Translated by Allan Bloom. Ithaca, NY: Cornell University Press.

Ruskin, John. 1903–1911. *The Poetry of Architecture; or The Architecture of Europe Considered in its Association with Natural Scenery and National Character, by Kata Phusin*, and *Modern Painters IV*. In *The Complete Works of John Ruskin (Library Edition)*, edited by E. T. Cook and Alexander Wedderburn, vols. 1 and 6. London: George Allen.

Schiller, Friedrich. [1967]1982 *On the Aesthetic Education of Man. In a Series of Letters. English and German Facing*. Edited and translated by Elizabeth M. Wilkinson and L. A. Willoughby. Oxford: Clarendon Press.

Shaftesbury, Earl of (Anthony Ashley Cooper). [1711] 2001. *Characteristicks of Men, Manners, Opinions, Times*, 3 vols. Indianapolis: Liberty Fund.

Stewart, Dugald. 1856–1860/1810. "Essays Relative to Matters of Taste." In *Philosophical Essays. The Collected Works of Dugald Stewart*, vol. 5, edited by Sir William Hamilton, 189–406. Edinburgh: Thomas Constable.

Tolstoy, Leo. [1904] 1996. *What is Art?* Translated by Aylmer Maude. Indianapolis: Hackett.

Townsend, Dabney. 2001. *Hume's Aesthetic Theory: Taste and Sentiment*. New York: Routledge.

CHAPTER 7

THE KNOWLEDGE THAT JOINS ETHICS TO ART IN YORÙBÁ CULTURE

BARRY HALLEN

"We will tell our stories ourselves."
—Adeyẹyẹ̀ Ẹnitan Bàbátunde Ògúnwusi, Ọjàjà II, Ọọ̀ni of Ifẹ̀[1]

THE Yorùbá are an ethnic group of roughly 40 million located primarily in southwestern Nigeria. Their culture has been described as "traditional." "Traditional" is a term that is used to characterize the cultures of sub-Saharan Africa, most specifically before the advent of European colonialism. Such cultures were then said to be genuinely indigenous. Thereafter, foreign influence via European conquest and colonial occupation would inevitably effect significant changes in them.

The model of traditional African cultures that was constructed by scholars is reasonably straightforward. They are characterized as less than rational in "modern" terms because their beliefs and practices do more to satisfy their inhabitants' emotional needs than to provide objective understanding of why things really happen as they do in the world. Furthermore, the dominant attitude toward those beliefs and practices was that they were wisdom inherited from past generations ("ancestors"), were not subject to challenge, and would therefore be preserved and honored unchanged in the present and future. As such, critical thinking and reflection were not prioritized. When such cultures' members were asked to explain *why*, for example, they valued a particular form of behavior, or *why* they valued art styled in a certain way, the responses

---

[1] Cited in Parkes 2017.

would themselves be an appeal to *tradition*—because this is what we inherited from the forefathers.

In this chapter, I am going to begin with art and then consider some of the ethical values involved in its creation, appreciation and use in Yorùbá culture. The art objects produced by traditional cultures and eventually prized by European museums and private collectors (primarily sculpture-masks and figurative carvings) were said to have been made for more than decorative purposes: to serve instrumental ends, to worship, to perpetuate the memory of an ancestor, to serve as one component of a masquerade. It was when severed from the indigenous context and hung on a museum or gallery wall that they were supposedly transformed into primarily artistic works.

Given the limited explanatory responses from traditional peoples, the obstacles to understanding Africans and their cultures were obvious. There was a need for specially trained observers, so-called fieldworkers, who would learn the languages and spend serious time living in the cultures. They would then use their own firsthand *observations* and experiences as well as secondary sources like the culture's oral literature (myths, poetry, song) to construct accounts that tried to bridge the gap and explain why things like the art were styled in certain ways or why certain forms of behavior were valued. In the case of the Yorùbá, much of this would take place when Nigeria was already a British colony or after it became an independent nation-state. There therefore had to be a presumption on the part of fieldworkers and researchers that enough of traditional Yorùbá culture had survived into the colonial and postcolonial eras for them to observe and analyze.

In the case of the Yorùbá, the amount of scholarship devoted to the study of the culture is substantial. If there is any insecurity on the part of the non-Yorùbá researchers involved, it is that explanations arising from *observation* are also by definition secondhand. There is therefore an enduring desire to find a way to have more direct access to the minds, the consciousnesses, of the traditional Yorùbá that fieldworkers can only observe. Are Yorùbá *experiences* of art and behavior defined exclusively by "traditions"? Do they have a *conscience*? How do their *minds* work when it comes to art and acceptable or unacceptable behavior? Do they have a sense of *artistic creativity*?

What will be of special interest here is that, as time passed, members of the culture who were themselves professionally trained chose to undertake comparable studies of these things in their own right. In this chapter, I want to concentrate on selections from the work of two Yorùbá scholars who did this when they were based at the University of Ife, Nigeria. Rowland Abiodun is now distinguished professor of art, history of art, and Black studies at Amherst College, and is the author of *Yorùbá Art and Language: Seeking the African in African Art*. Wole Soyinka is an internationally acclaimed novelist, essayist, and dramatist who won the Nobel Prize for Literature in 1986.

When Rowland Abiodun writes about art in Yorùbá culture, he primarily has sculpture in mind. He very much agrees that the role of such pieces—including all of those objects on display in international museums—*is* more than decorative. Nevertheless, a limitation arises: *thinking* of the objects as serving instrumental functions is still observation if it arises from the consciousness of the observer rather than the consciousnesses of the observed. The external forms of the objects do matter, of course. But to understand the Yorùbá point of view on, for example, a mask that features in a masquerade, one has to revisit the masquerade as participant rather than observer. To begin with, Wole Soyinka tells us that in a proper masquerade there is no division between the masqueraders and the "audience." Everyone, in effect, is involved as performer:

> The moment for choric participation [by the "audience"] is well-defined, but this does not imply that until such a moment participation ceases. The so-called audience is itself an integral part. (Soyinka 1976, 39)

There are no passive observers. The entire community is actively engaged as participants. In that setting, the mask is alive; it dances, it speaks, it has a personality. It can tell stories that enunciate moral values:

> Who owns the child, who owns the pregnancy?
> Pregnancy causes a fight in the house of Ajẹlẹ
> Who owns the child, who owns the pregnancy?
> Pregnancy caused a fight in the house of Ajẹlẹ
> *O yi ṣe nan pe ji l'ọjọkọ rẹ [bis]*[2]
> You can't have one pregnancy by two persons
> Wife of Ajẹlẹ, to whom does the pregnancy belong?
> You can't have one pregnancy by two persons! (Drewal and Drewal 1990, 52)

Yorùbá culture itself is distinctive for the importance attached to knowledge obtained and evidenced via firsthand experience (Hallen 2000). This in turn reinforces the impact art objects can have upon people's lives. They are not things. They have being, and, as such, can articulate values that are foundational to the culture. In this case on the occasion of the performance the entire assembly, mask and "audience," affirm the sanctity of marriage and that adultery and infidelity are unacceptable.

Abiodun tells us that what is truly essential about such art objects in the culture is expressed by the Yorùbá phrase *ìwà l'ẹwà*. In standard bi-lingual dictionaries, one finds *ìwà* translated as *nature* or *character* and *ẹwà* as *beauty*. Abiodun acknowledges that the phrase can be used in ordinary everyday terms with moral intent to compliment a person's character as beautiful/good. But there is a whole other dimension to its use involving art objects that has a meaning that is profound and metaphysical.

Art objects are invested with a deeper identity and meaning by the artists who create them. It is this deeper identity that is responsible for and critical to their *nondecorative* roles in the culture. A mask is not able to play a vital role in a masquerade simply because of the way it looks. It is able to *be* the masquerade because of the more special *ìwà* (*nature* now as *essential nature*) that provides its inner *meaning* as *that* mask in *that*

---

[2] The Yorùbá-language original of the succeeding line.

masquerade. It is the artist's creative responsibility to ensure that identity and meaning are instilled in and expressed by the form of the created mask or piece, and so it is what it should be. This is then its *ẹwà*. It is when *ìwà* and *ẹwà*, the inner and the outer, are successfully combined that a piece has true *ìwà l'ẹwà* and succeeds in being and thereby expressing the truth of its existence.

This essence or deeper identity finds subtle expression via a remarkable genre of chanted oral literature known as *oríkì*:

> It is said that everything in existence has its own *oríkì*. . . . for *oríkì* are felt to en-capsulate the essential qualities of entities. . . . They evoke a subject's qualities, go to the heart of it and elicit its inner potency. They are a highly charged form of utter-ance. Composed to single out and arrest in concentrated language . . . their utter-ance energises and enlivens the hearer. They are "heavy" words, fused together into formulations that have an exceptional density and weight. . . . All . . . are felt to evoke the essence of their subjects. (Barber 1991, 12–13)

Oríkì themselves come alive when they are chanted and thereby manifest the vital force (àṣẹ), the power, that the object *is*. Karin Barber, emeritus professor of African cultural anthropology at the University of Birmingham in the United Kingdom, puts it this way:

> For an *oríkì* . . . to be apprehended . . . it must be heard and seen in action. . . . They are fully realized only in the moment of performance. There is a sense in which they are simply not accessible at all viewed as words on a page. . . . because it is what they are *doing* that animates them and gives them their form and significance. (Barber 1991, 7)

They may be obscure and robbed of their power if recorded here in English translation, but that will at least provide some idea of their form and content. The first example is said by Abiodun to be applicable to a sculpture of the god Ẹshù, one of the very few divinities the Yorùbá allow to be represented in graven-image form. Ẹshù is respon-sible for communications between the gods and humankind, a process that can become perilous because of his own mischievous and unpredictable nature. His *oríkì* therefore serves to forewarn us of the morally weighted possibility that things in life don't always work out the way we expect them to:

> Ẹshù turns right into wrong, wrong into right. When he is angry, he hits a stone until it bleeds. When he is angry, he sits on the skin of an ant. When he is angry, he weeps tears of blood. Ẹshù slept in the house—but the house was too small for him. Ẹshù slept on the verandah—but the verandah was too small for him. Ẹshù slept in a nut—at last he could stretch himself. Ẹshù walked through the groundnut farm, the tuft of his hair was just visible. If it had not been for his huge size, he would not be visible at all. Lying down, his head hits the roof. Standing up, he cannot look into the cooking pot. He throws a stone today and kills the bird yesterday. (Abiodun 2014, 261–262)

The Ẹshù here is more than a subtle and amusing personification of life's surprises and disappointments. More importantly, the point is to promote attitudes that can be prepared for and can cope with such developments.

People, as well as objects and gods, may have *oríkì*, so the second example concerns Lagbai, a successful Yorùbá carver:

> Child of "One who transforms a piece of wood, turns it into a person"
> Carving is your métier, child of Ajibogunde
> What happened on the very first day? The child of Ajibógundé
> He lived in the town, he went into the forest
> The mahogany bean trees knocked against each other, the *ìrókò* trees ran into each other in their fright
> Nobody knows which one Lagbai will pick on.
> He carved a piece of wood and made it smooth and round
> The wood had no eyes, the wood had no mouth
> The wood had no big toe on either of its feet
> But the third time round
> What did the true-born son of Ọjẹ do? He lived in the town, he went into the forest
> He went and carved a piece of wood and brought it out on view
> The wood hard arms, the wood had a mouth, and it had a big toe on each of its feet
> He cut *pélé*[3] marks on the wood's right cheek
> He cut *àbàjà* marks on the wood's left cheek
> Child of Ikújẹnrá, his carving took him as far as Ọyọ-ile. (Barber 1991, 141–142)

One wonders how Lagbai came by the special abilities that allow him to transform and create "life." Abiodun answers this question by identifying select articulated intellectual and moral attributes that the Yorùbá use to, in effect, define the *ìwà* or essence of the person who is a superior artist or artistic critic. They are articulated concepts that occur in the discourse of people who make and talk about art in Yorùbá culture. If some of their English-language translations appear awkward, that is because Abiodun is working with the English language to communicate the nuances of Yorùbá meanings. He lists the following: clear thinking (*làákàyè*), design consciousness (*ojú-ọnà*), insight (*ojú-inú*), sensitivity (*ìmọjú-mọra*), teachableness (*ìlutí*; involving one's capacity to learn as well as educate), calmness (*ìfarabalè*), gentle character and imperturbability (*ìwàpèlé*), patience (*sùúrù*), and steadfastness (*títọ*). Then there are the supplementary terms used to refer to the knowledge itself that is thereby acquired: wisdom (*ọgbọ́n*) and understanding (*òye*).

There is both epistemological and ethical content to these attributes. Clear thinking, design consciousness, insight, sensitivity and teachableness indicate superior cognitive, communicative, and artistic abilities. By contrast, being calm, gentle, imperturbable, patient, and steadfast entail a character that is stable, self-controlled, and observant. These

---

[3] Marks that serve to identify someone as belonging to a group of people (Abiodun 2019, 39).

are moral values that the Yorùbá believe support optimal cognition, and thereby optimal artistic expertise. Mastering the creative processes involving inner essences (*ìwà l'ẹwà*) and *oríkì* involves considerably more than learning how to handle a hammer and chisel. The superior moral character of the artist becomes a prerequisite to the superior quality of their work.

Facial expressions associated with these virtues and their artistic representation can relate to some very famous examples of Yorùbá art. This is in regards to the thousand-year-old, life-size, copper-alloy Ife heads that some critics consider the finest art objects ever produced by the traditional cultures of sub-Saharan Africa. The problem for some of those critics was that, given the age of the objects, the advanced casting technology required for their production, and the high degree of life-like representation, they were a clear anomaly for a culture that was supposed to be traditional. By definition, a traditional culture was not capable of such refinement. At first, the heads were therefore thought to be the creations of ancient Phoenicians or Greeks who had been shipwrecked on the shores of West Africa.

There is now agreement that they are products of indigenous "ancient" Yorùbá culture. The suggestion here is that the premium placed on knowledge by the culture via the articulated endorsements of things like clear thinking, design consciousness, insight, and teachableness, allow for technological innovation and refinement. In addition, the facial expressions of these pieces are more than compatible with attributes like calmness (some commentators say "serenity"), imperturbability, and patience. Those portrayed may have been rulers or otherwise important figures in the society of the time, but Abiodun tells us that "the artist's *ìwà*, incidentally, is also the type that Yorùbá culture demands of chiefs, kings, diviners, and family heads for their works or activities to possess *ẹwà*" (Abiodun 2014 255).

The preceding serves to highlight the fact that Yorùbá culture places as much emphasis on the *ìwà* or essential nature of the artist as it does upon the *ìwà* or essential nature of the objects the artist creates. Indeed there is a causal relationship between the two, as an artist whose words and actions do not express and exhibit these intellectual and moral values would not be thought capable of producing superior works of art. (See Matthes, this volume) In academic philosophy, this blending of the moral with the intellectual has come to be known as *virtue epistemology* (see Snow, this volume)—the point being that moral values can have cognitive consequences.

There is another unusual category of art objects in Yorùbá culture that has profound ethical ramifications. Abiodun describes it as sculpture that represents "destruction . . . injury . . . blemishes . . . imperfections . . . diseases . . . unwholesomeness . . . [and] sickness" (2014, 241). His point being that art objects are about more than beauty or what people find to be pleasing. They are about life, and there are things in life that involve disgust, fear, destruction, and death. But the message underlying such art is that these things can be overcome and provide inspiration for existential renewal.

Soyinka tells us that to appreciate the ethical implications of this art it is necessary to understand something of the Yorùbá cosmos. That cosmos is inhabited most importantly by the gods and humans. These gods are not transcendent—they coexist and interact with humanity. They also are not exempt from the kinds of trials and tribulations that trouble human beings: "Finally, it is the innate humanity of the gods themselves, their bond with man through a common animist relation with nature and phenomena" (1988, 30).

One form of experience in that cosmos which provides a key insight into the human condition is tragedy. One of Soyinka's most famous essays is titled "The Fourth Stage: Through the Mysteries of Ògún to the Origin of Yorùbá Tragedy" (1988). Tragedy arises from real-life situations that can be painful and even disastrous for both gods and humans. What Soyinka wants us to understand is that Yorùbá art, both as sculpture and as literature, does not avoid the tragic. Yorùbá art faces it head-on and tells us by example how it must be dealt with ethically if we are to surmount tragedy and thereby regain control of our lives.

> This is the fourth stage, the vortex of archetypes and home of the tragic spirit . . . nothing rescues man . . . from loss of self within this abyss but a titanic resolution of the will . . . when disasters and conflicts (the material of drama) have crushed and robbed him of self-consciousness and pretensions, he stands in present reality at the spiritual edge of this gulf. . . . It is at such moments that transitional memory takes over . . . his struggle and triumph over subsumation through the agency of will. (1988, 32)

Tragedy is latent in the cosmos and therefore a possibility for human and divine life. A prototypical example involves the god Ògún:

> Ògún in his wanderings came to the town of Ire where he was well received, later returning its hospitality when he came to its aid against an enemy. In gratitude he was offered the crown of Ire. He declined and retired into the mountains where he lived in solitude, hunting and farming. Again and again he was importuned by the elders of Ire until he finally consented.
>
> When he first descended among them, the people took to their heels. Ògún presented a face of himself which he hoped would put an end to their persistence. He came down in his leather war-kit, smeared in blood from head to foot. When they had fled he returned to his mountain-lair, satisfied that the lesson had been implanted. Alas, back they came again. They implored him, if he would only come in less terrifying attire, they would welcome him as king and leader. Ògún finally consented. He came down decked in palm fronds and was crowned king. In war after war he led his men to victory. Then, finally, came the day when, during a lull in the battle, our old friend Èshù the trickster god left a gourd of palm wine for the thirsty deity. Ògún found it exceptionally delicious and drained the gourd to the dregs. In that battle the enemy was routed even faster than usual, the carnage was greater than ever before. But by now, to the drunken god, friend and foe had become confused; he turned on his men and slaughtered them. This was the possibility that had haunted him from the beginning and made him shrink from the role of king over men (MLAW 29).

Those who have not experienced the culture in depth might see this as a story about an unpredictable and warlike African deity who wreaks havoc on a vulnerable humanity.[4] Going back to the identity of the Ẹshù and its role in unpredictable human and divine misfortune a similarly simplistic *deus ex machina* causal mechanism might seem to be involved. For Soyinka, such interpretations would fail to appreciate the essential underlying ethical maxim that can restore a positive meaning to existence and is the raison d'etre for the story. That maxim relates to the role of the will as what enables god or human to survive and surmount the tragic and thereby reaffirm their existence in a positive manner.

With tragedy, the bottom can drop out of our lives as we emotionally and metaphysically transition into an abyss. According to Soyinka, the lesson to be learned from the Yorùbá worldview about how to deal with and survive this transitioning into the abyss is to rely upon the exercise of one's will. Exercising one's will in the sense of reasoned resolution and actions that represent "man's penetrating insight into the final resolution of things and the constant evidence of harmony" [58] (TFS 33). Such resolve enables those involved to return from the abyss and resume a life of "normalcy," even if now on a bed of tragedy. And it is that experience of tragedy that can also provide creative inspiration for the artist:

> Ògún is the embodiment of *Will*, and the *Will* is the paradoxical truth of destructiveness and creativeness in acting man. Only one who has himself undergone the experience of disintegration . . . can understand and be the force of fusion between the two contradictions. The resulting sensibility is also the sensibility of the artist, and he is a profound artist only to the degree to which he comprehends and expresses this principle of destruction and re-creation. (TFS 32–33)

The moral both of the unpleasant sculptures and of the Ògún in Ire story is that the deity and the town of Ire do not self-destruct after their shared disaster. Ire still exists and might even be said to be thriving. Ògún continues on as a respected deity. That is because both sides picked themselves up and reconstituted their existence in a life-affirming manner. The deity, human being, or community involved have no choice but to become self-determining if they are to survive. There are no external saviors. They must face the fact that they ultimately have responsibility for themselves and muster the resolve to endure and fashion a life that restores a positive balance to the cosmos. The alternative would be to surrender to disaster and annihilation, an absence of will that amounts to self-destruction. In fact by transitioning out of the abyss and back into life, one emerges as a stronger, more sensitive, and even inspired person or deity.

The consequences of all of this for sculpture and aesthetics in the Yorùbá cosmos are profound. In real life, tragedy is something we definitely want to avoid. What is distinctive about the Yorùbá cosmos is that it makes a point of emphasizing that ignoring or pretending the tragic is not part of life is a form of bad faith. As would be failure to recognize that recovery from tragedy depends, most importantly, on the choice of the

---

[4] "The traditional one-dimensional conception of African reality, a largely anthropological creation" (MLAW 124–125).

individual. The tragic demands artistic representation. Art must therefore involve itself with the tragic in an immediate and direct manner.

There is something existential about all of this. The importance assigned to the will as the ultimate arbiter in life shares some similarities with Sartre's views on the human condition. There too, it is up to individuals to accept responsibility for their freedom—for the choices that define their lives—so they can thereby live in an authentic manner. The fact of the matter is that most people are not strong enough to do this and therefore live their lives in an inauthentic manner. Soyinka's assessment of that choice in the Yorùbá cosmos appears to be a bit more severe. Inauthenticity—the failure to muster sufficient strength of self and character to take responsibility for one's life in a positive manner—is viewed as a form of self-destruction.

To go back to the beginning of this chapter, if Yorùbá culture were to adhere to the model of traditional culture, one would not expect to find such insightful and refined understanding of the role of art and its attendant ethical values. When he was assessing the role of the "traditional" in anthropology, the philosopher Ludwig Witttgenstein wrote the following: "In a case like this we often say: 'this practice is obviously age-old.' How do we know that? Is it only because we have historical evidence regarding ancient practices of this sort? *Or is there another reason, one that comes through interpretation. . . . So that* [historical] depth lies *solely* in the *thought* of that ancestry" (Wittgenstein 1979, 15e; my emphasis). He is suggesting that "tradition" may be the product of the observer's thought rather than the observer's experience, since experience must be of the present rather than the past. Perhaps what happened in the case of the Yorùbá was that if one encounters a culture with the predisposition that it is "traditional," one's observations will tend to confirm that predisposition.

See also: Snow, Song, Clavel-Vázquez, this volume

References

Abiodun, Rowland. 2014. *Yoruba Art and Language: Seeking the African in African Art*, Cambridge: Cambridge University Press.

Abiodun, Rowland. 2019. "Ogun, the Orisa Whose Fame is Worldwide." In *Striking Iron: the Art of African Blacksmiths*, edited by Allen F. Roberts, Tom Joyce, Marla C. Berns, 36–41. Los Angeles: Fowler Museum at UCLA.

Barber, Karin. 1991. *I Could Speak Until Tomorrow: Oríkì, Women, and the Past in a Yoruba Town*. Washington, DC: Smithsonian Institute Press.

Drewal, Henry J., and Margaret T. Drewal. 1990. *Gelede: Art and Female Power among the Yoruba*. Bloomington: Indiana University Press.

Hallen, Barry. 2000. *The Good, the Bad, and the Beautiful: Discourse about Values in Yoruba Culture*. Bloomington, IN: Indiana University Press.

Parkes, Phoebe. 2017. "Ọ̀ọ̀ni of Ifẹ̀: We Will Tell Our Stories Ourselves." *CNN African Voices*, March 29, 2017. https://www.cnn.com/2017/03/29/africa/ooni-of-ife-london-visit.

Soyinka, Wole. 1976. *Myth, Literature and the African World*. Cambridge: Cambridge University Press.

Soyinka, Wole. 1988. "The Fourth Stage: Through the Mysteries of Ogun to the Origin of Yoruba Tragedy." In *Art, Dialogue, and Outrage: Essays on Literature and Culture*, 27–39. New York: Pantheon Books.

Wittgenstein, Ludwig. 1979. *Remarks on Frazer's Golden Bough*. Translated by A. C. Miles and Rev. Rush Rhees. Retford, Nottinhamshire, UK and Atlantic Highlands, NJ: The Brynmill Press Ltd and Humanities Press.

CHAPTER 8

ART AND ETHICS IN INDIA IN THE NINETEENTH AND TWENTIETH CENTURIES

NALINI BHUSHAN AND ARVIND KRISHNA MEHROTRA

INTRODUCTION

ARTISTIC traditions like dance-drama (theatre), poetry, music, architecture, sculpture, and painting have always been at the center of ancient and contemporary Indian philosophical, ethical, and religious life. At the same time, *ethical* lessons regarding good and evil characters, and explicit and implicit conventions of morality have been an integral part of the ancient and contemporary Indian artistic tradition. The link between art and ethics was taken to be seamless and self-evident.

In Indian modernity in the late nineteenth and early twentieth centuries, however, and especially in the context of colonialism, the link between arts and ethics became more contested for artists in India, involving choices whose outcomes in the ethical domain were less certain. Traditional ethical preoccupations with good and evil and with right and wrong actions expanded to include newly situated ethical choices and dilemmas for members of Indian society. In a politically unfree India there were, for instance, active disagreements regarding which actions were ethically conducive to obtaining freedom at the level of the individual, consistent with the wider nation-in-the-making. Practitioners of the arts hence faced new artistic choices—regarding subject, style, and method—that were connected to the ethics of identity, authenticity, and creativity. This creative ferment generated by these ethical dilemmas for the arts in this historical and cultural period—in pre- and post-Independent India—are our focus in this chapter.

In the next section, we provide some background on the relation between ethics and the arts in ancient and medieval India, limiting our analysis to painting and the literary arts. This sets the stage for a more focused attention on the new kinds of ethical questions that troubled artists and their publics in the late nineteenth, twentieth, and early twenty-first centuries. We will conduct our analysis via case studies of a couple of prominent painters and poets during this period, whose work generated a lively public debate among artists, art critics and philosophers.

Ethics and Art in Ancient and Medieval India

A robust religious sensibility permeated human activities in all walks of life in ancient and medieval Hindu India. These included the personal, familial activities of daily living and people's lives in all public social settings. This meant that the norms that governed these groups of activities and practices—ethical, social, and political— were themselves further governed by an overarching religious or transcendental goal.[1] While the norms specific to ethical conduct were different in kind from norms specific to the craft of artisans[2] and artists, both sets of norms were, in the end, useful instruments, valued for their role in helping individuals achieve another, more intrinsically valuable goal. All manner of societal norms were, in this sense, ultimately just useful conventions.

Nonetheless, in an actual world of separation and division, societal conventions were necessary to maintain order and stability. Ethical norms played a critical intermediate role in helping individuals achieve the discipline and stability that would put them on the path to achieve a higher, more transcendental freedom. For this reason, Hindu society required its members to participate fully in these traditionally established and clearly articulated norms of behavior.[3]

The ethical life for Hindu India was the *right* life, which required the rigorous performance of ethical *duties*. The ethical duties of daily life were caste-bound and additionally, bound by one's stage in life. According to the *Bhagavad Gītā*, a central text on ethical practice (circa second to fifth century BCE), the philosophical heart of the epic

---

[1] The narrative we provide here is overly simple. A disruptive element was very much around in medieval times, for instance, through the poetry of Kabir and others, aimed at dismantling the dominant religious and caste hierarchies.

[2] Interestingly, many of the bhakti (devotional) poets were from the lower castes (including the Baul singers) and several were artisans: Janabai was a sudra, Tukaram a kunbi; Kabir was a weaver, Ravidas a cobbler, and they all wrote in the vernaculars rather than Sanskrit.

[3] Again, these also left room for those who wished to break away to do so. Here is Tukaram in Kolatkar's translation: "An emigrant now, I'm / A citizen of No Land." See Mehrotra (2010, 315).

Mahābhārata, "It is better to do one's own duty imperfectly, than it is to do another's duty perfectly" (18.47). This strict code of duty applied not only to warriors, but to other members of society as well: merchants, laborers, and including artisans and artists (who each belonged to a particular caste with their own clearly articulated caste duties). The goal was to maintain social and natural order and avoid chaos.

In addition to caste-based rules, additional ethical rules governed individuals as they progressed through different stages of their lives, from birth, through student, to house-holder, to the life of the sanyasi.[4] Hindu ethics was thus based on a clear and strict assignment of duties for every individual who lived within Hindu society, specific both to the unchanging caste context and to the changing developmental status as they lived their lives.

As was the case in the ethical lives of the people, Indian art was understood to serve the transcendental goal of liberation. Much of Indian art of the ancient and medieval period of Hindu India, therefore, was valued for its depictions of the Gods, of mythological themes, or of the relation between the divine and secular realms. This raised specific aesthetic questions: What were the right ways to depict these subjects? Who were the best artists? Why create art at all? Individual self-expression was not a goal. Language, color, form, and content for artists was constrained by the larger goal and by iconographic accounts of soteriologically efficacious images. Therefore, the arts were intended to give, to those who attended in the right way, a taste (*rasa*[5]) of liberation, which was a taste—an aesthetic experience—of freedom from the mundane. This experience was the closest that an ordinary human being could come to realizing that transcendental goal outlined in the philosophy of the Vedas and Upaniṣads. Art was therefore thought to make transcendental human experiences possible, and, critically, to make it possible for any member of Indian society regardless of caste.[6] For this reason, art was always central to Indian conceptions of a fulfilling life.

Painting and the literary arts in India each have ancient ancestries. From the third century BCE to 1100 CE, painting was used in interior decoration in palaces, temples and shrines; it was also used to illustrate both sacred and secular texts. Thus we have many palm leaf manuscripts and mural paintings from this period. The content primarily involved depictions of legends of religious figures (e.g., of the Jain prophet Mahavira) and

---

[4] Celibacy, for instance, was prescribed for a student and a sanyasi, but not for a householder.

[5] In Hindu mythology the oft-cited example is of Valmiki (author of the epic *Ramayana*), whose personally felt grief, beholding the death of one of a pair of birds shot down by a hunter and witnessing the shrieks of its mate, moved him to write what are arguably the first lines of poetry known to humankind. His personal emotion of *karuna* was transformed into karuna *rasa* as embodied in his epic poem. While the personal emotion belongs to a single and singular self, *rasa* itself does not and is in this sense impersonal, possible only because of human subjectivity but not reducible to the uniquely personal feeling of any particular subject.

[6] The traditional paths to liberation (knowledge, action, devotion) were open only to the upper castes. But the aesthetic route generated possibilities for all Indians regardless of caste. For this reason, the earliest treatise on aesthetics in India, the *Natya Sastra* by Bharata, is regarded by many as the fifth Veda (sacred text), although in fact there are only four.

the celebration of aesthetic beauty by a painterly elucidation of the Hindu *rasas* (e.g., a twelfth-century Nepalese manuscript cover illustrating scenes from Kalidasa's secular play *Sakuntala*). Overall, though, in this premodern period, it is religious expression that inspires the art of painting.[7]

The literary arts occupy a central place in oral and written traditions in early India. The greatest epic literatures of India, the *Ramayana* (c. fifth century BCE) and the *Mahābhārata* (composed between fourth century BCE and second century CE), were therefore understood and taken in by their ancient audiences as dance-dramas (or theater), where song and word were inextricably linked in their narrative retellings. This underscores the *aesthetic* power of these epic literatures as integral to their ethical effects. At the same time, the *content*, or the specifically moral lessons having to do with good and evil characters, and with the role of custom and convention in regulating moral behavior, are integral as well to these epic literatures.

In sum, the relation between Ethics and Art in Ancient and Medieval India was self-evident, although by no means unproblematic. Art had its prescribed role to play in contributing to a religiously oriented Indian society. In colonial Indian modernity, however, the role of art and the artist, and the relation between art and ethics, became less certain.

In a newly uncertain world, epistemic blindness rather than immoral action was the primary affliction that needed correction. One had to ask the question "Who am I?"—though not as Descartes might have asked it—that is, as a question for the mind to answer, focused on its own interiority. Rather, it was a question one needed to ask about one's embodied subjectivity in an often fraught personal, social, and political context, before one's own ethical duties and societal duties could possibly be ascertained.

The philosopher K. C. Bhattacharyya, in a powerful address to his students, argued for exactly this focus: he asked, "Who *are* we, the educated Indians under colonial rule? And which caste ought to matter for us in twentieth-century colonial India, and which we ought to undermine?" His answer was equally radical: the "caste" that, he argued, had to be contested, was the one ushered in by English education. The "caste" divide that therefore had to be overcome was the newly created divide between the English-educated Indian intellectual and the masses (1930).

As a result of this questioning of what it meant to be an authentic person in India, new ethical debates took place in the world of philosophy and art regarding the relation between individual and political identity, of the meaning and value of subjectivity, freedom and autonomy of a newly aware citizenry in-the-making.

---

[7] This is not to say that there were no erotic paintings (or indeed erotic sculpture) during this period. It is only to emphasize that the dominant trend in art and its subject matter was transcendentally inspired (and acts of sexual intimacy in art were not sharply separated from divinity.) In effect, the erotic *was* the religious.

THE PAINTER IN MODERN INDIA

Four Art Schools were set up by the British in colonial India to retrain Indian artists to paint in ways that reflected European taste: Calcutta and Madras (1854), Bombay (1857), and Lahore (1875). The prevailing view among the British aesthetes was that the formal techniques of the Indians were primitive, even barbarous, and their choice of content overly constrained by depiction of religious and mythological figures.[8] Birds and human portraits are good examples of this early shift in the painterly practices of artists newly educated in the four art schools, works that demonstrated the ways in which the primitive artistic excesses of the Indian approach to art were reigned in and artfully domesticated.

At the same time, there was resistance to this shift. One strand of resistance came from Orientalist scholars and art historians who operated outside the sphere of the art schools. In several essays, A. K. Coomaraswamy argued for the superiority of ancient Indian crafts and artistic styles (1913; 1994; 2003; 2004). He called for a *revival* of craft traditions, which also meant a return to strict rules governing craft making. Rather than creativity, he argued, artistic success was entirely a matter of following the traditional rules that governed different kinds of ancient crafts, with the right mental attitude attuned to the larger (spiritual) goal (2004, 164–169). He argued that art was a yoga or discipline that enables the artist to embody an intuition of the divine in their artwork.

A second strand of responses challenged the divide between traditional and modern art styles presumed by the revivalists. This response came from artists themselves, who lived and worked in India during the colonial period. Artists were attracted to a number of artistic methods and influences from Indian tradition and European modernity, challenging the dichotomy. (Mitter 1994; 2007)

The most influential of the visual artists in pre–independent India include Ravi Varma, Abanindranath Tagore, Binodbehari Mukerjee, Nandanlal Bose, and Amrita Sher-Gil. In a post-Independence India, many more prominent women artists like Nalini Malani, Arpita Singh, and Nasreen Mohamedi, including other artists such as M. F. Hussain, K. G. Subramanyan, F. N. Souza, Tyeb Mehta, and Bhupen Khakhar, continued the interrogation of subjectivity, freedom, and belonging begun in the earlier generation. Each, in their own way, creatively integrated their artistic Indian heritage with globally inspired artistic methods in fashioning their uniquely individual forms of expression.

---

[8] Even before the formal establishment of the four art schools, a significant shift in style and content had occurred in "Company Style" paintings (so-called because these were commissioned by the East India Company, not by the British Crown). Company painting was being done in the early 1800s by artists trained in the Mughal workshops, now underemployed after the disintegration of the Mughal Empire. They catered to the prevailing taste for Company paintings—Indian occupations, Indian flora and fauna. (See, for instance, the work of the Scottish brothers William and James Fraser.)

We will take Sher-Gil as our case study for the colonial period, illustrating certain kinds of ethical issues that arose for painters as it relates to embodied subjectivity. For the postcolonial period, Bhupen Khakhar will be our case study, as we continue with the thematic exploration of subjectivity and the body, this time within the Indian avant-garde. In each case, we consider their work as a response to ethical challenges that emerged in their respective historical moments.

Amrita Sher-Gil (1913–1941)

Amrita Sher-Gil was the daughter of a Sikh aristocratic painter-philosopher from Lahore, India, and a Hungarian Jewish mother. Her artistic sensibility was forged in the artistic-intellectual circles of India and Hungary; she trained at Paris's Ecole des Beaux Arts, absorbing the writings of Dostoevsky and Baudelaire, as well as mastering the then-current painterly techniques of Gauguin, Matisse, and Cezanne. She settled in Shimla—then the summer capital of the British government in India—and rose to national prominence as a painter, winning a gold medal from the Bombay Art Society for her painting *Group of Three Girls* (1935) in 1937, when she was twenty-four years old.

Amrita Sher-Gil died in 1941, age twenty-eight. Sher-Gil's work had a profound impact on painting and provides particularly illuminating material for reflecting on the ethics of identity, the concept of artistic integrity, and the ethics of stylistic and formal choices of method. (Dalmia 2006; 2014)

We will approach the relationship between ethics and art in this period by taking as central a specific notion that characterizes some of the most creative artwork by artists of this period, namely, *integrity*. Integrity is often glossed as "authenticity" in popular and self-help culture. For an artist, this may include authenticity in self-expression (being true to oneself or one's experience), or authenticity in capturing-creating the artistic object (rather than romanticizing it, being sentimental, or forcing it into false categories). In British India, some influential artists and art critics argued that authentically Indian art involved the appropriate relation to Indian tradition. This required that artists with integrity depict their subject matter—the country, the history, and women in particular—in ways that reflected their status as emblems of Indian valor, religiosity, domesticity, spirituality, or suitably idealized female beauty. But this relation of the authentic to the nation was contested as well, as we will see in the case of Sher-Gil.

Etymologically, integrity is what makes a *thing* whole. Christine Korsgaard (2002) extends the notion to apply to a *person, subject*, or *self*, conceived of as *self*-integration, from which one creates a stable and unified identity capable of consistent speech and action. But, as many scholars in the field of post and decolonial literature, for instance, have shown, the identity of a colonized or otherwise subaltern self involves the fracture or disunity of different aspects of self (Bhaba 1994; Spivak 1999). While some argue that such a disunity is *disabling* to healthy functioning (Raghuramaraju 2006; 2009), we will demonstrate via the work of artists that self-hood and disunity are not incompatible.

Sher-Gil's artwork provides ample scope to manifest this sort of complex whole-some integrity. We chose for analysis one of her best-known paintings, *Self-Portrait as Tahitian*. It embodies a multilayered and hybrid subjectivity that respects the reality of fracture. It is also a splendidly creative exercise in self-integration.

Despite its provocative title, *Self-Portrait as Tahitian* (Figure 8.1), Sher-Gil's identity is at first hard to read. She is nude from the waist up; she seems to represent herself as an exotic other (Tahitian) and is framed against a shadowy figure. We cannot immediately ascertain her relation to the male figure in the shadow (is he a voyeur?). Her un-self-conscious representation of herself as a partially nude woman (from an ostensibly conservative India) is unsettling. The reference to Gauguin as well is impossible to ignore although difficult at first to decipher.

Self-Portrait as Tahitian is illuminating in several ways. Consider, again, its title. What might it mean, in the context of self-identity, for Sher-Gil to portray herself as something she is clearly *not*? On one level, we could argue that the self-portrait reflects her desire to exoticize *herself*, much as Gauguin, in his portrayals of his Tahitian subjects, exoticized *them* to a Western public. Thus, Sher-Gil might be taken to portray herself as a pure, simple, innocent, and primitive other. On the basis of this analysis, we would arguably have a failed artwork, for a number of aesthetic and ethical reasons: mimicry, failure of self-integration, an inauthentic self-representation.

This analysis is overly simple. Sher-Gil in fact *is* a racial hybrid (by her own lights and by those who saw her through the lens of race). Here is a more convincing reading: in *Self-Portrait as Tahitian,* Amrita Sher-Gil is revealing the non-European facet of herself (the Tahitian being at the time the aesthetic non-European prototype par excellence). To see this self-portrait as an instance of ethically problematic mimicry is therefore to misunderstand the nature of her subjectivity.

It is instructive to compare the aesthetics of Gauguin's own well-known depictions of Tahitians with Sher-Gil's version. In situating the two in their respective biographies (and geographies), Gauguin's own self-persona was that of a rootless cosmopolitan who belonged nowhere, an aesthete in exile, and an outsider to the Tahitian people and culture. Sher-Gil, in contrast, is a multiply rooted cosmopolitan. While Gauguin claimed to belong to no place, we might say that Sher-Gil belonged to many places.

Given these differences between the two artists' situations, the occasion of Sher-Gil painting a Tahitian woman (who happens in this case to be herself) has an aesthetic power that even as it self-exoticizes, rests on its being simultaneously a critique of orientalism and its exoticization of the other.[9]

This work has an additional link to contemporary feminist art projects.[10] *Self-Portrait as Tahitian* puts Sher-Gil in a position of active and creative interrogation with different

---

[9] Edward Said in his *Orientalism* (1978) first gave voice to this double role of representation and critique in literature and the arts.

[10] The North American artist Cindy Sherman's self-portraits come to mind in this connection. Sherman herself considers photographs to be a mask, but the viewer is struck more by the performative and freeing aspects of her work rather than the elusive dimension of her self-portrayals.

FIGURE 8.1 Amrita Sher-Gil. *Self-Portrait as Tahitian.* 1934. Oil on canvas (56x90 cm). Collection of Navina and Vivan Sundaram. Artwork in the public domain; image courtesy of the estate of the artist. Reproduced with permission from Sher-Gil Sundaram Arts Foundation (SSAF).

parts of herself. Her identity is both complicated and freeing. In portraits of her own self we see, *not* a unified integrated whole, but fragments that—even while remaining separated—evoke in the viewer a rich and robust person in all her complexity. The integrity we assign to her work is due in part to our recognition of the artist's *intention* to certify the portrait as a portrait *of self* (the label matters)—this is who I am—and a *responsibility* to the public to stand ready to be accountable for that certification.[11]

The political context in which Indian artists such as Sher-Gil worked is instructive as well, as we seek to better understand their aesthetic choices and ethical anxieties. The political context of pre–independent India suffused the artistic consciousness of most artists in colonial India. Indian artists had to face existential questions regarding the authenticity of their work *as Indians* even as they struggled to be individually creative and to produce works that would be recognizably relevant on a global stage. The imagined future independent Indian nation provided raw material for many artists of the time.

Both Ravi Varma and Abanindranath Tagore, for example, kept national identity at the center of their aesthetic oeuvre, with Tagore's painting of *Bharat Mata* (1905, translation: Mother India) serving as a powerful image of Indian Independence for a nationally inspired public. In sharp contrast, Sher-Gil shunned the symbolic political narratives of the nation in her art, focusing explicitly on ordinary scenes of people and their lives in rural India. In paintings such as *Brahmacharis* (1937) and *Hill Women* (1935), Sher-Gil evokes the sensibilities of actual local communities rather than explicitly depicting the imagined nation of India-in-the-making. This sets her oeuvre apart from much of the art that received public and specifically art-critical discourse at the time.

In the next generation, the artist we choose for our case study is Bhupen Khakhar. We choose him for several reasons. First, like Sher-Gil, Khakhar is responsive to techniques and styles of artistry in the West, productively appropriating them for his own ends, and adapted to his Indian context. Second, his explorations of his own subjectivity are dramatic and transgressive, as were Sher-Gil's.

At the same time, they are very different artists, drawn to very different styles, themes and forms of transgression in their work. Khakhar's individual subjectivity is complicated as was Sher-Gil's, but he is working in a context of political freedom and in a generation facing an influx of even more global artistic styles.

Bhupen Khakhar (1934–2003)

Bhupen Khakhar was a prolific painter, poet, playwright, and short-story writer in Gujarati. He came of age as an avant-garde artist in India in the 1960s, finding his global muse in the American pop artist Robert Rauschenberg. Khakhar came from India's

---

[11] Sher-Gil's portrayal of the many different women she encountered in Europe and India are some of her most interesting, powerful, and evocative works. (Bhushan, 2020) Consider for instance *Sleep* (1932); *The Professional Model* (1933); *Group of Three Girls* (1935); *Bride's Toilet* (1937); *Child Wife* (1939); and *Woman on Charpoy* (1940). All are accessible online.

middle class and interpreted the genre and artistic language of "pop" broadly, reading the Indian *popular* into his pop art, which included calendars, posters, and the graffiti street art of the cities. (Kapur, 2000)

The Indian popular was also connected with the religious-political-popular and Khakhar's work in this decade reflected his own irreverent comfort with the hyphenated popular. He often mixed the profane with sacred conventions in his pop representations of Hindu deities, saints, and Indian national heroes.[12] A ritualistic symbolism pervades even his most descriptive and secular paintings.

In the 1970s Khakhar's interests shifted from the style and language of popular culture, to, more specifically, the subjects of his work, and, ultimately, in the 1980s, to an exploration of his own subjectivity. As Geeta Kapur observes, in the 1970s, Khakhar was drawn to representing people in ordinary professions like fishing, accounting and watch repair, "a vulnerable form of representation that highlighted a cast of characters whose identities did not depend on the privilege of authority" (2007, 4). In this way he provided access to and humanized his subjects across class divides. His fascination with the popular-sacred infused these works as well, but with a transgressive twist. Here again is Kapur:

> Khakhar translated . . . the visual recitation of a saint's or hero's good deeds . . . *into a voyeur's pleasure.* He turned the narrative inset into a peep-hole, revealing the 'secret' life of the neighbour—fragments of a neat house, of middle-class homes with swing-beds and eating tables in rooms painted green, rose and sky-blue that are also mini-theatres for routine forms of male intimacy. (2000, 5)

Khakhar also had a penchant for masquerade and satirical role-playing. These included him posed as James Bond at one end of the spectrum and Lord Krishna at the other. In the 1980s, however, Khakhar's self-portraits began to shift from satirical masquerade to works that revealed more of his identity and sense of being in the world. In a series of works he began to explicitly represent and, in this way, acknowledge, gay male sexuality. Same-sex intimacy is presented almost matter-of-factly, in the context of the everyday.[13]

This inclusion in his art normalizes for the viewer a form of belonging to a society, a society in which such belonging was not sanctioned. In its visual descriptive appeal, it shows, rather than tells. Rather than being told what a society ought to be, we *see*, via his

---

[12] Rauschenberg's *Canyon* (1959) and *Black Market* (1961) are productively seen alongside Khakhar's *Paan Shop* (1965); *Paan Shop* is a blend of Rauschenberg's textured and layered surface and style of assemblage with Indian subject matter, itself an assemblage of the sacred, the caricature, the crude, and the kitsch. It also demonstrates Khakhar's life-long fascination with the Indian street market or bazaar. (See Khullar (2015), Chapter 5, titled "Paan Shop for People" for an in-depth discussion of Khakhar's work, as well for his intriguing connection to the writer Salman Rushdie, for whom Khakhar was a muse for his novel *The Moor's Last Sigh*.)

[13] See *Two Men in Benares* (1982) and *Yayati* (1987) for further depictions of same-sex love.

FIGURE 8.2 Bhupen Khakhar. *You Can't Please All*. 1981. Oil on canvas (28.5x30 cm). Collection of the Tate Modern, UK. Copyright @ Bhupen Khakhar. Reproduced with permission from the Kapil Jariwala Gallery.

work, what a more inclusive society might *look* like. His work thus persuades its viewer with a prescriptive force, but a force that is aesthetic rather than didactically moral.

We choose for our case study a work that is regarded as a self-portrait, and for which Khakhar is most well-known: *You Can't Please All*, from 1981 (Figure 8.2).[14]

One is immediately struck by the juxtaposition: sharply etched miniature scenes of conventional daily life in an Indian town, below, and, almost hovering above, a life-sized figure of an unadorned and quite naked man, who leans over a balcony, taking in the

---

[14] *You Can't Please All* was also used as the title of an exhibition at The Tate Modern in 2016 devoted to Khakhar's work.

view. The exquisitely crafted miniatures occupy much of the composition and seem at first to be the primary purpose of the painting. But then one's focus shifts to the naked man, and then back again to the different scenes below. At a second go round, one sees much more. The juxtaposition of the viewer and viewed does an about-turn as their more complex relationship comes to the fore.

The connections between public and private, and between the individual and his society, are revealed at two levels. First, the naked man is in his own private space, on a balcony, above the town. But this private space is in public view. Nonetheless, there is a literal screen: a towel hangs over the balcony, so that his frontal nakedness is hidden from the public below.

In each vignette, the people in the town are in public space, working or having social interactions. And the man on the balcony above is in a position to observe it/them all. If the people below were to look up in his direction, they would happen upon what would likely be a familiar sight: a bare-chested, apparently informally dressed man in the comfort of home, relaxing and people-watching on his balcony at the end of the day. His total nakedness is obscured from view—they do not know this, and, related to this unknowing of the true nature of his naked body, they do not know *him*.

As viewers of the painting, we can observe with more attention both the man's body and what the naked man observes. We observe that his back functions as a screen for us, just as the towel functions to screen him from the people in the town below. His frontal nakedness is hidden from both sets of (actual or possible) prying eyes. At the same time, in a vignette below and within clear public view, is an elongated penis belonging to a donkey on which two men are seated. It is hard not to see this as the displaced penis of the man on the balcony; we see the relation between these fragmented body parts.

And so, while the man's complete nakedness is *literally obscured* from view, both inside and outside the painting, we, the viewers of the painting, *know* a fuller truth. He really *is* naked, although no one can *see* that. And, judging from the orientation of his limbs as he rests over the balcony, he is comfortable in his nakedness as we take him in again, not just as an observer apart from his town, but as a part of that slice of Indian dailyness. He is both a part of the community and apart from it. The composed scenes of daily life are, on the one hand, external to him, but are also part of his own interior world, one where he comfortably belongs.

Khakhar's *You Can't Please All* is, at first blush, spectacularly different from Sher-Gil's *Self Portrait as Tahitian* in several respects. One, Sher-Gil presents herself at the center of the painting. Her bodily orientation is outward facing and has the effect of challenging the viewer to confront her complexity as a subject. Khakhar, in contrast, is off to one side in the painting. We are privy only to his back, as he leans over a balcony facing away from the viewer, and we are invited to confront the complexity of a scene rather than of a person. Second, Sher-Gil's portrait is transparently gendered (her breasts are uncovered), while the gender of the nude in Khakhar's painting must be inferred from the back of his head and the elongated body-type. The penis that is *absent* from view—the evidence of gender that one would see if the viewer were privy to the front of the naked man—is at the same time *present*, in the clearly visible penis of the donkey in the scene surveyed below.

Third, and linked to the first point, each work requires different kinds of interpretive labor. For Sher-Gil, our first reaction is "who is she, really?"; for Khakhar, our first reaction is "what am I looking at, really?" Thus, for Sher-Gil the question is one about her *as a subject*, while for Khakhar the question is primarily about *place* and specifically about one's role and location in society. The parallel question—"who is *he*, really?"—lurks in the background, leaping into focus as one contemplates further the rationale behind the visual details and placements within the entire scene of which the naked man is a part.

We also see that Khakhar's artistic irreverence for certain kinds of dichotomies is not (at least explicitly) shared by Sher-Gil: between the serious and the trivial in culture; between high and low art; between the sacred and the profane. Khakhar famously blurs these divides and questions the value of these separations explicitly in his artwork in a way that we find at best obliquely in Sher-Gil.[15]

And yet there is a continuity that is evident in their work. Both artists are conscious of and aim to enact an embodied subjectivity-at-the-margins via their self-portraits. Both hint at a held back sexuality and the loneliness it brings, the narrow bed that Khakhar has just risen from to view the street scene below. Ripping the curtain off middle class respectability would have been no easier for Khakhar in 1981 than it was for Sher-Gil in 1934. They each have no interest in the nationally inflected modernisms of their respective eras. Sher-Gil and Khakhar taken together offer us a powerful case study of the ethical and epistemological challenges that painters faced in their time.

THE POET IN MODERN INDIA

With the literary arts comes language. While a poet has a choice of which language she would like to use as her mode of expression, this choice was determined in pre–independent India by several interlocking factors. These included the opportunities a particular language presented for stylistic and contentful expression, as well as by the ease of thought and feeling of a particular language. In the colonial context, this choice of medium was also in part determined by politics, by a sense of patriotism and nationalist loyalty.

Just as the painters in the colonial period struggled with the content and style of their works of art, feeling these artistic choices as *ethical*, poets in pre- and post-Independent India struggled with content, style, but most prominently with their linguistic medium.

---

[15] Much has also been made of the surrealist inflection in much of Khakhar's work; we get none of that in Sher-Gil.

For many Indian poets educated in the university system set up by the British, the default language of expression was English. The "Minute on Education," written in 1835 by Thomas Macaulay, led to the passage of the English Education Act of 1835 and determined the status of English and of the Anglophone Indian over the next century and a half.

For better or worse, it is no surprise that those of us who were educated under the Indian university system are sometimes referred to as "Macaulay's children." For the Indian literary intelligentsia in this period of political and cultural ferment, anxieties regarding the use of English as one's professional language of choice as an ethical choice and its attendant shadow of paternalism, inauthenticity and false consciousness as a psychological reality are understandable.[16] These anxieties continued well into the twentieth century.

We choose for analysis the work of two poets from overlapping generations.

Rabindranath Tagore (1861–1941)

Rabindranath Tagore won the Nobel Prize for Literature in 1913. Apart from being a highly renowned poet, composer, and playwright, Tagore founded Visva-Bharati at Shantiniketan in West Bengal. He conceived of Visva-Bharati as an experimental college, an alternative to the universities (referred to earlier) that had been set up by the British. Here he put the Indian arts at the core of a student-centered curriculum. Unlike his art-historian colleague Coomaraswamy, however, his conception of Indianness had little to do with the idea of the Nation but rather with a vision of a universal humanity to which all human beings belonged. In underscoring the presence of a universal aesthetic sensibility within the traditional Indian religious arts, he blended the secular with the sacred.

Tagore advanced a conception of national identity grounded not in religion, caste, creed, or a moral code, but rather in the possibility of a shared aesthetic experience. He saw the ethical as flowing organically from the aesthetic, and he saw shared delight among humans as organically linked to a shared truth regarding the unity of the universe. Tagore was convinced that aesthetic education and shared participation in the arts would lead naturally to a higher ethical consciousness. He puts it this way in *Creative Unity* (1922):

> Therefore it is . . . that this world is a creation; that in its center there is a living idea that reveals itself in an eternal symphony, played on innumerable instruments, all keeping perfect time. We know that this world-verse, that runs from sky to sky, is not made for the mere enumeration of facts . . . it has its direct revelation in our delight. That delight gives us the key to the truth of existence. (Tagore 1994, 507)

---

[16] See, for instance, K. C. Bhattacharyya, "Svaraj in Ideas" (1930). See also Bhushan and Garfield (2017).

Tagore presupposes here an ancient Indian idea, namely, that the world is more than what it seems. The universe is not reducible to just the mundane, delineated by custom and habit. Truth is more than this; sources of delight lie in something larger than this. At this level of active participation in the world, the realm of the creative (the aesthetic) is no different from the realm of truth (the ethical). Thus Tagore's ethics—as a philosopher and as a poet—transcend traditional Hindu ethics and modern Indian politics, as Tagore takes as central a universalist humanism that is, at bottom, aesthetic. From an aesthetic perspective that sees all human beings as equal in value and in their capacity for evoking delight, attachments to narrow Hindu caste hierarchies and to a nationalist politics simply fall away.[17]

Tagore's Nobel-prize winning prose poem was named *Gitanjali,* which means "song-offering." While offerings are traditionally made to gods, the referent of the reverential demonstrative *Thou* in Tagore's verses is delightfully ambiguous. *Thou* occurs in many different contexts where he addresses in turn a God, or a friend, or a parent, or a lover. Is *Thou* my Lord, the creator of the universe? Or my friend? Or my lover? Or are these false dichotomies to begin with?

Consider for instance Tagore's Bengali poem titled "Ami" or "Myself" translated into English verse by Chaudhuri:[18]

> It's the colour of my consciousness that's made
>   the emerald green,
>   the ruby has become red.
> I looked up at the sky:
>   light began to shine
>   in the east and west,
> Turning to the rose, I said, "Beautiful,"
>   beautiful it became.
> You'll say, This is information,
>   not a poet's words.
> I'll say, It's truth,
>   that is why it's poetry.
> This is my pride;
>   we all have a pride of our own.
>
> (1994, 231)

This poem, that prefigures by several decades Wallace Steven's idea that poetry was the supreme fiction, is noteworthy for several reasons in the context of the relation between ethics and art. It is hard not to see the allusion to the title of Whitman's famous poem *Song of Myself* (1855). What is gained by this closeness in denotation of the title

---

[17] A fundamental source of disagreement between Tagore and M. K. Gandhi lay in where they located the source of value: for Tagore it was aesthetic; for Gandhi, it was moral. See Bhattacharya (1997).

[18] Amit Chaudhuri (2021) is a well-known novelist, scholar of English literature and a musician of Bengali heritage who grew up in the cosmopolitan Indian city of Bombay.

of Whitman's poem? Tagore creatively does two things at once: he aligns himself with Whitman's *focus* on the subject or subjectivity; at the same time, he distances himself from Whitman's *conception* of the subject or self. For, as Chaudhuri eloquently puts it, in Tagore's poem "when the self empties itself, it becomes the world" (Tagore 1994, 291). Whitman's song of *my*self is different from Tagore's song of my*self.*

Tagore takes individualized self to be illusory. In keeping with the Indian idealist spiritual tradition, Tagore's self transcends anything captured by the modern idea of a subject. Its identity is not to be explored by viewing it as individualized, as substantially distinct from others. Tagore also dismisses the scientific realist view that objects have their properties independent of our consciousness. In Tagore's poem, as Chaudhuri puts it, one "both surrenders to and creates what is true: the 'fact' that the rose is a rose, and that it's beautiful" (231–232).

Arun Kolatkar (1931–2004)

Perhaps nowhere has the globally networked world of poetic and artistic creativity, and, by implication, the ethical that flows out of this universally shared experience of reading and listening, of delight and pleasure, been invoked more mischievously than by the bilingual poet Arun Kolatkar. He wrote in both Marathi and English and was once asked by an interviewer from a Marathi little magazine who his favorite poets and writers were. "You want me to give you their names?" Kolatkar replied and then taking a deep breath rattled them off the top of his head, it would seem (there were eighty such names, from the world over). He was of course being dead serious. "Whitman, Mardhekar, Manmohan, Eliot, Auden, Hart Crane," he begins, and he ends with "Eisenstein . . . Truffaut, Woody Guthrie, Laurel and Hardy" (Mehrotra 2010, 14).

In another of his rare interviews, this one to Eunice de Souza, Kolatkar said:

> I want to reclaim everything I consider my tradition. I am particularly interested in history of all kinds, the beginning of man, archaeology, histories of everything from religion to objects, bread-making, paper, clothes, people, the evolution of man's knowledge of things, ideas about the world or his own body. (2010, 32)

Kolatkar's desire to "reclaim everything," his interest in "history of all kinds," is not very different from Tagore's "eternal symphony, played on innumerable instruments." Kolatkar's "world-verse," the litany of names, does not mention Tagore, but it does several of the Marathi saint poets—"Dnyaneshwar, Namdev, Janabai, Eknath, Tukaram"—and also Kabir, whom Tagore translated, and, while playing fast and loose with chronology, he starts the enumeration with Whitman (2010, 34–35).

Based in the frame story of the *Mahābhārata*, Kolatkar's long poem *Sarpa Satra* (2004) is a contemporary tale of revenge and retribution, mass murder and genocide, and one person's attempt to break the cycle. In the story, the divine hero Arjuna decides, "Just for kicks, maybe," to burn down the Khandava forest. In a passage of great lyrical beauty, Kolatkar describes the conflagration in which everything gets destroyed, "elephants, gazelles, antelopes" and

> people as well.
> Simple folk,
>
> children of the forest
> who had lived there happily for generations,
> since time began.
>
> They've gone without a trace.
> With their language
> that sounded like the burbling of a brook,
>
> their songs that sounded like the twitterings of birds,
> and the secrets of their shamans
> who could cure any sickness
>
> by casting spells with their special flutes
> made from the hollow
> wingbones of red-crested cranes.

Among those who die in the "holocaust" is a snake-woman, to avenge whose loss her husband, Takshaka, kills Arjuna's grandson, Parikshit. Parikshit's son, Janamejaya, then holds the snake sacrifice, the Sarpa Satra, to rid the world of snakes: "My vengeance will be swift and terrible. / I will not rest / until I've exterminated them all."

Though the mass killing of snakes symbolically represents the many genocides of the last century, Kolatkar, by taking a story from an ancient epic, brings the whole of human history under the scrutiny of his moral vision. In the original *Mahābhārata*, Aasitka, whose mother is herself a snake-woman and Takshaka's sister, is able to stop the sacrifice midway, but Kolatkar's poem offers no such consolation:

> When these things come to an end,
> people find
> other subjects to talk about
>
> than just
> the latest episode of the Mahabharata
> and the daily statistics of death;
>
> rediscover simpler pleasures—
> fly kites,
> collect wild flowers, make love.
>
> Life seems
> to return to normal.
> But do not be deceived.
>
> Though, sooner or later,
> these celebrations of hatred too
> come to an end

like everything else,
the fire—the fire lit for the purpose—
can never be put out.

CONCLUSION

The relation between Ethics and Art in a predominantly caste-conscious Ancient and Medieval India was relatively clear. Art took its cue from ethical norms that governed a religiously circumscribed Indian society.

In colonial Indian modernity, however, the role of art and the artist, and the relation between art and ethics, became looser and less self-evident. In a newly configured world, it was the possibility of epistemic blindness and of false consciousness that produced anxiety, rather than the risk of immoral action as traditionally understood. The awareness of one's own subjectivity and existential situatedness was essential to this new generation of Indians. Their integrity as artists and as human beings depended on this awareness.

We saw this demonstrated in colonial India in the work of Amrita Sher-Gil and Rabindranath Tagore. In the next, overlapping generation of Indian artists, the two case studies of the painter Bhupen Khakhar and the poet Arun Kolatkar provide us with a measure of thematic continuity across generations even as each evoke in their work a decidedly different situatedness, this time in a free India (after 1947).[19]

See also: Lamarque, Schellekens, Clavel-Vázquez, Taylor, this volume

REFERENCES

Bhabha, Homi. 1994. *The Location of Culture*. New York: Routledge.

Bhattacharyya, Krishna Chandra. [1930] 2011. "Svaraj in Ideas." Reprinted in *Indian Philosophy in English: From Renaissance to Independence*, edited by Nalini Bhushan and Jay L. Garfield, 103–111. New York: Oxford University Press.

Bhattacharya, Sabyasachi, ed. 1997. *The Mahatma and the Poet: Letters and debates between Gandhi and Tagore 1915–1941*. Delhi: National Book Trust.

Bhushan, Nalini. 2020. "Amrita Sher-Gil: Identity and Integrity as a mixed-race woman artist in Colonial India." In *Portraits of Integrity: 26 Case Studies from History, Literature and Philosophy*, edited by Charlotte Alston, Amber Carpenter, and Rachael Wiseman, 195–206. London: Bloomsbury Academic.

---

[19] One of us, Arvind, is a celebrated poet and translator of poetry in twenty-first century India. One strand of continuity in his work with the previous generations of poets from India is touched on by Chaudhuri (2020), who describes how Arvind *inhabits* the mystic poet Kabir (as his translator). Chaudhuri regards Mehrotra's remarkable ability as an "accidental multiplicity - rather than strategy" (2020, xxxvi). "Accidental multiplicity," as an embodied subjective contingency, aptly characterizes the position occupied by many prominent artists in colonial and postcolonial India and its diverse diasporic communities [NB].

Bhushan, Nalini, and Jay Garfield. 2017. *Minds Without Fear: Philosophy in the Indian Renaissance*. New York: Oxford University Press.

Chaudhuri, Amit. 2021. *Finding the Raga: An Improvisation on Indian Music*. New York: New York Review Books.

Coomaraswamy, Ananda K. 1913. *The Arts and Crafts of India and Ceylon*. London: T. N. Foulis.

Coomaraswamy, Ananda K. 1994. *Art and Swadeshi*. New Delhi: Munshiram Manoharlal Publishers, Private Limited.

Coomaraswamy, Ananda K. 2003. *The Dance of Shiva: Fourteen Indian Essays*. New Delhi: Munshiram Manoharlal Publishers, Private Limited.

Coomaraswamy, Ananda K. 2004. *The Transformation of Nature in Art*. New Delhi: Munshiram Manoharlal Publishers, Private Limited.

Dalmia, Yashodhara. 2006. *Amrita Sher-Gil: A Life*. New Delhi: Penguin India.

Dalmia, Yashodhara, ed. 2014. *Amrita Sher-Gil: Art and Life (A Reader)*. New Delhi: Oxford University Press.

Kapur, Geeta. 2000. *When Was Modernism: Essays on Contemporary Cultural Practice in India*. New Delhi: Tulika Books.

Khullar, Sonal. 2015. *Worldly Affiliations: Artistic Practice, National Identity, and Modernism in India, 1930–1990*. California: University of California Press.

Korsgaard, Christine. 2002. *Sources of Normativity*. Cambridge: Cambridge University Press.

Mehrotra, Arvind Krishna, ed. 2010. *Arun Kolatkar. Collected Poems in English*. Northumberland: Bloodaxe Books.

Mehrotra, Arvind Krishna. 2020. *Selected Poems and Translations*. New York: New York Review Books.

Mitter, Partha. 1994. *Art and Nationalism in Colonial India*. Cambridge: Cambridge University Press.

Mitter, Partha. 2007. *The Triumph of Modernism*. London: Reaktion Books.

Tagore, Rabindranath. 1994. *The English Writings of Rabindranath Tagore* (ed. S. K. Das). Delhi: Sahitya Akademi.

Tagore, Rabindranath. 1922. *Creative Unity*. New Delhi: Macmillan.

Raghuramaraju. 2006. *Debates in Indian Philosophy: Classical, Colonial, and Contemporary*. New Delhi: Oxford University Press.

Raghuramaraju. 2009. *Enduring Colonialism: Classical Presences and Modern Absences in Indian Philosophy*. New Delhi: Oxford University Press.

Said, Edward. 1978. *Orientalism*. New York: Pantheon Books.

Spivak, Gayatri. 1999. *A Critique of Postcolonial Reason*. Cambridge, MA: Harvard University Press.

CHAPTER 9

....

ART AND ETHICS

Formalism

....

MICHALLE GAL

THE contemporary predominantly visual age grants aesthetic formalism a new role in philosophical analysis. According to the visual turn in aesthetics, philosophical attention ought to focus on the visual sphere as the correct context for addressing the concepts of human nature, culture, and ontology. Sensuous forms and captivating constructions abound in modern life. Observe, for instance, the excessive use of screens and media nets, the ubiquitous image-making use of mobile phones, the spread of emoji-based communication, and the aggressive exploitation of the public sphere by vested industries.[1] Seemingly, it is in terms of these sensuous forms and constructs, rather than internal conceptual contents, that our ontology and perception is constructed. Consequently, vital questions about the ethical commitments of the visual disciplines, to which art is unique and central, arise with pressing force. To this end, I consider *formalism* as the main theory of art to emphasize the power of art's form, composition, and appearance, and to demand that art's forms should enjoy creative autonomy and institutional freedom. It is thus imperative to revisit the formalist view of the ethical status of art, aptly captured in the famous slogan that "art is above morals" (Bell 1958, 24).

"Aesthetic formalism" refers both to an abstract characterization of art (and adjacent aesthetic realms) and a prominent Anglo-American school in the modernist philosophy of art. In various forms, aesthetic formalism operated from the closing decades of the nineteenth century to the middle of the twentieth century, growing concomitantly with the development of formalist art, curation of exhibitions, and art criticism. The present contribution thus addresses the formalist definition of art, in conjunction with a historicist account of the ethical status of art arising from the formalist movement. Formalism in aesthetics is often presented in the literature as a movement devoid of ethical content and theoretically indifferent to ethical questions; in other words, as a nonmoral theory

---

[1] For a discussion, see Cross, this volume.

of art. Nevertheless, not only did formalism thoroughly address the relations between art and ethics, and art and life (against the relations between ethics and the extra-artistic visual realm), but it also defined art as an ethical model of life. I therefore argue that aesthetic formalism is *not* indifferent to ethics but, on the contrary, forms a cogent ethical stance, which is dialectical yet orderly, along the lines of modernist social liberalism. It is true that the formalist liberalist thought of the nineteenth century moved in the twentieth century toward a "revolt against formalism," as claimed in 1957 by the pragmatist philosopher and historian of ideas Morton White (White 1957). Nevertheless, throughout modernism, art was granted an exceptional status, and aesthetics did not entail that liberalist ethics and formalism were mutually exclusive. On the contrary, aesthetic formalism was committed to the paramount natural right defended by liberalism, namely individual freedom and fulfillment.

The aesthetic moralism of the nineteenth century, which grew alongside formalism, emphasized art's didactic message in order to advance a moral conception of actual action, "to forward the right action," as highlighted by the formalist critique (Fry 1920, 14). At the same time, formalists rejected the use of artistic forms in spheres extraneous to art. For example, John Ruskin's influential Victorian moralism endorsed the use of the "moral part of imagination" in art, claiming in *Modern Painters* that "perfect taste is the faculty of receiving the greatest possible pleasure from those material sources which are attractive to our moral nature in its purity and perfection" (Ruskin 2018, 62). Similarly, Leo Tolstoy's socialist version of moralism enlisted the content or art to the moral progress of the community to produce a model fit for evaluative purposes: "The evolution of feelings takes place by means of art, replacing lower feelings, less kind and less needed for the good of humanity, by kinder feelings, more needed for that good. This is the purpose of art. And therefore art is better in its content in so far as it fulfills this purpose better, and is worse in so far as it fulfills it less" (Tolstoy 1995, 143). In their writings, the contemporary nineteenth-century formalists explicitly addressed Ruskin's and Tolstoy's approaches to art, arguing that the captivating power of art ought to be expended on the production of new ontological spheres, allowing art's forms to remain free from political or social message, and to become a model for freedom and self-fulfillment (Gal, 2015, Ch. 2). These formalist proposals formed an alternative to what the aestheticist-formalists Oscar Wilde and Roger Fry respectively called "poor, probable, uninteresting human life" (Wilde 2013, 1515) and "actual life" (Fry 1920, 12). In short, life is inferior to art, according to formalism. While Wilde argues that "Life imitates Art far more than Art imitates Life" (Wilde 2013, 1516), Fry offers an imperative regarding imaginative life, "the expression and a stimulus" of which is art: "We should rather justify actual life by its relation to the imaginative . . . since the imaginative life comes in the course of time to represent more or less what mankind feels to be the completest expression of its own nature, the freest use of its innate capacities, the actual life may be explained and justified in its approximation that freer and fuller life" (Wilde 2013, 1259–1260; Fry 1920, 14–15). Formalism thus sees art as dwelling in the depths of our nature and argues that the flourishing human being is an aestheticist at heart. It is through art that we may reach "freer and fuller life," at once the constitutive principle and mainstay of modern liberalism.

The significant moral status of art as a model, according to aesthetic formalism, becomes clearer if we bring out what I see as its four main propositions, to be elaborated in the subsequent discussion:

a. Art's moral status is "internal"; that is, art has an independent value and is self-justified.

b. Art is committed to its medium and internal normativity—named, for example, "the spirit of the picture" by Henri Matisse, or art's "own special responsibilities to its material" by Walter Pater—rather than to extra-artistic goals.

c. The foregoing does not render art nonmoral or detached from life. Rather, owing to its internal normativity, art serves as a model for individual freedom, autonomy and aspiration to self-fulfillment and the ideal.

d. Thanks to its internal normativity, art is able to create ontological possibilities through free forms, enabling the viewer to access spheres beyond the familiar.

THE PROPER AREA OF ART

General philosophical formalism holds that the identity of a thing is determined by its form, a prototypical form when referring to groups, and that knowing a thing involves an acquaintance with its form. In the case of systems or languages, such as logic, mathematics, or law, formalism abstracts normativity and standards of judgment from the internal or syntactic, often rule-bound, set of relations between the elements of the system. Aesthetic formalism is closely related to the ontological, epistemological, and syntactic aspects of general formalism. It focuses on *aesthetic form*, namely, a composition organized around aesthetic principles. Aesthetic form is considered the essence of an artwork and the foundation of artistic experience and judgment. The formalist idea regarding art was expressed as early as the eighteenth century by Immanuel Kant, and again in the mid-nineteenth century by Eduard Hanslick in "The Beautiful in Music."[2] As a distinct modernist movement, formalism was inaugurated in Europe of the late nineteenth century by the aestheticist anti-moralist and partly anti-Victorian Walter Pater and his student Wilde, who championed aestheticist art and the budding of abstraction in art (as exemplified, for example, by James Whistler). It progressed in the early twentieth century mainly through the efforts of A. C. Bradley and members of the Bloomsbury group such as Clive Bell and Roger Fry, who dedicated themselves to defending post-Impressionist art. In the American mid-twentieth century, it gained adherence from Clement Greenberg and Michael Fried, who supported Abstract-Expressionist art. The formalist movement ended with the anti-formalist linguistic turn in aesthetics, and the emergence of Pop Art and Conceptual Art. Yet formalism remains an influential and

[2] For more detailed discussions, see Costelloe and Shapshay, both in this volume.

much discussed school of thought. As a general theory of art, formalism is a prominent force in areas pertaining to design and the aesthetics of the everyday world.

For aesthetic formalism, as proper to other kinds of formalism also, the subject of judgment is not the correspondence between system and life or external reality, but rather the consecutive or mutual relations between artworks, styles, or methods within the larger frame of art. Thus, formalism demarcates the limits of art as independent from society, culture, or ethics. The characterization of the ambit of art as internal to the sphere of art is proposed by Wilde in his aestheticist and early formalist "The Critic as Artist" from 1891:

> I would call criticism a creation within a creation. For just as the great artists, from Homer and Aeschylus, down to Shakespeare and Keats, did not go directly to life for their subject matter, but sought for it in myth, and legend, and ancient tale, so the critic deals with materials that others have, as it were, purified for him, and to which imaginative form and colour have been already added. (Wilde 2013, 1317)

According to the formalist theory of art-criticism sketched by Wilde in this brilliant essay, the critic's task is not to extract a message from an artwork, reapplying it to life, but to advance beyond the ordinary reaches of life using the artwork's forms to create new ones.[3] It is evident that Wilde's proposition is normative, implying that the power of art does not emerge from correspondence to a notion of life or reality extraneous to life. Indeed, a salient feature of aesthetic formalism is its normative character and emphasis on the power of aesthetic form. The power of aesthetic form is the foundation of the relation between art and ethics: if genuinely free, it may inspire us to achieve freedom and self-fulfillment, but it may also draw responses of wanting to co-opt or defuse its forms.

The celebrated formalist label of aesthetic form, "significant form," was coined in 1909 by Bradley in "Poetry for Poetry's Sake." Drawing upon the aestheticist imperative "art for art's sake," which enjoins art to free itself through composition from external justification, moral obligation and moral ends, Bradley defined "mere form in poetry" as possessing intrinsic value, freed from "ulterior ends" (Bradley 1965, 16). In realizing that mere form is rare in poetry, he follows Pater, the founder of aestheticism ("an authority whom the formalist will not despise") as he develops his proposal (Bradley 1965, 16). Like Pater, Bradley claims that free poetry is an art form whose *telos* is internal, and its structure immune to recruitment for external purposes, because its content and form are absolutely united by an expressive style: namely, by an aesthetically significant form. Bradley elaborated the aestheticist-formalist anti-mimesis theory that Wilde presented in his 1891 "The Decay of Lying." These ideas are centered on the notion of ontological independence from reality and its imitation, and the artificial creation of a novel and superior alternative sphere. Aestheticism and Formalism argue that the visual and artistic composition of the arts comprehensively contain all that there is in it—a crucial

---

[3] For more about the distinction between interpretive vs. formalist criticism, see Chapter 6, "Criticism versus Interpretation" in my Gal,2015, 119–130.

condition for art's autonomy.[4] For Bradley, too, the aim of poetry is to stay clear of adventitious goals, or goals extrinsic to art, which is a necessary condition for grasping art's ontological structure and underpins our ability to judge art's real value. Moreover, the need to respect the autonomy of poetry is related to resisting the impositions of ordinary existence, and applies to both artist and reader:

> The consideration of ulterior ends, whether by the poet in the act of composing or by the reader in the act of experiencing, tends to lower poetic value. It does so because it tends to change the nature of poetry by taking it out of its own atmosphere. For its nature is to be not a part, nor yet a copy, of the real world (as we commonly understand that phrase), but to be a world by itself, independent, complete, autonomous; and to possess it fully you must enter that world, conform to its laws, and ignore for the time the beliefs, aims, and particular conditions which belong to you in the other world of reality. (Bradley 1965, 7)

The term "significant form" was transferred from poetry to visual arts by Bell in his 1913 book *Art*, which became a canonical formalist text. "Lines and colours combined in a particular way, certain forms and relations of forms, stir our aesthetic emotions. These relations and combinations of lines and colours, these aesthetically moving forms, I call 'Significant Form'; and 'Significant Form' is the one quality common to all works of visual art" (Bell 1958, 17). Thus, Bell claims, significant form is the essential quality that constitutes the group of visual art and design works, comprising elements as diverse as the mosque of Hagia Sophia, the windows at Chartres, Mexican sculpture, a Persian bowl, Chinese carpets, Giotto's frescoes, the paintings of Poussin, Piero Della Francesca, or Paul Cézanne. All these possess "moving arrangements and combinations": a significant form, which according to formalism, is internally related to ethical character. When the organizing principle is the aesthetic rightness of the interrelations between its elements, the artwork's commitment is internal, or better yet, it is a commitment to the autonomy of its medium. It exempts the artwork from external moral commitments, but at the same time, it, the formalists believe, a point overlooked by many, construes art as a model of internal normative consistency, self-fulfillment, autonomy, and freedom—one's being for one's sake.

However, that is not to say that according to the formalist view of art, an exemption from external moral commitment entails a vacuous moral status. Rather, for the formalist, it is the very character of art that attributes to it ethical status and significance. By contrast, moralism in art deprives art of its unique ethical status. Bell's formulation, stressing the difference between moralism and autonomy of art with respect to the creation of positive ethical value, is clear on this score:

> Art is above morals, or, rather, all art is moral because, as I hope to show presently, works of art are immediate means to good. Once we have judged a thing a work of

---

[4] The term "aestheticism" has been used in multiple ways. See Rothfeld, this volume, for more discussion.

art, we have judged it ethically of the first importance and put it beyond the reach of the moralist. (Bell 1958, 24)

Bell's comments reveal that behind formalism's apparently purist lack of substance lies a deep understanding of human nature and a commensurate commitment to ethical flourishing. Insofar as it is a modernist movement, aesthetic formalism, from its aestheticist beginnings in the 1870s up to its final reverberations on the 1960s American art scene, was committed to the natural right of personal freedom, and to humanism and democracy. Certainly, the ethical stance of formalism is complex and sometimes needs refinement and elaboration. Nevertheless, formalism explicitly argued that art is the avant-garde of culture, and indeed the outstanding formalist avant-garde art movement of the first half of the twentieth century made a point to resist any public, social or moralist pressure in order to serve at the cultural vanguard. The resistance practiced by the avant-garde culture rested on "a superior consciousness of history, the appearance of a new kind of criticism of society" (Greenberg 1984, 4). Accordingly, Greenberg, the chief formalist of the last stage of modernist aesthetics, writes in his 1939 "Avant-Garde and Kitsch" that formalist philosophy of art and art collaborated to maintain this regulative model:

> The true and most important function of the avant-garde was not to "experiment," but to find a path along which it would be possible to keep culture moving in the midst of ideological confusion and violence. Retiring from public altogether, the avant-garde poet or artist sought to maintain the high level of his art by both narrowing and raising it to the expression of an absolute in which all relativities and contradictions would be either resolved or beside the point. "Art for art's sake" and "pure poetry" appear, and subject matter or content becomes something to be avoided like a plague. (Greenberg 1984, 5)

On these lines, the very model of individual freedom is free and autonomous art. As explained, the formalist construes artistic form as a distinct perspective on freedom and commitment, in opposition to the preordained content mandated by the structures of oppression. It is the freedom to concentrate on the artistic form, and not the obligation to convey meaning or ethical beliefs, that liberates art from external commitment, rendering it autonomous and immune to being co-opted by the power structures of the day (Gal 2022, 26–27). Nevertheless, general autonomy will not suffice; art's freedom is dialectically achieved by devotion to its *explicit medium*, organized in an aesthetic form. This is the "unique and proper area of competence of each art," as Greenberg calls it in his retrospective 1960 "Modernist Painting." Since, as Wilde had argued, "each art has its grammar and its material," formalism refers to the form created within the limits of each artistic medium (Wilde 2013, 1595). That is to say, each individual form of art ought to be freed from commitments external to itself, eschewing the dominion or even influence of rival arts. If art is exploited to "deliver the message," its medium loses autonomy and distinct character. To secure art's freedom and its status as a model of freedom, each medium of art should be free to operate within its own framework. In this relation, formalism endorses Lessing's canonical account of the essential difference between spatial and temporal arts presented in *Laocoön, or the Limitations of Poetry* from 1765. Pater elaborates these ideas in a more general application in his 1877 edition of *Renaissance*: "The sensuous material of each art brings with it a special phase or quality of beauty, untranslatable into the forms of any other, an order of impressions distinct in kind" (Pater 1998, 83). If art is but the 'translation' of a message, as many critics mistakenly assume, then "the sensuous element in art, and with it almost everything in art that is essentially artistic, is made a matter of indifference" (Pater 1998, 83). Following Pater, Wilde presents the dialectical structure of art in *The English Renaissance of Art*, delivered on his American lecture tour: "This limitation is for the artist perfect freedom: it is at once the origin and the sign of his strength. So that all the supreme masters of style—Dante, Sophocles, Shakespeare—are the supreme masters of spiritual and intellectual vision also" (Wilde 2013, 1450).

The dialectical relations between the limitation imposed by the medium and the freedom of art does not end here. In a celebrated passage, Pater explains the nature of these relations by adverting to music as the freest art, given its relatively abstract medium in which content and form reach the completest fusion: "*All art constantly aspires towards the condition of music*" (Pater 1998, 86, emphasis in original). He adds that painting incurs the highest risk of colonization by other arts, mainly by literature or poetry ("it is in popular judgments of pictures that the false generalization of all art into forms of poetry is most prevalent"), hence of being co-opted in the service of external goals (Pater 1998, 86). This claim is echoed by the late formalist Greenberg in "Towards a Newer Laocoön," in which he portrays the rule of literature as the "dominant art" from the seventeenth century onward (though music was said to be the "greatest art"), causing the arts that had surrendered it to "deny their own nature," that is, to forego their essential qualities and self-fulfillment (Greenberg 1988, I:26). The overtaking by literature sent the special nature of other arts into deep concealment. Given that literature is an obstacle to the freedom of the various arts, Greenberg (like Pater before him) calls for the musicality of the arts as immunity against the inroads of literature. This sheds a light on the musical titles chosen by some formalist painters for their works, such as Whistler's *Nocturnes* series, Matisse's *Harmony in Red*, or Wassily Kandinsky's *Composition* series. Resorting to musicality is thus not aimed at substituting the dominion of music for that of literature, but at freeing the other arts to attain their individual essential nature.

These formalist ideas have important consequences for the practice of criticism in art. Thus, artistic criticism should allow art to achieve its self-justification and self-standing moral status. Not only is art able to demonstrate its unique power of composition, but each art should demonstrate what it alone can supply. According to Pater, art criticism should endorse the independent moral status of each individual art, rather than becoming unduly focused on the "message" of the artwork, at the cost of treating the art's medium as a mere instrument. Note that Pater characterizes the activation of the unique formal power of each artistic medium of art as its responsibility:

> One of the functions of aesthetic criticism is to define these limitations; to estimate the degree in which a given work of art fulfils its responsibilities to its special material; to note in a picture that true pictorial charm, which is neither a mere poetical thought nor sentiment, on the one hand, nor a mere result of communicable technical skill in colour or design, on the other; to define in a poem that true poetical quality, which is neither descriptive nor meditative merely, but comes of an inventive handling of rhythmical language—the element of song in the singing; to note in music the musical charm—that essential music, which presents no words, no matter of sentiment or thought, separable from the special form in which it is conveyed to us. (Pater 1998, 83)

In brief, criticism ought to align with the project of artistic freedom by pushing art to reach its "special form." The benefit of embracing the proper function of criticism is the acquisition of "new ontological spheres," to the disambiguation and explication of which I now turn.

ALTERNATIVE ONTOLOGY

Fin-de-siècle aestheticists and formalists were accused by contemporary critics of yielding to decadence, and of making an undue appeal to the exemption of art from external morality in favor of "responsibility to its special material" (Pater 1998, 83). Whether the objection bears weight is moot; in explaining that "to those who are preoccupied with the beauty of form nothing else seems of much importance," Wilde for example was certainly toying with decadent ideas of a marvelous but morally declining art (Wilde 2013, 1264). Wilde's critique of Victorian moralism and the didactic realist art movement of his time was taken a step further: "There is no essential incongruity between crime and culture. We cannot rewrite the whole of history for the purpose of gratifying our moral sense of what should be" (Wilde 2013, 1274). Truth-based or "useful" art was distinguished from beauty, as he claims in "The Decay of Lying"—a canonical anti-realist constructivist essay in which he clamored for autonomy on behalf of art. The protagonist of his 1885 essay "Pen, Pencil and Poison: A Study of Green," T. G. Wainewright, who also happened to be a notorious dandy and suspected serial-killer of the Victorian era, is depicted both as a poisoner and a brilliant artist, whose value as an artist is defended by Wilde, who contended that "the fact of a man being a poisoner is nothing against his prose" (Wilde 2013, 1293). The expression of extreme views was no doubt for Wilde a direct affront to moralism as promoting low-value art: "The domestic virtues are not the true basis of art, though they may serve as an excellent advertisement for second-rate artists" (Wilde 2013, 1293).

Though more irenic in their pronouncements, subsequent formalists belonging to modernist aesthetics supported Wilde's sharp distinction between artistic spirit and moralism. However, they did not fail to grapple adequately with the idea of an internal normativity granted to art. Bell, for example, made it a point of not evading the question "what is the significance of anything as an end in itself? What is that which is left when we have stripped a thing of all its associations, of all its significance as a means? What is left to provoke our emotion?" His answer is "that which philosophers used to call 'the thing in itself' and now call 'ultimate reality'" (Bell 1958, 45). In his review of Bell's *Art*, Fry adds that his idea of significant form, "with all its possible implications of ultimate reality . . . rises to genuine artistic passion, is a thing of passionate import" (Fry 1996, 160). Bell's formalism is clearly metaphysical, first and foremost. In the chapter titled "The Metaphysical Hypothesis," he contends that reaching the "deeper" levels of reality is enabled through form, and that "visual artists come at reality generally through material form" (Bell 1958, 47). This explains why the creation of autonomous forms may lead to an expanded ontology. The artist sometimes sees reality as made of pure forms: "the perception of forms and formal relations" (Bell 1958, 48). Bell does not endorse extreme aestheticism according to which the artist merely aims to create significant form, subject to few or no material or intellectual constraints. Formalism, for him, is not wholly abstract and unconstrained. Medium, intention, and feeling for reality constitute the substance of the form.

Yet formalism goes beyond the claim that art is a model for individual freedom. Formalism stresses that due to its own self-regulated form, freed from external values, art exposes the viewer to an "ultimate reality"; that is, to alternative ontological spheres. This ability of art is closely related to modernism's congruence with aspects of liberal humanism. Wilde's inversion of the mimetic model of art is based on the proposition that "art has flowers that no forests know of, birds that no woodland possesses. She makes and unmakes many worlds, and can draw the moon from heaven with a scarlet thread. Hers are the 'forms more real than living man,' and hers the great archetypes of which things that have existence are but unfinished copies" (Wilde 2013, 1260). That is to say, art possesses metaphorical and ontological abilities to create new realms, which in their turn prove to be the "model" of life—the symbolized rather than the symbol.

Here Wilde sets out the bold claim that art when free can fracture the impression of necessity inherent in our experience of the familiar everyday life, in both a personal sense, and for society as a whole. For an illustrative use of metaphor, note that to "draw the moon from heaven with a scarlet thread" should not be dismissed as an escapist fantasy since it denotes no feasible action and thus seems to be content-free. On the contrary, the image is one that we are meant to take seriously, insofar as it perfectly illustrates the fracture in the obviousness of the "given," that is, in what we take for granted in ordinary life. Furthermore, it is a perspective for the practice of humanist critical thought, a release from oppression, in Immanuel Kant's words "man's emergence from his self-incurred immaturity" (Perry 2012, 60). To the enlightenment's emphasis on reason, formalism, influenced by romanticism, opposes a constructivist imagination. Imaginative life, Fry explains in his "Essay in Aesthetics," is one in which, thanks to the absence of "responsive action," which narrows the ambit of consciousness down to mere necessities, individuals can practice a contemplative oversight of their surroundings. Imaginative life opens the inner gaze beyond what is relevant to the established demands of ordinary life, and trains it to attend to elements and relations reorganized in new forms. This is the aesthetic life, said to be superior to real life, and led by art. Wilde formulates a similar view in "The Critic as Artist" with due force and eloquence:

> Art can lead us away from surroundings whose beauty is dimmed to us by the mist of familiarity, or whose ignoble ugliness and sordid claims are marring the perfection of our development. It can help us to leave the age in which we were born, and to pass into other ages, and find ourselves not exiled from their air. It can teach us how to escape from our experience, and to realize the experiences of those who are greater than we are. (Wilde 2013, 1334)

Art, as proposed above, has a significant and unique role in "materializing" humanist, liberalist ideas of freedom, by giving them concrete expression in the medium of each art form. This is the happy meeting point of autonomy, the power of composition to create what Bell calls a "sense of reality," and ethics.

Note that historically, philosophical formalism was deeply immersed in modernist aestheticist-formalist art. Formalists were invested in curating exhibitions of post-Impressionist (a term coined by Fry) and later abstract-expressionist art, generating new conceptions of art to fit formalist art. At the same time, it highlighted the workings of artistic freedom through art, which stood as a model of individual freedom, presenting new ontological spheres. The catalog of the second post-Impressionist exhibition of 1912 organized by Fry reveals (according to him) the difficulties faced by visitors, accustomed to the realist-mimetic model of art, encountering the free ontological aspirations manifested by artists who participated in the first exhibition two years earlier. "These artists do not seek to give what can, after all, be but a pale reflex of actual appearance, but to arouse the conviction of a new and definite reality. They do not seek to imitate form, but to create form; not to imitate life, but to find an equivalent for life" (Fry 1920, 157). Masters such as Paul Gauguin, George Braque, Matisse, and Cézanne were suspected of manipulating the public through fictitious attempts at art. The formalists, therefore, took it upon themselves to bring the public closer into relation with formalist art. Within the framework of modernism, formalist art was regarded as having philosophical, humanist, and liberal ambitions, whose goal was to secure art's internal normativity and ethical status as a model of individual freedom. "What modern art has to do in the service of culture," said Pater, is "to rearrange the details of modern life, so to reflect it, that it may satisfy the spirit. And what does the spirit need in the face of modern life? The sense of freedom" (Pater 1998, 148).

Fry, too, aims to investigate "the relation of the modern movement in art to life" (Fry 1920, 6). To understand this relation, we need to return to the burgeoning of the impressionist movement in 1870. The early impressionists followed two main ideas, Fry claims in "Art and Life":

On the one hand they upheld, more categorically than ever before, the complete de-tachment of the artistic vision from the values imposed on vision by everyday life—they claimed, as Whistler did in his "10 o'clock," to be pure artists. On the other hand, a group of them used this freedom for the quasi-scientific description of new effects of atmospheric colour and atmospheric perspective, thereby endowing painting with a quite new series of colour harmonies. (Fry 1920, 7)

Fry stresses the fact that the most significant result of the new impressionist manner in art is the exposure of the public to new ontological spheres. "The effects thus explored were completely unfamiliar to the ordinary man, whose vision is limited to the mere recognition of objects with a view to the uses of everyday life" (Fry 1920, 7–8). While this gradually brought out a whole new tolerance in the viewing public, as Fry tells us, the public remained in constant need of aesthetic education to acknowledge and observe art's aspiration to autonomy. Recall that Wilde held deep misgivings about the public's desire to control art, usurping its autonomy time and time again. Public opinion, Wilde warns us in "The Soul of Man Under Socialism," tries to dictate "to the artist the form he is to use, the mode in which he is to use it, and the materials with which he is to work" (Wilde 2013, 1519). The progress of art, he adds, is enabled "entirely due to a few indi-vidual artists refusing to regard Art as a mere matter of demand and supply" (Wilde 2013, 1519).

Reissuing Wilde's warnings, Bell and Fry note that many works to the public's liking are only "fictitiously" moral. Because one cannot respond to a work of art through ac-tion, an ethical response to a work of art is in fact fictitious, proving that morality in art is an inappropriate exploitation of the medium. Bell's distinction between the sub-ject matter of an ethical judgment and the status of art as ethical by itself is drawn con-jointly with the related contrast between "descriptive" and "real" works of art, to the extent that the latter contrast sheds light on the former. Descriptive work, according to Bell, is subordinate to an external referent, holding out an invitation to participate in a nonaesthetic experience that falls outside the remit of art. Sir Luke Fildes's popular artwork *The Doctor* is presented as an illustration. *The Doctor* is supposed to infect the viewer with the doctor and parent's worry about a very sick child. However, Bell and Fry disparage its sentimentality, claiming that it is not a work of art since it is about emo-tion rather than being itself an object of emotion. *The Doctor* is labeled as a descriptive painting by Bell, thus "not being a work of art, The Doctor has more of the immense ethical value possessed by all objects that provoke aesthetic ecstasy" (Bell 1958, 24). Fry further asserts in his "The Meaning of Pictures" that it is "false" and "profoundly wrong," inviting us to participate in an "extra-artistic" and inauthentic moral experience. As he explains, "we feel here an invitation to identify oneself with the doctor; we feel that we, too, are capable of this devotion, and we get a certain moral satisfaction which we have done nothing to earn. I suspect that a great deal of the attraction of sentimental art and sentimental stories comes from an indulgence in this fictitious sense of one's moral worth" (Fry 1996, 398). Descriptive forms are but imitations of familiar forms, bringing the viewers back to their familiar lives, devoid of aspiration to freedom.

By contrast, Cézanne's oeuvre, much discussed and admired by the formalists, is said to bring about a paradigmatic presentation of new values through new forms. Cézanne produced "the new conception of art," Fry claims. Cézanne's creation of new forms constituted a denunciation of the conventional use of perspective in painting and was deemed definitive of the modernist emphasis on autonomous forms. His endorsement of multiple viewpoints broke with tradition and insulated his works from outside influence. The "deformation" of objects, as formalist artist and thinker Maurice Denis called it, or "distorted forms of objects," as Erle Loran, a salient critic of Cézanne, calls it (Loran 1943, 29), could exist only in painting. In analyzing Cézanne's various still lifes with plates and pitchers, Loran argues that the practice of distortion was central to anti-mimetic formalist art, explaining the role of the distortions of forms in creating an ontological independent space. He asserts that abstract art was deeply influenced by Cézanne's intentional distortion. The presence of distortions in the picture plane was deemed forceful and dynamic, putting it in a relation of tension to other visual planes present in the picture. Loran tells the readers that "the result is a new, more exciting illusion of space than any mechanical perspective drawing could give. The distortion of natural shapes is thus seen as a positive 'form-conditioning' factor" (Loran 1943, 32).

This practice of art brings us directly to the problem of its ethical status. What Loran names "illusion of space" is not an illusion for Fry, but a space that belongs to the imaginative life. Its centrality to actual life reveals it to be intimately related to ethics. Where one can react, one is ethically committed to doing so, if a situation arises in which it is required to act. Conversely, the lack of "responsive" reaction in imaginative life exempts it from external moral commitment: "Responsive action implies in actual life moral responsibility. In art we have no such moral responsibility—it presents a life freed from the binding necessities of our actual existence" (Fry 1920, 14). But this makes art free and in so-doing allows it to body forth one of the central values of ethical life. Art thus presents us with new ontological spheres, by creating opportunities for viewers to view the world in new ways—to actually enter new worlds. "Art transports us from the world of man's activity to a world of aesthetic exaltation. For a moment we are shut off from human interests; our anticipations and memories are arrested; we are lifted above the stream of life," Bell famously claims (Bell 1958, 27, 29). Do viewers wish to be free? The viewers who cannot but look behind the artistic medium for traces of their own lives are called "weak" by Bell: "Instead of going out on the stream of art into a new world of aesthetic experience, they turn a sharp corner and come straight home to the world of human interests" (Bell 1958, 29).

It is hard to resist the conclusion that it is the responsibility of the viewer to allow art to lead them to new horizons: to conclude this chapter, it is apt to raise a few questions to set new directions consonant with the main thrust of the discussion. Do human beings aspire to be lifted from the quotidian "given," the stream of life, to the unfamiliar? Do they truly aspire to freedom? The fragility of democracy raises the deep worry that the freedom that liberalism offers humanity is not always desired. For the weak viewers, Bell claims, "the significance of a work of art depends on what they bring to it; no new thing is added to their lives, only the old material is stirred" (Bell 1958, 29). However, Fry strongly claims that imaginative life is an integral part of our nature and our deepest ful-fillment. Grasping and delighting in compositions is natural for us as the kind of species we are: a species dedicated to and permeated by the visual. In this sense, Fry was one of the most visionary figures among the formalists. Long after formalism had reached its zenith, Michael Fried reviewed Fry's aesthetics in relation to the ethical status of art, claiming "this is the core of his so-called formalist esthetics, the conviction that all per-sons capable of experiencing esthetic emotion in front of paintings are responding when they do so to relations of pure form—roughly, of ideated volumes in relation both to one another and to the surface and shape of the canvas" (Fried 2001, 6).

See also: Shapshay, Song, Stear, Lamarque, this volume

REFERENCES

Bell, Clive. 1958. *Art*. New York: Capricorn Books.

Bradley, A. C. 1965. *Oxford Lectures on Poetry*. New York: St Martin's Press.

Fried, Michael. 2001. "Roger Fry's Formalism." *The Tanner Lecture on Human Values*, 1–40. Talk delivered at the University of Michigan, Ann Arbor.

Fry, Roger. 1996. *A Roger Fry Reader*. Chicago: University of Chicago Press.

Fry, Roger. 1920. *Vision and Design*. London: Chatto and Windus.

Gal, Michalle. 2015. *Aestheticism: Deep Formalism and the Emergence of Modernist Aesthetics*. Bern: Peter Lang.

Gal, Michalle. 2022. "The Inauguration of Formalism: Aestheticism and the Productive Opacity Principle." *Journal of Comparative Literature and Aesthetics* 45 no. 2: 20–30.

Greenberg, Clement. 1984. *Art and Culture: Critical Essays*. Boston: Beacon Press.

Greenberg, Clement. 1988. *The Collected Essays and Criticism, Volume 1: Perceptions and Judgments, 1939–1944*, edited by John O'Brian. Reprint ed. Vol. I. Chicago: University of Chicago Press.

Loran, Erle. 1943. *Cézanne's Composition: Analysis of His Form with Diagrams and Photographs of His Motifs*. Berkeley: University of California Press.

Pater, Walter. 1998. *The Renaissance: Studies in Art and Poetry*. Edited by Adam Phillips. Oxford: Oxford University Press.

Perry, Marvin. 2012. *Sources of the Western Tradition: Volume II: From the Renaissance to the Present*. 9th ed. Boston: Cengage Learning.

Ruskin, John. 2018. *Modern Painters: Volume I*. Frankfurt: Books on Demand.

Tolstoy, Leo. 1995. *What Is Art?* London; New York: Penguin Books.

Wilde, Oscar. 2013. *The Complete Work of Oscar Wilde*. EBook: Delphi Classics.

Morton White. 1957. *Social Thought in America: The Revolt Against Formalism*. Boston: Beacon Press.

CHAPTER 10

....

HARLEM RENAISSANCE
An Interpretation of Racialized Art and Ethics

....

JACOBY ADESHI CARTER AND
SHEENA MICHELE MASON

INTRODUCTION

....

THE Harlem Renaissance was a cultural, political, philosophical, and philanthropic burgeoning that happened primarily between 1915 and 1940. Participants worldwide promoted and produced visual, theatrical, literary, and musical art that sought to (re)define and (re)imagine people racialized as Black. The New Negro movement refers to the cultural, aesthetic, and civil rights efforts that continued from earlier movements and through the subsequent civil rights movement of the 1950s–1960s. Many writers, musicians, actors, and visual artists alike challenged racism through their art.

The Great Migration out of the rural South, the experiences during World War I of African American soldiers abroad of different racial ideologies, increased federal funding of the arts inclusive of African American artists, and a putatively less rigid system of racial segregation and greater economic opportunity in the North all contributed to the cultural rebirth of a "New Negro" type and character. Although the renaissance expanded across and included all types of art, in the 1920s and 1930s, there was an extraordinary deluge of publications by African Americans. Artists identified, described, and renamed themselves, each other, and many of their imagined characters as "New Negroes," a distinction from America's "Old Negro" that had come to represent America's Frankenstein, a boogieman, everything monstrous, and inferior when compared to "white" refinement and Victorian morals.

African American artists are compelled to do their work within a cultural context that not only devalues them as artists, but devalues them as human beings. This circumstance alone gives rise to myriad ethical questions and normative and aesthetic debates among African American artists. Some problems germane to the New Negro movement concern ethical questions about the responsibility of artists racialized as white toward subjects and subject matter of those racialized as Black.

The Old Negro was a literary aesthetic phantasm, often a minstrel presentation of Afrodescendant people, created through racialized white ignorance, stereotypes, and phobias of African American people and their experiences in the United States.[1] Several varieties of misrepresentation were common from Mammies and Uncle Toms to happy-go-lucky buffoons and shiftless slaves, but what is represented are racialized white fears, false beliefs, and intentional disregard. African American aesthetic production has always taken place within a cultural backdrop of white supremacist racism that imposes normative constraints on an already oppressed population. One normative problem is whether to let the mischaracterizations stand; that is, whether racialized Black artists are required to counteract the racist tropes propagated by racialized white artists. Another normative problem involves the unfair comparison of racialized Black and white art, without attention to the differing effects of racism on the two groups. Finally, there is the obvious fact that devaluing African American aesthetic culture normalizes a context that upholds and perpetuates ideas about the Old Negro and undermines that of the New Negro.

Those racialized as Black are made to confront the existential and political question of "the role of the Negro artist." Artists working within the Harlem Renaissance were often preoccupied with questions of authenticity and representation. The ethical implications of authenticity and representation are necessarily intertwined. Authentic representation of racialized Black people and their experiences has ethical import. Authentic depictions of racialized Black people and their experiences need not always flatter but should avoid the perpetuation of empirically unfounded stereotypes. The authenticity that was demanded of the Harlem Renaissance participants reflected a desire for freedom from the constraints created by racism and a demand for artists to be true to themselves and those they depicted in their art. Where our moral assessment of "Black" authenticity gets more complicated is when artists and consumers are not permitted or willing to see racialized Black people outside of the bounds of racism and racist frameworks.

If a person is racialized as Black, one's identity is often considered representative of racialized Black people. (See also Taylor, this volume.) That reflects the violent nature of the Old Negro, as racialized white people too often rendered those stereotypical images of African Americans as true and accurate depictions of the entire population. Any racialized Black artist contradicting such homogenous and racist images, regardless of how they contradict racist ideology, were interpreted as also and necessarily representing African Americans. The debates of the period were infused with the understanding that much was at stake, a burden and fact less often imposed on racialized

---

[1] For example, the popularity of blackface minstrelsy, a genre that mocked and ridiculed what was perceived to be "Black culture" and was interpreted as accurately reflecting the culture of people racialized as Black from approximately the 1830s to the 1960s.

white artists. In this way, racialized Black artists have grappled with ethical and existential implications of both authenticity and representation, working to reshape the racist gaze and normative presumptions imposed onto them by American society. African American artists interrogated the unethical practices of their society and called racialized white and Black people alike to action.

Many artists and critics recognized that the New Negro they were reconstructing from the Old Negro was, indeed, a work of fiction, a utopic version of racialized subjects. It is from within the paradoxical nature of creating, defining, sustaining, and willing into the American imagination a New Negro that participants of the Harlem Renaissance dared to (re)create a race. Ultimately, the writers and artists presented and debated the blueprint for what is now commonly known as the "Black Aesthetic" (Fuller 1976 and Gayle 1970, 78). Artists found themselves arguing over what an "authentic" representation of Blackness should be, how it should look in art, and, by extension, theories for development beyond racism in a society consumed by race and color.

The question of racialized art and its interpretation was at once a metaphysical, epistemic, and moral issue contested by the artists themselves. With greater artistic freedom and novel forms of cultural expression came a demand to wrestle squarely with the historical interpretive constraints on racialized Black people's creativity and subjectivity. Even in its nascent stage, the most fecund period of artistic expression ever seen to that point, African American artists grappled with the question of the very existence of racialized Black (Negro) art. The racialization of the art and the artists has resulted in the obfuscation of both, particularly in cases where the art and artist were viewed as being on the fringes of their required and externally ascribed racialization. Nella Larsen, Jessie Fauset, George Schuyler, Zora Neale Hurston at the end of her career, Jean Toomer, and so on were all figures whose art, in part or in total, was placed in noncanonical dustbins or otherwise heavily critiqued for even attempting to extend outside of what it meant to be racialized in the United States. Others, like Walter White and James Weldon Johnson, who employed the popular literary tropes of the period, were embraced, in significant part, because their imagining of the New Negro was more aligned with the expectations of racialized art.

Participants both during and after the movement engaged in debates, unsettled to this day, about the operation of racism within and outside of the United States, the prominence and role of race in American culture, the existence of African American culture, and the relationship of the latter to mainstream American culture. That the movement was from its very inception mired in these debates has left some of its interpreters, including Weldon Johnson, with the impression that the Renaissance failed. A reexamination of the Harlem Renaissance, especially uncanonized artists and texts, results in an expanded understanding of the underlying philosophies of race and racialization and the correlation between philosophical positions and ongoing civil rights efforts. In this chapter, we survey the period's most common tropes and genres that arose from participants' aesthetical and ethical inclinations, and that coincide with the fight for civil rights.

KNOW THY *RACIAL* SELF

The proliferation of African American culture that came to be known as the New Negro movement required for its occurrence the existence of historical transformations of consciousness and sociological conditions requisite for forms and instances of Negro expression theretofore unseen. At the outset of the movement, World War I (1914–1918) engendered for many racialized Black people an understanding of the difference between America's and Europe's racial codes. Racialized Black people were increasingly aware of the discrepancy between America's demands of the Negro and what the country was willing to give in return for satisfaction of those demands. This shift in both awareness and attitude resulted in a raised consciousness of people racialized as Black and in their artistic and literary productions. The Harlem Renaissance was not possible in its aspirations until a certain historical point had been reached.

These historical transformations brought the possibility of novel and corrective forms of expression by African Americans, including the partial amelioration of social conditions that constrained African American artists. Those conditions included the erosion of barriers that prevented racialized Black people from being properly known and understood. For racialized white artists the question may well have been whether an artist has a moral obligation to "Know thyself" and derivatively to "Know the selves" one invokes in their art. But for racialized Black artists, one must inquire a step further whether there is a moral obligation to "Know thy '*racial*' self." This was itself a normatively contentious issue for Harlem Renaissance artists. Some pressed for an obligation on the part of artists to "uplift" the race through their work. Others thought the ethical responsibilities of racialized Black artists laid elsewhere and problematized the imposition of a racial burden on African American artists in the absence of a similar imposition on racialized white artists.

Here, one hits upon an ethical dilemma that is ubiquitous throughout African American experiences and the experiences of other marginalized populations; namely, the stultifying condition of being forced to reify the very same pernicious social constructions one seeks to oppose. Racialized white Americans no longer held an unmitigated and unqualified authority over representations of racialized Black populations. With greater freedom of artistic expression came the ability to construct the consciousness, character, and aspirations of the group through its art. Racism has been a limiting condition on the artistic possibilities of racialized Black people, confining them for much of their history to the domain of folk expression and art. Artists racialized as Black were able to speak from their own perspective and worldview, sometimes as immigrants to the United States, rather than being burdened with the yoke of championing the race and responding to the challenge of racist supremacy through advocacy of race specific social policies.

Alain Locke observed that though many racialized Black artists were first and foremost engaged in a universal human endeavor of creative expression, for Harlem

Renaissance poets and other artists, a significant aspect of that endeavor is racial. That raises what is undoubtedly one of the most vexing philosophical questions that emerge from the New Negro movement. In the words of the heralded "Dean of the Harlem Renaissance:"[2] "Who and What is 'Negro'?" If racial categories are thoroughly pernicious and divisive, then it would seem that it is not morally permissible to consciously and intentionally perpetuate belief in or identification with those categories. Alternatively, consequentialist justifications may be given for qualified invocation of racial categories where that is serviceable to the realization of moral outcomes.

Many Harlem Renaissance figures, including Alain Locke, Zora Neale Hurston, George Schuyler, Countee Cullen, and Sterling Brown, were skeptical about the ethical propriety of racially demarcated art. African American art and literature was, in the view of some scholars, a subset of American national art and literature. One worry is that the desire to treat African American art as segregated from national art and literature fostered the potential marginalization of the genre.[3] People racialized as Black were not well known or accurately understood either to themselves or the larger racist culture. This results in a twofold failure, first, of racialized Black artists to see themselves as contributing to American national art, and second the failure of racialized white American artists and audiences to understand African American art as part of the broader culture. The practical entailment of these combined failures is that African American art is seen as separate and a special province for racialized Black artists alone. A further consequence of this separation, according to Locke, is the designation of African American art as inferior to that of the cultural mainstream, and the subsequent relegation of the artists who produced it and their works themselves to artistic ghettos of special, provincial, and chauvinistic group interest.

Locke, for example, appreciated that racialized Black artists created art against a sociocultural backdrop of exclusion and aesthetic derision. (See also Clavel-Vázquez, this volume.) Arguably, this motivated the desire to represent their work and art as characteristically distinct and superior to aesthetic representations of racialized Black people and their experiences by others, and even to claim, in some cases, that their work and art were products of a separate and unique culture. Reasonable though this perspective may be, Locke and Schuyler worried that this kind of move invited the racist counter assertion by the dominant group of the propriety of marginalizing those artists and their work. This could be done either by claiming that the artists themselves agree that the work is separate, or that by instantiating different technical elements, and culture specific themes and idioms, the work was not a part of mainstream American culture. This says nothing of course about the indefensible pernicious position of racialized whites who sought to exclude the art from the mainstream American canon because it was racialized as Black or African, by extension. This also creates a circumstance in which it is easier to segregate racialized Black artistic contributions and circumscribe its full

---

[2] See Locke (1942).
[3] See, for example, Locke (1939) and Schuyler (1926).

aesthetic potential. Because it is not recognized as American art, it can be marginalized, subjugated, and relegated to an aesthetic ghetto.

Situating African American art as a culturally distinct phenomenon was understandable against the backdrop of a white supremacist culture. Yet given the consequences outlined by Locke and others, normative questions arise not only of the practical efficacy of such a move, but its moral justifiability. If explicit invocations of race have detrimental consequences for the very racialized populations made victim by racism, then it would seem that such invocations are not warranted. However, ethical dictates against the use of race by negatively racialized groups seems to place an additional and indefensible burden on those populations. Racialized Black people are thus twice victimized, once as the targets of negative racialization, and then again in being handicapped in the range of morally permissible responses to that racialization.

For Locke, much of the work of New Negro artists had ethical consequences—counteracting racist beliefs, affirming autonomy, respecting persons as such. However, he did not believe that ethical considerations underwrote the artistic enterprise, nor did he see the ethical implications of the artists' works as their primary motivation or mode of assessment. Locke observed that though African American artists were engaged in a universal human endeavor of creative expression, a significant aspect of that endeavor is racial. Locke counts the direct representation of the "characteristic idioms of thought, feeling and speech" (Locke 2012, 69) of folklife and folk types among the various modes of racial artistic expression. Yet there are subtler forms of African American expression that capture a race temperament; the "tempo and moods of Negro life" (Locke 2012, 69). Another form of expression is that which contends that there is a separate historical African American culture and tradition, "a racialist trend that is the equivalent of a nationalist background and spirit" (Locke 2012, 69). Yet another form is personal expression where racial situations elicit a "spiritual reaction" and embody a "particular philosophy of life" (Locke 2012, 69). Then there is the poetry that directly expresses a group sense and experiences common to it, either as a form of protest, advocacy, or group propaganda. Although Locke perceives African American art to be characteristically unique, this distinctness is a matter of degree and flavor. As the longest standing minority literary tradition in the United States, he contends that African American literature has coalesced with the larger national literature to produce a uniquely American amalgamation.

In "The Negro-Art Hokum" (1926), Schuyler agrees, in part, with Locke's position with one key distinction. Whereas Locke argues that there is a racially distinct "Negro art," Schuyler says there is no such thing existing in America. He writes, "Negro art there has been, is, and will be among the numerous black nations of Africa; but to suggest the possibility of any such development among the ten million colored people in this republic is self-evident foolishness" (Schuyler 1926, 1219). In Schuyler's view, the forces that shape the character and temper of aesthetic contributions by racialized populations are primarily national, economic, and political. For Schuyler, the assertion of racial distinctiveness is a reactionist stance to the immoral imposition of racialization. He points out that the Harlem Renaissance works taken to be racially representative and expressive of the racialized Black soul and character are in fact alien to many African cultures and nationalities. Hence, they could not be representative or characteristic of the entire race. The lacuna in Schuyler's argument, with which Locke would agree, is that race cuts across culture in many instances, with most putative racialized populations being composed of multiple ethnicities or cultures.

Schuyler does not deny that African descendants in the United States have produced notable artistic contributions. He is quick to point out that they have been assisted in those endeavors by the contributions of racialized white Americans. Here, again, is a point that he shares with Locke, and one that raises interesting normative questions about cultural appropriation. The spirituals, ragtime, jazz, and blues rhythm inflected poetry (e.g., Vachel Lindsey) are all artistic contributions putatively attributed to Negro aesthetic genius that have definite influences of European culture if not outright participation by racialized white artists.

Schuyler is adamant in denying that the art of diasporic African descendant peoples, the Harlem Renaissance, or any art produced by a subset of an ostensibly racial population is representative of the race as such. Yet in making these denials, Schuyler is committed to the belief that art can be nationally representative. For Schuyler, the question of whether or not to adhere to and promote ideas of racialized art is an ethical one. He believed that upholding the idea of racial difference, ultimately, upholds the practice of racism. He offers a brief survey of African descendant artists from his contemporary Harlem Renaissance writers and artists such as Henry Ossawa Tanner, to historical figures like Alexander Dumas. He claims that in every case, these artists fit squarely within the national aesthetic vogue that prevailed in their day. Schuyler contends that African descendant peoples in the United States, though presumably racially different from European descendant Americans, do not differ in how they are influenced by and respond to prevailing economic, political, and social conditions within the country. More than that, he maintains that racialized white and Black Americans alike are subject to the same set of economic, political, and social conditions. This, of course, was a significant point of departure between Schuyler and Locke.

A question that arises when considering Schuyler's view is why national representation is possible where racial representation is not? Locke, for instance, claimed that racial consciousness and identification could be stronger than patriotism and national identification, and within certain constraints neither was of necessity morally objectionable. If art must speak for an entire racialized population to be characteristic of a racialized group, then it would seem that to be nationally representative, art must speak for the nation writ large. But this may be as difficult for an artist to achieve as it would be to speak for an entire racialized group, which Schuyler believed was a morally bankrupt conclusion or expectation.

This is further complicated by Schuyler's contention that regionally representative art exists. He gives as examples Appalachian and Dalmation song and dance, the Charleston, blues, and so on. Schuyler defends his assimilationist and integrationist positions against critics by illustrating how, from his perspective, African Americans created and popularized spirituals, work songs, blues, and "rag-time known as jazz"

(Schuyler 1926, 1219). Such cultural creations cannot and should not be presumed "racial" any more than "the music and dancing of the Appalachian highlanders or the Dalmation peasantry are expressive or characteristic of the Caucasian race" (Schuyler 1926, 1219). Similar to Locke's thinking, Schuyler says that African Americans are American and participate within broadly cultural contexts so that anything they produce is, by default, American and should be examined and understood from within an American context. Belaboring perceived "racial" differences in art results in the idea that "there are fundamental, eternal, and inescapable differences" (Schuyler 1926, 1221) between racialized white and Black Americans, insisting on "racial" difference results in the upholding of racist ideas and racism. W. E. B. Du Bois and Langston Hughes replied to Schuyler's essay with their own essays, blueprinting their ethical positions related to creating and recognizing racialized art as necessarily racial.

In "Criteria of Negro Art" (1926), Du Bois espouses his ideas about the distinctive artistic traditions and cultural expressions of racialized Black people, and what he thought was the racialized Black artist's moral obligation to create identifiably racial art. (See also Clavel-Vázquez, this volume.) As a commentary on the significance and historical importance of the Harlem Renaissance, Du Bois's essay rejects the assimilationist position of Schuyler. Du Bois emphasizes the racialized aspects of music and folklore as reflecting the spiritual aspirations of racialized Black folk.

Du Bois contends that all art is propaganda. This is not intended as a diminutive statement. In his view, the pertinent ethical question is not whether a particular aesthetic work is propagandistic or not, but whether it exists in consequence of an artist having the freedom to express the aspirations of a people. He testified to the violence of racism and encouraged other racialized Black artists to use their art as weapons against colonialism, racism, capitalism, and the like. Du Bois seems at times simply to presuppose what for Schuyler is a point of contention that is, that art is racially expressive. Du Bois observes, "Just as soon as true art emerges; just as soon as the Black artist appears, someone touches the race on the shoulder and says, 'He did that because he was an American, not because he was a Negro'" (Du Bois 1926, 777). Thus, Du Bois problematizes Schuyler's contention that African American art is just American art. Whereas Schuyler was lambasted for his assimilationist and integrationist inclinations, Du Bois argued for integration and against assimilation: "We want to be Americans, full-fledged Americans, with all the rights of other American citizens. But is that all? Do we want simply to be Americans" (1926, 772). The answer is no.

Pace Schuyler, Du Bois is attuned to a particular way that racism functions in the estimation and reception of artwork by racialized artists. Earlier in the essay he remarks that racism clouded the American public's recognition of Roland Hayes as a talented vocalist until he received critical acclaim from European audiences. Racism functions here not only to unethically deny artistic freedom and recognition to racialized Black artists but, as Du Bois further imagines it, engenders cries of "he was born here; he was trained here; he is not a Negro—What is a Negro anyhow? He is just human; it is the kind of thing you ought to expect" (Du Bois 1926, 772). On Du Bois's understanding of race at the time, particularly his contention that there are "racial gifts," one ethical dimension that ought not to be missed or underplayed is the harm to racial groups as such. Racism then in such instances functions as a kind of erasure when a recognized talent is deemed to be rac*eless*, which is often conflated with whiteness, in an otherwise racialized context.

There is the further issue of the normalization of racialized whiteness to which Hughes is attuned. Implicit in the perspective of Du Bois's imagined interlocutor is the view that to be human is to be white. Hence, as Hughes will observe, claims by African American poets to be seen simply *as poets* are implicitly appeals to be viewed in terms of white normality. Racialized white Americans would, upon European acceptance, recognize Roland Hayes as a talented *American* singer, but not as a talented *African* American vocalist. Consider further the significance of the difference between Du Bois's fictional racialized white American's answer to the query: "What is a Negro anyhow?" and Locke's answer to the query: "Who and What is 'Negro'?"

The second article penned in response to Schuyler was Hughes's "The Negro Artist and the Racial Mountain" (1926). For Hughes, racialized art is a cultural output of the masses, as opposed to middle- and upper-class Victorian elites. African American culture is replete with nascent aesthetic material—language, spirituals, jazz, blues, film, and theater—suitable for novel idioms. The "bellowing voice of Bessie Smith" (Hughes 1926, 1324), the dramatic performances of Paul Robeson, and the visual compositions of Aaron Douglass are evidence of the kind of racial expression Hughes champions. Hughes claims that African American artists are confronted with a "racial mountain." African American artists must either accept the imposition of racialized whiteness, or scale the mountain in the hope of finding culturally distinct standards of beauty, appropriateness, values, and beliefs in their own communities and experiences as racialized Black people in the United States.

Hughes takes a psychologically insightful and thoroughly critical posture toward Schuyler's contention that racialized Black artists are, in point of fact, American artists. His criticism is twofold and entails, in part, an agreement with Schuyler concerning the predicament of racialized Black people in the United States. Hughes interprets the racelessness Schuyler promotes as indicative of one's subconscious desire "to be white" (Hughes 1926, 1321). First, he contends that the social pressure exerted by externalized and internalized white supremacy engendered beliefs about the normalcy of racialized whiteness and pathology of racialized Blackness leading, Hughes contends, to the subconscious desire to achieve a level of racialized whiteness in order to find acceptance as an artist. A consequence of this is the unwillingness or inability to see the richness of African American culture as a source of beauty and prime material for novel forms of creative expression. Second, Hughes contends, similarly to Du Bois, that American racism imposes normalized "white" standards of beauty, values, and beliefs on African American artists. Hughes views the reception of racialized white audiences of African American aesthetic contributions as a kind of bribe, one in which recognition, professional accolades, and profit are bestowed in exchange for renouncing any claims to cultural or racial distinctiveness.

AMERICAN INTEGRATIONISM

In 1946, approximately thirty-two years after his request for a course on race and race relations was rejected, Locke wrote an essay titled "The Negro Minority in American Literature." Locke contends that a more enlightened pedagogical approach to minority literatures would add to curricula "the integrated consideration of the minority literature with the main stem of the literature of the majority" (Locke 1946, 315). He says that racialized Black American literature is, simply put, American literature and should be taught within courses centered on American literature. The question of an integrated view of African American literature and culture, or any minority literature and culture, is salient and distinct from that of racialized art because the extent to which it is achieved constitutes a method of testing the erosion of racism in American society. If the impediments to such a view are various forms of racism and discriminatory practices and beliefs, then the degree to which a pluralistic and integrative view is attained would seem to be an indication of the lessening of those very practices and beliefs. Reflective of the changing same, contemporary writers still write within the integrationist tradition.

Processes of integration and assimilation do not necessarily track popular beliefs regarding the incorporation of a minority culture into the cultural mainstream. Locke argued that racialized Black Americans were in fact an integral part of the national and cultural development, despite contrary chauvinistic and provincial assertions. Locke poignantly observed that racialized Black Americans have had a profound impact on the national culture, and been among the avant-garde of cultural innovation, despite the persistent refusal of racialized white Americans to recognize this fact. Failure to recognize states of affairs does not negate their existence. American national culture is thoroughly infused with the humor, mood, language, and temperament of African American culture.

The failure of recognition, Locke argued, is due to the endemic nature of American racism. African American contributions to mainstream American culture have been denied because the racial creeds and practices of the United States have made possible the wholesale denial of that contribution. Color, and putative biological racial categorization of European descendant immigrants to the United States, have not been the persistent bulwark to assimilative integration into American society that African descent has been. But Locke presciently observes that politically motivated racial beliefs are not a failsafe against the underlying social and cultural mechanisms that account for exchanges between cultures.

But the question of assimilation of African American culture into mainstream American culture is distinct from the notion of an integrated view of American art and literature. Integration should not be misinterpreted as assimilation, though some integrationists believe in assimilation. As Locke points out in his essay, most integrationists think that viewing racialized American art as American art still requires methodological frameworks that take historical, social, cultural, economic, and political contexts into consideration for productive conversations regarding the literature.

Three approaches to interpreting minority group literature suggest themselves. First, as a representation of the minority mindset toward itself and the broader culture. Second, as a reflection of the majority's understanding of, and attitude toward, the minority. Third, the position that Locke advocated, as a lens through which to understand minority-majority interactions and their alterations over time. It is worth noting that these interpretative approaches are not mutually exclusive, neither are they necessarily at odds with approaches that interpret minority literatures as separate and distinct. The difference is a matter of emphasis and focus and reflects an understanding that what is commonly held to constitute a given body of literature, is as much a consequence of our pedagogical and interpretive practices, as it is an assessment of a wide range of literary contributions. Locke suggests two practical applications of the integrative view for use in teaching minority literature and more broadly. First is the inclusion in general anthologies and collections, as well as in course syllabi, the works of nonracialized white artists. This, for Locke, would suggest the use of more "objective criteria" for understanding national literature. Second is the interpretation of African American and other minority literatures as representative of regional or national art and literature, rather than as racially expressive, even though it may be that as well. This would likely involve the use of "common cultural denominators" that put such aesthetic contributions in proper perspective. Perhaps by painting African American art as solely separate, distinct, and "Black," African American artists were unintentionally reifying the underpinnings of racist discourse that insists on writing "Otherness" onto racialized Black people and oppresses them based on these alleged differences, which signify inferiority. While some integrationists write against the labeling of "Blackness" and distinctiveness in art, others maintain that there are indeed differences between different forms of racialized American art. In other words, there is not just one or even two ways to be an integrationist.

CULTURAL "BLACKNESS"

During and after the Harlem Renaissance, many participants and critics attempted to find and make correlations between African American art and cultural remnants from Africa. In "One Phase of American Literature" (1892), Anna Julia Cooper writes, "A race that has produced for America the only folk-lore and folk-songs of native growth, a race which has grown the most original and unique assemblage of fable and myth to be found on the continent, a race which has suggested and inspired . . . the outside world" (Cooper 2007, 171). Prominent anthropologist and writer, Zora Neale Hurston and her books, like *Mules and Men* (1935) and *Folklore, Memoirs and Other Writings* (1995), were uplifted as proof positive that folklore and folk songs emanate from African American culture and emphasize linkages between "Black" America and Africa. Artists like

Hughes, Aaron Douglas and Hurston were increasingly inspired to create art that incorporated and centered the folk.

Additionally, the Négritude movement, an international movement during the 1930s that was aimed toward cultivating "Black consciousness," edged American artists even closer toward recognizing and embracing their African heritage, which was deeply connected with elevating the folk in the public's imagination. The Négritude movement and Harlem Renaissance coinformed each other and inspired artists to (re)connect with their African heritage and history. Marcus Garvey, Hurston, Paul Robeson, Douglas, Weldon Johnson, William Grant Still, and Claude McKay, for example, focused on, theorized about, imagined, and created art that incorporated aspects closely related to the folk: spirituals, folklore, ragtime, jazz, blues, and what was labeled African American English or "Black" English. Some critics have dubbed these artistic happenings "the vernacular tradition" (e.g., spirituals, secular rhymes and songs, ballads, work songs, blues, folktales).

From within and extending beyond the vernacular tradition, jazz and blues motifs and themes appear regularly in the poetry of the Harlem Renaissance. Read aloud, many Harlem Renaissance poems convey the rhythm and cadence of racialized Black musical forms of the day. This is especially noteworthy when one considers that these musical forms are among the few native forms of American musical expression. By invoking these motifs and themes New Negro artists were able to simultaneously assert the originality of Afrodescendant contributions to American art, and elevate unique forms of racialized Black expression to the domain of formal art. Harlem Renaissance artists sought to link contemporary music of the Negro with other genres of artistic production through works like Hughes's "Song for Billie Holiday," "Weary Blues," "Jazzonia," "Danse Africaine," "Jazz Band in a Parisian Cabaret," "Homesick Blues," and "Dream Boogie," or Sterling Brown's "Memphis Blues," "Ma Rainey," and "Cabaret," or Grant Still's collaboration "And They Lynched Him on a Tree." This stemmed in part from an effort to infuse African American creativity with folk elements.

This dependence on the motifs and themes of folk expression was not limited to poetry. In prose, the likes of Weldon Johnson featured the performance of Ragtime by his protagonist in *Autobiography of an Ex-Colored Man* (1912). Nella Larsen's protagonist in *Quicksand* (1928) frequented bars, lounges, and parties where blues and jazz played. Walter White's protagonist in *Flight* (1926) went to bars, lounges, and parties, too, where racialized Black music played. She and her father frequently eavesdropped on neighbors singing spirituals and are depicted as experiencing deep and meaningful rejuvenation from hearing the songs. Hurston was commissioned to record blues singers and other folk artists in Florida. Her recordings, including a recording of herself, lends to an often obscured history of blues in Florida. Jazz and blues scenes were frequent themes in the paintings of the period, like Douglas's "Songs of the Towers" (1934). Jazz and blues themes were an integral part of "Shuffle Along," a Broadway performance largely held to have given early energy to the Harlem Renaissance movement.

Jazz and blues also impacted the fashion of the period, which was prominently featured by visual artists. James Van Der Zee's *Garveyite Family, Harlem* (1924) chronicled life and fashion in Harlem. The syncopated rhythms and improvisation in blues music influenced various art forms and led to musical innovation. Duke Ellington, Ma Rainey, Ella Fitzgerald, Louis Armstrong, Bessie Smith, and Billie Holiday popularized blues and jazz. Pianist James P. Johnson and Smith popularized a new way of playing the piano called the "Harlem Stride" style in their song "Backwater Blues," indicating the expansiveness of the impact blues and jazz had on its own medium and on theater, literature, and visual art.

THE TRAGIC MULATTO/A & PASSING

During the Harlem Renaissance, the so-called mulatto/a, as seen in Victor Séjour's *Le Mulâtre* (1837), Harriet Wilson's early iteration in *Our Nig* (1859), and Frances E. W. Harper's *Iola Leroy, or Shadows Uplifted* (1892), continued to proliferate in American art and haunt imaginations. The "tragic mulatto/a" is a stereotypical, fictional, "biracial" character that emerged in African American literature during the late nineteenth century and remains a character trope used in contemporary African American literature. Intertwined then with the "mulatto/a" is the idea of "passing" and what have been labeled "passing novels."

Racial passing is when a person of a particular race is perceived or accepted to be of a different race. "Mulattoes" are, more often than not, described, again, stereotypically as appearing near-white, the phenotype of the mulatto/a often conflicts with their revealed inner "Blackness" and reflects their fated tragic ending. They are often interpreted as tragic not only because the racialized white society rejects them after discovering their "Blackness" but also because "Black" communities (both fictional and literal) view them as the writer's attempt to appease a racialized white readership or as a rejection of "Blackness" and an elevation of "whiteness" and so-called white ideals. Hence, the figure of the mulatto/a emphasizes many of the underlying philosophical issues in the Harlem Renaissance. Through an examination of the mulatto/a trope one can further investigate the questions of racialized art; the effects of racism on African American literature and art; the integrative view of African American art and literature, and many other subthemes germane to the Harlem Renaissance.

Scholars like Cherene Sherrard-Johnson explain that the tragic mulatto/a highlights a gap between the ideology of the one-drop rule and integration. This also tracks observations made by Locke concerning the shifts in social attitude present in white literature from successive times leading up to and including the Harlem Renaissance. Locke observed that the mulatta character was present in Southern racialized white American literature, but that the onset of Northern criticism of the hypocrisy of having intimate relations with the very persons one held in bondage had a chastening effect on Southern racialized white literary production. This manifests the second of two psychological tendencies he observes over the course of American literary history of authors seeking to avoid identification with stereotypical roles and portrayals of racialized Black characters that failed to jive with the social conscience of the time.

People feared "racial mixing" that was no longer founded and controlled by enslavement or laws, not just regarding miscegenation but in terms of integration and assimilation. The "mulatto/a" reflects the literal and figurative "interracial" mixing that society had to, by necessity, work through and accept. Interestingly, many "mulatto/a" figurations were created to counter negative depictions of both "Black" people and "biracial" people. Such interpretations diminish the oppression and conflict these characters experience, interpreting them as simply appeals to a racialized "white" audience supports the discourse of colorism, which operates both ways, and silences the various forms of oppression that exist both within and without of racialized "Black" communities, which writers like Larsen, Hurston, Weldon Johnson, and others recognized and resisted. Contemporary literary critics have argued that the "mulatta," has two primary functions: as a vehicle for an exploration of the relationship between the races and, at the same time, an expression of the relationship between the races. Such an understanding emphasizes "interraciality" and upholds a "Black" and "white" racial binary that the "mulatto/a" character trope is intended to interrogate and subvert. Many contemporary critics fail to see the possibility of interpreting the biracial or transracial characters as antitheses of race itself, as the ultimate undoing of racism.

Locke understood the mulatto/a trope, and the phenomenon of passing, "as a sort of internal projection of the outside prejudice of the majority" (Locke 2012, 63–64). He claims that "the fact that North American racial prejudice makes no difference in treatment between blacks and mulattos" is evidence of the artificiality of color distinctions (Locke 2012, 64). Locke is here attuned to the importance of critically assessing the ways in which racism can naturalize and reify racial conceptions. Importantly, there is nothing unique about the depiction of mulatto/a characters by "biracial" authors compared to "nonbiracial" Black authors, other than the frequency with which the work of the former contains mulatto/a characters. The vast majority of these depictions of the "mulatto" were stereotypical, even as many artists worked against stereotypical characterizations. A survey of a few writers and artists and their characterization of the "tragic mulatto/a" provides further insight into the debates about art and ethics that artists and critics alike grappled with before, during, and after the Harlem Renaissance.

Writer after writer explored the psychological, cultural, and social trauma of American racism through the trope of the mulatto. In *Quicksand* (1928) and *Passing* (1929), Larsen explores "intraracial," "interracial," and cross-cultural themes. In "Mulatto" (1925), Hughes illuminates the ironic implications of "miscegenation," calculating whiteness, and race ideology, broadly speaking. He would return to the trope in the realm of theater with *Mulatto: A Play of the Deep South* (1935) and "Father and Son" (1934), a short story. Oscar Devereaux Micheaux wrote and produced what are now lost films titled *The Virgin of the Seminole* (1922) and *The House Behind the Cedars* (1927), the latter inspired by Charles Chestnutt's book *The House Behind the Cedars* (1900), indicating the synergy that existed between the literary and visual arts. Richard Bruce Nugent, a contributor to Locke's anthology *The New Negro* and a writer and visual artist, created *Drawings for Mulattoes Number 1–4* (1927–1928). *Drawings for Mulattoes Number 2* was an illustration for Charles S. Johnson's anthology *Ebony and Topaz* (1927). The interconnection between the various types of art, which included mixed media, during the Harlem Renaissance influenced artists with varying views of race and race consciousness to create art that embodied their philosophies of race. The likes of Larsen, Hughes, Micheaux, and Nugent counter notions of "racial uplift," "race," and "race pride" by highlighting, through their characterization of "mulattoes," the quicksands caused by concepts of and demands for representation, authenticity, and reconstruction, especially as it pertains to racialized groups of people. Paradoxically, the same artists created art that implicitly and explicitly upholds the normative modes of racialization and interpretations of racialized art. But much of the literature from the Harlem Renaissance reveals more complicated philosophies of race that are easy to miss under the constraints of racialization, which continues to be a privileged way to consume such art and artists.

FUTURE INTERPRETATIONS

Traditionally, African American literature has been presupposed and expected to always be about race and racism either with "realistic" portrayals of what it means to be racialized within a racist society or with more complex portrayals of racialized Black people. Implicit in this assumption is the normative judgment that racialized Black artists have a moral obligation to represent the race, and champion a racialized conception of African American art. Also implicit in this assumption is that the primary ethical responsibility of depicting and tending to racism falls on racialized Black people, the people most negatively and violently impacted by the very system presumed to inform their art. Consequently, the Harlem Renaissance is often mistakenly understood exclusively along racialized lines.

Although many scholars examine and identify art from this period as that which racialized Black writers and artists created, people generally understood to be outside the bounds of "Blackness" also participated in discourses regarding racialization and racialized art. Undoubtedly the existence of such figures contributed to the intense debates of the movement and the continuation of such discussions thereafter. Importantly, the philosophical underpinnings of the marginalized voices were mostly overlooked or ignored, having been misidentified as "anti-Black" writings and thereby unethically positioned. These same philosophies (i.e., the likes of Schuyler, writers of "passing" narratives, and assimilationists or integrationists) are more accurately identified as "anti-racialized" writings or even anti-racist art. It was at once a movement and anti-movement because it encouraged and necessitated a push and pull dialogue about what it means to be racialized in America; what it means to be a racialized Black artist; what racialized Black art does or should do for racialized people; and what ethical obligation racialized Black artists have to their larger societies, if any.

Often missed is the fact that these contentious issues were always already bound up with normative ethical considerations, such that in many cases where one came down on these issues often presupposed certain ethical commitments or constituted a rejection of putative moral obligations. But the art and literature produced during the period extends far beyond the bounds of racialization and racism. No pretense is made herein to the single correct interpretation of the Harlem Renaissance, the existence and role of racialized art, or the ethical obligations of racialized Black artists.

See also: Taylor, Clavel-Vázquez, Nguyen and Strohl, this volume

References

Cooper, Anna Julia. [1892] 2007. "One Phase of American Literature." *The New Negro: Readings on Race, Representation, and African American Culture, 1892–1938*, edited by Henry Louis Gates Jr. and Gene Jarrett, 157–172. Princeton, NJ: Princeton University Press.

Du Bois, W. E. B. 1926. "Criteria of Negro Art." WEB Du Bois, http://www.webdubois.org/dbCriteriaNArt.html (accessed February 12, 2023).

Fuller, Hoyt. 1976. "From a Decade of Triumph to the Next Stage: Where We Were: Where We Must Go." Unpublished keynote address given at the 1976 Afro-American Writers Conference at Howard University, Washington, DC.

Gayle, Addison. 1970. "The Harlem Renaissance: towards a Black Aesthetic." *Midcontinent American Studies Journal* 11, no. 2: 78–87.

Hughes, Langston. 1926. "The Negro Artist and the Racial Mountain." Poetry Foundation, https://www.poetryfoundation.org/articles/69395/the-negro-artist-and-the-racial-mountain (accessed February 10, 2023).

Hurston, Zora Neale. 1995. *Folklore, Memoirs, and Other Writings*. Edited by Cheryl A. Wall. New York: The Library of America.

Locke, Alain. 2012. "The Message of the Negro Poets." In *The Works of Alain Locke*, edited by Charles Molesworth, 68–78. New York: Oxford University Press.

Locke, Alain. 1939. "The Negro's Contribution to American Culture." *Journal of Negro Education* 8, no. 3: 521–529.

Locke, Alain. 1942. "Who and What Is 'Negro'?" In *The Philosophy of Alain Locke: Harlem Renaissance and Beyond*, edited by Leonard Harris, 209–228. Philadelphia: Temple University Press.

Locke, Alain. 1946. "The Negro Minority in American Literature." *The English Journal* 35, no. 6: 315–20.

Schuyler, George. 1926. "The Negro-Art Hokum." In *The Norton Anthology of African American Literature Third Ed.*, *Vol. 1*, edited by Henry Louis Gates Jr. and Valerie A. Smith, 1219–1222. New York: Norton.

CHAPTER 11

EVOLUTION OF ART AND MORAL CONCERNS IN NEW CHINA

From Mao Zedong's Yenan Talks to Xi Jinping's Speech on Artistic Practice

EVA KIT WAH MAN

BACKGROUND: THE YENAN FORUM ON LITERATURE AND ART IN CHINA IN 1942

MAO Zedong hosted three meetings in the city of Yenan in May 1942 as part of the *Yenan Rectification Movement* (1942–1944) launched by the Chinese Communist Party (CCP), which controlled this city in northern Shaanxi at the time. The meetings later became commonly known as the *Yenan Forum on Literature and Art*.

Over one hundred leading figures in literature and the arts attended the Forum, many of whom took the floor to speak, and Mao delivered the introductory and concluding speeches. The attendees included Ding Ling, a modern revolutionary writer; He Qifang, a modern poet, essayist, and literary critic who taught at the Lu Xun Academy of Fine Arts in Yenan; and Ouyang Shanzun (1914–2009), a founding father of modern Chinese drama. Ouyang began his career in the Shanghai Save-the-Nation Troupe after the start of the War of Resistance against Japanese Aggression before relocating to Yenan, which was a revolutionary base of the CCP at the time. There, he directed numerous revolutionary dramas and received letters of praise from Mao (*China Pictorial* 2015). Mao organized the Yenan Forum to address the numerous debates and disagreements between artists and literary writers of the CCP. Some argued for the primacy of art over politics, while others asserted that art should be independent of Marxism-Leninism to which the CCP referred, to ensure freedom of individual expression positions. Others stated that art should serve politics by revealing political incorrectness and social "darkness" and by presenting issues and characters to be criticized, praised, and confirmed, and some advocated the ironic style of the literary master Lu Xun.

Mao invited these prominent figures to the Forum to exchange views regarding artists' positions in society, art strategies, stylistic issues, readers' issues, and subject matter. Most of the participants were from the Lu Xun Academy, while others worked in CCP propaganda and cultural affairs. The three meetings of the Forum were held in 1942 on May 2, 16, and 23, and their details and the content continue to be discussed and interpreted, with the focus mainly on how Mao reacted to and reconciled the various positions and finally stated his own views on the future direction of art and literature in Communist China (Sun 2007).

Mao's introductory and concluding speeches addressed the five main problems that had been hotly debated by the party's literary and art circles: the obsession with expressing "darkness"; the production of works that were divorced from reality and the masses; debates over whether Marxism hindered literary and artistic creation; excessive tolerance of intellectual shortcomings; and the lack of solidarity among literature and art experts (*China Pictorial* 2015). Mao concluded that art and literature were for the people, and primarily for workers, peasants, and soldiers. Art should speak to the masses and be easily comprehended. Instead of being abstract and serving individual egos, art and literature should aim to change society by elevating the thoughts and appreciation levels of the people.

Before the Yenan Forum, Mao issued a policy statement in his article "On New Democracy" in 1940, addressing the culture and ideas of the proletariat. His championing of ideological unity through the CCP was later referred to as Maoism, as distinct from the Soviet-style Marxism–Leninism. Critics have concluded that Maoism was aimed at addressing the specifics of the Chinese Revolution, while Marxism-Leninism was intended to be universally applicable. Mao's contributions to Communist thought have been identified as his analysis of social class divisions, development of the revolutionary situation, establishing the party's theory of knowledge and strategy, method of party leadership in the revolutionary war, attitude toward the enemy, view of the people as a source of power, modern revisionism in socialist and imperialist countries, dialectical materialism, and so on (Nicola 2007).

Ellen Judd succinctly identifies the decisive aspect of the Yenan Talks as the linking of urban intellectuals and peasants to create an effective political force. Many intellectuals who had come to Yenan in the late 1930s attended the talks. Mao called upon them to move to the countryside to promote their mental transformation (Judd 1985, 377). The talks were gradually developed into a series of policy documents by cadre leaders over the following two to three years. Once implemented, these policies resulted in artists venturing into the countryside and visiting factories and front lines, where they created works based on their living experiences of their venturing that enhanced the popularity of their work among the masses. These creations included the populist opera *The White-Haired Girl*, which first performance was in Yenan in 1945, and novels such as *The Marriage of Young Blacky* and *Rhymes of Li Youcai*, addressed the moral support needed by the people during the Sino-Japanese war (1937–1945) and the revolution movements that follow. The spirit of Mao's Yenan Talks was said to have guided China's literary creativity and development for decades, and their effects persisted until well into the era of Xi Jinping.

Critics including Judd, note the influence of the Yenan period, during which the CCP won large-scale peasant support, and soon after that led to its political and military victories in 1947–1949. This success was not only the product of the oppressive Japanese occupation, but also a result of Mao's creative formulation of policies and organization methods. It directly followed the mass line policy of Marxism-Leninism in the beginning but has developed further its nationalistic fervors. Judd suggests that the sending of intellectuals to Yenan was the decisive move in linking urban intellectuals with peasants to create an effective political alliance (Judd 1985, 390). The Japanese occupation of large areas of China, including the entire seaboard, led to tremendous social, economic, political, and military changes, which had also become the basis for literary and artistic creativity.

Wylie notes that the theoretical path to Chinese socialism was confronted directly and explicitly after 1938 with the commitment of major Party leaders to Marxism-Leninism (Wylie 1980). Over the next few years, specific policies for art and literature were developed. In 1939, the CCP called for the absorption and training of larger numbers of intellectuals to create a proletarian intellectual order. Mao then directly addressed questions about a new democratic culture in his "On New Democracy" in 1940 with strong China fervors. Judd quotes Mao in fragments: "The anti-imperialist anti-feudal new democracy of the popular masses [is] led by the culture and thought of the proletariat. This kind of new democratic culture is national . . . National in form and new democratic in content, this is our new culture of today" (Mao 1940, 201–202; Judd 1985, 391). Mao emphasized the importance of cultural workers being closely connected to the masses and of delivering political messages rather than individual experimentation, for his beliefs that art should be nurtured in the real soil of living. These ideas soon spread from the Lu Xun Academy in Yenan to other border regions, even when many institutions of higher learning in the coastal cities fell under the Japanese control (Judd 1985, 392).

The Lu Xun Academy had been active in research and producing creative outputs in Yenan before the Yenan Talks, focusing on subjects such as the classics of Western drama (Judd 1985, 394). The rectification movement soon provided relatively clear and detailed guidelines to intellectuals and artists in the revolution about how to create "New Democratic" literature and art from local and national soils, and the political values of the arts recognized by the CCP. Judd suggests that the Yenan Talks can be viewed as the site of an important delivery of policy statements by Mao on the positions and functions of art and literature (Judd 1985, 3973). The first two talks included discussions and debates about the nature of art and literature, and participants who held Western modernist views were identified and denounced at the occasion.

In the final talk of the Forum, Mao stated that all artists should serve the masses creatively and create work intended for the masses. Popularization was key, and artists could learn from the masses by living and laboring with them via their venturing. The Yenan Talks are viewed as summarizing the basics of China's revolutionary literature and art movements. The three talks were later edited and published as the *Talks at the Yenan Forum on Literature and Art* (在延安文艺座谈会上的讲话), and they became the main reference and foundation of literature and art censorship in the new China. These had immediate effects on the form and content of Chinese music, performing arts, literature, films, visual arts, and design, demonstrating the dominant socialist spirit and approaches with new respects for folk and mass styles emerged.

The Yenan Talks have remained culturally relevant in recent times, with reports recalling the details of the members photographed, the setting, the weather and the environment, and Mao's gestures and reactions to the speakers (Sun 2007). It is as if the event was sacred, and the talks are like the manuscripts of a holy book that prescribed what artists should and should not do. Mao's views of art delivered at the Forum have been reinforced, as the anniversary of the Yenan Talks has been marked, and they are celebrated every five years (Melvin 2012).

ART AND POLITICS IN MAO'S SPEECHES AT THE YENAN TALKS

The Ministry of Culture announced a month of celebrations for the 70th anniversary of the Forum in 2012, in which the main art and literature political agenda set out by Mao in his lectures was reviewed. The main points included how artists were obliged to achieve an understanding of the lives of the people through living with them and reflecting their real lives in their work, and that popularizing art for the masses should be prioritized over concerns about artistic quality (Melvin 2012). One of the most renowned quotations from Mao's speeches at the Forum is "In the world today all culture, all literature and art belong to definite classes and are geared to definite political lines. There is in fact no such thing as art for art's sake, art that stands above classes or art that is detached from or independent of politics" (Mao 2004, 21).

Mao outlined the relationship between politics and art in the context of revolution, arguing that there were only contextual and pragmatic rather than absolute criteria for judging the value of art. Mao believed that art could transform reality via reflection (Sorace 2019). He stated:

> Although man's social life is the only source of literature and art and is incomparably livelier and richer in content, the people are not satisfied with life alone and demand literature and art as well. Why? Because, while both are beautiful, life as reflected in works of literature and art can and ought to be on a higher plane, more intense, more concentrated, more typical, nearer the ideal, and therefore more universal than actual everyday life. (Mao 2004, 16)

When everyday life is chaotic and complex, art can project a better version of the future. Mao pointed out that the masses did not need art to remind them of their daily experience of "hunger, cold, and oppression" but to depict the possibility of transcending their sufferings. In revolutionary terms, art should remind the masses of their own collective power and future (Sorace 2019). Thus, artwork should be "bright," positive, and progressive. At the talks, Mao discussed attitude in art:

> From one's standpoint there follow specific attitudes towards specific matters . . .
> With regard to the enemy, that is, Japanese imperialism and all the other enemies of
> the people, the task of revolutionary writers and artists is to expose their duplicity
> and cruelty and at the same time to point out the inevitability of their defeat . . . As for
> the masses of the people, their toil and their struggle, their army and their Party, we
> should certainly praise them. (Mao 2004, 2–3)

> Many petty-bourgeois writers have never discovered the bright side. Their works only
> expose the dark and are known as the "literature of exposure." Some of their works
> simply specialize in preaching pessimism and world-weariness. (Mao 2004, 27)

These attitudes remained central to the guidelines of artistic creativity in China today. The Yenan Talks reveal conflicts and disagreements about the purposes of art and artistic creativity within the Chinese Marxist circle in the 1940s, and Mao realized that he would need to address such issues at the Forum to ensure "rectification" (Fu 2015). The attitudes were closely correlated with the parallel strengthening of the CCP's power. Goldman notes that the talks focused more on the importance of the educational transformation of literary intellectuals than on the Russian Marxist literary theory that was circulating at the time. The Chinese Communists used moral persuasion and indoctrination against those who did not comply (Goldman 1967, 49). Fu points out the unconventional Marxist ideas found in the Yenan Talks and in the notion of culture as a powerful revolutionary tool. Examples include Mao's notions on the classist nature of Chinese and Western literature and art, and his references to both traditions. The implications were that art and literature should be integrated into the revolutionary movements and be subordinated to the Party. Thus it is important to transform the thoughts of artists and intellectuals through criticism and self-criticism, as suggested in the Yenan Talks. These had also become central to the resolution of cultural disagreements and contradictions (Fu 2015).

Fu reviews how the Yenan Forum was received and read in the West, and identifies three waves of development since its publication (Fu 2015). First was during the 1950s and 1960s, when Sinologists took a negative view based on social, political, and ideological critiques instead of any in-depth analyses of the text. Then came the second wave of criticism in the 1970s and 1980s, which followed Richard Nixon's 1972 visit to China. This brought about the "gradual normalization" of the Sino-Western relationship, which led to a shift in critical theory among Sinologists, who began to study Mao's texts of the Yenan Talks from the perspective of neo-Marxist literary theory, which considered central issues of modern and contemporary literature. The texts were thus read more seriously, leading to the discussions of Chinese Marxist literary theory, and they were related to the works of earlier Chinese Marxist critics such as Qu Qiubai. The third wave is within the context of globalization in China, during which Mao's talks were examined in English-language scholarship, when the attitudes and methods changed. Fu attributes this latest development to the advancement of market socialism and China's emergence in global markets, through which various discourses of knowledge about modernity and postmodernity are involved. He suggests that with the rise of critical theory in the English-speaking world, Mao's notions of cultural hegemony and the mediation between aesthetics and politics are reevaluated against the discourse of Western Marxist aesthetics and postcolonial theories (Fu 2015).

However, the dominant reading of the Yenan Talks was of Mao's authoritarian sense of control and emphasis on social function over individual expression or artistic exploration. Critic Liu Kang provides a deeper level of the reading, arguing that the national form played a major role by mediating Mao's interpretation of Marxism. Mao associated international Marxism with specific Chinese practices, thus resolving the tensions between modern urban intellectuals and rural peasants. The solutions came through the process of learning from intellectuals, who, by living with the masses, would take a stand for the proletarians. Liu suggests that popularization through a national form was not merely a process of aesthetic creation, but was first and foremost a process of political, ideological, and moral transformation by the urban intellectuals (Liu 2000, 90).

THE TEXTS AND THE CONTENT OUTLINE OF THE YENAN TALKS

Bonnie McDougall provides a very detailed account and reading of the text of the Yenan Talks. She has high regard for Mao's grasp of literary issues, the ways he remained close to traditional literature and saw no issue in merging traditional Chinese elite and popular cultures (McDougall 1980, 4). First, she notes the problem of the texts to adopt. They were first published in October 1942, and then in numerous other editions. Mao published a collection of his pre-1950 writings with drastic revisions, including the talks, after the establishment of the PRC in 1949, and they then appeared in a later edition of his collected works in the 1960s (McDougall 1980, 7). McDougall compares the pre- and post-1953 versions and finds that the revised text was not as clear-cut as the initial version, as the revisions indicate a wider audience of workers, soldiers, and peasants than the original, thus demonstrating considerations of the actual historical context, including the Cultural Revolution. She therefore suggests that the original version be referred to, also because the sources of Mao's remarks on literature and art may have been derived from the literary policies adopted in the Soviet Union at that time and thus drew on Leninism, which had been circulating in China since the 1920s. McDougall mentions Qu Qiubai's influences on Mao in particular (McDougall 1980, 8).

The Yenan Forum illustrated how Mao wanted to organize the loose collection of literary doctrines by declaring a clear and firm literary policy for the situation, thus uniting the whole country. The CCP was stationed at Yenan, which was at the time a remote north Shaanxi town from which the Communists could mobilize the peasants in guerrilla warfare against the Japanese. The nationalist spirit reached its peak, and as McDougall described, intellectuals visited from the cities to observe and participate in a type of social change that represented to them the only possible path to a vigorous and independent new China, one that would be free of the Japanese invasion and the corruption of the Nationalists (McDougall 1980, 10).

In his speeches, Mao discussed the nature and the origin of literature and art. He made strong appeals to traditional Chinese poetry, including the Confucian social functions of poetry, which involved changing, observing, uniting people, and criticizing society. McDougall clearly identifies the Confucian utilitarian approach to art and literature in Mao's words (McDougall 1980, 10). Mao covered five main topics in the first speech he delivered on May 2, 1942: positioning whom art and literary work should serve, the artist's attitude, the audience, the work, and the educational value of art and literature. Mao can be regarded as narrowing his focus to the basic and essential problem: the question of the audience. Mao's inclination toward realism in literature reflected his focus on the audience and how he regarded literary figures as social leaders (McDougall 1980, 14). Issues regarding the audience were discussed in both the first speech and the final speech, which was delivered three weeks later on May 23, 1942, and a development of his ideas is discernible. Art and literature had to serve the masses and were for the masses only, with no focus on the individual in the creative process. Artists had to be guided by the "budding forms of literature and art" within the masses through living and working with them, as all forms of art emerged from the basic nature of people's lives (McDougall 1980, 18).

While Mao was of the opinion that art and literature should be more organized, typical, ideal, and universal, he removed the emphasis on organization or technique in the later versions and replaced it with the idea of effectiveness through intensity, which could be read as more comprehensible to the masses (McDougall 1980, 20–21). In the original version, Mao stated that literature and art were not independent of politics, but in the later versions, he made this more specific, suggesting that art should not simply follow the political demands of class but should serve the masses and the revolution. In contrast to the approaches of Lenin and Marx, Mao imposed party discipline, regarding the arts as a matter of state policy and apparatus that remained, as McDougall notes, exclusive, binding, and universal. Thus, the art and literary works during Mao's time were viewed as stereotypical and black-and-white in character and storytelling, as typified by "revolutionary model operas" (McDougall 1980, 26).

Mao was more concerned with philosophical or ideological attitudes and political needs than the relationship between form and content. According to McDougall, Mao twice mentioned socialist/proletarian realism as the required literary style, although he had not clearly defined it (McDougall 1980, 29). In section 4 of Mao's first speech at the Forum, he emphasized developing a new mentality of resistance, self-reliance, self-sacrifice, generosity, and courage, and he asked the group to ensure that any romantic or moral elements were within this critical context, to defend against the harsh social realities (Mao 2014). McDougall further points out that Mao only conceded that artists and writers had talent in terms of their contribution to the masses, without any sense of their artistic superiority or freedom (McDougall 1980, 34).

In the fifth and the final sections, Mao summarized the previous literary debates in Yenan, stressing that a writer's work should be judged by its social effect (Mao 2004). This explains the success of the revolutionary opera *Bai Munu* (White-Haired Girl), which combined traditional narrative techniques and ballads with ballet. McDougall points out that after 1950, the Yenan Talks were referred to when justifying the application of Chinese classical tradition and adaptations of folk literature to the political and moral development of society, which led to a limited revival of the cultural modes of the May Fourth movement, particularly in literature (McDougall 1980, 38). The freedom that the CCP granted to art and literature after it became the ruling party did vary. After the 1950s, the policies derived from the Yenan Talks were relaxed, but they again represented the dominant guiding principles for creativity in the Cultural Revolution movement of the late 1960s. Revolutionary operas that had been previously produced that featured workers, peasants, and soldiers as the protagonists remained in production until Mao's death in 1976 (McDougall 1980, 40). The talks had varying practical effects after the 1970s, when Western modern and contemporary art influenced China through its open-up policies. The most intense censorship and persecution of individual artists and authors occurred after the Yenan Talks were widely circulated in China during the Cultural Revolution in the late 1960s to the mid-1970s.

THE YENAN SPEECHES: ART AND MORALITY IN CHINA AFTER MAO'S REGIME

The Gang of Four radicalized the Yenan Talks during the Cultural Revolution era in the 1960s, led to a new Party-sanctioned form of political art and revolutionary operas and the condemnation of the "bourgeois decadence" of the oppositional art camps, claiming that they were not serving the people. Only after Deng Xiaoping's condemnation of the Cultural Revolution in 1979 were the talks reassessed. As Mackerras points out, Mao's doctrine that literature and art were subordinate to politics became regarded as "incorrect" in 1982, but it was reaffirmed that art should reflect the reality of the lives of the workers and peasants (MacKerras 1983, 171). This restated the principle of artistic practices in China. Artists who aim to express themselves through art are expected to serve the masses as the audience of their work, particularly if projects are funded by the government.

The content of art and literature in China are still following the correct political morality and the guidance of the CCP. Arts and entertainment could not be too "dark" or superstitious; this guideline explains why the horror film genre has been so limited in China and ghosts and gore are not featured. Films should not be excessively satirical or mock public figures, and definitely not the police, soldiers, party members, or the government. Art must convey a "realistic" view of history, and any depiction of historical figures must emphasize their heroic qualities. Productions made for export must convey a positive sense of the Great China. Those works that involve ethnic populations, particularly those from border regions like Tibet, Xinjiang, and Mongolia, remain extremely sensitive. Art and entertainment aimed at children must be morally uplifting, or at least not viewed as negative. This direction was reinforced by Xi Jinping's policy on art and literature following the opening policy of Deng Xiaoping in the 1980s.

Xi Jinping's "Speech at the Forum on Literature and Art" in Beijing in 2014

On October 15, 2014, Xi Jinping gave his "Speech at the Forum on Literature and Art" in Beijing, which echoed Mao's agenda delivered at Yenan, but was appropriated and idealized to emphasize the development of a strong China. His speech was regarded as putting less emphasis on the historical revolution and Communism, but as encouraging artists to celebrate Party-sanctioned morality, cultural heritage, and nationalist sentiment (Sorace 2019). Xi stated that the main purpose of art was to infuse reality with optimism for the future: "If literature and art creation is only pure recording and description of the status quo, and the first-hand display of hideousness, there would be no eulogising of the light, not expression of ideals, no guidance of morality, and so it would be impossible to inspire the people to progress" (Xi 2014).

He also said that art must combine "a realist spirit" with "romantic feelings," "to shine light on real life, use the light to dispel darkness, use the beautiful and good to vanquish the ugly and the bad, let people see beauty, see hope, and see that their dreams are ahead" (Xi 2014). The text was published a year later in 2015, enriched by examples from art and literature in both the Chinese and the Western classics and with more detailed discussion.

In October 2015, new rules were issued days after the release of the full text of Xi's speech, in which he asked artists to put material returns aside and create works that embodied both artistic quality and political correctness. Xi said that "creating shoddy works is not only a kind of injury to the arts, but also a kind of injury to the moral life of society. Entertaining the simple sense organs will not equate to a happy spirit. The arts must win the people's approval, fancy but ineffectual work is not acceptable and egotistical self-promotion is not acceptable" (quoted in Canavas 2015). His office added more information and examples to his 2015 edition to present a conservative and patriotic view of the arts: "Our contemporary literature and art must ever more make patriotism into the main melody of literature and art creation, guide the people in establishing and upholding correct view of history, views of the nation, views of the country and views of culture, and strengthen the backbone and confidence of the Chinese people" (Xi 2015). Xi also claimed that the market value of the arts is secondary to social value, and he set rules to strengthen and improve the CCP's leadership of artistic practices in his speech.

This agenda deviated from Mao's historic Yenan Talks, in which Mao said that creative ambitions must first serve the people and the revolutionary clause. In addition, Xi's approach was informed by the "moral high ground," which differed from Mao's propaganda tactics in 1940s China (Sorace 2019). The moral high ground is undoubtedly a sign of patriotism. The same agenda was restated during Xi Jinping's speech at the Party's 19th Congress in October 2017. Xi followed Mao in his arguments against formalistic art and the mentality of "art for art's sake," though Xi recognized that the global art market was developing rapidly in China and that artifacts were becoming cultural commodities. (See Gal, "Formalism," this volume.) His priority was that art must contribute to the rejuvenation of the great Chinese nation. The critical function of art was to condemn anti-social or anti-Chinese phenomena. Xi used the term *meihao* to describe a "better life" in China, meaning that life is aesthetically pleasing and morally ordered. The duty of an artist is to produce visions of a good life, and the responsibility of the CCP is to create the socioeconomic conditions for its realization. Through the *meihao* principle, art can promote a positive image of the nation and address any negative connotations with strong patriotism. Josh Chin suggests that the essential point here is a potential halting of artistic creativity and practice, which can dictate a cultural world driven by popular tastes but that is in constant battle with the direction of the Communist Party (Chin 2015).

Xi's comments were noted when he delivered his speech in 2014. These included Xi's concerns about the quality of the new art and literature, as he commented that these works attained no "high peaks," and there were problems of plagiarism, imitation, stereotypes, and mechanistic production. Xi warned that literature and art would lose its direction when absorbed into the market economy (Xi 2014). In contrast to the subsequent rules and censorship he imposed, Xi, in this earlier speech, urged artists to hold high ideals, step with the times, and to innovate through the individuality of their art. He suggested that they should construct a vigorous, healthy, tranquil, and harmonious atmosphere, and advocated discussion between different viewpoints and schools of thought, and that styles, themes, forms, and methods should be fully developed (Xi 2014).

Xi proposed that art and ethics should focus on artistic virtue and should present beauty and virtue to the world, and that artists should strive to win the love of the people and embrace noble professional integrity while presenting a good social image. His speech echoed the ideas of Mao's Yenan Talks, which suggest that literature and art must reflect society through serving the people and Socialism by satisfying the spiritual and cultural needs of the people. He said that of the various ways of creating art, the most fundamental is "taking root among the people and taking root in life." His message about the "bright side" of art can be discerned in his earlier pronouncements, when he suggested that artists and authors should "use light to disperse darkness, use the beautiful and the good to vanquish the ugly and the evil, let the people see that beauty, hope and dreams are ahead" (Xi 2014). Xi was of the opinion that art should be aimed at integrating social and economic effects, and that ideological and artistic success would be well received in the market, when the logical relation between the two was not clarified.

Xi felt that literature and art could guide the people by strengthening their moral judgment, and that morals and moral awareness could be nurtured through art. As long as the Chinese nation pursues the moral plane of the true, the good, and the beautiful throughout, the nation will continue to be healthy and make progress (Xi 2014). Xi related contemporary creativity to Chinese traditional culture, which he claimed to be the spiritual lifeline of China and represented a firm foothold within increasing cultural globalism. He said, "We must integrate the conditions of the new age with inheriting and carrying forward China's excellent traditional culture, and inheriting and carrying forward the spirit of Chinese aesthetics" (Xi 2014). He viewed foreign culture as a resource that could benefit the Chinese through comprehensive study. Officials had added numerous Western and Chinese art titles and author names as examples to the 2015 version of Xi's speech. At this time, he appeared to respect the individual creative labor of literature and art workers:

> We must, through deepening reform, perfecting policies and completing mechanisms, create a vivid dimension for the incessant production of excellent works and emergence of talent. [We must] use historical, popular, artistic and aesthetic viewpoints to criticize and praise works, dare to seek truth from facts concerning artistic qualities and levels, dare to declare their stand with regard to all kinds of harmful literature and art works, phenomena and thinking trends, dare to make their position clear on great questions of right and wrong, speak the truth, speak reason, and create a conducive atmosphere for the launch of literature and art criticism. (Xi, 2014)

DIFFERENCES BETWEEN MAO ZEDONG AND XI JINPING REGARDING ART AND MORALITY

Chinese Marxist scholar Ma Yue concludes that Xi Jinping inherited and developed Mao's theory on literature and art (Ma 2018). His comparison between the Yenan Talks and Xi's talk on literature and art reveals that both adhered to the ideas of people holding principal positions in the country, advocating the leadership of the party and the guidance of Marxism. Both referred to traditional Chinese culture as the foundation of creativity. Xi, however, under the economic and social context of China in his era, developed new ideas, judgments, and requirements. The Yenan Talks took place during the new democratic revolution in the 1930s, when China faced battles with the Nationalists, the Sino-Japanese War and political revolution. Ma's reading is that the ideological fluctuation and debates meant that it was timely to define the roles of artists and the social functions of literary and artistic work at the Yenan period. The unity and alliance of the masses, writers, and artists were of vital importance, and no split or differences were to be tolerated. Xi's speech in 2014 was delivered when China was becoming more economically wealthy and at the time Xi was promoting the "China Dream" (Ma 2018). The Beijing Olympics of 2008 also signaled the "great rejuvenation" of the nation.

Xi's speech was delivered seventy-two years after the Yenan Talks. According to Ma, the so-called socialism with Chinese characteristics had entered into a new era, and the Chinese people had higher expectations of material and cultural life. However, rapid economic development and consumerism brought the need for artistic and cultural developments, and directions were provided to writers and artists regarding the value of literary and artistic work. Ma's reading of this new era stresses that writers and artists should not be distracted by material gain but should remain true to their original aspirations. They should create works that meet the needs of the people, carry forward the core values of socialism and enhance the cultural identity of the Chinese nation, as Xi stated clearly in his speech (Ma 2018).

Did Xi inherit Mao's literary and artistic thoughts? Ma admits that there were a few. The first being the common assumption that art and literature should serve the people. Artistic creativity was based on the understanding of the lives of the masses and aimed to reflect their broad social life (Ma 2018). These were emphasized and adhered to when the old social conflicts and contradictions of Mao's era were replaced by new economic changes and social developments. Second, there was the recognition that the needs of the people represented the fundamental values of art and literature. Third, art and literature were for the people, and so artists must love the people. Other commentators suggested that Xi did not stress the agenda of art as serving politics or the Party to the same extent as that of Mao. In the Yenan Talks, the virtues of art and literature lay with the politics of the proletariats and the masses, rather than the politics of an individual artist. Xi mentioned in his speech that the leadership of the Party guarantees the support and development of socialist arts and literature, and that writers and artists should hold strong political beliefs and have a keen political consciousness. Xi was also more alert to Western ideologies and urged Chinese artists to develop a nationalistic and cultural stance for the people.

In the Yenan Talks, Mao promoted the important position of literature and art as basic revolutionary causes, and regarded them as the tools and operation of ideological changes and political revolution. I agree with Ma's reading that Mao used art and literature to win the hearts of the people, to represent the national spirit, and to promote the victory of the democratic revolution. During Xi's era, they were important means of enhancing cultural confidence and realizing the China Dream of national rejuvenation with prosperity through market economics. They have also become important manifestations of the country's soft cultural power and comprehensive national strength. These factors continue to be directed at supporting China's current economic, political, and social development (Ma 2018).

Xi's further developments based on Mao's agenda for literature and art related more to social functions than artistic achievements. Mao was more concerned with the relationship between art and politics in the context of the revolutionary war and the people's liberation cause, and the antagonistic, oppositional approach and polarization were the attitudes that Mao advocated, as he concluded that literature was subordinated to politics. Xi wanted art and literature to reflect the times, and he thought that outstanding works should be produced to demonstrate the greatness of China and its people. According to Xi, the virtue of art is to illustrate the good lives people can attain, and to motivate them to achieve a better life. He cares very much about how people perceive China and wants to promote the *meihao* side of its culture (Xi 2014). Art was to represent socialist core values, therefore literary and artistic works should be realistic and effective in promoting what are regarded as the correct values and national views, which embody the sense of patriotism that he endorses. Truth, goodness, and beauty could be conveyed through art for the moral enhancement and education of the people, although the specifics of these general terms are not articulated clearly (Ma 2018).

Another point of comparison is the relation of art and literature to the masses or the people. Mao emphasized the understanding of the ideological, emotional, and real lives of the subjects, implying that the work had to be comprehensible and for the people. Xi also stresses serving the people and Socialism by grasping what people would want to read and appreciate, which could change along with their living standards, ways of living and spiritual needs, in addition to the improvement and advancement of their artistic taste and style preferences (Xi 2014). Thus, artists and writers should develop a deep understanding of the taste and perceptions of their readers (Xi 2014). This line of thought suggested to commentators that Xi was promoting realism in art and literature. However, what is more notable is his preference for the bright side of life in China, and that it should be depicted in art and literature. Xi's agenda concerning correctness in artistic creativity and its relation to morality was thus different from that of Mao's.

Ma read the Yenan Speech as an example of emerging Marxist literary thought in China in the 1940s, and Xi's speech as a "cultural construction in the governance of the country under the new era" (Ma 2018). He commented that Xi had progressed with the times and put forward new ideas, perspectives, artistic and moral requirements for artistic creativity (Ma 2018). Xi's image is read as a new type of Chinese leader, instead of a traditionally rigid leader of the Communist Party (Rudolph 2015).

Some of Mao's thoughts in the Yenan Talks, along with Lenin and Marx, were mentioned in Xi's speech, and also Mao's key word, "revolution," was replaced with Xi's "rejuvenation." Xi said, "without the flourishing and prosperity of Chinese culture, there will be no great rejuvenation of the Chinese nation. The rejuvenation of a nation requires major material strength, it also requires major spiritual strength. Without the vigorous guidance of advanced culture and the great wealth of the people's spiritual world, and without the incessant strengthening of the nation's spiritual strength, a country and a nation cannot stand tall among the forest of the nations of the world" (Xi 2014). The arts should therefore serve to make Chinese culture a global force and position China in the world map, according to Xi. He noted the irreversible trend of globalization and how it would affect art. He aimed to control and monitor art in China, and to keep it within the principles and the moral codes that he proposed. This included encouraging patriotism and restrictions on incoming foreign art products like films, and that imported arts had to comply with China's censorship under Xi's regime (Rudolph 2015).

Michel Hockx mentioned that Xi's speech reiterated and confirmed the moralistic view of literature and art, which in Deng's regime since 1978, had been well received and acknowledged. This can be viewed as Mao's legacy or influences also. Xi's proposal to promote "truth, goodness, and beauty" represents a triad that is common in the history of European philosophy, and Xi and his speechwriters have awkwardly combined the traditional European view with a call for greater adherence to native Chinese traditions, and for patriotism (Hockx 2018). Comparing the moral agendas in Mao and Xi's speeches on literature and art, along with how morality clauses were applied and interpreted by artists in China, one can see how artistic creativity has developed in China, following the grand presentation of "the bright side" of people's lives in China as requested and enforced.

See also: Hutton, Soucek, Gal, this volume

REFERENCES

"A Glance Back at Yan'an Forum on Literature and Art." 2015. *China Pictorial*, March 2, 2015, http://www.chinapictorial.com.cn/en/features/txt/2015-02/03/content_667021.htm.

Canavas, Sky. 2015. "Chinese President's Speech on the Arts: The Hollywood Connection." *China Film Insider*, last modified October 20, 2015. http://chinafilminsider.com/chinese-pre sidents-speech-on-the-arts-the-hollywood-connection/.

Chin, Josh. 2015. "A Year After Xi's Landmark Speech on the Arts, Some Things Get Left Out." *Wall Street Journal*, last modified October 15, 2015, https://blogs.wsj.com/chinarealtime/2015/10/15/a-year-after-xis-landmark-speech-on-the-arts-some-things-get-left-out/.

Fu, Qilin. 2015. "The Reception of Mao's 'Talks at the Yan'an Forum on Literature and Art' in English-Language Scholarship." *Comparative Literature and Culture* 17, no. 11. https://doi.org/10.7771/1481-4374.2567.

Goldman, Merle. 1967. *Literary Dissent in Communist China*. Cambridge, MA: Harvard University Press.

Hockx, Michel. 2018. "Censorship, Morality, and Cultural Policy under Xi Jinping." Talk presented at the 2017/2018 School of Chinese Public Lecture Series, University of Hong Kong, May 10, 2018, http://web.chinese.hku.hk/main/2018/04/16/censorship-morality-and-cultural-policy-under-xi-jinping/.

Judd, Ellen. 1985. "Prelude to the 'Yan'an Talks.'" *Modern China* 11, no. 3: 377–408.

Liu, Kang. 2000. *Aesthetics and Marxism: Chinese Aesthetic Marxists and Their Western Contemporaries*. Durham, NC: Duke University Press.

Ma, Yue. 2018. "Discussing Xi Jinping's Inheritance and Development of Mao Zedong's Literary Thought." *Advances in Social Science, Education and Humanities Research* 204,

Conference proceedings of the 4th International Conference on Economics, Social Science, Arts, Education and Management Engineering (ESSAEME 2018): 555–560.

MacKerras, Colin. 1983. *Chinese Theatre: From Its Origins to the Present Day*. Honolulu: University of Hawai'i Press.

Mao, Zedong. 2004. "Talks at the Yenan Forum on Art and Literature." In *Selected Works of Mao Tse-tung*. Transcription by the Maoist Documentation Project, https://www.marxists.org/reference/archive/mao/selected-works/index.htm (accessed February 10, 2023).

Mao, Zedong. [1940] 1976. "Xin minzhuzhuyi lun" (On New Democracy). In *Mao Zedong Ji* (Collected Works of Mao Zedong), 7. Tokyo: Uchiyama tosho.

McDougall, Bonnie S. 1980. Mao Zedong's "Talks at the Yan'an Conference on Literature and Art": A Translation of the 1943 Text with Commentary. Ann Arbor: Centre for Chinese Studies, University of Michigan.

Melvin, Sheila. 2012. "Commemorating Mao's 'Yan'an Talks.'" *Arts Journal* blog, last modified May 15, 2012. https://www.artsjournal.com/china/2012/05/commemorating-maos-yanan-talks/.

Nicola, P. 2007. "The Five Main Contributions of Maoism to Communist Thought." La Voce del (nuovo)Pci, ast modified October 18, 2007. http://www.nuovopci.it/arcspip/article7019.html.

Rudolph, Josh. 2015. "Xi's Arts Speech: Context and Cultural Implications." *China Digital Times*, last modified October 27, 2015. https://chinadigitaltimes.net/2015/10/xis-arts-speech-historical-context-and-soft-power-implications.

Sorace, Christian. "Mao on the Relationship between Politics and Art in the Context of Revolution." *In Afterlives of Chinese Communism Political Concepts from Mao to Xi*, edited by Ivan Franceschini, Nicholas Loubere, and Christian Sorace, 11–17. London: Verso Books.

Sun, Guolin. "Details of the Yenan Forum on Art and Literature." *News of the Communist Party of China*. Beijing: People Daily, http://cpc.people.com.cn/BIG5/64162/64172/85037/85038/6691780.html (accessed April 21, 2021).

Wylie, Raymond. 1980. *The Emergence of Maoism: Mao Tse-Tung, Ch'en Po-ta, and the Search for Chinese Theory 1935–1945*. CA: Stanford University Press.

Xi, Jinping. "Xi Jinping's Talks at the Beijing Forum on Literature and Art." China Copyright and Media, October 16, 2014, https://chinacopyrightandmedia.wordpress.com/2014/10/16/xi-jinpings-talks-at-the-beijing-forum-on-literature-and-art/.

Xi, Jinping. "Speech at the Forum on Literature and Art." Speech presented at the Beijing Forum on Literature and Art, Beijing, October 14, 2014. China Copyright and Media. Last modified December 5, 2015. https://chinacopyrightandmedia.wordpress.com/2014/10/15/speech-at-the-forum-on-literature-and-art/#more-4034.

PART II

THEORETICAL APPROACHES TO ETHICS AND ART

CHAPTER 12

META-ETHICS AND META-AESTHETICS

ALEX KING

METAETHICS (or meta-ethics) and meta-aesthetics are about, respectively, the nature of morality and the nature of aesthetics. They are concerned with questions about the metaphysical status of moral or aesthetic facts, the epistemological status of moral or aesthetic belief and knowledge, the psychological status of moral or aesthetic judgments and attitudes, and the linguistic status of moral or aesthetic statements. They are not concerned with what are sometimes called normative or first-order questions, including what is right or wrong or what is beautiful or ugly. Rather, they are concerned to ask questions about how it could come to be that *anything* really is right or beautiful, how we could come to know that, what is involved in thinking it, and what it would mean to say so.

Metaethics is a live and flourishing subdiscipline of ethics, and meta-aesthetics flourishes in aesthetics, but only infrequently under that title. Still, in the long history of aesthetics and the philosophy of art, a great many thinkers have delved into these issues. The nature of aesthetic judgment, for example, is one of the most frequently recurring topics in premodern and modern European aesthetics. Given their different histories and focal points, metaethics and meta-aesthetics have gone in somewhat different directions. As a result, both would benefit from more contemporary cross-pollination. This chapter will investigate four epicenters of debate that should be of importance to anyone working in meta-aesthetics. It will also provisionally defend realism, partly to illustrate how the arguments work, but partly to show that aesthetic realism isn't the nonstarter it is sometimes taken to be.

THE TRADITIONAL OPTIONS

The most obvious motif in the tapestry of metaethical views is realism versus antirealism. Each of these views comes in many varieties, and there are views that are not obviously on one side or the other: relativism, subjectivism, constructivism, and even sophisticated expressivism. Considering how aesthetics would fit into this entire taxonomy is not my present goal. This is in part because metaethicists have spent a lot of time and effort trying to carefully delineate these views and the boundaries between them, so much so that even this taxonomical project is its own subgenre of metaethics. It is also in part because I think that these taxonomies translate very straightforwardly to aesthetics. Metaethics textbooks usually contain a flowchart one can follow, using yes-or-no questions, that maps out the major options and illustrates how the views are related to one another. But you can pick up any metaethics textbook and replace all moral terminology with aesthetic terminology, and the chart works just as well[1]—even if you might want to answer some of the questions differently.

It is thus not my aim to give a detailed guide to these flowcharts; in other words, my central aim is not taxonomical. Instead, we will look at the most significant debates in metaethical discussions. These debates often don't appear transparently as decision points on these flowcharts, but they are crucial in defending and rejecting different metaethical views. These are importantly diagnostic, too, in that they help or force us to answer the flowchart questions one way or another. We will look at how such debates would in principle or do in fact manifest in aesthetics. By differently framing the existing space of meta-aesthetic theory, this chapter will hopefully provide some new ways into old debates.

Still, in order to understand the broad debates discussed below, we need a working understanding of some major classificatory distinctions. Four classes will be essential in what follows: realism and antirealism, and cognitivism and noncognitivism.

The definition of realism is itself a matter of some controversy, but we need not concern ourselves here with that. In its simplest form, *realism* (for a given normative domain) holds that there are genuine facts (in that domain). It also holds that we can get it right or wrong about those facts, and we do so insofar as our judgments match or fail to match the facts. Typically, those facts must also be mind-independent, that is, not dependent on our beliefs or attitudes. For example, the fact that I like olives depends on my attitudes and so is not mind-independent, but the fact that olives grow on trees does not depend on anybody's beliefs or attitudes and so is mind-independent. *Antirealism* is just the denial of realism.

In holding that we can get it right or wrong about the normative facts, realists are committed to saying that these normative judgments can be true or false. That is, they are committed to *cognitivism*. Cognitivism for a given normative domain holds that those normative judgments are fundamentally representational or belief-like: they contain contents whose standard for correctness is truth or fit with the way the world is.[2] Because they can be true or false, they are called truth-apt. *Noncognitivism*, on the other hand, holds that those normative judgments do not have representational

---

[1] Miller (2013) and Van Roojen (2015) contain good instances.

[2] An important note about the usage of "judgment": I will use this word for mental states that correspond to statements like "Acting callously is immoral," or "The sunset was beautiful." "Judgment" is therefore neutral between cognitivism and noncognitivism in a way that "belief" is not.

content and are not truth-apt.[3] Instead, they more closely resemble desires or even commands. They are more akin to wants, wishes, likes, dislikes, and emotions or affective states than they are to ordinary beliefs. One's wanting a glass of water cannot be false, nor can one's dislike of olives, but one's belief about the number of chairs in the room certainly can be.[4]

We've already seen that realism entails cognitivism. However, the reverse is not true. It might be that we all have beliefs about what is and isn't beautiful, but that nothing *really is* beautiful, and so all of those beliefs are false. Such a view is called *error theory*. It is broadly analogous to atheism. The error theorist thinks that, in the same way that theistic thought and talk presuppose the existence of deities with certain properties, aesthetic thought and talk presuppose the existence of objects with real value properties like beauty. But just as the atheist thinks that deities don't exist, and that therefore our theistic beliefs are systematically false, the error theorist thinks that aesthetic properties don't exist, and that therefore our aesthetic beliefs are systematically false. So cognitivism does not entail realism.

Finally, noncognitivism entails antirealism. If our normative judgments cannot be truth-apt, then they cannot be right or wrong about how the world is. Our judgments might be beholden to other standards—they can *make sense* or *be appropriate*, but noncognitivism precludes their being *correct* or *true*, something realism is committed to. There are also hybrid cognitivist-noncognitivist views, which see the normative judgments in question as involving both a belief-like component and a desire-like component. The penultimate section will return to hybrid views and the realism-antirealism distinction, but we now have enough foundation to examine some of the exciting live debates.

The Debates

This section will focus on four topics: disagreement, testimony, internalism, and strangeness. Though testimony gets a lot of attention in both aesthetics and metaethics, the other three topics are substantially more popular in metaethics. We will survey how they arise in the context of meta-aesthetics, paying special attention to what an aesthetic realist should say about them.

Disagreement

Aesthetic disagreements are ubiquitous. People disagree about how good, how beautiful, and how subtle or playful things are. But what does any of this say about meta-aesthetics?

---

[3] Although sophisticated "quasi-realist" versions of noncognitivism do try to accommodate truth-aptness.
[4] See Scruton (1974) for a noteworthy presentation of aesthetic noncognitivism.

On the one hand, disagreement supports cognitivism. Looking more closely at the phenomenon of disagreement, we find that the very fact that two people can disagree means that they each assert propositions, both of which cannot be correct. Suppose we are looking at the same landscape painting. I say, "This painting is beautiful," and you say, "No, it isn't beautiful." Or perhaps I say that it is the best landscape by this painter, and you say the one next to it is better. In either case, it seems we have a disagreement; we cannot both be right. The painting cannot be both beautiful and not beautiful, or both better and worse than the one next to it. Of course, it can be better in one respect and worse in another, and if that is what we mean, then we can resolve this disagreement. But notice that even that assumes that there was an apparent disagreement that needed resolving, and that its resolution comes about when we agree about the respects in which one is better than the other. That is, we agree insofar as we both believe that this painting has superior composition, but that the one next to it has better use of color. But it seems we would disagree if I maintained that this painting had superior composition and you thought the one next to it did. As Peter Kivy (2015) argues, such genuine disagreements are not only possible, but actual and even frequent. They occur all the time in discussions about art.

Why does this support cognitivism? Parties to an aesthetic disagreement make incompatible claims about how things are. Compare a nondisagreement: If we are both in the gallery when they install the painting, and I cheer for it and you boo at it, we don't have a disagreement. Neither of us asserts anything truth-apt. A cheer can't be true, nor can a boo. I might then say to you, "I like this painting," and you might say, "Well, I don't like it." Here, too, although we assert propositions, we say two things that can both be true, and so we aren't having a disagreement. In contrast, if I say that the painting was made in 1735, and you say that it was made in 1738, we clearly do have a disagreement. We assert incompatible propositions and at least one of us (perhaps both of us) are wrong. If the cases in the previous paragraph constitute genuine disagreements, then we assert incompatible propositions and cannot both be right. So the very possibility of disagreement in aesthetics supports cognitivism, at least about the statements that constitute the disagreement.

The most common replies to this argument involve either denying that these are genuine disagreements, which undercuts the alleged support for cognitivism, or else revising the definition of disagreement so that noncognitivism is compatible with it. To the first, suppose I say that the painting is large and you say that it isn't. Though it appears we have a disagreement, perhaps we find that we are using different standards for what counts as large. In that case, we had a merely apparent disagreement. Once we notice this, both our claims can be true because the painting can be large relative to one standard and not relative to another standard. To make use of this reply, notice that the noncognitivist must also hold that the judgments involved in the alleged disagreement are purely representational, rather than genuinely normative (as the latter are not truth-apt at all). The realist response is to maintain that disagreements can persist even when suitably clarified, as in the earlier example of clarifying the disagreement over which painting is better. The second avenue revises the definition of disagreement so that noncognitivists can explain it. This usually proceeds by saying that there *is* a kind of disagreement implicit in my cheering and your booing the painting, or in my liking and your not liking it. I won't get into these sophisticated attempts,[5] but I will note that they involve giving up some of what seems intuitive about when we do and don't have disagreements.

Although Kivy argues for cognitivism, he does not argue for realism. Remember that cognitivism is consistent with error theory, according to which all aesthetic assessments are systematically false. And the disagreement argument itself makes no additional realist assumptions. Two parties to a disagreement can both be incorrect, as is implied in the disagreement about the year the painting was created. Similarly, if you say that ghosts are mean and I say that ghosts are kind, we are both wrong because there are no ghosts. In the former case, although we were both wrong, there was a possibility of getting it right; in the latter case, there's no way to get it right about what ghosts are like. Realists think that aesthetic disagreements are at least sometimes like the former kind, whereas error theorists think that aesthetic disagreements are all like disagreements about ghosts: we're trying to get it right about beauty, but there is no such thing.

Disagreement has also been used to argue directly against realism. In particular, realism seems to have trouble accommodating how widespread aesthetic disagreement is, even among people who are experts. There are two different arguments to this effect. On the first, the bare fact of widespread expert disagreement, where these experts are understood to be in equally good epistemic positions, suggests a disanalogy with classically realist domains of inquiry. In domains that we acknowledge as realist, the argument goes, we do not face widespread disagreement among experts or the generally well informed. People certainly do disagree about, for example, what Australia's capital city is or whether the earth is flat. However, in neither case is there widespread expert disagreement. People who have pretty good access to evidence and are equally well informed will tend to converge in their judgments. Such people will tend to agree that Canberra is the capital and that the earth is round. But when it comes to aesthetic matters, we appear to face widespread expert disagreement: how good a book Elizabeth Gilbert's *Eat, Pray, Love* is, how good Kanye West's music is, how good Bob Ross's paintings are.

There are a few replies to this. One is that there is more convergence on aesthetic matters than this argument acknowledges. We can find contentious cases that provoke disagreement, but we can also find cases where experts are in near or even complete agreement: that *Citizen Kane* is a good movie, that *Beloved* is a good novel, that Japanese gardens are beautiful. Furthermore, we still find widespread expert disagreement in perfectly realist domains. Well-informed and competent mathematicians might disagree about whether a certain proof works. Well-informed and competent historians might disagree about the cause of a certain uprising. In reply, the antirealist might maintain that we have ways of resolving these questions, at least in principle, but that this doesn't

[5] See, e.g., Evers (2018).

hold in aesthetics. This reply, however, begs the question by assuming the aesthetic realist has no account of how to resolve disagreements.

To defend against this, the aesthetic realist needs to provide such an account. This doesn't look impossible. When we disagree with others about aesthetic matters, we often trade reasons: we point out trite narratives or underdeveloped characters; we point out musical innovation or formal complexity; we point out visual composition and fine brushstrokes. And we do seem to be able to convince others by bringing them to see or be aware of such things. In short, we seem to have some ways to resolve aesthetic disagreements, at least in principle.

A second, more insidious problem for realism posed by widespread disagreement is typically traced to Mackie (1977). It argues that the best explanation for widespread disagreement is something cultural or evolutionary, rather than any tracking of would-be aesthetic facts. We believe that certain things are beautiful, have artistic merit, and so on because it is to our cultural and economic advantage to believe that. Those with power and influence prize "good taste" and so we try to learn what good taste is, deploy it well, and reap the benefits. Take body aesthetics as an example: We are taught by those in power how to look at bodies and that certain bodies are more beautiful than others. We communicate to others that we endorse those standards, verbally and socially and even personally by trying to make our bodies conform to them. And we are rewarded if we succeed, which reinforces the whole system.

Notice that this problem actually does not require disagreement for its force. It could be that we all *agree*, but that the best explanation for our widespread agreement has nothing to do with the aesthetic facts. The point of such arguments, often called *debunking* arguments or *genealogical undermining* arguments, is that the best explanation of our disagreement or agreement—of why our aesthetic judgments are the way that they are—makes absolutely no reference to aesthetic facts. Compare our beliefs about the earth's shape. The best explanation for why we believe that the earth is round makes reference to facts about its shape: we have evidence concerning its shape, including satellite images, time zones, astronomical observations. But we have believed that blue eyes are beautiful because those historically in power have had blue eyes. As it happens, this often comes up in the case of disagreement because we want to find out who is right. And, if this argument is correct, then nobody is right and it's all a social power game.

We can separate two versions of these arguments, one specific to aesthetics and one not. Some evolutionary arguments, such as Street (2006) and Joyce (2007), are mainly targeted at moral realism and may implicate epistemic normative realism too. Because these arguments are not a problem for aesthetic realism specifically, I won't discuss them in detail here.[6] The cultural line in aesthetics is famously pushed by Pierre Bourdieu (1987), among others. Realists should defend themselves by arguing that we are not hopelessly boxed in by our cultural baggage. It often clouds our judgment about what is and isn't good, of course, just as ravenous hunger makes it hard to detect what's truly delicious. But we can make efforts to correct our cultural predispositions. In fact, the

---

[6] See Vavova (2015) for a useful survey.

contemporary body positivity movement does just this, and it is not premised on the falseness of all beauty claims about the body. Instead, it often carries the slogan that all bodies are beautiful. In other words, there is beauty there, but culture has obscured our access to it. We should also take seriously those who disagree with us, that we might better understand their perspective. And we should reevaluate our judgments if we find ourselves hewing too closely to upper-class tastes or assessing European art as better than everything else. Because we know who has historically been in power, we know in which directions prejudice will operate. On this view, we are admittedly boxed in but perhaps not without hope.

To take stock, we've seen three arguments from disagreement. The first argues that the possibility of genuine disagreement supports cognitivism. The second and third argue that the fact of widespread disagreement supports antirealism, and I have suggested realist replies to such arguments.

Testimony and Acquaintance

At bottom, the antirealist disagreement arguments concern the epistemology of aesthetic judgments. They doubt that we could reliably have access to aesthetic facts, even if they did exist. A further set of issues arises when thinking about the epistemology of aesthetic judgments, and these concern aesthetic testimony and the role of acquaintance in aesthetic knowledge.

The familiar debate examines whether we can get justified beliefs or knowledge through testimony concerning aesthetic matters, which I'll call *aesthetic testimony* for short. The nature of aesthetic testimony is thought to reveal many things: what it is aesthetically virtuous to do, whether there are aesthetic experts, or how central perception is to the formation of aesthetic judgments. In meta-aesthetics, it has an additional purpose as a potential diagnostic tool for aesthetic cognitivism and noncognitivism. Nonnormative testimony can quite clearly provide justification for beliefs, so that if a weather forecaster or someone standing outside says that it's raining, then we ordinarily have sufficient reason to believe that it's raining. We can form justified beliefs and even obtain knowledge this way. However, it has seemed to many that aesthetic testimony does not work this way. A friend or even well-regarded critic may say that Mexican architect Luis Barragán's Casa Gilardi is beautiful, but that can never give us justification for judging or believing that it is beautiful.

These observations about aesthetic testimony can seem best explained by noncognitivism.[7] If aesthetic judgments are purely cognitive or representational, as they seem to be in the case of testimony about the rain, then we should be able to arrive at justified beliefs through aesthetic testimony. But it seems to many that we can't. Noncognitivism explains this by saying that aesthetic judgments are not belief-like; they are partially or wholly desire-like or affective. And

---

[7] On this issue, see Hopkins (2001) and Todd (2004).

affective or desire-like mental states cannot engage at a mere description of the beautiful thing or at a mere assertion of beauty. If I say that Casa Gilardi is vibrant, serene but playful, emotionally alive, or simply beautiful, those things cannot engage your affective states in the way that the noncognitivist thinks is requisite for forming an aesthetic judgment.

This is related to the well-known but controversial Acquaintance Principle. According to one version of this principle, we need firsthand experience of an object (i.e., acquaintance with it) to form a justified aesthetic judgment about it, and that is why aesthetic testimony can never provide justification. A stronger version claims that we need firsthand experience to form any aesthetic judgment about the object at all, and that is why aesthetic testimony can never provide justification.

Each version requires a different cognitivist response. The first version of the Acquaintance Principle is completely consistent with cognitivism. A cognitivist can concede that affective engagement and therefore firsthand experience are necessary for the justification of aesthetic judgments. But that only entails that acquaintance is necessary for justification, not that it is necessary for the truth of the aesthetic judgment. Compare a hypothetical case where firsthand perceptual acquaintance is requisite for being justified in one's color judgments. Testimony wouldn't give us justification for color judgments, so we would have to perceive the object ourselves to form a justified belief about its color. But that would not entail that the judgment thus justified is noncognitive.

To this, the noncognitivist may redouble the attack. The fact that acquaintance and affect are necessary for our aesthetic judgments to be justified cries out for explanation. Why would this be true? Only the noncognitivist can offer a good explanation: because our aesthetic judgments are partly or wholly constituted by affective states. (Note that this is not strictly entailed by the stronger version of the Acquaintance Principle, but very closely allied to it.) Here, the cognitivist can either deny that acquaintance and affect are necessary for the justification of aesthetic judgments, and thus obviate the need for that explanation; or they can concede a limited version of this but deny that noncognitivism does indeed offer the best explanation of it.

In line with the first option, we can argue that it is our norms of aesthetic *assertion* that require acquaintance, not norms about the *justification* of our aesthetic judgments.[8] On this view, I can't under normal circumstances assert that Casa Gilardi is beautiful if I haven't seen it. I instead have to say, "I've read that Casa Gilardi is beautiful," or "Casa Gilardi is supposed to be beautiful." But that doesn't undermine my having beliefs, even justified ones, regarding its beauty. And special circumstances or verbal cues might even allow me to say, "Casa Gilardi is beautiful, and I really hope to see it in person someday." If such utterances make sense, this suggests that we can form aesthetic judgments without acquaintance (e.g., via aesthetic testimony), but we have to be careful what we assert to others because normal aesthetic assertions carry a strong implication of acquaintance.

---

[8] See Robson (2015) for discussion.

In keeping with the second option, we can admit that firsthand acquaintance is often, though not always, in fact required to arrive at justified beliefs. But the cognitivist explains this by pointing out that we often lack reasonably unequivocal and reliable aesthetic testimony (reliable in the sense that it issues from unimpeachably informed and sincere testifiers whose status as such we are *ourselves* able to discern). In other words, the quality of testimonial evidence in aesthetics is typically not very good, although it may occasionally be much better. As a result, acquaintance is often required to form a justified belief about the object in question. In cases where we have reasonably unequivocal reliable testimony, as with *Citizen Kane*, we can form justified beliefs. But such cases might be the exception rather than the rule. Notice, too, that nothing here is necessarily unique to aesthetics. It is generally true that it's rational to withhold from forming beliefs when there is rampant testimonial conflict and a lack of firsthand evidence. And in such cases, firsthand experience usually helps in the formation of justified beliefs— though it isn't guaranteed to, since one's firsthand evidence might also be indecisive. In their preferred explanation, the cognitivist just applies these general observations to aesthetic testimonial phenomena.[9]

A final dialectical note: These arguments assume that our aesthetic judgments *are* sometimes justified and examine whether testimony can provide justification. Because error theorists typically think that none of our aesthetic beliefs is justified, we can think of these arguments as interesting only to the noncognitivist and the realist cognitivist.

Internalism

Turning away from epistemological issues, we come to an influential metaethical topic concerning the psychology of moral judgments. This debate, like the first disagreement argument for cognitivism, is of interest to the realist and error theorist alike. A consideration that often motivates metaethical noncognitivism is that it usually seems like, when we make a normative judgment, our motivations are somehow activated. This thought is captured under the label *motivational internalism*. In the moral case, it says that if we sincerely judge that a certain action is the morally right one, then we are thereby at least a little bit motivated to perform that action. The problem for cognitivism is that, if beliefs are *purely* representational, they cannot as such engage our motivations or our affect in any way. To believe that it's a sunny day does not itself involve any motivation to go outside. One is only motivated to go outside if one wants to get vitamin D, get a tan, or feel the warm, fresh air. But those desires are all contingent. In contrast, the connection between moral beliefs and motivations does not seem contingent. Noncognitivism, the argument goes, has a much better explanation for internalism, since only noncognitivism presents the connection between moral judgments and motivations as being necessary.

---

[9]   See Meskin (2004) for a related deflationary strategy.

Translated to aesthetics, the internalist holds that judging something to be aesthetically good necessarily entails having corresponding motivational or at least affective states like pleasure. If the entailed mental state is motivational, then we have a close parallel of the metaethical debate. If the state is instead something affective, then we have a thesis which we might call *affective internalism*. This makes for a looser parallel, but one that many will find better suited to aesthetics. And affective internalism will be very cleanly explained by a form of aesthetic noncognitivism that resembles strong aesthetic hedonism: the view that aesthetic judgments are partly or wholly constituted by the experience of pleasure.[10] Both forms of internalism seem prima facie plausible. If I sincerely judge that *The Miseducation of Lauryn Hill* is a beautiful album, aren't I thereby at least somewhat motivated to listen to it? If I sincerely judge that it is beautiful, aren't I thereby at least somewhat pleased by it? Answering yes to either question poses a problem for cognitivism.

Notice that a premise of this argument construes beliefs as purely representational and thus bridges internalism and noncognitivism. One style of reply denies this assumption. This view, often tacit because it is so widely accepted, is the *Humean belief-desire psychology*. According to the Humean, beliefs alone cannot motivate us; desires or something desire-like (potentially including positive affect) is required for motivation. The cognitivist might deny this Humean view, and in doing so, make cognitivism perfectly compatible with internalism. But it will come at the expense of making cognitivism harder to characterize as distinct from a hybrid cognitivist-noncognitivist view. Fortunately, there are other options for those who prefer not to reject this popular psychological model.

A better strategy is to deny internalism as stated.[11] This can be done through counterexamples, and supplemented by offering a compelling cognitivist explanation of the residual correlation between aesthetic judgments and motivational or affective states. To provide counterexamples, notice first that not all positive aesthetic judgments are judgments of something's being beautiful. Aesthetic objects may be good because they are playful, sublime, tragic, or campy. If the staunch defender of "beauty" as the most general term of aesthetic praise wants that concept to encompass all the others, we should at least bear that very clearly in mind when assessing what sounds natural to say or which examples seem plausible. Building on that, the cognitivist can argue that we often judge something to have positive aesthetic qualities without feeling any corresponding motivation or pleasure at all.[12] One might judge that conceptual artworks like Joseph Kosuth's *One and Three Chairs* is a good artwork but have no desire to see it,

[10] According to the taxonomy in the first section, partial constitution views are technically hybrid cognitivist-noncognitivist views.

[11] Notice that it won't do to respond by saying that we don't always act or intend in accordance with these motivations. All the internalist requires is that we are *at least somewhat* motivated, and it happens all the time that we are a little bit motivated to do things that we don't in fact do.

[12] For arguments against aesthetic motivational internalism, see Strandberg (2016), King (2018). Archer (2017) defends a weaker version of internalism that what I examine here, but holds that it does not conflict with cognitivism.

or alternatively experience no pleasure in seeing it. Or one might recognize that punk music is very rich, interesting, and good, but just not like the sound of it and so not be at all motivated to listen to it, or again take no pleasure in listening. Or one might judge that Krzysztof Kieślowski's *Dekalog* is beautiful, but it is tragic (in a way that plausibly enhances its beauty), and so one might in many circumstances not be at all motivated to watch it. If one watches it, one might take no pleasure in the experience. These examples are made more plausible once we emphasize that beauty—at least narrowly understood—is not the only way for an artwork to be aesthetically valuable. Thus, even if motivation or pleasure is a frequent accompaniment to judgments of beauty, it is not a constant and conceptually necessary companion.

The second half of the reply acknowledges and offers some explanation for why motivation or pleasure is in fact a frequent companion to positive aesthetic assessments. A typical experience of beauty produces a belief (that of the object's being beautiful), but it also produces motivation or pleasure because we are usually motivated to pursue what we deem beautiful and usually take pleasure in the experience of beauty. This dual-effect view holds that the belief and motivation or pleasure are always in principle separable, even if they are often empirically co-occurrent.

There is a final, more conciliatory reply that works even if the counterexamples above are denied. It works along the lines of the earlier remarks on testimony. Maybe pleasure is always necessary for the justification of (positive) aesthetic judgments, but the judgment itself is still only a belief. This in effect endorses a weakened version of internalism. The noncognitivist's version says that, in judging something aesthetically good, we are *thereby* a bit motivated or pleased by it, but the weakened version says only that, when we judge something aesthetically good, we are *in fact always* a bit motivated or pleased by it. In other words, the former holds the judging itself to require motivation or pleasure, where the latter asserts only a perfect correlation between the two. If pleasure is necessary for the justification of our positive aesthetic judgments, then we have a plausible cognitivist explanation for why pleasure always appears alongside positive aesthetic assessments.

Strangeness

The final debate I'll touch on is a direct challenge to forms of realism. It concerns the metaphysical strangeness of aesthetic value properties and the epistemological strangeness of aesthetic knowledge on a realist view. Let's call this the *strangeness challenge* to realism.[13]

The strangeness challenge comes in two forms: metaphysical and epistemological. The metaphysical challenge is that, as J. L. Mackie puts it, "if there were objective values,

---

[13] A terminological note: Mackie's influential presentation uses the word "queerness," which the literature has to large extent followed, but which I will not follow.

then they would be entities or qualities or relations of a very strange sort, utterly different from anything else in the universe" (Mackie 1977, 38). In other words, if there were objective aesthetic values, they would be very strange things. Among objective aesthetic value properties are the balanced, the sublime, the dynamic, the playful, the beautiful, or the just plain (aesthetically) good. The realist thinks that such things exist, but what kind of a thing could these properties be? They don't have mass or extension, and they aren't empirical or physical properties. It seems like we can't use our normal methods to measure or test how much of them is present, the way we can test how much lead is in a water supply. Even in the case of the balanced, which contains a descriptive and measurable component (symmetry or compositional weight), the property still has some value "in it," so to speak. Therefore, if aesthetic goodness is a real property of things, that property has to be very different from all the other, more familiar properties that exist. This is a problem for the aesthetic realist.

The epistemological challenge, as Mackie describes it, is that "if we were aware of [the objective values], it would have to be by some special faculty of moral perception or intuition, utterly different from our ordinary ways of knowing everything else" (1977, 38). Where he talks about moral perception or intuition, we can substitute talk of aesthetic perception and intuition. Now, perhaps it's not at all strange to imagine how we might know about aesthetic properties through perception: we see the balance. However, remember that we aren't talking about purely descriptive aesthetic properties like symmetry (which we do know through perception), but value-laden properties like balance or beauty. We see colors and textures arranged in a certain way, but we don't see beauty directly. We taste sourness and sweetness, but we don't taste deliciousness. So, although we can perceive the descriptive components that go into balance or beauty or other value-laden aesthetic properties, it seems that we can't directly *see* such properties, nor *taste* or *feel* or *hear* them. If they exist, how could we possibly know about them? In short, the metaphysical strangeness challenge is to explain how value properties can exist, and the epistemological strangeness challenge is to explain how we can know anything about them.

The strangeness challenge is in a way both the most serious and the least serious obstacle for the realist. Those struck by its power will think, "Golly, believing in value properties is like believing in ghosts or supernatural powers." Those unfazed will think, "Yep, value properties are very different from other kinds of properties. So what?" Both responses are worth taking seriously.

The strength of the metaphysical challenge rests on its deployment of ontological parsimony. If we don't have to posit a new type of entity (inherently value-laden properties), then we shouldn't. Because this is a widely agreed-upon metaphysical principle, the challenge is quite powerful. However, the reply can then take more solid shape: the realist must argue that we *do* need to posit such entities. Defenders of this line of thought can move in several directions.

One is to argue that aesthetic properties simply are not strange. This brand of realism will take value-laden properties to be constituted by, grounded in, or identical to naturalistic properties, that is, properties that are broadly compatible with a scientific worldview. Such a view faces the impressive but perhaps achievable task of fleshing out the details of how this view works. The next section of this chapter examines one such prospect.

A second response is to rally other normative companions in guilt. It's not just aesthetic properties, but other value-laden properties that we have to deny if we accept this line of argument. We have to deny moral properties and many epistemic properties, too, since normativity and value also find a home in epistemology.[14] This reply may seem question-begging. Since the problem is that you have to posit the existence of strange properties, it doesn't help to posit *more* of them. However, if we understand the challenge as maintaining that we don't need to posit such entities, this reply argues that, well, we do need to. At least, we sacrifice a lot more than just aesthetic properties if we reject the existence of all value properties. And if we don't sacrifice moral and epistemic value properties, then there's no special reason to sacrifice the aesthetic ones.

Third, the realist can rally non-normative companions in guilt. Sometimes we do add entities to our working ontology. The realist can argue that whatever happens to a theory to make the addition of an entity to our ontology necessary is also present in this case. This is the strategy adopted by some moral realists to defend the existence of moral properties. They argue that, much as we are justified in positing scientific entities to explain all of the empirical phenomena we observe, so too we are justified in positing moral properties to explain all of the phenomena we observe. Injustice *causes* riots. Kindness *causes* people to help others. The aesthetic realist could attempt something analogous. Beauty causes pleasure. Good novels cause us to have insights. This is related to the first response, in that it argues that value properties may seem strange, but they are actually an ineliminable part of our best explanations of observable phenomena.

A fourth reply takes an offensive rather than defensive position. Perhaps Mackie's starting assumptions are flawed and stack the deck in the antirealist's favor. Take a different starting point. It is very hard to deny the existence of human consciousness. Indeed, consciousness can seem to be the only thing we really do experience directly. It is similarly hard to deny the existence of qualia—colors, sounds, and pain. It is comparatively easier to deny the existence of the external physical world, lead and water and all. Value-laden experience may be more like consciousness and qualia in that we have clearer and firmer access to it. Indeed, maybe our experience of beauty and playfulness and sublimity—and therefore their existence—is more certain than the existence of trees. The mistake was thinking that we needed something resembling a scientific, physicalistic vindication of aesthetic properties. This is a difficult line to push, but not an impossible one.

Last is the "So what?" reply. Here, the realist simply bites the bullet. Value-laden properties, including aesthetic properties, *are* very strange—even in the technical,

---

[14] The core epistemic concepts of rationality, reason, justification, knowledge, and even belief warmly invite normative or evaluative analysis.

preferred sense of being different from other things. But the universe is a strange place. The human condition is strange. Consciousness is strange. Life is strange. Emotions and love and friendship are strange. Biology and physics and math are strange. Looking over this list, one wonders: Why should something's strangeness speak against its existence?

THE PECULIAR ROLE OF
RESPONSE-DEPENDENCE

So far, we have looked at realism, antirealism, cognitivism, and noncognitivism as largely exclusive and exhaustive categories. But certain popular meta-aesthetic theories sit uneasily along these divides. Response-dependence theories and hybrid cognitivist-noncognitivist theories may seem to resist categorization, and thus resist analysis in the above taxonomy or even, optimistically, to evade the above problems. Alternatively, such theories risk being skewered on both sides of such arguments. Spelling out the details of such theories is therefore of the utmost importance.

This chapter has touched on hybrid cognitivist-noncognitivist theories throughout. Such theories hold that aesthetic judgments involve a belief component *and* a desire-like or affective component.[15] These theories will resemble noncognitivism in that they will be able to endorse internalism, but they will not be able to fully endorse truth-aptness. After all, if it is unclear what it could be for a desire to be true, it will not become clearer if we say that a desire is a *component* of aesthetic judgment rather than the whole of it.[16] The truth-aptness problem might be resolved by saying that the belief component of aesthetic judgment is sufficient for truth-aptness, but then the cognitivist and hybrid theorist appear to have only a terminological dispute over which mental state gets to be dubbed "aesthetic judgment": is it the belief or the belief-plus-affect? The cognitivist is not committed to the existence of the latter, but it is perfectly compatible with cognitivism that such a state exists. Furthermore, if they endorse truth-aptness and moreover think that sometimes aesthetic judgments are *true*, hybrid theorists will have to face the strangeness challenge alongside realists because they too will have to offer an account of what makes the judgments true. They will also incur additional explanatory burdens. They must explain how the belief and nonbelief components are related, why we should think of them as a single state, and why *both* components function in all the ways that the arguments above require.

---

[15] See Gorodeisky and Marcus (2018).

[16] Compare slurs, which combine descriptive and evaluative components. Are there truth-conditions for what makes someone a spinster? Are all unmarried women of marrying age spinsters? It's a complex matter that isn't obviously made easier by the presence of a descriptive component. (Feel free to substitute your least favorite slur to get the intuition more strongly.)

Response-dependence theories are even more difficult to classify.[17] At the simplest level, response-dependence about a property or set of properties is modeled on color. We perceive certain apples as red and thereby attribute redness to those apples. We maintain that they are red even though many people are red-green colorblind, even though many people see them under odd lighting, and even though people see them as some other color if hallucinating. Response-dependence theories in aesthetics more or less say that aesthetic properties are *like that*.

Aesthetic response-dependence most commonly takes the form of ideal observer theory, the Hume-inspired view that what makes something beautiful (or balanced or good) is that an ideal observer would have a certain response to it. Such views have the apparent advantages of being realist and being able to meet the strangeness challenge. Let's look in slightly more detail at each of these advantages.

Whether such views count as realist depends crucially on how we characterize realism and how we characterize the particular response-dependence theory in question. I cannot hope to address this issue in all its complexity,[18] but we can get some idea of how this might work if we assess response-dependence according to the criteria given earlier in our characterization of realism. If we understand realism as involving a claim to the existence of facts, then we might say yes (after all, there are color facts). Insofar as realism includes our ability to get it right or wrong about those facts, then we can say yes, too (after all, we can get it wrong about colors). But if we understand realism as committed to mind-independence, then we may have to surrender (after all, colors aren't completely independent of our minds). This final verdict depends on how we define mind-independence, but regardless, mass seems mind-independent in a way that color does not. Perhaps this isn't a problem, though. Would it be so awful if aesthetic value were as real as color, but not as real as mass? Response-dependence modeled on color thus captures the intuitive thought, if unhappily vague, that we should be realists—but only of a relatively mild sort—about aesthetic value.

What of the other advantage, the ability of response-dependence to meet the strangeness challenge? On its face, this seems trivially easy. What makes the apple red is that suitably placed observers would perceive it in a certain way. One version of response-dependence is modeled on this, saying that what makes something beautiful is just that observers would respond to it in a certain way (with pleasure or a special kind of feeling). This account analyzes aesthetic value properties in purely descriptive terms—in terms of what would in fact produce certain responses under certain descriptively specifiable conditions. For color properties, it just is the case that suitably placed observers would respond in certain ways, and that's what makes something the color it is. So too with

---

[17] Influential presentations of aesthetic response-dependence theories are Hume (1777), McDowell (1985), and Wiggins (1998).

[18] What constitutes realism is a matter of much debate; I've only given a very rough approximation here. For more on whether response-dependence is compatible with realism, see Pettit (1991).

beauty, the proposal goes. If beauty works just like color, then there's nothing strange about it.[19]

However, it then becomes difficult to explain the *value* of aesthetic value and why it seems like we *should* respond in certain ways to balance or beauty.[20] Notice that response-dependence about color does not try to explain why we should respond in a certain way to redness. If someone is under odd lighting conditions and sees the red apple as yellow, we don't think that they should see it as red or that they have any reason to get into the right lighting conditions to see it as red. In contrast, if I'm not in the right viewing or experiential conditions to have the beauty-response to an aesthetic object, we generally think I should get into the right conditions so that I can appreciate its beauty. Such response-dependence theorists fundamentally lack an account of what makes aesthetic value worth pursuing or promoting. Think of this as the reverse side of the strangeness challenge: the current version of response-dependence does not make value strange *enough* or sufficiently *different* from regular empirical properties. This view makes it unclear how aesthetic value is valuable or worth pursuing at all.[21] In noticing this, we should ask whether this view is truly a version of realism. On this view, it is unclear if any aesthetic *value* gets to be real, or if such accounts render it value in name only.

CONCLUSION

This chapter has covered four central debates in metaethics and meta-aesthetics. We have seen disagreement used to defend cognitivism and to undermine realism. We have seen testimony and internalism used to defend noncognitivism. And we have seen a strangeness challenge to realists. I have made suggestions throughout for how the realist might deflect some of these worries. I hope it is now clear that aesthetic realism need not be a free-for-all where opinions become reality. None of this is meant to suggest that— even if the gestural and controversial defenses of realism I've offered work out—realists are home free. Many more obstacles await them. But many more obstacles await any meta-aesthetic theory. And this is as it should be for a burgeoning area in which there is still much fruitful work to be done.

See also: Nannicelli, Song, this volume

---

[19]   For more on response-dependence theories, see Watkins and Shelley (2012) and King (2023).

[20]   See Levinson (2002), Shelley (2011).

[21]   An alternative response-dependence approach analyzes aesthetic value properties using normative terms—in terms of what *should* produce certain responses under certain conditions. One *should* feel certain feelings in response to the beautiful. This signifies a slight but important departure from the parallel with color properties. Such views can more easily explain value and normativity and are perfectly compatible with realism, but will not meet the strangeness challenge. See D'Arms and Jacobson (2000) and Gorodeisky (2021).

REFERENCES

Archer, A. 2017. "Aesthetic Judgements and Motivation." *Inquiry* 60, no.6: 656–674.

Bourdieu, P. 1987. *Distinction: A Social Critique of the Judgment of Taste*, Translated by Richard Nice. Harvard, MA: Harvard University Press.

D'Arms, J., and D. Jacobson. 2000. "Sentiment and Value." *Ethics* 110, no. 4: 722–748.

Evers, D. 2018. "Expressivism and Arguing About Art." *British Journal of Aesthetics* 58, no. 2: 181–191.

Gorodeisky, K. 2021. "On Liking Aesthetic Value." *Philosophy and Phenomenological Research* 102, no. 2: 261–280.

Gorodeisky, K., and E. Marcus. 2018. "Aesthetic Rationality." *Journal of Philosophy* 115, no. 3: 113–140.

Hopkins, R. 2001. "Kant, Quasi-Realism, and the Autonomy of Aesthetic Judgement." *European Journal of Philosophy* 9, no.2: 166–189.

Hume, D. [1777] 1987. "Of the Standard of Taste." In *Essays, Moral, Political, and Literary*, edited by A. Miller, 226–249. Indianapolis: Liberty Fund.

Joyce, R. 2007. *The Evolution of Morality*. Cambridge, MA: The MIT Press.

King, A. 2018. "The Amoralist and the Anaesthetic." *Pacific Philosophical Quarterly* 99, no. 4: 632–663.

King, A. 2023. "Response-Dependence and Aesthetic Theory." In *Fittingness*, edited by C. Howard and R. Rowland, 309–326. Oxford: Oxford University Press, 2023.

Kivy, P. 2015. *De Gustibus: Arguing About Taste and Why We Do It*. Oxford: Oxford University Press.

Levinson, J. 2002. "Hume's Standard of Taste: The Real Problem." *Journal of Aesthetics and Art Criticism* 60, no. 3: 227–238.

Mackie, J. L. 1977. *Ethics: Inventing Right and Wrong*. London: Penguin.

McDowell, J. 1985. "Values and Secondary Qualities." In *Morality and Objectivity*, edited by T. Honderich, 110–129. London: Routledge.

Meskin, A. 2004. "Aesthetic Testimony: What Can We Learn from Others About Beauty and Art?" *Philosophy and Phenomenological Research* 69, no. 1: 65–91.

Miller, A. 2013. *An Introduction to Contemporary Metaethics*, 2nd ed. New York: Polity.

Pettit, P. 1991. "Realism and Response-Dependence." *Mind* 100, no. 4: 587–626.

Robson, J. 2015. "Norms of Belief and Norms of Assertion in Aesthetics." *Philosophers' Imprint* 15, no. 6 : 1–19.

Scruton, R. 1974. *Art and Imagination*. London: Methuen.

Shelley, J. 2011. "Hume and the Value of the Beautiful." *British Journal of Aesthetics* 51, no.2: 213–222.

Strandberg, C. 2016. "Aesthetic Internalism and Two Normative Puzzles." *Studi di estetica* 6: 23–70.

Street, S. 2006. "A Darwinian Dilemma for Realist Theories of Value." *Philosophical Studies* 127, no. 1: 109–166.

Todd, C. 2004. "Quasi-Realism, Acquaintance, and the Normative Claims of Aesthetic Judgement." *British Journal of Aesthetics* 44, no. 3: 277–296.

Van Roojen, M. 2015. *Metaethics: A Contemporary Introduction*. New York: Routledge.

Vavova, K. 2015. "Evolutionary Debunking of Moral Realism." *Philosophy Compass* 10, no. 2: 104–116.

Watkins, E., and Shelley, J. 2012. "Response-Dependence about Aesthetic Value." *Pacific Philosophical Quarterly* 93, no. 3: 338–352.

Wiggins, D. 1998. "A Sensible Subjectivism?" In *Needs, Values, Truth: Essays in the Philosophy of Value*, 3rd ed., 185–214. Oxford: Blackwell.

FURTHER READING

Budd, M. 2003. "The Acquaintance Principle." *British Journal of Aesthetics* 43, no. 4: 386–392.

Elton, W. 1954. *Essays in Aesthetics and Language*. Oxford: Basil Blackwell.

Hampshire, S. 1954. "Logic and Appreciation." In *Essays in Aesthetics and Language*, edited by W. Elton, 161–169. Oxford: Basil Blackwell.

Hanson, L. 2018. "Moral Realism, Aesthetic Realism, and the Asymmetry Claim." *Ethics* 129, no. 1: 39–69.

Harold, J. 2008. "Can Expressivists Tell the Difference between Beauty and Moral Goodness?" *American Philosophical Quarterly* 45, no.3: 287–298.

Levinson, J. 1998. *Aesthetics and Ethics: Essays at the Intersection*. Cambridge: Cambridge University Press.

Loeb, D. 2003. "Gastronomic Realism—A Cautionary Tale." *Journal of Theoretical and Philosophical Psychology* 23, no. 1: 30–49.

Lord, E. 2016. "The Rational Power of Aesthetic Testimony." *British Journal of Aesthetics* 56, no. 1: 1–13.

Meskin, A., and Robson, J. 2015. "Taste and Acquaintance." *Journal of Aesthetics and Art Criticism* 73, no. 2: 127–139.

Pettit, P. "The Possibility of Aesthetic Realism." In *Pleasure, Preference, and Value*, edited by E. Schaper, 17–38. Cambridge: Cambridge University Press.

Railton, P. 1998. "Aesthetic Value, Moral Value, and the Ambitions of Naturalism." In *Aesthetics and Ethics: Essays at the Intersection*, edited by J. Levinson, 59–105. Cambridge: Cambridge University Press.

Schaper, E. 1983. *Pleasure, Preference, and Value*. Cambridge: Cambridge University Press.

Shafer-Landau, R. 2021. *Oxford Studies in Metaethics*. Oxford: Oxford University Press.

Sundell, T. 2010. "Disagreements About Taste." *Philosophical Studies* 155, no. 2: 267–288.

Whiting, D. 2015. "The Glass Is Half-Empty: A New Argument for Pessimism about Aesthetic Testimony." *British Journal of Aesthetics* 55, no. 1: 91–107.

Wodak, D. 2021. "Approving on the Basis of Moral and Aesthetic Testimony." In *Oxford Studies in Metaethics*, edited by R. Shafer-Landau, 183–206. Oxford: Oxford University Press.

CHAPTER 13

....

DISTINGUISHING BETWEEN ETHICS AND AESTHETICS

....

MOONYOUNG SONG

RECENT discussion of the relationship between the aesthetic and the ethical has focused on whether and how the two realms *interact* with one another, and thus it is often called the value interaction debate.[1] Behind this debate lies the implicit assumption that the aesthetic and the ethical are distinct in some sense—generally only things that are distinct from each other can be said to interact.[2] A question, then, naturally arises: Are the two realms distinct and, if so, in what ways? This chapter surveys existing discussions related to this question and explores the implications that they might have for the value interaction debate.

In doing so, the chapter focuses on three specific questions that correspond to three ways in which the aesthetics and the ethical may not be fully distinct: (1) Are the aesthetic and the ethical identical? (2) Do they partly overlap? (3) Is one of them part of the other? The third question will require the longest consideration, as it has the most important implications for the value interaction debate.

ARE THE AESTHETIC AND THE ETHICAL IDENTICAL?

....

Many would consider that the answer to this question is obviously no. However, some philosophers seem to have argued that the aesthetic and the ethical are identical.

---

[1] See Stear, Carroll, Jacobson, and Rothfeld in this volume for the value interaction debate.

[2] I am using these broad terms "the aesthetic" and "the ethical" to cover all of the relevant entities, including the relevant kinds of values (ethical, moral, aesthetic, and artistic) as well as our evaluations of them. More fine distinctions will be made where necessary. I will also use the terms "ethical" and "moral" interchangeably in this chapter, as nothing of importance for our purposes hinges on the distinction between the two.

Shaftesbury, for instance, famously claimed that "Beauty" and "Good" are *one and the same*" (2001 [1709], 399). This certainly looks like an explicit claim of the identity of the beautiful and the good, but it is under debate what Shaftesbury actually meant. While some philosophers think that he was indeed making the identity claim, others believe that Shaftesbury was merely claiming that the good is a species of the beautiful or that he was just drawing an analogy.[3]

It is unnecessary for our purposes to settle this interpretative issue. Nor do we need to discuss other philosophers who have made a similar claim. This is because there are independent reasons to consider the aesthetic and the ethical as not identical. First, it is hard to deny that there are some dissimilarities between the two. The precise nature of the dissimilarities depends on many on-going debates in aesthetics and ethics, as we will see in the following section. However, regardless of how those debates are settled, it is very unlikely that there will ultimately be no dissimilarity at all between the aesthetic and the ethical. Therefore, assuming that identical things must share the same properties, we have good reason to think that the aesthetic and the ethical are not identical. Second, there is an interesting intuitive asymmetry between the two. While many philosophers have argued that what is moral is beautiful,[4] few have argued that what is beautiful is moral. Our ordinary linguistic usage exhibits a similar asymmetry. We often say that a moral person or action is beautiful, and when we do so, we seem to imply that the person or action is beautiful in virtue of being moral. But few would say that a beautiful person—such as a beauty pageant winner—is moral in virtue of being beautiful. To put it another way, while the word "beautiful" is applicable to moral objects that are not beautiful in the narrow, nonmoral sense, the word "moral" is not applicable to beautiful objects that are not moral.[5] These considerations strongly suggest that the aesthetic and the ethical are not identical. However, there are other ways in which they might be less than completely distinct. Let us now turn to those possibilities.

DO THE AESTHETIC AND THE ETHICAL OVERLAP?

How far, if at all, do the aesthetic and the ethical overlap? They may do so in different senses. To begin with, some *bearers* of aesthetic value may also have ethical value. This

---

[3] For a brief overview of the debate, see Gill (2021, Section 3.1).

[4] See Gaut (2007, 116–119) for a discussion of those philosophers.

[5] We should, of course, be careful when making a philosophical point based on an observation about our ordinary linguistic usage, and I am not claiming that this asymmetry offers a conclusive argument that the aesthetic and the ethical are not identical. It is worth mentioning, however, that at the very least, the asymmetry is not restricted to contemporary English. As a native Korean speaker, I can attest that Korean exhibits the same asymmetry, and Yorùbá seems to do so as well (Hallen 2000, Chapter 5; see also Hallen, this volume).

seems obviously true—for instance, a person can possess both aesthetic and ethical values—and thus a rather uninteresting way that the two might overlap.

Another way to understand the overlap relation is to see whether there are any *specific virtues or vices*, or evaluations of those virtues or vices, that concern both aesthetic and ethical values. Sentimentality, which is considered both aesthetically and ethically bad, is often mentioned as such a vice. It is debatable, however, whether sentimentality merely has separate aesthetic and ethical dimensions or whether those dimensions overlap in a more interesting way.[6]

Yet another way to unpack the idea of an overlap between the aesthetic and the ethical is in terms of the *properties or characteristics* that may be shared or not shared by the aesthetic and the ethical. In other words, we could ask what similarities and dissimilarities there are between the two.[7] It would be impossible, however, for us to reach a definite answer to this question in this chapter. This is because any candidate for a similarity or dissimilarity would be highly controversial and its plausibility would crucially depend on how various on-going debates in aesthetics and ethics are settled, if they are ever settled. Thus, instead of seeking a final answer to the question, I will just list some of the issues with respect to which the aesthetic and the ethical are often considered dissimilar.[8]

Realism

It appears common to think, at least pretheoretically, that the ethical is more amenable to various forms of realism than the aesthetic or, at least, that the ethical is real in a more robust sense than the aesthetic. But some philosophers think otherwise (e.g., Hanson 2018). King in this volume discusses this topic in depth.[9]

Naturalism

In aesthetics, there is a strong tendency to understand aesthetic value and aesthetic properties in terms of the natural, such as the general human tendency to respond in a certain way to objects with certain characteristics. Naturalism comes in different forms,

---

[6] Eaton (2001, Chapter 9) argues that the dimensions are not separate.

[7] Hampshire (1979) is a well-known early attempt to address this question, which touches on some of the issues that are mentioned below including generalism and practicality. For a critical discussion, see Zemach (1971).

[8] See Harold (2020, Chapter 7) for a more in-depth discussion on the similarities and dissimilarities between the aesthetic and the ethical. My list below owes a significant part to his discussion.

[9] For a related discussion on how expressivists can distinguish between the ethical and the aesthetic, see Harold 2008. Locke (1935)'s value taxonomy based on feeling-types is also relevant to this question.

but in general, it tends to face less resistance in aesthetics than in ethics, although some philosophers are naturalists in both domains (e.g., Railton 1998).

Generalism

Generalism, which is the view that, roughly put, there are general principles on the subject matter in question, is often considered more plausible in the ethical than in the aesthetic domain. People tend to find the idea that there are general principles about aesthetic or artistic value counterintuitive. By contrast, it may seem that morality almost requires general principles by its nature. It is unclear, however, whether this common line of thinking is on the right track. The debate between generalists and their opponents, particularists, is still ongoing in both aesthetics and ethics.[10]

Practicality

The ethical is commonly considered to be more practically oriented than the aesthetic, in the sense that it is more closely tied to actions. For instance, although this is controversial, action-motivation is often considered to be an important part of moral judgments but not of aesthetic judgments.[11] Also, while few would deny that there are such things as moral obligations, we do not usually speak of aesthetic obligations (and even if there were such things, they would probably be weaker in some sense than moral obligations).[12] This asymmetry in practicality has recently been challenged, as several philosophers have emphasized the practicality of the aesthetic (e.g., Cross 2017; King 2018; Lopes 2018).

Acquaintance

It is often claimed that knowledge or judgment about an object's aesthetic or artistic value requires acquaintance, that is, experiencing the object first-hand. This is called the acquaintance principle. On the other hand, it seems less plausible that moral knowledge or judgment would require acquaintance. It is debated whether the acquaintance principle is true and, if so, what grounds it, as well as whether the apparent asymmetry regarding acquaintance between the aesthetic and the ethical really holds (e.g., Budd 2003; Konigsberg 2012; Hills 2020; Livingston 2003; Lord 2018).

---

[10] For an overview of the debate in ethics, see, e.g., Ridge and McKeever (2020). For an overview of the debate in aesthetics, see, e.g., Tsu (2019).

[11] Strandberg (2011) makes a claim roughly in this vein.

[12] Kubala (2020) provides an overview of the debate on aesthetic obligations.

Is the Ethical Part of the Aesthetic?

This section discusses whether one of the two domains, the aesthetic and the ethical, is part of the other. We will focus on whether the ethical is part of the aesthetic rather than the other way around. This is because, first, it seems less plausible that the aesthetic would be part of the ethical, given the asymmetry I noted above—while we often describe what is moral as beautiful, we rarely say that what is beautiful is moral. Also, the question of whether moral value is part of aesthetic or artistic value, especially when the value bearer is a work of art, has important implications for the value interaction debate. This debate has mostly focused on whether and how an artwork's moral value affects its aesthetic or artistic value, not the other way around,[13] and one way in which an artwork's moral value may affect its aesthetic or artistic value is by being part of the work's aesthetic or artistic value.

Interestingly, despite its clear relevance to the value interaction debate, this question of whether an artwork's moral value is part of its aesthetic or artistic value has rarely been foregrounded in the literature. Instead, as Hanson (2019) notes, most arguments for value interaction seek to forge a connection between an artwork's moral value and its aesthetic or artistic value through an intermediary factor, such as the work's cognitive value or ability to secure its audience's uptake. The possibility of a direct connection without an intermediary factor has been little explored. This possibility is precisely what the question of whether an artwork's moral value is part of its aesthetic or artistic value is about. Or, at least, that is how I will understand the question in this chapter. The notion of being part of a value could be cashed out in different ways, but to maintain the link to the value interaction debate just mentioned, I suggest that being part of a value can be understood to mean directly contributing to the value without an intermediary factor. Why we need the qualification here of a *direct* contribution should be clear. All sorts of features of an artwork—for instance, the patch of red color in a painting—may indirectly contribute to its aesthetic or artistic value, but we would not want to say that they are all part of the work's aesthetic or artistic value.

Now, being a direct contributor to aesthetic or artistic value (and, accordingly, being part of the value) may mean one of two different things, depending on the nature of aesthetic or artistic value. First, suppose that aesthetic or artistic value, whichever one is at issue, is not identical or reducible to a single unified entity. Instead, it consists of multiple components, and no unified entity ties all of its components together. Let us call this a strictly pluralistic account of aesthetic or artistic value. If this account is correct, then being a direct contributor to aesthetic or artistic value would amount to simply being one of those components of aesthetic or artistic value. Call this the *strict* sense of being part of aesthetic or artistic value.

---

[13] See Rothfeld in this volume for how the aesthetic might affect the ethical.

What if the strictly pluralistic account is wrong and aesthetic or artistic value, whichever one is at issue, is identical or reducible to one single unified entity, for instance, the value of (a certain kind of) pleasure that the work provides? In this case, the moral value of an artwork cannot be a component of its aesthetic or artistic value, but it can still be a direct contributor to the value if it makes the work more aesthetically or artistically valuable without involving an intermediary factor. Call this the *loose* sense of being part of aesthetic or artistic value.

Why should we understand being part of a value in this broad way, including both the strict and loose senses? This allows us to avoid making our inquiry of whether an artwork's moral value is part of its aesthetic or artistic value hinge on whether the strictly pluralistic account is correct or not. This is especially important in that the existing discussions related to our inquiry that I will survey below are not committed to a specific account of aesthetic or artistic value. Thus, I will below adopt the broad sense of being part of a value, although, where necessary, I will distinguish between the strict and loose senses.[14] I will also call an account of aesthetic or artistic value according to which the value is identical or reducible to one unified entity but has multiple direct contributors a loosely pluralistic account, to be opposed to the strictly pluralistic account discussed above, according to which aesthetic or artistic value, whichever one is at issue, is not identical or reducible to one unified entity.

With these clarifications in hand, let us now consider whether an artwork's moral value is part of its aesthetic or artistic value. This question has not received much attention, at least not in this exact form, but some existing discussions can be found on related topics. I will survey those discussions and explore other possible ways of approaching the question.

Moral Beauty

One topic related to our inquiry here is moral beauty. Because this topic is more closely related to aesthetic value than artistic value, due to the closer relationship of beauty to aesthetic value, I will limit the discussion of moral beauty to aesthetic value for the sake of simplicity.

The notion of moral beauty or something close to it has a long history, from Plato to Shaftesbury and Hume.[15] One contemporary philosopher who argues for moral beauty in the context of the value interaction debate is Berys Gaut, so let us focus on his view.

---

[14] One possible implication of this distinction is that when we speak of one value being part of another in the strict sense, we seem to be concerned with value *types* (e.g., moral value and aesthetic value), whereas what is at issue in the case of the loose sense seems to be *instances* of the values (e.g., a particular artwork's moral value and aesthetic value). This is because when something is a component of a value, it is natural to think that it should be a part of any instantiation of the value (I will say more about this later), but something can be a direct contributor to a value without being its component only in certain instantiations of the value.

[15] For a brief discussion of the history, see Gaut (2007, 116–119).

He uses moral beauty as an argument for his position on value interaction, which he calls ethicism. Ethicism is the view that an artwork is aesthetically meritorious (flawed) insofar as it has a moral virtue (defect) that is aesthetically relevant. He summarizes his argument for ethicism from moral beauty as follows:

> If a work of art manifests ethically good attitudes [and if the attitudes are aesthetically relevant], then it possesses in that respect a kind of beauty; and, since beauty is undoubtedly an aesthetic value, it follows that a work has aesthetic value in so far as it manifests ethically good attitudes. Conversely, if a work manifests ethically bad attitudes [and if the attitudes are aesthetically relevant], then it possesses in that respect a kind of ugliness; and it follows that the work has an aesthetic flaw in so far as it manifests such attitudes. (2007, 115)[16]

First, a clarification is in order regarding this argument's relevance to our question of whether an artwork's moral value is part of its aesthetic value. If beauty is not identical with aesthetic value, this argument could not show, even if it were successful, that an artwork's moral value is part of its aesthetic value, as beauty would be an intermediary factor.[17] So, beauty has to be identical to aesthetic value for this argument to count as an argument for the claim that an artwork's moral value is part of its aesthetic value. In relation to this, it is worth mentioning that although the term "beauty" is indeed sometimes used interchangeably with aesthetic value, this is not how Gaut understands aesthetic value; instead, he identifies the aesthetic value of an artwork with its value qua art (2007, 34–41). So, it is safe to say that Gaut himself does not intend this argument to be an argument that an artwork's moral value is part of its aesthetic value, assuming that he would agree with me about what being part of a value amounts to. His aim is to argue for ethicism, and ethicism can be true even if an artwork's moral value is not part of its aesthetic value. However, his argument could be used to argue that an artwork's moral value is part of its aesthetic value, if beauty is identical to aesthetic value, or if we simply replace the term beauty with the term aesthetic value in his argument. Thus, this argument remains relevant to our inquiry.

Various objections could be raised against Gaut's argument, but many of them are not directly relevant to our inquiry.[18] What is most important for our purpose of evaluating this argument as an argument for the claim that an artwork's moral value can be part of its aesthetic value is the aesthetic relevance condition. By adding this condition, Gaut allows that an artwork's moral value may not be relevant to its beauty and aesthetic value in some cases. That is, it is not enough for a work of art to manifest ethically good attitudes for it to be beautiful in that respect; the attitudes should also be aesthetically relevant. Gaut adds this condition because there are some artworks whose

---

[16] I have added the aesthetic relevance condition to reflect a refinement made by Gaut. See Gaut (2007, 129).

[17] I owe this point to Hanson (2019, 6).

[18] See Gaut (2007, 114–132) for his response to possible objections.

ethical attitudes intuitively seem irrelevant to their beauty. However, adding this condition creates some challenges if Gaut's argument is understood as an argument that an artwork's moral value can be part of its aesthetic value.

First, if we understand the notion of being part of a work's aesthetic value here in the strict sense discussed earlier (i.e., being a component of the value), which requires the strictly pluralistic view of aesthetic value (the view that aesthetic value is not a single unified entity) to be true, then there is a tension between this view and the existence of some artworks whose moral value is irrelevant to their aesthetic value. If moral value is irrelevant to aesthetic value in some artworks, moral value is certainly not a component of aesthetic value in those cases. The moral beauty argument with the aesthetic relevance condition, then, implies that moral value is a component of aesthetic value in some works but not others. However, it is unclear what would explain this variance and how the different combinations of components could be all instances of aesthetic value, if, as the strictly pluralistic view of aesthetic value implies, aesthetic value is not a unified entity but merely is the combination of its components.

On the other hand, if we understand the notion of being part here in the loose sense discussed earlier, according to which being part of a value means being a direct contributor to the value without being its component, the challenge is to explain how moral value is a direct contributor to aesthetic value in some works when, in other works, it is not even relevant to aesthetic value. If moral value is a direct contributor to aesthetic value in one work, which means there is no intermediary factor that connects moral value to aesthetic value there, then its irrelevance to aesthetic value in other works cannot be because of the absence of the intermediary factor. Another explanation is needed, such as that there is an additional necessary, but a nonintermediary, factor. That is, moral value directly contributes to aesthetic value only when combined with an extra factor. This is what Gaut seems to be thinking when he suggests that we understand the aesthetic relevance condition in terms of manifestation through the artistic means of expression (2007, 129). The challenge, then, is to show that moral value itself, and not just the artistic means of expression or the combination of moral value plus the artistic means, makes at least part of the contribution to the work's aesthetic value.

The Value of Art Qua Art

Another existing discussion relevant to our inquiry of whether an artwork's moral value is part of its aesthetic or artistic value is that on how an artwork's artistic value, which is widely understood to be the work's value *qua art*, is to be distinguished from the other values that the work has. An artwork may have many values, including aesthetic value, moral value, cognitive value, therapeutic value, financial value, political value, decorative value, entertainment value, and value as a status symbol or even as a doorstop. Not all of these values intuitively appear to be the values an artwork might have qua art. How, then, can we distinguish artistic value from the other values an artwork might have? If we can find a principled answer to this question, it could be used to help judge whether moral value is part of artistic value.

It is tempting to approach this question by appealing to the *purpose* with which an artwork was made. That is, one might argue that an artwork's value is artistic just when the work was made to realize that value.[19] This suggestion rightly excludes some of intuitively nonartistic values, such as the value as a doorstop, from artistic value. It is not fully satisfactory, however, because an artwork can be made with a purpose that is intuitively irrelevant to its artistic value, such as to spread propaganda. And restricting the relevant purposes to *artistic* ones would not help us unless we found a way to elucidate what purposes can count as artistic.

How, then, can we distinguish a work's artistic value from its other values? Lopes (2011) considers and rejects four possible approaches and uses this result to motivate his conclusion that there is no artistic value that is distinct from aesthetic value. This conclusion itself is not directly relevant to our inquiry, but it is helpful to look at the approaches he rejects.[20]

The first of these approaches derives a theory of artistic value from a theory of art. In this approach, a work's artistic value is a value realized by the features that make it a work of art. As Lopes notes, however, this connection between the two kinds of theories might not exist. This becomes clear if you consider the institutional theories of art. According to the institutional theories, what makes an object a work of art is, roughly put, its institutional features, such as its being conferred a certain status by the so-called artworld, which is not part of what realizes its artistic value (Dickie 1974; 1984).

The second approach that Lopes rejects equates artistic values to the values with which art criticism is concerned. If this were the case, we need only look at art criticism to determine which values are artistic ones. As Lopes rightly points out, however, this approach is not satisfactory, as evaluative discourse on art might concern the nonartistic values of a work as well. Thus, to follow this approach, we would first need to find a way to distinguish art criticism—evaluative discourse about artistic value—from other evaluative discourse about art, which would probably require us to distinguish a work's artistic value from its other values in the first place.

The third approach that Lopes considers and rejects is inspired by Walton's seminal paper "Categories of Art" (1970). According to this approach, an artwork's artistic value is the value it appears to have when appreciated in the category of art, namely, the category whose membership is all and only artworks. Lopes's objection to this is that we do not appreciate artworks in this category; we only appreciate artworks in subcategories, such as songs, dances, and paintings. It is debatable whether Lopes is right about this. However, even if he is wrong and we do appreciate artworks in the broad category of art, understanding an artwork's artistic value to be its value when appreciated in the category of art would not be very helpful for our purposes. This is because before we can

---

[19]   Lopes (2011) discusses this suggestion, calling such a value a value *in* art (520–521).
[20]   For criticisms of Lopes's view, see, e.g., Hanson (2013) and Huddleston (2012).

determine whether an artwork's moral value is an artistic value, we would first need to know what it means to appreciate an artwork in the category of art. This task seems no less daunting than the task of analyzing the notion of artistic value itself.

Lastly, Lopes considers and rejects the approach of equating an artwork's artistic value to its value as the product of an artistic achievement. The largest challenge for this view would be to elucidate what an *artistic* achievement is, as distinguished from other kinds of achievement involved in the production of the work. Lopes is skeptical that this challenge could be met, on the grounds, very roughly put, that an artist, when making a work of art, does not conceive of what they are doing as making *art*; they only conceive of their act as making a work of a *particular art form*, such as painting. As in the case of his rejection of the third approach, it is debatable whether Lopes is right in rejecting this achievement-based approach for this particular reason.[21] However, even if the particularities of Lopes's reasoning are wrong, it would remain the case that this achievement-based approach has difficulty elucidating what an artistic achievement is.[22] Appealing to a prior notion of artistic value is not an option, at least for the purpose of elucidating artistic value through artistic achievement. However, if that is not an option, it is unclear how we could distinguish artistic achievement from the other kinds of achievement involved in making artworks.

It seems that none of the four approaches that Lopes discusses could provide an easy solution to the problem of delineating artistic value. However, another approach is not discussed by Lopes. Stecker (2019, 52) proposes the following test for artistic value:

> A property of an artwork is artistically valuable if knowing or recognizing that the work has the valuable property requires grasping the work's meaning (usually by interpretation).

According to this test, an artwork's cognitive value is an artistic value because in order to recognize that this work has cognitive value, one needs to grasp the work's meaning. On the other hand, Stecker argues, the test rightly excludes a work's financial value from its artistic value, as knowing its financial value does not necessarily require grasping its meaning.

It is under debate, however, whether this test always generates the correct results. One objection to the test is that it would count intuitively artistic values as nonartistic ones once we accept that one can know or recognize that a work has a certain valuable property through testimony (Dodd 2014). For instance, Dodd argues, if one can know that Jeff Koons's *Travel Bar* (1986) is kitsch through testimony without grasping the work's meaning, it follows, according to Stecker's test, that the property of being kitsch is not a (negative) artistic value, which is counterintuitive (2014, 404).

It would take us too far afield to discuss whether this objection could be met. However, what it suggests is that although Stecker's test does not require a substantive analysis of

---

[21] See Huddleston (2012) for a criticism of Lopes.
[22] For a critical discussion of achievement-based accounts of artistic value, see Grant (2020).

artistic value and is, in that respect, superior to at least some of the above approaches that seem to require, in one way or another, such an analysis, Stecker's test requires a substantive analysis of a different topic, namely, what it is to grasp a work's meaning and to know or recognize that a work has a valuable property. Thus, the existing literature on how to delineate the value of art qua art does not seem to provide an immediate answer to our inquiry as to whether an artwork's moral value is part of its artistic value.

Invariance

Another possible approach to the question of whether an artwork's moral value is part of its aesthetic or artistic value is to think about whether moral value has an invariant relationship with aesthetic or artistic value. It is tempting to think that there should be some close connection between something being part of a value and its having an invariant relationship with the value. In other words, invariance might be a mark of being part of a value.[23]

I examine this idea below, clarifying exactly how invariance is related to being part of a value. This examination will demonstrate that the relationship is in fact more complicated than it may seem at first glance; thus, the notion of invariance is not very helpful for figuring out whether an artwork's moral value is part of its aesthetic or artistic value. Yet it is still worthwhile to understand why the relationship is complicated. For the ease of exposition, I will mention only artistic value in this part of the chapter, although what I discuss is applicable to aesthetic value as well.

Let me begin by clarifying the relevant notion of invariance. There are different senses in which the relationship between moral and artistic values can be invariant, but what is most relevant to our purposes would be invariance in terms of moral value's *valence* with respect to artistic value. The question, then, is what implications it has for the question of whether an artwork's moral value is part of its artistic value if an artwork's moral value always has a positive valence with respect to its artistic value (we can ignore the possibility of an artwork's moral value always having a *negative* valence, as few would think this is the case).[24]

The first thing to note is that invariance in this sense is *not sufficient* for an artwork's moral value to be part of its artistic value, either in the strict or loose sense of being part of a value discussed earlier. This is because moral value might always positively contribute to some intermediary factor, which in turn always positively contributes to

---

[23] I have expressed an idea roughly in this vein elsewhere (Song 2018), where I distinguished between two kinds of value interaction, which I called intrinsic and contextual value interaction. Intrinsic value interaction has to do with a moral defect or a virtue's intrinsic artistic valence that is invariant whereas contextual value interaction is variant as it happens by virtue of the ways in which a moral defect or virtue interacts with other features of the work in the particular context.

[24] I will not attempt to answer here whether an artwork's moral value always has a positive valence with respect to its artistic value, for this is one of the highly controversial issues in the value interaction literature. See Jacobson in this volume for a related discussion on immoralism, which is the view that an artwork's moral defect (virtue) is sometimes an aesthetic or artistic merit (defect).

artistic value, in which case moral value would have an invariant positive valence with respect to artistic value. This disqualifies moral value from being part of artistic value in both the strict and loose senses.[25]

Next, is the invariance of moral value's valence with respect to artistic value *necessary* for an artwork's moral value to be part of its artistic value? The answer is rather complicated. To see this, we should distinguish between two senses of valence. That an artwork's certain feature, call it X, has a positive valence toward the work's artistic value might mean two different things, given that X may affect the work's artistic value via multiple routes (X, for instance, might positively contributes to the work's artistic value by contributing to the work's aesthetic value while negatively contributing to the work's artistic value by undermining its originality). The first sense in which X has a positive valence toward the work's artistic value, then, is that the *overall* contribution of X to the work's artistic value is positive. That is, the sum of all the multiple ways in which X affects the work's artistic value is positive. The second sense is that there is at least one positive route from X to the work's artistic value. This is compatible with X's overall valence being negative. I will call this second sense of valence the *pro tanto* valence of X.[26]

Now, the invariance of moral value's *pro tanto* valence seems necessary for an artwork's moral value to be part of its artistic value at least in the strict sense of being part of a value (i.e., being its component). If moral value is a component of artistic value, it is reasonable to think that there is at least one positive route from moral value to artistic value in any work of art (this is perhaps just part of what it is to be a component of a value), assuming that which components constitute artistic value does not vary from work to work. What about the loose sense of moral value being part of artistic value (i.e., an artwork's moral value directly contributes to its artistic value without being its component)? In this case, the invariance of moral value's pro tanto valence does not seem necessary for an artwork's moral value to be part of its artistic value. Even if moral value directly contributes to artistic value in one work of art, which means that there is at least

---

[25] One might think that, if the two links (between moral value and the intermediary factor and between the intermediary factor and artistic value) are both constitutive, moral value should still count as part of artistic value. I doubt that this is the case. Suppose, for instance, that newness partly constitutes originality and that originality partly constitutes artistic value (and the two links are invariantly positive). My intuition is that newness would not be part of artistic value, although others might disagree.

[26] I am following how Gaut (2007, 57–66) uses the term "pro tanto" when he characterizes ethicism in terms of what he calls pro tanto principles. As I understand it, his claim is that an artwork's moral virtue (defect), when aesthetically relevant, always has at least one positive (negative) route to aesthetic value, not that an artwork's moral virtue (defect), when aesthetically relevant, always has an overall positive (negative) aesthetic valence. Note, however, that the term "pro tanto" is not always used this way. A pro tanto principle may refer to a principle regarding a consideration's invariant *overall* valence. In this case, a pro tanto principle is contrasted with an absolute principle, according to which a consideration always makes an action conclusively right, for example, not just always has an overall positive valence toward an action's rightness. The latter is compatible with the action being wrong if this consideration is outweighed by other considerations.

one positive route from moral value to artistic value in that work, that route might not exist in some other works of art where a necessary factor for that route to exist is absent.

On the other hand, the invariance of moral value's *overall* valence with respect to artistic value is not necessary for an artwork's moral value to be part of its artistic value in either the strict or loose sense. Even if moral value is a component of artistic value, which I take to imply that there is at least one positive route from moral value to artistic value in any work of art, moral value might, in some works of art, negatively interact with other component of artistic value and end up having an overall negative valence. Similarly, even if moral value is a direct contributor to artistic value in one work of art, in some other works of art, that direct connection might not exist or, even if it exists, might be outweighed by a negative route from moral value to artistic value that might exist in some works.

Let us take stock. The relationship between moral value having an invariant valence toward artistic value and moral value being part of artistic value turns out to be more complicated than what might have seemed at first glance. The only relationship that seems to hold between the two is that the invariance of moral value's pro tanto valence toward artistic value is necessary for an artwork's moral value to be part of its artistic value in the strict sense (that is, for moral value to be a component of artistic value). This means that if we can find a work in which moral value has no positive route to artistic value, we would be able to reject the view that moral value is a component of artistic value. However, whether such a work exists would be highly controversial itself. Settling this issue might well require a substantive account of artistic value. Also, recall that I am assuming that artistic value always has the same components on the strictly pluralistic account. This assumption might be questioned. These complications suggest that the notion of invariance would not offer a straightforward answer to the question of whether an artwork's moral value is part of its artistic value.

Might the Question Not Have an Answer?

We have thus far looked at existing discussions on several topics related to our inquiry of whether an artwork's moral value is part of its aesthetic or artistic value. Unfortunately, none of the discussions have provided immediate help with our inquiry. It seems that we will eventually need a substantive theory of artistic value to answer our inquiry. Surveying all existing theories of artistic value is beyond the scope of this chapter, but let me briefly discuss one interesting and not much discussed possibility that we will need to take seriously if we accept certain kinds of theories of artistic value—namely, the possibility that there might not be an answer to our inquiry.

Some theories of artistic value index artistic value to individual art forms (e.g., Stecker 2019; Lopes 2014), and those theories might have the implication that there is no *single* answer to the question of whether an artwork's moral value is part of its aesthetic or artistic value. That is, the answer might vary from one art form to another. In fact, if such a theory turns out to be plausible, not just our inquiry, which concerns direct interaction between moral and aesthetic or artistic value, but also the value interaction debate in general, which concerns indirect interaction as well, might have to be indexed to each individual art form.[27]

Another type of theory of artistic value that might imply there is not an answer to our inquiry is a theory that makes the boundary of artistic value indeterminate. Unlike the previous kind of theory, which still allows a definite answer to exist with respect to each individual art form (assuming that the artistic value of each art form is not indeterminate), on this type of theory, there is simply no definite answer to the question as to whether an artwork's moral value is part of its artistic value. On such a theory, some values of art would lie at the core of artistic value—aesthetic value would be a good candidate—while other values lie near or at the borderline. Moral value might be one of those values. Such indeterminacy could be due to the indeterminacy of the *term* or *concept* of artistic value, in which case there might still be a fact of the matter as to whether an artwork's moral value is part of its artistic value, or due to the indeterminacy of artistic value itself, in which case there is no fact of the matter regarding the question. A related option is to think that being a part of artistic value is a degree notion. On such a theory, there is no answer to the question as to whether an artwork's moral value is part of its artistic value, but we could say that an artwork's moral value is part of its artistic value to a lesser degree than the work's aesthetic value is part of its artistic value. Developing these various forms of indeterminate theory of artistic value seems like a project worth pursuing, considering that how we think about artistic value does exhibit some forms of indeterminacy. That might explain why it is difficult to find a straightforward answer to our inquiry of whether an artwork's moral value is part of its artistic value.[28]

See also: King, Carroll, Stear, Jacobson, Rothfeld, Hallen, this volume

REFERENCES

Budd, Malcolm. 2003. "The Acquaintance Principle." *British Journal of Aesthetics* 43, no. 4: 386–392.

Cross, Anthony. 2017. "Art Criticism as Practical Reasoning." *British Journal of Aesthetics* 57, no. 3: 299–317.

Dickie, George. 1974. *Art and the Aesthetic: An Institutional Analysis*. Ithaca, NY: Cornell University Press.

Dickie, George. 1984. *The Art Circle*. New York: Haven.

Dodd, Julian. 2014. "On a Proposed Test for Artistic Value." *British Journal of Aesthetics* 54, no. 4: 395–407.

---

[27] To my knowledge, the value interaction debate has not paid much attention to the relevance of artistic categories to the debate. An exception is Sauchelli (2013).

[28] I'm grateful to the editor of this volume, James Harold, for his helpful suggestions and feedback. This work was supported by the American Society for Aesthetics Postdoctoral Fellowship. Any views, findings, conclusions, or recommendations expressed in this publication do not necessarily reflect those of the American Society for Aesthetics.

Eaton, Marcia Muelder. 2001. *Merit, Aesthetic and Ethical*. New York: Oxford University Press.

Gaut, Berys. 2007. *Art, Emotion and Ethics*. New York: Oxford University Press.

Gill, Michael. 2021. "Lord Shaftesbury [Anthony Ashley Cooper, 3rd Earl of Shaftesbury]." In *The Stanford Encyclopedia of Philosophy* (Spring 2021 Edition), edited by Edward N. Zalta. https://plato.stanford.edu/archives/spr2021/entries/shaftesbury/.

Grant, James. 2020. "Art and Achievement." *Philosophical Studies* 177, no. 9: 2517–2539.

Hallen, Barry. 2000. *The Good, the Bad, and the Beautiful: Discourse About Values in Yoruba Culture*. Bloomington: Indiana University Press.

Hampshire, Stuart. 1979. "Logic and Appreciation." In *Art and Philosophy: Readings in Aesthetics*, 2nd ed., edited by W. E. Kennick, 651–657. New York: St. Martin's Press.

Hanson, Louise. 2013. "The Reality of (Non-Aesthetic) Artistic Value." *Philosophical Quarterly* 63, no. 252: 492–508.

Hanson, Louise. 2018. "Moral Realism, Aesthetic Realism, and the Asymmetry Claim." *Ethics* 129, no. 1: 39–69.

Hanson, Louise. 2019. "Two Dogmas of the Artistic-Ethical Interaction Debate." *Canadian Journal of Philosophy*: 1–14.

Harold, James. 2020. *Dangerous Art: On Moral Criticisms of Artwork*. New York: Oxford University Press.

Harold, James. 2008. "Can Expressivists Tell the Difference Between Beauty and Moral Goodness?" *American Philosophical Quarterly* 45, no. 3: 289–300.

Hills, Alison. 2020. "Aesthetic Testimony, Understanding and Virtue." *Noûs*. https://doi.org/10.1111/nous.12344

Huddleston, Andrew. 2012. "In Defense of Artistic Value." *Philosophical Quarterly* 62, no. 249: 705–714.

King, Alex. 2018. "The Amoralist and the Anaesthetic." *Pacific Philosophical Quarterly* 99, no. 4: 632–663.

Konigsberg, Amir. 2012. "The Acquaintance Principle, Aesthetic Autonomy, and Aesthetic Appreciation." *British Journal of Aesthetics* 52, no. 2: 153–168.

Kubala, Robbie. 2020. "Aesthetic obligations." *Philosophy Compass* 15, no. 12: 1–13.

Livingston, Paisley Nathan. 2003. "On an Apparent Truism in Aesthetics." *British Journal of Aesthetics* 43, no. 3: 260–278.

Locke, Alain. 1935. "Values and Imperatives." In *The Philosophy of Alain Locke: Harlem Renaissance and Beyond*, edited by Leonard Harris, 34–50. Philadelphia: Temple University Press.

Lopes, Dominic McIver. 2011. "The Myth of (Non-aesthetic) Artistic Value." *Philosophical Quarterly* 61, no. 244: 518–536.

Lopes, Dominic McIver. 2014. *Beyond Art*. New York: Oxford University Press.

Lopes, Dominic McIver. 2018. *Being for Beauty: Aesthetic Agency and Value*. New York: Oxford University Press.

Lord, Errol. 2018. "How to Learn about Aesthetics and Morality through Acquaintance and Deference." *Oxford Studies in Metaethics* 13: 71–97.

Railton, Peter. 1998. "Aesthetic Value, Moral Value, and the Ambitions of Naturalism." In *Aesthetics and Ethics: Essays at the Intersection*, edited by Jerrold Levinson, 59–105. Cambridge: Cambridge University Press.

Ridge, Michael, and Sean McKeever. 2020. "Moral Particularism and Moral Generalism." In *The Stanford Encyclopedia of Philosophy* (Winter 2020 Edition), edited by Edward N. Zalta. https://plato.stanford.edu/archives/win2020/entries/moral-particularism-generalism/.

Sauchelli, Andrea. 2013. "The Merited Response Argument and Artistic Categories." *Journal of Aesthetics and Art Criticism* 71, no. 3: 239–246.

Shaftesbury, the third Earl of (Anthony Ashley Cooper). [1709] 2001. *Characteristicks of Men, Manners, Opinions, Times*, edited by Douglas den Uyl. 3 vols. Vol. 2. Indianapolis: Liberty Fund. https://oll.libertyfund.org/title/uyl-characteristicks-of-men-manners-opinions-times-vol-2

Song, Moonyoung. 2018. "The Nature of the Interaction between Moral and Artistic Value." *Journal of Aesthetics and Art Criticism* 76, no. 3: 285–295.

Stecker, Robert. 2019. *Intersections of Value: Art, Nature, and the Everyday*. Oxford: Oxford University Press.

Strandberg, Caj. 2011. "A Structural Disanalogy between Aesthetic and Ethical Value Judgments," *British Journal of Aesthetics* 51, no. 1: 51–67.

Tsu, Peter Shiu-Hwa. 2019. "Of Primary Features in Aesthetics: A Critical Assessment of Generalism and a Limited Defence of Particularism." *British Journal of Aesthetics* 59, no. 1: 35–49.

Walton, Kendall. 1970. "Categories of Art." *Philosophical Review* 79, no. 3: 334–367.

Zemach, Eddy. 1971. "Thirteen Ways of Looking at the Ethics-Aesthetics Parallelism." *Journal of Aesthetics and Art Criticism* 29, no. 3: 391–398.

CHAPTER 14

RELATIVISM AND THE ETHICAL CRITICISM OF ART

TED NANNICELLI

INTRODUCTION

OVER the last several years, appreciators of all sorts of art, from popular music to painting to sculpture, have become increasingly attuned to ways in which the moral norms operative in the context of an artwork's creation (its generative context) clash with the moral norms prevalent in the here and now (the work's reception context). Consider, for example, recent debates about how mid-twentieth-century Hollywood movies featuring sexist and racist stereotypes ought to be handled by contemporary streaming services like Netflix, Disney+, and so forth. Whatever practical measures one endorses for dealing with such movies, most people probably have the intuition that, in this case, the moral norms of the reception context trump those of the generative context. That is, most readers will probably agree that the sorts of racist stereotypes featured in, say, *Gone with the Wind* (1939) are simply *wrong* despite not having been widely recognized as such by white audiences at the time it was made—and that the film is, thus, morally flawed.

On the face of it, this sort of case is grist for the mill of moral objectivists. For the present purpose, we can think of moral objectivism as a cluster or family of views that hold there are mind-independent or subject-independent moral facts. According to moral objectivists, one of the advantages of this view is its ability to account for the normative force or "objective purport" (Railton 1998, 60; Railton 2010, 299) that seems to characterize ordinary or folk evaluative discourse. As Michael Smith puts it, "it is a distinctive feature of engaging in moral practice that the participants are concerned to get the answers to moral questions *right* . . . Such concern presupposes, for example, that there are correct answers to moral questions to be had. And the natural interpretation of that presupposition is that there exists a domain of moral facts; facts about which we can form beliefs and about which we may be mistaken" (1994, 5). In other words, the idea is that because moral objectivism offers the most straightforward way of accounting for the apparently objectivist nature of our ordinary moral discourse, we have *prima facie* reasons to prefer it to competing views (also see Brink 1989; Shafer-Landau 2003; for discussion see Björnsson 2012). And the apparently unassailable judgment that it was (and still is) wrong for Hollywood to traffic in harmful racial stereotypes seems like just another case in which ordinary folk behave as if morality is objective—as if their ethical evaluations of artworks are straightforwardly true or false.

However, our encounters with the art of distant societies raise questions about this objectivist picture. In this chapter, we will briefly consider just one example: ancient Greek poetry and vase-painting that celebrates pederasty and the beauty of young boys. Notwithstanding scholarly debates about the details of this practice, including how the ancient Greeks themselves conceived of it, there is sufficient evidence to indicate that pederasty was widely accepted and often extolled throughout the ancient Greek world from the archaic period to as late as the fifth century BCE (Lear 2014).

On the one hand, these poems and vases raise moral psychological questions: Is it really the case that ordinary folk tend to regard these artworks as ethically flawed because they glorify pederasty? If it is, then why do we not see the same sort of public outcry over their exhibition as the exhibition of contemporary artworks that sexualize minors—say, the photographs of Bill Henson or paintings of Graham Ovenden (see Nannicelli 2020)? If not, then why—and what accounts for our departure from our putative objectivist default position?

On the other hand, as the case for objectivism makes clear, the moral psychological questions are not entirely separate from meta-ethical questions. Moral objectivists begin their argument with a putative fact about folk moral psychology and move to the claim that objective purport of our moral discourse lends prima facie support to objectivism. Yet moral relativists might, for their part, begin their brief with the observation that moral practice varies considerably across cultures and societies, and then move to the claim that this diversity, along with our apparent reticence to morally judge those other cultures and societies, lends prima facie support to moral relativism (e.g., Prinz 2007a). Although we'll refine the concept as we proceed, we can, initially, think of moral relativism as a cluster or family of views that hold that evaluative moral discourse is true or false relative to some specified standard or context.

Moral relativism is not a popular view in philosophy, and it is viewed as an anathema in most places outside of academia. One might worry that if moral relativism were true, it would lead to all sorts of unpalatable and pernicious conclusions. And for both philosophers of art and ordinary, "art-interested" (Kivy 2015) folk, moral relativism might seem like a threat to the common and, arguably, important practice of ethically appraising art. Wouldn't moral relativism hold, one might ask, that there is no objective fact of the matter about whether films that traffic in harmful sexist and racist stereotypes are ethically flawed? Wouldn't it mean that disputes about, say, whether it is morally acceptable to harm nonhuman animals as part of the creation of art are ultimately unresolvable? In this chapter I will not answer these questions directly, but I will try to make the case for a very limited, moderate version of moral relativism in the context of the ethical criticism of art.

The chapter begins by outlining several kinds of relativism in the two fields that concern us here: philosophy of art and moral philosophy. It then turns to a brief review of the recent literature in experimental folk moral psychology which suggests the folk are meta-ethical pluralists—objectivists in some contexts and relativists in others. Taking the case of ancient Greek art that celebrates pederasty as a touchpoint, I suggest empirical work on the moral appraisal of art is likely to mesh with and lend additional support to this idea. I conclude with a discussion of Bernard Williams's "relativism of distance," and the argument that there are, independent of the empirical findings, good meta-ethical reasons for considering a limited form of relativism about the moral standing of artworks.

RELATIVISM IN THE PHILOSOPHY OF ART AND MORAL PHILOSOPHY: A VERY BRIEF OVERVIEW

Before proceeding any further, it is worth reviewing some of the ways that relativism has been advanced and critiqued in relation to particular topics in the fields that concern us here: the philosophy of art and moral philosophy. Needless to say, the literature is voluminous, so I will be painting in broad strokes, and, even then, will not be able to address either the history of relativism within philosophy or the central debates about relativism within philosophy in general.[1]

Alethic Relativism

At the most general level, one can identify a tradition of relativism pertaining to the meta-theoretical questions about the conception of truth, knowledge of which is the ostensible aim of our inquiries about the arts. As Maria Baghramian and J. Adam Carter describe it, "The central claim of alethic relativism is that 'is true,' despite appearances to the contrary, is (at least, in some relevant domains of discourse) not a one-place but a two-place predicate such that 'P is true' should correctly be understood as (*modulo* differences in particular ways of developing this idea) shorthand for 'P is true for X,' where X is a culture, conceptual scheme, belief framework, etc." (2020, n.p.). In the context of aesthetics, the tradition that has embraced this sort of thoroughgoing, global

---

[1] Useful general overviews of relativism can be found in Harré and Krausz (1996); Baghramian (2004); Baghramian and Clark (2020). Helpful handbooks and anthologies of important papers include Krausz (2010), Hales (2011), and Kusch (2020).

relativism has roots in the Continental poststructuralist thought of François Lyotard and Jacques Derrida, as well as American philosopher Richard Rorty's distinctive version of (neo-)pragmatism (e.g., 1990; 1998; 1999).[2]

The borrowing and refashioning of the claims of these philosophers by literary theorists such as Stanley Fish (1980) and Barbara Herrnstein Smith (1988) gave such global relativism significant currency within literary studies, where ambitious critics "applied" the idea, variously, such that in specifying "*P* is true for *X*," *X* was held to be an interpretive community, a conceptual scheme, a cultural formation, and so forth. In every case, however, the crucial thesis concerned the nature of truth, which was held relative to some "framework," to borrow the term philosopher of art Paisley Livingston (1988, 55–65) uses in his incisive and devastating critique of these views.[3]

Relativism in Interpretation

Despite some of the sweeping pronouncements of poststructuralists like Derrida, literary theorists often appealed to global relativism about truth strategically, en route to the sort of relativism with which they were principally concerned: relativism about literary interpretation. As mentioned above, the figure perhaps most associated with relativism about literary interpretation is Stanley Fish, who claims that there are no interpretations that are true *simpliciter* because literary meaning is constructed by particular interpretive communities; it is thus only relative to an interpretive community that interpretations have truth value. Fish's arguments have been soundly rebutted by numerous philosophers of art (e.g., Currie 1991; Stecker 1997), but this has not stopped them from permeating adjacent disciplines such as cultural studies, film studies, and television studies (see Nannicelli 2013; 2022).

Within philosophy of art, more careful arguments for relativism about interpretation have been advanced by Joseph Margolis (1980; 1999) and Michael Krausz (1993). For these philosophers, relativism about the interpretation of art is warranted—indeed, demanded—by the particular ontology of artworks. There are some complex issues at stake here, which we cannot broach in the present context, but it is worth noting that one motivation these philosophers have for embracing relativism about interpretation stems from the recognition that interpretation plausibly involves a diverse assortment of different aims and purposes—only one of which is the pursuit of a single, true meaning of an artwork. The recognition of this "critical pluralism" (Stecker 2003) opens up space for the possibility of interpretive practices that issue in interpretations whose acceptability is relative to some other criterion—say, for example, the maximization of the work's value.[4]

---

[2] There are recent, more developed accounts of alethic relativism. See, for example, MacFarlane (2014).

[3] For a sustained critique of global relativism about truth and knowledge, see Boghossian (2006).

[4] It should be noted that this point can be accepted by philosophers who are not relativists. See, for example, Stecker (2003) and Davies (2007, Chapters 10–13).

Nevertheless, there are reasons to think that when the purpose of interpreting an artwork is to ethically evaluate the work, we are indeed (and should be) pursuing the work's actual (true) meaning. One important consideration here is the fact that sometimes the ethical judgments of artworks have real consequences for their artists: we blame and hold morally responsible artists whose artworks endorse or solicit defective moral views. But it is only coherent for us to do this if there is a truth about what such artworks mean—one that is not relativized to an interpretive community, a reading strategy, or whatever. A general relativism about the interpretation of art would seem to be a nonstarter for ethical criticism: How could we hold an artist morally responsible for the apparently blameworthy views his artworks endorse or solicit if the interpretation of the work as endorsing or soliciting such views is only correct relative to a particular interpretive community, a particular interpretive aim, reading strategy, and so forth (see Nannicelli 2017)?

Relativism about Value: Aesthetic Value

Relativism about value can be formulated as a metaphysical thesis or a semantic thesis. The metaphysical thesis starts by casting doubt on the idea that values (whether aesthetic or moral) could be entirely mind-independent—"out there" as part of the "fabric of the world" (Mackie 1977, 15). In contrast, it is plausible that values are dependent on *us* in some sense that requires further explication. Possibilities here range from various forms of subjectivism, by which we either construct values or project them onto the world (e.g., Hume; Blackburn 1984), to various sorts of response-dependence theories of a more realist flavor (e.g., Zangwill 2001), including sensibility theories (e.g., Wiggins 1987; McDowell 1998; D'Arms and Jacobson 2000; D'Arms 2005; Prinz 2007a. For further discussion see King, "Meta-Ethics and Meta-Aesthetics," this volume.)

At this point, the value relativist can argue that if we construct value or if value consists in our dispositions to respond in certain ways, then value is relative to the person(s) doing the constructing or having the disposition to respond in those ways.[5] This has not been a popular argument in moral philosophy, and, to my knowledge, it has not been advanced by any contemporary philosopher of art with regard to aesthetic value, although Prinz (2007b; 2011; Fingerhut and Prinz 2020) has flirted with it as a kind of parallel to his (2007a) argument for the relativism of moral value.[6]

---

[5] There is a distinct but related argument to relativism that starts with "internalism"—the idea, roughly, that moral judgments (or beliefs) are intrinsically motivating: "Moral goodness is such that sincere judgment about it intrinsically motivates. But, which properties motivate depends on the psychology of the judging agent. So, which properties are the moral ones depends on the psychology of the agent" (Dreier 2006, 259). The upshot for the relativist is a kind of agent-based relativism. See Harman (2000). This issue is also discussed in King, this volume.

[6] For a general discussion, see Matravers (2010). Alan Goldman (1995) is sometimes described in the literature as endorsing aesthetic relativism, but his view (which is better described as Humean) is rather different to what I describe here—to wit, he argues that aesthetic properties and value are best conceived as relative to the taste of ideal critics. The sort of full-blooded aesthetic relativism I have in mind does, however, have its advocates in literary and cultural studies (e.g., Smith 1988).

Instead, it is the semantic version of value relativism that has recently attracted the most interest in philosophy of art. A number of philosophers have argued that relativism offers the best account of apparently "faultless disagreements" (Wright 1992; Köbel 2004). A faultless disagreement is simply a dispute in which one party judges *p*, the other party judges not-*p*, and, *ex hypothesi*, neither party has made an error in formulating the judgment. Faultless disagreements tend to appear within particular domains of evaluative discourse; for example, recent work on the topic in philosophy of language has focused on "predicates of personal taste" (Lasersohn 2005; Stephenson 2007). The sort of case under examination here might be along these lines: Ted says: "Beers brewed with Cascade hops are delicious." Aliza says: "Beers brewed with Cascade hops are not delicious."

If we accept, for the sake of argument, that Ted and Aliza are rational, and neither has made an error or embraced a false belief in formulating this judgment, there are a few ways of analyzing this exchange. On an expressivist analysis, Ted and Aliza are merely expressing non–truth-evaluable attitudes; roughly put, they are each simply expressing how they each feel about beers with Cascade hops, so there is no real disagreement (see Ayer [1946] 1971). A second, related option, also dissolves the apparent disagreement, but in a different way. Consider the statement: "July is a winter month." The statement is truth-evaluable, but its truth depends on the context of utterance: uttered in the northern hemisphere it is false; uttered in the southern hemisphere it is true. Likewise, "indexical relativism" or "contextualism" (Wright 1992; Köbel 2004) would hold that Ted's statement is elliptical for, say, "Beers brewed with Cascade hops are delicious to me [or to people who share my taste for Cascade hops]," and Aliza's statement is elliptical for "Beers brewed with Cascade hops are not delicious to me [or to people who don't like Cascade hops]." Both statements are true, and there is no genuine disagreement. Finally, a fuller-blooded relativist analysis would insist that there is genuine disagreement— since, otherwise, it's not clear why people debate matters of taste (cf. Kivy 2015)—but claim that the truth-value of the propositions is itself relative (e.g., Lasersohn 2005). As Köbel puts it, this view "involves not just relativity at the level of sentences. Rather the same proposition (content of belief, assertion, etc.) is true in some perspectives, and not in others. This form of relativity is not eliminated by placing a sentence in a context of utterance" (2004, 71).

Seemingly in part because of the focus on faultless disagreements and in part because of the discussion of taste, some philosophers have suggested that relativism offers a plausible semantics for aesthetic discourse (MacFarlane 2005; Egan 2010; for objections, see Evers 2021). However, several philosophers of art have argued that aesthetic concepts are *not* the same "predicates of personal taste," and that it would be a mistake to infer the plausibility of a relativist semantics for aesthetic concepts from the putative plausibility of a relativist semantics for predicates of personal taste (e.g., Young 2009; Brogaard 2017; Davies 2017; Lopes 2017). For there are reasons to think that aesthetic judgments—or the predication of aesthetic properties—aspire to track objective features of the object of evaluation and to demand intersubjective agreement. On this view, aesthetic discourse appears less akin to taste discourse than to moral discourse.

Moral Value

Interestingly for our purposes, philosophers of art have had relatively little to say about the metaphysics of moral value or semantics of moral judgments despite the fact that the nature of the interaction between moral and aesthetic (or artistic) value has been a central topic within the field over the last several decades. Of particular note here is that although there might be good reasons to take a unified view of the metaphysics of value or the semantics of value judgments, it is nevertheless a conceptual possibility—one that numerous philosophers and folk embrace—that one sort of value (e.g., moral) is objective and the other (e.g., aesthetic) subjective (or that one is *more* objective than the other), and that we need a distinct semantics for each sort of value judgment. This possibility would seem to raise questions about the nature of value interactionism in art that have yet to be addressed. In the rest of this discussion, however, focus will be limited to assess the moral value of artworks.

Before proceeding, we should briefly outline the central varieties of metaethical relativism in the literature. (Normative moral relativism will be left to the side, and descriptive moral relativism will be addressed in the next section.) As with aesthetic relativism, moral relativism can be formulated as a metaphysical or semantic thesis, although in practice the two are often intertwined. For example, Gilbert Harman insists that "moral relativism is not by itself a claim about meaning . . . Moral relativism is a thesis about how things are and a thesis about how things aren't! Moral relativism claims that there is no such thing as objectively absolute good, absolute right, or absolute justice; there is only what is good, right, or just in relation to this or that moral framework" (1996, 17). Nevertheless, Harman's case for moral relativism focuses on the semantics of moral claims and judgments. In his words, "moral judgments contain an implicit reference to the speaker or some other person or some group or certain moral standards, etc." (2000, 22). Likewise, David Wong's early work on moral relativism is largely dedicated to the analysis of moral statements of the form "A ought to do X"—statements, he argues, are always implicitly (if not explicitly) relativized to a certain set of conditions and an "adequate moral system" (1984).

As one might have anticipated from the above discussion of indexical relativism about the semantics of aesthetic discourse, the relativism of Harman and Wong can be thought of as indexical relativism, contextualism, or "content relativism" about the semantics of moral discourse since it holds that the content of moral statements partly depends upon—and varies with—the contexts in which the statements are made (see also Drier 1990; Brogaard 2008; Björnsson and Finlay 2010). On this view, just as the content of "I live in Brisbane" varies with the context in which it is uttered, so too does the content of moral statements like "Incest is wrong." A standard objection to indexical relativism, which often motivates an argument for what is called "truth relativism" or "genuine relativism," is that it fails to adequately account for the *prima facie* evidence that in cases like the one described above the participants genuinely disagree. As the above analysis shows, indexical relativism posits that there is no genuine disagreement between the disputants since the content of their claims is not actually the same; this indexical relativism collapses into a kind of error theory that it is not supposed to be and that brings with it another group of problems (Dreier 2009). "Truth relativism" or "genuine relativism" attempts to address this problem by claiming not that the content of moral statements is relativized to context, but that the truth conditions for those statements are relative to some standard or parameter. As Max Köbel puts it, the idea is that "moral sentences express the same contents in all contexts of utterance (unless they are indexical for the usual reasons), but that these contents have their truth-values relatively, that is, vary in truth-value with parameter of evaluation" (2014, 298).

Without wading into the debate, we might merely note that with reference to the matter at hand, the indexical relativist might simply reply that their analysis *does* seem to capture at least some cases of disagreement that might in fact only be apparent. Moreover, this need not commit the indexical relativist to a general error-theoretical account of moral discourse. Rather, it may be the case that the moral systems of some societies might diverge so significantly that there is insufficient common ground for them to be disagreeing (but see Moody-Adams 1997 for objections). Consider a discussion in which my claim, "Having sexual relations with pubescent boys is wrong" is relativized to me and the moral system in which I am embedded, and Phaedrus's claim, "Having sexual relations with pubescent boys is not wrong" is relativized to him and the moral system in which he is embedded. Indexical relativism holds that the content of these two statements is different in virtue of the different contexts in which they are made, and that seems exactly right in this sort of case: the action under the description "having sexual relations with pubescent boys" means something quite different to me (and members of my society) than it did to Phaedrus (and members of his society) (cf. Lear 2006; Rovane 2013; Velleman 2015). For this reason, we might describe this apparent dispute, in Bernard Williams's terms, as a "notional confrontation" rather than a "real confrontation" ([1985] 2011, 178). We shall flesh out the meaning of these terms presently.

Versions of moral relativism that perhaps more directly or overtly concern "how things are and how things aren't" tend to start with a commitment to naturalism, which, for the present purposes we can roughly characterize as a metaphysical doctrine with methodological implications. As a metaphysical doctrine, naturalism holds that there are no entities, forces, laws, properties, values, and so forth that exist or operate outside of nature. Flanagan, Sarkissian, and Wong describe naturalism's methodological implications for moral philosophy as involving the idea "that moral philosophy should not employ a distinctive a priori method of yielding substantive, self-evident and foundational truths from pure conceptual analysis. The claims of ethical naturalism cannot be shielded from empirical testing . . . [and] ethical science must be continuous with other sciences" (2008, 5). For such ethical naturalists, moral facts are not *sui generis*; on the contrary, morality is a human construction—one that has evolved to fit the specific needs and purposes of particular societies. Thus, morality has certain shared characteristic features across societies, but its specific features (norms and values) also vary across societies, and there is no single morality that applies universally (see Westermarck 1932; Wong 2006; Prinz 2007a; Flanagan, Sarkissian, and Wong 2008).

Naturalist moral relativism (of which Wong's (2006) "pluralistic relativism" is a prominent example) provides a good segue to a discussion of folk moral psychology. If one starts with the naturalist assumption that morality is a human construction, folk moral psychology is worth taking seriously even if no philosophical conclusions follow directly from what the folk think about morality.

EXPERIMENTAL FOLK MORAL PSYCHOLOGY AND META-ETHICAL PLURALISM

As mentioned earlier, there is evidence to suggest that professional philosophers and nonexperts (the "folk") both tend to regard moral value as more objective than aesthetic value. This is perhaps unsurprising; there is no expression equivalent to "de gustibus non disputandum est" that pertains to morality. What may be somewhat surprising is the recent empirical research that suggests people also regard the objectivity of moral judgments as variable depending upon contextual features of those judgments.

For example, Sarkissian and his colleagues (2011) conducted several studies that showed folk metaethical intuitions tend toward objectivism when presented with scenarios involving individuals from their own culture, but strongly shifted toward relativism when those scenarios involved individuals from distant cultures. Sarkissian and his colleagues randomly assigned 223 US college students to one of three conditions—same-culture, other-culture, or extraterrestrial—and presented them with two scenarios. In the first scenario, "Horace finds his youngest child extremely unattractive and therefore kills him." In the second, "Dylan buys an expensive new knife and tests its sharpness by randomly stabbing a passerby on the street" (2011, 487). In each case, students were asking to imagine a student from their class finding the actions described as morally wrong and another individual—either from the same culture, another culture (an Amazonian warrior culture with "quite different values"), or an extraterrestrial culture (the "Pentars . . . [which] have a very different sort of psychology from human beings [and] are not at all interested in friendship or love" [2011, 488])—judging the actions as morally acceptable. The students were asked to record their agreement (on a scale of 1–7) with the proposition that since the disputants had different judgments about these cases, at least one of them must be wrong. Subsequent studies varied the experiment design slightly to control for different variables.

In short, the authors concluded from the studies:

> as long as [people] are thinking only about individuals who are fairly similar to themselves—say individuals from their own cultural groups—their intuitions might look more or less objectivist . . . [But] as they come to think more and more seriously about people who are deeply dissimilar—individuals with radically different cultures, values, or ways of life—their intuitions move steadily toward a kind of

relativism. They gradually come to feel that even if two individuals have opposite opinions on some moral question, it could still turn out that neither one would have to be wrong. (Sarkissian et al. 2011, 486)

Obviously, one study (or set of studies) hardly warrants any general conclusions about folk moral psychology. However, Sarkissian's findings have been replicated (Khoo and Knobe 2018), and similar findings, reported in a variety of studies, suggest, taken as a whole, that the folk are meta-ethical pluralists—objectivists about some moral issues in some contexts and relativists about other moral issues in other contexts (e.g., Goodwin and Darley 2012; Beebe 2019; Beebe et al. 2015; Wright 2018). In a 2013 study, Wright, Grandjean, and McWhite summarized:

> People do not conceive of morality as a unified (meta-ethically speaking) domain, but rather as a domain whose normative mandates come in different shapes and sizes. They view the wrongness of some moral actions as clear and unquestionable, unaltered (and unalterable) by the feelings/beliefs/values of the individual or culture. They view the wrongness of other actions (though still genuinely moral in nature) as more sensitive to, and molded by, the feelings/beliefs/values of the actor and/or the people whose lives would be (or have been) affected by the action. (354).

In another context, it could be useful to enumerate the different ways in which folk meta-ethical intuitions vary. For the present purpose, however, it will be sufficient to note the fact that one significant way they seem to vary is in proportion to perceived cultural distance.

The implications of these findings for meta-ethics are not self-evident. Moral objectivists could argue that the data shows that people's moral intuitions are inconsistent and irrational, which hardly impeaches objectivism (see Colebrook 2021). However, the relativist could here point out that, when it suited them—that is, when the folk appeared to be objectivists—moral objectivists claimed folk moral psychology as *prima facie* evidence for their view and that it was the explanandum for which their view offered the most plausible explanans. Thus, it would seem the empirical findings from experimental moral psychology undermine the moral objectivist's claim that the *prima facie* evidence suggests the folk are moral objectivists. Thus, the claim that moral objectivism is the most straightforward and parsimonious explanation of the evidence is also undermined.

The empirical evidence from experimental folk moral psychology stands in need of an explanation that moral objectivists have yet to offer, but which is at least suggested in some versions of relativism—that is, indexical relativism or contextualism (Beebe 2010; Khoo and Knobe 2018; Beebe 2021). Recall that, according to indexical moral relativism, the content of moral propositions is relativized to a context of utterance. Thus, if moral propositions like "incest is wrong" and "incest is not wrong" are uttered by speakers in the same moral system (or in different moral systems with relevant shared standards), the propositions express mutually exclusive contents and one of the speakers must be wrong. If they are uttered in different contexts, where different moral systems or standards are operative, the contents of the propositions might not be contradictory and both could be true. In this way, indexical moral relativism offers a plausible account of the way in which folk moral psychological intuitions seem to oscillate from objectivism to relativism in proportion to perceived distance between cultures or societies.

PEDERASTY IN ANCIENT GREEK ART

Studying folk intuitions about the moral standing of artworks from a heterogeneous group of generative contexts could provide an interesting complement to the extant experimental research on folk moral psychology. If nothing else, it would ground folk intuitions in actual, concrete social practices and contexts. On the one hand, it might seem likely that moving from the realm of thought experiments about imaginary societies and alien forms of life to the actual, human context would shift folk intuitions back toward meta-ethical objectivism. On the other hand, an informal survey of our actual practices of the ethical criticism of art might suggest that the findings would mesh with the extant research. Here is one reason to think so.

As mentioned earlier, there is very little tolerance for the sexualization of children in contemporary, Western society. Consider, for example, relatively recent uproars about the photography of Bill Henson and David Hamilton, the painting of Graham Ovenden, or the films of Larry Clark, all of which have condemned for depicting children as the proper objects of sexual attraction. To be sure, there are complexities to some of these cases. But the point is that if we were to encounter an artwork from our own generative context that represented, let alone celebrated, sexual relations between a man and a boy between the ages of twelve and seventeen, most of us would think that it was morally wrong of the artist to create such a work and that the work was morally blemished in virtue of its celebration of something that is morally wrong. It is less clear that this is how we think about the actual ancient Greek artifacts—or that it is how we *should* think about those artifacts—partly because it is hard for us to imagine being part of a society in which pederasty was normal.

The term "pederasty" comes from the Greek word *paiderastia,* which joins the terms *paid-,* meaning "child or boy," and *erôs,* meaning "love." So, the term's literal meaning—"boy-love"—is more or less continuous with the meaning of the contemporary term. What bears further explanation, though, is the complex cultural practice this term described. As one would imagine, it involved an older partner or lover (the *erastês*) who courted a pubescent beloved (the *erômenos*). Thus, the *erastês* is often portrayed as pursuing the *erômenos* through the offering of gifts, which he hopes will result in the *erômenos* "grant[ing] favors," which would have included favors of a sexual nature (Robson 2013, 39). On some accounts, including Phaedrus's speech in Plato's *Symposium,* such relationships can extend well beyond the realm of physical desire, instilling courage and honour in the erômenos—and thus be "ethically educative" as Andrew Lear puts it (2014, 118; also see Nussbaum 2002, 63–64).

Two fragments below, from works of Straton, offer an indication of how the desires of *erastai* and the beauty (*kalon*) of young boys were represented in poetry of the time.

> In the case of a young girl there is no sphincter, there is
> no simple kiss, no natural fragrance of the skin,
> none of that lascivious chat so sweet to the taste, no seductive
> glance, and even when she has been taught how, she is worse!
> Finally, when being joined from behind, they are frigid. But, what is of greatest import,
>   there is nowhere you can put your wandering
> hand. (qtd. in Johnson and Ryan 2005, 117)

> In the prime of a twelve-year-old boy I take the utmost delight.
> One of thirteen, however, is even more desirable.
> He who is fourteen is an even sweeter bloom of the Loves.
> More delightful is he not far from the beginning of his fifteenth.
> The sixteenth year is the property of the gods. The seventeenth
> it is not for me to seek, but Zeus.
> But if anyone has a craving for one even older, he no longer sports,
> but is now in need, and "answers him back." (qtd. in Johnson and Ryan 2005, 123)

If anything, vase-painting offers more explicit depictions of pederasty (Lear 2014, 111). One well-known, conventional depiction of pederastic courtship features what has been termed "the up and down position" (see Nussbaum 2002, 55; Lear 2014, 110): the *erastês* reaches up with one hand to touch the *erômenos*'s chin and down with the other hand to touch his genitals. Another conventional scene depicts "intercrural intercourse," a kind of nonpenetrative sex which involves the *erastês* thrusting his penis between the closed thighs of the *erômenos* (Dover 1978, 98–99).

Whether or not empirical research would support my hypothesis that the folk lack confidence about an objective truth about the moral standing of these ancient Greek artworks, there are considerable independent reasons to think those artworks were just as morally acceptable for the Greeks as they would be morally unacceptable if they were created in our contemporary context—and that this should give us pause before ethically appraising them. Recall that, according to indexical relativism, the apparent dispute is dissolved by relativizing moral statements to the context in which they are uttered. Indexical relativism is criticized on this count for failing to preserve the sense that there is a real disagreement. But in this case, there are reasons to think that, in fact, there is no real disagreement at all.

Here we can usefully draw upon Bernard Williams's suggestion regarding clashing ethical outlooks to "not simply draw a line between ourselves and others . . . but recognize that others are at varying distances from us" ([1985] 2011, 178). Moreover, he encourages us to recognize, "Some disagreements and divergences matter more than others. Above it, it matters whether the contrast of our outlook with another is one that makes a difference, whether a question has to be resolved about what life is going to be lived by one group or the other" (Williams [1985] 2011, 178). In this case, there is not a live question about whether we are going to carry on living life our way or changing to the ancient Greek way. In Williams's terms, the ancient Greek outlook, like many outlooks of the distant past, is not a "real option" for us: "The life of a Bronze Age chief or a medieval samurai are not real options for us: there is no way of living them" ([1985] 2011, 179).

If we acknowledge that ancient Greek life is not a "real option" for us—that there is, for us, no way of living it—then there is reason to think the clash in ethical perspectives is in some sense moot. It amounts to what Williams calls a "notional confrontation" in contrast to a "real confrontation": "A real confrontation between two divergent outlooks occurs at a given time if there is a group of people for whom each of the outlooks is a real option. A notional confrontation, by contrast, occurs when some people know about two divergent outlooks, but at least one of those outlooks does not present a real option" ([1985] 2011, 178).

Williams's "relativism of distance" suggests that "the vocabulary of [ethical] appraisal" is in some sense inappropriate or incoherent in the context of notional confrontations. In fact, he says that in such contexts, "it will not be possible" for a "reflective person" to "raise . . . questions in the vocabulary of appraisal" (Williams 1975, 225). By this, Williams seems to mean that upon considered reflection, one ought to recognize the incoherence or inappropriateness of such questions when there is no "real confrontation." In his words, "to stand in merely notional confrontation is to lack the relation to our concerns which alone gives any point or substance to appraisal: the only real questions of appraisal are about real options" (Williams 1975, 225). Thus, Williams at least offers a plausible explanation of the documented folk intuition that we are less confident that our ethical norms apply to distant societies, like ancient Greece, than to our own society and relatively proximate societies.[7]

CONCLUSION

Of course, many of us spend most of our time with the art of our own society or relatively proximate societies. It bears emphasis, therefore, that the moderate relativist line I have sketched here does not lead us down a slippery slope to "anything goes" relativism: it does not, for example, imply that the racist stereotypes in Hollywood films like *Gone with the Wind* are not "really" wrong, as a matter of fact. They surely are. Indexical moral relativism about the ethical criticism of art can hold onto this conclusion by pointing to the overlap in the moral system of its generative context (the mid-twentieth-century United States) and its reception context (the early twenty-first-century United States). (Or, if one takes a sufficiently coarse-grained view of moral systems, one could say that, in this case, there is a single numerically continuous moral system with some qualitative differences across time.) A fuller defense of this view would, accordingly, need to say something

---

[7] For objections, see Moody-Adams (1997) and Fricker (2010).

more about the identity and individuation conditions of moral systems. Assuming some adequate account of moral systems could be offered, indexical moral relativism about the ethical criticism of art might very well offer a promising account of folk moral intuitions about the moral standing of art and the semantics of moral judgments of art.

See also: King, Song, Destrée, this volume

REFERENCES

Ayer, A. J. [1946] 1971. *Language, Truth, and Logic*. 2nd ed. London: Pelican.

Baghramian, Maria. 2004. *Relativism*. London, Routledge.

Baghramian, Maria, and J. Adam Carter. 2020. "Relativism." In *The Stanford Encyclopedia of Philosophy* (Spring 2021), edited by Edward N. Zalta. https://plato.stanford.edu/entries/relativism/#RelAboTruAleRel.

Beebe, James R. 2010. "Moral Relativism in Context." *Noûs* 44, no. 4: 691-724.

Beebe, James R. 2019. "How Different Kinds of Disagreement Impact Folk Metaethical Judgments." In *Advances in Experimental Moral Psychology*, edited by Hagop Sarkissian and Jennifer Cole Wright, 167–187. London: Bloomsbury Academic.

Beebe, James R. 2021. "The Empirical Case for Folk Indexical Moral Relativism." In *Oxford Studies in Experimental Philosophy, Volume 4*, edited by Tania Lombrozo, Joshua Knobe, and Shaun Nichols, 81-111. Oxford: Oxford University Press.

Beebe, James, Runya Qiaoan, Tomasz Wysocki, and Miguel A. Endara. 2015. "Moral Objectivism in Cross-Cultural Perspective." *Journal of Cognition and Culture* 15, no. 3–4: 386–401.

Björnsson, Gunnar. 2012. "Do 'Objectivist' Features of Moral Discourse and Thinking Support Moral Objectivism?" *Journal of Ethics* 16, no. 4: 367–393.

Björnsson, Gunnar, and Stephen Finlay. 2010. "Metaethical Contextualism Defended." *Ethics* 121, no. 1: 72–36.

Blackburn, Simon. 1984. *Spreading the Word: Groundings in the Philosophy of Language*. Oxford: Oxford University Press.

Boghossian, Paul. 2006. *Fear of Knowledge: Against Relativism and Constructivism*. Oxford: Oxford University Press.

Brink, David O. 1989. *Moral Realism and the Foundations of Ethics*. Cambridge: Cambridge University Press.

Brogaard, Berit. 2008. "Moral Contextualism and Moral Relativism." *The Philosophical Quarterly* 58, no. 232: 385–409.

Brogaard, Berit. 2017. "A Semantic Framework for Aesthetic Expressions." In *The Semantics of Aesthetic Judgments*, edited by James O. Young, 121–139. Oxford: Oxford University Press.

Colebrook, Ross. 2021. "The Irrationality of Folk Metaethics." *Philosophical Psychology* 34, no. 5: 684–720.

Currie, Gregory. 1991. "Text without Context: Some Errors of Stanley Fish." *Philosophy and Literature* 15, no. 2: 212–228.

D'Arms, Justin. 2005. "Two Arguments for Sentimentalism." *Philosophical Issues* 15: 1–21.

D'Arms, Justin, and Daniel Jacobson. 2000. "Sentiment and Value." *Ethics* 110, no. 4: 722–748.

Davies, David. 2017. "The Semantics of Sibleyan Aesthetic Judgments." In *The Semantics of Aesthetic Judgments*, edited by James O. Young, 106–120. Oxford: Oxford University Press.

Davies, Stephen. 2007. *Philosophical Perspectives on Art*. Oxford: Oxford University Press.

Dover, K. J. 1978. *Greek Homosexuality*. London: Duckworth.

Drier, James. 1990. "Internalism and Speaker Relativism." *Ethics* 101, no. 1: 6–26.

Drier, James. 2006. "Moral Relativism and Moral Nihilism." In *The Oxford Handbook of Ethical Theory*, edited by David Copp, 240–264. Oxford: Oxford University Press.

Drier, James. 2009. "Relativism (and Expressivism) and the Problem of Disagreement." *Philosophical Perspectives* 23: 79–110.

Egan, Andy. 2010. "Disputing about Taste." In *Disagreement*, edited by Richard Feldman and Ted A. Warfield, 247–286. Oxford: Oxford University Press.

Evers, Daan. 2021. "Relativism and the Metaphysics of Value." *British Journal of Aesthetics* 61, no. 1: 75–87.

Fingerhut, Joerg, and Jesse J. Prinz. 2020. "Aesthetic Emotions Reconsidered." *The Monist* 103, no. 2: 223–239.

Fish, Stanley. 1980. *Is There a Text in This Class? The Authority of Interpretive Communities*. Cambridge, MA: Harvard University Press.

Flanagan, Owen, Hagop Sarkissian, and David Wong. 2008. "Naturalizing Ethics." In *Moral Psychology, Volume 1: The Evolution of Morality: Adaptations and Innateness*, edited by Walter Sinnott-Armstrong, 1–25. Cambridge, MA: The MIT Press.

Fricker, Miranda. 2010. "The Relativism of Blame." *Proceedings of the Aristotelian Society Supplementary Volume* 84, no. 1: 151–177.

Goldman, Alan H. 1995. *Aesthetic Value*. Boulder, CO: Westview Press.

Goodwin, Geoffrey P., and John M. Darley. 2012. "Why Are Some Moral Beliefs Perceived to Be More Objective than Others?" *Journal of Experimental Social Psychology* 48, no. 1: 250–256.

Hales, Steven D., ed. 2011. *A Companion to Relativism*. Oxford: Wiley-Blackwell.

Harman, Gilbert. 1996. "Moral Relativism." In *Moral Relativism and Moral Objectivity*, edited by Gilbert Harman and Judith Jarvis Thomson, 3–64. Oxford: Blackwell.

Harman, Gilbert. 2000. *Explaining Value*. Oxford: Clarendon Press.

Harré, Rom, and Michael Krausz. 1996. *Varieties of Relativism*. Oxford: Blackwell.

Johnson, Marguerite, and Terry Ryan. 2005. *Sexuality in Greek and Roman Society and Literature: A Sourcebook*. London: Routledge.

Khoo, Justin, and Joshua Knobe. 2018. "Moral Disagreement and Moral Semantics." *Noûs* 52, no. 1: 109–143.

Kivy, Peter. 2015. *De Gustibus: Arguing about Taste and Why We Do It*. Oxford: Oxford University Press.

Köbel, Max. 2004. "Faultless Disagreement." *Proceedings of the Aristotelian Society* 104, no. 1: 53–73.

Köbel, Max. 2014. "Indexical Relativism versus Genuine Relativism." *International Journal of Philosophical Studies* 12, no. 3: 297–313.

Krausz, Michael. 1993. *Rightness and Reasons: Interpretation in Cultural Practices*. Ithaca, NY: Cornell University Press.

Krausz, Michael, Michael, ed. 2010. *Relativism: A Contemporary Anthology*. New York: Columbia University Press.

Kusch, Martin, ed. 2020. *The Routledge Handbook of Philosophy of Relativism*. New York: Routledge.

Lasersohn, Peter. 2005. "Context Dependence, Disagreement, and Predicates of Personal Taste." *Linguistics and Philosophy* 28, no. 6: 643–686.

Lear, Andrew. 2014. "Ancient Pederasty: An Introduction." In *A Companion to Greek and Roman Sexualities*, edited by Thomas K. Hubbard, 106–131. Malden, MA: Blackwell.

Lear, Jonathan. 2006. *Radical Hope: Ethics in the Face of Cultural Devastation*. Cambridge, MA: Harvard University Press.

Livingston, Paisley. 1998. *Literary Knowledge: Humanistic Inquiry and the Philosophy of Science*. Ithaca, NY: Cornell University Press.

Lopes, Dominic McIver. 2017. "Disputing Taste." In *The Semantics of Aesthetic Judgments*, edited by James O. Young, 61–81. Oxford: Oxford University Press.

MacFarlane, John. 2005. "Making Sense of Relative Truth." *Proceedings of the Aristotelian Society* 105, no. 1: 321–336.

MacFarlane, John. 2014. *Assessment Sensitivity: Relative Truth and its Applications*. Oxford: Oxford University Press.

Mackie, J. L. 1977. *Ethics: Inventing Right and Wrong*. London: Penguin.

McDowell, John. 1998. "Aesthetic Value, Objectivity, and the Fabric of the World." In *Mind, Value, and Reality*, 112–130. Cambridge, MA: Harvard University Press.

Margolis, Joseph. 1980. *Art and Philosophy*. Atlantic Highlands, NJ: Humanities Press.

Margolis, Joseph. 1999. *What, After All, Is a Work of Art?* University Park: Penn State University Press.

Matravers, Derek. 2010. "Aesthetic Relativism." *Postgraduate Journal of Aesthetics* 7, no. 2: 1–12.

Moody-Adams, Michele. 1997. *Fieldwork in Familiar Places: Morality, Culture, and Philosophy*. Cambridge, MA: Harvard University Press.

Nannicelli, Ted. 2013. *Appreciating the Art of Television: A Philosophical Perspective*. New York: Routledge.

Nannicelli, Ted. 2017. "Ethical Criticism and the Interpretation of Art." *Journal of Aesthetics and Art Criticism* 75, no. 4: 401–413.

Nannicelli, Ted. 2020. *Artistic Creation and Ethical Criticism*. Oxford: Oxford University Press.

Nannicelli, Ted. 2022. "Interactive Documentary, Narrative Scepticism, and the Values of Documentary Film." In *Truth in Visual Media: Aesthetics, Ethics and Politics*, edited by Marguerite La Caze and Ted Nannicelli, 167–188. Edinburgh: Edinburgh University Press.

Nussbaum, Martha C. 2002. "*Erôs* and Ethical Norms: Philosophers Respond to a Cultural Dilemma." In *The Sleep of Reason: Erotic Experience and Sexual Ethics in Ancient Greece and Rome*, edited by Martha C. Nussbaum and Juha Sihvola, 55–94. Chicago: University of Chicago Press.

Prinz, Jesse J. 2007a. *The Emotional Construction of Morals*. Oxford: Oxford University Press.

Prinz, Jesse J. 2007b. "Really Bad Taste." In *Knowing Art: Essays in Aesthetics and Epistemology*, edited by Matthew Kieran and Dominic McIver Lopes, 95–108. Dordrecht: Springer.

Prinz, Jesse J. 2011. "Emotion and Aesthetic Value." In *The Aesthetic Mind: Philosophy and Psychology*, edited by Elisabeth Schellekens and Peter Goldie, 71–88. Oxford: Oxford University Press.

Railton, Peter. 1998. "Aesthetic Value, Moral Value, and the Ambitious of Naturalism." In *Aesthetics and Ethics: Essays at the Intersection*, edited by Jerrold Levinson, 59–105. Cambridge: Cambridge University Press.

Railton, Peter. 2010. "Realism and its Alternatives." In *The Routledge Companion to Ethics*, edited by John Skorupski, 297–320. New York: Routledge.

Robson, James. 2013. *Sex and Sexuality in Classical Athens*. Edinburgh: Edinburgh University Press.

Rorty, Richard. 1990. *Objectivity, Relativism, and Truth: Philosophical Papers, Vol. 2*. Cambridge: Cambridge University Press.

Rorty, Richard. 1998. *Truth and Progress: Philosophical Papers, Vol. 3*. Cambridge: Cambridge University Press.

Rovane, Carol. 2013. *The Metaphysics and Ethics of Relativism*. Cambridge, MA: Harvard University Press.

Sarkissian, Hagop, John Park, David Tien, Jennifer Cole Wright, and Joshua Knobe. 2011. "Folk Moral Relativism." *Mind and Language* 26, no. 4: 482–505.

Shafer-Landau, Russ. 2003. *Moral Realism: A Defence*. Oxford: Oxford University Press.

Shusterman, Richard. 1992. *Pragmatist Aesthetics: Living Beauty, Rethinking Art*. Oxford: Blackwell.

Smith, Barbara Herrnstein. 1988. *Contingencies of Value: Alternative Perspectives for Critical Theory*. Cambridge, MA: Harvard University Press.

Smith, Michael. 1994. *The Moral Problem*. Oxford: Blackwell.

Stecker, Robert. 1997. *Artworks: Definition, Meaning, Value*. University Park: Penn State University Press.

Stecker, Robert. 2003. *Interpretation and Construction: Art, Speech, and the Law*. Oxford: Blackwell.

Stephenson, Tamina. 2007. "Judge Dependence, Epistemic Modals, and Predicates of Personal Taste." *Linguistics and Philosophy* 30, no. 6: 487–525.

Velleman, J. David. 2015. *Foundations for Moral Relativism*. 2nd expanded ed. Cambridge: Open Book Publishers.

Westermarck, Edward. 1932. *Ethical Relativity*. London: Kegan Paul, Trench, Trubner & Co.

Wiggins, David. 1987. "A Sensible Subjectivism?" In *Needs, Values, Truth*, 185–214. Oxford: Basil Blackwell.

Williams, Bernard. 1975. "The Truth in Relativism." *Proceedings of the Aristotelian Society* 75: 215–228.

Williams, Bernard. [1985] 2011. *Ethics and the Limits of Philosophy*. Oxon: Routledge.

Wong, David B. 1984. *Moral Relativity*. Berkeley: University of California Press.

Wong, David B. 2006. *Natural Moralities: A Defense of Pluralistic Relativism*. Oxford: Oxford University Press.

Wright, Crispin. 1992. *Truth and Objectivity*. Cambridge, MA: Harvard University Press.

Wright, Jennifer Cole. 2018. "The Fact and Function of Meta-Ethical Pluralism." In *Oxford Studies in Experimental Psychology, Volume 2*, edited by Tania Lombrozo, Joshua Knobe, and Shaun Nichols, 119–150. Oxford: Oxford University Press.

Wright, Jennifer C., Piper T. Grandjean, and Cullen B. McWhite. 2013. "The Meta-Ethical Grounding of Our Moral Beliefs: Evidence for Meta-Ethical Pluralism." *Philosophical Psychology* 26, no. 3: 336–361.

Young, James O. 2009. "Relativism, Standards, and Aesthetic Judgments." *International Journal of Philosophical Studies* 17, no. 2: 221–231.

Zangwill, Nick. 2001. *The Metaphysics of Beauty*. Ithaca, NY: Cornell University Press.

CHAPTER 15

KANTIAN APPROACHES TO ETHICAL JUDGMENT OF ARTWORKS

SANDRA SHAPSHAY

It is difficult to capture a distinctively Kantian approach to the ethical evaluation of artworks since Kant's own aesthetic concerns are arguably first and foremost about the aesthetic experience of *nature,* and only secondarily about art. This is because the systematic purpose of the third *Critique* is to bridge the "great chasm" (*die große Kluft*) between the domain of nature (as governed by scientific laws) and the domain of freedom (as governed by the supersensible causality of the rational, autonomous subject) (5:195).[1] Within this systemic context, natural objects—especially *organisms*—and how we may judge them aesthetically and teleologically, take center stage.

On that stage, for Kant, we learn that a flower, bird, crystal, or some patch of intertwining foliage are paradigmatically apt to afford *pure* judgments of taste (a.k.a. pure judgments of beauty). These are judgments that express a disinterested, intellectual pleasure in a "free play" (*freies Spiel*) of the faculties of the imagination and understanding in a perceptual engagement with an object's formal features, "the spatial shape or three-dimensional outline of an object" (Reiter and Geiger 2018, 74). Pure judgments of taste have the greatest systematic importance for Kant, since they reveal the transcendental, regulative principle for the power of judgment—the principle of the purposiveness of nature—precisely the principle that is supposed to offer that mediating bridge between the domains of nature and freedom.

Most important for the concerns of this *Handbook,* however, is that in the process of offering an analysis of the pure judgment of beauty, Kant gives fodder for formalists and autonomists about *fine art.* This is because, *pure aesthetic judgments* according to Kant

---

[1] All citations to the third *Critique* utilize the Guyer and Matthews translation of *The Critique of the Power of Judgment* (Kant, [1790] 2000) with parenthetical notations to the standard Akademie edition.

are based on a subject's response to *perceptual form* and *pure aesthetic pleasure* is autonomous from interests of all kinds (moral, utilitarian, religious, political, etc.) as well as from concepts of what the object is supposed to be. Thus, it is fitting to see Kant as the forerunner of contemporary formalist and autonomist approaches to thinking about relationships between art and ethics. Yet as Paul Guyer has rightly stressed, Kant, as well as other eighteenth-century theorists of the disinterestedness and autonomy of the aesthetic, "did not intend to make a problem for ethical criticism of art" and did not argue for "the autonomy of *art* and the judgment of *art* from all ethical concerns and criticism" (Guyer 2008, 16; emphasis added).

Indeed, Kant was not an opponent of the ethical criticism of art for two main reasons: First, he seems to hold that judgments about fine art (*schöne Kunst*) are all *impure* judgments of taste—it seems we can only make judgments of "adherent beauty" (*anhängende Schönheit*) not judgments of "free beauty" (*freie Schönheit*) about art. This is because in judging art one always, and it seems ineluctably, takes into consideration notions of the perfection of its kind or subkind *qua* work of art. That is to say, we always judge a work of fine art at least in part for how it succeeds as a member of its kind, and thus we are always cognizant of the concept and purpose of art in the judging of any work, which leads to a merely adherent rather than pure judgment of taste.

Second, all genuine fine art for Kant expresses *content* in the form of aesthetic ideas, paradigmatically, *moral ideas*. These are aimed at provoking a pleasurable free play of the cognitive faculties and much open-ended thought. Prima facie, these two elements of Kant's theory of fine art—that all judgments about art are (merely) adherent judgments of beauty, and all genuine fine art involves the expression of content-full aesthetic ideas—make it much friendlier to anti-formalism, moralism and ethicism. Putting this point quite nicely, Guyer writes, "in fine art, the intended purpose of a work as well as its intended content clearly both constrain the form of the object but also enter into free play with the form and matter of the object, in such a way that ethical considerations do not remain external to the work's character as a work of art but become part and parcel of it" (Guyer 2008, 20).

Thus, on the one hand, Kant's theory of the pure judgment of taste (centered on natural objects) lends support to formalists and autonomists about art; but, on the other hand, Kant's own theory of fine art, lends support to anti-formalists, moralists, and ethicists about art! Complicating matters further, there is another wrinkle in this story: Ultimately Kant seems to be operating with *two conceptions of fine art* (Danto 2013, 117). The first conception is indeed formalist and in Danto's terms, "ornamentalist" (and includes wallpaper borders, free musical fantasias, and in general visual works of art that display taste but lack "spirit"), and the second is proto-Romantic: it is art with "spirit" (*Geist*) (5:313–314), that is to say, art that animates the mind through an aesthetic idea, "which purposively sets the mental powers into . . . a self-sustaining play" (5:313). While the former notion of art marks out similarities between works of art and the "free beauties of nature," the latter notion marks out those works which stimulate to a much greater extent our cognitive powers, pushing the boundaries of thought via the subject's free play with sensible "counterparts" of rational ideas (5:314). I call this second, proto-Romantic conception of fine art the "official" conception, and the first, the "unofficial one" (Shapshay 2020, 210).

On the official conception, artworks are representational works of genius that animate the mental powers of the spectator through aesthetic ideas; and on the "unofficial" conception, works of art are decorative, nonrepresentational works that animate the spectator's mind in free play along the lines of natural "free beauties," that is, through spatial shape or form. So it seems that at least some twentieth- and twenty-first-century formalists (Eduard Hanslick, Clive Bell, Clement Greenberg, and more recently Nick Zangwill) as well as various sorts of *autonomists* about art (e.g., Oscar Wilde and the "art for art's sake" movement, Theodor Adorno, and more recently Peter Lamarque, James C. Anderson and Jeffrey T. Dean, Adriana Clavel-Vázquez, and James Harold), might very well be called "Kantian" insofar as they may be developing aspects of the "unofficial" theory of art on offer in Kant's aesthetics rather than his "official" theory of fine art.[2]

In what follows I'll consider a contemporary formalist (Nick Zangwill) and a contemporary autonomist (James Harold) to investigate to what extent their approaches to the ethical judgment of artworks may be justifiably termed "Kantian." Next, I shall discuss some wider, suggestive connections that Kant drew between the overall domains of the aesthetic and the ethical:

- The experience of *the sublime*—more directly than beauty—makes vivid to the subject, her rational-moral vocation (see esp.§29 CPJ).
- Interest in the beauty of nature (though notably *not* in art) is the mark of a morally good soul (esp. §42 CPJ).
- The experience of imaginative freedom in pure judgements of the beautiful constitutes a *symbol of morality* (§59, CPJ).

I focus on these connections in order to explore what further ramifications Kant's theory may have for the central topic of this *Handbook*, connections between ethics and art.

KANT AND CONTEMPORARY FORMALISM

Nick Zangwill has defended a "moderate formalism" that lies, predictably enough, between extreme formalism, which holds that all works of art have only formal properties, and anti-formalism, which holds that no works of art have purely formal properties. Moderate formalism, on Zangwill's account, holds that "many works of art are purely formal works [where] all of their aesthetic properties are formal aesthetic properties" though some works have no formal aesthetic properties (e.g., purely

---

[2] For a discussion of the formalists and the art for art's sake movement, see Gal (this volume) and also Lamarque (this volume).

conceptual works) and "many [other] works of art, including most representational and contextual works . . . have both formal and non-formal aesthetic properties" (Zangwill 2000, 493; see also Zangwill 1999). The works that he is keen to defend as purely formal—versus what he sees as Kendall Walton's global anti-formalism about art (Walton 1970)—are especially abstract works such as "mature Mondrians," absolute music, and nonrepresentational works of art such as "Islamic decoration" (Zangwill 2000, 480–482).

While the issue of formalism, on the one hand, and the question of the legitimacy of the ethical criticism of art, on the other, are not directly connected, it stands to reason that if some works of art are purely formal, as Zangwill holds, at least these works seem inapt for any intrinsic ethical evaluation. This is because purely formal aesthetic properties wouldn't prescribe any unmerited because immoral attitudes (Gaut 2007), and *a fortiori* would not prescribe any immoral attitudes that might for that reason prevent uptake by a suitably situated spectator (Carroll 1996), thus leading to "interaction" between the moral and aesthetic value of the work (Stecker 2005).

Would it be accurate to say that Zangwill's moderate formalism—which would secure a kind of autonomy from legitimate ethical evaluation for at least some purely formal works—is a "Kantian approach"?

I think it would be, insofar as Kant does imply that there is a "select class" of artworks that are purely formal and thus apt for a pure judgment of taste. In fact, one of the first mentions of works that we and Kant's contemporaries would generally class as works of fine art in the 3rd *Critique* comes in §16 where he first distinguishes "free beauty" (*freie Schönheit*) from "merely adherent beauty" (*die bloß anhängende Schönheit*). As sketched at the outset of this chapter, the former type "presupposes no concept of what the object ought to be" whereas the latter type "does presuppose such a concept and the perfection of the object in accordance with it" (5: 229). And while natural objects are the paradigm cases of free beauties, abstract and decorative works of art also factor among the free beauties that Kant lists in this section: "designs à la grecque, foliage for borders or on wallpaper . . . and music fantasias (without a theme), indeed all music without a text" (5:229). These works of art seem to be appreciated in precisely the same manner as the free beauties of nature, that is, not under the description of a definite concept—not even under the concept of "work of art"—but rather for their formal, perceptual properties alone.

The conceptual coherence of this class of purely formal works within Kant's overall aesthetic theory, however, seems to depend on whether the judger can (or can appropriately) abstract away from the status of the work qua work of art, *in order to treat it just like a free beauty of nature* (Dowling 2010, 112).

Now, Kant does allow for this kind of abstraction from the object's purpose or kind in the case of the aesthetic appreciation of a flower by even a trained botanist. Accordingly, he writes, "flowers are free natural beauties. Hardly anyone other than the botanist, knows what sort of thing a flower is supposed to be; *and even the botanist, who recognizes in it the reproductive organ of the plant, pays no attention to this natural end if he judges the flower by means of taste*" (5: 229, emphasis mine). Yet somewhat puzzlingly, Kant seems to disallow this kind of abstraction from the object's end or purpose when judging the beauty of a horse or a church (5: 230).

What seems to make all the difference in whether this abstractive move is or is not possible (or more mildly, appropriate) on Kant's aesthetics, is whether the end or purpose is intrinsic or extrinsic to the thing. In other words, it depends on whether the object being judged is an organism (a "natural end") whose purposive form comes from itself, or whether the object is an artifact—like the church—or *more like an artifact*, in the case of a horse who has been bred by humans over centuries to have certain desirable traits. Thus, what seems to make this abstractive move possible/appropriate for Kant in the case of *free artistic beauties* like musical fantasias and designs à la grecque is that these works are abstract and nonrepresentational. Even in the case of "foliage for borders or on wallpaper," the point of these works is not to represent actual plants, or to spark a free play with aesthetic ideas, but rather to present the viewer with a pleasing, seemingly *internally purposive form* that has *no obvious extrinsic purpose* (unlike the horse or the church). Insofar as these free artistic beauties do not clearly bring to mind any definite *extrinsic* purpose for their form, abstraction from their status as works of art in their aesthetic appreciation is possible and, it seems, comes rather easily. Whereas, in the case of the horse, church, or representational work of art, there is an obvious extrinsic purpose to each of these objects: In the case of the horse, it is to serve human needs for transportation, work or sport; in the case of the church, it is to afford a congenial place for worship; and in the case of representational work of art, it is to represent an object in the world more or less faithfully and to spark a pleasurable free play of ideas. These extrinsic purposes, for Kant, make the abstractive move at best inappropriate and at worst, impossible.

Accordingly, we see how Zangwill's moderate formalism may be seen as genuinely Kantian, for his select class of purely formal works coincides rather well with Kant's "unofficial" theory of art that sees certain works as akin to "free beauties" of nature. But can the same be said for autonomist views of art? May these be justifiably termed "Kantian" approaches? To investigate this question, we will need to go a bit deeper into Kant's *official* theory of fine art.

KANT ON REPRESENTATIONAL FINE ART

When Kant gets down to the official theory of art (in §43), we find a view that cannot be reasonably interpreted in an extreme or even a moderate formalist way. This is for several reasons. First, in these sections of CPJ, all fine art seems to be representational, and arguably, all representational art needs to be appreciated in light of its proper arthistorical category in order to appreciate it appropriately. Since art-historical categories are nonperceptual aesthetic properties, we should not be formalists about representational art (Walton 1970, 345; Zangwill 2000, 480–481).

Second, and very much in line with this Waltonian anti-formalist argument, for Kant, all judgments about fine art are impure/adherent judgments of taste. This means that they inevitably involve evaluations of the perfection of the object's kind and perhaps also subkinds such as genres. As treated above, the ineluctable "impurity" of our *artistic* judgments stems from the fact that when we experience and judge a work of art, we seem not to be able to abstract away from its status as an intentional product of an artist with a certain purpose. Accordingly, Kant writes that "in a product of art one must be aware that it is art, and not nature" (5: 306). Thus, as discussed earlier, in these sections— when dealing with representational art—Kant suggests that the abstractive move with respect to designs à grecque, music without a text, and the like is not even possible.

Notwithstanding, Kant adds that fine art should still "seem to be as free from all con-straint by arbitrary rules *as if it were a mere product of nature*" (ibid., emphasis mine). Thus, the work of fine art should seem to have an intrinsic purposiveness (like an or-ganism) though we must be aware of it as an artifact (with extrinsic purposiveness, like a church). In order for an artist to pull off this complicated balancing act, namely, the creation of a work that seems at once natural and artifactual, the artist must have ge-nius—"the talent (natural gift) that gives the rule to art" (5: 307). Genius allows an artist to create a work that, in addition to displaying taste and academic correctness (which are also necessary features for a work of fine art on his theory), also enjoys originality and exemplarity, by virtue of the "natural gift."

Even with the addition of the natural gift of genius to his official theory of art, Kant holds that the work of fine art *cannot* be experienced exactly like a free beauty of na-ture, "for something in it must be thought of as an end, otherwise one cannot ascribe its product to any art at all; it would be a mere product of chance" (5:310).[3] The upshot is that insofar as we are judging a work of fine (representational) art *qua* work of art at all, we cannot judge it aesthetically merely on the basis of pleasurable engagement with its perceptual formal features. Rather, we must also judge it on the basis of how "perfect" it is as a member of its kind. Its kind is "fine art" or a subkind of art like "sculpture" or "painting." Thus, in Kant's terms, we can make only an "adherent judgment of beauty"— an impure judgment of taste—with these works, one in which a judgment of beauty is comingled with a judgment of perfection (5:311). This official theory makes Kant an anti-formalist about artworks insofar as one must utilize nonperceptual properties of the work such as art-historical properties in order to engage and judge it aesthetically in an appropriate manner.

Third, and perhaps most important for establishing Kant's anti-formalism on his "official theory" of art, *all genuine fine art expresses aesthetic ideas*. Recall that an aes-thetic idea is a "representation of the imagination that occasions much thinking though without it being possible for any determinate thought, that is, concept, to be adequate to it, which, consequently, no language fully attains or can make intelligible" (5:314). Aesthetic ideas are responsible for producing the pleasurable free play (*freies Spiel*)

---

[3] For an argument that runs counter to my interpretation here, see Tuna (2018).

of the mental faculties in which genuine artistic-aesthetic experience and pleasure consists. And they necessarily import content into the appropriate experience of works of fine art.

To make matters even less promising for a "Kantian formalist" about art, aesthetic ideas tend to be moral ideas; as Reiter and Geiger nicely put it, "the great subject of art [for Kant] is the idea of humanity and the breadth and variety of human freedom" (Reiter and Geiger 2018, 83). Recently, Samantha Matherne has made a strong case for a more "inclusive" interpretation whereby aesthetic ideas "can present not only moral and purely rational concepts but also empirical concepts and emotions related to our ordinary experience" (Matherne 2013, 21). Nonetheless, Kant himself goes so far as to suggest that if a work of art lacks *moral content*, the subject will find the work ultimately trivial or worse repulsive, writing "if the beautiful arts are not combined, whether closely or at a distance, with moral ideas, which alone carry with them a self-sufficient satisfaction" then they will "makes the spirit dull" and the object will become "loathsome" (5:326). Thus, with respect to his official theory of art, it is largely *moral content,* and the subject's reflection on and response to that content, that is integral to genuinely artistic-aesthetic experience.

Thus, it seems that Kant's official theory of art gives fodder to contemporary moralists and ethicists. But before putting Kant's official theory clearly on the side of "team moralism," I'd like to consider a test case for whether Kant could still be considered an autonomist about artworks that fall outside of the select class of purely formal works à la Zangwill. I'd like to focus on a compelling, nuanced case for autonomism made recently by James Harold, and ask: might this "moderate autonomist" approach be legitimately termed "Kantian"?

KANT AND AUTONOMISM

In her illuminating analysis of Leni Riefenstahl's Nazi propaganda film *The Triumph of the Will*, Mary Devereaux (1998) frames her discussion of the ethical judgment of the film in terms of the valuer's evaluative conflict. Should the viewer who finds the film formally beautiful and artistically innovative adjust her positive aesthetic judgment on the basis of her moral judgment that the film is evil, insofar as it clearly idealizes Hitler and endorses the genocidal ideology of the Third Reich? Taking his lead from this way of framing the issue, James Harold seeks to reconsider and defend a version of autonomism that foregrounds just this kind of evaluative conflict.[4]

Harold defines autonomism as "the view that a person who makes a global moral judgment *u* and a global aesthetic judgment *a* of the same object or event is not rationally required to adjust *a* in light of *u* or to adjust *u* in light of *a*" (Harold 2011, 140; see also

---

[4] For a detailed discussion and evaluation of formalism, see Stear, this volume.

Harold 2020, Chapter 8). And he sees as distinctive of autonomism the idea that it is "not itself a failure on the agent's part" if one does not "integrate one's moral and aesthetic evaluations" (ibid.). In other words, the subject who is experiencing such evaluative conflict is not "required to modify an aesthetic judgment because of a moral judgment or the other way around" (ibid.).

Could this version of autonomism be construed as a Kantian approach? After all, didn't Kant argue for the autonomy of the pure aesthetic judgment?

Unlike the class of art that Zangwill focused on in his defense of moderate formalism, the kind of artistic case that Harold is focusing on is not a work that has only formal aesthetic properties. On the contrary, the paradigm case of evaluative conflict for Harold is one that involves a work of representational, narrative, even morally engaged art—one that aims to marry formally beautiful scenes with "aesthetic ideas" of a moral/political sort. In other words, the case at issue falls squarely under Kant's official theory of art.

In attempting to answer the question of whether this form of autonomism can be aptly classed as "Kantian," let us grant that the appreciator in this case is engaging the film in an appropriately disinterested way, and in doing so is responding to the formal beauty of the film as well as the fact that the aesthetic ideas expressed in it—tied as they are to moral and political ideas—are morally evil and disgust her. Would Kant's theory necessitate the modification of her global, formal aesthetic judgment on the basis of her global moral judgment of the film? If she just didn't care to make these two judgments cohere with each other, would there be, on the Kantian theory, a failure of rationality on her part if she refused to do so?

I believe a Kantian analysis of this situation would proceed along the following lines: insofar as a film like *The Triumph of the Will* is *not* like a musical fantasia, it is not apt for a pure judgment of taste grounded on pleasurable engagement with purely formal features. In other words, it is not an abstract film—it is not merely a design or decoration; rather, it is a representational, narrative work that is expressive of aesthetic ideas. And thus, the film *should not be judged globally merely on its formal aesthetic properties;* it should rather be judged at least in part on the basis of its *kind*, *qua* work of fine art and on how well it serves its function as a work of art. The function of a work of fine art, for Kant, is to produce a pleasurable free play of the cognitive faculties via the expression of aesthetic ideas that are in some way connected to moral ideas. Given the morally repulsive nature of the aesthetic ideas expressed in the film, the (morally alert) viewer will meet with some imaginative resistance in engaging with it.[5] If she didn't experience some morally motivated imaginative resistance, of course, she wouldn't be in the position of evaluative conflict in the first place!

But this imaginative resistance (even perhaps to the point of disgust) would, on Kant's official theory of art, diminish the goodness of the film qua work of art, since it diminishes the pleasurable, sustained, and self-sustaining free play of the cognitive faculties. The morally evil content thus blocks to some extent that free play, and the

---

[5] For a treatment of Kant's views on imaginative resistance see (Tuna, n.d.).

spectator should accordingly factor that fact into her *adherent judgment* of the beauty or aesthetic value of the film as a whole.

In tension with this adherent judgment of beauty, however, is her attempt to make a pure judgment of beauty on the formal features of the film. In this way, one could see the evaluator as attempting to make that abstractive move away from the work's concept or purpose (along the lines of the botanist, who judges the flower aesthetically in abstraction from her knowledge of its purpose within the organism). But should the appreciator of Riefenstahl's film be seen as rationally required to adjust her positive global aesthetic judgment in light of the negative global moral judgment? This is Harold's key question.

I think Kant would say "yes"; she is rationally required to harmonize these judgments because it is inappropriate in the first place to try to render a global, pure judgment of beauty on a work of fine art of this sort. This narrative film is just not the kind of artwork that is appropriate to judge in this purely formal manner. In other words, the valuer is rationally required to adjust her formal aesthetic judgment in light of her ethical judgment of the work because the work is simply not the kind of thing that ought to be judged in a purely formal manner at all.

One might retort, however, that since Kant allows for even a trained botanist to render a pure aesthetic judgment of a flower—in abstraction from her knowledge of its purpose—his theory should similarly allow even a trained film critic legitimately to render a pure aesthetic judgment of *The Triumph of the Will* in abstraction from its status as a work of representational, narrative art (with its purpose of sparking pleasurable, sustained imaginative free play via aesthetic ideas). Are there any principled reasons on which Kant could ground this asymmetry? I think Kant's answer to this goes pretty deep into his system—and may be unsatisfying for this reason, but my job is to discuss Kantian approaches so I shall forge ahead. I think the principled grounds for this asymmetry relate to the organism/artifact distinction.

Flowers, as parts of organisms, have an *intrinsic purposiveness* that will, for Kant, remain ineluctably mysterious. Given Kant's commitments in the second part of the third *Critique*, he proclaims "we can boldly say that it would be absurd for humans . . . to hope that there may yet arise a Newton who could make comprehensible even the generation of a blade of grass according to natural laws that no intention has ordered" (5:400). In other words, organisms or "natural purposes" certainly don't seem to be explicable from merely mechanical, natural laws; rather, they seem *designed*, like human artifacts. But we can have no knowledge of a celestial artisan (by virtue of the arguments of the first *Critique*) who could have designed these organisms, so their status as "natural purposes" *must remain mysterious.*

By contrast, works of representational art—even the genial ones that *seem natural*—have an extrinsic purposiveness that is imposed on them by the artist. Because genius involves a *natural*, inborn talent giving the rule to art, artistic creation is more mysterious than, say, the creation of an artifact like a watch, but a work of fine art is still clearly something that is *made* intentionally by a human being for a purpose. If we try to abstract away from the status of Leni Riefenstahl's film as an intentional human product with a determinate purpose, we would then consider it as something that is the "mere product of chance" (5:310). But this is ridiculous. The film is manifestly not a mere product of chance. If we were to judge the film *as if* it were a free natural beauty—which is what we'd be doing in judging it merely on the basis of its formal beauty—we would be treating it as something it is manifestly not. Since this is a work of representational fine art, by definition for Kant, it is necessarily in the business of expressing aesthetic ideas. To treat it as a "free natural beauty" is to treat it as something it is not and makes little rational sense. Thus, at the end of the day, I don't think Harold's autonomist proposal would be well described as "Kantian." Of course, this makes little difference to the theoretical virtues of Harold's proposal. My only point here is that I don't think that one could legitimately say that Kant is on "team autonomism" about works of representational art.

SUBLIME ART AND THE MORAL

Kant's theory of the sublime has some perhaps surprising ramifications for the question about the ethical judgment of art. The experience of the sublime, for Kant, consists in a mixed painful/pleasurable (but, overall positively valenced) free play of the cognitive faculties, which differs from the experience of the beautiful in ways that connect it *more directly* to the moral. Especially in sublime experiences of the dynamical kind[6]—though some scholars would argue for the moral dimension of the Kantian sublime *tout court* (cf. Merritt 2012)—that is, with overwhelmingly powerful forces, typically storms at sea, cascades, tornadoes and the like, there transpires a free play between the cognitive faculties of imagination and *reason,* which enlivens the sense of our (supersensible) rational-moral vocation. If artworks can provoke a sublime response, for Kant, then these artworks will thereby spark morally uplifting thoughts. Thus, prima facie, on a Kantian view, *sublime art is to that extent and for that reason always morally salutary art.* In order to resolve whether such a view is entailed by Kant's aesthetic theory, however, we need to wade into a scholarly controversy: Can art be sublime on Kant's theory? (Crowther 1989; Abaci 2008, 2010; Clewis 2009, 2010; Wicks 1995; Pillow 2000).

As in pure judgments of the beautiful, the paradigm cases of pure judgments of the sublime are *natural* objects (though in the case of the sublime, this is better described as

---

[6] In the mathematical sublime, a subject is *cognitively* frustrated and humbled by objects that are too vast to comprehend, and whose appearances "[bring] with them the idea of its infinity" (5:255). In this way, Kant explains, the feeling of the sublime in nature, "makes intuitable [*anschaulich*] the superiority [*die Überlegenheit*] of the rational vocation of our cognitive faculty over the greatest faculty of sensibility" (5:258).

"raw nature" (5:253), that is, formless, vast, overwhelming "environments" and "forces" rather than discrete "objects" with purposive forms). And it seems that the context of nature is quite important to the moral connection. Accordingly, Kant writes, "the feeling of the sublime in nature is respect [*Achtung*] for our own vocation [*Bestimmung*], which we show to an object in nature through a certain subreption (substitution of a respect for the object instead of for the idea of humanity in our subject), which as it were makes intuitable the superiority of the rational vocation of our cognitive faculty over the greatest faculty of sensibility" (5:257).

But strictly speaking, no object in nature is truly sublime, for Kant. Rather, only the human mind is properly sublime:

> We express ourselves on the whole incorrectly if we call some object of nature sublime, although we can quite correctly call very many of them beautiful; for how can we designate with an expression of approval that which is apprehended in itself as contrapurposive? We can say no more than that the object serves for the presentation of a sublimity that can be found in the mind; for what is properly sublime cannot be contained in any sensible form, but concerns only ideas of reason. (5:245)

Thus, it seems that nature and art are in the same boat here: *Neither may be properly termed sublime* (Clewis 2010). Being in the same boat, however, would seem to imply that *both should be able to occasion responses that reveal the sublimity of the human mind*. Yet Kant implicitly deploys his pure/impure distinction in the case of judgments of the sublime to suggest that we may only make adherent judgments of the sublime with respect to art (5:252–253).

It stands to reason, though, that if we utilize Kant's unofficial theory of art, there may be free, artistic sublimities (along the lines of the free artistic beauties). In such cases, we might be able to abstract from the purpose of the work of art, and to judge it in a purely sublime way. So, for example, so long as the Egyptian pyramids are appreciated for their formal qualities alone (in this case, their overwhelming scale, which makes them from a certain vantage point seem formless or contra-purposive for our cognitive faculties), they can arguably be numbered among "free sublimities" along with vast and/or overwhelming natural environments. In cases where the purpose of a sublime work qua work of art cannot be abstracted away, it seems that the work of art could be classed as an "impure" or "adherent sublimity" (Clewis 2010, 168) along the lines of Kant's official theory of fine artworks. In any case, it seems that works of art may nonetheless still occasion enough of a sublime response to enliven a sense of our moral vocation. And thus, in the final analysis, it seems that while nature is more apt to provoke a sublime response, artworks on Kant's view may provoke at least an "impure" sublime response, and perhaps with the relevant, appropriate abstractive move, a pure one as well. Therefore, it seems that if a work of art provokes a dynamically sublime response in the subject, it is thereby and to that extent, on Kant's theory, always morally educative.

BACK TO NATURE

Kant makes a rather large deal out of the moral importance of the appreciation of *natural beauty* over artistic beauty.[7] Although artistic beauty is important for promoting "the cultivation [*Cultur*] of the mental powers for sociable communication" (Ak. 5:306) and brings the rational ideas closer to perception (via their aesthetic embodiments) (Ak. 5: 314), it is *natural beauty* that seems to hold greater *moral importance* for Kant, overall.

The main textual evidence for this comes in §42, "On the intellectual interest in the beautiful," where Kant contrasts the lovers of beautiful art with the lovers of beautiful nature. He "gladly concede[s] that the interest in the beautiful in art . . . provides no proof of a way of thinking that is devoted to the morally good or even merely inclined to it" (5:298) whereas he does "assert that to take an immediate interest in the beauty of nature . . . is always a mark of a good soul, and that if this interest is habitual, it at least indicates a disposition of the mind that is favorable to the moral feeling" (5:299).

Kant goes so far as to say that even if *the forms* of art were to surpass those of nature in their beauty,

> if a man who has enough taste to judge about products of beautiful art . . . gladly leaves the room in which are to be found those [artistic] beauties that sustain vanity and at best social joys and turns to the beautiful in nature, in order as it were to find here an ecstasy for his spirit in a line of thought that he can never fully develop, then we would consider this choice of his with esteem and presuppose in him a beautiful soul, to which no connoisseur and lover of art can lay claim on account of the interest that he takes in his objects. (5:299–300)

The ultimate reason for why it is morally better to be a lover of natural over artistic beauty, for Kant, is that the lover of natural beauty takes an interest in the signs that nature seems to give via its beauty that it "contains in itself some sort of ground for assuming a lawful correspondence of its products with our satisfaction that is independent of all interest (which we recognize a priori as a law valid for everyone, without being able to ground this on proofs)" (5:300). In other words, the lover of natural beauty takes an interest in the aesthetic hints that nature is amenable to our moral ends (Baxley, 2005). Only *nature's* beauty—not the beauty of art—can show "some trace" or "give a sign" that we will be able to realize our moral ends in this world (Henrich, 1992). By contrast, the beauty of art can bespeak "at best social joys" (Ak. 5:300). The disinterestedness of a

---

[7] Whether Kant *did* make this distinction in the moral value of natural beauty versus artistic beauty is not really disputed by Joseph Cannon (Cannon, 2011:113), but Cannon argues that Kant *should not* have made such a distinction "because his account of fine art as the joint product of the 'natural gift' of genius and the discipline of taste commits him to the claim that artistic beauty expresses . . . a harmony between nature and freedom."

pure judgment of taste means that the *actual existence* of the beautiful object—and, accordingly, whether it is natural or artistic—is beside the point, only the perceptual form matters. But from the perspective of the moral interest we take in beauty, that the beauty emanates *from nature itself* is crucial, insofar as we are keen to read the purposive signs that nature (not art) seems to be sending.

That said, there is another deep connection that Kant draws between beauty (again, paradigmatically *but not exclusively the beauty of nature*) and ethics: An experience of (pure, formal) beauty is the symbol of morality (section 59, 5: 353). In aesthetic judgment, "judgment does not find itself subjected to a heteronomy from empirical laws" rather, "concerning objects of such a pure liking it legislates to itself, just as reason does regarding the power of desire" (5:353). In this way the autonomous judgment of beauty has an indirect, symbolic connection with morality.[8] This, for Guyer, is "the heart of Kant's connection between aesthetics and morality": "the view that it is only by preserving its freedom from direct constraint by concepts, even didactic concepts of morality itself, that the experience of beauty can serve the purpose of giving us a palpable experience of freedom, which is its deepest service to the needs of morality" (Guyer 1996, 18). If Guyer is correct that this symbolic function provides the most morally educative link between aesthetics and ethics, in Kant's aesthetic theory, then, somewhat ironically, it seems that free natural and free artistic beauties—precisely the ones *not* subject to ethical criticism—turn out to be the most potent aesthetic-moral educators.

CONCLUSION

I hope to have shown that (1) the Kantian analysis of the pure judgment of taste and his unofficial theory of art does indeed lend support to moderate formalism about art; but that (2) Kant's official theory of fine art lends support to the anti-formalists, moralists, and ethicists; and that (3) sublime art, for Kant, would always be morally uplifting by virtue of its sublimity. Finally, (4) an *overall*, systematic Kantian approach to the relationship between aesthetics and ethics suggests that the aesthetic experience of nature is more morally beneficial than an aesthetic experience of art. This is for several reasons: nature is much more apt to provide a pure experience of the beautiful and the sublime. Accordingly, nature is more apt to afford those experiences of beauty that involve imaginative autonomy and thus symbolize moral autonomy. In the end, then, a Kantian approach to aesthetic moral education would urge us to quit the art galleries and get out to the park instead!

See also: Costelloe, Gal, Stear, Carroll, this volume

---

[8] For a canonical analysis of Kant's claim, see Cohen (1982, 2002).

REFERENCES

Abaci, Uygar. 2008. "Kant's Justified Dismissal of Artistic Sublimity." *Journal of Aesthetics and Art Criticism* 66, no. 3: 237–251.

Abaci, Uygar. 2010. "Artistic Sublime Revisited: Reply to Robert Clewis." *Journal of Aesthetics and Art Criticism* 68, no. 2: 170–173.

Baxley, Anne Margaret. 2005. "The Practical Significance of Taste in Kant's *Critique of Judgment*: Love of Natural Beauty as a Mark of Moral Character." *Journal of Aesthetics and Art Criticism* 63, no. 1: 33–45.

Cannon, Joseph. 2011. "The Moral Value of Artistic Beauty in Kant." *Kantian Review* 16, no. 1: 113–126.

Carroll, Noël. 1996. "Moderate Moralism." *British Journal of Aesthetics* 36, no. 3: 223–238.

Clewis, Robert R. 2009. *The Kantian Sublime and the Revelation of Freedom*. Cambridge: Cambridge University Press.

Clewis, Robert R. 2010. "A Case for Kantian Artistic Sublimity: A Response to Abaci." *Journal of Aesthetics and Art Criticism* 68, no. 2: 167–170.

Cohen, Ted. 1982. "Why Beauty Is a Symbol of Morality." In *Essays in Kant's Aesthetics*, edited by Ted Cohen and Paul Guyer, 221–236. Chicago: University of Chicago Press.

Cohen, Ted. 2002. "Three Problems in Kant's Aesthetics." *British Journal of Aesthetics* 42, no. 1: 1–12.

Crowther, Paul. 1989. *The Kantian Sublime: From Morality to Art*. Oxford: Clarendon Press.

Danto, Arthur. 2013. *What Art Is*. Yale University Press.

Devereaux, Mary. 1998. "Beauty and Evil: The Case of Leni Riefenstahl's *Triumph of the Will*." In *Aesthetics and Ethics: Essays at the Intersection*, edited by Jerrold Levinson, 227–256. New York: Cambridge University Press.

Dowling, Christopher. 2010. "Zangwill, Moderate Formalism, and Another Look at Kant's Aesthetic." *Kantian Review* 15, no. 2: 90–117.

Gaut, Berys. 2007. *Art, Emotion, and Ethics*. New York: Oxford University Press.

Guyer, Paul. 1996. *Kant and the Experience of Freedom: Essays on Aesthetics and Morality*. Cambridge: Cambridge University Press.

Guyer, Paul. 2008. "Is Ethical Criticism a Problem? A Historical Perspective." In *Art and Ethical Criticism*, edited by Garry L. Hagberg, 3–32. London: Blackwell.

Henrich, Dieter. 1992. *Aesthetic Judgment and the Moral Image of the World*. Stanford, CA: Stanford University Press.

Harold, James. 2011. "Autonomism Reconsidered." *British Journal of Aesthetics* 51, no. 2: 137–147.

Harold, James. 2020. *Dangerous Art*. New York: Oxford University Press.

Kant, Immanuel. [1790] 2000. *Critique of the Power of Judgment*. Translated by Paul Guyer and Eric Matthews. Cambridge: Cambridge University Press.

Matherne, Samantha. 2013. "The Inclusive Interpretation of Kant's Aesthetic Ideas." *British Journal of Aesthetics* 53, no. 1: 21–39.

Merritt, Melissa McBay. 2012. "The Moral Source of the Kantian Sublime." In *The Sublime: From Antiquity to Present*, edited by Timothy M. Costelloe, 37–49. Cambridge University Press.

Pillow, Kirk. 2000. *Sublime Understanding: Aesthetic Reflection in Kant and Hegel*. Cambridge, MA: The MIT Press.

Reiter, Aviv, and Ido Geiger. 2018. "Natural Beauty, Fine Art and the Relation between Them." *Kant-Studien* 109, no. 1: 72–100.

Stecker, Robert. 2005. "The Interaction of Aesthetic and Ethical Value." *British Journal of Aesthetics* 45, no. 2: 138–151.

Tuna, Emine Hande. 2018. "Kant on Informed Pure Judgments of Taste." *Journal of Aesthetics and Art Criticism* 76, no. 2: 163–174.

Tuna, Emine Hande. N.d. Unpublished manuscript. "Kant on the Puzzle of Imaginative Resistance."

Walton, Kendall. 1970. "Categories of Art." *Philosophical Review* 79, no. 3: 334–367.

Wicks, Robert. 1995. "Kant on Fine Art: Artistic Sublimity Shaped by Beauty." *Journal of Aesthetics and Art Criticism* 53, no. 2: 189–193.

Zangwill, Nick. 1999. "Feasible Aesthetic Formalism." *Noûs* 33, no. 4: 610–629.

Zangwill, Nick. 2000. "In Defence of Moderate Aesthetic Formalism." *Philosophical Quarterly* 50, no. 201: 476–493.

CHAPTER 16

CONSEQUENTIALIST APPROACHES TO ETHICAL JUDGMENT OF ARTWORKS

SCOTT WOODCOCK

IT might seem as if a consequentialist perspective on the ethical evaluation of art will be nothing but straightforward. If consequentialism claims that the rightness and wrongness of our actions ought to be judged according to the goodness of their consequences, then an application of this theory to art looks uncomplicated: promote art that generates good outcomes and suppress art that does the reverse. Case closed. Yet, as with most issues related to practical applications of consequentialism in realistic circumstances, the details that determine which of our choices will actually promote the most good turn out to be very difficult to evaluate.

In this respect, evaluations of art serve as a helpful case study to illustrate the tension between applying consequentialism to realistic contexts and its aspirations to provide a secure foundation for ethical inquiry. For the main appeal of consequentialism is parsimony. It offers a simple, intuitive foundation for ethics by recommending that we evaluate options according to what promotes more rather than less goodness. Its potential downfall, however, is trying to match this foundation with the unsettling complexity of the circumstances that agents face in their ordinary lives. What begins as a clear directive to make the world a better place becomes complicated to the point of being unviable, if its critics are correct, and the ethical evaluation of art provides a revealing look at how a consequentialist perspective invites this difficulty.

In this chapter, I begin by outlining the simplest possible interpretation of how we ought to evaluate art according to consequentialism. After putting forward this overly simple view of how consequentialism should approach the ethical evaluation of art, I proceed by adding more and more of the complexity associated with the empirical considerations that would need to be addressed for a robust application of consequentialism to art and the impact that it has on our lives. By the end of the chapter, it should be clear that consequentialism would require mind-boggling levels of complexity in its calculations of how we ought to promote and respond to art in ways that maximize goodness. By way of conclusion, I concede that this complexity fuels the so-called cluelessness objection to consequentialism, yet I argue that the way consequentialism recognizes the complexity of our evaluations of art ought to be viewed as an advantage for the theory because it reflects how genuinely complicated it is to account for the ethical dimensions of art in our lives.

HEDONISTIC UTILITARIANISM

Of the many possible formulations of consequentialism, the simplest is a hedonistic version of utilitarianism. Consequentialism tells us that a right action is the action available to us that will promote the most goodness, and utilitarianism narrows our understanding of what is good for its own sake to nothing but *well-being*. Many other things in the world are obviously good (e.g., knowledge, health, virtue, friendship), but they are only good, according to utilitarianism, insofar as they contribute to our well-being. As J. S. Mill claims in his defense of the view, we admire the sacrifice of a hero if their virtue contributes to the well-being of others, but if their virtuous actions fail to increase the well-being of anyone affected by them, then these actions cease to be worthy of our admiration (Mill 1998, 63–64). Similarly, all goods like friendship and knowledge are valuable, according to utilitarianism, to the extent that they promote well-being and not for their own sake. Moreover, hedonistic forms of utilitarianism narrow this position even further by interpreting well-being purely in terms of *pleasure* and the absence of pain. A notoriously minimalist version of this view is defended by Jeremy Bentham (1996), who claims that all the different ways we experience pleasure contain some common attribute—a single unit of pleasure to be measured and promoted to the greatest extent possible.

It may seem unlikely that the pleasure we experience listening to a beautiful melody or reading a classic work of literature is the same type of sensation that we experience eating an ice cream cone, yet Bentham is careful to formulate his position so that quantities of this single unit of pleasure increase or decrease depending on a variety of circumstances. Moreover, Mill proposes a modified version of hedonism that allows qualitatively different types of pleasure to be identified and potentially ranked as inferior or superior to others. As simple as the view may appear, then, it has options that allow it to capture may of our intuitions about well-being, and contemporary advocates of hedonism (Feldman 2004; Crisp 2006; Bramble 2016) have kept it alive as a theory that can serve as the foundation for utilitarianism.[1]

---

[1] For a succinct overview of hedonism, see Heathwood (2013). A critical overview of different varieties of hedonism can be found in Sobel (2002). For more complex explorations of mixing hedonism into hybrid theories of well-being, see Heathwood (2006), Kagan (2009), and Lin (2020).

If we begin with this hedonistic utilitarianism as our initial version of consequen-tialism, an application of this view to the evaluation of art directs us to support those works of art that produce the most pleasure given all available alternatives. That may not seem so implausible, since we normally expect good art to elicit pleasure from its audi-ence. Yet the view appears to invite the *reductio* that we are ethically obligated to pro-duce and encourage as much art as we can that generates as much simple gratification as possible for as many people as possible. This is worrisome, since we presumably do not have an ethical obligation to fill the world with even more films by Michael Bay, novels by Danielle Steele, or songs by Justin Bieber. If singling out these artists seems unfair, perhaps the challenge can be stated as follows: Do we really have an ethical obligation to produce as many ten-second videos of cute animals as possible so that we can distribute them for mass consumption? I should hope none of us has anything against cute ani-mals, yet we still might reject the idea that an ethical perspective on art would require us to work tirelessly to distribute kitten memes if this was the most effective way for us to maximize pleasure in the world.

Faced with this concern, a hedonistic utilitarian will reply by considering the empir-ical details at stake and denying that their view would lead to a kitten meme *reductio*. To begin, even the cutest baby animal content gets boring after a while. Any human fortu-nate enough to live in comfortable socioeconomic circumstances and to have benefitted from an education that provides them with an ability to appreciate more complex forms of artistic expression will at some point grow tired of simple kitten memes. In fact, Mill famously claims that individuals with the ability to appreciate both simple and cogni-tively sophisticated pleasures will display such a decisive preference for the latter that they would not trade their capacity to appreciate these pleasures for any number of simple pleasures (1998, 57). One need not be persuaded by the depth of Mill's confidence in this empirical prediction to agree that a hedonistic approach to well-being will not necessarily lead to the *exclusive* promotion of immediate gratification at the expense of more complex pleasures. Thus, when we consider how hedonistic utilitarianism relates to the evaluation of art, it is reasonable to think that it would promote art that engages our cognitive faculties as well as our basic propensities for pleasure. A healthy diet of cute sea-otter videos is an effective way to promote pleasure in the world for humans who sometimes need fast relief in their lives, but the facts of human psychology are un-likely to drive hedonistic utilitarianism into promoting nothing but art that reflects only our simple desires. Instead, it is likely that hedonistic utilitarianism will recommend that we produce, and promote access to, a variety of both simple and cognitively sophis-ticated types of art that appeal to our divergent aesthetic preferences and the ways in which each of us requires ongoing novelty in the art we appreciate if we are to experience the most pleasure possible.

It may seem, then, that even the simplest form of consequentialism manages to deliver an intuitively reasonable result. Yet it is worth noting that the variety of different types of art that would be endorsed by hedonistic utilitarianism is ultimately contingent on empirical facts about what will generate the most pleasure for all agents. This leaves the view open to further questions about whether it can adequately capture the complexity of our relationship to art in cases where we seem to value aesthetic experiences in ways that are not obviously consistent with the maximization of pleasure. These questions have solutions according to contemporary advocates of hedonistic utilitarianism; however, they prompt some consequentialists to adopt competing, pluralistic versions of the view. At the very least, these questions about the "math" of calculating how we ought to respond to art reveal just how complicated the calculations will be if our aim is to promote the most good possible.

PARADOXES OF PAINFUL ART

The most straightforward of the challenges to hedonistic utilitarianism in our evaluations of art is the observation that we are sometimes drawn to art that is specifically designed to produce unpleasant feelings for its audience. The classic examples of this puzzle in aesthetics are cases of *tragedy* and *horror*. As odd as it may seem when we step back and think about why we find certain instances of art appealing, a great deal of art is premised on how effectively it can make its audience feel painfully sad or uncomfortably afraid and disgusted. For examples of the first type of art, one can look to any number of Shakespearean plays we commonly label *tragedies*, as strange as that category might be for Martian anthropologists, and examples from painting (Van Gogh's *At Eternity's Gate*), music (Radiohead's *Let Down*), or modern film (P. T. Anderson's *Magnolia* (1999)) are just as easy to find. Similarly, examples of art designed to elicit feelings of horror and disgust are easily found in comics (*Creepy*), literature (the works of H. P. Lovecraft), and streaming series (*The Haunting of Hill House*; directed by Mike Flanagan, 2018). In fact, this content is so ubiquitous that readers will probably be puzzled only by how I selected this list of examples from the multitude of possibilities. Yet this content is particularly difficult to explain for a hedonist. Why is so much art devoted to painful emotions? And if we cannot find an explanation that detects underlying pleasures in this art, is the hedonistic utilitarian committed to claiming that we have an ethical obligation to prevent it from being produced?

To avoid this counterintuitive result, advocates of hedonistic utilitarianism can refer to some of the most influential discussions of these puzzles in the literature from aesthetics. For example, Noël Carroll's (1990) landmark treatment of the paradox of horror proposes that we are not drawn to horrific imagery for the sake of unpleasant emotions themselves but for the sake of compensatory benefits in the form of unique feelings of curiosity and suspense related to the ways in which monstrous beings are discovered, confirmed and hopefully overcome. If Carroll is correct, no special problem is generated for hedonism by our interest in art that invites painful emotions like fear and disgust, since this art produces an overall net benefit of cognitive pleasures for its audience. Similarly, if one is persuaded by the analysis of horror put forward by Susan Feagin (1983), then our first-order painful responses like fear and disgust are compensated for by a meta-level appreciation of the way we respond sympathetically when we are exposed to depictions of violence and suffering. Hedonistic utilitarianism is thus consistent with this compensatory account of what makes horrific imagery appealing as long as the art in question offers a productive ratio of positive meta-level responses over our immediate feelings of terror, repulsion, and so on.

Difficulties arise, however, when we consider the criticism compensation accounts have received from philosophers who point out that audiences are not exclusively interested in the secondary benefits of tragedy and horror. Instead, audiences complain if the art in question is able to provide these benefits without being sufficiently distressing or frightening.[2] This brings us back to the heart of the paradoxes of tragedy and horror, and not all of the remaining solutions to these paradoxes match up well with a hedonistic standpoint. The rich experience theory, for example, locates the value of painful emotions in nonhedonic reasons agents have for having access to the experience of negative emotions without having to face the real consequences of tragic or horrific situations (Smuts 2007). Unless these reasons for gaining access to unpleasant experiences can be somehow linked to downstream pleasures in the future, it looks difficult for hedonistic utilitarianism to justify painful art according to a rich experience account of why we find it appealing.

More promising options for a hedonist approach to our evaluations of art can be found in accounts of tragedy and horror that propose special conditions under which art enables our otherwise negative emotions to be converted into positive responses. David Hume (1965), for example, famously claims that the aesthetic merits of art can modify our affective reactions so that our painful emotions are instead felt as positive experiences, and contemporary accounts offer a variety of different explanations for this conversion process (Eaton 1982; Morreall 1985; Neill 1992; and Gaut 1993).[3] Yet even if these accounts are persuasive, they propose rather *complicated* psychological mechanisms that allow our painful emotions to be converted into pleasure in the appreciation of certain types of art. Thus, even if hedonistic formulations of utilitarianism can account for our fascination with tragedy and horror, they cannot do so very easily. The calculations required to evaluate our ethical obligations to art according to their consequences are difficult enough, but the complex ways in which aesthetic contexts can shift the polarity of our affective responses make hedonistic approaches to this task that much more difficult. One might think to abandon hedonism for this reason, but, as we shall soon see, the complex nature of the math required for consequentialist evaluations of art is only amplified when we consider versions of the theory grounded in broader conceptions of the good.

---

[2] For example, you might not be so surprised if a friend communicated their disappointment with a film they had recently seen by saying, "It was a sad and interesting story, but it just didn't emotionally connect with me."

[3] For a helpful overview of more recent work on paradoxes of painful art, including pluralist views that combine some of the options above, see Strohl (2019).

AESTHETIC EVALUATIONS AND
VALUE PLURALISM

Moving past the paradox of painful art, hedonistic utilitarianism still faces problems originating from its narrow conception of what we ought to promote as valuable for its own sake. If goods like friendship, virtue, and truth are merely instrumental valuable, then utilitarianism can only justify their promotion by connecting them to some eventual production of pleasure. If no such connection is possible, then utilitarianism must regard the creation of these instrumental goods to be an unjustifiable course of action. Applied to art, this invites some counterintuitive results when we consider works of art that are created to convey information, or to induce emotional reactions, that relate to goods other than pleasure. Take, for example, Joshua Oppenheimer's surreal documentary *The Act of Killing* (2012). The film includes extravagant Hollywood-esque action set pieces and musical numbers, yet it is clearly not intended to generate pleasure for ordinary audience members. Instead, the film invites its audience to gain a terrifying perspective on the atrocities committed in Indonesia during 1965–1966 by interviewing the perpetrators of some of these atrocities and filming them re-enacting their participation as part of the documentary. It is an astonishing work of art, but it is anything but pleasurable. Can a utilitarian perspective on art grounded in hedonism endorse this film along with so many other works of art that prompt audiences to reflect on important themes without necessarily experiencing pleasure?

The standard reply to this type of concern is to rely on the long-term prediction that if a work of art facilitates the acquisition of knowledge or elicits sympathetic reactions, these goods are likely to promote pleasure, or at least decrease suffering, for someone at some point in the future. It need not be true for each instance of the impact that a work of art has on those who appreciate it; rather, the hedonistic utilitarian can count on the reasonable probability that art will tend to contribute to pleasure if it promotes other goods like knowledge, solidarity, and caring. The problem for this reply, however, is that it still gives counterintuitive results in cases of art that is created and distributed so that the ordinary connections between pleasure and these other goods fail to get purchase. For example, truth might *generally* be an important means of promoting pleasure, but we can imagine an alternate version of James Frey's memoir *A Million Little Pieces* that does a better job covering its tracks—a memoir that offers vast numbers of readers the pleasures of a "real-life" story of triumph over adversity without being uncovered as a hoax. Like an experience machine (Nozick 1974) guaranteed to never break down, if we could ensure that the memoir would never be fact-checked, then it looks like it would be justified as great art by the standards of hedonistic utilitarianism despite the counterintuitive nature of this result.[4]

---

[4] One may want to consider Darren Hudson Hick's chapter on forgery in this volume with this problem for utilitarianism in mind.

Moreover, even if artists recognize the risk of inaccuracies in their work being detected, it remains an open *empirical* question whether this risk is worth taking compared to the gain in pleasure that will result from deviating from the truth. In historical dramas, for example, there are often significant details that are ignored or altered for the sake of an overall product that is more pleasing to the broadest possible audience. Philosophers normally object to these cases when the errors are conspicuous, such as *A Beautiful Mind* (directed by Ron Howard, 2001), *300* (directed by Zack Snyder, 2006), or *The Imitation Game* (directed by Morten Tyldum 2014). Yet this is not an objection that can be voiced by a hedonistic utilitarian as an absolute complaint rather than, say, a concern about unjustifiable risk, especially when the variables at stake are affected by large numbers of viewers who, unfortunately, do not much care whether the films they see are accurate so long as they are suitably uplifting. In fact, depending on how the math unfolds, deviations from the truth may be morally *required* for hedonistic utilitarianism if inaccurate art will generate a sufficiently large amount of pleasure!

The consequentialist now faces a choice. They can bite the bullet and stay committed to hedonism as a foundational theory of value, or they can accept that goods other than pleasure are valuable for their own sake. The former option preserves the sense of parsimony that many consequentialists consider significant, but the latter option helps to block the counterexamples above by allowing us to value goods like truth and knowledge for their own sake. When a fake memoir is compared to a truthful one, rejecting hedonism in favor of a *pluralist* conception of value allows the consequentialist to judge that we ought to promote truth and integrity even if both memoirs generate the same amount of pleasure.

The move to pluralism in the consequentialist evaluation of art can be implemented in two different ways. First, one can reject hedonism *within* our understanding of aesthetic value so that the aesthetic merits of art can be influenced by factors beyond just its ability to produce pleasure. There is an established tradition of conceptualizing aesthetic value in hedonist terms (Levinson 1992; Walton 1993; Goldman 1995; and more recently Matthen 2018), but if critics of this view (Kieran 2005; Lopez 2018; and Shelley 2019) are correct, then the value of art is located in more than just the pleasurable experiences it provides.[5] Second, it is possible for a consequentialist to remain an aesthetic hedonist yet claim that other important goods beyond those classified as aesthetic ought to be valued for their own sake. So, for example, a historical drama with serious inaccuracies might exhibit the same aesthetic value as one that is accurate if the two produce the same amount of pleasure for their audiences, but a consequentialist can nevertheless value truth or knowledge for its own sake, aside from aesthetic evaluation, and be able to appropriately favor the accurate historical drama.

Thus, consequentialists can avoid some of the difficulties we have discussed by moving away from utilitarianism toward a pluralist theory of value that includes a list of goods beyond well-being that are valuable for their own sakes. This is not the value pluralism

---

[5] For an overview of aesthetic hedonism and its critics, see Vanderberg (2020).

advanced by critics of consequentialism who claim that some assortment of foundational values in ethics are incommensurable (Ross 1930; Williams 1985; Stocker 1990; Thomson 1997). Rather, this value pluralism *within* consequentialism proposes that goods beyond well-being (like truth, virtue or friendship) are not just instrumentally valuable, but each a source of intrinsic value that is worth promoting for its own sake within our overall obligation to create as much good in the world as possible.[6] Applied to art, pluralist forms of consequentialism can solve some of the difficulties above by noting the variety of obligations that arise in cases where art challenges us to gain new insights or experience new perspectives without necessarily feeling pleasure as part of this process. So, for example, when considering Lawrence Hill's emotionally wrenching novel *The Book of Negroes*, a pluralist consequentialist need not figure out a way to construct an account of how the story produces pleasure for the work to be significant. A hedonistic account of this kind might be possible, but the pluralist consequentialist has the advantage of offering a more straightforward justification for the book's primary value: it generates unique *knowledge* for its readers that cannot be communicated simply by learning the relevant historical facts on which it is based. (For more discussion of the value of knowledge from art, see also John, this volume.) One hopes that this knowledge will help humanity learn from its past and therefore increase well-being in the future, but pluralist consequentialism does not require this result to endorse this novel as a powerful and important work of art.

And yet the move to pluralism introduces its own problems for consequentialism: How can we compare the value of the different types of goods to be promoted in order for them to fit into a commensurable system that determines our overall obligations? When we judge that the knowledge we gain from reading *The Book of Negroes* is worth the sadness we experience, how are we comparing these two different goods at stake? It may be feasible to compare these goods and make reasonable estimations of their relative significance, but pluralist versions of consequentialism are that much more complicated in the way they require some sort of multivalue conversion system to make evaluations of overall goodness. Complexity is not necessarily a bad thing for an ethical theory, perhaps, but consequentialism already has enough complexity in the "math" of its evaluations to draw the attention of its critics.

FREE EXPRESSION AND ART AS A REAL THREAT

Our discussion of consequentialism and art has so far included examples that help us to obtain knowledge at the cost of experiencing shock and sadness, yet most of these

---

[6] Prominent examples of pluralism within consequentialism include Moore (1903), Hooker (1996), and Railton (2003).

examples are cases where causing shock and sadness is merely a byproduct of some other primary goal. Some art, however, is specifically designed to upset the existing social order and create feelings of shock, horror, or moral outrage. This type of what might broadly be described as *protest art* can take many forms, but the examples I have in mind are those that deliberately subvert our aesthetic expectations in order to provoke audiences into reconsidering the norms, traditions, and social policies they might otherwise take for granted. In the simplest form of this art, the content of a story's plot (George Orwell's *1984*), a painting's images (Faith Ringgold's *American People Series #20: Die*), or a song's lyrics (Gil Scott-Heron's *The Revolution Will Not Be Televised*) is arranged to provoke audiences into questioning background assumptions, while more elaborate versions of this art are designed to undermine the very formats in which it is presented to challenge its audiences, such as Yoko Ono's *Cut Piece*, Dead Kennedys' *Chemical Warfare*, Ai Weiwei's *Dropping a Han Dynasty Urn*, or Childish Gambino's music video for *This is America*. Whether it resists format conventions or just defies aesthetic expectations, the aim of protest art is to disrupt the status quo and invite reflection on its own unsettling impact.

Here again we have a challenge to a consequentialist approach to art for which there is an easy initial reply followed by a cascade of complex empirical predictions. The challenge that valuable protest art is not immediately productive of happiness (or straightforward knowledge, truth, etc.) can be met by the plausible connection between disrupting established social norms and the future good that can come from reflecting on the status of these norms once they have been revealed and subjected to scrutiny. Just as Mill (2015) famously argued for the long-term value of allowing an open exchange of political ideas within a liberal democratic society, we can plausibly estimate that overall goodness is promoted by encouraging a broad enough variety of art that it will include disruptive variants with no immediate promise of increasing goodness. In this respect we have, at least in broad outline, a persuasive way to justify protest art within the scope of consequentialism, since we have a precautionary interest in granting artists the space to find novel ways of prompting us to reflect on existing social norms.

So far so good. Things get complicated, however, when we consider the finer details of *how much* protection we want to grant provocative art in order to maintain the open exchange of ideas that we consider to be vital for promoting goodness in the long run. We might predict that legal protection for all types of artistic expression is warranted by consequentialist math, but the depths of violent pornography and racist propaganda could undermine our confidence in this prediction.[7] For the consequentialist is left at the mercy of the empirical details of what will ultimately promote the most good when it comes to questions of censorship to protect the vulnerable from hateful artistic expressions. It is notoriously difficult to decide

[7] See Sumner (2004) for an examination of hate speech legislation in Canada from a prominent consequentialist.

what counts as justifiable protest art and what, if anything, ought to instead face legal sanctions for instigating harm toward undeserving victims. From a consequentialist perspective, however, this difficulty is a matter of complicated empirical predictions about the policies we can adopt to promote as much good as possible, and no solution seems unequivocally optimal.

Furthermore, things get even more complicated when we move past the issue of legal sanctions and consider our responsibilities to speak out against immoral art that nevertheless deserves protection from censorship. (See also Soucek, this volume.) Even if our best consequentialist predictions reveal that, as a matter of general social policy, artists should never face legal penalties for their work, an interest in promoting the most good possible will surely require us to condemn art that carries a potential to cause unnecessary harm. In other words, I might think censorship is unjustifiable yet still feel a responsibility to tell anyone who will listen that Slayer's *Angel of Death* is morally problematic (no matter what Jeff Hanneman's intentions were in writing the song). Similarly, I might have a solid consequentialist basis for claiming that Balthus's most controversial paintings ought to be preserved and discussed by art historians without endorsing a public display of the works in museum settings that would grant them widespread credibility and influence. The list of potential examples here is endless. The point for consequentialism is that the theory invites complex empirical calculations regarding the circumstances in which it is appropriate to morally condemn art within a general commitment to the value of unrestricted artistic expression.

Moreover, the complexity at stake here has exploded in recent years with the growth of social media and new expectations of public accountability. The obligation to speak out against immoral art must now be balanced against the risk of subtleties in one's condemnation getting lost in a sea of deep cultural polarization and media formats that encourage extreme brevity in expression. Take, for example, the incendiary realm of stand-up comedy. (See Butterfield, this volume.) Some of the best art of this kind is transgressive in ways that help us critically reflect on social standards, and comics ought to be given appropriate space to push the boundaries of these standards. Yet we are all familiar with cases of comics using this space in ways that are hurtful to undeserving people, so consequentialists presumably ought to celebrate the opportunities we now have through social media to voice our disapproval when this occurs. Unfortunately, voicing disapproval using the tools of social media has become a notoriously blunt instrument, and consequentialists have to make difficult predictions about what will genuinely promote the good when they choose how and when to publicly call out comics who cross the line. Of course, some material is egregious enough that a blunt instrument might be perfectly appropriate, and the claims of rich, famous comics that they have been censored because they might lose access to prestigious distribution platforms seem, well, *comically* overstated. Nevertheless, some stand-up comedians might try out jokes that deserve condemnation despite mitigating factors like, say, the joke being a well-intentioned miscalculation, or the jokes being part of an overall body of work that is genuinely progressive.[8] Consequentialism has to evaluate this art according to how well it contributes to, or takes away from, the overall, long-term good *and* attempt to calculate how to best respond to this art in an era of media platforms that are not always receptive to nuance. These are not easy calculations to make.

ART AND EFFECTIVE ALTRUISM

Imagine we can set all of the previous complexity associated with consequentialist evaluations of art aside. In other words, imagine that it is unproblematic to evaluate how specific works of art contribute to the good in terms of their aesthetic merits and the ways in which they help, or hinder, progress on important social issues. Even if that were the case, a further complication arises for consequentialism because of the way it specifies a right action as the action that will promote *the most* good possible compared to all other available options. This maximizing part of consequentialism creates notoriously demanding obligations for agents who attempt to live by its recommendations. Given opportunities to efficiently promote the good by helping those in desperate need of aid, it looks like consequentialism will require that agents work tirelessly toward altruistic causes without ever being granted permission to indulge in their own personal projects (Williams 1973; Wolf 1982). Applied to our evaluations of art, the challenge is that agents seeking to live as consequentialists will never be given permission to create or appreciate art when they could instead be helping a food bank, writing letters for Amnesty International, or volunteering abroad for Médecins Sans Frontières. The benefits of creating and sharing art with others are, of course, considerable, but are they great enough to outweigh the good that could be done if we devoted our time and resources to helping those who are facing food and water shortages, insufficient medical care, and political persecution? The comparison clearly favors helping those in need. As a result, the relentless demands of consequentialism seem to imply that we ought to give up on art as a noble but comparatively frivolous luxury.

Some consequentialists are willing to bite the bullet in the face of this demandingness challenge and argue that we should reject our common-sense intuitions that morality cannot possibly ask so much of us. They insist that those of us fortunate enough to be living in affluent conditions ought to devote far more of our time and money to help others in more desperate circumstances (Kagan 1989; Unger 1996; Singer 2015). And yet it seems a safe bet that many of these consequentialists have art hanging on the walls of their offices,

---

[8] Providing examples is risky here, because I do not want disagreement about particular jokes to obscure the point at stake that consequentialism has to make difficult predictions about how to publicly respond to transgressive art in a deeply polarized cultural environment. Nevertheless, I would suggest Amy Schumer as an example of an artist who seems genuinely well-intentioned, has created sketches with insightful social commentary (e.g., *Football Town Nights*), but who has sometimes delivered jokes that legitimately deserve the criticism they have received (e.g., her joke about dating Hispanic men).

or that they have seen a movie or two in recent years. This might look like a contradiction, but consequentialists have generally replied to the demandingness challenge by noting how counterproductive it would be to suddenly sell all of one's belongings and try to work nonstop to help others without ever a moment to focus on oneself. It would be a recipe for burnout rather than maximum efficiency, so consequentialists emphasize that a *long-term perspective* will allow them to prioritize their own needs to some extent in order to maintain their health, sanity and thus an ongoing ability to help more people in the future. In the same way that we inevitably need to sleep to remain capable of functioning as effective vehicles for promoting the good, consequentialists predict that humans are the kinds of creatures who need at least some time for our own relationships and personal projects that give our lives meaning, since the alternative will leave us so broken that we are unlikely to be motivated to care for others (Railton 1984; Ashford 2000; Woodcock 2010). If this general strategy is sound, then art certainly seems like it fits with the kinds of vital personal projects that we need to retain our psychological integrity.

For the purpose of this chapter I will assume that this strategy is sound, because even if this is so, consequentialism faces another difficult empirical question: *How much* space for our personal projects is required to keep us psychologically intact? With respect to art, *how much* can we direct our time and resources to creating and appreciating art when we could instead be promoting the good more efficiently by helping those in need? It seems plausible that art is an important enough part of our lives that consequentialists can justify spending some of their time engaging with it to maintain their integrity, but it is extremely difficult to predict the limits of this justification. Can I purchase an expensive painting, rather than give the money at stake to Oxfam, if looking at it each day will inspire me to be more productive and volunteer in some way to help others (or work at a regular job and then redirect some portion of my income to aid organizations)? How many hours each week can I devote to writing poetry or music if it lets me express my frustrations about social injustices and share these frustrations with others so I can cope with the stress of continuing to fight against these injustices? Must I evaluate my odds of reaching only a handful of people versus becoming the next Tom Morello and reaching millions of people who respond to my work? How often am I permitted to watch a mindless comedy or action movie if I need to shut down my brain and intentionally *not* think about my obligations in order to cope with the overwhelmingly bleak state of the world and my limited power to find a way to change it? Questions like these scratch the surface of estimates that a consequentialist would need to make to determine what kind of role art can permissibly occupy in their life.

Moreover, consequentialists cannot let the difficulty associated with making these very complex estimates lead them to rationalize *status quo* judgments about the balance we ought to strike between appreciating art and taking more direct steps to promote the good. It can be tempting to think that common-sense morality has shaped our intuitions in such a way that we will unconsciously find the appropriate balance between self-care and promoting the good, but this would be irresponsibly optimistic. Thus, consequentialists need to routinely reflect on the choices they make when it comes to most effectively promoting the good. When we have, for example, an opportunity to donate to the restoration of architecture like Notre-Dame in Paris, we need to think carefully about whether that is truly our best option considering what those funds could do if given to aid agencies with demonstrable metrics of success. When your friend asks you to contribute to a Kickstarter effort to fund their independent film, this contribution to the arts might be perfectly good by itself yet massively inefficient compared to other possible opportunities you have to make the world a better place. Consequentialists must therefore be permitted to reserve some space for their personal integrity while simultaneously reflecting on the fact that our ordinary intuitions about what counts as generosity toward others cannot be tacitly endorsed and must instead be carefully scrutinized. These are, again, very complicated evaluations for us to make when it comes to art and its significance in our lives.

Conclusion

None of the challenges we have seen for a consequentialist approach to art are insurmountable if we consider each challenge individually. Yet each strategy that consequentialism proposes to reply to these challenges depends on complex empirical predictions, and the combined total of this complexity may lead some to abandon hope for consequentialism being able to offer any well-defined recommendations in the real world. In other words, once we recognize the extent of the calculations required for consequentialism to remain viable, it looks like its application to art provides that much more ammunition for the *cluelessness* objection. This objection claims that consequentialism leaves agents clueless when it comes to practical guidance because the calculations required to identify right actions are far too intricate to even estimate.[9] Indeed, if we consider the depth of the complexity that we have covered in only a brief discussion of art in this chapter, it certainly seems as if the practical details of our relationships to art can bring the cluelessness objection into sharp focus by situating it within familiar territory.

Faced with this challenge, how can consequentialism remain a viable option when we contemplate the ethical evaluation of art? I close by suggesting that consequentialism is not only viable but a *preferable* option when it comes to practical applications of ethical theory to topics like our evaluations of art. Though it may seem like hubris, my recommendation is for consequentialists to lean in to objections that focus on epistemic complexity and argue that any sensible ethical theory ought to reflect the *genuine complexity that we find in the details of our lives*. For it is not as if the ethical dimensions of art are initially uncomplicated and it is only if we apply consequentialism to this subject matter that things get intricate. It is truly difficult to know whether aesthetic value is reducible to pleasure, whether we ought

---

[9] Helpful discussions of this objection include: Lenman 2000; Mason 2004; and Greaves 2016. The strongest form of the objection draws on the fact that our choices might have unexpected consequences in the distant future, yet critics are also deterred by the blinding complexity of consequentialist math in the near future (and it is this latter form of the objection that I propose the practical details of art can highlight).

to publicly condemn art that tests the boundaries of current social norms, or whether we ought to devote as much time as we do to the creation and appreciation of art when we can instead help others in great distress. These are deep and serious questions, and the fact that consequentialism recognizes their complexity for what it is ought to be appreciated rather than rejected. A full articulation of this strategy for defending consequentialism is not possible here. Yet I hope the preceding discussion has captured some of the key features of a consequentialist approach to evaluating art, and that by doing so it has revealed some of the ways in which this approach provides an insightful perspective for detecting the complexity of the ethical issues that arise in this vital part of our lives.

See also: Butterfield, Hick, Soucek, John, this volume

REFERENCES

Ashford, Elizabeth. 2000. "Utilitarianism, Integrity, and Partiality." *Journal of Philosophy* 97, no. 8: 421–439.

Bentham, Jeremy. 1996. *Introduction to the Principles of Morals and Legislation*. Edited by J. Burns and H. L. A. Hart. Oxford: Clarendon.

Bramble, Ben. 2016. "A New Defense of Hedonism about Well-being." *Ergo* 3, no. 4: 85–112.

Carroll, Noël. 1990. *The Philosophy of Horror: Or, Paradoxes of the Heart*. New York: Routledge.

Crisp, Roger. 2006. *Reasons and the Good*. Oxford: Oxford University Press.

Eaton, Marcia M. 1982. "A Strange Kind of Sadness." *Journal of Aesthetics and Art Criticism* 41, no.1: 51–63.

Feagin, Susan L. 1983. "The Pleasures of Tragedy." *American Philosophical Quarterly* 20, no. 1: 95–104.

Feldman, Fred. 2004. *Pleasure and the Good Life: Concerning the Nature, Varieties, and Plausibility of Hedonism*. Oxford: Oxford University Press.

Gaut, Berys. 1993. "The Paradox of Horror." *British Journal of Aesthetics* 33, no. 4: 333–345.

Goldman, Alan. 1995. *Aesthetic Value*. Boulder, CO: Westview Press.

Greaves, Hilary. 2016. "Cluelessness." *Proceedings of the Aristotelian Society* 116, no. 3: 311–339.

Heathwood, Chris. 2006. "Desire Satisfactionism and Hedonism." *Philosophical Studies* 128, no. 3: 539–563.

Heathwood, Chris. 2013. "Hedonism." In *The International Encyclopedia of Ethics*, edited by Hugh LaFollette, 2370–2380. Oxford: Blackwell.

Hooker, Brad. 1996. "Ross-Style Pluralism versus Rule-Consequentialism." *Mind* 105, no. 420: 531–552.

Hume, David. 1965. "Of the Standard of Taste." In *Of the Standard of Taste and Other Essays*, edited by A. Lenz, 29–37. Indianapolis: Bobbs-Merrill Company.

Kagan, Shelly. 1989. *The Limits of Morality*. Oxford: Clarendon Press.

Kagan, Shelly. 2009. "Well-Being as Enjoying the Good." *Philosophical Perspectives* 23: 253–272.

Kieran, Matthew. 2005. *Revealing Art*. New York: Routledge.

Lenman, James. 2000. "Consequentialism and Cluelessness." *Philosophy and Public Affaeirs* 29, no. 4: 342–370.

Levinson, Jerrold. 1992. "Pleasure and the Value of Works of Art." *British Journal of Aesthetics* 32, no. 4: 295–306.

Lin, Eden. 2020. "Attitudinal and Phenomenological Theories of Pleasure." *Philosophy and Phenomenological Research* 100, no. 3: 510–524.

Lopes, Dominic McIver. 2018. *Being for Beauty: Aesthetic Agency and Value.* Oxford: Oxford University Press.

Mason, Elinor. 2004. "Consequentialism and the Principle of Indifference." *Utilitas* 16, no. 3: 316–321.

Matthen, Mohan. 2018. New Prospects for Aesthetic Hedonism. In *Social Aesthetics and Moral Judgment: Pleasure, Reflection and Accountability*, edited by J. A. McMahon, 13–33. New York: Routledge.

Mill, J. S. 1998. *Utilitarianism.* Oxford: Oxford University Press.

Mill, J. S. 2015. *On Liberty, Utilitarianism, and Other Essays.* Oxford: Oxford University Press.

Moore, G. E. 1903. *Principia Ethica.* Cambridge: Cambridge University Press.

Morreall, John. 1985. "Enjoying Negative Emotions in Fictions." *Philosophy and Literature* 9, no. 1: 95–103.

Neill, Alex. 1992. "On a Paradox of the Heart." *Philosophical Studies* 65, no. 1: 53–65.

Nozick, Robert. 1974. *Anarchy, State, and Utopia.* New York: Basic Books.

Railton, Peter. 1984. "Alienation, Consequentialism, and the Demands of Morality." *Philosophy & Public Affairs* 13, no. 2: 134–171.

Railton, Peter. 2003. *Facts, Values, and Norms: Essays Toward a Morality of Consequence.* Cambridge: Cambridge University Press.

Ross, W. D. 1930. *The Right and the Good.* Oxford: Oxford University Press.

Shelley, James. 2019. "The Default Theory of Aesthetic Value." *British Journal of Aesthetics*, 59, no.1: 1–12.

Singer, Peter. 2015. *The Most Good You Can Do.* New Haven, CT: Yale University Press.

Smuts, Aaron. 2007. "The Paradox of Painful Art." *Journal of Aesthetic Education* 41, no. 3: 59–76.

Sobel, David. 2002. "Varieties of Hedonism." *Journal of Social Philosophy* 33, no. 2: 240–256.

Stocker, Michael. 1990. *Plural and Conflicting Values.* Oxford: Clarendon Press.

Strohl, Matthew. 2019. "Art and Painful Emotion." *Philosophy Compass* 14, no. 1: e12558.

Sumner L. W. 2004. *The Hateful and the Obscene: Studies in the Limits of Free Expression.* Toronto: University of Toronto Press.

Thomson, Judith Jarvis. 1997. "The Right and the Good." *Journal of Philosophy* 94, no. 6: 273–298.

Unger, Peter. 1996. *Living High and Letting Die: Our Illusion of Innocence.* Oxford: Oxford University Press.

Van der Berg, Servaas. 2020. "Aesthetic Hedonism and its Critics." *Philosophy Compass* 15, no. 1: e12645.

Walton, Kendall L. 1993. "How Marvelous! Toward a Theory of Aesthetic Value." *Journal of Aesthetics and Art Criticism* 51, no. 3: 499–510.

Williams, Bernard. 1973. "A Critique of Utilitarianism." In Utilitarianism: For and Against, 75–150. Cambridge: Cambridge University Press.

Williams, Bernard. 1985. *Ethics and the Limits of Philosophy.* Cambridge, MA: Harvard University Press.

Woodcock, Scott. 2010. "When Will Your Consequentialist Friend Abandon You for the Greater Good?" *Journal of Ethics & Social Philosophy* 4, no. 2: 1–23.

Wolf, Susan. 1982. "Moral Saints." *Journal of Philosophy* 79, no. 8: 419–439.

CHAPTER 17

VIRTUE AESTHETICS, ART, AND ETHICS

NANCY E. SNOW

INTRODUCTION

VIRTUE aesthetics is a relative newcomer in the field of philosophical aesthetics. In brief, virtue aesthetics applies the frameworks of virtue ethics and virtue epistemology to aesthetics. Thus far, four main approaches are discernible: those of David Woodruff (2001) and Tom Roberts (2018), who draw on virtue epistemology to develop accounts of aesthetic virtues; Peter Goldie (2007; 2008; 2010), who draws on neo-Aristotelian virtue ethics; Dominic McIver Lopes (2008), who critiques Goldie's view from a virtue consequentialist perspective; and Matthew Kieran (2010; 2013), who explores the vice of snobbery and a range of appreciative virtues and vices. In this chapter, I offer a brief overview of the work in virtue ethics and virtue epistemology that has thus far influenced virtue aesthetics, then turn to work in virtue aesthetics.

A BRIEF WORD ON VIRTUE ETHICS AND VIRTUE EPISTEMOLOGY

The philosophical study of virtue is of ancient pedigree, harkening in the West to the ancient Greek philosophers Plato and Aristotle and to the Greek and Roman Stoics. (See Destrée, this volume.) In the east, ancient Confucians and Buddhists were also concerned with virtue. (See Hutton, this volume.) After the medieval period in the West, virtue became less central to the study of ethics, as views such as Kant's deontology and various conceptions of utilitarianism took pride of place in the modern era. (See Woodcock and Shapshay, this volume.) The rise of virtue ethics in contemporary philosophy is generally attributed to a seminal paper by Elizabeth Anscombe, "Modern Moral Philosophy" (1958). There she critiques deontology and consequentialism, laments the lack of an adequate philosophical psychology in ethics, and urges a return to Aristotle for inspiration.

Though many philosophers heeded the call, virtue ethics per se did not emerge until the publication of Rosalind Hursthouse's book *On Virtue Ethics* (1999). Hursthouse's project was to offer "virtue ethics" as a fully blown theoretical alternative to deontology and consequentialism. Deontology offers ethical theories according to which the concept of the "right," or "duty," is taken as the primary or fundamental concept in terms of which other moral concepts, such as the "good" or "virtue," are understood. Consequentialism takes "happiness," "pleasure," or some variant of the good to be central, and understands concepts such as the "right," and "virtue" to be derived from it. Hursthouse (1999) sought to develop a theory in terms of which "virtue" has pride of place, and other concepts, such as "right," "right action," and "good" are understood in terms of it. She was inspired by Aristotle, who was a eudaimonist. Both maintain that virtue contributes to but is also partly constitutive of human flourishing or *eudaimonia*. Both believe that goodness consists in having virtue and in acting virtuously because acting courageously, generously, and so on, is the right thing to do, or is good in and of itself. Right action consists in virtuous action. Moreover, virtue is a rational excellence that is acquired through guided habituation and the development of reason. *Phronēsis*, or practical wisdom, is required for fully developed virtue—one cannot have virtue without practical wisdom, and one cannot have practical wisdom without virtue. Virtue, in the Aristotelian tradition, is an entrenched disposition of character, reliably manifested across a wide range of types of situations and guided by practical wisdom. Virtue is the stable and controlling element in eudaimonia and is necessary for it, but not sufficient. Aristotle thought we also need external goods, such as wealth, good family and friends, good looks, and noble birth. Today we might update the list by not requiring good looks or noble birth but instead insisting on other goods as essential for living a flourishing life, for example, having clean air and water, food security, healthcare, and being and feeling safe. A further point merits mention. Aristotle held a strong "unity of virtues" thesis: we must have all of the virtues if we are to have any. In other words, if we lack even one of the virtues, we cannot be said to have any others. I take it this is because of his strong commitment to the role of practical wisdom in unifying virtues in a single character. That said, contemporary virtue ethicists shy away from this overly strong view. Hursthouse (1999) herself adopts a version of the limited unity of virtues thesis, according to which we need not have all of the virtues in order to have some.

Neo-Aristotelian virtue ethics is not the only version of virtue ethics on offer, but it is the one that Goldie uses as his framework for virtue aesthetics, so I have dwelt upon it here. Other approaches to virtue come from the consequentialist tradition. Here, virtue is not the primary concept, but has value only insofar as it enables us to attain the good. A variety of consequentialist theories of virtue have been developed. The one that influences Lopes's approach (2008) to virtue aesthetics, which is discussed below, is the recursive account of Thomas Hurka (2001). The account has two components: a recursive characterization of good and evil and a definition of virtue and vice in its terms (Hurka 2001, 11).

Hurka (2001) starts by identifying base-level intrinsic goods and evils: base-level intrinsic goods include pleasure, knowledge, and achievement; base-level intrinsic evils include pain, false belief, and failure in the pursuit of achievement. Attitudes toward these intrinsic goods and evils are then identified as intrinsically good or evil. These include states such as desiring, pursuing, or taking pleasure in what is intrinsically good. In short, loving what is intrinsically good, or more precisely, loving what is intrinsically good for itself apart from its consequences, is intrinsically good. Similarly, loving what is intrinsically evil is intrinsically evil. Hating what is intrinsically evil is intrinsically good and hating what is intrinsically good is intrinsically evil. Hurka goes on to add clauses about instrumental goods and evils. For example, "If x is instrumentally good because it promotes intrinsic good y, loving x because it promotes y is intrinsically good" (Hurka 2001, 17). Virtue and vice are then defined in terms of this recursive account: "The moral virtues are those attitudes to goods and evils that are intrinsically good, and the moral vices are those attitudes to goods and evils that are intrinsically evil" (Hurka 2001, 20). Hurka (2001, 21) comments that moral virtues are thus identified as higher-level goods in his multilevel theory and moral vices as higher-level evils, so that any intrinsic good above the base level is a virtue and any intrinsic evil above it is a vice. Of special interest is Hurka's (2001, 40ff) conception of a virtue. By contrast with the Aristotelian notion that virtues are stable dispositions, Hurka (2001, 42) notes: "Our definition, by contrast, treats virtue atomistically, finding it in occurrent desires, actions, and feelings regardless of their connection to more permanent traits of character."

So much for the ethical approaches to virtue that have thus far influenced virtue aesthetics. Virtue epistemology, too, has been influential. Virtue epistemology aims to understand the pursuit of knowledge and other epistemic goods, such as truth and understanding, in terms of virtues. There are two important variants of virtue epistemology, both of which have influenced virtue aesthetics. Reliabilism is the view, pioneered by Ernest Sosa (2007; 2009) and John Greco (2010), that epistemic or intellectual virtues are capacities such as perception, attention, deliberation, and memory. These are basic human faculties that can be "fine-tuned" to become excellences and reliably lead us in the pursuit of knowledge (justified true belief). Responsibilism takes epistemic virtues to be not capacities, but character traits for the development of which individuals are responsible. We are responsible for being open-minded, intellectually humble, appropriately curious, perseverant in our pursuit of knowledge, and so on. This view, pioneered by Code (2020) and Montmarquet (1993), has been given its most influential development in Zagzebski (1996). Virtue epistemology is of relatively recent vintage, but it has taken off in popularity, and boasts a lively and growing literature.

The ethical and epistemological perspectives just reviewed can readily be discerned in the approaches to virtue aesthetics discussed in the next three sections.

VIRTUE EPISTEMOLOGICAL INFLUENCES ON VIRTUE AESTHETICS

In this section, I discuss the views of two authors: David Woodruff and Tom Roberts.

Woodruff (2001)

Woodruff (2001) models his theory of the aesthetic virtues directly on Zagzebski's (1996) theory of virtue. Zagzebski defines a virtue as "a deep and enduring acquired excellence of a person, involving a characteristic motivation to produce a certain desired end and reliable success in bringing about that end" (Zagzebski 1996, 136, emphasis hers, quoted by Woodruff 2001, 24). Woodruff (2001, 24–26) argues that this definition is broad enough to include aesthetic virtues and that the root or core motivation of aesthetic virtues is appreciation. He then goes on to sketch the outlines of a comprehensive virtue theory of aesthetics with appreciation as the fundamental motivation. This theory consists of a hierarchy of aesthetic virtues, which Woodruff (2001) uses to define aesthetic properties and art, but is also sufficiently comprehensive, he thinks, to account for both fine and decorative arts as well as art criticism and the production of artworks.

According to Woodruff (2001), mere exposure to artwork is not enough to generate appreciation; appreciation is developed not only through the experience of interacting with art, but also through the development of certain character traits that foster ever greater sophistication of art appreciation. Woodruff (2001, 27–29) divides the aesthetic virtues by means of which we develop our capacities for appreciation, into lower-level and higher-level traits. Lower-level traits enable one to have an incomplete appreciation of a work but are important for developing higher-level traits. He (2001, 27) writes: "To exercise a trait of a higher level requires that one be at least competent in all of the lower level traits."

Woodruff (2001, 27–28) contends that three higher-level traits are necessary to be able fully to appreciate an artwork: insight, sensitivity, and vision. Insight is the ability to discern what is in a work and how it relates to other works. Blindness or missing the point is the vice of deficiency associated with this virtue; reading too much into a work is the vice of excess. Sensitivity is closely linked to insight, and is the virtue of allowing "the work to affect us and shape our understanding of the subject" (Woodruff 2001, 27). Though he does not explain them, he notes that vices associated with sensitivity are brashness and being overly affected (Woodruff 2001, 28). Vision, also at the highest level of the hierarchy, is the ability to see the work both in terms of the "big picture," and in terms of small detail—to appreciate its unity, contrast, and context. The vices associated with vision are the deficiency of a limited or narrow focus and the excess of abstractedness.

At the lower level of the hierarchy, and necessary for the full development and exercise of those at the higher level, are creativity, persistence, and courage. Woodruff (2001, 28) contends that: "Aesthetic creativity seeks the expression of ideas related to appreciation. The creative process as an aesthetic concern is directed at expression for the sake of appreciation. I put creativity at a level below sensitivity, insight, and vision, because each of these virtues requires the exercise of the creative process." Vices related to creativity are the defect of unimaginativeness, and an excess that he calls "disassociatedness" but does not explain (Woodruff 2001, 28). Persistence, also necessary for the development and exercise of the three higher level virtues, is the second virtue at the lower level of the hierarchy. Vices are being too easily distracted and being obsessive. Finally, Woodruff (2001, 29) includes aesthetic courage: "the motivation . . . to face what the work tells us about ourselves in order to appreciate the work." Vices are timorousness and recklessness.

As noted previously, Woodruff (2001) uses his theory to distinguish between fine art and decorative art and thinks it can account for art criticism and art production. I shall not comment on these claims here, but wish to raise questions for his theory that I believe reveal potential problems. One issue is his contention that aesthetic virtues are basic and that an essential element of his theory, namely, art, is defined in relation to them. He writes:

> I take the aesthetic virtues to be basic and the actions of reflecting on and producing art to be defined by reference to them. Furthermore, artworks are products of actions brought about by the exercise of aesthetic virtues. I define art in terms of the process of production and that, in turn, will be defined according to the aesthetic virtues. (Woodruff 2001, 29–30)

Art, for Woodruff (2001, 30–31) is what is produced for aesthetic appreciation with some degree of success, and I take it, the aesthetic virtues contribute substantially to that success.

The issue is one of potential circularity: we develop the aesthetic virtues in order to appreciate art, but we cannot appreciate art, nor develop the aesthetic virtues, unless art already exists and we can, in some sense, know that it exists *qua* art. Woodruff (2001) might define art in terms of the aesthetic virtues, but he could just as well define the aesthetic virtues as those qualities elicited in us by our encounters with art. Woodruff (2001, 31) could break the circle with his claim that "aesthetic appreciation is not a unique kind of appreciation that is limited to our response to art." But it would be odd to think that aesthetic appreciation, the core motivation of the aesthetic virtues, and aesthetic virtues themselves, were not developed through encounters with art, but instead, through other appreciation-eliciting factors, such as nature, the elegance involved in games like chess, or the physical grace displayed in some sports. Perhaps the solution is not to define art in terms of the workings of the aesthetic virtues in the production process, but instead, to conceptualize the relationship between art and aesthetic virtues as being in a kind of complex developmental dynamic, according to which encounters with art nurture aesthetic virtues, and aesthetic virtues contribute to the continued successful production of works of art.

A final comment on Woodruff (2001) is worth noting. It seems arbitrary to divide the aesthetic virtues into a hierarchy, since all seem to contribute to aesthetic appreciation. Placing creativity on the lower level seems especially open to challenge, unless one also allows that it appears again, perhaps in an enhanced or enriched way, in the higher level of the hierarchy. The most troubling claim, however, is the contention that exercising a higher-level trait requires at least competence in all of the lower-level traits. Surely this is a matter to be determined by the empirical study of the traits in question, how they are developed, and how they relate to one another.

Roberts (2018)

In a later approach to aesthetic virtue, Roberts (2018) draws on reliabilist and responsibilist accounts of virtue epistemology, as well as other explanations of traits, to offer a person-focused theory of aesthetic virtue. He considers aesthetic virtues to be comprised of both traits and faculties. He analyzes aesthetic trait virtues

> in terms of the aesthetically conscientious agent's possession of an overarching concern for the aesthetically good . . . The aesthetically virtuous person is one whose traits of character reflect a commitment to the promotion and appreciation of these goods; not merely through being dispositioned to act in characteristic ways, but by constituting engrained patterns of care, affect, and motivation. (Roberts 2018, 433)

Aesthetic trait virtues include virtues such as aesthetic courage, honesty, discipline, focus, patience, and enthusiasm, among others, that are needed for the creation and appreciation of art (Roberts 2018, 434). Aesthetic vices bespeak a lack of appropriate concern for the aesthetic good and can be driven by motives such as the desire for prestige, wealth, or approval. The aesthetically lazy, cowardly, or dishonest person allows her concern for aesthetic goods, such as the beautiful, to be displaced by these and other external incentives. Drawing directly on responsibilist epistemology, Roberts (2018, 434) writes that, "The aesthetic trait virtues are the responsibility of the agent who possesses them—they are features for which she can be held accountable, and which go some way towards constituting her character as a person."

Roberts's (2018, 435–437) conception of aesthetic faculty virtues draws on reliabilist virtue epistemology. He claims that, "Aesthetic faculties can be understood, in this context, as the broad class of relatively stable powers of the agent that contribute to her execution of some artistic activity, such as music-making, painting, or sculpture" (Roberts 2018, 435). They are reliable technical facilities—we can count on a reliable pianist to give good performances, all else being equal. Two points that Roberts (2018, 436–437) makes about aesthetic faculty virtues are important. The first is that they can be acquired with practice but need not be; some people are simply naturally endowed with these kinds of excellences. However, they are not available to all; some people, even with practice, will not have the natural excellence of a pianist or singer. Second, faculty virtues have no necessary connection to an agent's motivational or affective states.

These claims lead to the question of whether faculty virtues really are virtues. Roberts (2018, 437–438) holds that they are, and that aesthetic traits and faculty virtues are not separable but display three kinds of dependency. The first is the dependency of trait virtues on faculty virtues: an artist's honesty in portraying her subject relies on her technical ability to capture the subject's likeness—to use color, light, and so on. Without these technical abilities, she will be unable to render a faithful portrayal of her subject. The second dependency is that of faculty virtues on trait virtues. The ability to acquire technical facility in the first place demands certain virtues such as patience and determination, which would require a conscientious commitment to aesthetic goods. Finally, there is a reflective dependency between the two kinds of virtues. A conscientious artist must keep track of her faculty virtues in order to appropriately possess trait virtues. Without keeping proper track of her technical abilities, she might overestimate or underestimate her artistic abilities, undertaking performances that are too difficult for her, or refusing to take part in creative endeavors. Roberts (2018, 438) notes: "Part of what it is to be aesthetically conscientious—to be fully trait-virtuous—is thus that one be prepared to keep track of one's faculty qualities, and to deploy them appropriately in the pursuit of aesthetic goods."

In the rest of his article, Roberts (2018) addresses how his account explains the kinds of value that can accrue to works of art. Consistently with reliabilist virtue epistemology, faculty virtues allow us to recognize that art is a kind of achievement. Consistently with responsibilism, trait virtues allow us to see the value of art produced by appropriate motives, that is, conscientious concern for aesthetic goods. More could be said about this discussion, but I wish instead to focus more directly on some of Roberts's (2018) claims about aesthetic virtues.

He seems to focus his views on aesthetic virtue to the production of art. As we saw from Woodruff (2001), consumers or appreciators of art can also have more or less well-developed aesthetic virtues. The trait virtues of aesthetic courage and honesty, for example, could be needed truly to appreciate artworks that challenge one's preconceptions and comfortable worldviews, or force us to confront ugly realities. Picasso's *Guernica* has just this effect—forcing us to confront the horrors of war. Those who are not willing or open-minded enough to be honest or courageous will not be able to take this journey.

Recognizing that aesthetic faculty virtues can be possessed by consumers or appreciators of art would allow for new directions in the development of Roberts's (2018) theory. He veers in the direction of elitism when he recognizes that faculty excellences in the sense needed to be a good artist are not available to everyone. Though it is true, as he notes, that not everyone can have these abilities, and therefore cannot be blamed for not having them (Roberts 2018, 436–437), the case is different when we consider that, barring physical impairments, all of us are capable of attaining competence in at least some faculty virtues when it comes to art appreciation. As Kieran (2013) advocates and Goldie (2010, 836–837; 2007, 380–382) suggests, education in art appreciation can proceed through the cultivation of aesthetic virtues. This can have the effect of "democratizing" the practices of art appreciation and opening up the art world to a larger population. The cultivation of faculties as well as traits is essential for this. We will not be able fully to appreciate classical music unless we learn how to listen. Our eye needs to be trained in order to understand and appreciate the nuances of painting, sculpture, architecture, and dance. The "training up" of our faculties of perception requires the tutoring of other faculties, such as cognition and memory, for frequently it is necessary to grasp the cultural and historical context surrounding the development of some art forms and some artworks in order to enter into a full appreciation of their beauty, meaning, and value as art. Thus, books such as *What to Listen for in Music* by Aaron Copland (2009), *How to Look at Art* by Susie Hodge (2014), and *How to Look at Japanese Art* by Stephen Addis and Audrey Yoshiko Seo (2015) help the consumer or appreciator of art to acquire greater capacities for understanding and appreciation. Of course, reading books is not the only means by which our faculties can be enhanced. Experiencing art is central, but it is especially important to experience art in an informed way, lest opportunities for appreciation of aesthetic goods be missed. For example, guidance by a knowledgeable friend or tour guide upon visiting a cathedral can immensely aid one's appreciation of the architectural richness of the edifice and its historical transformations.[1] I doubt that Roberts would disagree with these observations. I raise them only to underscore the need for further analysis of the faculty virtues of consumers and appreciators of art, in addition to those of producers.

VIRTUE ETHICAL INFLUENCES ON VIRTUE AESTHETICS

Two approaches to virtue aesthetics that are informed by virtue ethics have come upon the scene. In three important papers, Goldie (2007, 2008, and 2010) sketches a neo-Aristotelian perspective on virtue aesthetics. Lopes (2008) responds to Goldie (2008) from a consequentialist vantage point by drawing on Hurka's (2001) recursive account. After an overview of Goldie's views, I will respond with my own observations before turning to Lopes (2008).

Goldie (2007, 2008, 2010)

Goldie's neo-Aristotelian account develops a viewpoint according to which the aesthetic, ethical, and intellectual virtues are interwoven (Goldie 2008, 188–190).

---

[1] As I learned from Michael Reed's enlightening comments during a visit to Ely Cathedral.

Aesthetic virtues are psychological dispositions that have the correct motivations and appropriate emotions. A virtue is an excellence; it is an entrenched and enduring disposition; and it is reliably manifested in behavior across various types of situations—it has breadth of scope (Goldie 2010, 831–832). Though this approach is avowedly Aristotelian, it also meshes with Zagzebski's (1996) responsibilist account of intellectual virtues. Goldie (2007, 372; 2010, 832–833) takes on board both art production and art appreciation, arguing that different virtues are involved in each form of activity. For example, courage and honesty are involved in the making of art, and having good taste or being a fine observer is required for appreciation. In the virtues of art production, he aligns with Woodruff (2001) and in those of art appreciation, with Lopes (2008). Moreover, he admits that there are aesthetic vices, among them, snobbery (see Kieran 2010).

One of the most striking aspects of Goldie's approach is how he conceptualizes art-making, art appreciation, and associated virtues within the broader Aristotelian landscape of human flourishing. According to this outlook, we can view art and its production and appreciation as parts of a complex Wittgensteinian "form of life" that is a characteristically human activity, one without which we cannot truly flourish as human beings. Goldie (2007, 372) writes that when artistic activities are chosen for their own sake, that is, "under the concept of art,"

> the activities are themselves partly constitutive of human well-being, along with other activities, including leading an ethical life, and what Aristotle called contemplation. With a virtue theory of art before us, we can begin to see the point of art, to see why art matters to us as human beings.

Why does art matter to human beings? And how can virtue aesthetics shed light on this question? In remarks that are tantalizing but brief, Goldie (2007, 385; 2008, 191–192) argues that art is a form of contemplative intellectual activity that is part of human well-being. A second briefly discussed but provocative idea is this: artistic activity involves emotional sharing (Goldie 2008, 192). According to Goldie (2008, 192), "Emotional sharing occurs when two or more people experience an emotion of a certain kind, directed to a particular shared object or to a shared kind of object, and those people are aware that they are experiencing the same emotion towards the same object." Art makes possible the permanent possibility of this kind of emotional sharing—when we appreciate *Guernica*, for example, we are aware that the artist speaks to our human responses, and that such responses are not confined to specific times, cultures, or generations, but are common to our shared humanity (Goldie 2008, 193). Goldie contends that, "This kind of emotional sharing, as part of artistic activity, is valuable in its own right, and, of course, it is also valuable in so far as it plays a role in the development of our ethical virtues, in leading a good ethical life in our interaction with others, and in our self-knowledge" (Goldie 2008, 193).

Thus, art is necessary for human well-being and helps us to develop our distinctively human capacities, both for contemplation and for meaningful emotional sharing. Emotional sharing, and I would add, the contemplation of art, help us to develop ethical virtues, which, according to Aristotelian virtue ethics, are partly constitutive of living well. In other words, the same kinds of finely tuned perceptual capacities that enable us correctly to identify occasions for virtuous action are also needed for appreciating art; likewise, the same kinds of emotional states associated with ethical virtues are necessary for us to participate in the shared human responses that art appreciation calls for. It is easy to see how intellectual virtues are also integral to this picture. Open-mindedness and curiosity, for example, can whet our interest in art and create a receptivity to new experiences of art—art from different genres and different cultures. Intellectual perseverance and care can enable us to delve into the history, context, and background of works of art and their traditions. Having and exercising all of these virtues as appreciators of art enhances human flourishing, both individually and collectively.

In addition to sketching the main contours of his view, Goldie also tackles several problems for virtue aesthetics, which track parallel problems for virtue ethics. I will discuss four here, since doing so will enable us to flesh out his position in greater depth.

First, he gives careful consideration to problems of motivation and intention, which lead to questions of justification (Goldie 2007, 376–381). As mentioned earlier, he takes a strongly Aristotelian view: aesthetic virtues are expressed if and only if they are chosen for their own sake, "under the concept of art" (2007, 372). Goldie (2007, 376–381) is well aware of the various interpretative difficulties that attend this view. I will not review his entire discussion here, but note only that Goldie's (2007, 380–382) remarks on aesthetic education—on how children are initiated into aesthetic engagement and appreciation through introduction to artistic practices—lead him to adopt a McDowellian perspective on issues of motivation and justification. McDowell (1998) famously interprets Aristotelian ethical naturalism as not relying on external foundations for justification. The justification for adopting the ethical way of life is to be found from inside the practice of ethics; likewise, our motivations for acting ethically and wanting to be moral are cultivated from within a virtue-oriented perspective. Goldie (2007, 380–381) takes a similar perspective on our relations to art and aesthetic virtues. He writes: "Looking for the point of ethics, or for the point of art, from outside the practices will at best reveal explanations of their origins, or of how they came to be what they are; it will not reveal their value, nor will it reveal the reasons—*our* reasons—why we value them" (Goldie 2007, 381, emphasis his).

In other words, we can only value art for its own sake from within the practices of art, or the forms of life constituted by art-making and art appreciation. Of course, these practices can also be instrumentally valuable. We engage in art dealership as a form of commerce, or in art therapy as a form of recovery from illness. But these instrumental benefits cannot express the intrinsic value of art-making and art appreciation as ways of life. People standing outside of these forms of life cannot appreciate the intrinsic value of art or why art matters to human life.

The second problem is whether virtues are skills. Goldie (2008, 180) frankly notes that this is "a real challenge" and that more needs to be said to show that aesthetic virtues are not reducible to skills, nor are they natural virtues in Aristotle's sense, that is, virtues uninformed by practical wisdom (Goldie 2010, 834–835). One issue on which he (2008,

180–181) insists is that skills have only instrumental value, whereas aesthetic virtues are not exercised for some further end, but have intrinsic value. Their intrinsic value lies in their being partly constitutive of a good life.

The third problem is whether the virtues of art are cross-situationally consistent. The phrase "cross-situational consistency" entered the philosophical lexicon with the situationist critique of philosophers such as Harman (1999) and Doris (2002). Situationists attacked Aristotelian virtue ethics on the ground that it lacks an adequate empirical psychology. The presupposition of Aristotelian virtues is that they are "global" or "robust" traits—that is, traits that are reliably manifested across a wide variety of types of situations. An honest person, for example, can be relied on to be honest on her tax forms, when under oath in court, in conversations with her spouse, and so on.

Goldie (2008, 184) frankly admits that we do not expect cross-situational consistency in aesthetic virtues, either of production or appreciation: we do not expect an excellent sculptor to be an excellent composer or pianist, nor do we consider someone who fails to appreciate German expressionism or baroque music, but appreciates other art forms, to be deficient in art appreciation. Cross-situational consistency in aesthetic virtues, Goldie (2008, 181, 185) argues, is a matter of degree. Despite this, we do expect a certain degree of consistency in aesthetic virtues, and there is more consistency than appears at first sight. He points out a wide range of traits associated with and contributing to the virtues of art, for example, imagination, insight, sensibility, vision, creativity, and so on (see Goldie 2008, 185). These traits, he thinks, will cluster around and contribute to the virtue of being a good producer or good appreciator of art. What is required for cross-situational consistency "is that the possessor of the trait, the putative virtue of art, has what might be summarized as a certain artistic *receptivity*, sensitivity, or openness outside their particular local domain of interest—such as sculpting or impressionism" (Goldie 2008, 184–185, emphasis his).

This is clearly less stringent than the demand that the honest person manifest or express that virtue in all of the situations in which she is required to do so, and more like the intellectual virtue of open-mindedness—a person possessing that virtue is open to all forms of knowledge, even to those that lie outside of her domain of interest or expertise, even if she does not actually undertake studies in those domains. However, should she choose to engage with other disciplines, she would, as an intellectually responsible person, be required to exercise virtues such as care, perseverance, and thoroughness in her efforts to understand the new area of study. Similarly, we might say that the sculptor or appreciator of sculpture who wished to understand baroque music should be not only receptive and open-minded but also careful and perseverant in his approach to an unfamiliar art form.

The final challenge I will discuss here is Goldie's (2008, 181–182; 186–187) version of the demandingness objection. The demandingness objection is usually leveled against utilitarianism's demand that we maximize utility. It is commonly thought too burdensome always to act in ways that maximize utility, as that would entail being able to have little or no pleasures for one's self. Goldie (2008, 181–182; emphasis his) gives this a different twist, writing: "If someone fails on an occasion to do what is required of his ethical virtue, honesty for example, then we will think the less of him, whereas this does not seem to apply where the artistic virtues are concerned. In this respect, again, they seem more like skills, which one can exercise on an appropriate occasion if one chooses, but which one is not *required* to exercise."

Against this, Goldie (2008, 186–187) argues that two kinds of demandingness are involved in aesthetic virtues. For one thing, a kind of demandingness is involved in the production of art, for example, violin-playing, when one is fully engaged, say at a concert performance. This is not required in less formal settings. Second, and more pervasively, there is the demand to care about what one is engaged in. A skilled performance is not enough. Following the neo-Aristotelian virtue ethicist Philippa Foot (1978, 7–9), Goldie (2008, 186–187) argues that aesthetic virtues must "engage the will." I believe the same can be applied to the virtues of art appreciation. To appreciate fully a work of art requires our full attention to it, whether that is in close listening to a musical piece or careful study of a painting or sculpture. The demands of art appreciation go even further—as noted earlier, sometimes the study of context, background, history, art forms, and cultural traditions is needed. In addition to these cognitive demands, our imagination and creative powers can also be called into play, as well as our willingness to respond emotionally to what the artist presents to us—what Goldie (2008, 192) calls "emotional sharing."

More can be said about Goldie's approach (e.g., Goldie (2008, 188–190) discusses the interweaving of ethical, intellectual, and aesthetic virtues). To close this overview, however, I would like to offer my own observations on several aspects of his rich and provocative theory.

First, though Goldie (2010, 834–835) mentions that aesthetic virtues are neither merely skills nor natural virtues in Aristotle's sense, he does not raise the possibility of an aesthetic counterpart to Aristotelian *phronēsis*, or practical wisdom. Practical wisdom is what transforms natural virtues into moral virtues, and ensures that virtues like justice, generosity, and courage are not simply luck or skill in meting out what is due, having a knack for giving appropriate gifts, or using little tricks for overcoming fears in difficult situations (e.g., envisioning one's audience naked when asked to speak in public). Growth in practical wisdom enables us to grow and deepen in virtue. Might it not be the case that a similar faculty could exist with respect to the aesthetic virtues of art production and appreciation? As we cultivate that faculty—which could be affective as well as cognitive—we also develop our aesthetic virtues in depth and breadth.

A second challenge is cultural. Goldie's account highlights the universality of aesthetic goods—contemplation and shared human responses. Of course, cultures shape contemplation and human responses. They also shape taste, which seems to lie at the heart of both art production and art appreciation. Learning how to appreciate the art of different cultures often requires shifting or changing our tastes, or at least being open and receptive to the norms and conventions that shape taste in other traditions and cultures. A similar point can be made about avant-garde art in a single culture, especially those movements that seek to challenge prevailing traditions or schools of taste, form, and expression. Numerous questions can be raised about these issues, not the least of which is whether human capacities for artistic expression, appreciation, and taste are infinitely malleable, or whether there are fixed limits. Might it be the case that past certain points in the development of our aesthetic sensibilities within certain traditions, we simply lose the ability to be flexible, so that some artistic expressions lie beyond the reach of what we are able to appreciate? If so, we can no longer speak with confidence of the universality of the aesthetic goods of contemplation and human response.

Finally, we must again raise the spectre of elitism. Even in First World countries, opportunities for the kind of aesthetic education that could develop aesthetic virtues are limited. More to the point, many people simply do not see the value of fine art, classical music, literature, dance, sculpture, or architecture, and are turned off by their mere mention. Are those who are outsiders to the forms of life that encompass art production and art appreciation doomed to aesthetic vice? Or are there ways to cultivate art production and art appreciation that appeal to audiences of more popular pursuits—to those attracted by video games instead of Vivaldi, by basketball instead of Balanchine?

Lopes (2008)

As mentioned previously, Lopes (2008) responds to Goldie by modeling virtue aesthetics on Hurka's (2001) recursive account. Lopes (2008, 197), like Goldie, starts with the idea that having a virtue is intrinsically good for its possessor, and seeks to establish that good taste is a virtue only if:

(V) Good taste is intrinsically good.

Whereas Goldie takes an Aristotelian approach to defend this claim, Lopes offers an alternative coming from what he calls a "neo-Moorean" perspective. Moore (1903, 204) finds intrinsic value in the "appreciation of what has great intrinsic value" (quoted in Lopes 2008, 197). Beginning with this notion, he suggests a base clause, which establishes that some good—in this case, beautiful states of affairs—has intrinsic value, then follows with several recursion clauses that map out various relations to beautiful states of affairs that also have intrinsic value. The basic idea is that if a beautiful state of affairs has intrinsic value, and we can establish this using some kind of isolation test, as Moore suggests, then good taste, which enables us to appreciate beautiful states of affairs, has intrinsic value, too.

Lopes (2008, 201) starts with a base clause and a series of recursion clauses that follow:

(B) p is intrinsically good,

where p can be substituted with a list of intrinsic goods, such as beautiful states of affairs. Recursion clause (R) follows:

(R) If p is intrinsically good then V-ing p for itself is intrinsically good, where V-ing is a pro-attitude toward p. So, if p is a beautiful state of affairs that is intrinsically valuable, and admiring p is a form of V-ing, then admiring a beautiful state of affairs is also intrinsically good.

Recursion clause (I) follows. Following Hurka (2001, 17), Lopes (2008, 202) claims:

(I) If x is instrumentally good at promoting intrinsic good y then V-ing x for promoting y is intrinsically good.

So if the Museum of Modern Art is instrumentally good at promoting beautiful states of affairs, admiring it for doing so is intrinsically good.

Two clauses referring to dispositions are introduced. Recursion clause (RD) states (Lopes 2008, 203):

(RD) If p is intrinsically good then a disposition for V-ing p for itself is intrinsically good;

(RD) establishes that if beautiful states are intrinsically good, then being disposed to admire them for themselves is intrinsically good.

Finally, Lopes (2008, 204) claims that:

(ID) If x is good at promoting intrinsic good y then a disposition for V-ing x for promoting y is intrinsically good.

So if the Museum of Modern Art is instrumentally good at promoting beautiful states of affairs, a disposition for admiring it for doing so is intrinsically good.

I take it that other recursion clauses could be added, but Lopes (2008) spends the rest of his article comparing and contrasting the merits of his approach with Goldie's.

Establishing the base clause is key for the neo-Moorean approach. As Lopes (2008, 199–201) knows, establishing the base clause relies on isolation tests that essentially pump our intuitions about what has value. Moore's classic version of this test is to ask us to imagine a world in which some x, a candidate for an intrinsic good, exists in isolation of everything else. If we still deem x to have value, the value it possesses is intrinsic. Lopes (2008, 199–201) suggests two other tests. One asks us to imagine two worlds, Felix and Oscar, which are identical except for the taste of their inhabitants. Felicians have good taste, appreciate beauty, and so on, whereas Oscaroons do not. However, neither world contains anything that is beautiful or ugly, so taste is exercised in neither world. Yet if we think Felix is the better world, our intuitions suggest that good taste has intrinsic value. A third and more decisive test is more ecological, focusing on situations in which good taste is actually exercised. The test relies on Kieran's work on snobbery.[2] Kieran asks us to

---

[2] Lopes (2008, 200) refers to a then-unpublished manuscript by Kieran, later published as "The Vice of Snobbery: Aesthetic Knowledge, Justification and Virtue in the Art of Appreciation" (2010).

consider two individuals, the snob and the amateur. Each arrives at the same judgments of artworks based on the same features of the works, yet they differ in their motivations. The snob appreciates art only for the sake of social prestige or to maintain a certain self-image as highly cultured. The amateur, by contrast, appreciates art for its own sake. If we judge the character of the amateur better than that of the snob, Lopes (2008, 200) believes that this, too, indicates that we intuitively support the belief that art has intrinsic value.

Lopes (2008, 200–201) mentions other considerations in favor of the idea that intuitions support (V) and claims that traditional theories of taste should be revised or supplanted if they do not provide resources to explain (V). More can be said about the neo-Moorean approach, especially about the conception of intrinsic value on which it relies. Lopes (2008, 199–200; 202–204) takes up some of these issues, especially in the context of aesthetic empiricism. Explaining the intrinsic value of beautiful states of affairs and of the virtues that enable us to produce and appreciate them is a central challenge of virtue aesthetics, and the neo-Moorean account provides interesting possibilities for thinking about them.

I will close with only one set of observations. Clarification is needed of the kinds of entities that are instrumentally good at promoting the intrinsic good of beautiful states of affairs, as specified in (I) and (ID). It makes sense to claim that admiring MoMA or being disposed to admire it are intrinsically good. But surely there are some entities—perhaps part of the institutions—that promote beautiful states of affairs for which our admiration would not be intrinsically but only instrumentally good. For example, I have an app on my iphone called "Google Arts & Culture." It enables me to explore museums and learn about artworks from the comfort of home. A similar technological innovation is the Chicago Symphony Orchestra's streaming service, which can allow me to stream concert performances on my iPhone or TV. I have especially enjoyed these during the pandemic. Should my admiration of these technologies really be called intrinsically good? Intuitions about these cases can be blurry, so consider another example. Before the pandemic, I was able to purchase a ticket to a concert of the Chicago Symphony Orchestra online. The online purchasing function is instrumentally good at promoting beautiful states of affairs, but my admiration of it for doing so seems to me to be instrumentally and not intrinsically valuable. This illustrates a larger and well-known point about the hazards of intuition pumping: intuitions can be blurry and can conflict.

THE VICE OF SNOBBERY AND APPRECIATIVE VIRTUES: KIERAN (2010, 2013)

An overview of recent work in virtue aesthetics would not be complete without mentioning two important papers, Kieran (2010) and (2013). In the former, Kieran gives a detailed account of the vice of snobbery and the problems it raises for justifying our beliefs about aesthetic claims, and in the latter, builds on this work. In essence, the issue is this. The snob makes seemingly correct aesthetic judgments about the value of works of art but does so from the wrong motives. Her judgments do not stem from a true appreciation of art, but, instead, from irrelevant motives—for the sake of social prestige, hoping to look knowledgeable in front of others, to be part of an "in" crowd, to be associated with a certain brand, and so on. As Kieran (2010, 244) puts it, "A snob's aesthetic appreciation or judgement is distorted by social considerations which are extraneous to proper aesthetic appreciation."

Kieran (2010, 255) goes on to argue that it is not just the snob's motivations that are awry: "The snob's skills, abilities and dispositions are manifested in vice-ridden ways in appreciation." In other words, the snob's corrupted motivations "feed through" into her appreciative activity, "so that aesthetically irrelevant social features play a causal role in forming the aesthetic judgements arrived at" (Kieran 2010, 262). This constitutes appreciative vice. Moreover, the snob is likely to possess other appreciative vices, such as cowardice, closed-mindedness, or a tendency to be formulaic. A true appreciator, by contrast, is likely to possess virtues such as courage, open-mindedness, and imaginativeness. Proper aesthetic appreciation is an achievement, requiring not only trait virtues, but also the development of a wide range of perceptual capacities and cognitive-affective responses that can be cultivated and refined (2010, 255; 2013, 18).

Kieran (2010, 252–254) examines how snobbery can undermine aesthetic justification and knowledge claims. Though I cannot discuss his views in detail here, he offers as a possible way forward an approach to education which includes the development of aesthetic virtues as excellences of character. This is a long-term solution which, if enacted well, could result in a number of valuable benefits. For one thing, snobbery would be discouraged, and this could go some way toward ameliorating the elitism of which the world of aesthetics and art appreciation has been suspected, and to which it often falls prey. Related to this is the benefit that art appreciation could become more "democratic"—more open to all as a result of early and continuous education. Finally, cultivating excellences of character as a way of appreciating the good of art cannot help but sensitize us to other goods in our lives. This, of course, echoes Goldie's view that ethical, intellectual, and aesthetic virtues are intertwined.

CONCLUSION

Virtue aesthetics is clearly in its infancy. Yet the approaches reviewed here give a sense of its richness and vigor in engaging with any number of fascinating topics—art creation and appreciation, the appreciation of art as a "form of life," how art and its appreciation contribute to human flourishing through contemplation and emotional sharing, the nature of art's intrinsic value, and the examination of a range of aesthetic virtues and vices. These and other virtue aesthetical themes are wide open for further exploration.

See also: Fisher, Woodcock, Destrée, Hutton, Shapshay, this volume

REFERENCES

Addiss, Stephen, and Audrey Yoshiko Seo. 2015. *How to Look at Japanese Art*. Brattleboro, VT: Echo Point Books & Media.

Code, Lorraine. 2020. *Epistemic Responsibility*. 2nd ed. Albany: SUNY Press.

Copland, Aaron. 2009. *What to Listen for in Music*. New York: New American Library.

Doris, John M. 2002. *Lack of Character: Personality and Moral Behavior*. Cambridge: Cambridge University Press.

Foot, Philippa. 1978. *Virtues and Vices and Other Essays in Moral Philosophy*. Berkeley: University of California Press.

Goldie, Peter. 2007. "Towards A Virtue Theory of Art." *British Journal of Aesthetics* 47, no. 4: 372–387.

Goldie, Peter. 2008. "Virtues of Art and Human Well-Being." *Proceedings of the Aristotelian Society, Supplementary Volumes* 82: 179–195.

Goldie, Peter. 2010. "Virtues of Art." *Philosophy Compass* 5, no. 10: 830–839.

Greco, John. 2010. *Achieving Knowledge: A Virtue-Theoretic Account of Epistemic Normativity*. Cambridge: Cambridge University Press.

Harman, Gilbert. 1999. "Moral Philosophy Meets Social Psychology: Virtue Ethics and the Fundamental Attribution Error." *Proceedings of the Aristotelian Society* 99: 315–331.

Hodge, Susie. 2014. *How to Look at Art*. London: Tate Publishing.

Hurka, Thomas. 2001. *Virtue, Vice, and Value*. Oxford: Oxford University Press.

Hursthouse, Rosalind. 1999. *On Virtue Ethics*. Oxford: Oxford University Press.

Kieran, Matthew. 2010. "The Vice of Snobbery: Aesthetic Knowledge, Justification and Virtue in Art Appreciation." *Philosophical Quarterly* 60, no. 239: 243–263.

Kieran, Matthew. 2013. "For the Love of Art: Artistic Values and Appreciative Virtue." *Royal Institute of Philosophy Supplements* 71 (October): 13–31.

Lopes, Dominic McIver. 2008. "Virtues of Art: Good Taste." *Aristotelian Society Supplementary Volume* 82, no. 1: 197–211.

McDowell, John. 1998. "Two Sorts of Naturalism." In *Mind, Value, and Reality*, 167–197. Cambridge, MA: Harvard University Press.

Montmarquet, James A. 1993. *Epistemic Virtue and Doxastic Responsibility*. Studies in Epistemology and Cognitive Theory. Lanham, MD: Rowman & Littlefield.

Moore, G. E. 1903. *Principia Ethica*. Cambridge, MA: Cambridge University Press.

Roberts, Tom. 2018. "Aesthetic Virtues: Traits and Faculties." *Philosophical Studies* 175, no. 2: 429–447.

Sosa, Ernest. 2007. *A Virtue Epistemology*. Oxford: Clarendon Press.

Sosa, Ernest. 2009. *Reflective Knowledge*. Apt Belief and Reflective Knowledge, volume 2. Oxford: Clarendon Press.

Woodruff, David M. 2001. "A Virtue Theory of Aesthetics." *Journal of Aesthetic Education* 35, no. 3: 23–36.

Zagzebski, Linda Trinkaus. 1996. *Virtues of the Mind: An Inquiry into the Nature of Virtue and the Ethical Foundations of Knowledge*. New York: Cambridge University Press.

CHAPTER 18

....

FEMINISM, ETHICS, AND ART

....

AMY MULLIN

INTRODUCTION

....

ARTWORKS can be objects, like sculptures or paintings, or processes, like dance performances or installations. Few believe that one can offer a detailed and definitive account of the necessary and sufficient conditions for being art or, what is more difficult, good art. However, artworks share a claim on their spectators' attention. In addition to making this claim, it is expected that if the art is good, then the attention will be rewarded, whether it is focused on how the work addresses the senses, how it is organized, its thematic content, its conceptual claims, or some combination of the above. This is in keeping with Noël Carroll's claim that artworks are created in order to advance their purposes, which can include advancing a thesis, stimulating emotions, or providing understanding. He adds: "Where the means of embodying the purposes of the work succeed, we appreciate the work and regard our experience of it as worthy of our attention" (Carroll 2015, 175). Of course, the fact that an experience is worthy of attention is insufficient to identify it as aesthetic. Paying attention to traffic can save one's life and paying attention to restaurant reviews can help one select appropriate meals, but in neither of those cases is the traffic or the restaurant review an artwork.

Artworks can be ethically evaluated by reflecting on the people who make them, the purposes, if any, their creators articulate in making them, and the ways in which they impact their audiences. They can be engaged with more specifically for the extent to which they lead their spectators to rethink taken for granted moral certainties. Sometimes this can be when an artwork articulates a contrary perspective, whether or not that perspective appears to be endorsed, and sometimes when it explores moral terrain. When artworks are ethically evaluated, this may be guided by a specific ethical theory, whether consequentialism or deontology or virtue ethics or care ethics, or it may be and typically is more informal, and guided primarily by intuitions. (See Shapshay, Snow, and Woodcock chapters, this volume.) In order for the analysis to be feminist, those critiquing the art must be committed to feminism, and hence both concerned with sex and gender and opposed to discrimination on the basis of these.[1] However, there are multiple understandings of what this involves when applied to art, from a focus on women's creation and reception of art, through a critique of the gendered nature of key concepts connected to art, such as genius and disinterested reception, to specific focus on the moral subject matter of artworks.

While a critical analysis would not be feminist if it had no concern with and opposition to sexism, a range of approaches, from those that focus primarily on sexist oppression, to those that also take up other harms and forms of oppression, are plausibly feminist. If anything, feminism understood as opposition to sexism is more congruent with forms of activism that also oppose other forms of prejudice and discrimination than those that focus exclusively on gender.

The extent to which at least some contemporary feminist art theory continues to overfocus on gender is documented by Zoe Lavallee (2016). Lavallee argues that some feminist art theorists base their critique of artworks or artforms on the assumption that the way that white bodies are depicted, or white audiences are addressed, can be generalized to be true of the impact of gender more broadly. More particularly, she describes A. W. Eaton as claiming that "the female nude in Western art promotes sexually objectifying, heteronormative erotic taste, and thereby has insidious effects on gender equality" (2016, 77). By contrast, Lavallee suggests that we need to attend not only to gender but also to the presence and absence of racialized bodies and recognize that different communities can respond quite differently to artworks because of other aspects of their identities. (See Clavel-Vázquez, this volume) Indeed, increasingly feminist theorizing recognizes identities as shaped by membership in multiple communities. Given the complexity of gendered identities, and the many different approaches that can be undertaken by feminist theorists engaging with artworks, it is hardly surprising that feminist approaches to the ethical evaluation of art will be heterogeneous. Furthermore, the venues in which this evaluation appears are equally heterogeneous—and include books and journals, whether in philosophy or gender studies, along with exhibit reviews and film criticism.

Relatively little scholarly attention has been devoted to questions about immoral means of art production, although there are occasional publications devoted to puzzles about the extent to which works produced by people guilty of substantial immorality should be examined or appreciated.[2] For instance, Joanna Burch-Brown (2017) argues that it can be the right thing to topple statues and rename schools in order to reject the immorality associated with the subject of the statue or founder of the school, but this is not to engage with ethical criticism of artworks, but instead of people. Similarly, Alfred Archer and Benjamin Matheson argue that it can be dangerous and disrespectful to honor artists guilty of significant immorality (2019). Their primary examples of

---

[1] Carolyn Korsmeyer and Peg Brand Weisner (2021, section 4) suggest that more recent work concerned with sex and gender should be labelled postfeminist rather than feminist, but also acknowledge that there is no consensus around this distinction.

[2] For a discussion, see Matthes, this volume.

immorality are sexual misconduct, and their argument is not focused on the worth of particular artworks but the dangers of admiring people who have significantly wronged others. Since people who are honored are often emulated, it is hard to argue with the idea that we should not encourage behavior that victimizes others. However, rejecting the idea that people who are guilty of significant immorality should be honored is not the same as asserting that artworks produced by people guilty of such immorality should routinely be destroyed or ignored.

In this chapter, I set aside questions about whether or not we should engage with art that has been produced by immoral people, in order to review some of the main strands of feminist ethical engagement with art, while focusing on ways to think about the moral subject matter of artworks. I explore connections between the ethical and aesthetic value of works of art, whether those works are physical objects or processes. While the normative content and aesthetic value of artworks can be in tension, such that a normative message can be simplistic and encourage a similarly simplistic, even if salutary, response, they can also be in productive relation. This is particularly likely when the normative content involves imaginative exploration, in a way that unsettles habitual responses and encourages more complex aesthetic engagement.

MISUNDERSTANDINGS ABOUT FEMINISM AND ART

One myth about feminist theorizing about art and feminist art-making is that these were originally driven by an understanding that all women had essential features in common, and that both the art-making and the theorizing were about a reclamation and celebration of these features. Laura Mulvey's influential essay "Visual Pleasure and Narrative Cinema" (1999) drew on psychoanalytic theory to posit a universalizing male gaze, which left no room for female audiences to take pleasure in film other than by identifying with the objectifying male gaze. However, the films that were produced were more varied, as were the audiences, than Mulvey supposed. bell hooks is one of several theorists who pointed out Mulvey's failure to appreciate the difference that features like race and social class make to the ways in which women are portrayed and the ways in which both women and men respond to films (2003).

Kimberlé Crenshaw's insistence on identities as intersectional (1991), which itself built on earlier work by feminists of color such as the Combahee River Collective, has become standard practice in feminist theorizing. For Crenshaw, we may fail to acknowledge the way that Black women, for instance, have been discriminated against, if we ask only whether a company has employed women and whether it has employed people who are Black. It may indeed have employed both, but not hired Black women, as it only employed Black men and white women. Now it is largely taken for granted that identities are shaped by the way that our various features and group memberships intertwine, resist, and reinforce one another. Any battle between essentialism, or the assumption that all women have features in common simply because they are women, and a theory of intersectional identities has been decided in favor of the latter. However, this does not mean that recognizing identities as intersectional provides detailed guidance as to how to think about them (see Carasthathis 2014).

Just as films were critiqued as addressing the male gaze, conceived of as universal, and hence failing to make room for and recognize more nuanced responses, artists who focused on female bodies, including their own, were sometimes seen as doing so in order to uncover features common to all women, often literally so when the bodies were nude. Examples include Carolee Schneemann's *Interior Scroll* (1975) in which she stood nude before an audience and unrolled a scroll from her vagina, and the large number of paintings of female nudes, including ones of the artist, painted by Jenny Saville.

However, this work does not present female bodies as alike, and it does not present the unclothed female body as equivalent to nature, another sexist trope. Instead, it explores the various meanings attributed to bodies, and how female bodies differ not only from one another but also and equally from idealized bodies presented as passive and fit to be the object of others' gazes. The performances and the paintings focused on exploring how bodies are shaped by their experiences and by others' expectations of them, along with what they can do, rather than simply presenting femaleness.

The complex relationship between the body, art, and feminism is explored in *Body Aesthetics*, which makes it clear that race and disability, along with other markers of social difference, shape how bodies are presented and how they are received (Irvin 2016). Multiple essays in this volume also explore connections between bodies, art, and either or both of beauty and disgust, a significant topic in contemporary aesthetics. Carolyn Korsmeyer and Peg Brand Weisner note that: "Possibly there is no topic more discussed in feminist art and philosophy today than 'the body' " (2021, Sec. 5) The body appears in art as a subject to be depicted, as a site of desire, and the source of the senses, which have recently been expanded from sight and hearing to include touch and taste as proper subjects for aesthetic experience (Korsmeyer and Brand Weisner, Sec. 5). Disabled bodies and maternal bodies (whether pregnant, giving birth, or caring for babies and toddlers), including disabled maternal bodies, challenge ideas about what bodies should look like and the relationship between beauty and desire (Betterton 2006). For instance, both the depiction of the pregnant and disabled artist Alison Lapper by sculptor Marc Quinn (*Alison Lapper Pregnant*, 2000) and her own self-portraits, such as *Angel* (1999), which combines photography and painting, portray her body as different (shortened legs and no arms) but also beautiful and productive. In *Angel*, rather than arms, Lapper has wings.

One important aspect of these feminist works focused on depictions of female bodies is that the body of the person depicted is contextualized and not presented as revealing universal features of women. Back in 1974, Lise Vogel argued that what makes art (and theorizing about art) feminist is not a celebration of a feminine essence but instead a commitment to feminism (Vogel 1988) and her position was shared by many other theorists (see, for instance, Breitling 1986 and Lauter 1990). Just as feminist art theorizing and feminist art-making are neither primarily nor simply a celebration of being female, other feminist commitments are not simply about combatting errors and omissions found in theorizing and art-making done by sexist men. For instance, the work of artists like Judy Chicago was sometimes misunderstood as about reclaiming female crafts like pottery and embroidery making as art, championing collaborative art-making, or celebrating women from history, as with *The Dinner Party* (1979) rather than all of the above, in a manner designed to challenge both what is perceived as art and how art is perceived.

Moreover, as Griselda Pollock noted in the late 1980s, what makes works feminist is not that they are made by women, but that such work "subverts the normal ways in which we view art and are usually seduced into a complicity with the meanings of the dominant and oppressive culture" (Pollock 1987). What makes activity feminist is that it is undertaken by feminists, whether men or women or gender variant persons, with feminist ambitions to identify and critique sexism, and to present alternative ways to interact with other people, oneself, and the world. Of course, as is true of other ambitions, they are not always realized by the activity. Nonetheless, so long as those ambitions can clearly be detected, the work can reliably be called feminist. Furthermore, in order to count as feminist artwork, the activity should aim at, and ideally be successful in, achieving attention that responds to multiple features of the work, such as sensuous features embodied by it, ideas explored in it, and emotions evoked by it.

Stephen Davies (2015) provides a "cladistics" definition of art, offering a number of alternatives which can qualify a work as art, all branching off from the first art ever created. For Davies, the first art is something that we interpret as fulfilling aesthetic goals, and these goals include: "Expressions of powerful emotions, compelling narrations, realistic or evocative depictions, dexterous or difficult to realize actions, vivid enactments of historical or imagined scenes, and complex abstracta, all executed with exceptional expertise" (378). The rest of his definition reflects the role that various artworlds, all ultimately branching off from art identified by its aesthetic features, play in defining art, in part by shaping a context that draws spectators' attention to certain features of that art. He writes that something is art "(a) if it shows excellence of skill and achievement in realizing significant aesthetic goals . . . or (b) if it falls under an art genre or art form established and publicly recognized within an art tradition, or (c) if it is intended by its maker/presenter to be art and its maker/presenter does what is necessary and appropriate to realizing that intention" (375). He further details that artworlds (which I interpret as multiple, even within one time period and one cultural setting) help establish what counts as falling under an art form and being publicly recognized within an art tradition, as well as shaping what makers take to be art (375).

While Davies clearly locates at least some "first art" in prehistory and discusses cave paintings, I do not believe we need to be quite so literal. I take "first art" to be art that was recognized, presumably in its time and certainly now, for its aesthetic qualities, and without the need to reflect on its relationship to other art movements or genres or theories. The other ways in which an object or process can be recognized as art respond to those relationships and include imaginative responses to other artworks as well as to topics of interest within whatever artworld they are engaging.

Davies's definition is not only valuable for outlining how both aesthetic values and artworlds contribute to shaping what makes something art, but also for stressing the importance of context in providing clues to spectators as to how to respond to an artwork. One classic example of the importance of context is Duchamp's *Fountain* (1917), in which he displayed a urinal as a work of art. Even though Duchamp did not regard this work as having particularly remarkable aesthetic properties, having one's attention drawn to them, by presenting the urinal in an artworld context, can legitimately engage spectators with those aesthetic properties—the smoothness of the enamel, the way light strikes the white urinal, and the tension between the uses to which urinals are typically put and the role *Fountain* plays when displayed as art. This last feature makes it clear that what counts as an aesthetic property can go beyond properties that present themselves to the senses and can include what spectators are encouraged to imagine. They can also go beyond what an artist either intends or signals that they intend. Davies's definition further makes it clear that the status of an object or a process, so far as qualifying as art, will vary with aspects of context that direct an audience's attention toward or away from some features of that object or process. Certainly, the role of context in shaping spectators' responses to artworks is something of which many feminist artmakers are keenly aware.

There is a problematic tendency in some theorizing about relations between feminism and art to separate more concrete work from a more theoretical project of rethinking how art interacts with its social context. The more concrete work included noting the extent to which women were excluded from art-making practices, and the reasons for it (Nochlin 1971/1988). It also included rediscovering relatively neglected women artists, appreciating women's crafts as art forms, and emphasizing sexist imagery in art. Gayle Austin writes about three chronological stages of feminist art theory: "1. working within the canon: examining images of women; 2. expanding the canon: focusing on women writers; and 3. Exploding the canon: questioning underlying assumptions of an entire field of study, including canon formation" (1990, 17). When we generalize from literature to the arts more broadly, this amounts to a claim that concrete work on how sex and gender relate to the content, production and reception of art is preliminary to and apart from more ground-breaking work. However, rather than seeing these as stages of increased theoretical sophistication, it is important to recognize that work on the production and reception of art is already theoretically engaged, and work on the assumptions of the canon should reflect thoughts about the creation and reception of art. Feminists writing in the 1970s often critiqued the exclusion of women from the production of art, the relegation of women to making crafts in contrast to more venerated male artists, and the extent to which works of art were marketed to men, particularly wealthy and privileged men, but this was part and parcel of thinking about how to conceive of art.

GENDER AND THE CONCEPTS USED IN THEORIZING ABOUT ART

In addition to critiquing who got opportunities to make art and whose activities were recognized as art, feminist critics pointed to the gendered nature of concepts used in theorizing about art, such as the notion of a solitary genius, and the expectation that responses to artworks should be disinterested. Immanuel Kant, for instance, argues that art is a product of the work of a solitary genius through whom nature works, that it does not respond to and is not guided by concepts, and that appreciation of art responds to the way art sets our faculties to work (Kant 1987; see also Shapshay, this volume). Feminist theorists and feminist artists, by contrast, reject the idea that art can only be produced by individuals working alone and that the production and reception of art are entirely separate from moral, political, and prudential concerns.[3] They emphasize that collaborative and cooperative forms of art-making can be as fascinating and engaging as the work of individuals working to a greater extent on their own. At the same time, they do not insist that the only good art arises from collective art-making.

Judy Chicago's massive work *The Dinner Party* (1979) was completed in cooperation with over four hundred other women. The base of the work is porcelain tiles linked to women throughout history, upon which is mounted a triangular table with thirty-nine place settings, done in different period styles, and each containing a sculpted or painted vagina. Each of the place settings is linked to a particular woman with the aim of insisting on women as worthy of remembrance. Since the hundreds of women represented by the porcelain tiles and the thirty-nine women represented by the place settings are distinct and distinctly presented, there is clearly no claim that women are all alike. Furthermore, since the artist worked with hundreds of other women in creating *The Dinner Party*, there is no claim that art must be the work of a lone genius. Each depiction of a woman's vagina is linked to a particular historical era, as bodies and accomplishments belong together. *The Dinner Party* is therefore a strong rejection of Kant's position on what is required for and represented in art.

Feminist artists and feminist art theorists stress that art-making can be motivated by moral and political concerns in addition to ones that focus more narrowly on aesthetic properties alone, particularly when these are thought to be limited to formal properties. Responses to art can combine emotions, ideas, and determinations to act. Furthermore, feminist theorists and artmakers often have an expanded understanding of what should be considered an aesthetic property of a work, as mentioned briefly above. In particular, exploration of connections between artists' lives and the way they are presented in mainstream culture, and of the complex pull of multiple communities are common themes

---

[3] Given the well-known feminist insistence on the idea that the personal is political, I do not aim to make anything like a sharp distinction between what is moral and what is political.

in works by artists such as Lorraine O'Grady. Her conceptual and performance pieces combine photos and videos to explore the different features that shape Black female identities (see, for instance, *Miscegenated Family Album*, 1994, juxtaposing O'Grady's family with Nefertiti and her family). The work consists of a number of diptychs drawn from and presented in a 1980 performance and suggests both similarities and contrasts among the different family members, and between members of O'Grady's family and those of the Egyptian queen.

The focus on the various communities to which an artist belongs, or is thought to belong, can make it sound as if feminist art is resolutely local. However, as Estella Lauter wrote: "Good art reaches beyond its society of origin to suggest alternative ways of being. Its aesthetic value arises in relationship to moral and cognitive values" (1990, 103). If anything, the more levels on which an audience is addressed, the more possibilities for complicated reception that can challenge the people interacting with the work to recognize new possibilities. This feminist claim has largely been incorporated into artworld responses to activist and political artworks which are far less likely than in the past to see moral or political engagement as a threat to the artistic quality of the art.[4]

FEMINISM AND ETHICAL ENGAGEMENT WITH THE CONTENT OF ARTWORKS

My focus in the remainder of this chapter is on productive ways in which feminists respond to artworks from a moral perspective, and I concentrate primarily on artworks that are plausibly read as feminist. I am particularly interested in emotional responses to those artworks and the ways in which spectators' imaginations are engaged. In speaking of emotional responses to art, I view them as appraisals of artworks, both regarding any messages the work might be thought to convey, and with respect to how the work functions as a result of the features that shape how its spectators are addressed. Emotions are responses to what we find salient, and works can provoke multiple emotions. I aim to suggest this in my discussion of a work by Carrie Mae Weems and others. By imagination, I mean our capacity to respond to ideas and images in a way that is flexible and not determined by past ways of thinking: "*To imagine* is to represent without aiming at things as they actually, presently, and subjectively are. One can use imagination to represent possibilities other than the actual, to represent times other than the present, and to represent perspectives other than one's own" (Liao and Gendler 2020). In what follows, I sketch different ways in which artworks can be imaginative, and then introduce the concept of the "moral imagination." (See also Shim and Liao, this volume.)

---

[4] Amy Mullin (1996) discusses the distinction between activist and political artwork. The production of activist work is almost always collective and generally involves considerable consultation with relevant communities.

One of the things that we regularly seek from artworks is engagement of our imaginations, such that we can think differently about a topic. One example of an imaginative artwork is Carrie Mae Weems's *I Looked and Looked to See What So Terrified You* (hereafter *I Looked*) from the *Louisiana Project* (2003). *I Looked* is a diptych self-portrait of the artist, in which she is presented in two mirror image photos. Weems is wearing a dress made from repurposed quilts, in an inverse of the more typical quilt made from repurposed clothing, holding a hand mirror, looking into it, and touching her face and hair. She looks elegant and puzzled and anything but threatening, and yet she is claiming space that is too infrequently claimed by Black women and challenging how she is perceived. The photos are beautifully composed, with a background that suggests an outdoor setting but also obscures it. Altogether *I Looked* both reveals and obscures, while presenting and implicitly critiquing Weems's reception by others, presumably especially White others, but not necessarily only them. It encourages spectators to admire Weems, to be puzzled by her, and to wonder if she indeed has terrifying aspects, at least to an audience that is neither feminist nor Black.

Weems primarily works as a photographer (and videographer) and has won many major awards and had her work displayed in multiple exhibitions. She is interested in the complexities of identity, not only hers but also those of others with complex backgrounds who belong to many different communities, only some of which are entirely comfortable embracing, rather than being terrified by, all of their members. She is committed to an intersectional understanding of identity, according to which, as discussed earlier, people's identities vary depending not only on whether they identify as male or female or trans or genderqueer, but also on their social class, race, religion, the country in which they live, and features of their embodiment that go beyond sex and gender. *I Looked*, like so many of Weems's other works, raises questions in an open-ended way rather than dictating exactly what her spectators should think.

Feminist art-making is not restricted to work that gets displayed in galleries and museums. Zoë Cunliffe (2019) presents a film written and directed by Greta Gerwig, *Lady Bird* (2017), as an example of a feminist mainstream film. The film narrates events in the life of a teenager named Christine, who goes by Lady Bird, as she finishes high school and moves on to university. While some of the standard tropes of the coming-of-age narrative are present in the film (Lady Bird chooses between two potential boyfriends, goes to the prom, and fights with her mother), the film twists these tropes. For instance, the prom is about a reconnection between Lady Bird and her best female friend Julie, rather than a connection with either of the young men in whom she is interested. Moreover, Lady Bird's relationship with her mother is really the central relationship of the movie, with both mother and daughter being strong-willed and worried and funny and resentful, often all at the same time. The complexity of the characters, particularly but not only the female characters, and the importance of their relationships with one another, along with reflections in the movie that love can be characterized by paying attention, make this a film that is perceptibly feminist, especially in so far as it pays attention to flawed and interesting girls and women.

While I ultimately reject most aspects of Kant's understanding of both beauty and art, his insistence that art conveys purposiveness without purpose does resonate (Kant 1987, 64). For Kant, what is purposive appears to its spectators as necessarily produced according to a determinate design and yet with art there is no such design and so he argues that art suggests purposiveness but is without purpose. When we think of imagination as going beyond what exists to explore what might exist, or could have existed if the world were different, and particularly when we think of it as open-ended, then imaginative artworks like those of Weems can appropriately be understood as encouraging a sense that the different aspects of those works function excellently together, even if we cannot provide a determinate account of exactly how.

Art can certainly be imaginative without being clearly feminist, sometimes because it encourages its spectators to imagine in ways that are at least partly sexist, and sometimes because it predates contemporary feminism and makes it hard to assess whether or not it should be interpreted as feminist. Marc Chagall's painting *Pregnant Woman* (1913) is an example of the former, and Emily Dickinson's poem "The Contract" (1896) is an example of the latter, both of them discussed in work by Amy Mullin (2004). In the former, Chagall paints a friend's pregnant wife. Although the woman is fully dressed, her womb is revealed in the painting as containing and not touching a figure resembling a fully developed male child, not curled and conforming to his mother's body but standing erect. At the same time the painting contains a cow floating in the sky, a sliver of a moon, some domestic dwellings, a worker leading a yoked animal, and the head of a man. The painting encourages us to interpret the woman as respectable and yet primarily as the container, perhaps animal-like, for a child reflecting his father. The colors in which it is painted are beautiful and yet also suggestive of decay, with the woman's face and shoulders, the man's head, and the lower part of the child's body all green, and not in a way associated with vegetation and new plant life, but instead potentially of disease or death. The fetus of this pregnant woman is presented as independent of his mother, and she seems only incidentally affected by his presence.

In "The Contract," Dickinson presents what is probably a sexual union, but could be a marriage or a metaphor for lasting human connection, as a contract in which each party gives themselves to the other, and accepts the other in turn. The poem concludes with the following:

> At least, 't is mutual risk,—
> Some found it mutual gain;
> Sweet debt of Life,—each night to owe,
> Insolvent, every noon. (1982, 96)

To be insolvent is to owe more than one possesses, and the note that only "some" found their mutual risk to be mutual gain combines hope and concern, emphasizing that there is indeed risk involved in this kind of a contract, even though people often sign contracts precisely in order to minimize risk. Another interesting feature about this poem is the minimal reference to sex or gender, other than the opening couplet: "I gave myself to him, And took himself for pay" (1982, 96) there are no references to men and women, and it is not even clear that the one who gave themselves to "him" is a woman. I interpret the attempt to find a relationship in which there is mutual risk and gain to be a feminist ambition, but this dimension of the poem is certainly not foregrounded.

Considerable contemporary work in art theory is structured around a debate between moralism and autonomism, especially moderate moralism and moderate autonomism, a debate that has seen numerous publications over the past three decades in particular.[5] This debate concerns whether or not we ought to view ethical flaws in an artwork as *ipso facto* aesthetic or artistic flaws and ethical virtues as likewise artistic virtues. The moralists maintain the former although they insist that only some moral flaws and virtues constitute aesthetic ones, given that they are moderate and not radical moralists. By contrast, autonomists maintain that something that is a moral virtue or a moral defect is never, simply in virtue of that fact, an aesthetic virtue or defect. Given that what makes something an aesthetic virtue or defect will generally depend upon how it functions within a whole, the autonomist position is easier to defend, but much will depend on the details of individual claims.

What might we mean by an ethical flaw? Well of course much will depend upon one's moral theory, but a standard example is Leni Riefenstahl's film *Triumph of the Will* (1935), which celebrates fascist dictator Adolf Hitler and is a documentary of his 1933 Nüremberg rally. Riefenstahl is very successful at portraying Hitler as a unifying figure, and the people who support him as finding a place in his vision (Deveraux 1998). This example also suggests the extent to which the "moral content" of an artwork can vary from a theme to a perspective and how formal features in the work help shape what it is thought to convey. There is nothing so simple as an endorsement of Hitler in *Triumph of the Will*, as instead the film goes beyond this to portray a world in which he dominates everyone in his surroundings, and they find joy in being included in his will.

Berys Gaut (1998) and Noël Carroll (2001, 2002) are two prominent examples of the moderate moralist position. (See also Carroll, this volume.) Both argue that there are ways in which moral virtues in artworks are at least sometimes simultaneously aesthetic merits and likewise moral defects can be simultaneously aesthetic defects. They offer quite distinct arguments for this view. Carroll, for instance, argues that artworks can provide rich and developed scenarios that can serve to make a case for a particular position (2002) in a way that advances moral understanding and aesthetic value, and also that moral defects can prevent or reduce aesthetic appreciation by causing imaginative resistance (2001, 2015). Gaut argues that some cognitive-affective responses called for by an artwork, which its audience cannot take up because of their immorality, thereby lead the artwork to also have an aesthetic defect (1998). By contrast, moderate autonomists like James Anderson and Jeffrey Dean (1998) insist that a moral defect is never, merely insofar as it is a moral defect, an aesthetic defect. (See Stear, this volume.) Instead, these

---

[5] See, for instance, Levinson's edited volume (1998) and Mullin (2002). See also Carroll and Stear, this volume.

are different registers of value, and this explains why we can find a work to be both artistically great and morally reprehensible (166). Of course, given that there can be multiple ways in which a work is artistically great, the potential conflict between the two all-things-considered judgments is not definitive in establishing their complete separation.

In addition to the moderate moralist and autonomist positions, which respectively favor the views that at least some ethical flaws advance or do not advance the artistic value of a work insofar as they are ethical flaws, some theorists have also advanced an immoralist view, that work can be aesthetically better precisely in virtue of advancing an immoral outlook (Kieran 2002; Jacobson, this volume). Anderson and Dean note that sometimes the combination of a moral transgression with some aesthetically valuable features of a work can draw us to it (1998, 160). While Kieran's position gains some plausibility from the greater novelty that may be associated with advancing an immoral outlook rather than one that conforms to current community norms, there are certainly also plenty of banal ways in which the latter can be done.

By contrast with moralist, immoralist, and autonomist positions, I think it is more illuminating to think of what I term the moral imagination as an important feature of many artworks. By moral imagination, I simply mean the application of the imagination to morally relevant subject matter. In this sense, "moral" is not a term of praise or an insistence upon ethical quality but instead a descriptor of what the imagination is directed toward, at least in part. An artwork that conforms precisely to what one independently conceives of as a valuable or correct moral outlook may be comforting but is unlikely to be engaging in that conformity. By contrast, a work that challenges or disputes or plays with expectations for what constitutes morally upright conduct and perspectives is more likely to repay attention. Of course, a work could be morally routine but fantastically imaginative in other respects (how bodies move in a dance or the perspective portrayed in a poem), and so art does not need to be morally imaginative in order to be imaginative overall, or to be good art.

To return to the examples discussed earlier, particularly Weems and Dickinson and Chagall, each of them is imaginative. The Chagall painting combines then standard views of pregnant women as containers for fetuses with unsettling colors and floating images, of heads and animals and buildings. The implicit contrast between the start of new life and the end of existing life, as suggested by the green tint to people's skin, would be especially resonant in 1913, a time shortly before the onset of a major world war. Dickinson's poem "The Contract" combines different emotional attitudes (including hope and concern), with an exploration of the mutuality, or lack thereof, of relationships, and the contrast of love and formal contracts. It is unsettled with respect to whether the kind of contract it contemplates will typically be worth undertaking. Weems's diptych contrasts the calm and regal artist with the terror she is said to invoke in others. Without its title, her photos could be interpreted in many different ways, and the use of quilts to make clothing, rather than the more typical use of clothes and rags to make quilts, is suggestive of the surprising uses to which material can be put. I take this to be a general feature of much art, in that it can inspire and reward attention to imaginative combinations of preexisting images and ideas. In specifically feminist artwork, these ideas and images include aspects of sex, gender, and either discrimination or oppression, along with, ideally, exploration of other aspects of people's identities and community memberships.

I conclude with one final artwork, *It's All About ME, Not You* (hereafter *Me*) by Greer Lankton (1996), completed and exhibited shortly before her death. Lankton was a transgender artist who worked in sculpture (often life-sized dolls), painting, and installations. *Me* is a recreation of her apartment and contains bottles of pills in a reflection of her drug addiction, extremely thin dolls of a variety of sizes, many of them created by the artist, some of them found, and a scale with a note declaring bulimia to be wasteful and three digits to be too significant a weight. The installation is so full and rich that it is difficult to take it all in, but the images of children, crucifixes, and her idols, along with many self-portraits in the form of dolls and paintings and photos, present a life that was full and alluring and threatening. Lankton was shaped by and herself contributed to an understanding of one ideal for transgender people as extremely thin and exaggeratedly feminine, with massive hair and considerable cosmetics, but *Me* also includes, alongside its many models conforming to this ideal, a doll that depicts, from the overflowing bust up, a smiling and plump woman, eyes closed. The suggestion that everything found in the apartment is "ME, Not You" reminds us that this doll, too, is an image of the artist. There is no singular message conveyed by this artwork, but it rewards sustained attention, and invites repeat visits and exploration.

CONCLUSION

There is no style of art-making that is feminist. Feminist artworks can be produced by artists working on their own or by groups. Feminist art can involve a reclamation of crafts, such as quilt-making and ceramics, or instead photography that depicts an artist wearing a dress made from a quilt. There is certainly no agreed upon list of essentially female characteristics, and feminist artists and feminist art theorists recognize that identities are intersectional, shaped by race and class and disability and religion and age, among other things, in addition to sex and gender. Furthermore, work by transgender artists reveals that what is considered female or feminine need not be tied to being identified female at birth. Instead, feminist art contests pigeon-holing based on sex or gender, and typically explores multiple aspects of identity and multiple strategies for resisting limits based on aspects of one's identity and the communities to which one belongs, whether willingly or at others' insistence. Feminist art appears in poetry, plays, novels, painting, photography, dance, performance, installation, and many other genres. It can be marketed to mainstream audiences, as with *Lady Bird*, or displayed in relatively small galleries, as with *It's All About ME, Not You*. It is imaginative, includes a focus on sex and gender, and, when it is good, it decidedly rewards attention.

See also: Matthes, Shapshay, Shim and Liao, Eaton, Clavel-Vázquez, Carroll, Stear, Jacobson, this volume

REFERENCES

Anderson, James, and Jeffrey Dean. 1998. "Moderate Autonomism." *British Journal of Aesthetics* 38, no. 2: 150–166.

Archer, Alfred, and Benjamin Matheson. 2019. "When Artists Fall: Honoring and Admiring the Immoral." *Journal of the American Philosophical Association* 5, no. 2: 246–265.

Austin, Gayle. 1990. *Feminist Theories for Dramatic Criticism*. Ann Arbor: University of Michigan.

Betterton, Rosemary. 2006. "Promising Monsters: Pregnant Bodies, Artistic Subjectivity and the Maternal Imagination." *Hypatia* 21, no. 1: 80–100.

Breitling, Gisela. 1986. "Speech, Silence and the Discourse of Art." In *Feminist Aesthetics*, edited by Gisela Ecker, 162–174. Boston: Beacon Press.

Burch-Brown, Joanna. 2017. "Is It Wrong to Topple Statues and Rename Schools." *Journal of Political Theory and Philosophy* 1, no. 1: 59–86.

Carastathis, Anna. 2014. "The Concept of Intersectionality in Feminist Theory." *Philosophy Compass* 9, no. 5: 304–314.

Carroll, Noel. 2001. "Moderate Moralism." In *Beyond Aesthetics*, 293–305. Cambridge: Cambridge University Press.

Carroll, Noel. 2002. "The Wheel of Virtue: Art, Literature and Moral Knowledge." *Journal of Aesthetics and Art Criticism* 60, no. 1: 1–36.

Carroll, Noel. 2015. "Defending the Content Approach to Aesthetic Experience." *Metaphilosophy* 46, no. 2: 171–188.

Crenshaw, Kimberlé. 1991. "Mapping the Margins: Intersectionality, Identity Politics, and Violence Against Women of Color." *Stanford Law Review* 43, no. 6: 1241–1243.

Cunliffe, Zoë. 2019. "Feminist Philosophy of Film." In *The Palgrave Handbook of the Philosophy of Film and Motion Pictures*, edited by Noël Carroll, Laura T. Di Summa and Shawn Loht, 652–675. London: Palgrave Macmillan.

Davies, Stephen. 2015. "Defining Art and Artworlds." *Journal of Aesthetics and Art Criticism* 73, no. 4: 375–384.

Devereaux, Mary. 1998. "Beauty and Evil: The Case of Leni Riefenstahl's Triumph of the Will." In *Aesthetics and Ethics: Essays at the Intersection*, edited by Jerrold Levinson, 227–256. New York: Cambridge University Press.

Dickinson, Emily. 1982. "The Contract." In *Collected Poems of Emily Dickinson*, edited by Mabel Loomis Todd and T. W. Higginson, 96. New York: Avenel Books.

Gaut, Berys. 1998. "The Ethical Criticism of Art." In *Aesthetics and Ethics: Essays at the Intersection*, edited by Jerrold Levinson, 182–203. Cambridge: Cambridge University Press.

hooks, bell. 2003. "The Oppositional Gaze: Black Female Spectators." In *The Feminism and Visual Culture Reader*, edited by Amelia Jones, 94–105. New York: Routledge.

Irvin, Sherri. 2016. *Body Aesthetics*. Oxford: Oxford University Press.

Kant, Immanuel. 1987. *Critique of Judgment*. Translated by Werner Pluhar. Indianapolis: Hackett.

Kieran, Matthew. 2002. "Forbidden Knowledge: The Challenge of Cognitive Immoralism." In *Art and Morality*, edited by S. Gardner and J. Bermudez, 64–81. London: Routledge.

Korsmeyer, Carolyn, and Peg Brand Weiser. 2021. "Feminist Aesthetics." In *The Stanford Encyclopedia of Philosophy*, edited by Edward N. Zalta. https://plato.stanford.edu/archives/spr2021/entries/feminism-aesthetics/

Lauter, Estella. 1990. "Re-enfranchising Art: Feminist Interventions in the Theory of Art." *Hypatia* 5, no. 2: 91–106.

Lavallee, Zoe. 2016. "What's Wrong with the (White) Female Nude?" *Polish Journal of Aesthetics* 41, no. 2: 77–97.

Levinson, Jerrold, ed. 1998. *Aesthetics and Ethics: Essays at the Intersection*. Cambridge: Cambridge University Press.

Liao, Shen-yi, and Tamar Gendler. 2020. "Imagination." In *The Stanford Encyclopedia of Philosophy*, edited by Edward N. Zalta. https://plato.stanford.edu/archives/sum2020/entries/imagination/.

Mullin, Amy. 1996. "Art, Politics, and Knowledge: Feminism, Modernity, and the Separation of Spheres." *Metaphilosophy* 27, no. 1–2: 118–145.

Mullin, Amy. 2002. "Evaluating Art: Morally Significant Imagining Versus Moral Soundness." *Journal of Aesthetics and Art Criticism* 60, no. 2: 137–149.

Mullin, Amy. 2004. "Moral Defects, Aesthetic Defects and the Imagination." *Journal of Aesthetics and Art Criticism* 62, no. 3: 249–261.

Mulvey, Laura. 1999. "Visual Pleasure and Narrative Cinema." In *Film Theory and Criticism: Introductory Readings*, edited by Leo Braudy and Marshall Cohen, 833–844. New York: Oxford University Press.

Nochlin, Linda. 1988. "Why Have There Been No Great Women Artists?" In *Women, Art, and Power*, 145–178. New York: Harper and Row.

Pollock, Griselda. 1987. "Feminism and Modernism." *Feminism: Art and the Women's Movement 1970–1985*, edited by Rozsika Parker and Griselda Pollock, 79–124. London: Pandora Press.

Vogel, Lise. 1988. "Fine Arts and Feminism: The Awakening Consciousness." In *Feminist Art Criticism: An Anthology*, edited by Arlene Raven, Cassandra Langer, and Joanne Frueh, 21–58. New York: Harper Collins.

CHAPTER 19

....

AUTONOMISM

....

NILS-HENNES STEAR

WHAT IS AUTONOMISM?

....

To the Ethical Question[1]—whether an artwork's ethical values bear on its aesthetic value, or its value "as art"—autonomism answers "no." Sometimes called "separatism" or "aestheticism," autonomism is both artistic ideology and philosophical theory. Some reach autonomism by a theoretical vehicle: explicit commitments regarding explanation (Anderson and Dean 1998), ethical or aesthetic properties (Harold 2020; Clavel-Vázquez forthcoming.; Dickie 2005), representation (Clavel-Vázquez forthcoming; Pérez Carreño 2006), or meta-normative obligation (Harold 2020). Others travel by art-driven modes of conveyance. One is formalism, whose spare evaluative machine traditionally bypasses ethical and social considerations (Bell 1914).[2] Another is the idea that art's value transcends practical affairs (Fry 1920; Bell 1914), or that allowing practical affairs to determine artistic value undermines it (Balfour 1910, 37; Pérez Carreño 2006, 72). Finally, some think subjecting art to ethical evaluation imperils it somehow (Gass 1987; Posner 1997)—that, to paraphrase Cleanth Brooks, the ethical lion and the aesthetic lamb will not so much lie down together as with one inside the other (Brooks 1962, 358).

In contemporary philosophical discussions, autonomism opposes interactionism, and is often pitched as doing so.[3] Roughly, interactionists claim that ethical values can determine aesthetic values in artworks somehow. Broadly, interactionism comes in two flavors: moralism and immoralism. Moralists claim that where ethico-aesthetic determination occurs, it obeys what Stephanie Patridge (2008) and James Harold (2008) respectively call the "consistency of valence thesis" or "valence constraint": ethical goodness only contributes to aesthetic goodness, and ethical badness only to aesthetic

---

[1] The name is from Lillehammer (2008).
[2] For another view of formalism on this topic, see the discussion in Gal, this volume.
[3] See Locke (1928), Anderson and Dean (1998), Posner (1997), and Pérez Carreño (2006).

badness. Immoralists deny this constraint: ethical badness *can* contribute positively to its aesthetic value and ethical goodness negatively. (See Jacobson, this volume) In short, autonomists think an artwork's aesthetic value is independent, or *autonomous,* of ethical value; interactionists think a work's ethical value sometimes contributes to, or *interacts* with, its aesthetic value.

Aestheticians addressing the Ethical Question distinguish two kinds of ethical value artworks might have, if any: intrinsic and extrinsic. Artworks bear intrinsic ethical values insofar as they "manifest," "express," "promote," and so on ethically charged perspectives or attitudes. This is ordinarily understood as resulting from the responses an artwork "prescribes"—that is, requires appreciators to undergo to fully appreciate the work.[4] To take a simplified example, Nikolai Gogol's *Dead Souls* (Gogol [1842]1998) prescribes (imagined) beliefs about a person named Chichikov, and (imagined) repugnance toward his scheme to acquire legal possession of dead serfs. It thereby manifests an ethically laudable attitude toward meretricious social aspiration (Nabokov [1944]2011, ch. 3). Artworks bear extrinsic ethical value, in contrast, insofar as they cause good or bad effects, such as the suicides inspired by *Die Leiden des Jungen Werther* (Goethe [1787]1986), or spring from good or bad causes, such as the animal slaughter for Hermann Nitsch's *Orgien Mysterien Theater* "actions" (Nitsch 1962–present). Aestheticians broadly agree that ethical criticisms of artworks are only properly directed, if ever, at their intrinsic ethical features, their effects or etiology being too incidental to the work (Gaut 2007 9–12; Jacobson 1997, 165; Eaton 2003, 174–175; Harold 2006b, 260; Clavel-Vázquez 2018, 2). Recent work, notably Nannicelli (2020) and Harold (2020), challenges this agreement, however.

Some in the literature address an artwork's *artistic,* and others its *aesthetic,* value. I treat the terms interchangeably. Whether and how these values differ likely matters to the debate (Dickie 2005). Nevertheless, since its participants are interested in the same thing—the value of the work *qua* artwork—and clearly mean to engage with one another's views, regardless of preferred term, the conflation is tolerable.[5] I likewise treat "ethical" and "moral" interchangeably.

If the literature's value language is unstable, its language about the disputed ethico-aesthetic relation is like a drunk on skates. Drawing from just four representative papers, authors talk variously about ethical properties that "are pertinent to" (Carroll 1996, 227–228), "detract from," "count against" (Carroll 1996, 232), "are detrimental to" (Smuts 2011, 48), "count as" (Carroll 1996, 234), "result in" (Smuts 2011, 48), "figure as" (Jacobson 1997, 158), "contribute to" (Carroll 1996, 236), "make a significant contribution to" (Eaton 2012, 281), "constitute" (Smuts 2011, 35), "are" (Carroll 1996, 232, 233, 236; Eaton 2012, 282, 283, 285, 287, 288; Jacobson 1997, 159), are "the cause of" (Smuts 2011, 45), and are "part of the causal story for" (Smuts 2011, 48) aesthetic values. I treat

---

[4] "Prescribe" is a technical but ambiguously used term in the literature. I ignore this here for simplicity. See Stear (2019, 465–466).

[5] See, e.g., Carroll (1996), Gaut (1998), Eaton (2003), Kieran (2006), Guyer (2008), and Hanson (2020).

these diverse locutions as getting at the same relation: ethical properties determining aesthetic ones. We should remember, however, that, strictly speaking, they express different ones.

Since Noël Carroll's germinal paper "Moderate Moralism" (1996), autonomism has been divided into two kinds: radical and moderate. Radical autonomism denies AMENABILITY (Giovannelli 2013, 336–338):

> AMENABILITY
> Artworks can bear ethical value and, accordingly, warrant ethical evaluation. (Carroll 1996, 224, 231)

Radical autonomism maintains that artworks are just not the kinds of things in which ethical properties inhere; an artwork can no more be immoral than driftwood, the set of all bicycles, the number 5, volcanic eruptions, or the flavor of beer (with the heinous exception of Bud Light). One who evaluates them ethically commits a kind of category error. Moderate autonomists, by contrast, accept AMENABILITY but deny INTERACTION (Clavel-Vázquez 2018, 2):

> INTERACTION
> An artwork's ethical value, if any, determines its aesthetic value—its value *qua* artwork—to some degree. (Carroll 1996, 231–232)

Moderate autonomism maintains that ethical value is somewhat like doorstop value; an artwork might stop doors well, though this is irrelevant to its aesthetic value.

Finally, there are the "robust" autonomists, who are radical and moderate in different respects.

I begin with radical autonomism and end with its moderate cousin, considering robust autonomism in between.

RADICAL AUTONOMISM

Radical autonomism, in the past, principally proffered a punching bag on which other theories honed their physique, rather than a genuine sparring partner. Elisabeth Schellekens, for instance, has described the view as "highly implausible," characterizing its separation of values as "excessively strong" (Schellekens 2007, 65). Its most glaring difficulty is accounting for the ethical and political ways artists and appreciators discuss art (Freeland 1997, 11–12; Carroll 1998, 132; Gaut 2007, 91–97; Giovannelli 2013, 337; Clavel-Vázquez 2018, 3–4). Nonetheless, it enjoys some serious defenders, contrary to at least one commentator (Giovannelli 2007, 118–119).

Various belletrists are sometimes trotted out to extol radical autonomism's virtues and demonstrate its literary cred. Oscar Wilde's quip that "There is no such thing as a moral or an immoral book" (Wilde [1891]1992, 3) is by now cliché. Richard Posner, ostensibly a radical autonomist, presents George Orwell as an ally for remarking that good art must embody a "sane," rather than a (morally) true viewpoint (Orwell [1946]2002b, 1107–1108; Posner 2009, 456). This chimes with a chorus of philosophers who, echoing Aristotle (1898), argue that a perspective's *plausibility*, not truth *as such*, matters aesthetically (Lamarque and Olsen 1994; Pérez Carreño 2006; Clavel-Vázquez forthcoming).[6] However, under interrogation, these literary figures often confess to more divided loyalties. Wilde's writings about sentimentality, which he sees as cynicism's other face (Eaton 2001, 114–115), and some of his short stories belie the quip (Eaton 2001, 141–143). Orwell's claims elsewhere that, echoing W. E. B. Du Bois, "all art is propaganda" (Du Bois 1926; Orwell [1940] 2002), or that his aesthetically weakest work is that written without a political point (Orwell [1946] 2002a) seem to cut in the opposite direction, too.

Within the last quarter-century of intense focus on the "Ethical Question," Posner's represents the first thoroughgoing defense of autonomism. Posner's is arguably also the first defense of radical autonomism, though it is hard to tell since he conflates AMENABILITY and INTERACTION. Unlike many in the debate, Posner is more interested in literature than art generally, and in literature's effects rather than its intrinsic ethical value (Posner 1997; 1998; 2009, 456–493).[7]

For all their literary erudition, Posner's arguments have proved as hardy as Blake's Sick Rose. Posner's first argument is that a work's prestige is "little damaged by the discovery that the work condones a morality that later readers find monstrous" (Posner 1997, 6). If Posner means that such works are still regarded as great, then this is inconsequential; interactionists could concede that the aesthetic differences moral values make are slight. Moreover, the argument's main premise is also false. An obvious, recent counterexample is Woody Allen's *Manhattan* (1979). The award-winning film was widely lauded when released. But its forgiving portrayal of a manifestly sexual relationship between its middle-aged protagonist (played by Allen) and a seventeen-year-old girl, paired with revelations of Allen's appalling behavior toward nonfictional girls and younger women, has clearly marred the work's prestige. As writer Ayelet Waldman (Brown 2021) puts it, "I think we can only view *Manhattan* now as a grotesquerie of Ephebophilia." Quite.

Posner's second argument concedes that moral affairs are often literature's raw material crafted into an artistic form. Yet this material is as irrelevant to an artwork's value as "the value of the sculptor's clay as a building material" is to "the artistic value of the completed sculpture" (Posner 1997, 7). One might respond, as suggested elsewhere, that when morality is its subject matter, this *does* make a work ethically amenable (Giovannelli 2013, 118). But that cannot be right; a novel about food is not thereby edible, nor flavorsome.

Nevertheless, Posner's excellent analogy may mislead. If Posner means "the value of the sculptor's clay as a building material" as a species of what Karl Marx calls "use value"

---

[6] Clavel-Vázquez's and Pérez Carreño's views are discussed below. See also Lamarque (2014, 138–139) and his examples of authors appealing to verisimilitude (126–127).

[7] Harold (2020) also does this, though deliberately.

(Marx [1867] 1990, 126)—that is, its utility as a medium—then the claim is false; the softness Gian Lorenzo Bernini realizes in marble would be unremarkable in clay. If Posner intends instead what Marx calls its exchange value (Marx [1867] 1990, 126–127)—what it trades for—then his point is more plausible, but inapt. For, what moralists, at least, appear to show is that ethical value *is* relevant to artistic form, and not merely in securing or jeopardizing coherence, as Posner suggests. Whether the artwork accomplishes its ends depends on the nature—including the moral nature—of the responses it enjoins appreciators to have. The moralists might be mistaken, but Posner needs more than an analogy to show how. Posner does marshal one datum—namely, that most readers accept "obsolete ethics in literature" as calmly as "obsolete military technology" (Posner 1997, 7). If Posner means the *representation* of immoral views, such as a character's, then this is correct but irrelevant. If he means the views the work *endorses*, then the enormous literature on "imaginative resistance" would beg to differ.[8]

Third, Posner says that "to devalue a work of literature because of its implicit or explicit politics, morality, or religion is to cut off one's nose to spite one's face." The implicit argument resembles those value maximizers give: insofar as an interpretative approach (in this case, worrying about the work's ethics) impedes aesthetic enjoyment, one should abandon it. Hence, ethical value is properly discounted.

But this is too quick. Posner is right that bracketing one's moral misgivings often makes a work's aesthetic delights accessible. However, I also have to bracket the dreadful orchestration in most early 1990s pop songs to appreciate their musicality without this making the orchestration aesthetically irrelevant. Posner must show how immoral works differ from such cases.

Finally, Posner criticizes the view that works that edify through their moral insights are thereby ethically good. He argues that such insights are, at bottom, merely psychological. Echoing a theme in Kant's *Groundwork* (Kant [1785] 1998, 4 [4:393]), he points out that they can be used for ill as well as good—for manipulation as well as compassion (Posner 1997, 20).

That psychological insight can be abused is correct but does not support autonomism. Knowing how to read crime scenes might help one plant evidence or conceal crimes as well as solve them—that is, help one be a worse detective overall. Nonetheless, knowing how to read crime scenes remains a *pro tanto* good-making feature of detectives, if only because such knowledge is necessary for being a good detective at all. Again, Posner needs to show how a work's furnishing moral knowledge differs from cases like these.

Others have challenged AMENABILITY. Harold (2020) questions the claim that artworks are ethically amenable (henceforth just "amenable") in virtue of manifesting attitudes. Harold agrees that artworks can manifest ethically charged attitudes. He also agrees that when people harbor unethical attitudes, say, this is criticizable on broadly virtue-theoretic grounds, even when they are not acted upon. But he denies that this

---

[8] See Tuna (2020) and Gendler and Liao (2016) for overviews, as well as Shim and Liao, this volume. Though see Stear (2015, 15) for the possibility of "morality fiction."

suffices for AMENABILITY. The attitudes artworks embody differ crucially from morally evaluable attitudes: the latter form part of a person's psychology; an artwork's do not:

> Artworks do not have attitudes in the sense that people do; artworks do not desire, hate, mourn, or intend that we respond in any particular way, or at all. We can speak of an artwork as having a particular "character," but we are not thereby ascribing a set of mental states to the artwork. Artworks do not have minds. (Harold 2020, 41)

Harold follows this up with a *reductio* via an analogy between *Pride and Prejudice* and an engagement ring:

> The way in which an artwork celebrates an engagement is like the way in which a ring celebrates one. Rings and artworks are both artifacts that we understand as having particular meanings, but the attitudes they manifest are not mental states, or aspects of a person's character or inner life. (Harold 2020, 42)

If an artwork is morally evaluable for its attitudes, then so is an engagement ring since they exhibit their attitudes in relevantly similar ways. But an engagement ring obviously is not morally evaluable in this way. So, nor is the artwork.

There are two ways to defend AMENABILITY against this argument: affirm that rings *are* morally evaluable; or deny the analogy. The former strategy seems tricky. What about the latter?

Typical rings celebrate their engagements only incidentally. A ring used to celebrate a child's betrothal to a middle-aged man, for instance, could equally serve an unproblematic engagement between consenting adults. But artworks do not possess meaning so incidentally. One could not redeploy a painting celebrating the child's engagement to commemorate the unproblematic one (imagine something like Carl Willhelm Hübner's *The Timid Suitor* [1853] or Vasili Pukirev's *The Unequal Marriage* [1863], but with the opposite tenor). That is, one could not do so unless the painting, like the ring, abstracted away from the engagement's particularity. The incidental attachment of a ring to any particular engagement—the attachment that exhausts what we take the ring to "mean"—is what makes morally evaluating it inappropriate. Arguably, the ring does not really celebrate anything (this is, after all, Harold's point); rather, *we* celebrate something with the ring. But a painting glorifying adult-child marriage bears its meaning inherently—as inherently as anything can bear a meaning.[9]

There is perhaps a deeper problem with Harold's challenge to AMENABILITY. His argument might appear to rest on this:

PERSONS ONLY
Ethical properties properly inhere only in the attitudes and characters of persons.

---

[9] Compare Paris (2021).

PERSONS ONLY cannot be true. Actions are neither attitudes nor characters of persons. But they are amenable, paradigmatically so. As Susan Feagin notes in outlining a similar argument to Harold's:

> Attributing moral properties to works of art is prima facie problematic: generally speaking, moral properties are attributable to persons *and their behavior*, but not to inanimate objects. (Feagin 2010, 20–21, my emphasis)

On closer inspection, however, Harold is committed to a narrower claim than PERSONS ONLY:

> When we say that an *agent* has a particular attitude, say, jealousy [*sic*] of his friend's success, we mean that this attitude is an aspect of that agent's mind, moral disposition, and character. It is this connection—the connection between an attitude and the mind and character that generated it—that grounds our moral judgment. (Harold 2020, 42)

Putting aside his aversion to framing the debate as concerning ethical properties (Harold 2020, 145), Harold is committed to a restricted version of PERSONS ONLY:

PERSONS ONLY^A
Ethical properties properly inhere in attitudes and characters only when these belong to persons.

Why accept PERSONS ONLY^A? Harold gives two reasons. First, we otherwise end up ethically evaluating bare artifacts, such as engagement rings (Harold 2020, 43–44). I have considered this worry already. Second, it makes sense to respond to a person's character and attitudes, but not an artwork's, with the reactive attitudes of "gratitude, resentment, forgiveness, love, and hurt feelings" and so on (Strawson 1962; Harold 2020, 43).

One way to deny PERSONS ONLY^A, then, is to simply deny this difference: it *does* make sense to respond to artworks with many of these reactive attitudes. I can certainly love an artwork and have my feelings hurt by it. I think I can also resent and maybe even feel gratitude toward an artwork. True, I cannot forgive one, but such differences may be unimportant ones grounded in, for instance, the differing capacities of artworks and persons to bear culpability and make amends.

Another is to accept that "the connection between an attitude and the mind and character that generated it" is what "grounds our moral judgment" but account for it differently. PERSONS ONLY^A requires attitudes to find themselves *inside* a person to be ethically evaluable. But perhaps the attitudes need only bear an appropriate *relation* to persons. This suggests the following alternative:

PERSONS NEEDED
Ethical properties properly inhere in attitudes and characters if and only if they are related to persons in the right way.

Whether PERSONS NEEDED is true depends on what relating "in the right way" means. That said, I am optimistic about some reasonable account making the claim plausible. PERSONS NEEDED explains why the attitudes and character manifested in actions are ethically evaluable, even ignoring their effects. Like artworks, actions lack minds. But in both cases, their relation to agency imbues them with a potential for rich, contextually mediated, representational meaning that *seems* amenable.

Now, if one squints, one can see how PERSONS ONLY[A] and PERSONS NEEDED might be confused. Both entail that erasing people from the picture means erasing any ethically evaluable attitude. This makes it tempting to see people as the real repositories of value. This is a natural way to read PERSONS ONLY—that is, as claiming that attitudes and character are only ethically evaluable when part of a person. But this inference is fallacious. Depending on a person need not rob something of its value any more than such dependence must rob behavior of its action-status, or an object of its artwork-status. Agential involvement in both actions and artworks make them eligible for ethical evaluation much as formally entering a diving competition makes one's dive eligible for an official score. Still, ethically evaluating actions and artworks is not therefore merely an indirect or figurative way of evaluating the agent any more than officially scoring the diver's entry into the water is *really* scoring her entry into the competition.

The autonomist might retort that this is precisely the point: the dive is *not* inherently scorable, just as an artwork is not inherently amenable. In both cases, the properties are relational, not intrinsic. As such, the ethical value is not the artwork's. But this argument is truly nuclear. Marie-Gabrielle Capet's *Self-Portrait* (Capet ca. 1783) depends upon Capet in order to be a portrait of her. Her dress is blue only because of how our visual system is constituted. Most troubling, the painting is only vivacious, barring the naivest aesthetic realism, because of how it strikes beings like us. So, in a strict sense of interest to metaphysicians, being a portrait of Capet, blue, and vivacious are all relational properties not intrinsic to the work.[10] So, though this argument disposes of an artwork's ethical properties, it also annihilates almost everything else. This cannot, then, be the sense of "inhere" relevant to the debate (Zheng and Stear, 2023).

Perhaps I have dented Harold's arguments against AMENABILITY. Are there arguments *for* it? I will gesture at some positive reasons.

First, as an aside, one might worry that "character" and "attitude" apply only figuratively to artworks, while literally to people. Interestingly, the terms' etymologies flip this worry on its head. "Attitude" is an early eighteenth-century term of art for a sculpted or painted figure's posture (OED 2021a). "Character," meanwhile, comes from χαρακτήρ, a mark, engraving, or stamp and an engraving tool in Ancient and Hellenistic Greek, respectively (OED 2021b). If anything, characters and attitudes are literal features of artworks applied figuratively to persons.

---

[10] See Lewis (1983).

Second, if one accepts that actions can manifest attitudes and character in ethically evaluable ways, then one has reason to accept this for artworks, too. Arthur Danto noted that art and action exhibit "parallel structures," which he exploited for his theory of art. And with reason (Danto 1981, esp. 4–6). Whether Danto's theorizing hits the mark, his most famous insight is bang on: both artworks and actions can be indiscernible from mere objects and behaviors, respectively;[11] a spasm might be materially indistinguishable from a dance move, just as a urinal might be from a Duchamp. The differences in both ontology and significance depend on various contextual and agent-internal features.

Various philosophers treat this as more than a parallel. Gregory Currie has argued that artworks are action-types (Currie 1989), David Davies that they are performance tokens (Davies 2004), and Berys Gaut takes ethical assessment specifically to address "the artistic acts performed in the work" (Gaut 2007, 7). At the very least, artworks are meaningful entities in virtue of their nonaccidental relation to context and agency in ways strikingly similar to full-fledged actions.

ROBUST AUTONOMISM

The "robust autonomists," as Adriana Clavel-Vázquez calls them (Clavel-Vázquez 2018; Clavel-Vázquez forthcoming), appeal to the nature of representation to motivate their conclusions.[12] While some artworks may be amenable, they claim, lots of them are not, or at least not in aesthetically relevant ways. This is due to the nonamenability of representation as such.

Francisca Pérez Carreño, for instance, begins her argument from the abovementioned Aristotelian insight that art, unlike history, aims at "verisimilitude": a plausible depiction of events and their causes "according to the law of probability or necessity" (Aristotle 1898). Against the moralists, therefore, a work's immorality need not mar it, provided the work presents a coherent narrative in this Aristotelian sense. And insofar as an artwork is a *fiction*, its veracity, and thus its *moral* veracity, has no bearing on its verisimilitude, except insofar as true stories are *ipso facto* verisimilar; its veracity is thus aesthetically irrelevant (Pérez Carreño 2006, 82–83). This also applies, she argues, to nonfictional works, whose genre constraints require veracity for verisimilitude (Pérez Carreño 2006, 89–91). Even here, it is Aristotelian verisimilitude that matters aesthetically—the genre constraints merely restrict the ways of achieving it. Such works can, therefore, be evaluated ethically insofar as the work's ethical perspective adheres to or deviates from moral reality. Nonetheless, to put it in terms other autonomists have used, it is *qua* verisimilitude, not *qua* truth or moral truth, that such works succeed or

---

[11]   And from other artworks; see Borges (1939).
[12]   Pérez Carreño describes her autonomism as "moderate."

fail aesthetically (Clavel-Vázquez 2018, 6). Since Pérez Carreño's crucial claim hangs on this *"qua"*'s viability, I will postpone discussing it until I consider the so-called *qua* problem in the next section.

Clavel-Vázquez takes a similar line to Pérez Carreño, restricting her claim to works of fiction, or "fictional artworks": fictional artworks lack intrinsic ethical value. Now, this argument does not cover every artwork. However, intrinsic value is the kind of ethical value interactionists care about. Moreover, fictional artworks comprise most of the works subject to the Ethical Question. Thus, Clavel-Vázquez's arguments, were they to work, would support autonomism for *most* artworks relevant to the debate.

To reach her destination, Clavel-Vázquez travels via Alessandro Giovannelli's "Ethical Fittingness Theory" (EFT). On EFT, to be intrinsically amenable, a representational artwork must embody (a) an ethical perspective and (b) a commitment to that perspective's befitting the actual world (Giovannelli 2013, 338–339).[13] *The Reluctant Fundamentalist* (Hamid 2007), for instance, is intrinsically amenable not because it presents an ethically charged perspective on post-9/11 attitudes toward South Asians, but because it also *endorses* it.

The crucial premise in Clavel-Vázquez's argument is that fictional artworks *qua* fictions lack such actual-world pretensions. Fiction *qua* fiction is "quarantined" from actuality. Here, Clavel-Vázquez draws on Neil Van Leeuwen's argument that the inferential relation between beliefs and the kinds of imaginings fictions prescribe—attitude imaginings—is asymmetric; beliefs feed information to these imaginings, but the imaginings do not reciprocate (Van Leeuwen 2014, 794–795). So, the kinds of imaginings they prescribe are themselves quarantined from our remaining psychological economy, including those parts—beliefs, desires, and so on—that reach out to actuality. This dovetails with the idea that any perspectives fictions embody, *qua* fiction, are merely part of the representation (Pérez Carreño 2006, 85). Accordingly, *qua* fiction, a fiction's prescriptions concern its representational content only.

Clavel-Vázquez offers a powerful case for thinking that, in an important sense, fictions *as such* lack the extra-fictional ambitions they are widely assumed to have. The flipside is, as noted, that the argument applies only to fictional artworks. As such, Clavel-Vázquez has built a large ark to accommodate most works subject to the Ethical Question. But not all; works like Leni Riefenstahl's *Triumph des Willens*, to take a prevalent example, are left at sea.

Another difficulty with both forms of robust autonomism is that structural, sociopolitical considerations threaten to puncture the hull, as Clavel-Vázquez, to her credit, acknowledges. Some fictional artworks lack ethical value when considered in isolation. Yet they may nonetheless exhibit such value by having what Susan Feagin calls "*de facto* significance" as part of a pattern of works (Feagin 1995). A work welcome socially advantaged characters to its deep center and abandoning the disadvantaged to its shallow periphery, for instance, might be ethically mute by itself. But as part of an enduring

---

[13] Cooke (2014) also endorses this claim. See also Tamar Gendler's discussion of "export" (Gendler 2000).

tradition of similar works, it may contribute vociferously to a roar of *marginalization* and *privileging* (Clavel-Vázquez forthcoming).[14] Similarly, even wholly fictional works that stake no claim beyond the fiction's borders can instantiate problematic social meanings (Patridge 2011) or contribute constitutively to oppressive ideologies (Zheng and Stear 2023.).

Perhaps Clavel-Vázquez's biggest difficulty, however, is that the Ethical Question concerns *artworks*, not just fictions. Even granting her conclusion that fictions *qua* fictions are not amenable, the question remains whether fictional artworks *qua artworks* are amenable. Wooden chairs might not seat people *qua* wooden thing, but they do *qua* chair, and perhaps *qua* wooden chair. Similarly, a fictional artwork might be eligible for inclusion in a museum exhibition *qua* artwork, or even *qua* fictional artwork, for instance, even if not *qua* fiction. Nothing in Clavel-Vázquez's otherwise compelling arguments shows that being amenable is any different from being so eligible.

MODERATE AUTONOMISM

Moderate autonomism, recall, is the view that accepts AMENABILITY (artworks can have ethical value) but denies INTERACTION (such ethical values contribute to their aesthetic value). One of the most enduring arguments for autonomism has been given by moderates James Anderson and Jeffrey Dean. Their argument responds to Carroll's so-called uptake argument (Carroll 1996; see also Carroll, this volume).

Carroll observes that many artworks require appreciators to meet them halfway. For instance, a film depicting its protagonist in grave danger ordinarily prescribes vicarious fear, a farcical novel prescribes laughter, and so forth. Sometimes, however, artworks fail to elicit such responses. If the protagonist is obnoxious or the scene unfunny, appreciators may fail to "take up" the prescription to feel afraid or laugh. Where the audience is blameless for such failures, this typically indicates an aesthetic flaw in the work.

From this Aristotelian blueprint, Carroll builds his argument: one way works can induce uptake failure is by being morally flawed. A work prescribing sympathy for a monstrous protagonist, for instance, is (so the argument goes) ethically criticizable. But it also makes sympathy barely possible for the same reason. One way to rob a scene of humor is by making it one for which laughter is ethically inappropriate, to take another kind of case. When this happens, Carroll argues, the reason for both the aesthetic and ethical failures is the same. Thus, the uptake argument shows how "a moral problem *qua* moral problem is an aesthetic defect in an artwork" (Carroll 1996, 234).[15]

Anderson and Dean disagree. They do not dispute that the immoral artworks Carroll describes suffer an aesthetic flaw. Nor do they oppose the Aristotelian structure relating

---

[14] For a vividly described example of this kind of phenomenon, see James Baldwin's discussion of the maid (Baldwin [1976] 2013, 69–70).
[15] Gaut's "Merited Response Argument" is structurally similar (Gaut 1998, 2007).

the moral and the aesthetic flaw, broadly speaking. What they dispute is that the works are aesthetically flawed *qua* immorality; there are distinct arguments for the work's moral and aesthetic failures, respectively, which share just one premise. As such, no common reason supports both flaws.[16]

One might dismiss this argument as a technicality. But that would be rash. In denying that the ethico-aesthetic relation Carroll establishes is of the right kind, the "*qua* problem," considered carefully, suggests a question vital to the debate at hand: what kind of ethico-aesthetic relation would be of the right kind? I suggest the "*qua*" at issue, and thus the answer to this question, concerns virtues in explanations, even if Anderson and Dean do not frame things this way.[17]

Suppose I drink lots of limoncello and get drunk. If you ask me the next day why I was drunk, I might muster that I drank lots of limoncello. If, unmoved by my hangover, you probed further, you might object that the explanation is too strong. After all, it includes information surplus to explanatory need (just as the explanation that I ingested something would be too weak, since it includes too little information). A better, if still imperfect, explanation would be that I ingested lots of *alcohol*. The fact that I drank limoncello specifically is no more relevant to the explanation than the fact that I drank with my right hand, or on a Tuesday, or with exactly eighty-three sips, or while Venus was in retrograde.[18]

I propose the problem with Carroll's account mirrors the problem with my explanation. An artwork prescribes pity for a morally repugnant protagonist. Soliciting pity for such a character mars the work morally, let us grant. And because the solicitation is unsuccessful, it also blemishes the work aesthetically. But what matters here, say Anderson and Dean, is the failure to secure uptake, not the immorality. Another way to put this: what *explains* the failure is the uptake, not the immorality. One way to motivate this thought is through what we might call a "substitution argument":[19] being immoral might be how the work induces uptake-failure, much as drinking limoncello was how I in fact became drunk. But there are many ways works can induce uptake-failure, just as many kinds of drink will get me drunk. We can substitute them without loss because each is germane to explaining the aesthetic failure *only insofar as* it is uptake-failure-inducing.

I believe this is also a good way to understand Pérez Carreño's aforementioned argument: there are many ways to achieve the aesthetic merit of verisimilitude. (Moral) veracity is just one of them and so does not interestingly explain the merit.

Worse still for Carroll, the above discussion indulges the confusion that his argument connects the immorality to the failed uptake to the aesthetic disvalue in linear

---

[16] One can, (as Anderson and Dean partway do) raise more or less same objection to Gaut's "ethicism," by replacing all causal talk with constitutive talk and substituting "meriting a response," "giving cognitive insight," or "being beautiful" for "being uptake-frustrating," depending on which of Gaut's arguments one considers (Gaut 2007; Stear 2022).

[17] On the multifarious senses of "*qua*," see Bäck (1996) and Loets (2021).

[18] See Weatherson (2012), for a helpful discussion of these issues.

[19] For an example of such an argument, see Harold (2020, 173).

fashion. Analyzed more carefully, however, the explanatory structure is a fork, not a line (Clifton 2014). Calling on appreciators to pity a despicable protagonist grounds a moral flaw (if it does) and it causes (or, alternatively, grounds) the uptake failure. But these are two distinct branches on an explanatory tree. My rose bush might blossom on one branch and leak sap on another, owing to a common mechanism: transpiration through the xylem. But it would be madness to therefore *identify* the blooming and the dripping. Similarly for the ethical and aesthetic disvalue, though they stem from the same artistic choice.[20]

In fact, this suggests that Anderson and Dean do not make as strong an argument as they could. Even where a work's aesthetic and ethical values *are* rooted in a common reason, nothing interesting need follow. *Atlas Shrugged* (Rand [1957] 2005) advocates selfishness in a tedious way. As such, it suffers at least one ethical and one aesthetic flaw for the same reason: the novel's tedious advocacy of selfishness. Yet each type of flaw is grounded in a different facet of this common reason: the tedium explains the aesthetic flaw; the advocacy explains the ethical one. No one would argue on this basis that *Atlas Shrugged* demonstrates moralism's truth. After all, the two features—tedium and selfishness advocacy—have been conjoined arbitrarily to create a common reason for the two flaws. If, as has been argued elsewhere, the uptake argument rests similarly, if less obviously, on arbitrarily conjoined features (Stear 2020), then Carroll really will not have shown that "a moral defect can be an aesthetic defect" (Carroll 1998, 419, 423). Anderson and Dean's objection will stand.

One might wonder whether any of this really matters. Have the moralists not answered the Ethical Question? Well, yes. But whether autonomists or interactionists appreciate it or not, the troubled waters on which the *qua* problem floats are profound. The worry is, or ought to be, that the kind of ethico-aesthetic relation interactionists have established is fairly trivial.

Take some potential feature of an artwork of dubious aesthetic interest: containing RGB hue 255,15,135 (hot pink); featuring the name "Pubert" seventy-four times; depicting a Wankel rotary engine; playing frequency 1396.913 Hz, being made while a Norwegian sneezes, or whatever. I might similarly ask whether such features could affect the work aesthetically (causally or constitutively). The answer is: of course! Using hot pink might make a work garish where before it was reserved; being made while a Norwegian sneezes might, if the Norwegian is close by, jog the artist's hand, deforming the final composition; playing frequency 1396.913 Hz (F6) might introduce dissonance if the piece is written in C# minor. Once one permits the "contextual" (Gaut 2007; Song 2018) or "indirect" (Hanson 2020) accounts of determination like Carroll's, and the bridge properties they invoke in their explanatory stories—garishness, deformity, dissonance, uptake-failure—then, in principle, *any* property of an artwork can determine its aesthetic value and, *a fortiori*, any ethical value can do so too. Moreover, it is clear that the valence constraint will not hold across all such determinations, which means

---

[20]   See Song (2018, 291) for a similar worry raised against Eaton (2012).

allowing them gives us a straightforward answer to the Ethical Question: immoralism is true. But surely the interactionist aspired to show, and the autonomist did not mean to deny, *this* sort of ethico-aesthetic relation! (Stear n.d.).

On the other hand, there is something to the protest: what more could an interactionist *do* to establish an ethico-aesthetic relation? The *qua* problem is, in effect, a problem afflicting any theory invoking a third property bridging the explanatory gap from moral to aesthetic value (Hanson 2020; Stear 2022). So, avoiding it means establishing a more intimate ethico-aesthetic relation, perhaps even identity. In that respect, the moderate autonomist's *qua* problem sets a high price. Yet if the interactionist does not pay up, she walks away with a ubiquitous item of dubious value: a fairly trivial, indirect, ethico-aesthetic relation.[21]

AN EVALUATIVE TURN

If ethical values determine aesthetic values in artworks, then presumably, ethical values in artworks also determine standards of correctness for aesthetic judgments. Inspired by Mary Devereaux (1998), Harold has mobilized an argument for autonomism that denies this inference (2006a, 2020).

Harold's argument appeals to a constraint on reasons, which he borrows from reasons internalism. On this view, whether one has a reason to do something is constrained by one's motivational psychology. Its progenitor, Bernard Williams, for instance, writes that a person has a reason to perform some action "only if he could reach the conclusion to [perform that action] by a sound deliberative route from the motivations he already has" (Williams 1995, 35). If an action serves no end that one recognizes or could come to recognize as in any way desirable, then one has no reason to do it.[22] Harold adopts just as much of this meta-normative theory as he needs to defend autonomism.

To accommodate internalism, Harold changes register. Rather than discussing values, he considers reasons.[23] Autonomism is correct, he states, if there are appreciators for whom the ethical value of an artwork does not count as a reason. This is because, if interactionism is true, everyone must have a reason, in the appropriate cases, to reconcile their aesthetic and ethical evaluations of a work.

> The interactionist must show that there is some norm (or set of norms) regulating how we make evaluations of art that all of us must accept, no matter what our values are. (Harold 2020, 152)

---

[21] See Hanson (2020, 218–221) for some suggestions about how to get around this dilemma.

[22] The view's original defense is in Williams (1981). For further discussion of internalism in aesthetics, see King, this volume.

[23] Halvard Lillehammer, not an autonomist, also outlines such an approach (Lillehammer 2008, esp. 384–394).

Put differently, interactionism entails that anyone refusing to alter relevant aesthetic judgments in light of conflicting ethical ones commits a rational error.

The question of whether interactionism is true, then, becomes the question whether revising one's aesthetic judgments in such cases is rationally required. Enter internalism. On internalism, a work's ethical value counts as a reason to amend one's aesthetic judgment only if it speaks to one's psychology in the right way. Harold considers Julia, who has come to differently valenced ethical and aesthetic judgments of a work.

> Julia does not commit any error at all if she doesn't reconcile ethical and aesthetic judgments with different valences. The reasons to which interactionist appeal do not move her, and there is no sense in which they should. As Williams emphasizes, any reason that a person can be said to have must be able to figure in an explanation of that person's action. And something can only figure in an explanation of a person's action if it has some purchase on his psychology. (Harold 2020, 150)

In short, reasons internalism concerning aesthetic judgment gives us autonomism: some people unmoved by ethical considerations do nothing irrational in sticking with their morally indifferent aesthetic judgments.[24]

On first hearing, Harold's demand that the interactionist provide norms "that all of us must accept, no matter what our values are" sounds reasonable. One might reason as follows: if interactionists can show that ethical values sometimes determine aesthetic ones, then, with some caveats, the rational requirement to weigh ethical considerations in one's aesthetic evaluations follows. Rationality in evaluation follows the value facts; establish these and the rational constraints on aesthetic evaluation drop out for free.

However, listening carefully, the demand seems more strident. The problem is that once reasons internalism enters the room, the intimacy between value and rationality is disturbed. For, if some aesthetic knave cannot be made to care about whatever ethical facts there are, reasons internalism allows her to keep her discordant aesthetic and ethical judgments without rebuke. In other words, once we accept reasons internalism, the demand that the interactionist establish norms rationally binding on *everyone* is a huge ask. Any account shy of the transcendental kind Kant gives for ethics, in which the norms of morality are grounded explicitly in the norms of rationality itself, will always be susceptible to an aesthetic knave. The interactionist could protest that since she has shown how things stand with the values, she has shown how things stand with the relevant norms. Asking her to show that everyone could come to accept these norms as authoritative, while allowing for internalism's truth, is unreasonable. The

---

[24] In this respect, Harold's autonomism is logically weaker than classic autonomism (Harold 2020, 148–149). The latter quantifies universally: *no* artwork's ethical value determines its aesthetic value. Harold quantifies existentially: there is at least one appreciator for whom failure to revise an aesthetic judgment is rational.

interactionist could complain that Harold is no longer playing the same game. It is as though interactionists and autonomists had been debating whether the ball crossed the line when Harold rolled out his meta-normative Panzer, obliterated the goal, and started executing doughnuts on the turf.

One way to see why Harold's demand seems too strong is to consider whether we would accept an analogous application of reasons internalism to another debate. Suppose, as seems fair, that "everyone ought to keep their promises" is true only if everyone has a reason to keep promises. Would we accept the argument that, since reasons internalism basically rules out this conditional's consequent, there is no obligation to keep promises? I should think this would be as unpersuasive as the argument that 3 is not prime because mathematical nominalism is true. Using second-order conclusions to settle first-order debates is suspect because of the way each level is independent of the other.

Harold could retort that, even granting the independence of first-order ethics from meta-ethics, his argument is different. Suppose promise-keeping could not be validated nor invalidated by an argument with a meta-normative premise. Nevertheless, the Ethical Question concerns the reconciling of two distinct kinds of value. It is thus a second-order question to which reasons internalism is entirely pertinent.

Even granting that questions transcending value domains are second-order in the way needed, the problem with this argument is that it appears to beg the question against interactionism. That ethical and aesthetic values occupy entirely distinct domains in the cases in question is effectively what the interactionist denies. Or, to put it more carefully, whether ethical value counts among the aesthetic good or bad making considerations—whether it is part of aesthetics—is precisely what is under dispute. This is not relevantly different to asking whether any kind of property—such as elegance, originality, or vividness—counts among the aesthetic good or bad making considerations. To justify deploying internalism on the grounds that autonomism is a meta-normative position, then, begs the question against interactionism.

Harold can counter. Interactionists (and, we should add, traditional autonomists) have their own meta-normative commitments—namely, to value realism or quasi-realism (Harold 2020, 160). So, if Harold's internalism begs the question against interactionism, the interactionist's realism begs the question against Harold's autonomism. In other words, what the interactionist mistook for a football match had been a panzer battle all along.

CONCLUSION

Having been reimagined as a position allowing ethical considerations a restricted role, whether as internal reasons, or in nonfictional artworks, autonomism has mellowed in its riper years. Whether this signals a broad movement toward détente, or just a repositioning of increasingly subtle positions remains to be seen.

Mellow or not, I have shown that autonomism faces some difficulties. Though in that respect, it enjoys ample company.[25]

See also: Carroll, Jacobson, Lamarque, King, Gal, this volume

REFERENCES

Allen, Woody, dir. *Manhattan*. 1979. United Artists. Produced by Charles H. Joffe.

Anderson, James, and Jeffrey Dean. 1998. "Moderate Autonomism." *British Journal of Aesthetics* 38, no. 2, 150–166.

Aristotle. 1898. *The Poetics of Aristotle*, edited by S. H. Butcher. Translated by S. H. Butcher. London: Macmillan.

Bäck, Allan. 1996. *On Reduplication*. Leiden: Brill.

Baldwin, James. [1976] 2013. *The Devil Finds Work*. New York: Vintage International.

Balfour, Arthur James. 1910. *Criticism and Beauty: A Lecture Rewritten*. Oxford: Clarendon Press.

Bell, Clive. 1914. *Art*. New York: Frederick A. Stokes Company.

Borges, Jorge Luis. 1939. "Pierre Menard, Autor del Quijote." *Sur* (May): 7–16.

Brooks, Cleanth. 1962. "A Note on the Limits of 'History' and the Limits of 'Criticism'." In *Seventeenth-Century English Poetry: Modern Essays in Criticism*, edited by William R. Keast, 352–358. New York: Oxford University Press.

Brown, Hannah. 2021. *Another Look at Woody Allen's Manhattan: What We Should Have Seen All Along*. NextTribe, March 3, 2021.

Capet, Marie-Gabrielle. ca. 1783. *Self-Portrait*. The National Museum of Western Art, Tokyo.

Carroll, Noël. 1996. "Moderate Moralism." *British Journal of Aesthetics* 36, no. 3, 223–238.

Carroll, Noël. 1998. "Moderate Moralism Versus Moderate Autonomism." *British Journal of Aesthetics* 38, no. 4, 419–424.

Clavel-Vázquez, Adriana. 2018. "Rethinking Autonomism: Beauty in a World of Moral Anarchy." *Philosophy Compass* 13, no. 7, 1–10.

Clavel-Vázquez, Adriana. Forthcoming. "On the Ethics of Imagination and Ethical-Aesthetic Value Interaction in Fiction." *Ergo*.

Clifton, Scott. 2014. "Non-Branching Moderate Moralism." *Philosophia* 42, no. 1, 95–111.

Cooke, Brandon. 2014. "Ethics and Fictive Imagining." *Journal of Aesthetics and Art Criticism* 72, no. 3, 318–319.

Currie, Gregory. 1989. *An Ontology of Art*. London: Palgrave MacMillan.

Danto, Arthur C. 1981. *The Transfiguration of the Commonplace: A Philosophy of Art*. Cambridge, MA: Harvard University Press.

Davies, David. 2004. *Art as Performance*. Oxford: Blackwell.

Devereaux, Mary. 1998. "Beauty and Evil: The Case of Leni Riefenstahl's Triumph of the Will." In *Aesthetics and Ethics: Essays at the Intersection*, edited by Jerrold Levinson, 227–256. Cambridge: Cambridge University Press.

Dickie, George. 2005. "The Triumph in 'Triumph of the Will'." *British Journal of Aesthetics* 45, no. 2, 151–156.

[25] Special thanks to Rohan Sud, Boris Hennig, James Harold, and Keren Gorodeisky for their help with this chapter.

Du Bois, W. E. B. 1926. "Criteria of Negro Art." *The Crisis* (October): 290–297.

Eaton, A. W. 2003. "Where Ethics and Aesthetics Meet: Titian's Rape of Europa." *Hypatia* 18, no. 4, 159–188.

Eaton, A. W. 2012. "Robust Immoralism." *Journal of Aesthetics and Art Criticism* 70, no. 3, 281–292.

Eaton, Marcia Muelder. 2001. *Merit, Aesthetic and Ethical*. Oxford: Oxford University Press.

Feagin, Susan. 1995. "Feminist Art History and De Facto Significance." In *Feminism and Tradition in Aesthetics*, edited by Peggy Zeglin Brand and Carolyn Korsmeyer, 305–325. University Park: Penn State University Press.

Feagin, Susan. 2010. "Film Appreciation and Moral Insensitivity." *Midwest Studies in Philosophy* 34, no. 1, 20–33.

Freeland, Cynthia. 1997. "Art and Moral Knowledge." *Philosophical Topics* 25, no. 1, 11–36.

Fry, Roger. 1920. "An Essay in Aesthetics." In *Vision and Design*, by Roger Fry, 11–25. London: Chatto & Windus.

Gass, William. 1987. "Goodness Know Nothing of Beauty." *Harper's*, April: 37–44.

Gaut, Berys. 1998. "The Ethical Criticism of Art." In *Aesthetics and Ethics: Essays at the Intersection*, edited by Jerrold Levinson, 182–203. Cambridge: Cambridge University Press.

Gaut, Berys. 2007. *Art, Emotion and Ethics*. Oxford: Oxford University Press.

Gendler, Tamar Szabo. 2000. "The Puzzle of Imaginative Resistance." *Journal of Philosophy* 87, no. 2, 55–81.

Gendler, Tamar Szabó, and Shen yi Liao. 2016. "The Problem of Imaginative Resistance." In *The Routledge Companion to Philosophy of Literature*, edited by Noël Carroll and John Gibson, 405–418. New York: Routledge.

Giovannelli, Alessandro. 2007. "The Ethical Criticism of Art: A New Mapping of the Territory." *Philosophia* 35, no. 2, 117–127.

Giovannelli, Alessandro. 2013. "Ethical Criticism in Perspective: A Defense of Radical Moralism." *Journal of Aesthetics and Art Criticism* 71, no. 4, 335–348.

Goethe, Johann Wolfgang von. [1787] 1986. *Die Leiden des Jungen Werther*. Stuttgart: Reclam.

Gogol, Nikolai. [1842] 1998. *Dead Souls*. Oxford: Oxford University Press.

Guyer, Paul. 2008. "Is Ethical Criticism a Problem? An Historical Perspective." In *Art and Ethical Criticism*, edited by Garry L. Hagberg, 3–32. Hoboken, NJ: Blackwell.

Hamid, Mohsin. 2007. *The Reluctant Fundamentalist*. London: Penguin.

Hanson, Louise. 2020. "Two Dogmas of the Artistic-Ethical Interaction Debate." *Canadian Journal of Philosophy* 50, no. 2, 209–222.

Harold, James. 2006a. "Autonomism Reconsidered." *British Journal of Aesthetics* 51, no. 2, 137–147.

Harold, James. 2006b. "On Judging the Moral Value of Narrative Artworks." *Journal of Aesthetics and Art Criticism* 64, no. 2, 259–270.

Harold, James. 2008. "Immoralism and the Valence Constraint." *British Journal of Aesthetics* 48, no. 1, 45–64.

Harold, James. 2020. *Dangerous Art*. New York: Oxford University Press.

Hübner, Carl Wilhelm. 1853. *The Timid Suitor*. Private Collection.

Jacobson, Daniel. 1997. "In Praise of Immoral Art." *Philosophical Topics* 25, no. 1, 155–199.

Kant, Immanuel. [1785] 1998. *Groundwork of the Metaphysics of Morals*. Cambridge: Cambridge University Press.

Kant, Immanuel. 2006. "Art, Morality and Ethics: On the (Im)Moral Character of Art Works and the Inter-relation to Artistic Value." *Philosophy Compass* 1, no. 2: 129–143.

Lamarque, Peter. 2014. *The Opacity of Narrative*. Lanham, MD: Rowman & Littlefield.

Lamarque, Peter, and Stein Haugom Olsen. 1994. *Truth, Fiction, and Literature: A Philosophical Perspective*. Oxford: Oxford University Press.

Lewis, David. 1983. "Extrinsic Properties." *Philosophical Studies* 44, no. 2, 197–200.

Lillehammer, Halvard. 2008. "Values of Art and the Ethical Question." *British Journal of Aesthetics* 48, no. 4: 376–394.

Locke, Alain. 1928. "Art or Propaganda?" *Harlem* (November): 12–13.

Loets, Annina. 2021. "Qua Qualification." *Philosophers' Imprint* 21, no. 27: 1–24.

Marx, Karl. [1867] 1990. *Capital: A Critique of Political Economy*. Vol. 1. London: Penguin.

Nabokov, Vladimir. [1944] 2011. *Nikolai Gogol*. London: Penguin.

Nannicelli, Ted. 2020. *Artistic Creation and Ethical Criticism*. New York: Oxford University Press.

Nitsch, Hermann. 1962–present. *Orgien Mysterien Theater*.

Orwell, George. [1940] 2002. "Charles Dickens." In *Essays*, by George Orwell, 135–185. New York: Knopf.

Orwell, George. [1946] 2002a. "Why I Write." In *Essays*, by George Orwell, 1079–1085. New York: Knopf.

Orwell, George. [1946] 2002b. "Politics vs. Literature: An Examination of Gulliver's Travels." In *Essays*, by George Orwell, 1088–1108. New York: Knopf.

Oxford English Dictionary. 2021a. "attitude, n." *OED Online*, June. https://www.oed.com/view/Entry/12876 (accessed July 27, 2021).

Oxford English Dictionary . 2021b. "character, n." *OED Online*, June. https://www.oed.com/view/Entry/30639 (accessed July 27, 2021).

Paris, Panos. 2021. "Review of 'Dangerous Art' by James Harold." *Philosophy in Review* 41, no. 4, 236–240.

Patridge, Stephanie. 2008. "Moral Vices as Artistic Virtues: Eugene Onegin and Alice." *Philosophia* 36, no. 2, 181–193.

Patridge, Stephanie. 2011. "The Incorrigible Social Meaning of Video Game Imagery." *Ethics and Information Technology* 13, no. 4, 303–312.

Pérez Carreño, Francisca. 2006. "El Valor Moral del Arte y la Emoción." *Crítica* 38, no. 114, 69–92.

Posner, Richard. 1997. "Against Ethical Criticism." *Philosophy and Literature* 21, no. 1, 1–27.

Posner, Richard. 1998. "Against Ethical Criticism: Part Two." *Philosophy and Literature* 22, no. 2, 394–412.

Posner, Richard. 2009. *Law & Literature*. Cambridge, MA: Harvard University Press.

Pukirev, Vasili. 1863. *The Unequal Marriage*. Moscow: State Tretyakov Gallery.

Rand, Ayn. [1957] 2005. *Atlas Shrugged*. New York: Penguin.

Schellekens, Elisabeth. 2007. *Aesthetics and Morality*. London: Continuum.

Smuts, Aaron. 2011. "Grounding Moralism: Moral Flaws and Aesthetic Properties." *Journal of Aesthetic Education* 45, no. 4, 34–35.

Song, Moonyoung. 2018. "The Nature of the Interaction between Moral and Artistic Value." *Journal of Aesthetics and Art Criticism* 76, no. 3, 285–295.

Stear, Nils-Hennes. 2015. "Imaginative and Fictionality Failure: A Normative Approach." *Philosophers' Imprint* 15, no. 34, 1–18.

Stear, Nils-Hennes. 2019. "Meriting a Response: the Paradox of Seductive Artworks." *Australasian Journal of Philosophy* 97, no. 3, 465–482.

Stear, Nils-Hennes. 2020. "Fatal Prescription." *British Journal of Aesthetics* 60, no. 2, 151–163.

Stear, Nils-Hennes. 2022. "Immoralism is Obviously True: Towards Progress on the Ethical Question." *British Journal of Aesthetics* 62 no. 4, 615–632.

Stear, Nils-Hennes. n.d. *Beyond Moralism*.

Strawson, P. F. 1962. "Freedom and Resentment." *Proceedings of the British Academy* 48, 1–25.

Tuna, Emine Hande. 2020. "Imaginative Resistance." *The Stanford Encyclopedia of Philosophy*, April 13. https://plato.stanford.edu/entries/imaginative-resistance/.

Van Leeuwen, Neil. 2014. "The Meanings of 'Imagine' Part II: Attitude and Action." *Philosophy Compass* 9, no. 11: 791–802.

Weatherson, Brian. 2012. "Explanation, Idealisation, and the Goldilocks Problem." *Philosophy and Phenomenological Research* 84, no. 2, 461–473.

Wilde, Oscar. [1891] 1992. *The Picture of Dorian Gray*. Ware, UK: Wordsworth.

Williams, Bernard. 1981. "Internal and External Reasons." In *Moral Luck: Philosophical Papers 1973–1980*, by Bernard Williams, 101–113. Cambridge: Cambridge University Press.

Williams, Bernard. 1995. "Internal Reasons and the Obscurity of Blame." In *Making Sense of Humanity and Other Philosophical Papers*, by Bernard Williams, 35–45. Cambridge: Cambridge University Press.

Zheng, Robin, and Nils-Hennes Stear. 2023. "Imagining in Oppressive Contexts, or, What's Wrong with Blackface?" *Ethics* 133, no. 3, 381–414.

CHAPTER 20

MORALISM

NOËL CARROLL

THROUGHOUT history art and morality have been linked, sometimes indissolubly. In early human times, through its service as a vehicle for religion and other social ideals, art has functioned to express, inculcate, and sometimes to refine and expand ideas of right and wrong, and of virtue and vice. If caregivers served as humankind's first moral exemplars, soon afterward the characters, often heroes, in stories, songs, and images were recruited to augment the ethical education of children and later, in more sophisticated ways, their elders as well.

Traditionally, art has been a leading source for the social dissemination of morality. And even in the modern period (see Costelloe, this volume), where the link between art and morality has been questioned and sometimes denied, large numbers of artists have still continued to embrace the founding, originally natural, allegiance of art to the exploration of morality as part of their commitment to the ongoing conversation of culture. In our own times, this is especially evident across the arts in their frequent, pronounced concern with issues such as social justice and injustice.

"Moralism," although sometimes associated with the notion of being overly censorious in ordinary language, is, for philosophical purposes—less pejoratively and more neutrally—an umbrella term for views that, roughly speaking, regard as appropriate the ethical evaluation of artworks *qua* art (where this notion of "*qua* art" will have to be clarified in various ways as this chapter moves on).

Initially in Western philosophy (with parallels in other traditions), all art as such was considered to be subject to moral evaluation. Plato granted that artists would be allowed to practice in his Republic so long as the pleasure in which they trafficked was beneficial, where the benefit he had in mind was to contribute to the character of the citizenry (Plato 1997, Book X).[1] Art, most notably *mimesis* in his view, that undermined the character of the populace by inflaming the unruly appetites and the ungovernable emotions

---

[1] For a detailed discussion of Plato's views, see Destrée, this volume.

that are inimical to reason could be condemned and suppressed. Art, on the other hand, that tutored virtue had a role to play in the ideal polis.

Likewise, art that by parable and image was in the service of Christian doctrine, including its moral doctrine, was defended by figures like Pope Gregory the Great, whereas art that interfered with the communication of the Catholic ethos—such as melismatic singing—was condemned because it rendered the articulation of the credal message of the lyrics unintelligible to the listener (Gregory the Great 2004, 47).

Indeed, through the eighteenth century, most philosophers, including David Hume, would have considered the moral evaluation of the arts unexceptional. That is, most (or possibly all?) Western philosophers, if they held a view on the matter, were probably moralists, in the sense we are using it. (See Costelloe, this volume, for a discussion.)

Moralism itself can come in different forms. Some moralists may regard all art as morally suspect. Some of Plato's arguments seem to have this conclusion. In Book X of his *Republic*, he maintains that all *mimesis* destabilizes the rule of reason in the soul of the citizen and that it does so as the result of the very nature of what we would call the art market, since the poet *must* address the worst emotions of the audience in order to sell his/her wares (Gregory the Great 2004, 47).

At other times, including in his *Laws,* as well as in other parts of his *Republic,* Plato seems to weaken his conclusions and modify his position to the more reasonable view that some art is morally bad while some can be good in relation to the cultivation of character (Plato 1997). Nevertheless, we can still imagine moralists who might condemn all art. This is often how we use the word "puritan," even if it is not precisely historically accurate.

In stark contrast to such *puritans*, there are some who regard all art as morally good. Among these are the *utopians*. For example, Herbert Marcuse, in virtue of his belief that in the capacity of the arts—given their possession of features that afford aesthetic experiences and fictive imagining—to support conceiving that things could be otherwise, commends the arts for fostering faith in the possibility of morally positive liberation (Marcuse 1978). This too seems an overly ambitious perspective. Artworks replete with aesthetic features—such as Leni Riefenstahl's *Triumph of the Will*—are in actuality utterly morally condemnable.

Between the puritans and the utopians, the most radical of alternative moralist positions, the more plausible moralist stance is to regard all artworks as either morally good, or bad, or an admixture of both. This is probably what most philosophers in the Western tradition through Hume would have said, if they had been asked. However, this viewpoint—call it *variable radical moralism*—itself can also be thought "extreme" insofar as it supposes that all art is morally assessable, albeit it variably so. That is, every artwork is either morally good or morally bad.

Yet this view also comes to be challenged by a position that notably begins to emerge gradually especially in the West in the eighteenth century, that takes hold in the nineteenth century, and that, in modified form, continues to exert influence philosophically into the present. We can label this view *autonomism*. (For a full discussion, see Stear, this volume.) So, one way to clarify what is at stake philosophically in moralism is to consider the ways in which it, and certain of its variations, contrasts with autonomism, and its corresponding variations.

As the label "autonomism" suggests, this is the view that maintains that art is autonomous—that is, separate from the pursuits of other sorts of value: moral, cognitive, political, religious, and so forth. As already indicated, this view begins to emerge in the eighteenth century, a century obsessed with drawing distinctions. Arguably, autonomism emerges at the intersection of two such endeavors—the quest for an account of aesthetic experience, on the one hand, and the codification of the system of the fine arts, on the other hand.

In 1746, Charles Batteux published his *The Fine Arts Reduced to a Single Principle* (Batteux 2015). That alleged principle was the imitation of the beautiful in nature. The key word for our purposes in that formula is "beautiful," for the definition of aesthetic experience was initially pursued in terms of the experience of beauty.

Francis Hutcheson, for example, proposed that beauty was the experience of disinterested pleasure, where "disinterested" meant "without personal interests"—as we might expect of a judge ruling in a civil lawsuit.[2] Immanuel Kant then expanded the notion of disinterested pleasure with respect to what he called free beauty in terms of the absence altogether of cognitive, moral, religious, political, social, and instrumental interests. Given the identification of the arts with beauty and beauty with disinterested pleasure, the possibility for the emergence of autonomism was conceptually ripe.

Moreover, this was not only a possibility. Something like it actually happened. A student named Henry Crabbe Robinson who was taking a course with Schelling on Kant's aesthetics told Benjamin Constant about it. In his journal, Constant (mistakenly) interpreted Kant's theory of disinterested pleasure as *l'art pour l'art* in order to signify that art has no purpose other than to be beautiful (Wilcox 1953, 363; Singer 1954, 343–359). Thus, the idea of "Art-for-Art's sake," sometimes expressed by the phrase *l'art pour*, gained currency in Paris through the influence of the famous salon of Madame de Staël whose consort Constant was. Subsequently, the popular philosopher Vincent Cousin lectured on the concept, and Theophile Gautier defended it in his introduction to his novel *Mademoiselle de Maupin*. The idea had sufficient caché that Tolstoy attacked it at length in his book *What is Art?*

In England, autonomism was known as aestheticism and was represented by the likes of Walter Pater, James McNeill Whistler, and Oscar Wilde. Indeed, Wilde proposed what is probably the shortest, if not the best known, proclamation of literary autonomism in the preface to his book *The Picture of Dorian Gray*, where he stated that "There is no such thing as a moral or an immoral book. Books are well written, or badly written. That is all." Undoubtedly, that sounds like a strange way to introduce that novel, given its apparently moralistic ending. However, I suspect that Wilde regarded the struggle between

---

[2] Hutcheson, however, was not the first philosopher to employ that concept; the Earl of Shaftesbury was in his book *Characteristics*. For context, see Stolnitz (1961, 97–113).

good and evil as a merely convenient way to organize his drama structurally—means, as the Russian Formalists would say, of "motivating the device."[3]

Indeed, Wilde maintained in response to criticism of his novel that "An artist, Sir, has no ethical sympathies at all. Virtue and wickedness are to him simply what the colours on his palette are to the painter. They are no more, and they are no less. He sees that by their means a certain artistic effect can be produced, and he produces it" (Wilde 2021, 29–30).[4]

As a statement of autonomism, Wilde's slogan is very extreme. Call him a *radical autonomist* with regard to not only literature but with regard to the arts in general. But a cursory review of the history of the arts will immediately reveal that radical autonomism is empirically false. Considering film history: surely Charlie Chaplin's *The Great Dictator* is morally good, and D. W. Griffith's *The Birth of a Nation* is morally bad. Even if one is a formalist, like Clive Bell, one must concede that many artworks have ethically relevant features that they are intended to endorse and that they can be evaluated *morally* in light of those endorsements. The first season of the television program *24* condoned the use of torture and was in fact (and, arguably, legitimately) criticized ethically for that reason.

One way for the autonomist to negotiate such historical facts is to allow that artworks have moral properties, but then to go on to claim that these moral properties are not relevant for consideration when the artwork is being regarded as a work of art *qua* art (i.e., art *as* art). When contemplating and evaluating a work of art *qua* art, only attention to the aesthetic properties of the work is appropriate.[5]

Moralists are free to evaluate works of art ethically, but they are not approaching the artwork aesthetically when they do so. They are not treating it as a work of art *qua* art. Just as the historian may from a nonaesthetic perspective scrutinize an artwork for evidence of how people furnished their homes in seventeenth-century Holland, so the moralist can assess the work from an ethical perspective. But neither the historical nor the ethical perspectives are treating the work as art *qua* art.

This move allows the autonomist to disavow the excessive claims of radical autonomism. Call this form of autonomism *moderate autonomism*.

Moderate autonomism then is the position that although artworks can have ethically relevant properties—including moral defects or blemishes and/or moral excellences—and can be evaluated in terms of them, those ethical properties *qua* morality are *never* aesthetically pertinent in the evaluation of the work as art *qua* art. For example, it is

---

[3] For a longer discussion of formalism, see Gal, this volume.

[4] As the case of Wilde might suggest, autonomism may be very attractive, despite its dubious philosophical heft, to lovers of art as a useful brake against censorship. Indeed, Nietzsche suspects that all "art-for-art-sake" sloganeering is motivated to act as a buffer against the censors. See Friedrich Nietzsche (1997, section 24).

[5] I frame the issue here in terms of "aesthetic properties" rather than "artistic properties," as often occurs in the literature. I do this since, under certain construals, moral properties are counted as artistic properties, and this way of setting up the debate courts the danger of begging the question against the moderate autonomist. This problem arises with some of Berys Gaut's arguments for ethicism. See my "At the Crossroad of Ethics and Aesthetics" (2010b, 248–259).

never the case that a moral defect in an artwork counts as an aesthetic defect in an assessment of the work as art *qua* art.

One eminently reasonable moralist response to moderate autonomism is to grant that sometimes morality is aesthetically irrelevant to the appreciation and evaluation of artworks. Radical moralism is certainly mistaken. Patently, many abstract designs, predicated solely upon eliciting visual pleasure, and many works of music, predicated only upon affording auditory delight, are not candidates for moral evaluation. But is it plausible to maintain that a moral defect is *never* a defect in an artwork? Isn't a moral defect at least *sometimes* an aesthetic defect in an artwork? The *moderate moralist* answers that question affirmatively (Carroll 1996, 223–238; 2010a, 235–271; 2017, 68–78; 2020, 534–546).

According to moderate moralism, in some cases a moral defect in an artwork is an aesthetic defect, thereby contradicting the central claim of moderate autonomism. The moderate moralist defends this view by means of the uptake argument. The uptake argument begins by noting that many artworks are intended to raise certain emotions from their readers, viewers and/or listeners and that the failure to raise that emotion is a failure in the work *qua* work of art. A mystery story, for example, that failed to engender curiosity would be a failure on its own terms.

Often, the emotion that a work is intended to evoke is directed at a character in the work. For example, in his *Poetics,* Aristotle notes that in order to raise fear in the audience of a tragedy, the tragic character should be neither saintly nor utterly evil. For if the character is a saint, her destruction will provoke disgust rather than fear, whereas if the character is utterly evil, his destruction will prompt joy—he's gotten his just desserts. The character should be like the audience member—neither completely good nor bad—since the point of tragedy, according to Aristotle, is that we all should be made to fear for the contingency of our well-being; bad things can happen to moderately good people (Aristotle 1996, 1453a). Anyone can be brought low by calamity.

What this example shows is that characters—like situations—are *designed* to effect certain outcomes, notably emotional outcomes in audiences. Moreover, certain emotional outcomes depend upon the moral features of the relevant stimuli (e.g., for me to be angered by a character or a situation, I must feel an injustice has been done to me or mine), and, furthermore, certain other emotions are straightforwardly moral, such as indignation.

Consequently, in order to design various characters and/or situations in such a way that emotions like anger and indignation will be elicited, those characters and/or situations must be constructed in such a way that they satisfy the criteria for the emotions that they are intended to elicit. Failure to do so is an aesthetic failure. It is an aesthetic failure because it is a formal failure, since, according to a functional view of form, the formal features of a work are those choices that are implemented or designed with the intention to realize the constitutive purposes of the artwork.[6] If a choice that

---

[6] The constitutive purpose of the work is the purpose that makes the work the artwork it is. For a discussion of this notion, see my "Some Stabs at the Ontology of Dance" (2019) and my "Forget Taste" (forthcoming).

is designed to realize the constitutive purpose of the work blocks the attainment of the constitutive purpose of the work, that is a formal defect of the work.

The constitutive purpose of many artworks is to arouse emotional responses. That is, such artworks invite, mandate, or prescribe definite emotional responses, as horror fictions mandate fear as an appropriate affective reaction. Furthermore, certain emotional responses may require satisfying certain moral criteria in order to obtain or, in other words, in order to secure uptake. Consequently, a moral blemish in the relevant affective moral stimulus can thwart the goal of the intended design of pertinent characters and/or situations if it undermines the satisfaction of the requisite affective criteria.

For example, in *The Birth of a Nation*, there is a scene representing Black legislators during the Reconstruction era in the South behaving in an unmannerly (they put their feet on their desks) and disgusting fashion (they eat greasy food with their hands). The intended construction of these characters in this way is designed to elicit a form of comic amusement, namely ridicule, from the audience. However, morally sensitive viewers are apt to respond to the representation with outrage rather than comic amusement as a result of their recognition of it as an outright calumny. Their indignation, in other words, derails their emotive uptake of the representation as an occasion for comic amusement because they detect a moral flaw in the design of the scene—namely, it is libelous.

Here it is important to emphasize again that characters and scenes in artworks are *designed*; they are constructed in order to realize certain ends. Morality can be an ingredient in such designs. Sometimes, the flaw in such designs *can be* a moral defect, for instance, in cases where it defeats the realization of one or more of the intended ends of the work. Design flaws are formal flaws where *form* is understood as the assembly of choices intended to secure the constitutive purpose of the work.

Form is the "how" of the work—the way in which the content is intended to be presented. Moreover, traditionally formal properties have been considered to be paradigmatic aesthetic properties. So, sometimes a moral feature of a work can be an aesthetic property and thus be an appropriate subject for evaluation on the moderate autonomist's own terms.

To summarize the uptake argument: if something is a formal feature of an artwork, it is an aesthetic feature, as has been supposed at least since Kant. If something is a formal defect, then it is an aesthetic defect. Design features are formal features—they are choices intended to present the content or constitutive purpose of the work effectively. Design features are *how* the constitutive purposes of the work are embodied. If something is a design defect, it is a formal defect.

Character and/or situation design-features are among the kinds of design-features that can be elected with the intention of realizing the constitutive purpose or purposes of the work. A constitutive purpose of a work can be to elicit a positive affective response to the presentation of a character and/or situation. The design of a character and/or situation may fail to realize (and even thwart) a positive affective response because the character and/or situation has been designed with morally blemished attributes. It may fail because it engenders imaginative resistance in the audience; that is, they are unable to muster the emotion the work endorses because they find it immoral.

Furthermore, this design failure is a formal failure. And a formal failure is an aesthetic failure. Hence, sometimes a moral blemish in a work is an aesthetic failure. Therefore, it is false that a moral defect in a work is never aesthetically relevant to the evaluation of a work *qua* art. That is, sometimes a moral defect is aesthetically relevant to the negative evaluation of a work *qua* art.

The uptake argument, just sketched, is one way in which to defend certain versions of moralism against moderate autonomism.[7] However, even though this presentation is already somewhat elaborate, a few further clarifications are still in order.

First, the moral defects that are being invoked in the uptake argument are only *pro tanto*. In other words, they are defects only to the extent that they are attempting to realize their intended function. For example, if there is one audience-alienating, homophobic joke in a long and complex novel that is otherwise ethically inoffensive, the novel would not be evaluated as defective overall, but only to the extent that the existence of that joke in the text is a bad-making feature. That is why for the moderate moralist it is possible that a work can possess a moral defect and yet still be good, all things considered (although moderate moralism does not offer a theory of how to make all-things-considered judgments).

Also, the uptake argument presupposes that the intended audience is a morally sensitive audience. I suspect that if you could have interviewed Griffith about it, he would have said that he made *The Birth of a Nation* for a morally sensitive audience, as would most artists.[8] But, of course, empirically, not all audiences are morally sensitive. So, this presupposition is an idealization, a sort of regulative assumption. Nevertheless, *some* audiences are morally sensitive. And that is all the argument needs to go through.

As just discussed, the argument does presuppose morally sensitive audiences, but it is not being presupposed that the audience is *perfectly* sensitive—that is, that they will omnisciently detect every moral/aesthetic defect in the work. Artworks are frequently extremely complicated and elaborate objects. Some moral blemishes in a work can fly under the morally sensitive audience member's radar.

As Paul C. Taylor has pointed out, there is a short interaction in the musical *Hamilton* where the character Sally Hemmings is treated in a morally degrading way.[9] But there is a lot of action and noise going on in that fleeting moment and many viewers may have missed the morally dubious exchange. I know I did. So, if I count as a morally sensitive viewer, then it is possible for one to be a morally sensitive viewer and

---

[7] There is no presumption that it is the only way, nor is being presupposed that the only dimension of art that concerns the moderate moralist is the affective address of an artwork. The uptake argument is just one line of attack in my attempted philosophical reenfranchisement of the relevance of morality to art—one expressly tailored to defeat moderate autonomism.

[8] Of course, the qualification "most" is necessary here. I doubt that the producers of abusive, child pornography could claim with a straight face that their intended audience was morally sensitive. However, some—even most—artists would claim their work is meant for the morally sensitive and "some" is all the Uptake Argument requires.

[9] See Taylor (forthcoming); also Taylor, this volume.

yet not notice certain moral blemishes in a work because they are not sufficiently salient.[10] That is, for uptake to be blocked—for imaginative resistance to erupt—one must notice the defect in question. So, again, it is possible that a moral defect in a work may not amount to an aesthetic defect because it is not pronounced.

Historically, most moralists not only negatively evaluated morally defective artworks for their messages, but they also suspected that such artworks had the power to shape the behavior of audiences in their everyday lives. Indeed, one of the reasons they condemned morally compromised art was precisely because they believed that it had behavioral consequences. Plato questioned the ethical credentials of poetry because he believed that it would worsen the characters of the citizens, just as commentators worry today that violent pornography will encourage harm to women. Moderate moralism as such, in contrast, implies no position about the behavioral consequences of art whether for good or for ill. Logically speaking, someone could be a moderate moralist and go either way on the behavioral issue.

One recurrent objection to the uptake argument—first presented by James Anderson and Jeff Dean—is that it fails because it does not show that a moral defect can be an art *qua* art defect (Anderson and Dean 1998, 150–166).[11] For example, consider the case of the Brazen Bull of Phalaris, the ancient Sicilian tyrant. He had constructed a torture chamber in the shape of a great metal bull in which he imprisoned his enemies. Underneath the chamber was a great fire which gradually incinerated the prisoners inside the sculpture.

As they died, they moaned and shrieked in pain. But the apertures in Brazen Bull were sonically engineered so that their laments were transformed into pleasing, melodious tunes whose ghastly provenance was unrecognizable. Guests to Phalaris's court were smitten by them, and praised their delightful cadences—that is, until they learnt from whence the airs issued. At that point, the guests were outraged.

Anderson and Dean would agree that the moral condemnation of the Brazen Bull was warranted. It was warranted as moral criticism. But, for them, it wouldn't count as aesthetic criticism, since it wasn't relevant to evaluating the work *qua* art—that is, wasn't

---

[10] As we will see shortly, this distinguishes moderate moralism from ethicism. This also diverges from radical moralism which would count any moral defect—whether detected by viewers or not—in the work as defect in the work *qua* art.

[11] The objection that Anderson and Dean mount is related to what is sometimes called the "qua problem." This view argues against moderate moralism on the grounds that the relevant uptake is the result of a moral defect qua moral defect in the pertinent works. But the problematic moral properties are not aesthetic properties and, therefore, the audience's response to them are not a matter of aesthetic experience. In response, I argue that the moderate moralist maintains that when the moral defects are seen to play a negative role in our attention to the formal structure of the work, they are aesthetic defects. Its being a moral defect does not cause it to be a formal problem; its being a moral defect in the context of the relevant sort of artwork is constitutive of its being a formal problem. When we isolate a moral defect in an artwork, our powers of moral detection are patently operative. However, that does not entail that when we assess its defectiveness from the viewpoint of aesthetic experience, it is evil that is the object of our experience. Rather it is its formal unsuitability to the aim of the work upon which we are focusing. See Carroll (2015, 171–188).

relevant to evaluating it as *music*. Evaluating music as music is a matter of evaluating it sonically—are the sounds as sounds pleasing?

The question of the moral status of how those sounds were produced is external to evaluating them *qua* the art of music, just as would be evaluating them negatively because they had been produced by incredibly expensive instruments paid for by unjustly taxing the poor.

This argument against the uptake argument can be bolstered by an analogy to guns. Guns have many purposes. Not all of those purposes are intrinsic to guns *qua* guns. Let's say that the intrinsic purpose of guns is to launch projectiles. But some guns are also decorative. However, a gun *qua* gun is not defective if it is ugly. Decorativeness is not internal to evaluating guns *qua* guns. Likewise, morality is not internal to evaluating art *qua* art.

It is not clear whether the preceding analogy is as compelling as it initially appears to be. Surely it is the purpose of some artworks first and foremost to engage our imaginations affectively. Indeed, some artworks, like horror fictions, are labeled in terms of the very affects whose imaginative engagement they are designed to support. If a feature of that design, whose constitutive purpose is to invite a certain emotion, instead engenders imaginative resistance, the feature is relevant to—internal to—the negative evaluation of the work *qua* the kind of artwork it is. Similarly, if a work is constructed in a way meant to engage our imagination comically but provokes affective resistance in the form of indignation, that too is internal to a negative, *pro tanto* evaluation of the work as the artwork it is.

To this, the moderate autonomist may respond that this only applies to some works. But isn't that also true of the guns in their analogy? Only some guns are designed to launch projectiles; not all guns, such as many toy guns, are not.

Or, are the moderate autonomists claiming that there are certain features that are essential to the evaluation of all artworks *qua* artworks? If so, they owe us the as yet elusive account of which ones those are.[12] Without that, simply declaring that moral defects are not among them amounts to little more than a restatement of moderate autonomism, thus assuming what it is supposed to prove and thereby begging the question against moderate moralism.

The moderate moralist does actually offer a reason to think that some moral defects can be internal to the evaluation of the work qua the artwork it is. The design of characters and/or scenes in a work can be unavoidably connected to the intended realization of the constitutive purpose of the work—the purpose that makes the work the artwork it is. If the design defect impedes or undermines by, for example, provoking imaginative resistance, the realization of a constitutive purpose of the work, then regarding

---

[12] Perhaps, needless to say, the aim of distinguishing in general what is internal as opposed to external in the matter of evaluating artworks *qua* art is as fraught a venture as trying to say in general what is inside as opposed to outside a work of art.

it as a *pro tanto* aesthetic demerit is an internal evaluation of the artwork *qua* the art-work it is.[13]

The preceding objection was advanced by moderate autonomists. But oddly, some of the most dismissive responses to moderate moralism come from other positions within, broadly speaking, the moralist camp, specifically from ethicism and immoralism (including robust immoralism).

Ethicism is the view defended by Berys Gaut (Gaut 2009). On this view, a moral defect is *always* pro *tanto* an artistic defect in contrast to moderate moralism which maintains only that a moral defect may *sometimes* be an aesthetic defect.

On behalf of ethicism, Gaut presents three positive arguments: the character argument, the cognitive argument, and the merited response argument, the last of which is also an argument against moderate moralism.

The first argument, the character argument, might also be called the beauty argument. It has a very eighteenth-century ring to it.[14] It presupposes that it makes sense to speak of the beauty of a virtuous person and the ugliness of the vicious person. Here, Gaut seems to have in mind the beauty/or ugliness of a person's soul, perhaps best understood as an amalgam of personality traits. For Gaut, we can call a person's character beautiful or ugly. Moreover, the artist manifested in an artwork may evince a beautiful character or an ugly character. Gaut thinks that, in *Anna Karenina,* Tolstoy manifested a companionate character, whereas in *120 Days of Sodom,* the Marquis de Sade exhibits an ugly character. Beauty and ugliness are also aesthetic assessments. So, contra moderate autonomism, an ethical assessment is also an aesthetic assessment.

This argument seems dubious, however, because it appears to ride on an equivocation. Since Plato's dialogue *Hippias Major,* it has been obvious that there are a number of different concepts that go by the name of *beauty.* In Plato, *kalon* could mean the fine or the excellent as well as *the beautiful.* Clearly the same polysemy obtains in English. One may say that Quasimodo, Ghandi, and Mother Theresa had beautiful characters in the sense of fine characters, but they were not beautiful in the narrow aesthetic sense of being pleasing to sight. Consequently, personal characters or souls are not beautiful in the relevant aesthetic sense, and Tolstoy cannot be commended for being aesthetically beautiful because of the morally excellent compassion he displayed in his portrayal of Anna Karenina.

Gaut's second argument in favor of ethicism is the cognitive argument. This argument presupposes that artworks can promote moral understanding. Given that, Gaut goes on to argue that manifesting understanding, most particularly moral understanding, and teaching it nontrivially (or not) can count as an aesthetic merit (or demerit). That

---

[13]   A. W. Eaton recognizes this feature of my version of moderate moralism when she observes that the moral blemishes that concern my view are identified as structural features of the work and, therefore, not extraneous to judgments of the work *qua* artwork. See Eaton (2016, 448).

[14]   The Earl of Shaftesbury thought the virtuous person was beautiful because his character was *harmonious* which Shaftesbury thought was also an essential feature of beauty. In this, he influenced several eighteenth-century authors. See Stolnitz (1961).

is, where artworks manifest understanding and/or teach it in the relevant way, that supports (pro tanto) a positive aesthetic assessment; and where the work manifests cognitive deficiencies or misunderstandings in a certain way, that grounds a negative aesthetic assessment. Therefore, inasmuch as an artwork may manifest and/or teach ethical understanding (or fail to do so), artworks may in the relevant cases always be aesthetically commended or disparaged (pro tanto) on the basis of their ethico-cognitive dimension.

But why accept the preceding claim? In its defense, Gaut appeals to critical practice. Practicing critics in diverse arts can be shown to quite commonly invoke ethical considerations in their evaluation of artworks. Critical behavior is our best objective evidence for what counts as aesthetic. So, citing ethical defects and achievements can count as aesthetic defects and achievements because they figure in artistic evaluation.

However, it is unlikely that any moderate autonomist would accept this argument. They would accuse it of begging the question. Although they might accept critical practice as a useful guide to what counts as an *artistic* evaluation—an evaluation of the work qua artwork (where an artwork can possess many art-relevant dimensions, including moral ones)—they would deny that critical practice is a neutral guide to what counts as *aesthetic*. They would do so if only because critics disagree among themselves about what kinds of criticism qualify as aesthetic criticism. Moderate autonomism may concede that feminist criticism is a legitimate form of criticism but deny that it counts as aesthetic. To do so without further argument is to fallaciously conflate the entire domain of appropriate art criticism and aesthetic criticism.

Gaut's major argument for ethicism is the merited response argument. For Gaut, it functions not only as an argument in support of ethicism, but also as an argument against both moderate autonomism *and* moderate moralism (by claiming that moderate moralism in fact reduces without remainder to ethicism).

Like the uptake argument, the merited response argument focuses upon the affective response the artwork prescribes or mandates that the audience should mobilize.

Emotions have certain criteria of appropriateness—conditions that must be satisfied if the emotion in question is appropriate. Fear, for example, must be a response to a perceived threat, if it is to be appropriate. If the object of the response does not meet that condition, it is not adequate to that specific emotional response. If an emotion is appropriate or adequate to its object, for Gaut it is *merited*—that is, it is worthy of that response; it deserves that response. Artworks prescribe responses. The question then arises when those responses are merited.

The Birth of a Nation prescribes comic amusement as the appropriate response to its portrayals of the Black legislators. But those portrayals do not deserve that response. It is not merited. It is not merited because it is ethically vile.

The moderate autonomists will, of course, grant that the portrayal is morally defective. But they will deny that it is defective *qua* art. They will accuse Gaut of begging the question. After all, Gaut seems to be assuming that a moral blemish is an artistic defect, whereas that is what he should be demonstrating.

Yes, the portrayals of the Black legislators are unmerited—but are they unmerited *qua* art (or *qua* comic art/amusement)? That's what the ethicist needs to prove; it can't merely be presupposed under the broad, unqualified rubric of *unmerited*. It must be shown to be *unmerited* in the right way. But Gaut has not done that.[15]

Yet what of the ethicist's charge that moderate moralism is really just a version of ethicism? Consider the arguments recruited to advance each of the two positions: the uptake argument and the merited response argument. Both focus upon prescribed emotions; both issue merely *pro tanto* judgments. But the uptake argument proposes only that sometimes the moral defect is an aesthetic defect because it blocks a constitutive purpose of the work to arouse some prescribed affective response. On the other hand, for the ethicist the moral defect is always an artistic defect because it is always unmerited—unmerited whether or not anyone notices it or whether or not it blocks anyone's uptake of the prescribed affect response due to imaginative resistance.

With respect to the uptake argument, it is conceivable that a morally sensitive audience member could miss some minor moral defect in a very complex artwork and, as a result, not resist the mandated response. For the moderate moralist, although the defect would still count as a moral defect, it would not be an aesthetic defect, since it did not contribute *pro tanto* to undermining a constitutive purpose of the work.

On the other hand, on the merited response argument even an overlooked moral defect still also counts as a *pro tanto* artistic defect. Therefore, the extension of candidates for the status of moral *qua* art defects is potentially larger by ethicism's lights than the comparable extension of moderate moralism. So, moderate moralism is a less encompassing form of moralism than ethicism.

Another criticism of moderate moralism issued from fellow-travelers—called *immoralists*—in the moralist camp amounts to the charge that the moderate moralist doesn't go far enough.[16] The immoralist agrees with the moderate moralist that sometimes a moral defect can be an aesthetic defect and that sometimes a moral excellence can be an aesthetic excellence; but then the immoralist goes on to add that a moral defect can sometimes be an aesthetic excellence. This view clearly is in principle compatible with moderate moralism. The issue is whether there are any compelling examples of the phenomenon.

One example advanced by immoralists in support of their view has been *Triumph of the Will*. The film is inarguably compromised, but the immoralist claims that it is an artistic achievement because it gives antifascists insight into the attractions of Nazism. This example, of course, would be rejected by moderate autonomists on the grounds

---

[15] One problem here may be that Gaut's conception of the artistic properties is rather broad—it is broader, for example, than the sum of aesthetic properties. Gaut will accept as an artistic property, any property that critics invoke in evaluating artworks. But that will countenance moral features traditionally barred by autonomists from the exercise of evaluation. See Gaut (2009).

[16] This position was first advanced by Daniel Jacobson (1997). See also Matthew Kieran (2003). For a discussion, see Jacobson, this volume.

that what is being called an artistic achievement—insights about fascism—are not internal to the evaluation of the film as a work of art.

The film is about making fascism attractive; it is not about exhibiting the attractions of fascism for scrutiny. That insights about fascism can be gleaned from *Triumph of the Will* is true, but that is not what *Triumph* is offering the viewer—no more than a cigarette advertisement is offering smokers a lesson in marketing.

And in this, the moderate moralist agrees with the moderate autonomist inasmuch as it is not a constitutive purpose of *Triumph* to offer a diagnosis of Nazi imagery. The constitutive purpose is to present Nazi imagery as seductively as possible.

Another example of the immoralist's central point is supposedly Shakespeare's play *Macbeth* insofar as it is claimed that the play elicits sympathy for Macbeth, a character who finally turns out to be an irretrievably evil character.

But this account overlooks the function of Macbeth in the unfolding design of the play. Macbeth is a case of the good man gone bad. One constitutive purpose of the play is to illustrate how easily this can happen to even a person good enough to deserve our initial sympathy. A primary theme of *Macbeth* is that the road to perdition is a slippery slope. As Shakespeare says: "It will have blood, they say. Blood will have blood"—that is, murder breeds murder.

Whatever sympathies we may entertain for Macbeth serve as a warning to us that even someone like us can descend into evil, once one takes the first bite of the apple. The design of the character has to be assessed in terms of the way it functions not in one scene but, if the character develops, over the course of the narrative. And in that light, whatever sympathy we feel for Macbeth is not morally defective in the way that the immoralist needs him to be. Rather, it plays a key role in delivering a moral message which includes, among others, that sympathy unchecked can muddy the moral waters.

A. W. Eaton, who refers to her position as robust immoralism, has entered the debate arguing that she has discovered a systematic lode of examples that will confirm the immoralists' convictions once and for all (Eaton 2012, 281–292; 2013, 376–380; 2015, 433–450). What she has in mind is what Hume called "rough heroes." For Hume, these are characters worthy of "blame and disapprobation." Of them, Hume contends "we cannot prevail on ourselves . . . to bear an affection to characters which we plainly discover to be blamable" (Hume 1993, 152).

But Eaton disagrees with Hume in this matter; she believes that we can "bear an affection" for at least some rough heroes. Tony Soprano from the HBO television series *The Sopranos* is her leading example. Indeed, the rough heroes of his ilk have become a staple on television in the twenty-first century.

Eaton makes two claims. First, there are characters who are clearly marked in the fictions in which they appear as evil—as morally defective—but for whom viewers nevertheless feel sympathy, affection, and admiration where these reactions themselves are morally dubious.

And second, Eaton believes this counts as artistically excellent because disarming or defeating imaginative resistance to the pertinent rough heroes is an achievement since putatively the odds are against this occurring where the rough heroes are as unmistakably and obviously bad as Tony Soprano is. Our allegedly ambivalent state of affection-for-versus-disapproval-of him can be compelling, where *compelling* is taken to be a good-making aesthetic property. And this supposedly shows that an aesthetic excellent feature can be rooted in evil.

One thing to question regarding Eaton's presentation of her rough-hero phenomenon is whether there really is the kind of ambivalence that she claims. She claims that we can feel sympathy, affection, and admiration toward someone while simultaneously judging them to be evil. But there need be no contradiction or even tension here.

One feels sympathy and continued affection for the brother who is in prison for life for being a contract murderer; you can admire a hacker's ingenuity while disapproving of its use in disabling a philanthropy's charitable benefactions.

Thus, we can sympathize, without ambivalence, with Tony Soprano's suffering his son AJ's misadventures—surely the boy is the most tiresome, inept, and hopeless adolescent in the history of television—while simultaneously morally disapproving of Tony's murder of his best friend Big Pussy.

Likewise, with respect to *Breaking Bad*, one can surely admire Walter White's brilliant technical solutions to various of his "business" problems while morally condemning his abetting the self-destruction of countless drug addicts. There is no contradiction or tension between admiring someone's genius while morally deploring the way in which it is used.

And, perhaps most obviously, it is possible to like—even to love—people that you know are morally compromised. Affection isn't governed by moral law. Mothers don't say "I shouldn't love my son, the terrorist." Perhaps the viewer's affection for Don Draper on *Mad Men* is based on his good looks.

So, one problem with Eaton's robust immoralism is that the objects of the sympathy, admiration, and affection of which she speaks may not be of the right sort needed to advance her case. That is, they are not necessarily directed at moral defects. They may be directed at morally neutral properties, like Walter White's scientific wizardry, Tony Soprano's parenting, or Don Draper's beauty.

Eaton claims that with respect to her rough heroes in the relevant fictions we are led to take their side in their immoral pursuits.[17] Does this constitute a moral defect in the work? Once again, whether or not it is a moral defect in the design of the character depends upon the function the character and his/her actions are playing in the unfolding narrative. That is, what contribution are the character's behavior and our reactions to it over time making to the realization of the constitutive purpose of the work.

That we sometimes seem to give Tony Soprano a pass when he is engages in immoral activities and accept his rationalizations ("I do it for my family") is not a moral defect in the work, because by momentarily seducing viewers in that way (if they are seduced), it

---

[17] Does Eaton think that viewers ever endorse Tony Soprano's immoral actions? I'm not sure. If they don't ever endorse his immoral actions, is there a moral defect? If they do endorse the action, accepting it as immoral, why are they ambivalent?

provides them with a cautionary moral tale regarding how easy it is to, as Tony does, rationalize away moral flaws in our own lives.

A constitutive purpose of *The Sopranos* is to unmask such rationalizations as the psychiatrist Dr. Krakower does literally and relentlessly in the episode titled "Second Opinion" where he refuses to take Tony's wife as a patient until she stops claiming that Tony is a good man—a man who takes care of his family—and admits he is, without the slightest qualification, utterly, irredeemably evil. It is as if Krakower is speaking directly to the audience, telling them the central admonition that they are intended to take away from the series.[18]

So far, I have been arguing that the character design and the accompanying prescribed emotional responses, like affection, to Eaton's rough heroes need not be regarded as moral defects because, on the one hand, the reactions may not be morally relevant (admiring Walter White for his brains) or, on the other hand, do not count as moral defects in the design of the pertinent characters because they make a positive contribution the ultimately moral, constitutive purpose of the work. But if these features of the character design and the accompanying affective responses are not moral defects, then moral defects have not given rise to aesthetic excellences.

Yet furthermore, I also want to question whether eliciting the reactions Eaton cites is really a significant aesthetic achievement. Eaton believes that it is because it solves an allegedly formidable artistic problem—that of enlisting some sort of positive attitude toward rough heroes. Yet I question this, because it seems to me that there are a good number of tried-and-true, ready-to-hand, routine strategies for engineering this effect. That is, it is not as if recent work has solved any artistic problems. The supposed problems were solved long ago, often in genres. Indeed, many of "solutions" are pertinent to the presentation of the rough heroes found in contemporary television shows.

Here are a few; there are more.

The first relies on the principle "out of sight, out of mind." Basically, keep most of the really horrible things the rough heroes do outside of the audience's purview. For instance, don't show any of the misery Walter White wreaks on the lives of the consumers of his methamphetamine. Another useful device is to surround the rough hero with comparable figures who are even more evil than he is. Tony Soprano's nemeses get successively worse: Richie Aprile, then Ralph Cifaretto, then Phil Leotardo. A similar

---

[18] Immoralists, like Eaton, say that attracting us to a character like Tony Soprano makes the work better. Arguably, if it makes it better, then it does so because it encourages moral reflection. But this is paradoxical. Is encouraging moral reflection immoral? Also, there seems to be a problem with focusing narrowly on the character of Tony Soprano rather than on the function that the character serves in realizing the morally positive, constitutive purpose of the work—promoting the recognition of immorally self-serving rationalizations like Tony's. If the apparent moral defectiveness of a character is effectively designed to elicit genuine moral insight, how can it be judged in the final analysis to be immoral? That is, Tony's initial seductiveness is a crucial part of the strategy of unmasking our easy acceptance of rationalizations like his and, thus, cannot be counted as straightforwardly evil within its artistic context.

gambit is at work in the construction of Walter White through his rivals, like Gus, until the last bunch he faces are neo-Nazis!

Furthermore, it is important to realize that not everything that is illegal is immoral and that audiences are alert to this. Thus, rough heroes who are vigilantes because the authorities are too incompetent or too corrupt to meet their responsibilities will not be regarded as morally suspect if they deliver the justice that the relevant institutions are failing to provide. Indeed, audiences may regard certain behaviors as moral even if the law does not. Perhaps many feel that when Tony Soprano brutally beats up the gangster Coco Cogliano (who had earlier menaced Tony's daughter Meadow), Tony was morally justified in the extreme revenge he exacted because the law would never have dealt as definitively as Tony did to the threat that a criminal like Cogliano represented to Tony's daughter.

And lastly, as we have already seen, another strategy for making rough heroes attractive is to invest them with positive nonmoral traits, like intelligence or courage or beauty, or to give them morally positive traits that are not substantively connected to their evil deeds, like devotion to their families or generosity. It hardly seems as though there was the artistic problem Eaton thinks that television programs like *The Sopranos* finally solved. The solutions were there before there was an HBO.

For a concluding objection, let's turn back to autonomism. James Harold has challenged the view of moderate moralism presented in this entry. He has charged that this view, among others, on the grounds that they imply that autonomism is irrational; that they require that autonomists adjust or reconcile their moral and aesthetic judgments of artworks; and that they are committed to metaphysical realism—where this glossed as the view that "the values are really out there in the world" (Harold 2011, 141).

In his article, Harold introduces a different definition than the one that has governed most of the debate so far. He takes autonomism to be the view about making global judgments about artworks (judgments regarding the work as a whole). When global judgments involve global moral judgments and global aesthetic judgments of the artwork, autonomism, according to Harold, does not rationally require that the judgments be adjusted or reconciled. He says: "The autonomist rejects only the view that we are required to modify an aesthetic judgement because of a moral judgement, or the other way around" (Harold 2011, 140).

I am not sure from where this view of autonomism derives. However, it is not a position that moderate moralism contradicts, since the judgments discussed in the present version of moderate moralism are *pro tanto* judgments, not global judgments.[19] A similar observation would apply to ethicism.

Moderate moralism is compatible with someone saying that *Triumph of the Will* is morally defective in various respects and, in many other respects, aesthetically excellent. Many of the shots are beautiful and exquisitely composed. According to moderate

---

[19] Moderate moralism has not presented a general view of how to reach all-things-considered judgments of artworks. Elsewhere I have argued that these should be essayed on a case-by-case basis. See my forthcoming essay, "Forget Taste."

moralism, there would be nothing *irrational* in saying the endorsement of hero-worship by various strategies in the film is evil and some of the visual strategies are stunning and just leaving at that. Many have done just that. Nor would the moderate moralist require the autonomist, on pain of irrationality, to reverse their estimation of the tracking shots in light of their condemnation of the hero-worship. So, to that extent, moderate moralism seems at least compatible with Harold's version of autonomism.

Moderate moralists will, of course, say that various moral defects in *Triumph of the Will* are, at the same time, aesthetic defects. But the moderate moralist will not charge the autonomist with irrationality if they disagree with this, but only with error.

According to Harold, moderate moralism is committed to metaphysical realism in the strong sense, as previously quoted. I would argue that one can be a moderate moralist and maintain not that the values are "out there in the world" but only that the relevant properties for the moderate moralist be response-dependent properties. Indeed, a commitment to response-dependent properties is all that moderate moralism requires.

In conclusion, much of this chapter has been devoted to characterizing moderate moralism and defending it against a selection of objections to it. The reason for that is that is where with respect to moralism the action has been in the recent literature. Undoubtedly that is likely to continue to a greater or lesser extent, at least in the near future. But at some point, that is apt to change and the debate about moralism will take a different direction. No one can say with any certainty what that direction will be. But my own hunch is that it will be about something that the current debate has left on the back burner—a discussion of the behavioral effects of art.

See also: Lamarque, Stear, Jacobson, Destrée, Gal, and Costelloe, this volume

REFERENCES

Anderson, James, and Jeffrey Dean. 1998. "Moderate Autonomism." *British Journal of Aesthetics* 38, no. 2: 150–166.

Aristotle. 1996. *Poetics*, translated by Malcolm Heath, 1453a. London: Penguin.

Batteux, Charles. 2015. *The Fine Arts Reduced to a Single Principle*, translated by James O. Young. Oxford: Oxford University Press.

Carroll, Noël. 1996. "Moderate Moralism." *British Journal of Aesthetics* 36, no. 3: 223–238.

Carroll, Noël. 2010a. "Art and Ethical Criticism." In his *Art and Three Dimensions*, 235–271. Oxford: Oxford University Press.

Carroll, Noël. 2010b. "At the Crossroad of Ethics and Aesthetics." *Philosophy and Literature* 34, no 1: 248–259.

Carroll, Noël. 2015. "Defending the Content Approach to Aesthetic Experience." *Metaphilosophy* 46, no. 2: 171–188.

Carroll, Noël. 2017. "Architecture, Art, and Moderate Moralism." *Nordic Journal of Aesthetics* 25, no. 52: 68–78.

Carroll, Noël. 2019. "Some Stabs at the Ontology of Dance." *Midwest Studies in Philosophy* 44, no. 1: 70–80.

Carroll, Noël. 2020. "I'm Only Kidding: On Racist and Ethnic Jokes." *Southern Journal of Philosophy* 58, no. 4: 534–546.

Carroll, Noël. Forthcoming. "Forget Taste." *Journal of Aesthetic Education.*

Eaton, A. W. 2012. "Robust Immoralism." *Journal of Aesthetics and Art Criticism* 70, no. 3: 281–292.

Eaton, A. W. 2013. "Reply to Carroll: The Artistic Value of a Particular Kind of Moral Flaw." *Journal of Aesthetics and Art Criticism* 71, no. 4: 376–380.

Eaton, A. W. 2016. "Literature and Morality." In *The Routledge Companion to the Philosophy of Literature*, edited by N. Carroll and J. Gibson, 433–450. New York: Routledge.

Harold, James. 2011. "Autonomism Reconsidered." *British Journal of Aesthetics* 51, no. 2: 137–147.

Hume, David. 1993. "Of the Standard of Taste." In *David Hume: Selected Essays*, edited by Stephen Copley and Andrew Edgar, 133–153. Oxford: Oxford University Press.

Gaut, Berys. 2009. *Art, Emotion, and Ethics.* Oxford: Oxford University Press.

Gregory the Great. 2004. "Selected Epistles." In *Theological Aesthetics: A Reader*, edited by Greta Elsbeth Thiessen, 47–48. Grand Rapids, MI: Eerdmans.

Jacobson, Daniel. 1997. "In Praise of Immoral Art." *Philosophical Topics* 25, no. 1: 155–199.

Kieran, Matthew. 2003. "Forbidden Knowledge: The Challenge of Immoralism." In *Art and Morality*, edited by Jose Luis Bermudez and Sebastian Gardner, 56–73. New York: Routledge.

Marcuse, Herbert. 1978. *The Aesthetic Dimension: Toward a Critique of Marxist Aesthetics.* Boston: Beacon.

Nietzsche, Friedrich. 1997. *Twilight of the Idols or How to Philosophize with a Hammer.* Translated by Richard Polt, section 24. Indianapolis: Hackett Publishing Company, Inc.

Plato. 1997. *Republic*, translated by G. M. A. Grube, revised by C. D. C. Reeve in *Plato: Complete Works*, edited John Cooper, Book II, III, and X. Indianapolis: Hackett.

Singer, Irving. 1954. "Aesthetics of Art for Art's Sake." *Journal of Aesthetics and Art Criticism* 12, no. 3: 343–359.

Stolnitz, Jerome. 1961. "On the Significance of Lord Shaftesbury in Modern Aesthetic Theory." *The Philosophical Quarterly* 11, no. 43: 97–113.

Taylor, Paul C. Forthcoming. "Understanding (Mis)understanding: Sally Be a Lamb." In *Screen Stories and Moral Understanding*, edited by Carl Plantinga. Oxford University Press.

Wilcox, John. 1953. "The Beginnings of l'art pour l'art." *Journal of Aesthetics and Art Criticism* 11, no. 4: 363.

Wilde, Oscar. 2021. "Oscar Wilde Replies." In *Art and Morality: A Defence of "The Picture of Dorian Gray"*, edited by Stuart Mason, 29–30. San Francisco, CA: Blurb, Inc.

CHAPTER 21

IMMORALISM AND CONTEXTUALISM

DANIEL JACOBSON

UNTIL about twenty years ago, the literature on the ethical criticism of art assumed a dichotomy between two familiar views, autonomism and moralism.[1] *Autonomism* holds that the aesthetic value of an artwork is wholly independent from its "extrinsic" or "ulterior" values—such as its economic, cognitive, and particularly its moral value—which do not make it any better or worse, considered as art. The autonomist thesis is clearest and most compelling when made specifically about economic value. Although Van Gogh famously could not sell his paintings during his lifetime, they are now worth a fortune. Yet no one thinks that the massive increase in their economic value affects their aesthetic value. They were great art all along, even when they had no economic value and their aesthetic value went unappreciated. According to autonomism, something similar holds of moral value: the moral defects and virtues of an artwork do not bear on its value as art. If this view is correct, then the ethical criticism of a work of art as morally good or bad, praiseworthy or blameworthy—regardless of whether this criticism is correct in its own terms—is as irrelevant as the work's economic value to its aesthetic evaluation.

The revival of ethical criticism at the end of the twentieth century rekindled philosophical interest in a conflicting view which has since become pervasive, especially in popular culture. *Moralism* holds that the moral defects and virtues of an artwork contribute to its aesthetic value by counting as aesthetic defects and virtues, respectively—at least whenever they are aesthetically relevant.[2] In Berys Gaut's version of the view, "a work is aesthetically meritorious (or defective) insofar as it manifests ethically admirable (or reprehensible) attitudes" (Gaut 1998). This quotation also illustrates Gaut's conception of when and how the moral qualities of art are aesthetically relevant: it is a

---

[1] Although the term "autonomism" is relatively new, the position is one of several familiar tenets of the formalist tradition. For discussion and some historical representatives of these tenets, see Jacobson (1997, 155–199). See also Gal and Stear, this volume.

[2] See Carroll, this volume.

matter of the attitudes manifested in the work. This conception is central to what I'll call *Humean moralism.*

While the moral defects of an artwork need not completely efface its aesthetic value, moralism claims that they are blemishes, aesthetic defects, which make it worse as art. Though the analogous claim about moral merits is less frequently argued, it follows from what James Harold has helpfully termed the *valence constraint* implicit in the view: "If a moral flaw of a work affects that work's aesthetic value, it reduces that value; if a moral virtue of a work affects that work's aesthetic value, it increases that value" (Harold 2008, 46–47).[3] This constraint remained implicit in the work of *fin de siècle* moralists who focused on arguing for the aesthetic relevance of the moral qualities of artwork, against their autonomist opponents.

The tacit assumption in this debate was probably not that autonomism and moralism were exhaustive, but that the remaining logical space was uninhabitable. This is evident from Nöel Carroll's characterization of his own view, which he calls "moderate moralism":

> Moderate moralism maintains that in some instances a moral defect in an artwork can be an aesthetic defect, and that sometimes a moral virtue can count as an aesthetic virtue. This opposes the view of moderate autonomism which admits that artworks can be morally defective and morally bad for that reason, but then goes on to say that the moral badness of a work can never count as an aesthetic defect. (Carroll 1996, 419)

This claim is too modest to count as moralism, because it neglects the possibility that some such defects might contribute *positively* to the work's aesthetic value. As stated, without the valence constraint, Carroll's central claim merely contradicts autonomism.

The problem is not that it allows some moral defects to be aesthetically irrelevant. If artworks can possess moral properties otherwise than by manifesting ethically admirable or reprehensible attitudes, then Gaut's claim too is compatible with this possibility; and he seems to endorse the suggestion in later work.[4] This is one respect in which moralism can be more or less modest. Another is that it can hold either that moral defects count as *pro tanto* aesthetic defects, which allows that a morally flawed work nevertheless might be great art, or that such moral defects entirely undermine its aesthetic value. But neither Carroll and Gaut nor Kendall Walton—all of whom seem to have independently arrived at similar views—initially considered the possibility that a moral defect of an artwork might figure as an aesthetic virtue (Walton 1994, 27–50).[5] Although their

---

[3] As Harold notes, his formulation of the constraint as a conditional makes it inapposite for characterizing the dispute between moralism and autonomism, since autonomism denies the antecedent; but this problem can be avoided with a slightly different framing.

[4] Gaut later writes, "a work of art is always aesthetically flawed insofar as it possesses an ethical flaw which is aesthetically relevant." See Gaut (2001, 349); Gaut (2007).

[5] Only Gaut would go on to straightforwardly defend moralism against the contextualist challenge to the valence constraint, rather than retreating to agnosticism. Although it seems clear that Carroll is more amenable to moralism, he would later write: "I'm not convinced that a moderate moralist must

contemporaneous development of Humean moralism revived a moribund debate, it is far from obvious what conclusion to draw from their novel argument.

That was the dialectical situation when I argued, in a paper called "In Praise of Immoral Art," that the contemporary debate between moralism and autonomism perpetuated a false dichotomy. It is possible for both moralism and autonomism to be false, because the moral *defects* of artworks sometimes contribute to their aesthetic value (contrary to autonomism) by figuring as aesthetic *virtues* (contrary to moralism). These were the terms in which I praised some immoral art: by suggesting that the recent arguments against autonomism can be turned on moralism. Perhaps moral virtues can figure as aesthetic defects, analogously, but there is no pressure to make this claim unless one advances a theory of the relationship between the moral and aesthetic qualities of artworks—as do both autonomism and moralism.

Although the claim that a moral defect in an artwork can figure as an aesthetic merit has been called "immoralism," that is a misnomer similar to "moderate moralism." No one argues for a systematically valence-inverted relationship between moral and aesthetic qualities. That position is logically possible but incredible.[6] Unlike both autonomism and moralism, which offer universal generalizations, the view sometimes called immoralism makes merely an existential claim: that the moral defects of an artwork *sometimes* figure among its aesthetic virtues. Hence, it is better to call the view anti-theoretical or *contextualist*—since when and how the moral qualities of artworks affect their aesthetic value differs across contexts.

The positions on the relationship between the moral qualities of an artwork and its aesthetic value that have actual advocates are autonomism, moralism, and contextualism. Autonomism differs from both its rivals by claiming that moral qualities of artworks are aesthetically irrelevant. Moralism is unique in accepting the valence constraint (not merely by denying the antecedent of its conditional). Contextualism rejects both the irrelevance claim and the valence constraint. Strictly speaking, a single counterexample would belie both these claims and thereby vindicate contextualism. This admittedly overstates matters, since it seems unlikely that there is one unique case where a moral quality is aesthetically relevant and yet has inverted valence. Nevertheless, it is important to note the difference in the strengths of these positions and the corresponding difference in what suffices to make them compelling.

A few peculiar problems surround the debate between these views, some of which are philosophically superficial but rhetorically significant, others more deeply problematic. First, there is no consensus about what count as moral defects and virtues in art. The obvious answer, familiar from Plato's banishment of the tragic poets, concerns its

be antecedently committed one way or another on [the valence constraint] on the basis of what the moderate moralist has said so far" (Carroll 2000, 350–387). And Walton would opine that he did not find the question interesting.

[6] I do not think that its mere logical possibility is "all that is needed" to vindicate contextualism (Stecker 2008, 157, fn. 18). Rather, it is all that is needed in order to show that the debate over moralism had previously assumed a false dilemma between moralism and autonomism.

effects. (See Destrée, this volume.) Plato held that tragedy rouses the base parts of the soul, which have been pining to weep and lament, and gives them a seemingly safe place to release these negative emotions (Nehamas 1982, 47–78).[7] Plato's worries are more serious than is often appreciated, in my opinion, especially when they are framed in terms of the sort of narratives that are dramatically effective, which typically play to common empathic biases (Jacobson 2008). Recent popular worries about the effects of art, and the revival of enthusiasm for banishing artists, focus on what works depict rather than what they make fictional—though of course they diverge from Plato about the nature of these harms.[8]

Nevertheless, philosophers tend to be concerned less with the practical effects of art than with its inherent moral defects and merits. Perhaps the fact that *Uncle Tom's Cabin* aroused popular support for abolitionism makes it the most felicific American novel, but no one argues that it is a great art. That observation raises another question: What makes an artwork not just dangerous but vicious, not just beneficial but virtuous? Although our central question concerns the inherent moral and aesthetic qualities of art rather than its consequences, there is no consensus about how these qualities are to be assessed. Yet this example illustrates a crucial point. It is not just that *Uncle Tom's Cabin* galvanized support for abolitionism; the novel itself—or its "postulated" author— condemns the enormities of slavery and endorses abolition.[9] As Gaut puts it, the work manifests an admirable (though by now entirely uncontroversial) attitude.

The idea that narrative artworks have inherent moral qualities, which are manifest in the responses and attitudes they prescribe, trades on their status as communicative artifacts. I accept this foundational idea, on which Humean moralism depends. These are complex issues, however, and we will have to grant certain assumptions for the sake of argument. I will also avoid controversial moral claims as much as possible, even though this understates the ethical significance of art—since we hardly need *Uncle Tom's Cabin* to repudiate slavery. But we will not be able to avoid controversy about the morality of engaging with transgressive artwork.

Second, there is widespread disagreement in aesthetic judgment. Philosophers typically grant that canonical artworks are aesthetically valuable, but the examples that get used in this debate range from high literature to popular film, and sometimes disparate evaluations of the works in question distract from the debate. The issue is not whether *Triumph of the Will* is tedious, for example, but whether such aesthetic value as the work possesses is diminished by its glorification of the fascist aesthetic and Hitler's cult of

---

[7] In Plato's view, the theater is not in fact a safe place to express these emotions, as doing so seduces the virtuous into vicious habits.

[8] For example, the likes of *Huck Finn* and *To Kill a Mockingbird* have been banned not because of what the works make fictional or the attitudes they prescribe. The popular enthusiasm for regimenting art and banishing artists picks up on the worst aspect of Plato's view.

[9] For explanation of the notion of a postulated author, as well as an argument that this term is unnecessary, see Nehamas (1986, 685–691). I will follow Nehamas in speaking simply of works and authors, with the understanding that this is an interpretive construct, not the flesh-and-blood creator(s) of the work.

personality. Before his conversion to contextualism, Matthew Kieran put the moralist thesis most perspicuously by claiming that *Triumph of the Will* "would have been better, *qua* art, if it had vilified just as well that which it seeks to glorify" (Kieran 1996, 348). That is the crucial claim—not whether the film is overrated, or whether some moralists underrate the aesthetic value of the works they criticize as morally flawed, such as *Pulp Fiction* and *American Psycho*.

The relevant aesthetic judgments are comparative, and the relevant comparison is between the value of an actual work and the value the work would have if it lacked some moral defect or virtue. (The hypothetical is further complicated by the fact that some of these changes would fundamentally alter these works.) The central claim of moralism only makes sense on the assumption that some such comparative judgments between actual and hypothetical, morally altered works are coherent. And the same goes for contextualism.

Were these judgments always incoherent, then perhaps autonomism would be the only tenable view. But simple cases suffice to demonstrate that some hypothetical comparisons of aesthetic value make sense and can be evaluated. The cases I have in mind are judgments like this: if someone slathered red paint on the Mona Lisa, that would diminish its aesthetic value. The red paint would be a blemish on the painting. That isn't perfectly analogous to the judgments on which this debate turns, but we can imagine that someone has already defaced the Mona Lisa. (Such acts of vandalism are surprisingly common.) Then one could say, "This painting would be better, aesthetically, if it lacked one of its actual properties—if it weren't slathered with red paint." Since this seems not just coherent but obviously true, autonomism does not win by default.

There is also a persistent problem with arguments in the philosophy of art raised by the lack of a common body of artwork with which one can assume familiarity. I have mostly used works that could be reproduced in an essay, such as short poems by Emily Dickinson and Philip Larkin, but this severely diminishes the stock of available examples.[10] Worse yet, there are interpretive disputes even about commonplace works. This is not merely an adventitious difficulty. Moralists tend to trump up their moral criticism of artwork they dislike, and to interpret artwork they like in ways that exonerate it morally. The crucial claim is not that morally defective artwork is aesthetically bad, however, but that it is made worse by its moral defects (when they are aesthetically

---

[10]   Contrary to the inference of some readers, I do not think that Dickinson's "Tell All the Truth" is morally flawed. I used that poem first to argue against autonomism, and then to suggest that readers with a different moral view than mine, who reject the poem's moral perspective, would have a hard time arguing that this *putative* moral flaw constitutes an aesthetic defect. I'm not even inclined to criticize Larkin's "This Be the Verse" as morally flawed. (But I would make that argument about John Lennon's nadir, the song "Imagine," which some people seem to love largely for what I find pernicious about it.) My point about Larkin's poem is that a common sort of moralist—those who claim that works with "life-affirming" attitudes are morally praiseworthy—must think it vicious, on pain of inconsistency. Surely their view would render Larkin's antithetical poem morally defective.

relevant). The suggestion that immoral art has no aesthetic value is considerably easier to refute—though it too must rely on an inevitably controversial conception of what constitutes a moral defect in an artwork.

The final rhetorical difficulty arises from the fact that the best examples for making the "immoralist" claim—that is, the best examples of valence inversion—are morally defective by their job description. Yet it has grown increasingly risky to use truly offensive jokes and artworks, whatever skeptical attitude philosophers adopt in theory. Worse, the argument requires not only telling these jokes in an unfavorable context for eliciting amusement (a philosophy paper), but also on insisting that their offensiveness contributes to their funniness. That is not a career-affirming choice. Hence, I will mostly use my opponents' examples and arguments, and challenge their claims in the abstract, without giving my best cases.

THE ARISTOTLE-HUME MODEL OF MORAL DEFECTS AND VIRTUES IN ART

Aristotle famously characterized tragedy in terms of the tragic emotions, which he identified as fear and pity. Whether or not this characterization holds for the tragedies of antiquity, it seems too narrow to capture Shakespearean and other tragedy, which elicit a wider range of emotion and other affect-laden attitudes.[11] Despite these complications, it seems safe to say that comedies aim to amuse. At any rate, *comedians* have this aim in producing comedy. Yet real-life comedians have various motives, and sometimes the aims of making the audience laugh, being liked, and selling tickets diverge from the aim to be funny. Perhaps the best thing to say is that, *qua* comedian, they aspire to amuse *by being funny*—while acknowledging that some care more about being funny and others about eliciting amusement, regardless.

Jokes offer a useful test case, because on one hand they are easy to interpret and relatively straightforward in their intent; on the other, they form part of complex and aesthetically valuable comedies. Hence, the success of a comedy—and for that matter a Shakespearean tragedy—hangs in some part on its humor. "Look for me tomorrow and you shall find me a grave man," Mercutio's dying line, is quite witty. Moreover, its wit contributes (positively) to the aesthetic value of the scene, and thereby to the play. Notwithstanding the two previously noted problems, concerning how to identify the aims of artists and when they can be attributed to artworks, this much should be uncontroversial.

---

[11] It is even controversial whether many of our emotional responses to fiction—specifically those that seem to have fictional objects—are genuine or make-believe. See Walton (1990). Although I agree with Walton's conclusion, I think the issue is largely orthogonal to this argument, since moral objections can be raised toward various forms of make-believe as well.

It is easiest to consider the most significant complication for the Aristotelian dictum by thinking first about jokes. This complication arises from the fact that sometimes bad jokes elicit amusement and good jokes—that is, comically valuable, *funny* jokes—do not. Something analogous happens with art too, of course, as illustrated by the case of Van Gogh and many others. Good art requires a good audience, as it is said; and not all audiences are good. This point is likely to raise the hackles of some philosophers, who will be inclined to dismiss the notion of the funny, as opposed to the (relativist) funny-for-you. Yet our debate presupposes that artworks have moral qualities as well as intersubjective moral and aesthetic value; otherwise dispute over whether and how these qualities affect their value as art would be pointless.[12] Despite the philosophical attraction of treating the funny as a "predicate of personal taste," doesn't everyone think that some people have a better sense of humor than others? My children like puns excessively, for example, and many people enjoy banal sit-com humor.

Although there are foundational questions that cannot be addressed here, I will continue using the realist locutions and assumptions standardly adopted in this literature. This is in keeping with the dilemma at the heart of Hume's essay "Of the Standard of Taste." Despite the theoretical attractions of relativism and skepticism, no one really believes that all jokes, comedies, and sophisticated works of narrative art are equally good.

If we adopt this stance, then the complication for the Aristotelian dictum becomes clear. The funniness of a joke is a normative matter, about whether a joke *merits* amusement rather than whether it *elicits* amusement from any real-life audience. One way to bridge the gap between the natural and the normative is by appeal to an idealized audience, which is amused only by what is genuinely funny, and so forth. This seems to be the strategy employed by Humean moralists, and I consider it promising—to some extent. The details of the idealization matter, though, and I will argue that the debate has missed a crucial point: that moral sensitivity and aesthetic sensitivity are different notions, which can come apart. The Aristotelean aspect of aesthetic success can be summed up with the claim that success of (some) artwork depends (partly) on whether it merits certain emotional responses and other affect-laden attitudes.

Hume's contribution arises from a stray remark in "Of the Standard of Taste." It is a tribute to the richness of the essay that even this claim, which I doubt any Humean moralist accepts as stated, has inspired an original and important argument. The relevant passage from Hume asserts, "where vicious manners are described, without being marked with the proper characters of blame and disapprobation; this must be allowed to disfigure a poem, and to be a real deformity" (Hume 1757, 246).[13]

As with Aristotle and the distinction between elicited and merited emotions, Hume's claim needs modification. It should be recognized that the overt marking of vicious

---

[12] But compare Harold (2011, 137–147), who recasts the argument in terms of rational requirements on evaluation. This seems to me like a different question, but I will not pursue the issue here. See Stear, this volume, for a discussion.

[13] At least Gaut and Walton seem to accept some version of this view. See Gaut (2007, 227).

characters with disapproval is unnecessary and often heavy-handed. Even when sincere, it can be an aesthetic defect; moreover, such explicit markings cannot simply be taken at face value.[14] But we can suppose that Hume meant something less literal by "marked"— something more like what the Humean moralists refer to as the attitudes manifested by the work. All sides grant that the mere depiction of vice isn't vicious, and it should be similarly uncontroversial that the depiction of vice without explicit disapprobation need not constitute a moral defect. Artworks can implicitly adopt disapproving attitudes toward the vice they depict. The crucial question concerns the perspective the work takes on the characters and events depicted: what attitudes and responses it *endorses* or *prescribes*.

Here then is the revised Aristotle-Hume model of moral defects and virtues in art. Many works of narrative art prescribe certain affective attitudes and emotional responses to their depicted events. The aesthetic success of these artworks depends in part on whether they merit these prescribed responses. Aesthetically good comedies are funny, for example, and good tragedies tragic. The central insight of the Humean moralists is that the moral qualities of the characters and events depicted can affect whether the work merits these responses, since—as both Aristotle and Hume note in their own fashion—the downfall of a hero and a villain prescribe different responses.[15] Hence, the Humean moralists conclude:

> The moral defects in works of art, when they result in audiences being unable to se-cure psychological uptake of the aimed-at responses, are aesthetic defects in those works. Conversely, moral merits, when they enhance uptake of the works' aimed-at responses, such as when the moral merits of a work increase one's absorption in it, are aesthetic merits of these works. (Gaut 2007, 228)[16]

Suppose though that some moral defects in works of art *enhance* uptake of the works' aimed-at response, perhaps by increasing one's absorption in it; and that some moral virtues detract from it, for instance by being heavy-handed and tedious. If so then the Humean moralist's argument can be turned upon itself. There would be as much reason to consider *these* moral virtues to be aesthetic defects in the work, and analogously for moral defects. In that case, the Aristotle-Hume model of the nature of (some) aesthetic virtues and moral defects belies autonomism, as the Humean moralists claim, but it does so by supporting contextualism. There are still details about the view and its central claim left to be developed, but that will be the crux of my argument.

---

[14] Among the many delights of *Lolita* is Nabokov's repeated demonstration of this point, at increasing levels of complexity: bogus preface (by an "extradiegetic" character, John Ray Jr., PhD), unreliable narrator (Humbert), and afterword (by the postulated author, "Vladimir Nabokov").

[15] The idea of heroes and villains is grossly simplistic, of course, especially when it comes to the most interesting literature. This point will prove crucial to the argument for contextualism, but I start with the simplest cases for purposes of illustration.

[16] Carroll's argument rests on essentially the same idea. See Carroll (1996, 231–237); also Carroll, this volume.

There is a substantial lacuna in the moralist argument, since sometimes a work's inability to secure uptake is not an aesthetic defect but reflects the flaws of the audience. An audience of six-year-olds will not be amused at some witty material, whether because they don't get it or it isn't to their (crude) taste. There is a similar explanation for Van Gogh's failure to be appreciated during his lifetime, except by a few avant-garde artists and critics. People are conformist and look to others—now tellingly called "influencers"—to dictate many of their responses. This is an obvious insight with significant implications for Humean moralism. It is inadequate to claim that the fact that an artwork fails to secure uptake of its prescribed responses in unspecified audiences manifests any aesthetic flaw in the work. But if the dictum concerns *most* audiences, then it makes aesthetic value into a popularity contest. Surely Van Gogh was not a mediocre painter when living who became a genius posthumously.

The central dictum of the Aristotle-Hume model cannot be applied to actual audiences without generating absurd results. Yet if we instead apply it to an idealized audience, the claim threatens to become either trivial or question-begging. A *morally* ideal audience, which never responds to jokes (or artworks) in ways that are contrary to virtue, will fail to be amused whenever amusement would be vicious—whether or not the joke is funny. Hence, the dispute between autonomism, moralism, and contextualism must concern whether an *aesthetically* ideal or sensitive audience will respond to an artwork as prescribed. It is trivial that an aesthetically ideal audience will respond to artwork in ways that reflect its aesthetic value: they will be thrilled by thrilling works, amused by the funny, and disgusted by the disgusting. But then the debate between autonomism, moralism, and contextualism simply gets recast as a dispute over how an aesthetically ideal audience would respond to morally flawed artwork. This makes no progress.

Carroll offers two main arguments for moralism. First, he does not find plausible the contextualist's supposed counterexamples to the valence constraint. We will presently consider the question of which view best coheres with our considered aesthetic judgments. Second, he claims that an artwork is aesthetically defective "if it is such that it would daunt the work's prescribed responses for ideally morally sensitive audiences because it is ethically defective" (Carroll 2000, 378). But this argument seems to assume that morally sensitive audiences will have the same responses as aesthetically sensitive audiences—and that begs the question. Moreover, it is dubious on independent grounds, since there are reasons to think that, in real-life circumstances, the virtuous (morally sensitive) emotional response can deviate from the *fitting* emotional response, where fitting emotions are those that correctly appraise their object.

A similar problem attends the central case for moralism made by Gaut, which he calls the *merited response argument*. One sense of a "merited" emotional response is a notion of correctness: in this sense, to say that an emotion is merited is just to say that it is fitting. Funny jokes merit amusement and scary films merit fear. If there is a dedicated response to beauty, then it is merited when directed at the beautiful. It is not clear whether this is what Gaut means by a merited response, however, since he says that merit concerns "whether it is appropriate or inappropriate to respond in the way the work prescribes"

(Gaut 2007, 231). The trouble is that "appropriate" is vague as between (at least) assessing an emotional response as virtuous and as fitting. One can say that it is inappropriate to be amused by even a very funny offensive joke, toward which amusement is fitting, because that response would nevertheless be vicious.[17] (For a discussion of the ethics of jokes, see Butterfield, this volume.)

Consider such offensive but funny jokes. While an extreme moralist can deny that there are any such jokes—at the cost of making the view more obviously vulnerable to counterexamples—Gaut grants that they exist.[18] His more modest form of moralism is committed to holding that the joke is nevertheless rendered *less funny* by its offensiveness.[19] But how is it "appropriate" to feel toward such a joke? In order for the merited response argument to track the comic value of jokes, funny jokes must merit amusement. Yet the crucial premise of Gaut's argument claims: "One way in which [prescribed responses] can be unmerited is in being unethical . . . So, if the prescribed responses are unmerited because unethical, that is an *aesthetic* failure of the work—that is to say, is an aesthetic defect in it" (Gaut 2007, 233). It might be true that unethical responses are always inappropriate, in the moralized sense of appropriateness; but then the merit of a response can deviate from its fittingness, and what is at issue in this debate is whether unethical responses are always unfitting. If a joke can be offensive but funny, and if it is unethical to be amused by offensive jokes, then amusement at them is fitting despite being unethical.

Suppose it is always wrong or vicious to be amused by offensive jokes, regardless of how funny they are. This is not my view, but it is a position endorsed or suggested by comic and aesthetic moralists. Let's call this claim *moral inaccessibility*, since it holds that whatever comic value offensive jokes have is rendered morally inaccessible to a virtuous audience.[20] If so then it is morally inappropriate but fitting to be amused by such a joke, since the joke is funny by stipulation. These arguments founder in similar ways. Virtue or moral sensitivity might preclude comic and aesthetic sensitivity in such cases. Then we would face a forced choice between having fitting emotional responses (e.g., being amused by what is funny) and having virtuous ones. This may pose a practical dilemma, but it obscures matters to call this not just a moral defect but a comic defect in the joke.[21]

---

[17] See D'Arms and Jacobson (2000).

[18] Gaut thus writes that his view "does not entail that a work cannot be funny because it manifests immoral attitudes"; and he allows that moral defects of art are pro tanto aesthetic defects, which is expressly compatible with their retaining aesthetic value (Gaut 2007, 245–246).

[19] Carroll correctly notes that in order to assess this claim, one would have to make the hypothetical comparison, which is "extraordinarily difficult" (Carroll 2014, 108). It is odd that he does not draw the same conclusion about the analogous case of morally flawed art.

[20] Both Gaut and Walton have suggested that moral inaccessibility is an aesthetic (or comic) defect in an artwork (or joke). See Gaut (2007, 241); Walton (1994, 30). But this is a different sort of defect than the debate concerns.

[21] Some argue that we morally should not engage with artwork created by (putatively) evil artists, such as Richard Wagner, Woody Allen, or Roman Polanski. If so then their work is similarly morally inaccessible—regardless of its aesthetic quality. However that may be, it obscures matters to conflate this

This demonstrates the difficulty with modest forms of moralism: they allow morally flawed artworks to have aesthetic value—to be beautiful, funny, tragic, and the like—which raises the possibility that their prescribed responses may be vicious but fitting. Moralists are pushed to the more modest claim because the stronger claim, which entails that there are no offensive but funny jokes or morally flawed but great artworks, is so vulnerable to counterexample. Indeed, autonomists such as Arnold Isenberg claim precisely that aesthetic judgment must ignore the moral qualities of artworks to be plausible (Isenberg 1973, 85). The core tenet of autonomism is that only this stance issues in correct aesthetic evaluation. Whereas the Humean moralists claim, to the contrary, that aesthetic judgment comes out correct when it is sensitive to the moral qualities of artworks—at least those that reach some threshold of significance. How are we to adjudicate between such competing first-order aesthetic (and moral) claims?

Isenberg's argument works best for the positive case, where moralism would be refuted by examples of artworks that are aesthetically worse in virtue of their morally good properties. Consider Hume's unrevised claim that rough heroes need to be marked with disapprobation. This needed revision partly because many didactic works fail to merit the virtuous responses they prescribe, because they do so in heavy-handed ways that discourage absorption in the work. Then the artistic means by which the work prescribes attitudes and responses amounts to a blemish, though there might be no other sufficiently directive means available. This will be so when a less didactic version of the work would be morally ambiguous, perhaps detracting from the admirability of its perspective but making it better as art.

What about negative cases, where contextualists argue that moral defects can count among a work's aesthetic virtues? This is where the examples developed by philosophers I'll call *Humean immoralists* come into their own. Their argument takes Hume's case of rough heroes and uses them to turn the argument of the Humean moralists back upon itself. Despite my reservations about the term "immoralism," it has been embraced by A. W. Eaton and Matthew Kieran, in their arguments for contextualism, and Nils-Hennes Stear makes a similar argument about "seductive works" (Keiran 2003, 56–73; Eaton 2012, 281–292; Stear 2019, 465–482). At the heart of these arguments is an observation that poses a deep problem for moralism.

Their crucial observation complicates the point that to depict vice is not thereby to endorse it. This is of course true. Nevertheless, the Humean immoralists offer examples designed to show that works of narrative art *often* trade on engaging the audience's sympathy for Hume's rough heroes: characters who do bad things without guilt, let alone atonement. It would be a gross interpretive error to claim that *The Sopranos* endorses the actions and attitudes of Tony Soprano; that the ethical perspective of *Lolita* is Humbert Humbert's perspective; or that *Mad Men* prescribes admiration of Don Draper. And yet what is so fascinating about those works is the cleverness with which they seduce the

---

sort of defect with an aesthetic criticism, concerning the nature of the work, such as has been leveled at *Manhattan*, especially in retrospect. See Matthes, this volume, for a discussion.

reader into caring about their flawed heroes. These points are more often acknowledged by artists than by philosophers, though I find the Humean immoralists to be especially perceptive critics. As the playwright David Mamet notes, drama affects us in part because often "we identify *sub*consciously (uncritically) with the protagonist" (Mamet 1987, 13). Those works succeed in part because Draper is so cool and, not coincidentally, extremely handsome; Tony is the boss and acts like it; and Humbert has, as he famously declares, a fancy prose style.

In my view, the most sophisticated position recognizes that the dramatic success of these works depends upon making the reader care about these rough heroes—and not merely in a censorious way. This makes the reader complicit with their viciousness, as being amused by an offensive joke may make one complicitous. This is *not* to say that the depiction of vice is vicious, or that readers really adopt the attitudes of the rough heroes. On the contrary, these works stop readers short by acidly illustrating how we have been seduced into caring for morally problematic characters—even moral monsters.[22] These seductive works prescribe conflicting, ambivalent responses, some of which seem morally suspect precisely because they involve absorption in the psychology of the vicious. If they did not, then the aesthetic effect of implicating the reader would not come off. As Isenberg notes, we often do not respond to fictions as if we were real-life spectators to their depicted events, somehow constrained to inaction: "In practical life it would be our business to correct the distorted evaluations which result from the nearness and prominence of certain objects [in works of art] . . . and not to bother about the conflicts in the soul of Macbeth when he is every day murdering innocent people" (Isenberg 1973, 84).

This point about the disparity between commonplace responses to narrative art and to real-life reveals another class of case, more mundane (and perhaps less controversial) than that of rough heroes. We are not brainwashed by fiction but remain aware that its characters are not actual people; in fact, some of them resemble plot devices. Take Polonius, for example, who gets murdered by Hamlet while eavesdropping behind an arras. No one cares about the pompous Polonius, who is mainly a figure of ridicule, and it would detract from the work to mourn his death. The point of his murder is to demonstrate that Hamlet is not squeamish about dispatching people other than his uncle, even for far lesser crimes. Does *Hamlet*, the work, endorse being amused by Polonius's absurd death? Perhaps that goes too far, but it is more than I need. Rather, I claim that the aesthetic success of *Hamlet*—as Isenberg says about *Macbeth*—requires us to refrain from expending emotional resources on characters who serve primarily as plot devices. Moreover, the inner workings of the minds of deeply flawed characters are often more absorbing and dramatic than those of the virtuous. This is a Platonic insight.

My argumentative strategy accepts the Humean moralist's characterization of moral defects and virtues of art. It remains possible for the moralist to deny that these examples are moral defects, for instance by putting forward strained interpretations or making

---

[22] Perhaps the greatest literary example of this is the final line of Part I of *Lolita*: "You see, she had absolutely nowhere else to go." To be sure, Draper is flawed but no monster, unlike the others.

moral claims that would not otherwise be tempting. But the more frequently such arguments are mounted, the more they look like ad hoc maneuvers designed to save the theory. The same holds of the moralist argument that an artwork's moral flaw is an aesthetic defect even though the work would not be improved, aesthetically, were the defect removed. This is the argument from value interaction, considered in the final section.

Why Contextualism?

The central moralist claim is that the moral defects and merits in an artwork count as aesthetic defects and merits, respectively, at least if we put aside trivial blemishes that would not deter a virtuous audience. When it comes to jokes and wisecracks, the claim is that "humour is aesthetically flawed in so far as" it is vicious (Gaut 2007, 246).[23] Although some vicious jokes might be funny, this implies that they must nevertheless be rendered *less funny* by their viciousness. The question is: less funny than what? There is an obvious answer that renders the correct result in simple cases: A joke is comically flawed by a moral defect when a sanitized version of the joke, lacking the morally defective feature, would be funnier than the original.

Some jokes are gratuitously offensive. For example, consider a racist joke that works just as well without the racial element, because it does not trade on any specific stereotype. As Carroll puts the point, it might instead have been told as a moron joke (Carroll 2014, 85–86).[24] That joke is comically flawed because the moron version is funnier than the racist version. Notice that this is true *even if the offensive version amuses some actual audiences more* specifically due to its racism. We should not be naïve about the transgressive nature of humor. Comedy often joins some of us together, in laughter at a common object, by casting others out: making them the butt of the joke. A joke that gratuitously ridicules a group toward whom some specific audience is hostile is likely to elicit more amusement from them than does the inoffensive version.

It is hard to deny that the gratuitous slur counts as a moral defect in the joke. Then the moralist claim that the moral defect of this joke is a comic blemish, which makes it less funny, has determinate content. The crucial claim is that the racist version merits less amusement than does the morally sanitized version. The "less funny" claim makes sense, and seems true, because there is an obvious comparison. It is *less funny than the same joke without the moral defect.*

[23] Note that this claim is not qualified with, "whenever the viciousness of the humor is comically relevant." On the contrary, the "insofar as" clause implies that a joke's viciousness always makes it at least somewhat less funny.

[24] I think he underestimates the tenacity of moralism, as shown by the fact that 'moron' too is now considered offensive by Miriam-Webster, due to its "history of clinical use." It is a challenge to ride the moralist tiger, now more than ever.

Notice that this discussion trades on the idea that these are two different versions of "the same joke." People often say things like that without having a theory of joke-identity. Although this thought does not seem problematic here, it may make trouble in more complex cases such as works of art. But there are easy cases there too, such as the defaced Mona Lisa. Whether or not we say that these are two different versions of the same painting does not matter. The crucial point is that the claim of a blemish or aesthetic flaw is similarly coherent and plausible: the work is better art without the red paint (or this work is better than that one). The challenge for moralism is to make sense of more difficult and interesting cases. When there is no obvious answer to the question "Less aesthetically valuable than what?," this exposes a lacuna in the theory. By developing this challenge, I can also clear up a misunderstanding of contextualism and answer an objection to how I've previously developed it.

Recall the quintessential moralist claim that *Triumph of the Will* "would have been better, qua art, if it had vilified just as well that which it seeks to glorify" (Kieran 1996, 348). I've previously noted that I find it hard to imagine such a work, because the glorification of fascism is so central to the film. "Whatever such a work would be," I wrote, "it would not be *Triumph of the Will*" (Jacobson 1997, 193). This was too strong, unnecessarily. One can imagine a repentant Leni Riefenstahl releasing a "director's cut" of the documentary that adds voice-over narration designed to vilify the Nazi rally it depicts. I don't know if such a version of the film would count as the same film or not, and I don't think it matters; what matters is that this version would be ridiculous, aesthetically worse than the original.

However, my previous overstatement has led Harold to attribute to me what he refers to as the *identity argument*, on which "a necessary condition for X's being an aesthetic defect in work Y would be that the absence or alteration of X in Y would leave Y's identify unchanged" (Harold 2008, 49). Since I have no theory of the identity conditions of artwork and doubt that any such account can be given, this had better not be my argument. Let me try again. My view is that for x to count as a blemish or aesthetic defect in a work, it must be the case that this claim is coherent and compelling:

(*) The work would be aesthetically better if it lacked x.

This is not a logical point about what moralism entails. Rather, (*) is controversial and expressly denied by Gaut. But it seems quite plausible about many commonplace claims about aesthetic value, and not because "the work" entails an identity claim. Consider another toy case. A version of *Lolita* in which the narrator's name is Hamburg Hamburg would be a worse novel, because this silliness would be a blemish on the work, like the gratuitously offensive joke and the defaced Mona Lisa. Since these alterations are minor—as well as being obviously for the worse—it seems safe to call these different versions of the same work, but I don't think anything hangs on this terminology. We could call these imagined versions "counterparts" to the work instead, but I won't bother to do that more than once. As applied to *Triumph of the Will*, the point is that (*) challenges the moralist to put flesh on the bones of the claim that the film or its counterpart could vilify rather than glorify fascism, and that it would be aesthetically better for doing so.

In response, Gaut (in his defense of moralism) and Stecker (in his argument against contextualism) embrace *value interaction*: the claim that the presence of one evaluatively relevant property can affect the presence of another, such that a work is made aesthetically worse by some moral flaw though there is no way to remove the blemish, even in principle, without decreasing the work's aesthetic value.[25] I can grant the coherence of the value-interaction claim, which resembles Moore's claim about the organic unity of value. The question is whether the possibility of value interaction suffices to justify the claim that *x* counts as a blemish on the work, when it is granted that removing *x* would in fact make the work aesthetically worse. Absent an explanation of *why* such moral defects inevitably exhibit precisely the sort of value interaction required by moralism, this seems like an ad hoc maneuver designed to save the theory from counterexample.

It is also possible to reject the Aristotle-Hume model of moral defects in art, which focuses on how they can manifest vicious attitudes and prescribe vicious responses. Some philosophers do this by noting that one doesn't have to adopt such an attitude to have the relevant response. This is true: you don't need to be a sexist to be amused at a sexist joke. But some go further by suggesting that it is always morally benign to imaginatively entertain attitudes and emotional responses in aesthetic contexts. I think this claim goes too far, and that *sometimes* one should refrain from amusement at jokes and other prescribed responses of artworks.

However that may be, all that the debate between moralism and contextualism requires is that works of art can have morally appraisable qualities, and that their aesthetic value can be assessed and compared. I find both these claims extremely plausible. For purposes of this chapter, however, I must be content to have argued that the assumptions and arguments of Humean moralism better support contextualism.

See also: Carroll, Stear, Matthes, Butterfield, Costelloe, Destrée, this volume

REFERENCES

Carroll, Nöel. 1996. "Moderate Moralism." *British Journal of Aesthetics* 36, no. 3: 223–238.

Carroll, Nöel. 2000. "Art and Ethical Criticism." *Ethics* 100, no.2: 350–387.

Carroll, Nöel. 2014. *Humour: A Very Short Introduction*. Oxford: Oxford University Press.

D'Arms, Justin, and Daniel Jacobson. 2000. "The Moralistic Fallacy: On the Appropriateness of Emotion." *Philosophy and Phenomenological Research* 61, no.1: 65–90.

Eaton, Anne. 2012. "Robust Immoralism." *Journal of Aesthetics and Art Criticism* 70, no.3: 281–292.

Gaut, Berys. 1998. "The Ethical Criticism of Art." In *Aesthetics and Ethics: Essays at the Intersection*, edited by Jerrold Levinson, 182–203. Cambridge: Cambridge University Press.

---

[25] By "in principle" here, I meant to exclude the possibility of an ineradicably defaced Mona Lisa, where the only techniques available to remove the red paint would further degrade the painting.

Gaut, Berys. 2001. "Art and Ethics." In *The Routledge Companion to Aesthetics*, edited by Berys Gaut and Dominic Lopez, 341–352. London: Routledge.

Gaut, Berys. 2007. *Art, Emotion and Ethics*. Oxford: Oxford University Press.

Harold, James. 2008. "Immoralism and the Valence Constraint." *British Journal of Aesthetics* 48, no. 1: 45–64.

Harold, James. 2011. "Autonomism Reconsidered." *British Journal of Aesthetics* 51, no. 2: 137–147.

Isenberg, Arnold. 1973. "The Aesthetic Function of Language." In *Aesthetics and the Theory of Criticism: Selected Essays of Arnold Isenberg*, 70–86. Chicago: University of Chicago Press.

Jacobson, Daniel. 1997. "In Praise of Immoral Art." *Philosophical Topics* 25, no. 1: 155–199.

Jacobson, Daniel. 2008. "Review of Berys Gaut, *Art, Emotion and Ethics*." *Notre Dame Philosophical Reviews* https://ndpr.nd.edu/reviews/art-emotion-and-ethics/

Kieran, Matthew. 1996. "Art, Imagination, and the Cultivation of Morals." *Journal of Aesthetics and Art Criticism* 54, no. 4: 337–351.

Kieran, Matthew. 2003. "Forbidden Knowledge: The Challenge of Immoralism." In *Art and Morality*, edited by J. Bermudez and S. Gardiner, 56–73. London: Routledge.

Mamet, David. 1987. "Radio Drama." In his *Writing in Restaurants*, 11 17. New York: Penguin.

Nehamas, Alexander. 1982. "Plato on Imitation and Poetry in *Republic* 10." In *Plato on Beauty and the Arts*, edited by Julius Moravcsik and Philip Tempko, 47–78. Lanham, MD: Rowman & Littlefield.

Nehamas, Alexander. 1986. "What an Author Is." *Journal of Philosophy* 83, no. 11: 685–691.

Stear, Nils-Hennes. 2019. "Meriting a Response: The Paradox of Seductive Artworks." *Australasian Journal of Philosophy* 97, no. 3: 465–482.

Stecker, Robert. 2008. "Immoralism and the Anti-Theoretical View." *British Journal of Aesthetics* 48, no. 2: 145–161.

Walton, Kendall. 1990. *Mimesis as Make-Believe*. Cambridge, MA: Harvard University Press.

Walton, Kendall. 1994. "Morals in Fiction and Fictional Morality." *Proceedings of the Aristotelian Society* (Suppl. Vol. 68): 27–50.

CHAPTER 22

....

AESTHETICISM

....

BECCA ROTHFELD

MORALISM, the view that aesthetic evaluations sometimes depend wholly or partially on ethical evaluations, is the most widely defended alternative to *autonomism*, the view that aesthetic evaluation is insulated from other sorts of evaluation.[1] Against the autonomist's insistence that an artwork's moral merits or defects are irrelevant to its aesthetic successes or failures, a moralist might maintain that a portrait is majestic because it is compassionate, or that a novel is inelegant because it is sexist.[2] For instance, many critics and commentators have argued that the lechery of Woody Allen's *Manhattan*, a film in which a forty-two-year-old man conducts an affair with a seventeen-year-old girl, makes the movie aesthetically repellent (Dederer, 2017; see also Matthes, this volume).

This chapter will treat the inverse view, *aestheticism*, according to which moral evaluations sometimes depend wholly or partially on aesthetic evaluations. An aestheticist might hold that a painting is objectifying because it is garish, or that a poem is respectful because it is melodic. Some aestheticists have argued, for instance, that Gustave Flaubert's 1856 novel *Madame Bovary* is morally sensitive by dint of its aesthetic sensitivity. The book's lyrical depiction of its female protagonist's suffering renders the text considerate: a cruder, more sensationalist portrayal of Emma Bovary's humiliation might be trivializing or even voyeuristic, constructed so as to dispose readers to delight in the woman's pain. It is because of *Madame Bovary*'s aesthetic virtues, claims the aestheticist, that the work proves ethically commendable.

Aestheticism is a relative newcomer to the scene, at least within recent analytic philosophy, and its champions have not yet marked out much consolidated territory. Because the view does not yet have many self-professed adherents, much of the taxonomizing in this chapter will be somewhat speculative. The term has been used in the past, often in reference to the autonomism of thinkers such as Oscar Wilde: thinkers in this camp

---

[1] See Carroll in this volume for a discussion of moralism; see Stear for a discussion of autonomism.
[2] Throughout this chapter, I use "moral" and "ethical" interchangeably.

regard the aesthetic and the moral as quarantined from one another but take the aesthetic to trump the moral. This is, for instance, the way in which Alexander Nehamas uses the term in *Nietzsche: Life as Literature*, where he argues that Friedrich Nietzsche looks at the world "as if it were a literary text" (Nehamas 1985, 3). Still, my usage of "aestheticism" is new—and the various philosophers I survey in this chapter, who have not been put into conversation with one other before, may not think of themselves as belonging to a meaningfully unified group. Accordingly, there is greater diversity among aestheticism's proponents (or those I enlist as its proto-proponents) than there is among thinkers often grouped together under the moralist umbrella.

Aestheticists differ about almost everything. They disagree about both the dependence-relation in question and the relevant relata. Some aestheticists hold that aesthetic value *gives rise* to ethical value, while others hold that aesthetic evaluations *imply* ethical evaluations. And, though aestheticism is most often formulated as a thesis about the aesthetic and ethical value of artworks in particular, it is sometimes formulated as a thesis about aesthetic value and ethical value more generally, or even a thesis about how artworks aid or incite the moral development of persons.

In the first part of this chapter I will identify what, if anything, is at the heart of the heterogenous views that I regard as aestheticist in spirit: I will distill some central theses at the core of the aestheticist project, sketch the position's boundaries, and motivate the view with reference to a few cases. Broadly speaking, I will distinguish between possible variants of aestheticism with reference to two questions, one about the nature of the proposed relation between the moral and the aesthetic, the other about the nature of the entities that stand in this relation. In the next section, I will explore the range of forms that aestheticism has taken, surveying both aestheticist theses and views that are adjacent to aestheticism but not quite iterations of it. I begin with a brief discussion of the view's historical antecedents, then proceed to categorize contemporary views on the basis of the objects on which they center; my discussion is divided between views that primarily treat artworks and views that are more expansive.

I will proceed with several assumptions in mind. First, with the exception of my historical detour, I limit my discussion to aestheticism as it manifests within contemporary philosophy. As I note briefly in the second section, aestheticism has some precedent, but few of the thinkers who lend themselves to aestheticist elaboration are uncontroversial defenders of the view. It would take a great deal of interpretive legwork to motivate the notion that Martin Heidegger or James Baldwin can be plausibly read as aestheticist, and in this chapter, I will stick to discussion of philosophers whose views can be parsed more straightforwardly.

Second, I focus on challenges to aestheticism that target the view uniquely, rather than objections that apply equally to moralism. For this reason, I take for granted both that autonomism is false and that there is some workable distinction between the aesthetic and the ethical, though I will not attempt to spell out what this distinction amounts to and will proceed as if it is at least reasonably intuitive.[3] I will also help myself to the

---

[3] For a discussion of different approaches to distinguishing ethics from aesthetics, see Song, this volume.

assumption that artworks can be bearers of moral value. That is, I will suppose that it is at least sometimes intelligible and apt to speak of "the moral value of an artwork"—to say that *Manhattan*, not its director, is lecherous, or that *Madame Bovary,* not its author, is morally good. What I (and other aestheticists) have in mind when we make claims like these is not that the artworks can have harmful or salutary effects, nor that artworks can be produced under morally good or bad conditions, though of course both an artwork's composition and its consequences can be evaluated in moral terms. Rather, the idea is that the artwork's internal commitments are morally evaluable in some way. I take it that this kind of talk, a staple of everyday critical discourse, is familiar enough to make some basic sense. After all, articles attributing moral value or disvalue to art itself regularly appear in publications like the *New York Times*, where Cristopher Buckley has deemed the novel *Less* "humane," (Buckley 2017) and *Marie Claire*, where Kayleigh Roberts has examined "movies that were dragged for sexism" (Roberts 2017). Though I will gesture at accounts of the moral value of artworks in what follows, an argument for any particular approach is beyond the scope of this chapter.[4] Hopefully, however, the cases I explore in the latter third of the first section will give skeptics more of a concrete idea of what it might mean to say that an artwork is morally good or bad.

What Is Aestheticism?

Like moralism, aestheticism admits of different formulations. Some aestheticists maintain that formal relations, such as implication-relations, obtain between moral and aesthetic evaluations; others hold that metaphysical relations, such as grounding-relations, obtain between moral and aesthetic values, properties, or concepts. I class members of the former camp as defenders of *weak aestheticism* and members of the latter camp as defenders of *strong aestheticism*. Call the question of the relation in which the moral and aesthetic stand to one another *the relation question*. Different answers to the relation question, along with additional considerations, yield different answers to *the relata question*, which asks after the nature of the entities that stand in the relation.

Weak Aestheticism

According to *weak aestheticism*, some aesthetic evaluations imply moral evaluations. A weak aestheticist might hold, for instance, that an evaluation of a portrait as vivid implies an evaluation of it as empathetic. Weak aestheticists take their cue, to some extent, from the preeminent moralists, who also tend to speak in terms of evaluation. For

---

[4] For discussion of the moral value of specific artforms, such as paintings and films, see various chapters in Part III of this volume.

instance, Noël Caroll, a seminal moralist, defends "moderate moralism," the view that "sometimes the moral defects and/or merits of a work may figure in the aesthetic *evaluation* of the work" (Carroll 1996, 236, emphases mine).

Weak aestheticism is perfectly compatible with the corresponding iteration of moralism: it may be that some aesthetic evaluations imply moral evaluations *and* that some moral evaluations imply aesthetic evaluations.[5] Perhaps an aesthetic evaluation of one portrait as vivid implies a moral evaluation of it as empathetic, while a moral evaluation of another portrait as voyeuristic implies an aesthetic evaluation of it as lurid. Indeed, weak aestheticism, as formulated, is even consistent with a picture on which aesthetic and moral evaluations relate bi-conditionally, implying each other. Still, few have argued for aestheticism with a bi-conditional structure, and in any case, the aestheticist part of such a structure would concern only one half of the bi-conditional: the half in which an aesthetic evaluation implies a moral one.

The weak aestheticist answers the relation question by maintaining that the relevant relation is one of *implication*, and she answers the relata question by maintaining that the relevant relata are moral and aesthetic *evaluations*. But how, exactly, we are to parse weak aestheticism hinges on the knotty question of what aesthetic evaluations (and, for that matter, moral evaluations) amount to. On some pictures, an aesthetic evaluation consists in an evaluator's attitude; on competing pictures, an aesthetic evaluation consists in the object of an evaluator's attitude. If aesthetic evaluations are indeed attitudes, there is a further question of which attitudes they are. They might be beliefs about aesthetic value (perhaps beliefs characteristically accompanied by experiences or emotions), such that to evaluate *Madame Bovary* as beautiful is to believe that it is beautiful; or, alternatively, they might be special sorts of experiences or emotions, such that to evaluate *Madame Bovary* as beautiful is to take a particular kind of pleasure in it, or to respond to it with a special brand of appreciation.[6] On the other hand, if aesthetic evaluations are objects of attitudes, then they might consist in propositions, such as the proposition that *Madame Bovary* is beautiful, or they might consist in something nonpropositional, such as a perception of *Madame Bovary* as beautiful. We are left with four possibilities as to what aesthetic evaluations might be: beliefs, emotions or attitudes, propositions, or nonpropositional contents of some kind.

Canonically, implication is a relation between propositions. If aesthetic evaluations (and moral evaluations) turn out to be propositions, then weak aestheticism is straightforward: it is the view that some aesthetic propositions imply moral propositions. If,

---

[5] See also the discussion of contextualism in Jacobson, this volume.

[6] Related debates in aesthetics tend to center not on "aesthetic evaluation" but on "aesthetic judgment," but I take discussions of the latter to apply, *mutatis mutandis*, to discussions of the former. For a defense of the notion that aesthetic judgment (or evaluation) is a matter of believing a proposition about aesthetic value, see Nguyen (2017); for a defense of the notion that an aesthetic judgment (or evaluation) is a matter of appreciation, see Gorodeisky and Marcus (2018); for a defense of aesthetic sentimentalism, the view that an aesthetic judgment (or evaluation) is a question of emotional response, see Schellekens (2017).

however, aesthetic evaluations turn out to be either sort of attitude, or if they turn out to be nonpropositional, weak aestheticism may become more complicated.[7] Still, even if aesthetic evaluations are attitudes or nonpropositional contents and do not imply moral evaluations per se, they could still *rationally commit* those who make them to certain moral evaluations, such that forming the belief that *Madame Bovary* is beautiful rationally commits me to forming the belief that it is morally good. The upshot is that even the weak aestheticist who regards aesthetic evaluation as attitudinal or nonpropositional can nonetheless hold that aesthetic evaluation is always (or ought always to be) accompanied by moral evaluation. Whether or not such a relation is, strictly speaking, a species of implication, or is merely something adjacent, does not strike me as terribly important.

Weak aestheticism is a view about how the moral and the aesthetic relate to one another, not a view about *why* aesthetic evaluations imply moral ones. As stated, the view is consistent with many explanations. It could turn out that there is no direct connection between the aesthetic and the moral, but that certain aesthetic properties are always accompanied by certain descriptive properties that in turn always yield certain moral properties. Still, if it turned out that moral properties sometimes *depended on* aesthetic properties, the weak aestheticist would find herself in a comfortable position. After all, if some aesthetic properties give rise to moral properties, then it is obvious that the corresponding aesthetic evaluations imply the corresponding moral ones.[8]

Strong Aestheticism

It is therefore unsurprising that many weak aestheticists suppose that there is a relation of *metaphysical dependence* between the aesthetic and the moral. In other words, weak aestheticism is often accompanied by hints of *strong aestheticism*, the view that ethical value sometimes depends on aesthetic value. Like weak aestheticism, strong aestheticism is compatible with its moralist analog: in some cases, aesthetic value may depend on ethical value, and in others, ethical value may depend on aesthetic value.

How we fill in the details of the strong aestheticist picture hinges on how we answer several further questions. For one thing, it hinges on how we answer the relation question—on which sort of dependence-relation we take to yoke the aesthetic to the ethical. To say that A stands in a relation of metaphysical dependence to B is to say that

[7] We could keep it simple by maintaining that the propositions that stand in an implication-relation are propositions about holding beliefs: < Becca believes that Madame Bovary is beautiful> might imply that <Becca believes that *Madame Bovary* is morally good>. But this picture is so implausible as to make for an unsatisfactory solution.

[8] At least if we assume that the aesthetic properties in question necessitate the moral properties, and that necessitation is sufficient for implication. If these assumptions are denied, then there could be strong aestheticism without weak aestheticism, for it would be possible to think that moral value depends on aesthetic value but that corresponding aesthetic evaluations do not imply corresponding moral evaluations.

B is the source of A. For instance, my conscious experience depends on my brain (although, as we shall see shortly, someone else's conscious experience could depend on something else), and a particular statue depends on the specific hunk of stone from which it is carved (although another statue could depend on a different hunk of stone). The chemical composition of my brain is what affords my sensations the phenomenological flavor they have, just as the slab of marble from which Auguste Rodin's *The Kiss* is carved is what makes the sculpture as it is.

Contemporary metaphysicians have the benefit of working with a large repertoire of dependence-relations. *Grounding* and *constitution* are just some of the many options at their disposal, but a quick comparison of the two will suffice to illustrate some of the different forms that strong aestheticism could take. To say that one thing *grounds* another is to say that the latter obtains in virtue of the former, whereas to say that one thing *constitutes* another is to say that the former makes up the latter. We might think that the brain *grounds* consciousness: the brain is not itself consciousness, nor is it the material from which consciousness is made, but it gives rise to (and, in some sense, explains) consciousness. In contrast, we might think that a piece of marble *constitutes* a sculpture: the marble is conceptually separable from the sculpture, but it is the material of which the sculpture is composed. Moreover, different dependence relations admit of different relata. Only entities, like marble and statues, can enter into constitution-relations, for only an entity can serve as the material for another entity. In contrast, many philosophers believe that grounding-relations can obtain not only between entities but also between facts. For instance, we might think that the fact that setting cats on fire causes them pain grounds the fact that it is morally wrong to set cats on fire. Metaphysical dependence-relations of all kinds, however, share several formal features. They are all asymmetrical, which is to say that if A depends on B, then B does not depend on A. At least for our purposes, they are also all irreflexive, which is to say that a thing cannot depend on itself.[9] Finally, metaphysical dependence of all sorts can be partial. One quadrant of a hunk of stone partially constitutes the statue but does not constitute the whole of it; one neuron is a partial ground of consciousness but is not enough to independently instantiate experience without the other portions of the brain.

Accordingly, there are many possible versions of strong aestheticism—some on which the aesthetic grounds or partially grounds the moral, some on which the aesthetic constitutes or partially constitutes the moral, and some on which the moral depends on the aesthetic in some other way. A strong aestheticist could hold that moral values or properties sometimes depend on aesthetic values or properties, or she could hold that facts about moral value depend on facts about aesthetic value. What unites these views—what makes them all versions of strong aestheticism, rather than versions of

---

[9] There are practically no philosophical theses that *someone* has not taken the trouble to dispute, and while many metaphysicians assume that metaphysical dependence is irreflexive, there are a few dissenters: e.g., Jenkins (2011). Still, aestheticists and moralists alike are interested in the relation between two different things, the aesthetic and the moral, so it is safe to say that the brands of dependence to which they appeal are irreflexive.

something else—is that all of them have it that the aesthetic is sometimes the source of the moral. That is, for strong aestheticists of all sorts, the aesthetic and the moral do not merely happen to covary: rather, there is a robust connection between the two domains.

Of course, most aestheticists also hold that moral properties are *multiply realizable* (or, more aptly, multiply groundable or multiply constitutable), which is to say that moral properties sometimes obtain in virtue of aesthetic properties and sometimes obtain in virtue of something else. Analogous claims are often made in philosophy of mind. According to many philosophers of consciousness, experience is sometimes instantiated by the brain, but it could also be instantiated by something else, for instance a robot or a mind that takes an unfamiliar, nonbrain form. A given instance of consciousness, for example mine, would blink out if the brain on which it depends were destroyed, God forbid. But another instance of consciousness, for example an alien's or a ghost's, might depend on some other structure. Similarly, an aestheticist could hold that *Madame Bovary* is morally good because it is aesthetically good but that setting a cat on fire is morally bad not for aesthetic reasons but simply because cats suffer when they are on fire. Even strong aestheticists needn't defend the implausible view that *all* moral values depend on aesthetic values (or, if they prefer fact-talk, that *all* moral facts obtain in virtue of aesthetic facts).

Strong aestheticists can also offer a range of answers to the relata questioning, defending an assortment of views about what, exactly, stands in the relevant dependence-relation. We have already seen that aestheticists can take metaphysical dependence-relations to obtain between either facts or entities. But even those who take aestheticism to target a relation between entities can differ about the entities in question. Famously, Bernard Williams distinguishes between *thin* moral properties, such as goodness, and *thick* moral properties, such as courage (1985). Thin properties are wholly normative: to describe an act as "good" is to make a claim about its moral valence but no descriptive claims about what it is like. In contrast, thick properties wed the normative and the descriptive: to call an act "courageous" is to gesture both at its moral valence and at its properties. We might make the same sort of distinction in aesthetics, as Roman Bonzon has (2009). Thin aesthetic properties include beauty and ugliness; thick aesthetic properties include grace, garishness, and magniloquence. Thus, aestheticism might pick out a relation of dependence between thick properties or between thin properties. Maybe *Madame Bovary*'s goodness depends on its beauty (thin-on-thin dependence), but maybe its generosity depends on its lyricism (thick-on-thick dependence).

Motivations for Aestheticism: Two Cases

What makes aestheticism appealing? Why should you think that it is true? In the following section, I will survey some of the considerations that have in fact swayed the view's defenders; here, however, I will content myself with glossing two cases that support it.

The first is that of *Madame Bovary*. Flaubert's 1856 novel caused a sensation when it was published: it defies the norms of nineteenth-century France in depicting the trials and travails of an adulterous woman with precision and beauty. Emma Bovary finds herself in unbearably stifling circumstances. The wife of a provincial doctor, she is unable to pursue a career or even to engage in any compelling pursuits outside her home. She is left to sit around, awaiting her husband. For much of her youth, her reading diet consisted of romance novels that promised her excitement and diversion. But her husband is deflatingly frivolous, and the dullness of her adult life is an acute disappointment. It is unsurprising that she turns to a series of extramarital affairs for fulfillment, then ends by killing herself. When she realizes that she would prefer a son over a daughter, Emma thinks,

> a man, at least, is free; he can explore each passion and every kingdom, conquer obstacles, feast upon the most exotic pleasures. But a woman is continually thwarted. Both inert and yielding, against her are ranged the weakness of the flesh and the inequity of the law. Her will, like the veil strung to her bonnet, flutters in every breeze; always there is the desire urging, always the convention restraining. (Flaubert 1992, 82)

Madame Bovary is a book that confers dignity upon its protagonist *because* of its tastefulness—its lyricism, its richly detailed descriptions, and its resistance to bombast. A novel with a similar plot but a sensationalist savor would not express respect toward women suffocated by their oppressive circumstances; instead, its vulgarity would render it exploitative, and it would only serve to cheapen the suffering it depicts.

Another case is that of heterosexual pornography, often charged, in my view rightly, with sexism. (See Eaton, this volume) It is not pornography's graphic content that makes it objectifying or obscene; after all, plenty of works of erotic art are at least as explicit, among them the gorgeous novels of D. H. Lawrence. Lawrence's prose is so luscious and rapturous that it conveys something more than respect for the characters whose ecstasies it describes. He writes, for instance, of Lady Chatterly in *Lady Chatterely's Lover*, "there awoke in her new strange thrills rippling inside her. Rippling, rippling, rippling, like a flapping overlapping of soft flames, soft as feathers, running to points of brilliance, exquisite and melting her all molten inside. It was like bells rippling up and up to a culmination" (Lawrence 1994, 133). The passage conveys not just respect but rapture and awe precisely because it is so exquisitely rendered. Pornography, in contrast, is devoid of lyricism, and it is objectifying because it is lurid and salacious.

AESTHETICISM IN THE WILD

As I have already had several occasions to note, there is great heterogeneity among aestheticists. In the previous section I explored different versions of the view with reference to two questions: the question of the exact relation between the ethical and the aesthetic (the relation question), and the question of the nature of the relata (the relata question). Here, I survey views in the wild—views that have been advanced by actual contemporary philosophers—with reference to the *object question*, which asks which sorts of objects are taken to display an aestheticist structure. While some philosophers focus on art, often on specific kinds of art, others regard aestheticism as a thesis about aesthetic and moral value as they manifest in a wider range of contexts. First, however, I take a brief detour so as to gesture at some of the view's historical antecedents.

Aestheticism about Art

Arguably, versions of aestheticism have been advanced both by figures throughout the history of philosophy and by those in distinct traditions, for instance by novelists and critics. Confusingly, however, some of the figures and traditions designated as "aestheticist" are not aestheticist in the sense at hand. For instance, Nietzsche has been called an aestheticist by both Alexander Nehamas and Sebastian Gardner. The former holds that the German maverick approaches life as he would a literary text; the latter holds that in the philosopher's work, "art and the aesthetic" play "a necessary, internal, privileged role in the task of philosophy" (Gardner 2013, 600). Nietzsche's commitment to these brands of aestheticism is disputed by other Nietzsche scholars (Leiter 1992), but even if we were to accept Nehamas or Gardner's accounts, it remains an open question whether we should understand Nietzsche as an aestheticist in my sense—that is, whether we should understand him as thinking that moral value depends on aesthetic value. Even if Nietzsche believed that we should approach the world as we approach literature, he might not think that the moral value of literature depends on its aesthetic value; and even if Nietzsche believed, as Gardner argues, that "in the final instance justification can *only* be aesthetic," he might not think that moral value depends on aesthetic value, for he might think moral value reduces to aesthetic value, or that moral value does not exist at all (Gardner 2013, 600).

Gardner has also used the term "aestheticism" in connection with a particular Continental tradition, one he sees as beginning with the Romantics and resurfacing in the work of thinkers like Martin Heidegger. "Aestheticism," on this definition, is the view that "art and affect are not merely central topics of philosophy, but must be included among the very *grounds* of philosophical thought" (Gardner 2007, 81). Defenders of this view, fascinating as it is, are not necessarily aestheticists in my sense, either. Even if the aesthetic perspective enriches or enables philosophical rationality, it is not clear that aesthetic *value* does so, such that aesthetic value gives rise to moral value in particular.

There are readings, however, on which Nietzsche and Heidegger are aestheticists in my sense. Neither thinker puts much stock in ethical value as it is traditionally understood, but both can be read as regarding self-authentication as a moral imperative, and, further, as regarding aesthetic value as a ground of and means to self-authentication. Similarly, it is possible to read some of the Romantics, such as Friedrich Schiller, as the sort of aestheticists that concern me, for many of them can be understood as claiming that aesthetic sensibility and even aesthetic value are necessary components of the good life.

Just as there are figures in the history of philosophy whom we might conscript as aestheticist, there are figures in the history of literature on whom we might drape the mantle. In "Everybody's Protest Novel," James Baldwin maintains that *Uncle Tom's Cabin* is morally bad because it is aesthetically bad: its crudeness renders it self-congratulatory (Baldwin 1998, 11–19). Henry James often proposes that characters who act "beautifully" thereby act morally—that aesthetic merit, in persons, is a source of moral merit (James 1987, 69). Unfortunately, however, a fuller discussion of aestheticism in the work of these thinkers and authors would require a great deal of interpretive work that is beyond the scope of this chapter.

Aestheticism about Art

To date, I am the only contemporary analytic philosopher to use the word "aestheticist," in the sense in which the term is employed in this chapter, to describe my view (Rothfeld, 2022). My view is that aesthetic values partially ground moral values at least sometimes. The view is a species of strong aestheticism, and I defend it by appealing to two cases, one in which aesthetic value is a partial ground of moral value and one in which aesthetic disvalue is a partial ground of moral disvalue. Both cases center on artworks. One concerns *Madame Bovary,* discussed at some length earlier: by my lights, Flaubert's masterpiece is respectful toward women by dint, in part, of its lyrical treatment of its protagonist's plight. The other case is that of *Grand Budapest Hotel,* Wes Anderson's cutesy 2014 movie. The film's palate is pink, and each shot is highly stylized. Its sets are as ornate as dollhouses, and it features quaint costumes that have a confectionary quality. The film's overall affect, in sum, is twee. Yet *Grand Budapest Hotel* is about the advent of World War II and thus indirectly about the Holocaust. Its cloying romanticization of prewar Europe papers over the virulent anti-Semitism and noxious nationalism that in fact prevailed in the lost world it glorifies. Hence the proviso that aesthetic value (or, in this instance, aesthetic disvalue) is merely a partial ground of moral value (or, in this instance, moral disvalue): *Grand Budapest Hotel* is disrespectful because it is precious *and* because it is about the Holocaust. Its callousness, I maintain, is jointly grounded in its subject matter and its aesthetic failings. More generally, then, I maintain that aestheticism is structured like this:

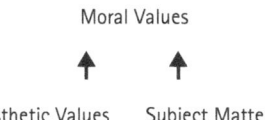

Moral Values

Aesthetic Values   Subject Matter

This formulation, of course, makes no mention of artworks in particular. The omission is intentional: in principle, I am not committed to the idea that aestheticism manifests only in art. Still, the cases I treat concern art, and the structure that emerges from my analysis seems if not specific to art, then at least applicable primarily to it. After all, I maintain that (certain) artworks are able to bear moral value—and thus able to display an aestheticist structure—because they are capable of expressing morally evaluable attitudes or emotions: on my account, *Madame Bovary* is morally good in that it evinces respect toward women, and *Grand Budapest Hotel* is morally bad in that it evinces callousness toward the Holocaust. Of course, not all artworks express attitudes or emotions about subject matter, and artworks are not the only things that do; still, art is the paradigm case.

Maria José Alcaraz León has defended a similar version of aestheticism, though she does not use the term. Her central claim is nonetheless recognizably aestheticist: she argues that "aesthetic properties or merits play a significant role in explaining moral or cognitive value" (León 2018, 21). Cognitive value is not part of the aestheticist thesis, but the rest of León's view is aestheticist in spirit. Some aspects of her position remain to be clarified. For one thing, it is not obvious how she answers the relation question. Sometimes she writes of aesthetic properties or merits *explaining* moral value, but sometimes she opts instead for talk of how "aesthetic properties substantially *contribute* to other values" (2018, 21, emphasis mine). It is not clear that contribution and explanation are different: both words might pick out something like the grounding-relation, which is often described in terms of explanation. But it is not obvious that they are the same: "contribution" might refer to a relation of determination, such that aesthetic merits inform moral merits in much the way that the application of a filter informs (but does not ground) the quality of a photograph.

Nor is it clear how León answers the relata question, for she switches between talk of "aesthetic properties" and talk of "aesthetic merits." She is cognizant of this ambiguity, which she has retained on purpose. Although she concedes that there are important differences between "aesthetic properties, values, or merits," she chooses to "address the problem without entering into these distinctions." For her, "the main issue . . . is whether an object's aesthetic aspects can have a role in explaining other non-aesthetic features" (León 2018, 22). Only some of her examples involve aesthetic *values* specifically, and only some of her examples involve the relation between aesthetic and *ethical,* rather than cognitive, values. Thus, only some of her examples support a strictly aestheticist picture.

What is clear, however, is that León is a strong aestheticist of some kind: contribution, explanation, and constitution are all forms of metaphysical dependence, however "contribution" is parsed. It is also clear that her account centers on artworks (although as we shall see, she also takes it to extend to a wider class of objects): her argumentative strategy is to flesh out some cases, by far the most persuasive of which involve art. For instance, she argues that the moral value of the still-lifes of Jean-Baptiste-Siméon Chardin—their propensity to elicit respectful attention—depends on their aesthetic value—on their dynamic mode of depiction.

By León's own admission, she does not aspire to offer a wholly systematic account of how the moral relates to the aesthetic (2018, 25). Still, she has commitments when it comes to the nature of moral and aesthetic value, and these commitments in turn yield an account of how aestheticism might come about. She understands aesthetic merits and demerits in terms of their "affective character," which is to say, in terms of the emotions they prescribe or merit (2018, 21). And for her, as for me, an artwork counts as morally valuable or disvaluable in virtue of "the attitudes that the artwork embodies, or expresses, toward the content presented" (2018, 27). Because she believes that the attitudes an artwork embodies or expresses are a question of the affective responses it prescribes, the moral depends on the aesthetic: aesthetic properties contribute to moral properties by determining an artwork's "expressive content" (2018, 27). Though León is explicit that aestheticism could function differently in different contexts, this is the only account of its workings she offers. In the end, her view targets things that express attitudes—and, further, things constituted such that their attitudes are a function of the responses they prescribe. As we shall see, perhaps artworks are not the only things that satisfy these two conditions. Nonetheless, artworks certainly make up the bulk of the things in this class.

An aestheticist (or perhaps proto-aestheticist) who restricts his view even further is Dominic Lopes, whose discussion is limited not only to pictures but to representational pictures. Like León, Lopes is interested in how the aesthetic interacts with both the moral and the cognitive. His view is that "aesthetic evaluations of pictures, while distinct from cognitive and moral evaluations, *sometimes imply* or are sometimes implied by non-aesthetic evaluations of those pictures" (Lopes 2004, 5, emphasis mine). Lopes's answer to the relation question is that of the weak aestheticist: he takes the aesthetic and the moral to relate to one another by way of implication. His answer to the relata question is that moral and aesthetic evaluation are at issue. Be all this as it may, his primary focus is still on implication-relations that flow in the familiar moralist direction. The major example he explores, that of pictures catering to the so-called male gaze, is more standardly moralist: on his account, the "moral condemnation of the male gaze in a picture implies aesthetic condemnation" of the picture, not the reverse (Lopes 2004, 186).

Another aestheticist who limits his discussion to specific kinds of artworks is Roman Bonzon. On Bonzon's view, "the value of a literary work for moral reflection depends entirely upon its value as a work of art" (Bonzon 2003, 167). He goes on to argue that in some works of fiction, "experiential moral content" is "made available through—and only through—an aesthetic experience" (2003, 170). In Henry James's *Portrait of a Lady*, for instance, it is "the aesthetic experience that affords us the moral insight" (Bonzon 2003, 170). "Experiential moral content" is something like moral know-how. Thus, the claim is that a work of fiction is disposed to teach moral lessons of a certain kind just in case it is aesthetically rich. Bonzon's central thesis is, at least arguably, not wholly aestheticist, for it is a thesis about how epistemic or cognitive value can depend on aesthetic value: Bonzon's account has it that literary fiction is sometimes ethically elucidating in virtue of being aesthetically valuable, but his account does not have it that fiction is ethically *valuable* in virtue of being aesthetically valuable. Now, it may be that ethically elucidating fictions are in turn ethically valuable. (Indeed, this claim strikes me as plausible.) If so, then they are ethically valuable in virtue of being ethically elucidating, and ethically elucidating in virtue of being aesthetically valuable—and if the in-virtue-of relation is transitive, then Bonzon's account qualifies, nominally, as aestheticist. After all, there is a sense in which a fiction can be said to be ethically valuable *because* it is aesthetically valuable. But this picture does not capture the spirit of the view, for a fiction's aesthetic value alone will not explain its ethical value without an intervening appeal to epistemic value.

Bonzon is inspired by—although he departs from—Martha Nussbaum, who can also be fruitfully read as a proto-aestheticist. On Nussbaum's view, certain works of fiction are morally elucidating. This is because some kinds of moral knowledge involve more than an "intellectual grasp of propositions": moral knowledge of this sort involves "perception," "seeing a complex, concrete reality in a highly lucid and richly responsive way" (Nussbaum 1992, 152). She illustrates this thought via appeal to Henry James's *Golden Bowl,* in which a character performs an act of sacrifice in renouncing his daughter so that she can lead an independent life with her husband. A sacrifice, for Nussbaum, "*is* an act of imaginative interpretation" (1992, 152): the character makes a sacrifice, rather than some other thing, because he pictures his daughter as a glorious sea creature floating away; a different mental picture would have transformed his sacrifice into some other act, for renunciation unaccompanied by the right sorts of mental images (and perhaps also by the right sentiments) would not qualify as such. Fiction therefore coaxes us to moral achievement because it elicits certain sorts of mental images by dint of its aesthetic qualities. Now, none of this is to say that the images in question are only effective if they are aesthetically valuable, though it is to say that the moral character (and thus the moral value) of an action depends upon its aesthetic qualities. The crucial question for Nussbaum is whether it is the content of our mental images that confers moral value, or whether their aesthetic value plays a role. Nussbaum sometimes seems to suggest that their value is relevant. The father's imaginings of his daughter would not betoken *sacrifice* were they less resplendent: "It is relevant that his image was not a flat thing but a fine work of art" (Nussbaum 1992, 152).

Aestheticism about More Than Art

Is aestheticism only a view about artworks? Both León and I suggest that aestheticism may apply to more than art, but neither of us marshals any decisive arguments for this conclusion. Although León claims that the aesthetic properties of a person's actions can influence our moral evaluations thereof, it is not clear that the aesthetic *contributes* to the moral in such cases. To illustrate her point, she asks us to consider two people who perform a morally praiseworthy action, one of whom does so in a "dry and mechanical" fashion and one of whom does so with delicacy. She concludes that "the aesthetic character with which the agent performs the action can improve an action's overall value" (León 2018, 23). It may be that we should prefer the delicate action to the mechanical one, but it may be that the two actions are morally equivalent and we have aesthetic reason to prefer the former, or that we take the aesthetic properties of the action as evidence of morally relevant facts that in turn bear on our moral evaluations.

Marcia Eaton offers a more promising account of an extra-artistic aestheticism (though she ultimately rejects it). Her aim is to investigate a claim that the poet Joseph

Brodsky made in his Nobel address. "On the whole," he remarked, "every new aesthetic reality makes man's ethical reality more precise. For aesthetics is the mother of ethics." The question, as Eaton has it, is whether the "aesthetic is in some sense *prior* to the ethical": (Eaton 1997, 356) she takes herself to be asking after "a strong sense in which the ethical comes into existence only when an aesthetic system is already established" (1997, 357).

Though Eaton's account seems like a strain of strong aestheticism—after all, she asks whether the ethical "*comes into existence* only when an aesthetic system is already established" (1997, 357, emphasis mine)‾it is unclear exactly what relation Brodsky, on her reading, takes to obtain between them, or what exactly the relata are. Does ethical value, in general, depend on aesthetic value, in general? Or does the ethical, whatever that consists in, depend on the aesthetic, whatever that consists in? And if the ethical depends on the aesthetic—if there is some conceptual connection between the two domains, for instance—does this imply that ethical value depends on moral value?

Eaton, who ultimately rejects Brodsky's aestheticism, does not answer these questions, but she does precisify matters in the course of asking whether various thinkers can be read as aestheticists. Though she concludes that many fall short of embracing the stronger thesis she attributes to Brodsky, her survey yields two sorts of pictures in which "priority is given to the aesthetic over the ethical" (Eaton 1997, 361). Both fail to establish the priority of the aesthetic, in general, over that of the ethical, in general, for both speak to the priority of the aesthetic in circumscribed domains. Importantly for our purposes, however, neither focuses on art.

The first has it that, "in making a moral decision, one first chooses style and then content" (Eaton 1997, 357). Eaton locates this view in the writings of Charles Peirce, who once wrote that "ethics rests . . . on a foundation of esthetics" [*sic*] (1997, 357). He takes ethics to "rest on" aesthetics "because answering the question 'What conduct will achieve certain ends?' requires answering the question 'What are or should our ends be?' And this last question can only be answered in terms of intrinsic desirability—an aesthetic matter, he thinks" (1997, 357–358). This view is highly implausible. Pierce's conceptions of both the moral and the aesthetic are, if not wrong-headed, then at least controversial: the question of what ends we should value strikes me as at least in part a moral one, and the ethical strikes me as involving more than answers to the question of what conduct will bring about certain ends. Eaton rejects the view not for these reasons but rather because it assumes a Kantian conception of aesthetic value as autonomous. "The priority Peirce gives to aesthetics depends upon his separating off the feeling from the object of the feeling," she writes. "Ultimately then, Peirce gives priority to the aesthetic only by separating the aesthetic completely from the ethical" (Eaton 1997, 358).

The second strain of aestheticism that Eaton explores has it that "one who fails to engage in aesthetic activity will not be a moral person," or, in a weaker incarnation, that "people who engage in aesthetic activity are more likely to be moral people" (1997, 359). Glimmers of these sorts of views are to be found in the work of Foucault, who suggests that the formation of the self is a function of the style one adopts, and in the writings of several analytic philosophers, who suggest "that art plays a crucial role in developing moral lives" (1997, 359). It is not wholly clear, however, that these accounts are aestheticist. Claims of this species are sometimes about conceptual links, but they are sometimes about causal connections. Some of the thinkers Eaton surveys, for instance, advance the claim that artworks make their audiences more moral—a claim that seems distinct from the notions of conceptual or metaphysical connection. In the end, Eaton abandons aestheticism altogether, concluding that Brodsky's position, as she interprets it, is untenable (1997, 361). Perhaps future aestheticists will take up the challenge implicit in her account, developing and defending the versions of aestheticism at which she gestures so tantalizingly.

Conclusion

Whether or not you find aestheticism plausible will hinge on your background views. If you are compelled by the popular challenges to moralism, you likely will remain unpersuaded of aestheticism: if the aesthetic is hermetically sealed from the moral, then moral value cannot depend on aesthetic value; and if artworks cannot be bearers of moral value at all, then many of the cases that lend aestheticism its plausibility are undercut. Moreover, if you are strongly committed to a moral theory in which aesthetic properties do not appear, you may find it hard to swallow aestheticism. For instance, if you are an act-utilitarian, then you will think moral goodness is just a matter of maximizing utility. (See Woodcock, this volume) How, then, could aesthetic properties ever be among the grounds of moral properties?

Still, for many, aestheticism is an exciting newcomer to the scene. Debates about moralism and autonomism have been ongoing for decades, but comparatively few philosophers have considered the many ways that the moral may depend on the aesthetic. Whether aesthetic evaluations imply moral evaluations or moral values depend on aesthetic values—and whether aestheticism is a view about artworks or about persons—there is fecund ground for future cultivation.

See also: Carroll, Stear, Jacobson, Song, Matthes, this volume

References

Anderson, Wes, dir. 2014. *Grand Budapest Hotel*. Century City, CA: Fox Searchlight, 2014. DVD.
Baldwin, James. 1998. "Everybody's Protest Novel." In *Baldwin: Collected Essays*, edited by Toni Morrison, 11–19. New York: Library of America.
Bonzon, Roman. 2003. "Fiction and Value." In *Imagination, Philosophy, and the Arts*, edited by Matthew Kieran and Dominic McIver Lopes, 160–176. New York: Routledge.
Buckley, Chris. 2017. "June's Bookclub Pick: 'Less' by Andrew Sean Greer." *New York Times*, July 2017. https://www.nytimes.com/2017/07/24/books/review/less-andrew-sean-greer.html
Carroll, Noel. 1996. "Moderate Moralism." *British Journal of Aesthetics* 36, no. 3: 223–238.
Dederer, Claire. 2017. "What Do We Do with the Art of Monstrous Men?" *Paris Review*, November 2017. https://www.theparisreview.org/blog/2017/11/20/art-monstrous-men/

Eaton, Marcia. 1997. "Aesthetics: The Mother of Ethics?" *Journal of Aesthetics and Art Criticism* 55, no. 4: 355–364.

Flaubert, Gustave. 1992. *Madame Bovary*. Translated by Geoffrey Wall. New York: Penguin Books.

Gardner, Sebastian. 2013. "Nietzsche's Philosophical Aestheticism." In *The Oxford Handbook of Nietzsche*, edited by John Richardson and Ken Gemes, 599–629. Oxford: Oxford University Press.

Gardner, Sebastian. 2007. "Philosophical Aestheticism." In *The Oxford Handbook of Continental Philosophy*, edited by Michael Rosen and Brian Leiter, 75–122. Oxford: Oxford University Press.

Gorodeisky, Keren, and Eric Marcus. 2018. "Aesthetic Rationality." *Journal of Philosophy* 115, no. 3: 113–140.

James, Henry. 1987. *The Golden Bowl*. New York: Penguin Classics.

Jenkins, C. S. 2011. "Is Metaphysical Dependence Irreflexive?" *The Monist* 94, no. 2: 267–276.

Lawrence, D. H. 1994. *Lady Chatterley's Lover*. New York: Penguin.

Leiter, Brian. 1992. "Nietzsche and Aestheticism." *Journal of the History of Philosophy* 30, no. 275: 275–290.

León, Maria José Alcaraz. 2018. "Aesthetics Makes Nothing Happen? The Role of Aesthetic Properties in the Constitution of Non-Aesthetic Value." *Journal of Aesthetics and Art Criticism* 76, no. 1: 21–31.

Lopes, Dominic. 2004. *Understanding Pictures*. Oxford: Clarendon Press.

Nehamas, Alexander. 1985. *Nietzsche: Life as Literature*. Cambridge, MA: Harvard University Press.

Nguyen, C. Thi. 2017. "The Uses of Aesthetic Testimony." *British Journal of Aesthetics* 57, no. 1: 19–36.

Nussbaum, Martha. 1992. *Love's Knowledge: Essays on Philosophy and Literature*. Oxford: Oxford University Press.

Roberts, Kayleigh. 2017. "11 Movies That Were Dragged for Sexism in 2017." *Marie Claire*, November 20, 2017. https://www.marieclaire.com/celebrity/g13792399/sexism-in-movies/.

Rothfeld, Becca. 2022. "The Good, the Bad, and the Ugly." *British Journal of Aesthetics* 62, no. 4: 653–670.

Schellekens, Elisabeth. 2017. "Value Judgements and Standards of Normative Assessment." In *The Semantics of Aesthetic Judgment*, edited by James O. Young, 140–159. Oxford: Oxford University Press.

Williams, Bernard. 1985. *Ethics and the Limits of Philosophy*. Cambridge, MA: Harvard University Press.

FURTHER READING

Nannicelli, Ted. 2020. *Artistic Creation and Ethical Criticism*. Oxford: Oxford University Press.

Shim, Joy. 2022. "Literary Racial Impersonation." *Ergo* 8, no. 31: 219–245.

PART III

ETHICAL ISSUES IN INDIVIDUAL ARTS

CHAPTER 23

....

PAINTING

....

ELISABETH SCHELLEKENS

THE ETHICAL DIMENSIONS OF PAINTING

EVER since the earliest categorizations of the arts, and the emergence of painting as an artform in its own right, works of pictorial art have confronted us with ethical questions. They have spoken to us about kindness, injustice, goodness, and evil. They have illustrated cruelty, compassion, nobility, and courage. And they have been boycotted, censored, propagandized, and canceled. In ways not entirely unlike life itself, paintings have presented us with endless moral, cognitive, and emotional possibilities by provoking, shocking, bolstering, and challenging our ethical perspective on the world.

Despite occupying an eminent role in the history of moral education through art, not least in religious contexts in the Western tradition, painting might in some respects be seen as less ethically galvanizing than, say, literature or poetry.[1] One reason for this is that a depiction might be considered more static or inert than the more extensive stories or scenes offered by literary works. According to this line of thought, what we are presented with in a painting is a highly specified event, frozen in time and stagnant in space, separated both from a broader narrative and a critical commentary. Another reason might be that the visual impressions afforded by pictorial representations are thought to overwhelm us or even blind us to more cerebral involvement with the themes central to the work. Mere size, color, and shape, and possibly even the visceral effect on us of the event, person, or scene depicted, may be seen to detract from a proper exploration of the work's ethical features.

Clearly, not all paintings have a strong, or even an interesting, ethical dimension. Some works are only speculatively connected to the sphere of ethics and morality, if at all, and call for an altogether different kind of appreciative engagement. Nonetheless, where a painting is characterized by a certain set of ethical features—where there is

---

[1] For example, see Eldridge (1989), Gibson (2007), John (1998), Nussbaum (1990).

ethics in painting so to speak—any artistic appreciation isolated from this dimension seems both difficult to achieve in practice and conceptually misguided in theory. How and why, one may well ask, would one engage with Artemisia Gentileschi's *Judith Slaying Holofernes* (1612–1613) or Picasso's *Guernica* (1937) without taking the ethical element of the painting into account? What would it even mean to say that we value these two masterpieces in isolation from their moral content?

It is, of course, important to bear in mind that the way we look at paintings today tends to differ in salient respects from the way people have looked at paintings in earlier epochs, certainly in the Western tradition. The fact that most of the paintings we see and engage with now hang in museums and galleries automatically privileges our attention to their distinctly aesthetic qualities. In simple terms, museums and galleries encourage us to engage with and enjoy paintings *as* art or *as* objects of aesthetic appreciation. A piece originally intended as an object of religious devotion and moral contemplation, such as an altarpiece triptych depicting the Second Coming, for example, here becomes an *oeuvre d'art* to be admired as such. However, when paintings hang in churches or palaces, say, other aspects of the painting are foregrounded in our experience of them. A battlefield depiction detailing the heroic exploits of our noble host's great-grandfather, say, may principally direct our attention to concepts such as bravery, sacrifice and tenacity in the settings of the ancestral home. In these kinds of cases, it is likely that our awareness and relation to the putative moral content occurs more naturally. Thus, while it seems right to concede that the literary arts are nowadays more easily construed as kindling our moral attention than painting, for the larger part of the history of Western art, paintings were intended and used to tell stories by highlighting events, virtues, legends, and individuals from which the viewer could learn and, by emulation, aspiration, or meditation, guide their actions and develop their character.[2]

In this chapter, I shall defend the view that the art of painting presents us with a rich and significant range of ethical implications, and that it does so in a large variety of ways. This puts them right up there as sources for learning about moral and philosophical concepts (John 1998), human psychology (Gibson 2007), and the development of our imagination or emotional sensitivity (Robinson 1997; Currie 1998), alongside, for example, the great novels that tend to be cited in the context of moral learning through art (Currie 2020). This is not to say, of course, that every such painting will be ethically relevant or interesting in the same way or to the same extent. Nor is it necessarily the case that all the particular features of paintings which challenge us ethically will carry equal weight in our evaluative assessments, for some will be more central to the artistic character of the work than others. For this reason, it will be helpful to begin by drawing a few distinctions about the concerns we are about to address.

---

[2] For more on this point, see McNeill (2014, 34): "In 'Early Modern' painting (1500–1800 CE) . . . painting fulfilled a didactic role as public art." There are several excellent art historical studies addressing questions to do with the ethical dimensions of religious art in the Western tradition. See for example D'Elia (2005).

Let us begin our inquiry into the ethics of painting by distinguishing between two kinds of issues. First, there are concerns pertaining to the general relation between art and ethics, relevant to painting in virtue of being an important artform. Second, there are questions of an ethical nature specific to painting. Whereas the former set out to tackle issues that apply to most if not all kinds of representational art (see, for example, this collection's chapters on the interaction of moral and aesthetic value, cultural appropriation, and racism[3]), the latter aims to capture areas particular to paintings. Furthermore, and straddling this division, is another distinction between what I shall call *internal* and *external* ethical issues. By *internal* I mean to identify ethical aspects that can be found in the work itself, so to speak, or in the mere experience of it and principally relating to the work's thematic content. By *external*, in contrast, I intend to pinpoint concerns more directly connected to factors beyond the immediate experience of the work. This will include the artist's moral character or political commitments, a painting or collection's provenance, copyright or intellectual property issues, and factors to do with the social context in which the work is either made or viewed (such as when a historical work is used for current political purposes or when an entire artistic tradition is reevaluated in line with contemporary moral standards).

The main focus of this chapter will be the ethical issues *specific* and *internal* to painting. That is to say, our emphasis will not lie on philosophical queries of a general nature about art and ethics, nor issues to do with ethical features external to the work. Instead, I will be concentrating on a couple of closely related concerns which arise specifically in connection with painting: the *content* question, and the *value* question. The content question addresses *how* we find ethics in painting, or what it means to say that a painting can have moral content. On this point, I shall show that there are several ways in which a painting can represent ethical concerns. This, in turn, will lead us to the value question which targets the relation between moral content and the overall value of the artwork *qua* painting.[4] I shall defend the view that engaging with art's moral content is central to the artistic appreciation of painting, and that paintings can be sources of moral learning. Moreover, I will hold that the more complex or interesting the moral content of the painting, and the more cognitive explorative possibilities are open to us morally speaking, the more likely it is that the work will have significant artistic value. In this respect, the moral content of paintings, in their delicate interplay with the visual manifestation or expression of this content through a particular representation, ought to be seen as one of the main sources of the value of painting as an artform.[5]

---

[3] See Stear, Carroll, Jacobson, Rothfeld, Nguyen and Strohl, and Clavel-Vázquez, this volume.

[4] This investigation will lead us to reflect on the moral potential of painting by emphasizing the complexity and variety of its moral content (rather than how the presence of aesthetic qualities can add to its moral depth, see Armstrong [2003] and Gaut [2007]).

[5] Some theorists have argued that only figurative painting can be said to have moral content (for example McNeill [2014]). Although the examples I will discuss are indeed figurative, I do not wish to claim that some more abstract forms of representation cannot also be seen to have some moral content. Nonfigurative painting is often self-reflexive, but such reflection can be manifested in morally charged ways, as in many of Mark Rothko's works, for example.

THE CONTENT QUESTION

How can we find ethics in painting, or what does it mean to say that paintings can have moral content? In what follows, we will begin by discussing examples of ethically relevant works in order to get a better understanding of the various ways in which paintings can be said to have moral content. A brief survey reveals that paintings can be said to have moral content in at least a dozen ways. Although this list should not necessarily be taken as exhaustive, it is nonetheless instructive to lay out the groundwork in this way in order to better grasp the complexity and variety of the moral content of painting. As we shall see, this richness also lays the foundations for the artistic value of such paintings.

Representation of a Virtue or a Vice

Historically speaking, one of the more prominent ambitions of much European painting from antiquity until, broadly speaking, the mid-nineteenth century, was to illustrate generalized moral character traits and corresponding behavior.

In Jacques-Louis David's *Belisarius Begging for Alms* (1781), for example, we find an embodiment of the virtues of charity and mercy, as we see the once lionized Byzantine general Belisarius, now blind and reduced to begging on the street (Figure 23.1). A woman passing by ignores the protesting soldier and stops to give alms to Belisarius. The painting thus provides a clear illustration of someone who holds the virtue of charity over that of social propriety. Similarly, Rembrandt's *The Good Samaritan* (1633) represents the virtue of compassion by depicting the final scene in the parable. Exuding an extraordinary calmness, the painting depicts the moment at which the Samaritan, who has borne a wounded man from the place he was left by a band of robbers, places payment in the innkeeper's hands with instruction to care for him. Rembrandt chooses to show the orderly, almost dispassionate carrying through of the act of compassion as if to remind us that genuine kindness must outlive the passion that inspires it.

Representation of a Moral Ideal or State of Affairs

At a more abstract level perhaps, some paintings can be seen to have moral content in virtue of representing an optimal state or moral ideal. In one of the most well-known paintings of the early nineteenth century, Eugène Delacroix's *Liberty Leading the People* (1830), we see a woman holding the flag of the French revolution in the aftermath of the riots which led to the toppling of King Charles X (Figure 23.2).

FIGURE 23.1 Jacques-Louis David. *Belisarius Begging for Alms* (1781). Palais des Beaux-Arts, Lille. Image reproduced under GNU Free Documentation License.

Personifying liberty, one of the three moral ideals of the revolution, the figure leads men from different social echelons and walks of life forward to a shared future of brotherhood, equality, and political freedom. Again, in *Earthly Paradise* (1916–1920) by the French post-Impressionist Pierre Bonnard, a pastoral scene captures a man and a woman, both nude, enjoying the abundant and colorful nature around them, in a state of profound repose. The intensely peaceful scene, echoing a long tradition of bucolic motifs in Western painting but rendered in Bonnard's ecstatically intense color palette, seems to call us, reminding us that the untroubled harmony of the Garden of Eden is still within reach.

Representation of a Moral Dilemma or Problem

The Garden of Eden of course also features prominently as the site of one of the most recognizable depictions of a moral dilemma, the biblical legend of the Fall of Man, in

FIGURE 23.2 Eugène Delacroix. *Liberty Leading the People* (1830). Louvre, Paris. Image courtesy Dennis Jarvis, reproduced under Creative Commons License.

which Adam hesitates to take the forbidden fruit offered to him by Eve while the snake, embodying temptation and evil, looks on. In Cornelis van Haarlem's painting *The Fall of Man* (1592), for example, Adam and Eve are represented just at the moment when temptation, embodied by a serpent with the head of a cherub who reaches down from the tree with a second apple, overwhelms them (Figure 23.3).

Eve's gaze, as she passes the apple to her beloved, is entranced, while Adam's is more searching. Similarly, Frans Francken the Younger's allegorical painting *Mankind's Eternal Dilemma, The Choice Between Virtue and Vice* (1633) also focuses on the deciding moment. The setting represents the three regions of Heaven, Earth, and Hell, using a mixture of Christian and pagan symbolism to illustrate the myriad choices the virtuous person must make and vanities she must eschew, such as the pleasures of the table, the bed, and the field of victory, in order to avoid eternal damnation. An innocent-looking young man, surrounded by cherubs and angels, is seen to be in the throngs of difficult moral deliberation.

FIGURE 23.3 Cornelis van Haarlem. *The Fall of Man* (1592). Rijksmuseum, Amsterdam. Image US public domain .

Representation of the Resolution of a Moral Dilemma or Problem

A closely connected theme in painting is that of a moral problem which has been over-come and where the path of progress was taken. In John Trumbull's *Declaration of Independence* (1818), we find the draft of the 1776 Declaration stating the nation's inde-pendence from Britain being presented to the Second Continental Congress by Thomas Jefferson, the draft's principal author, together with his coauthors (John Adams, Benjamin

Franklin, Robert Livingston, and Roger Sherman). Turnbull represents the grim, determined faces of the congressmen all looking toward the document. Commissioned for display in the US Capitol Rotunda, the painting seeks to remind its occupants of the unifying act of overcoming and defiance on which their power rests. A comparable dignified resolve is exuded by a work by an unknown artist, housed in the State Capitol at Salt Lake City, of Seraph Young Ford, the first woman to vote in the United States in 1870 under an equal suffrage law. Though the grandeur of the Trumbull scene is absent, the sense of moment and occasion is captured in the quietly resolute faces of the female onlookers who wait, some with their husbands, others grouped on the staircase, for their turn to cast their ballots. Their activism has not been in vain and moral resolve has led to a historic victory.

Representation of a Social Moral Phenomenon

Another common way for painting to have moral content is by drawing attention to more widespread social phenomena. A good example of this is Norman Rockwell's *The Problem We All Live With* (1964). The painting depicts six-year-old Ruby Bridges, walking to school, escorted by four deputy US marshals. Racist tokens and slurs are inscribed on the wall, together with the remains of a tomato, which has just been thrown at the group. The marshals are shown only up to their shoulders as if to indicate that it is neither their authority, nor even Ruby's courage as she makes her way to her previously all-white school, that is the primary focus of the painting. Rather, it is the historical situation itself which is presented as a point of tension in need of recognition and political action. Likewise, a case of remarkable change in need of recognition can be found in the first work of Adrienne Grandpierre-Deverzey. *The Studio of Abel de Pujol* (1822) depicts the painter's husband teaching a group of women. The scene is notable for the way it depicts the seriousness with which Pujol, one of the most celebrated religious painters of his day, engages with the work of his female students and treats them as fellow artists. The paraphernalia of the studio, including a nude male torso the front of which is turned tastefully, for the occasion, toward the wall, suggests that there are still aspects of the artist's world which remain beyond the grasp of women.

Representation of an Emotional Moral Phenomenon

Unsurprisingly, human suffering has been one of the major motifs in art in all its forms, as often as not held up as something the contemplation of which will engage our moral sensibilities. Renaissance and Baroque depictions of the crucifixion increasingly emphasize blood and physical disfigurement, for example in Matthias Grünewald's *Isenheim Altarpiece* (1512–1516), which uses the physical violence of Christ's execution to prompt us to focus on his suffering as the cornerstone of Christian morality (Figure 23.4).

A contrasting depiction in Velazquez's masterpiece *Christ Crucified* (1632) achieves a similar moral aim through highlighting the dignified and serene resignation in the

FIGURE 23.4 Matthias Grünewald. *Isenheim Altarpiece* (c. 1515). Unterlinden Museum at Colmar, Alsace. Image courtesy of Joregens.mi/Wikipedia, reproduced under Creative Commons License.

posture and facial expression, as if pointing to the theological tenet that just as Christ was ready to die for our sins, so should we be willing to suffer for the good of others. A more personal approach can be found in Frida Kahlo's painting *The Wounded Deer* (1946), where the artist's face seems to dare us to return her gaze with equal intensity and take in her stag's body, in pain and pierced by numerous arrows. Interestingly, the animal's posture remains proud and healthy, suggesting that the wounds are a condition of existence for the artist, a state of suffering which, as the artist herself put in the painting's dedication, "cannot be fixed."[6]

Representation of an Everyday Scene or Event with Moral Character

Artists have, however, not always relied on exceptional events, or depictions of acute suffering, to express moral qualities. The depiction of everyday scenes, an increasingly

---

[6] From a handwritten note given by the artist together with the painting to her friends Linda and Arcady Boitler, May 1946 (The Wounded Deer by Frida Kahlo, n.d.) .

prominent feature of painting in the modern era, is often used to draw attention to the pervasiveness of political and moral concerns. Mary Cassatt's *A Woman and Girl Driving* (1881), for example, quietly asserts the normality of a woman—in this case the artist's sister—taking the reins for a drive through the park. Her passengers, an inscrutable young girl and an indistinct groom facing the rear, are entirely at ease. Similarly, in Cassatt's *Reading "Le Figaro"* (1878), the artist's mother is portrayed as an autonomous and intellectually active person engaging with the traditionally male preserve as a matter of course. The cool-headed scrutiny expressed in her attitude to her reading matter suggests a woman fully in possession of her critical faculties. Less subtly perhaps, Paula Rego's *The Maids* (1987), inspired by Jean Genet's 1947 play with the same name, depicts a latent violence as the two servant sisters tend to their employer and her daughter. The clawing branches of a tree outside the window, and the piglet scuttling across the foreground, hint at the bloody resolution to come.

Representation of a Person Expressing a Moral Attitude

Another common device in painting to represent moral themes is the depiction of subjects expressing specific attitudes, often in a way that challenges the viewer actively to identify themselves with or against that attitude. A case in point here is the famously provocative gaze of Edouard Manet's controversial *Olympia* (1863). Painted on a canvas much greater in size than traditionally used for genre-paintings of this kind, the courtesan's confident and entirely shameless stare seems designed to call the viewer's own perhaps illicit interest into question, reversing the traditional power structure implicit in depictions of female nudes. By contrast, a painting like the recent *Mare Nostrum* (2015), by the Swiss artist Miriam Cahn, depicts a group of the naked and in some cases mutilated bodies of refugee mothers and children against the background of the sea. The weakened refugees cover their genitalia as best they can, their eyes and faces smudged in embarrassment. As with Manet's *Olympia*, however, those returning the blurred gaze in the act of looking at the painting are forced to ask whose shame is really being expressed here. (See also Eaton, this volume.)

Representation of a Person Symbolizing a Specific Moral Character

Paintings excel perhaps better than any other artform in getting us to see their subjects as possessing particular character traits. In portraiture, the use of symbols, props and attributes are central to the way in which artists have succeeded in representing individuals as, say, powerful, learned, or virtuous. An interesting example is the portrait of Nelson Mandela by Cyril Coetzee. In some respects the depiction contrasts with more iconic images of Mandela by presenting him neither as gripped by inimitable good humor or as striving for justice, but rather as embodying wisdom. Seated in a high-sided armchair, at ease but with one hand raised in a gesture suggesting he is waiting for an opportunity to interject, the subject emerges as a man of good judgment and experience. Aiming to capture an altogether different kind of moral character, Marlene Dumas's portrait of Osama Bin Laden, intimately titled *Osama* (2010), depicts its subject by highlighting the fickle and unpredictable, nearly childish, side of a malevolent fanatic. Here, the Al Qaeda leader's soft look, the half-smile playing on the lips, opts out of caricature and represents a more realistic and human side of evil.

Representation of a Morally Charged Atmosphere

In many cases the moral content of a painting is best understood in terms of a mood or atmosphere. In Elizabeth Butler's *The Roll Call* (1874), we see the tired remnants of a battalion of the Grenadier Guards after the Battle of Inkerman with little or no reference to martial virtues such as valor, leadership, or strategic brilliance. Somber and cheerless, the ambience is instead one of steadfast endurance, with ordinary soldiers supporting their injured comrades, looking around in the cold dawn light in a dazed fashion to see how many of their comrades made it through against the odds. Similarly, in George Grosz's *The Funeral* (1918), the group depicted is one for whom the virtues of loyalty and fortitude have become entirely strange. Echoing the hue and composition of a medieval depiction of hell, Grosz shows a funeral procession making its way through a modern city. The mourners are presented as monstrous in their chaotic decadence, their faces scarred by the effects of alcoholism and syphilis, and the atmosphere is one of chaotic and anarchic frenzy.

Representation of a Morally Significant Place

Sometimes, the places and locations depicted in paintings have a strong moral character in their own right. This tends to be because of an event which unfolded there some time ago. Notwithstanding the tragic biographical details surrounding the artist (who was murdered by the Nazis shortly after completing the painting), Peter Kien's study of Theresienstadt, *Terezin* (1944), shows the concentration camp lit up in the pinkish hue of the evening light with the mountains rising behind. No people can be seen, and there is no obvious sign of the horrors going on there. Despite this, the dead tree rising from the courtyard, the blank windows and tangled lines succeed in revealing a space in which human design has in some way clearly transgressed the laws of nature. Luc Tuymans's more recent *Gas Chamber* (1986) shares many features with *Terezin*. Here, the muted colors and largely anonymous features—including the drain in the center of the floor and the vents in the ceiling—are displayed as neutrally as possible in order to emphasize the room's likeness to the cellar of any other modern building. Simultaneously ordinary and eerie, the painting exudes a firm sense of the wrongs committed in what now looks like an airless vacuum, the moral injustice of past events somehow impregnated in the very walls.

Representation of a Morally Charged Event Implicating the Viewer

Finally, a famous example of a painting which openly seems to implicate the viewer in the situation depicted is Rembrandt's *Susanna and the Elders* (1647) (Figure 23.5). Rembrandt's version differs markedly from previous paintings of the biblical scene from the Book of Daniel, in which Susanna is accused of committing adultery by two Hebrew elders who tried to seduce her after having spied on her bathing naked.[7]

FIGURE 23.5 Rembrandt van Rijn. *Susanna and the Elders* (1647). Monochrome print by Richard Earlom. Image reproduced under Creative Commons License.

---

[7] For a longer discussion on this point, see Gaut (2007), Eaton (2013).

In contrast to the sensuous tones of his predecessors, Rembrandt emphasizes the lecherous intent of the elders and the pained and fearful expression of Susanna, who looks directly at the viewer as if to demand that we make our intention plain. Will we side with the elders or with her? Have we come to defend her honor or take advantage of her complete vulnerability? Of course, voyeurism is itself a relatively common theme in paintings, both in the guise of intending to highlight its morally questionable nature, such as Louis Emile Adan's *Les Voyeurs* (ca. 1900), as well as those more obviously directed at titillation, such as the "What the Butler Saw" series (early twentieth century) of Hans Zatzka.

THE VALUE QUESTION

Paintings such as these, and many more like them, tend either to capture the moral themes of specific importance to their age, or to express those themes in ways suitable or intelligible to their time. In this, painting as an artform has served to shape our awareness of many different ethical concerns by inviting us to conceptualize these visual manifestations of moral ideals, dilemmas, prejudices, personality traits and more. Many of these conceptualizations have then been refined or adapted to fit in with our continually evolving ethical reflections. It is here that we find a different angle on the idea mentioned above, namely that paintings tend to be less morally rewarding because they tend to offer more particularized representations than the literary arts. The thought there had been that painting has a less privileged moral educational status in virtue of being limited to presenting *one* scene, person, or event to the viewer (as opposed to a series of such scenes, persons or events described even in a short story). Also, we saw that one may think that the strong perceptual character of pictorial representations might be assumed to divert us from moral messages requiring more intellectual kinds of involvement with the painting. But this is an overly simple view of the moral content of painting on both counts. Both descriptive and immersive, paintings such as these tend to rely heavily on symbolism, contextual, and art-historical knowledge, aesthetic sensibility, emotional association, and imagination. As a result, at least some works succeed perfectly well in epitomizing considerable narrative depth and interpretative variety in ways which do enable them to play an important role in our moral training through art. The moral and philosophical concepts we refine by engaging with Delacroix's *Liberty Leading the People,* the insight into human psychology we gain by looking at Rembrandt's *Susanna and the Elders,* and the emotional sensitivity we attune by contemplating Cahn's *Mare Nostrum* or Kahlo's *Wounded Deer* all add to our ethical perspective on the world.

In addition to the consideration outlined above that there is not merely *one* way in which painting can be said to have moral content—the moral phenomena depicted are diverse, as are their mode of articulation—three further observations can be made.

First, paintings can have more than one kind of morally relevant content along the lines sketched above. It would, for example, be unfair to think of Rembrandt's *The Good Samaritan* as presenting us merely with moral content in the way described in the section "Representation of a Virtue or a Vice," that is to say as representing the virtue of compassion, and not simultaneously also as depicting the resolution of a moral dilemma in the way characterized in the "Representation of an Everyday Scene or Event with Moral Character," in an everyday scene with a strong moral undertones. Again, Tuymans's *The Gas Chamber* represents moral content both in so far as it depicts a morally significant place ("Representation of a Person Symbolizing a Specific Moral Character") and a morally charged atmosphere ("Representation of a Morally Charged Atmosphere"). In such cases, the different moral representations can affect one another in interesting ways. The prosaic way in which the Samaritan hands over money to the inn-keeper, say, reinforces the commitment to virtue displayed by the man and, if anything, strikes us as even more far-reaching under the circumstances. Similarly, our experience of the gas chamber's moral atmosphere is profoundly affected once we come to realize the moral meaning of the place in question. In general, disentangling moral layers of this kind in our analyses of artistic experience adds depth to our moral explorations of the work and the lessons we stand to gain from it.

Second, there can be ambiguity or room for interpretation about exactly what the moral content of a work amounts to or consist of. This applies especially to works from the very end of the nineteenth century onward, when painting moved away from more didactic or doctrinal forms of moral expression toward less conclusive or explicit ones. For while there are cases where the relevant moral perspective is apparent even from a quick glance at the painting (such as with Francken the Younger's *Mankind's Eternal Dilemma*), there are others for which this is a more gradual process (such as in Grandpierre-Deverzey's *The Studio of Abel de Pujol*). And, of course, there are also works for which no matter of effort or time can lead us to establish with certainty precisely what the moral message amounts to. Representations of morally charged atmospheres, albeit more interpretatively ambivalent than the paintings discussed above, might serve as a case in point here.

Third, knowing precisely how to relate to a painting's moral content, even if it is not thematically ambiguous, is not always straightforward. Most pertinently perhaps, taking on a work's moral content can be made more difficult by other issues that are close to hand to do, for example, with the identity of the artist and their political convictions,[8] or one's own views about quite how far a work ought to be allowed to push the boundaries of our moral imagination. This point brings us back to the first section of this chapter and the distinction drawn there between internal and external ethical issues in painting. But can external ethical issues in fact be kept separated from the internal issues we have been focusing on? Is our grasp of a painting's moral content not affected by our ability or inability to endorse the perspective supported by that content if, say, we find that the work crosses the line of what is even imaginatively morally acceptable? If we were to

---

[8] For an excellent discussion of this topic, see Harold (2020).

find out that Rockwell's *The Problem We All Live With* were painted ironically by a sympathizer of racism, or that Dumas's *Osama* were painted by a supporter of Al Qaeda, could we be sure that that which we see in the painting morally speaking would not be affected?[9] Other factors which might be difficult to keep apart from how we perceive a painting's moral content includes the use of controversial materials (such as Vincent Castiglia's use of blood in many of his paintings).

It cannot be denied that at least some ethically relevant paintings can allow for more than one kind of moral content, that any such content can be open to more than one interpretation, and that assessing which factors ought to be allowed to influence our perception of this moral content can at times be perplexing. But it doesn't follow from any of these observations that the prospects of moral learning from painting are necessarily weakened or abrogated. Rather, one might argue that the opposite is true. Of course, paintings such as David's *Belisarius Begging for Alms* or Cassatt's *A Woman and Girl Driving* present us with a clear moral focus which is presumably not in tension with our personal convictions. In this way, their moral content and our uptake of them is fairly unproblematic. However, less morally specific paintings, perhaps such as Grosz's *The Funeral* and Rego's *The Maids,* also present us with ample opportunity to flex our moral muscles. To be sure, the moral content is less determined, our reflections and moral deliberations less channeled, and there may be a variety of angles and attitudes to explore. There may be complex multidimensional themes to unravel, and wildly opposing approaches to try to reconcile. Yet it is precisely these features, one might suggest, which make for one of the paintings' main strengths. Ethics in painting, where we find it, is not always a simple encounter, but then neither are the ethical dimensions of the events, persons, and scenes they represent. To that extent, complex moral content does little other than mirror the moral situations we come across in real life and this, in itself, is an important contributing factor to the value of painting.[10]

SOME CONTEMPORARY ACCOUNTS OF THE VALUE OF PAINTING

In many respects, the topic of ethics in painting has been conspicuously absent from analytic aesthetics, at least as an area discussed independently of the wide-ranging

[9] Note that this is a separate issue from challenging cases to do with whether we should cancel or otherwise boycott pieces painted for example by Adolf Hitler or the representations of young Tahitian girls by Paul Gauguin. There is little to no moral content in these paintings in isolation from the moral issues raised by the moral character of the artists. See Matthes, this volume, for a discussion of these kinds of cases.

[10] To this extent, such paintings are not unlike the great literary works which we tend to cite *in support* of moral learning through art. After all, we rarely hear Dostoyevsky's *Crime and Punishment* or Flaubert's *Madame Bovary* praised for their didacticism or monolithic meaning, nor do we agree with every moral perspective displayed.

themes applicable to the relation between art and ethics in general (such as moralism or ethicism[11]). That said, much work has been done on pictorial representation in general during the last thirty years or so, some of which has succeeded in placing the philosophy of pictures on the map as an area of great interest in contemporary aesthetics. Most importantly, perhaps, considerable progress has been made in connection with how best to conceive of the relation of representation itself or how pictures represent, and the ways in which pictorial representations are similar or dissimilar to other kinds of representation.[12] Some of these analytic philosophers have developed accounts of the value of this wider category of pictures (which tends to include not only paintings but also drawings, murals, photographs, commercial images, etc.) with a focus on understanding the theme depicted, often in connection with the work's potential for artistic expression. Although these theories tend to emphasize different aspects of our experience of thematic paintings and why they matter to us, and do not always make the distinctly ethical or moral content of the work their main focus, it will be instructive to review some of the most influential positions in this field.[13]

In his *Values of Art: Pictures, Poetry and Music*, Malcom Budd suggests that when we see a picture and look at what it depicts, the appreciation of a picture's subject-matter is pertinent to our appreciation of the work *qua* art in so far as it would be rewarding to have the perceptual experience of that which the picture represents (Budd 1995, 46). When we look at a picture as a picture, however, and we are aware of certain differences in appearance between the depiction and that which is depicted, our experience of the picture may be more valuable than any face-to-face experience of that which is represented. The underlying reason for this difference in value, Budd argues, cannot be pinned down to one factor alone, since seeing a real scene and looking at a representation of that scene in a picture are two entirely distinct phenomena, sharing only the two-dimensional aspect of the appearance of the scene as depicted (Budd 1995, 81). That said, the nature of the subject-matter is relevant to our assessment of it as art in so far as understanding the subject is necessary for a proper evaluation of its success as a manifestation of it. Understanding the moral content of pictures is, then, pertinent to an evaluative assessment of a painting in that such understanding is central to whether the picture manages to represent that very content in the first place.

Addressing this same concern,[14] namely how best to explain why a depiction can be more valuable than a face-to-face experience of that which is depicted, Dominic McIver Lopes turns to understanding and the notion of "seeing-in" a picture (roughly the experience of seeing in a picture what it represents while also seeing the picture's surface)

---

[11] For more on this topic, see for example the important work of Berys Gaut, especially Gaut (2007).

[12] See, for example, Hopkins (1998), Hyman (2006), Lopes (1996), Rudd (2017), Walton (1991; 2008), and Wollheim (1990).

[13] This is by no means an exhaustive study of recent work in the philosophy of pictorial representation. For more, see for example, Armstrong (2003), Robinson (2017a; 2017b), Maynard (2005), Rancière (2007), and Pelletier and Voltolini (2019).

[14] Lopes refers to this concern as the "puzzle of mimesis."

(Lopes 2005). According to Lopes, a picture's expressiveness is the result not only of the depicted event, person, or scene, but also of the picture's design. Rather than stemming from a person's (or *persona's*) psychological state,[15] a picture's expressiveness is explained in terms of "the physical configuration of a picture's design, or the figure or scene a picture depicts" (Lopes 2005, 78). Furthermore, cognitive, moral, and aesthetic evaluations have in common that they are assessments of pictures *qua* pictures, or evaluations of pictures as vehicles for seeing-in. Moral value can, then, influence the aesthetic value of a picture in so far as the structure of some moral evaluations of pictures can be said to match the structure of aesthetic evaluations and, to that extent at least, a moral merit such as fostering or "boosting" our moral sensibility can be converted into an aesthetic merit. Pictures can contribute to the development of our moral sensibility by allowing us to acquire or recalibrate our moral concepts, and the moral value of pictures correspondingly depends on how their representational contents influence our moral training or refinement in this way.

One of the main questions in *Marvelous Images: On Values in the Arts*, a collection of essays assembling some of Kendall Walton's most important work, targets the following moral problem: How should we relate to works which present us with moral content with which we disagree, where this ruins our pleasure in the work and leads us to assess it negatively?[16] Set against the background of Walton's general theory of representation, whereby representation in the arts is to be understood in terms of make-believe and props prescribing imaginings rather like how toys operate in children's games, the question becomes one of whether our moral imagination has limits in artistic experience.[17] For Walton, a prop generates fictional truths which, collectively, constitute fictional worlds. What moral possibilities are genuinely open to us in such fictional worlds? Walton's position is clear: whereas it is possible to imagine almost any factual content in fiction, some moral content is simply not accessible to us in this way. In contrast with factually untrue things—which can be made to be true in fiction—immoral things can't be made moral in fiction. To this extent, fictional worlds cannot differ morally from the real world (or if they can, this does not happen often).

In Continental aesthetics, an important strand in philosophy's engagement with painting and its value is the connection between art and truth, and the potential our phenomenological experiences of artworks have to reveal this truth. Art, as Heidegger puts it in his essay "On the Origin of the Work of Art," can be understood as the "working of truth" in the sense that it brings into the open something that was previously hidden. Jacques Derrida's main aim in the four essays collected in *Truth in Painting* is the way in which both the philosophical and art-historical discourses around painting share the goal of trying to subordinate the visual sphere to that of written discourse (Derrida 1987). The "silence" of the painting is, according to Derrida, itself a kind of writing which

---

[15] For a defense of this view, see Robinson (2017a) and (2017b).
[16] The collection's most important article for our purposes is "Morals in Fiction and Fictional Morality."
[17] See also Shim and Liao, this volume.

ultimately breaks down the text which seeks to make sense of it. Paintings, in this way, obey the logic of deconstruction in precisely the same way as textual entities, by offering within themselves the grounds for dismantling the hierarchies and structures that we use for making sense of them. The ethical dimension of this emerges in the idea that the qualities of respect and modesty are essential to any meaningful encounter with painting—respect both for the otherness of the painting as well as for our engagement in it, and modesty with respect to our desire to speak on its behalf. For Derrida, making something explicit always involves making it complicit, and the value of painting, therefore, lies to a significant extent in the indissolubility of the philosophical problems it poses.

Approaching painting with the aim of developing a general theory of expression, Maurice Merleau-Ponty describes perception as an expressive and creative act deeply connected to artistic practice (Merleau-Ponty 1993). Painting, he argues, has ontological priority (in comparison to music and the literary arts) in virtue of its power to reveal the "there is" of the world occluded by science. Painting reminds us of what it actually means to see, and to that extent it can be characterized as extending or amplifying our perception. Through their works, artists can express a more fundamental realm of human experience where the moral dimension of what it is to be a human being becomes tangible. By rendering the human world visible to us in painting, and shedding light on among others moral themes, artists reveal the structure which underlies a seemingly chaotic world.

More recently, Paul Crowther has argued that certain pictures have a unique kind of beauty and sublimity in that they evoke a sense of the divine. When we explore these pictures imaginatively, we develop a relationship with them which is best described as a form of "aesthetic transcendence." Such a transcendent experience, Crowther holds, is embodied in pictorial structures and styles and "complete" us psychologically. By engaging with a picture's thematic content and its particular idealized expression in the work we may hope to elevate ourselves to a more "universal level" (Crowther 2016, 25).

CONCLUDING REMARKS

For a complex variety of reasons we can only speculate about, painting has been largely absent from the forefront of morally provocative and politicized art of late. With a few exceptions, murals, video documentaries and photographs have instead become the expressive means of choice of artists creating works with morally charged content. The rise of modernism and the move away from realistic motifs toward renditions of our perceptual experiences of the world will undoubtedly figure in any explanation of this phenomenon, as will the concomitant desire to use innovative media instead of what might be seen as an old-fashioned artistic form. Also, paintings might be thought too detached from the communities they represent, criticize, or defend by hanging—framed and cut off—on the white walls of galleries and museums.

Precisely how painting can continue to develop technically in order to address the ethically relevant themes it has been exploring ever since its inception will be a matter for artists to address. But as historically informed philosophers of art and appreciators of paintings, we can offer a broader picture of what the moral content of paintings can look like in all its diversity and intricacy. Ranging from Cassatt's subtle and unassuming yet unapologetic moral messages about women's rights to Grosz's brutal and macabre hellscape about a society of man gone insane, painting is no less "done" with ethics than the events, persons, and scenes it depicts. Engaging with the moral content of a painting is inseparable from engaging with the artwork as such, as is the possibility of learning from it.

The main aim of this chapter has been to reflect and shed light on ethical issues specific to painting and internal to its thematic content. More specifically, what does it mean for a painting to have moral content, and how does this content influence the value we accord the work *as a painting*? Many interesting topics, not least about the interplay between internal and external ethical concerns, call for further examination. A heterogeneous moral universe, in many respects lacking a shared symbolic language, no doubt presents unique challenges to the pictorial representation of specific, perhaps context-dependent moral perspectives. Nonetheless, just as ethical and moral issues have been central to the art of painting for most of its history, and just as these issues have been addressed by artists in a wide variety of different ways, it may certainly be supposed that paintings will remain a site of ethical and moral work in the future.

See also: Matthes, Shim and Liao, Stear, Carroll, Eaton, Clavel-Vázquez, Bhushan and Mehrotra, this volume

References

Armstrong, John. 2003. "Moral Depth and Pictorial Art." In *Art and Morality*, edited by Sebastian Gardner and Jose Bermúdez, 170–184. London: Routledge.

Budd, Malcolm. 1995. *Values of Art: Pictures, Poetry and Music*. London: Penguin.

Carroll, Noël. 2020. "Literature, the Emotions, and Learning." *Philosophy and Literature* 44, no. 1, 1–18.

Crowther, Paul. 2016. *How Pictures Complete Us. The Beautiful, the Sublime, and the Divine*. Stanford, CA: Stanford University Press.

Currie, Gregory. 1998. "Realism of Character and the Value of Fiction." In *Aesthetics and Ethics: Essays at the Intersection*, edited by Jerrold Levinson, 161–181. Cambridge: Cambridge University Press.

Currie, Gregory. 2020. *Imagining and Knowing*. Oxford: Oxford University Press.

D'Elia, Roman Una. 2005. *The Poetics of Titian's Religious Paintings*. Cambridge: Cambridge University Press.

Derrida, Jacques. 1987. *The Truth in Painting*. Translated by Geoffrey Bennington and Ian McLeod. Chicago: University of Chicago Press.

Eaton, A. W. 2013. "What's Wrong with the (Female) Nude?" In *Art and Pornography: Philosophical Essays*, edited by Hans Maes and Jerrold Levinson, 277–308. Oxford: Oxford University Press.

Eldridge, Richard. 1989. *On Moral Personhood: Philosophy, Literature, Criticism, and Self-Understanding*. Chicago: University of Chicago Press.

Gaut, Berys. 2007. *Art, Emotion, and Ethics*. Oxford: Oxford University Press.

Gibson, John. 2007. *Fiction and the Weave of Life*. Oxford: Oxford University Press.

Harold, James. 2020. *Dangerous Art. On Moral Criticism of Artworks*. New York: Oxford University Press.

Hopkins, Robert. 1998. *Picture, Image and Experience: A Philosophical Inquiry*. Cambridge: Cambridge University Press.

Hyman, John. 2006. *The Objective Eye*. Chicago: University of Chicago Press.

John, Eileen. 1998. "Reading Fiction and Conceptual Knowledge: Philosophical Thought in Literary Context." *Journal of Aesthetics and Art Criticism* 56, no. 4, 331–348.

Lopes, Dominic McIver. 1996. *Understanding Pictures*. Oxford: Oxford University Press.

Lopes, Dominic McIver. 2005. *Sight and Sensibility: Evaluating Pictures*. Oxford: Oxford University Press.

Maynard, Patrick. 2005. *Drawing Distinctions: The Varieties of Graphic Expression*. Ithaca, NY: Cornell University Press.

McNeill, Paul. 2014. *Ethics and the Arts*. New York: Springer.

Merleau-Ponty, Maurice. 1993. *Philosophy and Painting: The Merleau-Ponty Aesthetics Reader*, edited by Galen Johnson. Evanston, IL: Northwestern University Press.

Nussbaum, Marta. 1990. *Love's Knowledge: Essays on Philosophy and Literature*. New York: Oxford University Press.

Pelletier, Jerome, and Alberto Voltolini, eds. 2019. *The Pleasure of Pictures: Pictorial Experience and Aesthetic Appreciation*. London: Routledge.

Rancière, Jacques. 2007. *The Future of the Image*. Translated by Geoffrey Elliott. London: Verso.

Robinson, Jenefer. 1997. "L'Education Sentimentale." In *Art and Its Messages*, edited by Stephen Davies, 212–226. University Park: Penn State University Press.

Robinson, Jenefer. 2017a. "Missing Person Found. Part One." *British Journal of Aesthetics* 57, no. 3, 249–267.

Robinson, Jenefer. 2017b. "Missing Person Found. Part Two." *British Journal of Aesthetics* 57, no. 4, 349–367.

Rudd, Anthony. 2017. "Why Painting Matters: Some Phenomenological Approaches." *Journal of Aesthetics and Phenomenology* 4, no. 1: 1–14.

The Wounded Deer by Frida Kahlo. n.d. kahl.org (website). Accessed April 24, 2023. https://www.kahlo.org/wounded-deer/

Walton, Kendall. 1991. *Mimesis as Make-Believe: On the Foundations of the Representational Arts*. Cambridge, MA: Harvard University Press.

Walton, Kendall. 2008. *Marvelous Images. On Values and the Arts*. Oxford: Oxford University Press.

Wollheim, Richard. 1990. *Painting as an Art*. Princeton, NJ: Princeton University Press.

CHAPTER 24

ETHICS AND LITERATURE

PETER LAMARQUE

NARRATIVES where even remotely human-like characters and actions are depicted will of necessity have, if only implicitly, an ethical dimension. That is, they will elicit from readers reflections grounded in an ethical vocabulary: for example, actions conceived as selfish, kind, mean-spirited, generous, irresponsible, heartless, cruel, beyond the call of duty. In this sense, we can speak of such narratives, including most literary narratives, as having an ethical content. We should ask how this ethical content is to be evaluated. Readers might be moved by depicted acts of kindness or outraged by the display of heartless cruelty and such responses will feed into judgments of character and incident. However, at a higher-order level, literary readers will ask what functions, within an artistic design, are served by actions so characterized. Is the cruelty gratuitous or meaningfully integrated? Is the kindness subtly displayed or merely sentimental? On such issues are literary judgments grounded. But these judgments must be sharply distinguished from instrumental values: whether, for example, reflecting on work content in these ways can encourage empathy in readers, or improve their moral sensibility, or enrich their understanding of moral behavior. These are no doubt benefits of some literary narratives, but they are not, it will be argued, at the core of where narrative content manifests its ethical dimension or where its deeper values reside.

There are multiply varied ways in which ethics and literature intersect. Here are more sample claims made. Works of imaginative literature (novels, plays, poems) are sometimes praised for the acuity of their moral vision (George Eliot's *Middlemarch*), or others denigrated for their moral depravity (de Sade's *Juliette*). Individual characters and episodes in particular works are subject to moral appraisal: readers of *Tess of the d'Urbervilles* (1891) are likely dismayed by the cruel treatment of Tess by her newly wedded husband Angel Clare, while admiring Tess's own moral strength and honesty. As noted, claims are sometimes made for the moral benefits of reading literature, emphasizing what might be learned from doing so: such as coming to know what it is like to be a person of a certain kind or in a certain kind of predicament; or acquiring a deeper grip on, or clarification of, fundamental moral principles. However, it is also claimed that overt forms of moral didacticism in literature can detract from a work's aesthetic value, or more strongly that the highlighting of a moral message in fiction or drama tends to be crude and reductive. This in turn engages a wider debate about whether, or how, a work's moral stance does, or should, affect aesthetic judgments of the work. Is the aesthetic realm distinct from, or intertwined with, the ethical? Ethics and literature seem inescapably linked but there is little agreement about the substance or consequences of the connections.

It might be thought that canonical works of literature, by the very fact of their canonicity, will attain a threshold of ethical probity, sufficient to make them candidates at least to be timeless exemplars of the good and the enlightened. But that is far from clear. Richard Posner offers a colorful picture of something far less ennobling:

> The classics are full of moral atrocities—as they appear to us today, and sometimes as they appeared to the more enlightened members of the author's own society—that the author apparently approved of. Rape, pillage, murder, human and animal sacrifice, concubinage, and slavery in the *Iliad*; misogyny in the *Oresteia* and countless other works; . . . anti-Semitism in more works of literature than one can count, including works by Shakespeare and Dickens; racism and sexism likewise; homophobia (think only of Shakespeare's *Troilus and Cressida* and Mann's "Death in Venice"); . . . colonialism, imperialism, religious obscurantism, militarism, gratuitous violence, torture (as of Iago in *Othello*), and criminality; . . . The world of literature is a moral anarchy. (Posner 1997, 5)

Let us assume for the sake of argument that this indictment is broadly correct. The question is what follows from it. In an age of culture wars, where serious challenges are made to the status of any literary "canon," the matter might seem pressing. Of course, it is always possible for teachers of literature, or those who devise reading lists in other capacities, to weed out works that offend contemporary moral sensibilities. But that can in turn be viewed negatively as a kind of censorship. More importantly, though, these controversies do little to clarify the different kinds of values sought in literature or what the priorities should be.

Posner's own stance with regard to his list is to historicize and aestheticize it.[1] The "moral anarchy," he thinks, can largely be overlooked given that "most readers accept the presence of obsolete ethics in literature with the same equanimity that they accept the presence of obsolete military technology or antiquated diction or customs" (Posner 1997, 7). In other words, ethical failings of the kind listed are just what one might expect from works of earlier periods. Posner's position is not just about what "most readers accept" but is also normative. They are right, he thinks, to adopt this nonchalant attitude:

> A work of literature is not to be considered maimed or even marred by expressing unacceptable moral views; by the same token, a mediocre work of literature is not

---

[1] See Stear, this volume, for another discussion of Posner's views.

redeemed by expressing moral views of which we approve. The proper criteria for evaluating literature are aesthetic rather than ethical. (Posner 1997, 2)

The Autonomy of the Aesthetic

The point of view that Posner is expressing stresses the autonomy of the aesthetic over other kinds of value, with the insistence that in the literary case aesthetic value has precedence. It is a view held by critics like Harold Bloom (1994) or Frank Kermode (2006), for whom the literary canon is and ought to be founded on strictly aesthetic criteria alone. Bloom writes: "Aesthetic choice has always guided every secular aspect of canon formation . . . [which is] founded upon severely artistic criteria" (Bloom 1994). For Kermode, "aesthetic pleasure" should be the grounding principle, although the pleasure he approves is one tinged with "dismay" (Kermode 2006, 28–29).

It is noteworthy that a somewhat similar point of view prevailed in two famous twentieth-century cases of literary censorship: the trials of James Joyce's *Ulysses*, in the United States (1933), and D. H. Lawrence's *Lady Chatterley's Lover* in the United Kingdom (1960). In both cases, prosecutors sought to show that the works should continue to be banned for obscenity, while the defence, in both, rested in effect on "severely artistic criteria." In fact, the ruling of the trial judge, John M. Woolsey, in the *Ulysses* case, deeming the novel not to be obscene, was an eloquent defence of the novel as a work of art (Morgan and Peters 2006, 10). In the *Lady Chatterley's Lover* trial, similar points were made, with expert witnesses for the defence including the critics Helen Gardner and Richard Hoggart, and the novelists E. M. Forster and Rebecca West. The trials—along with others in a similar period, including John Cleland's 1749 erotic novel *Memoirs of a Woman of Pleasure*, Henry Miller's *Tropic of Cancer*, and William S. Burroughs's *Naked Lunch*—helped to establish that aesthetic and literary merit can, properly identified, override perceived immorality in literature.

Anticipating this line of thought, the art critic Clive Bell, writing in 1914, claimed for works of art a special kind of ethical status that placed them somehow outside the scope of first-order moral judgments and unaffected by consequences flowing from them: "Once we have judged a thing a work of art, we have judged it ethically of the first importance and put it beyond the reach of the moralist. . . . The habit of introducing moral considerations into judgments between particular works of art would be inexcusable" (Bell 1914, 20, 115).

Bell was a formalist and an aestheticist. For him, the highest good to which art can aspire is to produce "aesthetic emotion" and to do so, not through what it represents, but through its "significant form." We need not pursue Bell's theory—it is more concerned with painting than literature—but should note that it marks an extreme form of autonomism, setting aesthetic quality radically apart from morality. It has echoes of Oscar Wilde's often quoted dictum: "There is no such thing as a moral or an immoral book. Books are well written, or badly written. That is all" (Wilde [1891] 1965, Preface).

But Wilde did not discount the subject matter of art, nor indeed the depiction of moral life in art, rather he held that judgments of art should focus less on moral probity than on perfection of form: "The moral life of man forms part of the subject-matter of the artist, but the morality of art consists in the perfect use of an imperfect medium" (Wilde [1891] 1965, Preface).

This brief sketch of aesthetic autonomism leaves many questions unanswered, not least what exactly the aesthetic criteria are, and what becomes of other dimensions of literature such as content and meaning. It should be emphasized from the outset that it is not necessary to be a formalist (certainly not of the Wilde or Bell kind) to defend the autonomy of the aesthetic. As will be shown later, a work's content, even its moral content, plays an essential role in its aesthetic value.

Formalism, broadly the view that aesthetic features of literary works are grounded in, even identical to, formal features of texts (verbal, rhetorical, stylistic, structural) was, in different versions, a dominant force in literary criticism throughout the twentieth century. (See Gal, this volume, for a detailed examination.) The influence of linguistics in this critical trend was evident, as was a tendency to downplay political, cultural, or ideological aspects of literature, including moral aspects. Distinctively literary qualities came to be associated with formal qualities. An underlying (partial) motivation was to ground criticism in scientific and objective methodologies. However, throughout the century there were also counterformalist undercurrents, including Marxism, feminism, and cultural humanism (those influenced by Matthew Arnold), where ethical values were not subsumed.

It seems clear that Posner, in spite of claiming allegiance to Wilde, and in spite of stating that "the moral content of . . . a work of literature has little to do either with the value of the work . . . or with the pleasure to be derived from the work" (Posner 1998, 394), does not commit himself to a strict formalism. He writes, for example: "In reading literature we are also learning about the values and experiences of cultures, epochs, and sensibilities remote from our own . . . We are acquiring experience vicariously by dwelling in the imaginary worlds that literature creates" (Posner 1997, 19).

The autonomy of the aesthetic might separate the aesthetic from the ethical but it does not eschew literary *content*, even content of a moral nature. Furthermore, it is important to recognize that purely formal (linguistic) features of a text are not *intrinsically* of literary (or aesthetic) value. What matters is the aesthetic function assigned to such formal features within an overall conception of a work. A formal feature *emerges* as salient only within the context of a literary reading, that is, a construal or interpretation of the content. The feature is assigned significance relative to some function fulfilled. In other contexts, a similar feature might remain merely inert, or assigned a different function. An example might be the narratorial style of Peter Carey's award-winning novel *True History of the Kelly Gang* (2000). The first-person narration in the novel is in the voice of the protagonist, Ned Kelly, a semiliterate outlaw and fugitive. The prose itself appears illiterate, misspelt, and syntactically awry. However, the story recounted in the narration is engaging and disturbing. The surface illiteracy in other contexts might be a serious aesthetic weakness, while here it is clever and effective in its exploration of the protagonist's pained attempt at self-exculpation.

It might seem obvious that the aesthetic value of a literary work must include reference to the work's content, what the work is about, over and above the linguistic forms in which the content is presented. But what is meant by content? Is it truly distinct from the form? Or does not the form, as in the Ned Kelly case, substantiate both the nature and identity of the content? (Lamarque 2021)

It is useful to distinguish between a work's *subject matter* and the work's *themes*. These invite answers of two different kinds to the question "What is the work *about*?": a subject-based and a theme-based answer. At its simplest, the subject matter of a work includes the story told and the characters described. In turn, themes are ideas that arise out of the treatment of the subject, bringing wider significance and interest to it. Characteristically, literary themes involve some of the deepest issues that confront human beings, such as love, death, envy, power, ambition, the pursuit of happiness, moral conflict, unfulfilled desires, hope and despair, chance and necessity, the trials of faith, self-understanding, self-doubt, and so forth. The great enduring works of literature are not just those that tell good stories but do so through the creation of an intricate linguistic design that gives both unique structure to the story and a perspective for thinking more deeply about just such thematic ideas.

In summary, we can think of three pillars of literary works, broadly conceived, as *form*, *subject*, and *theme*. Every literary work exemplifies each of these. They are the basis of literary or aesthetic value. Rather than limit aesthetic value to form alone we should see it as arising out of and based on the consonance of these three. A great work of literature is one where form, subject, and theme effectively cohere to produce something of interest, originality, and power: *this* subject perfectly suited as a vehicle for this theme, and *this* presentation of the subject capturing precisely the essence of the subject itself and the thematic implications realized through it. Thus is an overall aesthetic value attained, but each of the three elements is itself also subject to critical evaluation. Shallowness and cliché at any level (which might include, say, crude racist or anti-Semitic tropes, endorsed and unassimilated in the work) will be aesthetic as much as moral weaknesses in subject or theme. In the light of this broadening of the aesthetic it seems far more plausible to think of the canon of great works as resting on aesthetic criteria so defined.

THE REENTRY OF ETHICS: MORAL CONTENT

Once we include subject and theme, as well as form, in the sphere of the aesthetic it is easy to see ways in which the ethical can become involved. Moral content can be identified both at a subject level and at a thematic level. At subject level, moral content is present in different forms: sometimes overtly, where a fictional scenario takes a directly moral turn, as when Mr. Knightley in Jane Austen's *Emma* (1815) reprimands Emma for her tactlessness; sometimes in less overt forms, where situations are characterized, as suggested earlier, in such a way as to invite ethical appraisal, as in the scene from *Tess of the d'Urbervilles*. In another Hardy novel, *The Mayor of Casterbridge* (1886), the principal character Michael Henchard, in a drunken state, auctions his wife and baby daughter at a country fair. Although he soon shows remorse for the act, and it eventually destroys him, there is no escaping the moral abhorrence of what he has done, both invited by the narrative and shared by the reader. In both cases the scenes are offered not neutrally but with a strong moral valence. A reader who fails to recognize the moral perspective inherent in the scenes has failed to understand them.

Of course, not all fictional situations or actions are so clearly delineated ethically. Indeed, the more interesting cases are those where there is moral ambivalence. For example, the reader of F. Scott Fitzgerald's *The Great Gatsby* (1925) is invited to share the narrator Nick Carraway's ambivalent moral perception of Jay Gatsby's behavior: a repugnance tinged with sympathy. Ethical judgments arising from subject level content can be complex and contested, in just the way familiar with judgments of real people. However, it is important to see that there are fundamental differences between judgments of the two kinds. Fictional characters, at least those of a realist nature, seen from the internal perspective as people in an imaginary world, might seem to live and act exactly as do real people, and thus be subject to precisely the same kinds of moral appraisal. In fact, many of the judgments readers do make accord with that assumption.

But there is another perspective that can and should be taken on subject level content when the focus is on literary evaluation and interpretation. This is the external perspective from which we view characters not just as imaginary people but as artifacts in an aesthetic construct (Lamarque 2014). This makes a difference in several ways. One involves a re-emphasis on form. Our judgments under this perspective are responsive not just to (fictional) actions *as actions* but to the actions as presented to us in *this* form, with *this* function. *How* the actions are described is as important as *what* is described. It is the form that partially dictates the nature of our judgments as well as the ethical character of the acts described. Vocabulary, syntax, implicature, and tone, contribute to the emergence of moral salience. A consequence is that the ethical stance we take to a scene or incident is partially controlled by the narrative modes of its presentation. We respond as we do partly because we recognize the intention that we should respond that way.

Here is an example from Muriel Spark's novel *The Prime of Miss Jean Brodie* (1961), in a passage where some of the "Brodie set" of girls at the school are being grilled by the Headmistress Miss Mackay, who dislikes everything that Miss Brodie stands for and is always looking for grounds to dismiss her, believing she is both corrupting the girls and undermining the ethos of the school. Miss Mackay addresses the girls:

> You are very fortunate in Miss Brodie. I could wish your arithmetic papers had been better. I am always impressed by Miss Brodie's girls in one way or another. You will have to work hard at ordinary humble subjects for the qualifying examination. Miss Brodie is giving you an excellent preparation for the Senior school. Culture cannot compensate for lack of hard knowledge. I am happy to see you are devoted to Miss Brodie. Your loyalty is due to the school rather than to any one individual. (Spark 2000, 66)

The writing is clever. The sentences self-consciously (hints of Mark Antony praising Brutus?) oscillate between fulsome but insincere praise for Miss Brodie, and sharp but implied criticism of her methods. Each alternate sentence effectively contradicts the preceding one. The tone is one of menace and resentment. What the passage sets up nicely are the two powerfully opposing moral forces in the arc of the novel: the sensible but unimaginative and priggish Miss Mackay, and the charismatic but irresponsible Miss Brodie. The characters each stand for something wider, more symbolic, than just their contrasting personalities.

While little sympathy is extended to Miss Mackay, the reader's attitude to Miss Brodie remains equivocal throughout, her rebelliousness appealing, her manipulation of the girls, her arrogance, and her support for Mussolini, much less so. The self-consciousness and control of Spark's writing keeps readers constantly alert for irony and moral nuance.

The external perspective on character and incident also allows for radically different kinds of explanation for action in a fictional setting. It means that there are distinct kinds of answers to the question: "Why did such-and-such a character act that way?" One answer, from the internal perspective, in terms of motives, desires, and beliefs, is grounded in familiar worldly forms of action explanation. The other answer, from the external perspective, appeals to the role of the action in an artistic design.

Take Maggie Tulliver in George Eliot's novel *Mill on the Floss* (1860). Why did she enter the flood to try to save her brother Tom, an effort that in the end killed them both? One answer: she hoped to rescue him and find some reconciliation in their strained relationship ("Along with the sense of danger and possible rescue for those long-remembered beings at the old home, there was an undefined sense of reconcilement with her brother" [Eliot [1860] 1965, 542]). She acted through hope, love, and the desire to make up, an action that invites moral praise.

Another answer, though, has a far less direct moral dimension: her action with its fateful outcome was the inevitable end of the story, given the tragic trajectory of her life, fulfilling the epitaph "In their death they were not divided," an end long anticipated, not least by earlier references to storms and floods. George Eliot speaks of Maggie in the terms of classical tragedy: she was "essentially noble but liable to great error—error that is anguish to its own nobleness" (Eliot 1965, 555).

Moral content appears not only at subject level but also at a thematic level. Familiar over centuries of literary output, recurrent literary themes, as listed earlier (love, death, envy, power, ambition, the pursuit of happiness, unfulfilled desires, and so on) all have an ethical aspect. It is common to speak of works "exploring" themes of these kinds. The thought is that such general concepts can be marshalled in interpretation to help establish connections and commonalities across the particulars of the work: character, incident, dialogue, reflection. By forging these connections under a concept, a reader can find salience in the details suggesting unity or significance where at first this might not be evident.

Sometimes, although not always or necessarily, themes are characterized as propositions. This can support another form of moral content. Here, for example, is a comment from a literary critic about Dostoyevsky's *Crime and Punishment* (1866): "It is unjust to deny to the criminal that responsibility that raises him above the beasts, and also to deny him the punishment that purifies him and gives him new being" (Ivanov 1975, 584). It is important to note the status of a claim like this. It is not offered by the critic as a statement in moral philosophy but rather as an interpretation of a strand of thought in the novel that helps make sense, in broad summary, of Raskolnikov's predicament.

The difference can be starkly registered when we ask what kind of support might be proposed to establish its truth under these different aims. As a statement in moral philosophy the support would come from arguments about the justifications for punishment in a philosophical or jurisprudential context. As an interpretative thematic statement about the novel, the only relevant support would have to involve citing evidence from the novel itself. We ask: is this a significant theme that emerges in the novel, supported by, and helping to make sense of, the novel's particulars? These are radically different exercises, and the difference is important in a discussion of moral content. While the latter (the interpretative context) is grounded in aesthetic appreciation of the novel, the former (the philosophical context) belongs in moral philosophy and could be assessed entirely independently of the novel.

THE REENTRY OF ETHICS: MORAL EDUCATION AND EDIFICATION

It is important to distinguish these two roles that could be assigned to thematic statements because they all too easily get run together. Indeed, the merging of these roles becomes a central pillar in the moralist's response to aesthetic autonomy. For the moralist, the value of literature is not to be confined or reducible to aesthetic qualities revealed through literary analysis. (See Carroll, this volume.) The moralist viewpoint sees deeper values in the morally educative function that the great literary works can serve (for illuminating applications, see John 2010, 2018). There are many strands to this thought, and it is helpful, for expository purposes, to keep them distinct even if there is a shared element that unites them.

One strand in the moralist's case rests in the idea of a moral lesson derivable from a literary work, and often expressed in propositional form as a candidate for moral knowledge. From this moralist perspective, the critic's statement about *Crime and Punishment*, quoted earlier, "It is unjust to deny to the criminal that responsibility that raises him above the beasts," can be taken both as a derived moral statement and as a critical thematic statement, with both encapsulating a moral "insight" delivered by the novel.

But there are problems with this. One is that the truth-conditions under these two construals might be different. As a thematic statement by a critic we should understand it as implicitly prefixed by "It is a theme in *Crime and Punishment* that," but in the second construal (about the real world) there is no such implied prefix, so one might be true, the other false. In fact that is not uncommon. In certain novels, perhaps by Franz Kafka or Samuel Beckett, thematic statements might be characterized in pessimistic or nihilistic terms that many would want to reject as a true description of human life. Nor need this disconnect impugn the literary value of such novels, which could be of interest precisely for exaggerating the dark side of human nature in an illuminating and aesthetically rewarding manner.

Our example has focused on a critic's statement about thematic content, but thematic propositions can also occur within literary works. Here is an example from Dostoyevsky's novel *Notes from Underground* (1864), being reflections from the narrator, the "man from underground":

> Where did all the sages get the idea that a man's desires must be normal and virtuous? Why did they imagine that he must inevitably will what is reasonable and profitable? What a man needs is simply and solely *independent* volition, whatever that independence may cost and wherever it may lead. (Dostoyevsky [1864] 1977, 34, italics in original)

These reflections become salient thematically as the protagonist's life takes an increasingly dark and erratic turn. However, it would be a mistake for the moralist to latch onto these propositions too quickly as extractable worldly truths. In fact, as the autonomist would see it, by pointing inwardly to the dynamics of the novel, rather than outwardly to the world at large, they afford seemingly more significant insight into the protagonist himself. What we see in the novel is the terrible cost of following "solely *independent* volition, . . . wherever it may lead."

This comes to a head at the end of the novel with the protagonist's painfully cruel and humiliating treatment of the prostitute Liza, who had offered her love to him. His actions, as he recognises himself, are gratuitous, unkind, and almost inexplicable. But as if to emphasize his "independent volition" he refuses any temptation to apologize and seek forgiveness. His justification adds to the cruelty and perversity: "Isn't it better if she carries away with her now an everlasting wound to her pride? Humiliation, after all, is purification . . . now the insult will never die within her, . . . her humiliation will elevate and purify her . . . through hate" (Dostoyevsky [1864] 1977, 121). The "man from underground" himself is clearly not a reliable source of moral wisdom! Nor of course are we invited to suppose he is. Indeed, the reader who focuses too eagerly on what looks like a profound existentialist principle of free will, will be chastened to realize through the novel just how devastating its consequences can be. Perhaps that is the extractable moral lesson.

However, another problem immediately arises, casting doubt on the idea of novels as conveyors of moral truths, namely that the purported moral lessons often conflict with one another, as happens with the simple "morals" in folktales ("Look before you leap," "He who hesitates is lost"). Existentialist novels might offer a theme of radical free will, where more deterministic works (Greek tragedies, perhaps) might support a picture of destiny or fatalism. When powerfully realized, both contradictory visions can be compelling. Yet from a literary perspective, not only is there no serious conflict here but there is no compulsion to choose or to suppose that literary value must be guided by philosophical or theological truth. Again, aesthetic judgment takes precedence; how the theme is developed in consort with subject and form provides a sounder ground of literary interest.

Finally, extracting worldly moral truths from works of literature raises an issue of generality and specificity (Stolnitz 1992). In the two recent examples (from the Dostoyevsky novels), the propositions, either derived (in the first case) or explicit (in the second), are generalities with no mention of the particulars of the work. This is what makes them seem candidates for moral lessons (beyond the work) but it potentially cuts them loose from the work, assessable apart from it. As suggested earlier, that moves the discussion away from literary appreciation toward moral philosophy. While, in some contexts, that might seem a useful move, it weakens the claim that the work is playing an essential role as a vehicle for the moral lesson. After all, the very same generalization could have occurred in other, nonliterary, contexts. And we have seen how in the second case the particularities offer a striking challenge to the generalization. However, if the moral lesson is tied too specifically to the details of the work, its claim to be a generalizable moral principle is compromised.

The emphasis on extracting moral propositions from literature as a route to enhancing moral knowledge can seem reductive and at odds with the nuance of literature. (See also John, this volume.) A refinement of the view proposes that literature affords not necessarily new moral knowledge but a clarification and deepening of what readers know already. Here is Noël Carroll:

> Clarificationism does not claim that, in the standard case, we acquire interesting new propositional knowledge from artworks, but rather that the artworks in question can deepen our moral understanding by, among other things, encouraging us to apply our moral knowledge and emotions to specific cases. (Carroll 2001, 283)

In reflecting on the characters and incidents in a work, readers can "put together previously disconnected belief fragments in a new gestalt in a way that changes their moral perception" (Carroll 2001, 283). This, Carroll believes, is itself a form of moral learning, albeit not via the acquisition of moral knowledge. The phenomenon is familiar, whereby reading a work of literature helps to sharpen understanding of principles that readers implicitly but unreflectively endorse (what does it *really* mean to treat people as equals?). This is what it is for a work to "hit home," to shake us out of complacent thinking. The way in which the particulars are described, the attitudes and judgments we are prompted to make, the themes we are invited to reflect on, contribute to this eye-opening effect. But as this way of putting it indicates, the first and foremost "deepening" of understanding must be directed to the work itself. Close attention to the work—its form, its subject, its themes—is a prerequisite for any subsequent moral benefit in a reader, such as acquiring clearer moral understanding in a broader context. However, the latter, if it occurs at all, seems entirely contingent on extraneous factors.

The "clarification" that matters rests fundamentally with attention given to the work itself; and that is an aesthetic response.

The idea of "moral perception" suggests a further way for the moralist to characterize the moral learning potential of literature. This is the appeal to "vision." It is common to speak of a novel's vision and one way of taking this is quite literally as offering a new way of looking at the world. The idea is that when we read the great novels our perspective on the real world can change and do so in a morally beneficial manner: we come to see things differently, more clearly. The novelist and philosopher Iris Murdoch puts it like this:

> What we learn from contemplating the characters of Shakespeare or Tolstoy . . . is something about the real quality of human nature, when it is envisaged, in the artist's just and compassionate vision, with a clarity which does not belong to the self-centred rush of ordinary life. (Murdoch 1970, 65)

For Murdoch our "ordinary life" is "self-centred," in the sense that almost inevitably we see and judge things (including other people) through an egotistic lens. Great art can mitigate this by presenting us with an imagined world conceived through the "just and compassionate vision" of an artist, able, as we might say, to "take us out of ourselves." As Martha Nussbaum elaborates: "We find here love without possessiveness, attention without bias, involvement without panic" (Nussbaum 1990, 162). Perhaps this is another form that clarification can take.

The philosopher D. Z. Phillips has argued that a change in moral perspective need not be explained in terms of a change in beliefs or even principles, so much as a change in ways of looking at the world (Phillips 1982). He too held that literature can bring about such change.

The moralist is right to focus on a work's moral vision, but this should not be seen as a challenge to the autonomist. The vision offered by a work is embodied in the work's subject and themes, as realized through its form. Giving close aesthetic attention to this vision can be intrinsically rewarding. But, as we noted earlier, the vision that emerges from a literary work is not always one that readers want to endorse. The nihilistic vision of, say, *Notes from Underground*, is not convincing as a picture of "the real quality of human nature." Perhaps Murdoch and Nussbaum are thinking only of morally enlightening cases. But neither philosopher, it might be supposed, would reject such nihilistic novels as flawed works of literature. The novels' literary (aesthetic) value does not depend on a reader's endorsement of the vision offered. This position seems to extend more support to the autonomist than the moralist.

Another common line of thought for the moralist draws on the idea of readers adopting a perspective that is not their own. In this case it centers on coming to know *what it is like to be a person of a certain kind or in a certain kind of predicament*. David Novitz puts it like this, referring to readers of *Anna Karenina* (1877): "They imagine what it is like to be assailed by such problems, they feel the fright and despair that accompany them, and, arguably as a result, they are able to discern their overwhelming complexity"

(Novitz 1987, 135). Note that this is not asking a reader to imagine him or herself *to be* Anna Karenina, a kind of identification, which makes little sense taken literally, but rather to imagine facing moral conundrums similar to those attributed to the character, not just in thought but experientially and emotionally.

But there is a danger that any moral reward delivered through this experience will move beyond the specific detail in the novel and yield to a focus on peculiarities in a reader's own life. My simulated experience of Anna's predicament might reflect on features more pertinent to me than to her. The sense we are learning something *from the novel* might be weakened. Also, there is no guarantee that the moral reward will be positive when we imagine what it is like to be a certain kind of person: for some readers learning (experientially and affectively) what it is like to be, say, a serial killer, a pedophile, or a torturer might have seriously harmful consequences (for further concerns, see Harold [2003]).

Related to the idea of readers taking up different perspectives is that of empathy. It is not uncommon to find claims that literary fiction can, for example, "intensify empathy" (Smith 2017, 192–193) or lead to "empathetic knowledge" (Novitz 1987, 136). There is also empirical work by psychologists which suggests such a connection (Mar and Oatley 2008, 173; Kidd and Castano 2013), although the findings have been challenged. If true, the encouragement of empathy might look like a moral benefit of reading literature. But much in this debate is contested: not only whether there is a significant increase in empathy as a result of reading literature but even whether it has any essential connection to ethics. The latter has been disputed, for example, by Jesse Prinz (Prinz 2011, 221) and Posner (Posner 1997, 19). Nussbaum prefers to speak of "compassion" rather than "empathy" (Nussbaum 1998, 352).

Gregory Currie, having reviewed some of the empirical studies on empathy as well as the philosophical debates, is skeptical. Addressing the hypothesis "Reading fiction makes us more likely to experience empathy and to behave empathetically towards real people," he concludes that there is just as much evidence for the "opposing tendency," namely that reading fiction actually decreases empathetic behavior (Currie 2020, 213).

Such an "opposing tendency" might recall the advice given to Dorian Gray (in Wilde's *The Picture of Dorian Gray* [1891]) by the aesthete Lord Henry Wotton at the death of Dorian's actress girlfriend, Sibyl Vane: "Mourn for Ophelia, if you like. Put ashes on your head because Cordelia was strangled. Cry out against Heaven because the daughter of Brabantio died. But don't waste your tears over Sibyl Vane. She was less real than they are" (Wilde [1891] 1965, 117). The position is extreme and repellent. But it is not too fanciful to suppose that sustained immersion in certain kinds of (romantic, sentimental) fiction is more likely to harm than enhance real-life empathy or the ability to cope well with the feelings of real people.

Currie's skepticism is not, of course, the last word on literature and empathy but it is a salutary restraint on those who think it is just *obvious* that reading fiction enhances empathy in a positive way.

Conclusions

There are other considerations where the autonomist clashes with the moralist. Analytical aestheticians have characterized and debated numerous positions that could be, and have been, adopted: radical versus moderate autonomism (Anderson and Dean 1998, Carroll 1998), radical versus moderate moralism (Carroll 2000, 2001), "ethicism" (Gaut 1998, 2007), "immoralism" (Eaton 2012), and further refinements of these. As these positions are discussed in detail elsewhere in this *Handbook* (see Carroll, Stear, and Jacobson, this volume) they will not be analyzed here.

One point of fairly widespread agreement, however, takes us back to Posner's charge of "moral anarchy" in the literary canon, with its rollcall of murder, cruelty, deceit, and torture, in canonical works. There is agreement that in the moral appraisal of a literary work is not just subject content itself, but the attitudes adopted to it in the work that matters. Posner himself qualifies his list to "moral atrocities . . . that the author apparently approved of." It is the apparent endorsement, or failure to censure, immoral behavior that is the focus for judgment. Undoubtedly, readers can feel uncomfortable with, for example, unchallenged negative attitudes or stereotypes (anti-Semitism in Shakespeare's Shylock or Dickens's Fagan, or sexism in *Taming of the Shrew*, or the abuse of power in *Measure for Measure*). The autonomist acknowledges this. One path of potential mitigation is to historicize the offending attitudes (Posner's acceptance of "obsolete ethics" in historic works). Another more interesting route is to seek ways of interpreting the works which offer aesthetic justification for the depictions (ways of integrating or making sense of them in a larger vision or design of the work); this is common in productions of Shakespeare's plays. Needless to say, it does not always remove the discomfort.

Posner's own approach might seem complacent and cavalier. Parts of the canon are indeed disturbing in the attitudes and depictions presented. Perhaps it is not enough just to assert, as Posner does, that "the proper criteria for evaluating literature are aesthetic rather than ethical." As moderate autonomists acknowledge, it is perfectly proper to make moral evaluations of literary works. What is more questionable is to infer aesthetic evaluations directly from those, in the manner of the moralists. Much will depend on the account given of aesthetic evaluation. As suggested earlier, a good starting point is to ask how form, subject, and theme are coordinated in a literary work: is each component appropriate to the others, and in itself coherent and reflectively worked out? That might seem too abstract to be helpful. But returning to those obscenity trials it was precisely such considerations that swayed the case. Whatever obscenity was found in individual scenes was justified, so it was argued, by their integration in the whole. This was how the aesthetic was seen to override the ethical.

This chapter has offered a broadly sympathetic presentation of a (moderate) autonomism that gives priority to aesthetic values, broadly conceived, in literature. Unlike less moderate forms of autonomism, it has not endorsed Wildean aestheticism or Clive Bell-style formalism, nor does it deny a role for moral judgments in assessments both of complete works of literature and of individual aspects of such works. It has also taken a mildly skeptical stance toward views that associate literature with moral learning or edification, the idea that reading literature encourages moral sensitivity, empathy, and moral knowledge.

By broadening the idea of aesthetic value beyond merely formal aspects of literature to encompass different models of content, notably subject-level and thematic-level content, the position allows for ethical interests to penetrate in a fine-grained manner into standard literary critical protocols for responding to literature. Thus, an ethical vocabulary will play a central part in the characterization of subject and theme and standard procedures of explication and interpretation will issue in the identification of ethical perspectives and moral valence.

Interestingly, the moderate moralist Noël Carroll agrees with the autonomists that "It is not the function of a narrative artwork to provide moral education" (Carroll 2001, 292). And he further agrees that "typically, the purpose of a narrative artwork is to absorb the reader, viewer, or listener" (Carroll 2001, 292). Where he potentially disagrees is in finding a central place within such absorption for the "enlisting" of a reader's "moral understanding," which in turn can "bequeath moral learning to the audience" (Carroll 2001, 292). But it is not clear how great the differences are here. The reader who identifies and shares the moral valence in the passages from the Hardy novels mentioned earlier or from *Notes from Underground* could well be described as enlisting moral understanding even if the emphasis for the autonomist is more on the reader's critical acuity than moral sensitivity. The question is only what place there is for "moral learning," especially when the function of "moral education" is set aside. In a perfectly anodyne sense, we might say that a reader who engages deeply with the subject and themes of a work where moral perspectives are presented has *learned* something about such perspectives, if only by bringing them to mind. But the instrumental value of that, as a byproduct of reading, is likely to vary significantly across different kinds of readers, with different backgrounds, experience, and interests.

In fact, moralists of different kinds are surprisingly keen, like Carroll, to play down the instrumentality of moral understanding in relation to literature. Berys Gaut, for example, states unequivocally: "The ethicist claim concerns the intrinsic ethical qualities of works, not their empirical consequences or accompaniments" (Gaut 2007, 80) and also "the ethical value of an artwork is not to be understood in terms of the ethical effects of the work on actual audiences" (Gaut 2007, 9). Attending to the "intrinsic ethical qualities" of works is precisely what the aesthetic autonomist demands, for they will manifest themselves in form, subject, and theme. Nussbaum adds this: "The activities of imagination and emotion that the involved reader performs during the time of reading are not just instrumental to moral conduct, they are also examples of moral conduct, in the sense that they are examples of the type of emotional and imaginative activity that good ethical conduct involves" (Nussbaum 1998, 355). Again, the autonomist is unlikely to object to the thought that reading literature and "good ethical conduct" are both types of "emotional and imaginative activity."

As so often in philosophical debates, after careful reflection and compromise, differences can come to seem less extreme. In this debate, all sides agree that ethics and literature are indeed deeply and indivisibly connected. It is inconceivable that anyone should have a serious interest in literature—notably in narrative and dramatic forms— without an interest in ethical reflection as it emerges from the very fabric of the works they enjoy. That is the common ground on this topic.

See also: Stear, Carroll, Jacobson, Gal, and John, this volume

REFERENCES

Anderson, James, and Jeffrey Dean. 1998. "Moderate Autonomism." *British Journal of Aesthetics*, 38, no. 2 (April): 150–166.

Bell, Clive. 1914. *Art*. London: Chatto & Windus.

Bloom, Harold. 1994. *The Western Canon: The Books and School of the Ages*. New York: Harcourt, Brace & Company.

Carroll, Noël. 1998. "Moderate Moralism versus Moderate Autonomism." *British Journal of Aesthetics* 38, no. 4 (October): 419–424.

Carroll, Noël. 2000. "Art and Ethical Criticism: An Overview of Recent Directions in Research." *Ethics* 110, no. 2: 350–387.

Carroll, Noël. 2001. *Beyond Aesthetics*. Cambridge: Cambridge University Press.

Currie, Gregory. 2020. *Imagining and Knowing: The Shape of Fiction*. Oxford: Oxford University Press.

Dostoyevsky, Feodor. [1864] 1977. *Notes from Underground*. Translated by Jessie Coulson. Harmondsworth: Penguin Books.

Eaton, A. W. 2012. "Robust Immoralism." *Journal of Aesthetics and Art Criticism* 70, no. 3 (Summer): 281–192.

Eliot, George. [1860] 1965. *The Mill on the Floss*. New York: Signet.

Gaut, Berys. 1998. "The Ethical Criticism of Art." In *Aesthetics and Ethics*, edited by Jerrold Levinson, 182–203. Cambridge: Cambridge University Press.

Gaut, Berys. 2007. *Art, Emotion, and Ethics*. Oxford: Oxford University Press.

Harold, James. 2003. "Flexing the Imagination." *Journal of Aesthetics and Art Criticism* 61, no. 3 (Summer): 247–257.

Ivanov, Vyacheslav. 1975. "The Revolt Against Mother Earth." In Feodor Dostoevsky, *Crime and Punishment*, edited by George Gibian, 577–585. New York: Norton.

John, Eileen. 2010. "Literature and the Idea of Morality." In *A Companion to the Philosophy of Literature*, edited by Garry L. Hagberg and Walter Jost, 285–299. Oxford: Blackwell Publishing Ltd.

John, Eileen. 2018. "Allegory and Ethical Education: Stories for People Who Know Too Many Stories." *Journal of Philosophy of Education* 52, no.4: 642–659.

Kermode, Frank. 2006. *Pleasure and Change: The Aesthetics of Canon*. Oxford: Oxford University Press.

Kidd, D., and E. Castano. 2013. "Reading Literary Fiction Improves Theory of Mind." *Science* 342, no. 6156 (October): 377–380.

Lamarque, Peter. 2014. *The Opacity of Narrative*. London: Rowman & Littlefield International.

Lamarque, Peter. 2021. "Literary Form and Ethical Content." *Disputatio* 13, no. 62: 245–263.

Mar, R., and K. Oatley. 2008. "The Function of Literature is the Abstraction and Simulation of Social Experience." *Perspectives on Psychological Science* 3, no. 3: 173–192.

Morgan, Bill and Peters, Nancy J., eds. 2006. *Howl on Trial: The Battle for Free Expression*. San Francisco: City Lights Books.

Murdoch, Iris. 1970. *The Sovereignty of Good*. London: Routledge & Kegan Paul.

Novitz, David. 1987. *Knowledge, Fiction and Imagination*. Philadelphia: Temple University Press.

Nussbaum, Martha C. 1990. *Love's Knowledge: Essays on Philosophy and Literature*. Oxford: Oxford University Press.

Nussbaum, Martha C. 1998. "Exactly and Responsibly: A Defense of Ethical Criticism." *Philosophy and Literature* 22, no. 2: 343–365.

Phillips, D. Z. 1982. *Through a Darkening Glass. Philosophy, Literature, and Cultural Change*. Oxford: Blackwell.

Posner, Richard A. 1997. "Against Ethical Criticism." *Philosophy and Literature* 21, no.1: 1–27.

Posner, Richard A. 1998. "Against Ethical Criticism: Part Two." *Philosophy and Literature* 22, no. 2: 394–412.

Prinz, Jesse. 2011. "Is Empathy Necessary for Morality?" In *Empathy: Philosophical and Psychological Perspectives*, edited by A. Coplan and P. Goldie, 211–30. Oxford: Oxford University Press.

Smith, Murray. 2017. *Film, Art, and the Third Culture*. Oxford: Oxford University Press.

Spark, Muriel. 2000. *The Prime of Miss Jean Brodie*. London: Penguin Books.

Stolnitz, Jerome. 1992. "On the Cognitive Triviality of Art." *British Journal of Aesthetics* 32, no. 3: 191–200.

Wilde, Oscar. [1891] 1965. *The Picture of Dorian Gray*. Harmondsworth: Penguin.

CHAPTER 25

FILM

CARL PLANTINGA

VISUAL narratives, and especially that sort of popular film we sometimes call "the movies," have been thought to have an especially acute power over audiences. Soon after the movies became popular in the early twentieth century, concerns rose about their capacity to influence "morals and manners" and to interfere with, and perhaps nullify, formal education and religious instruction (Jowett 1976, 77). Jane Addams, cofounder of the Hull House and winner of the Nobel Peace Prize in 1931, dubbed the movie theater the "House of Dreams" and worried that movies filled young minds with "absurdities which certainly will become the foundation for their working moral codes" (quoted in Jowett 1976, 78). While concerns about the purported morally deleterious effects of the movies have been largely replaced by worries about social media, visual narratives of all sorts—movies, television, and streaming—still maintain their power. The kinds of experiences offered by moving image narratives and their effects on viewers and on culture have long been a central concern; we might call this an ethics of spectatorship.

The relationship between film and ethics, which is fast becoming a central concern of film theory and philosophy, can be approached from varied angles. Two recent edited collections on the topic bear this out. *What Film is Good For: On the Ethics of Spectatorship* (Hjort and Nannicelli 2022) gathers essays by thirty-five films scholars, with discussions ranging from political activism, human rights, and films as cultural rituals to the benefits of aesthetic delight and visions of the good life. *Motion Pictures and Public Value* (Hanich and Rossouw 2023) also centers on what film is good for, though it uses different terminology. Its twenty-six authors discuss, among other subjects, the cultivation of ethical attention, the ethics of representativeness, the poetics of karma and transcendence, and issues of sustainability.

While all of the chapters in these two books are centered on ethics and the public good in relation to motion pictures, they are remarkably varied in subject matter. To narrow the focus somewhat, this chapter will discuss the film spectator's experience in relation to ethics. In other words, ethics in this case asks the question, "What kind of experience do films (or does a particular film) offer, and how can that experience be evaluated from an ethical perspective?" What sorts of stories on screens are to be praised or condemned in relation to our ethical commitments? What sorts of screen stories might be thought to have salutary social benefits? And does the medium itself, in the broad contours of the sort of experiences it offers, have ethical significance?

As a mass art form thought to wield substantial rhetorical power, film has attracted a great deal of attention since its invention in the late nineteenth century, but primarily for the potential ethical *harms* it might bring. It is often thought that films have powerful means to motivate thought and action and to assure a high degree of attention and retention. Noël Carroll contends that the movies derive their particular power from two sources. The first is their elicitation of intense engagement, derived from their capacity to focus attention through framing, editing, and what Carroll calls the erotetic narrative, which proceeds in a neat question/answer progression. The second source of the power of movies is their widespread accessibility, stemming from their use of moving photographic images and sound that require little by way of literacy (Carroll 1996, 78–93). Concerns about the medium thus relate to its mass audience. As the MPPDA Production Code of 1930 reads, while "most arts" appeal to the mature, the motion pictures appeal to "every class of persons" (Motion Picture Producers and Distributors of America 1930, 322–323). And so a concern with film and ethics has, in the past, often taken the form of moral hectoring, production code "lists of don'ts and be carefuls," and censorship.

This chapter will focus on discussions of film and ethics as they developed among film theorists and philosophers of film, often responding to the same or similar concerns as some of the institutions and individuals mentioned above, but also taking examinations of film and ethics in wholly new directions. These are fruitful discussions of the sorts of embodied experiences films offer and the activities and responses they elicit. They include, for example, the kind of thinking and feeling that audiences have while they watch a film, the way that film narratives encourage later reflection, and the skills, proclivities, and affective responses films may cultivate.

CLASSICAL FILM THEORY

Early film theory, traditionally called "classical film theory," was understandably preoccupied with the nature of a then relatively new medium. Much of this discussion emerged in relation to medium specificity, with attempts to identify the nature of the film medium and the artistic commitments that were thought to stem from its nature. While debates about medium specificity are largely beyond the scope of this chapter (see Andrew 1976 and Carroll 1988), such debates had ethical implications that I will comment on here. Classical film theorists were not merely interested in how the medium could reach its artistic potential, but also its potential to impart ethical goods.

Classical film theorists are often put into three camps: the formalists, realists, and revelationists. The formalists were primarily concerned with promoting film as an art form, and thus advocated the use of formal techniques that would rescue films from their supposed propensity to become a bastardized form of theater, or else a mere imitation of the phenomenal world through motion picture photography. Realists, on the other hand, believed that what is special and important about movies is their relationship to the material world. Siegfried Kracauer, who has often been identified as a realist, believed that film was essentially a photographic medium. For Kracauer, this had ethical dimensions. He believed that movies, when made right, had the capacity to reconnect people with the physical reality around them and to deepen their relation to their native habitat, the Earth. In place of traditional religions and mythologies, films can follow nature's own patterns. Ideally, film works on us from the bottom up. As J. Dudley Andrew writes, for Kracauer, film "begins in the earth and shapes our imaginative patterns to the earth" (Andrew 1976, 127). As a realist medium connected to materiality via the photographic image, film can thus assist humanity in developing "imaginative patterns" that derive not from religion or mythology but from nature itself.

André Bazin is by far the most influential realist theorist. For Bazin as for Kracauer, the realism of the movie medium begins with its connection with photography. In "The Ontology of the Photographic Image," Bazin likens a photograph to a fingerprint, footprint, the shadow cast by a sundial, or an embalmed body (Bazin 1967, 9–16). All register a trace of the reality that they signify. Like footprints and fossils, the photograph is related by causality to its referent (what it stands for or represents), because it is created by a mechanical device, the camera, which eliminates at least some aspects of human subjectivity (Bazin 1967, 12). This has ontological, psychological, and ethical implications; the physical nature of moving image photography granted the movies the capacity to connect viewers with nature in a psychologically powerful way (Nagib 2011).

Bazin argued that filmmakers, for both ethical and aesthetic reasons, ought to use techniques and styles that put viewers into a relationship with the movie that is somewhat like their relationship to the outside world. Thus Bazin favored the long take aesthetic, consisting of long takes with camera movement, over the montage style of the Soviets or the classical cutting of Hollywood. At the same time, Bazin also favored narrative techniques that incorporated indirection, ambiguity, and ellipsis, arguing that such realist storytelling managed to respect the ambiguity of reality; this style allowed the viewer a certain amount of freedom of interpretation and required that the spectator actively fill in narrative gaps. Making sense of the right sort of film is much like making sense of the world around us. Spectators must sort through ambiguous information, make hypotheses about missing events, and so on.

Aside from the formalists and realists, Malcolm Turvey has identified what he calls the "revelationist" tradition, an approach to the medium that seems to draw from elements of both formalist and realist theory in its approach to how film ought to be conceptualized vis-à-vis reality (Turvey 2008). For Turvey, theorists such as Jean Epstein, Dziga Vertov, Bela Balázs, and Siegfried Kracauer should be seen as neither formalists ("modernists," as he terms it) nor realists. Like the realists, the revelationists take the capacity of the motion picture medium to reproduce reality to be a valuable one and the starting point for an ethics of film. Unlike André Bazin, however, the revelationists distrust human vision. As Turvey notes, the revelationists "view those stylistic techniques that depart from everyday sight as most likely to reveal reality as it really is" (Turvey 2010, 88). Dziga Vertov, for example, believed that cinema's ability to record people in various locations *and* link the shots together through editing (as human vision cannot normally do), could, as Turvey puts it, "broaden the moral horizons of human beings beyond . . . family and village . . . to include unknown persons connected by geographical location, class, ethnicity, race, and ultimately humanity" (Turvey 2010, 125–126). The revelationist tradition thus effected a kind of compromise between realist and formalist film theories. But most importantly for our purposes, it prefigured the contemporary interest in the capacity of screen stories to extend the range of the viewers' sympathies, as will be detailed further below.

Critique and Interrogation

When film studies emerged as an academic discipline in the 1970s, ethical issues were first subsumed under Marxist concerns about the ideological effects of film viewing. The field at that time more or less presumed a Marxist standpoint such that the words "moral" and "ethical" and their association with personal behavior, were thought to distract us from pressing concerns with political formations and ideology. Neither was film theory at that time particularly concerned about "art," except insofar as the arts had a political function. Film theory in the 1970s and 1980s was intensely interested in the question of what sorts of films and film techniques could lead to emancipation from bourgeois complacency and lead to a distanced, politically savvy spectatorship (Stam 2000, 130–178). This led to a celebration of films and techniques that elicited "critique" and "interrogation," or in other words, the spectator's distanced and reflective response.

This interest came in two major strains. The first is the so-called apparatus theory that melded Lacanian psychoanalysis with an Althusserian Marxism that posited the "subject positioning" by which mainstream films were thought to "reproduce" obedient capitalist subjects. The "subject" was lured by the seductive emotional pleasures of classical Hollywood cinema into a state of regressive and infantile passivity. Whether one accepts the Marxist/psychoanalytic framework or not, it should be noted that contemporary media psychologists tend to agree that the most persuasive narratives are those capable of generating the spectator's immersion or absorption in the story-world. Timothy Brock and Melanie Green, for example, use the term "psychological transportation" rather than immersion, arguing that transporting narratives inhibit "counterarguing" and other forms of potential resistance to the perspectives of the story (Green and Brock 2002).

For the apparatus theorists, film ethics was seemingly a matter of film form and not content, because apparatus theory largely rejected the possibility of objective realism or the idea that spectators might find an opportunity for learning about the world from filmic representation. Mainstream films and classical forms were thought to work hand in hand with bourgeois ideology, conspiring to immerse the spectator into an unthinking state of passivity and mesmerization. The publication of Laura Mulvey's

"Visual Pleasure in the Narrative Cinema" (1975) extended these concerns to the ethics of spectatorship in relation to gender, arguing that the means by which movies instantiate the male gaze embodied both male desire and the idea of femininity as passive, to-be-looked-at. Mulvey's essay generated ongoing discussions of "the gaze" in mainstream film and the gendered nature of film viewing.

On the other hand, modernist, reflexive, and disruptive formal techniques such as those manifested in many of the films of Jean-Luc Godard, Sergei Eisenstein, or Robert Bresson, were held to be emancipatory in their self-consciousness and distancing techniques. Instead of the seamless style and narrative closure characteristic of the classical Hollywood film, theorists celebrated an alternative aesthetics as seen in the films of the various avant-gardes (Dada, expressionism, Surrealism), the exploding anarchy of the Marx Brothers, the disruptive techniques of political modernists like Jean Luc Godard, or the so-called Third Cinemas of developing countries (Stam 2000, 151–157).

The ethics and politics of apparatus theory were often coupled with that of the second strain of 1970s film theory, critical theory. Critical theory emerged from the Frankfurt school and also, like apparatus theory, drew from the theories of playwright, poet, and filmmaker Bertolt Brecht (Stam 2000, 145–150). Theodore Adorno and Max Horkheimer regarded the "culture industry" as the producer of mass art characterized by conformity and the encouragement of passivity, all in the service of bourgeois ideology. The works of the culture industry are seen as stilted and formulaic, stunting the viewer's powers of imagination. As Adorno contends (and with a clear remembrance of the then-recent experience in Nazi Germany), "the power of the culture industry's ideology is such that conformity has replaced consciousness" (Adorno 1975, 13). Adorno favored avant-garde art that was autonomous from the culture industry and that promoted reflective and creative mental activity rather than the predigested passivity of mass art.

As I have argued elsewhere, both of these strains of theory bordered on a kind of ideological (or ethical) formalism, whereby certain formal techniques, especially those that favored reflexivity, disruption, contradiction, and counterpoint, are held to be inherently progressive. An ethical formalism that favors disruptive over realist techniques, however, would have to contend with the apparent ethical benefits of a realist documentary such as Barbara Kopple's *Harlan County, U.S.A.* (1976), and on the other hand, the ethical shortcomings (or at least, irrelevance) of reflexive television programs like *Beavis and Butthead* (1993–2011) and juvenilia like the extremely self-conscious *Wayne's World* (1992). Film form in itself cannot fully determine the ethical significance of a film (Plantinga 2016, 378–379).

Apparatus theory also invoked Bertolt Brecht to advocate for "ideological stoicism," a rejection of emotion as inherently mystifying and the enemy of reflective reasoning. If you want to encourage critical, active, reflective spectatorship, perhaps the fostering of emotional estrangement is the right strategy. Apparatus theorists found mainstream film to be both critically numbing and reactionary, and tended to see pleasure—much of which, I would add, is obtained through emotional experiences—as a trap or lure. The unspoken premise was that emotion and empathy were opposed to reason and were the enemy of distanced, critical thought that enabled the spectator to escape the narrative pleasures that brought on complacent acceptance of bourgeois ideology.

Yet the dichotomy between reason and emotion is simplistic and misleading, as Brecht himself came to recognize. Brecht's thinking about emotion and reflective thought evolved through his life. While the early Brecht often wrote with disdain about "the scum who want to have the cockles of their hearts warmed" (Brecht 1964 [orig. 1927], 14), later in his career he insisted on the *importance* of certain types of emotions and emotion-elicitation strategies in encouraging the sort of savvy spectatorship he favored (Plantinga 2018a, 123–127). Brecht came to realize that reason and emotion were not necessarily opposed, but that practitioners of both film and theater needed to understand how to enlist emotion in the service of the sorts of disruptions and contradictions that might lead to reflective thought and criticism.

Both apparatus and critical theory presumed a Marxist, anti-bourgeois, countermainstream perspective that favored emancipation from the oppressive norms of capitalism and bourgeois morality. One legacy of both apparatus theory and critical theory is, in some forms of poststructuralist ethical theory, the celebration of "interrogation" and "critique" as properly ethical responses to films. Lisa Downing and Libby Saxton, in their book *Film and Ethics: Foreclosed Encounters* (2010), celebrate "interrogative energies" and "a mobilization of the power of questioning" over the adherence to clearly demarcated ethical principles and moral certitudes. Their book examines the ethical implications of films and genres in light of the ethical theories of Levinas, Derrida, Foucault, and others. They write that a "properly critical interrogation of our investments, our belief systems, and our identifications may ultimately be the most ethical academic and political gesture we can make" (159). This interrogatory approach, supposedly, will avoid the problem of personal agency and a unified conception of the self, which they see as endemic to virtue theory approaches to cinema such as that of Joseph Kupfer in his *Visions of Virtue in Popular Film* (1999).

While this "critique and interrogation" approach is certainly preferable to an unthinking adherence to conventional morality, it does not escape moral agency or personal commitment, nor should it attempt to do so. The ethical commitments of Downing and Saxton are clearly present in every chapter of the book; at some point, even in the midst of interrogation, we must define our commitments. Presumably our choices about what to interrogate stem from our sense of what a film gets wrong or where we need to extend our understanding, and that sense depends on ethical beliefs and moral commitments.

The interrogatory approach tends to be less interested in the kind of ethical thinking embodied in a film and more in its capacity to elicit a reflective response after the screening ends. In a piece on *Borat*, for example, Robert A. Clift notes that the film solicits viewers to take pleasure in the ethical violation of others, as Sasha Baron Cohen, as Borat, pranks and offends his way through racist segments of the American public. Yet Clift is less interested in any unethical practices undertaken in making the film, or in ethical evaluations of the film's meaning or solicitations. For Clift, the film's epistemological and ethical work "is not performed *in* the film but *after* the film; it is played out in the conversations, arguments, and inquiries incited by the experience of viewing *Borat*" (Clift 2014, 108).

In making this claim, Clift draws from theorist Michelle Aaron's argument that an ethics of spectatorship directs us not to think about the moral framework developed *in* a film, but rather about "those films that require us to reflect upon our moral framework and those that do not" (Aaron 2007, 114). As with other theorists of critique and interrogation, Aaron favors self-reflexivity and distanced self-reflection to the mesmerization of immersion and the emotions elicited by the design of the narrative. She writes that "involuntary emotion is the opposite of reflection" (116) and holds a catharsis view of emotion whereby having an emotion, for example, about the horrors of war or of cruelty, absolves us of responsibility for those horrors. Having sympathy for a character, likewise, merely proclaims our innocence. In short, the spectator's emotional responses insulate them from responsibility.

Aaron's theory arguably partakes of a questionable reason/emotion dichotomy, however, such that the cool distance of reason is able to see its way through the mesmerization of "involuntary" emotions. But our anger about injustice can also be an involuntary emotion, and may be the result of a largely prereflective appraisal of the unjust situation. And still, our anger may be both justified and beneficial. Aaron also assumes that the affective experiences elicited by the film placate us but prevent us from thinking critically. This view of affect as inherently misleading is open to question, as is the theory of catharsis that underlies these claims (Plantinga 2009, 177–179). And in relation to Clift's article on *Borat*, we can agree that the importance of postfilm reflection and discussion is certainly important in any theory of ethics in film spectatorship; such reflection and discussion, however, may depend in part on the strength of the emotions elicited *in* the film and *during* the viewing. Emotions are not necessarily opposed to reason, and are not necessarily mystifying, but are accompanied by all sorts of cognitive processing, both in consciousness and in the cognitive unconscious (Plantinga 2009, 49–53). And strong emotions elicited during a viewing may well initiate postfilm reflection, discussion, and action.

Elsewhere I argue that although the engendering of critical self-reflection is ethically laudable, theories of critique and interrogation may focus on this single good-making quality at the expense of other ethical benefits (Plantinga 2018a, 104–107) such as aesthetic and other forms of delight, experimentation and imagination, the promotion of justice, empathy and kindness, various communal values and goals, virtue, moral understanding, and the inspiration to act ethically. For an alternative theory that values and seeks to understand *attachment* to works of art, see Rita Felski's *Hooked: Art and Attachment* (2020) and *The Limits of Critique* (2015). It should also be noted that the argument that narrative form has inherent ethical significance can be made from a cognitive perspective as well. Nitzan Ben Shaul (2012) has more recently argued that narratives that offer alternative narrative paths promote "optional thinking," thus potentially opening minds to choices and possibilities.

THE BURDEN OF REPRESENTATION

The issue of the representation of race, ethnicity, sexual orientation, and gender has been an enduring concern of film and television ethics; the associated problems are sometimes called "the burden of representation." The presumption is that screen narratives have the capacity to affect how viewers see types of people. There is good reason for this concern. Aristotle claimed that poetry (by which he meant fiction, broadly speaking) is "a more philosophical and a higher thing" than history because it deals with what "may happen" rather than what "has happened," and thus with the universal rather than the particular (Aristotle 1971, 53). Thus the wizard in *The Wizard of Oz* (1939) or John Wayne's cowboy Ethan Edwards in *The Searchers* (1956) can become, in the minds of the audience, representative of all wizards and all cowboys. And these kinds can, in some cases, become harmful stereotypes, reflective of demeaning ways dominant groups conceive of others. The concern with stereotypes is the most obvious manifestation of the ethics of representation. A veritable cottage industry of books and articles (too numerous to fully cite) has examined representations of various racial and ethnic groups, genders, sexual orientations, and several other "types" by which we slot people into familiar roles and categorize those around us. These types can become stereotypes, rigid categorizations that prevent us, through sheer repetition, from seeing the diversity and complexity of humanity.

Stereotypes are also sometimes demeaning, leading to the dehumanization of the group so portrayed. For example, Thomas Bogle identifies common stereotypes of Black characters as toms, coons, mulattos, mammies, and bucks (2001). And as Molly Haskell writes in her book *From Reverence to Rape: The Treatment of Women in the Movies* (2016), "images" of women in films (1) reflect ways society sees women, (2) teach viewers how to view women, and (3) participate in the social construction of gender. Aside from the obvious ethical importance of stereotypes, they also raise the underexplored problem of representativeness. How do some characterizations become rigid stereotypes, while others do not? How does a character come to be seen as representative of a type rather than as a singular and unique individual? What kinds of social forces and power relationships are at work in representativeness?

The interest in characters and/or stereotypes as representative, while valuable, can be reductive when it fails to recognize the contexts in which such representations occur. A narrative film unfolds temporally, and is in many cases designed to encourage changes in perspective toward the characters as the narrative progresses. In their simplest form, characters can become rigid stereotypes. But filmmakers can also create expectations or assumptions only to thwart them. Too much emphasis on the static stereotype may lead to a misunderstanding of one of the fundamental characteristics of narrative, that it unfolds in time, an evolving narrative in which circumstances and characters change over time.

Ella Shohat and Robert Stam offer a helpful account of stereotypes in their book *Unthinking Eurocentrism: Multiculturalism and the Media* (2014), in which they both celebrate the importance of stereotype criticism and recognize its limitations. They claim that an undue focus on stereotypes can be moralist and individualist and lose sight of both narrative development and the complex "voices" or positions that come together in the film. It may ignore the issue of how stereotypes are meant to function in their narrative and cinematic context. And it may ignore issues of "perspective and the social positioning both of the filmmakers and the audience" (205). Shohat and Stam argue that it makes more sense to speak less of "images" and "stereotypes" and more of "voices" and "discourses," to get beneath the surface features to the social voices and positions being promoted, imagined, or considered in the film (214–215).

FILM AS PHILOSOPHY AND ETHICAL EXPERIENCE

Adherents of the film-philosophy movement emphasize the capacity of films to lead the spectator through a complex temporal experience that often has ethical import. Some claim that films "do philosophy" or "philosophize." As a figure of speech, such a claim is not controversial. Most would agree that in some cases, films can elicit complex thinking and feeling about a range of philosophical issues. Whether it is the films doing philosophy or else the filmmakers doing philosophy through their films is the question. Films can certainly serve as prompts for complex embodied experiences, including ethical thinking elicited through the spectator's engagement with characters and the following of the narrative. Whatever the case, however, debates about whether films *do* philosophy are merely terminological in part. The important question is whether films can become prompts for and/or lead the spectator through a philosophically and ethically beneficial experience.

Many scholars have argued that they can. Film-as-philosophy approaches have significant points of content with the cognitive/analytical approaches described in the next section. For our purposes here, suffice it to say that film-as-philosophy approaches demonstrate the ethical significance of a film primarily through close analysis and interpretation, while cognitive/analytic approaches foreground philosophical concepts and psychological research, also often employing these within interpretive claims about the experience or thinking films may elicit.

Robert Sinnerbrink is an important advocate of the potential for films to offer profound ethical experiences to the viewer, arguing that films can "evoke ethical experience and invite philosophical reflection" not only through a unified thematic and emotional experience, but also by complexities "through which conflicting, clashing, or incompatible ideas, commitments, or beliefs can be revealed" (Sinnerbrink 2016, 8). Filmic worlds that are "morally ambiguous, ethically intolerable, or politically extreme" may prompt conflicting responses, which can themselves be productive, however unpleasant.

For Sinnerbrink, cinema and ethics are related in at least these four ways: (1) we can find ethical significance in cinema, that is, in the experience offered the spectator through morally charged scenarios; (2) the ethics and politics of representation focuses on ethical issues raised by film production or by spectator response; (3) the ethics of cinema as a cultural medium focuses on symptomatic expressions of beliefs, social values, and ideology, as in the issues of representation discussed above; and (4) we can study the aesthetic dimensions of cinema as a way of evoking ethical experience and expressing ethical meaning (Sinnerbrink 2019, 15–16). Sinnerbrink writes that the challenge is to think these four together. Ever the pluralist, Sinnerbrink also wants to bring together four theoretical approaches to cinematic ethics: Cavellian, Deleuzian, phenomenological, and postphenomenological, and cognitivist film theory. Thus Sinnerbrink aims to "explore the idea of cinema as a medium of ethical experience with a transformative potential to sharpen our moral perception, challenge our beliefs through experiential means, and thus enhance our understanding of socio-moral complexity" (Sinnerbrink 2016, 16).

Sinnerbrink argues that one of the chief ways that films can encourage philosophical and ethical thinking is through what he calls "cinempathy"; he offers an analysis of the brilliant Iranian film *A Separation* (2011) to illustrate his point. As it reveals its story of a husband and wife at loggerheads and headed for divorce, the film "provides a powerful means of enacting the affective temporal dynamic between empathy and sympathy, emotional engagement, and multiple perspective-taking." Thus films have the potential to offer "experientially rich, context-sensitive, and ethically singular forms of imaginative engagement in social situations that reveal the complexities of a cultural-historical world" (Sinnerbrink 2016, 80).

Although Sinnerbrink has gone farther than most in explicitly examining the nature of the ethical experience offered through films in this tradition, he is certainly not alone (see the essays in Jones and Vice 2007, for example). Although practitioners of the film-as-philosophy position will appeal to theoretical argument to make their case, they normally rely on close analysis and interpretation to carefully show how films embody ethical thinking. Here I mention just a few examples. Joseph Kupfer (1999) and Philip Gillet (2012) show how various narrative films highlight issues of ethics and virtue theory. Jane Stadler's book *Pulling Focus: Intersubjective Experience and Narrative Film* (2012) argues that films have the capacity to helpfully reframe ethical issues for spectators. Tom Wartenberg's writing on film as philosophy often focuses on film as ethics, for example in his chapter on Orson Welles's *The Third Man* in *Thinking on Screen: Film as Philosophy* (2007). Finally, Martin Rossouw's recent *Transformational Ethics of Film* (2021) traces debates in the film-as-philosophy movement and discusses film spectatorship as a practice of self-transformation.

COGNITIVE/ANALYTICAL APPROACHES

M. H. Abrams writes that when we become interested in a story, "we are interested in a way that brings into play our entire moral economy and expresses itself continuously in attitudes of approval or disapproval, sympathy or antipathy." The storyteller attempts "to persuade us to concur with the common-sense and moral positions" presupposed by the work, and when the story is done well, "contrives which of our beliefs will be called into play, to what degree, and with what emotional effect" (Abrams 1958, 17). The reading or viewing process puts the ethical selves of viewers and readers into play, and has the potential for ethical persuasion, instruction, or corruption. Both cognitive film theory and analytic aesthetics have focused squarely on the moral psychology of the viewer's encounter with visual narratives. Film theorist Wyatt Moss-Wellington, in his two recent books (2021 and 2019) challenges cognitive film theorists and philosophers to go beyond a naturalistic concern with what is to address questions of what ought to be, and to adopt what he calls a "humanist consequentialism."

Some good work on questions of ought in relation to film and ethics has already been accomplished. Approaches to film and ethics from the perspective of aesthetic cognitivism would tend to make the following assumptions, adapted from an account by Cynthia Freeland of the relation to art in general to cognition (Freeland 1997, 19):

1. Narrative film may stimulate cognitive activity, here broadly conceived of as both thinking and feeling, in ways that can teach us about the world.
2. This cognitive activity is central to the functioning of films as works of art.
3. As a result of this stimulation, we can learn from narrative films: "We acquire fresh knowledge, our beliefs are refined, and our understanding is deepened."
4. We enjoy and value narrative films in part due to what we learn from them.

One sort of learning obtainable from films would be moral learning. We have already considered the possibility that screen stories can mislead us through stereotyped representation. On the other hand, narrative films have the capacity to teach us about varieties of characters in sometimes complex or ambiguous circumstances through which they plot their course of action. Narrative films can embody clear moral positions and principles, or perhaps more interestingly, they can offer complex narratives in which various stances, positions, and characters are brought together in what could only be described as a kind of thought experiment.

One influential account of moral learning from art is Noël Carroll's "clarificationism" (Carroll 1998, 319–342). Carroll holds that artworks like screen stories may confer moral learning not by teaching us new propositions, but by clarifying and enhancing moral understanding we already possess. This learning occurs chiefly because viewing screen stories can enable us to apply moral knowledge we already possess to novel situations. Carroll notes that narratives are inherently incomplete, and that when viewing narratives, audiences are required to fill in the gaps as a means of completion. As an example, Carroll discusses *A Raisin in the Sun* (1961) which, as he notes, "addresses white audiences in such a way as to incite vividly their recognition that African Americans are persons, like any others, and, therefore, should be accorded the kind of equal treatment of persons that such audiences already verbally endorse as a matter of moral principle" (326).

This example, however, does suggest one difficulty for Carroll's notion of clarificationism. If *A Raisin in the Sun* does elicit this sort of recognition in a viewer, and if said viewer did not previously believe that African Americans are persons, it is hard to see why this new understanding should not be counted as *new* propositional knowledge. On the other hand, if we were to say that the film made vivid this proposition and motivates audiences to take action with regard to propositional knowledge they already had, namely that African Americans are persons, then this outcome is not an epistemological clarification so much as an *inspiration* to act on our already-existing knowledge stock, or at least to put this propositional knowledge at the front of one's mental queue such that plays a larger role in one's thought and action going forward. Perhaps this is what Carroll means when he writes that clarification in his sense involves a "gestalt switch," in which seeing a film can cause a viewer to "reorganize and reshuffle" one's moral beliefs (327).

In *Screen Stories and the Ethics of Engagement* (2018a), I distinguish between moral learning (which I refer to as the "transfer" of knowledge from a fictional to the actual world) and moral cultivation. Fictional stories can increase our moral knowledge because while the particular characters they deal with do not actually exist, such characters (and other entities in the fiction such as event structures, perspectives, and patterns of social interaction) are often representative of types that *can* exist in the actual world. From a film like *A Raisin in the Sun* we can learn something new about what it entails to be the object of racial prejudice, if the fictional events represented are characteristic types of events that actually occur. Just as important as moral learning, however, is the cultivation of skills and sensitivities, or "habits of the heart" (Plantinga 2018a, 70–71). Thus even if the viewer were already fully cognizant of the humanity of others, fiction may cultivate a sensitivity to that fact, moving this knowledge to the front and center of one's mental architecture such that it informs one's everyday thought and action as a kind of disposition to act or sensibility of thought. We could call that a moral commitment.

Moral learning must be distinguished from moral persuasion, of course. For it is possible that screen stories might function as persuasive prompts for the uptake of harmful perspectives, as I claim is the case in regard to the "fascist affect" of the 2006 film *300*, for example (Plantinga 2019). Fictions often make an implicit case for various moral perspectives. The case is embedded in the nature of the viewing experience the film attempts to elicit, in the very emotional responses the unfolding narrative is designed to arouse—anger and disdain toward an antagonist, sympathy for the protagonist and relief and happiness when she overcomes obstacles and achieves her laudable goals. The search for pleasure is a strong motivation for the viewer to allow the film to do its work, and much of that work is to elicit a pleasurable affective experience that evolves through the course of the story's unfolding. I divide the proximate and immediate pleasures of screen stories into three categories: (1) cognitive, such as the pleasure in coming to know or understand, (2) affective, such as the sensory pleasure we take in looking, the experience of positive emotions, and sympathy or empathy for favored characters (more to be said on this below), and (3) therapeutic pleasures we take when a story seems to aid us in coping with our fears, doubts, or anxieties; renews our sense of the world as a place of beauty and/or inspiration; and/or confirms our sense of the nature of an issue or problem (Plantinga 2018a, 47–51). Social scientists have found that the most persuasive screen stories are those that are immersive, encourage strong engagement with one or more protagonists, exhibit a high level of craftsmanship, elicit a participatory response, and are socially attuned to relevant cultural discourses (Plantinga 2018a, 52–53).

To better understand how the emotions are central to the potential for screen stories to persuade, consider Noël Carroll's account of the emotional rhetoric of *Philadelphia* (1993), a film which tells the story of a young lawyer Beckett (Tom Hanks) who is illegally terminated from his law firm because he suffers from HIV/AIDS. Suppose that a viewer opposed to or made uncomfortable by homosexuality then views the film *Philadelphia*. Further suppose that said viewer is moved by the film, allowing himself to feel the emotions and sympathies it attempts to elicit. Following Jesse Prinz, Carroll claims that a film such as *Philadelphia* has the capacity to *recalibrate* our emotions, in part by causing us to "refile" objects from one mental category to another (Carroll 2014). Thus if the viewer associates homosexuals with the disgust response, a film like *Philadelphia* can put Beckett into the context of a loving family. In the film's final scenes, as the deeply loved Beckett lies on his deathbed, his family members say their good-byes one by one, exchanging their moving last words with their son and brother. If successful, the film changes attitudes toward homosexuals by recalibrating Beckett, and by extension homosexual men generally, as beloved family members.

The viewer's psychological entry into a story is most often through its major characters, and thus the viewer's engagement with characters has important implications for the ethics of spectatorship. Murray Smith has argued that spectators develop allegiances with characters largely based on a moral evaluation of the character (Smith 1995). If a character possesses moral virtues, or engages in morally salutary behavior, the spectator will, all things being equal, tend to sympathize with the character. We like Becket's lawyer, Joe Miller (Denzel Washington), not only because he defends Beckett, but because he overcomes his own distaste for homosexuality and comes to respect and love the stricken man, becoming a kind of moral exemplar. But sympathies for characters are not necessarily instructive. I have argued that films can sometimes encourage allegiances with characters based on nonmoral traits such as appearance, similarity, and style, which can potentially lead to a form of moral confusion or dumbfounding whereby spectator attitudes toward characters are not rooted in moral criteria, but may be interpreted as such (Plantinga 2018a, 206).

The viewer's sympathy and empathy for characters has clear ethical importance. As we have seen, several observers find that the development and expansion of empathy is a key potential of screen stories (Sinnerbrink 2019; Stadler 2012). Visual narratives have unique means of eliciting empathy for characters through cinema through framing, lighting, editing, music, and pacing. For example, in what I call a "the scene of empathy," typically occurring well into a narrative, the pacing slows considerably and the camera rests in a close-up shot, usually comparatively long in duration, of the face of an emoting character (Plantinga 1999). Examples include Charlie Chaplin's embarrassed smile at the end of *City Lights* (1931) and the close-up of replicant Roy Batty (Rutger Hauer) at the end of *Blade Runner* (1982) as he gives his dying soliloquy. Such scenes, in their narrative placement and use of cinematic techniques, are employed in such a way as to maximize empathetic responses in viewers. In fact, Vittorio Gallese and Michele Guerra call their account of relationships between cinema and neuroscience in the elicitation of "embodied simulation" *The Empathic Screen* (2020), illustrating the centrality of empathy for screen storytelling.

Empathy and sympathy in film viewing are regularly regarded as one of the key ethical features of screen stories (See also Coplan 2004; Coplan 2009; Plantinga 2018a, 191–210). Some scholars make a sharp distinction between empathy as feeling with, and sympathy as feeling for, a character. Yet most of the time when we sympathize or empathize with characters, we both feel with them by having similar and congruent emotions, and sympathize with them because we can never wholly share the experience of a fictional character from the inside (Plantinga 2018a, 198–199). Antipathy would then be opposed to sympathy and empathy, and rooted largely in the moral disapproval of a character. The capacity of screen stories to enlarge our sympathies, to train our antipathies, or else to confound and confuse us in that regard, has tremendous ethical implications. For as primatologist Frans DeWaal argues, sympathy and empathy are the pillars of morality, helping to ensure that reciprocal altruism will occur and be rewarded by the pleasures of human feeling" (DeWaal 2009). To the extent that engagement with screen characters in fictions can alter our real-world sympathies and antipathies, screen fictions have vital implications for an ethics of spectatorship. The key going forward will be to relate the moral psychology of sympathy and character engagement with cultural understandings of stereotypes and representativeness, as discussed in the third section of this chapter.

See also: Carroll, Clavel-Vázquez, Destrée, John, this volume

References

Aaron, Michele. 2007. *Spectatorship: The Power of Looking On*. London: Wallflower Press.

Abrams, M. H. 1958. "Belief and the Suspension of Disbelief." In *Literature and Belief: English Institute Essays 1957*, edited by M. H. Abrams, 1–30. New York: Columbia University Press.

Adorno, T. W. 1975. "Culture Industry Reconsidered." *New German Critique* 6: 12–19.

Andrew, J. Dudley. 1976. *The Major Film Theories: An Introduction*. Oxford: Oxford University Press.

Aristotle. 1971. "Poetics." In *Critical Theory Since Plato*, edited by Hazard Adams, 47–66. New York: Harcourt Brace Jovanovich.

Bazin, André. 1967. In *What is Cinema?* Vol. 1., edited and translated by Hugh Gray. Berkeley: University of California Press.

Bogle, Thomas. 2001. *Toms, Coons, Mulattos, Mammies, and Bucks: An Interpretive History of Blacks in American Films*. London: Bloomsbury Academic.

Brecht, Bertolt. 1964. *Brecht on Theatre*, translated by Jay Willet. New York: Hill and Wang.

Brereton, Pat. 2015. *Environmental Ethics and Film*. London: Routledge.

Carroll, Noël. 1988. *Philosophical Problems of Classical Film Theory*. Princeton, NJ: Princeton University Press.

Carroll, Noël. 1996. *Theorizing the Moving Image*. Cambridge: Cambridge University Press.

Carroll, Noël. 1998. *A Philosophy of Mass Art*. Oxford: Oxford University Press.

Carroll, Noël. 2014. "Moral Change: Fiction, Film, and Family." In *Cine-Ethics: Ethical Dimensions of Film Theory*, edited by Jinhee Choi and Mattias Frey, 43–56. New York: Routledge.

Clift, Robert A. 2014. "Uncomfortable Viewing: Deauthorized Performances, Ethics, and Spectatorship in Sasha Baron Cohen's *Borat*." In *Cine-ethics: Ethical Dimensions of Film Theory, Practice, and Spectatorship*, edited by Jinhee Choi and Mattias Frey, 96–110. New York: Routledge.

Coplan, Amy. 2009. "Empathy and Character Engagement." In *The Routledge Companion to Philosophy and Film*, edited by Paisely Livingston and Carl Plantinga, 97–110. London: Routledge.

Coplan, Amy. "Empathic Engagement with Narrative Fictions." 2004. *Journal of Aesthetics and Arts Criticism* 62, no. 2: 141–152.

De Waal, Frans. 2009. *The Age of Empathy: Nature's Lessons for a Kinder Society*. New York: Harmony Books.

Downing, Lisa, and Libby Saxton. 2010. *Film and Ethics: Foreclosed Encounters*. New York: Routledge.

Felski, Rita. 2020. *Hooked: Art and Attachment*. Chicago: University of Chicago Press.

Felski, Rita. *The Limits of Critique*. 2015. Chicago: University of Chicago Press.

Gallese, Vittorio, and Michele Guerra. 2020. *The Empathic Screen: Cinema and Neuroscience*. Oxford: Oxford University Press.

Gillett, Philip. 2012. *Film and Morality*. Newcastle upon Tyne: Cambridge Scholars Publishing.

Green, Melanie C., and Timothy C. Brock. 2002. "In the Mind's Eye: Transportation-Imagery Model of Narrative Persuasion." In *Narrative Persuasion: Social and Cognitive Foundations*, edited by Melanie C. Green, Jeffrey J. Strange, and Timothy C. Brock, 315–341. Mahwah, NJ: Lawrence Erlbaum.

Hanich, Julian, and Rossouw, Martin P., eds. 2023. *What Film Is Good For: On the Ethics of Spectatorship*. Berkeley: University of California Press.

Haskell, Molly. 2016. *From Reverence to Rape: The Treatment of Women in the Movies*. 3rd ed. Chicago: University of Chicago Press.

Hjort, Mette, and Ted Nannicelli, eds. 2022. *Motion Pictures and Public Value*. New York: Routledge.

Jones, Ward E., and Samantha Vice, eds. 2007. *Ethics at the Cinema*. Oxford: Oxford University Press.

Jowett, Garth. 1976. *Film: The Democratic Art: A Social History of American Film*. Boston: Little, Brown, and Company.

Kupfer, Joseph. 1999. *Visions of Virtue in Popular Film*. Boulder, CO: Westview Press.

Moss-Wellington, Wyatt. 2021. *Cognitive Film and Media Ethics*. Oxford: Oxford University Press.

Moss-Wellington, Wyatt. 2019. *Narrative Humanism: Kindness and Complexity in Fiction and Film*. Edinburgh: Edinburgh University Press.

Motion Picture Producers and Distributors of America. 1982. "The Motion Picture Production Code of 1930." In *The Movies in Our Midst*, edited by Gerald Mast, 321–333. Chicago: University of Chicago Press.

Nagib, Lúcia. 2011. *World Cinema and the Ethics of Realism*. New York: Continuum Books.

Plantinga, Carl. 2019. "Fascist Affect in *300*." *Projections: The Journal for Movies and Mind* 13, no. 2: 20–37.

Plantinga, Carl. 2018a. *Screen Stories: Emotion and the Ethics of Engagement*. Oxford: Oxford University Press.

Plantinga, Carl. 2018b. "Brecht, Emotion, and the Reflective Spectator: The Case of *BlacKkKlansman*." *NECSUS: European Journal of Media Studies* 8, no. 1: 151–169.

Plantinga, Carl. 2016. "Notes on Spectator Emotion and Ideological Film Criticism." In *Film Theory and Criticism*, 8th ed., edited by Leo Braudy and Marshall Cohen, 374–393. New York: Oxford University Press.

Plantinga, Carl. 2009. *Moving Viewers: American Film and the Spectator's Experience*. Berkeley: University of California Press.

Plantinga, Carl. 1999. "The Scene of Empathy and the Human Face on Film." In *Passionate Views: Film, Cognition, and Emotion*, edited by Carl Plantinga and Greg M. Smith, 239–255. Baltimore: Johns Hopkins University Press.

Rossouw, Martin P. 2021. *Transformational Ethics of Film: Thinking the Cinemakeover in the Film-Philosophy Debate*. Leiden: Brill Rodopi.

Shohat, Ella, and Robert Stam. 2014. *Unthinking Eurocentrism: Multiculturalism and the Media*. 2nd ed. London: Routledge.

Sinnerbrink, Robert. 2019. *Terrence Malick: Filmmaker and Philosopher*. London: Bloomsbury Academic.

Sinnerbrink, Robert. 2016. *Cinematic Ethics: Exploring Ethical Experience Through Film*. London: Routledge.

Smith, Murray. 1995. *Engaging Characters: Fiction, Emotion, and the Cinema*. Oxford: Clarendon Press.

Stadler, Jane. 2012. *Pulling Focus: Intersubjective Experience, Narrative Film, and Ethics*. London: Continuum.

Stam, Robert. 2000. *Film Theory: An Introduction*. Malden, MA: Blackwell.

Turvey, Malcolm. 2010. "Balázs: Realist or Modernist?" In *The Film Theory Reader: Debates and Arguments*, edited by Marc Furstenau, 80–89. New York: Routledge.

Turvey, Malcolm. 2008. *Doubting Vision: Film and the Revelationist Tradition*. Oxford: Oxford University Press.

Wartenberg, Thomas E. 2007. *Thinking on Screen: Film as Philosophy*. London: Routledge.

....

CHAPTER 26

ETHICS AND MUSIC

....

KATHLEEN HIGGINS

Music is ubiquitous, and so is the tendency to connect it with extra-musical aspects of human life. Across cultures it is an integral part of socially significant activities, and many traditions consider it ethically significant because of its powers to influence, to further relationships among people, and to enable human flourishing. Plato and Aristotle consider musical training a means for developing virtue. The Confucian tradition similarly sees harmonious music as conducive to social harmony, while Daoist thinkers associate music with attunement to the larger world. Many societies use music to teach moral lessons (for example, see Ellis 1985, 17). Anthropologist John Miller Chernoff describes Ghanaian drum music as articulating a moral system and creating opportunities for ethical interaction within "the music-making situation itself" (1979, 37; cf. Amegago, 2000). Music educator Marissa Silverman describes ethical benefits of West African drumming even outside its cultural context, reporting ways in which drumming students at Montclair State University develop caring relationships, mutual respect, and feelings of community (2018, 16 and 22).

While music is cross-culturally used in the service of moral education and social improvement, it is not always considered ethically beneficial. Whole musical styles have been subjected to moral criticism. Historically, Plato and Confucius both argue that the wrong sort of music could have a harmful effect on character and behavior. (See Destrée, Hutton, this volume.) The same conviction seems to animate modern moral critics of particular musical idioms, who have variously condemned crooning, the blues, jazz, rock 'n' roll (and rock more generally), rap (and hip/hop), punk, and probably other popular forms of music. Although blanket rejections of types of music may be unjustified, it would be difficult to defend music as an unmitigated ethical good. Music is utilized to wage war, inflict torture, incite violence, rally support for vicious projects, and control people in questionable ways.

Some of the ethical issues related to music are similar to those raised in connection with the other arts. Among these are: whether the ethical character of the artist (or the presented persona) should be considered in assessing the art (e.g., Gracyk 2017, Matthes, this volume); whether engaging with particular artworks can make us morally worse (e.g., Smuts 2019; Woodcock, this volume); whether immorality represented in the work has a deleterious influence on the audience (e.g., Taruskin 2009); whether art should be censored and, if so, on what grounds (e.g., Korpe, Reitov, and Cloonan 2006; Soucek, this volume); when appropriation of another culture's music is wrong (e.g., Feld 2000; Nguyen and Strohl, this volume); when the production, reproduction, and/or marketing of artworks is exploitative and what should be done to redress such injustice (e.g., Inawat 2015). A case involving the last of these issues is what Amiri Baraka terms "the Great Music Robbery," in which white musicians who performed African American music became prominent and fabulously wealthy while the music's originators were not appropriately compensated (see Baraka 1987, 328–333; Rudinow 2010, 131ff.; Taylor 2016, 175). The extreme rewards of musical stardom in the era of widespread distribution of recordings makes this an especially egregious example. Nevertheless, debates about what should be done to right past wrongs is an issue that extends well beyond cases involving music.

In this chapter, I will focus on distinctive features of music that give it potency for ethical good or ill. I will begin by drawing attention to music's effects on the human body and psyche, indicating the ways in which they affect our sense of interpersonal connectedness. I will go on to consider three ways in which music is used in moral education, each of which builds on the relational character of musical experiences. I will then discuss ways in which music can serve unethical projects, noting that the mechanisms involved are often the same as those used by moral educators. Considering whether we should consider music "itself" ethically neutral and direct moral evaluation at the ways it is used, I explain why this approach will not always be helpful. We typically encounter music with a penumbra of associations that must be recognized to make responsible ethical choices in using it. I will conclude, however, that while music on its own cannot produce good people and good societies, we should make choices that will actualize its potential to contribute to human flourishing.

THE POWER OF MUSIC OVER BODY AND MIND

How to define "music" is debated. I am inclined toward a broad definition, along the lines of John Blacking's "humanly organized sound," but allowing for the inclusion of some vocal productions of nonhuman animals as well (1973, 10). Even if one does not define music so permissively, music's characteristically involving sound does not seem up for debate.[1] Music's sonic aspects have physiological and psychological effects that make it serviceable for both ethical and unethical projects.

---

[1] Even in the atypical case of John Cage's 4' 33," the silence of the performance ambient sound draws attention to ambient sound.

"More than any other art form," Marcel Cobussen and Nanette Nielsen observe, "music has the potential to invade personal spaces" (2012, 8). Music penetrates the body, entering it directly through the ears and through the membrane of the skin. The whole body resonates with music, and when not technologically channeled through earphones or contained through soundproofing techniques, it causes the body and the environment to resonate together. Music also engages the motor system, which we use to navigate external space (see Nussbaum 2007). This bodily activation is evident when we feel the urge to move to a beat or to dance in response. Rhythmic music also entrains us, regulating the pace of our activity, and synchronizing our behavior with that of others who are experiencing the music.

By virtue of rhythmic entrainment, the sonic features of music also promote social bonding. Sound, in fact, is our primary means for detecting the presence of others, for the auditory system relays information to the brain much more rapidly than does the visual system, which is also more limited in directional scope (see Bregman 1993). We are alert to sounds as indicators of others who are present, and we hear musical sound as intentional as well.

When not technologically restricted, music's reach is extensive and multidirectional, and thus it is always at least potentially shared with others. Musical synchronization of many individuals' physical movements can be a means for coordinating activities, and the coordination itself can provoke feelings of connectedness. Cobussen and Nielsen point out that music draws attention to our participation in a larger world, for it involves "an experiential sensing of the world as life-world," in which we attend and respond to other people (2012, 163).

Chernoff links the relationality of music to ethical functions, including the aforementioned objectification and manifestation of moral systems, the development of community cohesion, and the promotion of relationships based on mutual respect (1987). While his account is focused on the specific musical practices he encountered in Ghana, it illuminates three basic ways in which music functions in moral education: it articulates moral ideas, provides occasions for interacting in ethically desirable ways, and engenders pro-social attitudes and motivations. In the next several sections we will observe some of the aspects of music that suit it to serving these three functions.

Music as Moral Model

Music can reveal a society's ideals for interpersonal interaction because it is itself inherently social. To see this, we do best to depart from the tendency common in Western aesthetic theorizing to focus on the experience of the individual listener. Music's social dimension becomes more visible if we consider the broader range of activities that fall into the category of "musicking," defined by Christopher Small as taking part "in any capacity, in a musical performance, whether by performing, by listening, by rehearsing or practicing, by providing material for performance (what is called composition), or by dancing" (1998, 9). This definition of musicking emphasizes the similarities between listening and more performative modes of musical engagement, which is apt in light of the fact that the brain activity of attentive listeners resembles that of performers (see Zatorre and Halpern 2005). It also recognizes the solitary music-maker's engagement in gestures that are implicitly social and directed outward, toward a larger world.

Much musicking involves the interaction of distinct (human or instrumental) voices with each other. This interaction can serve as a model for ways that human beings relate in any situation, and ethnomusicologists have noted similarities between social and musical organization within societies, suggesting that musical structure embeds the patterns that are taken to be norms for interaction. Pioneering this type of theorizing, Alan Lomax drew correlations between various societies' typical musical forms and profiles of societal structure. He considered features of musical structure that are typically emphasized in Western analyses (such as pitches, rhythms, interval size), but also other features, such as desired vocal quality, characteristic embellishments, and the organization and typical behavior of music-making groups (such as their size, composition, relative egalitarian or authoritarian organization, gender distribution, etc.) (Lomax 1976). Although the details of his theory and certain features of his methodology have been rejected, ethnomusicologists continue to recognize parallels between musical organization and forms of social institutions (cf. Feld 1984a, 384).

The idea of isolated cultures and musical traditions, unaffected by external influences, is anachronistic, given the global dissemination of music and the rarity of isolated societies. Nevertheless, we can still see correspondences between social patterns and musical ones and parallels between social groups' ideals for interpersonal interaction and their preferred ways of organizing music. Musical structure displays and implicitly endorses broad features of social organization through patterns in the ways that parts interact, the tolerance of noise elements and heterophony, the encouragement or discouragement of spontaneous participation by those not part of a fixed ensemble, the degree to which performers are subordinated to a controlling authority (such as a conductor), and so forth (cf. Cobussen 2012, 104). Performance conventions for a musical idiom may also legitimize a particular style of comportment through the degree to which it allows for overt emotional expression and bodily movement, as opposed to subordination to more "rational" control.

The structures of extended musical form can also objectify certain ethical visions. Musical genres with characteristic sequential developments can utilize their development to suggest ethically significant possibilities. The sonata-allegro form in Western classical music, for example, is designed to reflect the reconciliation of opposites in a higher synthesis. While the form as such does not provide specific guidance on interpersonal interaction, it suggests a vision in which sharp tensions and contrasts can be reconciled in ways that preserve the distinct character of contrasting elements. This vision may have inspirational ethical force, encouraging acceptance of differences by presenting them as not ultimately antagonistic (cf. Berman 1993; Higgins 2012, 130). Some forms of musical interaction in performance, such as jazz improvisation, also manifest distinct parts whose contribution to the overall achievement depends in part on their preserving their uniqueness, suggesting possibilities for harmonious social interactions beyond the musical context (Higgins 2011, 149–151; Cobussen and Nielsen 2012, 62–65).

Musicologist Robert Hatten suggests another way that musical structure can contribute to moral education. He draws attention to works in Western art music whose structures present virtual dramas with a dramatic arc and an outcome. According to Hatten, these dramas involve the interactions and gestures of virtual agents, with whom we identify when listening (2018, 79). He submits that attending to such virtual agency can occasion moral insight.

> Emotions are not simply represented or expressed as singular emotional packets; rather we engage with the continuously unfolding development of a character or subject through its virtual emotional life (with implications for thinking, for moral awareness, and for psychological *Bildung* as the growth of an individual character). And that engagement . . . involves not only identifying with familiar characters but coming to understand new identities. As we continue to learn from their journeys, we develop our own subjective and intersubjective competencies. (197)

Hatten's contention that the tracking of a virtual agent's trajectory through music can expand the listener's consciousness in ways that enhance moral awareness points us toward a second way in which music serves moral education. Music can help one to develop virtues that promote interpersonal harmony. We will consider music's cultivation of particular virtues in the following section.

THE MUSICAL ENCOUNTER
DEVELOPING VIRTUE

To see how engaging with music can foster virtue, let us begin by considering Chernoff's account of his moral discoveries while studying with a drumming teacher in Ghana. He describes a discussion about morality and respect that he had with his teacher, Ibrahim, after he had lost his temper with another drummer, Alhassan. The day after this conversation, Ibrahim, Alhassan, and Chernoff played together for a gathered group. While polyrhythmically interacting with the other drummers, Chernoff realized that Ibrahim was testing him by feeding him challenging rhythms and that this test was designed to bring out his best: "Ibrahim did not want to knock me off the beat but was rather giving me the *better chance to succeed*" (1979, 139).

Chernoff describes this experience as helping him to understand "principles which can best be described as ethical." Specifically, these had to do with paying close attention to others and rising to the occasion in response. Chernoff observes, "It was only by listening to Ibrahim and Alhassan that I knew what to do," that is, how to interact with the others' rhythms, so that "with each single beat I threw in, each of us became stronger in himself and in relationship perfecting the form" of the music. "Precision" was "essential." If he had not grasped that what was at stake in Ibrahim's test was his understanding of ethical principles of interaction, Chernoff tells us, "I would not have been able to listen for, look for, and judge the proper moment. I would have demonstrated through a random gesture my lack of concern for the people there" (1979, 139–140).

Broadly, Chernoff came to see the music as geared to "socialization" and the virtues he developed (presence of mind, respect, consideration, and responsiveness) as applying beyond the musical situation (154, 166–167).[2] Although his account focuses specifically on his experiences of drumming, other forms of musicking, too, provide training in virtues that facilitate good interpersonal relationships. Music contributes to participants' ethical development because engaging with well-performed music involves the actual *exercise* of virtues that matter both within and beyond the musical context. Stefan Caris Love points to a number of virtues that are involved in good straight-ahead jazz solos. Besides compositional skill, the soloist, according to Love, should exemplify commitment to the spirit of improvisation, which involves courage—displayed through taking musical risks—as well as independence and spontaneity (2016, 65).

Although the virtues Love considers involve individual assertion, Love emphasizes their relational character. The risks taken, he observes, are impressive only when they are integrated into a coherent design, and when performing with others, sensitivity and "discretion—not getting in the way" are also important (2016, 71–72). William Day similarly considers the importance of a balance between individual creativity and responsiveness, stressing the importance of subordinating the ego in the service of a collective goal. Analyzing Thelonious Monk's admonitions to Steve Lacy that he should not just repeat Monk's own line and that he should "make the drummer sound good," Day observes that Monk was indicating Lacy's "moral confusion" as well as his musical difficulties. Lacy describes his moral discovery as follows: "I learned to stick to the point, and to not lose the point, and not get carried away. And to play with the other musicians and not get all wrapped up in my own thing, and not to just play interesting notes just to be interesting, you know, weird notes just to be weird" (Day 2000, 108). Day characterizes the ideal balance as a matter of both attending to what the others are doing and nourishing them with ideas by "reshaping his experience of the present moment" (110).

Some of the virtues that Chernoff, Love, and Day discuss in relation to improvisatory musical forms can also be recognized in other kinds of musical performance. The performance of any kind of music involves presence of mind, for example, a "liveness" that contrasts with mechanical playing, and attentive responsiveness to what others are doing. Meilin Chinn considers the attentive responsiveness required for good musical performance in her account of a line from the ancient Confucian *Yue Ji* ("Record of Music"): "Only music cannot be faked." Chinn draws attention to the importance of a virtue she calls "timeliness," the arrival of musical events at precisely the right moment. Timeliness is attained only when the performer attentively responds to all the specifics

---

[2] Presence of mind may not strike everyone as a moral virtue, but it is certainly a characteristic that facilitates other virtues, such as attentiveness to others' behavior and the virtue of timeliness as Meilin Chinn (2017) describes it, a matter that will be considered in what follows.

of the particular musical occasion, including the other performers' musical gestures. Performances that exhibit timeliness also affect the skills of listeners, who become more sensitive in the process of recognizing it. The musical experience thus develops the receptivity of both performers and listeners, enabling them to become more adept at sensing and responding within their specific situations. In the idealized Confucian vision of musical performance, all are involved and attuned to what is happening, so "faking" is impossible (Chinn 2017, 341–354).[3]

Cobussen and Nielsen elaborate on some of the moral skills that can be developed specifically through listening. They discuss these ideas in terms of hospitality, drawing on Jacques Derrida's idea that ethics includes an "unconditional hospitality" toward everyone, however "foreign" a person might seem (Derrida 2000). Cobussen and Nielsen consider the possibility of an analogous musical hospitality through attentive listening, which would involve "preserving the space of the other as other" within the music and "having an ear for the singular in music" (Cobussen 2012, 20–21 and 30).

> Music can teach us to listen more carefully; it can make us receptive and responsive to the voices of others and to the voice of otherness, to other voices and the otherness of the voice, and thus not only to alternative messages, opinions, and ideas, but also to subtle timbres, tonalities, *Stimmungen* [Moods], atmospheres and associations which might influence and regulate human action. Attentive listening means to allow otherness to enter us, to be able and willing to relinquish our usual defence mechanisms that all too often lead us to exclude that which appears strange to us. (Cobussen and Nielsen 2012, 155)

Some see the kind of openness that listening can involve as a means of developing empathy. Deniz Peters sees empathy as being appreciative of otherness, yet he suggests that musical empathy is built upon our awareness of our bodily similarity to others. We each recognize our body's vital rhythms being affected by the music we experience, and we typically recognize that the music affects others in a similar manner. Relating our own embodied responses to those of others, a generalized sense of empathy results. However, Peters thinks that this vague sense of empathy is only occasionally associated with specific others (such as composers, performers, audience members, or a whole social group). Typically, in musical empathy we embrace "otherness" in general (2015), and a nonradical otherness at that.

Peters's analysis raises questions about the extent to which musically generated empathy translates to concern for actual people. This question becomes especially salient in light of the fact that music-lovers have sometimes displayed a shocking lack of concern for others. Nazi officials who were moved by musical performances in concentration camps but were willing to murder the prisoner-performers provide an obvious case in point. Such cases draw attention to what Bruce Johnson and Martin Cloonan

---

[3] The fakery that the Confucian text describes as impossible in music differs from musical "faking" in jazz, which is a synonym for improvising an accompaniment part.

describe as "the darker side" of music (2009). Ironically, some of music's more vicious involvements make use of certain mechanisms that make it serviceable as a moral educator, specifically those that promote prosocial attitudes such as solidarity and willingness to cooperate.

Affinity Through Music

Music makes our connectedness with others evident on an affective level, and this contributes to social bonding. We have already considered ways in which experiencing music in tandem with others encourages feelings of solidarity.[4] We are aware of sharing intimately felt bodily effects, and if Peters is correct, this facilitates empathy (2015). Phenomenologist Alfred Schutz also draws attention to the intimacy created through sharing music, not only through rhythmic entrainment, but also by virtue of the fact that "different dimensions of time" are "simultaneously lived through by the participants" (1951, 96). He contends that tracking the same sequence of specific musical events as other engaged listeners generates strong feelings of connection. The fact that we typically identify with the impression of agency in music, too, may be transitive, enabling us to feel connected with other people whom we take to be sharing this identification.

Psychologist Daniel Stern suggests that as infants, we learned to distinguish our caregivers as distinct agents and mutually attune with them by means of dynamic features of their behavior, which he terms "vitality affects." By attending to these vital dynamics, we developed feelings of rapport and security (1985, 11), and throughout our lives we feel that we are "with" another person by virtue of these features.[5] Stern has argued that music creates experiential conditions akin to those experienced when we attended and attuned to others in infancy, for the patterns of music involve dynamic features and opportunities for attunement that are similar to those utilized in early life. The vitality affects, accordingly, may be among the bases for feeling rapport in the context of music. Another is suggested by the finding that music generates the production of oxytocin, a neuropeptide that facilitates bonding (Freeman 2000, 411–424; Machin and Dunbar 533–537).[6]

By generating feelings of connectedness with others, music has the potential to motivate a spirit of cooperation. Work songs demonstrate that it can support active cooperative efforts. By galvanizing the participant's willingness to contribute constructively to a collective project, music motivates dispositions that promote ethical interaction and

---

[4] I will assume in this context that the music shared is relatively enjoyable for the participants.

[5] To give an impression of the qualities of experiences involved in the vitality affects, Stern suggests utilizing terms "such as: 'surging,' 'fading away,' 'fleeting,' 'explosive,' 'crescendo,' 'decrescendo,' 'bursting,' 'drawn out,' and so forth," terms that are readily applied to dynamic features of music (1985, 11). For further discussion, see Higgins (2012, 110–111 and 152–153).

[6] For further discussion of this and the other bases for solidarity developed through music, see Higgins (2012 and 2018).

social harmony. Roger Scruton praises music's ability in making one feel a member of something larger, a potential that is actualized when a society uses music to allude to itself and provide its members "a way of 'joining in' " (1997, 478).

Nevertheless, we may be skeptical about whether the musical promotion of camaraderie with other members of one's society is an unmitigated ethical good. Music may promote solidarity with others, but we can ask which others are involved, and who is being excluded. Musical experience can bridge social divides, but it can also reinforce them. This is because, as Scruton appreciatively notes, particular music can be linked to group identity, and group identity depends on clearly defining who is in the group. Martin Stokes observes that "ethnic boundaries define and maintain social identities, which can only exist in 'a context of opposition and relativities' " (1994, 6, citing Chapman, Tonkin, and McDonald 1989). Identity of any kind depends on a logic of exclusion. Identifying as a member of the audience for jazz or for Indian classical music is intelligible only to the extent that other types of music exist from which the preferred type of music can be distinguished. Such identifications are not necessarily mutually exclusive, for the same person can be a member of more than one musical audience. However, group identities themselves depend on making clear in-group/out-group distinctions, and music can play a role in creating or reinforcing such distinctions, and it can do so beyond the musical context.[7]

The fact that music can consolidate social groups is not itself an ethical problem. It may be ethically beneficial, for example, when it asserts collective identity within marginalized social subgroups and expresses the perspective and needs of the group in a public arena. Ethical concerns arise, however, when music assists the consolidation of an in-group that takes hostile or vicious attitudes toward the out-group. Music's significance for group identity can sometimes contribute to such attitudes even when there is no intention of stoking antagonism. Cobussen provides a nice illustration in his discussion of a documentary named *Whose Song?* The filmmaker, Adela Peeva, chronicles a road trip she took through southeast Europe, talking with members of various nations about a song that each group claimed as its own. "In each country," Cobussen summarizes, "the reactions . . . are the same: people display shock, anger or disbelief when Peeva suggests that the same tune is also claimed by their neighbours." They respond with so much vituperation and acrimony toward the other groups that claim the song that Peeva asks, "How can one song cause so much hatred?" (Cobussen 2012, 91–92). The case shows the intensity of feeling and sense of ownership that can be connected with music that one perceives as emblematic of one's group identity.

Presumably, the associations with group identity that Peeva documents were developed organically, but such associations can also be deliberately cultivated, sometimes with viciously exclusionary aims. Nancy Love discusses a neo-Nazi group's use of music in the folk tradition to promote their white supremacist ideology. Love points out that

---

[7] Simon Frith (1996, 111) suggests that cultural identities, at least, depend on music and other cultural activities, since they help enable a group to see itself as a group.

although American folk music is "most typically associated with protest songs of social justice movements," white nationalists have drawn on the relative "whiteness" of the folk music scene to interpret the idiom "as a racially pure expression of white culture and use it to reinvoke an imagined . . . white community" (Love 2018, 3–5). Supporting their feelings of connection with each other, the music is exploited to reinforce racial divisions and to express refusal of fellowship with members of other racial groups.

Ironically, the musical promotion of hostile attitudes toward the out-group depends on the same mechanisms as those that make music an effective means to develop pro-social feelings. Rhythmic entrainment, the bonding character of sharing the intimacy and intensity of musical experience, the revival of deep-seated feelings of secure rapport developed in infancy, and the stimulation of neurotransmitters that encourage social bonds can all help to bridge social divisions, but they can also be utilized to promote solidarity within a group that promotes hatred and ill-treatment of those viewed as "other."

In addition to encouraging hostile attitudes toward those outside one's group, music is utilized for a large range of other morally problematic uses. Cobussen mentions the infliction of bodily harm (by damaging the inner ear, for example, or by inducing dizziness, lack of balance, sleeplessness, and/or nausea) or psychological harm (using music to disorient, humiliate, insult, or cause anxiety or terror). Such acts of violence may be connected with group identity, as is the case when they are directed against perceived adversaries or prisoners of war, but they need not be. Cobussen also draws attention to the morally questionable character of music used to exert control through "acoustic design." Some of these are employed without consideration of particular group affiliation, as in the case of environmental music aimed at affecting the pace of consumer movement (encouraging shoppers to linger and patrons of restaurants to eat more quickly). However, others are premised on reinforcing social divisions by chasing away those considered undesirable or keeping social strata from mixing by playing styles of music that are expected to seem differentially alienating or welcoming to members of different socioeconomic classes (Cobussen 2012, 106–112).

Love's observation that music within the same idiom (such as folk music) can be used to very different ends suggests the potential fruitfulness of distinguishing "the music" from the uses to which it is put. Such a distinction is important and serviceable, for indicating that the "same" music is used in multiple ways (e.g., for religious purposes in one context and secular purposes in another), for example, or for pointing out that it can acquire new associations (by being used as a part of a soundtrack or an ad campaign, for instance). Similarly, we might distinguish "the words" from the "music," since words are sometimes a vehicle for linking a piece of music with a particular group or agenda.

If what we mean by "the music itself" is an abstract sound structure, the strategy of evaluating music separately from its uses and associated texts makes considerable sense. In practice, however, we never encounter an abstract sound structure. We always experience music in a context, and we engage in interpretive acts to make sense of it (see Feld 1984b, 8). As we will see, the consequence is that we cannot easily extricate the music "itself" from the penumbra of uses, texts, and other associations connected to it, and this has repercussions for its role in unethical projects.

Blurry Distinctions between Music and Its Others

Sometimes it makes good sense to give separate moral evaluations to a piece of music and to the uses to which it is put. The same music (even the same recording of a piece of music) might be an enjoyable diversion in one context, while torturous when played at a deafening volume in another. Causing others to hear the music will have different moral significance in the two cases, and the music "itself" seems morally indeterminate.

Let us consider a case in point. Paul McCartney describes the Beatles' song "Helter Skelter" as his effort to write a song with a raucous, noisy sound, and he says that the title referred to a fairground ride called a "helter skelter," in which one slides in a spiral around a tower. Charles Manson idiosyncratically interpreted the song as anticipating a race-war in the United States, and he used it to inspire a group of his followers to commit a mass murder, in which the song's title, misspelled, was written in blood on a refrigerator in the home of some of the victims (Grow 2019). It seems reasonable to see the ethical status of McCartney's song as independent from that of the horrific use to which Manson and his followers put it. McCartney does not seem blameworthy for writing it, even though Manson's use of it contributed to ghastly crimes.

This judgment seems fair enough, but the case also demonstrates that associations that become attached to particular pieces of music can be quite strong. For listeners who recall the mass murder and Manson's use of "Helter Skelter," it is probably hard to completely ignore this fact when responding to the song, demonstrating how difficult it can be to completely disconnect a piece of music from associations, however much one might wish to do so.

Pieces of music can be burdened by their histories because particular music readily absorbs associations. Particular pieces assist memorization, as will be evident to all who have made use of the "ABC song" to learn the alphabet, and they can become psychologically linked to particular activities, helping one to stay on track (cf. Sacks 1985). Charles Nussbaum points out that because music makes use of the motor system, the very means through which we interact with the external world, we easily associate music with much that is not intrinsically musical. "Musical modeling of nonmusical domains . . . is pervasive," he says, "because musical experience is fundamentally bodily, gestural, and simulational in significance" (2007, 141).

Anthropologist Judith Becker draws on Gerald Edelman's theory of neuronal group selection in a pertinent account of trance behavior. According to Edelman, bundles of neurons that are habitually activated together can form "classification couples," in which the excitement of one prompts the excitement of the other, and the same bundle can be coupled with multiple others. Becker sees this as an explanation of the strength and specificity of acquired associations with music. The auditory system involves neuronal groupings that respond to particular features of a sonic signal, with "synaptic connections to many other parts of the brain." So in addition to the sound that we hear, "we are simultaneously, or so it seems, aware of the last time we heard the piece, or one like it, as well as concomitant feelings of joy, sadness, or even fear." The musical stimulus "acts as a physiological metonym," with associations that are engaged automatically when we hear the music (Becker 2004, 114–115).

Thus, we do not easily shed cognitive and/or affective associations with particular music. Associations are acquired, but once formed they are reliably activated and deeply entrenched, and they can be cultivated across a cultural group. Becker emphasizes that while not in conscious control of themselves, trancing individuals each enact the cultural scripts associated with the trance-inducing music. Long-standing cultural mythologies are invoked in the cases Becker considers, but associations can also become widespread simply by virtue of frequent use. In Richard Wagner's opera *Lohengrin,* the "Bridal Chorus" is sung as wedding guests lead the bride and groom from the wedding celebration to the bridal chamber. However, its use as an instrumental for the procession of the bride at a wedding has become such a prevalent practice that the song is commonly referred to in many English-speaking nations as "Here Comes the Bride." Associations can be more personally specific, too, as is the case in the "our song" phenomenon, in which two people associate a song with their romantic relationship, or when one connects a song with a particular period in one's life (cf. Koopman and Davies in Davies 2011, 81–83).

Similar points can be made with respect to the relationship between words and music. When we speak of "the words and the music," we mean by the latter what is constituted by pitches, rhythms, and timbres, as opposed to text. But once music has become associated with specific words, the words often seem to be mentally implied even when they are not sung. An instrumental version of "The Star-Spangled Banner" seems to profess the words for those who know them. One may wonder whether associated words have such force in the case of contrafactums, in which an alternative text is attached to music already associated with another.[8] But even in the case of a listener who knows both, an instrumental version of the music is likely to call to mind one text or the other, or at least one at a time. Having distinct and even contrasting associations may complicate one's experience of a piece (for example, when one knows both secular and religious texts associated with the music of "Greensleeves"), but if it does, that only shows the associations' strength.

David Davies also suggests that separate evaluation of music and associated texts may be both difficult and inappropriate. He suggests that song is a "compositionally composite" art form, in which words and music are designed to work together, with the consequence that the meanings of the two cannot be disconnected if one is to evaluate properly (Davies 2013, 13–22). While uses and contexts may be less integral to a piece of music's ontological identification, in practice they still contribute to ascribed meaning, which suggests that they should also be factors when evaluating.

---

[8] In fact, "The Star-Spangled Banner" is a contrafactum of "To Anacreon in Heaven," a song about Anacreon, a Greek poet renowned for his love poems and drinking songs.

Approaching Music Ethically

A further reason to attend to the many associations and practices linked to particular pieces and idioms is that these are relevant if we are interested in the way music reflects and affects human relationships. This becomes particularly clear when we consider that engaging with music does not occur in a political vacuum. Particular pieces and styles of music have histories and associations that affect their meaning for particular groups, and this has relevance for taking an ethical approach to music, as Jeannette Bicknell points out.

Bicknell compellingly argues that when a song is "valued by a group, whether for musical or extra-musical reasons," this fact should guide decisions about how to perform it (2015, 83). She draws on Laurence Thomas's account of moral deference, which involves respecting the authority of others for determining what matters in their own experience and foregoing the temptation to make one's own experience the standard for judging what is morally significant (Thomas 1992–1993). Accordingly, Bicknell contends that when performing a song that has value to a group of people, "a morally sensitive singer must try to understand why it has the significance that it does, and must shape the details of her performance so as to respect or honor that significance. If she does not, then she risks giving offense" (83).[9]

While uses of music can exemplify moral deference, they can also manifest and reinforce power inequalities. An ethical approach to music should be alert to ways that it is used to perpetuate injustice so as to be able to counteract them. Sometimes music's reinforcement of chauvinism and inequity is concealed behind practices whose political impact may not seem obvious. Christopher Jenkins analyzes institutional practices within the classical music industry that marginalize the music of African Americans. He argues that this marginalization is manifest even in the musical aesthetic values that dominate conservatory curriculums and classical performance. Institutions of classical music prize harmony and melody over rhythm, which is given primacy in the music of the African diaspora. They also encourage a "clean" sound, which contrasts with the "percussive sound quality" that is salient in African American music. To resist the supremacist judgments lurking within the reigning aesthetic paradigm, Jenkins calls for "a more integrated aesthetic" within the classical music industry. This would involve teaching the sound ideals of both traditional European and African diaspora music, without treating one as superior to the other, and also "the teaching of basic tools for improvisation" (Jenkins 2020).[10]

---

[9] Moral deference might also figure in decisions about what not to perform. The German decision after World War II to make only the third stanza of the *Leid der Deutschen* their national anthem takes account of associations some saw between the first two stanzas and the Nazi agenda. Although the first stanza, beginning with "Deutschland, Deutschland über alles" (Germany, Germany above everything) had at one time been understood as a call for German unification, the change of the anthem acknowledges that it now calls up associations with Third Reich militarism and atrocities.

[10] My thanks to the author for sharing the manuscript. Cf. Amegago (2000) on the importance of revising music and dance curriculums to overcome the dominance of European aesthetic paradigms.

Awareness that music can be implicated in unethical projects should inform our decisions about using it, especially music that has associations with particular groups of people. It should also motivate efforts to find ethically constructive alternative approaches. We might take heart from the fact that music and musical practices change as musicians encounter and draw inspiration from each other. And perhaps there are grounds for optimism toward the future, given that contemporary technology makes it possible for people around the globe to engage with each other through music.

Preventing musical reinforcement of unjust arrangements is not, however, an easy task. Power dynamics affect the way music is disseminated, what is recorded, and how much artistic control musicians have over their music, as well as how particular music is received in particular contexts. While music can build bridges among communities, it does not always do so on equal terms. Given that mutual influence among musicians is a basic part of music, an ethically responsible approach would act in a respectful way toward sources (both as individuals and as groups) while contributing something of one's own (cf. Rudinow 1994). David Hesmondhalgh, however, cautions that we cannot assume that coming to appreciate otherness through music will automatically translate into respect for those seen as other than oneself. In connection with the international proliferation of distinct national "pop-rock" styles, he observes that it is not obvious that "the integration of foreign styles and tastes into local hybrid styles involves any engagement with the otherness of foreign styles in a way that would meaningfully establish commonality and equal moral standing across peoples" (2013, 154).[11] Like Bicknell, he calls for moral deference, urging us to guard against using music as a basis for projecting one's own fantasies on others (2013, 138–139).

Yet Hesmondhalgh also stresses music's positive ethical potential to help us to feel human connection and "our mutual dependence and obligation" in a way that "can inform our contributions to political life" (2013, 146). He rightly observes that "the right social, economic and institutional conditions" are necessary for music to fulfill this potential (171). Music alone cannot produce good societies or good people. But it can help develop motivations and virtues, and that can help us to build flourishing relationships. It can also help us envision ways of relating in which we contribute to each other's thriving by being both strong in ourselves and open-heartedly hospitable.

See also: Hutton, Woodcock, Clavel-Vázquez, this volume

References

Amegago, Modesto Mawulolo Kwaku. 2000. *An Holistic Approach to African Performing Arts: Music and Dance Curriculum Development and Implementation*, PhD diss., Simon Fraser University.

Baraka, Amiri. 1987. "The Great Music Robbery." In *The Music: Reflections on Jazz and Blues*, edited by Amiri Baraka and Amina Baraka, 328–333. New York: William Morrow.

[11] Hesmondhalgh is referring here to Motti Regev's analysis of aesthetic cosmopolitanism in Regev's (2007), noting that this aesthetic cosmopolitanism does not obviously coincide with ethical cosmopolitanism.

Becker, Judith. 2004. *Deep Listeners: Music, Emotion, and Trancing*. Bloomington: University of Indiana Press.

Berman, Laurence. 1993. *The Musical Image: A Theory of Content*. Westport, CT: Greenwood Press.

Bicknell, Jeannette. 2015. *Philosophy of Song and Singing: An Introduction*. New York: Routledge.

Blacking, John. 1973. *How Musical Is Man?* Seattle: University of Washington Press.

Bregman, Albert S. 1993. "Auditory Scene Analysis: Hearing in Complex Environments." In *Thinking in Sound: The Cognitive Psychology of Human Audition*, edited by Stephen McAdams and Emmanuel Bigand, 10–36. Oxford: Clarendon Press.

Chapman, Malcolm, Elizabeth Tonkin, and Maryon McDonald. 1989. "Introduction." In *History and Ethnicity*, edited by Elizabeth Tonkin, Maryon McDonald, and Malcolm Chapman, 1–21. London: Routledge.

Chernoff, John Miller. 1979. *African Rhythm and African Sensibility: Aesthetics and Social Action in African Musical Idioms*. Chicago: University of Chicago Press.

Chinn, Meilin. 2017. "Only Music Cannot Be Faked." *Dao* 16, no. 3: 341–354.

Cobussen, Marcel. 2012. "Affect." In *Music and Ethics*, by Marcel Cobussen and Nanette Nielsen, 91–116. London: Routledge.

Cobussen, Marcel, and Nanette Nielsen. 2012. *Music and Ethics*. London: Routledge.

Davies, David. 2013. "The Dialogue between Words and Music in the Comprehension and Composition of Son." *Journal of Aesthetics and Art Criticism*, Special Issue: Song, Songs, and Singing 71, no. 3: 13–22.

Davies, Stephen. 2011. *Musical Understandings and Other Essays on the Philosophy of Music*. Oxford: Oxford University Press.

Day, William. 2000. "Knowing as Instancing: Jazz Improvisation and Moral Perfectionism." *Journal of Aesthetics and Art Criticism* 58, no. 2: 99–111.

Derrida, Jacques. 2000. *Of Hospitality*. Translated by Rachel Bowlby. Stanford, CA: Stanford University Press.

Ellis, Catherine. 1985. *Aboriginal Music, Education for Living: Cross-cultural Experiences from South Australia*. St. Lucia: University of Queensland Press.

Feld, Steven. 1984a. "Sound Structure as Social Structure." *Ethnomusicology* 28, no. 3: 383–409.

Feld, Steven. 1984b. "Communication, Music, and Speech about Music." *Yearbook for Traditional Music* 20: 1–18.

Feld, Steven. 2000. "A Sweet Lullaby for World Music." *Public Culture* 12, no. 1: 145–171.

Freeman, Walter. 2000. "A Neurobiological Role of Music in Social Bonding." In *The Origins of Music*, edited by Nils. L. Wallin, Björn Merker, and Steven Brown, 411–424. Cambridge, MA: The MIT Press.

Frith, Simon. 1996. "Music and Identity." In *Questions of Cultural Identity*, edited by Stuart Hall and Paul du Gay, 108–127. London: Sage.

Gracyk, Theodore. 2017. "Performer, Persona, and the Evaluation of Musical Performance." *Contemporary Aesthetics* 15. https://digitalcommons.risd.edu/liberalarts_contempaesthetics/vol15/iss1/13/.

Grow, Kory. 2019. "Charles Manson: How Cult Leader's Twisted Beatles Obsession Inspired Family Murders. *Rolling Stone*, August 9, 2019. https://www.rollingstone.com/feature/charles-manson-how-cult-leaders-twisted-beatles-obsession-inspired-family-murders-107176/.

Hatten, Robert. 2018. *A Theory of Virtual Agency for Western Art Music*. Bloomington: University of Indiana Press.

Hesmondhalgh, David. 2013. *Why Music Matters*. Chichester, UK: Wiley Blackwell.

Higgins, Kathleen. 2018. "Connecting Music to Ethics," *College Music Symposium* 58, no. 3: 1–20. https://doi.org/10.18177/sym.2018.58.sr.11411.

Higgins, Kathleen. 2012. *The Music between Us: Is Music a Universal Language?* Chicago: Chicago University Press.

Higgins, Kathleen. [1991] 2011. *The Music of Our Lives*. Philadelphia: Temple University Press; reissued Lanham, MD: Lexington Books.

Inawat, Ronald J. 2015. "Music as Cultural Heritage: Analysis of the Means of Preventing the Exploitation of Intangible Cultural Heritage." *John Marshall Review of Intellectual Property Law* 14, no. 2: 228–248.

Jenkins, Christopher. "The Aesthetics of Classical Music: Assimilation vs. Integration." Unpublished manuscript (accessed November 21, 2020).

Johnson, Bruce, and Martin Cloonan. 2009. *Dark Side of the Tune: Popular Music and Violence*. Farnham: Ashgate.

Koopman, Constantijn, and Stephen Davies. 2011. "Musical Meaning in a Broader Perspective." In *Musical Understandings and Other Essays on the Philosophy of Music*, edited by Stephen Davies, 71–87. Oxford: Oxford University Press.

Korpe, Marie, Ole Reitov, and Martin Cloonan. 2006. "Music Censorship from Plato to the Present." In *Music and Manipulation: On the Social Uses and Social Control of Music*, edited by Seven Brown and Ulrik Volgsten, 239–263. New York: Berghahn Books.

Lomax, Alan. 1976. *Cantometrics: An Approach to the Anthropology of Music*. Berkeley: University of California Extension Media Center.

Love, Nancy S. 2018. "From Settler Colonialism to Standing Rock." *College Music Symposium* 58, no. 3. https://doi.org/10.18177/sym.2018.58.sr.11412

Machin, A. J., and R. I. M. Dunbar. 2011. "The Brain Opioid Theory of Social Attachment: A Review of the Evidence." *Behaviour* 148 no. 9/10: 985–1025.

Nussbaum, Charles O. 2007. *The Musical Representation: Meaning, Ontology, and Emotion*. Cambridge, MA: The MIT Press.

Peters, Deniz. 2015. "Musical Empathy, Emotional Co-Constitution, and 'the Musical Other.'" *Empirical Musicology Review* 10, no. 1–2: 2–15.

Regev, Motti. 2007. "Ethno-National Pop-Rock Music: Aesthetic Cosmopolitanism Made from Within." *Cultural Sociology* 1, no.3: 317–341.

Rudinow, Joel. 1994. "Race, Ethnicity, Expresssive Authenticity: Can White People Sing the Blues?" *Journal of Aesthetics and Art Criticism* 53, no. 3: 127–137.

Rudinow, Joel. 2010. *Soul Music: Tracking the Spiritual Roots of Pop from Plato to Motown*. Ann Arbor: University of Michigan Press.

Sacks, Oliver. 1985. "The Man who Mistook his Wife for a Hat." In *The Man Who Mistook His Wife for a Hat and Other Clinical Tales*, 8–22. New York: Harper and Row.

Schutz, Alfred. 1951. "Making Music Together: A Study in Social Relationship." *Social Research* 18, no. 1: 76–97.

Scruton, Roger. 1997. *The Aesthetics of Music*. Oxford: Oxford University Press.

Silverman, Marissa. 2018. "I Drum, I Sing, I Dance: An Ethnographic Study of a West African Drum and Dance Ensemble." *Research Studies in Music Education* 40, no. 1: 5–27.

Small, Christopher. 1998. *Musicking: The Meanings of Performing and Listening*. Middletown, CT: Wesleyan University Press.

Smuts, Aaron. 2019. "The Ethics of Singing-Along: The Case of 'Mind of a Lunatic.'" *Journal of Aesthetics and Art Criticism* 71, no. 1: 121–129.

Stern, Daniel. 1985. *The Interpersonal World of the Infant*. London: Academic Press.

Stokes, Martin. 1994. "Introduction: Ethnicity, Identity and Music." In *Ethnicity, Identity and Music: The Musical Construction of Place*, edited by Martin Stokes. 1–27. Providence, RI: Berg.

Tarusukin, Richard. 2009. "The Danger of Music and the Case for Control." In *The Danger of Music and Other Anti-Utopian Essays*, 168–180. Berkeley: University of California Press.

Taylor, Paul. 2016. *Black Is Beautiful: A Philosophy of Black Aesthetics*. Hoboken, NJ: Wiley.

Thomas, Laurence. 1992–1993. "Moral Deference." *The Philosophical Forum* 24, no. 1–3: 233–250.

Zatorre, Robert J. and Andrea R. Halpern. 2005. "Mental Concerts: Musical Imagery and Auditory Cortex." *Neuron* 47, no. 1: 9–12.

....

CHAPTER 27

SOME MORAL FEATURES OF THEATRICAL ART

....

JAMES R. HAMILTON

In this chapter, I undertake three main tasks. I show, where possible, the current state in theater and performance studies as well as philosophy concerning moral worries about theater. I distinguish between worries due to specific styles of presentation within theater from those due, instead, to the art-form itself. And I argue that some of these concerns are, in the end, not genuine moral worries at all. While I do not take a stand on how any of the moral issues are to be resolved, I do take a stand on whether those issues are real.

The focus in the entry is on moral issues about theatrical performances per se rather than the *contents* presented in them. For example, I will discuss issues that can arise in the rehearsal process; but I make only brief remarks on moral issues arising out of the *contents* of scripts, even though those are important areas in which moral problems arise, because they receive focused attention elsewhere in this volume.

In the introductory essay to the collection *Acting (Re)Considered*, Philip Zarrilli argues that "every time an actor performs, he or she implicitly enacts a 'theory' of acting—a set of assumptions about the conventions and style which guide his or her performance, the structure of actions which he or she performs, the shape that those actions take (as a character, role, or sequence of actions as in some performance art), and the relationship to the audience" (Zarrilli 2002, 3). In a later essay, he adds that "implicit in each specific theory of acting are metaphysical questions, that is, principles or perspectives that invite us to step back from, and to reflect more generally on, the nature, practice, and phenomenon of acting" (Zarrilli 2007, 637). Such reflection is often less metaphysical than moral. That is the perspective I take in this chapter.

A number of moral issues that are thought to occur in acting, and in theater more generally, are not explicitly articulated in the *acting process theories* Zarrilli discusses but are there nonetheless. As Zarrilli indicates, they lie within those theories as assumptions both performers and spectators make about processes of performing, ways of preparing for a performance, obligations that hold among the performers, the sites of their performances, and obligations that performers have to spectators.

The big question regarding theater and ethics, as stated by Plato (and perhaps also by Emmanuel Levinas), can be put this way: "Can theater justify itself in terms of the contribution it makes to a moral life?" (Plato c.380/1992, Books III and X; Levinas 1930/1989, 129–142).[1] Alan Read responds to this big question by asserting that "theatre is worthwhile because it is antagonistic to official views of reality" (Read 1995, 1).[2] It is for this reason that Read thinks theater is a justifiably ethical practice. But while the issue is of concern to theater and performance theorists, to philosophers it is largely inconsequential because the question is only interesting to the extent the underlying metaphysical picture that it presents and relies upon is solid. But only a very few philosophers endorse Plato's metaphysical picture, involving forms, realms of forms, eternal abstract objects, and so on, and even then, in very limited circumstances. Much the same can be said of most theater people. In fact, one is more likely to find a philosopher than a theater or performance theorist who is a metaphysical Platonist. (For more discussion of Plato, see Destrée, this volume.)

On the other hand, what underlies Levinas's view is not a metaphysical but rather a moral view. Many people, including a great number of philosophers, hold that the ground of our lives is related to other people, even though it is unlikely that the influence is that of Levinas per se (Levinas 1930/1989, 83; Ridout 2009, 54). This may indeed be the lay idea of what justifies an ethical life; it is a life aimed at securing the fulfillment of others. However, as Nicholas Ridout notes, there are real problems connected with a theater that aims to use Levinas (Ridout 2009, 54–56), not least of which is Levinas's well-known "suspicion of the purely aesthetic" (Ridout 2009, 56). For Levinas, the crucial question is not whether art, including theatrical art, can tell us truths but whether it can be efficacious in changing people's habits, beliefs, and lives. We will address this question directly in the final section of the chapter.

Moral Problems That Concern the Process of Theatrical Performance Itself

Iris Vidmar Jovanovic (2019) notes that there are some fairly standard moral issues concerning the *contents* of narratives. And as I remarked earlier, this source of moral issues is also commonly dealt with in philosophy of literature, and so on. However, narrative performances are only a small part of theater, considered as a worldwide

---

[1] See also Ridout (2009, 16–24, 51–56).

[2] Read also notes, and argues, that "questioning dogmatic positions does not unthinkingly embrace every possible alternative" (Read 1995, 3).

phenomenon. Nevertheless, it is a useful question whether anything that is specifically germane to theater is among these moral issues. In answer, one may notice that whenever a moral problem arises in the context of consuming art there will also be a moral problem arising with the production of that art, especially when at least a large part of the means by which the art is produced is, as it seems to be theater, the performer's own body and voice. In other words, this kind of moral problem arises precisely because theater requires agents (or things that can be made *by* agents to act like agents) to present the narrative contents encountered.

Tzachi Zamir (2013) notes the following are frequent areas of moral tension with this kind of theater: violence, erotic acting, "emotional recall" and "imaginative substitution," and character- and individual-identity "percolation." The first is probably self-explanatory. Moral issues distinctive to performing in theater occur when one performer is called upon to strike another, for example. The same kinds of worries can arise in cases of erotic acting, especially when erotic acting is hard to distinguish from cases of violence among performers. These kinds of issues seem to arise no matter what acting process theory the actor has adopted.

Yet many moral issues arise only for certain acting process theories. For instance, the kinds of moral questions Zamir raises concerning emotional recall and imaginative substitution can arise only for those theories that call for the use of these techniques (the so-called Method, for example). Consider first emotional recall. In Method acting, a practice aimed at revealing the so-called inner psychological structures involved in personal conflicts, a performer may be called upon to recall a real memory that occasioned a past emotion in order to resurrect and feel that emotion in a performance. The case of imaginative substitution, where "the actor is encouraged to infuse into an enacted situation aspects of a nonfictional relationship, drawing genuine responses from the imagined scenario," is similar in that the moral issues that occur only in performances guided by so-called mimetic or representational acting process theories, ones that seek so-called psychological realism (Zamir 2013, 355). A good example of the moral problem involved in emotional recall concerns a memory used in the service of acting, when the memory itself may be cherished by the actor and seen as debased in some fashion when so used. A good example of the moral problem involved in imaginative substitution might involve an actor imagining a horrific instance involving a loved one so as to yield a genuine emotional reaction to whatever horrific thing is happening onstage, only to have that image stick in the mind of the actor for many subsequent years. Yet another instance is provided by Goff (2016) in discussing one of Sarah Ruhl's plays with novice actors in a university setting:[3] "The Ibsens and Chekhovs and Millers and Mamets that these students know so well traffic in deep subtext and correct answers that are hidden away by the playwrights in the characters' complex background stories, just waiting for the diligent actor to mine them. Ruhl, on the other hand, writes worlds without

---

[3] The play in question is *Dead Man's Cell Phone* (Ruhl 2008) and the location and date of the discussion is Wayne State University in September 2013.

certainties or answers, and this proved to be unsettling for my two casts of young actors" (Goff 2016, 2). The opening for moral problems lies in how a young actor, raised by seeing only so-called realistic acting, is supposed to react to this new style.

The same moral problems do not arise in so-called presentational, or detached, theories, such as Brecht's or Diderot's (Rouse 1984; Konijn 2002). According to those theories, the "actor feels nothing at all in order to get the audience maximally involved in the staged character-emotions" (Konijn 2002, 62). Nor do they arise in theories that focus on the tasks of performer where "the actor's point of view onstage is performing a particular task—conveying an image of a character['s emotion]—as convincing[ly] and believab[ly] as possible to the audience" (Konijn 2002, 65). Neither of these acting processes require emotional recall or imaginative substitution, and there is good empirical support for the claim that the moral problems attached to emotional recall and imaginative substitution do not arise in the detached or task-oriented styles of acting.[4]

However, moral worries arising from the fact that, as Zamir puts it, there is "percolation" between characters and performers' identities seem to cut across acting process theories. No matter what the theory involves, exactly insofar as a performer portrays a character, there is likely to be room for the following kind of thing: "Actors are urged to deflate value-laden acts such as kissing and embracing into mere value-neutral bodily operations" (Zamir 2013, 356). An illustration of this, perhaps, concerns a vegetarian actor who is asked to represent joy or fulfillment in eating meat in character. Quite apart from any effect the meat-eating (even if it is "faux" meat) might have on the audience, the moral issue arising here is that just insofar as the action would be value-laden and negatively valanced for an individual in actual life, portraying that same action as a positively valanced action of the portrayed character may well require it to be treated as value-neutral for that individual actor.

MORAL PROBLEMS IN PREPARING FOR A PERFORMANCE

If there are moral problems within the practice of acting, one should expect the same issues to arise in *preparing* the actor's performance. And indeed they do. Concern about these problems has been around for quite some time (Burgoyne et al. 1999). According to Burgoyne and her colleagues, "the blurring of boundaries between actor and character may be a significant condition for impact, and that the actor's ability to control that blurring may influence whether an acting experience leads to growth or emotional distress" (Burgoyne et al. 1999, 157). How, precisely, this affects students who are studying the craft may depend on acting styles, for as Burgoyne and colleagues also note: "Since some inside-out approaches to acting [such as the Method] encourage the actor

---

[4] Much of this empirical material is adduced in Konijn (2002, 69–76).

to use her own personal experience in building a character, thus facilitating boundary blurring, this theory has major implications for theatre pedagogy" (Burgoyne et al. 1999, 157). But, as mentioned in the previous section, the kinds of moral concerns one might have about performances is not limited to only one specific set of acting practices or acting styles, nor should it be so limited when discussing preparation.

Shawyer and Shively offer us a case of this kind of worry. In a *Saturday Night Live* video from 2019 that has been widely shared among high school teachers of theater, a group of drama students eagerly await their drama teacher's cast list for a show. To delay, while also surreptitiously watching their expressions of anxiety, the director, Mr. Koenig, asks a Christian student if he would "tongue" another student actor while kissing her in the show even if his parents object, and he also demands that two students have sex before they appear at the first rehearsal.[5] This kind of situation may not be unusual, especially in university settings, as is revealed in the arguments for safeguards against these very same kinds of worries (Shawyer and Shively 2019). Shawyer and Shively call these "boundary-establishment protocols," and their goal is to "advocate for continuous conversation in the acting class about managing personal boundaries" (Shawyer and Shively 2019, 100).

Adopting "boundary-establishment protocols" may assist with addressing these kinds of situations in rehearsal, but one might ask whether there is something about contemporary rehearsal processes themselves that raises moral issues. Such a concern is suggested by the following: Richard Schechner once stated the goal of rehearsal was to provide "living behavior treated as the film-director treats a strip of film," and that it does not matter where "strip of behavior was made, found, [or] developed" because "the strips of behavior are . . . things, items, 'material' " (Schechner 1981, 2). Regarding a set of rehearsed behavior and the people who engage in that behavior as strips is not dependent only on one style of acting, codified in one kind of "acting process theory." However, it *does* rely on *practices* of theater in which directors are thought to function something like auteurs, treating human behavior as though it, and the people who behave in those ways, were mere strips of material to be selected by a director for display.

Such cases as these involve discrepancies of power, where the teacher or director is in the position of power over the student-actors and able, because of it, to make what are at least questionable demands. And this position may be fairly innocently entered into; one does not have to assume all acting coaches or directors are like the aforementioned Mr. Koenig. It may be that it is the very possibility of such power imbalances that raises the moral issue: what are the responsibilities of those in power to those not in power?

But is that all there is? One might ask, if not reliant on particular acting *styles* nor on particular *practices* of theater (such as arise when directors are thought to function something like auteurs), are there any moral issues that occur due to the rehearsal

---

[5] Available on YouTube at https://www.youtube.com/watch?v=Ve1kmdHTY24 (accessed April 19, 2021).

process itself? In this context, consider the following from Peter Brook: "The actor allows a role to 'penetrate' him; at first he is all obstacle to it, but by constant work he can allow the barriers to drop . . . so that the act of performance is an act of sacrifice, of sacrificing what most men prefer to hide - this sacrifice is his gift to the spectator" (Brook 1968/2019, 59–60). The idea here is that performing is risky behavior and actors *must learn* to take those risks. Moreover, people learn to do this within the *rehearsal process*.[6] Brook claims, "It is not the fault of the holy that it has become a middle-class weapon to keep children good," and "we do not know how to celebrate, because we do not know what to celebrate." Nevertheless, he claims that "more than ever, we crave for an experience that is beyond the humdrum" (Brook 1968/2019, 46, 47, 48). In the passages quoted, Brook is presenting an account of a particular form of theater that he calls "The Holy Theatre," a term he borrows from Jerzy Grotowski in order to discuss the theater of Merce Cunningham, Grotowski, Samuel Beckett, and, much later, the Living Theatre of Julian Beck and Judith Malina. So a particular style of acting *may* be responsible for these moral worries. For these are expressed as worries one might have about rehearsing to produce performances in *that particular style*.

But suppose there is a risk that anyone who portrays another undertakes, and that learning how to portray another is, to varying degrees, what rehearsals are all about. Rehearsals—whether in groups or by actors singly and alone—can be about many other things: blocking, stage business, as well as lines and pronunciation of words (if any). Tiffany Stern notes that lines and pronunciation of words were the only things that were thought about in an actor's "study" of his or her "part" that took place in the sixteenth and seventeenth centuries in England (Stern 2000 63, 77). Group rehearsals were rare and indeed the first night's "performance" was in fact usually the only group rehearsal; and it was the prompter who governed what we now call "blocking" and other stage business (Stern 2000, 10–15; see also Marshall 2004, 32–33). Yet it is not these details Gay McAuley has in mind when she writes "there is something utterly fascinating about the openness and fluidity of the meaning making process in rehearsal" (McAuley 2006, 10). And even if she goes on at some length in what follows this passage to focus upon "fluidity," it is noteworthy that she remarks upon the "openness" of the process.[7] If not about technique and the fluidity it can enhance, what does she have in mind by the openness that contemporary forms of rehearsal offer apart from risk?

---

[6] Brook presents what may be only a partial picture of the relationship between actor and spectator wherein all the risk-taking is done by the actors. N. R. Helms has argued it is at least as plausible that "through the self-conscious use of empathy and critical insight, spectators can become active participants in theatre, risking themselves by using their identities as material for an understanding of performance" (Helms 2012, 91).

[7] McAuley notes "the way a tiny detail like the turn of a head, a look, a gesture can transform the meaning of a moment or a phrase, the way a tiny textual detail can lead the actors to major creative decisions concerning character, action or emotion, the way a prop or design decision or proxemic relationship can introduce a whole new direction and unleash a new wave of inventiveness." None of these have much to do with "openness" but all have to do with the "fluidity of the meaning making process in rehearsal" (McAuley 2006, 10).

So again, suppose there is a risk that at least any contemporary actor undertakes. The nature of the risk is what Zamir has in mind when he discusses the "percolation" between characters and a performers' identity that occurs in any style of acting (Zamir 2013, 356).[8] And, in consequence, learning to be vulnerable to such risks seems to be what contemporary rehearsal practices are centered upon to varying degrees. Certainly, setting up so-called boundary protocols and finding ways of protecting actors from those who would act as auteurs helps to reduce the vulnerability of actors and acting students against others who would abuse their power. But these strategies seem not to reduce the risk posed by the percolation between characters and a performers' identity that occurs in any style of acting. Nor does it mitigate the learning that takes place in rehearsals of how to accommodate the vulnerabilities to those risks.

Obligations That Hold Among the Performers

A youthful actor in an amateur production, suddenly aware that her father is in the audience, changes a word at the end of her line. The scripted word is one she knows her father would hate to hear coming out of her mouth, no matter that he will realize it was assigned to her and would recognize it as accurate to the character his daughter is playing. Inspired, she hits on an alternative word equally appropriate to the character. As delivered by this performer on this occasion, the word change is a fortunate improvement because the company wanted a laugh to occur at that moment in the performance but had been unable to induce it. And now, for the first time, the laugh actually does occur, right on spot. But the word she changed is a fellow performer's cue. He pauses, a look of panic crosses his face followed closely by a look of recognition, and that combination—of a pause, a moment of panic and a moment of recognition—turns out, given the content of the scene, to be quite funny. The spectators laugh because they are tracking the changes in his expression. Fortuitously, the changes in his mental state which registered on his face can plausibly be interpreted by spectators as consistent with the *content* of the scene. In fact, however, he is pausing because he is trying desperately to remember a cue that consists of the new word. He is suddenly wondering where exactly they are in the scene. His look of panic followed immediately by a look of recognition, or perhaps of hope, marks what he is currently thinking and feeling, concluding with his decision to go on, precisely where and how he should. Lucky perhaps, but these things do happen. The case is not all that unusual. Many performers inadvertently change many things in their performances. What makes this case a bit unusual is that the word was a cue and that one of the consequences of the word change was a change in spectator response.

---

[8] This "percolation" is similar to what Currie (1995) calls "leakage."

The moral problem raised by this case applies to pretty much every scripted performance, including all types of scripted theatrical performances in whatever styles. It calls our attention to the fact that performers rely on other performers to act in concert with them, to keep to the routines they have planned together. But because the planning is absent for that crucial moment, the case also reveals that even when such things happen actors still *feel* they must go on to act in concert. Yet we have no principled explanation of why that feeling is justified.

There is no contractarian, act-utilitarian, deontological, or virtue ethics solution to this. We actually have no clear and compelling *explanation* for why performers should expect others to rely on them, why performers have reason to rely on their fellow performers, and why spectators are right to expect the show will go on. There usually has been no kind of explicit or implied agreement to that effect among the performers. Nor is it clear how we could make that out, without appealing to some sort of social contract that is covertly entered into. It is not enough to suggest performers owe it to each other because they are other human beings. The relevant comparison classes are not readily made out so we could assess this from an act-utilitarian point of view. And since the case involves at least two people, two performers at least, it is unclear how a virtue ethicist might make headway here, short of endorsing collective intentions.[9]

The contractarian would be onto something were it not for the stubborn fact that there really has been no prior explicit agreement. But there is a tradition, going back to at least David Hume, that envisages agreements that are *de facto* rather than *de jure* (see, e.g., David Lewis 1969/2002; Brian Skyrms 2004; Christina Bicchieri 2018).[10] According to this tradition, the obligation to engage in a cooperative enterprise, or joint project, is a result of individuals acting according to their own calculations about what is reasonable.[11]

Other obligations among theatrical performers might include the moral problems encountered in the first two sections of this chapter, by saying that performers have, for example, whatever obligations we determine they actually have to other performers with respect to violence, erotic theater, and so on. But there has been no discussion among theater theorists, performance theorists, or

[9] The idea that spectators appear to attribute intentions to collective groups of performers is also one of the issues raised by this case. But, since that is not a moral issue, I will not discuss it here.

[10] There is no general agreement among philosophers that this is true. Indeed, in private correspondence, David Davies (of McGill University) has written that "an actor's moral commitment to accord with what was rehearsed falls under a more general *ceteris paribus* moral obligation covering any collective agreement to proceed in a certain way to realize a (morally permissible) shared end - an obligation that would seem to make sense on both deontological and consequentialist lines" (email dated April 19, 2021). But the point made here is that apart from the game-theoretic extension of Hume cited in the body of this text, there really is little discussion of how any "collective agreement to proceed in a certain way" gets started in the first place.

[11] There is a considerable literature concerning each of these elements: what it means to say that engagement in a cooperative enterprise or joint project is a *result*; whether it is the result of what *individuals* calculate: what a *calculation* is and what that presupposes about human capacities; and what it means to say that individuals calculate what is *reasonable*.

philosophers beyond thinking about those kinds of obligations. Even thinking about the obligation to engage in cooperative enterprises or joint projects turns out to be something new.

POSSIBLE MORAL ISSUES CONCERNING SITE-SPECIFIC THEATRICAL PERFORMANCES

Among the new practices of theater, so-called site-specific performances have generated a fair amount of controversy. This controversy is generated by the persistent belief among many theater and performance theorists, if not also among practitioners, that theater provides effective tools for impacting or changing spectator habits and beliefs. And, even though many do not acknowledge this fact, much of this controversy has to do with moral issues, at least if "moral issues" is broadly construed to include the social effects of theater (Snyder-Young 2013).

What is a "site-specific theatrical performance"? As David Wohl puts it, "the term 'site-specific' has been tossed about rather loosely to describe any performance that doesn't take place in a conventional theatre space" and furthermore "scholars and critics have different views about what 'site-specific' really means" (Wohl 2014, 29). Wohl quotes Rand Harmon, the director and cofounder of St. Louis' (Missouri) Specific Gravity Ensemble, a group that performed a series of four "elevator plays" in 2007 and 2009, as saying that the company "intended to provide an experience that changed our audience once they'd completed a performance. We didn't feel that was always the case when they were sitting comfortably in a cushy seat in dark anonymity" (Wohl 2014, 30). Immediately one thinks the company had some specific moral agenda, some moral point of view they hoped to change in the audience. But as Wohl states it, when he began to investigate and produce site-specific theater, his "intent was to push the boundaries of traditional theatre and offer audiences something different. We also wanted to explore new spaces so that . . . the space itself might become part of the performance text." This is what is going on when performances consist of "freeing space from traditional use and reclaiming sites as they metamorphose into wildly appealing artistic environments" (Cordileone and Whorton 2015, 299). From this we derive one of the currently popular senses of "site specificity," namely, that it is a matter of "finding a site" that fits the technical needs of a preexisting play or a devised performance, but usually ignores the actual history of the site.

But consider what might happen when a practitioner or theorist does consider the fact that a site has an actual history that may be at odds with the play? Two responses are possible. One response is that the play may transform the place so that its actual history does not matter but its space becomes "transformed" or "interrogated." In this context, a critique of the motives of the National Theatre of Scotland might provide a useful perspective. Fiona Wilkie writes:

It is clear that the artistic team of the NTS . . . finds something of value in site-specific theatre for the devolved and fluid model that it seeks to establish. In this case the value, I suggest, lies not in the opportunity to interrogate spatial relationships that has attracted many other site-specific practitioners . . . Rather, site-specificity offers a convenient marker of a set of ideas with which the NTS wants to be associated: experiment, accessibility, the connection between art and everyday life, and a shift away from the primacy of the metropolitan theatre building. (Wilkie 2013, 87–88)

The other possible response to the fact that a site already has a significant history is that the "elements of imagined worlds are suddenly non-negotiable when an existing space becomes the intended performance location" (Cordileone and Whorton 2015, 298). This is the view that whatever the site is for a performance, the actual history of a site can lead to stories about the site itself. This response is more closely associated with devised performances rather than prescripted performances, but that need not be so.

We have now encountered at least three senses of site specificity that seem to govern the discussion: a) finding spaces that will fit the technical needs of a play, b) finding spaces that the play transforms or "interrogates" in some way, or c) performing in spaces and allowing the histories of those spaces to have a voice, so to speak, in the performance. The first of these is part of what is deemed, in a deprecating move by theater and performance theorists, a "merely aesthetic interest." That deprecatory label is also sometimes given to performances of the second kind. But in the third cases, where a performance in a "site" is aimed at giving the history of that site voice in the production, then it merits a kind of approbation, at least from theater and performance theorists. And this is what the controversy has been about.

Why should it be? The answer is given by reflecting on why the actual history of a site could be important to either an already written play or a devised piece. One might think the importance is due to some antiquarian interest in the site. An antiquarian interest could be material relevant to a description of the performance but not normally material meriting critical approbation. Instead, what makes sense of the approbation among many theater and performance theorists is a commitment to the idea that theater provides effective tools for changing spectator habits and beliefs. For without that commitment, it is difficult to see why one should care.

MORAL PROBLEMS ABOUT OBLIGATIONS PERFORMERS HAVE TO SPECTATORS

Two sources of moral issues underwrite putative obligations performers have to spectators. One is the view, widely accepted among theater and performance theorists, that performances can be socially efficacious. They do not merely *express* ideologically inflected agendas, they can actually bring those agendas about. The other is the less contentious view, widely accepted among philosophers of the imagination, that narratives (including theatrically presented fictional narratives) "prescribe" certain imaginings to spectators. If either view is correct, then performances have power to change the habits, the beliefs, or the imaginings of spectators. In that case, performers should take special care that both the performances themselves and the contents of a set of theatrical performances are morally worthy in some way.

Many textbooks and articles concerning acting or performance theory make the assumption that whatever else they may do, performances can be efficacious in changing the habits or beliefs of spectators. Because so much theater in the West is narrative in structure, it is worth examining the hypothesis in the context of the *presentation of narratives*. The theatrical mode of presenting narratives may be thought more likely to be efficacious than forms requiring only reading are likely to produce. Here we are concerned less with the *contents* of narratives than with the modes of presenting narratives. Note also that whereas the so-called liveness issue could be important to this discussion, we will not focus upon it.[12]

It is an empirical question whether narratives can be and are efficacious for spectators. Greg Currie has argued that there is very little empirical evidence for this (Currie 2016). The kinds of narratives Currie discusses are not theatrical and one might find fault with his failure to remark the differences between theatrical and nontheatrical modes of presentation. Nevertheless, "down-playing fiction's role as a giver of moral reasons," Currie "emphasizes instead its (presumed) capacity to inculcate skills, with fictions providing models of human behavior analogous, some say, to those simulators of flight used to train pilots, [even though] fictions do sometimes offer moral reasons" (Currie 2016, 50). And it seems the kinds of skills learned by reading that he discusses could easily be imagined to be learnable by spectators who witness a performance of a fictional theatrical narrative.[13] But, as it turns out, the evidence of fiction's efficacy in this regard is weak: "It's only ever some literary works, in some contexts, for some readers, which promote this kind of learning" (Currie 2016, 51). In short, we might well conclude that *single* performances are not efficacious at changing the habits and beliefs of spectators.

However, perhaps a culture of immersion in a great many fictional narrative theatrical performances makes one more likely to be a sensitive person. But the evidence for this is also uncertain. An important reason is the variation in kinds of spectating that takes place in theater. Dennis Kennedy has noted that "audiences are not (and probably never have been) homogeneous social and psychological groups" (Kennedy 2009, 1). In addition, "a good deal of the history of audiences, especially after records improved in the eighteenth century, reveals that spectators often attended the theatre without attending to the play" (Kennedy 2009, 12). Kennedy elaborates, "The unwilling spectator, the

---

[12] The "liveness issue" is often taken to be that there is an efficacy to live presentations that fails to be achieved in so-called mediated presentations. But, as Philip Auslander has argued, this is simply not true (Auslander 2012). This is somewhat beside the point discussed here.

[13] Anna Ichino and Greg Currie also provide empirical evidence showing that even when we consider fictions that *do* offer moral reasons, those reasons are not necessarily adopted by readers (Ichino and Currie 2017).

reluctant spectator, the spectator in a bad mood or feeling poorly, the accidental spectator, the snoring spectator; I cannot put statistics or proper names to this roll call but
they are not fictitious creatures" (2009, 13).

Nevertheless, some support may be given to the hypothesis by the vagaries of
spectating. As Kennedy noted in an earlier essay, "the approbative and disapprobative
audience gestures conventionally available in theatre are limited—applause, laughter,
shouting encore, booing, weeping—and they confine spectators to predetermined and
relatively compliant roles . . . the physical and vocal passivity of the spectator, frequently
condemned in the avant-garde tradition of the twentieth century, is partly necessary if
the performance is to proceed: audience participation is workable on a continuing basis
only when it occurs inside the producer's plan" (Kennedy 2001, 277). So, if spectating in
theater is constrained in these ways, it is at least possible that a culture of immersion in
fictional narrative theatrical performances might actually be efficacious in changing the
habits or beliefs of spectators. If so, then the moral claim is that performers should take
special care that both the performances themselves and the contents of a collection of
theatrical performances are morally worthy in some way.

One of the reasons for doubting the moral claim is that in fact, we do not take this
particular kind of care. A quick counter to this skeptical viewpoint might consist in
the observation that we are often blind to hypotheses we do not think are true. Explicit
arguments in favor of this hypothesis, in contrast, are many. But an even more cynical
skeptic might point out that the actual reason actors prefer to present morally worthy
theatrical performances may only be that, by doing so, they may be better liked or get
better box office numbers. An appeal to evidence seems in order. And the evidence is
that neither individually nor collectively are presentations of fictional narratives *always*
efficacious in bringing about the conditions for improvement or even in bringing about
any effect on the habits and beliefs of spectators (Braddock and Dillard 2016). So, perhaps there is no genuine moral problem here. As Dani Snyder-Young put it, in a rare acknowledgment of this fact, "Most artists [including theater artists] are aware that theatre
projects cannot, generally, stop wars, start revolutions, prevent the rise of regimes, stop
the proliferation of nuclear arms, or put an end to global warming" (Snyder-Young 2013,
16–17).

The second view that underlies a moral constraint on performances is the less contentious view, widely accepted among philosophers of the imagination, that narratives
(including theatrically presented fictional narratives) "prescribe" certain imaginings to
spectators. Ever since Kendall Walton's *Mimesis and Make-Believe* (1990), most imagination theorists have held that narratives and other works of art "prescribe" certain imaginings to spectators. If this is true then the moral implications of such prescriptions
must be considered.

Suppose you go to see Shakespeare's *A Merchant of Venice* and there encounter a
representation of the character named "Antonio." Throughout the course of the play,
Antonio is revealed to be little more than a self-pitying lump of clay; indeed he is unable or unwilling (depending on the actor) to gather the resolution required to defend
himself against execution. Also, his anti-semitism combined with his self-pity suggests

that the dominant threads of his character are melancholy and cruelty. Does imagining Antonio have any effect on your habits and beliefs? Of course it does, insofar as you can imagine that people behave as he does. But does it change your orientation to the world? Probably not, unless naively you had not imagined the world to have such people in it.

There may also be such a phenomenon as "imaginative resistance" which would, should it occur in our example case, be a cause that might explain why a given spectator resisted the prescription of the problematic attitude or belief (Walton 1990, 154–155; see also Walton 1994, 27–50: 2006; Gendler and Liao, 2019; Shim and Liao, this volume). This is because to resist imagining what a narrative has prescribed is either to be unable or to refuse to imagine it (Walton 2006, 142–144). But it is not clear why, naiveté aside, the phenomenon of imaginative resistance should occur in the *Merchant* case.

It might also be that Waltonian "prescriptions" to imagine should be taken as little more than "invitations" for reflection. As Zamir points out, in an essay on Shakespearean tragedy and ethics, "tragedy *invites* the audience to reflect on various links and ties [among "home," "family," and "status" and the ways we live] not as givens, but as entities that demand repeated, conscious, active sustaining" (Zamir 2016, 82, my emphasis). However, if what we are "prescribed" to imagine is only what we are "invited" to reflect upon, the moral issue disappears. One can always decline an invitation. So, no reason derives from the fact a narrative is morally questionable or contains morally obnoxious elements to suppose we should be cautious about presenting that narrative. So, again, perhaps there is no real moral problem here after all.

CONCLUSION

At the outset of this chapter, I asserted that it would undertake three tasks. The first was to present the state of discussion in theater and performance theory as well as philosophy on moral issues concerning theatrical presentations. The fact is that most theater and performance theorists do not discuss morality directly and when they do, as in the case of site-specific performances, they tend to discuss the issues in terms of social effects and ideology rather than in terms of morality. Among philosophers, with the exception of Tzachi Zamir, there is little more.

The second task undertaken was to distinguish among those moral issues those which occur only because a theater company has adopted a particular performance or acting style and those which occur because of the nature of theater itself. My initial statement of that second task was a bit disingenuous because "the nature of theater itself" was taken to mean only one form of theatrical performances, that containing characters whose stories are conveyed theatrically. Other forms, by analogy with the difference between lyric rather than narrative poetry, are not narrative at all. Indeed non-narrative forms may well be in the majority of theatrical performances worldwide (Zarrilli et al. 2010). But narrative theater is the most common form of theater in the West, so I did not make more of this.

The third task was to distinguish between areas in which genuine moral issues arise and areas where they do not. I do not believe that all the practices in which moral (social, or ideological) problems are thought to arise actually do. Instead, as we saw in the previous section, it turns out that many moral issues are only thought to arise because the beliefs they rest upon are mistaken or do not have the consequences they might be thought to have.

See also: Destrée, Shim and Liao, Whalen, this volume

REFERENCES

Auslander, Philip. 2012. "Digital Liveness: A Historico-Philosophical Perspective." *PAL: A Journal of Performance and Art* 34, no. 3: 3–11.

Bicchieri, Christina. 2018. "Social Norms." In *The Stanford Encyclopedia of Philosophy*, edited by Edward Zalta (Winter 2018). https://plato.stanford.edu/archives/win2018/entries/social-norms/.

Braddock, Kurt, and James Price Dillard. 2016. "Meta-Analytic Evidence for the Persuasive Effect of Narratives on Beliefs, Attitudes, Intentions, and Behaviors." *Communication Monographs* 83, no. 4: 446–467.

Brook, Peter. [1968] 2019. *The Empty Space*. New York: Simon & Schuster.

Burgoyne, Suzanne, Karen Poulin, and Ashely Reardon. 1999. "The Impact of Acting on Student Actors." *Theatre Topics* 9, no. 2: 157–179.

Cordileone, Amy, and Rachel Tuggle Whorton. 2015. "Site-Specific theatre: New Perspectives on Pedagogy and Performance." *Research in Drama Education* 20, no. 3: 298–301.

Currie, Gregory. 1995. "The Moral Psychology of Fiction." In *Art and Its Messages: Meaning, Morality, and Society*, edited by Stephen Davies, 49–58. University Park: Penn State University Press.

Currie, Gregory. 2016. "Does Fiction Make Us Less Empathic?" *Teorema* 35, no. 3: 47–68.

Gendler, Tamar Szabo, and Shen-Yi Liao. 2019. "The Problem of Imaginative Resistance." In *The Routledge Companion to Philosophy of Literature*, edited by Noel Carroll and John Gibson, 405–418. New York: Routledge.

Goff, Jennifer. 2016. "Two Dead Men, One Director." *Theatre/Practice* 5: 1–20.

Helms, N. R. 2012. "'Upon Such Sacrifices': An Ethic of Spectator Risk." *Journal of Dramatic Theory and Criticism* 12, no. 1: 91–107.

Ichino, Anna, and Greg Currie. "Truth and Trust in Fiction." In *Art and Belief*, edited by Ema Sullivan-Bissett, Helen Bradley, and Paul Noordhof, 1–24. New York: Oxford University Press.

Kennedy, Dennis. 2001. "Sports and Shows: Spectators in Contemporary Culture." *Theatre Research International* 26, no. 3: 277–284.

Kennedy, Dennis. 2009. "The Problem of the Spectator." In *The Spectator and the Spectacle*, 1–72. Cambridge: Cambridge University Press.

Konijn, Elly A. 2002. "The Actors' Emotions Reconsidered." In *A Theoretical and Practical Guide*, 2nd ed., edited by Philip Zarrilli, 62–81. New York: Routledge.

Levinas, Emmanuel. [1930] 1989. *The Levinas Reader*, edited by Sean Hand. Oxford: Blackwell.

Lewis, David, [1969] 2002. *Convention*. Oxford: Blackwell.

Marshall, C. W. 2004. "'Alcestis' and the Ancient Rehearsal Process." *Arion: A Journal of Humanities and the Classics* 11, no. 3: 27–45.

McAuley, Gay. 2006. "The Emerging Field of Rehearsal Studies." *About Performance* 6: 7–13.

Plato. [380 BC] 1992. *The Republic*. Translated by Grube, G. M. A, and C. D. C. Reeve. Indianapolis: Hackett.

Read, Alan. 1995. "Introduction." In *Theatre and Everyday Life: An Ethics of Performance*, 1–18. Milton Park, UK: Taylor and Francis Group.

Ridout, Nicholas. 2009. *Theatre and Ethics*. London: Palgrave Macmillan.

Rouse, John. 1984. "Brecht and the Contradictory Actor." *Theatre Journal* 36, no. 1: 25–42.

Ruhl, Sarah. 2008. *Dead Man's Cell Phone*. New York: Theatre Communications Group, Inc.

Schechner, Richard. 1981. "Restoration of Behavior." *Studies in Visual Communication* 7, no. 3: 2–45.

Shawyer, Susanne, and Kim Shively. 2019. "Education in Theatrical Intimacy as Ethical Practice of University Theatre." *Journal of Dramatic Theory and Criticism* 34, no. 1: 87–104.

Skyrms, Brian. 2004. "Evolution of Inference." In *The Stag Hunt and the Evolution of Social Structure*, 49–64. Cambridge: Cambridge University Press.

Snyder-Young, Dani. 2013. "Why do we want to use theatre to make social change?" In *Theatre of Good Intentions*, 1–17. Palgrave Macmillan.

Stern, Tiffany. 2000. *Rehearsal from Shakespeare to Sheridan*. Oxford: Oxford University Press.

Vidmar Jovanović, Iris. 2019. "Cognitive and Ethical Values and Dimensions of Narrative Art." In her *Narrative Art, Knowledge and Ethics*, 17–85. Rijeka: Filozofski fakultet Rijeka.

Walton, Kendall. 1990. *Mimesis and Make-Believe*. Harvard University Press.

Walton, Kendall. 1994. "Morals in Fiction and Fictional Reality." *Proceedings of the Aristotelian Society, Supplementary Volumes* 68: 27–50.

Walton, Kendall. 2006. "On the (So-called) Puzzle of Imaginative Resistance." In *The Architecture of the Imagination*, edited by Shaun Nicholls, 137–148. Oxford: Oxford University Press.

Wilkie, Fiona. 2013. "The Production of 'Site': Site-Specific Theatre." In *A Concise Companion to Contemporary British and Irish Drama*, edited by Nadine Holdsworth and Mary Luckhurst, 87–106. Hoboken, NJ: Wiley-Blackwell.

Wohl, David. 2014. "Site Specific Theatre." *College of Visual and Performing Arts Faculty Publications* 32: 28–35. h5ps://digitalcommons.winthrop.edu/cvpa_facpub/32.

Zamir, Tzachi. 2013. "Unethical Acts." *Philosophical Quarterly* 63, no. 251: 353–373.

Zamir, Tzachi. 2016. "Ethics and Shakespearean Tragedy." In *The Oxford Handbook of Shakespearean Tragedy*, edited by Michael Neill and David Schalkwik, 71–88. Oxford: Oxford University Press.

Zarrilli, Phillip. 2002. "General Introduction: Between theory and practice." In *Acting (Re) Considered: A Theoretical and Practical Guide*, 2nd ed., edited by Phillip B. Zarrilli, 1–6. London: Routledge.

Zarrilli, Phillip. 2007. "An Enactive Approach to Understanding Acting." *Theatre Journal* 59, no. 4: 635–647.

Zarrilli, Philip, Bruce M. McConachie, Gary Jay Williams, Carol Fisher Sorgenfrei, eds. 2010. *Theatre Histories: An Introduction*, 2nd ed. London: Routledge.

CHAPTER 28

DANCE ETHICS

AILI WHALEN

INTRODUCTION

DANCE is one of the arts that is typically physically embodied in a moving, engaged, powerful, and corporeal way that involves one or more persons together in a shared, interconnected, active and dynamic space (see also Hamilton, this volume). As such, it involves all the sensory modalities of sight, hearing, smell, and touch (as well as kinaesthetic and somaesthetic feelings of vibrations and movement energy) that belong to sports, physical combat, love-making, and therapy. It also allows for the conceptual and cognitive awarenesses that belong to the more physically remote fine arts. This means that dance provides great possibilities for love, connection, harmony, and healing, as well as for its ethical opposites of abuse and harm. In addition, dance can deliver these at all of the physical, emotional, and mental levels where we think, live, feel, and breathe.

My primary goal in this chapter is to focus on some of the special responsibilities that the embodied nature of dance can bring into ethical relationships, honing in on the idea of dancers as ethical agents and actors who must navigate issues of personal space, touch, consent, closeness, and care for those who are sharing a professional, social, or community dance space. I will start with a discussion of the personal nature of embodiment, moving out from there to a discussion of one-on-one connections with another person that are illustrated in dance, comparing these to what I will call "romantic entanglements." Next, the chapter expands outward from on-one-one dancing to "ethics writ large"—what some might call social and political philosophy—and briefly touch on some research being done on dance-specific cultural appropriation, authorship, copyright, personal identity discrimination and exclusion, and decolonization. Finally, I will provide a conclusion and coda that discusses new issues for dance that have arisen due to the COVID-19 global pandemic.

Dance, Embodiment and Ethics

Dance, whether for social, performative, art, exercise, or therapeutic purposes, is typically embodied in a *person who dances*. A person, as opposed to a *homo sapiens*, exists at the level of culture (see Margolis 2004 for more on moral agents as encultured rather than biological). They are an ethical agent when they act in an intentional way that—in very broad strokes—is aimed to either further some idea of the good for human beings or to avoid or alleviate some harm. Bodily actions have long been treated as ethically relevant because physical care and injuries provide clear, universalizable examples of pleasure and pain on a basic utilitarian calculus. Not punching one's sibling or grabbing a toy away from them or petting or holding the baby or family pet nicely are among the earliest childhood examples many of us have of a physical, body-based code of ethics. Protecting one's body from unwanted touching, gazes, and issues of consent, sexual touch, assault, and rape arise in childhood and adolescence and into adulthood. Here issues of sexual ethics combine with issues of identity, vulnerability, power, and fear as a result of imbalances of physical (as well as social) strength, power, and control. When these issues become sexualized, gendered, racialized, colonized, and able-ized (and all of these institutionalized), it is often the case that what is being policed and controlled are people's bodies and the expressions of those bodies, including dance. It is for this reason that a discussion of the body is not only relevant to understanding human ethics but crucial. Perhaps dance's intimate connection with the body can help in this endeavor. This is the hope behind writing about dance ethics: that it will have something to say not just about dance but about human ethics through dance.

Most of the existing work in dance ethics exists in the dominant forms of discourse of dance studies, which are currently dance history and cultural studies. These issues are large and societal; they are embodied in societal structures although the burdens are often borne at bodily and individual as well as collective bodies. I will canvass some of these later in the chapter. But first, I will discuss ethics at the person-to-person bodily level, beginning with the example of partnered dance.

Dance Ethics One-on-One

This chapter will take as its guiding image the example of a close, coupled partnered dance, whether an artistic dance to be rehearsed and performed in a competition or on stage or whether in a social dance form, like salsa, rumba, or bachata, to be performed in a club arena with potential partners who are virtual strangers. These encounters mirror the real-life dating situation for many people (which for ease of reference I'll simply call, perhaps quaintly, "romantic entanglement," not to be confused with Romantic philosophy). Here the situation in both cases is one in which encounters with potential partners can range along a physical and emotional continuum of light and relatively uninvolved (a hand-holding day-time date, say) to passionate and intense (full-on sexual intercourse, however one chooses to define that), with either a near-stranger and involving a short duration and little commitment or with someone one knows well with whom one might develop a long relationship over time.

And as with romantic entanglement, partnered dance typically involves issues of power imbalances of physical, emotional, and mental kinds where the potential for harm exists. In partnered dance, for example, a larger, stronger partner can crush a smaller one, drop them from a height in a lift, or lift them in a way that causes damage. Consider the situation, for example, where a partner tries to lift another under their rib cage and grabs them by the ribs instead, breaking a rib in the process and puncturing a lung.[1] Collisions or kicks with feet wearing hard-shanked pointe shoes are other possible physical harms that can occur either deliberately, with malice, via negligence or failure to pay attention, or just by accident.

There are also issues of emotional and mental vulnerabilities that can be exploited that have to do with societal, economic, or structural rather than physical power imbalances. One contemporary dancer and choreographer, Lewys Holt, told me that he started his own company in part in reaction to his own discomfort with feeling physically vulnerable in relation to the power dynamics of relationships with company directors as a dance-for-hire. He explained that it was his experience that sometimes a company director would ask a dancer to rehearse or perform something that is outside of their physical comfort zone or otherwise injury-risking—such as asking them to rehearse or perform without adequate warm-up—and that the dancer might feel uncomfortable saying "no" because of their job vulnerability in that employment context. In response to this, Holt has employed a counselor to whom the dancers he works with in his company meet as a group on a regular basis and with whom they can go individually and confidentially if they so choose to raise issues of discomfort during the rehearsal or performance process (Lewys Holt, Zoom interview with author, February 12, 2021). This is a new process for a fledgling company, but so far Holt reports that some conscious attention to climate and comfort of the dancers has created emotionally safe outlets for issues that might otherwise harm the dancers that they have been making use of in various ways. (And one can presume that if a director is showing awareness for the dancers' feelings in this way that says at least something about directorial intentions not to be autocratic and dictatorial.) Here the issue has to do with a one-on-one relationship issue— that of a dance company or production member and their director—even though it's not in the course of a *pas de deux* dance necessarily.

Dancer, choreographer, dance-partnering expert, coach, and philosopher Ilya Vidrin has helped dancers to attune to one another in partnering for some fifteen years (as of this writing) and he believes that explicit ethical norms are needed to guide their

---

[1] This example is the true-life experience of a ballet dancer with whom I have lost touch so her name and former ballet company affiliation will remain anonymous. Suffice it to say that this accident ended her career.

interactions so that they can keep positive goals of their partnering in mind and avoid harm. His choreographic projects include (among others) these explicit norms:

- Communicate with care and consistency in ways that invite dialogue.
- Honor our commitments and ask for help when we need it.
- Create a culture that welcomes critique and feedback that promotes learning.
- Assume best intentions.
- When conflict occurs, ask questions to seek clarity and understanding.
- Make room for personal growth by speaking from first-person perspective and allowing for changing interpretations and choices. (Ilya Vidrin, email communication with the author, February 4, 2021)

Vidrin's view is that even though the body can be trained to have a certain degree of bodily sensitivity and awareness, explicit norms must be kept in mind to guide this training and development. He thereby subscribes to a "communicative, inter-relational, norm-based care ethics" for partnered dance and cites his influences as Paul Grice, Nelson Goodman, Catherine Elgin, Margaret Gilbert, and classical care ethics (Ilya Vidrin, Zoom conversation with the author, February 16, 2021).

Vidrin's full ethics of partnered dance is fleshed out in his essay "The Conditions and Norms of Partnering," in which his guiding question, asked in an ethical sense but with some aesthetic overlays, is "What makes a good dance partner"? (Vidrin 2020) Vidrin's answer, in short, is that good ethics consists of norm-based communication includes "a physical exchange of information on the basis of ethically-bound conditions" (proximity, orientation, and points of contact) which constrain agency and predictability (Vidrin 2020, 2 and 7). He also says that these norms govern what it means to communicate *well*, which requires both *listening* and *response* to change (14).

Vidrin denies that dance is a language and wants to hold onto norm-based ethical theories that use verbal communication to guide dance (Vidrin, Zoom conversation with the author, February 16, 2021; cf., Vidrin 2018). He is aware, however, that the best-laid verbal intentions don't always cash out in physical practice. This may be due to a number of factors, including lack of a partner's "refined awareness" to "attend to what they are communicating" due to lack of training and competence (Vidrin 2020, 11). A dancer's values are part of whether or not they are sensitive to others but so are how their interactions are negotiated in practice, including "aesthetic conventions of the form" (12). In short, they might say the right things, the verbal rhetoric might be there, but in practice the ethical responsibility and agency that would match what they are saying in partnered interaction is physically absent. This means that the ability of each partner to perform and to recognize the ethical effects of their actions is key to the success of their dance partnering, not just the ability to know what the principles are and agree to them (14). Vidrin concludes that this means that a dancer must have the right disposition, which I think means the dancer has to have the right character or virtue—putting this into the virtue ethics camp. As Vidrin concludes, they "must always be listening and responding to change" (14).

While it seems reasonable to use cognized norms to visualize moral intentions and to communicate boundaries with others, one can also imagine power-imbalance situations in one-on-one dance ethics situations—again using the romantic entanglement situation as our thought-help visual guide—where expressed intentions are silenced by fear or intimidation. Holt brought up one example, above, but fear of violence or social disapproval or both can be another. In the romantic entanglement arena, for example, the immediate and obvious examples that come to mind are of all the intricacies around consent to sexual intercourse and whether or not someone has "said yes"—with "saying yes" now the preferred explicit norm for consent rather than yes being inferred unless someone "says no," explicitly, given that in many situations (such as in cases of intoxication, fear, deception, intimidation, or lack of mental capacity) saying "no" may not happen and yet full and free ethical consent may not be presumed accordingly. There are also many other micro-aggressive romantic entanglement situations that may not rise to rape-assault levels but that are coercive and involve ethical harm and communication nevertheless where a bodily awareness might be helpful to determine whether touch or closeness is wanted or not. How to read these cues might involve a bodily sensitivity beyond understanding of verbal norms that is analogous to dancer-trained bodily sensitivity. Imagine, for example, that it starts to drizzle on a date and person A rushes over to person B and puts their arm around person B's shoulder while holding an umbrella over their head. Their faces might be close, breath on the other's cheek, bodies touching. Does this harm the person being touched? Here are some cues that might tell A that it does cause B harm:

- Bodily stiffening of person B's shoulders
- B's wriggling out of the shoulder grasp of A
- B turning their face turning away from person A
- Other movements of B to distance themselves from A
- B "going dead" and otherwise showing no positive response

And if any of these things happen, person A can respond with sensitivity and awareness—saying something like, "I'm sorry, I'm clumsy—I don't know if you want to share this umbrella—is it ok?" Or they can double-down and press closer (an insistent and unethical act if the physical response were any of the above).

When I was the Aesthetics editor for *The Philosophers' Magazine*,[2] I asked amateur Latin dancer and professional philosopher Joshua M. Hall to write an article for us considering issues of consent in social Latin dance clubs and he did so in an article titled "Consensuality: Joshua M. Hall on what Latin dance can teach us about unwanted touch" (2018a). When writing this piece, he informally asked his friends and acquaintances in the Latin dance world via social media to weigh in on social codes of

---

[2] The reader should note here that prior to July 2022 my name was Aili Bresnahan. It is now Aili Whalen.

ethics and consent in Latin social dance and some of the responses he got are reported in the excerpts that follow.

> One male dancer said that "leaders" (usually male) must have significant leeway to "teach" partners to accommodate new and challenging touches and that if a "follower" (usually female) shows up at a social dance she has consented to anything the leader chooses to happen in the dance, one song at a time. (Hall 2018a, 35)

In his article, Hall challenges this view as unethical and not true of how all male dancers (or all "leaders") see the norms of social Latin dance (35). He also points out that there is no historical basis for the man's view—that in the West African traditions from which Latin dance derives improvisation is key and touch is forbidden (36). A female dancer Hall interviewed reported her discomfort with this sort of attitude, explaining to Hall how she and other female dancers she knows try to handle it in bodily rather than verbal ways:

> Instead of telling someone we aren't comfortable with the level of touch they enacted, we plaster on tight smiles and try to manoeuvre to a more comfortable position without our partners noticing, shifting in increments or hoping he'll notice how still and unresponsive we've become and correct himself on the next turn. (Hall 2018a, 33)

Another dancer pointed out to Hall that unwanted or offensive touch can just be by clueless or inexperienced dancers rather than on purpose: "by male 'leaders' who are inexperienced with dance (which makes it harder for them to perceive cues of discomfort in their typically-female 'followers') or who have difficulty interpreting social cues in general" (Hall 2018a, 33–34). This tracks Vidrin's note in his work on partnering that there is a physical sensitivity and awareness that must accompany cognized ethical rules if ethical norms are to be implemented effectively in one-on-one dance.

Hall's own suggestion is one that he attributes to his dance training in Tango:

> The dancer (leader or follower) makes a gentle gesture, then pays careful attention to how their partner responds. If the partner enthusiastically joins the new movement, or at least gives no indication of discomfort, that can be interpreted as a tentative acceptance of the invitation (for the time being). But if the partner responds negatively—either verbally, or with body language indicating discomfort—that should be interpreted as the invitation being declined. (Hall 2018a, 36)

He then goes on to say that instead of consent being a one-time thing, as the male dancer who responded to his question reported, that it is an ongoing process (much like in romantic entanglement) of communication, one in which consent can be revoked at any time (37). He likens this ongoing interaction to a continuous electric circuit that can be continued with ongoing consent or broken when it is revoked by one of the dancers during the course of the giving and receiving of energy.

The ethical standard Hall thus ends up adopting for one-on-one social dance involves "feeling-with" one's partner, or what he calls "consensuality"—a "mutual sensuality of consensual togetherness" (37). Supplementing all this discussion of bodily aware-ness, however, is a verbalized ethical norm that Hall provides at the end of the article in the form of advice: "If you are currently touching your partner, but you feel no en-ergy from them sustaining that touch—or if you're so detached from any awareness of their movements that you've no idea whether such energy is present—then you should reattune your awareness in search of that energy" (38).

The above examples of one-on-one dance ethics, which I have likened throughout to one-on-one romantic entanglements, show the promise that further work in embodied dance ethics might have for further work in sexual ethics, consent, and interpersonal ethics of relationships more broadly. There is more work to be done in these areas by connecting this work on dance partnering in particular to ethics in these areas, but these pieces are a start.

There is a great deal of additional opportunity for dance philosophers to help to lo-cate research in dance studies that bears on ethical issues and connect it to the relevant discourses in academic philosophy. In the next section, I will survey a couple of the pri-mary works which have done this explicitly, as well as highlight some additional areas for further work.

DANCE ETHICS WRIT LARGE: COMMUNITIES, COLLECTIVES, COMPANIES, AND SOCIETY IN BACKGROUND: LITERATURE REVIEW

In this section I first provide a literature review of two pieces on dance ethics proper. Next, I list some areas of dance scholarship and practice that are related to dance ethics broadly construed. These include issues of cultural appropriation, authorship, and cop-yright as well as of identity, discrimination, and decolonization.[3]

Bresnahan, Katan-Schmid, and Houston: Dance as Embodied Ethics

"Dance as Embodied Ethics," a chapter for the *Routledge Companion to Performance Philosophy*, treats dance as embodied ethics from three perspectives: (1) where dance

---

[3] Other dance-related health and safety concerns (which are ethical in the sense of affecting the well-being and flourishing of dancers) arise in the industry that I do not have time or space to research or address. These include physical concerns such as amenorrhea and bone-density due to overtraining and lack of proper nutrition, mental and emotional health concerns such as the emotional toll of constant striving, injuries and work-life balance, body image and eating disorder concerns, and safety issues related to work conditions of travel, stage, and public environments.

can serve as a performative metaphor that can guide ethical reflective activity (Katan-Schmid), (2) how some dance practices, such as those in political protest dance, exemplify applied ethical action in virtue and consequentialist ethics (Bresnahan), and (3) how dance practices in community dance, such as those serving vulnerable populations, involve an ethics of care (Houston) (Bresnahan et al. 2020).

Einav Katan-Schmid's work draws on that of Mark Johnson and George Lakoff, "to suggest that 'dance' enables thinking of decision-making in terms of embodied comprehension of dynamic interrelationships. Thus, tacit and contemplative decisions are made beyond rigid definitions" (Bresnahan et al. 2020, 379). She then develops this view with the help of John Dewey, Fiona Bannon, Rosemary Tong, and Nancy Williams to show how " 'dancing' holds three characteristics, which are significant for human understanding: it is personal, cultural and reflective at the same time" and that these features are deeply connected to personal ethics and embodied agency (380–381).

My section connects Aristotle's virtue ethics theory with his view of how human flourishing can result from a *katharsis* of emotions in tragedy (Aristotle 1984). I do this by applying his view to a theatrical dance performance during a Black Lives Matter protest where dancers reenacted twelve-year-old Tamir Rice's shooting by a Cleveland police officer (Bresnahan et al. 2020, 382). John Dewey's brand of ethical consequentialism is then brought in to argue that if dance is a practice that can create societal good (like the BLM dance, above) then it can be ethical action as well (383).

Finally, Sara Houston's section draws on the care ethics philosophy of Nel Noddings, Joan Tronto, and James Thompson, supported by examples of her community dance work with vulnerable populations, such as examples of persons in political refugee camps, with Parkinson's disease, and with cognitive disability and impairment. Her claim is that ethics in community dance requires care and an ethical attitude that is attuned to accessibility and flexibility of societal resources for vulnerable populations—one that requires those who engage in community dance to be sensitive and attuned to the needs and boundaries of differently abled and situated persons (Bresnahan et al. 2020, 383–385).[4]

Together the Einav-Katan, Bresnahan, and Houston sections provide three alternatives for how dance ethics might be embodied: (1) reflectively and metaphorically, (2) as a form of human flourishing in the service of human life, and (3) as a form of embodied sensitivity and care for vulnerable populations in a way that recognizes autonomy. A Kantian account was left out here just because a rationalist view seems intuitively less embodied than the others (see Kant 1994). But there is no reason that I can think of why one couldn't develop a Kantian view along a formulation, like Vidrin's

---

[4] For a survey piece on dance and disability see Hall (2018b). For a good primer text on care ethics see Held (1995). For a piece that connects care ethics with virtue ethics and disability see O'Shea (2018).

perhaps, in which a rational principle guides embodied interactions or helps people to live in a kingdom of ends. (See also Shapshay, this volume.)

Fiona Bannon's work can be read in line with this view, coextensive in particular with (and cited by) Katan-Schmid's section of the piece. What she adds is an additional affective element and an emphasis on interrelationality and avoidance of institutional norms.

Fiona Bannon: Collective, Relational, Affirmative, and Affective Dance Ethics

In one of the few books on dance ethics that refers to ethics specifically to date, *Considering Ethics in Dance, Theatre, and Performance*, Fiona Bannon argues for an ethics that is not about moral imperatives as principles but is instead

> an adaptive framework of ethics, as a practice that emerges through those elements gained from our responsible, responsive, and affective engagement with others. In this sense, the discussion revolves around our capacity to engage with variation, in terms of the circumstances in which we each find ways to facilitate positivity, satisfaction, and fulfilment. (Bannon 2018, 3)

In short, in this book she is seeking what she calls an "affirmative ethics" (5). For Bannon, ethics is "about all matter of behaviours towards being-in-community with others, and towards ourselves" (11). It concerns (at least): co-creation, collaboration, self-expression, self-determination, and collectivity, integrated through shared reliance. Bannon connects her view with Spinoza's ethics in finding that the identity of the human being is achieved through striving to survive in a way that is connected to our relation with others and that this is an ideal that is realized in relation with others (15).

A theme throughout is her view that dance collectives show us that ethics ought not to be institutionalized:

> We need to acknowledge the institutional tendency to think of ethics and ethical protocols as mechanisms through which we accommodate a set of prescriptive, protective, and administrative rules. Once acknowledged as such, they can be thought to offer little more than constraint in terms of our freedom to act. (26)

Instead, Bannon is specifically interested in cultivating and managing ethical behaviors in a "dialogic ethics" and "an ethics that embraces *being-with-others*" in an ongoing way (27).

Besides Spinoza and Deleuze and Guattari, Bannon's major influences are John Dewey, Antonio Damasio, and Hans-Georg Gadamer, among others. She sees these philosophers as being not just interested in avoiding institutional, rational ethics but as being sensitive to *affect*, noting the following:

> The science of affect for Spinoza—and later, for Deleuze—is ethics, where the quest is to seek to organize one's world so as to produce joyful encounters, or affects of the "joy increasing type"—those which arguably increase our capacity to act in the world. Performance in this regard could be thought of as an arena of encounters in which ethics, aesthetics, and creativity act together through affective compositions, offering different potential outcomes through varied routes to thought. (41)

Thus, Bannon's contribution to dance ethics brings dance philosophy into Continental philosophy and cognitive psychology in a way that the prior pieces have not in connection with some of the postmodern and contemporary dance collectives and companies that her book discusses.

Additional Dance-Ethics Concerns

Bannon took pains to show how dance groups have worked to exemplify relational ethics and avoid what they see as top-down dictates. Following are some further areas of ethical issues that are located in societal phenomena and structures, and will be highlighted briefly with some sample sources cited. The purpose is not to provide a full literature review but just to give the reader a general lay of the land and provide some starting resources for further research.

Cultural Appropriation, Authorship, and Copyright Concerns

Here ethical concerns have to do with who gets proper attribution, credit, and in many cases social and actual capital as a result of the creation of dance art. The ethical issues in this category include outright theft, exploitation of a less powerful social group for the benefit of a more powerful group, deceit, fraud, false promises, and the silencing and erasing of the contributions of artists who deserve recognition for their work. For pieces on cultural appropriation and appropriate racial boundaries and sharing in dance see Zink (2017), Sreevathsa (2019), and DeFrantz (2019); for issues of correct attribution of authorship to dancers versus choreographers see Van Camp (1980), Alpert (2016), Bresnahan (2014), and Bresnahan (2021).[5] Anthea Kraut's book *Choreographing Copyright: Race, Gender, and Intellectual Property Rights in American Dance*, which won the American Society for Aesthetics' Selma Jean Cohen Prize for best book in dance aesthetics for 2017, is a particularly strong and extended work on copyright and dance (2016). In it, Kraut discusses how race and gender biases have operated in the seeking,

---

[5] For a general discussion of cultural appropriation, not just in dance, see Nguyen and Strohl, this volume.

bestowal and operation of copyright for dance choreography and how this has played out through case studies of how dance choreographers have sought to handle these institutional injustices and uncertainties.

Identity, Discrimination, and Decolonization Concerns

There are more excellent books on these topics in dance scholarship than there is time or space to describe but in general, and in overbroad strokes, ethical issues arise around personal identity when the standard for judging dance is one that privileges any or all of the following: the male gaze, white Europeans, an ableist classical ideal, and where those dancers who do not meet the standard of acceptable by the gatekeepers are excluded, harmed, misunderstood, or treated negatively as a result. A classic on the male gaze on the female dancing body is Sally Banes's *Dancing Women*. Brenda Dixon Gottschild's *The Black Dancing Body: A Geography from Coon to Cool* provides a cartography of how the Black dancing body has been seen through a societal lens. Petra Kuppers's work, both as a community dance activist for persons with disabilities and a poet and scholar, has been a leader for mapping the terrain for dance and disability (Banes 1998, Dixon Gottschild 2003, Kuppers 2000, 2003, 2011, and 2014).[6]

In the wake of civil rights violations in the United States that came to a head after George Floyd was murdered by police officer Derek Chauvin, the Dance Studies Association issued a strong condemnation of anti-Blackness and white supremacy, publishing a booklet dedicated to conversations about how to further anti-racism and decolonization within dance studies (Banerji and Mitra 2020). There such topics as the politics of Indian dance and the caste system, silencing within the dance studies field itself, gender binaries and care, Filipino martial arts, Black dance, Mayan performance practice, and the benefits of immersion versus sight were discussed, among other topics pertaining to anti-racism and decolonization of dance and dance institutions. (This *Conversations* booklet is worth reviewing for those interested in mining these issues for dance ethics issues pertaining to decolonization and an extensive cumulative bibliography is provided at the end for all the entries.)

All of this dance scholarship is handling "ethics-writ-large" in the sense that something having to do with dance is being focused on in a scholarly way, often via case studies, and this close scrutiny highlights something about how persons who are dancing are being treated in ways that has bearing on their ability to flourish and perform as dancers and as human beings. In the next and final section to follow, I will take us back to the embodied nature of the ethical human agent with which this piece began, looking at it now in light of how dancers and dance ethics have had to adjust due to the global COVID-19 pandemic.

---

[6] For more on dance and disability see Albright (2013), Houston (2005, 2015) and Houston and McGill (2019), Whatley (2007) and Whatley et al. (2018), and Bresnahan and Deckard (2019). For more on the male gaze, see Mullin, this volume.

Coda and Conclusion: Dance Ethics in Times of Public Health Crises

Public health crises that require people to limit or drastically alter social and physical contact often have devastating consequences for all of the live performing arts, including, and perhaps especially for dance as a one-on-one social and communal practice. This is due to the obvious fact that dancing closely with other person(s) puts the dancers in the sort of close physical proximity to one another that can harbor the spread of infectious and contagious diseases and viruses. In terms of dance ethics, this means that during a public health crisis, the positive dance ethics goals of attunement and sensitivity to others must take second place to the competing ethical goal of preserving public health and safety. To demonstrate how and why this is true, I'll be using the global COVID-19 pandemic that began in or around March of 2020 as a paradigm example in the discussion below.

Dance is a practice that typically involves physical exertion. This means that it involves frequent and deep intake and outtake of breath. After some brief confusion at the beginning, the COVID-19 virus was soon determined to be transmissible via airborne particles, this meant that people could no longer dance together safely. Dance studio spaces that were considered "exercise studios and gyms" were banned by many quarantine and lock-down ordinances, with exceptions made for university-run dance and theatre programs in some cases. Many dance performance venues, typically enclosed theatres, were closed down altogether, and dance social clubs were shut down as well along with pubs and bars.

The consequences of these changes were dire for both dancers and dance organizations that rely on the revenue from dancing. It also took a toll on the physical, mental, and emotional well-being of dancers who could not dance in a space with other dancers. Zoom dance classes and performances sprung up immediately, and TikTok dance challenges became more popular, but in-person sense and one-on-one dancing was lost to a large degree. Dancers and dance-lovers struggled to stay dance-fit and to maintain a sense of community with others outside of their normal dance classes and routines. (See Bresnahan 2020 for a popular piece advocating the benefits of dancing for children during the pandemic on ethics-as-well-being and flourishing grounds.)

Dance companies and choreographers also rushed to make new dances for film, oftentimes having to create pieces that video-edited dances together from pieces that were filmed in isolation by dancers in different locations and then spliced together. This created an opportunity for new kinds of dance-film creations but this sort of dance-art making obvious changes the one-on-one bodily ethical dynamics that were discussed in the one-on-one dance section, and would shift the focus onto the ethics of dance-film editing. This can involve power dynamics and ethical issues of consent as well (as in the famous Sharon Stone situation in the film *Basic Instinct*, in which she claims she was not told initially told that her genitals were visible to the camera during that famous short-white-dress legs-uncrossing interview scene), but it does not involve the sort of physical sensitivity and communication on which that section focused.

The COVID-19 pandemic also led to some speculation in the dance-world as to how our perceptions of what is ethically appropriate in terms of physical space, touching, and distance would change as a result of how we were reconditioned, culturally and socially, to see distance between people due to the pandemic restrictions. Even a year later, as vaccines were developed and introduced to the public en masse, it was unclear how well the vaccines would work and whether a vaccinated person could still transmit the virus. This meant that even though dance classes and spaces were allowed to open up to some degree, most still had to include the early pandemic restrictions of requiring dancers to wear masks and keep six feet between dancers (in the United States) or two metres (in the United Kingdom) while dancing. This closed off some possibilities for "reads" of another person's facial expressions as well as created another source of fear in another person's closeness, breath, and touch.

Public health crises like COVID-19 add a layer of ethics of social responsibility and possible autonomy invasion, as one wonders to what extent it may be ethical for a dance company or collective to require mandatory testing for infection or antibodies, or vaccinations, or how much power any individual may feel they have if someone with more power than they have violates mask-wearing or protocols in ways that put them at risk. Here we are back, again, at romantic entanglement ethics, heightened now with the prospect of a new element of risk that affects all close bodily entanglements.

At the beginning of the COVID-19 pandemic, Gia Kourlas, former professional ballet dancer and dance critic for the *New York Times*, wrote about a trained dancer's usual heightened awareness of navigating space and how this has become a skill all people would now have to develop:

> Stay six feet away from others. As choreographic intentions go, that's not remotely vague. Yet during my runs and walks in Brooklyn over the past few days, I've noticed that six feet doesn't mean the same thing to everybody....
>
> That feeling and control of where we are in space is important right now; dancers, through years of training and sensorial alertness, grasp this inherently. If this pandemic is teaching us anything, it is that we need to return to our bodies. (Kourlas 2020)

Dance studies scholar, dramaturg, curator, and choreographer Kate Elswit followed this up with a *Dance Magazine* piece where she canvassed some of the strategies that people have used to measure and manage the distance requirements necessitated by the pandemic (Elswit 2020). Here she suggested that dancers, especially with the aid of Rudolph Laban-inspired geometric space around them which she calls a "coronasphere" can help to create such a sphere for public as well as dance spaces. But Elswit also warned against the idea that we ought to give in too quickly to the idea that dancing closely with others is to be avoided as dangerous or non-navigable, fearing the loss of intimacy and connection and *care* that may result when we are afraid to connect with one another in the physical and bodily ways that dance can provide. As she put it:

> At a moment in which breath already seems to make the body too permeable, and our relation to that porousness is often ruled by fear or, at best, mutual care, expanding sensory awareness outward might seem to add another layer of vulnerability. Early in the pandemic, I noticed how many people on the street had stopped making eye contact, even physically closing in on themselves as though any connection might somehow translate through the textured air between them.
>
> There are similar anxieties in shared space but across time: I enter places that other people and their breath have previously occupied, and I wonder about the others who will reuse my questionable air before it falls to the ground. . . . Once breath functions as a kind of touch, we need new skills to manage the intimacy that results. (Elswit 2020)

Elswit went on to describe and to accurately predict many of the ways that dancers, dance schools, and dance companies would have to go about figuring out and carving up space and distance, managing the embodied interrelationships accordingly. These would come to include taped marks on the floor, "hoops, inflatable bubbles and wing[s]," putting up barriers between dancers—all designed to keep people away from one another (Elswit 2020). Even so, Elswit found reason to hope that dance would choreograph its way around even these problems and that dance might lead the way. She said:

> But new public choreographies—ones that let us feel the pleasure or passion of moving with others, while minimizing risk—will only emerge once more people hone their capacity to sense the contours of changing breath forms that extend beyond the skin, and to move attentively in proximity to other coronaspheres.
>
> Every person outside has a responsibility as a dancer, to train to better exist at this moment in which we are engaged in more communal movement, not less. This demands a shift toward moving with the space around us—instead of through it—and with all of the breathers that share it. Dancers know how to make physical choices in response to sensed imagery, and they are also accustomed to building kinesthetic connections to other moving bodies. Public life now depends on these skills, and we as dancers can help. (Elswit 2020)

The public health crisis scenario sketched out above suggests a way that dance ethics is not siloed off in its own special dance space but might be relevant to ethics overall. We all have bodies, do we not? We all move in our bodies, do we not (at least to some degree)? In some sense then, to write about dance ethics is just to write about human ethics—about the embodied ethics of sensitive, moving, feeling, living, breathing, and interconnecting persons.

See also: Hamilton, Mullin, Clavel-Vázquez, Nguyen and Strohl, this volume

REFERENCES

Albright, Ann C. [1998] 2013. "Strategic abilities: Negotiating the Disabled Body in Dance." In *Engaging Bodies: The Politics and Poetics of Corporeality*, 297–317. Middletown, CT: Wesleyan University Press.

Alpert, Lauren R. 2016. "Co-Authorship and the Ontology of Dance Artworks." Presentation at the American Society for Aesthetics 74th Annual Meeting, Seattle, November 18.

Aristotle. 1984 [c. 335 BCE]. "Poetics." In *The Rhetoric and the Poetics of Aristotle*. Translated by I. Bywater, with an introduction by Edward P. J. Corbett, 221–266. New York: The Modern Library, McGraw Hill Inc.

Banerji, Anurima, and Royona Mitra, eds. 2020. *Conversations Across the Field of Dance Studies: Decolonizing Dance Discourses* XL: 20–21. Dance Studies Association. https://www.dancestudiesassociation.org/conversations-across-the-field-of-dance-studies

Banes, Sally. 1998. *Dancing Women: Female Bodies on Stage*. London: Routledge.

Bannon, Fiona. 2018. *Considering Ethics in Dance, Theatre, and Performance*. London: Palgrave MacMillan.

Bresnahan, Aili. 2014. "Toward A Deweyan Theory of Ethical and Aesthetic Performing Arts Practice." *Journal of Aesthetics and Phenomenology* 1, no. 2: 133–148.

Bresnahan, Aili. 2020. "A Philosopher Explains Why Dance Can Help Pandemic-Proof Your Kids." *The Conversation* (US), May 29, 2020. https://theconversation.com/a-philosopher-explains-why-dance-can-help-pandemic-proof-your-kids-138398.

Bresnahan, Aili. 2021. "Interpretation in Dance Performing." In *The Bloomsbury Handbook to Dance and Philosophy*, edited by Rebecca Farinas and Julie Van Camp, with Aili Bresnahan and Craig Hangs as consulting editors, 139–149. London: Bloomsbury Academic Publishing.

Bresnahan, Aili, and Michael Deckard. 2019. "Beauty in Disability: An Aesthetics for Dance and for Life." In *Dance and Quality of Life*, edited by Karen Bond, 185–206. Cham, Switzerland: Springer Nature.

Bresnahan, Aili, Einav Katan-Schmid, and Sara Houston. 2020. "Dance as Embodied Ethics." In *The Routledge Companion to Performance Philosophy*, edited by Laura Cull Ó Maoilearca and Alice Lagaay, 379–386. Abingdon: Routledge.

DeFrantz, Thomas F. 2019. "What Is Black Dance? What Can It Do?" In *Thinking Through Dance and Performance*, edited by Maaike Bleeker, Adrian Kear, Joe Kelleher, and Heike Roms, 87–99. London: Methuen Drama.

Dixon Gottschild, Brenda. 2003. *The Black Dancing Body: From Coon to Cool*. New York: Palgrave MacMillan.

Elswit, Kate. "Dancing With Our Coronasphere to Navigate the Pandemic." *Dance Magazine*, July 21, 2020. https://www.dancemagazine.com/six-feet-distance-2646412593.html.

Hall, Joshua M. 2018a. "Consensuality: Joshua M. Hall on what Latin dance can teach us about unwanted touch." *The Philosophers' Magazine* 82 (3rd Quarter): 32–38.

Hall, Joshua M. 2018b. "Philosophy of Dance and Disability." *Philosophy Compass* 13, no. 12. https://doi.org/10.1111/phc3.12551.

Held, Virginia, ed. 1995. *Justice and Care: Essential Readings in Feminist Ethics*. Boulder, CO: Westview Press.

Houston, Sara. 2005. "Participation in Community Dance: a Road to Empowerment and Transformation?" *New Theatre Quarterly* 21, no. 2 (May 2005): 166–177.

Houston, Sara. 2015. "Feeling Lovely: An Examination of the Value of Beauty for People Dancing with Parkinson's." *Dance Research Journal* 47, no. 1: 27–43.

Houston, Sara, and McGill, Ashley. 2019. "Understanding Quality of Life Through the Experiences of Dancers with Parkinson's." In *Dance and Quality of Life*, edited by Karen Bond, 281–292. Cham, Switzerland: Springer Nature.

Kant, Immanuel. 1994 [1785]. "Grounding for the Metaphysics of Morals." In *Ethical Philosophy, Second Ed.*, translated by J. W. Ellington, Book I: 1–65. Indianapolis: Hackett Publishing Company.

Kourlas, Gia. "How We Use Our Bodies to Navigate a Pandemic: Your Partner Is a Stranger, and the Sidewalk Is a Stage. Our Dance Critic Asks: Will Social Distancing Bring Us Back to Our Bodies?" *New York Times*, Critics' Notebook, March 31, 2020. https://www.nytimes.com/2020/03/31/arts/dance/choreographing-the-street-coronavirus.html.

Kraut, Anthea. 2016. *Choreographing Copyright: Race, Gender, and Intellectual Property Rights in American Dance*. New York: Oxford University Press.

Kuppers, Petra. 2000. "Accessible Education: Aesthetics, Bodies, and Disability." *Research in Dance Education* 1, no. 2: 119–131.

Kuppers, Petra. 2003. *Disability and Contemporary Performance: Bodies on the Edge*. New York: Routledge.

Kuppers, Petra. 2011. *Disability Culture and Community Performance*. New York: Palgrave Macmillan.

Kuppers, Petra. 2014. *Studying Disability Arts and Culture: An Introduction*. New York: Palgrave Macmillan.

Margolis, Joseph. 2004. *Moral Philosophy After 9/11*. University Park: Penn State University Press.

O'Shea, Tom. 2018. "Civic Republican Disability Justice." In *Oxford Handbook of Philosophy and Disability*, edited by Adam Cureton and David Wasserman, 1–19. https://doi.org/10.1093/oxfordhb/9780190622879.013.20.

Sreevathsa, Sammitha. 2019. "Classical Dance and Appropriation: How to Think about a Field Whose Foundations Rest on Cultural Violence." *Firstpost.com*, December 1. https://www.firstpost.com/living/classical-dance-and-appropriation-how-to-think-about-a-field-whose-foundations-rest-on-cultural-violence-7708381.html.

Van Camp, Julie. 1980. "Anti-Geneticism and Critical Practice in Dance." *Dance Research Journal* 13, no. 1 (Autumn, 1980): 29–35.

Vidrin, Ilya. 2018. "Partnering as Rhetoric." In *A World of Muscle, Bone & Organs: Research and Scholarship in Dance*, edited by Simon Ellis, Hetty Blades, and Charlotte Waelde, 112–130. Coventry: C-DaRE.

Vidrin, Ilya. 2020. "Embodied Ethics: The Conditions and Norms of Communication in Partnering." In *Thinking Touch in Partnering and Contact Improvisation: Pedagogy, Philosophy, Practice*, edited by Malaika Sarco-Thomas, 1–15. Newcastle upon Tyne: Cambridge Scholars Press.

Whatley, Sarah. 2007. "Dance and Disability: The Dancer, the Viewer and the Presumption of Difference." *Research in Dance Education* 8, no. 1: 5–25.

Whatley, Sarah, Charlotte Waelde, Shawn Harmon, Abbe Brown, Karen Wood, and Hetty Blades, eds. 2018. *Dance, Disability and Law: InVisible Difference*. Chicago: Intellect Books.

Zink, Shereen. 2017. "Twerking and Cultural Appropriation: Miley Cyrus' Display of Racial Ignorance." *MacEwan University Student EJournal* 3, no. 1 (May 2017): 15–20.

FURTHER READING

Burt, Ramsay. 2016. "Violence, Performance, and Relationality." In *Choreography and Corporeality: Relay in Motion*, edited by Thomas F. DeFrantz and Philipa Rothfield, 261–272. London: Palgrave MacMillan.

Fischlin, Daniel, Ajay Heble, and George Lipsitz. 2013. *The Fierce Urgency of Now: Improvisation, Rights, and the Ethics of Cocreation*. Durham, NC: Duke University Press.

Houston, Sara, and Monica Gillette. 2022. *Soft Skills in Dance: A Guidebook to Enhance your Practice*. Empowering Dance. http://empowering2.communicatingdance.eu/guidebook/en/.

Jackson, Naomi M. 2022. *Dance and Ethics: Moving Towards a More Humane Dance Culture*. Chicago: University of Chicago Press.

Rowe, Nicholas. 2011. "Dance and Political Credibility: The Appropriation of Dabkeh by Zionism, Arabism, and Palestinian Nationalism." *The Middle East Journal* 65, no. 3: 363–380.

Nwankpa, Uzoamaka, and Stephanie Bevill. 2019. "Dance and Well-Being: Honoring Caroline Plummer." In *Dance and Quality of Life*, edited by Karen Bond, 293–306. Cham, Switzerland: Springer Nature.

Tarah, Manjulika. 2020. "Women Dancers and Morality in Bangladesh." In *Conversations Across the Field of Dance Studies: Decolonizing Dance Discourses* XL: 20–21, edited by Anurima Banerji and Royona Mitra, 43–45. Dance Studies Association. https://journals.publishing.umich.edu/conversations/issue/72/download/16.

CHAPTER 29

···

ARCHITECTURE

···

SAUL FISHER

Introduction

···

As built structures, architectural objects envelop us, guide us, prevent us, and may well outlast us. They are generally unavoidable and constant in their presence and our sensations of them. These features of architectural objects mark architecture as an artform or design medium with not only aesthetic impact but persistent moral impact as well. How so? What about these or other aspects of built structures mark them as ethically significant—and what is the nature of that significance? Further, how much is that significance tied up with architecture's aesthetic or artistic character or capacity?

Much contemporary discussion of architectural ethics centers on the plausibility of connections between aesthetic and ethical features of architectural objects, as mooted in the moralism-autonomism debate. Those deliberations, following the broader aesthetics debate, generally turn on whether ethical flaws we might ascribe to a building are in some way propagated by aesthetic flaws, or the other way around. These are valuable matters to sort, yet there are considerably more, and more *basic*, questions for architectural ethics to address. To get at the fullest terrain, one place to start is to ask what sort of work we want an ethical theory of architecture to do. A full-service theory, I propose, should touch on these matters:

1. How ethical value, virtues, rights, and responsibilities—and perhaps other dimensions of moral life as relate to justice, fairness, equity, inclusion, and other social desiderata—attach to architectural objects, factor into "architectural acts" (creating or implementing a design); and how objects and actors relate to one another as concerns assignment of agency, responsibility, and "reception."

2. How ethical value relates to other sorts of value attached to architectural objects, which includes aesthetic value (as typically construed, this is a broad concern

beyond artistic value in architecture, given the range of non–art-architecture); artistic value (relative to art-architecture); and architectural value in an omnibus, all-inclusive sense (cf. Baumberger 2015)—or as importantly, the different component values thereof.

3. How ethical values, virtues, rights, and responsibilities attendant to architectural objects relate to one another (viz. autonomism vs. interactionism).[1]

4. How we should *apply* ethical reasoning to specifically architectural problems, such as as related to preservation, restoration, zoning, adaptive re-use/re-purposing, and intellectual property rights.

In what follows, I focus on (1), with particular attention to this question: if we take architectural objects to have moral agency, how does that shape our notions of architectural ethics more generally? In particular, I propose that architectural objects have a moral agency in ways discernible from that of their creators, and that this is in addition to other morally relevant features of architecture as we identify in choices, actions, and outcomes of its practitioners and other stakeholders. I begin, however, with an overview of architecture's moral dimensions, to identify distinguishing features that ethical questions may have in the domain. The sorts of questions we ask, and that our best theory will address, are likely only as distinctive as the nature of agency, values, virtues, or other moral dimensions are in architecture, in contrast with other artforms, artifactual classes, environmental features, and so on.

Contours of the Moral Terrain

Accounts of architectural ethics often leave a number of assumptions unexamined. Even before accounting for architecture's ethical features, a preliminary question is what to count as architecture and its objects. Here I assume an inclusivist stance: architectural objects range over not simply the built structures we take as exemplary of artistic practice but all built structures. The reason to assume inclusivism in this discussion is that relevant differences as the exclusivist asserts between "art architecture" and "non art architecture" are not likely significant for the purposes of understanding the ethics of architecture and its objects *qua* things with aesthetic properties. If that is correct, then any ethics for architecture as art should line up closely with an ethics for architecture not merely as art.

The sorts of basic assumptions that should guide exploration of architectural ethics define a moral terrain not quite identical to that of the other arts, or to design generally, or to the worlds of artifacts or technologies, though there are shared elements with each of those domains. Here is a brief overview of some primary

[1] See Stear, Carroll, this volume.

aspects that give us the contours of that terrain, with its particularities and defining characteristics:

a. *How architects conduct themselves as moral agents.* Architects' roles comprise a range of moral dimensions, including the professional and the practical as well as those entailed by their roles as artistic creators or, more modestly, generators of aesthetic properties. Nonartistic or aesthetically related roles entail ethical choices and actions that are special to architecture[2] where those choices and actions bear on perspicuously ethical questions regarding architectural objects, as may concern, for example, conservation, conflicts of context, or social liabilities particular to built structures. If my account of architectural objects as moral agents is correct, then their conduct, too, merits our moral attention. But even if that account does not work, nonetheless those objects bear ethical properties or express moral values as a result, in part, of architects' ethical choices and actions. To be sure, this is a partial relationship: architectural objects may be as they are *generally* because the architects make them so, yet the ethical properties or moral values of architectural objects are not entirely tied to those of their creators. After all, the character and uses of built structures change as time marches on. Architectural objects frequently outlast their creators all told and always outlast the creative act. While some moral valence may endure over the life of the object, that is subject to shifts with change of context and use. However, architectural objects *sometimes* are morally endowed in ways reflective of their creators' moral input or ethical considerations. In such cases, aspects of architects' concerns and actions—possibly extending to the professional and practical— may fall within the scope of ethical evaluation of the objects themselves. (See Matthes, this volume.)

b. *Values special to architecture and its objects.* There are specifically architectural values if, beyond a standard range of values associated with art or other artifactual or environmental domains—whether aesthetic or nonaesthetic (e.g., use, historical, functional, cognitive, cultural, etc.)—there are yet other values not common or applicable to those other domains. These might include safety, security, or other such values associated with structural integrity; defensibility (Crippen and Klement 2020); or "publicness" (how publicly accessible created spaces are, or the degree to which they promote public interaction) (Spector 2014). Some such values may be folded into use-value yet are special to architecture, particularly in light of how they articulate with aesthetic value. On one alternative view, architectural value is a composite of all values special to architecture as well as those aesthetic or nonaesthetic values characteristic of other sorts of art objects (Baumberger 2015). That view readily counts ethical value in overall evaluations of architectural objects, and connects the morally positive or negative valence of those objects to standard architectural functionality

---

[2] And not merely, as Taylor and Levine (2011, 26) put it, "ethical issues pasted on to architecture."

(e.g., effects on users or communicative function). Still, the task remains of identifying values special to architecture, why that is so, and what they contribute in particular to architectural evaluations—whether as primarily of ethical, aesthetic, or yet other focus.

c. *Temporal characteristics and life-cycle.* Like sculptures, built structures exist in space, with all that entails for shaping experience and even engaging physically in the causal nexus.[3] But unlike sculptures, architectural objects are also characterized by temporal factors in morally significant ways. For one, it is a specified intention of most architects and builders that the structures for which they are responsible remain standing for a long time, and many of them do. As a consequence, the choices of architects today can shape lives for hundreds or more years in the future; those initial choices can also be defeated by users and others who engage with their built structures over its life span. For another, architectural objects have life-cycles with demarcated stages. The ways that people engage with built structures or those structures affect them vary over the frequently lengthy course of planning and creation, as well as in the initial use, subsequent phases of use, and decline and demise or ruin of the structures. As a simple example, consider that the Great Pyramid of Giza served the pharaoh Khufu and others observing the rites and mores of the Fourth Dynasty was viewed and treated very differently by subsequent dynasties, kingdoms, empires, and caliphates governing Egypt, and, as a tourism destination and an ongoing subject of scientific research, presently affects lives of the local population in altogether distinct ways. Over its very long life span with discrete life-cycle stages, the same built structure has exercised shifting influences, been subject to shifting obligations, and experienced greatly varying evaluations of its moral worth as seen through spiritual or material lenses.

d. *Physical contextuality (engagement with the environment).* Built structures frequently live among other built structures, whether at some remove or in direct contact; and they always live among *some* environmental elements, whether built or natural. This contextual character results in built structures affecting, and being affected by, other objects in their surroundings—for example, by shaping further development in virtue of changing the existing physical configuration of the landscape. Just as built structures promote or hold back human behavior, they open up new possibilities or foreclose options for present and future neighboring structures. In this way, they contribute to defining the broader built and social environment and, with that, the modes of conduct and commerce among the people who occupy those environments. *How* built structures engage with their built or natural surroundings thus constitutes a range of options with potential moral significance.

e. *Systemicity.* Within the systems that built structures represent, actions upon one element generate effects upon other elements, behaviors of subsystems

---

[3] I say more about this in the "Moral Agency" section.

affect those of other subsystems, and the whole of built structures interact caus- ally with connected systems—as include other built structures, yet other entities comprising the built or natural environment, and social, political, or still other artifactual systems. The more familiar systems of built structures are physical in- frastructure: drainage, plumbing, electricity, and the like. Their functioning (or malfunctioning) may have ethical import, as can other, less apparent systematic aspects of built structures such as the social groupings of a structure's occupants or connected series of hallways and passages as permit or restrict the flow of a structure's users. As an example of the former, consider the alteration of part of a façade by a single occupant of a shared ownership building, which then promotes alteration of the rest of the façade by other occupants, whether in concert or suc- cession. The behavior of one network node trips the behavior of all others, and the entire façade changes as a result. Beyond relatively minor costs and anguish of façade alteration, the range of possible ethical issues may concern instigating, pursuing, or resisting a restorative or preventative alteration, or may concern impinging on or promoting aesthetic rights of others relative to a shared built structure.

f. *Behavioral, social, and cultural impact.* As persons engage with built structures, those structures may prompt, catalyze, direct, constrain, prevent or otherwise in- fluence the nature and rate of those persons' behaviors and actions. As I propose, these are kinds of influence on not only our individual behaviors but as well social choices and cultural developments and tendencies, with potential for direct and indirect moral significance.

g. *Functionality and user cohorts.* Built structures are typically working artifacts. Indeed, with the exception of apparel and food, few other artifacts whose aes- thetic properties constantly command our attention have the same claim on utility—and only architectural objects (among the trio of clothing, sustenance, and shelter) are as pervasive and persistent in their appearance to us. The marriage of utility and ubiquity introduces a need for awareness and special responsibilities relative to how we use and care for them and how their use shapes us, as well as whether and how their aesthetic properties are connected to their functional properties.

In sum, architecture's distinctive features among various domains of which it is a member (arts, design, environment, etc.) shape the ways that built structures en- gage the people who build them, live with them, work in them, or visit them. These sorts of engagement, distinctive by degree or kind—along with the characteristic moral agency of architects and architectural objects, and the embedded values of built structures—mark the special moral terrain of architectural objects. Ethical issues regarding built structures arise, then, from questions specific to architecture as well as concerns more common to other domains (such as, per the moralist/au- tonomist debate, how the ethical interacts with the aesthetic). (See Carroll, Stear, this volume.)

MORAL AGENCY

The key to a full account of architectural ethics, I suggest, is identifying who or what counts as architecture's moral agents, as well as those upon whom they act. In this, I take it as uncontroversially true that architects are moral agents within the architectural domain as well as in society broadly. The debate instead focuses on whether moral agency in architecture extends to architectural objects, primarily (and most relevantly in the current context) built structures. One feature distinguishing most architectural objects from many other art objects is the degree to which they have some pronounced intended utility, which is dependent on their capacity to participate in the causal nexus: to act on people, and to act on other objects and on phenomena and events. Otherwise put, they act upon their audience and environment, with a constancy and pervasiveness generally unmatched by most art objects. This may or may not make architectural objects agents (depending on one's view of agency), and possibly so in some moral sense (also as depends on criteria for such). I consider arguments for and against architectural object moral agency, and in the end suggest that we cannot block the assignment of such agency given the relationship of architects and other architectural creators to the objects created and sustained, and the moral import of the behavior of those objects. Though we may start with (1) taking architects or other persons (including developers, contractors, regulators, and preservationists) as responsible for effects of their architectural programmes and designs, we end up with (2) architectural objects as responsible for morally suffused actions and behaviors in the world around them.

In favor of assigning moral agency to architectural objects, Annabel Jane Wharton appeals to key features of built structures and how they engage with their environment (Wharton 2015).[4] Built structures, she proposes, have unique, noninterchangeable features that are structural, spatial, locational, and historical. The historical character of built structures—that they last over time—has agential force because in doing so they develop histories that can have causal effects. As a historian of Jerusalem's architecture, Wharton is keenly aware that a building's history can instigate wars. A further core feature she cites is the materiality of built structures (being "embodied") which, together with spatiality, certainly puts such structures in the causal nexus as *recipients* of actions. But can they give as much as they get? Together, she argues, these features yield agency in architectural objects, as manifest in their capacity to influence, shape, and modify human behavior.

The significance of Wharton's uniqueness claim is that the noninterchangeable features, in establishing a unique identity for each built structure, allow responsibility

---

[4] She also appeals to historical precedent, noting an old tradition of ascribing agency to architectural objects, viz. the English law tradition of the "deodand," by which objects found responsible for harms were assessed for fines to the Crown. In more recent times, she points out, there are analogous ascriptions of agency to corporations, nature, animals, etc.

to be assigned to particular buildings for the behaviors that they causally influence. Moreover, this way of putting matters explains how architectural objects that are multiples—designs built out over and again in different locations, or even in the same location over a temporal sequence—sustain a unique, morally significant identity. The materiality claim is significant for possibly differentiating architecture relative to questions about objects of other art forms having causal agency: though, say, poetry or music might fail to have agency as a consequence of their immateriality, that would not be a point against built structures. That said, if this argument works, it's because materiality and uniqueness are sufficient to moral agency and not only required by it, and this is where things get murkier. The central problem for sufficiency is that all agency requires intentions and any such intentions as we might ascribe to architectural objects really belong to the architects, builders, developers, users, and other stakeholders who create or otherwise interact with those objects.

To establish the sufficiency of materiality and uniqueness to the moral agency of built structures, we can appeal to an "architectural determinism," the view that physical modalities (shape, size, location, etc.), aesthetic properties, and yet other features attached to particular built structures determine, in part, social and psychological behaviors along with other environmental effects. In short, the built environment determines or, more minimally, influences social behavior of its users.[5] The ready-to-hand arguments for architectural determinism are empirical: studies in environmental psychology and related disciplines point to the nature and shape of our environments as affecting our physical and psychological well-being, our modes of behavior, our sense of self, our relations with others, and other modalities of being.[6] So architectural objects, as significant interventions in the environment, look to be causally responsible for determining a wide range of behaviors, mental states, and physical engagements. If, accordingly, determinism is correct, then sufficiency is established. There may well be an a priori reason available, too. For if determinism were entirely wrong, then we could say that architects were largely wasting their time on design pseudo-problems, insofar as

---

[5] Unsurprisingly, sociologists of architecture take a particular interest in the possibility that built environments influence or determine behavior, or otherwise reflect their social context, inclusive of social values. Lipman (1969) associates architectural determinism with modernist architects who, following Ruskin and Morris, see design of the built environment as a means of promoting social ideals. It is as well their bid at social engineering, Lipman proposes. (As such, he holds, it is unlikely to succeed, especially given "administrative distance" between architects of public structures and their mass clientele or user base.) Delitz (2010) offers an even stronger thesis, positing that built structures not only influence or determine social behavior, but contribute to the very constitution of society and its values in material form.

[6] Early critics noted that empirical results show people are adaptive to the built environment and in any case equally or more susceptible to cultural or other influences on their behaviors (for a recent iteration, see Till 2009). In short, architectural determinism, if true, is weakly so. Half a century later, however, more refined studies identify spatial arrangements likely to shape behaviors—and many institutional settings since the 1970s are designed on the premise that behaviors of users can be thus oriented. For the early research, see Gutman (1972); recent overviews of the empirical literature, with lessons for architectural design include Kopec (2012) and Sloan Devlin (2018).

we could not optimize the built environment to the ends of improved behaviors, mental states, and physical engagements. But architects do not think this is an insignificant or unimportant task for them to pursue, nor does anyone else. More needs to be said here, though ostensibly the reason no one thinks this is an unimportant task is that—as utility is concerned—architectural objects are not exclusively designed to meet *shelter* requirements.

Against the notion that architectural objects have moral agency, the critic can run several lines of argument. For one, we could allow that they have some role in the causal nexus but it's not agential. Thus, it's fair to say that if built structures *were* causally responsible agents, their causation would be indirect and passive. The only way they could be *active* agents is if they were in motion, and few buildings are capable of moving to any relevantly significant degree. So one available move against moral agency is to deny that passive agency counts as agency altogether. For another, we could point to their lack of intentionality and insist on that as a requirement for agency. As Harold (2020) puts the matter—relative to artworks overall—such objects don't have relevant attitudes, psychological states, or intentions hence are not responsible agents. For a third—as consonant with rejection of intentionality—we could say that we just don't need architectural objects to have moral agency to explain how there are ethically charged events that occur involving built structures. It's sufficient to point to the human actors, or even other affected things (natural or otherwise) thus engaged. When generic apartment blocs that stretch on for entire neighborhoods are said to cause blight, a visible scar on the urban landscape, we can simply put the blame on the architects or city planners, without any need to point to the buildings themselves as morally responsible.

The critic's first two strategies may be dispatched thus: we can stipulate that one sort of agency is passive and that this holds for moral agency in particular; and we can equally well stipulate a sort of agency that does not require intentions or other mental states. While this may be stipulative in the architectural case, it's not fantastical: first, the biological world is filled with agents that cause events in the world by passive means and without any mental states; and second, once we've deemed mental states irrelevant to moral agency, it makes no difference whether the entities said to be moral agents act passively or actively. What is important is that they can act and that such actions have morally significant consequences in the world, or communicate morally significant content to users and appreciators.

The third strategy is addressed differently: we need to show that the moral agency of architects or other human actors is insufficient to characterizing the moral phenomena for which the proponent of object agency is trying to account. Here are two such cases. In the first case, over the course of several centuries, a number of buildings have been built next to one another on both sides of a street. As those buildings have been built, they run right up to the street, leaving no room for sidewalks and, in the modern day, not much room for cars, either. As a result, cars must tightly navigate these streets and share them with pedestrians. Occasionally a pedestrian is injured, as a result. None of the architects are to blame for these accidents, and there weren't any urban planners around when the buildings were built, anyway. The problem has arisen strictly because of (a) the accretive, compositional nature of grouped architectural objects, and (b) the way the buildings frame the street, perhaps some more egregiously jutting into the street than others. In the second case, a viaduct bridge has empty spaces below its arches, and these are populated by restaurants, bookshops, and other small businesses, as in modern-day Berlin and Paris. The architect designed the bridge for trains; its arches merely presented the best structural support of the day. When the train line was discontinued, small business owners employed contractors to hastily retrofit the spaces under the arches for commerce (i.e., without employing architects). Now the businesses are quite popular, leaving the viaduct as a lively shopping area but without any relationship to any train, role as a bridge, or remnants of the original architect's design intentions. If we praise this small business district as charming, and for generating positive results for city life and the urban economy, we might well apportion some of our acclaim to the viaduct structure, but we can't apportion any to the viaduct architect because they had nothing to do with its repurposing and present, adaptive use. The need for ascribing moral agency to built structures can be seen in such instances where there aren't any architects whose agency is pertinent, or primary, to an account of the phenomena or events as morally inflected. It may be pertinent or primary in other situations as well.

The upshot of plausibly attributing moral agency to built structures is that we now can recognize a variety of moral phenomena as describe behaviors of such structures. As moral agents, architectural objects can do physical and psychological good or harm; they can produce, sustain, or defeat justice; they can produce, sustain, or diminish fairness or equality; and they can sustain or undermine individual autonomy, social affiliation, and social choice. They can have some such effects on individuals and groups of people, and others on their local environments—all in the present or future. Further, as moral agency comprises production of morally significant phenomena, architectural objects may display or exercise moral virtues, and they may produce, project, reflect, or communicate moral values. In the remainder of this chapter, I offer accounts of how built structures in particular have virtues, and so may be ethically evaluated accordingly.

VIRTUES

Any theory of architectural objects as morally significant—*qua* agents or otherwise—likely requires some account of the role of virtues. (See also Snow, this volume.) We get some notion of the centrality of virtues in this regard by the deep association of built structures with virtues in a range of ancient traditions around the world, in the Renaissance Latin West, and in contemporary perspectives on architecture.

A first question to address in this regard is who or what in architecture is considered as virtuous or vicious—the creator, the architectural object, or some other party (e.g., user). In classical architectural theories of the West, virtues of utility, beauty, and structural integrity (to cite the Vitruvian triad) are assigned to the architect as morally or professionally upstanding behavior. But, as it happens, these are virtues of the works themselves, and we evaluate them accordingly—and the architect, if at all, derivatively. For while the architect can ensure that a built structure has *firmitas, utilitas, et venustas*, there is no suggestion that these somehow map onto characteristics of the architect themself nor is it relevant if they do. They simply need to be, from the Vitruvian perspective, the sorts of well-trained architects who broadly ensure such virtues are in place. This may prompt a question as to how artifacts like architectural objects (built structures) have virtues, an idea with an animistic ring to it. The answer, I suggest, is that they have a sort of moral agency that allows us to talk about their behaviors, causal influences, and even improvement or deterioration over time. This is, to be sure, a crude approximation of the sort of moral agency which, complete with intentions and motivations, allows for conscious adjustments and therefore blame, praise, and likely richer gradations of virtuousness. But it is a moral agency marked by virtuousness—or its opposite—all the same.

The way that agents without any possible intentions or motivations nonetheless exhibit virtues or vices follows the traditional dispositional view. Thus, agents bearing such virtues or vices characteristically tend to perform the sorts of actions upon the world or give rise to sorts of actions in the world in ways that track particular values. The values of a built structure's architects may well inform its virtues but they will almost never be the only such values that a building's virtues track—unless, perhaps, the architect is the structure's builder, owner, and sole occupant. The virtues or vices of a built structure may track values from many sources, from the parties initially responsible for advancing or shaping its construction[7] to any parties who subsequently use, maintain, change, or otherwise live with those architectural objects as they structure their environment. Indeed—and independent of initial designer or user preferences—as built structures endure, they undergo changes in structure, programme, and appearance in accordance with changing values. A façade of stately marble that projects values of power and prominence may be found striking and influential on public attitudes in one generation, virtuous in its bold statement and beauty of a sort. Yet in a subsequent generation, the same marble façade may be found ostentatious and tired, reflecting a world weary of pomp and "muscular" design. While no motivations or intentions shifted, still the building's appearance moved—with values it tracks and its effects on users, appreciators, or passers-by—from a virtuous to a vicious design.

This picture of things raises several questions. For one, what sorts of virtues and vices are distinctive to, or distinctively prominent among, architectural objects? For another, are these *moral* or *aesthetic* virtues and vices, somehow both at once, or some other variety altogether? (See Song, this volume.) Relatedly, is there a single intrinsic good to which all architectural virtues contribute, in the manner that *eudaemonia* is relative to Aristotelian virtues? And further, how would we expect either the virtues and vices of built structures to relate, if at all, to those of architects or architectural users and appreciators?[8]

---

[7] Chan (2015) proposes that built structures track the values of the governing building codes.

[8] Thus, for example, Scruton (1979) and Taylor (2000) propose that attention to aesthetic detail reflects the virtue of architects caring for the aesthetic experience of the architectural user or audience. To be inattentive to such details is a lack of care, a form of neglect, on the part of the architect and as

Some such answers may be gleaned, or at least glimpsed, from the range of such virtues and vices as historically proposed. Architects have expended much effort to assess the constituent aspects of Vitruvian beauty,[9] or the numerous Albertian virtues as also relate to visual or formal properties,[10] and therefore it may seem that these are *the* architectural virtues, at least by Western lights. Some of these appear—notably symmetry and proportionality—as virtues in other architectural traditions as well, and such virtues may be grouped as aesthetic in nature. Yet other, nonaesthetic virtues, much discussed by a wide range of architectural writers across traditions, include the rest of the Vitruvian triad—utility and structural integrity—as well as modesty, sanctity, and honesty or authenticity. These last candidates are of particular interest, as they have been identified time and again across the history of architecture as characteristic of objects in the domain, though they are not associated with the Vitruvian, Renaissance, or various non-Western virtue traditions in architecture.[11] If viable *qua* virtues qualifying behaviors or consequences (or their "opposites" as vices), that would count as robust evidence—beyond cultural norms of architecture as canonize, for example, the Vitruvian triad—for a virtue-theoretic approach to architectural ethics that takes built structures as moral agents.

One such prospective virtue—*modesty*—is tied to scale and generally more discussed relative to its corresponding vice, *vanity*. As Christine Smith (1992) notes, among ancient cultures of the Mediterranean basin, as well as Renaissance authors, there is a common suggestion that the vast scale of some buildings is a vice.[12] This is true in the

then shows up in the architectural object. Taylor suggests, following Scruton, that in such cases the ethical tracks and is the product of the aesthetic. Perhaps so, but it is less clear that the virtues or vices of architects in this regard show up as virtues or vices of the corresponding architectural objects.

[9] These include *ordinatio* (appropriateness of magnitude among parts), *dispositio* (harmony or congruity of parts), *eurythmia* (fit or balance of parts in the whole), *symmetria* (fixity of ratio among parts), *decor* (propriety of design relative to custom and nature), and *distributio* (economy of materials and site use). Cf. Vitruvius (1999) and Pavlos Lefas (2000, 179–197); and discussion of his legacy in, e.g., Indra Kagis McEwen (2011, 255–282); Ingrid D. Rowland (2013, 412–425).

[10] These include *numerus* (precision of dimensions and forms), *finitio* (roughly, well-measured outline), *collocatio* (suitable arrangement or planning), *concinnatus* (harmony or congruity of parts), *proportio* (proportionality), and so on. Cf. Leon Battista Alberti, (1988); and discussion of his legacy in, e.g., Michel Paoli (2006, 62–89).

[11] Substantial review of architecture in non-Western ethical perspectives is beyond the scope of this chapter. However, certain prominent themes merit mention. In the Chinese tradition, built structures may be viewed as embodying or communicating Confucian virtues of humility, honesty, and gentility (Xiong 2017). The built environment is also taken to communicate Li (禮), that is, "rites," or as often rendered, "norms of social behavior"; buildings both connote Li and help structure life accordingly, or at least are intended to do so by design. Harmony, hierarchical order, and practicality are also guiding principles in traditional architectural design, particularly in ritual and royal architecture (Chen and Guo 2012). (See also Hutton, this volume.) In the Islamic tradition, both home and mosque may be characterized by virtues of modesty and moderation; the home may also be virtuous insofar as it promotes privacy and hospitality, two core values in the tradition (Mortada 2003; Omer 2008). (See also Leaman, this volume)

[12] Smith points to Horace, Ovid, and Plutarch among the Romans, and Plato among the Greeks. We can also find such sentiments regarding architectural vanity and grandiosity in the Tanakhic worldview,

Chinese tradition as well: Confucius praises the king who builds a humble palace and instead attends to civil infrastructure.[13] In the Western traditions, buildings that are too grand are taken to exhibit self-importance and efforts by human mortals to match divine capacities; in the Confucian tradition, they needlessly exceed their utility. However, as a candidate vice, we may ask whether such grandiosity is primarily characteristic of built structures or else derivative of the human vice of vanity as characteristic of building owners, the builders, or humanity overall. Moreover, many built structures are of great scale yet *not* characterized as vain, even in the ancient world and Renaissance period.[14] So, there appear to be circumstances where something *other* than the building's features (scale), namely those persons responsible for designing at great scale, track the relevant values and *they* are characterized by modesty (and not vanity).

A bit more promising is the proposal that some buildings have virtues related to particular functions. For example, much of the *preserved* built environment over all human civilizations comprises buildings that are built and maintained for spiritual or religious ends. The spaces so enclosed, the areas they occupy, and the people who pass through or stay for ceremonies all may be consecrated or otherwise endowed with spiritual or religious character. This endowment can be done well or poorly, and a building design might fail badly enough to desacralize a space, a site, or its users. For a built structure to do so well is for it to display the virtue of *sanctity*. Note that, if this sort of case works, it may suggest that architectural virtues are or can be indexed to types, as functionally defined in architectural theory. Thus, to be a school building well—for such a building to facilitate and contribute to teaching and learning—is to display educative virtue, to be a warehouse well is to display storage- and retrieval-related virtues, and so on.

The last putative virtue on this list, honesty, has been touted by a broad range of architects and architectural critics—from Laugier to Ruskin, Pugin, Viollet-le-Duc, Pevsner, and numerous others.[15] They suggest architectural objects exhibit a kind of honesty by reflecting design that is, for example, "true" to the materials, or "true" to the building's function, as in "honest expression of structure." "True to" here may be understood as "deployed in such a way as to not be illusory." Thus, the building displays this virtue if its users can tell what a building is actually made of, how it is made, what its function is, and possibly other dimensions of its structure or programme. We may question, per Carroll (2015), whether this counts as honest in the same way as a commitment to propositional truth or, say, emotional honesty. Or, following Carroll, we might not

---

regarding the story of Bavel (Breisheet (9–11:1 (בראשית)) and in the Quranic worldview, regarding the story of 'Ād (Surah Ash-Shu'ara (140–123 :26 (الشعراء)).

[13] Analects (論語) 8.21.

[14] Smith points out that Alberti, following a Renaissance humanist tradition, takes the scale of Brunelleschi's dome as a creative act that values human dignity, and its advancement through construction of culture, civilization, technical skill, ingenuity, and progress.

[15] Cf. Laugier's *Essai sur l'architecture* (1753); Pugin's *True Principles of Pointed or Christian Architecture* (1841); Ruskin's *Seven Lamps of Architecture* (1849); Viollet-le-Duc's *Entretiens sur l'architecture* (1863–1872); and, among the Modernists and their proponents, Pevsner's *Pioneers of the Modern Movement* (1936).

take this sort of "honesty" to be a *virtue* if we think that people don't want that kind of truth or such qualities in buildings, either because they prefer (aesthetically) artifice and deception or because this isn't a sort of honesty or truth about which they care, in the sense of carrying moral weight. However, and notwithstanding such practical concerns, we may yet hope for a prospective virtue of this sort. For one, we can't hold prospects for this sort of "honesty" hostage to examples provided for advocacy purposes on behalf of a particular style (by, e.g., Pugin or Pevsner); or to well-known failures to sustain "honesty," such as the bronze used in the mullions of Mies van der Rohe's *Seagram Building* (1958) for purely decorative purposes. For another, we can look to "honest expression of structure" or "truth to materials" as of a kind with relevantly similar virtues of *authenticity* that mark many or most built structures as not wholly illusory relative to structure, materials, and so forth. Even as illusion may be prized in built structures under the right conditions or to meet particular programmatic needs, the average built structure may well be more virtuous where it sustains such sorts of authenticity and thereby meets perceptual and aesthetic expectations of owners, users, and the public.[16]

These last candidates (sanctity, honesty) highlight ways that architectural virtues may characterize how built structures act upon us, and shape our attitudes, behaviors, habits, and our own actions. They can affect us well (effectively for the good) or poorly (ineffectively for the good, or effectively for the bad), and as they do so consistently, their character presents as virtuous or vicious. These are hardly distinctive to architecture as brands of virtue or vice, yet they are markers of moral character among architectural objects such as we do not find among other art objects, and possibly among other artifacts. Yet moral character is distinctive to architecture among the arts and design domains, with distinctive arrays of virtues and vices, because of the particularly comprehensive and persistent ways that architecture acts upon us and shapes our experience. While objects of other art forms and artifactual categories *also* act upon us or shape our experience, architecture is immersive, holistic, subliminal, and life-organizing, creating frameworks for our every activity and for the sum totals of our activities.

Revisiting earlier questions about the nature of specifically architectural virtues and vices, some brief thoughts are in order. To begin with, no clear candidate appears for a single intrinsic good to which all architectural virtues contribute. One Vitruvian candidate, through Henry Wotton's early modern translation, is the well-building of built structures.[17] That doesn't add much but does suggest a parallel with the well-lived or flourishing goal of the Aristotelian tradition. And perhaps flourishing is apt here, too, as architectural objects endure over time and, moving beyond how well they are *built*,

---

[16] This sort of visual authenticity is a virtue of built structures relative to the ways those structures succeed or fail to shape expectations of users in helping them determine their physical behavior in the built environment. A Mr. Wile E. Coyote may attest to the vicious nature of regularly eschewing such authenticity.

[17] In his phrasing, "Well building hath three Conditions. *Commoditie, Firmenes,* and *Delight.*" From Part I, "In Architecture as in all other Operative Arts, the end must direct the Operation. The end is to build well.," in Henry Wotton, *Of The Elements Of Architecture*, John Bill (1624).

are the poorer or richer for how they serve different needs and populations across their life spans. That said, the diversity among architectural virtues, along with the evolving functionality of any given built structure over time, may also point away from any single intrinsic good to which they contribute (or from which vices detract). Indeed, that diversity among architectural virtues and vices is all the greater because they weave together the *moral* and the *aesthetic*, tracking values such as structural integrity and utility but as well beauty and proportionality, and all in keeping with a sort of meta-virtue of equipoise. (See Song, this volume.)

Finally, as we scan across these putative virtues or vices, we may ask whether we might better understand the phenomenon in question, not as buildings tracking such-and-such values because they are virtuous or vicious in the right ways, but as built structures displaying or exemplifying the corresponding values through symbolic communication. In other words, if buildings are media for communicating or projecting values of, for example, power, glory, or piety, on behalf of the state, church, personas, and so on, it's not clear that we even need virtues and vices for the right analysis here. It might be sufficient to locate values in built structures on one hand and in persons responsible for the shape and content of those structures on the other, and indicate how the values of the former present or represent the values of the latter. Perhaps these differing analyses are not mutually exclusive. But if they are both correct and work in tandem, we need an account of why virtues and vices are explanatorily required on top of a story about architecture as a medium for values, and an account of how we would expect virtues and vices of built structures to relate, if at all, to those we may identify among architects or architectural users and appreciators.

Conclusion

I have argued that built structures, as architectural objects, have moral agency and that it is a bit different than that which we might ascribe to most other sorts of art objects. Built structures may count as art objects and generic artifacts at once, or as simply generic artifacts, but in either case bear aesthetic properties attendant to their own physical properties as well as to properties of the spaces to which they give shape, their relations to other elements (natural or artifactual) of their immediate environment, the behaviors they constrain or prompt, and yet other aspects of the ways they engage with the world around them. Further, and resulting from any moral weight associable with such aesthetic properties, we can ethically evaluate such architectural objects in terms of virtues as they may exhibit or realize, as well as consequences they may produce. In addition, built structures may inherit moral triumphs or failings of their creators as are encoded and passed on through plans or programmes corresponding to those structures. And while the moral portfolio of architectural objects does not comprise obligations per se (as they lack intentional agency), they plausibly bear rights incurring obligations of others toward them. This picture of architectural objects as morally endowed, morally causative, and morally invested lends support, if defeasible, to a moderate moralism. But that is only one corner of the territory of moral inquiry that architectural objects occupy.

See also: Song, Snow, Carroll, Stear, Matthes, this volume

References

Alberti, Leon Battista. 1988. *De Re Aedificatoria*. Translated by Joseph Rykwert, with Neil Leach and Robert Tavernor. Cambridge, MA: The MIT Press.

Baumberger, Christoph. 2015. "The Ethical Criticism of Architecture: In Defense of Moderate Moralism." *Architecture Philosophy* 1, no. 2: 179–197.

Carroll, Noël. 2015. "Architecture and Ethics: Autonomy, Architecture, Art." *Architecture Philosophy* 1, no. 2: 139–156.

Chan, Jeffrey. 2015. "Moral Agency in Architecture: The Dialectics of Spatializing Morality and Moralizing Spaces." In *Architecture, Materiality and Society: Connecting Sociology of Architecture with STS*, edited by Anna-Lisa Müller and Werner Reichmann, 198–214. London: Palgrave Macmillan.

Chen, Wan-qiu, and Guo, Ling-xi. 2012. "Human Ethics: Traditional Architectural Ethics" (人伦栖居：传统建筑伦理). *Philosophy Online* (哲学在线). October 22, 2012. https://www.csust.edu.cn/mksxy/info/1077/1768.htm

Crippen, Mathew, and Vladan Klement. 2020. "Architectural Values, Political Affordances and Selective Permeability." *Open Philosophy* 3, no. 1: 462–477.

Delitz, Heike. 2010. "Architektur als Medium des Sozialen: Zur soziologischen Theorie des gebauten Raumes." http://www.heike-delitz.de/Architektur_als_Medium_2010.pdf (accessed February 20, 2023).

Gutman, Robert, ed. 1972. *People and Buildings*. New York: Basic Books.

Harold, James. 2020. *Dangerous Art: On Moral Criticism of Artworks*. Oxford: Oxford University Press.

Kagis McEwen, Indra. 2011. "Virtù-vious: Roman Architecture, Renaissance Virtue." *Cahiers des études anciennes* XLVIII: 255–282.

Kopec, DAK. 2012. *Environmental Psychology for Design*, 2nd ed. New York: Fairchild Books.

Laugier, Marc Antoine. [1753] 2012. *Essai sur l'Architecture*. Paris: Hachette Livre BNF.

Lefas, Pavlos. 2000. "On the Fundamental Terms of Vitruvius's Architectural Theory." *Bulletin of the Institute of Classical Studies* 44, no. 1: 179–197.

Lipman, Alan. 1969. "The Architectural Belief System and Social Behavior." *British Journal of Sociology* 20, no. 2: 190–204.

Mortada, Hisham. 2003. *Traditional Islamic Principles of Built Environment*. London: Routledge.

Omer, Spahic. 2008. "Towards Understanding Islamic Architecture." *Islamic Studies* 47, no. 4: 483–510.

Paoli, Michel. 2006. "Fortune et Infortune Critique d'Alberti en France." In *Alberti humaniste, architecte*, edited by Françoise Choay and Michel Paoli, 62–89. Paris: Louvre/Ensba.

Pevsner, Nikolaus. 1936. *Pioneers of the Modern Movement, from William Morris to Walter Gropius*. London: Faber & Faber.

Pugin, Augustus W. N. [1841] 2014. *The True Principles of Christian or Pointed Architecture*. Cambridge: Cambridge University Press.

Rowland, Ingrid D. 2013. "Vitruvius and his Influence." In *A Companion to Roman Architecture*, edited by Roger B. Ulrich and Caroline K. Quenemoen, 412–425. Oxford: Wiley-Blackwell.

Ruskin, John. [1849] 1989. *The Seven Lamps of Architecture*. Mineola, NY: Dover Publications.

Scruton, Roger. [1979] 2013. *The Aesthetics of Architecture*. Princeton, NJ: Princeton University Press.

Sloan Devlin, Ann, ed. 2018. *Environmental Psychology and Human Well-Being: Effects of Built and Natural Settings*. Cambridge, MA: Academic Press.

Smith, Christine, 1992. *Architecture in the Culture of Early Humanism: Ethics, Aesthetics, and Eloquence, 1400–1470*. Oxford: Oxford University Press.

Spector, Tom. 2014. "Publicness as an Architectural Value." *Journal of Architecture and Urbanism*, 38, no. 3: 180–186.

Taylor, Nigel. 2000. "Ethical Arguments about the Aesthetics of Architecture." In *Ethics and the Built Environment*, edited by Warwick Fox, 163–206. London: Routledge.

Taylor, William M., and Michael P. Levine, eds. 2011. *Prospects for an Ethics of Architecture*. London: Routledge.

Till, Jeremy. 2009. *Architecture Depends*. Cambridge, MA: The MIT Press.

Viollet-le-Duc, Eugène-Emmanuel. 1863–1872. *Entretiens sur l'architecture*. Paris: A. Morel.

Vitruvius. 1999. *Ten Books on Architecture*. Translated by Ingrid D. Rowland and commentary and illustrations by Thomas Noble Howe. Cambridge: Cambridge University Press.

Wharton, Annabel Jane. 2015. *Architectural Agents: The Delusional, Abusive, Addictive Lives of Buildings*. Minneapolis: University of Minnesota Press.

Wotton, Henry. 1624. *Of the Elements of Architecture*. London: John Bill.

Xiong Chengxia. 2017. "Traditional Architecture as the Medium of Public Ethical Value." *Sociology Study* 7, no. 3: 168–178.

CHAPTER 30

....

ETHICS AND VIDEO GAMES

....

CHRISTOPHER BARTEL

ETHICS in video games is a divisive issue, one that gamers and even some academics dismiss as mere "moral panic." Certainly, moralizers can be a bit much at times. But how can we distinguish a mere moral panic from genuinely meaningful ethical criticism? Perhaps moral panics are cases where a critic's moral concerns are uninformed by evidence or experience. When critics become whipped into a frenzy over issues that they barely understand, then the label "moral panic" seems apt. However, the anti-moral-panic crowd can veer too far in the other direction, dismissing genuinely good moral questions. This chapter will draw attention to some key questions that have been raised by video games researchers. My account here will not be exhaustive; but nonetheless, my aim is to highlight some of the live debates while avoiding moral panic.

Ethical questions about video games can be divided into roughly two kinds: questions *internal* to a game and questions *external* to any specific game. This distinction equates to a distinction between the ethics *in* games and the ethics *of* games. The ethical issues internal to video games arise from both their status as fictions and their status as games. The first section will examine how moral values are inherent within games and some potential consequences. Players engage with the embedded moral values of games both at the level of their narratives and their rules. When playing a game, players deliberate and act within a value-laden system. Games therefore can be objects of moral reflection, not only through the stories that they tell, but also through the ways in which players are invited to engage actively with those stories. Finally, many games afford players the opportunity to perform violent and sadistic acts; however, these are of course fictional actions and are often contextualized as part of the game's competitive play. This raises the general question whether it can ever be morally wrong to perform some fictional action in a video game.

Alternatively, external ethical issues are those that focus on the nature of the gaming industry, gaming cultures, and gaming technologies. In the second section we will briefly survey some of these issues. First, the gaming industry has notoriously struggled with representations of gender and race, both in their workforce and in their games. Much has been written about such issues lately; however, change has been slow in coming. Second, the gaming industry is a major source of e-waste. The hardware used in gaming has a lifecycle that begins with the exploitation of resource-rich developing countries that produce the precious materials used in computer screens and processing chips and ends with those same products being dumped in toxic landfills in other developing countries. Additionally, gaming is a major source of energy consumption, particularly as cloud gaming servers are required to run continuously. When considering the ethics *of* games, such social and ecological concerns must surely figure in one's moral calculation. (See Woodcock, this volume.)

The distinction between internal and external moral questions offered above could be refined a bit further. Plausibly, the distinction comes down to whether the content of a game is itself the object of some moral question. For instance, the debate over violence in video games is fundamentally a debate about the content of certain games—whether that content is associated with any negative moral or psychological effects—while issues concerning the ecological impact of the gaming industry have nothing to do with the contents of any games. Additionally, when speaking of the "content" of a game, we should understand this broadly to include not only what the game fictionally represents (e.g., objects, characters, and events), but also its rules and affordances. Again, the debate over violence in video games is not just a debate about fictional representations of violence; it is also a debate about players acting out violent imaginings in games.

The internal-external distinction neatly divides some moral questions into their distinctive spheres; however, there are other moral issues that seem to straddle the line. These are cases where a game's content is not directly the object of moral investigation, but where it may yet have some relevant role to play in our philosophical analysis. In the third section we will consider four such "borderline" issues: multiplayer games, harassment, gamesmanship, and trolling. This section will consider what role a game's content may play in the moral analysis of such issues.

INTERNAL QUESTIONS

Video games are a form of representational media, many of which are works of fiction (but not all; see Juul 2005, Chapter 4). In many respects, video games are like paintings, animation, and cinema; and the philosophical debate over the moral criticism of these more traditional representational media is also appropriate in the case of video games. Some philosophers argue that our engagement with works of fiction are informed by our moral attitudes toward the characters and events represented in the fiction (Carroll 1996). Many philosophers have argued that works of fiction can be open to moral criticism, not for what they represent, but rather for what attitudes they suggest toward those representations (Eaton 2003, Gaut 1998, Giovannelli 2013, Harold 2003). Finally, some argue that we stand to gain something morally by engaging with immoral representations in fiction (Eaton 2010, Kieran 2003; see also Jacobson, this volume). As each of these debates concerns general issues about our engagement with works of fiction, they can be applied to video game fictions just as well. However, the interactive nature of video games raises further issues. Because the actions of the player-character are causally dependent on the player, we can ask, is the player ever morally responsible for their actions?

Concerns about the ethics of virtual actions can best be appreciated by considering the "gamer's dilemma," posed by Morgan Luck (2009). In brief, the dilemma goes like this: Many players commit gruesome acts of violence in video games. Such violence is often defended on the grounds that "no one is really harmed." Acts of violence in video games are mere fictional representations after all, and no one is really harmed by fictional representations of violence.[1] However, Luck suggests that the same inference could be used to defend fictional representations of pedophilic acts in video games. If it is morally permissible to commit acts of violence in video games because no one is really harmed, then it should be equally permissible to commit acts of pedophilia in video games on the same grounds. After all, both virtual murder and virtual pedophilia have the same status as fictional representations. Yet this seems intuitively wrong. Many gamers find it highly intuitive to believe that virtual pedophilia is morally impermissible while still maintaining that virtual murder is morally permissible. This intuition is predicated on the belief that there is some relevant distinction between virtual murder and virtual pedophilia that justifies the asymmetry. The dilemma, however, is that there seems to be no plausible way to explain that distinction. If this is right, then Luck suggests that we ought to treat both similarly: either both virtual murder and virtual pedophilia are morally permissible, or they are both morally impermissible (2009, 35–36). Luck's dilemma is one of the most substantial contributions to the ethics of video games and has proven to be a notoriously difficult dilemma to solve.

Numerous commentators have sought to address Luck's dilemma. Broadly speaking, one may either pursue a *conservative* resolution—where one seeks to conserve the gamer's intuition that there is some morally relevant distinction between virtual murder and virtual pedophilia (Bartel 2012 and 2020; Bourne and Caddick Bourne 2019; Kjeldgaard-Christiansen 2020; Luck 2022; Patridge 2011; Young 2016)—or one might instead pursue a *revisionist* resolution—where one argues that we must revise either our moral intuitions (Ali 2015; Ramirez 2020; Schulzke 2020; Tillson 2018) or our metaphysical intuitions (Davnall 2020 and Seddon 2013; for further discussion, see Bartel 2020, Chapter 6). While the gamer's dilemma is one specific puzzle concerning the morality of virtual actions, other philosophers have sought to address more general issues. Some recent accounts of the ethics and moral relevance of virtual actions are highlighted below.

Ian Bogost (2008) has argued that values are embedded in a game's design. Game designers create a fictional world using representations of things and events that are

---

[1] One could question this claim on empirical grounds. Some empirical studies suggest that violence in video games is harmful, but other social scientists have questioned these studies and offered evidence to the contrary. The empirical evidence pertaining to the effects of violence in video games is too large to survey here, and is also inconclusive. To save space, I will set aside these issues and ask the reader to take the gamer's dilemma at face value.

recognizable to the player. They are worlds of heroes, villains, and monsters where injustices must be righted and mysteries uncovered. Players quickly learn how digital objects in games work by taking cues from what those objects represent. Guns are things that can shoot, and items of food are things that can be eaten to restore health. No player makes the mistake of trying to kill their opponent with a roasted chicken or to eat a battle-axe. Game designers also create a world governed by rules. The rules of the game dictate how players may interact with the game's fictional representations. Bogost calls this the game's "possibility space," which refers to "the myriad configurations the player might construct to see the ways the processes inscribed in the system work. This is really what we do when we play video games: we explore the possibility space its rules afford by manipulating the symbolic systems the game provides" (121). Every possibility space is subject to various constraints—actions that the game affords to players, but also those actions that the game disallows—which structures the player's behavior. Thus, games become "procedural systems," which "generate behaviors based on rule-based models" (122). Bringing together the procedural and representational aspect of video games offers designers a tool to create dynamic and responsive models that can represent real-world scenarios or events. For instance, a game designer can create a world that models a real-world economic system. And by modeling a system, game designers are able to comment upon the values of that system. Bogost calls this the "procedural rhetoric" of games (125). Of particular interest for us is the way that games embed values in their design. Game designers decide what kind of behaviors are permissible and impermissible; which are rewarded and which are thwarted; and through developing a point-system, they decide what actions are more valuable relative to other actions. Players internalize these systems of reward-and-punishment, and by internalizing, they become better at deciding and strategizing within the game. Thus, games embed values within their design and players are responsive to those values.

With similar points in mind, Miguel Sicart (2009) argues that games can be tools of moral reflection, when they are ethically designed. Like Bogost, Sicart holds that games are systems of rules, which create "values we *have* to play by" (22); but importantly, game design (i.e., the rules and affordances) is ethically relevant because one cannot understand a game or how to engage with its fictional world without considering its rules (32–33). What a game represents superficially can have some ethical import for the player. This offers players the opportunity for moral reflection: Should I do this? Should I be allowed to do this? Are my actions right or wrong? An ethically designed game, for Sicart, is one where the affordances and embedded values of the game line up in the right way to offer players opportunities for moral reflection. However, many games fail at this. Some games constrain players' actions in ways that are incoherent. For instance, there are many games that offer players the opportunity to commit anarchic acts of violence, but prohibit friendly fire or harm to children. If the player is supposed to take the role of a senseless killer, then why can't I kill my teammates? Games that constrain the player's actions in incoherent ways do not afford the player an ethical game experience because they fail to allow the player to engage in ethical reasoning (58).

So, games are designed with ethical values in mind and players engage with those values partly by making decisions about how to behave within games. From this point, we can return to our earlier question: is it ever morally wrong to perform some virtual action in a video game? Marcus Schulzke (2020) offers a mixed answer, arguing that there is no genuine moral wrongness to virtual actions, and yet virtual actions can serve as useful tools of moral reflection. Schulzke does not defend amoralism, but rather defends a positive interactionism. Schulzke's rejection of the moral status of virtual actions is due squarely to their fictionality and their lack of real-world harms; and yet games effectively function as thought experiments, which can be beneficial when it leads the player to some moral reflection (2020, Chapter 3). Schulzke acknowledges that it can be reasonable to feel some disgust or discomfort about the actions that players perform in games, but such feelings are an insufficient basis to judge those actions as morally wrong.

By contrast, Christopher Bartel (2015; 2020) argues that it can be morally wrong to perform some actions in video games, under the right circumstances. Not all actions performed in games are morally relevant. Bartel suggests that virtual actions become morally relevant when we consider the player's motivation to commit such actions. Sometimes players are motivated to commit immoral acts in games for morally innocent reasons. For instance, players might wish to experiment with how the game works, to experience a complex and harrowing storyline, or to simply gain some advantage in competitive play. But sometimes, players commit immoral acts because they imaginatively identify with such actions (2015; 2020: 84–85; for criticism, see Kissel 2020). This is morally problematic because of the link between the player's actions and their desires. Bartel argues that we cultivate and reinforce our desires by acting out fictional scenarios in video games. Insofar as the motivating desires are themselves immoral ones, it is morally wrong to cultivate an immoral desire (2020, 105–107; see also Bartel and Cremaldi 2018, and Harold 2003). The controversial premise of Bartel's argument is the claim that desires can be objects of moral condemnation. Bartel, following McCormick (2001), defends this claim on Aristotelian grounds: the cultivation of immoral desires is bad for the player because it constitutes a harm to the player's moral character (Bartel 2020, 59–60, 100–103).

Garry Young (2013; 2016; 2020) comes to a similar conclusion as Bartel, but for different reasons. Where Bartel and Young agree is in the claim that the moral evaluation of virtual actions must be sensitive to the agent's motivations. Sometimes an agent might simulate taboo actions (e.g., murder or sexual assault) in a virtual world just because they take some delight in the moral transgression of a taboo. These sorts of cases are permissible. What is impermissible is virtually simulating a taboo action because one desires to perform the action in real-life (2013, Chapter 11; 2020, Chapter 7). A crucial disagreement, however, is that Young situates his account within an anti-realist meta-ethical theory, which he calls *constructive ecumenical expressivism* (2016 and 2020). Young's theory is *expressivist*, meaning moral declarations—like "Murder is wrong"—are expressions of disapproval; it is *ecumenical*, meaning that moral declarations also express the agent's belief that some wrong-making property is realized in some action; and the theory is *constructive*, meaning that the various moral statements that individuals give voice to can be taken to form a social norm (Young 2016, 107–112; 2020: 211–213).

EXTERNAL QUESTIONS

As previously discussed, some moral questions fall outside of the contents of games themselves. These typically are questions that focus on the nature of the gaming industry, gaming cultures, and gaming technologies. Drawing attention to external moral questions is important because many philosophers have largely ignored them in favor of the moral questions that more easily link up with longstanding philosophical interests. Some of the recent hot topics in philosophy of art concern the nature of fiction, the metaphysics of fictional entities, and the nature of the relationship between aesthetics and ethics (see Song, this volume). Given the broad interest in such questions, it is not surprising that, when looking at video games, philosophers turn their attention to the ethics of virtual actions, because that is a topic that clearly intersects with the issues identified above. By contrast, discussions of (e.g.) ecological problems have not figured strongly in the philosophy of art generally. So, ecological questions about gaming may not seem immediately relevant to philosophers of art just because such issues do not neatly fall into the existing debates in our field. By drawing attention to these issues here (however briefly), we may take some steps toward addressing their absence. In this section, we will consider some ethical problems associated with the lack of gender and racial representation (see Taylor, this volume) in gaming and some of the industry's material and ecological impacts.

Video games have long been associated quite narrowly with young, white, male, cisgender, and heterosexual players. However, many demographic studies have demonstrated that this perception is mistaken—people across the spectrum play a wide range of games (Yee 2014, Chapter 2). Scholarly attention to gender representation in gaming has focused on three main interrelated issues: the underrepresentation of female characters in games, the incorrect assumption that women and girls do not play games, and the underrepresentation of women in the gaming industry. I will focus on the first and second of these issues.

As many scholars have noted, female characters are greatly underrepresented in video games, especially when it comes to playable female characters (Williams et al. 2009; Gestos, Smith-Merry, and Campbell 2018). Additionally, when female characters are represented in games, they are often represented as subordinate to the male characters, in need of being rescued, are often targets of sexual violence, or they are hypersexualized in ways that male characters are not (Downs and Smith 2010; Lynch et al. 2016). The oversexualization of female characters is not a mere aesthetic choice that has no real-world impact. Rather, it solidifies sexist attitudes in male players (Stermer and Burkley 2015) and reinforces the acceptability of sexist behaviors (Dill, Brown, and Collins 2008).[2]

---

[2] See also Mullin, this volume.

The issue of gender representation in games should not only be understood as the underrepresentation of women and femininity in games, but also as the overrepresentation of men and masculinity in games. Putting the point this way recognizes that the issues identified above will not be solved merely by increasing the number of female characters in games, or even by representing femininity positively. Rather, the gaming industry and gaming communities must also face up to the damaging aspects of a "militarized masculinity" (Kline, Dyer-Witheford, and de Peuter 2003; for discussion of confronting masculinity, see Consalvo 2012 and Salter and Blodgett 2012).

Video gaming has long been perceived as being a male-oriented activity despite the fact that women and girls have been involved in gaming from its start. Kocurek (2015) attributes the alienation of girls from gaming to the early commercial development of the arcade and the console industries in the 1980s. It was during this period, Kocurek argues, that several factors peculiar to the culture of the United States came together to associate gaming with boys, which she summarizes as, "the greater relative freedom of young boys to move through and participate in public culture; the alignment of computer and video game technologies with both military interests and competitive male-dominated sports; the subsequent affiliation of video gaming with violent thematic content; and the ongoing association of technological skill with masculinity" (xiii). Despite the progress that has been made, the cultural groundwork laid there continues to reverberate through gaming today, sometimes in particularly ugly ways, as can be seen in the "GamerGate" controversy of 2014.[3]

While the lack of diverse gender representation in games may be bad enough, the issue becomes worse when we factor in representations of violence against women, particularly sexual violence. Undoubtedly, where themes of sexual violence appear in games, the victims are overwhelmingly women. Some games even afford the player the opportunity to commit acts of sexual violence against NPCs and against other players. An early example of this is the game *Custer's Revenge* (1982), where the player controls a caricature of General Custer, who is naked except for a cowboy hat. The player must walk across a field while dodging volleys of arrows toward a naked Native American woman who is tied to a post. If the player succeeds in reaching the woman, they then have the opportunity to rape her (for criticism, see Patridge 2011 and Shaw 2015, Chapter 1). While such games are obviously offensive, the harms perpetrated by it go beyond mere offense. Additionally, such games reinforce the attitude that video games are for boys, thus perpetuating the exclusion of girls from gaming. Furthermore, some empirical evidence suggests that it can be damaging for some gamers to consume such images. Gabbiadini et al. (2016) found that playing "violent-sexist" video games increased acceptance of masculine beliefs among male players who identify with dominant and aggressive male avatars (Beck et al. 2012; Stermer and Burkley 2015).

There is a growing body of work focusing on race and representation in games, though the existing literature is still quite small when compared to the existing literature

---

[3] For summary and discussion, see Mortensen 2018.

on issues of gender and sexuality (for a recent collection of essays at the intersection of these issues, see Malkowski and Russworm 2017). Just as female players and game designers have struggled for inclusion, gaming in the United States has long been associated with whiteness despite the facts that there have been nonwhite players from the early days of arcade gaming and that so many gaming companies and game developers hail from Japan, South Korea, and China. Nonetheless, nonwhite characters—playable or not—are also greatly underrepresented in video games (see Williams et al. 2009 for a content analyses of race representation in games). Additionally, the racial stereotyping of nonwhite characters is rampant. (See Taylor, this volume.) For instance, Black characters are often depicted as criminals (e.g., C. J. Johnson in *Grand Theft Auto: San Andreas* [2004] and Franklin Clinton in *Grand Theft Auto V* [2013]; see Dyer-Witheford and de Peuter 2009: 164–170) or they are exoticized (e.g., Sheva Alomar in *Resident Evil 5* [2009]). Nuanced nonwhite playable characters that challenge racial stereotypes are rare—two (still imperfect) exceptions being Lee Everett from *The Walking Dead* (2012) and Aveline de Grandpré from *Assassin's Creed III: Liberation* (2012; but see Murray 2017, Chapter 1).

The remainder of this section will briefly draw attention to some material and ecological problems (for more, see Apperley and Jayemanne 2012). The video game industry operates on two fronts: hardware and software. The hardware for video games—which includes not only consoles, but also all of the peripheral products like controllers, keyboards, and audio headsets—has a life cycle of only a few years in the primary consumer markets of North America, Europe, and Asia. Once these products become obsolete, broken, or just unfashionable, they either find their way into secondary markets (i.e., poorer regions of the world where many used earlier-generation consoles are still played) or they are loaded into landfills, often located in developing countries, where they release toxins into the groundwater as they slowly decay (Dyer-Witheford and de Peuter 2009, 223–224). Some gaming hardware have particularly short life cycles (e.g., controllers only last a few years of hard use) and some are designed to be used for a small number of games (e.g., the guitar-shaped controllers used with the *Guitar Hero* games or the floor pad controllers used for dance games).

Like most consumer digital technologies, video game consoles are manufactured using many rare and precious minerals—like tungsten, tin, gold, and coltan. Consumer demand for these materials has grown massively in recent decades as the production of new video game consoles, cellphones, and personal computers has increased. While some of these materials can be sourced through recycling efforts, many must be mined. Coltan is a particularly rare mineral. It is estimated that 70 percent of the world's coltan is in the Democratic Republic of Congo where control of the coltan mines has become a major point of conflict. Rebel militias have fought a bloody civil war over the mines killing thousands each year and displacing hundreds of thousands—sometimes called the "PlayStation War" (Shachtman 2008). Moreover, the mines are often worked using forced labor and child labor (Mantz 2008; see also Dyer-Witheford and de Peuter 2009, 222–223). The major console producers—Microsoft, Nintendo, and Sony—have taken to issuing "corporate social responsibility" (or CSR) reports detailing how they maintain their coltan supply lines and the steps taken to investigate whether their products have been produced using "conflict minerals" (for a summary of the 2020 reports, see Maxwell 2020).

Finally, consider the energy consumption associated with gaming. As Sean Cubitt vividly illustrates (2017, Chapter 1), it takes an enormous amount of electricity to run all the gaming computers, consoles, and servers required to maintain our online games, and the need for more is constantly growing. Energy must be produced from something—whether that is coal, nuclear power, or renewables—and the energy consumed produces something—not only heat, light, and sound, but also carbon emissions. Powering a persistent online game like *World of Warcraft* requires hundreds of servers that are rarely ever switched off. These not only consume great amounts of energy, but they must also be cooled using tens of thousands of gallons of water. One might think that the problems associated with e-waste discussed previously could be minimized by shifting the gaming industry away from a model based on console sales and their accessories and shifting to the digital delivery of games that are playable on a variety of hardware through services like Steam. However, following Cubitt (2017, 17–18), the benefits of this model must still come at the cost of increasing power consumption. Video games promise worlds of fantasy with endless possibilities, but they are dependent on a real world of consumable resources. The gaming industry's need to stay ahead of trends and offer novel forms of entertainment is contributing to global environmental problems that only get worse with each new generation of consoles.

Admittedly, these problems are not unique to video games. All forms of online media can be accused of the same thing. While it is estimated that online gaming produced 7 exabytes of internet traffic per month in 2020, internet video content produced 140 exabytes per month (Clement 2020). There is no telling how much energy is consumed each year by the worldwide consumption of videos of strangers' cats. More generally, the issues described above may strike some as problems that do not directly have much to do with video games. One might object that, while matters of representation, social responsibility, and environmental impact are certainly important, they do not directly bear on the ethics *of* games. So, why are these issues relevant?

In response, two quick points. First, concern over the material conditions and real-world impacts of gaming has received much attention outside of analytic philosophy. While analytic philosophers of art have spent much time in recent years concerned with internal moral questions, nonanalytic philosophers have done considerable work investigating these external questions. The attitude implied by the objection above—that some moral questions have greater bearing than others on understanding games—is an unnecessary factionalist distraction. Moral questions are moral questions. They are all worthy of investigation.

Second, the objection above is also likely motivated by a theoretical stance that places the fictionality (or virtuality) of video games above all else. This ignores that there is a "materiality to gaming that links digital games to the world and demands that they are also understood as objects in the world" (Apperley and Jayemanne 2012, 15). An honest account of the moral and social impact of gaming cannot ignore such issues.

BORDERLINE QUESTIONS

This section will survey some moral issues that straddle the line between "internal" and "external." As suggested above, these are cases where the object of moral concern is some real-world harm, but where the content of the game may broadly play some role in our moral assessment.

The ethics of multiplayer games is particularly interesting because of their porous nature. In multiplayer games, players perform virtual actions in a virtual space, and yet such actions impact other players. Such in-game actions can have multiple motivations—that is, while some in-game actions may be purely part of the game, other actions may be perpetrated for reasons that are external to the game. For instance, imagine a *World of Warcraft* player, Smith, whose older brother likes to bully her in real life. In the game, Smith's brother targets her avatar with friendly fire during battles in order to frustrate Smith. Imagine further that Smith's brother does this not for the sake of some in-game benefit like earning experience points, or collecting special loot, or gaining some strategic advantage. Rather, Smith's brother is "griefing" her (which is play that impedes or disrupts the normal play of others [Tavinor 2009, 108]) for reasons that fall outside of the game. Smith is being real-world bullied in a virtual space.

Helen Ryland (2019) has recently drawn attention to some moral implications of such cases. In some multiplayer games, players can team up together to take on difficult missions or to fight in group battles. While gamers typically play with teammates who are already familiar to them, it is also common for players to team up with strangers. Some unscrupulous players will invite a player to team up for a difficult mission and, once the mission is over, kill their teammate to take off with the loot and whatever other possessions the victim may have. The killing of other players is allowed in many multiplayer games and players (typically) consent to the risk of having their avatars killed in competitive multiplayer games. However, the invitation to team up creates a moral obligation, one where the consent to compete has been retracted. Ryland argues that these are cases of exploitation, which are morally wrong on straightforwardly Kantian grounds: the unscrupulous player treats the victim as a means to an end (2019, 111–113). To augment Ryland's account, one could describe such cases as an exploitation of the victim's labor. Completing a difficult mission can take many real-world hours of effort. When this is undertaken with the expectation of a reward, which is later denied, then the player's real-world effort has been stolen.

These cases are plausibly borderline moral issues, neither "internal" nor "external." While the actions are virtual, the moral repercussions concern real-world relationships (in cases of targeted bullying) and real-world losses (in cases of exploitation). The content of the game becomes a relevant factor in the moral analysis of these cases because it is the game's rules and affordances that creates situations where players can be bullied, harassed, and exploited in the ways described. Games are designed to make certain kinds of virtual interactions possible and to disallow other kinds of interactions. For instance, imagine if *World of Warcraft* were designed so that friendly fire was impossible and teams only break up once all teammates teleport away. These modifications would prevent many of the cases Ryland worries about.

Another interesting borderline case is that of trash-talking, which is a familiar feature of many competitive games. Trash-talk is commonly defended as "doing what it takes to win." Some theorists consider trash-talking as one manifestation of "gamesmanship" (Howe 2004), which is generally when competitors employ strategies of intimidation to break the will or the concentration of one's opponent. As Howe puts it, one "attempts to win one game by playing another" (2004, 212). The acceptability of trash-talking specifically, and gamesmanship generally, in traditional sports is debatable. However, it is also important to recognize that much of the trash-talking frequently found in video games is quite different from that of traditional sports in some important respects. First, online trash-talk is frequently anonymous. The anonymity of online games makes it easy to treat other competitors in ways that we never would in person. Indeed, anonymity is one source of online "moral fog"—an aspect of the technology that clouds our judgment and makes it harder for users to recognize the moral impact of their actions (Cocking and van den Hoven 2018, 48). Second, much of the trash-talking in video games, which often makes use of racist, sexist, and homophobic slurs, is often targeted at women and minority players (Hussain and Griffiths 2008). These factors together suggest that what happens in gaming is not really trash-talk but instead a more sinister form of trolling (more on this below).

Turning now to gamesmanship generally, there too we notice some important differences, which can be illustrated through the example of "tea-bagging." This is when the winner of a battle humiliates the loser by crouching over the face of the fallen player's avatar, thus crudely implying forcible oral sex. Strictly speaking, this is not an instance of gamesmanship. The purpose of tea-bagging is not to break will or the concentration of one's opponent. Indeed, it is not done for the sake of some in-game advantage. Once a battle is over, there is no strategic benefit. Tea-bagging is a form of humiliation that has a very different purpose from gamesmanship: it is to discourage the fallen player from ever wanting to play again. Additionally, the sexual nature of tea-bagging serves to enforce certain gendered norms about who gets to be a "gamer." Tea-bagging happens so commonly in games that many players just accept it as "what happens in games." However, such complacent attitudes overlook the offensiveness of tea-bagging. Imagine that a professional football player tea-bagged a downed player during a match in real life; they would almost surely be booted off the field and legal actions would likely follow.

A related phenomenon is trolling, which has been insightfully analyzed by Megan Condis (2018). Harassment is often a product of chance encounters online, generally unfocused in its targeting of specific individuals, and is not motivated by any goal or agenda. By contrast, trolling is more calculated. Condis's analysis begins with the observation (discussed above) that gaming has long been associated with boys and masculinity. Many young men feel that gaming is "their space" and any attempt (whether it is instigated by the industry, activists, or academics) to make gaming more inclusive will necessarily minimize the market dominance of male players. Trolls target unwanted individuals with the aim of dominating gamer culture, and thus with the hope of tamping down moves toward greater inclusivity. This sort of targeted harassment itself becomes a "metagame." According to Condis (Chapter 1), the trolling game works like this. Many gamers associate masculinity with coolheaded aloofness. A "real gamer" cannot be goaded into earnest or emotional outbursts. Trolls post inflammatory comments on gaming discussion boards or in live chat feeds that often contain racist, sexist, and homophobic language. This is intended as bait. The game is to remain cool-headed and aloof. The "noob" who reacts negatively to the offensive comment outs themselves not only as being a fake gamer, but also as one who exhibits the (perceived) quality of effeminacy. As Condis summarizes it, "some gamers frequently turn masculine policing into a metagame in its own right, a game in which one improves one's own standing both by enacting masculine performances of dominance and self-mastery, and by successfully baiting others into losing status by letting their mask of masculinity slip" (2018, 15).

Trash-talking, gamesmanship, and trolling are plausibly borderline moral issues, but for different reasons. Tea-bagging can be given a similar analysis to that of griefing or Ryland-cases of exploitation. Remember, these latter issues are borderline cases because they depend on certain affordances of the game. Similarly, tea-bagging is possible because of a number of features that are designed into games. Game designers could prevent players from tea-bagging by changing certain affordances, but which ones? The crouch-function is very important to many games where stealth is an option, so, removing that feature would be quite damaging to many games. But other options are available. Game designers could prevent players from standing over the bodies of fallen avatars, or they could program games so that fallen avatars always lie face-down, or they could disintegrate fallen avatars quickly from the battlefield. These fixes might detract somewhat from the "realism" of some games, but then we should question whether this degree of realism is worth the ethical costs.

By contrast, the same sort of analysis cannot be given straightforwardly to trash-talking and trolling because these issues do not depend strongly on the affordances of any game. Instead, these are factors of gaming culture. There are features that game designers could employ to prevent some instances of trash-talking and trolling. They could take steps to minimize anonymity, create an easy system to report offensive players, ban players with multiple offenses, make available audio recordings of player-to-player chat, and create programs that detect the use of certain words. However, many of these functions are implausible as they would likely be technically cumbersome and, more importantly, players who really wish to offend others will find creative ways to skirt the system.

Our moral analysis of trash-talking and trolling must instead center on the ways that gaming cultures form, police their members, and reinforce the group's values. While this might seem like an external moral issue, this is in fact a place where we might consider the relevance of a game's content. Gaming culture is not monolithic. There are numerous gaming subcultures (or "fandoms"), each with their own character and standards of behavior. Some fandoms can be quite exclusionary and hostile, while others relatively more inclusive. Why is that exactly? While much could be said, here is a brief sketch of how a game's content can contribute to the character of its fandom. The actions that are represented in a game, the affordances that a game offers its players, and the story that it tells are all laden with values (as described earlier). The differences that one finds when comparing various fandoms are plausibly driven (in part) by the values inherent within each game. Players respond to the values inherent within games and are attracted to games whose values align with their own interests. By attracting players with similar shared interests, the collective shared values of a fandom begin to coalesce around the inherent values of a game. While this sketch is certainly very brief, this topic generally is ripe for further philosophical exploration.

"But It's Just a Game"

This chapter has touched on potential ethical worries concerning many forms of game-play interactions. However, whether we are talking about virtual pedophilia, tea-bagging, or griefing, a thoroughgoing amoralist may nonetheless insist that nothing of real ethical importance is happening here. Two common amoralist arguments are that (1) games have special rules that stand outside of the normal rules of morality, or (2) games are works of fiction. I have criticized both of these arguments in detail elsewhere (Bartel 2020, Chapter 2); however, I will offer a brief rebuttal here.

First, many theorists have observed (rightly) that games are capable of suspending some moral rules. Consider boxing: it is normally morally wrong to punch people, but it becomes permissible—even laudable—to punch one's opponent in a boxing match. Games seem capable of suspending certain moral rules through a social convention: competitors consent to punch each other in boxing for the sake of developing their skills and athletic abilities (Weimer 2012). This claim is defensible, however, only in a limited sense. Some moral rules can be suspended, but some cannot. Performing an action in the context of a game is not sufficient to morally justify that action. Consider dogfighting: appealing to its status as a game does not make it right. Applying this to video games, it may be the case that certain kinds of actions are socially accepted in some games and gaming communities, but mere social acceptance is a weak basis for moral justification.

Second, some amoralists appeal to the "just a game" defense because of the fictional nature of virtual actions. No one is really sexually assaulted when players tea-bag each other; so, what's the big deal? This argument is appealing for two reasons: first, the fiction-ality of video game actions cannot be denied; and second, many people take an innocent pleasure in doing bad things in video games. We should not forget Young's (2013) point, that acting out taboos through the fiction of a game can be both pleasurable and valuable, nor Schulzke's (2020) point that games can offer opportunities for experimentation. But again, the fictionality defense is limited in its scope. There are some gamers who take an innocent pleasure in performing taboos in games, but there are other gamers who take a sadistic pleasure in the same actions. For some gamers, the actions they perform express something of their real-world values and attitudes. What is morally condemnable in these cases is not the fictional action, but instead is the player's values and attitudes. Think of the earlier example of Smith, whose brother likes to bully her: it is not "just a game" when the player's actions are motivated by their real-world vicious motivations.

See also: Carroll, Jacobson, Taylor, Woodcock, this volume

REFERENCES

Ali, Rami. 2015. "A New Solution to the Gamer's Dilemma." *Ethics and Information Technology* 17: 267–274.

Apperley, Thomas, and Jayemanne, Darshana. 2012. "Game Studies' Material Turn." *Westminster Papers in Communication and Culture* 9(1): 5–25.

Bartel, Christopher. 2012. "Resolving the Gamer's Dilemma." *Ethics and Information Technology* 14: 11–16.

Bartel, Christopher. 2015. "Free Will and Moral Responsibility in Video Games." *Ethics and Information Technology* 17: 285–293.

Bartel, Christopher. 2020. *Video Games, Violence, and the Ethics of Fantasy.* New York: Bloomsbury.

Bartel, Christopher, and Cremaldi, Anna 2018. "It's Just a Story: Pornography, Desire, and the Ethics of Fictive Imagining." *British Journal of Aesthetics* 58(1): 37–50.

Beck, Victoria, Stephanie Boys, Christopher Rose, and Eric Beck. 2012. "Violence Against Women in Video Games: A Prequel or Sequel to Rape Myth Acceptance?" *Journal of Interpersonal Violence* 27(15): 3016–3031.

Bogost, Ian. 2008. "The Rhetoric of Games." In *The Ecology of Games: Connecting Youth, Games, and Learning,* edited by Katie Salen, 117–140. Cambridge, MA: The MIT Press.

Bourne, Craig and Emily Caddick Bourne. 2019. "Players, Characters, and the Gamer's Dilemma." *Journal of Aesthetics and Art Criticism* 77(2): 133–143.

Carroll, Noel. 1996. "Moderate Moralism." *British Journal of Aesthetics* 36(3): 223–238.

Clement, J. 2020. "Data Volume of Global Consumer Internet Traffic from 2017 to 2022, by Subsegment." Statista.com, February 28. https://www.statista.com/statistics/267194/forecast-of-internet-traffic-by-subsegment/.

Cocking, Dean, and Jeroen van den Hoven. 2018. *Evil Online.* Hoboken, NJ: Wiley Blackwell.

Condis, Megan. 2018. *Gaming Masculinity: Trolls, Fake Geeks, and the Gendered Battle for Online Culture.* Iowa City: University of Iowa Press.

Consalvo, Mia. 2012. "Confronting Toxic Gamer Culture: A Challenge for Feminist Game Studies Scholars." *Ada: A Journal of Gender, New Media, and Technology* 1.

Cubitt, Sean. 2017. *Finite Media: Environmental Implications of Digital Technologies.* Durham, NC: Duke University Press.

Davnall, Rebecca. 2020. "What Does the Gamer Do?" *Ethics and Information Technology.* doi.org/10.1007/s10676-020-09558-8.

Dill, Karen, Brian Brown, and Michael Collins. 2008. "Effects of Exposure to Sex-Stereotyped Video Game Characters on Tolerance of Sexual Harassment." *Journal of Experimental Social Psychology* 44(5): 1402–1408.

Downs, Edward, and Stacy Smith. 2010. "Keeping Abreast of Hypersexuality: A Video Game Character Content Analysis." *Sex Roles* 62: 721–733.

Dyer-Witheford, Nick, and Greig de Peuter. 2009. *Games of Empire: Global Capitalism and Video Games*. Minneapolis: University of Minnesota Press.

Eaton, A. W. 2003. "Where Ethics and Aesthetics Meet: Titian's *Rape of Europa*." *Hypatia* 18(4): 159–188.

Eaton, A. W. 2010. "Rough Heroes of the New Hollywood." *Revue Internationale de Philosophie* 4 (no. 254): 511–524.

Gaut, Berys. 1998. "The Ethical Criticism of Art." In *Aesthetics and Ethics: Essays at the Intersection*, edited by Jerrold Levinson, 182–203. Cambridge: Cambridge University Press.

Gabbiadini, Alessandro, Paolo Riva, Luca Andrighetto, Chiara Volpato, and Brad Bushman. 2016. "Acting Like a Tough Guy: Violent-Sexist Video Games, Identification with Game Characters, Masculine Beliefs, and Empathy for Female Violence Victims." *PLoS ONE* 11(4): e0152121.

Gestos, Meghan, Jennifer Smith-Merry, and Andrew Campbell. 2018. "Representation of Women in Video Games: A Systematic Review of Literature in Consideration of Adult Female Wellbeing." *Cyberpsychology, Behavior and Social Networking* 21(9): 535–541.

Giovannelli, Alessandro. 2013. "Ethical Criticism in Perspective: A Defense of Radical Moralism." *Journal of Aesthetics and Art Criticism* 71(4): 335–348.

Harold, James. 2003. "Flexing the Imagination." *Journal of Aesthetics and Art Criticism* 61(3): 247–257.

Howe, Leslie. 2004. "Gamesmanship." *Journal of the Philosophy of Sport* 31(2): 212–225.

Hussain, Zaheer, and Mark Griffiths. 2008. "Gender Swapping and Socializing in Cyberspace: An Exploratory Study." *CyberPsychology and Behavior* 11(1): 47–53.

Juul, Jesper. 2005. *Half-Real*. Cambridge, MA: The MIT Press.

Kieran, Matthew. 2003. "Forbidden Knowledge: The Challenge of Cognitive Immoralism." In *Art and Morality*, edited by Sebastian Gardner and José Luis Bermúdez, 56–73. New York: Routledge

Kissel, Andrew. 2020. "Free Will, the Self, and Video Game Actions." *Ethics and Information Technology* 23: 177–183. doi.org/10.1007/s10676-020-09542-2.

Kjeldgaard-Christiansen, Jens. 2020. "Splintering the Gamer's Dilemma: Moral Intuitions, Motivational Assumptions, and Action Prototypes." *Ethics and Information Technology* 22: 93–102.

Kline, Stephen, Nick Dyer-Witheford, and Greig de Peuter. 2003. *Digital Play: The Interaction of Technology, Culture, and Marketing*. Montreal: McGill-Queen's University Press.

Kocurek, Carly 2015. *Coin-Operated Americans: Rebooting Boyhood at the Video Game Arcade*. Minneapolis: University of Minnesota Press.

Luck, Morgan. 2009. "The Gamer's Dilemma: An Analysis of the Arguments for the Moral Distinction between Virtual Murder and Virtual Paedophilia." *Ethics and Information Technology* 11: 31–36.

Luck, Morgan. 2022. "The Grave Resolution to the Gamer's Dilemma: An Argument for a Moral Distinction Between Virtual Murder and Virtual Child Molestation." *Philosophia* 50: 1287–1308.

Lynch, Teresa, Jessica Tompkins, Irene van Driel, and Niki Fritz. 2016. "Sexy, Strong and Secondary: A Content Analysis of Female Characters in Video Games across 31 Years." *Journal of Communication* 66(4): 564–584.

Malkowski, Jennifer, and TreaAndrea Russworm. 2017. *Gaming Representation: Race, Gender, and Sexuality in Video Games*. Bloomington: Indiana University Press.

Mantz, Jeffrey. 2008. "Blood Diamonds in the Digital Age: Coltan and the Eastern Congo." *Global Studies Review* 4(3): 12–14.

Maxwell, Jini. 2020. "Videogames Have a Conflict Mineral Problem." *Screen Hub*, November 24. https://www.screenhub.com.au/news-article/features/digital/jini-maxwell/videogames-have-a-conflict-mineral-problem-261507.

McCormick, Matt. 2001. "Is It Wrong to Play Violent Video Games?" *Ethics and Information Technology* 3: 277–287.

Mortensen, Torill Elvira. 2018. "Anger, Fear, and Games: The Long Event of #GamerGate." *Games and Culture* 13(8): 787–806.

Murray, Soraya. 2017. *On Video Games: The Visual Politics of Race, Gender and Space*. London: I. B. Tauris.

Patridge, Stephanie. 2011. "The Incorrigible Social Meaning of Video Game Imagery." *Ethics and Information Technology* 13: 303–312.

Ramirez, Erick Jose. 2020. "How to (Dis)Solve the Gamer's Dilemma." *Ethics and Information Technology* 23: 141–161.

Ryland, Helen. 2019. "Getting Away with Murder: Why Virtual Murder in MMORPGs can be Wrong on Kantian Grounds." *Ethics and Information Technology* 21: 105–115.

Salter, Anastasia, and Bridget Blodgett. 2012. "Hypermasculinity and Dickwolves: The Contentious Role of Women in the New Gaming Public." *Journal of Broadcasting and Electronic Media* 56(3): 401–416.

Schulzke, Marcus. 2020. *Simulating Good and Evil*. New Brunswick, NJ: Rutgers University Press.

Seddon, Robert. 2013. "Getting 'Virtual' Wrongs Right." *Ethics and Information Technology* 15: 1–11.

Shachtman, Noah. 2008. "Inside Africa's 'PlayStation War.'" *Wired*, July 15. https://www.wired.com/2008/07/the-playstation-2/

Shaw, Adrienne. 2015. *Gaming at the Edge: Sexuality and Gender at the Margins of Gamer Culture*. Minneapolis: University of Minnesota Press.

Sicart, Miguel. 2009. *The Ethics of Computer Games*. Cambridge, MA: The MIT Press.

Stermer, S. Paul and Burkley, Melissa. 2015. "SeX-Box: Exposure to Sexist Video Games Predicts Benevolent Sexism." *Psychology of Popular Media Culture* 4(1): 47–55.

Tavinor, Grant. 2009. *The Art of Videogames*. Hoboken, NJ: Wiley Blackwell.

Tillson, John. 2018. "Is It Distinctively Wrong to Simulate Doing Wrong?" *Ethics and Information Technology* 20: 205–217.

Weimer, Steven. 2012. "Consent and Right Action in Sport." *Journal of the Philosophy of Sport* 39(1): 11–31.

Williams, Dmitri, Nicole Martins, Mia Consalvo, and James Ivory. 2009. "The Virtual Census: Representations of Gender, Race and Age in Video Games." *New Media and Society* 11(5): 815–834.

Yee, Nick. 2014. *The Proteus Paradox*. New Haven, CT: Yale University Press.

Young, Garry. 2013. *Ethics in the Virtual World*. Durham, NC: Acumen.

Young, Garry. 2016. *Resolving the Gamer's Dilemma*. London: Palgrave Macmillan.

Young, Garry. 2020. *Fictional Immorality and Immoral Fiction*. New York: Lexington Books.

CHAPTER 31

ART AND PORNOGRAPHY

Ethical Issues

A. W. EATON

THIS chapter offers a critical overview of recent philosophical literature on erotic art and pornography as well as some suggestions about new directions for inquiry, all with an eye toward ethical issues that arise in these areas. The first section surveys philosophical discussions of the purported distinction between art and pornography. The next section considers new areas of inquiry that arise once we shift focus to the connections and similarities between erotic art and pornography. Once we put the pornography literature and the aesthetics-and-ethics literature into conversation with one another, new areas of inquiry open up, including: the harms and benefits that come from engaging with libidinous representations, applications of speech act theory to libidinous representations, and philosophical and ethical issues pertaining to fiction, imagination, and fantasy. Finally, the chapter concludes with a discussion of sex positivity and social justice issues related to libidinous representations.

Before we begin, I would like to make some remarks about terminology. Unless otherwise specified, "art" is here construed broadly to include popular culture, and "pornography" is treated not as a monolith, but rather as a diverse category of representation that includes queer porn and feminist porn, to name only a few. I also construe "ethics" and "ethical value" broadly to include social justice concerns such as (listed in alphabetical order) ableism, classicism, fatism, homo-negativity, racism, sexism, and trans-negativity.

Finally, there is a trigger warning for this chapter. At various points I will be mentioning rape and other forms of sexual violence, pedophilia, racialized violence, and eroticizing representations of these things, although I do not discuss any of this in vivid detail.

DISTINCTIONS BETWEEN ART AND PORN

What, if anything, is the difference between pornography and erotic art? While I have serious doubts about the value of asking this sort of question, it is true that most of the philosophical literature on erotic art and pornography focuses on the "line-drawing" problem, as Hans Maes calls it (Maes 2011; 2014; 2013; Mikkola 2019, sec. 6.3). Since it is one job of a handbook chapter to orient the reader toward relevant literature, I begin by briefly surveying philosophical discussions of the purported distinction between art and pornography. Only after surveying the literature do I turn to the question of the point and value of drawing such distinctions.

Let us begin with the candidate features that might demarcate erotic art from pornography:

(a) Representational content: pornography is sexually explicit whereas erotic art is merely sexually suggestive.
(b) Aesthetic quality: pornography is one-dimensional and lacks any "redeeming artistic value" whereas erotic art is complex and artistically valuable.
(c) Prescribed responses or function: pornography functions merely as an aid in sexual activity (often said to be "arousal and release") whereas erotic art serves to inspire imaginative activity and aesthetic appreciation of its forms.
(d) Ethical differences: whereas pornography is ethically flawed, erotic art is not, or at least is not to the same extent as pornography.

Given the topic of this volume, (d) will be our focus, but before we come to this we should briefly run through the first three. Nowadays most reject (a) because there exists pornography that is not sexually explicit—for example, foot fetish porn that represents only feet and does not depict any sexual acts (Mikkola 2019, sec. 6.3). Further, some works that are uncontestably considered "high art" are quite sexually explicit (Kieran 2001; van Brabandt and Prinz 2013), and not only contemporary works that intentionally transgress boundaries but also lots of older works in the European tradition (Eaton 2018). (b) has been widely rejected on similar grounds. Some pornography is artistically interesting (Maes 2011; 2011; 2014; 2013; van Brabandt and Prinz 2013). Further, there are many examples of erotic works whose artistic status is undisputed yet that are nevertheless formulaic and artistically flat; consider, for instance, some of the paintings in Titian's *Venus and Musician* series or many of Bouguereau's nudes.

A more promising, but also more complicated, way of drawing the distinction is (c). Recall that (c) distinguishes between pornography and erotic art in terms of function (where "function" may mean the purpose that the artist intended, the prescribed response, or "normal" or "reasonable" use).[1] Often, the idea is that pornography functions

---

[1] Michael Rea offers a definition that focuses on whether it is reasonable to believe that the work in question is used in ways that he specifies (Rea 2001).

as an aid or accompaniment to sexual activity whereas erotic art serves to inspire imaginative activity or aesthetic appreciation of its forms. Some argue that these two functions are incompatible (Levinson 2005; Mag Uidhir 2009; Scruton 2009). Others argue that these two functions can be compatible, thereby allowing that a single work can be both art and pornography (Sontag 1994; Kieran 2001; Maes 2013; Davies 2013). And some argue against a difference in function of this sort in the first place (Eaton 2018).

This brings us to (d), which posits an ethical distinction between erotic art and pornography. Some feminists, like Helen Longino and Andrea Dworkin and Catharine MacKinnon, may appear to implicitly resolve the question of the difference between art and porn terminologically by defining *pornography* as sexually explicit material that is ethically flawed in the sense that it plays a specifiable and significant role in perpetuating sexism.[2] One might expect these views to yield a crisp distinction between art and pornography, where erotic art would be sexually explicit material that is not ethically problematic in the very specific way that pornography is. It should be noted that this would not preclude the possibility that erotic art could be ethically problematic in other ways; that is, on such a view "erotic art" need not be defined or characterized as ethically pure. But even in cases where erotic art is ethically problematic, by stipulation, it would not be ethically problematic in the specific way that pornography is, at least on this view.

If such definitions aim to capture widely accepted understandings of "erotic art" and "pornography" and of the distinction between them, then they would appear to miss their mark. One problem is that such definitions do not appear to countenance feminist pornography and other kinds of porn that promote social justice (and so are ethically salutary in this way and to this extent).[3] Another problem is that such definitions appear to disregard works with undisputed high art status that arguably also participate in perpetuating gender injustice, such as Renaissance paintings that eroticize rape or works belonging to the European genre of the white female nude (Eaton 2013; Lavallee 2016).

However, I hold that antiporn feminism is most usefully and charitably understood not as stipulating necessary and sufficient conditions for "pornography," but rather as drawing our attention to and explaining ethically problematic features of the dominant form of mainstream heterosexual pornography, which I dub *inegalitarian pornography* (Eaton 2007). These ethically problematic features include the harms brought about through the production of pornography, the harms caused directly or indirectly through the use of pornography, and the subordination constituted by pornographic materials themselves.[4] On my view, if antiporn feminism is to single out (inegalitarian)

---

[2] I say "implicitly" because these thinkers are not explicitly concerned with distinguishing between "art" and "pornography." Further, when Catharine MacKinnon says that pornography is "not a moral issue," she means to distance her concerns with pornography from worries about obscenity, not to disavow the expanded sense of "ethics" employed in this essay.

[3] On feminist pornography, see Taormino et al. (2013), Eaton (2017), and Mikkola (2019, chap. 7).

[4] For thorough accounts of these, including analyses of criticisms, see Mikkola (2019, chaps. 1–5), and Altman and Watson (2018, pt. II).

pornography, it should be on the basis of its peculiarly egregious role in promoting gender injustice. This would allow feminists to locate porn on a continuum of other representational forms—coming from, for instance, high art and popular culture—that also promote gender injustice and would not commit antiporn feminists to the specious claim that among representational forms all and only pornography promotes gender injustice.

It is my view that most *art-distinction projects*—by which I mean, any project whose primary aim is to distinguish "art" from other kinds of artifact or practice—are themselves ethically problematic to some degree.[5] The ethical problem is this. Most art-distinction projects, whether explicitly or implicitly, take "art" to be a category of commendation, where it is argued that precisely those features that make art especially praiseworthy also distinguish it from other kinds of artifact or practice with which it might mistakenly be confused. Art-distinction projects invariably, in my experience, tell us that "art" is unique in one or more of a variety of ways: it encourages aesthetic appreciation (which is itself unique among modes of appreciation), it produces the highest sort of pleasure (again, distinct from other kinds of pleasure), it is produced by way of special and rarified skills, it is created for its own sake and lacks or at least is not characterized by practical function, and so on. The kinds of artifacts and practices that end up meeting the criteria for "art" almost never come from mass culture, popular culture, domestic spaces, indigenous traditions, non-European traditions, or traditions of enslaved peoples. This is no accident since, after all, the whole point of distinction projects (whether explicit or not) is to distinguish "art" from neighboring kinds of artifacts and practices with which it might be confused. But unlike other kinds of distinction projects that one might pursue—for example, distinguishing cars from trucks—*art*-distinction projects usually aim to explain not just how artworks are different from other kinds of things, but also how artworks are *better* than these other sorts of things. What, to my knowledge, always results is a class of artifacts and practices marked off as superior that coincide with works from the European tradition that are mostly produced by and for white upper-class men. In this way, art-distinction projects take their place as part of a larger machinery that supports, and sometimes even promotes, unethical gender, race, and class hierarchies.

Proponents of art-distinction projects may protest that this was never their aim. We should take them at their word. But good intentions do not redeem these projects. When one looks closely at the features that purportedly distinguish art from other artifacts and practices, and when one considers which traditions and kinds of artifact and practice fall on the "not art" side of the distinction, one always, to my knowledge, finds traditional class, racial, or (conjunctive) gender hierarchies being reinforced. This is as true of attempts to distinguish "erotic art" from "pornography" as it is of attempts to distinguish "art" from "craft." As I have argued elsewhere, we should think pragmatically about the

---

[5] To be clear, I do not mean to be singling out projects that aim simply at *definitions* of art. Definitions of art need not take *art* to be a category of commendation that picks out a special group of high-quality artifacts and practices; e.g., institutional definitions of art.

erotic art/pornography distinction and ask ourselves what work this distinction does (Eaton 2018). What does it accomplish?[6] If, as I have also argued, one primary function of the erotic art/porn distinction is to secure special exalted status for the artifacts and practices made by and for members of the upper classes, thereby reinforcing and maintaining class hierarchy, then we ought not spend any more time and energy trying to locate and shore up the distinction (Eaton 2018, secs. 4 and 5).[7] For this reason, in the remainder of this chapter I will be discussing the broader class of "libidinous works"— that is, works that have as a central function stimulating the audience's sexual appetite, which usually represent sexual acts and unclothed bodies (Eaton 2018, 417)—and when I use the terms *erotic art* and *pornography*, I mean not to be endorsing the distinction, but rather to refer to the libidinous works that have been conventionally labeled as such.

New Directions for Inquiry

I have just urged that philosophers stop worrying about the line-drawing problem altogether. Instead we should focus on other issues and on cross-pollination between relevant areas of research. For instance, might theoretical and empirical work on pornography shed new light on erotic art? Might work in philosophy of art and philosophical aesthetics, including philosophical thought about erotic art, promote a better and more nuanced understanding of pornography? The rest of this chapter is devoted to outlining some new directions.

Harms and Benefits

One fertile area of study for both philosophers interested in pornography and those working on erotic art is the question of whether and how a given libidinous work influences its audiences and the broader society with which work and audience interact. As it happens, however, this issue has been handled in quite different ways in the two literatures, and each field has investigated these questions in almost total ignorance of the other.[8] It is my view that each area of inquiry has much to offer the other, and it is my hunch that exchange between those who do empirical work on pornography, feminist theorists and philosophers, and philosophers of art would be extremely fruitful when it comes to thinking about how libidinous works affect their audiences.

---

[6] This is the sort of question that Haslanger recommends in her *ameliorative* or *revisionary* approach to thinking about these kinds of terms (Haslanger 2000).

[7] This thought owes much to Pierre Bourdieu's *Distinction* (Bourdieu 1984).

[8] Since there has been, to my knowledge, no work on how specifically *erotic* artworks affect their audiences, I discuss the literature on artworks more broadly and assume that whatever philosophers have to say about this also applies mutatis mutandis to erotic artworks.

For a long time, psychologists, sociologists, feminist theorists, and legal scholars who study pornography tended to focus almost exclusively on pornography's purportedly negative influence on its audience's beliefs, desires, and physiological responses (although these are not always so clearly distinguished) and, via these channels, its negative influence on the broader society in which it is used.[9] These negative influences are thought to pertain primarily to gender, although some also consider its connection with race, disability, age, and body size—all areas that deserve more attention. The bulk of this research amounts to incriminating or defending pornography by trying to prove or disprove these purported negative effects. The models employed in this research have traditionally been conditioning models (in particular desensitization and exposure effects) or imitation models, relying on different kinds of empirical evidence.[10] There have been two recent developments in this literature that are relevant to the matter at hand. First, there is a burgeoning industry of feminist porn that aims to promote gender and racial equity, body positivity, sex positivity, and trans and queer positivity. Scholars are beginning to investigate the potentially positive influence that these works may have on their audiences and beyond, although much more empirical work needs to be done (Taormino et al. 2013; Eaton 2017; Mikkola 2017, pt. IV; 2019, chap. 7). Second, feminist theorists and philosophers have proposed interesting models for how pornography affects its audiences, such as the silencing model (Langton 1993; MacKinnon 1996; Mikkola 2019, chap. 3) and the presupposition-accommodation model (Langton and West 2009; Langton 2012). So far as I know, no empirical work has been done on these models.

Whereas the scholarship on pornography has tended to focus on its purportedly *negative* effects on its audiences and beyond (by either supporting or denying claims about said effects), philosophers of art have for decades eagerly focused on artworks' *positive* impact on their audiences, with little attention to possible negative impacts. The models employed here include catharsis models, imitation models, and conditioning models (especially sensitization rather than desensitization which tends to be the focus in the pornography literature).[11] But the majority of the focus in the philosophy of art has been on what some call *aesthetic cognitivism*, the idea that artworks can be an important source of moral knowledge (propositional knowledge or, more often in this literature, nonpropositional sorts of knowledge).[12]

---

[9] See Eaton (2007), Mikkola (2019, chap. 2), and Altman and Watson (2018) for a discussion.

[10] See Eaton (2007) for a critical discussion of the empirical evidence, and Langton (2012) for a discussion of the different models employed. See Altman and Watson (2018) for a recent discussion of the evidence for and the evidence against these harms.

[11] See Eaton (2016) for an overview.

[12] At first blush, this might not seem to be a question of art's *effects* on its audiences, but I think that it is. A work or, if you prefer, an artist might provide, or aim to provide, various ethical lessons, but an audience can be said to *learn* these lessons only if they are absorbed, and this is a question of a work's impact on its audience. This, by the way, is an empirical question, although many do not appear to recognize it as such; exceptions are Gregorie Currie (2011; 2013) and Harold (2014; 2020).

These two fields of inquiry have much to learn from one another. To begin with, research on pornography should take seriously the idea that some pornography—perhaps certain genres or styles—can have a beneficial impact on its audiences and on the broader society in which they live, much in the way that philosophers of art claim that artworks do. Similarly, philosophers of art should give more attention to the idea that artworks, even some works considered to be "masterpieces," can do harm. In both cases, the various models for how libidinous works affect their audiences should be shared, compared, and studied across the board in all of their complexity. Those who study pornography would benefit from engaging the subtleties of aesthetic cognitivist models, especially given that young people turn to pornography to learn about sex.[13] Philosophers of art, on the other hand, would do well to take seriously imitation and conditioning models of influence rather than dismiss them as overly simplistic.[14]

Along these lines, philosophers of art should also be interested in Langton's accommodation model as a possible way that libidinous works can affect their audiences.[15] Langton's accommodation model should be of special interest to philosophers of art because it depends on the work in question having a certain amount of authority, and whereas some have questioned whether pornography has the requisite authority (Bauer 2015, Chapters 5 and 7), no one to my knowledge has considered whether works deemed "high art" might have the requisite authority in virtue of their exalted status.[16] Similar things could be said about the silencing arguments made by antiporn feminists (MacKinnon 1988; 1996; Hornsby et al. 2011; Hornsby 1993; Mikkola 2019, Chapters 2 and 3). Silencing arguments also require that the work purportedly doing the silencing have a certain amount of authority (Mikkola 2019, Chapter 4). Might some erotic artworks silence or subordinate? This area is ripe for exploration.

Speech Acts

A different feminist critique of pornography focuses not on porn's effects on its audiences, but rather on its *illocutionary actions*. This is what is sometimes called the *constitutive subordination* claim, as opposed to the causal subordination claim discussed in the previous section (Mikkola 2019, Chapter 2). Constitutive subordination accounts grow out of Austinian speech act theory, and in what follows I underline the actions that pornography purportedly performs. Rae Langton famously argues that pornography performs several speech acts: (1) it *ranks* women as inferior sex objects, and (2) it *legitimates* rape and other kinds of sexualized violence against women (Langton 1993). Although she appeals to Austin very little, Catharine MacKinnon also argues that what

---

[13] For summaries of aesthetic cognitivism, see Eaton (2016) and Harold (2020, chap. 4). See Rothman et al. (2015) for a critical overview of the sex research literature.

[14] See Harold (2020), especially Chapter 2, for a discussion of these models.

[15] For a recent critique of Langton's model, see Heck (2021).

[16] I briefly consider this in Eaton (2013; 2018), but much more needs to be said.

pornography, as well as hate speech and propaganda, does is *promote* and *enact* the power of one social group over another (MacKinnon 1996). More recently, Mary Kate McGowan develops an account of conversational exercitives that covertly *enact norms* for the conversations in which they contribute, and she uses this to show how pornography and racist speech *enact discriminatory norms* (McGowan 2019).

As I urged in the previous section, the philosophy of art would benefit from taking these arguments seriously and exploring their potential application—likely with modifications—to works considered to be "erotic art." How might artworks of various sorts, from high art painting to video games, rank women as inferior, legitimate sexual violence, and covertly enact discriminatory norms?[17] While there has been some exploration of these issues, much more needs to be done (Eaton 2003; 2013; Patridge 2013). As these issues are pursued, we should be wary of the extent to which speech act theory can be applied to pictorial representations; this, by the way, is a criticism that some have made of Langton and others using speech act theory to understand pornography (Antony 2011; Bauer 2015). Pictures represent in ways that are, on most any account, quite different from the ways that language represents (Hyman and Bantinaki 2021). Perhaps pictorial acts, if there can be such things, also work in ways or have characteristics that are importantly different from language?[18] This is a topic that the philosophy of art is especially well-suited to explore, and the fruits of this exploration, whatever they be, should be brought back to the feminist accounts mentioned above.

In the conclusion of her book, McGowan briefly considers the ways in which conversational exercitives can enact egalitarian and otherwise ethically positive norms (McGowan 2019, 184–189). This is something that it would be fruitful for everyone working on libidinous works to explore. If some libidinous works can, say, rank women as inferior, might others promote women and rank them as equals? How might libidinous works enact egalitarian norms for women, and especially for women of color, disabled women, trans women, and fat women (where of course these groups intersect)?

Fiction, Imagination, and Fantasy

Fiction, imagination, and fantasy are important topics when it comes to thinking about the contents, functions, and effects of libidinous representations.[19] (See also Bartel, this volume.) These are also topics that, at least with respect to libidinous representations, are not typically treated with the subtlety and sophistication that they merit. This is one

---

[17] For an art historical exploration of these topics in early modern European art, see Wolfthal (2000).

[18] On a related point, José Medina criticizes Jason Stanley's account of propaganda for its excessively linguistic focus and begins to outline a new way of thinking about how pictures can promote an ideology (Medina 2018).

[19] For the purposes of this chapter, I shall assume that fantasy is an especially vivid kind of imagining that usually involves some fictional elements and often is almost entirely fictional. However, for a subtle account of this issue, see Todd (2013).

of the ways in which the philosophy of art has much to offer our understanding of libidinous representations and how they work, since fiction and imagination have long been important topics in the field.

To begin with, it is not possible to cleanly sort libidinous works or libidinous imaginings into "fictional" and "nonfictional," nor is it a simple matter to sort the fictional elements of a given libidinous work from the nonfictional elements. For instance, while most mainstream pornographic videos rely on fictional plots, they also centrally involve real people having actual sex (McGlynn 2021, 12). Most works of erotic art, by contrast, tend to depict fictional persons in fictional scenarios, and yet as theorists of fiction have long noted, these often draw from and reflect real-word phenomena, something that may make a significant ethical difference when it comes to things like eroticizing representations of rape. So before we can even get off the ground with the interesting issues outlined below, more work needs to be done in sorting through the connections between fiction and fantasy with respect to libidinous representations.

It is common for defenders of violently misogynist pornography (and to a lesser extent violently misogynist erotic art) to argue that it is neither harmful nor constitutively subordinating precisely because said representations are or centrally contain fictions. Let us call this the *fiction defense*.[20] Fiction defenses tend to assume that imaginative activity is discrete from a person's character and real-world actions.[21] These defenses often rely heavily on intuition pumps and personal introspection. For instance, some men report that while they may have sexual fantasies about fictional rape, they have never raped anyone nor do they have any desire to actually do so. After all, the argument continues, women are known to have rape fantasies, and, of course, these women do not actually desire to be raped. It follows, so the argument concludes, that there is nothing ethically wrong, at least from the perspective of those who care about consequences, with fantasizing (sexually or otherwise) about harming others, nor is there anything ethically wrong with representations that prescribe or solicit such responses.

However intuitive, arguments like these move too quickly through complicated terrain, some features of which I now briefly unpack but which deserve much more careful attention.

First, it is not clear that fiction and imagination are exempt from ethical scrutiny, even when we bracket considerations regarding consequences. Is there anything ethically wrong with merely fantasizing about doing harm to others?[22] And is there anything ethically wrong with representations that prescribe, cater to, or otherwise encourage fantasizing about doing harm to others? Answering the second question depends on our answer to the first, yet not enough work has been done on the first question; further, the

---

[20] There are many versions of the fiction defense. See Langton and West (2009) for a perspicuous formulation and response and Mikkola (2019, Chapter 6) and McGlynn (2021, secs. 3 and 4) for recent analyses and responses.

[21] An example is Cooke (2013).

[22] We should be clear to distinguish here between fantasizing about doing immoral things and fantasizing about *simulating* the act of doing immoral things. See Hopkins (1994).

work that has been done has rarely been brought into conversation with work on libidinous representations.[23] Some argue on virtue-ethical grounds that it is ethically wrong to fantasize about doing immoral things (Bartel and Cremaldi 2018; Bartel 2020) while others argue from the structure of fantasy itself that it is usually not wrong to fantasize about doing immoral things (Kershnar 2005), and of course there are other positions worth developing and exploring.

Other difficulties arising with fiction defenses pertain to consequences. Does the fictional status of most fantasies prevent the fantasized content from making its way into our real-world psychology or from leafing out into action? This is a complicated question that the empirical literature has not settled.

Another problem with fiction defenses is that they tend to assume a *mimetic* relationship between (a) the content of the fantasies to which pornography caters or that it promotes and (b1) the content of the audience's actual beliefs and desires about real-world counterparts, or (b2) the audience's actions toward real-world counterparts.[24]

In some ways, it seems plausible to think about pornography's effects on its audiences as mimetic. For instance, there is mounting evidence that pornography, especially when used as sex education by young people (which it is in the United States because our formal sex education is terrible), does have a mimetic effect when it comes to things regarding the mechanics of different kinds of sex acts (Hare et al. 2015; Orenstein 2016; Jones 2018; Miller et al. 2019).

While positing a mimetic relationship may seem unobjectionable in such cases, it strikes many defenders of misogynistically violent pornography and erotic art as untenable in cases where the content of the fantasy is recognized by the subject to be immoral or is at least unequivocally prohibited in the society in which he finds himself. This is often said about pornography whose content is rape, racialized sexual violence, or pedophilia, all of which are at least in theory illegal or otherwise officially in the United States. The idea, then, is that the legal and moral prohibitions would work, perhaps in conjunction with the subject's own moral codes or ethical outlook, to prevent the fantasized content from (a) infecting the subject's actual beliefs, desires, and tastes, and (b) from leafing out into action.

However, things are rarely this simple. For one thing, people often do things that they know to be illegal or in violation of their own moral codes; indeed, there is an entire philosophical tradition built around trying to understand and explain this. For another thing, we must consider not just the subject's own explicitly acknowledged ethical codes and the applicable legal norms, but also the broader social context. Consider

---

[23] For philosophical work on the ethics of fantasy, see Corvino (2002), Neu (2002), Kreitman (2006), and Kershnar (2008; 2005). With the exception of Corvino, these treatments are not especially sensitive to issues of gender and race. For more recent treatments that are sensitive to issues of gender and race, see Bartel and Cremaldi (2018), Bartel (2020), and on a closely related topic, see Patridge (2013). An important recent work on the question of norms and sexual fantasy and practices is Alcoff (2018, Chapter 3).

[24] See also Hurley (2004) for a detailed defense of a more general mimetic paradigm. For a recent discussion of such matters with respect to art, see Harold (2020, Chapter 2).

the example of rape. While it is true that rape is illegal, it is also true that it is extremely common, woefully underpunished, openly advocated in some circles, and encouraged and eroticized in many aspects of our culture; this is what it means to say that we live in a *rape culture*.[25] My point is that we need to be very cautious about what we infer from the mere illegality of an act; an act may be simultaneously illegal yet widely tolerated and even promoted throughout a society, and so there might not be the forceful prohibitions to the expression of fantasy that one might have expected when considering only laws.

But this is not necessarily to endorse the mimetic picture. It is my view that assuming the mimetic picture undermines careful thought on all sides of the debate about the ethical status of libidinous representations. There is no reason to assume that the only way, or even the most common way, for fantasizing to have a lasting impact on the fantasizer is for the exact fantasized content to be absorbed into the fantasizer's actual beliefs and desires and imitated toward real-world counterparts. A man who masturbates to rape porn (or, for that matter, erotic art with rape themes) might never rape anyone, but he might be more prone to things like: sexual harassment (where this is a spectrum, and so they might harass severely or only mildly), micro-aggressions, taking women less seriously, or disbelieving women who report rape, sexual harassment, and other kinds of gender-based harms, to name only a few.[26] The diversity and subtlety of potential effects of our interactions with libidinous works needs spelling out and empirical research needs to take account of this.

The last thing to note is that the idea that a person's imaginative engagement with fiction influences their actual psychology (their beliefs, desires, hopes, likings, etc.), and perhaps also behavior, is a cornerstone of the ethics-and-aesthetics literature, and further, this literature rarely assumes a mimetic picture of the sort discussed above.[27] This should not, of course, stand in for empirical evidence, but those who want to explore the question of how, if at all, fantasizing with libidinous pictures affects the fantasizer would do well to consult the various sophisticated arguments for the idea that vivid imaginative engagement has lasting effects on the moral psychology of the imaginer.

SEX-POSITIVITY AND SOCIAL JUSTICE

I conclude with some final very important interconnected points. To begin with, everyone working on libidinous images—whether on those considered to be "art" or on those considered to be "pornography"—should take seriously arguments from sex-positivity and body-positivity to the effect that sexualization is not in itself necessarily a

---

[25] There is much to read on rape culture. Some recent works that I find especially helpful include: Harding (2015); Manne (2017); Alcoff (2018); Gay (2018).

[26] See Eaton (2007) for a discussion of the subtlety of the variety of possible effects.

[27] This literature is too vast to summarize here. See Eaton (2016, pt. I), Gregory Currie (2020, pt. III), and Harold (2020, Chapters 1, 2, and 4).

bad thing (Cahill 2012). There is not necessarily anything in itself ethically or politically wrong with vividly representing nudity or sex in ways that call for erotic responses from their audience. This is true even when the persons featured in such representations are members of minoritized or oppressed groups.

Libidinous representations can be harmful or otherwise ethically problematic in their promotion of ableist, fatist, homophobic, racist, sexist, and transphobic hierarchies. The kinds of libidinous works that we usually refer to as "erotic art" can participate in and promote these hierarchies just as fully as the works that we call "pornography," even if the modes of participation may be different. But libidinous representations can also be deeply liberatory and can promote social justice. Consider the case of feminist pornography discussed above, and there are many other kinds of libidinous works that undermine unjust social hierarchies by empowering oppressed groups through eroticization. How can being made into what some might call a "sex object" be empowering? As Robin Zheng puts the point, "if certain oppressed and marginalized groups have been deemed aesthetically and sexually unappealing, then pornography [and, I would argue, erotic art] depicting members of such groups as erotically desirable performs an especially important function in destigmatizing and normalizing such bodies in the way required for genuine social equality" (Zheng 2017, 188).

What makes the difference between the empowering and disempowering forms of libidinous image? We might begin by saying that some libidinous representations express or promote attitudes that disempower minoritized or oppressed groups whereas other libidinous representations express or promote attitudes that empower members of minoritized or oppressed groups, but this gets us only so far. A fuller explanation of the differences would have to take into consideration: (a) an analysis of numerous features of the representation in question including formal features, proper function, and its illocutions; (b) empirical information about the representation's effects on its audience, and (c) careful consideration of the role of sexualization and sexualizing representations, or lack thereof, in harmful stereotypes about the particular group in question.

This last point is important and subtle. Social exclusion from sexuality is a significant facet of the oppression of some groups, such as disabled persons (Boer 2015; Danaher 2020). On the other hand, hypersexualization plays an important role in the oppression of other groups, like Black women (Collins 2008; hooks 1992, chap. 4; Collins 2005). On still another (third?) hand, sexual fetishization plays a significant role in the oppression of still others, such as Asian women (Zheng 2016). (Also, please note that the literature on each of these is vast and rich. I tried to choose just a couple of sources that would be useful in orienting the reader.) But of course things are not this simple, first of all because these social identities intersect and second because the role of sexuality in oppression is often even more complex. For instance, sexual fetishization is also an aspect of the oppression of disabled persons, and some groups, such as deaf women, are routinely hypersexualized. In addition to being hypersexualized, Black women and men are routinely sexually fetishized, and Black women are also desexualized. So is a particular work of art that eroticizes a person at the interection of various oppressed groups empowering or disempowering? The answer likely come down to the particularities of the work in question interpreted against the backdrop of the broader patterns just mentioned. These are just a few examples of the complexities involved in thinking through the role of sexuality in stereotypes and other mechanisms of social injustice.

What these complexities mean for artists and producers is that any project of making libidinous representations that have liberatory and empowering functions must maneuver around many potential hazards.[28] One must, as Zheng notes, walk a "fine line between resistance and recapitulation, transgressive and regressive pleasures, fetishization and tokenization" (Zheng 2017, 192). But this is not to say that such projects are impossible; as the vibrant field of feminist pornography demonstrates, there are many ways to navigate this minefield.

See also: Mullin, Bartel, Taylor, Clavel-Vázquez, this volume

REFERENCES

Alcoff, Linda Martín. 2018. *Rape and Resistance*. Cambridge: Polity.

Altman, Andrew, and Lori Watson. 2018. *Debating Pornography*. New York: Oxford University Press.

Antony, Louise. 2011. "Against Langton's Illocutionary Treatment of Pornography." *Jurisprudence* 2, no. 2: 387–401.

Bartel, Christopher. 2020. *Video Games, Violence, and the Ethics of Fantasy: Killing Time*. London: Bloomsbury Academic.

Bartel, Christopher, and Anna Cremaldi. 2018. "'It's Just a Story': Pornography, Desire, and the Ethics of Fictive Imagining." *British Journal of Aesthetics* 58, no. 1: 37–50.

Bauer, Nancy. 2015. *How to Do Things with Pornography*. Cambridge, MA: Harvard University Press.

Boer, Tracy De. 2015. "Disability and Sexual Inclusion." *Hypatia* 30, no. 1: 66–81.

Bourdieu, Pierre. 1984. *Distinction: A Social Critique of the Judgement of Taste*. Translated by Richard Nice. Cambridge, MA: Harvard University Press.

Brabandt, Petra van, and Jesse Prinz. 2013. "Why Do Porn Films Suck?" In *Art and Pornography: Philosophical Essays*, edited by Jerrold Levinson and Hans Maes, 161–190. Oxford: Oxford University Press.

Cahill, Ann J. 2012. *Overcoming Objectification: A Carnal Ethics*. Reprint ed. New York: Routledge.

Collins, Patricia Hill. 2005. *Black Sexual Politics: African Americans, Gender, and the New Racism*. New York: Routledge.

Collins, Patricia Hill. 2008. *Black Feminist Thought: Knowledge, Consciousness, and the Politics of Empowerment*. New York: Routledge.

Cooke, Brandon. 2013. "On the Ethical Distinction Between Art and Pornography." In *Art and Pornography: Philosophical Essays*, edited by Jerrold Levinson and Hans Maes, 229–253. Oxford: Oxford University Press.

Corvino, John. 2002. "Naughty Fantasies." *Southwest Philosophy Review* 18, no. 1: 213–220.

Currie, Gregory. 2011. "Literature and the Psychology Lab." *The Times Literary Supplement*, August 31.

---

[28] Two really important and subtle accounts of these difficulties are Nash (2014) and Zheng (2017).

Currie, Gregory. 2013. "Does Great Literature Make Us Better?" *New York Times: Opinionator*, June 1. http://opinionator.blogs.nytimes.com/2013/06/01/does-great-literature-make-us-better/.

Currie, Gregory. 2020. *Imagining and Knowing: The Shape of Fiction*. New York: Oxford University Press.

Danaher, John. 2020. "A Defence of Sexual Inclusion." *Social Theory and Practice* 46, no. 3: 467–496.

Davies, David. 2013. "Pornography, Art, and the Intended Response of the Receiver." In *Art and Pornography: Philosophical Essays*, edited by Jerrold Levinson and Hans Maes, 61–82. Oxford: Oxford University Press.

Eaton, A. W. 2003. "Where Ethics and Aesthetics Meet: Titian's Rape of Europa." *Hypatia* 18, no. 4: 159–188.

Eaton, A. W. 2007. "A Sensible Antiporn Feminism." *Ethics* 117, no. 4: 674–715.

Eaton, A. W. 2013. "What's Wrong With the Female Nude?" In *Art and Pornography: Philosophical Essays*, edited by Jerrold Levinson and Hans Maes, 277–308. Oxford: Oxford University Press.

Eaton, A. W. 2016. "Literature and Morality." In *The Routledge Companion to Philosophy of Literature*, edited by Noël Carroll and John Gibson, 433–450. London: Routledge & Kegan Paul.

Eaton, A. W. 2017. "Feminist Pornography." In *Beyond Speech: Pornography and Analytic Feminist Philosophy*, edited by Mari Mikkola, 243–257. Oxford: Oxford University Press.

Eaton, A. W. 2018. "'A Lady on the Street but a Freak in the Bed': On the Distinction Between Erotic Art and Pornography." *British Journal of Aesthetics* 58, no. 4: 469–488.

Gay, Roxane. 2018. *Not That Bad: Dispatches from Rape Culture*. Illustrated ed. New York: Harper Perennial.

Harding, Kate. 2015. *Asking for It: The Alarming Rise of Rape Culture—and What We Can Do about It*. Boston: Da Capo Lifelong Books.

Hare, Kathleen A., Jacqueline Gahagan, Lois Jackson, and Audrey Steenbeek. 2015. "Revisualising 'Porn': How Young Adults' Consumption of Sexually Explicit Internet Movies Can Inform Approaches to Canadian Sexual Health Promotion." *Culture, Health & Sexuality* 17, no. 3: 269–283.

Harold, James. 2014. "Damn the Consequences." *Aesthetics for Birds* (blog), August 16. https://aestheticsforbirds.com/2014/08/16/damn-the-consequences-by-james-harold/.

Harold, James. 2020. *Dangerous Art: On Moral Criticisms of Artwork*. New York: Oxford University Press.

Haslanger, Sally. 2000. "Gender and Race: (What) Are They? (What) Do We Want Them To Be?" *Noûs* 34, no. 1: 31–55.

Heck, Richard Kimberly. 2021. "Pornography and Accommodation." *Inquiry* 64, no. 8: 830–860.

hooks, bell. 1992. *Black Looks: Race and Representation*. Boston: South End Press.

Hopkins, Patrick D. 1994. "Rethinking Sadomasochism: Feminism, Interpretation, and Simulation." *Hypatia* 9, no. 1: 116–141.

Hornsby, Jennifer. 1993. "Speech Acts and Pornography." *Women's Philosophy Review* 10: 38–45.

Hornsby, Jennifer, Louise Antony, Jennifer Saul, Natalie Stoljar, Nellie Wieland, and Rae Langton. 2011. "Subordination, Silencing, and Two Ideas of Illocution." *Jurisprudence* 2, no. 2: 379–440.

Hurley, Susan. 2004. "Imitation, Media Violence, and Freedom of Speech." *Philosophical Studies* 117, no. 1–2: 165–218.

Hyman, John, and Katerina Bantinaki. 2021. "Depiction." In *The Stanford Encyclopedia of Philosophy*, edited by Edward N. Zalta, Summer 2021. https://plato.stanford.edu/archives/sum2021/entries/depiction/.

Jones, Maggie. 2018. "What Teenagers Are Learning From Online Porn." *New York Times*, February 7, 2018. https://www.nytimes.com/2018/02/07/magazine/teenagers-learning-onl ine-porn-literacy-sex-education.html.

Kershnar, Stephen. 2005. "The Moral Status of Sexual Fantasies." *Public Affairs Quarterly* 19, no. 4: 301–315.

Kershnar, Stephen. 2008. "Rape Fantasies and Virtue." *Public Affairs Quarterly* 22, no. 3: 253–268.

Kieran, Matthew. 2001. "Pornographic Art." *Philosophy and Literature* 25. no. 1: 31–45.

Kreitman, Norman. 2006. "Fantasy, Fiction, and Feelings." *Metaphilosophy* 37, no. 5: 605–622.

Langton, Rae. 1993. "Speech Acts and Unspeakable Acts." *Philosophy & Public Affairs* 22, no. 4: 293–330.

Langton, Rae. 2012. "Beyond Belief: Pragmatics in Hate Speech and Pornography." In *Speech and Harm: Controversies Over Free Speech*, edited by Ishani Maitra and Mary Kate McGowan, 72–93. Oxford: Oxford University Press.

Langton, Rae, and Caroline West. 2009. "Scorekeeping in a Pornographic Language Game." In *Sexual Solipsism: Philosophical Essays on Pornography and Objectification*, 173–195. New York: Oxford University Press.

Lavallee, Zoey. 2016. "What's Wrong With the (White) Female Nude?" *Estetyka i Krytyka: The Polish Journal of Aesthetics* 2, no. 41: 77–97.

Levinson, Jerrold. 2005. "Erotic Art and Pornographic Pictures." *Philosophy and Literature* 29, no. 1: 228–240.

MacKinnon, Catharine A. 1988. *Feminism Unmodified: Discourses on Life and Law*. Cambridge, MA: Harvard University Press.

MacKinnon, Catharine A. 1996. *Only Words*. Cambridge, MA: Harvard University Press.

Maes, Hans. 2011. "Drawing the Line: Art Versus Pornography." *Philosophy Compass* 6, no. 6: 385–397.

Maes, Hans. 2013. "Who Says Pornography Can't Be Art?" In *Art and Pornography: Philosophical Essays*, edited by Jerrold Levinson and Hans Maes, 17–47. Oxford: Oxford University Press.

Maes, Hans. 2014. "Erotic Art." August. https://plato.stanford.edu/archives/win2018/entries/ erotic-art/.

MagUidhir, Christy Mag. 2009. "Why Pornography Can't Be Art." *Philosophy and Literature* 33, no. 1: 193–203.

Manne, Kate. 2017. *Down Girl: The Logic of Misogyny*. New York: Oxford University Press.

McGlynn, Aidan. 2021. "Blurred Lines: How Fictional Is Pornography?" *Philosophy Compass* 16, no. 4: e12721.

McGowan, Mary Kate. 2019. *Just Words: On Speech and Hidden Harm*. Oxford: Oxford University Press.

Medina, José. 2018. "Resisting Racist Propaganda: Distorted Visual Communication and Epistemic Activism." *The Southern Journal of Philosophy* 56, S1: 50–75.

Mikkola, Mari, ed. 2017. *Beyond Speech: Pornography and Analytic Feminist Philosophy*. New York: Oxford University Press.

Mikkola, Mari. 2019. *Pornography: A Philosophical Introduction*. Oxford University Press.

Miller, Dan J., Kerry A. McBain, Wendy W. Li, and Peter T. F. Raggatt. 2019. "Pornography, Preference for Porn-like Sex, Masturbation, and Men's Sexual and Relationship Satisfaction." *Personal Relationships* 26, no. 1: 93–113.

Nash, Jennifer C. 2014. *The Black Body in Ecstasy: Reading Race, Reading Pornography*. Illustrated ed. Durham, NC: Duke University Press.

Neu, Jerome. 2002. "An Ethics of Fantasy?" *Journal of Theoretical and Philosophical Psychology* 22, no. 2: 133–157.

Orenstein, Peggy. 2016. "Opinion | When Did Porn Become Sex Ed?" *New York Times*, March 19, https://www.nytimes.com/2016/03/20/opinion/sunday/when-did-porn-become-sex-ed.html.

Patridge, Stephanie L. 2013. "Pornography, Ethics, and Video Games." *Ethics and Information Technology* 15, no. 1: 25–34.

Rea, Michael C. 2001. "What Is Pornography?" *Noûs* 35, no. 1: 118–145.

Rothman, Emily F., Courtney Kaczmarsky, Nina Burke, Emily Jansen, and Allyson Baughman. 2015. "'Without Porn . . . I Wouldn't Know Half the Things I Know Now': A Qualitative Study of Pornography Use Among a Sample of Urban, Low-Income, Black and Hispanic Youth." *Journal of Sex Research* 52, no. 7: 736–746.

Scruton, Roger. 2009. *Beauty*. New York: Oxford University Press.

Sontag, Susan. 1994. "The Pornographic Imagination." In her *Styles of Radical Will*, 35–37. New York: Vintage.

Taormino, Tristan, Constance Penley, Celine Parrenas Shimizu, and Mireille Miller-Young, eds. 2013. *The Feminist Porn Book: The Politics of Producing Pleasure*. New York: The Feminist Press at CUNY.

Todd, Cain. 2013. "Imagination, Fantasy, and Sexual Desire." In *Art and Pornography: Philosophical Essays*, edited by Jerrold Levinson and Hans Maes, 95–115. Oxford: Oxford University Press.

Wolfthal, Diane. 2000. *Images of Rape: The "Heroic" Tradition and Its Alternatives*. Cambridge: Cambridge University Press.

Zheng, Robin. 2016. "Why Yellow Fever Isn't Flattering: A Case Against Racial Fetishes." *Journal of the American Philosophical Association* 2, no. 3: 400–419.

Zheng, Robin. 2017. "Race and Pornography: The Dilemma of the (Un)Desirable." In *Beyond Speech: Pornography and Analytic Feminist Philosophy*, edited by Mari Mikkola, 177–196. New York: Oxford University Press.

CHAPTER 32

....

HUMOR ETHICS

....

PAUL BUTTERFIELD

INTRODUCTION

SUPPOSE an acquaintance says something in conversation that you find offensive. Then, when you censure her for the content of her speech, she explains to you that she was "only joking." Provided that you take her claim to have been speaking humorously at face value, what ought you to make of her speech now? Should you disregard your prior moral judgment entirely and accept whatever she said in good humor? Or, if you keep your negative assessment, should you temper it somewhat now that you understand that her intentions were comical?

Pretheoretical instincts about this question vary widely. Some jokers earnestly believe that they should be permitted to say whatever they like when they speak humorously, on the grounds that humor is not serious and, accordingly, communicates no ethically assessable content. Others deem some examples of comic speech to be offensive indeed, occasionally even rising to the level of hate speech. In this chapter I survey the relevant academic literature to cite support for, and criticism of, the conclusions that jokes are harmless fun, and, alternately, that we all need to exercise a great deal of moral caution about the things we say in jest.

A different, and somewhat more widely researched, topic concerns the relationship between ethics and aesthetics in instances of humor. This is the question of whether being morally bad makes a given instance of humor *less funny*. On this score, comic moralists disagree with comic amoralists: the former believe that just such a relationship does hold, such that we can sensibly say of some jokes that they are not funny *because* they are morally bad, while the latter hold that a joke's moral value is unrelated to the question of how humorous it is.

This chapter details the claims made by proponents of each of the most prominent views related to the question of when a joke is morally acceptable or unacceptable, as well as those that concern the relationship between ethics and the funniness of an instance of humor. I will also consider why it can be difficult to make definitive ethical claims about particular instances of humor, and offer some practical guidance on how to come to conclusions about humor ethics despite these difficulties.

THE DISMISSIVE VIEW

One popular prephilosophical account of humor ethics is what I will call *the dismissive view*. Proponents of the dismissive view hold that there is simply no such thing as a morally bad instance of humor; if you criticize some piece of humorous speech on moral grounds, you have made a kind of category error. It is true that the issuing of sincere, nonhumorous speech can be morally wrong—such as when one stands on a soapbox in a public square and gives a racist diatribe, or when one gratuitously insults the host of a dinner party by declaring their food second-rate and their décor dreary—but *humorous* speech is just light-hearted play. Nobody can express hate or cause legitimate offense through humor, any more than they could kill you with a toy gun. Maybe it's true that lots of people get offended when they hear certain jokes, or that heads of states throughout history have tried to outlaw humor at their expense—but, if so, more fool them. They have imbued light-hearted tomfoolery with more power than any rational person would credit it with. They should lighten up, get a sense of humor, and accept that their correspondent was "only joking."

When professional comedians have engaged with the ethics of humor soberly, it has typically been to defend some version of the dismissive view (Gimbel 2018, 149). After controversies regarding offensive stand-up sets, comics often appeal to the fact that their material is comic in nature as an ethical defense, thereby implying that humorous speech is morally acceptable by default (Butterfield 2022). The view is also implicitly appealed to in the following anecdote, relayed in Dennis Howitt and Kwame Owusu-Bempah's "Race and Ethnicity in Popular Humour":

> A few years ago, a black person was inside a local shop when a man covered in coal dust entered and placed his hand next to the black person's. He then chanted "I wanna be like you, black like you . . . ." This was objected to on the grounds that, unlike the "joker," he was black and not dirty. Those in the shop joined in the denial of racism: "It's only a joke," they said, almost in unison. One of them actually counselled him (the victim) to cultivate a sense of humour in order to "get on in this world." This is not a hypothetical example. The incident involved one of the authors of this chapter. (2005, 45)

But the use of humorousness as some kind of ethical "magic bullet," whose presence immediately renders all behavior acceptable, is too strong an interpretation of the difference that joking makes. Instances of humor have too much in common with other forms of communication and expression to be entirely morally inert: jokes can demean, witticisms can insult, and interpersonal joshing can build rapport on the basis of admirable or objectionable shared interests. Playground bullying often takes place by means of targeted joke-telling, and it would be eccentric to believe that this kind of ridicule is immediately made acceptable by virtue of being comic. Additionally, the jokes we enjoy do seem to have some link to our sincere beliefs, which is why, for example, one can find archives of insulting jokes about Black people on white supremacist websites, as Simon Weaver does in his book *The Rhetoric of Racist Humor* (2008, 76–77). This is also why it is perfectly unremarkable for one to make judgments about a second party's character on the basis of the humor she shares. If I tell you one joke that makes fun of feminists, you will not necessarily think much about it; but if I tell you a joke that makes fun of feminists *every time you see me*, it will not take long for you to justifiably conclude that I really hold some anti-feminist views. Humor is too embedded in the rest of our lives, then, for it to be entirely without moral implications.

HUMOROUSNESS MAKES A DIFFERENCE

Pointing out that one was joking does not tidily absolve one of all possible wrongdoing in communication then. But the fact of having been speaking humorously is not morally irrelevant, either. "Only joking" is not a nonsequitur response to the accusation of having said something transgressive. On at least some occasions, whether or not we were speaking jokingly makes a difference to the moral value of what was said. Why is this?

Victor Raskin famously categorizes jokes as "non–bona-fide communication," in which a speaker does not attempt to convey information straightforwardly and unambiguously. In cases of bona-fide communication, "the speaker is committed to the truth and relevance of his text, the hearer is aware of this commitment and perceives the uttered text as true and relevant by virtue of [this] recognition" (1985, 100–101). Raskin expresses the process of issuing, and understanding, bona-fide communication in terms of H. P. Grice's "cooperative principle": that a speaker ought, in order to contribute to conversations that are maximally effective for the purposes of the parties involved, make their contributions "such as is required, at the stage at which it occurs, by the accepted purpose or direction of the talk exchange in which [they] are engaged" (Grice 1989, 26). Adhering to this principle involves speaking in a way that is accurate, relevant, and concise, such that conversational partners can easily read your beliefs and intentions from your speech. The point of non–bona-fide communication, however, "is not to convey any information contained in the text . . . but rather to create a special effect with the help of the text," which in the case of joking is typically "to make the hearer laugh" (Raskin 1985, 101). This will often involve conspicuously violating the cooperative principle, and issuing propositions that one knows are not informative, or not true, or not relevant, or ambiguous.

Now, since bona-fide communication involves a speaker attempting to disclose relevant, accurate information concisely, we are justified in understanding the judgments expressed under those parameters to reflect the speaker's actual view of the world. Contrastively, when a speaker jokes, we have no such justification. Suppose I told you this joke:

Q: *What do you call 500 lawyers at the bottom of the sea?*
A: *A good start.*

Well—you might not fall out of your chair laughing, and I cannot fault you for that. But you are also unlikely to believe that the telling of this joke reveals very much about my character: you would probably not warn your friends in the legal profession that I should be considered a threat to their safety, for example.

On the other hand, imagine that I told you, without any obvious joke format or any behavioral cues to indicate that I was trying to be funny, that I like it when lawyers die and would consider a killing spree at a series of legal firms to be good news. Or—to sharpen the sense that my speech was not just playful—suppose that there actually *was* just such a series of murders, and that you and I watched a news broadcast reporting the story together. Suppose that you commented on what a terrible incident it was, and I responded, "Well, I can see why someone might think that. Personally, I admire the killer, and can only hope that others follow in their footsteps." That would be an awful thing to say, and you would have reason to consider me, henceforth, a terrifying psychopath.

The distinction between these two speech acts—whereby one is an ethically unremarkable utterance, and the other is an appalling attack, despite each appearing to have similar content—lies in the fact that the latter can justifiably be taken to express my actual views, and the former cannot. In the second case, I reveal a violently hateful attitude toward lawyers, and in the first I do not. In fact, holding such an attitude would actually be an *impediment* to the success of the joke in question, because one does not find amusement in straightforward descriptions of the world as it actually is (or as one actually believes it to be) (see Carroll 1991, 296). This is the difference that speaking in a non–bona-fide way makes, and it is why pointing out that one was "just joking" will, at least on some occasions, serve as a legitimate moral excuse.

The Attitude-Endorsement Theory

So we should not think of humorousness as an ethical get-out-of-jail-free card, but it is also not morally irrelevant. What, then, are the conditions under which a joke is condemnable?

Philosopher Ronald De Sousa offers an answer to this question which is rather expansive, proscribing a large proportion of the jokes people share with one another in everyday life. De Sousa does not deny that humorous speech is non–bona-fide, but he contends that nevertheless, the telling, and enjoying, of jokes tells us a great deal about a speaker or hearer's attitudes. While a pun or shaggy dog story might be enjoyed independently of one's view of the world, De Sousa believes that tendentious jokes, like those based upon ethnic stereotypes or insult comedy, can only be enjoyable to those who really hold some negative view of the targeted group or individual.

A joke that makes fun of women, for example, is unlike a simple story-based gag (like those that begin "A man walks into a bar . . .") because, instead of simply asking us to follow a short fictional tale, it invokes some attitude toward women as a group. And when a joke invokes an attitude, "it does not allow of hypothetical laughter [and] makes us laugh only insofar as the assumptions on which it is based are attitudes actually shared. Suspension of disbelief in the situation can and must be achieved for the purposes of the joke; suspension of attitudes cannot be" (De Sousa 1987, 290).

Elsewhere, Hugh LaFollette and Niall Shanks develop a similar view of humor ethics, based upon their account of humor, more broadly. The pair take comic amusement to be a reaction to a cognitive "flickering," where the audience to some instance of humor alternate rapidly between two interpretations of, or perspectives on, an event or observation. This flickering is fundamental to finding something funny: when hearing a pun, we move between each sense of the word spoken; with slapstick physical comedy, we alternate from our understanding of how a character *intends* to carry out some task, to their erratic and inefficient approach to it, and back again. LaFollette and Shanks go on to give an explanation for why humor can be a tool of social oppression, on the back of this view:

> [The "flickering" account] helps explain what specifically is objectionable about racist or sexist "humor" . . . Recall that a person's belief that an event, action, or claim is humorous depends upon the higher order beliefs which she has and to which she currently attends. A joke which belittled women, then, could only be humorous to someone who had the appropriate sort of higher-order beliefs, in particular, beliefs that women are mentally or morally inferior to men. Hence, what is disturbing about this humor is not the bare joke, but what that joke indicates about those who find the joke humorous. (1993, 337)

Like De Sousa, then, LaFollette and Shanks think that we can draw a direct line between the jokes a person tells and the things she believes sincerely. They agree that pejorative jokes about some group of people amount to evidence that the joke-teller really has a bad attitude toward that group.

However, De Sousa's theory of attitude endorsement in humor has been criticized for failing to account for the possibility of merely *entertaining* an attitude, or *recognizing* a stereotype, in order to enjoy a joke (Benatar 1999, 2014; Carroll 2005; Lengbeyer 2005). That is: one does not need to be a bigot to appreciate some joke that paints an unflattering picture of (e.g.) Catholics; one only needs to be able to temporarily, for the sake of the joke, imagine what it is like to hold some anti-Catholic attitude. Likewise, no need to consider some (e.g.) anti-Semitic stereotype *true* in order to enjoy an instance of humor that makes reference to it; one only has to be able to acknowledge that the stereotype in question *exists*. A similar objection may be leveled against LaFollette and

Shanks's view: it is almost certainly true that some people get a particular kick out of pejorative humor about women because of genuinely held misogynistic beliefs; but there is no reason to suppose that it is not possible for others to find it funny on the back of simply humoring those beliefs. Whereas straightforward assent to a sincere proposition tells us that a person believes some particular thing, laughter in response to a joke tells us only that a hearer is in one of various epistemic states that would allow her to be amused by it. And while *some* of those states may be ethically troubling, it is very unlikely, for any particular instance of humor, that all such states are. After all, even the most lurid ethnic jokes can be repackaged, retold, and enjoyed ironically by members of the ethnic group in question—and nobody would sincerely claim that this is evidence of widespread self-hatred on the part of those groups (see Carroll 1991; Benatar 2016).

SKEPTICISM ABOUT HUMOR ETHICS

We are blocked, then, from claiming that any joke *requires* any specific belief or attitude from its listeners in order to be amusing. As such, it is not legitimate to say that some joke could only be funny to a racist or a sexist. And in light of this observation, some theorists have become skeptical about the very idea of theoretically grounded moral objections to comic speech: they believe that attempting to provide a principled argument for the wrongness of any joke is a fool's errand.

This skepticism can take different forms: the sociologist Christie Davies, for example, took a position similar to the dismissive view, holding that jokes are simply incapable of expressing bigotry or having any serious pernicious social effects (see Davies 1998, 2011). Ted Cohen, on the other hand, was perfectly willing to accept that there is such a thing as a racist comedy, a cruel prank, or a joke in poor taste; but he believed that it would remain impossible to prove this using reasoned argument. Any ethical complaint one might lodge against something humorous is an expression of one's personal distaste, rather than a description of the gag itself that could be demonstrated to be true or false. Calling to mind a joke that paints a particularly nasty caricature of Black men, Cohen writes: "If I were to offer some resounding moral condemnation of this joke, no doubt I would have to invoke some 'moral theory,' and then show that an implication of the theory is that this joke is Bad . . . I think [this] can't be done" (1999, 81). Instead of trying to come up with any such theory, Cohen advises concerned joke-hearers to adopt the following policy: "When you feel strongly that some joke . . . is no damned good, and especially when you don't like having that joke told, and it seems to you that the thing—either itself or the telling of it—is morally defective, hold on to that feeling, and continue to express the feeling in terms of moral condemnation." But, since a unified model of humor ethics is so elusive, "don't imagine that your dislike must be grounded in some stupefying Moral Theory" (82–83).

Something More Moderate?

But what if we are more optimistic about a codified humor ethics than Cohen? Can we offer principled ethical suggestions that go beyond the (unedifying) advice to treat one's views on the rights and wrongs of joke-telling as a mere matter of personal taste, but stop short of the (unlikely) claim that pejorative joking directly reveals one's sincere opinions?

One solution is to accept that we can never know *precisely* what views of the world are prescribed by examples of joke speech, and attempt to find some claims worth making about humor under that imperfect epistemic condition. Thus far we have noted that for any joke that trades upon some negative ethnic stereotype, it is possible for that joke to be enjoyed by nonracists, who might ironically enjoy the outrageous transgression involved in saying something so wrong-headed.[1] But of course, it is also possible for such jokes to be enjoyed by racists, as, in part, an indulgence of their racism. In "On Jokes," Noël Carroll identifies potential moral wrongdoing in the creation and performance of racial jokes in the following way:

> Ethnic, racist, and sexist jokes are very often used as insults, and insults customarily may take the form of hyperbole . . . Though they are literally and even intentionally false, hyperboles can figuratively point in the direction of an assertion. And where racist jokes are told with racist intent to racist audiences, tellers and listeners may regard their presuppositions as strictly and literally false—thereby appreciating them as merely jokes—while at the same time correcting the tropological figuration so that it accords with their prejudices. (1991, 296–297)

This results in an appreciation of racial insult humor, on the part of a racist audience, that involves understanding the humor as an exaggeration, rather than a straightforward falsification, of the way the world is:

> The racist [joker] will be understood by the racist listener as saying something stronger than the literal truth warrants, but also as saying something with the intention that it be corrected so that, though it will not be taken in its strongest formulation, it will still be taken as a strong statement that preserves the same initial polarity (say "major league" stupidity) that the hyperbole did. One might imagine the anti-Irish appreciator of [a joke about Irish stupidity] saying, after an initial burst of laughter: "Well, the Irish aren't that dumb; but they're really pretty dumb nonetheless." (296)

Carroll goes on to offer some action-guiding advice off the back of the potential for ethnic jokes to be understood variously as ironic or hyperbolic. He warns against the

---

[1] Almost all jokes will admit more than two angles for appreciation, but relying on a simplified "exaggeration"/"irony" dichotomy will be helpful for the present analysis.

assumption that just because I, myself carry no bigoted beliefs or attitudes, I need have no concerns when telling a joke at the expense of members of any social group. There is a risk that I might tell such a joke with honorable intentions (using irony to mock actual bigots, maybe, or innocently playing two recognized stereotypes off against each other), but that my joke might attract an audience that is genuinely antagonistic to my targeted group, and that it may read my joke as playing to, and offering support for, its prejudices. Members of that audience might not catch my irony, or they might read serious invective into my playful words. They might then have their hateful beliefs reconfirmed, or suspect that fledgling biases they hold are more widely shared than they actually are: "Ah, I see that I'm not the only one that finds *that lot* a bit shifty. This person's joking about it, so others must agree with me in secret." And, since our jokes have this potential, Carroll advises that we "should be morally concerned enough to refrain from telling them in contexts where they might stoke these sentiments; this probably applies to most of the social situations in which we find ourselves" (297–298).

There are, however, means by which one can make an educated guess that a joke has been told with innocent (or, alternately, malevolent) intent. The ambiguity of humorous speech—the possibility for a given instance of humor to be entirely inconspicuous, or an expression of genuine hostility—means that contextual clues regarding a speaker's likely intentions take on a greater role in predicting the moral value of jokes than of other forms of speech. One of the reasons that social identity plays such an important role in the etiquette of humor—such that a joke about a social group can be terribly offensive when told by someone outside of the group, but entirely benign when told by a group member—is that one's social group membership is a useful shorthand for one's probable beliefs and intentions when talking about the group (see Butterfield 2022). My being Catholic is a useful (though imperfect) signal that I am unlikely to be telling a Catholic joke from a place of actual antagonism against Catholics. Other contextual clues you could use to help determine the likely intentions associated with my joke include my tone and body language, details about my personal history, and even whether my joke was clever or not (Gimbel 2018, 133). In humorous contexts, then, actual textual content is of diminished moral relevance, while background factors regarding the identity of the speaker, the identity of the audience, and the context within which the speech takes place become unusually prominent when one is trying to make a normative assessment.

Another practical strategy one might adopt, in response to the difficulties one faces in determining the precise content and force of humorous speech, is to forego binary ethical categories in favor of something more nuanced. Luvell Anderson proposes an example of such a strategy in his article "Racist Humor." There, he suggests that instead of neatly categorizing racial humor as merely either "racist" or "not racist," it is better to introduce a third category: that of "racially insensitive humor" (2015, 505). While a racial joke is racist if it causes harm to members of a particular racial group by virtue of their membership of that group (or is intended to do so), and can be considered not-racist if it has the aim of subverting the hurtful stereotypes it invokes, racially insensitive humor occupies a middle ground, including, for example, cases in which jokers invoke negative stereotypes without intending to subvert them, but with care not to cause harm, either (506).

HUMOROUSNESS AS A BAD-MAKING
FEATURE OF SPEECH

So far we have considered the circumstances in which, and the reasons for which, an instance of humor may be morally preferable to its equivalent piece of nonhumorous communication. But there is an interesting question regarding the possibility of humorousness acting in the opposite direction. Can the fact that one was joking ever make one's speech *worse*?

One reason to believe that humorousness can act in this way is the fact that joke speech in conversation seems to allow for a certain amount of *sneakiness*. If an acquaintance gratuitously criticizes your dress sense to your face, then, however begrudgingly, you must credit her with honesty. If she instead makes a series of *jokes* about your new Bermuda shorts and Hawaiian shirt combo, however, she has failed to even have that decency. And, while humorous speech does not typically trade in literal assertion, that does not mean that it does not say anything about the world. Jokes zip along to their conclusion by leaving much unsaid—so when I make fun of a friend's clumsiness, I probably do not actually, explicitly mention the fact that she is clumsy (or that I consider her clumsy). Her clumsiness is something I *take for granted*, introducing it to the conversation without stating it explicitly. To the extent that jokes tell us anything about the world, then, they do so as what Rae Langton refers to as "back-door speech acts" (2018, 4): speech acts that rely on conversational inertia and rules of accommodation to make their point. Given this, jokes can be a rather good way of introducing a proposition to a conversation, without having to issue that proposition explicitly—and this can be useful to any speaker who wants to express some socially unacceptable sentiment. If I declare earnestly that I consider Scottish people to be violence-loving drunks, you are likely to upbraid me for my bigotry; but if, instead, I tell a joke which trades upon the idea of Scots as violent drunks, it becomes much more difficult for you to call me out for my prejudice. This is because, without explicitly assigning these attributes to Scottish people, I have not quite "signed my name" to that account of their character. I maintain some plausible deniability, should I choose to use it, in the event that someone objects to my speech. If you respond to my joke by telling me that this account of Scottish people is completely unfair, and that relative to population, Scotland has a rate of alcohol consumption and violent crime that is fairly unremarkable among similar nations, it is open to me to say: "Of course I know that—I was just telling a joke, for goodness' sake!" At this point, instead of me looking like a narrow-minded hater, it might instead be you who appears petty and humorless.

There are two potential advantages to this plausible deniability for someone with objectionable views. The first is a personal matter: one is less likely to receive social sanctions from one's interlocutors when the "just joking" excuse is in play. The second is strategic: if one can sneak (e.g.) a racist idea into conversation under the guise of playful joshing, then it is less likely that a right-thinking participant in the conversation will confront the idea and expose how wrong it is. Once the racist concept has been aired, and not confronted, it might then have a better chance of taking root among those agents who heard it. For this to work, however, it must be the case that jokes can be a vehicle for sincere, nonhumorous propositions. To draw a conclusion regarding how worried we should be about bigots using humor sneakily to proliferate their views, we need to know: can a joke making fun of a race of people actually influence a hearer's view of those people?

There is evidence from social psychology that jokes can, indeed, have this sort of effect. The psychologist Thomas Ford has conducted a series of experiments that have demonstrated that bigoted jokes are capable of influencing real-world behavior. In one study, groups of participants were primed with, alternately, sexist jokes, nonsexist jokes, and nonjoking sexist statements. They were then asked to roleplay a scenario in which they were the dean of a university, tasked with assigning budget cuts among a number of on-campus student groups. Ford's study found that respondents who had been shown examples of sexist humor tended to administer heftier cuts to the (fabricated) "National Student Council of Women," during the thought experiment, than those who had been told nonsexist jokes. More interesting for our current purposes, however, is that this group *also* cut more heavily into the budget of the women's organization than the group of respondents who had been presented with nonhumorous, sexist statements (Ford et al. 2008, 163–164). This suggests that there is something about the *humorousness* of the speech that correlated positively with subjects' willingness to defund the body supporting female students.

Ford and his colleagues hypothesize that these results are caused by the ability of bigoted jokes to introduce "prejudiced norms" into conversation, whereby humor implicitly sends a message, subsequently internalized by its audience, to the effect that "sexism (homophobia, racism, etc.) is a bit of a laugh; not something you need to seriously worry about" (Ferguson and Ford 2008). By comparison, nonhumorous expressions of bigotry are more clearly in violation of social conventions, and so no trivializing message is conveyed.

Finally, it may be worse to make a joke than to speak sincerely, in some contexts, because the very act of making a joke conveys an inappropriate attitude toward the situation one finds oneself in. Merrie Bergmann gives an example of how one can convey an insufficiently serious attitude toward an event by employing or appreciating humor in the following scenario:

> A professor comments that he would like to live the life of Socrates; the next day a student presents the professor with a bottle of hemlock. The professor finds this funny, as the student had intended, and, chuckling, carries the hemlock home. The following morning he discovers that his young daughter has crept into his study and drunk the hemlock. In this case, it would be an insult to the child (to put it mildly),

if the student, after hearing the news and offering sympathy, were to slap a classmate on the back and say, with a belly laugh, "Still, it was funny that I thought of giving him that hemlock, wasn't it?" It would also be an insult if the classmate laughed along. (1986, 78–79)

The point here is that showing one's appreciation of the gag, postmortem, conveys a disrespectful absence of solemnity. Note that while the link between the joke and the death—the fact that the funny provision of hemlock was what eventually *caused* the death of the professor's daughter—is an aggravating factor in the student's disrespectful behavior, it is not *required* in order for the student to be remiss. If the professor mentions that his daughter has recently died for unrelated reasons, and the student immediately segues into asking if everyone's heard the one about the actor and the bishop, she still conveys disrespect.

But Is It Funny?

Sometimes when we issue ethical criticism of joke speech, we comment on an instance of humor's *aesthetic* qualities, as a kind of shorthand. Thus one might indicate one's belief that rape jokes are morally impermissible by saying that "there's nothing amusing about sex crime," or chide an acquaintance over her repeated teasing of a third party by telling her that her jabs "just aren't funny anymore." We seem to imply, when we speak like this, that there is some strong link between the moral value of a joke and its success at inducing amusement. A prominent subtopic within the ethics of humor concerns the aptness of these claims: is objectionable comedy less funny? Is a bad joke a *bad joke*?

Comic moralism is the view that a joke being morally bad makes it less funny. Its proponents take the above logical moves between "this joke has some serious moral flaw" and "this joke is unfunny" at face value, and hold that there really is such a link between humor's ethical and aesthetic merits. (See also Carroll, this volume.) Comic moralism contrasts with *comic amoralism*, which is the view that an instance of humor's ethical and aesthetic merits are unrelated. (See also Stear, this volume.) For the comic amoralist, to call a joke "not funny" in reference to its cruelty or offensiveness is legitimate only as a figure of speech: suggesting that the two matters actually interact means being careless about the various ways in which speech can be good or bad.

Moralism's most strident form—which, following others in the field, I will call *strong comic moralism*—holds that an ethical flaw, like the manifestation of racist or sexist attitudes, will always render an example of humor entirely unfunny. It is impossible, according to strong comic moralism, for a morally imperfect joke to be funny.

It would be pretty startling if strong comic moralism was true. This would certainly require "funniness" to be a value detached from the fact of whether anybody is actually comically amused: after all, audiences definitely *can* find humor in ethically objectionable comedy, as evidenced by the career longevity of, for example, hateful working men's club comics like Bernard Manning and Roy Chubby Brown. This is not such a difficult premise to accept: most of us are comfortable with the idea that the funniness of some piece of comedy is not identical to the facts surrounding who was, or was not, actually amused by it. We understand, for example, that the question "what's the funniest television sitcom?" amounts to something different to the question "what's the most popular television sitcom?" Moreover, though, strong comic moralism seems to rely on an uncommonly restrictive view of what humor is. Instances of comedy can be funny because they reveal some as-yet unexamined aspect of everyday life, or because they demonstrate the quick-thinking of a protagonist, or because they expertly satirize some pompous public figure; or for a thousand other reasons. It is odd to think that the myriad potential aesthetic virtues of a piece of humor can *all* be undone, in one fell swoop, by the presence of some vicious attitude or expression. Suppose that a pejorative ethnic joke cleverly plays upon some link between two offensive stereotypes: by what process does the offensiveness of the stereotypes do away with the cleverness of the observation? An impersonator brilliantly lampoons some person of interest, but her bit goes too far, becoming personal and cruel: can we not enjoy the accuracy of the mimicry, as a quality separate from the tastelessness of the material? Even for those of us who are happy to accept that comedy has some significant ethical element, it is a problem that this view seems to reduce comedy to almost *nothing but* that element.

The strength of the moralist position can be moderated in two ways. *Comic ethicists* do not hold that wrongdoing in the creation, or enjoyment, of humor undoes its funniness completely, but, instead, believe that to some extent it *counts against* its funniness (Gaut 1998, 55). So while the strong comic moralist must deny that a morally compromised gag could ever be funny at all, the comic ethicist is able to say things like, "that was a very good joke you just told: it's just a shame that it was unethical, or else it would have been even funnier." On the other hand, *moderate comic moralism* is the position that moral flaws may detract from humorousness sometimes, but not necessarily on every occasion (Carroll 2014, 252). Moral wrongdoing of the right kind, in a joke of the appropriate sort, will make comic amusement difficult or impossible to achieve; but this is perfectly consistent with other vices, at other comic moments, being aesthetically irrelevant.

Noël Carroll argues in favor of moderate comic moralism by offering an explanation of the means by which an audience may be prevented from feeling amusement in response to an instance of humor, as a result of its perception of vicious attitudes on the part of the joke-creator (2014, 250–252). Humor is a mode of communication that necessarily involves some shared understanding between teller and hearer (see Cohen 1999, 12): the audience needs to be "in" on something with the joker, in order to "get" any joke. Recall that in discussion of ethnic humor, it has been suggested that we might sometimes need to entertain a certain attitude or recognize a certain stereotype in order to appreciate some joke. Sometimes, however, the ideas in question are so egregious that it is difficult to bring them to mind and still be in the mood to laugh. Carroll cites the attempts at comedy in D. W. Griffiths's *The Birth of A Nation* as an example of this phenomenon: sections of that film that are intended to be humorous will fall flat to a right-thinking audience, since, to enjoy them, one has to entertain a gruesomely racist perception of the story's Black characters (2014, 251).

The phenomenon Carroll identifies here is similar in nature to the experience of being put off of one's food. Even if your sirloin steak is perfectly flavorful, it may be tough to maintain your enjoyment of it if you sneak a glance into the kitchen and witness a chef sneezing into a stew. In the midst of your disgust, you are unlikely to still be in the appropriate state of mind to appreciate the positive qualities of your meal. Likewise, when we are overcome with moral disgust because we identify the joke we are being told as (e.g.) racist, that feeling can put us in a frame of mind that is not conducive to being comically amused.

Comic Immoralism

Perhaps it has occurred to you that while rejecting the moralist thesis, the comic amoralist has demonstrated a certain amount of restraint. There is a more extreme position that a person could hold in opposition to the idea that moral flaws make a joke less funny: namely, that they do quite the contrary, giving otherwise pedestrian gags an illicit bite and thereby making them funnier. (See also Jacobson, this volume.) Many of us consider ourselves to have a dark, or warped, sense of humor, via which we find special amusement in cases where an agent says the unsayable; cracks wise about That Which We Are Not To Joke About. We might experience schadenfreude at the expense of some comic foil, or simply get a kick out of flouting the ethical norms that surround most social interactions. If you have ever been chastened by a teacher for laughing during class, you may be familiar with the irresistibility of humor at precisely the times when it is forbidden. Doesn't it follow that ethical wrongdoing is exactly the kind of thing that would heighten comedy?

The view that moral flaws, such as the manifestation of a joke-teller's bigoted attitudes, in jokes makes them funnier is termed *comic immoralism* (Gaut 1998, 55). Definitional accounts of humor lend the theory a certain presumptive plausibility. When modern philosophers of humor have sought to explain what humor *is*, they have most commonly offered definitions that treat the presence of *incongruity* as a fundamental or essential feature of the comic (Morreall 2009, 10; Hurley et al. 2011, 45). According to these definitions, to count as humor, some piece of speech or work of fiction must present its audience with some object or phenomenon in a setting in which it is conspicuously out-of-place, or in a way that violates the audience's usual expectations about the world. We are not presently concerned with the answers to definitional questions about humor, except to the extent that they have normative import; but, even if incongruity is *not* at the heart of all instances of comedy, the popularity of these definitions tells us that occurrences that violate norms or expectations certainly *tend* to correlate with funniness. Thus, comic immoralism gains some theoretical grounding. After all, among the norms that exist are ethical norms. If humor is closely related to the flouting of norms, then, it makes sense that the violation of *ethical* norms should tend to induce comic amusement. Moral wrongdoing, being an exception to conventional standards for behavior, is exactly the sort of thing that incongruity theorists should expect to be funny.

However, in his paper "Do Moral Flaws Enhance Amusement?," Aaron Smuts contends that the first-blush plausibility of comic immoralism stems from two common mistakes. The first mistake is believing that mere examples of funny and ethically flawed jokes prove the immoralist thesis correct. It is likely that you have come across examples of humor that you consider to be morally flawed, but that you have—perhaps despite your better intentions—been amused by, and it is tempting to think that these examples are relevant to the question of whether comic immoralism is correct. But, as Smuts notes, "It is not enough merely to show that a funny joke is morally flawed. The immoralist needs to show that the joke is funnier *because* it is morally flawed" (2009, 152–153): the immorality of the joke itself must be a source of funniness. This is a tall order, indeed. Note that one could enjoy, say, a pejorative ethnic joke on the basis that it plays cleverly on some horribly offensive stereotype—but if we cannot show specifically that the horribleness of the stereotype is doing some of the joke work, we do not have any evidence in support of immoralism. As Berys Gaut, a comic moralist, has pointed out, we could even accept that some insult humor is made funnier by virtue of its aggressiveness—its in-your-face brashness; its teller's willingness to leap to confrontation during otherwise polite discourse—without accepting the immoralist thesis (1998, 61). This is because not all aggression is morally wrong: if the target is deserving and the attack is accurate, aggressiveness in insult humor can be an ethical virtue.

The second epistemic error lending credibility to comic immoralism is the tendency to mistake instances of humor that feature morally bad acts with morally bad instances of humor. The characters featured in a joke may engage in all sort of condemnable behavior, from infanticide to racism, and everything in-between. But while infanticide and racism are morally wrong, it does not follow that *depicting* infanticide and racism is morally wrong. Much as a character in a novel may be a murderer without the book itself amounting to an endorsement of murder, so too may a joke feature, for example, prejudice, without being an expression of that prejudice. So it is important to ask, of any putative example in favor of immoralism, whether one is really looking at an example of a morally bad joke, or merely a joke that depicts moral wrongdoing. Smuts writes that "a joke featuring immorality, however extreme, is not necessarily itself an immoral joke. Yes, outrageous content such as taboo subjects and wildly inappropriate behavior can clearly contribute to the humorousness of a joke, but it is not at all clear that moral flaws contribute positively in any way. It is important that one not confuse . . . the mere representation of an immoral character, attitude, or sentiment with a moral flaw" (2009, 153).

We can demonstrate this important distinction with reference to two of the most popular American sitcoms of the modern era. In the US version of *The Office*, overbearing manager Michael Scott learns that the office accountant Oscar Martinez is gay. Michael subsequently embarrasses Oscar with his over-the-top attempts to demonstrate acceptance of the latter's sexuality, culminating in his kissing him on the lips in front of their colleagues. The episode in question portrays homophobia, toxic masculinity, and harassment—but Michael, the perpetrator of the bad behavior, is the butt of the joke. The point of the scene is that the way he is acting is pathetic. The presumed position of the audience is that Oscar being gay is an unremarkable piece of personal biography, and humor arises from the fact that Michael does such a terrible job of dealing with news that ought not to make any employer uncomfortable. In *Friends*, on the other hand, there are many occasions in which the primary male characters are placed in compromising situations, at which their having homosexual desire is made to look plausible. A workmate attempts to set Chandler up on a date with a male friend, assuming that he dates men; Ross, stumbling over his words, accidentally proposes that he should kiss "random guys" to demonstrate his recovery from a break-up; Chandler, Ross, and Joey are discovered momentarily sharing a bathroom stall by a stranger. The main characters are the fall guys on all of these occasions; but, unlike in *The Office*, we are not invited to laugh at their small-mindedness. Instead, the presumed attitude of the audience is homophobic: we are supposed to believe that it is humiliating for a straight man to be perceived, for any period of time and from any perspective, as experiencing gay love or sexual desire. *The Office*'s material features prejudice, but the jokes in *Friends* actively express it. To provide evidence for immoralism, one would have to show something akin to the homophobia of *Friends* making that show more funny—not just that something like *The Office*'s depictions of homophobia do so. Ultimately, Smuts contends that once one understands just what is required for an example to prove the immoralist thesis correct, one will see that no such example is forthcoming.

The jokes we tell stand in some relation to our sincere beliefs and attitudes; but that relationship is complicated and ambiguous. The fact that speakers often communicate some version of their real opinion through humor—and that audiences often internalize some aspects of joke speech accordingly—means that a joke-teller cannot justifiably use "only joking" as an excuse to dismiss *all* possible moral criticism of her speech. At the same time, though, one would have to be willfully flat-footed and po-faced not to make *some* ethical allowances for speech on the basis of its being humorous. Clearly we do not mean everything we say comically: we variously exaggerate, use sarcasm, adopt fictional perspectives, and rely on shock tactics in pursuit of a laugh, and we ought to be given normative leeway to say things jokingly that it would be wrong to say seriously.

The ambiguity of intentions and consequences in jokes means that we rely on contextual clues when making ethical judgments about them. One's tone, timing, and social identity take on greater moral relevance in cases of humor than in cases of nonhumor, as do the circumstances in which one decides to speak. A joker can take herself to be permitted to say things she would not be permitted to say if she was being entirely literal; but she must also accept that the moral value of her speech is partially determined by nontextual factors, including some that will be out of her control. A conscientious humorist who tells an edgy race joke will do her best to convey, through contextual information, that she bears no ill will to the racial group about whom she jokes; and she will nevertheless have to anticipate the possibility that her clues fail, and her audience does not interpret her as joking innocently. Aside from the moral harm associated with this possibility, such an interpretation can also be the cause of aesthetic shortcomings: a joke which makes its audience entertain (e.g.) racist ideas can be difficult to access and find amusing, for right-thinking people.

See also: Carroll, Stear, Jacobson, Mullin, Clavel-Vázquez, Cross, this volume

REFERENCES

Anderson, Luvell. 2015. "Racist Humor." *Philosophy Compass* 10, no. 8: 501–509.

Benatar, David. 1999. "Prejudice in Jest: When Racial and Gender Humor Harms." *Public Affairs Quarterly* 13, no. 2: 191–203.

Benatar, David. 2014. "Taking Humour (Ethics) Seriously, But Not Too Seriously." *Journal of Practical Ethics* 2, no. 1: 24–43.

Benatar, David. 2016. "Reply to Paul Butterfield on 'Taking Humour (Ethics) Seriously, But Not Too Seriously.'" *Journal of Practical Ethics Letters*. http://www.jpe.ox.ac.uk/correspondence/

Bergmann, Merrie. 1986. "How Many Feminists Does It Take to Make a Joke? Sexist Humor and What's Wrong with It." *Hypatia* 1, no. 1: 63–82.

Butterfield, Paul. 2022. "Focusing on the Gap: A Better Approach to the Ethics of Humor." *Journal of Value Inquiry* 56, no. 2: 283 – 302.

Carroll, Noël. 1991. "On Jokes." *Midwest Studies in Philosophy* 16, no. 1: 280–301.

Carroll, Noël. 2005. "Humour." In *The Oxford Handbook of Aesthetics*, edited by J. Levinson. Oxford: Oxford University Press.

Carroll, Noël. 2014. "Ethics and Comic Amusement." *British Journal of Aesthetics* 54, no. 2: 241–253.

Cohen, Ted. 1999. *Jokes: Philosophical Thoughts on Joking Matters*. Chicago: University of Chicago Press.

Davies, Christie. 1998. *Jokes and their Relation to Society*. Berlin: De Gruyter Publishing.

Davies, Christie. 2011. *Jokes and Targets*. Bloomington: Indiana University Press.

De Sousa, Ronald. 1987. *The Rationality of Emotions*. Cambridge, MA: The MIT Press.

Ferguson, Mark, and Thomas Ford. 2008. "Disparagement Humor: A Theoretical and Empirical Review of Psychoanalytic, Superiority, and Social Identity Theories." *Humor* 21, no. 3: 283–312.

Ford, Thomas, Christie Boxer, Jacob Armstrong, and Jessica Edel. 2008. "More Than 'Just a Joke': The Prejudice-Releasing Function of Sexist Humour." *Personality and Social Psychology Bulletin* 34, no. 2: 159–170.

Gaut, Berys. 1998. "Just Joking: The Ethics and Aesthetics of Humor." *Philosophy and Literature* 22, no. 1: 51–68.

Gimbel, Steven. 2018. *Isn't That Clever: A Philosophical Account of Humor and Comedy*. New York: Routledge.

Grice, H. P. 1989. *Studies in the Way of Words*. Cambridge, MA: Harvard University Press.

Howitt, D., and K. Owusu-Bempah. 2005. "Race and Ethnicity in Popular Humour." In *Beyond a Joke*, edited by S. Lockyer and M. Pickering, 45–62. London: Palgrave Macmillan.

Hurley, Matthew, Daniel Dennett, and Reginald Adams Jr. 2011. *Inside Jokes: Using Humor to Reverse-Engineer the Mind*. Cambridge, MA: The MIT Press.

LaFollette, Hugh, and Niall Shanks. 1993. "Belief and the Basis of Humor." *American Philosophical Quarterly* 30, no. 4: 329–339.

Langton, Rae. 2018. "Blocking as Counter-Speech." In *New Work on Speech Acts*, edited by D. Harris, D. Fogal and M. Moss, 144–164. New York: Oxford University Press.

Lengbeyer, Lawrence. 2005. "Humor, Context, and Divided Cognition." *Social Theory & Practice* 31, no. 3: 309–336.

Morreall, John. 2009. *Comic Relief: A Comprehensive Philosophy of Humor*. Malden, MA: Wiley-Blackwell.

Raskin, Victor. 1985. *Semantic Mechanisms of Humor*. Dordrecht: D. Reidel Publishing.

Smuts, Aaron. 2009. "Do Moral Flaws Enhance Amusement?" *American Philosophical Quarterly* 64, no. 2: 151–162.

Weaver, Simon. 2008. *The Rhetoric of Racist Humor*. Aldershot, UK: Ashgate Publishing.

CHAPTER 33

....

MONUMENTS AND MEMORIALS

Ethics Writ Large

....

JEANETTE BICKNELL, JENNIFER JUDKINS, AND CAROLYN KORSMEYER

Every memorial in its time has a different goal."

—Maya Lin

MONUMENTS and memorials are designed to shape public consciousness for genera-tions, perpetuating and reinforcing a shared understanding of their subjects. Depending on their position, size, and subject matter, monuments can achieve considerable power when aesthetic, ethical, and political aspects merge. Because many monuments are erected in locations where they are seen daily, their familiar presence instills a shared commemorative atmosphere. If they are especially well-designed, their beauty enhances the landscape of daily life, which is one reason why their removal can be wrenching.

Insofar as the concepts overlap, the ethics of monuments and memorials invite joint treatment, prompting similar questions about the respect they enjoin or the harm they may represent or perpetuate. At the same time, the many differences that characterize specific memorials and monuments indicate that the ethical issues they raise cannot be addressed in quite the same ways. This chapter will review some of the history lying be-hind these kinds of artifacts; the civic, personal, and global value that they possess; the controversies that some provoke; possible ways to handle disputes that arise about their meanings; and questions that result when valued public artifacts are intentionally dam-aged or fall into disrepair.

REMARKS ON HISTORICAL CONTEXT

The urge to memorialize is ancient. It is impossible to determine exactly when it begins to manifest, but the creation of marked graves, a practice that extends deep into prehistory, is a good candidate. A grave marker serves as a reminder of the person buried beneath. It may be temporary, perhaps no more than a flower garland or a wooden stake, or durable, such as a tombstone. Sometimes, memorial markers are so large and elaborate that they are also monuments.

Memorials and monuments are built so that both we and those who come after us might remember what they signify, whether individuals, events, or historical movements considered momentous enough that they should remain objects of public attention and honor. Generations pass; monuments endure. However, such artifacts face particular indeterminacy as time goes by and assessment of the worth of their subjects changes. Susan Stewart (2019) observes that:

> Monuments are among the most controversial of built forms . . . We pose impossible goals for them when we expect them to last forever, to convey permanent meanings, to manifest all of our beliefs and ideas about the dead. . . . We face the unending, and very expensive, task of conveying to each new generation our knowledge of the past. We can put up monuments, assuming their messages will cohere, or pull them down, assuming their meanings will disappear. (269)

Meanings can disappear and change for at least two reasons. The first is time itself, for over a long enough period of history, recollection of an artifact's significance might fade. This is especially true of structures that have decayed to the point of ruination, a point that prompts thoughts about the vulnerability of even the most durable materials. In one of his famous Odes, the Roman poet Horace considered his poetry—which, being intangible, eludes physical destruction—to be a safer insurance that he would not be forgotten:

> I have crafted a monument more lasting than bronze,
> and loftier than the royal pile of the pyramids,
> a thing which neither biting rain nor the obstreperous
> North Wind can destroy, nor the countless run of years,
> the flight of time. (III:30)

Time and the forces of nature are enough to obliterate even the hardiest materials, but deliberate human action is also a source of monument destruction. The reasons behind such actions may be political, religious, ideological, or a combination of all three. Different motivations for destruction indicate ways in which the meanings attached to monuments vary, depending on who is assessing them and at what point in their history.

Demolition of the monumental artifacts of conquered peoples is a longstanding practice of imperial powers who target cultural heritage as a means of subjugation. The Spanish conquistadors, for example, laid waste to Aztec monuments and built churches over what had been Mayan temples in Mexico. In 2001, the Taliban destroyed with weeks of artillery fire the giant Buddhas of Bamiyan, Afghanistan, which had overseen their valley for 1,500 years (Nagaoka 2020). During the Balkan War of the 1990s, the Croatian army targeted the ancient Mostar Bridge in Bosnia, which was regarded as such an important historical artifact of global cultural heritage that it was quickly rebuilt. Ethical questions arise not only when monuments are deliberately damaged or destroyed, but also when predictable collateral damage is not averted, as in Baghdad in 2003 when military forces from the United States failed to protect ancient sites from conflict.

Changes within societies can also occasion willful devastation; over time, the events that monuments commemorate do not always sustain agreement about what merits honor and remembrance. The Cultural Revolution in China in the 1970s encouraged destruction of artifacts large and small in an ideological rejection of social systems that had reigned for centuries. (See Man, this volume.) Sometimes destruction targets specific fallen leaders. Hence the toppling of monuments to Lenin and Stalin after the demise of the Soviet Union throughout the former Soviet bloc; the elimination of memorials to colonial rulers erected in former subject states in Africa; and the defacement and removal of statues commemorating leaders of the Confederacy in the United States.[1]

Acts of war and protest have been responsible for the mutilation and destruction of memorials and monuments for thousands of years. Iconic artifacts may be damaged incidentally in battle, or they may themselves be the target of the attack because the defacing of monuments represents a negation of the cultural values they embody. Religious differences motivate the destruction of temples, mosques, and churches that are seen by some as heretical. On a smaller scale, statues may be toppled, set afire, or symbolically drowned (as a statue of Christopher Columbus in Richmond, Virginia in 2020); or decapitated (a bust of Cecil Rhodes, Cape Town, South Africa, also in 2020, shown in Figure 33.1).[2] (See Bacharach, this volume.) Statues that are spray-painted with graffiti or otherwise "amended" might still command public attention for a time, the mark of protest now exhibited and itself memorialized.

The question of what to do with controversial monuments and memorials is of immediate contemporary significance, but reflection on the outcomes of destruction raises longer term concerns. How can we be certain that present day values will endure sufficiently to justify changes we make today? In France, the Revolution of the late eighteenth century and the Commune of 1870 saw the demolition of many monuments in Paris. Fragmented remains from some of that destruction are now being reconstructed (as with the Cluny Abbey, now a museum), an endeavor that reminds us that assessments of worthiness are subject to ongoing change. When we recognize the losses perpetrated by

---

[1] Numerous examples of the willful destruction of monuments are to be found in Gamboni (1997).

[2] Some other infamous topplings include George III (New York, 1776), Joseph Stalin (Budapest, 1956), Saddam Hussein (Baghdad, 2003), and Vladimir Lenin (Kiev, 2013).

FIGURE 33.1 Cecil Rhodes. Cape Town, South Africa. Credit: Zaian.

previous revisionist movements, including destruction in the name of important causes, how do we maintain a perspective that acknowledges that future generations will doubtless form different views about the changes we perpetrate today in the name of justice?

DEFINITIONS AND CONCEPTS

Monuments and memorials raise ethical concerns in part because they embody meaning in ways that objects of nature, utilitarian items, and most other works of art do not. They are deliberate declarations of value made by individuals or (more often) groups to give honor and commemorate, and to shape public understanding. Thus, monuments reflect the values of those who commission, create, and sustain them. Like works of political art, they are intended to have a specific kind of effect on viewers. Public memorials may direct the viewer to remember a single individual, a group of individuals, or an event.

For most of this chapter, we understand "monuments" to be large works of public art created with the intention to honor and glorify the deeds of an individual or set of individuals, or, more abstractly, some political or moral cause. As Alois Riegl wrote in his foundational essay at the beginning of the twentieth century, "a monument in its oldest and most original sense is a human creation, erected for the specific purpose of keeping single human deeds or events (or a combination thereof) alive in the minds of future generations" (Riegl 1903/1982, 21).

Monuments, particularly those that Riegl labels "deliberate" monuments, are generally intended to endure far beyond the life spans of those who commission, create, and erect them. Examples include public statues in the likeness of significant persons, Hammer and Sickle monuments once found in communist countries, the Statue of Liberty in New York City, and obelisks such as the Washington Monument in Washington, DC. (The latter is a design copied from monuments of ancient Egypt, examples of which can be seen all over the globe.) Some monuments also carry religious significance, such as the colossal statue of Christ the Redeemer that overlooks Rio de Janeiro.

The word "monument" is also used to refer to old and imposing structures, especially those with cultural heritage significance. For example, the Palais Garnier in Paris is an opera house that was designated a historical monument by the French government in 1923; the Palace of Westminster, meeting place of the British Parliament, is considered a monument of British culture; and the Great Wall of China, a massive fortification, is recognized as a monument of Chinese civilization. We will call such structures "designated" monuments to distinguish them from "deliberate" monuments. The focus of most of our discussion will be deliberate monuments, as these have garnered the most controversy over their ethical implications.

Memorials have a narrower function than deliberate monuments; they mourn, honor, and commemorate the dead. As Noël Carroll (2010) observes, memorial art "celebrates the honored dead, underscoring their virtues, and calls upon the living to emulate them" (167). Nicholas Wolterstorff (2015) points out the "social practice" of memorials when he states that "memorial art often aims not just at honoring some person or event from the past but also at achieving the causal effect of preserving, enhancing, and shaping the public memory of the memorialized person or event" (124). Like monuments, memorials may be works of public art, although most memorials are private, as with the many gravestones in cemeteries around the world. Some memorials are intended to last in perpetuity, although this is not invariably the case. The Panthéon in Paris, a giant stone temple commemorating those considered the greatest citizens of France, is both a memorial and a monument that was built to last hundreds of years. In contrast, the AIDS Memorial Quilt may also deserve the adjective "monumental" because of its size (1.2 million square feet). Yet being made of fabric, it is much less durable than stone, and even with special preservation techniques, it will not last anywhere near as long. Similarly, impromptu roadside memorials at the scene of a car accidents, or "ghost bikes" tethered to places where cyclists have been killed, are not intended to last a long time. Indeed, their fate is often to be cleared away by officials soon after the events they commemorate.

When monuments are both figurative and individual, such as Admiral Nelson atop his column in London's Trafalgar Square, the achievements of a particular, recognizable person are kept alive. Figurative renditions may also stand for many, rather than for specific individuals. A figure dressed in uniform standing outside a Tomb of the Unknown Soldier represents the many unnamed soldiers who died in battle.

Another example is the Vietnam Women's Memorial, with three uniformed women commemorating the female soldiers and medical personnel who served in that conflict. This is one of the relatively few public monuments honoring women. In fact, monuments to individual women are few and far between. A contemporary exception is the monument to Mary Wollstonecraft by Maggi Hambling that was unveiled in 2020. This joins the only three percent or so of public statues in the United Kingdom that are of nonroyal women, and the percentage is only slightly higher in the United States (O'Grady, 2021). There is no lack of female-appearing statues (the Statue of Liberty, the Winged Victory, or the blindfolded Lady Justice with her scales, for example), but these are unnamed symbolic renditions, embodying a concept or a triumph, a goddess or an angel, but not a person. Megan O'Grady wryly observes that "if humankind vanished tomorrow and aliens arrived from another galaxy, they wouldn't be faulted for believing that the whole of human history was composed of men on horseback" (O'Grady, 2021).

The size of a monument of abstract, nonfigurative design might serve to indicate the immensity of an event. The 200,000 square foot expanse of the Memorial to the Murdered Jews of Europe in Berlin, with its grid of 2,711 concrete slabs, imparts a sense of the vast numbers who were killed in the Holocaust (Figure 33.2). Similarly, the memorial walls describing the giant footprints of the twin towers of the World Trade Center, listing the names of those who died there, evoke the magnitude of the destruction of the 9/11 attacks. The imposing memorial to Dr. Martin Luther King Jr. in Washington, DC by sculptor Lei Yixin combines both figurative and abstract design, as well as inscriptions. King's image advances from blocks of granite, whose position and bulk symbolize a

FIGURE 33.2 Memorial to the Murdered Jews Of Europe. Berlin, Germany. Credit: Dietmar Rabich

phrase from his famous "I Have a Dream" speech: "Out of the mountain of despair, a stone of hope."

When text is inscribed on a memorial, such as a list of those killed in a battle or a catastrophic event, the sheer number of names delivers an affective impact (Young 2020). When names cannot be discovered, other means may be found to signify the immensity of loss. Sometimes the memorializing is sweeping, as seen at the Douaumont Ossuary in France. There, forever mingled, are the bones of over 130,000 unidentified French and German soldiers who died during the protracted battle of Verdun in the First World War.

An important aspect of any monument's design is size. A large monument dwarfs passers-by, imparting a sense of political dominance. As Sandra Shapshay (2021) observes, monuments make us feel "small and insignificant in our own individual lives and virtue" yet at the same time ennobled by membership in a particular political or ideological community (9). In short, a monument's artistic design often possesses aesthetic features that resonate deeply with the ethical stance it enjoins. Sometimes memorial monuments even seem to emit a kind of moral directive, a feeling of obligation. They compel a sense that one ought to pause and attend to their meanings.

CONTESTED ARTIFACTS: MONUMENTS, MEMORIALS, AND HARM

The very nature of monuments and memorials, especially their inhabitation of large public spaces, privileges the status of the individuals or events celebrated. Monuments are meant to display a community's "group value commitments" (Nguyen 2019, 971). Perhaps in this way we can understand Arthur Danto's assertion that "With monuments we honor ourselves" (Danto 1985, 152). Although they are meant to speak for a community, monuments are designed and created by the few and then "set in stone." Members of the community who later find the values represented abhorrent, or who see themselves denigrated and depreciated, find not remembrance and honor, but frustration and anger.

Central to the ethical issues pertaining to monuments are the kinds of harm that they cause or that they are seen as representing. Monuments may honor but at the same time fail to note related harms. For example, a statue commemorating a victory in war is very unlikely to acknowledge so-called collateral damage that civilians suffered. This is probably inevitable with war memorials, which are sufficiently conventional in their remembrance of the fallen, whether in victory or defeat, that sins of omission may go unnoticed.

More troublesome are monuments that celebrate an individual or a set of ideas that harmed others on a large scale, or that now offend for their historical legacy. Monuments even to events of the fairly distant past can arouse feelings of offence or disrespect for a number of reasons: that the suffering of one's ancestors has been overlooked; that the community of the present still admires individuals who harmed one's ancestors; and that the attitudes that lead to suffering continue to be endorsed. Affronts include the continued veneration for the monument in question; the fact that one's own heroes are not known or celebrated by the community at large; and that the harm perpetrated in the past is denied or minimized today. These feelings are magnified to the extent that the monument is large, prominent, difficult to avoid, and plays a part in civic life (for instance, if parades start or end there).

Contested monuments vary so greatly, both as monuments and in how they are contested, that no one response is pertinent for all. There are few quick or simple ways to rectify the harms that contested monuments may perpetuate. The complex scope of their histories, as well as their often immense physical presence, make them challenging to modify or remove. These are pieces of civic art, controlled by governments, and disagreement about their disposition is inevitable. Contested monuments also accrue their own history of interventions, complicating any new revisions.

For example, the 35-foot-tall Battle of Liberty Place monument at the foot of Canal Street in New Orleans, Louisiana, honored the "White League" members who died fighting the police in 1874. After years of protests post-1970, the monument was moved in 1993 to a place further from public view. A new slab of granite was added to the base of the statue, with an inclusive message about the lessons from the past, to cover an earlier racist inscription that had been added in 1932. After numerous white supremacist rallies in its new location, which were answered by bonfires and threats of violence if the statue were not removed, the monument was finally declared a "nuisance" and carted off to storage in 2017.

Another example presents more complex issues that indicate how meaning alters over the years. The Freedman's Memorial in Washington, DC depicts Abraham Lincoln holding a copy of the Emancipation Proclamation, with an ex-slave in broken shackles kneeling at his feet. Some call for its removal, objecting to the obeisant stance of the slave. Others have found value in its expression of political self-assertion within the culture of the time (Moody-Adams 2022). Supporting the latter view is the fact that the memorial, which cost $20,000 in 1876, was funded by African Americans, many of whom had been slaves themselves. Former slave and abolitionist orator Frederick Douglass spoke at length at the dedication. David W. Blight points out that "No African American speaker had ever faced this kind of captive audience of the full government, and none would do so again until Barack Obama's inauguration as president in 2009" (Blight 2020).

There are four broad kinds of possible resolutions for contested monuments, each with its own assets and defects. The first and most conservative approach is to *preserve the status quo*: leave the contested monument as it is, and conserve it in its current state and location. Preserving the status quo, however, presents an ongoing affirmative evaluation of what the monument represents and seems oblivious to opposing voices in the community. Furthermore, one could argue that the full history of the monument includes the marks of protest against it, and that therefore these should not be cleaned or erased.

A second approach is *preservation with additions or alterations.* Leave the monument largely as is but add interpretations or additions, whether as forming part of the monument itself or situated nearby. However, it is difficult to know what kind of alteration would be adequate to fully contextualize the monument and blunt the harm it may still perpetuate. A new plaque at the base of the original monument may be inadequate. A new, separate monument situated nearby is not always practical and would often be secondary. When Maya Lin's now venerated Vietnam Veterans' Memorial was first erected, it prompted distress from those who saw its black, descending walls as an expression of defeat. To address this concern, another monument, a more traditional figurative one with three soldiers, was placed nearby. In this case, the controversy was successfully resolved.

Some amendments are highly successful, especially those that begin as impromptu efforts from the community. In Hungary, the public has continued to respond vehemently to the Memorial to the Victims of the German Occupation, because of its false implications: Hungary was in fact complicit in the Holocaust. A spontaneous "countermonument," including painful personal mementos from those war years, continues in front of the Memorial, as a new "living memorial" (Lowe 2020). Impromptu additions to contested monuments can also be humorous. The 1844 statue of the Duke of Wellington on horseback (outside of the Glasgow Museum of Modern Art) has had an orange traffic cone placed on top of his head since at least the 1980s. All attempts to foil this addition (including raising the height of the statue) have failed. Today this tongue-in-cheek comment is a beloved landmark and tourist destination.[3] Yet a fitting addition or alteration can likely not be found for every contested monument. Ivan Gaskell records the failed efforts to place the names of Harvard's Confederate dead in Harvard's Memorial Church, after they were completely excluded from the university's lists in the Memorial Hall (Gaskell 2020).

A third solution is to *remove the artifact and preserve it elsewhere, or destroy it.* Simple removal might seem an elegant answer, and indeed this has been a popular solution. Helen Frowe has strongly insisted that states have a duty to remove statues of wrongdoers from most public places, even including statues of "morally ambiguous" wrongdoers, who have positive accomplishments in addition to their "serious rights violations" (Frowe 2019). But remove them to where? The answer "to a museum" may come most readily to mind, but this proposal is also problematic. Museums today are quite socially conscious with regard to the history of their accessions and may resist the "gift" of a contested monument.[4] Even with very specific placement and annotation,

---

[3] Recent rallies and a social media campaign to "Keep the Cone" have successfully fought back government interference.

[4] For example, the Metropolitan Museum of Art announced that they would stop accepting gifts from the members of the Sackler family (linked to the maker of OxyContin). The Guggenheim has also distanced itself from the family tied to Purdue Pharma.

museums might flinch at giving any acknowledgment of artistic value or significance to highly contested statues.

Finally, a fourth approach is to erect "anti-memorials" or "countermonuments" that explicitly oppose contested commemorations. In the late twentieth and early twenty-first century, anti-monumentalism or countermonumentalism arose as a response to both the anti-individualism implicit in the tradition of monument-making, and to the embodiment of authoritarian social narratives in monuments. A prominent example is the Monument Against Fascism (Harburg, Germany) by Jochen Gerz and Esther Shalev-Gerz. It is a lead column twelve meters high that was gradually lowered into the ground over a period of seven years (Young 1992). Another example is Horst Hoheisel's Aschrott Fountain (1985). It commemorates a fountain gifted to the German town of Kassel by a Jewish donor that was later razed by the Nazis in 1939. Hoheisel re-created the fountain as a hollow shell, then buried it upside down in the same space the fountain had occupied. It is covered by glass and a grate. Hearing the water as it falls down the 12-meter depth reinforces the inversion and reminds us of the fountain's wanton destruction.

The Stolpersteine ("stumbling blocks")—an art project originated by Gunter Demnig in 1992 in Cologne, Germany, and now spread across Europe—is a smaller, more subtle example of a countermonument. It comprises a collection of cobblestone-sized stone cubes, each inscribed with the name and dates of victims of Nazi persecution. Cubes are usually set in the pavement near where the victims lived or worked, to be discovered by chance. These small stones, only understood by close examination, are searing memorials both to individuals and to the wrongs that millions suffered. The artworld continues to bring creative responses to the monument controversies (Lescaze 2020).

Critical assessments of Western memorial culture have been amplified by global anti-racist protests, including the Black Lives Matter movement, in the United States often targeting monuments that glorify the American Confederacy. Employing a traditional figurative style, the artist Kehinde Wiley sculpted a figure on horseback that echoes a notable monument to Confederate General J. E. B. Stuart. Titled *Rumors of War*, Wiley's statue depicts a young African American man in contemporary urban clothing (Figure 33.3). Significantly, this monument is located in Richmond, Virginia, known for its numerous monuments to the Confederacy.

A temporary monument with related subject matter was Kara Walker's *Fons Americanus*, a giant sculpture 42 feet high of a four-tiered fountain, which was installed in 2019 at the Tate Modern.[5] It was intended as a counterpoint to London's 1911 *Victoria Memorial*. In an inversion of a memorial's usual function of remembrance, *Fons Americanus* exposes the miserable history of the Atlantic slave trade, with numerous allegorical figures (such as a weeping boy half-submerged in a scalloped shell), topped with Venus gushing water from her slashed throat and bare nipples.

---

[5] This monument was meant to be recyclable and was later disassembled.

FIGURE 33.3 Kahinde Wiley, *Rumors of War*. Richmond, Virginia. Credit: Virginia Museum of Fine Arts, Richmond. Purchased with funds provided by Virginia Sargeant Reynolds in memory of her husband, Richard S. Reynolds, Jr., by exchange, Arthur and Margaret Glasgow Endowment, Pamela K. and William A. Royall, Jr., Angel and Tom Papa, Katherine and Steven Markel, and additional private donors, 2019.39. Photo: Travis Fullerton © Virginia Museum of Fine Arts.

The evident individuality of monuments and memorials makes general rules about contested monuments difficult if not impossible to determine in advance of the particular controversy. With this in mind, Jeanette Bicknell argues for a case-by-case examination for contested monuments, defining an anti-theoretical, highly particularized approach to each instance (Bicknell 2020). She favors strategies where the artifact is recontextualized or removed from public display. Complete destruction or alteration of the monument will always risk the loss of historical insight and perhaps aesthetic value.

THE TREATMENT OF MONUMENTS AND MEMORIALS

Despite recent controversies, as a rule, monuments and memorials are appreciated and even cherished by members of a community, whether local or global. They command public spaces and represent shared values, buttressing memory against the years, while themselves becoming prey to time. The upkeep of private memorials, such as gravestones in a cemetery, often falls to the family of the deceased. The public character of civic memorials and monuments, however, brings questions of their treatment into wider ethical concern. What significance does such an artifact have for continued awareness of the history that sustains a society? How does aesthetic value figure into what is good for social cohesion and common appreciation, and how is the expenditure of public monies to be weighed against other needs of a community?

National attitudes regarding the preservation of material culture differ widely. Some cultural traditions discourage sudden full restoration. In Japan, Shinto shrines are perpetually renewed, piece by piece over time, like living things flowering and dying on different branches. (See Saito, this volume.) Since the 700s, the Ise Grand Shinto Shrine has been completely dismantled and rebuilt over the course of every twenty years, alternating between two adjacent sites in a continual rebirth.

Political and economic attitudes also affect treatment of historic artifacts. In China, enormous development and population growth have proved ruinous for historic sites and structures. Tens of thousands of major artifacts have disappeared in just the last twenty years, significantly more than were lost in the Cultural Revolution. Today efforts are steadily growing to mitigate the effects of mass tourism, pollution, and climate change, as well as to preserve cultural heritage. Yet one can still see, for example, the mile of cement that was simply poured over some of the broken crenellations of the Great Wall, then smoothed out like a long sidewalk.[6]

Incidents of large-scale devastation also indicate that cultural resources and preferences vary across the globe, and that much can be lost when damaged artifacts are simply considered debris or rubble. Writing of the destruction wreaked by earthquakes in Nepal, Robin Conningham and Kai Weise (2020) describe some of the frustrating conflict between custodians' expectations and conservation norms:

> While many aspects of preparedness protocols cover planned responses to disasters and damage, the treatment of debris, waste and resultant ruins is less well defined. For example, while many retrieved fragments from the Bamiyan Buddhas in Afghanistan have been painstakingly recorded, scanned and consolidated in advance of potential reconstruction, the mudbrick debris from the Citadel of Bam [in Katmandu] after the earthquake was simply removed and dumped. (275)

Thus, questions of preservation tangle with practical urgencies as well as cultural norms and political exigencies.[7]

---

[6] See Buckley and Wu (2016) for more details and reactions.

[7] Other sorts of practical considerations also influence the treatment of monuments. Enhanced security measures post-9/11 have brought about changes in access to some major monumental icons, such as the Washington Monument. After being closed in 2016, it reopened in 2019 with a new blast-proof entry building, and a bank vault-like "interlock" room that visitors will pass through prior to boarding an elevator.

RUINS AS MEMORIALS

Even if left untouched by protest or war or earthquake, monuments are subject to ongoing deterioration. The gradual wearing-away of old gravestones may seem appropriate, for it is time itself that brings about their decay. On the other hand, any deliberate damage from human actions (as where gravestones are defaced or broken) seems morally wrong, showing disrespect both for the dead and the living.[8] If an artifact is left to ruin passively, are there ethical obligations to protect it from further destruction? Even a monument that is also a ruin requires upkeep if it is to serve as a focus of public attention.

Decisions about how to forestall or treat injury frequently involve difficult ethical, aesthetic, and political choices. The seemingly obvious "fix" for damaged monuments is repair and restoration, and perhaps replacement when all other measures fail. This strategy is not without difficulties. Large restorations (and even lesser repairs) often require the addition of new elements and the deletion of original materials, thereby altering the material identity of the artifact and raising questions as to exactly what has been "preserved" (Korsmeyer 2019).

One of the choices presented by large-scale tragedies is simply to let the damaged site remain, memorializing its devastation by leaving it on display. What is now the Hiroshima Peace Memorial, for example, is the remaining structure of the single building left standing after the atomic bomb was dropped on that city in 1945 (Figure 33.4). After years of consideration about what to do with the remains, the nation of Japan decided to preserve its ruined state as a memorial to those who died in the attack and as a symbol of hope that no such catastrophe would ever be visited again (Saito 2020). But the area could not simply be left alone; it required peripheral removal of debris and structural stabilization for public safety. What remains is the genuine artifact, but its material preservation demands ongoing attention.

Other damaged monumental buildings have been transformed into enormous memorials when they are incorporated into new structures. Old Coventry Cathedral is an instance of a historic ruin integrated with a new monument. The old cathedral, which was begun in the fourteenth century, was largely destroyed in the Coventry blitz of November 14, 1940, with only the tower, steeple and part of the side walls remaining. Rather than demolishing what was left, it was left as a ruin with a garden of remembrance. The new cathedral (of a modern design) was built next to the remains of the old one, using the same Great Gate sandstone to unify the two structures. The Kaiser Wilhelm Gedächtniskirche (Memorial Church) in Berlin actually incorporates into its modern structure the tower of the older church that suffered bombing in 1943. After

---

[8] In 2016, a two-mile stretch of erosion control along the Potomac was found to be full of grave markers from a historic African American burial ground (Columbian Harmony Cemetery), dug up in 1960 for commercial development. There are plans to recover, identify, and relocate as many headstones as possible.

FIGURE 33.4 Hiroshima Peace Memorial. Hiroshima, Japan. Credit: Oilstreet.

the war, large iron crosses were fashioned from long medieval nails salvaged from the Coventry ruin and presented as symbols of peace to a number of German churches that were damaged by Allied bombs, including this one.

For the visitor, being fully surrounded by a ruin, and moving in and around it, enables a full physical engagement with honoring and memory. One of the most striking examples where an entire area was transformed by violence into a memorial is the ruined village of Oradour sur Glane, in France (Figure 33.5). Here 642 people (including 246 women and 207 children) were killed by the Nazis; anyone trying to escape was machine-gunned. General (later President) Charles de Gaulle ordered that the burnt-out village never be rebuilt and instead be completely preserved as a memorial. Today, we can walk through those same streets surrounded by the forever broken shells of buildings and remember.

REPAIR AND RESTORATION

Even when a memorial is a ruin, decisions about repair and restoration are required. That necessity prompts controversy, for some argue that repairs of any kind wrong the monument by changing its material composition and thereby its identity (Sagoff 1978). Ethical concerns about cultural preservation are entangled with aesthetic and

FIGURE 33.5 Oradour-Sur-Glane, France. Credit: Calips.

ontological considerations. How much restoration can be undertaken before it results in loss of the original monument?

The repairs and reworkings themselves become part of the monument's history. Fixing "defects" that detract from essential aesthetic qualities is also a high priority, even if they are not causing significant physical deterioration. For example, the Taj Mahal (a memorial mausoleum) has undergone extensive repairs and cleaning recently. The back side faces a polluted river, the Yamuna, which causes green bacterial colonies to discolor but not damage the famous white stones. Cleaning the stones retains the characteristic aesthetic of the memorial, and, not insignificantly, impresses tourists.

If repairs are undertaken, even on a small scale, should they be invisible to visitors, or should they be somehow "marked" to reflect this crease in the object's history? Restoration, which often requires the manufacture and replacement of damaged parts of an artifact, raises even more questions. Many designated monuments are immense and have long histories of damage and renovation, and it is not clear to what historical point they should be restored. For instance, the architects overseeing repairs at Notre Dame Cathedral briefly considered adding a newly designed spire, before deciding to replicate the one burned in the conflagration of April 2019. That spire was itself designed in 1859 to replace the original spire of 1230, which had been removed in 1792 after collapsing. Notre Dame has been an icon of French history for so long that its appearance as it has evolved over time is fixed in national—indeed global—imagination. It is the loss of the familiar nineteenth-century steeple that is now mourned more than its original

FIGURE 33.6 Terracotta Warriors, Xi'an, China. Credit: Pavel Špindler.

thirteenth-century spire. The example of Notre Dame demonstrates that objects valued as cultural heritage are not always static or fixed.

While Notre Dame has been a part of civic life for centuries, cultural knowledge regarding other designated monuments has been interrupted. The now famous Terracotta Warriors in Xi'an, China (themselves a memorial to Qin Shi Huang, the first Emperor of China) were entombed in 210–209 BCE, rediscovered in 1974, and named a World Heritage Site in 1987 (Figure 33.6).[9] The army of around 8,000 statues is slowly deteriorating to dust, partially due to the environmental control systems in place that enable more than five million tourists to visit the immense excavated site each year (Dunne 2018).[10] Should those crumbled Terracotta Warriors be completely restored and repainted in shades of their original colors, armed with (now) shiny swords?[11] "Good"

[9] The designation "World Heritage Site" requires that a site be of outstanding universal value, and meet at least one out of ten selection criteria. Currently, there are 1,121 World Heritage Sites, of which 869 are cultural, 213 are natural, and 39 are "mixed." See "The Criteria for Selection," World Heritage Convention, UNESCO, https://whc.unesco.org/en/criteria/ (accessed December 19, 2020). UNESCO also provides stringent guidelines for the Protection of Cultural Property in the event of armed conflict.

[10] The entire army (including the horses and chariots) was painted in bright colors. Unfortunately, the moment they were unearthed, the pigment began fading. It is only very recently that the technology has been available to preserve the colors of newly unearthed warriors.

[11] Although we know that many of the white marble structures of classical antiquity, including its famous sculptures, were originally painted bright colors, to try to return familiar icons of civilization to what we now believe to have been their original appearance would violate the position they have come to hold in cultural history.

restorations use as much as is available of the original materials, and yet too often the act of restoration itself obliterates those materials. The risk is high in this case.

UNESCO (the United Nations Educational, Scientific, and Cultural Organization) identifies monuments much as they do archeological sites, as "immovable cultural heritage." The once dominant view of erring on the side of caution in regard to issues of restoration and reconstruction has progressed, and carefully documented reconstruction has found new favor (Matravers 2020). The reconstruction of the historic center of Warsaw and the Old Bridge of Mostar were justified on the basis of the restoration of cultural value, as well as practical use value. Both were damaged by acts of war. It is debatable whether their cultural value actually has been restored by their wholesale replacement and reconstruction. Does reconstruction of these sites count as a form of restitution? Derek Matravers asserts that "even though restoration does not fully compensate for injustice, it is the closest we can get to full nugatory compensation" (Matravers 2020, 194).[12] Even complete reconstruction of a monument that has been destroyed might be justifiable in order partially to mitigate malicious damage and restore cherished aesthetic character to a place (Bülow and Thomas 2020; Lamarque 2016).

Full restorations run the risk of becoming replicas, and in Western culture important aspects of the object's aesthetic properties (which may not be directly visible) are not sustained in replicas, nor is what Riegl termed "age value" (Riegl 1903/1982; Korsmeyer 2019).[13] Often, almost all that is original is the location, the place. When we walk through Dresden into the Frauenkirche (1743/2005), not understanding that it is a full-scale, monumental replica, we do have an affective experience of its Rococo exuberance. Yet it is still an essentially different experience than being nestled in the excesses of the original church—the *genuine* historic church as it stood before the bombings of World War II. This suggests that not only should there be demarcations between where the original object ends and any repair begins, but also that the repair should be such that it can itself be easily removed and redone later, at a time when new technology might offer more assistance.[14]

PRESERVING THE EPHEMERAL

Impromptu memorials present particularly difficult preservation issues. Even though they may feature fragile elements such as paper, flowers, and handwritten notes, they "are often

---

[12] Erich Hatala Matthes points out that some sites gaining an outsize focus for reconstruction (say, Palmyra) may be quite disassociated from the interests of the common people (who, in that case, were removed from the ancient site in the 1930s by French colonists) (Matravers 2020).

[13] In China, interestingly, "replication" includes two separate types of copies: obvious imitation and exact reproductions. The latter is often held to be of equal value to the original. See Han (2017).

[14] Sometimes the materials used in the repair are subsequently found to be inadequate or even dangerous, and must be replaced. Or, materials contained in the monument (for example, asbestos) are later understood to be toxic and must be substituted.

aggressively physical entities," erected in spaces that must be walked through or around, demanding our physical interaction (Doss 2008, 38). One of the largest examples would be the mountains of flowers (estimated at 60 million blooms) left throughout London after the death of Princess Diana in 1997. Impromptu memorials can also be small, such as the roadside memorials for private citizens. The intimate connection between these impromptu memorials and the grieving public means that disassembly may be experienced as a retraumatization (Bednar 2013, 340).[15] What is more, since they are not only ephemeral but also personal, what kind of consent for their display is mandated?

One of the saddest examples of an impromptu memorial is the Chelsea Jeans Memorial, now located within the 9/11 Memorial in New York.[16] It is a storefront that was painstakingly moved there after it was discovered that all of the clothing in the window was covered in ash and toxic dust from the disintegration of the nearby World Trade Center towers. The shelves of dusty jeans are all encased in plexiglass now, frozen in time. In this instance, a museum offered placement for what are undoubtedly human remains, now settled into the folds of a stack of blue jeans. This artifact is an impromptu memorial preserved in a monumental memorial museum that has now become, in part, a graveyard.

CONCLUDING REMARKS

Monuments and memorials raise a host of ethical questions. In a diverse society, the meaning of the past is likely to be contested. With this fact comes the question of which events, individuals, and ideas deserve to be commemorated and honored. The way in which the honor and commemoration is rendered must be appropriate, both aesthetically and morally. The use of public space (a limited resource) implies the need for some form of public consultation. Is it reasonable to seek consensus, and how is such a consensus to be achieved? Once a decision to erect a monument or memorial has been taken, further questions arise. These questions, which must be answered when new commemorative artifacts are contemplated, are no less urgent for monuments and memorials that already exist. The meaning of public monuments can change, just as our relationship to the events and people memorialized alters, and honor accorded may later be withdrawn. Hence some of the monuments we currently live with may afford historical figures a residue of public regard that some might reject. Yet at the same time, they might remain important tokens of a past we should not forget.

See also: Willard, Fisher, Bacharach, Soucek, Clavel-Vázquez, this volume

---

[15] Residents of Utøya Island, Norway, objected to erecting a memorial to the 69 people killed there in 2011 in a politically motivated killing spree. Their grounds included perpetuation of the trauma of the event.

[16] Other impromptu memorials including most of the tributes left at the Memorial are sent to storage facilities, but a few are catalogued and added to the official museum collection at the World Trade Center Memorial.

References

Bednar, Robert M. 2013. "Killing Memory: Roadside Memorial Removals and the Necropoliticsof Affect." *Cultural Politics* 9, no. 3: 337–356.

Bicknell, Jeanette. 2020. "The Physical Legacy of a Troubled Past." In *Philosophical Perspectives on Ruins, Monuments, and Memorials*, edited by Jeanette Bicknell, Jennifer Judkins, and Carolyn Korsmeyer, 253–261. New York: Routledge.

Blight, David W. 2020. "Yes, the Freedmen's Memorial Uses Racist Imagery. But Don't Tear It Down." *Washington Post*, June 25.

Buckley, Chris and Adam Wu. 2016. "Botched Repair to China's Great Wall Provokes Outrage." *New York Times*, September 22.

Bülow, William and Joshua Lewis Thomas. 2020. "On the Ethics of Reconstructing DestroyedCultural Heritage Monuments." *Journal of the American Philosophical Association* 6, no. 4: 483–501.

Carroll, Noël. 2010. *Art in Three Dimensions*. Oxford: Oxford University Press.

Coningham, Robin and Kai Weise. 2020. "Ruins and Debris: Cultural Heritage Practice,Resource Management, and Archeology." In *Philosophical Perspectives on Ruins,Monuments, and Memorials*, edited by Jeanette Bicknell, Jennifer Judkins, and Carolyn Korsmeyer, 275–290. New York: Routledge.

Danto, Arthur C. 1985. "The Vietnam Veterans Memorial." *The Nation* 241 (August): 152–155.

Doss, Erika. 2008. *The Emotional Life of Contemporary Public Memorials: Towards a Theory ofTemporary Memorials*. Amsterdam: Amsterdam University Press.

Dunne, Erin. 2018. "How Xi'an's past became a blueprint for its future." *The Diplomat*, May 8. https://thediplomat.com/2018/05/how-xians-past-became-a-blueprint-for-its-future/

Frowe, Helen. 2019. "The Duty to Remove Statues of Wrongdoers." *Journal of Practical Ethics* 7, no. 3: 1–31.

Gamboni, Dario. 1997. *The Destruction of Art: Iconoclasm and Vandalism since the French Revolution*. London: Reaktion Books.

Gaskell, Ivan. 2020. "For the Union Dead: Memorial Hall at Harvard University and theExclusion of the Confederate Fallen." In *Philosophical Perspectives on Ruins,Monuments, and Memorials*, edited by Jeanette Bicknell, Jennifer Judkins, and Carolyn Korsmeyer, 262–274. New York: Routledge.

Han, Byung-Chul. 2017. *Shanzai: Deconstruction in Chinese*. Translated by Philippa Hurd. Cambridge, MA: The MIT Press.

Horace, Ode III:30, lines 1–4. (c. 23 BCE). Trans. Terry Walsh. *The Classical Anthology*. https://classicalanthology.theclassicslibrary.com/2014/05/11/horace-odes-3-30-contributed-by-terry-walsh/

Korsmeyer, Carolyn. 2019. *Things: In Touch with the Past*. New York: Oxford University Press.

Lamarque, Peter. 2016. "Reflections on the Ethics and Aesthetics of Restoration and Conservation." *British Journal of Aesthetics* 56, no. 3: 281–299.

Lescaze, Zoë. 2020. "America's Monuments, Reimagined for a More Just Future." *T: The New York Times Magazine*, August 24.

Lowe, Keith. 2020. *Prisoners of History: What Monuments to World War II Tell Us About Our History and Ourselves*. New York: St. Martin's.

Matravers, Derek. 2020. "The Reconstruction of Damaged or Destroyed Heritage." In *Philosophical Perspectives on Ruins, Monuments, and Memorials*, edited by Jeanette Bicknell, Jennifer Judkins, and Carolyn Korsmeyer, 189–200. New York: Routledge.

Matthes, Erich Hatala. 2017. "Palmyra's Ruins Can Rebuild Our Relationship with History." *Aeon*. April 25. https://aeon.co/ideas/palmyras-ruins-can-rebuild-our-relationship-with-history.

Moody-Adams, Michele. 2022. *Making Space for Justice: Social Movements, Collective Imagination, and Political Hope*. New York: Columbia University Press.

Nagaoka, M., ed. 2020. *The Future of the Bamyan Buddha Statues*. Paris: UNESCO.

Nguyen, C. Thi. 2019. "Monuments as Commitments: How Art Speaks to Groups and How Groups Think in Art." *Pacific Philosophical Quarterly* 100, no. 4: 971–994.

O'Grady, Megan. 2021. "Why Are There So Few Monuments That Successfully Depict Women?" *T: The New York Times Magazine*, February 18.

Riegl, Alois. [1903] 1982. "The Modern Cult of Monuments." Translated by Kurt W. Forster and Diane Ghirardo. In *Oppositions* (Fall): 20–51.

Sagoff, Mark. 1978. "On Restoring and Reproducing Art." *Journal of Philosophy* 75, no. 9: 453–470.

Saito, Yuriko. 2020. "Reflections on the Atomic Bomb Ruins in Hiroshima." In *Philosophical Perspectives on Ruins, Monuments, and Memorials*, edited by Jeanette Bicknell, Jennifer Judkins, and Carolyn Korsmeyer, 201–214. New York: Routledge.

Shapshay, Sandra. 2021. "What Is the Monumental?" *Journal of Aesthetics and Art Criticism* 79, no. 2: 1–16.

Stewart, Susan. 2019. *The Ruins Lesson: Meaning and Material in Western Culture*. Chicago: University of Chicago Press.

Wolterstorff, Nicholas. 2015. *Art Rethought: The Social Practices of Art*. Oxford: Oxford University Press.

Young, James E. 1992. "The Counter-Monument: Memory Against Itself in Germany Today." *Critical Inquiry* 18, no. 2: 267–296.

Young, James O. 2020. "How Memorials Mean, or How to Do Things With Stones." In *Philosophical Perspectives on Ruins, Monuments, and Memorials*, edited by Jeanette Bicknell, Jennifer Judkins, and Carolyn Korsmeyer, 34–44. New York: Routledge.

FURTHER READING

Allison, David B., ed. 2018. *Controversial Monuments and Memorials: A Guide for Community Leaders*. Lanham, MD: Rowman & Littlefield.

Bicknell, Jeanette, Jennifer Judkins, and Carolyn Korsmeyer, eds. 2020. *Philosophical Perspectives on Ruins, Monuments, and Memorials*. New York: Routledge.

Bülow, William, Helen Frowe, Derek Matravers, and Joshua Lewis Thomas, eds. 2023. *Heritage in War: Ethical Issues*. Oxford: Oxford University Press.

Dementriou, Dan, and Ajume Wingo. 2018. "The Ethics of Racist Monuments." In *The Palgrave Handbook of Philosophy and Public Policy*, edited by David Boonin, 341–355. London: Palgrave.

Frankowski, Alfred. 2015. *The Post-Racial Limits of Memorialization: Toward a Political Sense of Mourning*. London: Lexington Books.

Farber, Lauren A. 2005. "Issues in the Collection and Conservation of American Vernacular Memorial Art." *The Book and Paper Group Annual* 24: 5–16.

Frowe, Helen and Derek Matravers. 2019. "Conflict and Cultural Heritage: A Moral Analysis of the Challenges of Heritage Protection." *J. Paul Getty Trust Occasional Papers in Cultural Heritage Policy*, no. 3. http://getty.edu/publications/occasional-papers-3/.

Gilbert, Catherine, Catherine Mary McLoughlin, and Niall Munro, eds. 2020. *On Commemoration: Global Reflections Upon Remembering War*. Oxford: Peter Lang.

Levinson, Sanford. 1998. *Written in Stone: Public Monuments in Changing Societies*. Durham, NC: Duke University Press.

Moody-Adams, Michele. 2019. "Episode 037: Michele Moody-Adams on Monuments and Memorials." Interview with Myisha Cherry (podcast), February 11. *UnMute Podcast*, https://unmutetalk.podbean.com/e/episode-037-michele-moody-adams-on-monuments-memorials/.

Nelson, Louis P. 2018. "Object Lesson: Monuments and Memory in Charlottesville." *Buildings & Landscapes: Journal of the Vernacular Architecture Forum* 25, no. 2: 17–35.

Richmond, Alison, and Alison Bracker, eds. 2011. *Conservation: Principles, Dilemma, and Uncomfortable Truths*. New York: Routledge.

Savage, Kurt. 2009. *Monument Wars: Washington, D.C., the National Mall, and the Transformation of the Memorial Landscape*. Berkeley: University of California Press.

Thompson, Erin L. 2022. *Smashing Statues: The Rise and Fall of America's Public Monuments*. New York: Norton.

Young, James E. 1993. *The Texture of Memory: Holocaust Memorials and Meaning*. New Haven, CT: Yale University Press.

CHAPTER 34

ETHICAL ISSUES IN INTERNET CULTURE AND NEW MEDIA

ANTHONY CROSS

INTRODUCTION

THE omnipresence of the internet in the twenty-first century has brought with it enormous changes in our everyday life; digital media have reconfigured our epistemic networks, altered our social relationships and our senses of self, and reconfigured our agency in ways that we have only recently begun to understand. It should be no surprise, then, that these media have also enabled new forms of aesthetic activity, many of which are rife with ethical significance.

This chapter focuses on the new media characteristic of internet culture: internet memes, viral videos, social media posts, and so on. These new media are largely participatory, ephemeral, and anonymous, yet they offer important new opportunities for everyday aesthetic expression which have, to date, largely been ignored by philosophers. This chapter highlights the ethical significance of these new media along three main dimensions. First, the chapter focuses on how the everyday aesthetic choices afforded by online curation, filters, and internet "aesthetics" provide new opportunities for the expression and creation of individual identities. Second, the chapter surveys the ways that internet memes and other participatory media contribute to the formation and expression of communities with shared values. Third, the chapter discusses ethical challenges associated with ownership and attribution of instances of these media: can anyone claim ownership of a meme? And what might such ownership consist in? The chapter concludes by considering the significance of these emerging media as a whole as a radically distributed, accessible, and powerful form of folk art.

Before going any further, it will be helpful to distinguish the focus of this chapter from what is often referred to as computer art, net art, and postinternet art. These labels are generally used to refer to the works of established artists that in some way or other take advantage of the affordances of digital media and the internet. Computer art is defined by reference to its interactivity—that is, its involvement of a user in the generation of the art's display (Lopes 2009). Net art consists in artists making work that in some way or other makes creative usage of internet technology (Ippolito 2002), while postinternet art consists in art-making that acknowledges and accommodates the role of the internet in artistic production and distribution (McHugh 2011). While these are useful categories for understanding contemporary developments in the artworld, they are less helpful in tracking the kinds of everyday aesthetic practices and activities that are common to many users of the internet. When creating an internet meme, reposting a viral video, curating a profile, or writing fan fiction, one engages in an exercise of what media theorist Jean Burgess has referred to as vernacular creativity: "everyday cultural production that makes sense in the context of contemporary transformations in culture and new media technologies" (Burgess 2007, 29). These everyday exercises of cultural production have largely fallen outside the focus of the philosophy of art—although the recent emergence of the field of "everyday aesthetics" represents an important corrective to this trend (Saito 2021). This chapter takes these practices to constitute a sphere of aesthetic activity which we can refer to as internet culture—a culture which combines features of more traditional forms of vernacular culture with the affordances of digital media and the internet.

Are there any distinguishing features of internet culture? One suggestion is that much internet culture shares a common aesthetic. According to critic Nick Douglas, much of internet culture is marked by a style he refers to as "Internet Ugly": an aesthetic encouraging pairing willful amateurism with absurd, surreal, or ambiguous content (Douglas 2014). By contrast, media theorists Whitney Phillips and Ryan Milner have argued that the distinguishing feature of much internet culture is *weirdness*—a kind of ambivalence and oddity that stands in marked contrast to predominant cultural values (Phillips and Milner 2017, 9–13). While these styles are prevalent, they aren't universal; there is a great deal of internet culture that fails to demonstrate the requisite ugliness or weirdness. Consider the aspirational content common to many Instagram accounts, consisting largely of "muted pastel palettes and washed-out backgrounds; flatlay still lifes, personal items painstakingly arranged for best visual appeal" (Leaver, Highfield, and Abidin 2020, 62). The aesthetic practices governing the curation, editing, and posting of such images could hardly be further from demonstrating an aesthetic of ugliness or weirdness.

Even so, these styles point us toward more promising means of distinguishing internet culture—not in terms of a unified style or content, but rather in terms of its primary modes of creation and dissemination. For one, a great deal of internet culture is *participatory*: users are encouraged to engage with internet culture by way of sharing, iterating and implementing it themselves (Jenkins, Ford, and Green 2013, 153–194). In making and sharing internet memes, for example, users alter and redeploy the meme to suit their interests and contexts, reposting it and sharing it to their own networks and communities (Shifman 2014a). The DIY amateurism of Internet Ugly flourishes in this context as both a reflection of participatory culture and a way of rendering participation more accessible.

Internet culture is also distanced from our ordinary, embodied identities—this means that much internet culture is either *anonymous* or *pseudonymous*. The distance afforded by digital mediation allows for a great deal of our participation in internet culture to be as isolated and distinct from our embodied selves as we wish; as the joke goes, "on the Internet nobody knows you're a dog." This distancing effect lends itself to the flourishing of the weird and sometimes even antagonistic culture Phillips and Milner refer to as the ambivalent internet (Phillips and Milner 2017, 50–51).

At the same time, much internet culture is *authorless*: users participate, share, and iterate collectively without any marks of authorship or attribution. In this respect, internet culture resembles more traditional forms of folk culture, such as oral traditions like joke-telling and folk-song: the culture is free to be shared and iterated as users see fit. This is not to say that there are no rules or norms for the production and dissemination of internet culture; as Ryan Milner argues, a great deal of internet meme culture is governed by both formal and informal gatekeeping, in which users collectively enforce norms surrounding the format of memes (Milner 2018, 36–37). However, all of this is compatible with much internet culture eschewing attribution to any particular individual (Davison 2012, 132).

A final feature of internet culture is its *spread*. Because internet media can be quickly replicated and disseminated across networks, internet culture can spread rapidly. An individual hashtag, GIF, or meme can be shared and iterated across many networks and redeployed in different communities or collectives for more specific purposes (Denisova 2019, 44–53). This "spreadability" is, in principle, not different from the way that more traditional vernacular culture spreads; what differentiates internet culture is only the speed and scale at which the spread occurs.

In the sections below, I highlight the ethical significance of the emergence of internet culture. First, I discuss the extent to which the development of our online identities through participation in internet culture is ethically significant. I'll then turn to the ethical significance of community and the extent to which internet culture facilitates community. Finally, I'll turn to questions surrounding the ownership of internet culture.

INTERNET CULTURE AND IDENTITY

It is a rather common notion that our aesthetic choices both express and construct our identities. We are beset by aesthetic opportunities, and as agents we must chart a path through our aesthetic lives on the basis of our judgments about aesthetic value. Most of these choices, as Kevin Melchionne argues, will have rather low stakes and will involve relaxed deliberation: we make such choices about which movies to stream, which outfits to wear, or how much salt to put in the soup (Melchionne 2017). Some might be more significant: everything can hang on a painter's selection of color or a poet's choice of words. But perhaps more important than any single aesthetic choice is the way that such choices, over time, come to express our identities: our choices might cohere into a broader pattern that reflects our individual sensibilities (Cohen 1998). As Nick Riggle has argued, matching our aesthetic choices to our personal ideals—aesthetic and otherwise—would be an achievement of individual style (Riggle 2015). It is arguably an aesthetic and perhaps even an ethical achievement to develop a *distinctive* style—one which sets us apart from others in notable or significant ways (Nehamas 2007, 84–91).

The internet presents a novel set of opportunities for making such aesthetic choices. The participatory nature of much internet culture actively involves users in aesthetic choices that go well beyond passive appreciation: users are invited to respond, to iterate, to share, and to curate. At the same time, the anonymity or pseudonymity of much internet culture encourages users to play with developing new identities and sensibilities. Finally, the affordances of digital media provide shortcuts to style—ranging from algorithmic suggestions to Instagram filters to ready-made internet "aesthetics." This section explores the ways in which the internet, considered as a context for aesthetic choice, can lead to ethically significant impacts on our identities.

Anonymity, Identity, and Play

As already noted, much of our interaction with internet culture is participatory; users are invited to actively engage by sharing, liking, iterating, and adapting. In this respect, internet culture is quite similar to more traditional forms of participatory culture, insofar as it creates extensive opportunities for vernacular creativity (Howard 2008). However, users' participation in internet culture is distinguished from more traditional cultural forms by its lack of embodiment and the anonymity and pseudonymity this invites; as argued below, this allows users to *play*—to try out different sensibilities and identities with a freedom not available in more traditional, embodied forms of cultural participation.

This is not to say that we should expect everyone to develop an online persona radically different from the one manifest in their embodied interactions and relationships; as Nancy Baym notes, although "the affordances of new media open up new possibilities for exploring and representing ourselves and others . . . it turns out that, with some significant exceptions, most people, most of the time, use new media to act in ways mostly consistent with their embodied selves" (Baym 2015, 118). What the absence of embodiment affords is a greater degree of freedom with respect to one's self-expression and self-disclosure: users have full control over whether to reveal certain aspects of themselves relevant to the sensibilities or styles they aim to cultivate. Such control may be lacking in embodied contexts, insofar as one lacks full control over what is disclosed through one's bodily appearance and activity (Cocking 2008).

At the same time, the platforms responsible for the creation and distribution of much internet culture allow users to mask their identities in ways that encourage departures from one's embodied self. Image boards like 4chan allow for complete anonymity in one's contributions, while message boards, Reddit, and social media platforms like Twitter and Instagram allow for pseudonymity—users are invited to post contributions under any username they choose.[1]

The combination of these features allows users greater freedom to play in their aesthetic choices by constructing new identities and presenting themselves to new communities. Consider the ease with which one can create new profiles on platforms such as Twitter, Instagram, or Reddit. These new profiles might be dedicated to particular aesthetic projects: creating and sharing niche memes, parodying public figures, or posting fan fiction. Just as easily, users can enter into networks and communities surrounding these aesthetic practices by subscribing to appropriate subreddits, following other users, or joining an interest-based internet forum. These choices and activities have very low stakes: if some particular aesthetic identity isn't working out, it can simply be abandoned in favor of something new. The benefit of this ease is that we're encouraged to think explicitly about and actively choose our identities through aesthetic experimentation and play, thereby expanding the range of our aesthetic agency.

At the same time, this sense of freedom and play is not without its downsides. Whitney Phillips argues that subcultural trolling is largely dependent on anonymity; negative and antagonistic engagement online is often dependent on maintaining a barrier between one's online activity and one's everyday embodied self (Phillips 2015, 25).[2] There's also little doubt that a great deal of racist, sexist, and otherwise morally repugnant content is created and circulated online due to a perceived insulation of users from any significant repercussions (Milner 2018, 115–149). Consider the example of an online community dedicated to sharing fan art of the Colorado movie theater mass shooter, James Holmes (Broderick 2012). Self-styled "Holmies" aren't alone; similar online fan movements have emerged surrounding other mass shooters and terrorists (Phillips and Milner 2017, 5–6). It's unlikely that individuals would participate in sharing this content without the perceived protections of anonymity and pseudonymity.

Online identity play also invites a risk of fragmentation of identity—the sense that one's online self is radically distinct from one's IRL self.[3] In some cases, the aesthetic choices and projects that we develop online may become central to our broader sense of our personalities. However, there may be cases in which these online projects and relationships fail to integrate with other aspects of our self-conception. This is especially likely when the sensibilities that we develop and cultivate online are at odds with one's other values; Phillips points out that many online trolls regard their trolling

---

[1] The exception to the rule is Facebook, which enforces a "real name" rule in which users must use the name they use in real life. For more discussion on the effects of real name rule, see Tufekci (2017, 139–146).

[2] For more on trolling and anonymity in the context of online gaming, see Bartel, "Ethics and Video Games," and Bartel, this volume.

[3] This is not to endorse the idea that there is a sharp distinction to be drawn between online and "in real life" (IRL) selves, or to endorse the idea that IRL projects and interactions are in any way superior. For an argument against "fetishism" of the IRL, see Jurgenson (2012).

selves—their identities as circulators of antagonistic and immoral internet culture—as radically distinct from their personal identity (Phillips 2015, 34–36). The risk of such fragmentation is plausibly exacerbated by the affordances of anonymity and pseudonymity; it is certainly easier to maintain distances between one's aesthetic identities insofar as they aren't publicly connected.

To what extent should we be concerned about such fragmentation? Some philosophers have argued that self-integration is a necessary constituent of the good life (Cottingham 2010). To the extent that such fragmentation makes total self-integration more difficult, there is perhaps some cause for concern that the ease of identity play online will undermine this ethical project. Then again, not all philosophers agree that complete self-integration is a necessary condition for living a good life; some argue that fragmentary and episodic lives are nevertheless consistent with individual flourishing (Strawson 2004).

Algorithms and Choice

By making decisions with respect to what we engage with aesthetically and how we do so, we exercise our autonomy by way of our aesthetic choices. C. Thi Nguyen has argued that we insist on such autonomy because we value the process of engaging with aesthetic objects—a process that involves individual discovery, exploration, and judgment (Nguyen 2020).

One salient feature of many of the platforms used to disseminate internet culture is their personalization. Platforms like Facebook, Twitter, Reddit, Instagram, and TikTok make use of algorithms which predict, on the basis of a user's past activity, what kinds of content will be most engaging to the user; content will then be provided to the user on the basis of these predictions. Many have raised epistemological, moral, and political concerns about the effects of personalized content filtering (Pariser 2011). What is less appreciated is the extent to which such filtering affects our online aesthetic activities and practices.

Kevin Melchionne argues that insofar as streaming services such as Netflix, Amazon, and Spotify provide algorithmic recommendations, they help us to solve a serious problem of aesthetic choice: how to navigate an overwhelming array of aesthetic opportunities in ways that will be productive to our aesthetic flourishing (Melchionne 2017). It's true that there is a similar problem of choice with respect to internet culture: we are awash in memes, viral videos, social media accounts, and online communities, and it can be quite difficult to know in advance what kinds of engagement will be worthwhile. By comparing our past choices on a platform to those of other users whose activity is similar, algorithmic filtering can often help direct us toward content that will be interesting or rewarding for us.

At the same time, the algorithms used to analyze our past choices can be helpful to us as a source of information about our sensibilities. Spotify, for example, provides year-end analyses of users' listening habits. It might be helpful to learn from this analysis that one has consistently engaged with a particular genre of music or video. If you learn, for example, that you've been listening to more and more art pop, this might help you to explicitly recognize this tendency as part of your sensibility, which you can then try to develop further.

However, this filtering might give us cause for concern for two reasons. First, insofar as an algorithm selects and presents content to you on the basis of your past behavior and choices, it may be less likely to provide you with opportunities to develop new aesthetic interests. Instead, the algorithm might lock you into what Eli Pariser has called the "you loop"—a cycle in which your initial actions trap you into an identity cascade in which you're served only content relevant to your initial identity cues. Engagement with this content further cements the algorithm's understanding of your identity, leading to more and more of the same kinds of content (Pariser 2011, 127). The result is that our aesthetic lives online are closed off from accident, happenstance, and surprise discovery; as a result, we are less likely to stumble into new opportunities for aesthetic appreciation and agency.

The second cause for concern about algorithmic filtering is that it is almost always opaque to users just how and to what extent their content is being personalized and filtered. Although some social media platforms are willing to publish the information collected about their users' past activity, almost no platforms disclose how their algorithms operate to select and filter content. Insofar as users are unaware of filtering, this can undermine users' ability to consent—and thereby compromise users' autonomy in engaging with internet culture.

How might we respond to these two concerns? There may be straightforward means of counteracting the first: users might take steps to "retrain" the algorithm by searching for and selecting content outside of their established areas of interest. Alternatively, users can rely on personal recommendations—from friends and family but also from critics and influencers. Finally, users might frequent online platforms such as internet forums and message boards that are not algorithmically filtered. Each of these strategies can lead to exposure to new and unexplored areas of internet culture. The second concern is only serious to the extent that users value complete autonomy in their aesthetic exploration. It may be that many users are willing to sacrifice some of their autonomy in the interest of an efficient solution to the problem of aesthetic choice; what ultimately matters may not simply be aesthetic autonomy, but rather which contexts for aesthetic choice lead to the most rich and rewarding lives.

Shortcuts to Style

A further affordance of internet culture is the extent to which individual platforms offer preconstructed stylistic choices. Consider the example of the Instagram filter: users are able to select between a variety of stylized filters to apply to images they post on the platform. These filters, featuring evocative names like "Nashville," "Toaster," and "Inkwell," each apply a preconfigured set of adjustments to images meant to be reminiscent of vintage analogue photographs (Leaver, Highfield, and Abidin 2020). This is one case of what we might call a "shortcut to style."[4]

Another case is the set of so-called internet aesthetics: online stylistic trends such as dark academia, cottagecore, VSCO, and goblincore spread largely through social media platforms like TikTok and Instagram. These styles are highly codified and standardized by practitioners, who publish guides focusing on fashion choices, visual style, media influences, and even typefaces. As such, it's fairly easy to adopt an internet aesthetic: one need simply string together a few themed and tagged posts on social media featuring one's internet aesthetic (Cross 2020).

Preexisting styles aren't a new phenomenon—examples of earlier stylistic templates include punk culture and queer ballroom culture. What distinguishes online styles and aesthetics is the ease with which users can toggle back and forth between different styles. This ease encourages the sort of play with respect to identity discussed above; because of the low stakes, one can easily try out a variety of different styles and sensibilities. Furthermore, users are encouraged to think of individual style as a matter of choice, open to revision through experimentation.

At the same time, insofar as these shortcuts to style are highly codified—and, in the case of Instagram filters, opaque in their operations to the user—there is a risk that settling simply for these prepackaged styles will circumscribe and constrain users' agency in developing individual style. This is especially a concern in cases where stylistic shortcuts are developed in a top-down way by various platforms, rather than through the activities of users themselves.[5]

INTERNET CULTURE, COMMUNITY, AND POLITICS

The previous section argued that participation in internet culture can have ethically significant impacts on an individual's identity. This section turns from the intrapersonal to the interpersonal: it focuses on the impact of internet culture on our relationships with others. Rather than taking up these issues at a highly general level, this section instead focuses on an in-depth case study of perhaps the most dominant form of internet culture—the internet meme. Drawing on resources from media theory as well as the philosophy of art, the section first develops a working theory of the nature of internet memes. Following this, I discuss the possibility that we might form ethically significant

---

[4] This is not to imply that posting photos without applying a filter represents a completely neutral, unstyled photograph; as Daniel Star argues, even "#nofilter" photos incorporate the default stylization of one's digital camera software (Star 2018).

[5] This worry is similar to that expressed by critics of Facebook, such as Zadie Smith, who argues that the platform offers a diminished and technologically constrained model of friendship and personal interaction (Smith 2010).

communities on the internet; I then argue that the creation and propagation of memes is an increasingly prevalent means of forming and maintaining such communities. Finally, I consider the political significance of internet memes.

A Working Theory of Internet Memes

Most discussions of internet memes—including this one—begin with a reference to Richard Dawkins's initial coinage of the term "meme" as the cultural analog of the gene: the smallest replicating unit of culture, transmitted from individual to individual through communication and observation (Dawkins 1989). While there is a vibrant discussion as to whether this notion of a meme is applicable to contemporary internet culture,[6] this chapter focuses on the slightly narrower categories of *internet* memes. This is a rather diverse category of internet phenomena that includes images, videos, animations, texts, and hashtags spread through social media, websites, and email. Especially popular examples of the category include Pepe the Frog (discussed further below), the Distracted Boyfriend meme, and the #yesallwomen hashtag. Most internet users will have encountered at least some members of this category through social media, online forums, browsing, or email; a somewhat smaller portion will have actively contributed to the propagation of internet memes by creating, sharing, or using them.

Internet memes are, in Ryan Milner's terminology, multimodal: they incorporate text, images, audio, video, and hypertext (Milner 2018, 25). However, many of the most notable examples are image-based—that is, they centrally involve some photographic or pictorial content, often paired with superimposed text elements (Shifman 2014a). Sometimes referred to as "image macros," these image-based memes began circulating among users of internet forums such as 4chan and Reddit around 2004 or 2005, although the practice—and the memes themselves—quickly spread beyond those communities (Börzsei 2013). Consider the well-known image-based meme of Pepe the Frog. This meme has its origins in a comic strip titled *Boy's Club* by artist Matt Furie. In around 2008, users of online message boards like 4chan began adapting one of the comic's characters, an anthropomorphic frog named Pepe, into a series of reaction images—most notably, Pepe saying "feels good man." Over time, users adapted the Pepe character into a number of increasingly bizarre contexts, and eventually the meme attained some measure of mainstream popularity.

What exactly *is* an internet meme? The past decade has seen the emergence of numerous definitions on the part of media theorists. Patrick Davison defines an internet meme as "a piece of culture, typically a joke, which gains influence through online transmission" (Davison 2012, 122). Davison's definition is largely in keeping with Dawkins's initial characterization of memes as transmissible units of culture; it also likens memes

---

[6] For in-depth discussion on whether internet memes are memes in Dawkins sense, see Shifman (2014b, 37–63).

to jokes. However, Davison's definition is extremely broad—it arguably encompasses all internet culture. Limor Shifman develops a more specific three-part definition, according to which internet memes are "(a) a group of digital items sharing common characteristics of content, form, and/or stance; (b) that were created with awareness of each other; and (c) were circulated, imitated, and/or transformed via the internet by many users" (Shifman 2014b, 7–8). Shifman's definition specifies that individual instances of a meme share common elements—either content, form, or "stance," which is understood in terms of the attitude or relation to the meme's content. Furthermore, Shifman makes clear the requirement that in order to participate in sharing or iterating an instance of a meme, users must be aware of the larger phenomenon of the meme itself. Ryan Milner expands on Shifman's definition, specifying five central "logics" of memetic media. These include the aforementioned quality of multimodality, along with what Milner refers to as reappropriation, resonance, collectivism, and spread (Milner 2018, 22–39). A quick gloss on these elements: memes generally involve reappropriation of existing media through processes of poaching and bricolage; they are the product of collectives, and lack specific authors responsible for their creation. They depend on an emotional effect, or "resonance" for their rapid spread through online networks.

Philosophers of art have appealed to the tools of analytic aesthetics to further theorize internet memes. Let us first distinguish between the instances of a meme—some particular images of Pepe the frog, say—and the Pepe meme itself. Borrowing from the ontology of music, Anthony Cross argues that internet memes themselves are indicated structural types: memes are thematic templates or sets of instructions for generating particular instances—in much the same way that a musical score indicates a structure governing the generation of individual performances (Cross 2017). However, Cross notes, internet memes differ from musical works in that memes are the product of collective authorship, and are furthermore open to collective revision over time. In a similar vein, Simon Evnine argues that memes are artifacts constituted by norms for producing instances; furthermore, Evnine provides a practice-based account of the concept "meme" (Evnine 2018).

Much more could be said about the nature of internet memes, but the above provides enough theory to explain how internet memes demonstrate each of the distinguishing features of internet culture: First, internet memes are participatory, in that they invite users not only to share instances of any particular meme but also to generate their own. Second, internet memes are authorless insofar as they are the product of collective practice rather than the fiat of any particular artist. Finally, internet memes are capable of rapid spread insofar as most instances of the meme can be easily replicated and shared among networks.

Memes, Communities, and Intimacy

Ted Cohen, writing about jokes, argues that all jokes are conditional: in order for a joke to land, and for an audience to find it funny, the audience must meet certain background conditions.[7] Some jokes require shared background knowledge, such as math jokes or philosophy jokes. Other jokes require a shared affective stance; the joke-teller and the audience have to have the same attitudinal orientation toward the subject matter of the joke. When the joke lands, the joke teller and audience are united by a kind of intimacy—what Cohen refers to as "the shared sense of those in a community" facilitated by both a shared outlook on the world and a shared appreciative response to the joke. (Cohen 1999, 28).

Philosophical consensus regards communities as normatively significant—although there is a disagreement about whether communities are significant because they are of instrumental value for individuals, or if communities have final value in their own right (Mason 2000, 42–63). If Cohen is right, jokes serve as an important means of constructing and maintaining normatively significant communities by generating intimacy.

Much the same story can be told about internet memes; a large part of the value of internet memes lies not so much in their content—which is often sophomoric or bizarre—but rather in their ability to generate precisely the sort of intimacy Cohen describes above. This makes internet memes an especially valuable means of creating and maintaining communities online. Consider the fact that in creating or sharing memes, users take on the role of collective authorship of the meme. Through their activity, they indicate that they are part of the group that understands and appreciates the meme. At the same time, in creating and sharing instances of the meme, users play a role in determining the nature of the meme itself. By creating new instances of the meme, users can shift community practice and ultimately alter or change the meme through their activity. The shared understanding of the meme as well as the resonance of each individual instance of the meme creates intimacy among members of this community.

Of course, one might object that the community of all the users involved in creating and sharing any particular meme is purely a notional one. The community of users of, say, the Distracted Boyfriend meme fails to correspond to any actual community, online or otherwise. Furthermore, some might express skepticism about the possibility that normatively significant *online* communities exist at all.

With respect to the first of these objections, consider Andrew Mason's definition of the ordinary notion of community as "a group of people who share a range of values, a way of life, identify with the group and its practices and recognize each other as members of that group" (Mason 2000, 21). Although massive, the global set of users of a particular meme does share in the common practice of appreciating and propagating the meme; to this extent, these global memes represent a sort of lingua franca uniting users across the internet (Denisova 2019, 44–53). At the same time, global memes are often localized in particular communities. Shifman points out that "global" meme templates are often customized for smaller communities—either by

---

[7] For more discussion, see Butterfield, "Ethics of Humor," this volume.

iterating the meme with contents relevant to the community's interests, or by altering, customizing, or translating the meme to make it more accessible (Shifman 2014b, 161–179). In such cases, although memes are deployed in preexisting communities, they are nevertheless able to play an important role in generating intimacy within these communities.

Some philosophers have also expressed skepticism about the possibility that online communities constitute genuine, normatively significant communities at all. Gordon Graham, for example, asks whether "a relationship restricted to electronic communication [is] capable of creating the sort of relationship between human beings that ordinary communities are expected to realize" (Graham 1999, 145). In particular, Graham expresses concerns about the prospects for a community that consists of anonymous participants, each of which has full control over their self-disclosure. Consider two responses to Graham's objection: first, many online communities aren't entirely online. Many social networking platforms provide us with new, mediated forms of communication with our preexisting, real-world communities. Even communities that form online may hold "meet-ups" or establish other forms of face-to-face interaction. Thus we shouldn't be so quick to assume a hard and fast distinction between online communities and real-world communities. A second response is to argue that even in cases where a community's interactions occur entirely online, this may nevertheless qualify a genuine, normatively significant community. Nancy Baym argues that these online communities often share features with more traditional communities, including a sense of a shared space and practices, shared identities and roles, common support structures, and interpersonal recognition (Baym 2015, 82–100).

Memes are therefore a kind of cultural glue, binding together online communities by generating intimacy. However, because of the ease with which memes are replicated, disseminated, and iterated, a meme based in one community can quickly spread to others. This raises interesting questions about ownership and appropriation of memes: Is it a breach of a community's intimacy when memes are appropriated by outsiders?[8] To consider a concrete example, let's return to the case of Pepe the Frog: as discussed earlier, the Pepe meme originated within the community of the image-posting message board 4chan. However, the meme spread virally until Pepe became—like the ubiquitous lolcat—a meme familiar to many mainstream internet users. Members of the original community out of which Pepe emerged took umbrage with the meme's new popularity and—likely out of a desire to troll mainstream internet users—began to associate Pepe with racist themes. Over time, their campaign worked. Pepe was taken up by white supremacists and those on the so-called alt-right on Twitter, Reddit, and other social networks. This ultimately led to the classification of Pepe as a form of hate speech by the Anti-Defamation League (Glitsos and Hall 2019).

[8] For more on cultural appropriation and its links to breaches of intimacy, see Strohl and Nguyen, "Cultural Appropriation," this volume.

Memes and Politics

The case of Pepe the Frog also demonstrates that internet memes, in addition to their role in developing and maintaining communities, can be *politically* significant. In the runup to the 2016 US presidential election, Pepe came to be seen as a figurehead for the alt-right—an outsider "deplorable" set apart from the "normies" of mainstream culture.[9] Pepe featured in numerous online communications, including a post from then-nominee Donald Trump's son's Instagram account. Hillary Clinton's campaign even went so far as to publicly denounce the meme and its associations (Cross 2017).

What, exactly, is the political significance of internet memes? As evidenced by the Pepe meme's significance for the alt-right, memes can be used as a tool to build *political* communities. Zeynep Tufekci notes that creation and dissemination of memes can help to create a sense of camaraderie and connection among members of a protest or political movement. What's more, given the ability to rapidly disseminate memes on a massive scale, these memes can function to draw outsiders into the political movement (Tufekci 2017, 111–112).

Some argue more broadly that internet memes have reconfigured the public sphere, allowing for the mass expression of viewpoints and perspectives outside the political mainstream. An Xiao Mina traces the use of internet memes in a number of different protest movements, arguing that memes contain the seeds of large-scale social change (Mina 2019, 189–190). Ryan Milner argues that any particular meme, because of its iterability and adaptability, is capable of supporting a vibrant public conversation in which numerous voices and views are expressed (Milner 2018, 151–184).

INTERNET CULTURE, OWNERSHIP, AND ATTRIBUTION

This final section will address ethical concerns about the ownership, attribution, and appropriation of internet culture alluded to in the previous section. Let's once again return to the case of Pepe the Frog: Recall that the meme is based on an image of an anthropomorphic frog appropriated from a comic strip by artist Matt Furie. Initially, Furie responded to the meme's popularity among the alt-right with a mixture of bemusement and resignation; he conceded that the meme itself didn't belong to him, and encouraged users to "save Pepe" by sharing positive or kind instances of Pepe (Serwer 2016). However, over time, Furie grew increasingly upset about how his character was being used in the meme; in 2017, he published a comic strip killing off the character of

---

[9] Nagle (2017) traces the alt-right's appropriation of 4chan's stance toward "normies" and its meme culture.

Pepe. He then began to file copyright infringement lawsuits against alt-right websites and publications using images of Pepe. He was ultimately successful in a number of these legal actions, winning financial compensation and take-down orders in a number of cases (Swinyard 2019).

Internet memes—and a great deal of internet culture more generally—involves reappropriation: users share reaction GIFs clipped from television shows and movies; memes draw on stock photographs or well-known pop cultural images; and users constantly appropriate and share images, clips, and texts via their social media accounts. These appropriations almost always occur without the consent of the original source, as in the case of Pepe. Even more notably, many memes feature likenesses of real persons, used against their will; this results in immense amounts of attention being directed toward the individuals who feature in the meme. Consider the well-known "Star Wars Kid" video—a private home video in which Canadian teenager Ghyslain Raza films himself awkwardly performing a mock light-saber duel with a golf club. Raza's classmates found the video and posted it online without his knowledge or consent; it quickly went viral, attracting an enormous number of views on Youtube and becoming the subject of numerous remixes. The effects on Raza's well-being were stark: he dropped out of school, was diagnosed with depression, and was ultimately admitted to a children's psychiatric ward. His parents ultimately sued the classmates who posted the video, leading to a settlement (Taylor 2020).

There are difficult and as-yet-unresolved ethical and legal questions concerning the control that individuals like Furie and Raza ought to have over their appropriated works and likenesses. The internet is an unruly place, and as Jonathan Zittrain notes, we currently lack "an infrastructure of meme propagation . . . capable of acknowledging and respecting preferences of the real people impacted by these virtual phenomena" (Zittrain 2014, 390). This hasn't stopped these individuals from trying: as mentioned, Furie has had some success in pursuing copyright infringement lawsuits as a means of controlling images of Pepe. Others have appealed to the legal right to be forgotten—the right to have private information about a person removed from the internet. This legal right has been affirmed in the EU and several other jurisdictions, although its implementation has been limited (Rosen 2011).

At the same time, many of these individuals have attempted to benefit from their status as the subjects of memes. For example, Matt Furie has recently taken to selling nonfungible tokens (NFTs) of Pepe the Frog (Cavna 2021). NFTs are crypto tokens, just like Bitcoins and other cryptocurrency: each NFT is a pointer to an address on a publicly verifiable and distributed blockchain. What differentiates NFTs from other forms of cryptocurrency is the fact that each NFT is unique and can't be interchanged with any other NFT. This makes NFTs especially well-suited to indicating ownership of specific objects, and recently NFTs have been the most favored mechanism for transferring ownership of digital objects like images and film clips. Furie is one of numerous individuals who have sold NFTs of digital content linked to memes; due to the supercharged cryptocurrency market, many of these NFTs have sold for hundreds of thousands of dollars (Rosenblatt 2021). Just what is being sold in these transactions? If you were to buy a licensed image of Pepe from Furie via NFT, what you'd be getting would be owner-ship of that single image. However, owning a one-off Pepe isn't the same thing as owning the meme itself; it's arguable that Furie, even if he owns the original image of Pepe, has no claim to the subsequent internet cultural phenomenon of iterating and sharing Pepe memes (Cross 2021).

Who owns the meme itself? Who deserves responsibility for it, and who should have the right to control it? There is an obvious parallel to draw between internet culture and more traditional forms of vernacular creativity and expression: like most folk art, internet culture is participatory, occurs against a background of cultural norms and traditions, and is largely authorless. In these contexts, the most reasonable claims to ownership lie with the members of the community responsible for creating and propagating these cultural forms. So perhaps we should regard internet memes and other forms of internet culture as a kind of cultural property, possessed in common by all users who are members of the community who iterate and propagate it (Matthes 2018). One problem for this approach has already been noted: much internet culture spreads rapidly, and what might begin as a shared practice among members of a small online community can easily expand into a part of global internet culture. This can make it difficult to individuate the particular culture or cultures responsible for the generation and propagation of a meme.

Can internet culture itself be subject to ethically problematic cultural appropriation? In 2010, the clothing retailer Hot Topic began selling a shirt featuring "Rage Guy"—a stick figure face central to the "rage comics" meme then circulating on 4chan, Reddit, and other online message boards. In retaliation for this perceived appropriation of their culture, users of these websites began a campaign of online harassment of the retailer—one which ultimately failed to prevent Hot Topic from continuing to sell the shirt. Nick Douglas points out that in this and other cases of corporate appropriation of internet culture, users object to what they perceive to be inauthentic usage of internet culture by those outside the community (Douglas 2014, 334–336). But is this outrage based on too narrow a reading of the community responsible for internet culture? If *all* users of the internet have a claim to internet culture, what's to stop any one of us from using its cultural forms for our own purposes?

Conclusion

Given its recent emergence, there is a tendency to write off much internet culture as a mere diversion: we go to social media merely to pass the time, and internet memes are only good for a quick laugh. However, even though most of our engagement with internet culture has low stakes, it nevertheless has major ethical significance: it provides us with important means of developing our identities and constructing communities. Given the ephemerality of most internet culture, its participatory nature, and our relative anonymity, we can approach these ethical projects with a level of freedom and play that we lack in more traditional, embodied contexts. At the same time, the collective nature of much internet culture gives rise to significant ethical concerns about cultural ownership and appropriation. Although worth taking seriously now, it's likely that these ethical considerations will only grow in significance as we shift even more of our attention and activity online.

See also: Butterfield, Willard, Bartel, this volume

REFERENCES

Baym, Nancy K. 2015. *Personal Connections in the Digital Age.* 2 ed. Malden, MA: Polity Press.

Börzsei, Linda K. 2013. "Make a Meme Instead: A Concise History of Internet Memes." *New Media Studies Magazine 7.*

Broderick, Ryan. 2012. "A Guide to the Dark World Of James Holmes Internet Fandom." *BuzzFeed,* July 31, https://www.buzzfeednews.com/article/ryanhatesthis/a-guide-to-the-dark-world-of-the-james-holmes-inte.

Burgess, Jean Elizabeth. 2007. "Vernacular Creativity and New Media." PhD Thesis, Queensland University of Technology.

Cavna, Michael. 2021. "Matt Furie Is Trying to Reclaim His Famous Cartoon Pepe the Frog — Through NFTs." *Washington Post,* May 30, https://www.washingtonpost.com/arts-entertainment/2021/05/30/pepe-frog-nft-matt-furie-crypto-art/.

Cocking, Dean. 2008. "Plural Selves and Relational Identity: Intimacy and Privacy Online." In *Information Technology and Moral Philosophy,* edited by Jeroen van den Hoven and John Weckert, 123–141. Cambridge: Cambridge University Press.

Cohen, Ted. 1998. "On Consistency in One's Personal Aesthetics." In *Aesthetics and Ethics: Essays at the Intersection,* edited by Jerrold Levinson, 106–125. Cambridge: Cambridge University Press.

Cohen, Ted. 1999. *Jokes: Philosophical Thoughts on Joking Matters.* Chicago: University of Chicago Press.

Cottingham, John. 2010. "Integrity and Fragmentation." *Journal of Applied Philosophy* 27, no. 1: 2–14.

Cross, Anthony. 2017. "The Curious Case of Pepe the Frog: On the Ontology and Value of Internet Memes." *Aesthetics For Birds,* January 26, https://aestheticsforbirds.com/2017/01/26/the-curious-case-of-pepe-the-frog-by-anthony-cross/.

Cross, Anthony. 2020. "Instagram Filters for the Self: Autonomy and Internet 'Aesthetics.'" *Aesthetics for Birds,* September 23, https://aestheticsforbirds.com/2020/09/03/autonomy-and-internet-aesthetics/.

Cross, Anthony. 2021. "Beeple and Nothingness: Philosophy and NFTs." *Aesthetics for Birds,* March 18, https://aestheticsforbirds.com/2021/03/18/beeple-and-nothingness-philosophy-and-nfts/.

Davison, Patrick. 2012. "The Language of Internet Memes." In *The Social Media Reader,* edited by Michael Mandiberg, 120–134. New York: NYU Press.

Dawkins, Richard. 1989. *The Selfish Gene.* Oxford: Oxford University Press.

Denisova, Anastasia. 2019. *Internet Memes and Society: Social, Cultural, and Political Contexts.* New York: Routledge.

Douglas, Nick. 2014. "It's Supposed to Look Like Shit: The Internet Ugly Aesthetic." *Journal of Visual Culture* 13, no. 3: 314–339.

Evnine, Simon J. 2018. "The Anonymity of a Murmur: Internet (and Other) Memes." *British Journal of Aesthetics* 58, no. 3: 303–318.

Glitsos, Laura, and James Hall. 2019. "The Pepe the Frog Meme: An Examination of Social, Political, and Cultural Implications Through the Tradition of the Darwinian Absurd." *Journal for Cultural Research* 23, no. 4: 381–395.

Graham, Gordon. 1999. *The Internet: A Philosophical Inquiry*. London: Routledge.

Howard, Robert Glenn. 2008. "The Vernacular Web of Participatory Media." *Critical Studies in Media Communication* 25, no. 5: 490–513.

Ippolito, Jon. 2002. "Ten Myths of Internet Art." *Leonardo* 35, no. 5: 485–498.

Jenkins, Henry, S. Ford, and Joshua Green. 2013. *Spreadable Media: Creating Value and Meaning in a Networked Culture*. New York: NYU Press.

Jurgenson, Nathan. 2012. "The IRL Fetish." *The New Inquiry* 28, https://thenewinquiry.com/the-irl-fetish/.

Leaver, Tama, Tim Highfield, and Crystal Abidin. 2020. *Instagram: Visual Social Media Cultures*. Cambridge: Polity.

Lopes, Dominic. 2009. *A Philosophy of Computer Art*. London: Routledge.

Mason, Andrew. 2000. *Community, Solidarity and Belonging: Levels of Community and Their Normative Significance*. Cambridge: Cambridge University Press.

Matthes, Erich Hatala. 2018. "The Ethics of Cultural Heritage." In *The Stanford Encyclopedia of Philosophy*, edited by Edward N. Zalta, https://plato.stanford.edu/entries/ethics-cultural-heritage/.

McHugh, Gene. 2011. *Post Internet*. Lulu.com.

Melchionne, Kevin. 2017. "Aesthetic Choice." *British Journal of Aesthetics* 57, no. 3: 283–298.

Milner, Ryan M. 2018. *The World Made Meme: Public Conversations and Participatory Media*. Cambridge, MA: The MIT Press.

Mina, An Xiao. 2019. *Memes to Movements: How the World's Most Viral Media Is Changing Social Protest and Power*. Boston: Beacon Press.

Nagle, Angela. 2017. *Kill All Normies: Online Culture Wars from 4chan and Tumblr to Trump and the Alt-Right*. Croydon, UK: Zero Books.

Nehamas, Alexander. 2007. *Only a Promise of Happiness: The Place of Beauty in a World of Art*. Princeton, NJ: Princeton University Press.

Nguyen, C. Thi. 2020. "Autonomy and Aesthetic Engagement." *Mind* 129, no. 516: 1127–1156.

Pariser, Eli. 2011. *The Filter Bubble: How the New Personalized Web Is Changing What We Read and How We Think*. New York: Penguin.

Phillips, Whitney. 2015. *This Is Why We Can't Have Nice Things: Mapping the Relationship Between Online Trolling and Mainstream Culture*. Cambridge, MA: The MIT Press.

Phillips, Whitney, and Ryan M. Milner. 2017. *The Ambivalent Internet: Mischief, Oddity, and Antagonism Online*. Malden, MA: Polity Press.

Riggle, Nick. 2015. "Personal Style and Artistic Style." *Philosophical Quarterly* 65, no. 261: 711–731.

Rosen, Jeffrey. 2011. "The Right to Be Forgotten." *Stanford Law Review Online* 64, no. 88, https://www.stanfordlawreview.org/online/privacy-paradox-the-right-to-be-forgotten/.

Rosenblatt, Kalhan. 2021. "Iconic 'Doge' Meme NFT Breaks Record, Selling for $4 Million." *NBC News*, June 11, https://www.nbcnews.com/pop-culture/pop-culture-news/iconic-doge-meme-nft-breaks-records-selling-roughly-4-million-n1270161.

Saito, Yuriko. 2021. "Aesthetics of the Everyday." In *The Stanford Encyclopedia of Philosophy*, edited by Edward N. Zalta, https://plato.stanford.edu/entries/aesthetics-of-everyday/.

Serwer, Adam. 2016. "It's Not Easy Being Meme." *The Atlantic*, September 13, https://www.thea
tlantic.com/politics/archive/2016/09/its-not-easy-being-green/499892/.

Shifman, Limor. 2014a. "The Cultural Logic of Photo-Based Meme Genres." *Journal of Visual
Culture* 13, no. 3: 340–358.

Shifman, Limor. 2014b. *Memes in Digital Culture*. Cambridge, MA: The MIT Press.

Smith, Zadie. 2010. "Generation Why?" *New York Review of Books*, November 25, https://www.
nybooks.com/articles/2010/11/25/generation-why/.

Star, Daniel. 2018. "#Nofilter: Philosophical Reflections on Photography in the Age of
Instagram." *Aesthetics for Birds*, July 27, https://aestheticsforbirds.com/2018/04/18/nofilter-
philosophical-reflections-on-photography-in-the-age-of-instagram/.

Strawson, Galen. 2004. "Against Narrativity." *Ratio* 17, no. 4: 428–452.

Swinyard, Holly. 2019. "Pepe the Frog Creator Wins $15,000 Settlement Against Infowars." *The
Guardian*, June 13, https://www.theguardian.com/books/2019/jun/13/pepe-the-frog-crea
tor-wins-15000-settlement-against-infowars.

Taylor, Chris. 2020. "Reconsidering 'Star Wars Kid,' the Early Internet's Meanest Moment."
Mashable, October 28, https://mashable.com/article/star-wars-kid-cyberbullying.

Tufekci, Zeynep. 2017. *Twitter and Tear Gas: The Power and Fragility of Networked Protest*. New
Haven, CT: Yale University Press.

Zittrain, Jonathan L. 2014. "Reflections on Internet Culture." *Journal of Visual Culture* 13, no. 3:
388–394.

PART IV

ETHICAL PROBLEMS IN THE ARTS

CHAPTER 35

....

ETHICS OF ARTISTIC
AUTHORSHIP

....

KAREN GOVER

WHEN we first consider "the ethics of artistic authorship," we probably think of artists who have made controversial works. The moral outrage surrounding, for example, Balthus and his erotically charged paintings of young girls, or Chris Ofili's use of elephant dung and pornographic imagery in his "The Holy Virgin Mary" (1996), or Damien Hirst's sculptures featuring decaying or embalmed animal corpses become focal points for questions about the nature, extent, and value of artistic freedom. In such cases, the focus is primarily on the content of the artwork. The author's role as the source of the work's controversial content is taken for granted.

A second, separate concern about the ethics of artistic authorship, also currently of great concern lately, makes a moral evaluation of the artist. It asks whether artworks are tainted by the moral turpitude of their authors. If the allegations that Michael Jackson molested children are true, for example, should we still enjoy his music? Even if the content itself is not objectively offensive, perhaps the art becomes tainted by association with its morally defective source. For some, this is an aesthetic issue—the artwork can no longer be pleasing to us once we know the moral deficiencies of its author. For others, the moral quandary manifests in the economics of art consumption: some say one should not reward a morally bad artist by consuming their work and thereby enriching them either materially or reputationally. In such cases, the locus of concern is on the moral worth of the artist, and only secondarily on the work. (See Matthes, this volume.)

In this chapter, I address the relatively unexamined and more fundamental question of the ethics of artistic authorship as such, setting aside morally questionable content or behaviors. I focus here on the ethical implications of the claim, "This is my artwork." The moral inquiry into the nature of artistic authorship also brings us into the domain of the law, insofar as authored works, including artworks, are regarded in the United States and in many other jurisdictions as a form of intellectual property. Property claims of all kinds, not just of artworks, have ethical implications because they involve the rights of owners to enjoin others from certain behaviors, and the corresponding responsibilities of others to respect those rights. Nevertheless, the ownership claims of authors with respect to their artworks are unique in some respects. This is because in contemporary Western culture we tend to regard artworks as a special kind of authored work, with a special tie to its author.

In order to unpack the ethical implications of claiming an artwork as one's own, we must first understand that there are multiple reasons for and contexts within which one might make such a claim: through creation; purchase; discovery; appropriation; delegation; collaboration; or heritage, to name a few. Some of these, but not all, are also claims of authorship. Consider for a moment the possible meanings of someone's credible assertion, "This artwork is mine":

- I made the artwork, and so I am its author.
- I own an artwork, but someone else authored it.
- I did not make or purchase the artwork, but it is part of my cultural patrimony and heritage, so it is mine.
- Someone else fabricated the art object, but at my behest and instruction, so I made the artwork, and I am therefore its author.
- I authored the artwork, which is a dance/play/musical work/set of instructions, so someone else must perform or execute my artwork.
- We authored the artwork.
- I made the artwork, so it is mine; but I do not like it, so it is not mine.

All these statements, in varying ways, involve the speaker asserting that they have a special proprietary relationship to an artwork. Most of the statements involve authorship claims. Hence, the simple statement "This is my artwork" can mean different things, depending on the context and circumstances in which it is uttered. And those different meanings will in turn entail different ethical entitlements and obligations. Since this chapter concerns the ethical implications of artistic authorship as opposed to simple ownership, I turn next to some general points before I return to the different permutations listed above.

At its most fundamental level, the modern Western concept of authorship revolves around the notion of responsibility. When we ask for the author of an artwork, at some basic level, we want to know who made it, or who directed its making. Philosophical theories of art authorship are remarkably consistent in defining authorship in terms of responsibility: "An author is one with the ultimate responsibility for the form and content of the work, including its artistic and, where applicable, moral qualities" (Hick 2014, 151); "The artist's authorship is defined by the fact that she bears ultimate responsibility for every aspect of the objectives she pursues through her work, and thus every aspect of the work itself" (Irvin 2005, 134); "Behind the question of authorship lies the interest we take in knowing who, on a specific occasion, has been proximally responsible for the intentional production of a given utterance" (Livingston 2005, 68); "To be an artist is to be directly responsible for a thing being an artwork, and to be directly responsible for a thing being an artwork just is to be the source of the intentions directing the activities constitutive of the successful art-attempt of which that thing being art is the product" (Mag Uidhir 2013, 85). While these philosophers' theories of artistic authorship may differ in their details, there is broad consensus that the authorship of artworks fundamentally involves responsibility for the work having the features it does. This is so even if someone else carried out the author's instructions for constructing it. For this reason, it is the author to whom we direct our praise and blame for the work's aesthetic or moral features. This account of authorship assumes that the artist has the creative agency, the autonomy, to determine the features of the work, and for that reason it is the author who should be credited as the source of those intentions.

Even if we accept that the authorship of artworks is defined by the artist's responsibility for the artwork being the way it is, this does not yet tell us what makes artistic authorship distinctive. People author all kinds of things in their daily lives that are not necessarily artworks: emails, essays, texts, grocery lists. If we expand authorship beyond the conventional association with texts so that it encompasses creating in general, the list is even broader: people make artifacts, meals, events, and messes, but it doesn't make them artists. We might ask, just what is distinctive about artistic authorship as opposed to other kinds? If we answer that in one case one has made an artwork and in the other case one has authored something else, the answer is vacuous. What is so special about authoring artworks, if anything?

There is no logical necessity to the answer. It is historically and culturally contingent. In contemporary Western culture, we understand works of art primarily to be expressions of their maker, made for their own sake. This does not mean that works of art are simply or even primarily vehicles for expressing the private thoughts and feelings of their makers. The works of art we as a culture tend to value the most are those which evince a deep engagement with their time, place, and history. Nevertheless, we see these works not as objects that fulfill some antecedent function in terms of which they are judged, such as a stapler or legal brief, but as artifacts that exist for their own sakes, and which answer to no other rules that determine their form other than the ones given by their maker. As philosopher Sherri Irvin puts it, "the artist, qua artist, has to choose her own objectives; the activity does not choose them for her" (Irvin 2005, 135). In other words, artworks are different from other kinds of artifacts because their makers are not constrained by a function or purpose that directs the artist's making. If I set out to make a functional object, such as a table, I can bring a great deal of creativity to my design, but it will still be constrained by the artifact's purpose. When I engage with the table, I might admire its aesthetic qualities, but I will also be judging it in terms of its function as a table. Not so with artworks, which are understood primarily as expressions of their maker rather than as useful objects. For this reason, the author's freedom to decide what the artwork will consist in—and therefore their responsibility—is highlighted in artistic authorship.

A classic expression of this idea can be found in Section 43 of Kant's *Critique of Judgment* (Kant 2000). Kant offers a theory of artistic labor as free play, and he distinguishes it from other kinds of skilled making. (See Shapshay, this volume.) He says that the artwork is a work, an opus, as opposed to an effect of natural instincts, like beehives. The artist freely, that is autonomously, chooses to make the work. But for Kant the artwork is free in another sense as well: it is not mercenary art. It is not paid labor, but rather it is done for its own sake. So, while the artwork is a "work," the nature of the work entailed and the motivation for making it are different from other kinds of human making. The labor of the artist consists of a serious but free play. This understanding of artistic labor as Kant articulates it, that art is a product of free play, done for its own sake, is still operative in our understanding of contemporary art. Artworks are a special, hypostasized form of authorship because they are seen as an expression made by their authors purely for their own sake, divorced from utility. We engage with artworks primarily as intentional expressions of their maker. And it is for this reason that we often treat artworks as having a special connection with the artist who made them.

The legal expression for this idea is the doctrine of moral rights. Moral rights are a collection of authorial rights, which vary by jurisdiction. They are called "moral" rights not because they are distinct from "immoral rights," but because they are designed to protect the artist's reputational interests in their work, in contrast with the artist's purely economic interests. In the United States, authors of visual works of art have two moral rights: the right of attribution, which protects the author's right to be associated with the work as its author, and the right of integrity, which prevents the intentional distortion or alteration of an artwork, and in some cases bars their destruction.[1] Artists retain moral rights to their authored works even after they have sold the work to another. They function in a way that is similar to an easement on land: one person may own the land, but another may retain certain rights-of-way to enter or use the owner's land. In some jurisdictions, though not the United States, the rights are inalienable. This is a reflection of the view that moral rights are rights of "personality": they are tied to the personhood of the artist and so they cannot be renounced through contract (Merryman 2009, 408).

According to the orthodox view of moral rights, they protect a special bond that artists have with their work that is deeply personal and emotional in character. To distort, misconstrue, or destroy the work is to inflict a psychological trauma on the work's maker: "Because the artist infuses her work with her own personality, a harm to the work or her relationship to the work may well harm the artist herself" (Liemer 1998, 43). However, although such accounts are commonplace in the legal scholarship on moral rights, there are good reasons to be skeptical of this account, for both empirical and normative reasons.[2] First, it is not clear that artists in general *do* experience their relation to their artworks in terms of deep spiritual or emotional bond. Second, even if they did, it is not clear why that should entitle them to a special category of property rights that the makers of other kinds of artifacts do not enjoy. Rather than resorting to metaphysical speculation about the nature of artistic creation, I think we should understand that the artist's name functions as a kind of brand or trademark.[3] It may sound crass to conceptualize art and the artist's interests in such commercial terms, since we tend to treat art as a

[1] 17 U.S.C. §106A.
[2] See for example Kwall (2009); Lee (2007); Ong (2003).
[3] See Ginsburg (2005); Tang (2012).

cultural sphere that transcends such venal concerns as money and status. This hearkens back to Kant's description of art-making as a kind of free play, done for its own sake rather than as a job.

The better way to think about the connection between artists and the works they make is not in terms of an emotional or spiritual bond but as a reputational interest. Artists have an interest in the works that bear their signature not being distorted or altered in such a way that their intentions are misrepresented, just as libel and slander laws protect people generally from attacks on their reputation and standing in the community (Beitz 2005, 343–344). Reputation is a kind of social capital, and it can have material effects, for example, on the value of an artist's work and the professional opportunities made available.

This means that the traditional characterization of moral rights as protecting artists' noneconomic rights in their work is misleading. Reputational interests are quite often tied to economic interests, especially in arenas of cultural production, like the fine arts, in which the object is understood primarily as an expression of its author, made for its own sake. This intertwining of moral and economic values is often present in the way we often talk about authorship. Consider, for example, the language we use when talking about plagiarism and attribution: we say that the author deserves to be "credited" for their work. We use the economic vernacular of credit and debt to describe a moral obligation to recognize the author's accomplishment.[4]

An authorship claim is not simply an account of who made the work; it is not just an assertion about some neutral fact of the matter. Rather, it is also a kind of ownership claim. And ownership claims are inherently ethical insofar as they implicate our relations with others, and our rights, entitlements, and duties with respect to the work and to one another.[5] In the arts, these relations are often formalized by the legal regime governing intellectual property, copyright, and moral rights in each jurisdiction. But the law does not have the last word on what artistic authorship entails. While the law may reflect a community's ethical values, it can also be at odds with them. Another example is the work-for-hire doctrine. Under US copyright law, if an artist makes an artwork within the scope of their employment by another, the employer, not the artist, is considered the work's author.[6] One might object that this legal fiction not only misrepresents the fact of the matter—who actually created the work—but that it is unfair to artists because it deprives them of the rights that naturally follow from the fact of their having created it. Furthermore, one can raise the ethical concern that such a law disadvantages artists who do not have the economic means to make their works independently, and who can only afford to create artworks under an employment relation.

---

[4] For a general discussion of the ways in which moral and economic concepts are intertwined, see Graeber (2014).

[5] Wesley Hohfeld is the leading theorist of legal interests in property as a bundle of rights with correlative duties in others. See Hohfeld (1978).

[6] 17 U.S.C. §101.

Hence, the authorship and ownership of a work of art can both overlap and come apart in multiple ways. One of the first questions we might ask when someone claims an artwork as theirs is whether this is an assertion that they authored the work, or merely that they own the art object or the rights to it in some way. Imagine, for example, that you purchase a painting at an art gallery or at auction. It is now your painting, your artwork. You take it home, hang it on the wall. You show it to your friends. One of them asks whose work it is. Your friend knows that you own the object (in one sense it is, of course, yours) but she wants to know who painted it. That's because in another sense the painting is still the author's, not the collector's. You own the material object, but the artist owns the immaterial element of the work, its design. This everyday example shows how two different people can own one and the same object, but in different respects.

Normally, these two ownership claims coexist compatibly. People purchase paintings, buy works of literature, listen to music, attend concerts, and all goes well. Or, in a less common but by no means unusual scenario, imagine that the painting in our hypothetical is by a living artist whose career is on the rise. She is getting positive reviews in major publications and museum shows. The painting's owner will probably not only accept but insist that the painting she purchased be recognized and documented as having been authored by the renowned artist. The artist, in turn, is probably glad that people and institutions are eager to acquire "her" paintings, because it enhances her reputation, and likely increases the monetary value of her works. In such a scenario, both the collector and the painter claim the work as hers, but in a different way, and each benefits from the ownership interest of the other.

Sometimes, however, this symbiotic relation between artist and collector can degrade into conflict. Imagine that the collector wants to lend the painting to an upcoming museum exhibition, but over the artist's protests. The artist objects to her work being shown publicly in that context for some reason, perhaps political or moral. Whose painting is it to lend? There is a legal answer to this question (which can vary with jurisdiction), but the law might be at odds with our ethical intuitions about who should have the right to determine where the work is displayed. Some might argue that the owner of the art object should have the right to lend it out to whomever they wish, as with any other material possession. Others might argue that the artist should retain control over where their artworks are displayed, even if the art object is owned by another. Under this theory, artworks are extensions of their makers, and it could harm the artists' reputation or subjective sense of well-being if their work were displayed in a context or manner that the artist did not approve.[7]

---

[7] There are a number of instances in which musicians have objected to their work being used in political contexts to which they object. A classic example is Dmitri Shostakovich's objection to the use of his music in Wellman's 1948 film, "The Iron Curtain" (Beitz 2005, 330). In more recent times, musicians such as Bruce Springstein and Neil Young have objected to the use of their songs in political campaigns. See Chao (2015).

Or imagine that a collector purchases a painting by a very famous, very beloved dead artist. She decides, perversely, to cut the painting into 1x1 inch squares and sell each one on eBay. One can imagine the public outcry that such a sale would provoke. When artworks become canonical, they often pass into the cultural imagination as communal property. We now have a third entity, the public at large, who can lay claim to artworks as "theirs." (See Willard, this volume.) Rather than an authorship claim, the proprietary stance stems from the belief that some artworks are so important to a culture or community that, in an important sense, it belongs to the collective: it is really "theirs," not the collector's, not even, perhaps, the artist's.[8]

The controversies surrounding the private sale of Banksy's graffiti are a useful real-world example of this. Because Banksy's art has become so valuable, some people whose property has been "vandalized" by one of his stenciled, spray-painted images have removed and sold them, to public outcry by the communities that enjoy having a Banksy in their neighborhood. Since graffiti is often viewed as an assault to property values and the beauty of the public realm, it is a wonderful irony that in the case of Banksy's art, people actually protest the *removal* of graffiti from the public realm—while the property owners remove it not in order to restore their property but in an attempt to cash in on their windfall!

Such a reaction attests to the fact that the public sometimes asserts ownership rights over beloved works, even when their claims are usually not recognized legally.[9] Another recent example is the controversy surrounding public monuments to Confederate heroes in the United States.[10] (See Bicknell et al., this volume.) In this situation, members of the public are demanding the removal of artworks from the public sphere, because they abjure the racism that the monuments represent. In neither the case of the Banksys nor the Confederate monuments does the public hold legal title as property owner, and yet it is asserting, as an ethical matter, certain proprietary rights over the presence of the artworks in the public realm. A third example of this kind of proprietary claim involves the calls for certain cultural artworks and artifacts to be repatriated to their country of origin, even though they are nominally the property of a collector or institution. The Getty Villa Museum in Malibu, for example, was ordered by an Italian court to return a two-thousand-year-old sculpture in its collection because, the court held, it was illicitly taken from Italian waters.[11]

[8] See Sax (1999).

[9] See Isaac Kaplan, "A Banksy Appears on a Building Overnight. Who Gets to Cash In?", Artsy, March 30, 2018, https://www.artsy.net/article/artsy-editorial-banksy-appears-building-overnight-cash-in.

[10] See "AHA Statement on Confederate Monuments," American Historical Association, August 2017, https://www.historians.org/news-and-advocacy/aha-advocacy/aha-statement-on-confederate-monume nts; Benjamin et al. (2020, 237–22). See generally Bicknell, Judkins, and Korsmeyer (2020).

[11] See Gaia Pianigiani, "Italian Court Rules Getty Museum Must Return a Prized Bronze," New York Times, https://www.nytimes.com/2018/12/04/arts/design/getty-bronze-italy-ruling.html.

Another common but infrequently discussed complication to the ethics of authorship concerns the relation between the artist and the employee-assistant.

The English artist Sir Anthony Caro is most famous for his abstract sculptures made from scrap metal, and yet he relied on other skilled assistants to weld the pieces together according to his instructions. No one questions whether the sculptures are authored by Caro himself, even if he did not lay hands on them, because they were designed and assembled under his direction. Jeff Koons is widely considered to be the author of his artworks, which include famous sculptures such as *Rabbit* (1986) and *Balloon Dog* (1994–2000), but he does not fabricate them himself.[12] In fact, Koons runs a large production studio in which he employs other people to paint his paintings and fabricate his sculptures. Nevertheless, Koons is regarded as their author because he directs the employees to make them the way he wants. While this way of working is not new— Rembrandt, after all, had assistants who helped execute his paintings—it does confound some peoples' expectations of what it means to be a fine artist. As Katerina Bantinaki puts it, "For some, commissioning has always been present in art in one form or other and so is irrelevant to artistic creation . . . but, for others, it is a scam of contemporary art at the (moral and financial) expense of the (supposedly) multiple creators of commissioned artworks" (Bantinaki 2016, 16). The difference in attitudes toward commissioned artworks may depend on the degree to which one identifies artistic achievement with technical skill. The prevailing contemporary attitude is that the artist is first and foremost a creative visionary, not a master technician. Art historians have described this turn in artistic making, in which the artist directs others rather than making the objects directly, as a "post-studio" practice.[13]

For some artists, such as Caro, the use of assistants to carry out the fabrication of his sculptures was simply a practice borne of necessity: he was not a skilled welder and did not need to be. For other artists, however, the choice not to fabricate one's own work became part of the artistic statement itself. In the 1970s, minimalist artist Donald Judd made artworks that consisted of a set of instructions for someone else to construct the art object. The collector Count Giuseppe Panza purchased Judd's "certificates," such as one called "Untitled [Seven plywood boxes: open back]" (1972–1973), which showed a rough sketch and the dimensions of the plywood cubes. They were, as collector Count Giuseppe Panza said, "works of the intellect that could become a reality at any time, in the near or distant future, just like a plan for erecting a building or making a machine"

---

[12] We can gain insight into Koon's artistic process from one of the lawsuits filed against him by the photographer Art Rogers, which became a landmark case in US copyright law. Koons took a greeting card with the photographer's image of a couple holding a litter of puppies, crossed out the copyright notice, and sent it to a fabrication studio in Italy with instructions to turn the image into a sculpture (*Rogers v. Koons*, 960 F.2d 301 [2d. Cir 1992]).

[13] See generally *The Studio* (Hoffman 2012).

(Panza 2007, 137). This mode of art-making seemed revolutionary at the time because it fully separated the act of conceiving the work of art from the material process of making it. It emphasized, in its very form, that an artist does not have to make the art object to be its author-creator.

Unfortunately, this revolutionary mode of art-making has also encountered pitfalls because it opens the possibility that the artwork will not be instantiated according to the artist's precise wishes and specifications. When Panza attempted to have some of Judd's artworks fabricated into objects, the artist protested that they were done improperly and without his approval, and he angrily disavowed their authenticity (Judd 1990). He was further incensed when Panza sold his collection, including his Judd certificates, to the Guggenheim twenty years later for millions of dollars. This put the Guggenheim in the awkward position of owning certificates for the fabrication of artworks that the artist himself was not prepared to authenticate (Karol 2020).[14] One might think that the natural consequence of Judd's choice not to make or oversee the making of the sculptures himself is that he might be dissatisfied with the way they look if the certificate's owner decides to instantiate them. Shouldn't Judd have to accept this as a real possibility, and if the artwork really is just the design, and not the object itself, then why should it matter? I think the simplest explanation is that Judd is protecting his artistic brand. He (understandably) does not want his name associated with works that don't satisfy his standards. Here we see the limits of utopian conceptual gestures such as Judd's hands-off sculptures: they reside in an art system that continues to prioritize provenance, authenticity, and authorship even as the system celebrates conceptual gestures that ostensibly undermine those very values.[15]

An extreme form of the hands-off approach to artistic creation is the found object, in which the act of artistic creation consists merely in the selection of an object and a presentation of that object as one's own. This radical approach to art-making was made famous by Marcel Duchamp's Readymades at the turn of the last century, but has become an established mode of artistic expression, even if it remains at times controversial. For example, Martin Creed is a contemporary artist who often makes artworks out of commonplace objects such as cactuses in pots, sticky-tak, or crumpled wads of paper. In 2011, he won the Turner Prize, an important award for early-career contemporary artists, for an artwork that did not even involve an object at all: it consisted of the lights turning on and off in the Turner Galleries.

While Duchamp and Creed have authored artworks that consist of everyday objects placed in a gallery, another, more controversial variation on this theme involves the appropriation of other authored works, making minimal changes, and indexing it as a new work, authored by the appropriator. (See Hick, this volume.) The artist Richard Prince, for example, is most famous for his appropriation of images from Marlboro Man cigarette ads. Sherrie Levine made artworks by appropriating images that were already

---

[14] See also Guggenheim Museum (2021).

[15] For a discussion of another case study concerning the performative contraction surrounding what the artwork *says* versus what it actually *does*, see Gover (2012, 46–58).

recognized as art: she is best known for rephotographing Walker Evans's iconic images of the rural poor during the Great Depression and presenting them as new works in a series titled *After Walker Evans* (1981). Works of appropriation art by Prince and Levine have been exhibited and collected by some of the most important art institutions in the world. There is no question that they are regarded as canonical figures in postwar American art because of their appropriative works.

At the same time, however, their work has been subject to moral objection and even legal challenge by the artists whom they appropriate. The legal problem, to put it simply, is that copying another author's image and presenting it as one's own has all the formal features of a copyright violation even when it is done for a philosophical purpose. If appropriation art is going to pass legal muster, there must be some way for courts to distinguish between illicit acts of copying and those that are justifiable. Generally speaking, in order for the appropriation of an existing artwork to fall under the "fair use" exception, courts ask whether the new use of the source material has transformed it into something new.[16] The legal system is not well-equipped to handle cases of appropriation in which the transformation is purely conceptual.[17] Because there is no bright-line standard for fair use, it can come down to the artistic tastes of the judge.[18]

And yet for defenders of appropriation art, the fact that there is no perceptual difference between the source material and the appropriation does not make the transformation any less real or philosophically significant. The difference—and for some this is a key moral difference—is that unlike the plagiarist, the appropriation artist has no intention to conceal the fact of the appropriation. On the contrary, the point of appropriation art is to foreground the copying as an artistic act in its own right. In Darren Hick's words, "appropriation art is *about* appropriation: the viewer is meant to know that the objects and images presented *are* appropriated, and this is meant to say something about the objects and the authorship of the original and new works" (Hick 2013, 124). For some, the fact that the appropriator foregrounds rather than conceals the fact of having taken another's image might not be enough to justify the act on moral grounds. After all, one might argue, robbing someone openly does not make the act any less blameworthy than robbing under cover of darkness. It just makes it brazen. For those who value art at least in part because of the accomplishment it represents on the part of the artist, whether for the originality or technical skill involved, appropriation art is an insult to the authors who are responsible for creating the source material. Others, however, see it as a radical gesture that undermines the Romantic ideology of the single-author-genius, perhaps by suggesting that all works of art, to some degree, borrow from the work of others.[19]

---

[16] See 17 U.S.C. §107 for the fair use limitations to copyright. This standard was established by the landmark case *Campbell v. Acuff-Rose Music, Inc.* 510 U.S. 569 (1994), holding that 2 Live Crew's song "Pretty Woman" was a parody of Roy Orbison's "Oh Pretty Woman," and as a form of commentary and criticism of the original work, it may claim fair use.

[17] There is a robust literature on the legal problems surrounding appropriation art. For a good overview, see Carlin (1988, 103–143).

[18] See McKenzie (2013, 83–105).

[19] See, for example, McLean (1993, 373–422).

When it comes to the moral imperative to respect the intentions of the artist by not misrepresenting their artwork, the performing arts offer a unique set of challenges. In the case of object-based works of visual art, US law requires that artworks not be deliberately altered.[20] But in the performing arts, the very structure of the work invites interpretation, variation, and inept renderings because the work does not inhere in a stable material object. In theatre, music, and dance the artwork consists of a score that must be instantiated in performance. Because of this natural separation between score and performance, these works are particularly vulnerable to misrepresentation. Unless the composer or choreographer is performing the work themself, there is always the possibility that the performance will fall short of the artist's intentions and misrepresent the work, which could in turn reflect poorly on the artist.[21]

One might regard the possibility of multiple interpretations of the original score or script to be a particular virtue of the performing arts, not a danger to be lamented. In theatrical productions, for example, we often expect the director and actors to make creative choices that will open new avenues for appreciating the work. But it is not clear just how much artistic license is permissible before such choices become distortions. The playwright Samuel Beckett was known for vigorously defending the integrity of his plays as he intended them to be performed. For example, in 1984 he objected to a production of *Endgame* at the American Repertory Theater because it was set in an abandoned subway station and not the empty room stipulated in the stage directions (Gussow 1984, 13). A few years later, he sued a Dutch theater company for mounting an all-female cast of *Waiting for Godot*. The Dutch judge sided with the theatre company, who found that it was impossible to establish that the work's integrity had been violated even with the all-female cast. Beckett responded by banning all productions of his work in Holland (Rajan 2011, 366–367).

The Beckett examples are interesting from a moral rights perspective because his objections seem to have been by pure principle. By the 1980s, Beckett had been well established in the literary and theatrical canon, so it is hard to imagine that his rigid insistence on fidelity to his scripts was motivated by monetary or reputational concerns, as might be the case with an unknown or emerging artist. At the same time, especially when the playwright's reputation is so well-established as Beckett's was, one might argue that one has a duty to uphold the artistic freedom of the *director* to make informed yet creative choices—after all, she also has a kind of authorship role and an interest in putting her own expressive mark on the production.

Hence, the performing arts offer another situation in which ownership claims over a work of art can overlap and conflict. The questions of who owns the work, and in what respects, must be carefully navigated. In some fields, such as theater, it might be generally expected that directors will make innovative choices when producing plays, particularly canonical works. In concert dance, on the other hand, the choreographer or their

[20] 17 U.S.C. §106A(3)(A).
[21] See Gover (2021, 61–77).

estate may insist that the dancers be personally coached by someone uniquely author-ized (usually a former dancer) to oversee performances of the work. The law may offer some guidelines, but it will often be a matter of appealing to extralegal cultural and com-munity norms or negotiating on a case-by-case basis.

While the single author-artist is the standard in contemporary Western culture, there are well-known artists who work in pairs or teams to jointly author their works. Gilbert and George, the Chapman Brothers, and Christo and Jean-Claude are collaborative pairs each with decades-long practices of coauthorship as a single unit. Although harder to find, there are collaborative artworks made by even larger groups: Haus-Rucker-Co (1967–1992) were an Austrian group who used inflatable structures and prosthetic devices such as the "Flyhead Helmet" (1968) to make humorous statements about con-temporary life and perception. The Guerilla Girls are self-described "feminist activist art-ists" who work anonymously on projects that seek to expose and bring critical light to inequities in the artworld, while also exhibiting in some of its most celebrated institutions (Guerilla Girls, 2021). One is tempted to infer that the choice to engage in anonymous, collective authorship of artworks is part of their critique of art world norms.

US copyright law defines joint authorship as "a work prepared by two or more authors with the intention that their contributions be merged into inseparable or interdependent parts of a unitary whole."[22] While philosophers of art disagree about the particulars of this intentional merging, they generally acknowledge that works of collective author-ship involve a mutual commitment to create a single, unified work (Bantinaki 2016, 21).[23] They distinguish collective authorship from mere contribution to an artwork, and they also distinguish it from the case of multiply authored works or collective works, such as Wikipedia (or this volume), which involve contributions by multiple authors but the in-dividual contributions do not comprise a single, unified work.

While such distinctions seem simple enough in theory, in practice it can be difficult to distinguish between mere contribution and coauthorship. If authorship really comes down to responsibility, and to giving credit where it is due, then it becomes more dif-ficult to justify our tendency to treat artworks as the expressions of single individuals in those cases where the collaborative process is highly collaborative and cooperative. Sometimes nominal authorship is a legal or cultural fiction that grossly oversimplifies the facts of a work's creation. Take, for example, the production of a film, which requires scores of people, each with different talents and contributions, to form the whole, even as we persist in attributing authorship to a single entity, usually the director (Gaut 1997, 150). And the creation of large works of visual art, such as contemporary art installations, often involve a team of assistants providing creative and logistical support whose contributions go officially uncredited. The tension between the cultural norm of the single author, on the one hand, and the pragmatic realities of such projects, on the other was very publicly and acrimoniously exposed in the case of *Massachusetts Museum of*

---

[22] 17 U.S.C. §101.
[23] See Bacharach and Tollefsen (2010, 23–32); Paisley (2011, 221–225); Hick (2014, 147–156); Bacharach and Tollefsen (2015, 23–32). See also Willard, this volume.

Contemporary Art (Mass MoCA) v. Christoph Büchel.[24] In that case, the artist angrily walked away from an unfinished art installation planned for the museum's football field sized gallery, and he blamed the museum for failure of the work's realization. What came to light in the ensuing litigation is that the museum had invested nine months of its staff's labor and $300,000 of its own money to make Büchel's installation, which he oversaw largely by email correspondence while living in Europe. While the museum was ostensibly producing the work at the artist's behest and for a work in his name only, the actual creative process was highly collaborative, as the judge in the case observed (Gover 2011, 356). Nevertheless, as far as the law and the court of public opinion was concerned, Büchel was the sole author. The question then became whether the museum had the legal or moral right to show the unfinished work over his protests.

The Mass MoCA controversy also brings us to our final category of ethically complicated authorship claims: when the artist both asserts and denies that it is "his" artwork. This is what happened in the case of Büchel's unfinished installation at Mass MoCA: on the one hand, he insisted that it was his artwork and that he had the right to discard it, unexhibited, if he so chose (and at the museum's expense). On the other hand, the reason why he wanted to discard it rather than oversee its completion and exhibition is that he was not happy with it and lost faith that it could be done to his satisfaction. In other words, it wasn't his work, not in the fullest sense. To make sense of this seemingly paradoxical state of affairs, that is to say, "It's mine and it's not mine," I have argued elsewhere that we must keep in mind that authorship claims are not just answers to the empirical question of who made the artwork, as the responsibility theorists would have it, but they are also a question of whether the author is willing to accept the work they made as their own, as part of their oeuvre (Gover 2018, 10–41). Artists, just like any other kind of author, are sometimes disappointed with their work. They seek to control the works that circulate in their name, just as Kafka asked that his works be destroyed upon his death. One of the ethical questions that can arise in such cases is whether we have a duty to respect their disavowal even when others, such as their supporters or the public at large, may insist on the right to savor their creations.

See also: Willard, Hick, Matthes, Soucek, Bicknell et al., this volume

References

Bacharach, Sondra, and Deborah Tollefsen. 2010. "'We' Did It: From Mere Contributors to Coauthors." *Journal of Aesthetics and Art Criticism* 68, no. 1: 23–32.

Bacharach, Sondra, and Deborah Tollefsen. 2015. "Co-Authorship, Multiple Authorship, and Posthumous Authorship: A Reply to Hick." *Journal of Aesthetics and Art Criticism* 73, no. 3: 23–32.

Bantinaki, Katerina. 2016. "Commissioning the (Art)Work: From Singular Authorship to Collective Creatorship." *Journal of Aesthetic Education* 50, no. 1: 16–33.

---

[24] See Gover (2011, 354–365).

Beitz, Charles. 2005. "The Moral Rights of Creators of Artistic and Literary Works." *Journal of Political Philosophy* 13, no. 3: 343–344.

Benjamin, Andrea, Ray Block, Jared Clemons, Chryl Laird, Julian Wamble. 2020. "Set in Stone? Predicting Confederate Monument Removal." *PS: Political Science & Politics* 53, no. 2: 237–242.

Bicknell, Jeanette, Jennifer Judkins, and Carolyn Korsmeyer, eds. 2020. *Philosophical Perspectives on Ruins, Monuments, and Memorials*. New York: Routledge.

Carlin, John. 1988. "Culture Vultures: Artistic Appropriation and Intellectual Property Law." *Columbia VLA Journal of Law and the Arts* 13, no. 1: 103–143.

Chao, Eveline. 2015. "Stop Using My Song: 35 Artists Who Fought Politicians over their Music." *Rolling Stone* July 8, https://www.rollingstone.com/politics/politics-lists/stop-using-my-song-35-artists-who-fought-politicians-over-their-music-75611/bruce-springsteen-vs-ronald-reagan-bob-dole-and-pat-buchanan-28730/.

Gaut, Berys. 1997. "Film Authorship and Collaboration." In *Film Theory and Philosophy*, edited by Richard Allen and Murray Smith, 149–172. Oxford: Oxford University Press.

Ginsburg, Jane C. 2005. "The Author's Name as a Trademark: A Perverse Perspective on the Moral Right of 'Paternity'?" *Cardozo Arts & Entertainment Law Journal* 23: 379–389.

Gover, K. E. 2011. "Artistic Freedom and Moral Rights in Contemporary Art: The Mass MoCA Controversy." *Journal of Aesthetics and Art Criticism* 69, no. 4: 354–365.

Gover, K. E. 2012. "Christoph Büchel v. Mass Moca: A Tilted Arc for the Twenty-First Century." *Journal of Aesthetic Education* 46, no. 1: 46–58.

Gover, K. E. 2018. *Art and Authority: Moral Rights and Meaning in Contemporary Visual Art*. Oxford: Oxford University Press.

Gover, K. E. 2021. "'You Stole My Work! And You Stole It Poorly!' Choreography, Copyright, and the Problem of Inexpert Iterations" *Dance Research Journal* 53, no. 1: 61–77.

Graeber, David. 2014. *Debt: The First 5,000 Years*. Brooklyn: Melville House.

Guerilla Girls. 2021. "Our Story." https://www.guerrillagirls.com/our-story (accessed July 23, 2021).

Guggenheim Museum. 2021. *Object Lessons: Case Studies in Minimal Art: The Guggenheim Panza Collection Initiative*. Edited with text by Francesca Esmay, Ted Mann, and Jeffrey Weiss. Preface by Nancy Spector and Lena Stringari. Text by Martha Buskirk and Virginia Rutledge. New York: Guggenheim Museum.

Gussow, Mel. 1984. "Stage: Disputed 'Endgame' In Debut." New York Times, December 20, https://www.nytimes.com/1984/12/20/arts/stage-disputed-endgame-in-debut.html.

Hick, Darren Hudson. 2013. "Appropriation and Transformation." *Fordham Intellectual Property Media & Entertainment Law Journal* 23, no. 4: 101–140.

Hick, Darren Hudson. 2014. "Authorship, Co-authorship, and Multiple Authorship." *Journal of Aesthetics and Art Criticism* 72, no. 2: 147–156.

Hoffman, Jens. 2012. *The Studio*, from Whitechapel: Documents of Contemporary Art. Cambridge, MA: The MIT Press.

Hohfeld, Wesley. 1978. *Fundamental Legal Conceptions*, edited by Arthur Corbin. Westport, CT: Greenwood Press.

Irvin, Sherri. 2005. "Appropriation and Authorship in Contemporary Art." *British Journal of Aesthetics* 45, no. 2: 124–137.

Judd, Donald. 1990. "Una stanza per Panza, Part I- IV." *Kunst Intern Magazine*.

Kant, Immanuel. 2000. *Critique of the Power of Judgment*. Translated by Paul Guyer and Eric Matthews. Cambridge: Cambridge University Press.

Karol, Peter. 2020. "Why Did the Guggenheim Decommission a Donald Judd?" Hyperallergic, May 31, https://hyperallergic.com/566854/why-did-the-guggenheim-decommission-a-donald-judd/.

Kwall, Roberta Rosenthal. 2009. *The Soul of Creativity: Forging a Moral Rights Law for the United States*. Stanford, CA: Stanford University Press.

Lee, Brian A. 2007. "Making Sense of 'Moral Rights' in Intellectual Property." *Temple Law Review* 84, no. 1: 71–118.

Liemer, Susan. 1998. "Understanding Artists' Moral Rights: A Primer." *Boston University Public Interest Law Journal* 7, no. 1 41–57.

Livingston, Paisley. 2005. *Art and Intention: A Philosophical Study*. Oxford: Oxford University Press.

Livingston, Paisley. 2011. "On Authorship and Collaboration." *Journal of Aesthetics and Art Criticism* 69, no. 2: 221–225.

Mag Uidhir, Christy. 2013. *Art and Art Attempts*. Oxford: Oxford University Press.

McKenzie, Liz. 2013. "Drawing Lines: Addressing Cognitive Bias in Art Appropriation Cases." *UCLA Entertainment Law Review* 20, no. 1: 83–105.

McLean, Willajeane. 1993. "All's Not Fair in Art and War: A Look at the Fair Use Defense After Rogers v. Koons." *Brooklyn Law Review* 59, no. 2: 373–422.

Merryman, John Henry. 2009. "The Refrigerator of Bernard Buffet." In *Thinking About the Elgin Marbles: Critical Essays on Cultural Property, Art, and Law*, 406–430. Alphen aan den Rijn, the Netherlands: Kluwer Law International.

Ong, Burton. 2003. "Why Moral Rights Matter: Recognizing the Intrinsic Value of Integrity Rights." *Columbia Journal of Law & the Arts* 26, nos. 3–4: 297–312.

Panza, Giuseppe. 2007. *Memories of a Collector*. Translated by Michael Haggerty. New York: Abbeville Press, 2007.

Rajan, Mira Sundara. 2011. *Moral Rights: Principles, Practice, and New Technology*. Oxford: Oxford University Press.

Sax, Richard. 1999. *Throwing Darts at a Rembrandt*. Ann Arbor: University of Michigan Press.

Tang, Xiyin. 2012. "The Artist as Brand: Toward a Trademark Conception of Moral Rights." *Yale Law Journal* 122, no. 1: 218–257.

CHAPTER 36

....

GROUP AGENCY,
ALIENATION, AND
PUBLIC ART

....

MARY BETH WILLARD

MUCH of the recent focus on the ethical dimension of public art has focused on the problem of monuments to the immoral. (See Bicknell et al., this volume.) Judging from the public discourse, the primary ethical problem of monuments lies in the discrepancy between the values of the past and the values of the present. In the past, when the monuments were commissioned and placed in the public sphere, the good that the honoree had done outweighed the evil he committed (or the evil was hidden, or not recognized as evil). Nowadays, we recognize that the person did wrong, and that we must reevaluate his accomplishments. The debates thus assume a common shape: weighing the good interred with the person's bones against the evil they wrought; arbitrating between the values of the past and the presumed more enlightened values of the present; and determining if and when a monument should be removed or altered.

As important as the problem of monuments to the immoral has become politically, it does not, I argue, exhaust the ethical challenges that arise because of public art. For example, sometimes public art is controversial because of its subject, but not because the subject is inappropriately praised. The frescos that comprise *The Life of Washington* depict episodes from the life of Washington, but not the sanitized version that every child learns in school. Artist Victor Arnautoff painted Washington's slaves in the background of his Mount Vernon estate in one mural, and the corpse of a Native American killed by Washington's frontier explorers in another. Art historians agree that Arnautoff, a communist, intended the murals to be critical of Washington, and by extension, the United States, by painting images of slavery and genocide at a time when those sordid facts were not generally acknowledged. The murals, which adorn the entryway of George Washington High School, are delightfully subversive, especially given that Arnautoff, a Communist, painted them at the behest of Works Progress Administration, a New Deal agency that provided public works jobs during the Great Depression. (One must imagine the look on the bureaucrat's face.) The murals used to be controversial for their unflattering portrait of a beloved Founding Father; now they generate controversy because of their purported negative effects on the student body.

Moreover, many examples of controversial art have nothing to do with the morality of the subject. Sometimes, public art just seems like a bad fit. *The Collective* is a sculpture of a large head made up of many faces constructed from old propane tanks. The faces are mask-like, evocative of ghosts, and their collective effect is both deeply intriguing and profoundly unsettling, a rusty writhing scream. The problem with the "Big Head" sculpture, as the Appleton residents have dubbed it, is that it stands in the intersection of a residential neighborhood. They do not mince words when describing it, comparing it to "a pile of dead people from a concentration camp," saying that it belongs in a landfill, or that it is "plain ugly, juvenile, and dumb" (Behnke 2019).

Neither of these cases fits neatly into the dominant way of evaluating monuments to the immoral. Big Head is unsettling, but residents who object to it do not find its subject matter inapt or offensive; they just want it out of *their* neighborhood. The *Life of Washington* might, at first glance, look like a case that concerns the moral character of the subject of the mural, but the ethical attitude prescribed by the murals is merited, as they invite the appreciator to be shocked and horrified at Washington's failings and then to reflect on the iconic stories of cherry trees and revolutionary glory. The murals do not invite the appreciator to glorify slavery or genocide. Further, the mural is not generally thought to be ambiguous. As the earlier controversies show, most people understand that Arnautoff intended the murals to be critical of Washington, but they find those intentions insufficient.

Here's what's missing from the standard ethical analysis of the monuments and other public art. Public art exists in public *space* and contributes to its sense of *place*. I borrow the terms from environmental and ecological philosophy, where they have a characteristic use. *Space* refers to the material features of a location: a mountain pass; a forested glade; a pool of tidewater that time and silt have separated from the larger bay. Space also can refer to the built environment of cities such as the plaza at the five-way intersection, the *Fußgängerzone* in Berlin, and the Washington, DC Metro.

Place, by contrast, involves the material setting—the space—but also the values, knowledge, aesthetic, and cultural practices of the humans who live there. Place is the "lived environment of embodied dwellers . . . loci of social meaning, felt relationality, and emotional attachment" (Chackal 2018, 220), and it depends on both space and human practice. A city's public fire hydrant is a feature of the space; its use by the community's children as a way of cooling off during hot sticky August summer days contributes to the sense of place. A suburban fire hydrant is likewise a feature of the space, but if no one uses it as a sprinkler because the suburban children play in their backyard sprinklers or their pools, it does not feature heavily in the community's sense of place.

Public artwork also contributes to a sense of place. The manicured lawns, statues of founders, and charming Georgian architecture of a small liberal arts college informs expectations of what it might be like to study there (and how much one should expect to pay); a city's choice of anodyne public art projects affects the image they hope to project to tourists and business investors; and the street-art inspired mural outside the new coffee shop projects ambitions of hipness. One can see the importance of art to place by imagining the above places with the art switched: a college with corporate art, a city festooned with edgy murals, and a coffee shop full of statues of toga-clad baristas and thousands of immaculate yellow mums.

A space may become contested when there are conflicting conceptions of place. In my own state of Utah, an interesting dynamic has evolved around the annual celebration of Pioneer Day, a public holiday that commemorates the arrival of Mormon pioneers into the Salt Lake Valley. It is in many ways an unremarkable American holiday with gatherings of family and friends, parades, and grilling, but it has distinctly religious overtones and coincides with religious observances and traditions. Utah's residents since its founding were overwhelmingly Mormon, but in the past twenty years the state has seen plenty of in-migration, such that Salt Lake City itself is no longer majority Mormon. Newer, non-Mormon residents developed an alternative tradition for the holiday: "Pie'n'Beer" day, which subtracts the religious elements and adds eating pie and drinking beer. The tradition is cheeky, but a way that newcomers to Utah assert that *this space is our place, too.*

To place an artwork in public is to change the space, and in so doing, shape the sense of place that grows out of the space. The installation at 5Pointz in Queens, New York is a striking example of the power of art to transform a space. 5Pointz originally consisted of twelve disused factory buildings, but in 1993, it became the home for legal graffiti art following an agreement between the Wolkoff family, who owned the site, and artists. Brilliantly colored graffiti and murals soon covered the buildings. The works were visible from the 7 train, and 5Pointz itself became known as "the world's premier graffiti mecca," with artists around the world contributing to the colorful mural and tags that adorned its external surface. The art changed a decrepit water meter factory into a cultural icon.

5Pointz, like all street art, turned out to be ephemeral. In 2013, the Wolkoff family won approval to demolish the buildings in order to build condos. Protests ensued, and in November of that year, the Wolkoff family painted the exterior of the building white, destroying the artwork (Buckley and Santora 2013). This resulted in a round of court cases, and damages of nearly seven million dollars awarded to the artists (Kinsella 2020). The factory buildings themselves were destroyed in 2014.

The evolution of the 5Pointz site shows how artwork, by changing the space, affects the sense of place. The old factory at 5Pointz had fallen out of use and out of the public consciousness. Had it been demolished in the early 1990s to put in a luxury condo complex, probably no one would have protested. The addition of the graffiti-inspired artwork, however, turned it into a tourist attraction and cultural site, and its destruction harmed not just the interest of the artists but the sense of place that had grown up around the site. Indeed, 5Pointz's contribution to place was so powerful that the developers wished to capitalize on it. The new condos will take their name from the installation and incorporate street-art inspired murals into the lobby and other public spaces. Artists' renditions of the proposed building show an "engraved graffiti logo" of the 5Pointz tag adorning the wall behind the reception desk (Voon 2017). 5Pointz was a brief flash of artistic creativity and autonomy; now its legacy appears to be a parasitic attempt to win hipster cred in a trendy new high-rise.

One might think therefore, that the controversy over public art simply amounts to a controversy between competing groups over the use of public space. To place a work of public art, as with 5Pointz, is to change the space, and in so doing, shape the sense of place that grows out of the space. It is to declare that the group that placed the monument has the right to define the place, that their values, relationships, knowledge, and practices will be passed on, and that those of the competing group will not. In cases where there are two distinct groups such as descendants of Utah pioneers and rootless cosmopolitans, or graffitists and developers this analysis is plausible. In other cases, however, there do not seem to be two distinct groups. Public art often appears to be placed anonymously, on behalf of the public. It suggests that *anyone* who belongs to the public values the artwork and what it does to the space.

To put it another way, when the high school community objects to *The Life of Washington* or the residents of Appleton lobby for *Big Head* to be relocated, they are not outsiders criticizing a group to which they do not belong. They are not a separate group contesting the space. Rather, they criticize the artwork as members of the public; they resist the implication that *being part of the public means condoning this art*.

I suggest therefore that there is a second, often overlooked ethical dimension of public art, the *problem of alienation*, which occurs when a work of art that was intended to embody the public's ideals instead has the effect of dividing the public into those who approve of the work and those who do not. Here is how I will argue this works. Public art contributes to the success of group agency because aesthetic practices encourage individuals to align their aims and attitudes with the aims and attitudes of the group. When an aesthetic practice of a group *fails* to engage someone, by contrast, they tend to resist identifying with the group. As a result, bad public art can diminish those who object to its placement, relegating them from "we" to "them." This is a subtler ethical claim, and to build the argument that leads to it we need to discuss group agency.

We're also going to need to talk about Reddit.

GROUPS, GROUP AGENCY, AND GAMESTOP

Let's start with the basics of groups and group agency. A *group* is distinct from a mere set of individuals. A set is defined by its membership yields a new set. The set of *people in my university classroom* is extinguished and replaced when students leave or enter. A group, by contrast, is a collection of individuals that can survive changes in membership. The group of *students enrolled in my aesthetics class* survives the changes in enrollment through the add and drop period.

Group agents are groups to which we ascribe beliefs, desires, aims, and moral responsibility. The group agent is something, in that maddening philosophical phrase, "over and above" the members that make up the group, but like many philosophical concepts, we more or less know it when we see it. Sometimes it makes sense to talk of groups of people as if they were people. We ascribe beliefs to the university ("the university believes that students want more face-to-face classes") even as the individual professors disagree. We can attribute the desire of the New England Patriots to make the playoffs even as several players are hoping to be traded to another team. We can hold developed nations morally responsible for affecting the climate even as we recognize that many individuals do what they can to reduce their impact on the climate.

Turning to the philosophy of art, Bacharach and Tollefsen (2010) understand artistic collaboration as resulting from a group of artists who have jointly committed to bringing about an artistic product. Hick (2014) considers the role of power, authority, and institutions in determining whether artists who collaborate are mere contributors or coauthors. For my purposes, the metaphysical specifications of what makes a group an agent will not matter much, so for the ease of exposition, I will follow an *interpretivist* definition of group agency.[1] According to interpretivism, a group counts as a group agent when it makes sense to ascribe agency to the group in order to explain its behavior. We can determine whether the group of *students enrolled in my aesthetics class* counts a group agent if we understand and interpret its behavior using the tools of folk psychology (Strohmaier 2020, 1904). List and Pettit write that groups are agents when they have the "capacity to mimic the more or less rational way in which individual agents act" (List and Pettit 2006, 85). Think of the interpretivist standard as an agency analogue to the Turing test.[2] There is a correlation between organizational complexity and agency, just as there is a correlation between computational power and artificial intelligence, but what makes something an agent is that its behavior is that of an agent, just as the robot is intelligent because it passes the Turing test, not because it has complex circuitry. The robot would not be intelligent without the particular arrangement of its circuits; likewise, the interpretivist should not be interpreted as denying that agency typically supervenes on the organizational structures and practices of the group. What they deny is that agency is determined by the complexity or organization of those structures.

One common concern with the interpretivist interpretation of group agency is that it overproduces agents because any group that appears to behave like an agent qualifies; there's no need to look at internal mechanisms or intentions. Responding to these objections is beyond the scope of this chapter, but here's a rough-and-ready rule for identifying group agents: the hallmark of a group agency is not that we *can* use folk psychology to make sense of the group's behavior, but rather that we *need* to use folk psychology to explain the behavior of the group because the phenomena cannot be explained by appealing to the individual agency of the members of the group. One can

---

[1] See Strohmaier (2020) for an excellent overview of the terrain. "Interpretivists" contrasts with "functionalists," who hold that group agency must be explained in terms of internal states over outward behavior.

[2] Indeed, List and Pettit introduce their version of group agency by asking us to imagine a robot interacting with a cylinder.

be certain that one has identified a group agent when one can judge that the beliefs, desires, motivations, and moral responsibility of the group differs from the sum of the beliefs, desires, motivations, and moral responsibility of the individuals that comprise the group.[3]

One reason to prefer a permissive conception of group agency is that we often ascribe agency to groups that are only minimally organized. Consider, for example, the group of Redditors who congregated on the subreddit/r/wallstreetbets and drove up the price of GameStop stock in early 2021. A subreddit is a loosely organized group.[4] Membership requirements in /r/wallstreetbets are minimal, for anyone with internet access can make a free account, join the subreddit, and post about whatever stocks they like. There is not a leader or a hierarchy, but instead a handful of volunteers who moderate posts and a community-decided set of norms about what content is allowed. Users post under pseudonyms, so that all anyone knows about each other is what they choose to reveal. One could read, however, news articles attributing to the group the *belief* that the hedge fund Citadel had heavily shorted the stock, the *desire* to drive up the price, the *motivation* to make the "one percent" pay, and the *moral responsibility* for inducing naïve investors to invest at the top.

One needs to appeal to group agency to explain the GameStop incident because of the conflict between the aims of the group and the interests of the individuals who had purchased the stock. As individuals, the Redditors wanted to make money gambling on stock prices. As a group, however, /r/wallstreetbets wanted to instigate a short squeeze. For a short squeeze to succeed, the price of the stock must rise sharply and quickly so that those who short the stock (those who bet that the price would fall) will be forced to buy shares at massively inflated prices to cover their bets. The new, higher price means that even more shares must be covered, which then drives the price even higher.

Creating a short squeeze pits the aims of the subreddit group against the aims of the individual subredditor. To make sense of the subreddit's behavior requires treating the subreddit as an agent distinct from the individuals who were posting. Individual speculators naturally want to realize a profit, which requires buying the stock and then selling it once it appreciates sufficiently. The aims of the group required that a large number of people buy the stock, and *then not sell it even if the price skyrocketed*. If individuals were to follow their own interest and take a profit, the squeeze would stall and quickly fizzle out.

The tale of the short squeeze illustrates a common problem with group agency. The group has aims and attitudes that may not match the aims and attitudes of the individuals who make up the group. Thus, if a group is to achieve its aims when they run contrary to the interests of the members who make up the group, members must be encouraged to adopt the group's priorities over their own. Group members must cooperate even when

[3] *Agentia non sunt multiplicanda praeter necessitatem?*
[4] For another discussion of online agency, see Cross, this volume.

doing so is contrary to their interests. Successful group agents, therefore, must have some means of encouraging individuals to cooperate.

More organized groups accomplish this through formal incentives such as contracts or bonuses. Suppose that individual faculty at a teaching university prefer to teach only general education classes that they've previously taught, so that they have more time for their own research. More updated and dynamic classes might attract more students, but then there would be more work. The university, however, wants to attract more students through advertising exciting new classes. To urge recalcitrant faculty to develop new courses, the university might offer additional funding or build the development of new courses into the tenure and promotion criteria.

List and Pettit note, however, that even formal organizational measures alone are not always sufficient to align the interests of individuals with the interests of the group. Groups might attempt to achieve cooperation through "educational, communicative, or social measures that change the group's informal norms and culture" (2011, 126). In our hypothetical university, we might expect brown bag lunches on teaching best practices, memos from the university president praising innovative teaching, and praise for those who develop new classes. We might describe the effect of those measures as "creating a culture of excellent teaching," which would not only indicate to the faculty how the university wants them to act but would encourage them to adopt the university's aims as their own.

Such social measures can be powerful. List and Pettit observe that members of a group can lead each other to adopt the perspective and attitudes of a group "just by being around to observe one another's behavior," but also that "activist members may remind their peers of their shared identity (2011, 128.) In the case of the GameStop squeeze, Redditors posted exhortations to each other to hold ("diamond hands," or stalwart refusal to sell even in the face of collapsing *or* skyrocketing prices), and argued that the stock would rise even higher than the 1700 percent it finally realized. The subreddit also has a culture of inside jokes (everyone declares that they are holding because they "just like the stonk" being one of the cleaner ones) and terms (they're in it for the "tendies," from "legal tender" but also joking that their winnings will go purchasing fast-food chicken tenders) that promote camaraderie.

They also posted memes. (See Cross, this volume, for a discussion.) Memes consist of text over images (or sometimes short animations), and it is characteristic of memes that the image is reused with the text varied to address the specific situation. As a result, the meaning of the meme derives not just from the text, but the meaning that has been collectively assigned to the image. For example, one meme posted during the GameStop squeeze featured a scene from the movie *Avengers: Endgame*, where the hero Iron Man defeats the villain Thanos, with the text "r/wallstreetbets" and "banks" superimposed over the hero and villain, respectively. To understand the meme presupposes a familiarity with the movie and the characters—one must know that the villain was thought to be unstoppable, and that he was defeated only by one, last, desperate heroic act. One also must know that in this scheme, /r/wallstreetbets are supposed to be the good guys. When a Redditor posts a meme to the subreddit, they temporarily take on the perspective of the group: */r/wallstreetbets are the heroes who are going to take down a hedge fund.*

Memes are hardly art, but they are aesthetic objects. Cross writes in his analysis of the aesthetic function of memes that "the real value of internet memes lies in their distinctive ability to generate a community: in creating or disseminating instances of memes, users take on a role in the community responsible for the collective authorship of the meme itself. Through their activity, they indicate that they are part of the group that understands and appreciates the meme" (Cross 2017). Sharing in the meme fosters intimacy between members of the group, and it also encourages members of the group to adopt the perspective of the group. Memes serve as reminders to the rest of the group of the group's aims, and the cumulative effect of seeing others react to the memes and affirm the group's desire to short the stock can lead individuals to adopt that desire.

Thus, not only does creating the meme lead one to identify with the group but *getting* the meme—engaging with it aesthetically—tends to reinforce one's identification with the group. A Redditor will not hold just because /r/wallstreetbets is holding, but if she identifies with /r/wallstreetbets because the memes and jokes bound her more tightly to the community, she may hold because being part of the group is *fun* ("like 4chan found a bloomberg terminal") and being part of the group requires *not selling.*

Reddit's use of memes to achieve cooperation illustrates a theme from recent work in aesthetics that highlights the way that aesthetic practices bring people together, setting aside the standard image of the solitary appreciator alone in contemplation of his art in favor of an account of aesthetic practices as inherently social activities. The specifics of the accounts vary, but whether they are understood as empowering us to venture forth and explore new aesthetic terrain, or creating social openings, or as a kind of joint achievement, aesthetic practices foster and strengthen social connections.[5] Examples of aesthetic practices as social glue abound. When we wait to watch the latest episode of *Game of Thrones* with our friends or share a new recipe for sourdough on social media, or dance in a silly conga line at a wedding, our aesthetic practices are social, drawing us beyond our individual interests so that we might share with others. Doing so strengthens our connection with the group.

Rejecting an aesthetic practice, conversely, often amounts to rejecting identifying with the group shares in that aesthetic practice. Imagine explaining "diamond hands" or YOLOing a large sum of money on a memestock to someone who understands none of those phrases; the memes and in-jokes make it hard for an outsider to see the appeal of belonging to the group. Moreover, if someone finds the chatter /r/wallstreetbets to be obscene and childish, it is reasonable to suppose that they will not identify with the aims of the group. (After all, should one really take stock advice from someone called byteman420 who posts vulgar memes followed by emojis of apes and bananas?)

The case of /r/wallstreetbets is thus instructive in two ways. First, it shows how even a loosely organized group agent can achieve cooperation through the use of aesthetic

---

[5] See, for example Lopes, Nanay, and Riggle (2022); Lopes (2018).

practices. Second, it shows that using an aesthetic practice to align individuals' aims and attitudes with those of the group also risks alienating those who do not or cannot participate in the prescribed aesthetic practice. Little, of course, turns on whether the memes of r/wallstreetbets appeal to philosophy professors, or for that matter whether teenagers' fashion is comprehensible to their parents; but it does matter ethically, I argue, when an artwork performs this function for a group agent that is the public.

ALIENATION, AGENCY, AND ART

Let's apply the lessons of Reddit to the cases of problematic public art. The relevant group is *the public*, which picks out the populace. Somewhat controversially, we may consider the public to be a group agent: we often make sense of the public by resorting to the concepts of folk psychology. We are inclined to attribute agency to the public especially in those cases where the public is morally responsible for an outcome, but where it is less clear that the individuals who make up the public share in the responsibility.[6]

On the assumption that the public is a group agent, it is at best only a loosely organized group agent, and thus we should expect that shared artistic and aesthetic practices are integral to getting individuals to identify with the public. I argue that one function of public art, especially but, importantly, not exclusively, monuments, is not just to memorialize momentous individuals and events, but to encourage individuals to identify with the group. My view thus dovetails nicely with Nguyen's view (2019) that groups embody their ethical commitments in monuments that speak to their future selves. Not only do groups speak to their future selves through monuments, but they sustain themselves as agents by encouraging members of the group to subordinate their own agency to that of the group.

Let's start with the clearest cases of troublesome public art: monuments to the immoral. Monuments represent the group's decision to honor someone. Monuments typically induce feelings of honor and awe toward their recipients, and they do so through their design. Statues typically stand on impressive pedestals, literally elevating the honoree. We can see the importance of this visual language of honoring when it is conspicuous by its absence. The recent monument to early feminist Mary Wollstonecraft, for example, fell afoul of this implicit constraint on monuments. It has drawn criticism because the statue does not depict her, but instead consists of a small female nude arising out of a silver wave-like eruption. One might admire it as artwork, but as a monument

---

[6] Some philosophers consider the fact that the public can be considered an agent to be a mark *against* the interpretive view. I am not convinced this is a problem. Arguably, we can see the value of attributing group agency to the public as a whole in addressing problems like climate change, or policy responses to global pandemics. I'm happy to bite this bullet, but I'm not going to make the case for it here. See Killoren and Williams (2013) for reasons to think that we need to posit groups as moral agents, and also Michael and Szigeti (2018) for a discussion of how people attribute agency to groups.

to a feminist icon, it falls short because it does not suggest to the appreciator that Wollstonecraft should be admired.

Sometimes the group that places monuments is explicit and exclusive ("the class of 1947"), but often the group is undefined or expansive ("a grateful nation"). In either case, however, the placement of the monument in the public space means that it enters the public's sense of place. As part of the public, one is *supposed* to adopt the prescribed attitude toward the subject of the monument as part of appropriately acting in public.

Consider, for example, the various monuments to J. Marion Sims, the so-called father of modern gynecology. In the 1840s, Sims developed novel surgical techniques to repair vesicovaginal fistula, a devastating childbirth injury to the bladder and vagina that caused great suffering. Sims's groundbreaking surgical technique won him great acclaim, and after his death, New York City erected a statue in his honor that proclaims his "brilliant achievement." The monument elides Sims's methods, which he perfected on the bodies of enslaved Black women, some of whom endured multiple surgeries without anaesthesia. The New York City Commission, in justifying their decision to remove the monument, wrote "the sculpture is clearly laudatory in itself, and the monument presents Sims on a high pedestal in a heroic pose . . . There is no ambiguity to the monument's glorification" (Walker and Finkelpearl 2018, 20).

Someone who knows the terrible story of Sims's discoveries will likely balk at honoring him. Honoring his achievements feels like condoning his crimes. (See Matthes, this volume.) In placing the monument, the group agent *the public* asserts that Sims is worthy of honor. Honoring Sims and feeling pride in his achievement tends to make one identify with the group agent. A New Yorker might think: his work is *our* gift to the world. Balking at admiring Sims, however, sets one apart from the public. The person who refuses to admire Sims tends to identify less with the group agent. *That is, aesthetic disagreement*, just as in the case of the Redditors who do not get the memes, *tends to lead some members of the public to resist identifying with the public*. The result is that the monument which was intended to speak to the public's pride in American surgery instead has the effect of dividing the public into those who approve of the monument and those who do not.

Sometimes when artistic and aesthetic practices define a group and, in doing so, exclude others, they do so blamelessly, with no cause for ethical complaint. It is unjust, however, when a monument's directive to admire someone leads a person who should feel at home in a public space to not identify with the public, and this is compounded when the injustice intersects with racism and sexism. We now have a fuller picture of the problem of monuments to the immoral. The public, as a group agent, implies when it honors Sims with a monument that the harms he did do not matter. There is, however, a second wrong. The prescribed aesthetic response alienates those who are unable or unwilling to engage the artwork, because failing to appreciate an artwork sets one apart from the public, a group which by definition *should* include all. The New York Commission gestures at this kind of aesthetic disenfranchisement when it notes that not only does the monument "represent a legacy of oppressive and abusive practices on bodies that were seen as subjugated, subordinate, and exploitable in service to his fame," but that the monument was located in a neighborhood consisting "of communities of color, predominantly Latino and Black," and that members of the community had been demanding the removal of the statue for *decades* (Walker and Finkelpearl 2018, 21). The continued existence of the statue suggests that "the public," wrongly, does not include people of color.

The Sims monument thus alienates those who object to the monument. One might object, therefore, that the problem of alienation that I have identified is nothing more than a mere side effect of the real problem, that we have chosen to honor the immoral, and that distinguishing the problem as a separate effect overstates the case.

Attending to the problem of alienation, however, helps explain cases like *The Life of Washington*. Recall that the frescos adorning George Washington High School in San Francisco depict slavery and the genocide of Native Americans among the more usual scenes of Washington's life. Unlike many works of public art which erase any mention of ethical wrongdoing, the Arnautoff murals center the wrongs of slavery and genocide. If the concern were only that viewers might misinterpret the mural's intent, one would expect that an instructive plaque or similar community education outreach would ameliorate the controversy completely.

Yet the controversy does not result from ignorance about Arnautoff's intentions or the history of the work. Students and community members know—as does anyone who follows the press coverage—that the work does not praise Washington's treatment of Black and Native Americans. In a museum, the work would shock, but it perhaps would not offend. It stands at the entrance of the school, however, so that students walk every day beneath the images of dead Native Americans and enslaved Black farmhands. As a fresco, it forms part of the surface of the wall. It is functional, so as impressive as it is, it is encountered not only as an artwork, but as part of the furniture of the educational system. While one can admire the artwork for its history and Arnautoff's cheeky iconoclasm, the practical effect is that students of color walk into a building every day that depicts people who look like them in bondage or as corpses.

The fresco's placement in the school, as a work of public art, suggests that the public thinks that the images are unobjectionable, or at least sufficiently contextualized that students should be assured that *everyone* understands that *no one means anything bad* by the depicted slaves and corpses. Suppose that a student reacts with distaste to the images. She will recognize that the public, as a group, has decided that they are unobjectionable, and that identifying as part of the public means agreeing that the frescos are unobjectionable. Given the circumstances, it is plausible that the presence of the mural will result in her identifying less with the community of the school. Moreover, the alienating effect persists even if the student believes that Arnautoff's murals succeed artistically in its criticism of the standard hagiographies of Washington. The alienation results from its ability to shape the sense of place in a space reserved for education, and it's not an effect that is easily canceled. Students who find the frescos unsettling will feel at odds with a public that has decided that the frescoes are appropriate for the space.

The resulting alienation may also be unjust. If promoting the identification with the public, or, more narrowly, with the community of scholars at the school is ethically laudatory, then undermining it is ethically troublesome, especially if the students who are alienated are otherwise marginalized. Fully analyzing what should be done in the case of *The Life of Washington* is beyond the scope of this chapter. One might argue, for example, that the pedagogical value of *The Life of Washington* outweighs the harm of the alienation it evokes, and that it should remain intact in the foyer of the school. The case is also complicated by the fact that the mural cannot be removed without being destroyed. There is not an easy answer here. My point is simply that a complete analysis of the ethics of public art must consider not just the ethics of the subject of the art, but the way that art is used by the public to define what it means to be part of the public.

Here's another example that shows how public art conveys what it means to be part of the public. In the waning days of the Trump administration, President Trump issued an executive order calling for a "National Garden of American Heroes," built "to reflect the awesome splendor of our country's timeless exceptionalism" (Federal Register 2021). The Garden was proposed as a reaction to a summer of demonstrations that saw many monuments to immoral men of the past torn down or defaced. Although the Garden will almost assuredly never come to exist, it would have been composed of statues of famous Americans. The eclectic list of heroes includes writers and artists, athletes and justices, politicians and capitalists. Despite the order's proclamation that the honorees were chosen for "embodying the American spirit of daring and defiance, excellence and adventure, courage and confidence, loyalty and love" (Federal Register 2021), one suspects that the primary criterion for inclusion was that it was likely to appear in a sixth-grade history textbook, plus Kobe Bryant and Alex Trebek.

It is reasonable to suppose that the intended aesthetic reaction would incorporate feelings of awe toward the honorees and pride in being American, but one suspects that the likely effect would be somewhat uncomfortable. Most of the proposed honorees are not particularly objectionable—at least by the standards of most American monuments—were they encountered singly or in another more appropriate context. When they are displayed together, however, the message is not just that these men and women are notable, but that *honoring them is just what it means to be American*. Objecting to the Garden is thus un-American. One might find that the call for group adulation alienating even if one agrees that the proposed honorees are worthy of admiration.

The strength of my analysis, however, lies in its ability to explain cases like *The Collective*, where the controversy stems not from ethical concerns about the content, but about what its placement says about the people who placed it there. *The Collective* isn't the first work of public art to result in controversy in Appleton. Dmitri Hadzi's *Fox River Oracle* is a work of abstract culture consisting of large concrete geometrical forms; the sculpture calls to mind nothing so much as monochrome shape-sorter blocks stacked as if by a giant toddler. Like *The Collective, Fox River Oracle* polarized the community when it was first placed; unlike *The Collective*, however, the work wasn't thought to be unusually uncanny or unsettling, just "ugly" modern art (Collar 2020.)

Placing art intentionally changes Appleton's sense of place. AcreofArt, a nonprofit organization that brought *The Collective* and other pieces to Appleton and the surrounding area and aims to "cultivate, promote, place and preserve public art in outdoor spaces throughout the Fox Cities" recognizes this explicitly in their mission statement, writing "in a way, public art is a direct reflection of who we are and who we aspire to be" (Schultz, n.d.). In hosting an annual exhibition of public sculpture, the city establishes itself as the kind of place where one can expect to find engaging, evocative artwork. The works, placed on behalf of the citizens of Appleton, declares that to be Appletonian is to want to live in a place with said engaging, evocative artwork. Or, to borrow the words of a resident who defended *The Collective* against objectors, to be Appletonian is to reject living in a city whose conception of art starts with Precious Moments and ends with Thomas Kinkade (Collar 2020).

In *The Collective*, and cases like it, the problem is that the placement of the work as public art suggests that the community *endorses it* as aesthetically and artistically valuable. One cannot say simply that one lives in a town with a strange artwork comprising many rusty heads; one says instead, "in *my* town, there is an artwork . . ." To state the problem in terms of group agency: the residents of Appleton form a group agent as it makes sense to understand Appleton's behavior—here, installing public art—as resulting from the goals, desires, and beliefs of the group. The group agent *Appleton* decided to install *The Collective* at a residential thoroughfare. Individuals who disagree with the decision, or who just dislike the sculpture feel alienated from their hometown. This changes Appleton's sense of place; it is not a mundane residential neighborhood, but a place where one might find edgy, challenging artwork. Arguments over the sculpture are arguments over the identity of Appleton.

Concluding Observations

Considering how group agents use artwork opens up new directions for the ethical criticism of art beyond the moral status of the subject of the work. Group agents use artwork to align the aims and attitudes of the individuals who make up the group with those of the group. When this is successful, the result is that the individual identifies with the group. When it is unsuccessful, public artwork risks alienating those who cannot or will not engage with the artwork. When the resulting alienation intersects with other forms of injustice, the placement of the artwork is unjust.

In closing, it seems to matter little to those who object that *The Collective,* and other statues similarly installed, were chosen as a result of a democratic process where presumably all voices had the chance to be heard. One might even speculate that having the imprimatur of democratic deliberation and assent makes the alienation from the group worse. Were a hated work of public art imposed by an external group, while one might dislike it and resent its intrusion on the space and place, it might not be alienating. The problem of some public art is that it is ours, whether we like it or not. Alienation then grows out of the conflict between the belief that one should have the power to ensure that one's place reflects one's values and reality that one's local street corner now boasts strange art. The broader lessons for democratic deliberation are suggestive.

See also: Cross, Bicknell et al., Matthes, Gover, Soucek, this volume

REFERENCES

Bacharach, Sondra, and Deborah Tollefson. 2010. "We Did It: From Mere Contributors to Coauthors." *Journal of Aesthetics and Art Criticism* 68, no. 1: 23–32.

Behnke, Duke. 2019. "Fuss Over Appleton's Big Head Sculpture Invigorates Artist Behind It." *Appleton Post-Crescent*, December 20, https://www.postcrescent.com/story/news/local/2019/12/20/fuss-over-appletons-big-head-sculpture-invigorates-artist-behind/2669386001/.

Buckley, C., & Santora, Marc. 2013. "Night Falls, and 5Pointz, a Graffiti Mecca, Is Whited Out in Queens." *The New York Times*, November 20, https://www.nytimes.com/2013/11/20/nyregion/5pointz-a-graffiti-mecca-in-queens-is-wiped-clean-overnight.html.

"Building the National Garden of American Heroes." 2021. *Federal Register*, January 22, https://www.federalregister.gov/documents/2021/01/22/2021-01643/building-the-national-garden-of-american-heroes.

Chackal, Tony. 2018. "Place, Community, and the Generation of Ecological Autonomy." *Environmental Ethics* 40, no. 3: 215–239.

Collar, Jim. 2020. "What Does the Sculpture Squabble Say about Arts in Appleton?" *Valley Review*, January 22, https://valley-review.com/2020/01/21/what-does-the-sculpture-squabble-say-about-arts-in-appleton/.

Cross, Anthony. 2017. "The Curious Case of Pepe the Frog: On the Ontology and Value of Internet Memes." *Aesthetics for Birds* (blog), January 26, https://aestheticsforbirds.com/2017/01/26/the-curious-case-of-pepe-the-frog-by-anthony-cross/.

Hick, Darren Hudson. 2014. "Authorship, Co-Authorship, and Multiple Authorship: Authorship, Co-Authorship, and Multiple Authorship." *Journal of Aesthetics and Art Criticism* 72, no. 2: 147–156.

Killoren, David, and Bekka Williams. 2013. "Group Agency and Overdetermination." *Ethical Theory and Moral Practice* 16, no. 2: 295–307.

Kinsella, Eileen. 2020. "A Stunning Legal Decision Just Upheld a $6.75 Million Victory for the Street Artists Whose Works Were Destroyed at 5Pointz." *Artnet News*, February 20, https://news.artnet.com/art-world/5pointz-ruling-upheld-1782396.

List, Christian, and Philip Pettit. 2006. "Group Agency and Supervenience." *Southern Journal of Philosophy* 44: 85–105. https://doi.org/10.1111/j.2041-6962.2006.tb00032.x.

List, Christian, and Philip Pettit. 2011. *Group Agency: The Possibility, Design, and Status of Corporate Agents*. Oxford: Oxford University Press.

Lopes, Dominic McIver. 2018. *Being for Beauty: Aesthetic Agency and Value*. Oxford: Oxford University Press.

Lopes, Dominic McIver, Bence Nanay, and Nicholas Riggle. 2022. *Aesthetic Life and Why It Matters*. Oxford: Oxford University Press.

Michael, John Andrew, and András Szigeti. 2018. "'The Group Knobe Effect': Evidence That People Intuitively Attribute Agency and Responsibility to Groups." *Philosophical Explorations* 22, no. 1: 44–61.

Nguyen, C. Thi. 2019. "Monuments as Commitments: How Art Speaks to Groups and How Groups Think in Art." *Pacific Philosophical Quarterly* 100, no. 4: 971–994.

Schultz, Alex. n.d. "Our Vision." Sculpture Valley, https://www.sculpturevalley.com/our-vision (accessed July 12, 2021).

Strohmaier, David. 2020. "Two Theories of Group Agency." *Philosophical Studies* 177, no. 7: 1901–1918.

Voon, Claire. 2017 "A Glimpse Inside the Street Art-Themed 5Pointz Condos." *Hyperallergic*, June 26, https://hyperallergic.com/386244/a-glimpse-inside-the-street-art-themed-5pointz-condos/.

Walker, Darren, and Tom Finkelpearl. 2018. "Mayoral Advisory Commission on City Art, Monuments, and Markers." Mayoral Advisory Commission, Report to the City of New York, https://www1.nyc.gov/assets/monuments/downloads/pdf/mac-monuments-report.pdf (accessed February 20, 2023).

CHAPTER 37

....

IMMORAL ARTISTS

....

ERICH HATALA MATTHES

INTRODUCTION

....

THERE are seemingly endless examples of successful artists who have committed morally condemnable acts, including rape, murder, and molestation, as well as those who have made morally condemnable statements espousing views that include racism, misogyny, fascism, and transphobia. What do the (im)moral lives of artists mean for our relationship to their artwork? While there is a long philosophical tradition focused on the relationship between ethics and artworks, philosophical focus on the specific problem of immoral artists is relatively novel.

This chapter will begin by briefly considering how the ethical criticism of artists relates to the existing philosophical literature on the ethical criticism of art. We will then turn our attention to moral and practical questions about how we should act in response to revelations about the immoral actions of artists, focusing specifically on questions about ethical consumerism, institutional responsibility, and fan culture. I argue that we have substantial moral latitude when it comes to our individual engagement with the work of immoral artists, but that arts institutions can and often should play a more active role in responding to the immoral behavior of artists. Finally, I briefly turn to questions about the emotional turmoil many fans experience when they learn that the creator of a beloved work has acted immorally, and argue that the artwork itself is a useful tool for grappling productively with these conflicting feelings.

ETHICAL CRITICISM OF ARTISTS

....

The central question motivating work on the ethical criticism of art is this: are the moral flaws of artworks also aesthetic flaws of those works? There are a range of answers to this question in the literature. Some deny the premise of the question (there's no such thing as a morally flawed artwork!).[1] Some propose a strong *pro tanto* relationship according to which the moral flaws of artworks are to that extent also aesthetic flaws (Gaut 1998; 2007). Others turn this relationship on its head and argue that the moral flaws of artworks can in fact be aesthetic merits (Eaton 2012; Clavel-Vazquez 2018b; Li 2020). These positions and others are discussed in the Stear, Carroll, Jacobson, and Rothfeld chapters in this volume. But we can also ask an analogous question about the ethical criticism of artists, namely: do the moral flaws in artists' lives generate aesthetic flaws in the artworks they create? The existing literature on the ethical criticism of art has offered a natural starting point for philosophers investigating the ethical criticism of artists. Can we use the frameworks developed in the former case to illuminate the issues that arise in the latter?

In his paper "Ordinary Monsters," Christopher Bartel attempts to do just this using Berys Gaut's ethicism as an organizing framework. Bartel begins his discussion by reflecting on another recent essay, "Art by Jerks" by Bernard Wills and Jason Holt, where the authors try to motivate an autonomist position according to which the moral lives of artists are independent from the aesthetic quality of their work (Wills and Holt 2017). However, Wills and Holt claim that there are exceptions to this position when the artist acts in ways that are particularly morally egregious. As Bartel notes, this exception belies the purported independence of the moral lives of artists from the aesthetic success of their work, suggesting instead that Wills and Holt's view might be characterized more accurately as accepting interaction between the moral and the aesthetic, but with a very high bar when it comes to evaluating whether the moral lives of artists are relevant to the aesthetic quality of their work (Bartel 2019, 5).

So, how are we to accurately characterize the contours of this interaction? According to Gaut's ethicism, when it comes to the ethical criticism of *art*, works that manifest immoral attitudes are *to that extent*, aesthetically flawed (Gaut 1998, 182). As Gaut notes, this is consistent with the work in question being all-things-considered aesthetically excellent. On the ethicist framework, the manifested attitudes of a work are a function of the attitudes that the work prescribes the audience to have. When the audience ought not have the prescribed response, because it would be unethical, that is a failure of the work on its own terms, and hence an aesthetic flaw. Bartel's aim is to see how we might expand the ethicist framework to account for the moral lives of artists, and not just the moral content of their work. The argument goes like this: understanding the attitudes prescribed by a work of art depends in part on understanding the work's point of view, which is produced within a particular sociohistorical context. This means that the point of view of the work is always underspecified when we confine our focus to the work alone; bringing this context to bear on the work's point of view requires a broader lens. As Bartel notes, it is common practice in art criticism to consider features related to the artist's biography in determining that sociohistorical context. Viewed in this light, it seems arbitrary to preclude the moral life of the artist from being considered as part of

---

[1] For discussion, see Carroll (1996), Harold (2011), Clavel-Vazquez (2018a).

the effort to fill in the point of view of the work. As Bartel puts it, drawing on a comment from Richard Wollheim (1980), "if we allow ourselves to consider some background knowledge from the artist's life, then why stop short at the artist's own personal morality?" (Bartel 2019, 8–9).

Bartel's discussion focuses on how our knowledge of the moral life of the artist can in turn inform our understanding of what attitudes the work prescribes (Bartel 2019, 9). Facts about the moral life of the artist can moreover influence whether the attitudes prescribed by the work are morally merited. For example, we might judge that a satirical perspective on violence is merited by a work until we learn of the artist's own predilection for violence; this wouldn't necessarily alter our understanding of what attitudes the work prescribed, but rather raise the bar for whether they would be morally acceptable for the audience to adopt (Matthes 2022, 21). This is particularly important for the advocate of a view such as immoralism, which is more friendly toward the potential of immoral artworks to present unique opportunities for aesthetic success, but wants to explain why such aesthetic merits might be undermined when the immorality in question extends beyond the artwork and into the artist's life. For instance, we might be perfectly open to the sadistic charms of Hannibal Lecter, but not if the role were portrayed by an actual cannibalistic serial killer (Matthes 2022, 38; cf. Wills and Holt 2017, 4).

On an approach such as this one, where we look to the moral lives of artists to aid interpretation of their work, the aesthetic significance of the artist's immorality will be limited (Harold 2020, 61). While there are some clear examples where an artist's life offers a plausible lens for interpreting their work, such as Woody Allen's *Manhattan* or R. Kelly's "Age Ain't Nothing But a Number" (performed by Aaliyah), these cases seem exceptional. This approach does not, for example, give us any clear reason for thinking that Hitler's egregious immorality has anything to do with his unobtrusive cityscapes. However, we might view this as a salutatory feature of the view rather than an objection. As we will see, there is a range of other moral questions we might ask about how we relate to the work of immoral artists, and we should be wary of trying to shoehorn that diverse set of issues into our account of the relationship between an artist's moral life and their work's aesthetic success.

CONSUMER ETHICS

Independently of whether or not the moral transgressions of artists compromise the aesthetic quality of their work in some regard, many art consumers have begun asking questions about whether this immoral behavior should influence their engagement with that work anyway. Should we stop listening to Michael Jackson hits such as *Thriller* due to the artists' alleged molestation of children? Should we give up on Morrissey because of his seeming embrace of fascism?

The first kind of answer to this question takes a consequentialist approach. Consider this comment by TV critic Emily Nussbaum: "My job is actually to respond to the art itself and find a way to do that. But I definitely understand the idea that, for instance, you don't want to fill Bill Cosby's coffers—that makes total sense to me" (Gross and Nussbaum 2019). Here, Nussbaum claims a moral permission to engage with Cosby's work due to her professional role as a critic, but acknowledges that another consumer might be disinclined to give their money to Cosby due to his history of serial sexual assault. You might think about this in terms of not wanting to *benefit* an immoral artist, of avoiding the *enabling* of future harms they might perpetuate, or *signaling* your disapproval to them. But each of these reasons seems to depend on the ability of your consumer decision to bring about a particular result, and the prospects for achieving those outcomes, especially when it comes to successful artists, are grim.

It's first worth acknowledging the limited scope of application for approaches to our individual relationships with the work of immoral artists that focus on our purchasing power. For one, they have no clear bearing on cases where the artist is no longer living, and those cases do comprise a substantial set of popular concerns about immoral artists. Moreover, plenty of our engagement with the work of beloved artists doesn't involve purchasing; rather, it concerns art that we already own. So, whatever other moral reasons might bear on our engagement with these works, considerations grounded in our market behavior don't seem to apply (Willard 2021, 35–36; Matthes 2022, 45–46).

Even for that subset of cases where we are concerned with *purchasing* work by *living* artists, the prospects for a good consequentialist reason to refrain will be weak. The explanation is familiar from other cases that share a similar structure concerning individual action and collective responsibility. We can assume that *everyone* deciding to boycott a particular artist's work would have a substantial impact on them, but your individual decision is such a minuscule contribution to that effort that it will have no discernible effect. And if it has no discernible effect, then from a consequentialist perspective at least, it will seem to lack moral significance. Even if you think the action retains some tiny amount of moral significance, it then seems easy for it to be outweighed by competing considerations. It's easy to boycott an artist's work if it's already meaningless to you, but as Mary Beth Willard explains, such decisions are often not *cost-free*, especially when they focus on artists whose work we care about, or that play a role in our individual aesthetic projects (Willard 2021, 22).

Moreover, if the strength of our moral reason to boycott an artist's work depends on our ability to make a difference to the artist, this will have the unintuitive consequence that our reason to boycott an unsuccessful immoral artist will be *stronger* than our reason to boycott a successful one. So, if you think there's a particularly important moral imperative to take a stand against the Bill Cosbys of the world, the consequentialist approach to our individual consumer behavior will have a hard time explaining that moral impulse (Matthes 2022, 45). (See also Woodcock, this volume.)

In a recent article, Bradley Elicker argues that we should take a page from the literature on collective harm to argue that even if my individual purchasing decisions make an imperceptible difference, this does not entail that they are "inconsequential" (Elicker 2021, 2). Elicker suggests that we can think of our decision to provide public or financial support to certain immoral artists as *enabling* the harm that they cause. In brief, predatory artists make use of their "wealth and influence" to engage in predation, and we enable their ability to do this through our support of their celebrity. We will return below to questions about the responsibilities of arts institutions that control some of the most direct means of affecting an artist's celebrity (through, for example, canceling the dissemination, performance, or support of their work). For now, though, we are faced with the same concerns about individual action and collective responsibility we have faced before: even if we grant that our decision to financially or publicly support an artist contributes to their celebrity and thus enables harm, it appears to do so in an inconsequential way (Elicker 2021, 7).

Elicker builds on Parfit's famous "Drops of Water" case to argue that "If I know that enough of us supporting a [harmful artist] enables them to cause a significant amount of harm (and that more of us supporting them would cause more harm) and I reasonably believe that others would withdraw their own support, then I have a moral obligation to withdraw my public or financial support [for that artist]" (Elicker 2021, 9). Elicker suggests that the increased attention to the moral lives of artists supports a reasonable belief that others will in fact withdraw their support, but this supposition is not clearly supported by the available evidence. For instance, the release of documentaries chronicling the alleged abusive behavior of R. Kelly and Michael Jackson seem to have substantially spurred engagement with those artists' work (R. Kelly streaming activity increased 116 percent the day the finale of "Surviving R. Kelly" aired) (Zellner 2019). Elicker suggests that even if we can't form this belief in the actions of others, we may still have an obligation to withdraw our support of harmful artists if that action is relatively low-cost (Elicker 2021, 10). However, as we have noted, this may further limit the applicability of this framework, since for many consumers the decision about what artists to engage with may play a significant role in their aesthetic projects: it's not as low-cost a sacrifice as Elicker seems to assume (Willard 2021, 22). Even if we are not already attached to a particular artist whose behavior turns out to be immoral, we may worry about the cost of making our aesthetic lives *subservient* to our moral lives in the way that this framework suggests (Matthes 2022, 59–60).

However, there are other, nonconsequentialist ways of thinking about consumer ethics that don't depend on your purchasing behavior on its own actually making a difference. We can divide these into considerations that focus on *complicity* and those that focus on *expressive significance*.

Standardly, attributions of complicity also depend on making a difference. For instance, if you fail to rescue the proverbial child drowning in the pond when it would only be a minor inconvenience to intervene, we might say that you are complicit in the child's death—you could have made a difference, but declined to act. However, more popular uses of the concept of complicity often move beyond contexts in which you can make an individual difference. It is common to hear objections to the effect that continuing to purchase the work of a predatory artist, for instance, makes you complicit in their behavior; the reasoning here is analogous to objections to purchasing clothing from companies that rely on child labor, or buying factory-farmed meat. You neither commit the wrong in question (being a sexual predator, exploiting child labor, cruelly slaughtering animals), nor do you make an individual difference with respect to whether these actions occur, and yet to many observers there seems to be something morally objectionable about your behavior. Adrienne Martin suggests that cases with this structure are akin to "contributing to an already flush collective fund to hire an assassin" (Martin 2016, 205). Because our contribution makes no difference, by hypothesis, we will need to employ alternative moral concepts to explain what, if anything, is wrong with our behavior in cases that share this structure.

Martin introduces the idea of "adopting a role" to address these cases. For the consumer of factory-farmed meat, "she willingly participates as a member of a consumer group that has the function of signaling demand" (Martin 2016, 210). So, in the case of immoral artists, we might consider the ethics of adopting a role as a fan of the artist. What exactly you're signaling as part of this consumer group may be unclear. For instance, we might think that in your role as a Kevin Spacey fan, you're just signaling demand for his acting, not for his alleged predatory behavior. However, what you signal through adopting a role might plausibly diverge from your intentions. James Harold, for instance, has argued that being part of an affective community surrounding the work of an immoral artist might plausibly shape the ethics of our engagement with that work (Harold 2020, 62). Harold notes that cases where an artist actively engages with their fan base, or where moral themes are key to their work, will provide natural avenues for the moral life of the artist to matter to their fans (Harold 2020, 63–65). These two considerations are primarily explanatory, offering an analysis of why fans might reasonably care about the moral life of the artist. To these, Harold adds a further normative consideration: the public salience of the affective community might shape what their actions communicate to others. As Harold puts it: "If an affective community is highly public, one's actions as a member of that community may communicate to others support for those artists, even if one privately disapproves of the artist's actions" (Harold 2020, 65). Adopting a role as a Kevin Spacey fan may well signal that concerns about his alleged predatory behavior simply don't matter, or at least are swamped by the quality of his acting.

Martin's idea of adopting a role still seems to be linked with the prospect of future harm, however. The moral weight of adopting a role that signals demand seems to rest on the role that such group demand will play in affecting future harms (such as further painful slaughter of animals, or further predatory behavior from an artist). This will limit the applicability of this model: in addition to not applying to deceased artists, it seems that it will also not apply to artists whose moral transgressions are agreed to be in the past. However, Harold's considerations about the role that affective communities might play in communicating both within and outside their group offer a way of thinking about the expressive significance of our consumer behavior that moves beyond the limits of the particular model proposed by Martin. As Willard notes, *condoning* is a moral sense of complicity that is "fully after the fact" and could be applied both to cases where there is the prospect of future harm (such as Spacey's) as well as to cases where there is not (such as Jackson's) (Willard 2021, 50). While Willard agrees that condoning sexual assault is definitely wrong, she is skeptical that actions such as refusing to boycott an artist accused of sexual assault should be interpreted as condoning their immoral behavior. As she notes, there are other straightforward explanations of such behavior (such as not believing the allegations or not thinking a boycott can do anything about them) that do not entail attributing condonation of sexual assault to fans who don't sign on for boycotts (Willard 2021, 53).

Alfred Archer and Benjamin Matheson, however, argue that we should not think about condoning as only a function of someone's beliefs or intentions. They identify two ways in which a decision to *honor* an immoral artist (which we'll return to below) might be interpreted as condoning their behavior: emotional prioritization and exemplar identification. While exemplar identification (picking out an individual for admiration and emulation) appears more specific to the bestowal of honors, the idea of emotional prioritization might be applied to our everyday public behavior. As the authors put it, "Honoring immoral artists involves choosing to identify them as people we ought to admire rather than as people we ought to be indignant about. Given that these attitudes and emotions are all fitting, honorers are thereby communicating that this is the correct way to prioritize these attitudes and emotions" (Archer and Matheson 2019, 251). In addition to cases where an honor is bestowed with the specific goal of prioritizing admiration over condemnation, Archer and Matheson explain that a decision to honor an artist can have a "public meaning," according to which social context makes condonation a justifiable interpretation, even where this goes beyond the "intended meaning" of the action (Archer and Matheson 2019, 251). Analogous reasoning might apply to our decisions to publicly engage with or support the work of an immoral artist, even if we have no intention of condoning their behavior. Even if there are alternative explanations, as Willard notes, a broader social context in which artists' immoral behavior is standardly treated as if it is somehow justified by the greatness of their art might exacerbate the risk that our actions are reasonably interpreted as condoning.

While Willard focuses primarily on what our actions might stand to communicate to artists or to victims, it may well also be morally significant for us to think about the expressive significance of our consumer behavior to our friends and family, which can come apart from moral analysis of the role we might play as part of a group that signals something to the artist or to victims or to the public in general (cf. Willard 2021, 33). If you know that your friend is deeply upset by the allegations against Woody Allen, for instance, then dictating that *Manhattan* will be the film for your group movie night seems like an obnoxious thing to do, an action that would open you to plausible moral criticism. However, cases such as this center more around the ethics of friendship than any independent norms concerning our engagement with the arts—the wrong in these cases is of a piece with serving an entirely meat meal to your vegetarian friend, even if we assume that meat-eating is permissible (Matthes 2022, 71).

At this point, we have tentatively established that other things being equal, individuals have substantial moral latitude in their individual engagement with the work of immoral artists, at least when that engagement is relatively private. In the quotation mentioned earlier, Emily Nussbaum claims this moral permission as a function of her professional role as a TV critic, but it seems that we all in fact share this permission. There may be reasons to avoid complicity with immoral artists, understood in terms of adopting a role as part of a group that signals demand with adverse consequences, but the application of this framework will be extremely limited, applying only to the exercise of your purchasing power in relation to artists causing ongoing harm. And even then, since your individual contribution makes no difference, it might plausibly be outweighed by the value of that artist's work to you and your aesthetic projects (Willard 2021, 42). The fact that considerations of complicity might, in certain circumscribed cases, give you a good moral reason to boycott an immoral artist does not entail that you have a decisive reason to do so. There are also ethical considerations arising from the expressive significance that our *public* artistic engagements might have for others, but these don't clearly bear on our *private* artistic preferences and behaviors.

INSTITUTIONAL RESPONSIBILITY AND CANCEL CULTURE

Beyond these considerations for individual choice and action, however, there are further questions to examine concerning the role of *institutions*.[2] What should those in positions of power in the art world do in response to revelations about the immorality of artists? Should exhibitions and concerts be canceled, books pulled from publication, songs stricken from the radio rotation?

Popular discussion of "cancel culture" tends to lump together individual and institutional responses to immoral artists, but it's worth prizing them apart for the purposes of moral analysis. "Canceling" a person via social media mobbing, for instance, has an overreaching metaphorical usage that can obscure more straightforward practical questions faced by institutions. For instance, the influential American painter Chuck Close was accused of sexual harassment by multiple models who sat for him. It can be difficult to answer the question posed by recent parlance "should Chuck Close be canceled?" since it remains unclear precisely what that means, whereas the meaning of the question "should the National Gallery cancel their planned special exhibition of Close's work" is unambiguous, however controversial the answer may be. The imprecision (and concomitant confusion) of questions about canceling a person are captured well in a recent *New York Times* article titled "Is it Time Gauguin Got Canceled?" (Nayeri 2019). Despite worries about boycotts expressed by curators, no one interviewed in the article actually advocates for a position stronger than making Gauguin's immoral behavior explicit as part of exhibiting his work. It thus behooves us to be as precise as possible in what practical action we're proposing when we ask after how we ought to respond

---

[2] I use "institutions" in a very broad sense here to refer to the many and varied organizations of the art world, including, but not limited to, publishing houses, record companies, radio stations, movie studios, magazines, museums, galleries, art schools, etc.

to artists' immoral behavior. I'll first discuss institutional decisions about whether to work with an immoral artist or publicize their work before moving on to the issues surrounding social media activism in response to artists' actions and statements.

The National Gallery did in fact cancel their special exhibition of Close's work, and other specific examples of institutional responses to artists' personal actions can be identified across artistic mediums. Hachette ultimately decided against publishing Woody Allen's memoir (following employee protests). Kevin Spacey was removed from the final season of *House of Cards*, the show he had been headlining on Netflix for years, and director Ridley Scott decided to reshoot Spacey's scenes in the movie *All the Money in the World*, recasting him with the late actor Christopher Plummer.

In considering these actions, we might start by asking what the relevant institutions aim to achieve. First, they might aim to stop abusive behavior. For instance, in the case of Spacey, the public removal of the actor from prominent roles plausibly undercuts his ability to take advantage of this celebrity in order to prey on others (a more direct version of the argument Elicker made about consumer behavior). We might see an analogy here in the steps that any institution should take to address abuses of power within their organization. When an employee abuses their power over a subordinate, a natural step is to remove the offending individual from their position of power. While the roles aren't formalized in the same way when it comes to celebrity artists taking advantage of their social standing, trying to undercut their social power to exploit might be justified through a similar pattern of reasoning (Matthes 2022, 95–96).

The aim of prevention, however, underlines a significant difference between artists whose immorality is a function of serial abuse and those whose immorality consists in espousing bigoted attitudes. As Willard notes, one of the problems with "cancel culture" is that it lacks a sense of proportionality and nuance, applying the same consequence no matter the nature or extent of the misdeed, an issue that we'll return to in relation to social media below (Willard 2021, 114–116). We might add to this that if the goal is preventing bad behavior, canceling an artist who has only made morally objectionable statements seems to approach this goal even more indirectly than in the case of predators; even if we thought it was appropriate and proportional for a bigoted comment to be career-ending for an artist, this would only socially sanction the expression of those beliefs, not having them. And even if we thought that such a strong social sanction was desirable, what counts as an immoral belief is often substantially more controversial than what counts as predatory behavior. We might well support strong social sanctions against sexual exploitation and predation but be warier of equally strong social sanctions against the expression of objectionable ideas.

Apart from trying to prevent any particular future behavior, though, an institution might decide that they don't want to *honor* an artist because of the artist's immoral behavior.[3] As noted earlier, Archer and Matheson argue that honoring an immoral artist

---

[3] For further discussion of Archer and Matheson's views on the ethics of honoring, see their 2021 book.

can involve an objectionable form of *exemplar identification*. Even if the honor is only meant to refer to the artist's aesthetic achievement, admiration has a tendency to spread; picking out an immoral artist as an exemplar may thus, even inadvertently, be read as condoning their immoral behavior or even encourage emulation of that behavior (Archer and Matheson 2019, 254).

Archer and Matheson also worry that honoring immoral artists can have ramifications for epistemic justice. In particular, they suggest that it can inflate the credibility of immoral artists and silence their victims (Archer and Matheson, 256–257). By singling out an immoral artist for praise, honoring can add to their sense of credibility, which can make listeners more inclined to believe their testimony, including denials of immoral behavior. This in turn contributes to an epistemic climate where victims reasonably fear not being believed, and so may decide not to come forward in the first place.[4]

However, a decision to cancel an artist's exhibition in order to avoid honoring them need not entail that institutions should all refuse to display their work. Declining to accord special honors to an immoral artist is compatible with making their work available for consumption, though navigating that line may be trickier in some artistic mediums than others. For instance, one might object that having an artist's work displayed in a museum or gallery is necessarily an honor, refusal to grant special exhibitions and awards notwithstanding. But depending on how the institution in question treats the accusations against the artist, this might not be the case. As Daniel Callcut puts it: "Fame is no longer a shield from moral scrutiny: it's a magnet for moral attention. The failings of famous artists are now examined and publicised to a degree far beyond the consideration paid to those who commit the same wrongs in ordinary life. The script, in this sense, has been flipped" (Callcut 2019). This is consistent with the actual calls for action highlighted in the *New York Times* article about "canceling" Gauguin; rather than wanting Gauguin's work removed from museums, the activists quoted there want explicit discussion of Gauguin's personal behavior alongside displays of his work. This highlights a way in which continued engagement with the work of an immoral artist can actually facilitate communicative actions that takes the artist's misdeeds seriously, rather than acting as if their artistic achievements should be understood as justifying or making irrelevant their immoral behavior, as the proffering of honors and awards might plausibly do. We might moreover believe that continued access to the work of immoral artists is important for the way it facilitates understanding of work by other artists that grapple with an immoral artist's legacy. For example, Kehinde Wiley has painted a portrait series of Tahitian subjects that has been described as a "riposte" to Gauguin (Rea 2019); understanding that artistic dialogue, and both its moral and aesthetic contours,

---

[4] Willard also discusses epistemic injustice, but her focus is on whether our individual engagement with the work of immoral artists risks contributing to a harmful epistemic climate surrounding sexual assault. Willard agrees that this culture should be addressed, but is skeptical that our personal decisions about what artists to engage with ought to play a key role in cultivating epistemic virtues (Willard 2021, 67–82).

would be challenging in the face of complete erasure of Gauguin's work (Matthes 2022, 84).[5]

The fact that institutions have an important role to play in addressing the immoral actions of popular artists does not mean they have consistently risen to this challenge. Reforming arts institutions and diversifying their leadership may offer productive routes for ensuring that these institutions will have policies and procedures for addressing the behavior of artists in a thoughtful way, as well as leaders who will be sensitive to the range of objectionable behaviors that might arise (Matthes 2022, 107). As is often the case with patterns of institutional failure, the public has sometimes stepped in to "cancel" artists in lieu of institutional action, typically employing social media as a vehicle. Ta-Nahesi Coates has observed that "canceling" is nothing new: powerful institutions have always had the ability to cancel, a power that they can also abuse, as he argues was the case with the NFL and Colin Kaepernick (Coates 2019). What we see in the "democratization" of cancellation via social media, he claims, is an understandable response to the failure of institutions to hold immoral actors responsible; but Coates also notes that this is a "suboptimal" situation. It would be better still if we developed trustworthy institutions that we could rely on to bring an understanding of moral accountability to their operations.

There are a number of reasons why social media cancellation is less desirable than institutional accountability. For one, as we've noted, social media cancellation lacks the ability to apply nuance or proportionality: it's all or nothing (Willard 2021, 114–16). Furthermore, it's very difficult to un-ring the bell of social media cancellation; it leaves little room to address mistaken accusations or provide avenues for reform since it lacks any procedures for appeal or accountability (Rini 2020). Third, the focus of social media cancellation on particular artists can actually undermine the cause of institutional reform. It is subject to "elite capture," where institutions can sacrifice a particular artist to appease activists without making any changes to institutional operations that might avoid similar situations in the future (cf. Táíwò 2020). Journalist Helen Lewis captures the concern perfectly when she writes: "Those with power inside institutions *love* splashy progressive gestures . . . because they help preserve their power" (Lewis 2020).

The point here is not to be dismissive of protest or the use of social media as a protest tool. Rather, it is to highlight the specific pitfalls of social media cancellation of particular artists as a mechanism for addressing the problem of predatory artists. Protest (including via social media) will no doubt be an important element in achieving the kind of institutional reform I have argued that we should pursue.

One further concern about social media cancellation focuses not on its effectiveness for creating appropriate forms of accountability but on ethical worries about participation in such social media campaigns and their effects on moral discourse. Building on work by Justin Tosi and Brandon Warmke (Tosi and Warmke 2016 and 2020), we might worry that social media cancellation involves an objectionable form of "moral

---

[5] For further discussion of the Gauguin case, see Nannicelli (2020), and Matthes (2023).

grandstanding" (Willard 2021, 123). When one "grandstands," one's contribution to public discourse aims primarily at demonstrating one's own moral respectability, which can hence corrupt the quality of public moral discourse: it becomes about you rather than about getting at the moral truth. Willard illustrates how "every single characteristic that Tosi and Warmke identify as characteristic of grandstanding is actively promoted by the structure of social media (Willard 2021, 125). Thi Nguyen and Bekka Williams have similarly defined the concept of "moral outrage porn" to describe expressions of moral outrage that aim primarily at making the person expressing the outrage feel good, a phenomenon familiar from social media as well (Nguyen and Williams 2020). So, to the extent that one is worried about the adverse effects of moral grandstanding and moral outrage porn, those concerns appear to carry over to the phenomenon of social media cancellation.

Beyond its purported effects on moral discourse, you might further worry that in the case of the arts in particular, grandstanding is objectionable because it instrumentalizes art. If grandstanding involves treating moral concerns about an artist and their work as an occasion just to demonstrate one's own moral respectability or make yourself feel good, then it turns the art into nothing more than a tool for one's own ends. At the beginning of this chapter, I argued that the moral lives of artists can bear in important ways on our understanding of their work; grandstanding, on the other hand, treats the work of immoral artists as an occasion for a moral statement about oneself that has no necessary relationship to the artwork as an object of aesthetic attention. While we have seen many ways that ethical considerations are salient to art and aesthetics, attending to ethical issues in a way that ignores or erases the fact that those issues involve artistic and aesthetic concerns is a failure to treat art as art. Morality matters to art, but if we treat our engagement with art as if it's *just* about morality, then something has gone awry (Matthes 2022, 59). To be sure, identifying instances of objectionable grandstanding may well be difficult. Practically, concerns about grandstanding and the instrumentalizing of art for purely moral aims may best be employed as a check on one's own thinking and actions. The point is not that aesthetic or artistic concerns should necessarily take priority over ethical ones, but that they shouldn't be completely eclipsed in our thinking about the problem of immoral artists.

FANS AND EMOTIONAL TURMOIL

Having considered various aspects of what we should do in response to the immoral behavior of artists, we will conclude by briefly considering the problem of how to feel. For many art fans, revelations about the immoral lives of beloved artists have been marked by emotional turmoil and conflict. Consider this passage from an essay by Constance Grady, where she reflects on her teenage love for *Edward Scissorhands* amidst allegations of domestic violence against actor Johnny Depp: "I loved this movie. It made me feel all kinds of deep and profound teenage feelings, and those feelings were real and I could not unfeel them. But now, whenever I thought about Johnny Depp, I felt a deep and profound disgust, a moral outrage. That was a real feeling too, and I couldn't unfeel it either" (Grady 2019).

What might fans do in the face of such emotional conflicts? One approach is to try to "separate" the art from the artist. This is what Daniel Radcliffe, the actor who played Harry Potter in the film adaptations of the series, recommended to fans who were hurt by author J. K. Rowling's transphobic statements. Focusing on the personal meaning that fans may have found in the books, he said: "That is between you and the book that you read, and it is sacred. And in my opinion nobody can touch that. It means to you what it means to you" (Radcliffe 2020). He thus suggested that the relationship between fan and artwork could be a private sphere protected from the artist themself. This may be a viable strategy for a fan who can perform such an emotional separation, but we should also not undersell its trickiness. Especially in genres such as film and television, many fans (such as Grady, above) report feeling *unable* to separate their experience of a beloved work from what they now know about the actors performing in it.

Another approach to the emotional turmoil in question is not to try to separate the art from the artist, but to throw out both together. Roxanne Gay, writing about Bill Cosby and *The Cosby Show*, adopts this approach:

> Every time I think of Cosby's work, I remember the women he victimized and how their silence was trapped by the gilded cage of his fame. To me, Cosby's artistic legacy is rendered meaningless in the face of the pain he caused. It has to be. He once created great art, and then he destroyed his great art. The responsibility for that destruction is his and his alone. We are free to lament it, but not at the expense of his victims. (Gay 2018)

So, for Gay, we might be saddened by the loss of the work, but the way forward is to reject the work altogether. Cosby "destroyed" it through his actions.

Whichever of these two approaches a fan might take, it's important to see that arriving at it as a potential solution to emotional conflict would be facilitated by actually engaging with the art. Are you, as an individual, able to separate the art from the artist? Might you train yourself to do so? Have the artist's actions destroyed their work for you, such that you need to reject both together? Revisiting the artwork in question has the potential to be pivotal in exploring this difficult emotional terrain. It also has the virtue of offering an opportunity to reflect on the ways that the artist's actions have (or perhaps haven't?) influenced the aesthetic experience of their work. Art has the potential to be *cathartic* in this regard; not in the sense of *expunging* your emotional turmoil, but rather, of *clarifying* your feelings. By engaging with the artwork, you may even find that you can still appreciate it while disdaining the actions of the artist who made it. In this case, you neither separate the art from the artist, nor reject both wholesale, but rather situate your emotions in a kind of balance, even if it remains an uneasy one (Matthes 2022, 135).

What we have seen throughout this discussion is that art has a central role to play in our grappling with the problem of immoral artists. Whether we're thinking about the influence that an artist's personal life might have on their work, the moral or expressive significance of our engagement with that work, or the responsibilities of arts institutions with respect to the artist's behavior, the artwork itself continually reemerges as a source of both moral and aesthetic guidance. The discussion here suggests that an adequate solution to the problem of immoral artists in these various contexts has ultimately less to do with *what* art we engage with, and whether we do so, than with *how* we engage with that art.

See also: Stear, Carroll, Jacobson, Rothfeld, Woodcock, this volume

REFERENCES

Archer, Alfred, and Benjamin Matheson. 2019. "When Artists Fall: Honoring and Admiring the Immoral." *Journal of the American Philosophical Association* 5, no. 2: 246–265.

Archer, Alfred, and Benjamin Matheson. 2021. *Honouring and Admiring the Immoral: An Ethical Guide.* London: Routledge.

Bartel, Christopher. 2019. "Ordinary Monsters: Ethical Criticism and the Lives of Artists." *Contemporary Aesthetics*, 17: 1–16.

Callcut, Daniel. 2019. "Paul Gauguin, the National Gallery and the Philosophical Conundrum of Exhibiting Immoral Artists." *Prospect Magazine*, October 16, https://www.prospectmagaz ine.co.uk/philosophy/paul-gauguin-the-national-gallery-and-the-philosophical-conund rum-of-exhibiting-immoral-artists.

Carroll, Noel. 1996. "Moderate Moralism." *British Journal of Aesthetics* 36, no. 3: 223–238.

Clavel-Vazquez, Adriana. 2018a. "Rethinking Autonomism: Beauty in a World of Moral Anarchy." *Philosophy Compass* 13, no. 7: 1–10.

Clavel-Vazquez, Adriana. 2018b. "Sugar and Spice, and Everything Nice: What Rough Heroines Tell Us about Imaginative Resistance." *Journal of Aesthetics and Art Criticism* 76, no. 2: 201–212.

Coates, Ta-Nehisi. 2019. "The Cancelation of Colin Kaepernick." *The New York Times.* November 22. https://www.nytimes.com/2019/11/22/opinion/colin-kaepernick-nfl.html

Eaton, A. W. 2012. "Robust Immoralism." *Journal of Aesthetics and Art Criticism* 70, no. 3: 281–292.

Elicker, Bradley. 2021. "Why We Should Avoid Artists Who Cause Harm: Support as Enabling Harm." *Journal of Applied Philosophy* 38, no. 2: 306–319.

Gaut, Berys. 1998. "The Ethical Criticism of Art." In *Aesthetics and Ethics*, edited by Jerrold Levinson, 182–203. Cambridge: Cambridge University Press.

Gaut, Berys. 2007. *Art, Emotion, and Ethics.* Oxford: Oxford University Press.

Gay, Roxanne. 2018. "Can I Enjoy the Art but Denounce the Artist?" *Marie Claire*, February 6, https://www.marieclaire.com/culture/a16105931/roxane-gay-on-predator-legacies/.

Grady, Constance. 2019. "What Do We Do When the Art We Love Was Created By a Monster?" *Vox*, June 25, https://www.vox.com/culture/2018/10/11/17933686/me-too-separating-artist-art-johnny-depp-woody-allen-michael-jackson-louis-ck.

Gross, Terry, and Emily Nussbaum. 2019. "We All Watch In Our Own Way: A Critic Tracks the 'TV Revolution.'" *NPR*, July 15, https://www.npr.org/2019/07/15/741146427/we-all-watch-in-our-own-way-a-critic-tracks-the-tv-revolution.

Harold, James. 2011. "Autonomism Reconsidered." *British Journal of Aesthetics* 51, no. 2: 137–147.

Harold, James. 2020. *Dangerous Art*. Oxford: Oxford University Press.

Lewis, Helen. 2020. "How Capitalism Drives Cancel Culture." *The Atlantic*, July 14, https://www.theatlantic.com/international/archive/2020/07/cancel-culture-and-problem-woke-capitalism/614086/.

Li, Zhen. 2020. "Immorality and Transgressive Art: An Argument for Immoralism in the Philosophy of Art." *Philosophical Quarterly*, 71, no. 3: 481–501.

Martin, Adrienne M. 2016. "Factory Farming and Consumer Complicity." In *Philosophy Comes to Dinner*, edited by Andrew Chignell, Terence Cuneo, and Matthew C. Halteman, 203–214. London: Routledge.

Matthes, Erich Hatala. 2022. *Drawing the Line: What to Do with the Work of Immoral Artists from Museums to the Movies*. Oxford: Oxford University Press.

Matthes, Erich Hatala. 2023. Paul Gauguin's *Manao Tupapau (Spirit of the Dead Watching)* (1892) in *Bloomsbury Contemporary Aesthetics*, ed. Darren Hudson Hick. London: Bloomsbury Publishing.

Nannicelli, Ted. 2020. *Artistic Creation and Ethical Criticism*. Oxford: Oxford University Press.

Nayeri, Farah. 2019. "Is It Time Gauguin Got Canceled?" *The New York Times*. November 18. https://www.nytimes.com/2019/11/18/arts/design/gauguin-national-gallery-london.html

Nguyen, C. Thi, and Bekka Williams. 2020. "Moral Outrage Porn." *Journal of Ethics and Social Philosophy* 18, no. 2: 147–172.

Radcliffe, Daniel. 2020. "Daniel Radcliffe Responds to J. K. Rowling's Tweets on Gender Identity." *The Trevor Project*, June 8, https://www.thetrevorproject.org/2020/06/08/daniel-radcliffe-responds-to-j-k-rowlings-tweets-on-gender-identity/.

Rea, Naomi. 2019. "Artist Kehinde Wiley's Latest Paintings Are a Progressive Riposte to Paul Gauguin's Primitivist Portraits of Tahitians." *Artnet News*, May 15, https://news.artnet.com/art-world/kehinde-wiley-tahiti-gauguin-1546054.

Rini, Regina. 2020. "The Internet Is an Angry and Capricious God." *Times Literary Supplement*, https://www.the-tls.co.uk/articles/the-internet-is-an-angry-and-capricious-god/ (accessed July 18, 2020).

Táíwò, Olúfẹ́mi O. 2020. "Identity Politics and Elite Capture." *The Boston Review*, May 7, http://bostonreview.net/race/olufemi-o-taiwo-identity-politics-and-elite-capture.

Tosi, Justin, and Brandon Warmke. 2016. "Moral Grandstanding." *Philosophy and Public Affairs* 44, no. 3: 197–217.

Tosi, Justin, and Brandon Warmke. 2020. *Grandstanding*. Oxford: Oxford University Press.

Willard, Mary Beth. 2021. *Why It's OK to Enjoy the Work of Immoral Artists*. London: Routledge.

Wills, Bernard, and Jason Holt. 2017. "Art by Jerks." *Contemporary Aesthetics* 15, no. 1: 1–11.

Wollheim, Richard. 1980. "Criticism as Retrieval." In *Art and Its Objects*, 185–205. Cambridge: Cambridge University Press.

Zellner, Xander. 2019. "'Surviving R. Kelly' Doc Finale Spurred 116% Gain in R. Kelly Music Streams." *Billboard*, January 10, https://www.billboard.com/articles/columns/chart-beat/8492984/r-kelly-docuseries-caused-gain-music.

FURTHER READING

Matthes, Erich Hatala. 2022. "How Museums and Arts Institutions Can Deal with the Problem of Immoral Artists: A Response to Willard." *British Journal of Aesthetics* 62, no. 4: 559–566.

Matthes, Erich Hatala. 2022. "Immoral Artists and Our Aesthetic Projects: A Commentary on Mary Beth Willard's *Why It's OK to Enjoy the Work of Immoral Artists.*" *British Journal of Aesthetics* 62, no. 4: 517–525.

Willard, Mary Beth. 2022. "Aesthetic Reasons, Aesthetic Value, and the Myth of the Aesthetic Meritocracy: Reply to Erich H. Matthes' Comments." *British Journal of Aesthetics* 62, no. 4: 577–586.

Willard, Mary Beth. 2022. "Institutional Responsibility and Aesthetic Value: Commentary on Erich Hatala Matthes' *Drawing The Line: What to Do with the Work of Immoral Artists from Museums to the Movies.*" *British Journal of Aesthetics* 62, no. 4: 539–548.

CHAPTER 38

CULTURAL APPROPRIATION

C. THI NGUYEN AND MATTHEW STROHL

"CULTURAL appropriation" is an umbrella term that encompasses several related but distinct forms of cultural transmission. This chapter concerns what is often called *style appropriation*.[1] Style appropriation is the use of some culturally specific style or practice, such as hairstyles, musical styles, or textile patterns, by individuals who are not part of the relevant cultural group. Prominent examples include the clothing chain Urban Outfitters selling imitation Native American headdresses and white Australian Iggy Azalea emulating musical styles developed by black Americans.[2] Most contemporary debates over cultural appropriation concern whether style appropriation is problematic in some way, and whether outsiders to a group should respect requests by insiders to refrain from style appropriation. To put it another way: What gives requests to refrain from style appropriation their normative force?

Style appropriation is distinct from *object appropriation*, which involves the literal taking of particular cultural objects, such as pottery or religious artifacts. Debates about object appropriation concern, for example, questions about how to redress the seizure of cultural artifacts during the colonial period.[3] Object appropriation is a special case of the familiar wrong of theft: one group suffers a tangible loss. An object has been taken away; the group no longer has access, or even legal ownership. The basis of restrictions concerning style appropriation is significantly harder to understand, because it does not involve this kind of clear, obvious loss.[4] When white musician Justin Bieber wears

---

[1] We take our use of "object appropriation" and "style appropriation" from Young (2010). Many of our examples focus on the standard cases in the popular discourse, or appropriation of styles associated with cultural groups. For a discussion of other forms of style appropriation, see James (2011), which discusses the appropriation of styles associated with gender, race, and sexual orientation.

[2] We choose not to capitalize "black" in light of Nicholas Whittaker's arguments in their (2021).

[3] See Young and Brunk (2009) for a range of views on the issue and Matthes (2017) for a more recent discussion.

[4] There is some overlap between the issues. Michel-Antoine Xhignesse, for instance, addresses in his paper "Retitling, Cultural Appropriation, and Aboriginal Title" (2021) the question of whether it is justifiable to retitle artworks with titles that are offensive to oppressed groups. He argues that such retitling is one avenue for addressing the harms of cultural appropriation.

dreadlocks, black people don't suddenly lose the ability to wear dreadlocks. He didn't "steal" dreadlocks in the way that you can steal a family heirloom. What, then, might be wrong with this sort of appropriation, if it is not reducible to the straightforward theft of an object?

For the rest of this chapter, we use the term "cultural appropriation" to refer narrowly to style appropriation, which is the way it is often used in popular discourse. We use the term in a value-neutral way: whenever one entity uses a style from some cultural group of which they are not a member, this counts as cultural appropriation, whether or not this appropriation is in any way worrisome. The real question, then, is: When is cultural appropriation wrong? And why might it be wrong?

All sorts of answers are possible, but here are the two extremes: First, one might take a stance of *universal permission* toward cultural appropriation, asserting that cultural appropriation faces no normative restrictions whatsoever. If you see something you like, you can help yourself. Universal permission is a common position in public discourse, but mostly among political reactionaries. We know of no serious academic defenses. Second, one might take a stance of *universal prohibition* toward cultural appropriation, and where one asserts that all cultural appropriation is wrong. Universal prohibition has no defenders whatsoever that we know of, although it has been a convenient straw man for some commentators.

Let's call any particular claim that some particular case of cultural appropriation is wrong an "appropriation claim."[5] If some black individuals claim that Justin Bieber's dreadlocks are wrongful appropriation, and that Bieber shouldn't wear them—that's an appropriation claim. If one thinks that some appropriation claims have normative force (as most, but not all, philosophers commenting on this issue do), one needs to provide an account of what grounds the normative force of particular appropriation claims, starting with two interrelated questions:

1) Why are some instances of cultural appropriation wrong?
2) Who is it, exactly, who is wronged (if anyone)?

The first question concerns the normative grounding of appropriation claims.[6] The initial difficulty, again, is in identifying grounds that do not depend on familiar notions of ownership and theft.[7] The second question concerns the group identity of the claimants. As Bruce Ziff and Pratima Rao put it, normative constraints on cultural appropriation

---

    [5] We originally introduced this terminology in Nguyen and Strohl (2019).

    [6] We mean here *moral* normativity, but there are also questions concerning *aesthetic* normativity. Do artists have aesthetic reasons to refrain from cultural appropriation? See Pearson (2021).

    [7] According to Thomas (2021), appropriation claims could only be justified given some coherent sense in which a given culture *owned* a given style—but, suggests Thomas, ownership is the wrong concept. If all of the ensuing accounts we discuss here fail, then perhaps Thomas is right. But, we think, Thomas is rather hasty here in dismissing the possibility of nonownership based normative justification, especially given the deep and rich literature about cultural appropriation, which almost never presumes an ownership relationship between a group and a style.

presuppose a distinction between insiders who are allowed to take part in some prac-tice, and outsiders who are (perhaps) not (Ziff and Rao 1997). But, sorting insiders from outsiders is not straightforward, especially in light of worries about racial and cultural essentialism. Race and ethnicity are vexed concepts, and the boundaries of ra-cial and ethnic groups are often unclear or under dispute. What's more, as Erich Hatala Matthes points out, boundary-setting is itself an expression of power. Trying to sort insiders from outsiders can enact problematic cultural dynamics—like having to explic-itly answer questions about who the "real" or "authentic" members of a group are, and privileging some voices while silencing others (Matthes 2016). Some Native American tribes, for instance, set formal boundaries using controversial blood quantum laws that are contested by many of the individuals they exclude (Holywhitemountain 2019).

Moreover, it is often difficult to establish which group a style belongs to. For example: Does reggae music belong specifically to Jamaicans, or to Rastafarian culture? Or does it belong to black people in general—or specifically to the black people standing in a cer-tain relation to colonialism and the colonial diaspora? Or does it belong to the fans and performers of reggae music, whoever and wherever they might be? The answers to these questions matter crucially for settling appropriation claims, since many cases of cultural appropriation involve attempts at cultural solidarity. A white reggae fan may play reggae music to express their solidarity with Rastafarianism—so the validity of any appropria-tion claim against the fan will depend on establishing whether the musical style belongs to, say, black people standing in a certain relation to a particular diaspora, and not, say, reggae fans or self-identified Rastafarians.

The discussion of cultural appropriation has been wide and ongoing, across many ac-ademic fields and in broader cultural discourse. We will briefly touch on the broader conversation;[8] however, our goal in this brief chapter is to summarize recent debates within analytic philosophy, focusing on the way philosophers have addressed the two questions we highlight.[9]

THE NORMATIVITY OF
APPROPRIATION CLAIMS

If cultural appropriation is sometimes wrong, what is the normative basis of that wrong? First, we need to be careful to separate the particular phenomenon in question from neighboring phenomena that it is often conflated with. For example, cultural appropri-ation is sometimes conflated with the demeaning portrayal of a cultural group, such as

---

[8] For surveys, within the philosophical literature, of the broader cultural discourse on cultural appropriation, see Young (2010), Matthes (2016), and Nguyen and Strohl (2019).

[9] There is a slightly longer history of discussion of object appropriation within analytic philosophy. Many of the chapters anthologized in Young and Brunk (2009) concern object appropriation.

the racist caricature in the logo of the football team formerly known as the Washington Redskins. Racist caricatures like this are obviously wrong, but not primarily because they involve appropriation. Some commentators have suggested that one of the wrongs of cultural appropriation lies in the likelihood of misrepresentation by outsiders.[10] But, as Joy Shim points out, the wrong of stereotyping isn't essentially linked with the identity of the stereotyper. Maxine Hong Kingston's *The Woman Warrior*, for example, was widely disparaged by the Chinese American community for trading on exoticizing stereotypes of Chinese Americans—even though Maxine Hong Kingston is, herself, Chinese American (Shim 2022).

In order to disentangle cultural appropriation from neighboring phenomena, it is helpful to focus on examples that are not obvious cases of racist stereotyping. For example: suppose a non-Native American wearing a replica of a Native American headdress as an expression of their support of the sovereignty of Native tribes. Or suppose a white athlete wears corn-rows—a hairstyle strongly associated with black American culture—because they find it a practical hairstyle for strenuous activity. So, what is the potential wrong in cases like this? We have previously suggested that there are three prominent accounts of the normative basis of informal restrictions concerning cultural appropriation: *harm*, *objectionable symbolism*, and *claim deference* (Nguyen and Strohl 2019).

First, one might claim that some instances of cultural appropriation *harm* members of the group appropriated from. There are a wide variety of potential harms that have been described. Some have argued that cultural appropriation dilutes key cultural practices.[11] Others have argued that cultural appropriation diverts attention and rewards away from the originators of a style, typically toward members of dominantly positioned social groups.[12] One might think, for instance, that Iggy Azalea took many of the stylistic innovations of black rappers, but also that as a blonde white woman, she was better positioned to attract a large audience. So, one might think, Azalea exploits advantages that are rooted in pernicious racial dynamics to divert compensatory resources to herself that otherwise might have gone to black artists.

Harm-based approaches have at least one clear advantage: they make the normative force of appropriation claims clear. (See Woodcock, this volume.) We have a reason to avoid cultural appropriation insofar as we have a reason to avoid harming others. But harm-based approaches typically have trouble providing empirical evidence of harm or quantifying the magnitude of harm. The harms cited are often quite diffuse. This leads to the following worry: using a harm-based approach, one might think that the normative force of an appropriation claim depends on the strength of our evidence for its

---

[10] See Nittle (2021); discussed in Young (2010, 107–113).

[11] See Baraka on cultural genocide discussed in Gracyk (2001, 113) and Young (2010, 118–120).

[12] See Briahna Joy Gray (2017) on cultural exploitation. See also Godoy and Chow (2016), as discussed in Young (2010, 114–118). See also, for a discussion of cultural appropriation and intellectual property theft, "Of Seeds and Shamans" and "Native American Intellectual Property Rights: Issues in the Control of Esoteric Knowledge" in Ziff and Rao (1997).

harmfulness. A reasonable response to an appropriation claim would, then, be: "Where's your evidence of harm? No evidence of harm, no respect for the claim!"

But many who take worries about cultural appropriation seriously think we should respect appropriation claims regardless of the strength of the empirical evidence they cite that the form of appropriation in question is harmful. A citizen of a Native American tribe may feel strongly that nontribal members should not appropriate traditional cere-monial garments but not be in a position to possess evidence that such appropriation is harmful. If one thinks that appropriation claims made in this sort of epistemic position can still have normative force, then we need to move beyond a harm-based approach.

The second approach to grounding normative restrictions concerning cultural appro-priation stresses the objectionable symbolism of appropriative acts. One might claim that cultural appropriation symbolically enacts problematic dynamics of oppression. For example: many black Americans are deterred from wearing dreadlocks by explicit corporate policy or implicit norms of professionalism in personal grooming. White Americans, on the other hand, can appropriate black hairstyles as a fashion statement with relative impunity. White Americans, one might think, can get away with wearing these hairstyles precisely because of unjust social power dynamics operating in the background. They are less likely to be read as unprofessional when they wear these hairstyles, and also less likely to be harassed by police, and this is due to an unjust store of social credibility.[13] When White Americans wear black hairstyles—and profit from them, socially—without having to pay the costs paid by black Americans for wearing these same hairstyles, then this form of appropriation can be seen as reenacting the power imbalance in a way that is distasteful or offensive.[14] The act of appropriation is ob-jectionable, we might say, because it visibly indulges in and vividly displays that power imbalance.

Notice a key difference between the objectionable symbolism account and, say, the Iggy Azalea story we used in the discussion of harm-based accounts. For its normative force, a harm-based account seems to owe us evidence of harm. In this case, we'd need to provide some sort of evidence that Azalea's success does, in fact, divert economic and social resources from black Americans. The objectionable symbolism account does not owe us any such evidence. The argument is not that the appropriation leads to some further harm, as a consequence down the road, but that the appropriation is itself of-fensive, in its ostentatious enactment of an unfair social dynamic. A significant diffi-culty that emerges for objectionable symbolism accounts is showing why offensiveness should, in and of itself, be sufficient to ground substantive prescriptions for action. Also, objectionable symbolism arguments might overgeneralize. One might worry

---

[13] See Briahna Joy Gray (2017) on cultural disrespect. See also Gaynor (2012). For a recent philosophical discussion of dynamics of the appropriation of black hairstyles, see Bacharach and Chavez (2021).

[14] James O. Young thinks that in addition to cases where it is harmful, cultural appropriation can be wrong when it causes *profound offense*, by which he means that it is *morally* offensive, especially to members of the group appropriated (Young, 2005).

that almost everything that happens in a structurally racist society enacts, in some way, the dynamics of unjust oppression. Why pick out hairstyles and textiles when there are so many more urgent enactments—such as structural injustice in job hiring, or in the criminal justice system?

Next: notice that the harm-based and objectionable symbolism account both seek to offer some particular justification, on a case-by-case basis, for the wrong of cultural appropriation. A third approach—claim deference—avoids offering such an explanation. One might think that when a member of an oppressed cultural group makes an appropriation claim, others should respect that claim by default. Adrienne Keene, a professor of Native American studies, gives such an argument on her blog, "Native Appropriations":

> But the thing that keeps bothering me is that we're expected, as community members, to have perfectly reasoned, calm, point-by-point rebuttals to your image and words. The burden of proof is on us, not you. Why can't we, as the cultures you're "respecting" simply say "no"? Why do we have to defend and fight and write 1400 words about why, and then listen while others mock our pain and hurt as being "overly sensitive"? Why can't you show us respect by just listening to us when we say, "Hey Christina, that headdress? It's not for you to wear." (Keene 2014)

In the case of oppressed groups like Native Americans, Keene suggests that the appropriation claim itself is all that is required; no further justificatory work needs to be done. By analogy: if a person asks you not to touch their knee, that the very claim, by itself, has normative force. Perhaps the person has experienced trauma that has given them an aversion to being touched in this way, perhaps they resent the intrusion and what it signifies about background social dynamics, or perhaps they just hate *you* in particular and seethe at your touch. They don't need to explain themselves for their command to not touch their knee to have normative force.

A worry, however, is that the claim deference approach—at least in the stark form proposed by Keene—gives too much power to the claimant. There is no recourse for the accused appropriator; any appropriation claim creates uncontestable normative constraints.

To sum up: each of these approaches is subject to some clear worries. Objectionable symbolism has difficulty grounding robust normative restrictions. The claim deference approach seems to put too much power in the hands of the claimant. The claimant can forbid whatever they wish, without having to provide an independent rationale; the rest of us simply have to defer. The claim deference approach, we might say, makes it too easy to get to normative force. Are we simply supposed to do what anybody asks us to do, and give up any practices that another asks us to give up, simply because they ask? The harm-based approach, on the other hand, seems to suffer from the opposite problem. If one thinks that at least some appropriation claims have normative force, then a harm-based approach might seem toothless. It places an uncomfortably high bar on what it takes to make a normatively significant appropriation claim: namely, that there must be good evidence of harm. And even if somebody can meet the evidential requirement, we might worry that harm-based approaches put the evaluation of the evidence in the wrong hands. Following a harm-based approach, one might think that one should really listen to social scientists and other empirical researchers, rather than to the voices of the oppressed communities themselves. For example, it might turn out that in the Iggy Azalea dispute, it is not black Americans who are best positioned to adjudicate the claims about harm. It might instead be, say, a bunch of economists and social scientists. This is worrisome if one is moved by the sorts of concerns that motivate claim deference accounts.

Of course, there are many ways of responding to these bullets. You could dodge them—by, for example, providing an account of the normativity of objectionable symbolism. You could bite one, and, say, accept that the claimant does indeed have the power to normatively ground an appropriation claim. Or, you could claim that the social sciences have a monopoly on standing to adjudicate appropriation claims. Alas, though, we expect that most interested parties will find all of the approaches on offer to be dissatisfying in some respect.

SPECIFIC APPROACHES

At this point, we turn to representative examples of the above categories that make some effort to address the set of worries we sketch above. Rather than survey the incredibly wide variety of arguments in the larger discourse, the goal of this chapter is to focus on a recent set of exchanges and accounts within analytic philosophy's relatively small literature on cultural appropriation.

Let's start with harm-based accounts. Philosophers have disagreed about the extent to which cultural appropriation is apt to cause harm. James O. Young has argued that cultural appropriation is wrong when it is harmful, but that is unlikely to be harmful (Young 2010, 6–7, 106–128). He acknowledges, for instance, that racist depictions of Native Americans in Hollywood movies are apt to cause harm, but is highly skeptical of more ambiguous cases (Young 2010, 107–108). Erich Hatala Matthes points to the pitfalls of Young's default skepticism (Matthes 2016, 348–349; Matthes 2019).[15] The relationship between cultural appropriation and structural oppression might be complex and indirect; we should not expect any causal connections to be clear and transparent. Perhaps Young is right that the vast majority of cultural appropriation is not harmful, but this is not something that one should feel confident declaring from the armchair. Philosophers have a role to play in articulating *possible* harms, but ultimately the question of the actual harmfulness of cultural appropriation must be investigated empirically by social scientists.

---

[15] For Young's rejoinders to Matthes and Nguyen and Strohl, see Young (2021).

Matthes offers a particularly well-developed version of a harm-based account. According to Matthes, cultural appropriation might contribute to the harms of epistemic violence and epistemic injustice. He calls this view the "oppression account" of cultural appropriation. Cultural appropriation is potentially harmful, suggests Matthes, because of the way it "interacts with dominating systems so as to silence and speak for individuals who are already socially marginalized." Drawing on recent work in social epistemology, Matthes argues that cultural appropriation is potentially harmful because, in many instances of cultural appropriation, members of oppressed groups are harmed by the unwillingness of audiences to properly listen or properly trust those members. In Kristie Dotson's terms, such groups are subject to epistemic violence, when their audiences fail to communicatively reciprocate their claims due to pernicious ignorance (Dotson 2011). In Miranda Fricker's terms, members of oppressed groups suffer from an unfair credibility deficit. This is exacerbated by a corresponding credibility excess granted to members of dominant groups (Fricker 2007). For example: in the contemporary United States, black Americans and women are typically trusted less, unfairly, simply because of the way their identity plays in with a network of stereotypes, biases, and prejudices, where white men are typically trusted more, for similar (unfair) reasons. That unfairly lowered trust is, in itself, a harm, says Fricker. Matthes adds that many acts of cultural appropriation enact such harmful silencing, and so are harmful in precisely this manner.

This is particularly apparent when, for example, the voices of members of marginalized groups are relatively distrusted even on the experience of being members of these groups, while the voices of dominant groups are relatively trusted on this form of experience. For example: many contemporary audiences seem to trust white American novelists writing about the African American experience or the Native American experience, over the voices of African Americans and Native Americans.[16] As Loretta Todd puts it, "Appropriation also occurs when someone else becomes the expert on your experience and is deemed more knowledgeable about who you are than yourself" (Todd 1990, 26).

Matthes argues that such cases of cultural appropriation are wrong because of their relationship with epistemic violence and epistemic injustice. Notice that if Matthes's account is right, then appropriation claims are more weighty when they are about cultural elements with testimonial content—most especially about the testimony about the experiences of marginalized groups. Interestingly, Matthes's account doesn't have a good explanation for worries about the appropriation of styles without testimonial content, like hairstyles and food. Matthes himself takes this to be a feature of the account. He says that his account explains why rarely we see charges of cultural appropriation over cuisine, as compared to film and literature. Nguyen and Strohl criticize Matthes's account on this point; they argue that there are many instances of appropriation claims

---

[16] Shim (2022) offers an extended analysis of this phenomenon, which she dubs "literary racial impersonation."

being lodged against forms of style appropriation that don't involve much in the way of testimonial content. For example, they point out, there have been many appropriation claims made concerning cuisine appropriation (Nguyen and Strohl 2019).

It's worth taking special note of two features of Matthes's view. First, if he is right, then appropriation claims only have weight when they are issued by an oppressed group. We have no reason to respect the appropriation claims of dominant groups. The normative power of appropriation claims arises from the specific epistemic harms enacted upon oppressed groups embedded in a structurally unjust society. That is, in America, say, Catholics and Scandinavians have no grounds to make appropriation claims, because they aren't being harmed by structural injustice. Black Americans, women, and queer people, on the other hand, do have grounds to make appropriation claims since they have been subject to oppression.

Second, Matthes has a very interesting prescription. According to Matthes, it is potentially counterproductive to focus on particular cases of cultural appropriation, since this risks bolstering essentialist tendencies that are worrisome in their own way. There are strong reasons for denying that there is a definite group of "black Americans" that is picked out by a list of shared essential qualities. Furthermore, trying to figure out what "black Americans" think, we need to decide who counts as a black American, and who does not—and the very process of making this determination threatens to enact problematic and oppressive power dynamics by privileging certain voices and excluding others.

Avoiding the need for such adjudication is, for him, a positive feature, but that does not mean that he thinks that we as individuals should simply ignore appropriation claims and do as we please. He suggests that we should take appropriate account of claims from marginalized groups in subjective deliberative contexts (Matthes 2016, 364–365). That is, although we should be hesitant to police particular instances of cultural appropriation by others on behalf of oppressed groups, we should take appropriation claims and the potential harms of a given form of appropriation to heart when making our own decisions about borrowing from other cultures. The difference is that policing the behavior of others involves implicitly or explicitly drawing boundaries around a culture, but making determinations about our own actions on the basis of self-identification need not.

We find a very different kind of view from C. Thi Nguyen and Matthew Strohl. They offer a version of a claim deference account. According to them, a claim deference account best fits widely shared intuitions about cultural appropriation (Nguyen and Strohl 2019). To them, the very act of making an appropriation claim (under certain specified conditions) does seem to carry *some* normative weight, which is not to say that we ought to automatically obey all appropriation claims from members of oppressed groups, since other considerations may be relevant. But what could explain the normative weight of appropriation claims?

Nguyen and Strohl suggest that the normative weight of appropriation claims can be grounded in considerations of *intimacy*. They draw on Julie Inness's work on the relationship between intimacy and rights of privacy. According to Inness, we protect all kinds of things under the aegis of "privacy": bodies, personal information, autonomy in decision-making. The only thing that could unite these, says Inness, is the concept of intimacy. Intimate acts, she says, are those that draw their meaning and value from the agent's motivational state of loving, liking, or caring for (Inness 1996, 90–92). When, for example, we share an old love letter or a diary entry to express love, like, or caring, that act is intimate, and so has special meaning and value for an agent. The various privacy protections, according to Inness, are justified in terms of that special meaning.

Inness's language seems to closely track common elements of nonacademic cultural appropriation discourse—especially the idea that acts of cultural appropriation threaten to dilute and undermine the specialness of certain practices. Nguyen and Strohl suggest that the normativity of appropriation claims can be grounded in group intimacy.[17] In the case of larger groups, a practice is intimate when it functions to embody or promote a sense of common identity and group connection among the practice's participants. In that case, we have certain reasons to refrain from cultural appropriation. Such appropriations can breach intimacy. Insofar as a group derives meaning from the intimacy of a practice, others have at least some (defeasible) reason to avoid breaching intimacy.

But intimacy is also flexible. Consider situations of individual intimacy. I can invite others to participate in my family's intimate practices. I can extend permissions for the short-term, for specific contexts, or in general. In that way, the intimacy account is supposed to explain the basic intuitions about claim deference. If I give you permission, or refuse to give permission, for you to view my intimate personal information, then it is my permission itself that creates the normative weight. Your right to access the intimate information isn't grounded in separate considerations, but in the permission itself.

A feature of this view is that unlike Matthes's view, members of any cultural group can make appropriation claims with normative force. In Matthes's view, it is *only* oppressed groups who can make appropriation claims with any normative force. In Nguyen and Strohl's view, any group can have an intimate practice, and so make claims protecting that intimacy with normative force. Nguyen and Strohl add that conditions of dominance and oppression can give us reason to amplify, or defeat, that normative force—but the default is that any group with intimate practices can lodge appropriation claims with at least some normative force.

Nguyen and Strohl take their view to be distinctive from—and more moderate than—Keene's version of claim deference. Keene seems to imply that the existence of a single, or small number, of appropriation claims gives us a good reason to avoid appropriation. But Nguyen and Strohl worry that this kind of policy opens the door to a certain kind of swamping effect, where the voices of few can outweigh the many. Imagine, for instance, a case where the majority of, say, a South Asian yoga community are in favor of permitting the appropriation of yoga by non–South Asians—but a very small

---

[17] Group intimacy is intended to be an analogous concept to the kind of smaller scale, interpersonal intimacy Inness describes. It is not a version of interpersonal intimacy. In particular, Nguyen and Strohl's argument doesn't depend on the truth of Inness's analysis of interpersonal intimacy.

but vocal minority are against it. Keene seems to suggest that we should defer to the small but vocal minority. Nguyen and Strohl are concerned that this kind of policy leads to the automatic dismissal of appropriation-friendly voices, so long as there are a few appropriation-opposed voices. This worry also goes in the other direction. Some appropriators act as if a small handful of appropriation-friendly voices can swamp a vast majority of appropriation-opposed voices, a.k.a. The "Well, My One Black Friend Says It's OK" effect. Nguyen and Strohl foresee that either version leads to, in practice, something almost identical to either universal prohibition or universal permission—since, in most cases, we can always find at least one refusing, or permitting, voice. They stress, instead, the importance of attending to the wishes of the larger group, to the extent that they can be ascertained.

This leads to a significant dilemma for them: How do we actually figure out what a group wants? And to figure that out, we need to figure out who counts as a member of that group. Matthes's account specifically avoids answering those questions, which points to what seem like the primary strengths and weaknesses (depending on where you stand) of his account. The primary strength (according to Matthes) is that we need not figure out what a group wants, or who is in the group. The primary weakness, one might think, is that Matthes's view seems to warrant our ignoring specific appropriation claims. Also note that a more radically deferential view, like Keene's, avoids the dilemma. Suppose we interpret Keene to be suggesting the following very strong principle: "If anybody thinks you should avoid appropriating some style, then you should." In that case, we need not figure out a group's wishes, or its boundaries—the existence of a lone voice is enough to normatively ground an appropriation claim.

Nguyen and Strohl's approach has a different set of strengths and weaknesses than other views discussed so far. According to them, their view has the advantage of avoiding worrisome swamping dynamics while at the same time granting that particular appropriation claims have normative force. But this places a very high burden on anybody who follows their theory: to respect appropriation claims, one needs to figure out the constitution of the relevant group as well as the group's wish. The wishes of a group can be difficult or impossible to determine—often because the group is unsettled in its views, or the boundaries of the group are unsettled. In such cases, they say, there isn't an easy solution about what to do. The question of what to do is genuinely unsettled—and sometimes, it's important to respect and treat a situation as unsettled, just as it's important to respect, say, the fact that one's friend's mind is unsettled about an issue. Again: whether this is a strength or weakness of the view depends on where you stand on certain questions. We view it as a strength. Matthes, on the other hand, has objected that our intimacy account depends on resolving the boundaries of groups— and without that, the intimacy account is sunk (Matthes 2019).[18]

---

[18] Nguyen and Strohl do offer a particular suggestion about how their intimacy account might sometimes solve this boundary problem: in some particular cases, the very sharing of an intimate practice might help to constitute a particular group.

Julian Dodd offers a further criticism of Nguyen and Strohl's intimacy account of cultural appropriation. According to Dodd, Nguyen and Strohl's view puts too much power in the claimant. In other words, if Dodd is right, then Nguyen and Strohl's intimacy account will turn out to have the same kind of problems that they themselves find in Keen's account.

Here is Dodd's worry: Nguyen and Strohl's account holds that certain appropriation claims are expressive. According to Nguyen and Strohl, this means that appropriation claims "stand without need for rationale" and are "not up for debate" (2019, 993). Dodd objects that Nguyen and Strohl's expressive account gives too much power to the appropriation claimant. Dodd here stresses a disanalogy between the kinds of social practices that are subject to appropriation claims, and bodies. It is, one might think, not possible to be wrong about one's body being one's own, but it is possible to be wrong about a practice genuinely being an intimate practice of one's group. Says Dodd: there are facts on the ground—independently grounded facts—about whether a practice is really a particular group's, or really intimate. Since, says Dodd, according to the intimacy account, a practice is only intimate if the participants derive meaning from that practice, it is possible for participants to be wrong about a practice's being intimate.

One possible defense for an intimacy account would be to show that the expressive nature of the claim is conceptually separable from the "facts on the ground" in a useful way. Returning to the analogy with physical touching, it's possible to be wrong about a particular body part's being yours. Imagine a sleepy bunch of people entangled with each other at a fireplace, after a long hike to a cabin. You see Tom moving to touch an elbow that you think is yours, and you tell him not to. But you were wrong: that elbow belongs to Stephane (who is in fact, Tom's husband). In the natural case, the expressiveness of the normativity of various refusals and permissions to bodily touch also depend on a presumption of some factual ground. Given the fact that this body part is actually mine, then the mere fact that I ask you not to touch that part gives you a reason not to touch it. The sensible solution for Nguyen and Strohl here might be to insist on the analogy: there are, in fact, independent facts on the ground about whether a practice is intimate, or if it is actually the group's. If C. Thi Nguyen, an Asian American, attempted to make an appropriation claim in which he claimed that the afro was an Asian American hairstyle and that others should not appropriate it, then obviously that claim would fail. The sensible claim to make here would be that given the facts on the ground about the practice's actually being intimate and actually being the relevant group's, then the further fact that a group makes an appropriation claim generates a reason to respect that claim. In other words: the claim is not that the appropriation claim constitutes the intimacy of the practice, but that the independent facts of the intimacy are the background against which appropriation claims can gain normativity, when they are actually made.[19]

---

[19] Speaking now as the authors of Nguyen and Strohl 2019: we take this view here to be implicit within our original discussion, when we said that expressive appropriation claims setting the *boundaries* of use for intimate practices. We did not claim that the intimacy and provenance of the practice was set expressively (991–992). The source of the confusion may be that we also think that groups can self-constitute through intimate practices—but this is a distinct issue.

The theoretical accounts of cultural appropriation discussed so far seek to ground its normativity in broader socioeconomic and cultural dynamics. Rebecca Tuvel argues that such approaches fall short in part because they do not yield sufficiently determinate guidance for action (Tuvel, 2021). A well-meaning appropriator is often not in the position to know the wishes of the relevant group or to understand how their particular act of appropriation might link up with larger power structures, and thus—according to the intimacy and oppression accounts—is often not in the position to know whether a given act of appropriation is permissible. If one thinks that it is a requirement for a theory of the normativity of cultural appropriation to offer clear action guidance in each case, then this is a major point in Tuvel's favor. Alternately, one might think, as Nguyen and Strohl do, that in many cases it is genuinely indeterminate whether or not an act of appropriation is permissible and that we should not expect a theory to offer clear action guidance in such cases. This turns out to be an important theory selection criterion.

Tuvel offers an alternate normative grounding for appropriation claims, which we can call the *respect account*. She says:

> In sum, accusers of cultural appropriation generally suspect that appropriators are guilty of a problematic way of regarding (or, rather, disregarding) members of the culture in question. These ways of disregarding can be many, but are captured by terms like disrespect, indifference, and culpable ignorance. (Tuvel, 25)

This account grounds the normativity of cultural appropriation not in external facts about group intimacy or the harmful consequences of appropriation, but in the state of mind of the appropriator. Her view is that if one is a well-meaning appropriator who does their due diligence in investigating the importance of the cultural element they appropriate and then acts in a way that expresses appropriate regard for the group appropriated from, then that's good enough. This theory offers much clearer guidance for action than any alternative discussed so far. Tuvel effectively lays out a procedure for determining whether or not an act of appropriation is permissible: investigate the context, consider the implications of one's act for the group one wishes to appropriate from, evaluate whether or not one's act is appropriately respectful, and then act (or refrain from acting) accordingly. For Tuvel, the permissibility of an act of appropriation does not directly depend on its harmfulness or on the wishes of the group appropriated from. It depends on the extent to which the act expresses respectfulness and regard for the group.

Two connected worries emerge for Tuvel's account. First, there is a worry about its coherence. On her account, being respectful as an appropriator entails taking appropriate account of some set of considerations that are prior to and independent of the appropriator's regard. When the appropriator does their due diligence in investigating the context, there must be some independent considerations that they are investigating. But then wouldn't these considerations—rather than the appropriator's respectful attitude—ground the normativity of cultural appropriation? If so, then it is possible in principle for the appropriator to reach the wrong conclusion about the permissibility of cultural appropriation while maintaining a respectful attitude.

The second worry is practical. Tuvel's account may be taken to leave too much to the discretion of the appropriator. People who think that it is acceptable to wear imitation Native American headdresses, for instance, often justify their actions by claiming that they are doing it out of respect and admiration for tribal culture. One might think that the appropriator shouldn't be the one who gets to set the standard for what counts as respectful, especially given that cultural outsiders may not be well-positioned to appreciate the reasons adduced by the tribe because they do not have the right sort of perspective (Keene 2014).

Tuvel is aware of this second worry, and responds:

> Especially because the concerns of cultural minorities have historically been trivialized or dismissed, refusing to even give them a hearing amounts to an objectionable form of disregard. However, if it turns out that anti-appropriation concerns are ultimately unreasonable—i.e., they lack an independent and compelling justification—then appropriators do not act wrongly. (Tuvel forthcoming, 29)

She clarifies here that a person who wishes to wear an imitation Native American headdress needs to do more than think of themselves as acting respectfully. Especially in cases where the group appropriated from is a historically oppressed minority, one needs to take special care to give the group's concerns a fair hearing. It is important to her view that the appropriator must investigate and earnestly take account of reasons offered by in-group members that outsiders should not appropriate a given cultural element, but she thinks that it is ultimately up to the appropriator's discretion to weigh these reasons. If the appropriator doesn't find them compelling, then they can simply dismiss them.

One might now criticize this aspect of her account with the resources of standpoint epistemology.[20] It is possible the appropriator is not in a position to understand the group's reasons and weigh them appropriately, and moreover is not even well-situated to recognize the limitations of their own perspective. Her view enables clear guidance for action because it holds that the appropriator's earnest determination (following upon appropriate investigation) that their action is respectful is sufficient for it to be permissible.

Tuvel's view contrasts with the picture suggested by Sondra Bacharach and Andrea Mejia Chaves in their paper "Hair Oppression and Appropriation" (2021). Bacharach and Chaves are concerned in particular with the case study of the appropriation of black hairstyles, but their account has broader implications. Bacharach and Chaves's view is an example of an objectionable symbolism view. They point to the ongoing ways in which black hair is a locus of oppression. Because black hairstyles function as a symbol of black cultural identity and solidarity in the face of the shared experience of oppression,

---

[20] For an excellent review overview of standpoint epistemology, see Toole (2019; 2022).

members of dominant groups should not appropriate these hairstyles. Wearing the relevant hairstyle is in part a way of expressing group solidarity in the face of hair oppression, and for a member of a dominant group to wear that hairstyle against the wishes of the group enacts the oppressive power dynamic all over again.

This view stands in sharp contrast to Tuvel's account. For Tuvel, it is enough if someone wears the hairstyle in a way that *they themselves* judge to be respectful. A potential appropriator might determine that the justifications that group members cite for their wish that outsiders refrain from a given form of appropriation give them sufficient reason to refrain, but they may also judge that the group does not have a compelling reason and thus that their wish can be ignored. Bacharach and Chaves think that the respectful attitude of the would-be appropriator is immaterial to the permissibility of appropriation. If they are a member of a dominant group and the cultural element they wish to appropriate is a symbol of identity for an oppressed group, then they shouldn't appropriate it, even if they imagine that to do so would be an expression of respect. Indeed, one might think that for the appropriator to act against the wishes of the group under the guise of self-proclaimed respectfulness just adds a further layer of objectionable symbolism.

Bacharach and Chaves's view is strongly restrictive concerning appropriation from oppressed groups by members of dominant groups. But what about outsiders to a group who are members of other oppressed groups? Consider, for example, the appropriation of black hairstyles by non-black persons of color. They write:

> But, the situation is more complicated when we turn to cases of Non-Black Persons of Colour (NBPoC) appropriating Black hairstyles by wearing them. Intuitively, NBPoC who wear Black hairstyles are wrongfully appropriating. Black hairstyles are intimately connected to their past, their oppression, their history and their identity. Wearing black hairstyles is a way for Black people to define, project and express this identity. For anyone who lacks this identity, wearing Black hairstyles should qualify as an act of wrongful cultural appropriation. (Bacharach and Chaves 2021, 344–345)

Bacharach and Chaves here indicate that historical oppression and the symbolic function of black hairstyles together yield the prescription that outsiders should not appropriate them, even if these outsiders are themselves members of oppressed minorities. This view faces the worry that it yields too strong and inflexible a prescription, but Bacharach and Chaves have a partial response. They identify the Natural Hair Movement as an intimate group that is not specifically tied to black identity and that creates a context in which individuals from a variety of ethnic backgrounds who experience hair oppression can forge bonds and express solidarity. Within the context of this intimate group, non-black individuals can be licensed to wear black hairstyles. This is, however, a highly specific case and it's not clear to what extent analogous consolatory alternatives exist for other sorts of cultural elements besides hairstyles. In any case, Bacharach and Chaves still need to answer the objection that their presumptively restrictive stance paternalistically limits the agency of members of oppressed groups concerning their prerogative to open their practices up to outsiders. How would they respond to a black hairstylist who serves customers from a variety of backgrounds and complains that restrictive hair appropriation discourse hurts her business? Does she not have the same standing as group members who have a more restrictive outlook?

CONCLUSION

In trying to think through specific cases of cultural appropriation, it's apparent that questions regarding the normative force of appropriation claims are deeply bound up with questions about who has the standing to make those claims and who has the standing to adjudicate them. In Matthes's harm-based account, the normativity of the claim depends on providing evidence of harm. This leads to a double bind. Matthes's account concerns the harm of silencing oppressed voices, and reducing our credence in them. But the upshot of his account is that in combating oppression, we should pay heed to the best empirical evidence—which threatens to silence oppressed voices in favor of traditional institutionally centered centers of discursive power. The account avoids the difficulties of figuring out who counts as part of a group, or what the group wants, at the expense of countenancing paternalism. Similarly, Tuvel's respect account avoids the difficulties of figuring out precisely who is in a group and whether they have standing to make an appropriation claim, focusing instead on the appropriator's own intentions and evaluative beliefs. Again, this avoids the problem of adjudicating the thorny issues group membership and group decision, but at the expense of privileging the evaluative perspective of the appropriator, above that of the group appropriated from.

On the flip side, views that place emphasis in respecting a group's wishes face a very different, but equally thorny, set of issues. Nguyen and Strohl's intimacy account centers the wishes of a group, which plunges into, rather than sidestepping, all the issues of adjudicating group membership and group belief. It also opens the door for genuinely unsettled group boundaries and group beliefs, which leads to unclear directives for action. Bacharach and Chavez's version of an objectionable symbolism account perhaps avoids the problems of adjudicating group beliefs, by simplifying the decision procedure. On their view, there is only one relevant normative feature: if a practice is a symbol of shared identity and solidarity in the face of oppression for an oppressed group, we ought not appropriate it, except in special localized circumstances. As a result, Bacharach and Chavez sidestep the need to ascertain a group's wishes—but at the cost of recommending a set of norms that are, as a default, extremely restrictive.

See also: Whalen, Taylor, Woodcock, Clavel-Vázquez, this volume

References

Bacharach, Sondra, and Andrea Mejia Chaves. 2021. "Hair Oppression and Appropriation." *British Journal of Aesthetics* 61, no. 3: 335–352.

Dodd, Julian. 2021. "Style Appropriation, Intimacy, and Expressiveness." *British Journal of Aesthetics* 61, no. 3: 373–386.

Dotson, Kristie. 2011 "Tracking Epistemic Violence, Tracking Practices of Silencing." *Hypatia.* 26, no. 2: 236–257.

Fricker, Miranda. 2007. *Epistemic Injustice: Power and the Ethics of Knowing.* Oxford: Oxford University Press.

Gaynor, Gerren Keith. 2012. "Dreadlocks VS. Corporate America: Real-Life Stories of Making the Choice." *Black Enterprise*, August 27, https://www.blackenterprise.com/dreadlocks-ban-corporate-success-stories/.

Godoy, Maria, and Kat Chow. 2016. "When Chefs Become Famous Cooking Other Cultures' Food." *NPR*, March 22, npr.org/sections/thesalt/2016/03/22/471309991/when-chefs-become-famous-cooking-other-cultures-food.

Gracyk, Theodore. 2001. *I Wanna Be Me: Rock Music and the Politics of Identity.* Philadelphia: Temple University Press.

Gray, Briahna Joy. 2017. "The Question of Cultural Appropriation." *Current Affairs*, September 6, https://www.currentaffairs.org/2017/09/the-question-of-cultural-appropriation.

Holywhitemountain, Sterling. 2019. "Sterling Holywhitemountain on Blood Quantum, Native Art, and Cultural Appropriation." *Aesthetics for Birds*, https://aestheticsforbirds.com/2019/01/31/sterling-holywhitemountain-on-blood-quantumnative-art-and-cultural-appropriation/ (accessed June 28, 2021).

Inness, Julie. 1996. *Privacy, Intimacy, and Isolation.* Oxford: Oxford University Press. James, Robin. 2011. "On Intersectionality and Cultural Appropriation: The Case of Postmillenial Black Hipness." *Journal of Black Masculinity* 1, no. 2. https://booklocker.com/books/5409.html

Keene, Adrienne. 2014. "Dear Christina Fallin." *Native Appropriations*, March 7, http://nativeappropriations.com/2014/03/dear-christina-fallin.html.

Lenard, Patti Tamara, and Peter Balint. 2020. "What Is (the Wrong of) Cultural Appropriation?" *Ethnicities* 20, no. 2: 331–352.

Matthes, Erich Hatala. 2016. "Cultural Appropriation without Cultural Essentialism?" *Social Theory and Practice* 42, no. 2: 343–366.

Matthes, Erich Hatala. 2017. "Repatriation and the Radical Redistribution of Art." *Ergo* 4, no. 32: 931–953.

Matthes, Erich Hatala. 2019. "Cultural Appropriation and Oppression." *Philosophical Studies* 176, no. 4: 1003–1013.

Nittle, Nadra Kareem. 2021. "A Guide to Understanding and Avoiding Cultural Appropriation." *ThoughtCo.*, February 4, https://www.thoughtco.com/cultural-appropriation-and-why-iits-wrong-2834561.

Pearson, Phyllis. 2021. "Cultural Appropriation and Aesthetic Normativity." *Philosophical Studies* 178, no. 4: 1285–1299.

Shim, Joy. (2022) "Literary Racial Impersonation," *Ergo* 8. https://journals.publishing.umich.edu/ergo/article/id/2232/

Thomas, Joshua Lewis. 2021. "When Does Something 'Belong' to a Culture?" *British Journal of Aesthetics* 61, no. 3: 275–290.

Todd, Loretta. 1990. "Notes on Appropriation." *Parallelogramme* 16, no. 1: 24–33.

Toole, Briana. 2019. "From Standpoint Epistemology to Epistemic Oppression." *Hypatia* 34, no. 4: 598–618.

Toole, Briana. 2022. "Demarginalizing Standpoint Epistemology." *Episteme* 19, no.1: 47–65.

Tuvel, Rebecca. 2021. "Putting the Appropriator Back in Cultural Appropriation." *British Journal of Aesthetics* 61, no. 3: 353–372.

Whittaker, Nicholas. 2021. "Case Sensitive—Why We Shouldn't Capitalize 'Black.'" *The Drift* 5, September 21, https://www.thedriftmag.com/case-sensitive/.

Xhignesse, Michel-Antoine. 2021. "Retitling, Cultural Appropriation, and Aboriginal Title." *British Journal of Aesthetics* 61, no. 3: 317–333.

Young, James O. 2005. "Profound Offense and Cultural Appropriation," *Journal of Aesthetics and Art Criticism* 63, no. 2: 135–146.

Young, James O. 2010. *Cultural Appropriation and the Arts*. West Sussex, UK: Wiley Blackwell.

Young, James O. 2021. "New Objections to Cultural Appropriation in the Arts." *British Journal of Aesthetics* 61, no. 3: 307–316.

Young, James O., and Conrad G. Brunk. 2009. *The Ethics of Cultural Appropriation*. Hoboken, NJ: Wiley.

Ziff, Bruce, and Pratima V. Rao, eds. 1997. *Borrowed Power: Essays on Cultural Appropriation*. New Brunswick, NJ: Rutgers University Press.

CHAPTER 39

FORGERY

DARREN HUDSON HICK

INTRODUCTION: MARCANTONIO AND ALBRECHT

IN 1568, when Georgio Vasari released the second edition of *Lives of the Artists*, he added a single chapter on printmaking—"as much on that subject as I may consider to be sufficient" (Vasari 1913, 91). The renowned German printmaker Albrecht Dürer is introduced early in the chapter, but serves primarily to kick off the story (and career) of the chapter's central figure, Marcantonio Raimondi of Bologna. Early in his career, Marcantonio sets out from Bologna to explore the world, making his first noteworthy stop eighty miles north in Venice:

> About the same time there arrived in Venice some Flemings with many copper-plate engravings and woodcuts by Albrecht Dürer, which were seen by Marc' Antonio on the Piazza di S. Marco; and he was so amazed at the manner and method of the work of Albrecht that he spent on those sheets almost all the money that he had brought from Bologna. [. . .] Marc' Antonio, having considered what honour and profit might be acquired by one who should apply himself to that art in Italy, formed the determination to give his attention to it with all possible assiduity and diligence. He thus began to copy those engravings by Albrecht Dürer, studying the manner of each stroke and every other detail of the prints that he had bought, which were held in such estimation on account of their novelty and their beauty, that everyone sought to have some. Having then counterfeited on copper, with engraving as strong as that of the woodcuts that Albrecht had executed, the whole of the said Life and Passion of Christ in thirty-six parts, he added to these the signature that Albrecht used for all his works, which was "A. D.," and they proved to be so similar in manner, that, no one knowing that they had been executed by Marc' Antonio, they were ascribed to Albrecht, and were bought and sold as works by his hand. (95–96)

In addition to the "A. D." monogram, Marcantonio had discretely added three marks to his otherwise meticulous copies: an "MAF" monogram of his own, and two marks indicating the Dal Jesus family, with whom he worked to produce his prints (Charney 2015, 11–12).

In 1506, when Marcantonio happened across his prints, Dürer was very probably the most copied living European artist. The market for replicas thrived in sixteenth-century Europe, and artisans turned a healthy trade in reproducing expensive works for a more general market (Pon 2004, 25–26). As apprenticing artists typically trained through direct imitation of the masters, this was simply the commodification of a familiar practice and skill set. But, when a friend sent Dürer one of Marcantonio's copies, the camel's back finally broke, and Dürer dragged the copyist and his printers to court in Venice. There, pointing at the three marks that Marcantonio had added to his prints, the court ruled that the prints were not exact copies, but were mere excellent imitations, adding that Dürer should be flattered to have been so copied (Charney 2015, 12–13). Dürer was *not* flattered, nor was he satisfied with the court's direction that Marcantonio remove the "A. D." monogram from his prints. Dürer famously added a notice to future printings of his work threatening both legal action and bodily harm to any "envious thieves" who should lay their hands on "works of ours" (Koerner 1993, 213).

Dürer based his legal complaint on a violation of his printer's privilege, an exclusive grant to print (in this case) his own works. But a printer's privilege was very narrow, both in jurisdiction and in subject, protecting only literal and exact copying, and only within a specified region. Art historian Lisa Pon suggests that, contrary to Vasari's characterization of it, Marcantonio's case is not one of clear-cut forgery: "These copies were produced in an ambience that did not always understand pictures as the artist's property, as 'works of ours' that could be stolen" (Pon 2004, 41). Although others at the time may have held more liberal views on artistic property, Dürer treated unauthorized copying of his works as a personal affront and used the legal means available to address the wrong that he believed had been perpetrated upon him. Unfortunately for Dürer, the means available to him did not so neatly align with his moral outrage. The court in Venice found that the offending prints, being inexact copies appreciable for their own qualities, were not forgeries. Rather, Marcantonio was selling his *own* works, and thus no substantive wrong had been done. Here, we find the two key philosophical questions that tend to weigh on forgery: what *is* it, and why would it be *wrong*? We also see how the matter is entwined with broader practices, both artistic and legal.

WHAT IS A FORGERY?

Contemporary philosophical discussion of forgery largely emerges from Nelson Goodman's *Languages of Art*, where he offers this definition: "A forgery of a work of art is an object falsely purporting to have the history of production requisite for the (or an) original of the work" (Goodman 1976, 122). In a simple case, a Picasso must be made by

Picasso's own hand. So, an object that purports to have been so made, when in fact it was made by the hand of another, is a forgery. Over his career as a master forger, Elmyr de Hory made hundreds—perhaps thousands—of drawings and paintings in the recognizable styles of Picasso, selling each as the genuine article (Horberry 2020). Insofar as each was sold as an object made by Picasso's own hand, each is a forgery on Goodman's analysis. The same is true of the pastel drawing that was sold for $2 million by Hollywood gallery owner Tatiana Khan. In 2010, Khan pleaded guilty to federal charges for the fraudulent sale of "La Femme Au Chapeau Bleu," a copy of a genuine Picasso in Khan's possession, which she had hired an art restorer to reproduce (FBI 2010). Each of de Hory's fakes is what Jerrold Levinson would call an *inventive forgery*, while Khan's reproduction is what he calls a *referential forgery* (Levinson 1980, 377). An inventive forgery is usually a *pastiche*: a new work that attempts to embody an artist's style, typically by incorporating recognizable features from an artist's global style, or elements of particular genuine works by that artist.[1] Referential forgeries, conversely, are straightforward copies of existing originals.

On Goodman's view, it does not matter how perfectly Khan's reproduction imitates the original; it cannot acquire the original's history of production, and so any presentation of it *as* the genuine article will be fraudulent. Curiously, however, the same does not apply across art forms. As Goodman notes, if I make a perfect reproduction of a literary work—say, Gregory McDonald's 1974 novel, *Fletch*—and present it *as* that work, I am telling no lie. A perfect reproduction—say, a photocopy or a complete and accurate retyping—of *Fletch* just *is* a genuine instance of *Fletch*. "La Femme Au Chapeau Bleu" is what Goodman calls an *autographic* work, while *Fletch* is an *allographic* work. On Goodman's analysis, an allographic work, like *Fletch*, allows for unlimited production of genuine instances, requiring only that a copy accurately reproduce the notation (in this case, words, punctuation, and the like) of the original. An autographic work, conversely, may not allow for more than one genuine instance. Or, if it does, it will require something more than mere notational adherence. Goodman suggests that we speak of a work of art as autographic "if and only if even the most exact duplication of it does not thereby count as genuine," and otherwise as allographic (Goodman 1976, 113). The difference between an allographic work and an autographic work, then, comes down to the question of how genuineness is determined. In the case of an allographic work like a novel, or poem, or song, or dance, one need only check the copy against the original for accuracy. In the case of an autographic work, like a painting or drawing, one needs to ask how the thing came to be. In the case of a drawing, like "La Femme Au Chapeau Bleu," there can only ever be one: only one drawing issued from Picasso's hand at that time, in that place, and in that way. That is, only one object has that drawing's unique history of production.

---

[1] Inventive forgery need not involve pastiche work. Sherri Irvin imagines a case involving an enterprising forger who is able to see a pattern in the work of a contemporary artist, and so predict what that artist's next work should look like, producing the target's next work before she does. The "preplica" is presented as the work of the target, and so is an inventive forgery without borrowing directly from any existing work (Irvin 2005, 127–128).

However, the autographic/allographic distinction does not neatly track the distinction between those artworks that only exist in a single instance, and those that allow for multiple genuine instances. There are plenty of genuine instances of Dürer's *Life of the Virgin* series. Prints, like these, are autographic, too.

The court in Venice, it seems, was treating Dürer's prints as being allographic in nature; since Marcantonio's reproductions were inexact, the court reasoned, they were Marcantonio's own works, and not illicit reproductions of Dürer's. Moreover, if Dürer's prints *were* allographic, and Marcantonio *had* made perfect reproductions of them, he would be committing no fraud when he sold them *as* genuine Dürer prints, just as I would be committing no fraud when I present my photocopy of *Fletch* as a genuine instance of McDonald's novel. But, if Dürer's prints were *autographic* in nature, even a perfect reproduction by Marcantonio would not save him from a complaint of forgery. And Goodman argues that prints are autographic, not allographic, in nature: "Even the most exact copy produced otherwise than by printing from that plate counts not as an original but as an imitation or forgery" (Goodman 1976, 114). That is, genuineness is found in the history of production of the object, tracing back to its interaction with the genuine template—the printing plate. Since Marcantonio's prints were made from engraving plates modeled on Dürer's prints, and not from Dürer's own plates, they came to be in the wrong way: they were not genuine Dürer prints, but mere imitations at best, and forgeries at worst.

However, while this would seem to be true if Dürer and Marcantonio were plying their trades today, Goodman notes that the boundaries of genuineness are culturally determined, arising from artistic practices and evolving technology (Goodman 1976, 121–122). Joseph Margolis similarly remarks that "authenticity is a distinction of an intentional and normative sort that is bound to reflect the shifting practices and technological possibilities of different societies" (Margolis 1983, 165). There is nothing like a *natural* and *atemporal* distinction between "genuine" and "forgery": what counts as genuine, and what counts as a forgery, are culturally emergent qualities, and subject to change as technology and attitudes change. On Goodman's view, while Marcanotio would likely qualify as a forger today, the Venetian court may well have judged rightly at the time. Things change. But evolving artistic practices are not the end for philosophical concerns about the nature of forgery.

HARD CASES

Typically, prints are sold in limited editions, each print being signed and numbered by the artist. The limiting of a print run would seem to be in service of the integrity of the work: however hardy the material used—wood, stone, zinc—every material degrades with use. So, rather than allow printing to run indefinitely, with each successive print getting muddier and blurrier, cutting off printing helps to ensure the integrity of the image. In practice, however, editions tend to be cut off long before the degradation of the image is a real concern. Rather, the artificial limit to a print run serves to enhance the perceived (and thus monetary) value of the few copies produced. Numbering a print "35/200" is meant to guarantee that only 200 copies of that work will ever be produced. As a standard practice, upon the completion of a series, the artist or printer will "cancel," "strike," or "cross out" the printing plate, literally marring the image to mark the end of the edition. Any prints outside the edition, such as artist's proofs and printer's proofs, are normally labelled as such. However, on occasion, an unscrupulous printer will run off a few extra copies without the artist's knowledge before the canceling of the plate. Visually and materially indistinguishable from the genuine article, these unauthorized prints will then be sold with false numbering and signature (*Metafisica* 2006, 585).[2] Contrary to Goodman's claim, one might reasonably expect that such prints, sold as genuine, would be treated as forgeries—that an authentic print must be *authorized* by the artist— and that our unscrupulous printer, once caught, would be charged with fraud. However, things in the artworld are still not so clear-cut. Matters become more complicated when the artist is complicit in the process.

In 1982, Salvador Dalí sued his former chief aide, Peter "Captain" Moore, for an exhibition of 426 paintings, sketches, and lithographs. Upon seeing a catalogue for the exhibition, the notoriously mercurial Dalí claimed that sixty of the works were fakes. Moore countersued, acknowledging that several of the works were not created by Dalí, but alleging Dalí had signed them and previously presented them as his own (Catterall 1992, 65). All of this is complicated by the fact that Dali had, over his career—including the fourteen years that Moore worked for him, signed a reported 350,000 blank sheets of paper, later to be printed with as-yet-unspecified Dalí prints (Catterall 1992, 61). Those sheets would be sold off by the thousands, and later adorned with "authentic Dalís" (mostly photographic reproductions of paintings, and not printing-plate impressions). In 1979, Arjomari, the company then responsible for most fine-art paper on the market, began printing its paper with watermarks. By 1980, Dalí was reportedly too ill to sign prints (Catterall 1992, 111). So, the thinking went, any Dalí editions produced after 1980 without a watermark would be fakes. The ontological question is, what makes a print pressed on presigned paper a fake? And, if a print made in 1978 on paper signed in 1976 is authentic, why not one made on the same 1976 presigned paper, but printed years after the artist's death? The worry seems to be that, unlike a blank cheque, one cannot preauthorize what art will be printed on paper. Dalí clearly thought otherwise.

Assuming that it would be difficult, at best, for an artist to authorize a print after his death, most editions of works printed posthumously would seem to be straightforward forgeries. However, posthumous editions are, at best, sketchy territory in the artworld. Several of Francisco de Goya's works continued to be printed in new editions long after his death. Goya sold only twenty-seven copies of his series, *Los Caprichos*, before

---

[2] This sort of activity is not limited to printmaking. In 2014, Brian Ramnarine, the owner of Empire Bronze Foundry in Long Island City, was sentenced to thirty months in prison for making and attempting to sell an unauthorized copy of a Jasper Johns sculpture, using the original mold in his possession (FBI 2014).

withdrawing the series from sale in 1799, out of fear of the Inquisition. Goya surrendered the plates to King Charles IV in exchange for the release of his brother from prison. From there, the plates made their way to the Royal Spanish Academy, which went on to produce a further eleven editions of the series, between 1855 and 1937, each edition being more visually degraded than the previous one.[3] Certainly, selling a print from the third edition as if it was from the first edition would be fraudulent. But what about selling a print from the tenth edition—or, for that matter, the second edition—as if it *was* a work from *Los Caprichos*? Here, art sellers are disinclined to use the "F" word:

> An undamaged print from the first edition of 'Los Caprichos' would be priced at $3,000 to $5,000, according to James Goodfriend, owner of New York's C&J Goodfriend Drawings and Prints. Prints from the posthumous second and third editions, dated 1855 and 1868, respectively, 'are very good and very hard to tell apart,' he adds, but sell for $1,500 to $2,000. Mr. Goodfriend says he sells prints from later editions, however, for $150. (Grant, 2017)

The question raised for unauthorized and posthumous editions isn't "is it genuine?" but rather "how much is it worth?" The problem is that the artworld generally prefers to avoid the term "forgery" altogether. Indeed, while art forgery is prosecutable in most jurisdictions under a range of offenses, "forgery" doesn't tend to be one of them, the term typically being reserved for cases of fraudulent documents (Casement 2020, 53–55 and Chappell Polk 2009, 393–412). Both the artworld and the legal world tend to prefer the term "fake," which has fuzzier boundaries. But even "fake" is a little blunt for the artworld and is used sparingly, especially when money is on the line.

As with the case of Dalí's presigned paper, artists tend to make the matter even blurrier, and this is not restricted to printmaking. Sol LeWitt is perhaps best known for his "wall drawings," hundreds of works for which LeWitt provided written instructions to be carried out by fabricators at the sites where the drawings (and sometimes paintings) would be instantiated. In many cases, LeWitt's designated assistants executed the actual on-site drawings, and LeWitt provided signed certificates of authenticity to those who had purchased the drawings (Galenson 2009, 194). Museums and auction houses in particular are fond of certificates of authenticity as a record of provenance. But LeWitt himself has stated that he would consider a wall drawing executed from his instructions by someone "without permission but with care to follow the instructions and in an appropriate site" as "authentic" (Weber 2000, 92). The wall drawings would seem to be, like *Los Caprichos*, autographic works admitting of multiple genuine instances, with "follow[ing] the instructions and in an appropriate site" as a restriction on genuineness.[4] That is, mere notational adherence is not enough for an instance to be genuine;

---

[3] Counting editions becomes difficult. See Glendinning (1989).

[4] Authentic prints are typically called "original prints," and there is an argument to be made that each, individual print from the first edition of *Los Caprichos* (and each instance of *Wall Drawing #545*) is a distinct work, rather than (like a poem) merely an instance of some work.

something more is required. But, unlike *Los Caprichos*, it seems, there is no upper limit to the number of genuine instances that might be authentically made.

A curious, complicating case for LeWitt—and talk of genuineness, generally—is *Wall Drawing #848*, which was painted on the wall of a Brooklyn apartment, where two of LeWitt's assistants, Jo Watanabe and Sachi Cho, lived. There is, indeed, a certificate of authenticity for the work, signed by LeWitt. What's curious, however, is that there are no instructions written by LeWitt for executing the work, as there are with his other wall drawings. This, Watanabe and Cho explained (when pressed), is because Watanabe produced the work without any involvement by LeWitt himself. LeWitt, they say, saw and liked the work, and produced the certificate of authenticity attributing #848 to himself, as a gift to the couple (Taylor 2007).

Paula Cooper, one of the major exhibitors of LeWitt's works, rejects Watanabe and Cho's story as fanciful, saying it was "not the way Sol worked. No one else made the drawings" (Taylor 2007). Gary Garrels, who curated the San Francisco Museum of Modern Art's 2000 LeWitt retrospective, disagrees: "As long as he signed a certificate, then however the work was generated, he [LeWitt] accepted it as a Sol LeWitt work" (Taylor 2007).

LeWitt would not be alone in this sort of practice. Celebrated Australian Aboriginal "dot painter" Clifford Possum Tjapaltjarri knowingly signed works made by other Aboriginal artists (Bowden 2001, 2). In the trial of his art dealer, John O'Loughlin, Tjapaltjarri stated that he only signed his name to the works while inebriated and intimidated by O'Loughlin (Barkham 2001).[5] However, the practice of signing dot paintings by family members is not unusual among Aboriginal dot artists, and is little different in kind from the practices of North American and European artists who employ fabricators and studios to make the art objects that the artists sign and present as their own works. Although they were commissioned to create it, and hold the copyright to it, Claes Oldenburg and Coosje van Bruggen did not actually *make* the towering *Spoonbridge and Cherry* installation that dominates the Minneapolis Sculpture Garden. Rather, the 51-foot, 7,000-pound steel-and-aluminum sculptural fountain was fabricated by a team at Merrifield-Roberts, then a yacht-making company. All that Oldenburg and van Bruggen made was a maquette (Taraborelli 2019). And of course, Marcel Duchamp famously made neither the urinal of which *Fountain* is composed, nor the bottle rack making up *Bottle Rack*. Now, I may well be accused of impropriety for dropping Duchamp into what was, until now, a civilized little discussion about art practices and ontology, but there is a lot of room between Duchamp's ready-mades and Picasso's "La Femme Au Chapeau Bleu," and artists fill that space.

Artistic practices are neither stable, nor simple, nor uniform. In practice, the rule for genuineness—and, by extension, for what qualifies as a referential forgery, and what

---

[5] A line commonly attributed to Picasso is that he would have happily signed a good forgery of his work if it were placed in front of him (Gorris and Röbel 2012). As Picasso rarely signed authorized prints of his *own* works, this may well be apocryphal.

qualifies as an inventive forgery—begins to fray around the edges. However, while the practices surrounding measures of authenticity are mercurial and fuzzy, the one factor that remains consistent across our cases is the question of whether the item's nature has been misrepresented: if there is no misrepresentation, there is no forgery. If, contrary to Vasari's account, Marcantonio had sold his copies *as* Marcantonios-after-Dürers, and *not* as authentic Dürers, then there would be no misrepresentation and no forgery. And, so long as the Royal Spanish Academy is transparent about how their prints of Goya's works came to be, and so long as James Goodfriend is transparent about the edition that a print is from, there is no forgery here either. So long as dealers are clear that the sheet of paper upon which a Dalí is printed was presigned by the artist, the print, it seems, is not a forgery.

GETTING IT WRONG

Goodman misspeaks when he says that a forgery is an object falsely purporting to have the requisite history of production: it is *people* who purport things, after all, not the objects themselves. Goodman's misspeaking is an innocent error, and we forgive those. Similarly, making false declarations of a work's origin is not enough to account for a forgery's nature *as* a forgery. A painting innocently mislabeled in a gallery is not thus a forgery, nor is a sculpture innocently misattributed to the wrong sculptor by an authenticator. Nor do I think we want to say that Gary Garrels makes *Wall Drawing #848* a forgery when he declares it a genuine Le Witt, whatever our ontological misgivings may be. After all, Garrels genuinely believes it is the genuine article. Michael Wreen thus offers a friendly and formal amendment to Goodman's definition. Where "X" is a variable that may be filled with, say, "Picasso," and "Y" with "painting":

> As I understand it, a forged XY isn't a genuine XY, but is represented as a genuine XY, and is so represented with the intention to deceive. That, in a nutshell, is my definition. A forged Picasso painting is not a genuine Picasso painting, but is represented as a genuine Picasso painting, and is so represented with the intention to deceive. (Wreen 2002, 152)

For it to count as a forgery, it is not enough that the object be falsely presented as a genuine Picasso; it must be *knowingly* falsely presented. It must be a *lie*, and lies are straightforward wrongs—or, at least, prime candidates for the title. But, if lying was all that was at the blackened heart of forgery, it probably wouldn't fascinate the artworld or the general public quite as much as it does.

While lying represents a failure of moral integrity, Alfred Lessing argues that forgery also represents a failure of *artistic* integrity. Specifically, the forger seeks to pass off "the inferior as the superior" (Lessing 1983, 65). By this, Lessing does not mean that a painting created as a replica of a Picasso will always be *aesthetically* inferior to the original; on the contrary, it may be far superior in this regard.[6] But it will never *be* a Picasso, with all that that implies. A forgery is pretended to be an artistic achievement that it is not: to be original when it is mere mechanical technique; to represent a step in an artist's trajectory which it isn't. The referential forgery seeks to take the rightful place of another work in the original artist's corpus and continuum. The inventive forgery seeks to wedge itself into a space that did not exist. A forgery may well be an aesthetic triumph, but it will always be an artistic pretender.

Following a similar line of thought, Denis Dutton argues that artworks are centrally appreciated as *performances*—as the doing or the artifact of the doing: "As performances, works of art represent the ways in which artists solve problems, overcome obstacles, make do with available materials" (Dutton 1983, 176). I might stand in sublime awe before a canyon or mountainscape, or marvel at the geometric intricacy of a snowflake's fractal pattern, but it would be weird to applaud such a thing. Artworks are achievements—products of human agency—and when I appreciate an artwork *as* an achievement, it is with some sense of the artistic challenge that has been surmounted. This is true whether the artwork is a dance, a drum solo, or a drawing. A forgery is presented as an achievement that it is not. Insofar as my appreciation of a work is grounded, in part, in an understanding of that thing as the performative answer to artistic challenges, Dutton suggests that the artistic failing is not so easily divorced from the aesthetic assessment as Lessing would like.

On the trail set out by Lessing and Dutton, the wrong of forgery does not end with the lie, but with the *repercussions* of the lie. For the dupe, the most pressing harm to come from forgery will likely be monetary in nature. And, while the forger, once caught, may plead all manner of purer motives, separating a fool from his money will usually be the forger's primary motive, as Vasari's account of Marcantonio suggests. Notably, Tatiana Khan's punishment for her fraudulent $2 million Picasso sale was not a court-mandated apology, but rather financial restitution to her victim.[7] With financial gain being what's on the mind of the forger, and financial harm on the mind of the dupe, it makes sense to prosecute art forgery under the established heading of fraud. However, monetary harms do not exhaust the possible harms that forgery may engender, nor account for the philosophical interest in the practice.

Philosophers have tended to frame the peculiar harms of forgery as aesthetic in nature. Insofar as knowledge is a prima facie good, artistic or aesthetic knowledge will be a species of this. Artistic or aesthetic misunderstanding, then, would be its opposite. Certainly, if I take the work before me to be an original Picasso, when it is not, I risk misunderstanding and so misappreciating the object. Of course, this is precisely the desired

---

[6] Goodman agrees, noting "a copy of a Lastman by Rembrandt may well be better than the original" (Goodman 1976, 109).

[7] And forfeiture of a painting by Willem de Kooning that Khan had purchased for $720,000 from the proceeds of the sale of "La Femme Au Chapeau Bleu"—Khan cannot be allowed a pleasure as the direct result of causing criminal harm. (Tran 2010).

outcome of misrepresenting the work. Sherri Irvin classifies this outcome as an "aesthetic harm"—a setback to my aesthetic interests (Irvin 2007, 284). Irvin argues, however, that the aesthetic harms perpetrated by forgery risk going well beyond corrupting my aesthetic understanding of the particular object in front of me. In my aesthetic judgment and appreciation of the work in front of me, Irvin suggests, I depend in part on my knowledge of, and experience with, other related works: other works by that artist, other works in that period, other works in that medium and genre. But, in this, I depend on the judgments of others, particularly the critics, historians, and connoisseurs who have contributed to the framework within which my judgment and appreciation of this work are situated. The whole structure is in flux, as present judgments may feed back into the framework, adjusting it as new understandings develop about how any one work relates to the others.

When forgeries are discovered to have worked their way into this system, it threatens the integrity of the whole apparatus. The system in which we understand and appreciate fine art is, Irvin suggests, a system built and wholly dependent on a sort of critical "bootstrapping." The system works to the extent that the experts can be trusted to be experts, and to the degree that the system can accommodate readjustment as it goes along. But once our understanding of a work or body of works as genuine becomes strapped to other clusters of understanding, forgery threatens the integrity of that system.

In 1945, when a celebrated corpus of paintings attributed to the seventeenth-century Dutch painter Johannes Vermeer were dramatically revealed to be the output of a twentieth-century forger named Han van Meegeren, the impact on the artworld was sudden. As one 1945 newspaper summed the matter up:

> Authorities are apprehensive. They fear that the phoney Vermeers may have been distributed by the gross throughout occupied Europe which fear, if a fact, would necessarily cast suspicion at all of the works attributed to the Dutch master. (*St. Louis Post-Dispatch* 1945)

In retrospect, we can ask, how deeply had the artworld misunderstood Vermeers between 1938, when van Meegeren had his first fake Vermeer authenticated, and 1945, when the ruse was uncovered? How much had we misunderstood Vermeer's place in the history of Western art? More to the point, how much do we misunderstand art right now? By one estimate, some 20 percent of the paintings in major museums around the world are forgeries (Sweeney 2018 and Glover 2011). On Irvin's view, this would imply a staggering instability in our bootstrapped system of appreciation.

Still, given the vagaries of what qualifies as a forgery, our concerns perhaps need not be quite so apocalyptic. Although, once revealed, the particulars of Salvador Dalí's art practices were scandalous, learning that the Dalí print in my possession is not the genuine signed print I thought it was is unlikely to require the sort of global recalibration that the van Meegeren forgeries threatened (Dietsch 1999). While such a revelation may well make me rethink the monetary value of my purchase, the impact on art history will probably be minimal. The same will be true for most referential forgeries: at worst, we misunderstand *where* the originals are.

The one individual who is certain to escape this particular sort of harm is the forger himself. But the forger is, perhaps, open to a distinct harm of his own, due to the very task of forgery. What distinguishes the forger from a true artist, Irvin suggests, is that the forger, "to count as a forger, cannot but pursue the nonartistic objective of producing an object that will pass as the work of the victim: this objective is constitutive of the role of forger" (Irvin 2005, 133). Everything that goes into the forgery is in service of the goal of forgery: producing a fake that will pass for the genuine article. Conversely, the artist is not so constrained: "There is no objective, particular method, set of activities, or set of goals (aside from the minimal goal of producing an artwork) that an artist must pursue in order to count as doing art. Insofar as a forger is pursuing forgery, she isn't pursuing art. How many cheaters have been admonished, "you're only holding yourself back"? The copyist who remains a copyist will never find her own originality, and that—we might say—is a shame.

According to the fragmentary accounts given by Han van Meegeren's own children, what drove him down the road of forgery was the art world's refusal to recognize his talent. After years of being slighted and overlooked, his plan was to "paint a Vermeer, get it accepted by the Rijksmuseum, and then announce triumphantly to an admiring throng: 'This Vermeer was painted by me, Han van Meegeren'" (Arnau 1959, 301). He wanted to show up all of the art critics, historians, and self-appointed experts who had dismissed him, rubbing their noses in their own snobbery (Arnau 1959, 308). Vindicated, van Meegeren would finally be free to pursue his own artistic objectives with the attention they warranted. The goal of forgery, however, dominated van Meegeren's life, with every spare moment spent preparing to create what would eventually be hailed as Vermeer's triumph, *The Disciples at Emmaus*. As Irvin would say, everything that went into *The Disciples at Emmaus* was in service of convincing the experts that it was genuine. The first step of the plan was a success, but van Meegeren's great reveal did not happen. Instead, having dug himself into a money pit, he made another forgery, and another, until he was forced to reveal the ruse in a less triumphant manner than he had imagined, having been arrested for selling one of his supposed Vermeers to Nazi Reichsmarschall Hermann Göring. Today, van Meegeren is not remembered as the great artist who brought down the ivory tower of art snobbery, but rather as the tragic forger whose surprising success only made the art world redouble its collective efforts at weeding out pretenders. As Lessing notes, van Meegeren's ruse was doomed from the start. The better the forger is at being a forger, the worse he is at being an artist. The very best that *The Disciples at Emmaus* might showcase is supreme technical ability.[8] But the closer the painter gets to perfect technique, the further he gets from the one quality that makes an artwork great: originality (Lessing 1983, 74).

---

[8] It doesn't. In the years since the ruse was uncovered, reassessments of van Meegeren's technique have not been kind.

Poor van Meegeren might protest, then, that the greatest harm in his whole situation was to not to the buyers of his fake Vermeers (it's hard to feel sorry for a Nazi), nor to the supposed art experts, whose claims to expertise had been rendered to tatters (shown, van Meegeren would say, to be the charlatans they were), nor to the art-loving public at large (who had been gifted the knowledge of how slipshod the bootstrapped system always was). Rather, van Meegeren might predictably claim, it was *he* who felt the greatest harm from his forgery, for, once entrenched, he had been unable to pursue his own artistic goals, to develop his own originality.

Van Meegeren's entreaty is unlikely to resonate with anyone but himself and other unsuccessful artists who feel they have been slighted by the art world. But one final party remains to be discussed, who is—perhaps surprisingly—typically overlooked in the philosophical debate about forgery. Necessarily, in any case of forgery, someone is lying: the forger, or the forger's representative. And someone is being lied to: the buyer, perhaps the public at large. But, in most cases, there is also someone being lied *about*: the artist to whom the work is being falsely attributed.[9]

In the case of a living artist, there is a reasonable possibility that such a person could suffer harm from an act of forgery. Certainly, Dürer appears to have been outraged by what he deemed an act of theft. Dürer's complaint likely rests in the income that the copies diverted from his hands to Marcantonio's. Dürer's letters from 1506, and his diary from 1520–1521, show a man acutely aware of his accounts (Dürer 2010). But money is not all that is at stake for an artist who discovers his works are being forged.

Given his name recognition, the layers that he has built up between himself and the public, and the skyrocketing market value of his work, the pseudonymous street artist Banksy has had to see more items fraudulently sold in his name than most living artists. However, Banksy's complaint about forgers is unlikely to be the same as Dürer's—that the forgery diverts income from the artist's hand to the copyist's. Banksy is not in the business of business: he does not typically sell his art, but rather leaves it on the sides of buildings and other structures. He is not represented by any gallery or institution, and has leaned on trademark law to restrict commercial sale of his work and use of his art (Bonadio 2019). Banksy's own website maintains a list of unauthorized exhibitions of his work with a request that his fans "treat them accordingly" (Banksy, n.d.). In 2008, Pest Control—the organization set up by Banksy to authenticate his art—found 226 works, including street art and screen printings, falsely attributed to him (Mendick 2008). A statement by Banksy's lawyer, Mark Stevens, sums up the artist's position: "The integrity of the work is being trampled upon, and it's being done for commercial purposes" (Cascone 2019). Given Banksy's aversion to commercialization of his work, the affront is personal. And, certainly, strong enough offense can rise to the level of psychological harm (Young 2008, 130).

---

[9] Not in all cases. A forgery may be fraudulently presented as being from a particular place, period, or even school or workshop, but without attaching the object to any particular individual.

Given the heightened risk of being caught forging the works of living artists, most forgeries will be of the works of dead artists, who are past suffering either financial or psychological harms. Still, there is room to think that we might wrong a person that cannot be harmed in the conventional sense. Where plagiarism involves the unjust taking of another's credit, central cases of forgery involve the unjust placement of credit, attributing to a person something for which he is not responsible. And if there is a wrong in misappropriating credit from a dead artist through plagiarism, then it seems feasible that there is a wrong in misattributing credit to the same dead artist through forgery. But, can the dead be wronged? Do we owe anything to the dead? Chilon of Sparta's admonishment to not speak ill of the dead is still commonly enough pointed to, some two and a half millennia after he, himself, passed (Diogenes Laertius 2018). The aphorism may simply embody a social nicety, but it may do more than that. There is a live philosophical debate about whether we can owe duties to the dead, part of a larger debate about whether we can owe duties to *anything* that isn't a living person (a larger category that includes animals, the unborn, and the environment). The debate emerges from the question of what grounds our rights.[10] Although weighing in on that debate outstretches the capacity of this chapter, recognition that one's interests might outlive the body may explain why we pay any mind to a decedent's last will and testament in distributing her property. Certainly, many an artist has an interest in her reputation that, while living, outweighs any interest she has in her material property. If the latter might outlive the artist, there seems at least a reasonable possibility that the former would as well. Indeed, outside of the United States, the copyright laws of most countries recognize robust "moral rights" in artists, including the right to not be attributed authorship of a work that one did not create, part of the right of paternity. (See Gover, this volume.) In most jurisdictions, moral rights either persist for the duration of copyright—usually fifty or seventy years after the author's death—or else are recognized in perpetuity. In most countries, then, works of forgery risk violating an author's legally protected rights even long after the author's death, provided someone is able to act on the decedent's behalf in court.[11]

SUMMA

As our examination of art practices illustrated the blurriness at the edges of art forgery, our examination of the wrongs of art forgery made things more complicated, not less.

---

[10] Interest Theory grounds rights in interests, but without restricting rights to those entities capable of understanding their own rights and interests. Will Theory demands that the rightsholder be "competent and authorized" to make rights claims. In other words, Interest Theory seems to at least leave some room for the dead to have interests, while Will Theory does not. For more on the debate over whether the dead may have rights, see Fabre (2008).

[11] For further discussion on posthumous moral rights, see McCutcheon (2016).

What is wrong with forgery is not one thing, and the wrongs attributable to forgery are not distributed uniformly.

The more contemporary the artist whose work is being forged, and the more quickly the ruse is uncovered, the less of an impact such a forgery is likely to have on the integrity of the bootstrapped framework that Sherri Irvin discusses, and so the less harm that will be done to our understanding of art history. And, where the forgery is not, like Han van Meegeren's fake Vermeers or Elmyr de Hory's fake Picassos, an inventive forgery, the impact is likely to be minimal regardless. As complicit parties, neither Dalí nor LeWitt are likely to suffer any undue psychological harm for willingly signing things they perhaps should not have signed. And most artists whose work is the subject of forgery are long dead, and past the ability to suffer psychological harm, though there seems room that they might be wronged just the same. However, the failure of moral integrity engendered by the lie at the heart of forgery, and the failures of artistic and aesthetic integrity pointed at by Lessing and Dutton respectively, do not depend on the impact of the fraud, but on the act itself. And while the forger's claim that he is most harmed seems beyond the pale, I do not think that we can simply dismiss the claim out of hand. The wrongs of forgery are no simple matter: at their heart is a lie, but the moral failing of the lie does not account for the constellation of wrongs that forgery may engender. In addition to the lie, any individual case of forgery may—but also may not—include wrongs done to the purchaser of the item, to the public at large, to the artist herself, and yes, perhaps to the forger.

See also: Gover, Soucek, Willard, this volume

References

Arnau, Frank. 1959. *The Art of the Faker: 3,000 Years of Deception*. Boston: Little, Brown.

Banksy. n.d. "PRODUCT RECALL—Art of Banksy." https://www.banksy.co.uk/shows.html

Barkham, Patrick. 2001. "Dealer Convicted of Fraud as the Aboriginal Art World Fights Back." *The Guardian*, February 24, https://www.theguardian.com/world/2001/feb/24/patrickbarkham.

Bonadio, Enrico. 2019. "Banksy Finally Goes to Court to Stop Unauthorised Merchandising, Despite Saying Copyright Is for Losers." *The Conversation*, February 25, https://theconversation.com/banksy-finally-goes-to-court-to-stop-unauthorised-merchandising-despite-saying-copyright-is-for-losers-112390.

Bowden, Ross. 2001. "What is 'Authentic' Aboriginal Art?" *Pacific Arts* 23/24 (July): 1–10.

Cascone, Sarah. 2019. "Banksy (and His Lawyer) Explain Why Fakes Have Forced the Artist to Go Into E-Commerce and Sharpen His Art." *artnet*, October 2, https://news.artnet.com/exhibitions/banksy-store-gross-domestic-product-1667449.

Casement, William. 2020. "Is It a Forgery? Ask a Semanticist." *Journal of Aesthetic Education* 54, no. 1: 51–68.

Catterall, Lee. 1992. *The Great Dalí Fraud and Other Deceptions*. Fort Lee, NJ: Barricade Books.

Chappell, D., and K. Polk. 2009 "Fakers and Forgers, Deception and Dishonesty: An Exploration of the Murky World of Art Fraud." *Current Issues in Criminal Justice* 20, no. 3: 393–412.

Charney, Noah. 2015. *The Art of Forgery: The Minds, Motives and Methods of Master Forgers*. London: Phaidon.

Dietsch, Deborah K. 1999. "Dali Prints: Are They Real, or Just Surreal?" *South Florida Sun-Sentinel*, March 29, https://www.sun-sentinel.com/news/fl-xpm-1999-03-29-9903290357-story.html.

Dutton, Denis. 1983. "Artistic Crimes." In *The Forger's Art: Forgery and the Philosophy of Art*, edited by Denis Dutton, 172–187. Berkeley: University of California Press.

Dürer, Albrecht. 2010. *Memoirs of Journeys to Venice and the Low Countries*. Translated by Rudolf Tumbo. Auckland: The Floating Press.

"Fake Paintings (Report to the Head of Police)." 2006. *Metafisica* 5–6: 582–587.

Fabre, Cecile. 2008. "Posthumous Rights." In *The Legacy of H. L. A. Hart: Legal, Political, and Moral Philosophy*, edited by Matthew H. Kramer, Claire Grant, Ben Colburn, and Antony Hatzistavrou, 225–238. Oxford: Oxford University Press.

Federal Bureau of Investigation. 2010. "Antiques Dealer Agrees to Plead Guilty to Federal Charges Related to Sale of Fake Picasso for $2 Million." Federal Bureau of Investigation news release, April 27, https://archives.fbi.gov/archives/losangeles/press-releases/2010/la042710.htm.

Federal Bureau of Investigation. 2014. "Foundry Owner Sentenced to 30 Months in Prison in $11 Million Scheme to Sell Fake Sculptures Attributed to Jasper Johns and Other Prominent Artists." Federal Bureau of Investigation news release, October 16, https://www.fbi.gov/contact-us/field-offices/newyork/news/press-releases/foundry-owner-sentenced-to-30-months-in-prison-in-11-million-scheme-to-sell-fake-sculptures-attributed-to-jasper-johns-and-other-prominent-artists.

Galenson, David W. 2009. *Conceptual Revolutions in Twentieth-Century Art*, 194. Cambridge: Cambridge University Press.

Glendinning, Nigel. 1989. "Nineteenth-Century Editions of Goya's Etchings New Details of their Sales Statistics." *Print Quarterly* 6, no. 4: 394–403.

Glover, Michael. 2011. "The Big Question: How Many of the Paintings in Our Public Museums are Fakes?" *The Independent*, October 23, https://www.independent.co.uk/arts-entertainment/art/news/big-question-how-many-paintings-our-public-museums-are-fakes-1946264.html.

"Goering's Hireling Painter Duped Him of $256,000 for 'Old Master.'" *St. Louis Post-Dispatch*, September 17, 1945.

Goodman, Nelson. 1976. *Languages of Art: An Approach to the Theory of Symbols*. New York: Bobbs-Merrill.

Gorris, Lothar, and Sven Röbel. 2012. "Geständnis eines ewigen Hippies." *Der Spiegel* 10 (March 5): 126–136.

Grant, Daniel. 2017. "Works Produced After Artists' Deaths Pose Challenges for Collectors." *Wall Street Journal Online*, February 13, https://www.wsj.com/articles/works-produced-after-artists-deaths-pose-challenges-for-collectors-1486955040.

Horberry, Max. 2020. "The Artist Beneath the Art Forger." *New York Times*, February 21, https://www.nytimes.com/2020/02/21/arts/design/elmyr-de-hory-art-forgery.html.

Irvin, Sherri. 2005. "Appropriation and Authorship in Contemporary Art." *British Journal of Aesthetics* 45, no. 2: 123–137.

Irvin, Sherri. 2007. "Forgery and the Corruption of Aesthetic Understanding." *Canadian Journal of Philosophy* 37, no. 2: 283–304.

Koerner, Joseph. 1993. *The Moment of Self-Portraiture in German Renaissance Art*. Chicago: University of Chicago Press.

Laertius, Diogenes. 2018. *Lives of the Eminent Philosophers*. Translated by Pamela Mensch. Oxford: Oxford University Press.

Lessing, Alfred. 1983. "What Is Wrong with a Forgery?" In *The Forger's Art: Forgery and the Philosophy of Art*, edited by Denis Dutton, 58–76. Berkeley: University of California Press.

Levinson, Jerrold. 1980. "Autographic and Allographic Art Revisited." *Philosophical Studies* 38, no. 4: 367–383.

Margolis, Joseph. 1983. "Art, Forgery, and Authenticity." In *The Forger's Art: Forgery and the Philosophy of Art*, edited by Denis Dutton, 153–171. Berkeley: University of California Press.

McCutcheon, Jani. 2016. "Dead Loss: Damages for Posthumous Breach of the Moral Right of Integrity." *Melbourne University Law Review* 40, no. 1: 240–287.

Mendick, Robert. 2008. "Banksy's? Don't Bet on It." *Evening Standard*, September 26.

Pon, Lisa. 2004. *Raphael, Dürer, and Marcantonio Raimondi: Copying and the Italian Renaissance Print*. New Haven, CT: Yale University Press.

Sweeney, Don. 2018. "'It's a Catastrophe.' French Museum Learns Half Its Paintings are Fake." *Miami Herald*, April 29, https://www.miamiherald.com/news/nation-world/world/article21 0101264.html.

Taraborelli, John. 2019. "Meet Paul Amaral, the Art World's Secret Weapon." *Rhode Island Monthly*, November 20, https://www.rimonthly.com/meet-paul-amaral-the-art-worlds-sec ret-weapon/.

Taylor, Kate. 2007. "A 'LeWitt' in Atlantic Yards's Path." *New York Sun*, May 25, https://www. nysun.com/arts/lewitt-in-atlantic-yardss-path/55245/.

Tran, My-Thuan. 2010. "L.A. Art Dealer Accused of Selling a Phony Picasso." *Los Angeles Times*, January 9, https://www.latimes.com/archives/la-xpm-2010-jan-09-la-me-picasso-2010jan09-story.html.

Vasari, Georgio. 1913. *Lives of the Most Eminent Painters, Sculptors, and Architects*, Vol. VI. Translated by Gaston Du C. de Vere, 91. London: Philip Lee Warner.

Weber, John S. 2000. "Sol LeWitt: The Idea, the Wall Drawing, and Public Space." In *Sol LeWitt: A Retrospective*, edited by Gary Garrels, 88–99. New Haven, CT: Yale University Press.

Wreen, Michael. 2002. "Forgery." *Canadian Journal of Philosophy* 32, no. 2: 143–166.

Young, James O. 2008. *Cultural Appropriation and the Arts*. Malden, MA: Blackwell.

CHAPTER 40

ART, ETHICS, AND VANDALISM

SONDRA BACHARACH

A common-sense intuition is that vandalism is never permissible (morally, historically, aesthetically, financially, etc.). For most cases of ordinary, run-of-the-mill
destructive vandalism, this seems right. But there is more to vandalism than the
stereotypical spray-painted tag on private property. This chapter explores some
central cases where vandalism is not only tolerated, but indeed celebrated. These
cases all concern *art* vandalism, and, in particular, vandalism that transforms an
existing artwork into something new and different. I call this "creative vandalism."
Vandalism is creative (and hence permissible) when it replaces or adds to an existing artwork.

In this chapter, I sketch three different forms of creative vandalism and what they
entail. First is *replacement vandalism*, an act of vandalism that destroys the physical
materials of the original artwork (and as a result, also destroys the existing artwork),
but also creates a new artwork. Second is *additive vandalism*, which leaves the physical materials of the existing work untouched, but vandalizes by *adding* to the existing
work. The result is the destruction of the original *artwork*, the preservation of the original physical materials that constitute the original artwork, and the creation of a new
artwork (consisting of the original physical materials plus the new vandalism overlayed
on top of the existing work). Finally, we have *invisible vandalism*, which destroys the
original artwork without altering the existing work of art or the physical materials that
constitute the work—instead this form of vandalism alters the nonphysical, or relational, features of a work, so that the artwork cannot be seen as originally intended. In
all three kinds of vandalism, the existing work can no longer be appreciated as it was
initially intended.

WHAT IS VANDALISM AND WHY IS IT
REGARDED AS WRONG?

Vandalism is usually understood generally as the destruction of physical objects.[1] A bus-stop is vandalized when someone smashes the glass shelter; a playground is vandalized when someone breaks the equipment; a building is vandalized when someone spray paints on it; a wall is vandalized when someone tags the public space with illegible scrawls; a car is vandalized when its tires are torn. These cases suggest that vandalism involves the intentional damage or destruction of physical objects.

Vandalism is usually limited to man-made objects, as the previous examples illustrate. But natural objects can be also vandalized, for example, trees, in whose bark people might carve their initials, or natural rock formations which are sometimes attacked with spray paint.[2] When those trees are part of a national park, or when those rocks are part of an archeological site, then we often say that the larger natural object, the site or park, is vandalized. In contrast, however, forests, lakes, beaches, and plants are destroyed, but not vandalized, which suggests that the difference between mere destruction and vandalism lies in the intentionality of the latter.

Intuitively, vandalism is morally wrong because it's wrong to destroy things. Destruction causes loss—a consumer loss of goods that could otherwise have been used; a financial loss for the property that no longer exists; a social loss for the degradation of the area in which the destruction occurs; an environmental loss for the now-wasted carbon footprint required for the object's creation. To the extent that vandalism involves damage or destruction, then, vandalism is wrong.

In addition to the material losses, vandalism is also a sign of disrespect—it is disrespectful to the people who created the now-destroyed physical objects, to the people who have to pass by the site of the destruction, to the people whose physical objects are destroyed, as well as to the materials and the environment. (See Gover, this volume.)

The specific case of vandalizing art is no different. Art vandalism also causes destruction and damage—both a physical kind and an artistic (nonphysical) kind. When Vladimir Umanets vandalized Rothko's *Black on Maroon* in 2012, everyone (including Umanets himself, who later offered a public apology),[3] denounced this act as bad,

---

[1] Special thanks to the audiences at the American Society for Aesthetics Annual Meeting (Phoenix 2019) and the London Aesthetics Forum zoom session in March 2021 for stimulating and valuable extensions of my thinking on this topic. Thanks also to Richard Joyce, for invaluable suggestions on an earlier draft. And, to James Harold for his thoughtful and constructive improvements.

[2] Rock art formations and petroglyphs are regularly vandalized, such as those in the Chattahoochee-Oconee National Forest (US), or the Range National Monument (US), Awiss in Lybia, Chile, Uluru, to name just a few.

[3] See Vladmimir Umanets, "I regret vandalising a Rothko but I remain committed to Yellowism" 14 May 2014. https://www.theguardian.com/commentisfree/2014/may/15/vandalising-rothko-yellowism-black-on-maroon-tate-modern

because it resulted in an important work being damaged. But art vandalism happens frequently, and every time, the media document our collective gasp of horror in response to these violent acts of destruction. Our most treasured, famous, and valued works of art from around the world have been attacked. Here is an abbreviated list of some of the most notorious acts of vandalism:[4] works by Da Vinci, Rembrandt, Picasso, Malevich, Rodin, Velázquez, Van Gogh, Poussin, Newman, Michelangelo, Warhol, Twombly, Mondrian, Matisse, Frankenthaler, Monet, Dürer, Rubens, and Rothko, to name just a few.[5] As is evident from this (still incomplete) list, the history of art is littered (pardon the pun) with famous cases of artistic destruction. The methods used to destroy vary widely: from dainty teacups to machetes and knives, from lipstick to sulfuric acid, from spray paint to vomit, from urine to explosives. The motives are equally diverse: from feminist rage against the representations of women to overwhelming expressions of tender love for an artwork, from a sophisticated intellectual political opposition to current affairs to random and unprovoked acts of violence. But the result—damage and destruction of art—is the same.

These cases of violent artistic destruction, and those like it, underwrite the common-sense view that it's never, ever permissible (morally, aesthetically, historically, financially, etc.) to vandalize art, understood as the intentional destruction of or damage to an artwork.[6] The same reasons that explain why it's wrong to vandalize physical objects also apply to art as well: destroying art is disrespectful to the artist, to the ideas that the artist is expressing, to the cultural heritage of the artist and their people, to the owner of the artwork (whether that's an individual or an institution like a museum), and to the viewers of the work (past, present and future). Respecting art requires valuing an artwork and acting in a way that recognizes the work's value. To vandalize art, then, is seen to *not* value an artwork appropriately and to *not* act in a way that recognizes or acknowledges the work's value.

The wrongness of vandalism is also formalized in the US legal system through the Visual Artists Rights Act. Introduced in 1990, it grants an artist moral rights over his or her art, even after selling it. These rights include an artist's right to prevent destruction, alterations or modifications to an artwork without the artist's approval, when these risk damaging the artist's reputation. It also gives artists the right to disavow a work if an artwork has been altered without the artist's permission. These rights are in force for the life of the artist, and cover most forms of visual art, such as paintings, limited edition photography, drawings, or sculptures.[7] Although this chapter is restricted to the ethical

---

[4] Note: For a discussion of the destruction of monuments and memorials see Bicknell et al. this volume. For the discussion of the destruction of public art, see Willard, this volume.

[5] For an updated list of artistic vandalism, consult the latest Wikipedia page at https://en.wikipedia.org/wiki/Vandalism_of_art (accessed May 3, 2021). For a thorough classification of the types of vandalism, see Thompson (2013).

[6] For the sake of clarity, accidental damage to artworks, by individuals or by acts of nature, are beyond the scope of this chapter. Vandalism requires the intention to damage an artwork.

[7] Most cases of vandalism occur with autographic works, works that admit a single object as its instance. Allographic works, like movies, music or books, are more difficult to vandalize due to the ambiguity over what the work is, and what would be involved in vandalizing it.

issues about vandalizing art, it is worth keeping in mind the legal debate around the act that runs alongside this discussion.

The wrongness of vandalism is so intuitively plausible that philosophers simply take it for granted—nobody has really bothered to provide a philosophical defence of the wrongness of vandalism, being so trivially obvious. Indeed, only a handful of philosophical papers even address the issue of vandalism, and those who have published on the subject tend to presuppose its wrongness.[8] For example, Fenner (2006) assumes that modifying works is wrong, and explores some of the reasons why. Likewise, van Camp (2011) has recently explored the rise of graffiti in the former Soviet bloc, arguing that the vandalism inherent in graffiti is not excused or justified by assigning it art-status— another position that presupposes the wrongness of vandalism.

Young (1989) has been one of the few to argue against this mainstream view that vandalism is always wrong. Focusing exclusively on art vandalism, he argues that it's permissible to vandalize bad art, when more value is gained by destroying the artwork than not. Even here, however, Young presupposes that for the most part and in most situations, it is wrong to destroy or vandalize art. His claim is quite restricted—he is simply suggesting that at least sometimes it's acceptable to vandalize *bad* art.

This chapter will question the received view about vandalism. The common-sense intuition is that vandalizing (whether it's an artwork or not) is wrong, where vandalism is understood to involve the intentional destruction of physical materials or objects. However, in the case of art, there are many interesting cases and situations where this common-sense view does not seem to apply. It turns out that our imagined stereotypical act of vandalism is narrow and limited: we imagine crass thugs lurking in the dark shadows angrily attacking a wall with simplistic scrawls. But famous, sophisticated artists also vandalize. Let us broaden our understanding of vandalism: the most philosophically interesting and challenging cases of vandalism engage in more than mere destruction.

BEYOND MERE DESTRUCTION: CREATIVE FORMS OF VANDALISM

The more creative forms of vandalism challenge our common-sense intuitions about what vandalism is—they go beyond mere destruction of physical materials. In these cases, vandals do not just destroy—the destruction also leaves something constructive in its wake. These are creative forms of vandalism.

---

[8] One exception here concerns the recent defense of vandalizing political monuments. See Daisy Dixon (2022), Chong-Ming Lim (2020), Ten-Herng Lai (2020), and Bicknell, Judkins, and Korsmeyer, this volume.

Broadening our conception of vandalism beyond the notoriously destructive acts that make news headlines allows us to recognize that at least sometimes, some acts of vandalism are morally permissible (and this extends beyond Young's restriction to the permissibility of acts of vandalism against bad art). In this section, I identify three different kinds of morally permissible, aesthetically creative vandalism: (a) replacement vandalism, which physically damages or destroys an existing artwork, leaving a new work in its place; (b) additive vandalism, which damages an existing artwork by overlaying a new artwork on top of the already existing work; and (c) invisible vandalism, which damages an existing artwork, not by damaging that work physically, but by damaging its nonphysical features. This chapter carves out these three forms of creative vandalism, and argues that they are morally permissible, in contrast to their ordinary, destructive counterparts.

Before moving forward, however, let's qualify the idea of invisible vandalism. It might seem magical, or even downright impossible, to imagine destroying an artwork without destroying the physical materials that constitute the work. But artworks are more than their mere physical materials. As Danto has taught us, an artwork's nonphysical properties are as important as its physical ones. As he famously proclaimed, "to see something as art requires something the eye cannot decry [*sic*]—an atmosphere of artistic theory, a knowledge of the history of art: an artworld" (Danto, 1964, 580). Visually indiscernible works made of the same physical materials do not always result in two identical artworks. For example, Walker Evans and Sherrie Levine both created photographs that look almost completely identical, though their related artworks are completely different. Moreover, even if they were *completely* visually indiscernible, they would still possess radically different nonphysical properties: one is a work of documentary photography, the other is a work of conceptual art; one is about poverty, the other is about the limits of art; one is emotionally poignant, the other is intellectual and distanced. A work of art is more than its physical materials—it includes both physical properties, as well as nonphysical properties. Obviously we can destroy an artwork by destroying its physical properties—that's what most forms of vandalism undertake to do. But if an artwork is more than its mere physical materials, then an entire new way of vandalizing art arises—we can vandalize art by destroying or altering its nonphysical materials, too.[9] We shall return to this in more detail when we consider invisible vandalism. But let's begin our examination of permissible vandalism with the more straightforward cases involving physical destruction.

Replacement Vandalism

Some art vandalism is not only permissible, but celebrated. This situation arises when great art is destroyed, but instead of lamenting the act as one of seriously wrong

[9] Daisy Dixon has also defended a form of metaphysical destruction through artistic (counter) speech in her "Artistic (Counter) Speech," *The Journal of Aesthetics and Art Criticism*, Volume 80, Issue 4, Fall 2022, Pages 409–419.

vandalism, the destructive act is acclaimed as possessing great artistic merit.[10] Consider some well-known examples. In 1953, Rauschenberg carefully and painstakingly erased a de Kooning sketch in order to make *Erased de Kooning*, which of course is now a famous work of art. In 1995, Ai Weiwei made *Dropping a Han Dynasty Urn*, by doing just that—dropping the culturally and historically valuable artwork. Ironically, in 2012, Salvisberg created another famous work, *Fragments of History*, documenting the art collector Uli Sigg as he drops a replica of Ai Weiwei's *Coca-Cola Urn*.[11] More recently, Bansky's *Girl with Balloon* autodestructed—at least, it mostly did. Perhaps we should consider it an incomplete (auto)destruction, given that the shredding mechanism didn't finish the job. For our purposes here, however, it's sufficient to acknowledge that Rauschenberg, Ai, Salvisberg, and Banksy have all destroyed great art, just like Umanets.

So why does Umanets get jail time for his vandalism, while Rauschenberg, Ai, Salvisberg, and Banksy ended up being celebrated as great artists? We can reject a few simple answers out of hand: it would be silly to say that it's somehow better to *completely destroy* art, as Rauschenberg, Ai, or Salvisberg have done, rather than *merely vandalize* art, as Umanets did—if a little bit of destruction is bad (*à la* Umanets, or other vandals who have done jail-time for their violent acts), then surely it's just as bad, if not worse, to engage in *total* destruction (*à la* Ai and Salvisberg). Perhaps instead Umanets's problem was that he didn't get permission from Rothko before vandalizing the work. But of course, neither Ai nor Salvisberg got permission to destroy either the ancient urn or its modern, appropriated counterpart, so that can't be the right explanation, either. If consent from the creator doesn't suffice to make vandalism permissible, then ownership also won't help either—owning the *Mona Lisa* or *Guernica* won't make it permissible to vandalize the works, and getting permission from their creators wouldn't either.[12]

---

[10] There is a class of artworks which are performances of objects (including art) being destroyed. These works are quite different to the cases of replacement, additive and invisible vandalism I consider here— for one, I am interested in cases of vandalism, which presupposes that some remnants of the work being vandalized, continue to exist, while in the cases of performances of destruction, usually nothing more is left of the work that was destroyed; for another, the cases considered here are of autographic artworks, while performances of destruction are allographic; finally, in the cases I am interested in, the result of vandalism is another work of art, while in the cases I am not interested in, the destruction itself *is* the artwork. This is a very interesting kind of example, even if it is not the one I am interested in here. For an extensive treatment of this issue, see Fisher (1974).

[11] This case is layered in ironic references: the urn that Sigg himself drops is a replica of Ai Weiwei's famous Coca Cola urns. Ai Weiwei, in turn, had purchased the urn himself to appropriate it, by painting the soda's famous insignia. Sigg is effectively appropriating Ai Weiwei's appropriation. A double appropriation, if you will. Likewise, Salvisberg's documentation of the dropping of Sigg's (replica) urn is designed to appropriate the documentation of the dropping of Ai Weiwei's urn—another double appropriation. See Victoria Woodcock, "Ai Weiwei and Me: the collector's tale," 9 July 2020, https://www.ft.com/content/951c11ae-2de0-411c-9732-e21884570834.

[12] Behind this intuition is the acknowledgment that famous works of art have a cultural heritage that prevents owners from doing whatever they want to these works. Indeed, part of the sheer disgust we might experience thinking about how the Chapman brothers vandalized the Goya *Disasters of War* prints stems from the intuition that ownership in no way justifies their vandalism. (as we'll see later, I think something *else* will justify their vandalism—but ownership does not).

Finally, one might think Umanets got in trouble because he was an unknown artist at the time, while Rauschenberg, Ai Weiwei, and Banksy are arguably world-famous. But that can't quite be right either, because Salvisberg is not world-famous (and by his own admission, not even a bona fide artist).[13] Likewise, Rauschenberg himself was, at the time of *Erased de Kooning*, still relatively unknown; indeed, Rauschenberg had wanted to erase his *own* work (a self-destructive act), but he didn't think he could get away with it, because he worried he wasn't sufficiently famous. At the time of Rauschenberg's violent act of destruction against the de Kooning, Rauschenberg was actually not in such a different position to Umanets in relation to fame. This leaves us back where we started, wondering why Umanets's mere vandalism is so much worse than Rauschenberg's total destruction.

Now, Rauschenberg denies that there was any destruction involved in making *Erased de Kooning*: "I remember that the idea of destruction kept coming into the conversation, and I kept trying to show that it *wouldn't* be destruction," said Rauschenberg, "although there was always the chance that if it didn't work out there would be a terrible waste."[14] But we shouldn't let Rauschenberg's metaphysical sleight of hand fool us. Any good aesthetician will see through this ontological equivocation: a work of art was most certainly destroyed (de Kooning's); however, there was also a new work of art created (Rauschenberg's). Rauschenberg's rationalization, however, offers an insight into understanding why we may be appalled at Umanets's vandalism, but delighted to be Banksy'ed by *Girl with Balloon*'s auto-destruction. Vandals merely destroy art leaving only damaged physical materials in their wake, while Rauschenberg, Ai, Salvisberg, and Banksy's destructions leave new works of art in place of ruins.

When vandals destroy art, leaving only damaged physical materials behind, we treat this as an immoral act and lament the resulting loss of art.[15] Its destruction is disrespectful to the work and its artist. But it is also disrespectful to the viewers, who are deprived of the ability to appreciate and value the work in the way that it deserves.

[13] See "Confessions of an Art Collector Turned Artist," Larry's List, http://www.larryslist.com/artmarket/the-talks/confessions-of-an-art-collector-turned-artist/ (accessed February 25, 2021).

[14] See Abigail Cain, "Why Robert Rauschenberg Erased a De Kooning," July 14, 2017, https://www.artsy.net/article/artsy-editorial-robert-rauschenberg-erased-de-kooning.

[15] What about when artists destroy their own work? Does that count as vandalism? Usually not (though we also lament the resulting loss of art.) Artists regularly destroy their own work: Agnes Martin, Michaelangelo, Georgia O'Keefe, and Monet are among the many artists who have physically destroyed their own earlier works. Many artists reject their earlier work, destroying it so that it cannot be seen or so that it no longer is included in their *oeuvre*. Even so-called vandals can vandalize their own work. Street artist Blu destroyed twenty years' worth of his own murals in Bologna upon discovering that they had been removed from their original site locations for inclusion in an art exhibition. It is permissible for artists to destroy their own work, as much as it may disappoint us viewers and appreciators. Since they are the creators of the works, they are also able to edit their *oeuvre*, including deleting works they don't want to include in their *oeuvre*. Here authorial status justifies the destruction, even when we may feel as if the world has lost access to potentially great art. But intuitively it's destruction, it's permissible, but it is not vandalism. As such, these cases are not considered in this chapter.

In contrast, all of the cases considered so far have involved the destruction of the existing work's physical materials, where the destruction of the existing artwork enables the replacement of what was destroyed with a new and different artwork. That is, these replacement vandals offer us an alternative object to appreciate and value in place of what they have destroyed. Their act of vandalism offers an ethical invitation to reevaluate how we value art—and to suggest that their replacements are comparably, if not more, valuable (either ethically or aesthetically) and deserving of respect.

One might object here that Rauschenberg and Banksy's destructions are relevantly dissimilar to Ai and Salvisberg. When Ai and Salvisberg destroy ancient Chinese Han Dynasty urns, they are not simply destroying an existing artwork, like Rauschenberg and Banksy. They are also thereby destroying artifacts of history, culture, and craft. Of course, that's part of the point of their work—to serve as an ironic commentary, about how we respect (or fail to respect) our past, whether that's seen as a criticism of the Chinese Revolution's lack of respect for its cultural and artistic heritage, or about the industrial, modern world's lack of respect for ancient craft, or perhaps they are laughing at us for revering vandalism.

Perhaps our considered response to replacement vandalism shouldn't be that the destruction itself is bad, so much as the destruction that leaves nothing else to appreciate. Cases like this support the intuition that acts of vandalism are bad when they destroy art and leave nothing else in its place, while they are permissible when such destruction results in the creation of a new work of art.[16] Replacement vandalism is one way of creating new works of art out of damaged materials. But not all vandalism necessarily involves damaging the physical materials of the existing works in order to create new works. Some creative vandals do not destroy existing materials, so much as *add* to them (though they destroy the existing artwork in the process of adding to them). Let us turn to these *additive vandals* next.

ADDITIVE VANDALISM

Additive vandalism brings a new perspective to the issues involved in vandalism: arguably, additive vandals purposefully avoid physical damage to the existing work of art and their additions are intended to be appreciated against the backdrop of the existing artwork. They vandalize the *artwork*, while leaving the *physical* materials that constitute the artwork untouched. Indeed, these vandals' works are designed to be understood in relation to the original work, so damaging or destroying that original artwork would undermine their goals. Their vandalism destroys the existing artwork by overlaying the artwork with a new work that cannot be appreciated without seeing the original work

---

[16] Fisher (1974) considers whether destruction can result in artistic creation, but limits his exploration to auto-destructive art.

in relation to the new work. They create new art not by destroying old art, so much as creating new art by adding to old art. Call this *additive vandalism*. Additive vandalism is vandalism that damages an existing artwork, by *adding* to it in ways that prevents us from seeing the work as it was meant to be seen.

Some artists' entire stock in trade consists of creating new artworks by adding to existing art, and thereby destroying the existing artwork while preserving its physical materials. Chris McMahon and Thryza Segal create new artworks by purchasing abandoned landscape paintings and then adding surreal and completely out-of-context alien monsters to the paintings in unexpected and unexpectedly humorous ways.[17] Obviously, in creating these strange monster paintings, these artists destroy the existing works. Likewise, the Chapman brothers have spent a lot of time destroying famous artists' works—adding ridiculous hippy motifs to Hitler's sappy landscape paintings (in an exhibit at the White Cube in 2008, aptly titled "If Hitler Had Been A Hippy How Happy Would We Be") and attaching disturbing puppy and clown heads to the etchings from Goya's *Disasters of War* (in the show "The Rape of Creativity," in 2003 at the Modern Art Oxford).[18] And Bansky has recently moved his usual vandalism from the streets into the artworld with his "Keeping It Spotless" (2007), which defaces one of Damien Hirst's spot paintings. Most yarn bombers also engage in additive vandalism, defacing an artwork without physically damaging it, by carefully encasing it in knitting or crochet: Agata Oleksiak yarn-bombed DiModica's *Charging Bull*, Marianne Jorgensen's delicate pink *Tank Cosy* to oppose the Iraq war in 2006. Cornelia Parker adds a mile of string, carefully wrapped around Rodin's *The Kiss*, in a way that completely hides much of Rodin's work, in order to create her 2003 work, *The Distance (A Kiss with String Attached)*. Glasgow's *Duke of Wellington* statue has been vandalized with a bright, orange traffic cone since the 1980s—originally a work of vandalism (worthy of a hefty fine), the cone has since been legally sanctioned (and arguably no longer an act of vandalism).

[17] "Adding Monsters to Thrift Store Paintings," April 13, 2012, https://twistedsifter.com/2012/04/adding-monsters-to-thrift-store-paintings/.

[18] One might think that it's perfectly permissible to destroy a print, because it's merely a token instance of an allographic work, rather than an irreplaceable singular autographic work of art. But this particular set of prints are treated as if they were unique, irreplaceable artworks (rather than a token of some other work). (See Hick this volume, for a discussion.) For example, according to the *Guardian*, "The Chapmans' series is from a—historically very significant—edition published directly from Goya's plates in 1937, as a protest against fascist atrocities in the Spanish civil war." This review treats these as if they are autographic, allographic reproductions, commenting that the Chapmans "do not destroy, but find something new in the *Disasters of War*. The Chapmans have remade Goya's masterpiece for a century which has rediscovered evil." See Jonathan Jones, "Jake and Dinos Chapman: Look What We did," March 31, 2003, https://www.theguardian.com/culture/2003/mar/31/artsfeatures.turnerprize2003. Those who find this work abhorrent often treat the prints as singular works of autographic art, rather than copies of a plate. An alternative explanation for why we find the additive vandalism abhorrent is that we may feel that the additions do not respect the value of the Goya. Adding vandalism to Hitler's work may be permissible because we do not see Hitler's work as worthy of respect; in contrast, adding vandalism to Goya's work does not seem appropriate because it does not respect to the value of Goya's work (and perhaps one might go further to suggest that some vandalism might be able to pull that off, but the Chapman's have not).

These replacement vandals vandalize art. But they do so without preventing us from seeing the original artwork—in all the cases, the original artwork is still there. We see the original work, but not as the artist originally intended. Indeed, the new works' power and force hinges on our ability to appreciate that there are *two* works here—the original work by the earlier artists, and a *new* work by the newer artists, who have added to that original work. Appreciating these new works involves seeing the original work and recognizing that the new work has been superimposed onto the earlier work, while leaving the original work intact and untouched. The old work is still there, in exactly the same state as it was after its initial completion. There's just more there now than there once was. Knowing what once was there is central to our appreciating what's now in its place.

But while there may not have been any *physical* destruction to the artworks, intuitively it seems right to insist that these artworks have been *vandalized*. After all, these new additions now prevent us from appreciating the earlier works as they were originally intended to be appreciated. They have been aesthetically destroyed, even if not physically destroyed—after the new artists add to them, we can no longer appreciate them as originally intended, in spite of the fact that the work underneath remains intact.

We can now pinpoint a key difference between replacement vandalism and additive vandalism: replacement vandalism alters and even damages the physical properties and materials of an existing artwork, while additive vandalism does not. Replacement vandalism creates new art, whose appreciation requires accepting that earlier work has been physically destroyed and hence no longer exists. Additive vandalism, in contrast, creates new art whose appreciation requires recognizing that the earlier work continues to exist physically, but the additions prevent us from seeing the earlier artwork itself as it was originally intended. Those additions have the consequence that, for all intents and purposes, we can no longer access the original artwork as initially intended, even though it is right there under our very noses.

The fact that an artwork can be aesthetically destroyed, even if not physically destroyed, offers valuable insights into how and why the loss involved in destruction is mitigated when a new artwork is created. We typically think vandalism's harm centers around the work's physical destruction. Replacement vandalism suggests that the physical destruction is mitigated in part by the new work that results. Additive vandalism expands this perspective: damage can come from the physical or aesthetic destruction, which destruction is also mitigated in part by the new work that results.

The force of additive vandalism stems from the fact that we are confronted with an artwork whose existence and aesthetic value depends crucially on its ability to distort another artwork. The new work requires appreciating the original work, but not in the way originally intended by the original artist. On the contrary, the added vandalism distorts and ruins what the original artist initially intended. Additive vandals are making a tacit commentary on the original work—it is not worthy of our respect. They offer their additions as an improvement to the work, an improvement to warrant our respect.

Moreover, because the new work is "simply" an addition, the additions haven't destroyed the original physical materials in any meaningful sense. The additive vandal's power stems from recognizing that the audience normally conflates *aesthetic* destruction with *physical* destruction. Additive vandals intentionally *aesthetically* destroy the original work without *physically* destroying it. By overlaying it with additional materials, additive vandals prevent us from seeing the original work as it is intended, ruining our experience of the work, even if they do not (strictly speaking) ruin the physical materials that constitute the work. In doing so, additive vandals flaunt their improvements as ones that enhance the work, designed to elicit our respect.

INVISIBLE VANDALISM

Like additive vandalism, invisible vandalism creates a new artwork that damages the existing artwork, all the while leaving the physical materials of the existing artwork untouched. To do this, invisible vandals damage the nonphysical properties of the work, rather than its physical ones.

To engage in invisible vandalism, a vandal must intentionally destroy the aesthetic properties of an artwork without altering its physical properties. Normally the traditional way of damaging the aesthetic properties of an artwork is to damage its physical properties. Rip the canvas, and you'll destroy the painting. Break the stone and you'll ruin the sculpture. Invisible vandals recognize the fact that many works of art have certain aesthetic features in virtue of their nonphysical properties. Altering these works' nonphysical features will damage these works. Let's consider some examples.

Site-specific works are vandalized by compromising their site-specificity. Richard Serra's *Tilted Arc* notoriously was carefully designed to occupy Federal Plaza in Manhattan in ways that would disrupt the path of pedestrians. This infuriated those who had to negotiate the space every day, which of course was part of Serra's point. After lengthy legal battles, Serra was required to relocate the work. He refused, however, arguing that to remove the work would be tantamount to destroying it.[19] To relocate a site-specific work is to destroy some of its key nonphysical properties that are constitutive of the work. Relocating *Tilted Arc* would damage the artwork, while leaving the physical materials that constitute the artwork untouched. The nonphysical property of the work, its site-specificity, is a feature that can be vandalized by being altered, just as the physical property of a painting can be vandalized by being torn. Moving a site-specific work elsewhere qualifies as a kind of invisible vandalism.

DiModica's *Charging Bull* is another example of a work that was invisibly vandalized by having its site-specificity compromised with the arrival of *Fearless Girl*. DiModica originally installed *Charging Bull* to inspire hope and optimism after the Wall Street

---

[19] See Hein (1996), Horowitz (1996), Kelly (1996).

crash of 1986. After *Fearless Girl* was installed a mere twenty-six feet from the bull, however, DiModica worried that his bull's meaning was corrupted, emasculated by the girl. *Charging Bull* is effectively invisibly vandalized by *Fearless Girl*: her arrival prevents us from being able to see the bull's machismo; her presence diminishes the bull's power; her site-specific feature, mere feet from the bull, is designed to prevent viewers from seeing the bull as originally intended.

Acts of invisible vandalism that hinge on site-specificity and proximity to other works have blurry boundaries—how close or far does a site-specific work have to be moved before it is destroyed? Presumably that depends on the specific relationship that work bears to its physical location. Similarly, how close a new work has to be to an existing work to vandalize it depends in part on the particular nature of the existing work, the new work, and how they are related.

A final instance of invisible vandalism that prevents us from seeing a work of art as it is intended without thereby altering the work itself is virtual reality. Jeff Koons, working with Snapchat, intended to use augmented reality to display his *Balloon Dog* in certain key geo-tagged locations. Upset at the takeover of virtual space by big technology giants, artist Sebastian Errazuriz created a vandalized augmented reality version of the Jeff Koons *Balloon Dog*, geo-tagged in the same location as where Jeff Koons's Snapchat version was meant to be. Again, although Errazuriz does not physically damage or destroy Jeff Koons's work (the physically or virtually instantiated ones), *Balloon Dog* has been (virtually, and thus invisibly) vandalized.

Invisible vandalism damages the *artwork* by preventing us from seeing and appreciating the work as it is meant or intended to be seen. Unlike generic vandalism, however, it leaves the physical materials that constitute the artwork untouched. Such vandalism involves altering the nonphysical or relational properties of an artwork. Taking away the site-specific location from a site-specific work like Serra's effectively destroys the work, even if the physical materials that constitute the work are undamaged. Changing the central features of the site of a site-specific work could also damage or destroy the work, even if the physical materials remain themselves untouched. These are nonphysical ways of damaging an artwork.

There are other ways of engaging in invisible vandalism for non–site-specific works. Arguably, disavowing authorship of a work is a form of vandalism that damages the work by altering its nonphysical or relational properties, that is to say, the relationship of the artwork to its creator. When Cady Noland disavows her *Milking Cowboys*, the works' physical materials remain the same, but nobody can see or appreciate the work in the same way. Indeed, her disowning of the work renders it unsellable, inauthentic, and authorless. When Richard Prince denounced his *Ivanka Trump* work from an Instagram series as "fake art," after learning that Ivanka Trump purchased it for her collection, its value became irreparably diminished—dissociated from its famous author, the picture returned to its status as mere Instagram feed material. A similar incident occurred when Büchel rejected the physical materials commissioned for *Training Ground for Democracy* in 2006—his rejection of those materials as constitutive of his artwork left the museum Mass MoCA with a random assortment of (ridiculously overpriced) objects to display, but no artwork (they did, somewhat successfully, display those materials as an unfinished work).[20]

Performance vandalism is also a case of invisible vandalism: a performance vandal's goal is to perform an act that leaves the original artwork untouched, but forever alters our understanding and appreciation of the work, by making it impossible to consider the work without considering the vandalistic act. For example, when Yuan Chai and Jian Jun Xi performed "Two Naked Men Jump Into Tracey's Bed" on Tracey Emin's *My Bed*, their actions become inextricably part of the history of Emin's work. Although the damage to the work is short-lived, temporary, and easily rectified, after that performance it becomes impossible to provide an account of Emin's work without referring to this event.[21]

When Parker Bright and Pastiche Lumumba stand intentionally in front of Dana Schutz's *Open Casket* in order to prevent viewers from seeing the work, they also perform an act designed to prevent viewers from seeing or appreciating the work, without necessarily physically destroying that work. Part of their point is to suggest that Schutz's work does not deserve respect, in part because she has not respected Emmett Till's death or what it represents to the Black community. By standing in front of it, they criticize the tacit respect given by the museum to the work simply in its display, and suggest that the work and its artist do not deserve our respect. Such performances are powerful because they illustrate the power of events and actions to impact and affect how we think about such works. They are designed to contribute to an ongoing political dialogue about racism in America and to underscore the role that the arts play in that discussion. (See Clavel-Vázquez, this volume.)

In a similar vein, Mary Richardson's violent attack on the *Rokeby Venus* embodies two distinct acts of vandalism:[22] first, the straightforward physical destruction of the artwork, an act of vandalism that has since been repaired (and hence rendered invisible), and second, the act of vandalism itself—a performance, whose impact is no longer seen in the work of art itself, but whose meaning and significance is now embedded in the narrative and history of the work, a permanent connection now between *Rokeby Venus*, conceptions of feminism and the male gaze (we cannot unsee the male gaze after her actions, even after that work is repaired).[23] Like Pastiche and Lumumba, Richardson's act is also designed to challenge the respect we give to works that objectify women. While no longer visible in the works themselves, Pastiche, Lumumba, and Richardson's

---

[20] See Gover (2012) for an interesting discussion of this issue.

[21] This invisible vandalism does not offer us any alternative ways of respecting the work, unlike additive or replacement vandalism, where the vandalism is done in ways to highlight new and different ways of respecting the work. Instead, it is simply a straightforward case of vandalism.

[22] A. W. Eaton (2012) offers an excellent analysis of "the problem of the female nude." See also Mullin, this volume.

[23] Notice an art historian's art criticism does not qualify as a form of nonphysical vandalism, because their writing does not involve any performance or actions done *to* or *on* the artwork. That's not to say that art critics' words don't profoundly shape how we see and think about art; simply that in so doing, they are not thereby engaging in invisible vandalism.

acts have all profoundly changed the narrative of these artworks in ways that challenge the respect accorded to them.

Altering a work's nonphysical properties can be done in lots of different ways—using virtual technology, or by changing its relational properties. The relational features can vary—how the work relates to its author (denouncing authorship), its site (altering the site for a site-specific work), and its history (causing the work to be permanently related; certain acts or performances that are intended to attack or alter its identity).

SPECIAL CASES OF VANDALISM: STREET ART AND GRAFFITI

So far, we have considered cases of artwork vandalism that we praise and admire. How should we think about tagging, graffiti, and street art? These works seem to awkwardly straddle the divide between the destruction of physical materials that we find morally objectionable, and the creative vandalism that we value. How we think about tagging, graffiti, and street art depends largely on the results. Some vandals are simply engaging in destructive acts that leave nothing but destruction behind; their works are simply run-of-the-mill destructive vandalism of the kind that we disapprove of. But many graffiti and street artists go beyond intentionally destroying physical materials.

Some graffiti and street artists create art by destroying their environment and the materials of the environment. When they create art as a result of their destruction, they are engaging in replacement vandalism—replacing what is destroyed with art. Vhils (Alexandre Manuel Dias Farto) destroys the sides of large buildings in order to create beautiful sculptural portraits of the local inhabitants. Brandalists intentionally vandalize advertisements in order to create art that raises awareness about consumer issues (challenging fast fashion ethics, objecting to photoshopping, promoting body positivity). Their destructive acts are rendered permissible, in part because they leave us with art to appreciate, just like the artists considered above. Moving to the streets does not change the nature of the act, though moving to the streets certainly complicates the discussion.

Many graffiti artists and taggers do not intentionally destroy property, either. Some, in fact, seek to repair and remediate public and private property that has been all but abandoned, calling attention to their fate. Of course, this officially qualifies as vandalism and even illegal vandalism, since it's altering someone else's property. But it's also improvement vandalism, because this vandalism uses vandalism to improve the property. Jan Voormann's LEGO street art creates art out of the damaged streetscapes that remain unrepaired. Juliana Santacruz Herrera repairs potholes with crocheted infill, taking the traditionally domestic craft into the streets. Guerilla gardeners bomb abandoned lands with wildflowers, plant out those strips between the street and the sidewalk with vegetables, and generally maintain public green spaces that often fall prey to the tragedy of the commons. Strictly speaking, these artists are intentionally damaging existing property. However, the art they make is designed to highlight that what already exists is so damaged that the street artists' further "damage" qualifies as an improvement over what is already there—a tacit indictment of the government's failure to maintain its public spaces. Improvement vandalism is a kind of replacement vandalism (specific to property, rather than artworks) that seeks to replace damaged property with something better. In these cases, the assumption that vandalism is disrespectful to the objects being damaged is overturned—improvement vandalism underscores the lack of respect accorded to the spaces, and the vandals themselves are, through their improvements, seeking to show their respect, and inviting others to do so as well.

Sometimes artists vandalize existing street art, graffiti, or tags by vandalizing them with other (better) street art, graffiti, or tags. Unlike in the museum contexts, replacement vandalism is the norm in the streets. Because the art is already illegal, replacing it with further illegal art is fair game. There are tacit social norms and rules of etiquette within the graffiti and street art community that govern the conditions under which it is socially acceptable to overwrite one work with another. Usually these concern the fame, skill or type of work being made, which again track the different kinds of respect we accord to different kinds of works and different levels of artistry and skill within the street art community. Sometimes tagging over is done in an attempt to establish respect. King Robbo and Banksy have famously engaged in dialogues through tagging over their works, notorious cases of vindictive replacement vandalism, replacing each other's works with one of their own in an extended game of one-upmanship.[24] These games are elaborate claims to respect.

More interesting are the cases where street artists engage in additive vandalism. Andy Leek, for example, praises existing street art by writing "good work" or "great job" below an existing work and adding a gold star, harking back to the kind and supportive words of primary school teachers on children's schoolwork.[25] This work of art builds on an existing work, to which his addition assigns praise. Many well-intentioned grammarians have engaged in additive vandalism, correcting the grammar of existing works; indeed there are a surprising number of grammar vigilantes, including Acción Ortográfica Quito (in Ecuador);[26] the self-proclaimed Apostrophiser (in Bristol, United Kingdom);[27] and the Tutor Company, which advertises its grammatical skills by editing graffiti (in the United Kingdom).[28]

A complex case of additive vandalism is Mobstr's works of vandalism involving an engagement with the council workers charged with painting over his works. In his series

[24] See Ben Davis, "King Robbo, Banksy's Rival, Has Died," Artnet, August 1, 2014, https://news.artnet.com/market/king-robbo-banksys-rival-has-died-71411 for an indicative account of the controversy.

[25] See Andy Leek, "Gold Start Project," http://www.andy-leek.com/gold-star/ (accessed May 6, 2021).

[26] Follow them on twitter at https://twitter.com/AccionOQ (accessed May 6, 2021).

[27] See Steven Morris, " 'Banksy of Punctuation' Puts a Full Stop to Bad Grammar in Bristol," April 3, 2017, https://www.theguardian.com/education/2017/apr/03/banksy-of-punctuation-puts-full-stop-bad-grammar-bristol.

[28] Zak Stone, "Ur Mom: Correcting the Grammar of Graffiti," March 26, 2013, https://www.fastcompany.com/2681661/ur-mom-correcting-the-grammar-of-graffiti.

"Shades of Grey," he appropriates the council paint used to cover his art as a backdrop to his existing work, or to future work. In this work, he vandalizes a wall whose previous vandalism has been overpainted in different shades of grey paint.[29] Writing "is this shade of grey acceptable?," he appropriates the background of grey paint as part of his own work. When it is overpainted with another shade of grey, he later returns to the site, to reclaim the most recent iteration of council paint as his own, to ask the question again (using, of course, a different shade of grey spray paint for his own lettering). One might be tempted to treat this as a case of improvement vandalism (the point of his work, after all, is to challenge the assumption that the council's ugly shades of grey are preferable to the existing graffiti on a wall). But the irony of Mobstr's work is better appreciated when we treat it as a case of additive vandalism: Mobstr appropriates the existing council paint jobs as the background art for his lettering. Additive vandalism best explains the humor of the graffiti, which unwittingly forces the council's painting to be treated as vandalism on a par with the vandalism it is designed to cover up.

A special case that arises exclusively in the area of street art and graffiti concerns whether one can vandalize a work of street art or graffiti, which itself is a work of vandalism. I think the answer is yes. Destroying a work of art in the street is still vandalism. When the city council paints over a work of street art, that qualifies as a case of destructive vandalism, since the council is destroying an existing work of art, leaving nothing in its place. In contrast, many street artists enjoy replacing an existing work with one of their own or adding to an existing work to create a new one. Anytime a street artist or graffiti artist paints over an existing work but leaves a new work in its place, they are engaging in replacement vandalism or in additive vandalism, just like regular artists.

CONCLUSION

Vandalism, understood as ordinary, run-of-the-mill destruction of physical materials is rarely ever permissible. In this chapter, we have considered many cases of vandalism that seek to exploit vandalism to create something better, whether that's a better environment or a better artwork. In these cases of creative vandalism, vandalism is permissible, because of the particular goals and functions to which vandalism aspires. We sanction creative vandalism, because we value the creation of new (and sometimes better) art. Works of replacement, additive and invisible vandalism all depend on their success to generate new works. These artworks made from vandalism are tacitly sanctioned by the artworld and its ordinary viewers, when they contribute to the art historical conversation—whether that's to challenge the artworld norms, to subvert art historical assumptions or challenge mainstream views about art. However, such artworks'

---

[29] See "Is This Shade of Grey Acceptable?", Mobstr, https://www.mobstr.org/acceptable-shade-of-grey (accessed May 6, 2021).

conversational power can extend beyond the museum walls. More recently, vandalism within the streets and public monuments have been used to engage in forms of social and political protest.[30] These acts of protest vandalism contribute to the conversations about art, politics and history.

If we take any lessons away from these more inspirational forms of creative vandalism, it is that destruction is neither necessary nor sufficient for vandalism, that vandalism is morally permissible when it is done in productive ways, and that many great works of art are the result of great acts of vandalism.

See also: Gover, Bicknell et al., Willard, Clavel-Vázquez, this volume

REFERENCES

Danto, Arthur. 1964. "The Artworld." *Journal of Philosophy* 61(19): 571–584.

Dixon, Daisy. "Artistic (Counter) Speech." The Journal of Aesthetics and Art Criticism, Volume 80, Issue 4, Fall 2022: 409–419.

Eaton, A. W. 2012. "What's Wrong with the (Female) Nude? A Feminist Perspective on Artand Pornography." In *Art and Pornography: Philosophical Essays*, edited by H. Maesand J. Levinson, 277–308. Oxford: Oxford University Press.

Fenner, David. 2006. "Why Modifying (Some) Works of Art is Wrong." *American Philosophical Quarterly* 43, no. 4: 329–341.

Fisher, John. 1974. "Destruction as a Mode of Creation." *Journal of Aesthetic Education* 8, no. 2: 57–64.

Gover, K. 2012. "Christoph Büchel v. Mass MoCA: A Tilted Arc for the Twenty-First Century." *Journal of Aesthetic Education* 46, no. 1: 46–58.

Hein, Hilde. 1996. "What Is Public Art? Time, Place, and Meaning." *Journal of Aestheticsand Art Criticism* 54, no. 1: 1–7.

Horowitz, Gregg M. 1996. "Public Art/Public Space: The Spectacle of the Tilted ArcControversy." *Journal of Aesthetics and Art Criticism* 54, no. 1: 8–14.

Kelly, Michael. 1996. "Public Art Controversy: The Serra and Lin Cases." *Journal ofAesthetics and Art Criticism* 54, no. 1: 15–22.

Lai, Ten-Herng. 2020. "Political Vandalism as Counter-Speech: A Defense of Defacing and Destroying Tainted Monuments." *European Journal of Philosophy* 28, no. 3: 602–616.

Lim, Chong-Ming. 2020. "Vandalizing Tainted Commemorations" *Philosophy and Public Affairs* 48, no. 2: 185–216.

Thompson, Erin. 2013. "Destruction of Art." In *The Oxford Encyclopedia of Aesthetics*, 2nd ed. Oxford: Oxford University Press.

van Camp, Julie. 2011. "Yes, But Is It Vandalism? Graffiti, Conceptual Criminals, Artists and Free Speech." *Aesthetic Pathways* 1, no. 2: 3–12.

Young, James. 1989. "Destroying Works of Art." *Journal of Aesthetics and Art Criticism* 47, no. 4: 367–373.

---

[30] See Bicknell et al., Willard, this volume.

CHAPTER 41

··

CENSORSHIP AND SELECTIVE SUPPORT FOR THE ARTS

··

BRIAN SOUCEK

INTRODUCTION

IF some works of art are morally better than others, or might either improve or harm the character of those who engage with them, the government may want to regulate works that are sufficiently immoral or harmful. Governments unwilling to go that far might instead want to support works they deem especially moral or character-building. Individuals too may decide to avoid some works of art and support others; when enough of them do so, their effect on the market or culture might be as great as direct government intervention would have been.

All of these interventions have, at times, been labeled "censorship." Narrowly defined, censorship refers to government officials banning the creation or distribution of expression—for our purposes here, of works of art. Book III of Plato's *Republic* provides a paradigmatic example: if a poet arrives, he should be honored as "wonderful and pleasing" but promptly sent away, for "it isn't lawful for there to be" someone like him in Plato's ideal city. (See Destrée, this volume.) Plato's poet is not the only one who raises the cry of censorship, however. Artists who have been denied government funding from the National Endowment for the Arts in the United States have claimed to be victims of censorship, as have authors and musicians who have been boycotted by consumer groups or dropped by their publishers.

This chapter takes these issues in turn, focusing on contemporary censorship of the arts in the United States. The sections that follow look first at government regulation, prohibition, and compulsion of private artistic expression; then, selective government support for the arts through contracts, grants, tax exemptions, and other means; and finally, restrictions private parties place on the arts, often making use of legal means (like copyright) that the state provides them.

Throughout, the focus here is on one particular type of censorship (if that is the right word for all the examples that follow): that based on moral judgments about art. To be sure, censorship on moral grounds is hardly the only kind there is. Expression gets censored for reasons of national security; for political reasons, as when a regime in power stifles dissent; for pragmatic reasons or reasons of efficiency or convenience, for example when evidence in court would distract or prejudice the jury, or an unnecessary comment would cause a meeting to drag on; and there are even, importantly, aesthetic arguments for censorship (Shusterman 1984). Most editing that writers receive probably falls within this last category. Censorship can also have more than one basis. Just think of the destruction of Richard Serra's *Tilted Arc*, which may have been torn down from the Federal Plaza in Manhattan because locals found it ugly, because it made it harder to get to the subway, or because it put the values of the artworld over those of the general public (Danto 2003)—aesthetic, pragmatic, and moral motivations, respectively.

This chapter is focused solely on limits placed on art—whether by direct restriction or a failure to receive support, and whether by government or by private actors aided by law—based on moral judgments. The "if" with which this chapter began is a hotly contested one—the subject, in fact, of most of this *Handbook*. To decide *if* artworks, or certain kinds of artworks, can or should be morally judged, or *if* the various arts can affect our own morality—these are questions for the rest of the book. The question here is: What in law, if anything, should follow from their answers?

Government Limits on the Arts

Throughout history and around the globe, government restrictions on writing, images, and music have been more the rule than the exception (Berkowitz 2021). In the United States, however, at least for the last century, the First Amendment to the US Constitution ("Congress shall make no law . . . abridging the freedom of speech") has been interpreted broadly to apply to all government action, not just laws made at the federal level by Congress, and not just to "speech," but to many other forms of artistic expression as well.

The US Supreme Court has described the "painting of Jackson Pollock, music of Arnold Schoenberg, [and] Jabberwocky verse of Lewis Carroll" as "unquestionably shielded" under the First Amendment (Hurley v. Irish-American Gay, Lesbian and Bisexual Group of Boston, 515 U.S. 557, 569 (1995)). But the Court has never explained why that should be so, or whether protection for the arts should be the same as, greater than, or perhaps less than other, nonartistic expression like newspaper articles, philosophy lectures, or campaign speeches. One place where these questions arise is in the law of obscenity—a type of expression that the First Amendment does not cover, and which state actors can thus censor at will. In addition to obscenity, this section will also discuss two less widely recognized areas where direct governmental censorship of the arts may still occur: through the demands that antidiscrimination law places on artists in the marketplace, and through various historic preservation laws that shape the possibilities of our lived environment.

Constitutional Protection for the Arts

Constitutional protection for artistic expression has always been something of a puzzle for theorists. Many, including the Supreme Court, find it unquestionably to be the case that artworks should be protected. This may be because of the way art and artists are generally valued; because of widespread (if often unexamined) beliefs about the autonomy of art and the freedom of artists from rules and conventions; or perhaps just in reaction to the fact that art has so long been subjected to government control. (One Supreme Court case about regulations on the volume of concerts in New York's Central Park notes that "from Plato's discourse in the Republic to the totalitarian state in our own times, rulers have known [music's] capacity to appeal to the intellect and to the emotions, and have censored musical compositions to serve the needs of the state" (Ward v. Rock Against Racism, 491 U.S. 781, 790 (1989).) Considerations like these might suggest that the arts merit even greater protection than ordinary expression.

But the standard rationales for protecting the freedom of speech apply awkwardly to many of the arts, especially those with nonrepresentational content (Tushnet, Chen, and Blocher 2017). It is not obvious how abstract art contributes to the marketplace of ideas or to democratic self-governance—two of the leading rationales for free speech. A third common rationale, that free speech facilitates self-realization, is far better at explaining why the arts should be protected, but it likely proves too much, as so many other nonartistic activities—from stamp collecting to pickleball playing—surely promote self-realization too, but without constitutional protection.

The Supreme Court's claim that painting, music, and verse are protected suggests the possibility that what is protected is not "art" as such, but what the Court has referred to as traditional mediums of expression. These mediums might be largely artistic (like painting), nonartistic (like billboards and handbills), or mixed (like photography and dance). Protecting mediums from government regulation has two consequences (Soucek 2021, 719–740). First, artistic and nonartistic expression get treated on par with each other. The traditional mediums of expression are generally protected because their dangers are mainly expressive ones, and the response to immoral or offensive or misleading speech is thought to be more and better speech, not limitations on expression. But second, medium-based protections mean that the government can treat mediums differently if their materiality tends to present different nonexpressive dangers. Bad architecture is dangerous in a way that bad poetry is not, and the law should be able to reflect that. So while mediums like books and music and painting that consist of little but expression will go largely unregulated, the nonexpressive components of arts like theater and architecture—the working conditions of actors, for example, and the stability of buildings and their effects on neighbors—mean that greater legal regulation may be needed, and permitted. Is it censorship when an architect can't build as high as she wants or if method actors aren't allowed to do drugs onstage? Perhaps not, but what if certain colors or architectural styles are not permitted by a city's zoning laws, or race discrimination is prohibited when hiring actors, just as it is when hiring ushers? Regulating the material aspects of a medium can be problematic if the medium is the message, and messages are not to be censored. This is not just a problem for the arts, however. It arises whenever expression and conduct intermingle, as when protesters express their views of the war by burning their draft cards. The law can prohibit arson or public fires; can it thus prohibit draft card burning?

The way certain expression achieves its effects can sometimes justify regulation. Take subliminal messages in film, television, and music. The few courts that have considered the issue—most famously in regard to a Judas Priest album said to cause a teenager's suicide—have said that subliminal messages are not covered by the First Amendment. But insofar as this is because subliminal messages surreptitiously influence us against our will, this argument seems little different than Plato's justification for censoring music and poetry. *How* various mediums move us might end up determining what protections they are or should be given.

Obscenity

Considerations of this sort perhaps motivate what is otherwise an inexplicable, anachronistic exception in American free speech law: its approval of censorship when it comes to obscenity. Current US doctrine, from the 1973 case *Miller v. California*, holds that depictions or descriptions of sexual activity can be censored if, taken as a whole, the works "appeal to the prurient interest in sex," "portray sexual conduct in a patently offensive way," and "do not have serious literary, artistic, political, or scientific value" (413 U.S. 15, 24 (1973)).

This doctrine is exceptional in allowing what seem like purely moral considerations to permit a prohibition on expression. One explanation on offer is that obscenity law, by exempting anything with communicative value, really just targets tools for titillation, not anything properly described as speech (Schauer 1979). Obscenity may have an effect, but it is not a communicative one.

Making this distinction, however, puts courts in the delicate position of having to decide whether works, taken as a whole, have "serious artistic value." And this despite Oliver Wendell Holmes's admonition, which courts never tire of repeating, that "it would be a dangerous undertaking for persons trained only to the law to constitute themselves final judges of the worth of pictorial illustrations" (Bleistein v. Donaldson Lithographing Co., 188 U.S. 239, 251 (1903); Soucek 2017). Much turns on these evaluations: works seen as lacking artistic value and deemed obscene can be destroyed; those who create or distribute them can be jailed. This is the one area where censorship in its most old-fashioned form is still permitted under US law.

Although one Justice famously said of judging obscenity that "I know it when I see it," the Supreme Court has actually interpreted the serious artistic value test in *Miller* as an objective one. Although prurience and offensiveness are to be judged by a jury applying contemporary community standards, a work's artistic value, the Court says, does not "vary from community to community based on the degree of local acceptance it has won" (Pope v. Illinois, 481 U.S. 497, 500 (1987). The *Miller* test asks not what an ordinary community member would think of an artwork's value, but what value a reasonable person would find in a work, taken as a whole—presumably after making an ontological judgment about what constitutes "a work": the story or the whole magazine, the exhibit or the individual photographs within in? Prominent obscenity prosecutions against *Penthouse* magazine and presenters of a Robert Mapplethorpe exhibit have turned on precisely these judgments. (See Eaton, this volume.)

Compelled Speech: Censoring Silence?

Censorship is generally considered a restriction on expression. But compelled speech too can operate as a restriction, at least when it prevents the compelled speaker from expressing contrary views. Those forced to express the government's message, including through their art, may not then be able to express their own beliefs without contradicting themselves. At the very least, their opportunity for expressive silence on a particular issue has been taken away—"censored" by the state.

This is the situation alleged in a spate of recent cases pitting artistic and religious freedom against nondiscrimination laws, particularly those protecting LGBTQ customers' access to the marketplace. In states where businesses are legally required to serve customers regardless of their sexual orientation, photographers, calligraphers, florists, website designers, and self-described cake artists have been punished for refusing to provide their artistic goods and services to same-sex couples getting married. These refusals are based not just on religious objections, but also on concerns about being made to endorse same-sex marriage through their art.

In some cases endorsement is said to come directly from the text written on an invitation, program, or cake. Other times the endorsement is said to come from, say, the form and feel of the photographs, or simply the use of a person's floral arrangements or cake within the celebration. The objection in these cases is that the maker's art will come to have immoral content, or (a different argument) be put to an immoral use with the artist's knowing complicity.

The wedding vendor cases raise a slew of difficult aesthetic questions, in addition to legal and moral ones. Does anything turn on whether the goods being made and sold properly count as art (Soucek 2021, 715–718, 747–750)? Should artists have any special ability, more than other vendors, to control what happens to the works they produce? (This is also the issue at stake in debates over so-called moral rights of artists (Gover 2018; see also Gover, this volume).) To what extent can subsequent use change their works' meaning—and potentially their moral character? Is the message expressed in words or through formal choices in commercially sold wedding cakes, photographs, movies, and floral designs properly ascribed to their creators, as opposed to those who purchase or commission them or put them to use in an expressive context like a wedding? If not, then perhaps the issue of censorship falls away, for artists actually haven't been forced to communicate messages of their own; they can speak out elsewhere as they wish without hypocrisy.

Historic Preservation

A similar dynamic arises in the context of historic preservation laws—laws that prevent the destruction of designated historic buildings, limit the choices of owners who want to renovate or expand their protected property, and sometimes regulate the architectural character of entire neighborhoods. When these laws apply, architectural expression is to a certain extent compelled, and the possibility of counter expression is thereby limited. Brutalist architects in Colonial Williamsburg will find themselves censored, and in the paradigmatic way: through direct government regulation of private expression.

Historic preservation limits on architectural expression differ, however, from other traditional censorship (like obscenity prosecutions, book burning, etc.) in at least two ways.

First, architecture may perhaps justify regulation to an extent that books and pictures and operas do not. One reason has already been mentioned: the dangers of bad architecture are importantly different than those of bad poetry. That is why building codes are far more common, and widely accepted, than poetry codes. But even beyond regulations needed to protect physical safety and environmental concerns, greater regulation of architecture may also be justified by the fact that it is harder to avoid bad architecture than bad poetry. The former forces itself on often captive audiences—neighbors and passersby—in a way that the latter rarely does. This provides a reason to regulate architecture's expressive elements more thoroughly than poetic expression.

Second, even if this first point is true, it may seem less plausible that expressive constraints on architecture, compared to those on other arts, should be rooted in moral concerns—as opposed to aesthetic or epistemic concerns, like protecting distinguished structures and providing access to history. And yet even preservation for history's sake requires morally freighted decisions about what histories are most worth preserving. Are historic preservation measures telling the stories just of history's "winners"? Are we preserving the history of the poor, of immigrants or native peoples or minority communities that may or may not still be present in the area? How are we balancing the desires of tourists with the needs of the present community? These are moral and political decisions that communicate values and can foster or destroy community—effects that modern historic preservation theory and practice count among their primary considerations (Rose 1981).

The moral stakes of preservation have become especially palpable in recent fights over public monuments, especially Confederate memorials in the American South. (See Bicknell et al., this volume.) There are almost two thousand monuments to the Confederacy across the United States, and state laws in a number of states prohibit their removal. That means that cities, counties, and public universities that morally object to maintaining statues and other monuments that valorize white supremacy cannot remove them from their property, or often even rededicate or otherwise alter them, at least without the state's permission. The following section will discuss how the government often expresses its own messages through the arts—and how its expression can potentially have a censoring effect by distorting, silencing, or crowding out expression by others. The problem here is more direct: these state laws flatly prohibit an important form of local dissent. The expressive act of tearing down or altering public monuments is barred, and given the scarcity of prominent public space, opportunities for local communities to express new messages is also thereby limited.

Since most of these monuments date from decades after the Civil War and few are artistically distinguished, it is clear that preservation laws in these states are not motivated by historic or aesthetic considerations. The fights here are over politics and morals, and for one side, censorship is among its weapons in the fight.

SELECTIVE GOVERNMENTAL SUPPORT FOR THE ARTS

Few would call it censorship if a public high school were to give an annual prize for the student artwork that best promotes social justice. Even fewer would call it censorship if the principal of the high school wrote a poem encouraging students to promote social justice, or if the high school itself were named after a social justice hero like Martin Luther King Jr. and featured a sculpture of its namesake outside the schoolhouse. If, however, the high school's art show included every senior's painting but one, which the school refused to exhibit because it was deemed insufficiently committed to social justice, cries of censorship would surely follow. And the cries would grow even louder if that student were suspended from riding the school bus for a while because the principal disliked her art.

Each of these examples involve selective subsidies for the arts: the prize money, the principal's salary, the commissioned statue of King, the exhibition space for the seniors' show, even the bus bringing students to (among other things) their arts classes. When it comes to the First Amendment, though—and surely to our intuitions as well—these selective subsidies are arrayed along a spectrum (Soucek 2017, 458–466), with the so-called government speech of the school and its principal at one end, the prize not much more problematic, and the student's exclusion from the show and bus down on the other, more worrisome end—seemingly closer to the examples from the last section, where the government directly banned certain art instead of simply refusing to subsidize it. Notice, however, that in commissioning the statue of King, the school was not required to spend equal money memorializing a prominent racist, so some other sculptor was denied a commission. Meanwhile, the prize money that was *denied* to every student but the winner of the contest may have been far more than what the suspended student spent on taxis after being kicked off the bus. What, then, makes the denial of subsidy seem like a regulation on speech in the last of these examples but not the others? This is the question to be addressed later in the chapter. Before that, however, are discussions of the somewhat less problematic examples: government art-making and commissioning of the arts and competitive funding, like that awarded by the National Endowment for the Arts. In each, subsidies are awarded, or not, based in part on moral considerations, whether in addition to or perhaps as a component of the aesthetic considerations that are also required.

Government Art-Making

No one thinks the government has to put up a monument to fascism every time it erects a monument to democracy, just to remain "viewpoint neutral." (This, in fact, is one of the reasons the memorials to the Confederacy in the United States are so egregiously racist. Absent a desire to express enduring support for white supremacy, there is no compulsion that states honor traitors in that way.) The First Amendment does not govern what the government itself says, as opposed to what the government allows or forces others to say. After all, the people elect leaders to take positions and express (and presumably act on) particular views, including through art-making.

Erecting monuments and memorials is one important way the government speaks on behalf of the community it represents. In Arthur Danto's words, public art isn't just art that is placed somewhere public; works of truly public art are those in which "the public has invested . . . its feelings, beliefs and values. They in effect *are* the public in the medium of art" (Danto 1985). Government architecture plays a similar role. In the last month of his presidency, Donald Trump issued an executive order making "classical architecture . . . the preferred and default architecture for Federal buildings." (See Willard, this volume.) Government builders were to notify the president before approving any "Brutalist or Deconstructivist architecture," explaining in detail "whether such design is as beautiful and reflective of the dignity, enterprise, vigor, and stability of the American system of self-government as alternative designs of comparable cost." The order justified these requirements by arguing that America's founders wanted public buildings that would "inspire the American people and encourage civic virtue." Visually connecting government buildings to antiquity would remind "citizens not only of their rights but also their responsibilities in maintaining and perpetuating [their government's] institutions." President Biden revoked Trump's order just five weeks into his presidency, highlighting how partisan public architecture can become, given its perceived capacity not only to convey messages, but to affect the virtue of a people.

Less clear is whether the government, in building as it chooses, engages in anything that can properly be called censorship. Was the Trump administration attempting to *censor* Brutalist architecture? Given that Brutalists remained free to build in their favored style, just not with federal contracts, the answer is probably no. That said, censorship worries may arise when the government's artistic expression sends messages of inequality, suggesting that some voices are more welcome, or more likely to be heard, than others (Brettschneider 2012). Consider a cross or Confederate flag placed atop city hall. Jewish or Black residents may (justifiably) feel less represented in that town, less willing to petition or participate in its government, even less likely to choose to live there. At the same time, more inclusive messages can also present challenges. The problem of representing neutral justice in courthouses—the standard iconography of a blindfolded woman having become less effective once actual women were allowed to participate in courts—is so daunting that US courts, which have commissioned a staggering amount of art in recent years, have largely turned to abstraction (Resnik and Curtis 2011).

Arts Grants and Other Competitive Funding

In addition to commissioning artists to express its message, the government also sometimes pays artists to engage in expression of their own. This gave rise to the most prominent controversy over censorship of the arts in recent US history: the fight in the 1980s and 1990s over funding by the National Endowment for the Arts (NEA). Responding to grants used to support Robert Mapplethorpe's sadomasochistic and homoerotic photography, Andres Serrano's *Piss Christ* (depicting a crucifix in urine), and other works it deemed morally objectionable, Congress voted in 1989 to prohibit funding for work that "may be considered obscene, including but not limited to, depictions of sadomasochism, homoeroticism, the sexual exploitation of children, or individuals engaged in sex acts" (Cole 2014). The following year, Congress established a new general standard for NEA grantmaking: "Artistic excellence and artistic merit are the criteria by which applications are judged, taking into consideration general standards of decency and respect for the diverse beliefs and values of the American public" (20 U. S. C. § 954(d)(1)). Denied a grant under the new criteria, Karen Finley and other performance artists sued, claiming that the standards were vague and viewpoint discriminatory. The eight years of litigation that ensued raised (at least) two philosophically interesting questions.

First, the new statutory requirement forced courts to ask whether, in Justice Scalia's words, "decency and respect are elements of what Congress regards as artistic excellence and merit, or [whether] decency and respect are factors to be taken into account in addition to artistic excellence and merit" (National Endowment for the Arts v. Finley, 524 U.S. 569, 591 (1998)). Most of the judges who considered the question chose the first option, with some adding the qualification that moral considerations would presumably be irrelevant to evaluating, say, symphonies. Does this mean that Congress in 1990 officially endorsed moderate moralism—the belief that, within some genres but not others, an artwork's moral value contributes to its artistic value (Soucek 2017, 393–394; Carroll, this volume)? And if so, is this itself a form of censorship, not just against individual works deemed immoral, but also against autonomists and immoralists and others who would presumably want their taxpayer dollars supporting a different set of works?

A second question: Do selective subsidies that benefit bluegrass music rather than Mapplethorpe, or moderate moralism at the expense of its philosophical rivals, count as viewpoint discrimination—which is roughly to say, as censorship? This was the primary question courts were asked to decide in *National Endowment for the Arts v. Finley*, and a fractured Supreme Court said no. Though it allowed that "a more pressing constitutional question would arise if Government funding resulted in the imposition of a disproportionate burden calculated to drive certain ideas or viewpoints from the marketplace" (*Finley*, 524 U.S. at 587), the Court found that the NEA was simply choosing to fund one thing rather than another, employing the kind of judgment that selective arts funding, by its very nature, requires. For liberals like Bruce Ackerman (1999), the selectivity was the problem: "The neutralist spirit of modern American liberalism strives to prevent either side in the ongoing culture war from using the state's coercive powers of taxation as a weapon in the struggle for our souls," Ackerman wrote at the time. On the other side, Justice Scalia saw no problem at all with letting they who pay the piper call the tune; voters who preferred a different tune, Scalia thought, should put their energy into winning elections.

Finley's not fully principled distinctions and sometimes tortured reading of the law make it an unsatisfying opinion, but its confusions and hedging might be the very thing that helped diffuse the culture wars being fought there. The opinion neither called for the end of arts funding nor gave funders free license to censor. So even after *Finley*, the question remained: Can denials of funding ever run afoul of the Constitution?

Nonsubsidy as Punishment

For an ongoing case that suggests the answer is yes, we need only look to the moral censorship enshrined in the Paycheck Protection Program (PPP). Part of the largest stimulus bill in American history, passed in response to the COVID-19 pandemic in March 2020, the PPP provided almost $1 trillion to small businesses to help them continue paying their employees and other costs during the pandemic. Excluded, however, were businesses that present "live or recorded performances of a prurient sexual nature" or "depictions or displays of a prurient sexual nature" (Soucek 2020). Strip clubs and adult movie theaters and bookstores were thus among the only small businesses denied this financial lifeline, all because the Small Business Administration decided that giving subsidies to these sorts of businesses was not in "the public interest"—a decidedly moral judgment against certain types of dance, movies, and books.

In lawsuits across the country, the government has defended its exclusion by invoking *Finley*, claiming that to deny someone a subsidy is not to censor them. The government wasn't shutting these businesses down, it argues; it was just refusing to pay their bills. (Query whether that distinction works in a pandemic world where no or few other sources of funding may have been available.) The adult business exclusion from the PPP calls for a more nuanced analysis than this. Two factors seem to be relevant for deciding when to treat nonfunding as punishment, discrimination, or censorship.

First is a matter of baselines. We need to ask: Is getting the subsidy the exception, as it is with competitive NEA grants, or the general rule—as in the PPP, which made all small businesses eligible *except* for a few listed categories? This is the intuition behind the school examples with which this section began. To give one student a prize is not to discriminate against or censor the others. But to exclude one student from a show, or a bus, made available to the rest of the class—that smacks of punishment, even if the show and bus are subsidies or benefits that the school district voluntarily provides.

Of course there will be hard cases in the middle. Take the sales tax exemptions commonly offered for tickets to see live "dramatic, choreographic or musical performances" (New York State) or "live performance[s] in any of the disciplines which are commonly regarded as part of the fine arts" (Chicago)—both of which have been interpreted to exclude pole dancing in strip clubs (Soucek 2021, 703–706). Do these tax schemes single out strip clubs for moral punishment, or are they just run-of-the-mill funding decisions to support some industries (like ballet and soybean farms) but not others (strip clubs and walnut growers)? Probably the latter, but that doesn't make these decisions any less important: some believe that the federal cabaret taxes during World War II spurred the growth of bebop (which was exempt) at the expense of big band jazz, which was taxed almost to death (Soucek 2021, 704).

A second factor to consider looks to the basis for the selection (or exclusion) and asks how relevant it is to the subsidy program's overall purpose. Had the NEA decided to start funding only Republicans, courts would have quickly and rightly struck that policy down. (A tougher question: What if the NEA refused to fund abstract expressionists or music for the banjo?) One problem with the PPP's exclusion of adult businesses is that the moral judgments motivating it are irrelevant to the PPP's legislative purpose: keeping small businesses and their employees afloat during the pandemic.

Here though the problem is that it is often possible just to redescribe the legislative purpose of some funding program to make the exclusion no longer irrelevant. (Is this what Congress did by adopting moderate moralism?) A good example comes from recent lawsuits in the United States over trademark protections. Until the Supreme Court stepped in, federal trademark law denied registration for marks that were scandalous, immoral, or disparaging. (The first major case on the subject was brought by the band "The Slants," whose name some saw as disparaging to Asian Americans.) To deny trademark registration is not to prevent the applicant from using their name or design; they just aren't given the same protections from potential infringers. So trademark law at least arguably operates like a subsidy—and an especially important one for the arts, as trademark affects the title of movies and books, the names of bands, and what can be depicted in paintings, movies, and video games. If the purpose of a trademark is just to prevent consumer confusion, the morality bars are irrelevant; but if its purpose is somehow also to elevate the tone of commerce, or to promote equality within the commercial sphere, then the bars become more germane.

As these examples show, moral judgments of the arts occur in areas of government—from the Trademark Office and Small Business Administration to state and local tax boards—where artists, art critics, and aestheticians seldom venture.

NONGOVERNMENTAL CENSORSHIP OF THE ARTS

So far we have seen the government directly restricting artistic expression and the government funding some artistic expression in ways that may limit or discourage art-making that goes unfunded.

Government actions aren't the only limits on art-making, though. Surely as or more important are the gatekeepers of the art world: the publishers, gallerists, studio heads, and impresarios who exert such enormous influence on what art gets made and seen or heard. The moral judgments made by these gatekeepers are sometimes explicit. Just think of the rating systems applied to movies, television shows, and video games, or the parental advisory labels on some audio recordings. Each rating system is industry-run rather than governmentally managed. And yet each "voluntary" program arose either to stave off direct governmental regulation or, as with the parental advisories on television, at the explicit instruction of Congress, which in 1996 also mandated that new televisions have V-chips capable of screening out objectionable content.

Consumer boycotts and so-called cancel culture also operate to limit what (or whose) art gets made, distributed, assigned in schools, and generally deemed socially acceptable (Matthes 2021; see also Matthes, this volume). When publishers respond to consumer protests by canceling a contract or pulling a book from its catalogue, or when private internet platforms like Facebook decide to bar certain content, cries of censorship are heard, even though the decisions were made private companies rather than the government—just as private companies had made the decisions about what to publish and promote in the first place.

Referring to the decisions of private companies, made (perhaps) at the behest of private citizens, as "censorship" is complicated by the fact that those citizens and companies are expressing themselves through their protests and choices—and such expression is itself protected by the First Amendment. Those wanting to stop cancel culture are themselves seeking to limit expression.

It would be wrong, though, to think that the government cannot or does not affect in this dynamic. For one thing, as the philosopher and artist Adrian Piper (1996, 201) has argued, the government could always step in to counter private—especially corporate—funding decisions that tend to limit "recognition or representation of views that compete with or criticize the status quo." Turning the previous section's concerns about government funding of controversial political art on their head, Piper (1996, 203) argues that instead of shying away from such art in order to better represent public preferences or avoid backlash, democratic governments have a "particular obligation to support works of art that offer critical alternatives to prevailing power relations".

Further, it is crucial to note that nongovernmental acts of censorship, if that is the right word, are often made possible by government action—or government inaction.

An important example of the former—government action that allows private actors to limit others' art-making—involves copyright. (See Hick, this volume.) Copyright law gives artists (and nonartists, including the author of this piece and the makers of the software used to type it) rights over who can exhibit or perform their works or adapt their expression in derivative works. Under the fair use doctrine, transformative use of someone else's expression is sometimes allowed, especially if it will have little effect on the market for the first work. Unless this is shown, however, those holding copyright in the first work can invoke the intellectual property rights they are given under federal law to stop other, infringing artistic expression. The choice to do this may often be economically motivated, but copyright holders also frequently shut down others' expression because of moral judgments about the infringing use—especially if the copyright holder sees the use as violating the copyright holder's privacy or conflicting with their political or religious views (Gilden 2019).

Copyright law is an example of the government empowering private actors' choices about what art and other forms of expression to censor. But individuals' ability to censor each other can also hinge on government *inaction*. An important strand of feminist thought on the regulation of pornography suggests one way this might play out, with important effects on women's equality and sexual autonomy. (See Eaton, this volume.)

The standard claim about censorship and pornography focuses on government regulation of pornographic movies or literature—the kind of direct, state-imposed limit on private expression that was discussed in the first section of this chapter. But some feminists claim that silencing also occurs when the government does *not* regulate pornography: when pornography, allowed to proliferate, reduces women's capacity for effective communication. According to Catharine MacKinnon (1987) and Rae Langton (1993), pornography creates an environment where "when a woman says 'No,' her 'no' sometimes fails to count as an act of refusal: it fails to achieve the necessary recognition—what [J. L.] Austin would call 'uptake'—on the part of the hearer" (Langton 1998). Pornography, on this view, legitimates an expectation on the part of certain hearers that a woman's "no" doesn't really mean no. Stripping women of their power to communicate refusal in this way is an important type of silencing—we might say, of censorship. And it is made possible by the government's own refusal to censor the pornographic material that produces this silencing effect.

Conclusion

Throughout this chapter, charges of censorship have mostly come with scare quotes and question marks attached. Is "censorship" the right word, I keep asking, as we move from cases where governments burn books to those where the government just refuses some authors funding or tax exemptions, to cases where publishers decide not to publish something, whether based on their own judgment or because of some public outcry? When we get, finally, to the notion that the government's refusal to censor can have censorious effects, some might think that the term has lost its usefulness. Perhaps, as Frederick Schauer (1998) has argued, we are only keeping the term because, at least in the United States, claims about limitations on speech have so much more rhetorical and political force than claims about inequality.

Schauer's broader argument is that "all human behavior both constitutes and restricts our communicative possibilities" (1998, 149), and therefore no subset of human behavior can properly be described as "censorship." The term proves less descriptive than *ascriptive*: "a conclusion masquerading as an analytic device" (1998, 160).

Some worry that we just ascribe the term "censorship" to speech restrictions we don't agree with, while finding other ways to describe speech restrictions we like. Thus, veterans of the Moral Majority can now be heard crusading against cancel culture. Schauer offers a more principled variation on that claim. Perhaps we do, or should, refer to restrictions on expression as "censorship" not because of our views about the content but because of our qualms about who is imposing the restriction. An editor shortening a book is seldom called censor, whereas government redactors clearly are. Professors deciding what artworks to show in Art History 101 are said to employ their disciplinary expertise, protected by academic freedom, whereas donors or legislators angry about what universities are teaching their students are flirting with censorship. Librarians spend their days picking and choosing what books to include in their schools' collections, but when parents and members of the school board try to get books pulled, the First Amendment gets invoked, or should.

In the many examples canvased throughout the chapter, it is worth asking whether charges of censorship turn more on who is restricting artistic expression as opposed to what is being restricted. The terminological agnosticism that runs throughout this chapter is meant to maximize the number of examples of censorship, not least so we can see the many contexts in which moral judgments of artworks get made, and the many people responsible for making them. Deciding which should be called "censors" may itself be one of the most important moral judgments to get made in the arts.

See also: Bicknell et al., Willard, Eaton, Matthes, Hick, Gover, Carroll, this volume

REFERENCES

Ackerman, Bruce. 1999. "Should Opera Be Subsidized?" *Dissent* 46, no. 3: 89–91.

Berkowitz, Eric. 2021. *Dangerous Ideas*. Boston: Beacon Press.

Brettschneider, Corey. 2012. *When the State Speaks, What Should It Say?* Princeton, NJ: Princeton University Press.

Cole, David. 2014. "Law and Art: Government-Funded Art and the First Amendment." In *Encyclopedia of Aesthetics*, edited by Michael Kelly, 160–162. Oxford: Oxford University Press.

Danto, Arthur C. 1985. "Public Art and the General Will." *The Nation* 241, no. 9: 288–290.

Danto, Arthur C. 2003. "The Removal of Tilted Arc." *Artforum* 41, no. 8: 106.

Gilden, Andrew. 2019. "Copyright's Market Gibberish." *Washington Law Review* 94, no. 3: 1019–1083.

Gover, K. E. 2018. *Art and Authority*. Oxford: Oxford University Press.

Langton, Rae. 1993. "Speech Acts and Unspeakable Acts." *Philosophy and Public Affairs* 22, no. 4: 293–330.

Langton, Rae. 1998. "Subordination, Silence, and Pornography's Authority." In *Censorship and Silencing: Practices of Cultural Regulation*, edited by Robert C. Post, 261–283. Los Angeles: The Getty Research Institute.

MacKinnon, Catharine A. 1987. *Feminism Unmodified*. Cambridge, MA: Harvard University Press.

Matthes, Erich Hatala. 2021. *Drawing the Line: What to Do with the Work of Immoral Artists from Museums to the Movies*. Oxford: Oxford University Press.

Piper, Adrian. 1996. "Government Support for Unconventional Works of Art." In *Out of Order, Out of Sight*, vol. 2: 201–206. Cambridge, MA: MIT Press.

Resnik, Judith and Dennis Curtis. 2011. *Representing Justice: Invention, Controversy, and Rights in City-States and Democratic Courtrooms*. New Haven, CT: Yale University Press.

Rose, Carol M. 1981. "Preservation and Community: New Directions in the Law of Historic Preservation." *Stanford Law Review* 33, no. 3: 473–534.

Schauer, Frederick. 1979. "Speech and 'Speech'—Obscenity and 'Obscenity': An Exercise in the Interpretation of Constitutional Language." *Georgetown Law Journal* 67, no. 4: 899–933.

Schauer, Frederick. 1998. "The Ontology of Censorship." In *Censorship and Silencing: Practices of Cultural Regulation*, edited by Robert C. Post, 147–168. Los Angeles: The Getty Research Institute.

Shusterman, Richard. 1984. "Aesthetic Censorship: Censoring Art for Art's Sake." *Journal of Aesthetics and Art Criticism* 43, no. 2: 171–180.

Soucek, Brian. 2017. "Aesthetic Judgment in Law." *Alabama Law Review* 69, no. 2: 381–467.

Soucek, Brian. 2020. "Discriminatory Paycheck Protection." *California Law Review Online* 11 (July 2020): 319–338.

Soucek, Brian. 2021. "The Constitutional Irrelevance of Art." *North Carolina Law Review* 99, no. 3: 685–752.

Tushnet, Mark V., Alan K. Chen, and Joseph Blocher. 2017. *Free Speech Beyond Words: The Surprising Reach of the First Amendment*. New York: NYU Press.

CHAPTER 42

....

ART, RACE, AND RACISM

....

ADRIANA CLAVEL-VÁZQUEZ

INTRODUCTION

IN contemporary philosophical aesthetics, much of the discussion surrounding the connection between ethics and art has centered on the ethical value that artworks have in virtue of their manifested attitudes, that is, the attitudes they express toward represented events and characters.[1] While this approach opens interesting avenues of inquiry, it misses the fact that artworks are neither created nor appreciated in a sociohistorical vacuum. Artworks, artists, critics, and appreciators are part of cultural patterns, institutions, and communities. The relevant context to approach and evaluate art is not simply one related to art-historical facts, but one that takes into consideration the network of social, cultural, and political systems of which the artworld participates. Artworks' ethical import, therefore, must also be examined on account of their relation to their sociohistorical context. The aim of this chapter is to take up questions surrounding the role of artistic practices in the formation of racial identity and the sustainment and legitimization of racial projects. Therefore, my focus is on the ethical value of art from a systemic perspective:[2] on the way art interacts with other social systems in specific sociocultural contexts in virtue of how artworks shape and are shaped by processes of racialization.

While the aim of the chapter is to focus on the ethical value of artworks in virtue of the role they play in racial formation and racial projects, it is important to emphasize that the aim is not to identify monolithic artistic practices that are determined by fixed racial identities. Instead, the focus is on how we can identify racial identity and racial projects as *themes* explored in and through artistic practices (Taylor 2010; 2016), and how these

[1] See Carroll and Stear, this volume.
[2] Sixto Castro (2004) argues for the systemic evaluation of artworks. Insofar as art is one among other social systems that make up our sociocultural world, its products should be evaluated in regards to how they contribute to global aims.

explorations are shaped by and shape other social practices. This involves questions surrounding how dominant artistic practices are partly constitutive of the white supremacist racial project, how aesthetic phenomena underwrite processes of racialization, and how artistic practices can emerge as sites for resisting racial oppression. Thus, throughout the chapter, a tension emerges between, on the one hand, art as a site for the assertion of agency and the resistance of racial hierarchy, and, on the other, as a site for the consolidation of white supremacy and the propagation of narratives that sustain racism.

I follow Paul Taylor in understanding race as a political category. Racial identities are constructed social categories that are created to give meaning to superficial differences among human individuals (e.g., Taylor 2004; Mills 1998). It might be that racial identity does not necessarily imply a hierarchical categorization. But it is important to note that as a political category, race is sociohistorically specific. This means that in the context that interests us, racial categorization involves the marking of differences in a "colour-coded ladder of human kinds," and is part of a racial project that puts white individuals at the top of a human hierarchy (Taylor 2010, 3).

From this understanding of race follows an understanding of racism in political terms. Racism involves a hierarchy that marks out superficial differences to illegitimately establish substantial intellectual, moral, and cultural differences by establishing members of white racial categories as superior. Moreover, racism is a tool in materializing this established racial hierarchy through access to social and material goods in a given context. Racism is, therefore, not simply a category that marks a set of morally repugnant attitudes toward members of nonwhite racial groups. Rather, it is a category that marks a *social and cultural project of racial hierarchy*. As such, it is something that marks not simply psychological attitudes of individuals, but social and cultural systems aimed at sustaining white supremacy.

The structure of the chapter is the following. In the next section, I examine how artistic practices are at the center of the racial project, and how they can contribute to the formation of racial identities that resist white supremacy.[3] The third section focuses on the role played by artistic representations of racialized individuals in how we engage with one another, and, therefore, how they impact the experience of concrete racialized subjects in and of the world. The fourth section moves on to focus on the social responsibility of artists and their work given art's role in processes of racialization. In the last section, I offer some concluding remarks.

Art, Racial Identity, and White Supremacy

As noted above, examining art's ethical import requires us to go beyond the attitudes expressed by artworks, to look at how artistic practices interact with the network of

---

[3] See also Carter and Mason, this volume.

social and cultural systems that make up human life. This, however, does not mean that art is just one among many other practices. Artistic practices play a central role in the construction of our social world. When it comes to racial identity and hierarchy, art is not just *one of* the realms in which a racial project is manifested. Rather, racial projects have an aesthetic dimension insofar as it is partly through artworks that they create the narratives on which racial hierarchy is built, and on which social cognition depends. For this reason, the philosophy of art should work hand in hand with critical race theory in "excavating the narratives and pictures that frame our reflective commitments and our deliberative practices" (Taylor 2019, 362).

The particular role of artistic practices in the formation of racial identity and the sustainment of racial hierarchy becomes evident when we consider what Taylor (2016) and Monique Roelofs (2014) call the race-aesthetics nexus, that is, the relation between processes of racial formation and aesthetic practices. Within this relation we find a double direction of interaction between race and aesthetics. First, the aesthetics-race interaction involves the way aesthetic phenomena—including aesthetic perception, aesthetic evaluation, and artistic practices—underwrite processes of racialization and racial hierarchy. By shaping how racialized agents are perceived and categorized by others, and how they engage with the world and other racialized agents, aesthetic phenomena also underwrite our experience in and of the world. Second, the race-aesthetics interaction refers to the role racial hierarchy and categorization play in defining the scope of aesthetic phenomena that are, in turn, available to structure racial thinking. This means that a specific racial project underwrites aesthetic perception and evaluation and determines what we regard as worthwhile artistic practices.

When we consider the race-aesthetics nexus, therefore, the ethical value of art emerges from two aspects. First, it emerges from the power of artworks in consolidating oppressive patterns by contributing dehumanizing narratives to the white supremacist project, and that result in the misrecognition of nonwhite agents as moral peers. Second, art has ethical value in virtue of its role in resisting the oppressive racial project by offering oppositional narratives that assert the agency of nonwhite individuals.

Art and Racial Hierarchy

Artistic practices play a central role in sustaining white supremacy. As said before, aesthetic phenomena underwrite processes of racialization and racial hierarchy. As such, artworks wield significant power in consolidating patterns of oppression by providing dehumanizing narratives that shape how racialized agents are perceived, how their actions are interpreted, and how they engage with their sociohistorical circumstances. Roelofs identifies two interrelated phenomena that sustain the central role of artistic practices in maintaining racial hierarchy: *aesthetic racialization*, the connection between racialized bodies' aesthetic value and other racial differences; and *racialized aestheticization*, the connection between racial identity and aesthetic sensibility (Roelofs 2014).

Aesthetic racialization refers to how the aesthetic value of racialized individuals is taken as a sign of other features relevant for determining access to social and material goods, such as intellectual or moral features (Taylor 1999; 2016; Yancy 2008; 2016). Insofar as beauty has been traditionally taken as the perfect realization of a human being, construing beauty as defined by whiteness carries the implication that the intellectual and moral credentials of members of other races are demeaned. White European artistic practices have thus contributed to the consolidation of white supremacy by racializing beauty, that is, by defining beauty in terms of the physical features that white individuals are considered more likely to have (Taylor 1999, 17–18). This means that the hierarchical evaluation of human beings along racial lines involves an aesthetic hierarchy too, one that is not simply derived from the assumed moral/intellectual hierarchy, but that sustains it. Establishing whiteness as an aesthetic ideal is as central to the racial project as establishing whiteness as a moral ideal.

Artistic practices sustain the racial project by providing representations of racialized individuals that justify oppression. On the one hand, artworks maintain the racialization of beauty by representing nonwhite individuals in ways that exclude them from positive aesthetic features, which involve the recognition of an individual's moral worth. On the other hand, this racialization of beauty goes hand in hand with the representation of racialized individuals in artworks as conforming to specific racial scripts that contribute to dehumanization. I come back to this point in the third section of the chapter.

White European artistic practices are allowed to play this role in sustaining racial hierarchy thanks to racialized aestheticization. This refers to the fact that racial hierarchy involves not only assumed moral and intellectual differences—which are reflected in bodily beauty—but also assumed differences in aesthetic sensibilities. This means that under the white supremacist project, it is the white European artistic tradition that is regarded as relevant to structure the racial project because the assumption is that nonwhite individuals lack the relevant intellectual and moral capacities to sustain proper aesthetic experience and, therefore, a valuable aesthetic production.

In the philosophical and aesthetic tradition we can thus identify, in addition to the racialization of beauty, the racialization of taste, in that whiteness and taste function together. Robin James (2009) explains the racialization of taste by noting that aesthetic sensibilities have been traditionally regarded as transcending bodily experience, even if they originate in the body, to be realized in noncorporeal domains, such as cognition. Nonwhite individuals are thought to lack the relevant aesthetic sensibilities because they are seen as exhausted by their corporality and concerned only with bodily sensations and pleasures. Moreover, because whiteness is construed as normative, it is regarded as the ultimate realization of a universal human aesthetic sensibility. As the ultimate realization of a universal human condition, whiteness is regarded as standard or neutral; white aesthetic sensibility is, thus, also the standard. According to James, this presumed "featurelessness" that follows from the normative, universal character of white identity becomes key to a central feature of the aesthetic: disinterestedness.

From this racialization of taste, the misconception that white aesthetic practices are the only ones that should be valued as relevant to impact sociohistorical systems easily follows. The assumption is that nonwhite aesthetic practices are exhausted by their dependence on bodily experience and pleasures, and, therefore, lack the necessary depth and complexity that would fully render them *Art*. This idea unfortunately remains pervasive in Anglo-American philosophical aesthetics to this day.

Nkiru Nzegwu (2019) shows how in contemporary aesthetics, and more specifically, in the philosophy of art of Arthur Danto, we find the idea that art is something that is only realized in the white tradition. In contrast, nonwhite artistic practices are regarded as mere artifact. This is clear in traditional approaches to African art.[4] The main problem is, Nzegwu argues, that racialized aestheticization involves the universalization of Western art schemes, which are then used to invalidate artistic traditions that emerge from different cultures. Moreover, for nonwhite artistic traditions to gain *Art* status they need to be appropriated and commodified by white culture. Nzegwu shows how this fulfils a doubly objectifying role. First, through appropriation and commodification, nonwhite artistic practices are only valued in relation to what they do *through* white artistic practices: "primitive" aesthetic motifs are transfigured into *Art* when touched by the white European artistic tradition. Second, appropriation and commodification render nonwhite artistic practices as valuable only on account of what they can do *for* white artistic practices: the inclusion of "primitive" aesthetic motifs transfigured into *Art* by white artistic practices transforms them, as they are changed by their encounter with what they regard as radically Other. I come back to these points later in the chapter. For now, it is important to note how racialized aesthetization in this way results in the denial of nonwhite artistic practices as a site for the assertion of agency of nonwhite individuals.

Rather than being marked by so-called disinterestedness, this reveals once again that artistic practices work with other cultural systems in maintaining racial hegemony. W. E. B Du Bois (1926) and Franz Fanon (2004) highlight that artistic practices are a racial phenomenon that is not divorced from moral, political and economic systems. Beyond the connection between beauty, truth, and goodness, which has a long tradition in philosophy, Du Bois emphasizes art's connection to world and agency. Art is inseparable from its political value, and beauty is "to set the world right" (Du Bois 1926).[5] But from this connection to political value also follows, as noted by Fanon, that art is partly constitutive of the racial project, and that it plays an important role in sustaining racial hierarchy and in colonization. The role of artistic practices in processes of colonization is also highlighted by Mariana Ortega (2019). Taking as a starting point María Lugones's claim that coloniality infiltrates every aspect of life, Ortega argues that artistic practices contribute to the creation of colonial imageries, directly built on aesthesis, and which involves the construction of particular kinds of beings, among which we find colonized and racialized subjects.

---

[4] See Hallen, this volume.
[5] See Carter and Mason, this volume.

Nevertheless, just as artistic practices play a central role in consolidating racial hierarchy, they can play a central role in challenging it too. Both Du Bois and Fanon, for example, think that racialized individuals need to change their aesthetic conduct to counter racial subjugation. Du Bois argues that white individuals need to learn to appreciate Black art, and Black individuals need to learn to measure themselves by criteria that do not originate from this racialization of beauty and taste. Fanon, on his part, argues that artistic practices must be directed toward efforts against racial hierarchy.

The racialization of beauty and taste by the white supremacist project means that an antiracist project calls for what bell hooks terms the "oppositional gaze" (2015, 117–125). This oppositional gaze consists in a critical engagement with artistic practices that examines their role in sustaining racial hierarchy. It should be constructed from an "understanding and awareness of the politics of race and racism" (hooks 2015, 123). If beauty really is to set the world right, therefore, artistic practices should be built in opposition to the racialization processes explored in this section and should be instead understood as places in which racialized individuals assert their agency through a critical engagement with racial scripts. I turn to this point next.

Art and Racial Identity

Let us now look at the role of artistic practices in the formation of racial identity in a way that confronts the white supremacist project by presenting artworks as the place for resisting essentializing racial narratives and for the assertion of agency. Artistic practices contribute to the formation of racial identity not because they are the result of racial essences manifested in specific aesthetic preferences and traditions; rather, they contribute to the formation and sustainment of racial identity because through artistic practices racialized individuals can confront white supremacist narratives on which hierarchy is established.

Adapting from Taylor's (2016) analysis of Black expressive practices, we can think about racialized artistic practices as tools in maintaining life-worlds in the face of the asymmetrical distribution of social goods that results from processes of racialization. This emphasis on life-worlds is crucial to avoid thinking about the relation between art and racial identity in essentializing terms. The formation of racial identity through artistic practices does not involve racialized artistic practices as cultural monoliths emerging from fixed racial essences. It involves, instead, a broad and diverse collection of artistic practices created by people categorized under a given racial group as they navigate life under a given racial project. In this way, artistic practices shape racial identity insofar as they involve ways by which agents "seek and create beauty and meaning from within the cauldron of racial formation" (Taylor 2016, 12).

In the context of the formation of racial identity, racialized artistic practices are the result of what bell hooks calls the "oppositional imagination," the capacity by which a subjectivity inhabiting specific social categories—not only race, but also gender and class—resists the status quo and breaks free from boundaries imposed by those socially constructed categories. Art as a creation of oppositional imagination becomes a way by which racialized individuals seek to transgress boundaries, take risks, and survive in their sociohistorical situation (hooks 2015, 47–48). This is also how Michelle Wallace (1989) conceives of art as partly constitutive of racial identity. Art's power in shaping racial identities should not be taken to provide essentializing narratives that emerge from a monolithic understanding of racialized aesthetic practices. On the contrary, art is a place in which we engage in an "unrelenting interrogation" of racial identity. Racial identities formed in and through artistic practices emerge as "autonomous essences." Not as identities that stand in simplistic opposition to white, but as complex and nonreductive identities forged by individuals as they negotiate their place in the social world (Wallace 1989, 51–52).

Consider, for example, Gloria Anzaldúa's (1987) "aesthetics of the shadow" as a renegotiation of Latinx identity in the United States, no longer simply in opposition to white identity. Anzaldúa develops the concept of the "new mestiza" as a new mode of selfhood that is characterized by a state of in-betweenness, and that is open to ambiguity and contradiction (Ortega 2016). In turn, this in-betweenness, what Anzaldúa calls Nepantilism, corresponds to a state of creativity and agency that involves the rejection of the racial script. The assertion and revalorization of the in-betweenness that characterizes the new mestiza, therefore, emerges too from the oppositional imagination, and it is expressed through the creative power of artistic practices. For Anzaldúa, then, art functions as a place for the formation of this new racial identity because its creative power allows it to challenge dominant epistemic frameworks through the introduction of resistant social imaginings (Pitts 2014, 96).[6]

Anzaldúa's aesthetics of the shadow highlights an important feature of how artistic practices can contribute to the formation of racial identity in a way that opposes the white supremacist project, as emphasized by hooks. There is an important difference between recognizing the cultural source of aesthetic practices that emerge from distinct racialized experiences, and a reductionist understanding of racialized artistic practices as resulting from essentialist racial projects (hooks 2015, 30–31). By regarding art as a place in which racial identities are shaped, hooks warns against the temptation of reducing the complex and diverse experience of individuals of colour, to the experience of only some of those racialized individuals. Art's role is not merely to become a place in which racial identities are shaped, but a place in which *resistant* racial identities are shaped. In the same way in which Anzaldúa thinks the value of art consists in the manifestation of agency and a creative impulse to reject racial scripts and embrace the ambiguity of in-betweenness, hooks thinks it is not enough to become subjects in/through art. The aim is to become *radical subjects* that resist racial scripts and essentializing racial norms (hooks 2015, 47).

<hr>

[6] See also María DeGuzmán (2012, 30–34) for an analysis of Anzaldúa's aesthetics of engagement and "excruciating aliveness" as a place for the transvaluation of darkness through art.

The emphasis on art's role in the formation of racial identity is, then, on its role in asserting agency. The only way in which art can contribute to the formation of radical subjects is, therefore, by representing the wide variety and complexity of racialized experience. Art is constitutive of racial identity not because it solidifies racial scripts, but because it embraces the ambiguity of racialized identities. Art fulfils this role by presenting racialized individuals as complex subjects that embody multiple locations. This further highlights that art is partly constitutive of racial identity not by offering features that characterize individuals belonging to specific racial groups, but by examining racial identities as themes. Artworks are central in the formation of racial identity, as noted by Wallace, as critical interrogations and negotiations of racialized life-worlds in the white supremacist project.

ART AND ENGAGEMENT WITH
RACIALIZED OTHERS

I noted earlier that the racialization of beauty goes hand in hand with the representation of racialized individuals in artworks of the white European tradition as conforming to specific racial scripts that contribute to dehumanization and racial hierarchy. When considering that racialized aestheticization involves the idea that aesthetic sensibilities are only properly realized in white individuals, and that therefore only the white artistic tradition is regarded as valuable and worthy of affecting processes of racialization, the result is that art's political value is placed at the service of racial hegemony.

The previous section focused on artistic practices at a systemic level to see how they interact in sustaining racial hierarchy. However, it is important to note that artistic practices underwrite processes of racialization not simply because they create and reinforce racial scripts that serve as theoretical justifications for racial hierarchy. Rather, art is partly constitutive of racial scripts that contribute to dehumanization by structuring our engagement with *concrete* racialized subjects. Artistic practices shape how racialized agents are perceived, how their actions are interpreted, and therefore, shape their interactions with other agents. In other words, strategies of what Taylor calls aesthetic depersonalization that are at the center of dominant artistic practices impact intersubjective recognition (Taylor 2016, 37–38).

Recall that the aesthetics-race interaction involves the fact that aesthetic phenomena underwrite processes of racialization by shaping how racialized agents are perceived by others and how they engage with their sociopolitical world. The ethical value of artistic representations of racialized individuals also emerges from how they structure our experience in and of the world and our engagement with others. This is possible because artistic representations do not simply present their content in a neutral way. On the contrary, artworks' aesthetic features bring our attention to certain aspects of representational content, while obscuring certain others. More importantly, perhaps, artistic representations dispose and invite appreciators to respond in specific ways to what is represented, and they represent objects as meriting the responses that are called for. This is what Noël Carroll (2003) calls artworks' "criterial prefocus." In the case of race, this means that artistic representations bring our attention to certain aspects of racialized individuals, they invite us to respond to them in specific ways, and they present those responses to racialized individuals as merited by deploying various aesthetic strategies.

Moreover, the way artistic representations structure our engagement with racialized others is reflected at different levels. First, artistic representations of racialized individuals impact how we aesthetically evaluate others. In the case of aesthetic evaluation of human bodies, artworks' criterial prefocus involves not just the foregrounding of specific features, but rather it involves racialized bodies being represented as having specific aesthetic properties: racialized human bodies are represented as being either ethereal or lewd, elegant or flamboyant, delicate or sexually aggressive. This is important because, as stated earlier, aesthetic evaluations impact the recognition of equal moral worth, and individuals' access to social and material goods. Establishing aesthetic superiority and inferiority goes hand in hand with establishing a moral and intellectual hierarchy.

Second, artistic representations of racialized individuals impact our affective disposition toward others. Our immersion in given artistic practices means that we come to see racialized others as conforming to the affective prefocus from which individuals are predominantly represented. We learn, therefore, to be affectively predisposed to interact with racialized others in ways that reinforce the racial project. This means that our exposure to criterially prefocused artistic representations of racialized individuals disposes us to regard each other as either aggressive and threatening, or comforting and trust-worthy. After all, these artistic representations teach us to pay attention to specific features of others and to regard these affective responses as merited by those highlighted features.

From their impact on aesthetic and affective evaluations, it is not difficult to see how artistic representations of racialized individuals might impact the attribution of mental states and intentions, and, therefore, how they can structure more meaningful interactions beyond mere perception. James (2013), for example, links these aesthetic and affective orientations to Linda Alcoff's (2006) interpretive horizons, that is, to the sociohistorical situation from which we interpret and engage with others, and which determines how we are seen and treated. More specifically, James argues that horizons foreground the role of the aesthetic because they are nonpropositional ways of engaging with the world and with others. In this way, James highlights the role of artistic practices as " 'pedagogies' of privilege and oppression" (2013, 106): we learn these horizons as we engage with artworks, and, therefore, our engagement with artistic practices underwrites our experience in and of the world.

The different ways in which artistic representations structure our perception and engagement with racialized others means that art has the power of either reinforcing dehumanizing racial scripts or opposing racial hierarchy. Let us then move to examine how these two roles of artistic representations have been explored in the literature.

Controlling Images

Taylor argues that artistic practices deploy objectifying aesthetic strategies in the service of the dehumanizing treatment of nonwhite subjects under the white supremacist project. One of these objectifying strategies concerns who and what we find represented in artworks, that is, which racialized subjects are depicted in what narrative contexts, and how they are represented by means of works' aesthetic features. Taylor notes that what we find are stereotypes and stock figures (Taylor 2016, 52): nonwhite individuals are represented in ways that confirm racial scripts at the service of racial hierarchy instead of offering representations of complex and deep individuals.

The representations in the service of racial hierarchy are what Patricia Hill Collins (2002) calls controlling images, racist and sexist stereotypical images that permeate popular culture and that attach to nonwhite folks, and that are used to justify oppression. As said before, controlling images in artistic representations are particularly well suited to play this role in justifying racial hierarchy due to how they are criterially prefocused, so that they not only represent racialized individuals with certain features that call for specific responses, but they represent them as meriting such responses. Hill Collins highlights, for example, controlling images associated with Black women that have been fundamental to their oppression: "mammies, jezebels, and breeder women of slavery to the smiling Aunt Jemimas on pancake mix boxes, ubiquitous Black prostitutes, and ever-present welfare mothers of contemporary popular culture" (Hill Collins 2002, 7). These controlling images have been created, repeated, and reinforced by the white European aesthetic tradition, and, as noted by Hill Collins, they play a central role in sustaining systems of oppression.

Controlling images not only conform to dehumanizing racial scripts. Rather, their complexity factors in interlocking social identities that are relevant for sustaining a racial project that is also marked by misogyny and class disparity. bell hooks notes how artistic representations of racialized bodies are gendered so that in addition to promoting dehumanizing racial scripts, they promote phallocentrism and harmful gender stereotypes. Prevalent representations of Black men as lazy, for example, are aimed at erasing the significance of Black male labor (hooks 2015, 90). At the same time, controlling images centered on phallocentric Black masculinity are those that are evoked when white supremacy attempts to justify genocidal assault on Black men (hooks 2015, 109). Likewise, controlling images of Black women have been central in their objectification and dehumanization by presenting their bodies as expendable. The fascination with the "exotic" appeal of Black femininity positions them as an exotic Other that is only there to satisfy the longings of white supremacist phallocentrism (hooks 2015, 73).[7]

Lugones and Ortega also highlight the central role that images play in promoting colonialist perceptions insofar as the work of colonization, as we saw before, is intimately

---

[7]   See Janelle Hobson (2003) and George Yancy (2016) for an analysis of the racist aesthetic perception of gendered Black bodies.

tied to sensory practices and, therefore, to the aesthetic. Lugones (2003) focuses on the role of the image in the constitution of the colonized self.[8] The subjectivity of colonized subjects is characterized by exile insofar as it is constituted by a denial of identity. This estrangement and the being in between colonized and colonizing perceptions results in a "ghostly subjectivity" in which the self is turned into an image.[9] Controlling images are the manifestation of these colonizing perceptions, and they are internalized in such a way that results in this state of in-betweenness.

Ortega examines how this is reflected in the use of photographic technologies in perceptual processes of colonization. Photographs are particularly well suited for racialized othering because they work at different levels of visibility and invisibility: they make racialized subjects overly visible and highlight racial difference, while at the same time transforming them into mere images, both to colonizers and to the colonized (Ortega 2019, 404).

Building on this idea of the ghostly subjectivities of colonized subjects, Ortega offers a helpful analysis of the *haunting* character of controlling images. They are haunting because there are no attempts by the racial project to hide or even attempt to disguise them. Controlling images fulfil their role by being out there for everyone to see. Their objectifying, dehumanizing, and invisibilizing strategies are meant to be out in the open. In this way that they "solidify and legitimize the subjectivity of the colonial gaze ... the colonial gaze asserts itself as the gaze to which all the gazes must return and the gaze through which all others must be seen" (Ortega 2019, 407).

However, it is important to note that these controlling images are not the only objectifying strategy. Ortega notes that *invisibilizing* strategies are also out in the open in the service of the white supremacist racial project. Controlling images, then, are not the only thing shaping our perception and engagement with racialized others. Rather, a lack of images that resist racial scripts is also responsible for skewing our interactions and experiences in and of the world. The fact that nonwhite subjects become invisible in our predominant artistic practices means that we do not have artistic representations as readily available as controlling images that could counteract their role in processes of racialization. So, in addition to the prevalence of controlling images, invisibility promoted by white European artistic practices also plays a significant role. For this reason, it is not enough to simply get rid of controlling images. These dehumanizing strategies must be resisted by artistic representations that assert racialized individuals' moral worth. I turn to oppositional images next.

---

[8] Lugones (2007) also emphasizes that these colonizing perceptions are gendered. Colonization involves the perception of light and dark sides of gender that shape how colonized subjectivity is built. The light side of gender corresponds to white bourgeois women, who are perceived and coded in images as fragile and passive; the dark side corresponds to colonized women of colour, who are perceived and coded in images as aggressive and violent.

[9] Alia Al-Saji (2019) provides an illuminating analysis of the "sticky" character of controlling images, i.e., their ability to fix identity to racial scripts that have already been written, in the light of Fanon's historico-racial schema.

Oppositional Images

When examining ghostly subjectivities and the haunting character of colonizing images, Ortega notes that they also represent a future possibility. As we saw earlier the oppositional imagination highlighted by hooks offers the possibility to reject the status quo and break free from dehumanizing racial scripts. Controlling images, therefore, call for a resistant response. While they might haunt them, racialized individuals are not doomed by artistic representations that reinforce oppression. On the contrary, Lugones identifies a tension emerging from being confronted by controlling images, a tension between "dehumanization and paralysis of the coloniality of being, and the creative activity of be-ing" (2010, 754).

Art, as a product of creativity and the oppositional imagination, offers the possibility of presenting what hooks calls "oppositional images." Contrary to controlling images that create and sustain racial scripts in the service of white supremacy, oppositional images are those that confront racial and sexual stereotypes and that aim at recognition. Instead of artistic representations that present subjects in ways that conform to racist stereotypes, oppositional images are those that highlight the complexity of racialized subjectivity, that focus on individuality rather than racial scripts, and that emphasize agency and self-expression (hooks 2015, 75–76). In other words, oppositional images are those artistic representations that depict radical subjectivities that actively resist racial scripts.

In addition to asserting agency, in rejecting racial rules, oppositional images introduce ambiguity. In her discussion of racializing images, for example, Al-Saji (2019) considers oppositional images of Muslims not so much in terms of how they represent racialized subjects, but in how they confront racialized appreciators by recentering open-ended questions. She highlights how oppositional images can fulfil their role in resisting racial hierarchy by exploiting representations' ambiguity and artworks' openness to multiple interpretations, which serve as mirrors for the complexity and multiplicity of racialized individuals' experience in and of worlds. Al-Saji shows that by embracing ambiguity in the representation of racialized individuals, artworks can aim at destabilizing the dominant racial project by inviting from audiences' oppositional readings and reinterpretations and reconfigurations of the past.

This brings us back to hooks's oppositional gaze. Resisting artistic practices that are partly constitutive of the white supremacist project involves acknowledging the role art plays in sustaining racial hegemony. For oppositional images to fulfil their role, appreciators must also be willing to embrace ambiguity and to regard their engagement with art as an active practice in which they interrogate, resignify, and reconfigure received representations of racialized others. Oppositional images and oppositional gaze go hand in hand. Yet this picture still leaves out another crucial element when examining art's role in a racial project: artists.

ART AND RACIALIZED ARTISTS

Given the role of artistic practices in either sustaining or resisting white supremacy, we must ask about the responsibilities of artists. What should or shouldn't they do when creating artworks? To conclude this entry, I focus on two aspects of the discussion regarding artists' responsibilities. First, the debate about whether they should regard political aims as central to their work; more specifically, I examine Du Bois and Alain Locke's debate on art and propaganda. Second, I examine what is wrong with cultural appropriation given art's role in sustaining racial hierarchy and in forming racial identity.

Artists and Political Aims

In addition to the aesthetics-race nexus, Taylor identifies the aesthetics-politics nexus, which partly concerns itself with the question of whether the value of artworks is independent from their political value. The first section highlighted the connection between artistic practices and other cultural systems. From this, it follows that art is inherently political. But from the fact that artistic practices are part of the cultural systems that sustain racial hierarchy and that artistic representations shape racialized subjects' experience in and of the world, it does not immediately follow that artists have a responsibility to create only artworks that support anti-racist projects. So let us turn to the debate between Du Bois and Alain Locke surrounding the responsibilities of artists under white supremacy.[10]

As Leonard Harris (2004) well notes, both authors recognize that an anti-racist project cannot thrive so long as artistic practices reinforce racial hierarchy. The debate among them, therefore, centers on how the goal of creating oppositional images should be achieved, as well as on the role of artists as agents for social change (Harris 2004, 15–16). At the center of Du Bois's argument is his understanding of Beauty as one with Truth and Right. Artists, as the apostles of Beauty, are bound by Truth and Justice. For Du Bois, Beauty is that which promotes the social project of racial uplift by presenting the Truth, namely, by asserting the absolute moral worth of Black people, and by promoting Justice, namely, the rejection of white supremacy. Art is propaganda because if it aims at Beauty, then it aims at Truth and Justice. Art's political aims are thus part of its aims *as art*.

This highlights the problem of racist artistic practices. If art aims at Beauty, Truth, and Right, racist artistic practices are propaganda in the service of the white supremacist project. Artworks create and sustain dehumanizing racial narratives that are presented *as* Beauty, Truth, and Right. Note that Du Bois's claim is not that art *should be* propaganda because it should be committed to racial uplift. Rather, his claim is that "all Art

---

[10] See also Carter and Mason, this volume.

is propaganda and ever must be" (Du Bois 1926) insofar as *qua art* it is committed to Truth and Right. What is at stake is what artists choose to present as Beautiful, True, and Righteous.

Locke's main argument against understanding art as propaganda is that instead of opposing white supremacy, it perpetuates racial injustice in two ways. First, by demanding artists to respond to the dominant racial project, it continues to grant that racialized subjects are to be defined in relation to white supremacy. Instead of being a site for the assertion of agency, artists' creative impulse is bound by the agenda set by white supremacy insofar as their art becomes nothing more than a response to its racist claims. Understanding art's inherently political dimension as propaganda "perpetuates the position of group inferiority even when crying out against it. For it leaves and speaks under the shadow of a dominant majority whom it harangues, cajoles, threatens or supplicates" (Locke 1928). Second, by demanding artists to subordinate artistic creation to an anti-racist project, it denies them of the opportunity for "free individualistic expression." Crucially, this is an opportunity that is afforded to white artists, who do not need to align their work with political aims, and who can then engage in a creative act of self-expression. This does not mean, however, that Locke chooses to ignore the political dimension of art. But, because he understands art's ultimate function as "a tap root of vigorous, flourishing living," he believes its political power lies in affording racialized agents the opportunity for self-expression outside the confines of racial scripts.

Locke's views, therefore, do not go against what this chapter has examined, but rather emerge from the emphasis he places on art as a site for the assertion of agency. Note that this is consistent with hooks's claim that art should be a place in which racialized subjects become radical subjects. The rejection of racial scripts involves a rejection of the reduction of racialized experience to the experience of some racialized subjects. Instead, art should represent different accounts of what it is like to be a racialized subject. This is what is at stake in what Harris calls Locke's aesthetic pluralism: the appreciation of racialized artistic practices as a changing phenomenon, and of racialized subjects as fully human, which is conveyed by complex personalities and different stories (Harris 2004, 34). Artistic practices can therefore contribute to the anti-racist project by focusing on openness and by "new perspectives unattached to old terms" (Harris 2004, 29), rather than by bounding artistic practices to propagandistic aims.

This, nevertheless, does not speak against Du Bois's argument. Insofar as artistic practices produce either controlling or oppositional images, all art is already propaganda. Therefore, artists should be mindful of whether their creative acts of self-expression work in the service of either racist or anti-racist projects. Rather than being in opposition, however, the difference between Locke's and Du Bois's views perhaps stems from the nature of their projects. While Du Bois is concerned with a descriptive claim about how all art *already is* propaganda, Locke is really concerned with a normative claim about how all art *should not be* propaganda: an anti-racist project should also center on offering racialized artists the opportunity of free self-expression so that they are not burdened with only creating representations that will speak against negative racial stereotypes.

Taylor, however, offers a finer understanding of artistic freedom that allows us to better see how it is compatible with the responsibilities that follow from art's place in the white supremacist project. Taylor argues that given that artistic practices are part of other cultural systems, artists are bound by their (racist) context and by the network of normative commitments that make up the dominant racial project. As a result, artistic freedom is not "an abstract possession" and does not involve a "complete detachment from ethical or political imperatives." Instead, artists should regard their activity as self-legislated, but "in the face of, and in recognition of, the wider resources for seeking the truth and pursuing the good" (Taylor 2016, 97). While this is important for nonwhite artists, this responsibility becomes all the more significant when considering white artistic practices. Let us turn to them now.

The Problem of Cultural Appropriation

Given the role of artistic practices in sustaining the white supremacist project, it should be clear that artists should refrain from contributing to dehumanizing racial norms and the creation of controlling images. But we can also question whether there should be other limitations in place. Earlier I looked at racialized aestheticization, by which only white artistic practices are valued. While resisting it should be at the center of an anti-racist project, an oppositional approach aimed at the valorization of nonwhite artistic practices should not simply be understood as a call to dominant white European artistic practices to bring them to the mainstream. Likewise, an oppositional approach to artistic representations of racialized subjects should not simply be understood in terms of the dominant artistic practices turning to racialized individuals as their subject matter in an effort to diversify the stories available in the mainstream. So let us finally look at the problem of appropriation in/through artistic practices.[11]

The problem of appropriation becomes evident when we consider that an anti-racist project can only be built on artistic practices as a site for the assertion of agency.[12] Nzegwu's analysis of the reception of African art by critics and philosophers of art reveals the wrongs of appropriation by highlighting a doubly objectifying character. First, through appropriation and commodification, the implication is that nonwhite artistic practices can only be valued in relation to what they do *through* white artistic practices, that is, once they have been transfigured into art proper by the intervention of white culture. Second, appropriation and commodification render nonwhite artistic practices valuable not in virtue of themselves, but in virtue of what they can do for white artistic practices, that is, in virtue of how they can "spice up" and transform white

---

[11] See also Nguyen and Strohl, this volume.

[12] Following hooks, I focus on the wrong of cultural appropriation in regards to commodification and the denial of agency. However, Thi Nguyen and Matthew Strohl's (2019) analysis of the wrong of cultural appropriation as a breach of intimacy is relevant when we consider the role of artistic practices in the formation of racial identity against white supremacy.

culture. Appropriation only results in the reaffirmation of nonwhite artistic practices as the absolute Other that is there to be exploited by the white gaze. In this way, rather than resisting racialized aestheticization, appropriation maintains the racist status quo.

The problem is that this support for the white supremacist project is disguised. Rather than being recognized as exploitation, appropriation is passed as genuine concern for the revalorization of nonwhite culture. hooks regards appropriation as a result of "imperialist nostalgia," as the result of a "yearning for what one has destroyed that is a form of mystification" (hooks 2015, 25) that promises reconciliation and is aimed at assuaging the guilt of the past. Appropriation, hooks argues, denies accountability and historical connection to oppressive practices, and, thus, deflects responsibility for the harm to the racialized Other.

For hooks, this reveals that appropriation is not part of an anti-racist project. The desire for so-called reconciliation through artistic practices only masks what she calls "consumer cannibalism": the emphasis is not on racial justice, but on "becoming" the Other (hooks 2015, 31). Racialized subjects' experience in and of the world is denied, only to be repackaged as "human" experience. Although disguised as good will, by emphasizing sameness in their effort to appropriate nonwhite culture, white culture assumes once again that it is solely in its hands to determine the nature of its relationship to nonwhite culture (hooks 2015, 27). Moreover, by decontextualizing racialized artistic practices, the emphasis on sameness erases "the specific historical and social context of black experience from which cultural productions and distinct black styles emerge" (hooks 2015, 30). As examined earlier, this is not to say that racialized artistic practices are the result of racial essences. But it means that racialized artistic practices emerge from specific experiences and are, in this way, constitutive of racial identity.

Appropriation involves the denial of agency in that it silences nonwhite voices again by denying the specificity of the experience from which specific artistic practices emerge. It robs racialized subjects from the opportunity to resist white supremacy by engaging in oppositional artistic practices that allow them to carve racial identity outside the racist racial project. Moreover, in this way, appropriation robs racialized subjects of the opportunity of becoming radical subjects through their unique artistic practices. Instead of a site for the assertion of agency, racialized artistic practices become just a backdrop for the cultural development of white people and a denial of their role in sustaining oppressive practices.

Concluding Remarks

Throughout this chapter, I have tried to emphasize the tension between artistic practices as a site for the assertion of agency and the resistance of racial hierarchy, on the one hand, and as a site for the consolidation of dehumanizing narratives that sustain white supremacy, on the other. First, while the racialization of beauty and taste in and through art contributes to sustaining racial hierarchy, the cultivation of an oppositional gaze, by which artworks become an unrelenting interrogation of racial identity, can lead to the construction of resistant racial identities. Second, although controlling images created and promoted by artworks structure our engagement with concrete racialized others, oppositional images in artworks can highlight the complexity of racialized subjectivity, and thus emphasize agency and self-expression outside of white supremacy. Third, while artworks as places for the assertion of agency highlight the importance of artists' self-expression outside the confines of racial scripts, artistic freedom should be understood within the context of the dominant racial project.

This should show that when examined from a systemic perspective, the ethical value of art cannot be separated from its political value, that is, from its place in the network of social, cultural, and political systems that make up human life. Beyond just looking at how ethical value emerges from artworks' manifested attitude, art's ethical import only becomes clear when considering what artworks do in specific sociohistorical contexts and as part of broader cultural patterns. The philosophy of art should aim at an oppositional approach to artistic practices that starts from the recognition of its inherently political nature.

See also: Hallen, Cater, and Mason, Taylor, Nguyen and Strohl, Carroll, Stear, this volume

References

Al-Saji, Alia. 2019. "Glued to the Image: A Critical Phenomenology of Racialization through Works of Art." *Journal of Aesthetics and Art Criticism* 77, no. 4: 475–488.

Alcoff, Linda Martín. 2006. *Visible Identities: Race, Gender, and the Self*. Oxford: Oxford University Press.

Anzaldua, Gloria. 1987. *Borderlands/La Frontera*. San Francisco: Aunt Lute Books.

Carroll, Noël. 2003. "Art, Narrative and Emotion." In *Beyond Aesthetics: Philosophical Essays*, 215–234. Cambridge: Cambridge University Press.

Castro, Sixto J. 2004. "Una Teoria Moral Del Arte. Moralismo Moderado Epistemico, Epistémico y Sistémico." *Contrastes. Revista Internacional de Filosofía* IX: 59–76.

DeGuzmán, María. 2012. *Buenas Noches, American Culture: Latina/o Aesthetics of Night*. Ebook Central. Bloomington: Indiana University Press.

Du Bois, W. E. B. 1926. "Criteria of Negro Art." *The Crisis* 32: 290–297.

Fanon, Franz. 2004. *The Wretched of the Earth*, edited by Richard Philcox. New York: Grove Press.

Harris, Leonard. 2004. "The Great Debate: W. E. B. Du Bois vs. Alain Locke on the Aesthetic." *Philosophia Africana* 7, no. 1: 15–39.

Hill Collins, Patricia. 2002. *Black Feminist Thought*. New York; London: Routledge.

Hobson, Janell. 2003. "The 'Batty' Politic: Toward an Aesthetic of the Black Female Body." *Hypatia* 18, no. 4: 87–105.

hooks, bell. 2015. *Black Looks*. New York: Routledge.

James, Robin. 2009. "In But Not of, of But Not in: On Taste, Hipness, and White Embodiment." *Contemporary Aesthetics* spec, no. 2.

James, Robin. 2013. "Oppression, Privilege, and Aesthetics: The Use of the Aesthetic in Theories of Race, Gender, and Sexuality, and the Role of Race, Gender, and Sexuality in Philosophical Aesthetics." *Philosophy Compass* 8, no. 2: 101–116.

Locke, Alain. 1928. "Art or Propaganda." *Harlem* I, no. 1. http://nationalhumanitiescenter.org/pds/maai3/protest/text10/lockeartorpropaganda.pdf.

Lugones, María. 2003. *Pilgrimages/Peregrinajes. Theorizing Coalition against Multiple Oppressions.* Lanham, MD: Rowman & Littlefield.

Lugones, María. 2007. "Heterosexualism and the Colonial / Modern Gender System." *Hypatia: A Journal of Feminist Philosophy* 22, no. 1: 186–209.

Lugones, María. 2010. "Toward a Decolonial Feminism." *Hypatia* 25, no. 4: 742–759.

Mills, Charles W. 1998. *Blackness Visible: Essays on Philosophy and Race.* Ithaca, NY: Cornell University Press.

Nguyen, C. Thi, and Matthew Strohl. 2019. "Cultural Appropriation and the Intimacy of Groups." *Philosophical Studies* 176, no. 4: 981–1002.

Nzegwu, Nkiru. 2019. "African Art in Deep Time: De-Race-Ing Aesthetics and De-Racializing Visual Art." *Journal of Aesthetics and Art Criticism*, 77, no. 4: 367–378.

Ortega, Mariana. 2016. *In-Between. Latina Feminist Phenomenology, Multiplicity, and the Self.* Albany.: SUNY Press.

Ortega, Mariana. 2019. "Spectral Perception and Ghostly Subjectivity at the Colonial Gender/Race/Sex Nexus." *Journal of Aesthetics and Art Criticism* 77, no. 4: 401–409.

Pitts, Andrea J. 2014. "Toward an Aesthetics of Race: Bridging the Writings of Gloria Anzaldúa and José Vasconcelos." *Inter-American Journal of Philosophy* 5, no. 1: 80–100.

Roelofs, Monique. 2014. *The Cultural Promise of the Aesthetic. The Cultural Promise of the Aesthetic.* London: Bloomsbury.

Taylor, Paul C. 1999. "Malcolm's Conk and Danto's Colors; Or, Four Logical Petitions Concerning Race, Beauty, and Aesthetics." *Journal of Aesthetics and Art Criticism* 57, no. 1: 16–20.

Taylor, Paul C. 2004. "Race: A Philosophical Introduction." Cambridge: Polity.

Taylor, Paul C. 2010. "Black Aesthetics." *Philosophy Compass* 5, no. 1: 1–15.

Taylor, Paul C. 2016. *Black Is Beautiful: A Philosophy of Black Aesthetics.* Oxford: Wiley Blackwell.

Taylor, Paul C. 2019. "Foreword: Toward a Critical Race Aesthetics." *Journal of Aesthetics and Art Criticism* 77, no. 4: 361–362.

Wallace, Michelle. 1989. "The Politics of Location: Cinema/Theory/Literature /Ethnicity/ Sexuality/Me." *Framework: TheJournal of Cinema and Media* 36: 42–55.

Yancy, George. 2008. *Black Bodies, White Gazes: The Continuing Significance of Race.* Lanham, MD: Rowman & Littlefield.

Yancy, George. 2016. "White Embodied Gazing, the Black Body as Disgust, and the Aesthetics of Un-Suturing." In *Body Aesthetics*, edited by Sherri Irvin, 243–260. Oxford: Oxford University Press.

CHAPTER 43

....

REPRESENTATION, IDENTITY, AND ETHICS IN ART

....

PAUL C. TAYLOR

INTRODUCTION: WE KNOW WHAT WE ARE, BUT KNOW NOT WHAT WE MAY BE

IT would be one thing to identify an Irish actress of Ethiopian descent as "the most fitting representative for the current Irish nation." It would be another thing entirely to cast this actress, for this reason, as Hamlet (Nakase 2021, 189–206). Depending on what one thinks the point of theater is, and, of course, depending on the actress, this casting choice would probably not produce the most fitting representation of Hamlet, or of at least some of what Hamlet is or means. Then again, one might think, as the leadership of Dublin's Gate Theatre seemed to in 2018, that casting Ruth Negga in this role would produce "a Hamlet for our time," which is nearly to say that it would capture or express or represent something crucial about that cultural moment (Nakase 2021, 189–206). At a minimum, Negga might represent certain citizens of Ireland who tend not to fit easily into standard notions of Irish national identity.

I've opened with a reference to the Gate Theatre's production of *Hamlet* because it quite economically introduces the guiding thought of this chapter. There is a great deal to say about the merits of and motivations for cross-racial casting, but that is not my topic here. I am interested in some of what gives cross-racial and otherwise nontraditional casting much of its claim on our attention. I am concerned here with the way a variety of issues in art and the ethics of social identity converge on the notion of representation, a notion that artworld actors and observers often use to raise questions of appropriation, inclusion, recognition, and more. The fitness of the notion of representation for this use occasions the inquiry.

Negga's Hamlet is a useful point of entry because it clearly implicates the four senses of representation that will shape the discussion. In one sense of the term, actors represent the characters they portray, and they participate in representations or depictions of the worlds those characters inhabit. In a second sense, institutions that sponsor these depictions and present them to audiences sometimes claim or are invited to accept that they represent some community the way the Gate apparently endeavors to represent Ireland. In addition, these institutions may find, in recent years in particular, that a more specific representational burden related to diversity and inclusion often complicates the general burden of civic representativeness: they may find themselves, in other words, and in the third sense of the term I'll consider, held to account for avoiding or correcting for certain historic patterns of *under*representation in relation to particular subgroups in the wider civic community. Finally, in a fourth sense of the term, artworld actors may aspire to create or designate certain art objects—where "object" includes performances and other events—as embodying, illuminating, or expressing a wider cultural ethos.

This chapter will explore these four conceptions of artworld representation and argue that attending to them can inform and deepen the practices of making, enjoying, and criticizing art. The aim is not to produce a rigid architectonic of artworld representation but to provide a preliminary mapping of some forms of representation that remain both underexplored in philosophical aesthetics and relatively undifferentiated in the heat of the political debates that invoke them. This preliminary mapping should begin to clarify the relationship between questions of representation and questions of appropriation, inclusion, and the like. It should also begin to clarify the way problems of artworld representation are bound up with political controversies related to social identities like race, gender, class, and national identity. I'll attempt to deepen these attempts at clarification by thinking through a few illustrative cases, one along the way and two more at the end.

Four Conceptions of Representation

The concept of representation has a long and complicated history in philosophy. More precisely, representation has a handful of complicated histories, each involving a particular refinement or conception of the underlying concept.[1] Thoughtful students of politics, language, cognition, law, art, and other subjects have had a great deal to say about what it means for one thing to represent another in some specific domain, and they continue to debate the various merits of different approaches to this topic. This results in several relatively distinct conceptions of representation, at least four of which bear directly on common questions and controversies in and around the artworld.

The first conception of representation concerns the semantic relation of aboutness, in something like the sense that organizes work on mental representations in the philosophy of mind and on theories of reference in the philosophy of language. This is most

---

[1] I am invoking here the familiar concept-conception distinction that appears in, among other places, the work of John Rawls, H. L. A. Hart, and, drawing on both in the context of race theory, Michael Hardimon (2003).

often what philosophical aestheticians have in mind when they talk about representation in art: a relationship between the work and (maybe) the world in virtue of which the work depicts, imitates, portrays, perhaps resembles, or otherwise contrives to be about something else. This is the sense of representation that Nelson Goodman (1968) famously endeavored to explain, and the sense that at least pretheoretically captures the relationship between pictures (and program music, and fictional narratives, and so on) and whatever the pictures (and so on) depict. It is also the sense that shows up most often in philosophical discussions of representation in art.

A second conception of representation concerns the broadly political or social relationship of fiduciarity. One finds this conception at work in democratic theory, political philosophy, and other fields that seek to understand how one entity can stand in for another in order to advocate for it or defend its interests. I use the notion of fiduciarity here to convey three ideas that routinely inform artworld discussions of this kind of representation: that the representative has duties of care or loyalty to the represented party, that the relation ought ideally to be rooted in something like trust, and that the representative may have to satisfy certain conditions to serve in this capacity. This is the sense in which galleries represent artists, but it is also the sense in which museums and other artworld institutions are sometimes expected, to the detriment in recent years of several elite institutions, to represent particular communities. If representation-as-aboutness dominates discussion among philosophers of art, representation-as-fiduciarity features much more prominently in discussion among artworld actors and real-world observers of artworld goings-on.

A third conception of representation concerns something like exemplarity or, perhaps better, inclusion or recognition, and, like fiduciarity, also figures more prominently in discussions outside of philosophical aesthetics than in discussions on the inside. In this sense, an entity represents another when it a) stands in something like a type-token relationship to it and b) is seen and accepted—*recognized*—as a stand-in for the type in a particular context and thereby, perhaps, c) helps confer recognition on or win recognition for the type. Artworld controversies related to representation-as-exemplarity have grown increasingly common as Western artworld institutions have faced demands to be more inclusive and to decolonize their holdings or programming. The charge in these cases, as we'll see, is that the institutions have failed to reflect in their programs and exhibitions the diversity of the populations they serve and of the artistic traditions that they aim to celebrate and advance. The worry, in other words, is that they have failed to make room for representative instances of typically excluded or underrepresented populations or traditions, and have therefore declined to recognize the relevant populations and traditions, or the persons who constitute and sustain them.

A fourth conception of representation involves expressiveness, by which I mean a broadly Hegelian kind of aboutness that goes deeper than mere reference or depiction. This sense of representation hovers behind claims about, say, a work of art representing an epoch or a movement or a zeitgeist. It is a way of saying that the work expresses what the moment is in some sense *really* about and does so by clarifying or embodying or articulating the deeper meaning that animates an age or a form of life.

Journalists and intellectual historians suggest this expressive representativeness when they suggest that someone or something embodies the spirit of an age. Expressiveness is closely related to exemplary inclusion, in part because one way to become an exemplar is to articulate the wider meaning that defines a form of life. The difference is that what I'm calling "exemplarity" can be a function of demography—a woman artist is, in this sense, supposed to represent women, and including the artist in a collection is supposed to be a way of recognizing women—while expressiveness should somehow go deeper than this. For example, the great writer Ralph Ellison, the iconic American writer, was an eminence in the 1960s and was still regarded as a token of the type "Black writer"; but his work was not *expressive of* the cutting edge of Black writing in the 1960s. It represented an earlier era, an era defined by, among other things, relationships between race, nationality, and class that had come in for withering criticism by the artists that many of us now regard as representing 60s-style American and Black American culture work.

Comforting Myths and an Illustrative Case

I have distinguished these four conceptions of representation for the sake of analysis and argument, but the distinctions may not seem hard and fast just yet. There are at least a couple of reasons for this. For one thing, the conceptual distinctions can probably do with some more refinement. For another, the different kinds of representation may overlap in practice in ways that may make it hard to operationalize the general accounts presented above. I'll refine the distinctions in this section by working through the areas of overlap using an illustrative case.

The case comes from the writer Rabih Alameddine. In a recent essay interrogating the idea of "world literature," he writes the following:

> This is not a discussion of authenticity. I'm not sure I believe in the concept. . . . What I'm talking about, in my roundabout way, is representation—how those of us who fall outside the dominant culture are allowed to speak as the other, and more importantly, for the other. (Alameddine 2019, 1–10)

This passage clearly puts the second and third conceptions of representation firmly in play. The elements of fiduciarity may be most prominent, as they give Alameddine's complaint its bite. But even apart from the ethical or political burden of fiduciary representation—of speaking *for* the other—there is the question of exemplarity—of speaking *as* the other, or of simply ensuring that some instance of a type is present in a space. On his way to a point like this, Alameddine notes that "world literature" works as a genre of writing in part by "adding another modifier, creating another box—Black writer, queer writer, and now the world literature writer" (Alameddine 2019)—that literature's gatekeepers and customers can check on their way to reassuring themselves of their cosmopolitanism and liberality. There are worse ways to cash out the idea of exemplarity than by reference to checking boxes. (The problem with this box-checking exercise, one problem, Alameddine says, is that the gatekeepers et al. don't work particularly hard at it, which is why the world lit lists tend to be filled with Western educated writers who work in English. We'll return to this.)

Alongside considerations of exemplarity and fiduciarity, Alameddine's complaint clearly also implicates questions of aboutness and expressiveness. One point of insisting on a world literature worthy of the name is to provide readers seeking to expand their horizons with access to the world, by depicting the parts of it that they don't know as well as their own and probably cannot visit with ease. Writing that aims to play this role will necessarily open itself to questions rooted in the first conception of representation, questions about the quality of its depiction, about how well, how faithfully, it manages to be about whatever it depicts.

Another reason to insist on a truly world literature, and a key element of Alameddine's complaint, emerges from considerations rooted in the fourth conception of representation-as-expressiveness. It takes a certain kind of world to have a world literature. This world must be urbane and cosmopolitan; it must avoid parochialism and invidious exclusion and remain open to the Other. Above all, and to Alameddine's point, this world must reassure itself that it is this kind of world, even at the cost of *mis*representing the degree and kind of Otherness that defines the actual world. A world like this will curate a comfortable world of *safe* Others, with Western educations and the ability to "cite Shakespeare with the best of them" (Alameddine 2019). All of which is, I think, to indicate what works of world literature are, in some sense, really about, or expressive of: a keen cultural hunger, a powerful sociopolitical neurosis, and the strikingly post-(post-)colonial dimensions of the contemporary moment (at least in places where people speak English and cite Shakespeare).

While this quick reading of Alameddine's critique of world literature helps clarify the differences between the four conceptions of representation, it is more valuable for my purposes because it begins to show how the various conceptions of representation intertwine to give shape to specific cases. The "speaking-for" of fiduciarity is rooted in the "speaking-as" of exemplarity: the presence of the token—the Lebanese writer, in Alameddine's case—not only ensures that the type is represented in the literary publishing ecosystem, but also carries presumptions of the token's authority as a kind of advocate, ambassador, or cultural diplomat. This happens in part because sensitivity to the demands of exemplarity and recognition—a rightful disdain for wrongful exclusions—has built demand for works that seem to express the spirit of a postcolonial, cosmopolitan world. And the works that satisfy this demand will depict the actual world in particular ways, using representations that, if Alameddine is right, support certain "comforting myths"—the title of his essay—about the accessibility and adequacy of an exotic but nonthreatening Otherness.

THE DIMENSIONS OF SOCIAL IDENTITY

This is not the place to defend or fully develop Alameddine's "comforting myths" argument. I offer it here in part for the reasons noted above—to help operationalize and clarify my sense of the four conceptions of representation. I offer it also, though, to show how the four conceptions converge and collide with rather striking intensity in cases involving social identities. In advance of considering the remaining cases, it may help to say a word about what social identities are and how they work, informed by the helpful reflections of K. Anthony Appiah and Linda Martín Alcoff (Appiah 2005; Alcoff 2015).

To talk about social identity in the ways that have become common among Western scholars and activists is to refine older, more general ideas of personal identity in light of certain specific conditions of social life. If personal identity has to do, as Appiah puts it, with who one truly is (Appiah 2005, 65), then social identity has to do with the way social forces and conditions shape who one is. We think of these forces most often in relation to the prominent axes of social differentiation in contemporary societies: race, ethnicity, class, gender, nationality, and so on. But these social identities are just particularly familiar and influential examples of the broader phenomenon whereby individuals form their self-conceptions in relation to the various options, opportunities, and meanings that societies make available for this task. Scholars of social life have attended with care to a variety of less familiar social identities, or identities that we less often think of as social identities per se, from butlers and *flaneurs* to soldiers and sports fans.

In relation to the more familiar options for self-conception that track the prominent axes of social differentiation, it is particularly important to note, as Alcoff does, that social identities have multiple aspects. They take shape and do their work in multiple contexts and registers, from the epistemic and the ethical to the material, discursive, and historical. The failure or refusal to understand this causes a great deal of trouble for people seeking effective engagements with, or edifying explanations for, the social and political dimensions of selfhood.

Social identities work in the epistemic register because they are bound up with accounts of the individual's relationship to a social environment, and these accounts are more or less explanatory or obfuscatory. To borrow an example from literary theorist Paula Moya, a Latina college student in Texas who declines to think of herself as a Latina is more likely to be puzzled by certain predictable encounters—people complimenting her on her English, even if she has never spoken anything else; people assuming she's a custodian rather than a resident of her dorm; and so on—than someone who accepts the relevance of the social identity category "Latina" to her life. In this spirit, one might think of social identities as micro-scale social theories, oriented specifically to the paths that specific individuals are likely to take through a social environment.

Categories like "Latina" also clearly work in the ethical register. They invite the people to whom they apply—more on this shortly—to think of themselves as linked to particular communities by ties of sentiment and obligation, or as rightful heirs of particular cultural practices, or as honor-bound to embrace particular political commitments. They may also advance or impair the individual's attempts to live well, whatever this comes to, perhaps by recommending more or less fruitful opportunities for building political coalitions or for constructing a meaningful life.

Social identities can do this epistemic and ethical work because they are discursive phenomena. They are rooted in systems of shared meaning that shape the regular parameters for meaningful human expression, imagination, and interaction. Identities are in this sense bound up with the networks of convention and habit and signs and symbols that assign social roles, define human relationships, and shape ideas about core human values. Put differently, as discursive phenomena, they take part in what Althusser called "the manifold of social reality," or the sets of lenses through which human subjects encounter and examine the world. What this means in practice is that social identities can carry with them quite robust scripts for perceiving, imagining, and interacting with the world. To think of oneself not simply as someone who happens to have been sexually assaulted but as a sexual assault *survivor* is—and for most people this is the point of making the concept "survivor" available for this use—to embrace a vision of the social world that offers one a community, the ethical high ground, and, depending on the depth of the analysis, some social-theoretic resources for making sense of one's suffering.

The epistemic, ethical, and discursive dimensions of social identity have rather direct material implications. The systems of meaning that inform identity categories use the categories to shape the distribution of social goods and the structure of human experience. Racially oppressive societies, for example, work in part by leveraging the discursive character and the material implications of their racial categories. On the discursive level, they encourage people to think of themselves just as inhabitants of different social locations, with different prospects for flourishing and different levels of entitlement to a good life. At the same time, though, this discursive work has real, material outcomes. For example, apartheid-style race-thinking inequitably distributes resources like income, wealth, opportunities for education or employment, and access to public space. Or, to return to the example of the assault survivor: once people have access to the idea of the assault survivor as a kind of person (or, if that language raises metaphysical hackles, as a kind of thing a person might be, or as a name for an identifiable property a person might have), people will build programming for survivors, or write songs about them, or raise money for foundations and centers to support them.

In a different but related sense of materiality, it is important to note that social identities also shape individual experience. This phenomenological dimension is quite clear in the kind of apartheid societies contemplated above. The literatures of protest and criticism from these societies are replete with stories about how it feels to be a second-class citizen, if one is a citizen at all; of how it feels to know, to feel, that one doesn't belong and is not supposed to feel like one belongs in a society that is still, somehow, one's own. This phenomenon of course goes beyond apartheid societies. Traditions of performance and aesthetic practice that are linked to social identity categories, like the Black aesthetic tradition, trade heavily on the modes of experience that different categories recommend to different people. Different ways of styling and moving—and hence experiencing—one's body, of cultivating and employing one's voice, of imagining one's possibilities as an embodied being on the athletic field or the stage, all emerge from the mobilization and refinement of social identity categories.

Finally, the dimensions of social identity discussed above all emerge from and reflect specific historical contexts. Humans are unavoidably encultured beings, which is to say that we enter the world (or are thrown into it, Heidegger would say) at points and in places not of our choosing. Once we're here, early on we're stuck using the cultural resources that happen to surround us to come to grips with what we find. If we survive long enough, we will eventually be able to reflect on the available resources and choose some over others. But accidents of history already constrain the possibility space even for those choices. Within this already-narrowed possibility space, those of us not endowed with heroic capacities for self-criticism and healthy appetites for cultural analysis, which is to say the vast majority of us tend to not to blaze new trails on the journey toward self-discovery. So the identities we adopt and embrace and resist and revise are artifacts of moments in the evolution of social life, and bear the marks of their creation. Or: identities like "race woman" or "homosexual" or "dandy" or "housewife" came into being at particular moments in time, in the context of specific social, political, and cultural dynamics. Grappling with these identities—for example, by making art that explores or presupposes them—means grappling with the contexts that produced them, and perhaps intervening in those contexts and contributing to the process of their ongoing development.

I've spoken so far of social identities, with their five dimensions, both as preexisting conditions of the social environment and as options for individuals to embrace or refuse. This duality is crucial to understanding how social identities work and how the controversies involving them get traction. On the one hand, social identity categories can get ascribed to individuals by others. If one's fellows discern that one satisfies the conditions for the application of an identity term—born in the right place to the right people, or possessing the right physiognomic traits, or displaying the right cultural preferences or sexual desires, or whatever—then they apply the term and that's that. On the other hand, social identity categories are resources that individuals can use or refuse. One may embrace the ascribed identity and identify with it or reject it and identify with something else. The challenges and implications of ascription and identification—and the tensions between them, when one declines to identify with the label that society ascribes—are rich sources of ethical controversy, as Alameddine's comforting myths essay makes quite clear. To be designated an ambassador for something called "world literature" is to play a role, or to occupy a space, in a network of meanings and practices that in some ways have very little to do with the individual writer. The individual writer might notice this and question the value and applicability of the category.

Transition: From Maps to Cases

Having completed a preliminary mapping of a few key forms of representation, we can now connect questions of representation to other issues—on the one hand, questions of appropriation, inclusion, and the like; on the other hand, to problems of artworld representation and the politics of social identity. To that end, it will be instructive to consider some more illustrative cases.

I've chosen these cases in part because they are timely, which has less to do with tracking current controversies than with tracking sea changes in the workings of certain artworlds. The controversies discussed below reveal particularly striking shifts in the broader social conditions under which artists both do their work and relate their work to the wider social world.

Newfields, New (Art)world

In the spring of 2021, Charles Venable, then the head of the Indianapolis Museum of Art at Newfields, resigned his post. He did this after the museum used some ill-advised language to advertise its search for a new director. The new director was supposed to free Venable from museum oversight duties so that he could run the wider complex. According to the job announcement, however, the new director was also supposed to carry out this work with a surprising goal in mind: to "attract a broader and more diverse audience while maintaining the museum's traditional core, white art audience." This genuflection to the "core, white" audience led hundreds of museum and art world stakeholders to complain and eventually publish a *j'accuse* open letter. This in turn led the Newfields board to publish a *mea culpa* open letter, acknowledging the misstep and the criticism and vowing to do better (Cascone 2021; Bahr 2021).

How did the board propose to do better? The following action items from the Newfields letter provide some insight.

- This morning, we accepted Dr. Charles Venable's resignation as President of Newfields. We thank him for his service and agree that his resignation is necessary for Newfields to become the cultural institution our community needs and deserves.
- We will engage an independent committee to conduct a thorough review of Newfields's leadership, culture and our own Board of Trustees and Board of Governors, with the goal of inclusively representing our community and its full diversity.
- We will expand curatorial representations of exhibitions and programming of/for/by Black, Latino/a/x, Indigenous, Women, People with Disabilities, LGBTQIA, and other marginalized identities. (Newfields Board 2021)

Notice that two of our four senses of representation appear in this list and a third is implicit. Starting at the top: the community, they say—"*our* community"—*deserves* something from Newfields, as, apparently, a fellow member of the community charged with some duties of care or loyalty. They follow this implicit acknowledgment of fiduciary representativeness by explicitly embracing "the goal of inclusively representing our community and its full diversity," which is to say that they had failed the test of inclusion and exemplarity. Then, finally, they pledge to "expand curatorial representations" of people with "marginalized identities." This pledge links the prospects for representation-as-depiction (or some such) to the work of representation-as-inclusion: including works *"of/for/by"* marginalized artists will not only break down barriers to inclusion and make the collection and programming more representative, but will also change the overall content profile of the museum, as the exhibitions and programs begin to feature work that takes up—is about, represents—topics in which previous curatorial regimes had little interest.

It may be useful to take a step back and flesh out the controversy these pledges mean to defuse. What is so wrong with the Newfields job posting? We talk all the time about Blackness; why not talk about whiteness? The core audience probably is white, if the museum is like most well-resourced museums in the United States. A responsible leader of such an organization will of course, other things equal, want to cultivate the core audience rather than alienate it.

What's wrong with the appeal to the white audience is its commitment to racial innocence. I use "racial innocence" more or less the way James Baldwin does, to denote the passionate attachment to a kind of willful ignorance by agents who "do not know . . . and do not want to know" about the human devastation that results from racial oppression (Baldwin [1962] 1998, 292). The force of appealing to innocence rather than simply to the epistemic failure of ignorance is to track the multiple layers of this condition. One layer is epistemic, rooted in social mechanisms for routinely producing ignorance and distorting inquiry. Another is ethical, rooted in the justice-relevant outcomes of the mechanisms for producing ignorance and in the states of character that allow people to play their roles in the operation of these mechanisms. A third layer is phenomenological, rooted in the affective and volitional states that leave people attached to and invested in the untruths and silences of racially oppressive social formations.

This account of racial innocence, or something like it, is essential to understanding the downfall of Charles Venable at Newfields. The museum's core audience surely is white, but for reasons that trace to the same historical dynamics that created wealth in white communities while declining to do so in, or removing it from, other communities. Wealth is the easiest factor to consider here, given its clear relevance to one's orientation to the artworld and its obvious connections to racial identity and membership in racialized populations. But it is not the only factor.

We might tell long, detailed stories here about the construction of cultural sophistication as a marker of middle-class status and, hence, given the white supremacist circumscription of US policies for building its middle class, as a marker of whiteness. Or about the exclusion of nonwhite communities from the kind of outreach that built museum audiences. Or about the conditions under which some people came by the opportunities to build and visit museums and sit on their boards while others did not and could not. (I recently heard a Black curator from working-class roots in the southern United States explain that she never set foot in a museum until she went to college, and that she owed her love of art largely to childhood experiences with her grandfather, who closely studied the images in newspaper articles about the museum exhibitions he couldn't attend.) But this is not that kind of essay. I'll write a blank check for all of those stories and turn in a direction more appropriate for an exercise in philosophical aesthetics.

It is important to remember who museums are for and what communities and populations they think they serve. Better put, it is important to remember to ask who particular museums are for, which is to say that the thing philosophers often call "the artworld" is an actual world of buildings and organizations, and this world must somehow map onto the regular social world. This mapping tends to be uneven and messy in ways that philosophers tend not to explore.

In this connection, it is probably worth noting that the Newfields campus of the Indianapolis Museum is named for a house on the former estate of the Lilly family, which it now occupies. This is the family of Eli Lilly, founder of what has over the last century become a wealthy and influential pharmaceutical concern. In the 1960s, the Lilly family donated the family estate to the organization that would eventually become the Indianapolis Museum (Newfields 2021). The museum and the campus are in the 46208 postal code, an area where the population is roughly half Black.

Under these conditions, to express concern, as Venable did, for the care and feeding of an arts organization's core, *white* audience is to make clear that the challenge of mapping the artworld onto the world-world is a challenge of ethics and representation. One has to join Venable in asking who and what these institutions really represent. And one ought to depart from him in asking it in a way that does not take the centrality of whiteness as a fait accompli, to be accommodated rather than interrogated. Of course, one way to read the appeal to the core whites is as a proxy for people with resources. But then one might think the question ought to be about the museum's business model, or about increasing public support for the arts, or about distributing resources more equitably so that whiteness ceases to serve as a proxy for resources. Considerations like these might productively supplant the impulse to find a director who can ensure the organization's continued alignment with white supremacist imperatives.[2]

We've made our way back to questions that go far beyond the scope of this piece, which means that it's time to turn to another case. A final observation is in order, though, about the artworld ethics of representation in the Newfields saga. We saw above that

[2] It is worth noting that Venable's downfall came less than a year after a Black woman named Kelli Morgan resigned as the Indianapolis Museum's associate curator. Morgan had been hired in part to promote diversity but, to hear her tell it, had taken that charge much more seriously than her employers meant for her to. She wrote about her experiences before leaving and on her way out and has spoken openly about them in the time since, charging in all these venues that the institution was not only not serious about diversity, but toxic for anyone who was or hoped to be (Bongiovanni 2020).

the saga clearly implicates three of the four kinds of representation. The museum board pledged to shift its curatorial energies toward inclusively representing different artists and art in its collection and programming, thereby presumably, inevitably, opening itself to supporting works and programs that represent the world differently than the core audience might expect. Their letter also nodded toward being a better representative of the community—toward more effectively discharging something like a fiduciary duty with respect to the (mostly Black, we now know) community that the museum claims to represent.

The appeal to racial innocence points also toward a role for the fourth conception of representation in our understanding of the Newfields controversy. Many race theorists argue that one of the defining features of racial politics in recent years is the growing influence of a kind of postracial sensibility (Taylor 2014, 9–25). Postracialism means different things to different people, but one of its critical meanings involves the determination to downplay the importance of race—on the theory that we've put all that behind us—while obscuring or ignoring the way racially oppressive and exclusionary dynamics continue to operate. It involves a kind of amnesia or myopia with respect to the ongoing operation of racially stratifying social forces, and it depends on racial innocence to persist and spread. The Newfields saga, with its enactment of a passionate attachment to willful ignorance, embodies what many people regard as the spirit of the age. One might say that this case is a clarifying expression of the political and cultural moment, in the sense of "expression" that informs the fourth conception of representation noted above.

Hamilton and the Hemings Cameo

After Lin-Manuel Miranda's *Hamilton* opened at the Public Theater in 2015, it went on to one of the most celebrated runs that any musical theatre piece has seen this century.[3] It may have enjoyed *the* most celebrated run if one considers White House invitations and crossover success beyond the Tony awards crowd. After a lucrative stint on Broadway, the production spawned an album-length cast recording, a "mixtape" album (of popular musicians performing the songs), a songbook, a crowd-sourced annotation project (think a Norton Critical Edition of the lyrics by way of Wikipedia), and an official book of annotations, blessed by Miranda himself. Along the way, the production became a famously hot ticket for US political and cultural elites, counting both Mike Pence (Donald Trump's vice president) and Barack Obama among its famous attendees. (Obama invited the cast to perform at the White House.)

The key to the production's success also makes it both controversial and relevant to our study of representation in art and ethics. *Hamilton* is a hiphop musical that uses cross-racial casting to reimagine America's founders as Black and brown people and

---

[3] See (Alemeddine 2019, 7).

that uses hiphop cultural references to insist on the continuities between the founders—including an immigrant from the Caribbean, Alexander Hamilton—and today's striving immigrants and people of color. One would be hard-pressed to design an artistic study of the issue of representation that would cue up the issues more effectively than this production.

Consider how clearly *Hamilton* puts three of the four conceptions of representation into play. The cross-racial casting of course immediately raises the issue of representation-as-depiction. Then there are Miranda's explicit efforts to advance the cause of inclusive representation, by doing, as one writer sees it, "what many history curricula fail to do: allow[ing] young people of color to see themselves in history" (James 2015). Finally, representation-as-expression might be central to the wider *Hamilton* phenomenon. Most commentators seemed to agree with some version of musicologist Philip Gentry's description of its cultural meaning, though fans of the production would surely object to his clearly negative, or at least skeptical, orientation: "Hamilton," he writes, "has . . . become a metonym for a certain kind of liberal identity politics characterized most of all by aspirational optimism tinged with nationalist fervor" (Gentry 2017, 273). It was, in other words, the perfect production for the Obama era, with its determination to desegregate America's mythology while reaffirming the enduring relevance of American values and the timeless heroism of the founders. How much mileage one gets from that will depend on what one thinks of America's values, explicit and implicit, and of its founders.

The different ways of reading and reacting to Miranda's integrationist patriotism point to the controversy that attended the production, and to the remaining conception of representation. Let's say that the three conceptions considered just above provide answers to three different questions: What is this about? Who gets a voice, or a seat at the table? And what is this *really* about, at the deeper level of underlying cultural significance? The first and third questions are also requests for interpretation and critical engagement, but a minimally responsible answer—skirting around the hermeneutic forests in which we could easily lose ourselves—will say something first about the persistent relevance of America's founding ethos, or about the continuities between the upstarts of the founding generation and the upstarts of today's postcolonial, postsegregation generations; and then about the achievement of something like multicultural liberalism. At this point the aboutness questions converge on the question of voice and inclusion: when a Black George Washington can sing to an actual US president who is actually Black about the burdens of democratic leadership, America has made room for some new voices.

What all of this leaves out is the question that representation-as-fiduciarity invites us to ask: Who, exactly, is all this for? Whose interests are being represented? The writer Ishmael Reed makes the relevance of this question clear with this pithy takedown of Miranda's production: "Can you imagine Jewish actors in Berlin's theaters taking the roles of Goering? Goebbels? Eichmann? Hitler?" This question grows out of the realization that Reed folded into the title of his essay: What does it mean when Black actors dress up like slave traders—Washington, Jefferson, apparently Hamilton, though the actual historical details here were a matter of some controversy, and so on—and it's not Halloween (Reed 2015)?

Another way to raise the worry about fiduciarity that Reed highlights is to ask what happens to the *actual* people of color people who shared the world of the founding with Hamilton and the rest. Sally Hemings makes a brief, ethically tone-deaf appearance, in a moment that threatens to unwind the entire production in ways I'll soon consider. But she is the only one. One historian sums up the difficulty this choice creates for the production by noting that someone watching Hamilton "could easily assume that slavery did not exist in this world, and certainly that it was not an important part of the lives and livelihoods of the men who created the nation" (Monteiro 2018).

It gets worse. Hemings was of course the enslaved woman who bore several of Thomas Jefferson's children in an arrangement that one might say, if one were inclined to treat Jefferson very generously, she had very little power to refuse. The historical record seems to show that she had and used some leverage, but the state of contemporaneous US policy with respect to forced labor and Black legal personhood was such that one might also be inclined to say simply that she was a rape survivor. However one characterizes the situation, it seems incongruous to have that woman make her only appearance in this egalitarian, multicultural reimagining of the founding moment by dancing into view—in the person of a member of the production's ever-present dance team and chorus—in response to Jefferson's impish request that she collect and bring him some papers. She complies, with a smile, and then dances away.

To which one has to ask: Who is this for? Who does this represent? If this production is supposed to help people of color see themselves in the founding, what does it mean that it invites them *not* to see the *actual* people of color who participated in the founding, and that it hauls into view and then downplays the sexual violence that was at the heart of the early republic's business model? Does this production represent Miranda's striving immigrants, people who share his own story of pluckiness, hard work, and democratic aspirations? Or does it represent something less lofty—like, say, the community of American elites, a community to which Miranda gained entry with *Hamilton*, a community of people for whom the cost of admission is subordinating worries about sexual violence and the afterlives of slavery to celebrations of America's democratic experiment?

CONCLUSION

I've undertaken this study of representation and identity in art in the hope of providing useful tools for the work of social criticism, art criticism, and cultural criticism. Tools like these are vital because identity-based forms of dominance and oppression are part of the fabric of contemporary social life, and because art and aesthetics help weave that fabric into its various configurations. The ethico-political function of art and the aesthetic is not obscure: it is a familiar aspect of social life. It nevertheless remains somewhat undertheorized, at least among Anglophone philosophical aestheticians. As a consequence, we've done less than we might have to fashion useful tools and practice employing them effectively.

The map and account of artworld representation introduced above is one contribution to the toolbox, and the cases discussed along the way show what it looks like when the tools are in use. If what I've said in this chapter is right, then questions of representation can take at least four forms. They can concern what a work is about, which is at least in part to say, what it depicts, how it depicts, and, perhaps, what it *ought* to depict. They can ask whose interests some artworld phenomenon serves, where "artworld phenomenon" can mean a work of art like *Hamilton* or an institution like the Indianapolis Museum. They can ask whether the artworld phenomenon adequately reflects the composition or character of some broader community, population, or social context, from civic contexts like the 46208 postal code to the national context of Lin-Manuel Miranda's excluded immigrants and people of color. Or they can pose the broadly phenomenological question of whether and how this artworld phenomenon captures or reflects the meaning of a particular cultural moment.

Earlier in the chapter I noted certain connections between the topic of representation and the ethically fraught topics that have made their way more securely into contemporary philosophical aesthetics. These other topics—appropriation and recognition, most saliently—have spawned their own cottage industries of commentary and analysis, so I've said little about them here. (See Nguyen and Strohl, this volume, for an overview of questions about cultural appropriation.) My aim was to explore the concept of representation to reveal the several layers of meaning that attach to it and to point toward points of convergence with these other subjects. Those points of convergence are not hard to locate—an easy reading of *Hamilton*, for example, or of what *Hamilton* means to be, might position it as a demand for recognition on the part of America's neglected peoples; and an easy critique might read it as an appropriation of hiphop culture for the benefit of the American empire. My aim has not been to add to the literatures on those more familiar topics, but to show the value of some notion of representation as a way of getting to those questions—by, for example, asking about the interests that *Hamilton* represents and about the costs of its demand for inclusive representation.

Having refined the notion of representation to a point at which the connections to recognition, appropriation, and other topics come more clearly into view, I can bring this study to a close. Scholars, critics, curators, and other culture workers in the orbit of art history, museum studies, and other fields talk routinely about the burdens of representation, but in ways that, at least in my experience, and for perfectly sensible reasons, roam freely across the distinctions that I've tried to introduce here. Perhaps this down payment on a more precise mapping of the conceptual space will make room for deeper interdisciplinary explorations of these topics, with philosophers working alongside colleagues in other fields to advance our shared purposes.

See also: Carter and Mason, Clavel-Vázquez, Nguyen and Strohl, this volume

REFERENCES

Alcoff, Linda Martín. 2015. *The Future of Whiteness*. Cambridge: Polity.

Alameddine, Rabih. 2019. "Comforting Myths." In *The Best American Essays 2019*, edited by Rebecca Solnit, 1–10. New York: Houghton Mifflin Harcourt.

Appiah, K. A. 2005. *The Ethics of Identity*. Princeton, NJ: Princeton University Press.

Bahr, Sarah. 2021. "Charles Venable Resigns as Head of Indianapolis Museum of Art." *New York Times*, February 17, https://www.nytimes.com/2021/02/17/arts/design/charles-venable-resigning-indianapolis-museum.html.

Baldwin, James. 1962. *The Fire Next Time*, in *James Baldwin: Collected Essays*, edited by Toni Morrison, 288–348. New York: Library of America, 1998.

Bongiovanni, Domenica. 2020. "Curator Calls Newfields Culture Toxic, Discriminatory in Resignation Letter." *Indianapolis Star*, July 18, https://www.indystar.com/story/entertainment/arts/2020/07/18/newfields-curator-says-discriminatory-workplace-toxic/5459574002/.

Cascone, Sarah. 2021. "Newfields Director Charles Venable Has Resigned After Posting a JobAd That Sparked Allegations of Racism." *Artnet News*, February 17, https://news.artnet.com/art-world/newfields-director-charles-venable-resigns-1944704.

Gentry, Philip. 2017. "Hamilton's Ghosts." *American Music* 35, no. 2 (Summer): 271–280.

Goodman, Nelson. 1968. *Languages of Art: An Approach to a Theory of Symbols*. Indianapolis: Bobbs-Merrill.

Hardimon, Michael O. "The Ordinary Concept of Race." *Journal of Philosophy* 100, no. 9(2003): 437–455.

James, Kendra. 2015. "Race, Immigration, and Hamilton: The Relevance of Lin-ManuelMiranda's New Musical." *The Toast*, October 1, https://the-toast.net/2015/10/01/race-immigration-and-hamilton/.

Monteiro, Lyra D. 2018. "Race-Conscious Casting and the Erasure of the Black Past in Hamilton." In *Historians on Hamilton: How a Blockbuster Musical Is RestagingAmerica's Past*, edited by Renee C. Romano and Claire Bond Potter, 58–70. New Brunswick, NJ: Rutgers University Press.

Nakase, Justine. 2021. "From White Othello to Black Hamlet: A History of Race andRepresentation at the Gate Theatre." In *A Stage of Emancipation: Change and Progress at the Dublin Gate Theatre*, edited by Corporaal Marguérite and Van Den Beuken Ruud, 189–206. Liverpool: Liverpool University Press.

Newfields. nd. "History: Newfields," https://discovernewfields.org/about/history (accessed February 21, 2023).

Newfields Board of Trustees and Board of Governors. 2021. "Letter from our Board of Trustees and Board of Governors." https://discovernewfields.org/statement.

Reed, Ishmael. 2015. "'Hamilton: The Musical:' Black Actors Dress Up like Slave Traders . . . and It's Not Halloween," *Counterpunch*, August 21, https://www.counterpunch.org/2015/08/21/hamilton-the-musical-black-actors-dress-up-like-slave-tradersand-its-not-halloween/.

Taylor, Paul, C. 2014. "Taking Postracialism Seriously: From Movement Mythology to Racial Formation." *Du Bois Review: Social Science Research on Race* 11, no. 1: 9–25.

CHAPTER 44

....

ETHICS AND IMAGINATION

....

JOY SHIM AND SHEN-YI LIAO

IT is difficult to overstate the disarrayed state of scholarship at the intersection of ethics and imagination. A vast range of methodologies and motivations across philosophical subdisciplines present quite the organizational challenge to providing a comprehensive overview of the field. Our goal in this chapter is to trawl through these issues at the intersection of ethics and imagination to identify and organize the predominant debates. In the following sections, we present a taxonomy of issues: the first section focuses on questions that ask whether our imagination can be constrained by ethical considerations; the next section asks whether imagination can contribute to the cultivation of ethical lives through engagements with narrative artworks; the third section applies similar questions to a real-world context; and the final section centers around the issue of whether imagination contributes to constructing new ethical or political frameworks.

Before delving into these issues, some terminological notes are in order: we work with deliberately broad construals of both ethics and imagination to better account for the diversity of issues at stake in their intersection. Articulating a precise account of either ethics or imagination is beyond the scope of this chapter. The following conceptions of ethics and imagination encompass the breadth of ideas we work with. First, we take *ethics* as the set of norms governing human lives that are concerned with how to live and what to do; they constitute the standards of good and bad, right and wrong, permissible and impermissible, and so on. (See also Song, this volume.) While we acknowledge that some moral philosophers, following Bernard Williams ([1985] 2006), use "ethics" to refer broadly to the subject matter of moral philosophy and "morality" to refer narrowly to a specific development of the ethical that came from the Western tradition, we will use these terms interchangeably. Second, we take *imagination* to be the capacity for representing possibilities other than the actual, times other than the present, and perspectives other than one's own (Liao and Gendler 2019). The use of imagination is pervasive to human lives, including engaging with artworks, understanding the perspectives of others, practical decision-making, and thinking about theoretical possibilities.

ETHICAL CONSTRAINTS ON IMAGINATION

Initially, one might think that ethics and imagination operate in separate realms: ethics seems to be grounded in the real world, but imagination is often thought to roam free in fantasy lands; we typically make moral assessments on publicly available behavior, but imagination happens inside one's head. However, important questions arise at the intersection, complicating any simplistic dichotomies. This section provides an overview of some of these challenges, including the moral evaluation of imagination, the potential for morality's constraining our imaginative abilities, and the possibility of moral norms' governing our imaginings.

When it comes to the moral evaluation of imagination, philosophers primarily focus on positive reactions to imagining morally reprehensible objects (Cooke 2014; Gaut 1998; 2007; Smuts 2013; 2016). Specifically, the question of moral evaluation arises when we assess certain responses to imagining egregious scenarios: Is it *wrong* to take pleasure in imagining the undeserved suffering of others, given that the suffering is purely imagined? If such imaginings have no real-world effects (for example, if they fail to change one's attitudes toward the real world or motivate immoral actions), it might seem strange to subject them to moral evaluation. Yet if one takes pleasure in imagining torturing children but never harms any in real life, it might intuitively strike us as wrong. (See the discussion of the "gamer's dilemma" in Bartel, this volume.) Why might this be?

A common approach locates an intrinsic wrong in enjoying evil, even in imaginary contexts. In other words, it is wrong to take pleasure in imagining things that are bad in themselves (Smuts 2013; 2016). Attitudes directed toward imagined states of affairs can likewise be subject to moral evaluation if they reveal negative aspects of one's character (Gaut 1998). Additionally, some argue that the attitudes directed toward imagined scenarios and characters are likely to manifest in attitudes toward real entities of the relevant type as well (Gaut 1998; 2007; Gendler 2006a; 2008a; 2008b). For example, even if a rape fantasist only imagines raping fictional women, it is integral to his fantasy that he is raping *women*, beings of a kind that exist in the real world.

An alternative solution distinguishes "imagination" from "fictive imagination" (that is, imaginings about fictional states of affairs) as a way to assess relevant moral differences between, for instance, taking pleasure in imagining murdering a fictional character and imagining murdering a real person.[1] Those who take this distinction

---

[1] For a related distinction regarding fantasies (that is, conscious, pleasurable imaginings), see Cherry (1985; 1988), who differentiates "surrogate fantasies" from "autonomous fantasies," where the former typically involves situations that the fantasist would like to take place in reality and the latter involves scenarios that the fantasist does not want actualized (for example, someone might enjoy rape fantasies but not want rape to occur in reality). Autonomous fantasies on his view are far less morally problematic, maybe even morally innocuous, because of this lack of desire for actualization. Alternatively, see Sher (2019) who argues that morality does not govern private thought in general, because prohibitions against thoughts lack discrete boundaries and an individual's subjective world is impermeable to others.

seriously suggest that any moral assessments we make about one type of imagining cannot transfer to the other: "Even if we grant that it might sometimes be wrong to imagine *x* or to take pleasure in imagining *x*, nothing follows about the ethical status of fictively imagining *x*, with or without pleasure" (Cooke 2014, 317). So, while it might be wrong to find pleasure in imagining murdering a real person, it might not be wrong to take pleasure in a similar imaginative act if it is directed toward a fictional one.

Another issue at the intersection of ethics and imagination is "the problem of imaginative resistance," which suggests that morality seems to impose constraints on imagination. *Imaginative resistance* occurs when an otherwise competent imaginer experiences a psychological tension when prompted to engage in an imaginative activity (Gendler and Liao 2016; Miyazono and Liao 2016; Tuna 2020). While we can easily imagine various things that do not exist in the real world, like flying castles, golden mountains, and grumpy ogres who befriend talking donkeys, it might be difficult, perhaps even impossible, for us to imagine forks that are indistinguishable from televisions, five-fingered ovals, and female infanticide being a paragon of ethical conduct, even in the context of fiction.[2] This contrast between easy and challenging cases gives rise to the following problem: Why is it that certain imaginative acts are met with resistance while others are not?

Although imaginative resistance seems to occur with a diverse range of imagined objects and scenarios (Kim et al. 2019; Walton 1994; 2006; Weatherson 2004; Yablo 2002), the initial cases that attracted philosophers' attention (and the cases we focus on here) tend to involve engagement with fictions that run counter to one's moral sensibilities (Gendler 2000; 2006b; Moran 1994; Walton 1990; 1994). Most people, for instance, experience difficulties trying to imagine the following: "In killing her baby, Giselda did the right thing; after all, it was a girl" (Walton 1994, 37).

This prompt has been subject to myriad analyses in the literature. It requires one to imagine that "Giselda did the right thing" in killing her baby on grounds of its gender; to accept the prompt, one must imagine having a positive moral evaluation of female infanticide. One possible explanation for why most people experience difficulty in imagining this prompt is because they do not endorse the moral evaluation in reality. However, as we have seen, we are typically able to imagine many things we do not believe exist in the real world, especially in the context of fiction. What makes the Giselda prompt any different, and why does this resistance arise? Various solutions have been proposed. For the purposes of this chapter, we expound the two main types of diagnoses on the nature of imaginative resistance.[3]

---

[2] Note that the imaginative resistance literature typically involves engagement with *fiction* in particular, but it is possible that the phenomenon can apply more broadly (see, for examples, Gendler 2006b).

[3] The two positions we outline are generally considered part of "first-wave" analyses of imaginative resistance, which take the mechanisms and psychological components of the phenomenon as the topics of disagreement. Some other approaches are worth noting: *eliminativists* stand in opposition to the majority theorists working in this tradition (who affirm the existence of imaginative resistance) by raising doubts about imaginative resistance's status as a *sui generis* phenomenon (Mothersill 2003; Sauchelli 2016, 2019; Tanner 1994; Todd 2009); and "second wave" analyses attempted to shed insight on

First, *cantian* theories of imaginative resistance locate the "resistance" in an *inability* to imagine—no matter how hard one tries to imagine certain things, one *can't* (Meskin and Weinberg 2003; Stear 2015; Walton 1990; 1994; Weatherson 2004; Weinberg and Meskin 2006; Yablo 2002). When it comes to prompts like the Giselda proposition, it seems like we simply lack the ability to imagine that female infanticide is morally right. To support this claim, cantians often appeal to a "Reality Principle," which posits constitutive relations between base-level and higher-order propositions that are fixed across worlds, including fictional worlds. Some variation of this principle is often invoked to impose limitations on authorial authority in determining what can be made fictional—authors lack authority to create fictional worlds that deviate significantly from some base-level facts (Walton 1990; 1994; Weatherson 2004; Yablo 2002). Just like how authors cannot make conceptual impossibilities such as square circles exist in their fictions, they cannot make moral impossibilities exist. Our inability to imagine results from an author's failed attempts to breach such laws.

Second, *wontian* theories maintain that we are not unable, but merely *unwilling* to engage with certain imaginative prompts—we simply *won't* imaginatively engage with a fiction that runs counter to our morals (Gendler 2000; 2006b; Currie 2002; Stokes 2006). Contrary to the cantian claim, wontians deny that conceptual impossibilities are what evoke imaginative resistance: conceptual impossibilities are not necessary because some stories seem able to make contradictory propositions hold true in the fictional context they build, and they are not sufficient because imaginative resistance can be evoked for stories that do not rest on conceptual impossibilities (Gendler 2000). On the wontian account, imagining turns out to be an act that exercises and engineers the imaginer's conceptual repertoire and appraisal habits. So morality imposes a constraint on our imagination, but not in the way cantians suggest. According to wontians, we can in principle imagine the fictional truth of the Giselda proposition, but we are unwilling to do so on moral grounds.

Further insight into the relationship between ethics and imagination can be drawn from adjacent literature that examines questions of ethical considerations bearing on other mental states. Surprisingly, attempts to bridge these literatures are currently rare, if not nonexistent. Here, we identify some parallels that have been overlooked thus far. For one, we could forge a connection between imaginative resistance and the burgeoning literature in moral encroachment of belief (Basu 2021; Bolinger 2020; Moss 2018). Moral encroachment tracks the idea that moral considerations can factor into epistemic phenomena, such as the justification of beliefs.[4] If this is right, it could potentially bolster the idea that moral factors bear on the imaginative realm as well, that is, features of

---

the phenomenon through examining both contextual differences (Black et al. 2018; Liao et al. 2014; Liao 2016; Nanay 2010; Weinberg 2008) and individual differences (Barnes and Black 2016; Clavel-Vazquez 2018; Peterson 2019).

[4] We note that although research in moral encroachment varies widely in methodology and motivations, this characterization of moral encroachment follows the general consensus of the concept in its most basic form. Going into the specificities of this debate is beyond the scope of this current chapter, but see Bolinger (2020) for an illuminating review of the varieties of studies that tend to fall under the label "moral encroachment."

imagination such as the ability to imagine or the authority to create scenarios to prompt imagination could be governed by moral norms. Indeed, we can plausibly construe the cantian theory as mapping onto a similar concept—the *moral encroachment* of imagination. As a tentative example, there might be parallel considerations between how authorial authority breaks down with significant deviations from moral constraints and how epistemic justification can be impacted by moral factors.

Next, in addition to the moral evaluation of the imaginings themselves (which we covered earlier in this section), we might draw further inspiration from the literature on *doxastic wronging* to investigate whether imaginings can *wrong others*. Proponents of doxastic wronging claim that beliefs in themselves can wrong others, even if they never get expressed or put into action (Basu 2021; Basu and Schroeder 2019). Specifically, beliefs can wrong in virtue of their content, for example, forming beliefs about someone based on stereotyped representations of their race can wrong them insofar as the believer fails to respect that person's individual agency. (See Clavel-Vázquez, this volume.) Turning to the imaginative realm, Robin Zheng and Nils-Hennes Stear (2023) argue that imaginings can wrong in virtue of their content when they realize a controlling image or normalizing oppressive behavior, in congruence with oppression, in a specific sociohistorical context. Thinking about the imaginative analogue of doxasting wronging could bolster the wontian theory by providing an explanation for why people resist imagining morally deviant propositions: perhaps we refuse to imagine certain prompts because we wish to evade moral culpability. Along these lines, we suggest that mining insights from adjacent literatures on ethics' bearing on other mental states can give us greater understanding of the interaction between morality and imagination.

THE FUNCTION OF NARRATIVE ARTS IN ETHICAL LIFE: A GUIDEBOOK FOR IMAGINATION?

Our next topic centers around the following question: to what extent can imaginative engagements with *narrative arts* (for example, literature, film, television, comics, etc.) influence people's morals?[5] Numerous theorists have offered accounts for ways in which imaginative engagement with narrative arts can morally educate or corrupt (Booth

[5] This debate has sometimes been referred to as the "moral persuasion" debate. Moral persuasion partially overlaps with, but is conceptually distinct from, the "value interaction" debate, which concerns the connection between aesthetic and moral values (see Liao and Meskin 2018, 659–662 for an overview; see also Giovannelli 2007 and McGregor 2014 for alternative taxonomies; and also see Carroll, Stear, Rothfeld, and Jacobson, this volume). The overlap occurs when, for instance, someone criticizes an artwork for morally corrupting its audience (moral persuasion) and that this ethical defect constitutes an aesthetic defect (value interaction). However, since one might endorse one claim but not the other (for example, one could affirm that an artwork morally corrupts its audience but deny that this constitutes an

1988; Depaul 1988; Jacobson 1997; Johnson 1994; Landy 2008; Mullin 2004; Robinson 2005; John, this volume).[6] In this section, we focus specifically on the role of imagination in *moral persuasion*, where narrative arts are thought to guide our imaginings in at least two ways: they facilitate the exploration and identification of morally significant patterns, and they can also prompt perspective-taking or the simulation of others' mental states. These imaginative mechanisms are thought to alter people's appraisal repertoire (that is, emotional, moral, and other responses) that can be deployed in real-life situations as well as merely fictional ones, providing another connection between the imaginative and ethical realms.

Narrative artworks can serve as "props" for testing, deepening, and refining our moral understanding in diverse scenarios without real consequences. Notably, Martha Nussbaum (1990; 1995) argues that imaginative engagement with literature helps people develop their ability to discern morally salient features of their situation; imagined scenarios enable emotional involvement without the taint of distorting self-interest. Given that narrative artworks are relatively self-contained in this manner, some have gone so far as to argue that they offer a *cognitively preferable* means to acquire epistemic benefits because of their simplicity (Elgin 2014).[7] This is because situations and people in real life are bound to be affected by endless connections to other features that could potentially merit consideration, while the nuanced depictions presented in fictional narratives are more tractable in typically being limited to descriptions of the story world.

Not all narratives guide imagination in the same way. Unfortunately, most philosophical discussions of narrative arts only examine examples in the *realist genre*, that is, the kind of fiction that is morally and psychologically realistic. James Harold (2007) critiques this narrow range of examples and uses the case of *Catch-22* to demonstrate how satire can guide imagination to cultivate our ethical lives in a distinctive way. Harold argues that while realistic narratives tend to invite readers to engage with the characters, *Catch-22* invites readers to maintain an ironic distance from the characters until the very end—this transition from disengagement to engagement encourages readers to reflect on the appropriate moral response to an absurd, unjust world. Generalizing Harold's observation, Shen-yi Liao (2013) analyses the genre of horror comedies such as *Evil Dead*

---

aesthetic defect) the two debates are conceptually distinct. This section sets aside the value interaction debate to focus on the role of imagination in the moral persuasion debate.

  [6] However, others have argued that narrative arts cannot offer any new, nontrivial moral knowledge (Lamarque and Olsen 1994; Posner 1997, 1998). In addition to the philosophical debate among these theorists, there is also a parallel empirical debate that occurs in fields such as psychology, communications, and media studies on the effect of narrative arts on cognitive attitudes (see Liao and Gendler 2011, 86–87 for an overview). See also John, this volume.

  [7] In this respect, narrative arts function similarly to thought experiments: both involve uses of imaginary scenarios for coming to new understandings of the real world (Gendler 2010). In fact, Jonathan Weinberg (2008) argues that philosophical thought experiments constitute a genre of narratives. One important difference is that while thought experiments primarily aim to generate new propositional knowledge, narrative arts (at least in the moral domain) also aim to generate other types of understanding, including a reconfigured appraisal repertoire.

2 to demonstrate that different narrative genres can guide imagination and cultivate our ethical lives in different ways. In addition, Paisley Livingston (2009) argues that the diversity of narrative artworks cautions against generic claims about narratives' capacity to educate and corrupt.

Another way narrative artworks can guide our imagination toward ethical ends is by prompting simulation (Currie 1995; Kieran 2003) or the adoption of a perspective (Camp 2009; 2017; Stueber 2008, 2016; von Wright 2002). Simulating a character's mental states involves cultivating a first-personal understanding of the character's mental states to imagine their experiences, rather than identifying or sympathizing with the character (Currie 1995). Narratives serve to orient readers in a manner appropriate for recreating another perspective by providing requisite information (Stueber 2008). Readers take the information that narratives provide to structure their understanding of characters and their way of experiencing the world.

Many theorists are optimistic about narrative artworks' capacity to foster empathy or compassion for others (Carroll 2000; 2002; Kieran 1996; Murdoch 1970). Martha Nussbaum (1990; 1995; 1997) is again a prominent advocate for the morally formative value of literature, advancing the view that literature can develop and exercise one's moral capacities via enhancing one's capacity for sympathetic understanding. This connection is well supported by empirical evidence (Djikic et al. 2013; Kidd and Castano 2013; Mar et al. 2006; 2009), particularly in developmental psychology (Gebhard et al. 2003; Melchiori and Mallett 2015; Vezzali et al. 2015).[8] The thought here is that children often acquire their moral capacities alongside exposure to stories by rehearsing empathetic responses to characters (Currie and Ravenscroft 2002; Ravenscroft 2012)—in rehearsing their empathetic responses, children recreate the emotional states of fictional characters and gain the ability to differentiate their own emotions from others', a skill they can also use to navigate real life situations.

However, this imaginative capacity also has the potential to *harm* moral development (Hurley 2004; Harold 2005). Matthew Kieran (2003) argues that narrative artworks espousing morally defective perspectives can be morally corruptive insofar as they invite one to imaginatively adopt dubious values and commitments. Using Martin Scorsese's crime film *Goodfellas* as a case study, he illustrates how the film entices audience members to absorb the values and commitments of the Mafia by rendering the deeply defective moral perspective intelligible. These values likely present a sharp divergence from the values the audience members hold in reality, creating a tension between the beliefs that they hold about the real world (for example, outgroup members are worthy of moral concern) and the ones they imagine holding about the fictional world (for example, outgroup members are morally insignificant).

---

[8] It is questionable that this moral formative value is unique to literature, and not common to all narrative arts: more recent experimental results show no measurable difference in empathizing abilities between groups that read literary fiction versus other reading materials (Panero et al. 2016). There also exists skepticism regarding the claim that children can transfer moral lessons from fictions to reality (Narvaez et al. 1998; Strouse et al. 2018).

A narrative artwork's power to edify can backfire when the work fails to meet epistemic standards, such as accuracy. When works present distorted depictions of marginalized groups, this can become particularly worrisome. For instance, *The Adventures of Huckleberry Finn* or *The Confessions of Nat Turner* can promote ignorance or arrogance on part of the reader in encouraging them to empathize with characters who have outlooks presented as representative of their social groups but actually deviate significantly from the group's actual outlook (Harold 2003; Shim 2022). This can in turn obscure the oppressive realities that the marginalized group faces, hampering progress in rectifying injustices. Thus, fiction plausibly serves as a guidebook for the imagination, but it can lead us to either morally enlightening or morally corrupt destinations. Although facilitating empathetic understanding is generally desirable, we ought to approach this ability with epistemic humility and caution for assessing the perspectives that a fiction prompts us to take.

SOCIAL COGNITION IN ETHICAL LIFE: IMAGINATION, FAST AND SLOW

Observing ethics and imagination in the context of fiction provides a relatively sterilized slate for theorists to distill the important features of their relation. However, ethics and imagination also interact in the absence of fictional prompts. Ethicists working outside of aesthetics have become increasingly interested in imagination as a facilitator for this kind of understanding toward real people and the implications it can have for our interpersonal relationships. In this section, we examine issues at the intersection of ethics and imagination that arise in real life, such as the function of imagination in moral deliberation and imagination's contribution to other mental states that are potentially subject to moral evaluation.

Moral theorists have identified imagination's role as providing us the means to view others as being worthy of serious moral concern (Jacobs 1991; Johnson 2016; Stueber 2016), as well as being a crucial element in moral decision-making (Biss 2014; Coeckelberg and Mesman 2007; Narvaez and Mrkva 2014). We can use imagination to explore different scenarios of moral significance without having to actually experience them. This can be applied in practice to various domains, such as medicine, in which imagination can play a practical role for medical practitioners in integrating an imaginative process into their decision-making processes. Here, imagination can help practitioners synthesize available information on the situation, empathize with the parties involved, and facilitate better outcomes for their patients after mentally exploring various possibilities for action (Coeckelbergh and Mesman 2007; Scott 1997).

In highlighting the practical applications of imagination, some theorists suggest that imagination is a skill that we can cultivate. Amy Kind (2020), for instance, argues that imagination can give us the ability to know what new experiences are like. If this is right, imagination can open radical possibilities for understanding others who have very different life experiences from ourselves, which can potentially foster greater care and empathy toward others. Some doubt the possibility that imagination has the ability to give us genuine understanding of situations that we have not actually experienced (Arpaly 2020; Elliot and Elliot 1991; Mackenzie and Scully 2007; Paul 2014). Moreover, others worry that taking this idea too seriously can promote epistemic arrogance, especially when dominantly situated imaginers claim that they can truly understand the experiences of marginalized people, even when they get it wrong (Frye 1992; Roelofs 2014; Shim 2022; Taylor 2014). So while imagination might help us achieve empathetic understanding, we might have reason to be sensitive to its potential limitations.

Another way that imagination can aid our moral development includes playing a role in autonomy, specifically in self-understanding, self-reflection, and practical deliberation about the self. On this point, Catriona Mackenzie (2000) suggests that failures of imagination that appear in stereotyped representations espoused in the dominant cultural repertoire of metaphors, symbols, and images could lead to failures in autonomy as well. Alternatively, we suggest that such failures in autonomy might not be caused by imaginative failures, but rather be *sustained* by imaginative practices: Our discussion so far has centered around imagination's role in "slow" moral cognition, that is, conscious, deliberate, and effortful ways of thinking. However, imagination might also play a role in "fast" moral cognition, that is, unconscious, automatic, and effortless ways of thinking. Traditional discussions of ethics have tended to focus on slow moral cognition, but in recent years fast moral cognition has gained traction. In what follows, we map out potential ways imagination can contribute to "fast" mental states that are potentially subject to moral evaluation, using implicit bias as a case study.[9]

The exact relationship between imagination and implicit bias is under debate. One approach is Ema Sullivan-Bissett's (2019) constitutive claim, in which implicit biases are unconscious imaginings. This account distinguishes two structures of implicit biases: associative implicit biases are constituted by multiple imaginings, and nonassociative implicit biases are constituted by single imaginings. Two major advantages of the imagination-based model of implicit bias are that the two different kinds of imaginings can accommodate the heterogeneity of the phenomenon, and since imagination is not constrained by truth, this model need not attribute contradictory beliefs to agents. Another approach follows an indirect causal claim proposed by Anna Welpinghus (2020), in which imagination plays a mediating role in turning implicit biases, whatever they turn out to be, into downstream effects. On this account, imagination is central to

---

[9] *Implicit bias* roughly encapsulates a cluster of representational mental states that can contribute to evaluative judgments and behavior (Brownstein 2019; Johnson 2020), which are typically assessed by implicit measures like the implicit association test (Greenwald et al. 1998). Given its heterogeneity as a concept, there remain numerous controversies in characterizing implicit bias, including its status as a psychological construct in the first place (Holroyd and Sweetman 2016; Machery 2022). Similarly, there remain controversies on agents' moral responsibility for implicit biases (Holroyd et al. 2017). We will set aside these controversies and focus on imagination's possible role in implicit bias.

decision-making because it is the mental activity with which we integrate a large array of social knowledge and elaborate the possibilities that we are considering.

If imagination is indeed linked to implicit bias in either of these ways, imaginings seem to be subject to moral assessment based on their downstream effects. Recently, moral theorists have shown special interest in the kind of implicit biases that might give rise to group-based discrimination, often based on negative stereotypes, for example, police officers are likely to associate Black bodies with criminality, which is plausibly connected to disproportionate levels of police violence against Black people (Correll et al. 2007; Eberhardt et al. 2004; Glaser and Knowles 2008; see Jost et al. 2009 for an overview). Such stereotypes tend to be intertwined with the dissemination of artworks—constantly depicting Black people as criminals in various media exposes audiences to this dangerous stereotype. If we combine this idea with the role of artworks in guiding imagination, we can see how imagination can be weaponized at a systemic level. So while imagination can, as we have shown, be cultivated for the betterment of ethical lives, it seems that it might also be utilizable for sustaining oppression. And this, perhaps, is yet another way in which imagination might be subject to further moral assessment.

MORAL AND POLITICAL IMAGINATION

So far, we have examined the interaction of ethics and imagination within the context of existing moral frameworks, either by applying them to the contents of imaginative attitudes or showing how imagination can facilitate the cultivation or transgression of them. In this final section, we examine yet another way in which imagination can bear on ethics: "moral imagination" or "political imagination" are thought to formulate or even constitute new moral, social, and political frameworks. This concept is typically invoked in highly heterogeneous ways—if imagination is the "junkyard of the mind" (Harpham 2017; see also Kind 2013), then moral and political imagination constitutes an especially messy area within.

We can begin tidying up this area of the junkyard by identifying an organizing principle behind disparate uses of the term: an emphasis on the creative and transcendental capacities of imaginings. To clarify this capacity, we can turn to a distinction posited by Gregory Currie and Ian Ravenscroft between *recreative* and *creative imagination*. Our focus until now has been on recreative imagination, that is, the capacity to cultivate or transgress existing moral (or political) frameworks. As we have seen, recreative imagination is exercised through engagement with narrative artworks or in ordinary social cognition. Creative imagination, by contrast, is the capacity for imagination to formulate or constitute new moral (and political) frameworks. It aims to combine ideas in unexpected and unconventional ways. Along these lines, some theorists argue that narrative artworks can stimulate an "imaginative leap" in its audiences to envision a morally better world (Kieran 1996; Stadler 2020).

Traditionally, morality has been conceived as a system of rational principles that seems *prima facie* at odds with the notion of imagination as unbound to reason. Accordingly, the earliest mentions of imagination in discussions of ethical reasoning tended to restrict imagination to the application of moral principles (Hare 1963; Werhane 1999; Williams 1997; see Fesmire 2003 for an overview). In particular, imagination was thought to play a role in moral deliberation by allowing us to imagine how requirements would play out in concrete situations. Such views tended to exhibit a wariness of imagination's potential to lead us to relativism if untempered by reason.

Recent thinkers have eschewed these concerns by demonstrating interest in developing a concept of *moral imagination* to delineate the means through which we explore and forge new values and commitments in the moral realm (Kekes 1991; 2006; Johnson 2016; Narvaez and Mrkva 2014). Moral imagination has been defined as "the expansive dimension of intelligence at work in the ongoing remaking of experience . . . a *process* of experiential transformation and growth" (Johnson 2016, 362) and "the operation of imaginative capacities by agents in pursuit of moral ends" (Biss 2014, 2). On these conceptions, moral imagination is intertwined with freedom by exhibiting the capacity to mentally explore what it is like to realize particular possibilities in the moral realm. John Kekes (1991) argues that the proper function of the moral imagination is not to free us from cultural conditioning, but rather to give us a tool to close the gap between what we consider to be reasonable beliefs about our possibilities and our actual beliefs. In other words, moral imagination should aim to help us explore or *imagine* different possibilities for action.

Some caution that moral imagination may not be intrinsically virtuous, insofar as it can also help us to contemplate and perform acts of evil (Jacobs 1991). However, as feminist philosophers have emphasized, moral imagination may be integral to circumventing dominant moral understandings that structure our interactions with the world (Babbitt 1996; Biss 2013; 2014; Clarke 2006; Cunliffe 2019; Murdoch 1992). For example, Bridget Clarke (2006) argues that exercising the moral imaginations entails envisaging alternative conceptions of people to the status quo. Following Iris Murdoch, she contrasts this with the notion of *fantasy*, which represents mere escapism—the moral imagination is not escapism, but rather a means by which we can generate new possibilities for our lived realities.

The literature on political imagination exhibits similar thematic commonalities. However, the concept of political imagination might have a distinctive origin, namely, C. Wright Mills's concept of *sociological imagination*, which "enables its possessor to understand the larger historical sense in terms of its meaning for the inner life and the external career of a variety of individuals. [The sociological imagination] enables [its possessor] to take into account how individuals, in the welter of their daily experience, often become falsely conscious of their social positions" (Mills [1959] 2000, 5). If we draw broad inspiration from this conception, we can construe *political imagination* as capturing the relationship between the mental lives of individuals and actual or possible sociopolitical arrangements. From this, we can identify two dimensions of variations to organize the diverse extensions of the concept.

First, political imagination can be internal or external. On the *internal* conception, political imagination concerns an individual's capacity to construct, critique, and challenge sociopolitical arrangements. For example, political theorist Hannah Arendt claims that radical social and political change "would be impossible if we could not mentally remove ourselves from where we physically are located and *imagine* that things might as well be different from what they actually are. In other words, the deliberate denial of factual truth-the ability to lie- and the capacity to change facts-the ability to act-are interconnected; they owe their existence to the same source: imagination" (Arendt 1972, 5). By contrast, on the *external* conception, political imagination exists as an emergent property of collective interactions, including ideologies and institutions that constitute social and political facts. For example, political philosopher Charles Taylor characterizes social imaginary as "the kind of common understanding that enables us to carry out the collective practices that make up our social life ... that is both factual and normative" (Taylor 2004, 24).

Second, political imagination can be *oriented* either conservatively or progressively. As Avshalom Schwartz notes, discussions of political imagination seem to ascribe contradictory capacities: "to both secure order and stability and encourage innovation and change" (Schwartz 2021, 2). Schwartz's diagnosis claims that imagination can have these seemingly contradictory uses because of differences in constraints (compare Kind and Kung 2016). On one hand, Taylor's conception exemplifies the *conservative* orientation, in which imagination is the social glue that enables institutions to sustain their structure. On the other hand, Arendt's conception exemplifies the *progressive* orientation, in which imagination is a central capacity that enables individuals to remake the world.

CONCLUSION

The terrain at the intersection of ethics and imagination is a particularly fecund area for scholarship. We have provided a sampling of the major issues that have garnered attention in recent years. Existing research provides great insight into the ways in which these realms interact: from morality's capacity to constrain our imaginative abilities, to imagination's role in cultivating moral understanding, to the way imagination can constitute moral frameworks. Though an impressive range of issues have been identified in the literature, this is by no means exhaustive of the field's potential. Several open questions remain: for example, where exactly moral assessment applies (that is, whether moral assessment should apply to the product of imagination, the imaginer, or the creator of the imagined object)? Are the "fast" and "slow" forms of imagination subject to the same level of moral assessment? What kinds of moral responsibilities do creators have when creating objects of imagination, and does this responsibility differ with varying levels of dissemination? We can look forward to further excursions in the field.[10]

See also: John, Clavel-Vázquez, Bartel, Eaton, this volume

[10] Both authors contributed to all aspects of this chapter. We thank Adriana Clavel-Vázquez, James Harold, and Nils-Hennes Stear for their incisive feedback.

REFERENCES

Arendt, Hannah. 1972. *Crises of the Republic: Lying in Politics; Civil Disobedience; On Violence; Thoughts on Politics and Revolution.* New York: Harvest.

Arpaly, Nomy. 2020. "What Is It Like to Have a Crappy Imagination?" In *Becoming Someone New: Essays on Transformative Experience, Choice, and Change,* edited by Enoch Lambert and John Schwenkler, 122–132. Oxford: Oxford University Press.

Babbitt, Susan. 1996. *Impossible Dreams: Rationality, Integrity and Moral Imagination.* Boulder, CO: Westview Press.

Barnes, Jennifer, and Jessica E. Black. 2016. "Impossible or Improbable: The Difficulty of Imagining Morally Deviant Worlds." *Imagination, Cognition and Personality: Consciousness in Theory, Research, and Clinical Practice* 36, no. 1: 27–40.

Basu, Rima. 2021. "A Tale of Two Doctrines: Moral Encroachment and Doxastic Wronging." In *Applied Epistemology,* edited by Jennifer Lackey, 99–118. Oxford: Oxford University Press.

Basu, Rima, and Mark Schroeder. 2019. "Doxastic Wrongings." In *Pragmatic Encroachment in Epistemology,* edited by Brian Kim and Matthew McGrath, 181–205. New York: Routledge.

Biss, Mavis. 2013. "Radical Moral Imagination: Courage, Hope, and Articulation." *Hypatia* 28, no. 4: 937–954.

Biss, Mavis. 2014. "Moral Imagination, Perception, and Judgment." *Southern Journal of Philosophy* 52, no. 1: 1–21.

Black, Jessica E., Stephanie C. Capps, and Jennifer L. Barnes. 2018. "Fiction, Genre Exposure, and Moral Reality." *Psychology of Aesthetics, Creativity, and the Arts* 12, no. 3: 328–340.

Bolinger, Renee J. 2020. "Varieties of Moral Encroachment." *Philosophical Perspectives* 34, no. 1: 5–26.

Booth, Wayne C. 1988. *The Company We Keep.* Berkeley: University of California Press.

Brownstein, Michael. 2019. "Implicit Bias." *Stanford Encyclopedia of Philosophy,* July 31, 2019. https://plato.stanford.edu/entries/implicit-bias/.

Camp, Elisabeth. 2009. "Two Varieties of Literary Imagination: Metaphor, Fiction, and Thought Experiments." *Midwest Studies in Philosophy* 33, no. 1: 107–130.

Camp, Elisabeth. 2017. "Perspectives in Imaginative Engagement with Fiction." *Philosophical Perspectives* 31, no. 1: 73–102.

Carroll, Noël. 2000. "Art and Ethical Criticism: An Overview of Recent Directions of Research." *Ethics* 110, no. 2: 350–387.

Carroll, Noël. 2002. "The Wheel of Virtue: Art, Literature, and Moral Knowledge." *Journal of Aesthetics and Art Criticism* 60, no. 1: 11–26.

Cherry, Christopher. 1985. "The Inward and the Outward: Fantasy, Reality and Satisfaction." *Canadian Journal of Philosophy* 11 (suppl.): 175–193.

Cherry, Christopher. 1988. "When is Fantasizing Morally Bad?." *Philosophical Investigations* 11, no. 2: 112–132.

Clarke, Bridget. 2006. "Imagination and Politics in Iris Murdoch's Moral Philosophy." *Philosophical Papers* 35, no. 3: 387–411.

Clavel-Vazquez, Adriana. 2018. "Sugar and Spice, and Everything Nice: What Rough Heroines Tell Us about Imaginative Resistance." *Journal of Aesthetics and Art Criticism* 76, no. 2: 201–212.

Coeckelbergh, Mark, and Jessica Mesman. 2007. "With Hope and Imagination: Imaginative Moral Decision-Making in Neonatal Intensive Care Units." *Ethical Theory and Moral Practice* 10, no. 1: 3–21.

Cooke, Brandon. 2014. "Ethics and Fictive Imagining." *Journal of Aesthetics and Art Criticism* 72, no. 3: 317–327.

Correll, Joshua, Bernadette Park, Charles M. Judd, Bernd Wittenbrink, Melody S. Sadler, and Tracie Keesee. 2007. "Across the Thin Blue Line: Police Officers and Racial Bias in the Decision to Shoot." *Journal of Personality and Social Psychology* 92, no. 6: 1006–1023.

Cunliffe, Zoë. 2019. "Narrative Fiction and Epistemic Injustice." *Journal of Aesthetics and Art Criticism* 77, no. 2: 169–180.

Currie, Gregory. 1995. "The Moral Psychology of Fiction." *Australasian Journal of Philosophy* 73, no. 2: 250–259.

Currie, Gregory. 2002. "Desire in Imagination." In *Conceivability and Possibility*, edited by Tamar Szabó Gendler and John Hawthorne, 201–221. Oxford: Oxford University Press.

Currie, Gregory, and Ian Ravenscroft. 2002. *Recreative Minds*. Oxford: Oxford University Press.

Depaul, Michael R. 1988. "Argument and Perception: The Role of Literature in Moral Inquiry." *Journal of Philosophy* 85, no. 10: 552–565.

Djikic, Maja, Keith Oatley, and Mihnea C. Moldoveanu. 2013. "Reading Other Minds: Effects of Literature on Empathy." *Scientific Study of Literature* 3, no. 1: 28–47.

Eberhardt, Jennifer L., Phillip A. Goff, Valerie J. Purdie, and Paul G. Davies. 2004. "Seeing Black: Race, Crime, and Visual Processing." *Journal of Personality and Social Psychology* 87, no. 6: 876–893.

Elgin, Catherine. 2014. "Fiction as Thought Experiment." *Perspectives on Science* 22, no. 2: 221–241.

Elliot, Carl, and Britt Elliot. 1991. "From the Patient's Point of View: Medical Ethics and the Moral Imagination." *Journal of Medical Ethics* 17, no. 4: 173–178.

Fesmire, Steven. 2003. *John Dewey and Moral Imagination*. Bloomington: Indiana University Press.

Frye, Marilyn. 1992. "White Woman Feminist." In *Willful Virgin: Essays in Feminism*, edited by Marilyn Frye, 126–127. Freedom, CA: The Crossing Press.

Gaut, Berys. 1998. "The Ethical Criticism of Art." In *Aesthetics and Ethics: Essays at the Intersection*, edited by Jerrold Levinson, 182–203. Cambridge: Cambridge University Press.

Gaut, Berys. 2007. *Art, Emotion, and Ethics*. Oxford: Oxford University Press.

Gebhard, Ulrich., Patricia Nevers, and Elfriede Billmann-Mahecha. 2003. "Moralizing Trees: Anthropomorphism and Identity in Children's Relationships to Nature." In *Identity and the Natural Environment: The Psychological Significance of Nature*, edited by Susan Clayton and Susan Opotow, 91–112. Cambridge, MA: The MIT Press.

Gendler, Tamar Szabó. 2000. "The Puzzle of Imaginative Resistance." *Journal of Philosophy* 97, no. 2: 55–81.

Gendler, Tamar Szabó. 2006a. "Imaginative Contagion." *Metaphilosophy* 37, no. 2: 183–203.

Gendler, Tamar Szabó. 2006b. "Imaginative Resistance Revisited." In *The Architecture of Imagination*, edited by Shaun Nichols, 149–173. Oxford: Oxford University Press.

Gendler, Tamar Szabó. 2008a. "Alief in Action (and Reaction)." *Mind & Language* 23, no. 5: 552–585.

Gendler, Tamar Szabó. 2008b. "Alief and Belief." *Journal of Philosophy* 105, no. 10: 634–663.

Gendler, Tamar Szabó. 2010. *Intuition, Imagination, & Philosophical Methodology*. Oxford: Oxford University Press.

Gendler, Tamar Szabó, and Shen-yi Liao. 2016. "The Problem of Imaginative Resistance." In *The Routledge Companion to Philosophy of Literature*, edited by Noël Carroll and John Gibson, 405–418. New York: Routledge.

Giovannelli, Alessandro. 2007. "The Ethical Criticism of Art: A New Mapping of the Territory." *Philosophia* 35, no. 2: 117–127.

Glaser, Jack, and Eric D. Knowles. 2008. "Implicit Motivation to Control Prejudice." *Journal of Experimental Social Psychology* 44, no. 1: 164–172.

Greenwald, Anthony G., Debbie E. McGhee, and Jordan L. K. Schwartz. 1998. "Measuring Individual Differences in Implicit Cognition: The Implicit Association Test." *Journal of Personality and Social Psychology* 74, no. 6: 1464–1480.

Hare, R. M. 1963. *Freedom and Reason*. Oxford: Oxford University Press.

Harold, James. 2003. "Flexing the Imagination." *Journal of Aesthetics and Art Criticism* 61, no. 3: 247–257.

Harold, James. 2005. "Infected by Evil." *Philosophical Explorations* 8, no. 2: 173–187.

Harold, James. 2007. "The Ethics of Non-Realist Fiction: Morality's Catch-22." *Philosophia* 35, no. 2: 145–159.

Holroyd, Jules, Robin Scaife, and Tom Stafford. 2017. "Responsibility for Implicit Bias." *Philosophy Compass* 12, no. 3: e12410.

Holroyd, Jules, and Joseph Sweetman. 2016. "The Heterogeneity of Implicit Biases." In *Implicit Bias and Philosophy: Volume 1, Metaphysics and Epistemology*, edited by Michael Brownstein and Jennifer Saul, 80–103. Oxford: Oxford University Press.

Hurley, Susan. 2004. "Imitation, Media Violence, and Freedom of Speech." *Philosophical Studies* 117, no. 1: 165–218.

Jacobs, Jonathan. 1991. "Moral Imagination, Objectivity, and Practical Wisdom." *International Philosophical Quarterly* 31, no. 1: 23–37.

Jacobson, Daniel. 1997. "In Praise of Immoral Art." *Philosophical Topics* 25, no. 1: 155–199.

Johnson, Gabbrielle M. 2020. "The Structure of Bias." *Mind* 129, no. 516: 1193–1236.

Johnson, Mark. 1994. *Moral Imagination: Implications of Cognitive Science for Ethics*. Chicago: University of Chicago Press.

Johnson, Mark. 2016. "Moral Imagination." In *The Routledge Handbook of Philosophy of Imagination*, edited by Amy Kind, 355–367. New York: Routledge.

Jost, John T., Laurie A. Rudman, Irene V. Blair, Dana R. Carney, Nilanjana Dasgupta, Jack Glaser, and Curtis D. Hardin. 2009. "The Existence of Implicit Bias is Beyond Reasonable Doubt: A Refutation of Ideological and Methodological Objections and Executive Summary of Ten Studies that No Manager Should Ignore." *Research in Organizational Behavior* 29: 39–69.

Kekes, John. 1991. "Moral Imagination, Freedom, and the Humanities." *American Philosophical Quarterly* 28, no. 2: 101–111.

Kekes, John. 2006. *The Enlargement of Life: Moral Imagination at Work*. Ithaca, NY: Cornell University Press.

Kidd, David C., and Emanuele Castano. 2013. "Reading Literary Fiction Improves Theory of Mind." *Science* 342, no. 6156: 377–380.

Kieran, Matthew. 1996. "Art, Imagination, and the Cultivation of Morals." *Journal of Aesthetics and Art Criticism* 54, no. 4: 337–351.

Kieran, Matthew. 2003. "Forbidden Knowledge: The Challenge of Immoralism." In *Art and Morality*, edited by José Luis Bermúdez and Sebastian Gardner, 56–73. New York: Routledge.

Kim, Hanna, Markus Kneer, and Michael T. Stuart. 2019. "The Content-Dependence of Imaginative Resistance." In *Advances in Experimental Philosophy of Aesthetics*, edited by Florian Cova and Sébastien Réhault, 143–165. New York: Bloomsbury.

Kind, Amy. 2013. "The Heterogeneity of the Imagination." *Erkenntnis* 78, no. 1: 151–159.

Kind, Amy. 2020. "What Imagination Teaches." In *Becoming Someone New: Essays on Transformative Experience, Choice, and Change*, edited by Enoch Lambert and John Schwenkler, 133–146. Oxford: Oxford University Press.

Kind, Amy, and Peter Kung. 2016. *Knowledge Through Imagination*. Oxford: Oxford University Press.

Lamarque, Peter, and Stein H. Olsen. 1994. *Truth, Fiction, and Literature*. Oxford: Oxford University Press.

Landy, Joshua. 2008. "A Nation of Madame Bovarys: On the Possibility and Desirability of Moral Improvement through Fiction." In *Art and Ethical Criticism*, edited by Garry L. Hagberg, 63–94. Oxford: Blackwell Publishing.

Liao, Shen-yi. 2013. "Moral Persuasion and the Diversity of Fictions." *Pacific Philosophical Quarterly* 94, no. 3: 269–289.

Liao, Shen-yi. 2016. "Imaginative Resistance, Narrative Engagement, Genre." *Res Philosophica* 93, no. 2: 461–482.

Liao, Shen-yi, and Tamar Szabó Gendler. 2011. "Pretense and Imagination." *Wiley Interdisciplinary Review: Cognitive Science* 2, no. 1: 79–94.

Liao, Shen-yi, and Tamar Szabó Gendler. 2019. "Imagination." *Stanford Encyclopedia of Philosophy*, January 22, 2019. https://plato.stanford.edu/entries/imagination/.

Liao, Shen-yi, and Aaron Meskin. 2018. "Morality and Aesthetics of Food." In *The Oxford Handbook of Food Ethics*, edited by Anne Barnhill, Tyler Doggett and Mark Budolfson, 658–679. Oxford: Oxford University Press.

Liao, Shen-yi, Nina Strohminger, and Chandra Sekhar Sripada. 2014. "Empirically Investigating Imaginative Resistance." *British Journal of Aesthetics* 54, no. 3: 339–355.

Livingston, Paisley. 2009. "Narrativity and Knowledge." *Journal of Aesthetics and Art Criticism* 67, no. 1: 25–36.

Machery, Edouard. 2022. "Anomalies in Implicit Attitudes Research." *Wiley Interdisciplinary Review: Cognitive Science* 13, no. 1: e1569.

Mackenzie, Catriona. 2000. "Imagining Oneself Otherwise." In *Relational Autonomy*, edited by Catriona Mackenzie and Natalie Stoljar, 124–150. Oxford: Oxford University Press.

Mackenzie, Catriona, and Jackie Leach Scully. 2007. "Moral Imagination, Disability, and Embodiment." *Journal of Applied Philosophy* 24, no. 4: 335–351.

Mar, Raymond A., Kieth Oatley, Jacob Hirsh, Jennifer dela Paz, and Jordan B. Peterson. 2006. "Bookworms versus Nerds: Exposure to Fiction versus Non-fiction, Divergent Associations with Social Ability, and the Simulation of Fictional Social Worlds." *Journal of Research in Personality* 40, no. 5: 694–712.

Mar, Raymond A., Keith Oatley, and Jordan B. Peterson. 2009. "Exploring the Link Between Reading Fiction and Empathy: Ruling out Differences and Examining Outcomes." *Communications* 34, no. 4: 407–428.

McGregor, Rafe. 2014. "A Critique of the Value Interaction Debate." *British Journal of Aesthetics* 54, no. 4: 449–466.

Melchiori, Kala J., and Robyn K. Mallett. 2015. "Using Shrek to Teach About Stigma." *Teaching of Psychology* 42, no. 3: 260–265.

Meskin, Aaron, and Jonathan M. Weinberg. 2003. "Emotions, Fiction, and Cognitive Architecture." *British Journal of Aesthetics* 43, no. 1: 18–34.

Mills, C. Wright. [1959] 2000. *The Sociological Imagination (Fortieth Anniversary Edition)*. Oxford: Oxford University Press.

Miyazono, Kengo, and Shen-yi Liao. 2016. "The Cognitive Architecture of Imaginative Resistance." In *The Routledge Handbook of Philosophy of Imagination*, edited by Amy Kind, 233–246. New York: Routledge.

Moran, Richard. 1994. "The Expression of Feeling in Imagination." *The Philosophical Review* 103, no. 1: 74–106.

Moss, Sarah. 2018. "Moral Encroachment." *Proceedings of the Aristotelian Society* 118, no. 2: 177–205.

Mothersill, Mary. 2003. "Make-Believe Morality and Fictional Worlds." In *Art and Morality*, edited by José Luis Bermúdez and Sebastian Gardner, 74–94. New York: Routledge.

Mullin, Amy. 2004. "Moral Defects, Aesthetic Defects, and the Imagination." *Journal of Aesthetics and Art Criticism* 62, no. 3: 249–261.

Murdoch, Iris. 1970. *The Sovereignty of Good*. London: Routledge & Kegan Paul.

Murdoch, Iris. 1992. *Metaphysics as a Guide to Morals*. New York: Penguin Books.

Nanay, Bence. 2010. "Imaginative Resistance and Conversational Implicature." *The Philosophical Quarterly* 60, no. 24: 586–600.

Narvaez, Darcia, Jennifer Bentley, Tracy Gleason, and Jay Samuels. 1998. "Moral Theme Comprehension in Third Graders, Fifth Graders, and College Students." *Reading Psychology* 19, no. 2: 217–241.

Narvaez, Darcia, and Kellen Mrkva. 2014. "The Development of Moral Imagination." In *The Ethics of Creativity*, edited by Seana Moran, David Cropley, and James C. Kaufman, 25–45. New York: Palgrave Macmillan.

Nussbaum, Martha C. 1990. *Love's Knowledge*. Oxford: Oxford University Press.

Nussbaum, Martha C. 1995. *Poetic Justice*. Boston: Beacon Press.

Nussbaum, Martha C. 1997. *Cultivating Humanity: A Classical Defense of Reform in Liberal Education*. Cambridge, MA: Harvard University Press.

Panero, Maria E., Deena S. Weisberg, Jessica E. Black, Thalia R. Goldstein, Jennifer L. Barnes, Hiram Brownell, and Ellen Winner. 2016. "Does Reading a Single Passage of Literary Fiction Really Improve Theory of Mind?" *Journal of Personality and Social Psychology* 111, no. 5: e46–e54.

Paul, L. A. 2014. *Transformative Experience*. Oxford: Oxford University Press.

Peterson, Eric. 2019. "Imaginative Resistance and Variation." *British Journal of Aesthetics* 59, no. 1: 67–80.

Posner, Richard A. 1997. "Against Ethical Criticism." *Philosophy and Literature* 21, no. 1: 1–27.

Posner, Richard A. 1998. "Against Ethical Criticism: Part Two." *Philosophy and Literature* 22, no. 2: 394–412.

Ravenscroft, Ian. 2012. "Fiction, Imagination, and Ethics." In *Emotions, Imagination, and Moral Reasoning*, edited by Robyn Langdon and Catriona Mackenzie, 71–89. Hove, UK: Psychology Press.

Robinson, Jennifer. 2005. *Deeper than Reason: Emotion and its Role in Literature, Music, and Art*. Oxford: Oxford University Press.

Roelofs, Monique. 2014. *The Cultural Promise of the Aesthetic*. New York: Bloomsbury Academic.

Sauchelli, Andrea. 2016. "Gendler on the Puzzle(s) of Imaginative Resistance." *Acta Analytica* 31, no. 1: 1–9.

Sauchelli, Andrea. 2019. "On the Study of Imaginative Resistance." Analytic Philosophy 60, no. 2: 164–178.

Schwartz, Avshalom M. 2021. "Political Imagination and its Limits." *Synthese* 199, no. 1: 1–19.

Scott, Pym, A. 1997. "Imagination in Practice." *Journal of Medical Ethics* 23, no. 1: 45–50.

Sher, George. 2019. "A Wild West of the Mind." *Australasian Journal of Philosophy* 97, no. 3: 483–496.

Shim, Joy. 2022. "Literary Racial Impersonation." *Ergo* 8, no. 31: 219–245.

Smuts, Aaron. 2013. "The Ethics of Singing Along: The Case of 'Mind of a Lunatic.'" *Journal of Aesthetics and Art Criticism* 71, no. 1: 121–129.

Smuts, Aaron. 2016. "The Ethics of Imagination and Fantasy." In *The Routledge Handbook of Philosophy of Imagination*, edited by Amy Kind, 380–391. New York: Routledge.

Stadler, Jane. 2020. "Imitation of Life: Cinema and the Moral Imagination." *Paragraph* 43, no. 3: 298–313.

Stear, Nils-Hennes. 2015. "Imaginative and Fictionality Failure: A Normative Approach." *Philosophers' Imprint* 15, no. 34: 1–18.

Stokes, Dustin R. 2006. "The Evaluative Character of Imaginative Resistance." *British Journal of Aesthetics* 46, no. 4: 347–405.

Strouse, Gabrielle, A., Angela Nyhout, and Patricia A. Ganea. 2018. "The Role of Book Features in Young Children's Transfer of Information from Picture Books to Real-World Contexts." *Frontiers in Psychology* 9, no. 50: 1–14.

Stueber, Karsten R. 2008. "Reasons, Generalizations, Empathy, and Narratives: The Epistemic Structure of Action Explanation." *History and Theory* 47, no. 1: 31–43.

Stueber, Karsten R. 2016. "Empathy and the Imagination." In *The Routledge Handbook of Philosophy of Imagination*, edited by Amy Kind, 368–379. New York: Routledge.

Sullivan-Bissett, Ema. 2019. "Biased by Our Imaginings." *Mind & Language* 34, no. 5: 627–647.

Tanner, Michael. 1994. "Morals in Fiction and Fictional Morality (II)." *Proceedings of the Aristotelian Society Supplemental* 68: 51–66.

Taylor, Charles. 2004. *Modern Social Imaginaries*. Durham, NC: Duke University Press.

Taylor, Paul C. 2014. "Taking Postracialism Seriously: From Movement Mythology to Racial Formation." *Du Bois Review* 11, no. 1: 9–25.

Todd, Cain S. 2009. "Imaginability, Morality, and Fictional Truth: Dissolving the Puzzle of 'Imaginative Resistance.'" *Philosophical Studies* 143, no. 2: 187–211.

Tuna, Emine Hande. 2020. "Imaginative Resistance." *Stanford Encyclopedia of Philosophy*, April 13, 2020. https://plato.stanford.edu/archives/sum2020/entries/imaginative-resistance/.

Vezzali, Loris., Sofia Stathi, Dino Giovannini, Dora Capozza, and Elena Trifiletti. 2015. "The Greatest Magic of Harry Potter: Reducing Prejudice." *Journal of Applied Social Psychology* 45, no. 2: 105–121.

Von Wright, Moira. 2002. "Narrative Imagination and Taking the Perspective of Others." *Studies in Philosophy and Education* 21, no. 4/5: 407–416.

Walton, Kendall L. 1990. *Mimesis as Make-Believe*. Cambridge, MA: Harvard University Press.

Walton, Kendall L. 1994. "Morals in Fiction and Fictional Morality (I)." *Proceedings of the Aristotelian Society Supplemental* 68: 27–50.

Walton, Kendall L. 2006. "On the (So-called) Puzzle of Imaginative Resistance." In *The Architecture of Imagination*, edited by Shaun Nichols, 137–148. Oxford: Oxford University Press.

Weatherson, Brian. 2004. "Morality, Fiction, and Possibility." *Philosophers' Imprint* 4, no. 3: 1–27.

Weinberg, Jonathan M. 2008. "Configuring the Cognitive Imagination." In *New Waves in Aesthetics*, edited by Kathleen Stock and Katherine Thomson-Jones, 203–223. New York: Palgrave Macmillan.

Weinberg, Jonathan M., and Aaron Meskin. 2006. "Puzzling Over the Imagination." In *The Architecture of Imagination*, edited by Shaun Nichols, 175–200. Oxford: Oxford University Press.

Welpinghus, Anna. 2020. "The Imagination Model of Implicit Bias." *Philosophical Studies* 177, no. 6: 1611–1633.

Werhane, Patricia H. 1999. *Moral Imagination and Management Decision-Making*. Oxford: Oxford University Press.

Williams, Bernard. [1985] 2006. *Ethics and the Limits of Philosophy*. New York: Routledge.

Williams, Oliver F. 1997. *Moral Imagination: How Literature and Films can Stimulate Ethical Reflection in the Business World*. Notre Dame, IN: University of Notre Dame Press.

Yablo, Stephen. 2002. "Coulda, Woulda, Shoulda." In *Conceivability and Possibility*, edited by Tamar Szabó Gendler and John Hawthorne, 441–492. Oxford: Oxford University Press.

Zheng, Robin, and Nils-Hennes Stear. 2023. "Imagining in Oppressive Contexts, or, What's Wrong with Blacking Up?" *Ethics* 133, no. 3: 381–414.

CHAPTER 45

....

MORAL LEARNING FROM ART

....

EILEEN JOHN

WE can think about moral learning in more and less ambitious terms, with the more ambitious end of the spectrum being a form of learning that is deeply transformative for the learner. The point of moral learning, in the ambitious sense, is to live morally, so it seems the learning would have to engage us in whatever processes enable a person to experience, care about, and act on morally significant terms. Can art help us to do that? There are sensible voices of caution and skepticism on this front (Currie 2020; Harold 2020; Gaut 2007; Hamilton 2003; Posner 1997). But given that there does not appear to be *any* reliable route to living morally, art may not be so bad within the field of potential contributors to moral learning. Perhaps we can only say art is patchily effective: "*Some* works of art . . . can, for *some* people *some* of the time, contribute to their moral education" (Hamilton 2003, 43). This chapter does not attempt to defend a more impressive record of success, but it takes the question of how art could contribute to moral learning, even some of the time, to be worth exploring. Where does art's potential for moral learning come from?

PRELIMINARIES ON MORALITY

....

To reach that question, let me first sketch some of the substance and complexity that the notion of moral learning inherits from the notion of morality. One complicating factor is that the term "morality" is used sometimes as a descriptive term and sometimes with normative force. Things that count as moralities are inculcated and learned and can play an important role in guiding individual and collective life. We might describe different moralities that have this role in different societies and could study how people learn a given morality. "Morality," especially in philosophical discourse, is also used to refer to a kind of ideal guidance, a domain of universally legitimate values and principles that should guide people's lives. In this usage, the social and cultural variability of moralities might be cast as contingent messiness or might fade from view. (See Nannicelli, this volume.) Kant sought "a pure moral philosophy completely cleansed of everything that can only be empirical and appropriate to anthropology" (Kant 1964, 57). From this perspective, a particular operative morality might be criticized as flawed or as possibly not really a morality at all. The normative usage sets the philosophical task of how to formulate and justify such a universal morality, and how to learn such a morality is also a question. I will not dwell here on the descriptive-normative ambiguity of morality. It seems unhelpful to uphold that distinction when focused on moral learning: moral learning is precisely a process that combines becoming inculcated into an available morality and becoming able to understand, justify, reflect critically on, and change one's moral commitments. Whatever is involved in learning a morality, concrete or ideal, includes becoming broadly apt for moral life, for grasping that there is such a thing as a moral value or norm. Moral learning is a best-we-can-do-with-what-we-have project, and, for that project, it is valuable to have resources that do not take established moral norms for granted but allow them to surface as things that might need justification and revision. We will here consider ideas about art that concern both acquiring a given morality and achieving reflective understanding of moral norms.

To set up these ideas, it is necessary to say something about the nature of morality. (See also Moon, this volume.) Descriptive accounts of morality construe it as a kind whose members have a shared broad function, for example, as a set of "social norms prescribing and prohibiting certain behaviors" (Decety and Yoder 2017, 7) or, more elaborately, behavioral norms "independent of any legal or social institution" that "typically engender *punitive attitudes* such as anger, condemnation, and blame" (Sripada 2008, 320). Norms focused on action, and morally significant emotional attitudes, are often at the core of normative accounts as well. Bernard Gert takes morality in the ideal sense to be crystallized in a system of rules, including "*Do not disable,*" "*Do not deprive of freedom,*" "*Do not cheat,*" where the system has "the lessening of evil or harm as its goal" and where "every feature of morality must be known to, and could be chosen by, all rational persons" (Gert 2005, 218, 14, 6). The rule-focused conception of morality, whether in descriptive or normative modes, has generated strong critiques of morality that cast it as a dogmatic system of obligations promoting unhealthy repression, blame, guilty consciences, and punishment (Nietzsche 2017; Williams 2011). One might try to respond to such critiques by tying morality to core positive values: "Morality is necessarily connected with such things as justice and the common good," such that a moral community would be united "to fight for liberty and justice and against inhumanity and oppression" (Foot 2002, 92, 167).

Meanwhile, sentimentalist accounts, which vary in their vulnerability to the unhealthy repression critique, ground morality essentially in the fact and significance of emotional concern and responsiveness. For example, in Hume's account, "corrected (sometimes rule-corrected) sympathy, not law-discerning reason, is the fundamental moral capacity" (Baier 1995, 55). More recent sentimentalist positions focus on the moral centrality of guilt and resentment or self- and other-directed blame (Gibbard 1990, 6; Prinz 2007, 90). Normative accounts also look inwardly in other ways, as Kant tied morality to the workings of an unconditionally good will (Kant 1964) and Iris Murdoch to the achievement of "just and loving" attention to reality (Murdoch 1970, 33).

Some accounts of morality focus less on function, feeling, and substantive values, and more on morality's scope of concern and its justificatory status. On scope, one widespread view is that morality specifically concerns "*other-regarding* actions, feelings and motives," where this regard is intrinsic, "a concern for the other . . . for his or her sake" (Gaut 2007, 45, 46). This coheres with the idea that a core aim of morality is to de-center the self and self-interested concerns. Putting the point negatively, Murdoch says, "In the moral life the enemy is the fat relentless ego" (Murdoch 1970, 51). In psychological research, "prosocial behavior" refers to "voluntary behavior intended to benefit another, such as helping, sharing, comforting, and donating," allowing the question of whether the behavior is "altruistic"—intrinsically motivated by a desire to help others—to remain open (Spinrad and Eisenberg 2017, 53). In any case, "prosocial" orientation to others' interests is taken as a marker of moral development. Annette Baier suggests the scope issue is more complicated, arguing that "the problem morality solves is . . . as much intrapersonal as interpersonal. It is the problem of contradiction, conflict, and instability in any one person's desires . . . as well as conflict among persons" (Baier 1995, 61).

Morality can also be held to be distinctive because its norms are treated as nonconventional: they have a seriousness and authority that "invite different kinds of justifications from conventional violations" (Nichols 2004, 6–7). This idea poses the question of how we might learn to take some norms to be especially authoritative. Finally, there are views that build in a kind of justificatory procedure or relationship into the realization of a morality, as in the idea that as moral beings we are "moved by the aim of finding principles that others, similarly motivated, could not reasonably reject" (Scanlon 1998 5). For Scanlon, "morality is not, fundamentally, a mechanism of control and protection but, rather, . . . a system of co-deliberation" (2000, 268). Margaret Urban Walker speaks of morality as "a socially embodied medium of mutual understanding and adjustment between persons. . . . moral problems are not cases to be closed by authoritative verdicts but conspicuous nodal points in histories of attempted mutual adjustment and understanding" (2003, 94). Broadly speaking, Walker and Scanlon take morality to be a project with mutual accountability at its core.

This quick survey holds a cornucopia of ideas relevant to what moral learning can encompass. It seems it could, for instance, be a matter of learning the rules that serve the relevant functions in a given community. In that case, it seems we could learn by being handed a list of rules and memorizing it, and art would not seem to be needed or helpful in this process. More challenging aspects of moral learning emerge if we think about how moral norms could acquire the right status and function, as, say, authoritative, motivating, tied to feelings. How would one come to see a morality as justified, whether in the terms of universal rationality or in terms of mutual accountability? How might one correct one's sympathy or learn to attend to reality in a just and loving way? Moral learning is perhaps starting to sound overwhelming and unrealistic. But it seems people do it, gradually and throughout life. Art has morally educative potential in part because it has some complementary complexity. Artworks can engage us in thought and

To be morally aware and active, it is not enough to deliberate rationally and not enough to respond with feeling; morality perhaps demands that we think with feeling or feel thoughtfully. Nichols says moral norms are rules "backed by an affective system" (2004, 21), suggesting they achieve normative salience and seriousness in part because we experience or feel them as serious and weighty. Continuing in a broad-brush fashion, this feeling-thinking combination is a point in art's favor. Art too is demanding, or rich, in that combined way. It is hard to make or appreciate art either by "simply feeling" or "purely thinking," though perhaps one or the other may seem appropriate to some works. Art prompts such responses as being moved due to understanding something, grasping the significance of a feeling, being struck forcefully by a question, laughing at a similarity, hoping for a resolution—the common occurrences of engaging with art are a jumble of affective and cognitive activity, not worth trying to tease apart. In this way, art seems to be a domain that meets us where we live, morally speaking.

When we turn to the substance of morality, it seems clear that artworks have often been intended to serve—and even when not intended can easily serve—to transmit the moral norms of a society. Experience with and responses to art can be an important vehicle of enculturation into those norms. The selection, composition, and elaboration of content in a work can hold wonderfully crystallized and concretely embodied moral ideals and norms. Grasping which characters count as good, which actions are wrong, or what morally significant emotions are appropriate to a situation can be integral to making sense of a work (Carroll 1998). Paintings of Florence Nightingale showed her as a steadfast, merciful carer for the wounded, with no frivolous vanity or pettiness. Michelangelo's *David* offers "an experience of an ideal recognized as such: one looks at courage" (Zamir 2006, 28; see Fehl 1972). Innumerable storylines contrast the shallowness of material success with the deeper excellence of moral achievement. Public art is now condemned for embodying moral norms that are no longer endorsed (e.g., the nobility of colonizing conquests or admiration for people who profited from enslavement of others). (See Bicknell et al, this volume.) As the latter examples illustrate, such crystallizing, manifesting power, if it is indeed effective in "imprinting" moral norms in its audience (Carroll 2004, 127), is a morally equivocal power. We may hesitate to call it moral learning, if, from our vantage point, it seems clear that a work would have transmitted distorting, prejudiced, or actively malicious meanings and norms.

As noted above, there is a sense in which this just is our predicament as moral learners, somewhere in a process of moral formation in which things can acquire normative status that may not be merited. The unintended, unreflective manifestation of operative moral norms is perhaps unavoidable in art, as artists cannot simply divest themselves of all assumptions and values they in fact use to "make sense" of the social world they inhabit. Some psychological research considers how cognitive biases can interact with transmission of normative content in morally problematic ways. If some norms are more cognitively "attractive," this can influence how norms are "copied" and transmitted in social learning processes: "Some normative rules might be easier to detect (i.e., they may be more salient), easier to infer, or easier to remember, store, or recall" (Sripada 2008, 333). One can see how evidentially shallow rule-content (e.g., *looks female, foreign, dark-skinned*) could ease cognition and transmission of norms. Sripada, however, also poses the question of how to explain fundamental changes in moral norms, if the models of cognition and transmission favor certain kinds of copying and simplifying trends. His example is what evolutionary psychologists cast as an evolutionarily deeply rooted norm that sanctions human males claiming women "as a valuable resource," suitable for control and ownership (2008, 340–341). That norm has been widely challenged and rejected (albeit not universally or fully effectively) over the past few hundred years. Sripada provisionally suggests that we can explain fundamental moral change by appeal to "other cultural processes," such as change in behavior of prestigious figures in a community (2008, 341–343). The next section will add to this quite abstract suggestion the idea that art, in its production and cultural presence, is one of these influential cultural processes.

One point that seems promising, when looking to art for morally progressive learning, is that moral learning itself is such a popular focus of artistic depiction. Especially in narrative genres, the plot arc that shows a character moving from a state of moral obtuseness or error to moral insight or strength is somehow deeply gripping and pleasurable (*Casablanca*, *Emma*, *The Remains of the Day*, *Pinocchio*). We like progress narratives in general (ugly to beautiful, poor to rich, undisciplined and self-sabotaging to dedicated, successful dancer/athlete/coach/teacher). But the moral progress story is, I would guess, the most beloved and is commonly entwined, implausibly or not, with all the others. Perhaps some fairly primitive psychological tendencies are at work here, as Freud (1983) points out that we would just as soon not be made aware of some of our fellow humans' drives and fantasies; the plotline in which morally salutary commitments triumph is an appealing gloss on humanity. But there are valid artistic reasons for choosing and developing moral learning narratives as well. The moral transformation, as typically imagined, involves deeper, more universally shared aspects of people: difficult choices, taking responsibility, responding to social expectations, experiencing care and neglect, and finding out which self-conceptions one can live with. Moral learning, as depicted in artistic narratives, is not likely to be a matter of changed behavior alone ("she used to follow that rule and now follows this one"), but involves internal, felt, reflective, and effortfully enacted shifts of concern, principle, self-conception, and social affiliation. All of this makes for interesting stories and provides ways to grip audiences with issues that overlap, more and less abstractly, with their own lives. How likely is it that immersion in such artistic depictions of moral learning would provoke moral learning in audiences?

A skeptical thought is that the enjoyment of these narratives may often hinge on audiences feeling they already know what the character misunderstands or fails to embody. We take ourselves to be morally secure in the relevant respect and cheer on the character's progress from a comfortably superior distance; we do not take it as an occasion for self-reflection and learning. Another skeptical thought is that being identifiable as "a story of moral learning" is no guarantee that the story in fact portrays an intelligible, morally warranted, insightfully registered transformation. Gregory Currie argues that works of fiction are not governed by constraints and expectations that would make them reliable sources of learning, including moral learning; he also suggests that people enjoy *thinking* they have learned something from fiction (2020, Chapters 10 and 11, 122–123). While these skeptical thoughts have merit (and merit more discussion), I take these dismissals to be too quick and general. As Noël Carroll has emphasized, even things we "already know" can call for reinforcement, deepening, and more astute and sensitive activation (1998; 2004). It seems possible that vicarious attention to a protagonist's moral failures and progress can provide an informative reawakening to what it is we are committed to and why it is important. Why a moral commitment can have "affective backing" seems related to being able to see the difference that having or lacking that commitment can make in a life, and an artistic depiction could bring such differences home to us. The individuality of our morally significant tendencies and weaknesses also makes it hard to generalize about what we can benefit from, even with regard to relatively formulaic stories of moral progress. We can be susceptible to shallow, biased, naïve, arrogant, and other morally problematic stances in relation to many different issues, and it seems impossible to rule out that a given artwork might allow a person, in the company of a depicted moral learner, to notice and unsettle some of these tendencies.

ART AND REFLECTIVE MORAL LEARNING

So far, I have been somewhat cautiously surveying the prospects for moral learning from art when the substance of the learning is to some extent taken for granted: a moral framework is on offer in an artwork, usually assumed to hold norms operative in the surrounding social world, and we can consider the work's potential to transmit that framework. Now we can consider some different models that do not assume the artwork will make that kind of offer or bear that relation to a given moral framework. I think of these as "nontransmission models," though transmission is never fully absent. These models can easily overlap and merge, but I will list them schematically as four items: (1) protesting the status quo, (2) expanding the moral community, (3) being a moral witness, and (4) initiating a conversation. As a list of activities, this approach is in sympathy with Joshua Landy's notion of "formative fictions," in which the educative potential "has less to do with content than it does with *process*" (2012, 12). These four models are suggestions for how art can be a resource for reflective understanding and change within moral life.

Some artworks set out to critique and protest against an operative moral norm or framework. (See also the discussion of protest art in Woodcock, this volume.) They may do this bluntly: Mary Beth Edelson, in *Some Living American Women Artists/Last Supper* (1972), superimposed the heads of women artists on the figures in Da Vinci's *Last Supper*, using the visual "disrespect" to a canonical work to call out the sexism that made women barely visible in the artworld. Adrian Piper, in part of her "Mythic Being" series, accompanies an image of herself as a Black man with the thought bubble, "I Embody Everything You Most Hate and Fear" (1975). The force of protest against racism is bluntly there, though the protest uses its visual and verbal means in a complex way (perhaps thrusting a claim at white viewers that they would want to disown but that feels sort of sickening to have to disown, and pointing to usually unspoken felt realities of racism). On the moral learning question, these sample works suggest rather different potential outcomes. Even to someone not already moved by feminist concerns, Edelson's act of artistic disrespect could be an effective way of at least raising questions—perhaps, in 1972, "can I even name a single woman artist?"—which could open the door for considering the oddness and eventually the injustice of that invisibility. Piper's work seems to be more directly, personally exposing and to go more deeply into what keeps racism "alive"; the learning potential might be more substantial (but see discussion in Harold 2020, 84–90).

These examples of Edelson's and Piper's work have the quality of swift critical blows, possibly experimenting to see what will have an impact. A different kind of project and a kind of moral risk in protest art are evident in Harriet Beecher Stowe's *Uncle Tom's Cabin* (1852). Stowe aimed the resources of a novel at convincing its audience—an assumed white, Christian audience—of the evil of slavery. Although it is hard to establish morally significant impact, this novel has one of the most convincing claims for it, as the best-selling novel of the nineteenth century and as a work that spawned an enormous response in the public press and popular culture. Goldner documents this response (e.g., citing a contemporary review that complained of " 'The Uncle Tom epidemic . . . No age or sex is spared, men, women, and children all confess to its power' ") and takes the novel to have helped form a fervent "imagined community" of abolitionists (Goldner 2001, 73, 72). Granted that this is speculation about complicated individual change, this novel may have met "the gold standard" for morally transformative power, actually rousing people to feel, believe, desire, and act on a moral view that—setting aside important qualifications to be considered in a moment—now seems obviously morally correct. The novel is known as a sentimental, tear-jerking work, but Michael Bell argues that it presses for a surprisingly astute entwinement of feeling and reflection: "The appeal to feeling is constantly problematized and mere kindness is no solution. For the kindness of individuals within the world of chattel slavery is not only defeated by the workings of the system, humane slave-owners give a specious moral cover for its evils" (2000, 122). Stowe manages the emotional force and real social relevance of her characters to facilitate the move from feeling to political commitment: the "exercise of feeling . . . finds a legitimate location in an object not just randomly individual, or religiously cosmic, but meaningfully typical" (Bell 2000, 123).

The moral qualifications, however, are inescapable. Charles Johnson reflects on the terribly mixed power of the novel; as a story, it is "fully imagined and deeply felt" and "brims with vivid characters now deeply inscribed in America's racial iconography" (Johnson 2003, 96). But exactly what the novel imagined and inscribed is the problem, as its images and narratively embodied ideas are "ineluctably racist. And truly beyond salvage" (Johnson 2003, 98). (See also Clavel-Vázquez, this volume.) Johnson views Stowe's work as the source of "the very images that I have fought, futilely, to correct and to change for the last thirty years in my own fiction" (Johnson 2003, 96). I will not go into the analysis that Johnson (along with many others) provides of how the novel helped to entrench "toxic racial thinking" (2003, 99). In a deep sense, then, *not* the gold standard. What can we say about this novel with regard to moral learning? It seems, on the one hand, an accident that this was the abolitionist work that was written and disseminated, and that we can imagine a better history in which a less morally contradictory artwork emerged—a different artwork could have helped us get from that past to a better present. Stowe's novel could nonetheless illustrate art's abstract potential for morally transformative learning, if a work can meld emotional vitality and intimacy with morally focused and cogent critique. But on the other hand, we should also consider whether moral change of this kind is just likely to be uglier and more blundering than seems necessary in hindsight. Could an artist's devastating, enlightening exposure of false conceptions of Black and white humanity have taken hold in 1852 America? Johnson speaks of the simultaneous painfulness of Stowe's work, as "we may wince at her half-blind progressivism," and its status as "a small step forward . . . a change for the better" (2003, 99). Perhaps the roots that have to be pulled out and examined for moral transformation are often deep and twisted. So a novel such as Stowe's risks a huge moral error in trying to dislodge elements of a moral framework without being able to see or understand the problem of what should take their place. While aiming to be a protest novel with a mandate for change, *Uncle Tom's Cabin* also transmits assumptions that partly sabotage its protest. As an exemplar of moral learning, it represents a risk taken by protest art: one might be ready to confront audiences with an evil without being ready to understand and promote a morally cogent alternative.

As a second model, we can think about the idea that morality involves expansion of one's sphere of concern. Although perhaps morality is not only other-directed concern—roughly because moral life seems to involve a good deal of wrestling with one's own commitments and self-understanding—it is crucially nonsolipsistic. Morality involves trying to relate myself well to other beings, giving myself and others the right weight in my attachments, decisions, and actions. There is evidence that as societies develop and become larger, "the moral community expands," with moral norms tending to take more beings and more kinds of beings into consideration (Nichols 2004, 143). This seems to reflect how moral concern ought to evolve, especially on conceptions of morality that put some kind of universalizing rationality at its core: "rationality not from the point of view of any particular individual," but counting equally "the interests of all potentially affected individuals" (Railton 1986, 190). Coming to inhabit a moral stance can be argued to generate "pressure to give fuller weight to the interests of more of those affected" (Railton 1986, 193). We can see Stowe's novel as operating under this pressure, if also revealing that an expansion of moral concern is not always a straightforward moral achievement. Scanlon's and Walker's conceptions of mutual reasonableness and adjustment are relevant to this model as well: moral life involves seeking forms of mutual recognition and responsiveness within a community. The process of incorporating more than myself into my sphere of concern seems commonly, and perhaps ideally, to combine cognitive and broadly affective capacities. We have to learn something about the beings we include in our moral community, to make sense of them being there at all, and we usually have to know more still about others' needs and interests in order to treat them in a morally decent way. We have to notice and think about the moral relevance of similarities and differences. But relating to someone as a member of one's moral community also seems to involve feeling that their needs, interests, and moral standing matter. That may not surface as a striking "feeling" very often, but is more like a dispositional commitment to be concerned: if you are in need, moral recognition means—or brings with it an expectation that—I cannot be indifferent to that fact.

The potential for art to contribute to expansion of an audience's moral community, bringing combined understanding and dispositional concern, is again difficult to generalize about and establish. The expansion of understanding seems likely, to the extent that people encounter art that shows others in a morally significant light, for example, as suffering, having interests and intentions, and being in some sense apt for mutuality. That we can reach that cognitive awareness may be controversial for anyone who challenges the epistemic value of creative production, especially fiction, but I think that challenge can often be met, especially if understanding of kinds is at stake ("would someone who had these characteristics belong in my moral community?"). The question of concern—feeling that others matter, not being indifferent to their needs—is more elusive. Can a work of art lead me not only to understand others' qualifications, as it were, for moral standing, but to have the corresponding concern for it? Perhaps not—especially if the focus of one's response to an artwork is solidly fictional (the sufferings of *this* heroine). It is hard to build a reliable bridge from the fact that people respond emotionally to the predicaments of characters to comparable response and concern for actual people. One kind of research related to this issue looks at the impact of reading fiction on real-world empathy (roughly, the grasp of another's situation that prompts one to feel what that person feels). Works of fiction very commonly seem to trigger empathetic responses to characters, but the moral impact of this is highly disputed. The moral role of empathy itself is disputed (Bloom 2017), and the evidence for a bridge from fiction-focused empathy to empathy for actual moral others is complicated and unclear, certainly not conclusive (Currie 2020, Chapter 11). In any case, empathy itself, as defined within such research, is not equivalent to moral concern; compassion is usually defined so as to be more directly pertinent to moral concern, with compassion but not empathy including motivation to help others (Spinrad and Eisenberg 2017, 53). Because we cannot act compassionately for fictional characters, this casts doubt on how directly a work of artistic fiction could prompt moral concern.

Granted that the path from understanding and felt response to art all the way to expansion of one's moral community cannot easily be traced and tested, nonetheless, it seems wrong to dismiss the broad phenomenon of feeling that artworks have opened one's mind and heart to morally significant others. This might be in Carroll's sense of deepening a recognition that one already had ("I already granted that people in general are members of my moral community but I did not really feel it, or understand the specific demands of it"). It might be via the fine-grained depiction of experiential perspectives that is common in fiction (John 2017). It might be due to artworks having the freedom to represent, and to imagine, beings that audiences may not directly know or share lives with, or whose moral status is denied or has not been contemplated:

nonhuman animals (Oerlemans 2018), forms of artificial intelligence (*2001, Bladerunner*), trees (Powers 2018). The expansion might also be through the fact of the artwork itself. I return here to the basic point made earlier, that artworks help us acquire some of the nuts and bolts of moral life: awareness that there are other people who think about the world, want things, suffer, and so forth. An artwork can occasion the awareness that someone made this who is really not me: I sense that I neither could make whatever it is nor would ever have thought of doing so. Artworks are often evidence that people with different pasts, reasons for action, and impulses to shape their environment, are or were occupying one's world. Why is this choreographer having the dancers dance on sand and coat themselves with a dark, shiny substance (Stéphanie Melyon-Reinette, *Kepone Dust*)? Why construct these dim, dreary corridors lined with fading photos and fragmentary writing (Ilya and Emilia Kabakov, *Labyrinth (My Mother's Album)*)? Such "why" questions have some regular chance of arising because of art's specific openness to creative and individual production. Though one may not find a given work's project gripping or worthwhile, an artwork still seems to be an unusually substantial exposure to another's reality. Robert Nozick takes "being a value-seeking I" to be our "basic moral characteristic," setting up the basic moral principle that we should "treat someone (who is a value-seeking I) as a value-seeking I" (1981, 462). Encounters with works of art will not reliably take us all the way to recognizing other value-seekers or treating them as such, but they are relevant to what we need to be aware of along the way.

The third model, being a moral witness, aims to capture the role of art in morally significant memory. Artworks are somewhat unusual in their temporal dimension, in that they can be intended to have and can achieve a relatively long and open-ended public presence. They can certainly outlast their initial makers and audience. But even in their moment of creation, they do not need to be construed as simply of their time but can be experienced as somehow vaguer or more expansive in how they fit into history. It seems that what we remember can have moral significance, though when and why that is true is itself a moral question. To the extent that artworks, when preserved and publicly available, support memory, they can serve as "moral witnesses." Avishai Margalit develops this notion suggestively: a moral witness has a "rather sober hope: that in another place or another time there exists, or will exist, a moral community that will listen to their testimony" (Margalit 2002, 155). This hope includes concern for oneself, as the "minimal moral community . . . is between oneself and the one's future self, who the current self hopes will retain a moral outlook" (Margalit 2002, 158–159). Commentators on Käthe Kollwitz's war-focused art discuss it explicitly in these terms (Sharp 2011, citing Margalit at 101–102; Kolb 2018). Though the works discussed have sources in Kollwitz's personal history, they are described as communicating something general and repetitive. Kollwitz presents "war as an ongoing and insurmountable experience of loss," of private suffering "replicated many times" (Sharp 2011, 97). Her works "invite communal remembrance" of history "repeating its tragedies" (Kolb 2018, 322). We might read a novel like Yaa Gyasi's *Homegoing* in terms of moral witnessing as well, as its readers reel through centuries of a family radically divided by the transatlantic slave trade, with each generation initiating life stories that rush into the past, often lost to the memory of their descendants. Though fictional, I think readers will take this as perhaps the best way we have to bear witness to lives that were consequential to the ones living them and are consequential to our present day, but that rarely left traces we can document.

Art that serves as a moral witness serves processes of moral learning in part through transmission. It would be hard to experience works such as Kollwitz's or Gyasi's without absorbing some basic, morally judgmental content: here is something, or a kind of thing, that happened, and that should not happen ever again. But the witnessing seems like a further activity that is not primarily judgmental, and that we could need to learn to do or to understand as worth doing. Within that activity, the point is not to assert the wrongness or to assign blame, but to make sure that there is a memory. There is something here—in these cases devastating harms to other humans—that we ought to remember about ourselves. There would be something morally negligent about not trying to remember these things and about, in Margalit's terms, not hoping to be listened to in the future. Artworks, in their capacities for generality and iconicity, and in their expansive temporal orientation, have good potential for inviting remembrance and for helping people to understand witnessing to be part of a moral life. The witnessing artwork can also leave much unsaid and, in particular, can leave open the question of what, beyond the somewhat blank fact of moral wrongness, is to be learned from what is remembered.

Finally, the admittedly vague idea of initiating a conversation is intended here to capture art's potential within processes of "attempted mutual adjustment and understanding" (Walker 2003, 94). Walker elaborates on this conception of morality:

> The resources of this medium of moral negotiation include shared moral vocabularies, common exemplars, familiar intuitions, and those deliberative styles recognized in some community. These starting points are renewable resources for the continuing construction and definition of social life. (Walker 2003, 94)

This casts moral life as a dynamic process that all participate in. It makes the idea that morality revolves around only one central construct, whether rules for behavior or sentiments of blame and guilt, seem too rigid. But where and how do we carry on such a complex construction? Philosophical ethics and political debate are obvious sites, along with ordinary conversation and problem-solving. I hope it sounds plausible that art is another site for developing and negotiating morally meaningful vocabularies, exemplars, intuitions, and styles of deliberation. In cycles of art-making, distribution, individual experience, and criticism, conversations relevant to morality can be initiated. These can come from diverse points of view using an unusual range of methods and capabilities. People whose experiences have not been well served in the moral negotiation to date can speak, protest, or bear witness in potentially mind-and-heart-opening ways. Ideas that are not yet accepted or acceptable, or not fully comprehended or articulated, can be provisionally floated in creative forms.

Let me gesture at a few examples of the sprawling activities that show such art-initiated conversations. There are morally freighted artistic responses to previous artworks, as in Johnson's project in response to *Uncle Tom's Cabin*. That novel has also triggered dance and theater adaptations explicitly incorporating critical debate (Parfait 2007, 1–2). The practice of "answer songs" includes morally pointed ripostes in song: Woody Guthrie's "This Land Is Your Land" responding to Irving Berlin's "God Bless America"; J. D. Miller's "It Wasn't God Who Made Honky Tonk Angels" talking back to Hank Thompson's "The Wild Side of Life." As an example of another form of unfolding artistic response, Dominic Lopes reads the history of visual illustration of Dante's *Divine Comedy* as showing visual media being used to variously interpret, obscure, and deepen understanding of Dante's moral concepts (2005, 170–181). Interpretive and critical conversation is relevant of course as well, as a given work or body of work can stimulate multiple interpretations that ascribe different kinds of moral significance (Robinson and Ross 1993; Lopes 2005, 187–190). One last kind of example involves artworks that initiate new, possibly outrageous visions of how things could be, for better and worse, in moral terms. This is sometimes a portrayal of moral extremity, as in works of dystopian fiction that implicitly ask (and fear) where we are headed as moral beings (Cormac McCarthy's *The Road*; Octavia Butler's *Parable of the Sower*). Butler's novel also holds a bold countering proposal to moral dissolution, as the central character, a fifteen-year-old girl, founds a radical religious faith ("God is Change"—"Shape God"). On the side of utopic extremity, Monique Roelofs discusses Pablo Neruda's poetic odes to things of all kinds (e.g., to the chair, the orange, bread) as holding out the promise of an equal, harmonious community (Roelofs 2014, Chapter 1). Roelofs reads Neruda's "Ode to Things" as trying to reclaim and reanimate something morally important: "The ode suspends the oblivion that had befallen past makers and owners. The love persons have felt is made decipherable" (2014, 17–18). Very broadly, such artistic projects use the freedom, experiential scope, and public reach of art—that art can make us gather around bold, intellectually and affectively challenging objects—to initiate morally significant conversations.

CONCLUSION

To think about moral learning from art means thinking about moral learning and morality itself. It does not seem that people have been able to gravitate toward a single model or conceptual framework on these topics. The relevant data-gathering—identifying and understanding what people actually do with art and whether it adds up to moral learning—is immensely difficult. I think we need to grant that art plays a complex role, with power to help us become moral beings of some kind, shaping habits of thought and feeling that matter to a given moral outlook, as well as having power to stimulate reflection, criticism, and moral change. In playing these roles, art's potential depends on many things: its ways of combining cognitive and affective communication and engagement; its ability to generalize, typify, and endow things with meaning; its ability to expand attention and concern; and its freedom to explore, share, and generate response to new problems and ideas. The conception of morality that I have slightly prioritized here involves thinking of morality as a continuous process in which we mutually adjust to and negotiate with each other. There is no simple story to tell about art's role in such a process, but I hope to have given reason to expect it to be a vital, if fraught, contributor.

See also: Clavel-Vázquez, Moon, Woodcock, Lamarque, Nannicelli, Carroll, Liao and Gendler, this volume

References

Baier, Annette. 1995. *Moral Prejudices*. Cambridge, MA: Harvard University Press.

Bell, Michael. 2000. *Sentimentalism, Ethics and the Culture of Feeling*. Basingstoke: Palgrave Macmillan.

Bloom, Paul. 2011. "Moral Nativism and Moral Psychology." In *Social Psychology of Morality: Exploring the Causes of Good and Evil*, edited by Mario Mikulincer and Phillip Shaver, 71–89. Washington, DC: American Psychological Association.

Bloom, Paul. 2017. "Empathy and Its Discontents." *Trends in Cognitive Sciences* 21, no. 1: 24–31.

Butler, Octavia. 2014. *Parable of the Sower*. London: Headline.

Carroll, Noël. 1998. "Art, Narrative, and Moral Understanding." In *Aesthetics and Ethics*, edited by Jerrold Levinson, 126–160. Cambridge: Cambridge University Press.

Carroll, Noël. 2001. *Beyond Aesthetics*. Cambridge: Cambridge University Press.

Carroll, Noël. 2004. "Art and the Moral Realm." In *The Blackwell Guide to Aesthetics*, edited by Peter Kivy, 126–151. Malden, MA: Blackwell.

Currie, Gregory. 2020. *Imagining and Knowing: The Shape of Fiction*. Oxford: Oxford University Press.

Cushman, Fiery, Liane Young, and Joshua Greene. 2010. "Multi-system Moral Psychology." In *The Moral Psychology Handbook*, edited by John Doris, 47–71. Oxford: Oxford University Press.

Feagin, Susan. 1996. *Reading with Feeling*. Ithaca, NY: Cornell University Press.

Fehl, Philipp. 1972. *The Classical Monument: Reflections on the Connection between Morality and Art in Greek and Roman Sculpture*. New York: College Art Association of America.

Foot, Philippa. 2002. *Virtues and Vices*. Oxford: Clarendon.

Freud, Sigmund. 1983. "Creative Writers and Daydreaming." In *Literature and Psychoanalysis*, edited by Edith Kurzweil and William Phillips, 24–28. New York: Columbia University Press

Gaut, Berys. 2007. *Art, Emotion and Ethics*. Oxford: Oxford University Press.

Gert, Bernard. 2005. *Morality: Its Nature and Justification*. Oxford: Oxford University Press.

Gibbard, Allan. 1990. *Wise Choices, Apt Feelings*. Cambridge, MA: Harvard University Press.

Goldner, Ellen. 2001. "Arguing With Pictures: Race, Class, and the Formation of Popular Abolitionism through Uncle Tom's Cabin." *Journal of American and Comparative Cultures* 24, no. 1–2: 71–84.

Gyasi, Yaa. 2016. *Homegoing*. London: Penguin.

Hamilton, Christopher. 2003. "Art and Moral Education." In *Art and Morality*, edited by José Luis Bermúdez and Sebastian Gardner, 37–55. London: Routledge.

Harold, James. 2020. *Dangerous Art*. Oxford: Oxford University Press.

John, Eileen. 2017. "Empathy in Literature." In *The Routledge Handbook to Philosophy of Empathy*, edited by Heidi Maibom, 306–316. London: Routledge.

Johnson, Charles. 2003. *Turning the Wheel: Essays on Buddhism and Writing*. New York: Scribner.

Kant, Immanuel. 1964. *Groundwork of the Metaphysic of Morals*. Translated by H. J. Paton. New York: Harper & Row.

Kolb, Martina. 2018. "Intimations of Mortality from Recollections of Atrocity: Käthe Kollwitz and the Art of Mourning." In *Women Writing War*, edited by Katharina von Hammerstein, Barbara Kosta, and Julie Shoults, 305–327. Berlin: De Gruyter.

Landy, Joshua. 2012. *How to Do Things with Fictions*. Oxford: Oxford University Press.

Lopes, Dominic McIver. 2005. *Sight and Sensibility: Evaluating Pictures*. Oxford: Clarendon Press.

Margalit, Avishai. 2002. *The Ethics of Memory*. Cambridge, MA: Harvard University Press.

Maynard, Patrick. 2005. *Drawing Distinctions*. Ithaca, NY: Cornell University Press.

Murdoch, Iris. 1970. *The Sovereignty of Good*. London: Routledge.

Nietzsche, Friedrich. 2017. *On the Genealogy of Morality and Other Writings*, 3rd ed. Translated by Carol Diethe and edited by Keith Ansell-Pearson. Cambridge: Cambridge University Press.

Nozick, Robert. 1981. *Philosophical Explanations*. Cambridge, MA: Harvard University Press.

Oerlemans, Onno. 2018. *Poetry and Animals: Blurring the Boundaries with the Human*. New York: Columbia University Press.

Parfait, Claire. 2007. *The Publishing History of Uncle Tom's Cabin, 1852–2002*. Aldershot, UK: Ashgate.

Posner, Richard. 1997. "Against Ethical Criticism." *Philosophy and Literature* 21, no. 1: 1–27.

Powers, Richard. 2018. *The Overstory*. London: Vintage.

Prinz, Jesse. 2007. *The Emotional Construction of Morals*. Oxford: Oxford University Press.

Railton, Peter. 1986. "Moral Realism." *Philosophical Review* 95, no. 2: 163–207.

Robinson, Jenefer. 2005. *Deeper Than Reason*. Oxford: Oxford University Press.

Robinson, Jenefer, and Stephanie Ross. 1993. "Women, Morality, and Fiction." In *Feminist Aesthetics in Perspective*, edited by Hilde Hein and Carolyn Korsmeyer, 105–118. Bloomington: Indiana University Press.

Roelofs, Monique. 2014. *The Cultural Promise of the Aesthetic*. London: Bloomsbury.

Scanlon, T. M. 1998. *What We Owe to Each Other*. Cambridge, MA: Harvard University Press.

Sharp, Ingrid. 2011. "Käthe Kollwitz's Witness to War: Gender, Authority, and Reception." *Women in German Yearbook: Feminist Studies in German Literature & Culture* 27: 87–107.

Smith, Murray. 1995. *Engaging Characters: Fiction, Emotion, and the Cinema*. Oxford: Oxford University Press.

Spinrad, Tracy and Nancy Eisenberg. 2017. "Compassion in Children." In *The Oxford Handbook of Compassion Science*, edited by Emma Seppälä, Emiliana Simon-Thomas, Stephanie Brown, Monica Worline, C. Daryl Cameron, and James Doty, 53–64 Oxford: Oxford University Press.

Sripada, Chandra Sekhar. 2008. "Nativism and Moral Psychology." In *Moral Psychology*, Vol. I, edited by Walter Sinnott-Armstrong, 319–343. Cambridge, MA: The MIT Press.

Stowe, Harriet Beecher. 1852. *Uncle Tom's Cabin*. Project Gutenberg, https://www.gutenberg.org/files/203/203-h/203-h.htm (accessed February 21, 2023).

Walker, Margaret Urban. 2003. *Moral Contexts*. Lanham, MD: Rowman & Littlefield.

Williams, Bernard. 2011. *Ethics and the Limits of Philosophy*. London: Routledge.

Zamir, Tzachi. 2006. *Double Vision*. Princeton, NJ: Princeton University Press.

INDEX

....

For the benefit of digital users, indexed terms that span two pages (e.g., 52–53) may, on occasion, appear on only one of those pages.

Figures are indicated by *f* following the page number

feeling on key elements of moral life: behavioral norms and their status, interests in self and other, conflict and negotiation around ideals. The encounter with works of differing moral significance across a lifetime can be an evolving source of moral stimulus and reflection.

MORAL LEARNING: BASIC COMPONENTS AND INCULCATION

Learning, very broadly, is a kind of change, in which the change leaves the learner in a new state of knowledge or with a new capacity. With respect to moral learning, the relevant knowledge and capacities include recognition and understanding that are not inherently moral: one has to be able to identify and to some extent understand aspects of reality such as the existence of other people and sentient beings, feelings and beliefs, causal relations, intentions, accidents, availability of goods, strengths and vulnerabilities, and interests and harms. These turn out to be important "moving parts" when making sense of moral claims. Psychologists point to the role of such components and basic theories of mind and action in children's development of moral norms (Sripada 2008, 321, 361; Spinrad and Eisenberg 2017). In terms of grasping such basic theories, artworks seem to have the potential to make tangible and intelligible the thinking, experiences, desires, and goals of whoever made them. The "handmade-ness" of some works shows in their signs of sculpting, drawing, organizing, moving, or making sounds. Artworks can serve as pointed, sophisticated evidence of intentional action and communication of thought and feeling (Maynard 2005, Chapter 14; Robinson 2005, Chapters 8 and 9). Artworks can also portray or represent these components of moral life and, especially in narrative art, the interactions of agents that often hold moral significance (Carroll 2001; Feagin 1996; Smith 1995). In this sense, art can contribute to learning to identify and comprehend basic constituents of moral meaning.

In empirical research aiming to identify the kinds of activity and competence relevant to moral development and life, there seems to be a consensus that morality draws on at least two broadly specified capacities: "Moral judgment is the product of both intuitive and rational psychological processes . . . what are conventionally thought of as 'affective' and 'cognitive' mechanisms" (Cushman et al. 2010, 48). "Emotions play a significant role in moral judgment—but so does deliberative reason" (Bloom 2011, 72). Philosopher Shaun Nichols echoes this in his view that morality engages us with "a normative theory prohibiting harming others and an affective system that is sensitive to harm in others" (2004, 20). Although these categories—emotional, intuitive sensitivity and rational, theory-informed deliberation—are broad brush, it is interesting that morality as enacted in our bodies and neurophysiology seems to have this duality. A philosopher might want to ground morality clearly in reason or in feeling, as a theoretical matter, but we appear to live as moral beings by drawing on both capacities.